ECONOMICS
Principles and Applications

ROBERT E.
HALL
Department of Economics
Stanford University

MARC
LIEBERMAN
Department of Economics
New York University

THOMSON
——— ✳ ———™
SOUTH-WESTERN

Australia · Brazil · Canada · Mexico · Singapore · Spain · United Kingdom · United States

THOMSON

SOUTH-WESTERN

Economics: Principles and Applications, Fourth Edition
Robert E. Hall and Marc Lieberman

VP/Editorial Director:
Jack W. Calhoun

VP/Editor-in-Chief:
Alex von Rosenberg

Sr. Acquisitions Editor:
Michael Worls

Sr. Developmental Editor:
Susanna C. Smart

Sr. Marketing Manager:
John Carey

Content Project Manager:
Tamborah Moore

Manager of Technology, Editorial:
John Barans

Marketing Communications Manager:
Sarah Greber

Sr. Manufacturing Print Buyer:
Sandee Milewski

Production House:
Lachina Publishing Services

Printer:
QuebecorWorld -Taunton
Taunton, MA

Art Director:
Michelle Kunkler

Cover and Internal Designer:
Albonetti Design/Lisa A. Albonetti

Cover Images:
© Dave Cutler/Images.com

Photography Manager:
Deanna Ettinger

Photo Researcher:
Susan van Etten

Library of Congress Control Number:
2006908997

For more information about our products,
contact us at:

Thomson Learning Academic
Resource Center

1-800-423-0563

Thomson Higher Education
5191 Natorp Boulevard
Mason, OH 45040

USA

Brief Contents

Contents

PART III: PRODUCT MARKETS

PART IV: LABOR, CAPITAL, AND FINANCIAL MARKETS

PART V: EFFICIENCY, GOVERNMENT, AND THE GLOBAL ECONOMY

PART VI: MACROECONOMICS: BASIC CONCEPTS

PART VII: LONG-RUN MACROECONOMICS

Preface

Economics: Principles and Applications is about economic principles and how economists use them to understand the world. It was conceived, written, and for the fourth edition, substantially revised to help your students focus on those basic principles and applications.

We originally decided to write this book because we thought that existing books often confused students about economics and what it is all about. In our view, the leading texts tend to fall into one of three categories. In the first category are the encyclopedias—the heavy tomes with a section or a paragraph on every topic or subtopic you might possibly want to present to your students. These books are often useful as reference tools. But because they cover too many topics—many of them superficially—the central themes and ideas can be lost in the shuffle.

The second type of text we call the "scrapbook." In an effort to elevate student interest, these books insert multicolored boxes, news clippings, interviews, cartoons, and whatever else they can find to jolt the reader on each page. While these special features are often entertaining, there is a trade-off: These books sacrifice a logical, focused presentation of the material. Once again, the central themes and ideas are often lost.

Finally, the third type of text, perhaps in response to the first two, tries to do less in every area—a *lot* less. But instead of just omitting extraneous or inessential details, these texts often throw out key ideas, models, and concepts. Students who use these books may think that economics is overly simplified and unrealistic. After the course, they may be less prepared to go on in the field, or to think about the economy on their own.

A DISTINCTIVE APPROACH

Our approach is very different. We believe that the best way to teach principles is to present economics as a coherent, unified subject. This does not happen automatically. On the contrary, principles students often miss the unity of what we call "the economic way of thinking." For example, they are likely to see the analysis of goods markets, labor markets, and financial markets as entirely different phenomena, rather than as a repeated application of the same methodology with a new twist here and there. So the principles course appears to be just "one thing after another," rather than the coherent presentation we aim for.

CAREFUL FOCUS

Because we have avoided encyclopedic complexity, we have had to think hard about what topics are most important. As you will see:

We avoid nonessential material.

When we believed a topic was not essential to a basic understanding of economics, we left it out. However, we have strived to include core material to *support* an instructor who wants to present special topics in class. So, for example, we do not have comprehensive treatments of environmental economics, agricultural economics, urban economics, health care economics, or comparative systems *as separate subject matter*. But instructors should find in the text a good foundation for building any of these areas—and many others-into their course. And we have included examples from each of these areas as *applications* of core theory where appropriate throughout the text.

We avoid distracting features.

This text does not have interviews, news clippings, or boxed inserts with only distant connections to the core material. The features your students *will* find in our book are there to help them understand and apply economic theory itself, and to help them avoid common mistakes in applying the theory (the Dangerous Curves feature).

We explain difficult concepts patiently.

By freeing ourselves from the obligation to introduce every possible topic in economics, we can explain the topics we *do* cover more thoroughly and patiently. We lead students, step-by-step, through each aspect of the theory, through each graph, and through each numerical example. In developing this book, we asked other experienced teachers to tell us which aspects of economic theory were hardest for their students to learn, and we have paid special attention to the trouble spots.

We use concrete examples.

Students learn best when they see how economics can explain the world around them. Whenever possible, we develop the theory using real-world examples. You will find numerous references to real-world corporations and government policies throughout the text. When we employ hypothetical examples because they illustrate the theory more clearly, we try to make them realistic. In addition, almost every chapter ends with a thorough, extended application (the "Using the Theory" section) focusing on an interesting real-world issue.

FEATURES THAT REINFORCE

To help students see economics as a coherent whole, and to reinforce its usefulness, we have included some important features in this book.

THE THREE-STEP PROCESS

Most economists, when approaching a problem, begin by thinking about buyers and sellers, and the markets in which they come together to trade. They move on to characterize a market equilibrium, then give their model a workout in a comparative statics exercise. To understand what economics is about, students need to understand this process, and see it in action in different contexts. To help them do so, we have identified and stressed a "three-step process" that economists use in analyzing problems. The three key steps are:

1. **Characterize the Market.** Decide which market or markets best suit the problem being analyzed, and identify the decision makers (buyers and sellers) who interact there.
2. **Find the Equilibrium.** Describe the conditions necessary for equilibrium in the market, and a method for determining that equilibrium.
3. **Determine What Happens When Things Change.** Explore how events or government policies change the market equilibrium.

The steps themselves are introduced toward the end of Chapter 3. Thereafter, the content of most chapters is organized around this three-step process. We believe this helps students learn how to think like economists, and in a very natural way. And they come to see economics as a unified whole, rather than as a series of disconnected ideas.

DANGEROUS CURVES

Anyone who teaches economics for a while learns that, semester after semester, students tend to make the same familiar errors. In class, in office hours, and on exams, students seem pulled, as if by gravity, toward certain logical pitfalls in thinking about, and using, economic theory. We've discovered in our own classrooms that merely explaining the theory properly isn't enough; the most common errors need to be *confronted,* and the student needs to be shown *specifically* why a particular logical path is incorrect. This was the genesis of our "Dangerous Curves" feature—boxes that anticipate the most common traps in economics, and warn students just when they are most likely to fall victim to them. We've been delighted to hear from instructors how effective this feature has been in overcoming the most common points of confusion for their students.

USING THE THEORY

This text is full of applications that are woven throughout the narrative. In addition, almost every chapter ends with an extended application ("Using the Theory") that pulls together several of the tools learned in that chapter. These are not news clippings or world events that relate only tangentially to the material. Rather, they are step-by-step presentations that help students see how the tools of economics can explain things about the world—things that would be difficult to explain without those tools.

CONTENT INNOVATIONS

In addition to the special features just described, you will find some important differences from other texts in topical approach and arrangement. These, too, are designed to make the theory stand out more clearly, and to make learning easier. These are not pedagogical experiments, nor are they innovation for the sake of innovation. The differences you will find in this text are the product of years of classroom experience.

Innovations In Microeconomics:

Scarcity, Choice, and Economic Systems (Chapter 2):

This early chapter, while covering standard material such as opportunity cost, also introduces some central concepts much earlier than other texts. Most importantly, it introduces the concept of *comparative advantage,* and the basic principle of *specialization and exchange.* We have placed them at the front of our book because we believe they provide important building blocks for much that comes later. For example, comparative advantage and specialization *within* the firm help explain economies of scale (Chapter 6). International trade (Chapter 16) can be seen as a special application of these principles, extending them to trade between nations.

How Firms Make Decisions: Profit Maximization (Chapter 7):

Many texts introduce the theory of the firm using the perfectly competitive model first. While this has logical appeal to economists, we believe it is an unfortunate choice for students encountering this material for the first time. Leading with perfect competition forces students to simultaneously master the logic of profit maximization *and* the details of a rather special kind of market at the same time. Students quite naturally think of firms as facing *downward*-sloping demand curves—not horizontal ones. We have found that they have an easier time learning the theory of the firm with the more familiar, downward-sloping demand curve.

Further, by treating the theory of the firm in a separate chapter, *before* perfect competition, we can separate concepts that apply in *all* market structures (the shapes of marginal cost and average cost curves, marginal cost equals marginal revenue, the shut-down rule, etc.), from concepts that are unique to perfect competition (horizontal demand curve, marginal revenue the same as price, etc.). This avoids confusion later on.

Monopolistic Competition and Oligopoly (Chapter 10):

Two features of our treatment are worth noting. First, we emphasize advertising, a key feature of both of these types of markets. Students are very interested in advertising, and how firms make decisions about it. Second, we have omitted older theories of oligopoly that raised more questions than they answered, such as the kinked demand curve model. Our treatment of oligopoly is strictly game theoretic, but we have taken great care to

keep it simple and clear. Here, as always, we provide the important tools to *support* instructors who want to take game theory further, without forcing every instructor to do so by including too much.

Capital and Financial Markets (Chapter 13):

This chapter focuses on the common theme of these subjects: the present value of future income. Moreover, it provides simple, principles-level analyses of the stock and bond markets—something that students are hungry for, but that many principles textbooks neglect.

Description vs. Assessment (Chapters 8–10 and 14–15):

In treating product market structures, most texts switch back and forth between the *description and analysis* of different markets on the one hand, and their *efficiency properties* on the other.

Our book collects the material on efficiency into two well-rounded chapters. Chapter 14 covers the concept and measurement of economic efficiency, using Pareto improvements as well as consumer and producer surplus. Chapter 15 deals with market failures and government's role in economic efficiency. They permit you to focus on *description and prediction* when teaching about market structures—a full plate, in our experience. Second, two chapters devoted to efficiency allows a more comprehensive treatment of the topic than we have seen elsewhere. Finally, our approach—in which students learn about efficiency *after* they have mastered the four market structures—allows them to study efficiency with the perspective needed to really understand it.

Comparative Advantage and the Gains from International Trade (Chapter 16):

We've found that international trade is best understood through clear numerical examples, and we've developed them carefully in this chapter. We also try to bridge the gap between the economics and politics of international trade with a systematic discussion of winners and losers.

Innovations in Macroeconomics:

Long-Run Macroeconomics (Chapters 20 and 21):

Our text presents long-run growth before short-run fluctuations. Chapter 20 develops the long-run, classical model at a level appropriate for introductory students, mostly using supply and demand. Chapter 21 then *uses* the classical model to explain the causes—and costs—of economic growth in both rich and poor countries.

We believe it is better to treat the long run before the short run, for two reasons. First, the long-run model makes full use of the tools of supply and demand, and thus allows a natural transition from the preliminary chapters (1, 2, and 3) into macroeconomics. Second, we believe that students can best understand economic fluctuations by understanding *how* and *why* the long-run model breaks down over shorter time periods. This, of course, requires an introduction to the long-run model first.

Economic Fluctuations (Chapter 22):

This unique chapter provides a bridge from the long-run to the short-run macro model, and paves the way for the short-run focus on spending as the driving force behind economic fluctuations.

Aggregate Demand and Aggregate Supply (Chapter 26):

One of our pet peeves about some introductory texts is the too-early introduction of aggregate demand and aggregate supply curves, *before* teaching where these curves come from. Students then confuse the *AD* and *AS* curves with their microeconomic counterparts, requiring corrective action later. In this text, the *AD* and *AS* curves do not appear until Chapter 26, where they are fully explained. Our treatment of aggregate supply is based on a very simple mark-up model that our students have found easy to understand.

Exchange Rates and Macroeconomic Policy (Chapter 29):

Many students find international macroeconomics the most interesting topic in the course, especially the material on exchange rates and what causes them to change. Accordingly, you will find unusually full coverage of exchange rate determination in this chapter. This treatment is kept simple and straightforward, relying exclusively on supply and demand. And it forms the foundation for the discussion of the trade deficit that ends the chapter.

ORGANIZATIONAL FLEXIBILITY

We have arranged the contents of each chapter, and the table of contents as a whole, according to our recommended order of presentation. But we have also built in flexibility.

In microeconomics:

- Chapter 5 develops consumer theory with both marginal utility and (in an appendix) indifference curves, allowing you to present either method in class. (Instructors will find it even easier to make their choice in this edition—see below.)
- If you wish to highlight international trade or present comparative advantage earlier in the course, you could assign Chapter 16 immediately following Chapter 3.
- If you wish to introduce consumer and producer surplus earlier in the course, all of Chapter 14 can be assigned after Chapter 9. And if you feel strongly that economic efficiency should be interwoven bit-by-bit with the chapters on market structure, Chapter 14 can be easily broken into parts. The relevant sections can then be assigned separately with Chapters 3, 4, 8, and 9.

In macroeconomics:

- Once the core chapters (17–26) have been taught, the remaining chapters (27–29) can be presented in any order.
- Some instructors may want to assign selections from Chapter 28 (Spending, Taxes, and the Federal Budget) along with Chapter 23 (The Short-Run Macro Model).

Finally, we have included only those chapters that we thought were both essential and teachable in a year-long course. But not everyone will agree about what is essential. While we—as authors—cringe at the thought of a chapter being omitted in the interest of time, we have allowed for that possibility. Nothing in Chapter 12 (economic inequality), Chapter 13 (capital and financial markets), Chapter 15 (government's role in economic efficiency), Chapter 16 (international trade), Chapter 21 (economic growth), Chapter 22 (economic fluctuations), Chapter 27 (inflation and monetary policy), Chapter 28 (fiscal policy and the budget), or Chapter 29 (international macro) is required to understand any of the other chapters in the book. Skipping any of these should not cause continuity problems. And in this edition, we've made our first discussion of monetary policy in Chapter 25 (The Money Market and Monetary Policy) more complete, so that an instructor can skip Chapter 27 (Inflation and Monetary Policy) with less sacrifice than previously.

In many cases, a chapter can be assigned selectively. For example, in Chapter 11 (labor markets), an instructor who feels rushed could focus on the equilibrium and comparative statics results in labor *markets*, and skip the analyses of the firm as a demander of labor. And in macroeconomics, an instructor who is anxious to get to the short-run macro model could freely select among the sections in Chapter 21 (economic growth and rising living standards) and Chapter 22 (economic fluctuations).

NEW TO THE FOURTH EDITION

For this fourth edition, we've done our most significant revision to date. We've incorporated many excellent suggestions from reviewers and adopters. We've also conducted lengthy interviews with some long-time users to refine their suggestions further. While the overall approach and philosophy of the book remain unchanged, you'll find that almost every chapter has been affected and significantly improved by the revision.

For example, we've worked hard to clarify and simplify figures. We've modified or deleted material that instructors identified as stumbling blocks for their students. We've added several new Dangerous Curves boxes, and removed some that seemed more trouble than they were worth. About a third of the "Using the Theory" sections are entirely new, and another third have been substantially revised. And, of course, we've updated all tables and figures with new data, adjusted content to reflect economic changes that have taken place over the past few years, and replaced or added dozens of end-of-chapter problems. In doing all this, we've kept our eye on the *essentials* throughout, resulting in a book that is about 100 pages shorter than the previous edition.

In addition, we've made some major changes that all instructors should know about in preparing their course.

- *Chapter 2 (Scarcity, Choice, and Economic Systems)* includes new PPF diagrams to illustrate economic growth.
- *Chapter 3 (Supply and Demand)* now includes a simple circular flow diagram.

- *Chapter 4 (Working with Supply and Demand)* has several important changes. First, based on popular demand, price elasticities are now given as *positive numbers*. Second, we've drastically cut back the material on income, cross-price and supply elasticities. Finally, we've replaced the difficult section on elasticity and tax incidence with an entirely new and more interesting section on the equivalence of taxes on buyers versus sellers. (Elasticity and tax incidence is treated more simply and intuitively in Chapter 14).
- *Chapter 6 (Production and Cost)* has been tightened. The lengthy discussion of why firms exist and the types of business firms has been deleted, and an (entirely optional) appendix on isoquants and isocost lines has been added.
- *Chapter 8 (Perfect Competition)* now includes graphs for all three types of industries: constant cost, increasing cost, and decreasing cost. However, we do this in a less complicated way, based on a shifting LRATC curve.
- *Chapter 10 (Monopolistic Competition and Oligopoly)* has additional game theory matrices to illustrate the case of only one dominant strategy, and of no dominant strategies.
- *Chapter 11 (Labor Markets)* has been reorganized to make the exposition clearer and shorter, and to make the key content stand out. We've deleted the separate treatment of the demand for labor with more than one variable input, instead incorporating this concept into the narrative when relevant. And our graphs of labor market changes no longer illustrate the firm and the market simultaneously. Users should find this chapter much more student friendly than in the past.
- *Chapter 12 (Income Inequality)* remains the location for our discussion of the minimum wage, but it's been expanded, and appears in a new context (as a frequently-proposed policy to address inequality at the bottom). We've also added an entirely new section on growing income inequality, incorporating recent research about incomes at the very top.
- *Chapter 13 (Capital and Financial Markets)* has new material on equilibrium in the bond market, and an expanded discussion of efficient markets theory.
- *Chapter 14: (Economic Efficiency and the Competitive Ideal)* and *Chapter 15 (Government's Role in Economic Efficiency)* were, in previous editions, combined into one chapter. Now, Chapter 14 focuses on efficiency, and the deadweight loss from

- The special topic "capstone chapter" on the stock market has been removed in this edition, to create an even greater focus on essentials. Instructors who would like to use this chapter with the fourth edition should contact their South-Western representative.

While we believe these are the issues mostly likely to affect your lectures, they are by no means an exhaustive list of changes in the revision. For those who would like a more extensive list, we have posted one on our Web site at **www.thomsonedu.com/economics/hall**.

TEACHING AND LEARNING AIDS

To help you present the most interesting principles courses possible, we have created an extensive set of supplementary items. Many of them can be downloaded from the Hall/Lieberman Web site **www.thomsonedu .com/economics/hall**. The list includes:

FOR THE INSTRUCTOR

- An *Instructor's Manual,* by Dennis Hanseman. The manual provides chapter outlines, teaching ideas, Experiential Exercises for many chapters, suggested answers to the end-of-chapter questions, and solutions to all problems.
- *Instructor's Resource CD-ROM.* This easy-to-use CD allows quick access to instructor ancillaries from your desktop. It also allows you to review, edit, and copy exactly the material you need. Or, you may choose to go to *Instructor Resources* on the *Product Support Web Site.* This site at **www .thomsonedu.com/economics/hall** features the essential resources for instructors, password-protected, in downloadable format: the *Instructor's Manual* in Word, the Test Banks in Word, and PowerPoint® Lecture and Exhibit Slides.
- *Macroeconomics Test Bank,* revised by Robert Guell, Indiana State University. This contains over 2,500 multiple-choice questions. The test questions have been arranged according to chapter headings and subheadings, making it easy to find the material needed to construct examinations.
- *ExamView® Computerized Testing Software.* Exam-View is an easy-to-use test creation package compatible with both Microsoft Windows and Macintosh client software, and contains all of the questions in all of the printed test banks. You can select questions by previewing them on the screen, selecting them by number, or selecting them randomly. Questions, instructions, and answers can be edited, and new questions can easily be added. You can also administer quizzes online-over the Internet, through a local area network (LAN), or through a wide area network (WAN).
- *PowerPoint® Lecture and Exhibit Slides.* Available on the Web site and the IRCD, the PowerPoint presentations consist of speaking points in chapter outline format, accompanied by numerous key graphs and tables from the main text, many with animation, which may be printed for use as transparency masters.
- *Principles of Economics Videotape. Principles of Economics* is a 40-minute videotape that offers students an insightful overview of ten common economic principles: Trade-offs, Opportunity Cost, Marginal Thinking, Incentives, Trade, Markets, Government's Role, Productivity, Inflation, and the Phillips Curve. *Principles of Economics* shows viewers how to apply economic principles to their daily lives. This video is filled with interviews from some of the country's leading economists, includes profiles of real students facing economic choices, and shows the economy's impact on U.S. and foreign companies. The video can be used at the beginning of a term to give students a general overview of economics, or used one section at a time prior to teaching each of these principles.
- *Favorite Ways to Learn Economics: Instructor's Edition.* Authors David Anderson of Centre College and Jim Chasey of Homewood-Flossmoor High School use experiments to bring economic education to life. This is a lab manual for the classroom and for individual study that contains experiments and problem sets that reinforce key economic concepts. The Instructor's Edition provides you the guidance and tips to ensure that these experiments are facilitated successfully.
- *MarketSim.* MarketSim, by Tod Porter at Youngstown State University, is an online simulation designed to help students in microeconomics classes better understand how markets work, by taking on the roles of consumers and producers in a simulated economy. In the simulations, students "make" and "accept" offers to buy and sell labor and goods asynchronously via the Internet. The goal

of MarketSim is to provide instructors with a flexible teaching tool that can be used to motivate students to better understand a wide variety of microeconomic concepts.

- *TextChoice.* TextChoice is a custom format of Thomson Learning's online digital content. TextChoice provides the fastest, easiest way for you to create your own learning materials. You may select content from hundreds of best-selling titles, choose material from our numerous databases, and add your own material. Contact your South-Western/Thomson sales representative for more information at **http://thomsoncustom.com.**
- *eCoursepacks.* Create a customizable, easy-to-use, online companion for any course with eCoursepacks, from Thomson companies South-Western and Gale. eCoursepacks give educators access to current content from thousands of popular, professional, and academic periodicals, including NACRA and Darden cases, and business and industry information from Gale. You also have the ability to easily add your own material-even collecting a royalty if you choose. Permissions for all eCoursepack content are already secured, saving you the time and worry of securing rights. eCoursepacks online publishing tools also save you time and energy by allowing you to quickly search the databases and make selections, organize all your content, and publish the final outline product in a clean, uniform, and full-color format. eCoursepacks are the best ways to provide your audience with current information easily, quickly, and inexpensively.
  http://ecoursepacks.swlearning.com.
- *WebTutor Toolbox.* WebTutor™ ToolBox provides instructors with links to content from the book companion Web site. It also provides rich communication tools to instructors and students, including a course calendar, chat, and e-mail. For more information about the WebTutor products, please contact your local Thomson sales representative.

FOR THE STUDENT

- *Hall/Lieberman ThomsonNOW:* Available for purchase with the textbook, access to this robust site provides a powerful set of multimedia learning tools.

  Pre- and Post-Assessment Quizzes offer students diagnostic self-assessment of their comprehension of each chapter and an individualized plan for directed study based on the areas in which they are found to have a weaker understanding. All testing is automatically graded as the instructor desires.

  Master the Learning Objectives give step-by-step instructions associated with each learning objective to guide students systematically through all the activities that will deepen their understanding of that particular concept.

  The Graphing Workshop is a one-stop learning resource to help students master the language of graphs — one of the more difficult aspects of an economics course for many learners. It enables students to explore important economic concepts through a unique learning system made up of tutorials, interactive drawing tools, and exercises that teach how to interpret, reproduce, and explain graphs. Key graphs are identified throughout the text.

  "Using the Theory" applications ask students to use the three key steps to analyze unique and real-world questions.

  Ask the Instructor Video Clips, presented via streaming video, explain and illustrate difficult concepts from each chapter. Featuring Dr. Peter Olson, an economics instructor from Indiana University, these clips provide extremely helpful review and clarification if a student has trouble understanding an in-class lecture or is more of a visual learner.

  ABC News Video Segments deliver the "real world" right to students' desktops, giving sudents a context for how economic topics affect world and national events as well as their own daily lives, and helping them learn material by applying it to current events.

  ABC News Video Segments within ThomsonNOW give students the context on how economic topics affect world and national events as well as their own daily lives.

- *Tomlinson Economics Videos.* Featuring award-winning teacher and professional communicator, Steven Tomlinson (Ph.D, Stanford), these new Web-based lecture video products—Economic LearningPath and Economic JumpStart®—are sure to engage your students, while reinforcing the economic concepts they need to know. Many of these videos are also part of ThomsonNOW.
- *Complete Online Economics Course.* Whether using these videos to deliver online lectures for a distance learning class or as the required text for your Principles course, *Economics with Steven Tomlinson*

presents and develops the fundamentals of economics. While this video text offers comprehensive coverage of economic principles, with more than 40 hours of video lecture, you can offer your students an exceptional value package and a richer learning experience by pairing the video text with one of Thomson South-Western's eight Principles of Economics texts. The videos are also available in Microeconomics and Macroeconomics split versions.

- **Economic LearningPath® and Economic JumpStart Videos.** Great online resources to accompany any Economics text, these segments are like unlimited office hours for your students!. Pre and post tests ensure that students are on track. The JumpStart product contains only the introductory building block principles chapters, while the LearningPath product contains all the topics in either a micro or macro course.

  Visit **www.thomsonedu.com/economics/tomlinson/videos** to learn more.

- *Aplia* is an on-line product developed by world-renowned economist Paul Romer and used by thousands of economics students at hundreds of colleges and universities. It includes online interactive problem sets that follow the order of topics within the text. To ensure the highest level of correlation with this textbook, the authors reviewed every Aplia question for suitability, modified hundreds of them for a closer fit, and wrote hundreds of new questions from scratch. And they reviewed each question for this new edition, making further changes whenever necessary. Their involvement has ensured consistency in pedagogical approach and technical language, and will allow students to move seamlessly from the text to Aplia and back again.

- The *Active Learning Guide,* by Geoffrey A. Jehle of Vassar College. This study guide provides numerous exercises and self-tests for problem-solving practice. It is a valuable tool for helping students strengthen their knowledge of economics, and includes a sample multiple-choice final exam, with answers and explanations.

- *WebTutor Advantage:* Available on WebCT and/or Blackboard, this interactive, Web-based student supplement harnesses the power of the Internet to deliver innovative learning aids that actively engage students. Instructors can incorporate WebTutor as an integral part of the course, or students can use it

on their own as a study guide. Benefits to students include automatic and immediate feedback from quizzes and exams; interactive, multimedia-rich explanation of concepts; online exercises that reinforce what students have learned; flashcards that include audio support; and greater interaction and involvement through online discussion forums. Visit WebTutor to see a demo and for more information: **http://webtutor.thomsonlearning.com.**

- *The Hall/Lieberman Web site* (**www.thomsonedu.com/economics/hall**). The text Web site contains a wealth of useful teaching and learning resources. Important features available at the Web site include *Interactive Quizzes* with feedback on answers—completed quizzes can be e-mailed directly to the instructor; a sample chapter from the *Active Learning Guide;* and links to other economic resources.

- *Economics: Hits on the Web.* This resource booklet supports your students' research efforts on the World Wide Web. The manual covers materials such as: introduction to the World Wide Web, browsing the Web, finding information on the World Wide Web, e-mail, e-mail discussion groups, newsgroups, and documenting Internet sources for research. It also provides a listing of the hottest economic sites on the Web.

- *9/11: Economic Viewpoints.* The shape, pace, and spirit of the global economy have been greatly impacted by the events that occurred on September 11, 2001. *With 9/11: Economic Viewpoints,* South-Western offers a collection of essays that provides a variety of perspectives on the economic effects of this event. Each essay is written by one of South-Western's economics textbook authors, all of whom are highly regarded for both their academic and professional achievements. This unique collaboration results in one of the most cutting-edge resources available to help facilitate discussions of September 11's impact within the context of economics courses.

- *The Economist's Handbook: A Research and Writing Guide,* 2nd Edition. This reference book, by Thomas Wyrick of Southwest Missouri State University, is designed to help students develop skills in conducting and interpreting economic research. *The Economist's Handbook* provides commonsense explanations, relevant examples, and focused assignments, as well as an extensive glossary of economic terms, information about economics careers, and other useful reference materials.

ACKNOWLEDGMENTS

Our greatest debt is to the many reviewers who carefully read the book and provided numerous suggestions for improvements. While we could not incorporate all their ideas, we did carefully evaluate each one of them. To these reviewers of past editions, we are most grateful:

Ljubisa Adamovich	Florida State University
Brian A'Hearn	Franklin and Marshall College
Rashid Al-Hmoud	Texas Tech University
David Aschauer	Bates College
Richard Ballman	Augustana College
Chris Barnett	Gannon University
Parantap Basu	Fordham University
Tibor Besedes	Rutgers University
Gautam Bhattacharya	University of Kansas
Sylvain Boko	Wake Forest University
Mark Buenafe	Arizona State University
Steven Call	Metropolitan State College
Kevin Carey	American University
Steven Cobb	Xavier University
Dennis Debrecht	Carroll College
Selahattin Dibooglu	Southern Illinois University
James E. Dietz	California State University, Fullerton
Khosrow Doroodian	Ohio University
John Duffy	University of Pittsburgh
Debra S. Dwyer	SUNY, Stony Brook
Stephen Erfle	Dickinson College
James Falter	Mount Marty College
Sasan Fayazmanesh	California State University, Fresno
Lehman B. Fletcher	Iowa State University
James R. Gale	Michigan Technological University
Sarmila Ghosh	University of Scranton
Satyajit Ghosh	University of Scranton
Scott Gilbert	Southern Illinois University-Carbondale
Michael Gootzeit	University of Memphis
John Gregor	Washington and Jefferson University
Arunee C. Grow	Mesa Community College
Rik Hafer	Southern Illinois University
Roger Hewett	Drake University
Andrew Hildreth	University of California, Berkeley
Shahruz Hohtadi	Suffolk University
Thomas Husted	American University
Jeffrey Johnson	Sullivan University
Jacqueline Khorassani	Marietta College
Philip King	San Francisco State University
Frederic R. Kolb	University of Wisconsin, Eau Claire
Kate Krause	University of New Mexico
Brent Kreider	Iowa State University
Viju Kulkarni	San Diego State University
Nazma Latif-Zaman	Providence College
Teresa Laughlin	Palomar College
Bruce Madariaga	Montgomery College
Judith Mann	University of California, San Diego
Mark McCleod	Virginia Tech University
Steve McQueen	Barstow Community College
William R. Melick	Kenyon College
Shahruz Mohtadi	Suffolk University
Paul G. Munyon	Grinnell College
Rebecca Neumann	University of Wisconsin, Milwaukee
Chris Niggle	University of Redlands
Emmanuel Nnadozie	Truman State University
Farrokh Nourzad	Marquette University
Jim Palmieri	Simpson College
Zaohong Pan	Western Connecticut State University
Yvon Pho	American University
Gregg Pratt	Mesa Community College
Teresa Riley	Youngstown State University
William Rosen	Cornell University
Alannah Orrison Rosenberg	Saddleback Community College
Thomas Sadler	Pace University
Jonathan Sandy	University of San Diego
Ramazan Sari	Texas Tech University
Ghosh Sarmila	University of Scranton
Edward Scahill	University of Scranton
Robert F. Schlack	Carthage College
Pamela M. Schmitt	U.S. Naval Academy
Mary Schranz	University of Wisconsin, Madison
Alden Shiers	California Polytechnic State University
Kevin Siqueira	Clarkson University
Kevin Sontheimer	University of Pittsburgh
Richard Steinberg	Indiana University-Purdue University Indianapolis

Martha Stuffler — Irvine Valley College
Mohammad Syed — Miles College
John Vahaly — University of Louisville
Mikayel Vardanyan — Oregon State University
Thomas Watkins — Eastern Kentucky University
Glen Whitman — California State University, Northridge
Robert Whaples — Wake Forest University
Michael F. Williams — University of St. Thomas
Dirk Yandell — University of San Diego
Petr Zemcik — Southern Illinois University, Carbondale

We are especially grateful to the reviewers of this fourth edition:

Gerald Scott — Florida Atlantic University
Thomas McCaleb — Florida State University
Jeff Rubin — Rutgers University
Mark Frascatore — Clarkson College
Arthur M. Diamond, Jr. — University of Nebraska at Omaha
Arsen Melkumian — West Virginia University
Richard Fowles — University of Utah
Frank Mixon — University of Southern Mississippi
Barry Bomboy — J Sargeant Reynolds Community College
Michael Heslop — Northern Virginia C.C.
Daniel Horton — Cleveland State
Barry Falk — Iowa State University
Kiril Tochkov — Binghamton University
Manjuri Talukdar — Northern Illinois University
William Doyle Smith — University of Texas - El Paso
Rose Rubin — U* of Memphis
Scott Redenius — Bryn Mawr College
Thomas Pogue — University of Iowa
Nick Noble — Miami University-Ohio
Jeff Gropp — DePauw
Dennis Debrecht — Carroll College
Ali Akarca — University of Illinois-Chicago

We also wish to acknowledge the talented and dedicated group of instructors who helped put together a supplementary package that is second to none. Geoffrey A. Jehle of Vassar College cowrote the *Active Learning Guide* and created numerous improvements to this edition making it even more user-friendly and *active*. Dennis Hanseman revised the *Instructor's Manual*, and the Test Banks were carefully revised by Robert Guell of Indiana State University. Finally, special thanks go to Dennis Hanseman, who was our development editor for the first edition; his insights and ideas are still present in this fourth edition, and his continued assistance has proved invaluable.

The beautiful book you are holding would not exist except for the hard work of a talented team of professionals. Book production was overseen by Tamborah Moore, Content Project Manager at South-Western, and undertaken by Katherine Wilson at Lachina Publishing Services. Tamborah and Katherine showed remarkable patience, as well as an unflagging concern for quality throughout the process. We couldn't have asked for better production partners. Two NYU students—Andrea Schiferl and Sara-Ashley Orr—helped to locate and fix the few remaining errors.

The overall look of the book and cover was planned by Michelle Kunkler and executed by Lisa Albonetti. Deanna Ettinger managed the photo program, and Sandee Milewski made all the pieces come together in her role as Manufacturing Coordinator.

We are especially grateful for the hard work of the dedicated and professional South-Western editorial, marketing, and sales teams. Mike Worls, Senior Acquisitions Editor, has once again shepherded this text through publication with remarkable skill and devotion. John Carey, Senior Marketing Manager, has done a first-rate job getting the message out to instructors and sales reps. Susan Smart, who has been Senior Development Editor on several editions, once again delved into every chapter and contributed to their improvement. With each new edition, she has shown greater patience, flexibility, and skill in managing both content and authors. Dana Cowden, Technology Project Editor, has put together a wonderful package of media tools and the Thomson South-Western sales representatives have been extremely persuasive advocates for the book. We sincerely appreciate all their efforts!

Finally, we want to acknowledge the amazing team at Aplia, who helped us as we modified existing Aplia problems, and wrote new ones, to create the closest possible fit with our textbook. In particular, Paul Romer (CEO and Founder), Kristen Ford (Managing Editor) and Perkin Chung (Senior Content Developer) showed remarkable skill, knowledge, and patience in working with us on content, and in coming up with clever ways to make our job easier. It was a pleasure to work with them.

A REQUEST

Although we have worked hard on the first three editions of this book, we know there is always room for
further improvement. For that, our fellow users are
indispensable. We invite your comments and suggestions
wholeheartedly. We especially welcome your suggestions for additional "Using the Theory" sections and
Dangerous Curves. You may send your comments to
either of us care of South-Western.

Bob Hall
Marc Lieberman

About the Authors

Robert E. Hall

is a prominent applied economist. He is the Robert and Carole McNeil Professor of Economics at Stanford University and Senior Fellow at Stanford's Hoover Institution where he conducts research on inflation, unemployment, taxation, monetary policy, and the economics of high technology. He received his Ph.D. from MIT and has taught there as well as at the University of California, Berkeley. Hall is Director of the research program on Economic Fluctuations of the National Bureau of Economic Research, and Chairman of the Bureau's Committee on Business Cycle Dating, which maintains the semiofficial chronology of the U.S. business cycle. He has published numerous monographs and articles in scholarly journals, and coauthored a popular intermediate text. Hall has advised the Treasury Department and the Federal Reserve Board on national economic policy, and has testified on numerous occasions before congressional committees.

Marc Lieberman

is Clinical Associate Professor of Economics at New York University. He received his Ph.D. from Princeton University. Lieberman has presented his extremely popular Principles of Economics course at Harvard, Vassar, the University of California, Santa Cruz, and the University of Hawaii, as well as at NYU, where he won the university's Golden Dozen teaching award and also the Economics Society Award for Excellence in Teaching. He is coeditor and contributor to *The Road to Capitalism: Economic Transformation in Eastern Europe and the Former Soviet Union*. Lieberman has consulted for the Bank of America and the Educational Testing Service. In his spare time, he is a professional screenwriter, and teaches screenwriting at NYU's School of Continuing and Professional Studies.

What Is Economics?

Economics. The word conjures up all sorts of images: manic stock traders on Wall Street, an economic summit meeting in a European capital, a somber television news anchor announcing good or bad news about the economy. . . . You probably hear about economics several times each day. What exactly *is* economics?

First, economics is a *social science*, so it seeks to explain something about *society*. In this sense, it has something in common with psychology, sociology, and political science. But economics is different from these other social sciences because of *what* economists study and *how* they study it. Economists ask different questions, and they answer them using tools that other social scientists find rather exotic.

ECONOMICS, SCARCITY, AND CHOICE

A good definition of economics, which stresses the difference between economics and other social sciences, is the following:

> *Economics is the study of choice under conditions of scarcity.*

Economics The study of choice under conditions of scarcity.

This definition may appear strange to you. Where are the familiar words we ordinarily associate with economics: "money," "stocks and bonds," "prices," "budgets," . . . ? As you will soon see, economics deals with all of these things and more. But first, let's take a closer look at two important ideas in this definition: scarcity and choice.

SCARCITY AND INDIVIDUAL CHOICE

Think for a moment about your own life. Is there anything you don't have that you'd *like* to have? Anything you'd like *more* of? If your answer is "no," congratulations! You are well advanced on the path of Zen self-denial. The rest of us, however, feel the pinch of limits to our material standard of living. This simple truth is at the very core of economics. It can be restated this way: We all face the problem of **scarcity**.

At first glance, it may seem that you suffer from an infinite variety of scarcities. There are so many things you might like to have right now—a larger room or apartment, a new car, more clothes . . . the list is endless. But a little reflection suggests

Scarcity A situation in which the amount of something available is insufficient to satisfy the desire for it.

that your limited ability to satisfy these desires is based on two other, more basic limitations: scarce *time* and scarce *spending power*.

> *As individuals, we face a scarcity of time and spending power. Given more of either, we could each have more of the goods and services that we desire.*

The scarcity of spending power is no doubt familiar to you. We've all wished for higher incomes so that we could afford to buy more of the things we want. But the scarcity of time is equally important. So many of the activities we enjoy—seeing a movie, taking a vacation, making a phone call—require time as well as money. Just as we have limited spending power, we also have a limited number of hours in each day to satisfy our desires.

Because of the scarcities of time and spending power, each of us is forced to make *choices*. We must allocate our scarce *time* to different activities: work, play, education, sleep, shopping, and more. We must allocate our scarce *spending power* among different goods and services: housing, food, furniture, travel, and many others. And each time we choose to buy something or do something, we also choose *not* to buy or do something else.

Economists study the choices we make as individuals and also the *consequences* of those choices. For example, over the next decade, the fraction of high school graduates choosing to attend college is expected to rise to record levels. What does this mean for state and federal budgets? What will happen to the wages and salaries of those with college degrees, and those without them? What are the implications for our ability to reform health care, to reduce poverty, and to deal with other problems? Economics is uniquely equipped to analyze these questions.

Economists also study the more subtle and indirect effects of individual choice on our society. Will most Americans continue to live in houses or—like Europeans—will most of us end up in apartments? As the population ages, what will happen to the quality and accessibility of health care for the elderly? Will traffic congestion in our cities continue to worsen or is there relief in sight? These questions hinge, in large part, on the separate decisions of millions of people. To answer them requires an understanding of how individuals make choices under conditions of scarcity.

SCARCITY AND SOCIAL CHOICE

Resources The labor, capital, land and natural resources, and entrepreneurship that are used to produce goods and services.

Now let's think about scarcity and choice from *society*'s point of view. What are the goals of our society? We want a high standard of living for our citizens, clean air, safe streets, good schools, and more. What is holding us back from accomplishing all of these goals in a way that would satisfy everyone? You already know the answer: scarcity. In society's case, the problem is a scarcity of **resources**—the things we use to make goods and services that help us achieve our goals.

Labor The time human beings spend producing goods and services.

The Four Resources

Economists classify resources into four categories:

1. **Labor** is the time human beings spend producing goods and services.

Capital A long-lasting tool that is used to produce other goods.

2. **Capital** is a long-lasting tool that we produce to help us make other goods and services.

    It's useful to distinguish two different types of capital. **Physical capital** consists of things like machinery and equipment, factory buildings, computers, and

Physical capital The part of the capital stock consisting of physical goods, such as machinery, equipment, and factories.

even hand tools like hammers and screwdrivers. These are all long-lasting *physical* goods that are used to make other things.

Human capital consists of the skills and knowledge possessed by workers. These satisfy our definition of capital: They are *produced* (through education and training), they help us produce *other* things, and they last for many years, typically through an individual's working life.[1]

Human capital The skills and training of the labor force.

Note the word *long-lasting* in the definition. If something is used up quickly in the production process—like the flour a baker uses to make bread—it is generally *not* considered capital. A good rule of thumb is that capital should last at least a year, although most types of capital last considerably longer.

The **capital stock** is the total amount of capital at a nation's disposal at any point in time. It consists of all the physical and human capital made in previous periods that is still productively useful.

Capital stock The total amount of capital in a nation that is productively useful at a particular point in time.

3. **Land** refers to the physical space on which production takes place, as well as useful materials—*natural resources*—found under it or on it, such as crude oil, iron, coal, or fertile soil.

Land The physical space on which production takes place, as well as the natural resources that come with it.

4. **Entrepreneurship** is the ability (and the willingness to *use* it) to combine the *other* resources into a productive enterprise. An entrepreneur may be an *innovator* who comes up with an original idea for a business or a *risk taker* who provides her own funds or time to nurture a project with uncertain rewards.

Entrepreneurship The ability and willingness to combine the *other* resources—labor, capital, and natural resources—into a productive enterprise.

Anything *produced* in the economy comes, ultimately, from some combination of these four resources. Think about the last lecture you attended at your college. You were consuming a service—a college lecture. What went into producing that service? Your instructor was supplying labor. Many types of physical capital were used as well, including desks, chairs, a chalkboard or transparency projector, the classroom building itself, and the computer your instructor may have used to compose lecture notes. There was human capital—your instructor's specialized knowledge and lecturing skills. There was land—the property on which your classroom building sits, and natural resources like oil or natural gas to heat or cool the building. And some individual or group had to play the role of innovator and risk taker in order to combine the labor, capital, and natural resources needed to create and guide your institution in its formative years. (If you attend a public college or university, this entrepreneurial role was largely filled by the state government, with the state's taxpayers assuming the risk.)

> As a society, our resources—land, labor, capital, and entrepreneurship—are insufficient to produce all the goods and services we might desire. In other words, society faces a scarcity of resources.

This stark fact about the world helps us understand the choices a society must make. Do we want a more educated citizenry? Of course. But that will require more labor—construction workers to build more classrooms and teachers to teach in them. It will require more land for classrooms and lumber to build them. And it will require more capital—bulldozers, cement mixers, trucks, and more. These very same resources, however, could instead be used to produce *other* things that we find desirable, things

---

[1] An individual's human capital is ordinarily supplied along with her labor time. (When your instructor lectures or holds office hours, she is providing both labor time and her skills as an economist and teacher.) Still, it's often useful to distinguish the *time* a worker provides (her labor) from any skills or *knowledge* possessed (human capital).

such as new homes, hospitals, automobiles, or feature films. As a result, every society must have some method of *allocating* its scarce resources—choosing which of our many competing desires will be fulfilled and which will not be.

Many of the big questions of our time center on the different ways in which resources can be allocated. The cataclysmic changes that rocked Eastern Europe and the former Soviet Union during the early 1990s arose from a very simple fact: The method these countries used for decades to allocate resources was not working. Closer to home, the never-ending debates between Democrats and Republicans in the United States about tax rates, government services, and even foreign policy reflect subtle but important differences of opinion about how to allocate resources. Often, these are disputes about whether the private sector can handle a particular issue of resource allocation on its own or whether the government should be involved.

Input Anything (including a resource) used to produce a good or service.

DANGEROUS CURVES

Resources versus Inputs The term *resources* is often confused with another, more general term—**inputs**. An input is *anything* used to make a good or service. Inputs include not only resources but also many other things made from them (cement, rolled steel, electricity), which are, in turn, used to make goods and services. *Resources*, by contrast, are the *special* inputs that fall into one of four categories: labor, land, capital, and entrepreneurship. They are the ultimate source of everything that is produced.

SCARCITY AND ECONOMICS

The scarcity of resources—and the choices it forces us to make—is the source of all of the problems you will study in economics. Households have limited incomes for satisfying their desires, so they must choose carefully how they allocate their spending among different goods and services. Business firms want to make the highest possible profit, but they must pay for their resources; so they carefully choose *what* to produce, *how much* to produce, and *how* to produce it. Federal, state, and local government agencies work with limited budgets, so they must carefully choose which goals to pursue. Economists study these decisions made by households, firms, and governments to explain how our economic system operates, to forecast the future of our economy, and to suggest ways to make that future even better.

THE WORLD OF ECONOMICS

The field of economics is surprisingly broad. It extends from the mundane—why does a pound of steak cost more than a pound of chicken?—to the personal and profound—how do couples decide how many children to have? With a field this broad, it is useful to have some way of classifying the different types of problems economists study and the different methods they use to analyze them.

MICROECONOMICS AND MACROECONOMICS

Microeconomics The study of the behavior of individual households, firms, and governments; the choices they make; and their interaction in specific markets.

The field of economics is divided into two major parts: microeconomics and macroeconomics. **Microeconomics** comes from the Greek word *mikros*, meaning "small." It takes a close-up view of the economy, as if looking through a microscope. Microeconomics is concerned with the behavior of *individual* actors on the economic scene—households, business firms, and governments. It looks at the choices they make and how they interact with each other when they come together to trade *specific* goods and services. What will happen to the cost of movie tickets over the next five years? How many management-trainee jobs will open up for college graduates? How would U.S. phone companies be affected by a tax on imported cell phones? These are all microeconomic questions because they analyze individual *parts* of an economy rather than the *whole*.

Macroeconomics—from the Greek word *makros*, meaning "large"—takes an *overall* view of the economy. Instead of focusing on the production of carrots or computers, macroeconomics lumps all goods and services together and looks at the economy's *total output*. Instead of focusing on employment of management trainees or manufacturing workers, it considers *total employment* in the economy. Instead of asking why credit card loans carry higher interest rates than home mortgage loans, it asks what makes interest rates *in general* rise or fall. In all of these cases, macroeconomics focuses on the big picture and ignores the fine details.

Macroeconomics The study of the behavior of the overall economy.

POSITIVE AND NORMATIVE ECONOMICS

The micro versus macro distinction is based on the level of detail we want to consider. Another useful distinction has to do with our *purpose* in analyzing a problem. **Positive economics** deals with *how* the economy works, plain and simple. If someone says, "Recent increases in spending for domestic security have slowed the growth rate of the U.S. economy," she is making a positive economic statement. A statement need not be accurate or even sensible to be classified as positive. For example, "Government policy has no effect on our standard of living" is a statement that virtually every economist would regard as false. But it is still a positive economic statement. Whether true or not, it's about how the economy works and its accuracy can be tested by looking at the facts—and just the facts.

Positive economics The study of how the economy works.

Normative economics concerns itself with what *should be*. It is used to make judgments about the economy and prescribe solutions to economic problems. Rather than limiting its concerns to just "the facts," it goes on to say what we should *do* about them and therefore depends on our values.

Normative economics The study of what *should be*; it is used to make judgments about the economy, and prescribe solutions.

If an economist says, "We should cut total government spending," she is engaging in normative economic analysis. Cutting government spending would benefit some citizens and harm others, so the statement rests on a value judgment. A normative statement—like the one about government spending above—cannot be proved or disproved by the facts alone.

Positive and normative economics are intimately related in practice. For one thing, we cannot properly argue about what we should or should not do unless we know certain facts about the world. Every normative analysis is therefore based on an underlying positive analysis. But while a positive analysis can, at least in principle, be conducted without value judgments, a normative analysis is always based, at least in part, on the values of the person conducting it.

Seemingly Positive Statements Be alert to statements that may *seem* positive but are actually normative. Here's an example: "If we want to reduce pollution, our society will have to use less gasoline." This may *sound* positive, because it seems to refer only to facts about the world. But it's actually normative. Why? Cutting back on gasoline is just *one* policy among many that could reduce pollution. To say that we *must* choose this method makes a value judgment about its superiority to other methods. A purely positive statement on this topic would be, "Using less gasoline—with no other change in living habits—would reduce pollution."

Similarly, be alert to statements that use vague terms with hidden value judgments. An example: "All else equal, the less gasoline we use, the better our quality of life." Whether you agree or disagree, this is *not* a positive statement. Two people who agree about the facts—in this case, the consequences of using less gasoline—might disagree over the meaning of the phrase "quality of life," how to measure it, and what would make it better. This disagreement could not be resolved just by looking at the facts.

DANGEROUS CURVES

Why Economists Disagree

The distinction between positive and normative economics can help us understand why economists sometimes disagree. Suppose you are watching a television interview in which two economists are asked whether the United States should eliminate all government-imposed barriers to trading with the rest of the world. The first economist says, "Yes, absolutely," but the other says, "No, definitely not." Why the sharp disagreement?

The difference of opinion may be *positive* in nature: The two economists may have different views about what would actually happen if trade barriers were eliminated. Differences like this sometimes arise because our knowledge of the economy is imperfect or because certain facts are in dispute.

In some cases, however, the disagreement will be *normative*. Economists, like everyone else, have different values. In this case, both economists might agree that opening up international trade would benefit *most* Americans, but harm *some* of them. Yet they may still disagree about the policy move because they have different values. The first economist might put more emphasis on benefits to the overall economy, while the second might put more emphasis on preventing harm to a particular group. Here, the two economists have come to the same *positive* conclusion, but their *different values* lead them to different *normative* conclusions.

In the media, economists are rarely given enough time to express the basis for their opinions, so the public hears only the disagreement. People may then conclude that economists cannot agree about how the economy works, even when the *real* disagreement is over goals and values.

WHY STUDY ECONOMICS?

If you've gotten this far into the chapter, chances are you've already decided to allocate some of your scarce time to studying economics. We think you've made a wise choice. But it's worth taking a moment to consider what you might gain from this choice.

Why study economics?

TO UNDERSTAND THE WORLD BETTER

Applying the tools of economics can help you understand global and catastrophic events such as wars, famines, epidemics, and depressions. But it can also help you understand much of what happens to you locally and personally—the worsening traffic conditions in your city, the raise you can expect at your job this year, or the long line of people waiting to buy tickets for a popular concert. Economics has the power to help us understand these phenomena because they result, in large part, from the choices we make under conditions of scarcity.

Economics has its limitations, of course. But it is hard to find any aspect of life about which economics does not have *something* important to say. Economics cannot explain why so many Americans like to watch television, but it *can* explain how TV networks decide which programs to offer. Economics cannot protect you from a robbery, but it *can* explain why some people choose to become thieves and why no society has chosen to eradicate crime completely. Economics will not improve your love life, resolve unconscious conflicts from your childhood, or help you overcome a fear of flying, but it *can* tell us how many skilled therapists, ministers, and counselors are available to help us solve these problems.

TO ACHIEVE SOCIAL CHANGE

If you are interested in making the world a better place, economics is indispensable. There is no shortage of serious social problems worthy of our attention—unemployment, hunger, poverty, disease, child abuse, drug addiction, violent crime. Economics can help us understand the origins of these problems, explain why previous efforts to solve them haven't succeeded, and help us to design new, more effective solutions.

TO HELP PREPARE FOR OTHER CAREERS

Economics has long been a popular college major for individuals intending to work in business. But it has also been popular among those planning careers in politics, international relations, law, medicine, engineering, psychology, and other professions. This is for good reason: Practitioners in each of these fields often find themselves confronting economic issues. For example, lawyers increasingly face judicial rulings based on the principles of economic efficiency. Doctors will need to understand how new technologies or changes in the structure of health insurance will affect their practices. Industrial psychologists need to understand the economic implications of workplace changes they may advocate, such as flexible scheduling or on-site child care.

TO BECOME AN ECONOMIST

Only a tiny minority of this book's readers will decide to become economists. This is welcome news to the authors, and after you have studied labor markets in your *microeconomics* course you will understand why. But if you do decide to become an economist—obtaining a master's degree or even a Ph.D.—you will find many possibilities for employment. The economists with whom you have most likely had personal contact are those who teach and conduct research at colleges and universities. But about equal numbers of economists work outside and inside of academia. Economists are hired by banks to assess the risk of investing abroad; by manufacturing companies to help them determine new methods of producing, marketing, and pricing their products; by government agencies to help design policies to fight crime, disease, poverty, and pollution; by international organizations to help create and reform aid programs for less developed countries; by the media to help the public interpret global, national, and local events; and by nonprofit organizations to provide advice on controlling costs and raising funds more effectively.

THE METHODS OF ECONOMICS

One of the first things you will notice as you begin to study economics is the heavy reliance on *models*.

You've no doubt encountered many models in your life. As a child, you played with model trains, model planes, or model people—dolls. You may have also seen architects' cardboard models of buildings. These are physical models, three-dimensional replicas that you can pick up and hold. Economic models, on the other hand, are built not with cardboard, plastic, or metal but with words, diagrams, and mathematical statements.

What, exactly, is a model?

Model An abstract representation of reality.

> *A **model** is an abstract representation of reality.*

The two key words in this definition are *abstract* and *representation*. A model is not supposed to be exactly like reality. Rather, it *represents* the real world by *abstracting* or *taking from* the real world that which will help us understand it. By definition, a model leaves out features of the real world.

THE ART OF BUILDING ECONOMIC MODELS

When you build a model, how do you know which real-world details to include and which to leave out? There is no simple answer to this question. The right amount of detail depends on your purpose in building the model in the first place. There is, however, one guiding principle:

> *A model should be as simple as possible to accomplish its purpose.*

This means that a model should contain only the *necessary* details.

To understand this a little better, think about a map. A map is a model that represents a part of the earth's surface. But it leaves out many details of the real world. First, a map leaves out the third dimension—height—of the real world. Second, maps always ignore small details, such as trees and houses and potholes. But when you buy a map, how much detail do you want it to have?

Let's say you are in Boston, and you need a map to find the best way to drive from Logan Airport to the downtown convention center. In this case, you would want a very detailed city map, with every street, park, and plaza in Boston clearly illustrated and labeled as in the map on the left in Figure 1. A highway map, which ignores these details, wouldn't do at all.

But now suppose your purpose is different: to select the best driving route from Boston to Cincinnati. Now you want a highway map such as the one on the right in Figure 1. A map that shows every street between Boston and Cincinnati would have *too much* detail. All of that extraneous information would only obscure what you really need to see.

The same principle applies in building economic models. The level of detail that would be just right for one purpose will usually be too much or too little for another. When you feel yourself objecting to a model in this text because something has been left out, keep in mind the purpose for which the model is built. In introductory economics, the purpose is entirely educational. The models are designed to help you understand some simple, but powerful, principles about how the economy

FIGURE 1

Maps as Models

These maps are models. But each would be used for a different purpose.

operates. Keeping the models simple makes it easier to see these principles at work and remember them later.

Of course, economic models have other purposes besides education. They can help businesses make decisions about pricing and production, help households decide how and where to invest their savings, and help governments and international agencies formulate policies. Models built for these purposes will be much more detailed than the ones in this text, and you will learn about them if you take more advanced courses in economics. But even complex models are built around very simple frameworks—the same frameworks you will be learning here.

ASSUMPTIONS AND CONCLUSIONS

Every economic model begins with *assumptions* about the world. There are two types of assumptions in a model: simplifying assumptions and critical assumptions.

A **simplifying assumption** is just what it sounds like—a way of making a model simpler without affecting any of its important conclusions. The purpose of a simplifying assumption is to rid a model of extraneous detail so its essential features can stand out more clearly. A road map, for example, makes the simplifying assumption, "There are no trees" because trees on a map would only get in the way. Similarly, in an economic model, we might assume that there are only two goods that households can choose from or that there are only two nations in the world. We make such assumptions *not* because they are true, but because they make a model easier to follow and do not change any of the important insights we can get from it.

A **critical assumption**, by contrast, is an assumption that affects the conclusions of a model in important ways. When you use a road map, you make the critical assumption, "All of these roads are open." If that assumption is wrong, your conclusion—the best route to take—might be wrong as well.

In an economic model, there are always one or more critical assumptions. You don't have to look very hard to find them because economists like to make these assumptions explicit right from the outset. For example, when we study the behavior of business firms, our model will assume that firms try to earn the highest possible profit for their owners. By stating this critical assumption up front, we can see immediately where the model's conclusions spring from.

Simplifying assumption Any assumption that makes a model simpler without affecting any of its important conclusions.

Critical assumption Any assumption that affects the conclusions of a model in an important way.

THE THREE-STEP PROCESS

As you read this textbook, you will learn how economists use economic models to address a wide range of problems. In Chapter 2, for example, you will see how a simple economic model can give us important insights about society's production choices. And subsequent chapters will present still different models that help us understand the U.S. economy and the global economic environment in which it operates. As you read, it may seem to you that there are a lot of models to learn and remember . . . and, indeed, there are.

But there is an important insight about economics that—once mastered—will make your job easier than you might think. The insight is this: There is a remarkable similarity in the types of models that economists build, the assumptions that underlie those models, and what economists actually *do* with them. In fact, you will see that economists follow the same *three-step process* to analyze almost any economic problem. The first two steps explain how economists *build* an economic model, and the last explains how they *use* the model.

What are these three steps that underlie the economic approach to almost any problem? Sorry for the suspense, but you'll have to wait a bit (until the end of Chapter 3) for the answer. By that time, you'll have learned a little more about economics, and the three-step process will make more sense to you.

MATH, JARGON, AND OTHER CONCERNS . . .

Economists often express their ideas using mathematical concepts and a special vocabulary. Why? Because these tools enable economists to express themselves more precisely than with ordinary language. For example, someone who has never studied economics might say, "When gas is expensive, people don't buy big, gas-guzzling cars." That statement might not bother you right now. But once you've finished your first economics course, you'll be saying it something like this: "When the price of gas rises, the demand curve for big, gas-guzzling cars shifts leftward."

Does the second statement sound strange to you? It should. First, it uses a special term—a *demand curve*—that you haven't yet learned. Second, it uses a mathematical concept—a *shifting curve*—with which you might not be familiar. But while the first statement might mean a number of different things, the second statement— as you will see in Chapter 3—can mean only *one* thing. By being precise, we can steer clear of unnecessary confusion.

If you are worried about the special vocabulary of economics, you can relax. All of the new terms will be defined and carefully explained as you encounter them. Indeed, this textbook does not assume you have any special knowledge of economics. It is truly meant for a "first course" in the field.

But what about the math? Here, too, you can relax. While professional economists often use sophisticated mathematics to solve problems, only a little math is needed to understand basic economic *principles*. And virtually all of this math comes from high school algebra and geometry.

Still, if you have forgotten some of your high school math, a little brushing up might be in order. This is why we have included an appendix at the end of this chapter. It covers some of the most basic concepts—such as interpreting graphs, the equation for a straight line, and the concept of a slope—that you will need in this course. You may want to glance at this appendix now, just so you'll know what's there. Then, from time to time, you'll be reminded about it when you're most likely to need it.

HOW TO STUDY ECONOMICS

As you read this book or listen to your instructor, you may find yourself following along and thinking that everything makes perfect sense. Economics may even seem easy. Indeed, it *is* rather easy to *follow* economics, since it's based so heavily on simple logic. But *following* and *learning* are two different things. You will eventually discover (preferably *before* your first exam) that economics must be studied actively, not passively.

If you are reading these words lying back on a comfortable couch, a phone in one hand and a remote control in the other, you are going about it in the wrong way. Active studying means reading with a pencil in your hand and a blank sheet of paper in front of you. It means closing the book periodically and *reproducing* what you have learned. It means listing the steps in each logical argument, retracing the flow of cause and effect in each model, and drawing the graphs that represent the model. It does require some work, but the payoff is a good understanding of economics and a better understanding of your own life and the world around you.

Summary

Economics is the study of choice under conditions of scarcity. As individuals, and as a society, we have unlimited desires for goods and services. Unfortunately, the *resources*—land, labor, capital, and entrepreneurship—needed to produce those goods and services are scarce. Therefore, we must choose which desires to satisfy and how to satisfy them. Economics provides the tools that explain those choices.

The field of economics is divided into two major areas. *Microeconomics* studies the behavior of individual households, firms, and governments as they interact in specific markets. *Macroeconomics*, by contrast, concerns itself with the behavior of the entire economy. It considers variables such as total output, total employment, and the overall price level.

Economics makes heavy use of *models*—abstract representations of reality. These models are built with words, diagrams, and mathematical statements that help us understand how the economy operates. All models are simplifications, but a good model will have *just enough detail for the purpose at hand.*

When analyzing almost any problem, economists follow a three-step process in building and using economic models. This three-step process will be introduced at the end of Chapter 3.

Problem Set   *Answers to even-numbered Questions and Problems can be found on the text Web site at www.thomsonedu.com/economics/hall.*

1. Discuss whether each statement is an example of positive economics or normative economics or if it contains elements of both:
   a. An increase in the personal income tax will slow the growth rate of the economy.
   b. The goal of any country's economic policy should be to increase the well-being of its poorest, most vulnerable citizens.
   c. Excess regulation of small business is stifling the economy. Small business has been responsible for most of the growth in employment over the last 10 years, but regulations are putting a severe damper on the ability of small businesses to survive and prosper.
   d. The 1990s were a disastrous decade for the U.S. economy. Income inequality increased to its highest level since before World War II.

2. For each of the following, state whether economists would consider it a *resource*, and if they would, identify which of the four types of resources the item is.
   a. A computer used by an FBI agent to track the whereabouts of suspected criminals.
   b. The office building in which the FBI agent works.
   c. The time that an FBI agent spends on a case.
   d. A farmer's tractor.

   e. The farmer's knowledge of how to operate the tractor.
   f. Crude oil.
   g. A package of frozen vegetables.
   h. A food scientist's knowledge of how to commercially freeze vegetables.
   i. The ability to bring together resources to start a frozen food company.
   j. Plastic bags used by a frozen food company to hold its product.

3. Suppose you are using the second map in Figure 1, which shows main highways only. You've reached a conclusion about the fastest way to drive from the Boston city center to an area south of the city. State whether each of the following assumptions of the map would be a *simplifying* or *critical* assumption for your conclusion, and explain briefly. (Don't worry about whether the assumption is true or not.)
   a. The thicker, numbered lines are major highways without traffic lights.
   b. The earth is two-dimensional.
   c. When two highways cross, you can get from one to the other without going through city traffic.
   d. Distances on the map are proportional to distances in the real world.

APPENDIX

Graphs and Other Useful Tools

TABLES AND GRAPHS

A brief glance at this text will tell you that graphs are important in economics. Graphs provide a convenient way to display information and enable us to immediately *see* relationships between variables.

Suppose that you've just been hired at the advertising department of Len & Harry's—an up-and-coming manufacturer of high-end ice cream products, located in Texas. You've been asked to compile a report on how advertising affects the company's sales. It turns out that the company's spending on advertising has changed repeatedly in the past, so you have lots of data on monthly advertising expenditure and monthly sales revenue, both measured in thousands of dollars.

Table A.1 shows a useful way of arranging this data. The company's advertising expenditure in different months are listed in the left-hand column, while the right-hand column lists total sales revenue ("sales" for short) during the same months. Notice that the data here is organized so that spending on advertising increases as we move down the first column. Often, just looking at a table like this can reveal useful patterns. Here, it's clear that higher spending on advertising is associated with higher monthly sales. These two variables—advertising and sales—have a *positive relationship*. A rise in one is associated with a rise in the other. If higher advertising had been associated with *lower* sales, the two variables would have a *negative* or *inverse relationship*: A rise in one would be associated with a fall in the other.

We can be even more specific about the positive relationship between advertising and sales: Logic tells us that the association is very likely *causal*. We'd expect that sales revenue *depends on* advertising outlays, so we call sales our *dependent variable* and advertising our *independent variable*. Changes in an independent variable cause changes in a dependent variable, but not the other way around.

To explore the relationship further, let's graph it. As a rule, the *independent* variable is measured on the *horizontal* axis and the *dependent* variable on the *vertical* axis. In economics, unfortunately, we do not always stick to this rule, but for now we will. In Figure A.1, monthly advertising outlays—our independent variable—are measured on the horizontal axis. If we start at the *origin*—the corner where the two axes intersect—and move rightward along the horizontal axis, monthly advertising outlays increase from $0 to $1,000 to $2,000 and so on. The vertical axis measures monthly sales—the dependent variable. Along this axis, as we move upward from the origin, sales rise.

The graph in Figure A.1 shows six labeled points, each representing a different pair of numbers from our table. For example, point *A*—which represents the numbers in the first row of the table—shows us that when the firm spends $2,000 on advertising, sales are $24,000 per month. Point *B* represents the *second* row of the table, and so on. Notice that all of these points lie along a *straight line*.

	Advertising Expenditures ($1,000 per Month)	Sales ($1,000 per Month)
TABLE A.1		
Advertising and Sales at Len & Harry's		
	2	24
	3	27
	6	36
	7	39
	11	51
	12	54

STRAIGHT-LINE GRAPHS

You'll encounter straight-line graphs often in economics, so it's important to understand one special property they possess: The "rate of change" of one variable compared with the other is always the same. For example, look at what happens as we move from point A to point B: Advertising rises by $1,000 (from $2,000 to $3,000), while sales rise by $3,000 (from $24,000 to $27,000). If you study the graph closely, you'll see that anywhere along this line, whenever advertising increases by $1,000, sales increase by $3,000. Or, if we define a "unit" as "one thousand dollars," we can say that every time advertising increases by one unit, sales rise by three units. So the "rate of change" is three units of sales for every one unit of advertising.

The rate of change of the *vertically* measured variable for a one-unit change in the *horizontally* measured variable is also called the *slope* of the line. The slope of the line in Figure A.1 is three, and it remains three no matter where along the line we measure it. For example, make sure you can see that from point C to point D, advertising rises by one unit and sales rise by three units.

What if we had wanted to determine the slope of this line by comparing points D and E, which has advertising rising by four units instead of just one? In that case, we'd have to calculate the rise in one variable *per unit* rise in the other. To do this, we divide the change in the vertically measured variable by the change in the horizontally measured variable.

$$\text{Slope of a straight line} = \frac{\text{Change in vertical variable}}{\text{Change in horizontal variable}}.$$

We can make this formula even simpler by using two shortcuts. First, we can call the variable on the vertical axis "Y" and the variable on the horizontal axis "X." In our case, Y is sales, while X is advertising outlays. Second, we use the Greek letter Δ ("delta") to denote the words "change in." Then, our formula becomes:

$$\text{Slope of straight line} = \frac{\Delta Y}{\Delta X}.$$

Let's apply this formula to get the slope as we move from point D to point E, so that advertising (X) rises from 7 units to 11 units. This is an increase of 4, so $\Delta X = 4$. For this move, sales rise from 39 to 51, an increase of 12, so $\Delta Y = 12$. Applying our formula,

$$\text{Slope} = \frac{\Delta Y}{\Delta X} = \frac{12}{4} = 3.$$

This is the same value for the slope that we found earlier. Not surprising, since it's a straight line and a straight line has the same slope everywhere. The particular pair of points we choose for our calculation doesn't matter.

CURVED LINES

Although many of the relationships you'll encounter in economics have straight-line graphs, many others do

FIGURE A.1

A Graph of Advertising and Sales

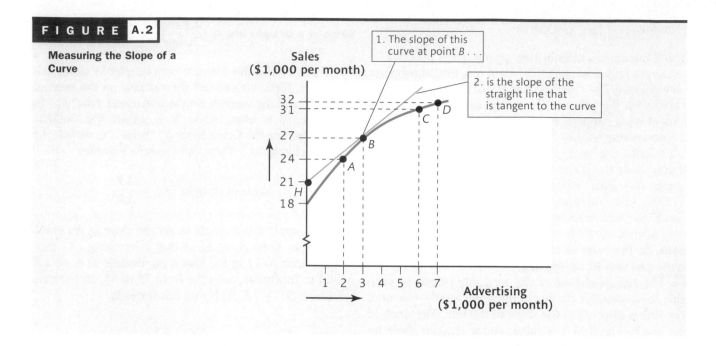

FIGURE A.2

Measuring the Slope of a Curve

not. Figure A.2 shows *another* possible relationship between advertising and sales that we might have found from a different set of data. As you can see, the line is curved. But as advertising rises, the curve gets flatter and flatter. Here, as before, each time we spend another $1,000 on advertising, sales rise. But now, the rise in sales seems to get smaller and smaller. This means that the *slope* of the curve is *itself changing* as we move along this curve. In fact, the slope is getting smaller.

How can we measure the slope of a curve? First, note that since the slope is different at every point along the curve, we aren't really measuring the slope of "the curve" but the slope of the curve *at a specific point along it*. How can we do this? By drawing a *tangent line*—a straight line that touches the curve at just one point and that has the same slope as the curve at that point. For example, in the figure, a tangent line has been drawn for point *B*. To measure the slope of this tangent line, we can compare any two points on it, say, *H* and *B*, and calculate the slope as we would for any straight line. Moving from point *H* to point *B*, we are moving from 0 to 3 on the horizontal axis ($\Delta X = 3$) and from 21 to 27 on the vertical axis ($\Delta Y = 6$). Thus, the slope of the tangent line—which is the same as the slope of the curved line at point *B*—is

$$\frac{\Delta Y}{\Delta X} = \frac{6}{3} = 2.$$

This says that, at point *B*, the rate of change is two units of sales for every one unit of advertising. Or, going back to dollars, the rate of change is $2,000 in sales for every $1,000 spent on advertising.

The curve in Figure A.2 slopes everywhere upward, reflecting a positive relationship between the variables. But a curved line can also slope downward to illustrate a negative relationship between variables, or slope first one direction and then the other. You'll see plenty of examples of each type of curve in later chapters, and you'll learn how to interpret each one as it's presented.

LINEAR EQUATIONS

Let's go back to the straight-line relationship between advertising and sales, as shown in Table A.1. What if you need to know how much in sales the firm could expect if it spent $5,000 on advertising next month? What if it spent $8,000, or $9,000? It would be nice to be able to answer questions like this without having to pull out tables and graphs to do it. As it turns out, anytime the relationship you are studying has a straight-line graph, it is easy to figure out an equation for the entire relationship—a *linear equation*. You then can use the equation to answer any such question that might be put to you.

All straight lines have the same general form. If *Y* stands for the variable on the vertical axis and *X* for the variable on the horizontal axis, every straight line has an equation of the form

$$Y = a + bX,$$

where a stands for some number and b for another number. The number a is called the vertical *intercept*, because it marks the point where the graph of this equation hits (intercepts) the vertical axis; this occurs when X takes the value zero. (If you plug $X = 0$ into the equation, you will see that, indeed, $Y = a$.) The number b is

the slope of the line, telling us how much Y will change every time X changes by one unit. To confirm this, note that as X increases from 0 to 1, Y goes from a to $a + b$. The number b is therefore the change in Y corresponding to a one-unit change in X—exactly what the slope of the graph should tell us.

If b is a positive number, a one-unit increase in X causes Y to *increase* by b units, so the graph of our line would slope upward, as illustrated by the line in the upper left panel of Figure A.3. If b is a negative number, then a one-unit increase in X will cause Y to *decrease* by

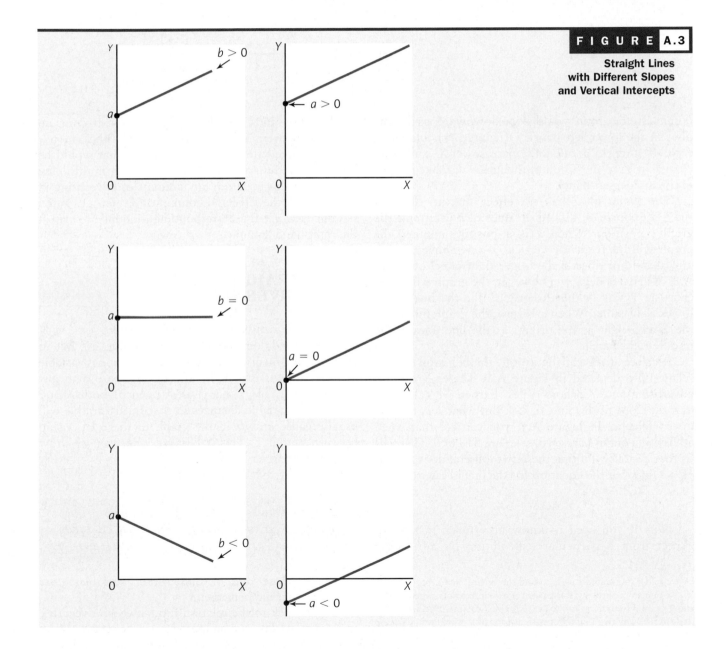

FIGURE A.3

Straight Lines with Different Slopes and Vertical Intercepts

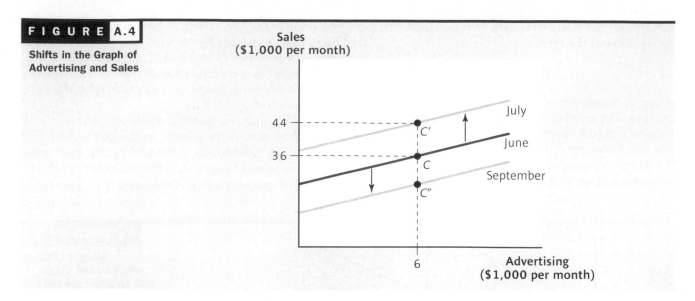

FIGURE A.4

Shifts in the Graph of Advertising and Sales

b units, so the graph would slope downward, as the line does in the lower left panel. Of course, *b* could equal zero. If it does, a one-unit increase in *X* causes no change in *Y*, so the graph of the line is flat, like the line in the middle left panel.

The value of *a* has no effect on the slope of the graph. Instead, different values of *a* determine the graph's position. When *a* is a positive number, the graph will intercept the vertical *Y*-axis above the origin, as the line does in the upper right panel of Figure A.3. When *a* is negative, however, the graph will intercept the *Y*-axis *below* the origin, like the line in the lower right panel. When *a* is zero, the graph intercepts the *Y*-axis right at the origin, as the line does in the middle right panel.

Let's see if we can figure out the equation for the relationship depicted in Figure A.1. There, *X* denotes advertising and *Y* denotes sales. Earlier, we calculated that the slope of this line, *b*, is 3. But what is *a*, the vertical intercept? In Figure A.1, you can see that when advertising outlays are zero, sales are $18,000. That tells us that $a = 18$.[2] Putting these two observations together, we find that the equation for the line in Figure A.1 is

$$Y = 18 + 3X.$$

Now if you need to know how much in sales to expect from a particular expenditure on advertising

(both in thousands of dollars), you'd be able to come up with an answer: You'd simply multiply the amount spent on advertising by 3, add 18, and that would be your sales in thousands of dollars. To confirm this, plug in for *X* in this equation any amount of advertising in dollars from the left-hand column of Table A.1. You'll see that you get the corresponding amount of sales in the right-hand column.

HOW STRAIGHT LINES AND CURVES SHIFT

So far, we've focused on relationships where some variable *Y* depends on a single other variable, *X*. But in many of our theories, we recognize that some variable of interest to us is actually affected by more than just one other variable. When *Y* is affected by both *X* and some third variable, changes in that third variable will usually cause a *shift* in the graph of the relationship between *X* and *Y*. This is because whenever we draw the graph between *X* and *Y*, we are holding fixed every other variable that might possibly affect *Y*.

> *A graph between two variables* X *and* Y *is only a picture of their relationship when all other variables affecting* Y *are held constant.*

But suppose one of these other variables *does* change? What happens then?

Think back to the relationship between advertising and sales. Earlier, we supposed sales depend only on advertising. But suppose we make an important discovery: Ice cream sales are *also* affected by how hot the

---

[2] We could also use direct logic to find the vertical intercept. In Figure A.1, locate any point—we'll use point *A* as our example, where $X = 2$ and $Y = 24$. From this point, to get to the vertical intercept, we'd have to decrease *X* by two units. But with a slope of 3, a two-unit decrease in *X* will cause a six-unit decrease in *Y*. Therefore, *Y* will decrease from 24 to 18. Summing up, we've found that when $X = 0$, $Y = 18$, so our vertical intercept is 18.

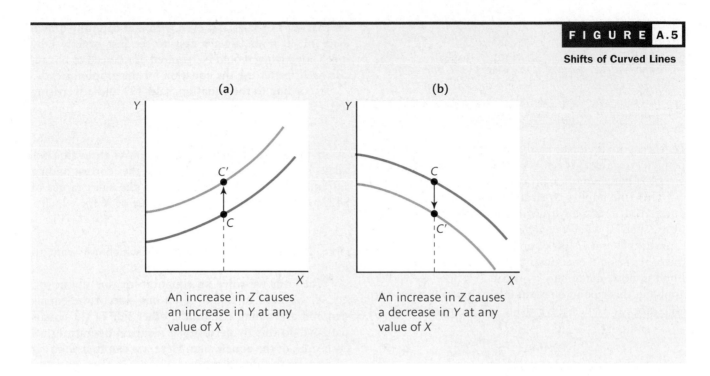

FIGURE A.5

Shifts of Curved Lines

(a)

An increase in Z causes an increase in Y at any value of X

(b)

An increase in Z causes a decrease in Y at any value of X

weather is. What's more, all of the data in Table A.1 on which we previously based our analysis turns out to have been from the month of June in different years, when the average temperature in Texas is 80 degrees. What's going to happen in July, when the average temperature rises to 100 degrees?

In Figure A.4 we've redrawn the graph from Figure A.1, this time labeling the line "June." Often, a good way to determine how a graph will shift is to perform a simple experiment like this: Put your pencil tip anywhere on the graph labeled June—let's say at point C. Now ask the following question: If I hold advertising constant at $6,000, do I expect to sell more or less ice cream as temperature rises in July? If you expect to sell more, then the amount of sales corresponding to $6,000 of advertising will be *above* point C, at a point such as C' (pronounced "C prime"), representing sales of $44,000. From this, we can tell that the graph will *shift upward* as temperature rises. In September, however, when temperatures fall, the amount of sales corresponding to $6,000 in advertising would be less than it is at point C. It would be shown by a point such as C" (pronounced "C double-prime"). In that case, the graph would shift downward.

The same procedure works well whether the original graph slopes upward or downward and whether it is a straight line or a curved one. Figure A.5 sketches two examples. In panel (a), an increase in some third variable, Z, increases the value of Y for each value of X,

so the graph of the relationship between X and Y shifts upward as Z increases. We often phrase it this way: "An increase in Z causes an increase in Y, *at any value of X*." In panel (b), an increase in Z *decreases* the value of Y, at any value of X, so the graph of the relationship between X and Y shifts *downward* as Z increases.

You'll notice that in Figures A.4 and A.5, the original line is darker, while the new line after the shift is drawn in a lighter shade. We'll use this convention—a lighter shade for the new line after a shift—throughout this book.

SHIFTS VERSUS MOVEMENTS ALONG A LINE

If you look back at Figure A.1, you'll see that when advertising increases (say, from $2,000 to $3,000), we *move along* our line, from point A to point B. But you've just learned that when average temperature changes, the entire line *shifts*. This may seem strange to you. After all, in both cases, an independent variable changes (either advertising or temperature). Why should we move *along* the line in one case and *shift* it in the other?

The reason for the difference is that in one case (advertising), the independent variable is *in our graph*, measured along one of the axes. When an independent variable in the graph changes, we simply move along the line. In the other case (temperature), the independent variable does *not* appear in our graph. Instead, it's been in the background, being held constant.

Here's a very simple—but crucial—rule:

> *Suppose Y is the dependent variable, which is measured on one of the axes in a graph. If the independent variable **measured on the other axis changes**, we move along the line. But if **any other** independent variable changes, the **entire line shifts**.*

Be sure you understand the phrase "any other independent variable." It refers to any variable that actually *affects* Y but is *not* measured on either axis in the graph.

This rule applies to straight lines as well as curved lines. And it applies even in more complicated situations, such as when *two different* lines are drawn in the same graph, and a shift of one causes a movement along the other. (You'll encounter this situation in Chapter 3.) But for now, make sure you can see how we've been applying this rule in our example, where the three variables are total sales, advertising, and temperature.

SOLVING EQUATIONS

When we first derived the equation for the relationship between advertising and sales, we wanted to know what level of sales to expect from different amounts of advertising. But what if we're asked a slightly different question? Suppose, this time, you are told that the sales committee has set an ambitious goal of $42,000 for next month's sales. The treasurer needs to know how much to budget for advertising, and you have to come up with the answer.

Since we know how advertising and sales are related, we ought to be able to answer this question. One way is just to look at the graph in Figure A.1. There, we could first locate sales of $42,000 on the vertical axis. Then, if we read over to the line and then down, we find the amount of advertising that would be necessary to gener-

ate that level of sales. Yet even with that carefully drawn diagram, it is not always easy to see just exactly how much advertising would be required. If we need to be precise, we'd better use the equation for the graph instead.

According to the equation, sales (Y) and advertising (X) are related as follows:

$$Y = 18 + 3X.$$

In the problem before us, we know the value for sales, and we need to solve for the corresponding amount of advertising. Substituting the sales target of $42, for Y, we need to find that value of X for which

$$42 = 18 + 3X.$$

Here, X is the unknown value for which we want to solve.

Whenever we solve an equation for one unknown, say, X, we need to *isolate* X on one side of the equals sign and everything else on the other side of the equals sign. We do this by performing identical operations on both sides of the equals sign. Here, we can first subtract 18 from both sides, getting

$$24 = 3X.$$

We can then divide both sides by 3 and get

$$8 = X.$$

This is our answer. If we want to achieve sales of $42,000, we'll need to spend $8,000 on advertising.

Of course, not all relationships are linear, so this technique will not work in every situation. But no matter what the underlying relationship, the idea remains the same:

> *To solve for X in any equation, rearrange the equation, following the rules of algebra, so that X appears on one side of the equals sign and everything else in the equation appears on the other side.*

Scarcity, Choice, and Economic Systems

What does it cost you to go to the movies? If you answered nine or ten dollars, because that is the price of a movie ticket, then you are leaving out a lot. Most of us are used to thinking of "cost" as the money we must pay for something. A Big Mac costs $3.15, a new Toyota Corolla costs $16,000, and the baby-sitter costs $8.00 an hour. Certainly, the money we pay for a good or service is a *part* of its cost. But economics takes a broader view of costs, recognizing monetary as well as non-monetary components.

THE CONCEPT OF OPPORTUNITY COST

The total cost of any choice we make—buying a car, producing a computer, or even reading a book—is everything we must *give up* when we take that action. This cost is called the *opportunity cost* of the action, because we give up the opportunity to have other desirable things.

> The **opportunity cost** of any choice is what we must forego when we make that choice.

Opportunity cost What is given up when taking an action or making a choice.

Opportunity cost is the most accurate and complete concept of cost—the one we should use when making our own decisions or analyzing the decisions of others.

Opportunity Cost for Individuals

Virtually every action we take as individuals uses up scarce money, scarce time, or both. This money or time *could* have been used for other things that you value. Thus, the true cost of any choice you make—the *opportunity cost*—is everything you actually sacrifice in making the choice.

Suppose, for example, it's 8 P.M. on a weeknight and you're spending a couple of hours reading this chapter. As authors, that thought makes us very happy, especially because we know there are many other things you could be doing: going to a movie, having dinner with friends, playing ping pong, earning some extra money, watching TV. . . . But, assuming you're still reading—and you haven't just run out the door to do something else—let's relate this to opportunity cost.

What *is* the opportunity cost of reading this chapter? Is it *all* of those other possibilities we've listed? Not really, because if you weren't reading for these two hours, you'd probably have time to do only *one* of them. And you'd no doubt choose whichever one among these alternatives you regarded as best. So, by reading, you sacrifice only the best choice among the alternatives that you could be doing instead.

> *When the alternatives to a choice are mutually exclusive, only the* next best *choice—the one that would actually be chosen—is used to determine the opportunity cost of the choice.*

For many choices, a large part of the opportunity cost is the money sacrificed. If you spend $15 on a new DVD, you have to part with $15, which is money you could have spent on something else (whatever the best choice among the alternatives turned out to be). But for other choices, money may be only a small part, or no part, of what is sacrificed. If you walk your dog a few blocks, it will cost you time but not money. Still, economists often like to attach a monetary value even to the parts of opportunity cost that *don't* involve money. By translating a sacrifice into a dollar value, we can express the opportunity cost of a choice as a single number, albeit a roughly estimated one. That, in turn, enables us to compare the cost of a choice with its benefits, which we also often express in dollars.

An Example: The Opportunity Cost of College

Let's consider an important choice you've made for this year: to attend college. What is the opportunity cost of this choice? A good starting point is to look at the actual monetary costs—the annual out-of-pocket expenses borne by you or your family for a year of college. Table 1 shows the College Board's estimates of these expenses for the average student (ignoring scholarships). For example, the third column of the table shows that the average in-state resident at a four-year state college pays $5,491 in tuition and fees, $894 for books and supplies, $6,636 for room and board, and $2,545 for transportation and other expenses, for a total of $15,566 per year.

So, is that dollar figure the opportunity cost of a year of college for the average student at a public institution? Not really. Even if the entries are what you or your family actually pays out for college, there are two problems with using these figures to calculate the opportunity cost.

TABLE 1 Average Cost of a Year of College, 2005–2006	Type of Institution	Two-year Public	Four-year Public	Four-year Private
	Tuition and fees	$ 2,191	$ 5,491	$21,236
	Books and supplies	$ 801	$ 894	$ 904
	Room and board	$ 5,909	$ 6,636	$ 7,791
	Transportation and other expenses	$ 2,791	$ 2,545	$ 1,986
	Total out-of-pocket costs	$11,692	$15,566	$31,917

Source: Trends in College Pricing, 2005, The College Board, New York, NY.
Notes: Averages are enrollment-weighted by institution, to reflect the average experience among students across the United States. Average tuition and fees at public institutions are for in-state residents only. Room and board charges are for students living on campus at four-year institutions, and off-campus (but not with parents) at two-year institutions.

First, the table includes some expenses that are *not* part of the opportunity cost of college. For example, room and board is something you'd need no matter *what* your choice. That's obvious if, as part of your best choice among the alternatives, you'd have lived in an apartment and paid rent. But even the alternative of living in your old room at home doesn't eliminate this cost: Your family *could* have rented out the room to someone else, or used it for some other valuable purpose. Either way, something is sacrificed. Let's suppose, for simplicity, that if you weren't in college, you or your family would be paying the same amount for room and board as your college charges. Then, the $6,636 for room and board expense should be excluded from the opportunity cost of going to college. And the same applies to transportation and other expenses, at least the part that you would have spent anyway even if you weren't in college.

Now we're left with payments for tuition and fees, and for books and supplies. For an in-state resident going to a state college, this averages $5,491 + $894 = $6,385 per year. Since these dollars are paid only when you attend college, they represent something sacrificed for that choice and are part of its opportunity cost. Costs like these—for which dollars are actually paid out—are called **explicit costs**, and they are *part* of the opportunity cost.

But college also has **implicit costs**—sacrifices for which no money changes hands. The biggest sacrifice in this category is *time*. But what is that time worth? That depends on what you *would* be doing if you weren't in school. For many students, the alternative would be working full-time at a job, something most students can't manage while attending college. If you are one of these students, attending college requires the sacrifice of the income you *could* have earned at a job—a sacrifice we call *foregone income*.

How much income is foregone when you go to college for a year? In 2005, the average total of an 18- to 24-year-old high school graduate who worked full-time was about $22,000. If we assume that only nine months of work must be sacrificed to attend college, and that you could still work full-time in the summer, then foregone income is about 9/12 of $22,000, or $16,500.

Summing the explicit and implicit costs gives us a rough estimate of the opportunity cost of a year in college. For a public institution, we have $6,385 in explicit costs and $16,500 in implicit costs, giving us a total of $22,885 per year. Notice that this is significantly greater than the total charges estimated by the college board we calculated earlier. When you consider paying this opportunity cost for four years, its magnitude might surprise you. Without financial aid in the form of tuition grants or other fee reductions, the average in-state resident will sacrifice about $90,000 to get a bachelor's degree at a state college and about $153,000 at a private one.

Our analysis of the opportunity cost of college is an example of a general, and important, principle:

Explicit cost The dollars sacrificed—and actually paid out—for a choice.
Implicit cost The value of something sacrificed when no direct payment is made.

> *The opportunity cost of a choice includes both* **explicit costs** *and* **implicit costs.**

A Brief Digression: Is College the Right Choice?

Before you start questioning your choice to be in college, there are a few things to remember. First, for many students, scholarships reduce the costs of college below those in our example. Second, in addition to its high cost, college has substantial *benefits*, including financial ones. In fact, over a 40-year work life, the average college graduate will make about \$2.5 million, which is about a million dollars *more* than the average high school graduate.[1]

True, much of that income is earned in the future, and a dollar gained years from now is worth less than a dollar spent today. Also, *some* of the higher earnings of college graduates result from the personal characteristics of people who are likely to attend college, rather than from the education or the degree itself. But even when we make reasonable adjustments for these facts, attending college appears to be one of the best *financial* investments you can make.[2]

Finally, remember that we've left out of our discussion many important aspects of this choice that would be harder to estimate in dollar terms, but could be very important to you. Do you *enjoy* being at college? If so, your enjoyment is an added benefit, even though it may be difficult to value that enjoyment in dollars. (Of course, if you *hate* college and are only doing it for the financial rewards or to satisfy your parents, that's an implicit cost—which is part of your opportunity cost—that we haven't included.)

Time Is Money

Our analysis of the opportunity cost of college points out a general principle, one understood by economists and noneconomists alike. It can be summed up in the expression, "Time is money." Those three words contain a profound truth: The sacrifice of time often means the sacrifice of money—in particular, the money that *could* have been earned during that time.

As a rule, economists have a simple technique to estimate the dollar value of time. First, we assume that working additional hours for pay is the best among the alternatives to the choice being considered. Then, each hour sacrificed for the choice is multiplied by the individual's hourly wage. (Even someone paid a monthly salary has an implied hourly wage: their total monthly income divided by the total monthly hours of work.)

For example, suppose Jessica is a freelance writer who decides to see a movie. The ticket price is \$10, and the entire activity—including getting there and back—will take three hours out of her evening. What is the opportunity cost of seeing this movie? Let's suppose that Jessica earns \$20 per hour as a freelance writer. We'll also assume that she can choose to take on additional work at that same wage rate. Therefore, each hour that Jessica chooses *not* to work causes her to give up \$20 in earnings. Then for Jessica, the opportunity cost is the sum of the explicit costs (\$10 for the ticket) and the implicit costs (\$20 × 3 hrs = \$60 in foregone income), giving her a total opportunity cost of \$70.

The idea that a movie "costs" \$70 might seem absurd to you. But if you think about it, \$70 is a much better estimate than \$10 of what the movie costs for Jessica. After all, she gives up three hours that *could* have been spent working on an article that, on average, would provide her with another \$60. Thus, in a very real sense, Jessica sacrifices \$70 for the movie.[2]

Our examples about the cost of college and the cost of a movie point out an important lesson about opportunity cost:

[1] Jennifer C. Day and Eric C. Newburger, "The Big Payoff: Educational Attainment and Synthetic Estimates of Work-Life Earnings," in *Current Population Reports* (U.S. Census Bureau), July 2002.
[2] If you are using the microeconomics or combined micro/macro version of this book, we'll revisit the value of college as an investment in the Using the Theory section of Chapter 13. In that chapter, you'll also learn the general technique economists use to compare future earnings with current costs.

> *The explicit (direct money) cost of a choice may only be a part—and sometimes a small part—of the opportunity cost of a choice.*

Indeed, the higher an individual's income, the less important is the direct money cost, and the more important the time cost of an activity. For example, suppose that Samantha is an attorney who bills out her time at $100 per hour. For her, the opportunity cost of the same movie—which entails three hours and the ticket—would be $310 dollars!

You might wonder if Samantha would ever see a movie at such a high cost. The answer for Samantha is the same as for Jessica or anyone else: yes, as long as the benefits of the movie are greater than the explicit and implicit costs. It's easy to see why Samantha might decide to see a movie. Imagine that she begins taking on more and more clients, working longer and longer hours, and earning more and more income. At some point, she will realize that leisure activities like movies are very important, while earning more income will seem less important. And taking time off to see a movie might be well worth sacrificing the $310 that she could have had.

The concept of opportunity cost also explains why you'll never see a rebate coupon like the doctored one in Figure 1. For most of us, the opportunity cost—including the cost of the stamp and the value of the time sacrificed to follow the instructions—is greater than the $1 that is being offered.

OPPORTUNITY COST AND SOCIETY

For an individual, opportunity cost arises from the scarcity of time or money. But for society as a whole, opportunity cost arises from a different source: the scarcity of society's *resources*. Our desire for goods is limitless, but we have limited resources to produce them. Therefore,

---

FIGURE 1

Something You'll Never See

The opportunity cost of this rebate (the value of the time lost plus the cost of a postage stamp) would exceed its benefit (one dollar).

We're sending some money to you!

$1 CASH BACK

OFFICAL REBATE MAIL-IN REDEMPTION FORM

Please complete the following information:
Name_____
Address:_____
City:_____State:_____Zip:_____

Please mail this card along with the original UPC code and a copy of the receipt to the address on the back. Please allow 6-8 weeks to receive your rebate check.

virtually all production carries an opportunity cost: To produce more of one thing, society must shift resources away from producing something else.

For example, we'd all agree that we'd like better health for our citizens. What would be needed to achieve this goal? Perhaps more frequent medical checkups for more people and greater access to top-flight medicine when necessary. These, in turn, would require more and better-trained doctors, more hospital buildings and laboratories, and more high-tech medical equipment. In order for us to produce these goods and services, we would have to pull resources—land, labor, capital, and entrepreneurship—out of producing other things that we also enjoy. The opportunity cost of improved health care, then, consists of those other goods and services we would have to do without.

An Example: Military versus Consumer Goods

Let's build a simple model to help us understand the opportunity cost we must pay to have more of something. To be specific, we'll look at a society's choice between producing military goods (represented here by tanks) and producing consumer goods (represented by wheat).

Table 2 lists some possible combinations of yearly tank production and yearly wheat production this society could manage, given its available resources and the currently available production technology. For example, the first row of the table tells us what would happen if all available resources were devoted to wheat production and no resources at all to producing tanks. The resulting quantity of wheat—1 million bushels per year—is the most this society could possibly produce. In the second row, society moves enough resources into tank production to make 1,000 tanks per year. This leaves fewer resources for wheat production, which now declines to 950,000 bushels per year. As we go down the left column, tank production increases by increments of 1,000. The right column shows us the maximum quantity of wheat that can be produced for each given quantity of tanks. Finally, look at the last row. It shows us that when society throws all of its resources into tank production (with none for wheat), tank production is 5,000 while wheat production is zero.

The table gives us a quantitative measure of opportunity cost for this society. For example, suppose this society currently produces 1,000 tanks per year, along with

TABLE 2 Production of Tanks and Wheat	Tank Production (number per year)	Wheat Production (bushels per year)
	0	1,000,000
	1,000	950,000
	2,000	850,000
	3,000	700,000
	4,000	400,000
	5,000	0

950,000 bushels of wheat (the second row). What would be the opportunity cost of producing another 1,000 tanks? Moving down to the third row, we see that producing another 1,000 tanks (for a total of 2,000) would require wheat production to drop from 950,000 to 850,000 bushels, a decrease of 100,000 bushels. Thus, the opportunity cost of 1,000 more tanks is 100,000 bushels of wheat. In this simple model with just two goods, the opportunity cost of having more of one good is measured in the units of the other good that must be sacrificed.

Production Possibilities Frontiers

We can see opportunity cost even more clearly in Figure 2, where the data in Table 2 has been plotted on a graph. In the figure, tank production is measured along the horizontal axis, and wheat production along the vertical axis. Each of the six points labeled *A* through *F* corresponds to a combination of the two goods as given by one of the rows of the table. For example, point *B* represents the combination in the second row: 1,000 tanks and 950,000 bushels of wheat. When we connect these points with a smooth line, we get a curve called society's **production possibilities frontier (PPF)**. Specifically, this PPF tells us the maximum quantity of wheat that can be produced for each quantity of tanks produced. Alternatively, it tells us the maximum number of tanks that can be produced for each different quantity of wheat. Positions outside the frontier are unattainable with the technology and resources at the economy's disposal. Society's choices are limited to points on or inside the PPF.

Production possibilities frontier (PPF) A curve showing all combinations of two goods that can be produced with the resources and technology currently available.

Now recall our earlier example of a change in production in Table 2: When tank production increased from 1,000 to 2,000, wheat production decreased from 950,000 to 850,000. In the graph, this change would be represented by a movement along the PPF from point *B* to point *C*. We're moving rightward (1,000 more tanks) and also downward (100,000 fewer bushels of wheat). Thus, the opportunity cost of 1,000 more tanks can be viewed as the vertical drop along the PPF as we move from point *B* to point *C*.

FIGURE 2

The Production Possibilities Frontier

Bushels of Wheat per Year

At point *A*, all resources are used for wheat.

Moving from point *A* to point *B* requires shifting resources out of wheat and into tanks.

At point *F*, all resources are used for tanks.

1,000,000
950,000
850,000
700,000

400,000

A *B*
C
D
W
E
F

1,000 2,000 3,000 4,000 5,000

Number of Tanks per Year

Increasing Opportunity Cost

Suppose we have arrived at point *C* and society then decides to produce still more tanks. Once again, resources must be shifted into tank production to make an additional 1,000 of them, moving from point *C* to point *D*. This time, however, there is an even *greater opportunity cost*: Production of wheat falls from 850,000 to 700,000 bushels, a sacrifice of 150,000 bushels. The opportunity cost of 1,000 more tanks has risen. Graphically, the vertical drop along the curve is greater for the same move rightward.

You can see that as we continue to increase tank production by increments of 1,000—moving from point *C* to point *D* to point *E* to point *F*—the opportunity cost of producing an additional 1,000 tanks keeps rising, until the last 1,000 tanks costs us 400,000 bushels of wheat. (You can also see this in the table, by running down the numbers in the right column. Each time tank production rises by 1,000, wheat production falls by more and more.)

The behavior of opportunity cost described here—the more tanks we produce, the greater the opportunity cost of producing still more—applies to a wide range of choices facing society. It can be generalized as the *law of increasing opportunity cost*.

> *According to the law of increasing opportunity cost, the more of something we produce, the greater the opportunity cost of producing even more of it.*

The law of increasing opportunity cost causes the PPF to have a concave (upside-down bowl) shape, becoming steeper as we move rightward and downward. That's because the slope of the PPF—the change in the quantity of wheat divided by the change in the quantity of tanks—can be interpreted as the change in wheat *per additional tank*. If we remove the minus sign from this slope and consider just its absolute value, it tells us the opportunity cost of *one more tank*.

Now—as we've seen—this opportunity cost increases as we move rightward. Therefore, the absolute value of the PPF's slope must rise as well. The PPF gets steeper and steeper, giving us the concave shape we see in Figure 2.[3]

Why should there be a law of increasing opportunity cost? Why must it be that the more of something we produce, the greater the opportunity cost of producing still more? Because most resources—by their very nature—are better suited to some purposes than to others. If the economy were operating at point *A*, for example, we'd be using *all* of our resources for wheat, even those that are much better suited to make tanks. People who would be better at factory work than farming would nevertheless be pressed into working on farms. And we'd be growing wheat on all the land available, even land that would be fine for a tank factory but awful for growing crops.

Now, as we begin to move rightward along the PPF, say from *A* to *B*, we would shift resources out of wheat production and into tank production. But we would first shift those resources *best suited* to tank production—and least suited for wheat. When these resources are shifted, an additional thousand tanks causes only a small

---

[3] You might be wondering if the law of increasing opportunity cost applies in both directions. That is, does the opportunity cost of producing more wheat increase as we produce more of it? The answer is yes, as you'll be asked to find in an end-of-chapter problem.

drop in wheat production. This is why, at first, the PPF is very flat: a small vertical drop for the rightward movement.

As we continue moving rightward, however, we are forced to shift away from wheat production resources that are less and less suited to tanks and more and more suited to wheat. As a result, the PPF becomes steeper. Finally, we arrive at point *F*, where all resources—no matter how well suited for wheat—are used to make tanks.

The principle of increasing opportunity cost applies to most of society's production choices, not just that between wheat and tanks. If we look at society's choice between food and oil, we would find that some land is better suited to growing food and other land is better suited to drilling for oil. As we continue to produce more oil, we would find ourselves drilling on land that is less and less suited to producing oil, but better and better for producing food. The opportunity cost of producing additional oil will therefore increase. The same principle applies if we want to produce more health care, more education, more automobiles, or more computers: The more of something we produce, the greater the opportunity cost of producing still more.

THE SEARCH FOR A FREE LUNCH

This chapter has argued that every decision to produce *more* of something requires us to pay an opportunity cost by producing less of something else. Nobel Prize–winning economist Milton Friedman summarized this idea in his famous remark, "There is no such thing as a free lunch." Friedman was saying that, even if a meal is provided free of charge to someone, society still uses up resources to provide it. Therefore, a "free lunch" is not *really* free: Society pays an opportunity cost by not producing other things with those resources. Therefore, some members of society will have to make do with less.

The same logic applies to other supposedly "free" goods and services. From society's point of view, there is no such thing as free Internet service, free broadcast television, or free medical care, even if those who enjoy these things don't pay for them as individuals. Providing any of these things requires us to sacrifice *other* things, as illustrated by a movement along society's PPF.

But there are some situations that seem, at first glance, to violate Freidman's dictum. Let's explore them.

Productive Inefficiency

What if an economy is not living up to its productive potential, but is instead operating *inside* its PPF? For example, in Figure 2, suppose we are currently operating at point *W*, where we are producing 2,000 tanks and 400,000 bushels of wheat. Then we could move from point *W* to point *E* and produce 2,000 more tanks, with no sacrifice of wheat. Or, starting at point *W*, we could move to point *C* (more wheat with no sacrifice of tanks), or to a point like *D* (more of *both* wheat and tanks).

But why would an economy ever operate inside its PPF?

One possibility is that, although all of its resources are being used, they are not being used in the most productive way. Suppose, for example, that many people who could be outstanding wheat farmers are instead making tanks, and many who would be great at tank production are instead stuck on farms. Then switching people from one job to the other could enable us to have more of *both* tanks *and* wheat.

That is, because of the mismatch of workers and jobs, we would be *inside* the PPF at a point like *W*. Creating better job matches would then move us to a point *on* the PPF (such as point *E*).

Economists use the phrase *productive inefficiency* to describe this type of situation that puts us inside our PPF.

Productively inefficient A situation in which more of at least one good can be produced without sacrificing the production of any other good.

> A *firm, an industry, or an entire economy is **productively inefficient** if it could produce more of at least one good without pulling resources from the production of any other good.*

The phrase *productive efficiency* means the absence of any productive *in*efficiency. For example, if the computer industry is producing the maximum possible number of computers with the resources it is currently using, we would describe the computer industry as productively efficient. In that case, there would be no way to produce any more computers except to use more resources and shift them from the production of some other good. For an entire *economy* to be productively efficient, there must be no way to produce more of *any* good except by pulling resources from the production of some other good.

Although no firm, industry, or economy is ever 100 percent productively efficient, cases of gross inefficiency are not as common as you might think. When you study microeconomics, you'll learn that business firms have strong incentives to identify and eliminate productive inefficiency, since any waste of resources increases their costs and decreases their profit. When one firm discovers a way to eliminate waste, others quickly follow.

For example, empty seats on an airline flight represent productive inefficiency. Since the plane is making the trip anyway, filling the empty seat would enable the airline to serve more people with the flight (produce more transportation services) without using any additional resources (other than the trivial resources of in-flight snacks). Therefore, more people could fly without sacrificing any other good or service. When American Airlines developed a computer model in the late 1980s to fill its empty seats by altering schedules and fares, the other airlines followed its example very rapidly. And when—in the late 1990s—Priceline.com enabled airlines to auction off empty seats on the Internet, several airlines jumped at the chance and others quickly followed. As a result of this—and similar efforts to eliminate waste in personnel, aircraft, and office space—many cases of productive inefficiency in the airline industry were eliminated.

Starbucks provides a recent example of reducing productive inefficiency.[4] In 2000, it created a special department of "store operations engineering," tasked with analyzing beverage preparation in order to identify and eliminate waste. Among the recommendations that were instituted: rearranging labor within each store, eliminating signatures on small credit-card purchases, and using larger scoops so that iced drinks can be made with one dip into the ice machine instead of two. These and other efforts—all using existing technologies—enabled more coffee drinks to be prepared each day with the same amount of labor and store space, thus eliminating a source of productive inefficiency. (For those in a hurry, the changes also reduced the average wait time from $3\frac{1}{2}$ minutes in 2000 to three minutes in 2006.)

[4] Steven Gray, "Coffee on the Double," *Wall Street Journal*, April 12, 2005.

Economists, logistics experts, and engineers are continually working to identify and design policies to eliminate cases of productive inefficiency. But many instances remain. Does that mean we are freed from having to pay an opportunity cost when we want to produce more of something?

Not necessarily. Many sources of productive inefficiency create benefits for individuals or groups who will resist changes in the status quo. For example, the government currently requires every taxpayer to file a federal tax return. About 40 percent of these returns are so simple that they merely provide the Internal Revenue Service (IRS) with information it already has, and contain calculations that the IRS duplicates anyway, to check for mistakes. Yet each taxpayer in this 40 percent group must spend hours doing his or her own return, or else pay someone to do it. Why not have the IRS send these people filled-out returns, requiring only a signature if they approve?

One economist[5] has estimated that this simple change would save a total of 250 million hours per year (for those who currently fill out their own returns), and $2 billion per year (for those who pay accountants). With resources freed up by this change, we could produce and enjoy more of all the things that we value. But if you reread this paragraph, you can probably guess who might lobby the government to oppose this change, if and when it is seriously considered.

Since political obstacles often make it difficult to reduce inefficiency, producing more of one thing we value typically results in taking resources away from something else we value, rather than getting "free" resources from greater efficiency. Productive inefficiency does create a theoretical possibility for a free lunch. But in practice, it does not offer as many hearty meals as you might think.

Recessions

Another reason an economy might operate inside its PPF is a *recession*—a slow-down in overall economic activity. During recessions, many resources are idle. For one thing, there is widespread *unemployment*—people *want* to work but are unable to find jobs. In addition, factories shut down, so we are not using all of our available capital. An end to the recession would move the economy from a point *inside* its PPF to a point *on* its PPF—using idle resources to produce more goods and services without sacrificing anything.

This simple observation can help us understand an otherwise confusing episode in U.S. economic history. During the early 1940s, after the United States entered World War II and began using massive amounts of resources to produce military goods and services, the standard of living in the United States did *not* decline as we might have expected but actually improved slightly. Why?

When the United States entered the war in 1941, it was still suffering from the Great Depression—the most serious and long-lasting economic downturn in modern history, which began in 1929 and hit most of the developed world. For reasons you will learn when you study macroeconomics, joining the allied war effort helped end the Depression in the United States. As shown in Figure 3, this moved our economy from a point like *A*, *inside* the PPF, to a point like *B*, *on* the frontier. Military production like tanks increased, but so did the production of civilian goods such as wheat. Although there were shortages of some consumer goods, the overall result

---

[5] Austan Goolsbee, "Why Tell the I.R.S. What It Already Knows?" *New York Times*, April 7, 2006.

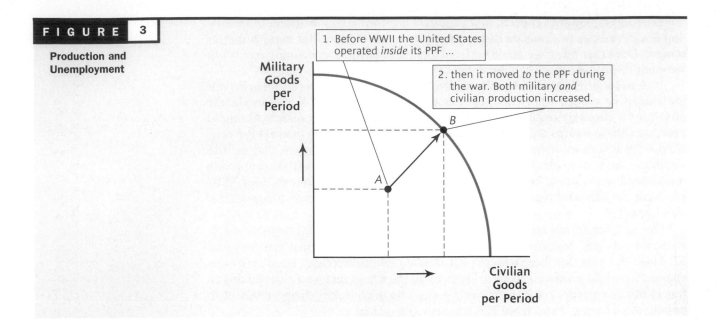

FIGURE 3

Production and Unemployment

1. Before WWII the United States operated *inside* its PPF ...

2. then it moved *to* the PPF during the war. Both military *and* civilian production increased.

Military Goods per Period

Civilian Goods per Period

B

A

False Benefits from Employment Often, you'll hear an evaluation of some economic activity that includes "employment" as one of the benefits. For example, a recent article in the online magazine *Slate*, after discussing the costs of email spam, pointed out that spam also has "a corresponding economic payoff. Anti-spam efforts keep well-paid software engineers employed."[6]

DANGEROUS CURVES

This is usually an error. True, when the economy is in a recession, an increase in employment can be regarded as a gain for those who get jobs. But in most years we are *not* in a recession. And once a recession ends, the software engineers—if not for the spam—would be employed elsewhere. At that point, employment in the spam-fighting industry—far from being a benefit—is actually part of the *opportunity cost* of spam: we sacrifice the goods and services these spam-fighting engineers would otherwise produce.

was a rise in total production and an increase in the material well-being of the average U.S. citizen.

An economic downturn, such as the Great Depression of the 1930s, does seem to offer the possibility of a free lunch. And a war is only one factor that can reverse a downturn. (In fact, no rational nation would ever *choose* war as an economic policy designed to cure a recession, since there are always economically superior alternatives to accomplish this goal.) Still, eliminating a recession is not *entirely* cost-free. When you study macroeconomics, you will learn that policies to cure or avoid recessions can have risks and costs of their own. Of course, we may feel it is worth the possible costs, but they are costs nonetheless. Once again, a truly free lunch is hard to find.

Economic Growth

If the economy is already operating *on* its PPF, we cannot exploit the opportunity to have more of everything by moving *to* it. But what if the PPF itself were to change? Couldn't we then produce more of everything? This is exactly what happens when an economy's productive capacity grows.

[6] Jeff Merron, "Workus Interruptus," *Slate*, posted March 16, 2006, 12:06pm ET.

Many factors contribute to economic growth, but they can be divided into two categories. First, the quantities of available *resources* can increase. An increase in physical capital—more factories, office buildings, tractors, or high-tech medical equipment—enables the economy to produce more of *everything* that uses these tools. The same is true for an increase in human capital—the skills of doctors, engineers, construction workers, software writers, and so on. In thinking about growth from greater resources, economists focus mostly on capital because, over time, increases in the capital stock have contributed more to higher living standards than increases in other resources (such as land or labor).

The second main factor behind economic growth is *technological change*, which enables us to produce more from a *given* quantity of resources. For example, the development of the Internet has enabled people to retrieve information in a few seconds that used to require hours of searching in a library. As a result, teachers, writers, government officials, attorneys, and physicians can produce more of their services without working longer hours.

These two main causes of economic growth—increases in resources and technological change—often go hand in hand. In order for the Internet (a technological change) to be widely used, the economy had to produce and install servers, Internet-capable computers, and fiber-optic cable (increases in capital). In any case, both technological change and increases in the capital stock have the same type of effect on the PPF.

Figure 4 shows three examples of economic growth, and how they might affect the PPF. Panel (a) illustrates the case of a technological change in wheat farming—say, the discovery of a new type of seed that yields more wheat for any given amount of land, labor, and capital. First, look at point *A*, which shows maximum wheat production when *all* of our resources are used to grow wheat, but without the new seeds. The introduction of the new seeds would enable us to grow even *more* wheat with all of our resources than before. For that reason, the vertical intercept of the PPF rises from point *A* to a point like *A'*, where the economy could produce 1,200,000 bushels per year.

Now consider point *F*, where we assume that *none* of our resources would be used to grow wheat, and all would be used to make tanks. The new seeds have no impact on this maximum possible tank production, so introducing them would not change the horizontal intercept of the PPF.

As you can see, the impact of the new seeds is to stretch the PPF upward along the vertical axis. Society could then choose any point along the new PPF. For example, it could move from point *D* on the original PPF to point *H* on the new one. For this move, all of the benefits of the new seeds would be devoted to giving us more wheat, with unchanged production of tanks. Or society could choose to move from point *D* to point *J* where, as you can verify, more of *both* goods are produced. Indeed, a society could choose to take advantage of the new seeds in a surprising way: more tanks and the same quantity of wheat as before. (See if you can identify this point on the new PPF.)

You may be wondering: How does a new type of seed enable greater production of *tanks*? The answer is: After the new, more productive seeds are introduced, society can choose to shift resources out of farming without decreasing wheat production at all. (Although there are smaller quantities of resources in the wheat industry, the new seeds make up for that.) The shifted resources can be used to increase tank production.

One more thing about panel (a): It can also be used to illustrate the change in the PPF from an increase in resources that can be used *only* in wheat farming. For example, an increase in the quantity of farm tractors would shift the vertical intercept of the PPF as in panel (a) but leave the horizontal intercept unchanged because tractors have no direct impact on tank production.

Panel (b) illustrates the opposite type of change in the PPF—from a technological change in producing tanks, or an increase in resources usable only in the tank industry. This time, the *horizontal* intercept of the PPF increases, while the vertical intercept remains unchanged. (Can you explain why?) As before, we could choose to produce more tanks, more wheat, or more of both. (See if you can identify points on the new PPF in panel (b) to illustrate all three cases.)

Finally, panel (c) illustrates the case where technological change occurs in both the wheat and the tank industries, or there is an increase in resources (such as workers or computers) that could be used in either. Now both the horizontal and the vertical intercepts of the PPF increase. But as before, society can choose to locate anywhere along the new PPF, producing more tanks, more wheat, or more of both.

Panels (a) and (b) can be generalized to an important principle about economic growth:

FIGURE 4

Economic Growth and the PPF

All three panels show economic growth from an increase in resources or a technological change. In panel (a), the additional resources or technological advance directly affect only wheat production. However, society can choose to have more wheat and more tanks if it desires, such as at point J. In panel (b), the additional resources or technological advance directly affect only tank production. But once again, society can choose to have more of both goods. In panel (c), the additional resources or technological advance directly affect production of both goods.

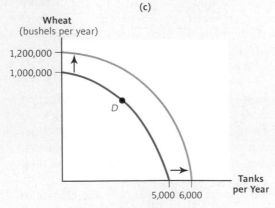

> *A technological change or an increase in the capital stock, even when the direct impact is to increase production of just one type of good, allows us to choose greater production of **all** types of goods.*

This conclusion certainly *seems* like a free lunch. After all, if we can produce more of the things that we value, without having to produce less of anything else, haven't we escaped from paying an opportunity cost?

Yes . . . and no. Figure 4 tells only *part* of the story because it leaves out the steps needed to *create* this shift in the PPF in the first place.

CONSUMPTION VERSUS GROWTH

In the previous section, you saw that increases in capital or technological advances can shift the economy's PPF outward along one or both axes, enabling us to produce more of everything we desire. Clearly, economic growth gives us benefits. But in this section, we'll see that it also entails an opportunity cost.

Consider the case of having more capital. First, note that capital plays a dual role in the economy. On the one hand, capital is a *resource*—a long-lasting tool that we use to produce goods and services. On the other hand, capital is itself a good and needs to be produced using . . . resources. A tractor, for example, is produced using land, labor, entrepreneurship, and *other* capital (a tractor factory and all of the manufacturing equipment inside the factory).

Each year, society must choose how much of its available resources to devote to producing capital. The more long-lasting capital we produce this year, the more we will have available in future years to help us produce the goods and services that we enjoy. But there is a tradeoff: Any resources used to produce capital this year are *not* being used to produce *consumer goods*—food, automobiles, movies, health care, books, and other things that we enjoy right now and that contribute to our current living standard. For example, food (a consumer good) that we produce this year contributes directly to this year's standard of living. But the tractors (a capital good) that we produce this year contribute to our standard of living only indirectly, over time, as the tractors are used to produce more food.

The tradeoff in having more capital is illustrated in Figure 5. In each panel, the quantity of capital goods is measured on the horizontal axis, and consumption goods are measured on the vertical axis. (Notice that we've lumped all capital goods together into one broad category and all consumer goods into another. Our purpose is to illustrate the general tradeoff between one type of good and the other, rather than make statements or measurements involving specific goods.) In each panel, the solid curve shows the economy's PPF this year—the maximum production of one type of good for any given production of the other type.

Now look at panel (a). Point *A* on the PPF shows one choice that society could make this year: relatively high production of consumer goods and little production of capital goods. This choice gives us a relatively high standard of living this year (lots of consumer goods) but adds little to our total stock of capital. As a result, next year's PPF—shown by the dotted line—does shifts outward (because we have more capital), but not by much.

Panel (b) illustrates a different choice. By locating at point *A'* on this year's PPF, we sacrifice considerably more consumption goods now, and shift even more resources toward capital than in panel (a). Living standards are lower this year. But next year, with considerably more capital, the PPF shifts outward even more. As a

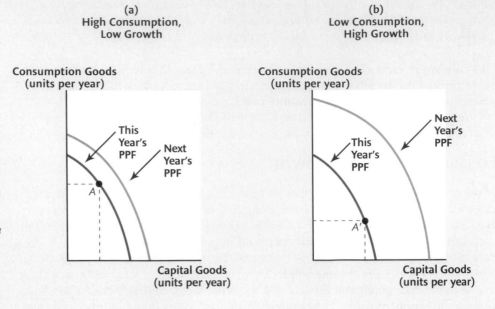

FIGURE 5

How Current Production Affects Economic Growth

In panel (a), production is tilted toward current consumption goods, with relatively few resources devoted to production of capital goods. As a result, in the future, there will not be much of an increase in productive resources, so the PPF will not shift out much in the future. In panel (b), production is tilted more toward capital goods, with a greater sacrifice of current consumption. As a result, there will be a greater increase in productive resources, so the PPF will shift out more in the future.

result, we can choose a point on next year's PPF, with much greater production of consumer goods than we could have chosen in panel (a). Panel (b), while requiring greater sacrifice this year, leads to a greater rise in living standards next year.

A similar tradeoff exists when we look at technological change as a cause of economic growth. Technological change doesn't just "happen." Rather, resources must be used to create it—mostly by the research and development (R&D) departments of large corporations. In 2003, corporations used about $200 billion worth of resources for R&D, and the federal government kicked in about another $100 billion.[7] These resources *could* have been used to produce other things that we'd enjoy right now. For example, doctors who are working in the R&D departments of pharmaceutical companies trying to develop drugs for the future could instead be providing health care to patients right now.

We could illustrate the sacrifice needed for technological change using a pair of PPFs similar to those in Figure 5. The vertical axis would still measure consumer goods production. But on the horizontal axis, instead of capital goods, we'd have a measure of "Research and Development Production"—such as the expenditures made by corporations and government agencies to run scientific laboratories or design new products. And we would come to the same conclusion we came to earlier about economic growth from more capital.

[7] For data on R&D in U.S. industries, see "Increases in U.S. Industrial R&D Expenditures Reported for 2003 Makes Up for Earlier Decline," *National Science Foundation Brief*, December 2005 (at http://www.nsf.gov). For the government's contribution, see "Federal Funds for R&D: FYs 2002, 2003 and 2004" *National Science Foundation* (at http://www.nsf.gov).

> *In order to produce more goods and services in the future, we must shift resources toward R&D and capital production, and away from the production of things we'd enjoy right now.*

We must conclude that although economic growth—at first glance—*appears* to be a free lunch, someone ends up paying the check. In this case, the bill is paid by those members of society who will have to make do with less in the present.

ECONOMIC SYSTEMS

As you read these words—perhaps sitting at home or in the library—you are experiencing a very private moment. It is just you and this book; the rest of the world might as well not exist. Or so it seems. . . .

Actually, even in this supposedly private moment, you are connected to the rest of the world in ways you may not have thought about. In order for you to be reading this book, the authors had to write it. Someone had to edit it, to help make sure that all necessary material was covered and explained as clearly as possible. Someone else had to prepare the graphics. Others had to run the printing presses and the binding machines, and still others had to pack the book, ship it, unpack it, put it on a store shelf, and then sell it to you.

And there's more. People had to manufacture all kinds of goods: paper and ink, the boxes used for shipping, the computers used to keep track of inventory, and so on. It is no exaggeration to say that thousands of people were involved in putting this book in your hands.

And there is still more. The chair or couch on which you are sitting, the light shining on the page, the heat or the air conditioning in the room, the clothes you are wearing—all these things that you are using right now were *produced by somebody else*. So even now, as you sit alone reading this book, you are economically linked to others in hundreds—even thousands—of different ways.

Take a walk in your town or city, and you will see even more evidence of our economic interdependence: People are collecting garbage, helping schoolchildren cross the street, transporting furniture across town, constructing buildings, repairing roads, painting houses. Everyone is producing goods and services for *other people*.

Why is it that so much of what we consume is produced by other people? Why are we all so heavily dependent on each other for our material well-being? Why don't we all—like Robinson Crusoe on his island—produce our own food, clothing, housing, and anything else we desire? And how did it come about that *you*—who did not produce any of these things yourself—are able to consume them?

These are all questions about our *economic system*—the way our economy is organized. Ordinarily, we take our economic system for granted, like the water that runs out of our faucets. But now it's time to begin looking at the plumbing—to learn how our economy serves so many millions of people, enabling them to survive and prosper.

SPECIALIZATION AND EXCHANGE

If we were forced to, many of us could become economically *self-sufficient*. We could stake out a plot of land, grow our own food, make our own clothing, and

Specialization A method of production in which each person concentrates on a limited number of activities.

Exchange The act of trading with others to obtain what we desire.

build our own homes. But in no society is there such extreme self-sufficiency. On the contrary, every economic system has been characterized by two features: (1) **specialization**, in which each of us concentrates on a limited number of productive activities, and (2) **exchange,** in which most of what we desire is obtained by trading with others rather than producing for ourselves.

> *Specialization and exchange enable us to enjoy greater production and higher living standards than would otherwise be possible. As a result, all economies exhibit high degrees of specialization and exchange.*

There are three reasons why specialization and exchange enable us to enjoy greater production. The first has to do with human capabilities: Each of us can learn only so much in a lifetime. By limiting ourselves to a narrow set of tasks—fixing plumbing, managing workers, writing music, or designing Web pages—we are each able to hone our skills and become experts at one or two things instead of remaining amateurs at a lot of things. It is easy to see that an economy of experts will produce more than an economy of amateurs.

A second gain from specialization results from the time needed to switch from one activity to another. When people specialize, and thus spend more time doing one task, there is less unproductive "downtime" from switching activities.

Adam Smith first explained these gains from specialization in his book *An Inquiry into the Nature and Causes of the Wealth of Nations*, published in 1776. Smith explained how specialization within a pin factory dramatically increased the number of pins that could be produced there. In order to make a pin . . .

> *One man draws out the wire, another straightens it, a third cuts it, a fourth points it, a fifth grinds it at the top for receiving the head; to make the head requires three distinct operations; to put it on is a [separate] business, to whiten the pins is another; it is even a trade by itself to put them into the paper; and the important business of making a pin is, in this manner, divided into about eighteen distinct operations, which, in some manufactories, are all performed by distinct hands.*

Smith went on to observe that 10 people, each working separately, might make 200 pins in a day, but through specialization they were able to make 48,000! What is true for a pin factory can be generalized to the entire economy: Total production will increase when workers specialize.

Notice that the gains from specialization we've been discussing—and that Adam Smith described so well—do *not* depend on any differences in individuals' capabilities. Even in a society where initially everyone is *identical* to everyone else, specialization would still yield gains for the two reasons we've discussed: People would develop expertise over time, and there would be less downtime from switching tasks.

Of course, in the real world, workers are *not* identically suited to different kinds of work. Nor are all plots of land, all natural resources, or all types of capital equipment identically suited for different tasks. This observation brings us to the *third* source of gains from specialization—one based on individual differences.

FURTHER GAINS TO SPECIALIZATION: COMPARATIVE ADVANTAGE

Imagine a shipwreck in which there are only two survivors—let's call them Maryanne and Gilligan—who wash up on opposite shores of a deserted island.

	Labor Required for:			TABLE 3
	1 Fish	**1 Cup of Berries**		**Labor Requirements for Fish and Berries**
Maryanne	1 hour	1 hour		
Gilligan	3 hours	$1\frac{1}{2}$ hours		

Initially they are unaware of each other, so each is forced to become completely self-sufficient. And there are only two kinds of food on the island: fish and berries.

Table 3 shows how much time it takes for each castaway to pick a cup of berries or catch one fish. For simplicity, we'll assume that the time requirement remains constant no matter how much time is devoted to these activities.

On one side of the island, Maryanne finds that it takes her 1 hour to catch a fish and 1 hour to pick one cup of berries, as shown in the first row of the table. On the other side of the island, Gilligan—who is less adept at both tasks—requires 3 hours to catch a fish and $1\frac{1}{2}$ hours to pick a cup of berries, as listed in the second row of the table. Since both castaways would want some variety in their diets, we can assume that each would spend part of the week catching fish and part picking berries.

Suppose that, one day, Maryanne and Gilligan discover each other. After rejoicing at the prospect of human companionship, they decide to develop a system of production that will work to their mutual benefit. Let's rule out any of the gains from specialization that we discussed earlier (minimizing downtime or developing expertise). Will it still pay for these two to specialize? The answer is yes, as you will see after a small detour.

Absolute Advantage: A Detour

When Gilligan and Maryanne sit down to figure out who should do what, they might fall victim to a common mistake: basing their decision on *absolute advantage*.

> *An individual has an **absolute advantage** in the production of some good when he or she can produce it using* fewer resources *than another individual can.*

Absolute advantage The ability to produce a good or service, using fewer resources than other producers use.

On the island, the only resource being used is labor time, so the reasoning might go as follows: Maryanne can catch a fish more quickly than Gilligan (see Table 3), so she has an *absolute advantage* in fishing. It seems logical, then, that Maryanne should be the one to catch fish.

But wait! Maryanne can also pick berries more quickly than Gilligan, so she has an absolute advantage in that as well. If absolute advantage is the criterion for assigning work, then Maryanne should do *both* tasks. This, however, would leave Gilligan doing nothing, which is certainly *not* in the pair's best interests. What can we conclude from this example? That absolute advantage is an unreliable guide for allocating tasks to different workers.

Comparative Advantage

The correct principle to guide the division of labor on the island is comparative advantage:

Comparative advantage The ability to produce a good or service at a lower opportunity cost than other producers.

> *A person has a **comparative advantage** in producing some good if he or she can produce it with a smaller opportunity cost than some other person can.*

Notice the important difference between absolute advantage and comparative advantage: You have an *absolute* advantage in producing a good if you can produce it using fewer *resources* than someone else can. But you have a *comparative* advantage if you can produce it with a smaller *opportunity cost*. As you'll see, these are not necessarily the same thing.

Let's see who has a *comparative* advantage in fishing, by calculating—for each of the castaways—the opportunity cost of catching one fish. For Maryanne, catching a fish takes an hour. This is time that could instead be used to pick one cup of berries. Thus, for Maryanne, the *opportunity cost of one more fish is one cup of berries*. It takes Gilligan three hours to catch a fish, time which he could use to pick two cups of berries instead. Thus, for Gilligan, the *opportunity cost of one more fish is two cups of berries*. These opportunity costs are listed in the first column of Table 4. As you can see by comparing the entries, the opportunity cost for one more fish is lower for Maryanne than for Gilligan. Therefore, *Maryanne has a comparative advantage in fishing*.

Now let's determine who has a comparative advantage in berries. From Table 3, Maryanne needs an hour to pick a cup of berries, time that could be used to catch one fish. Thus, for Maryanne, the *opportunity cost of one more cup of berries is one fish*. For Gilligan, it takes $1\frac{1}{2}$ hours to pick a cup of berries, time that could be used instead to catch one-half of a fish. Thus, for Gilligan the *opportunity cost of one cup of berries is one-half fish*. (Of course, no one would ever catch half a fish unless they were using a machete. The number just tells us the rate of tradeoff of one good for the other.)

These opportunity costs are listed in the second column of Table 4. As you can see, when it comes to berries, it is *Gilligan* who has the lower opportunity cost. Therefore, Gilligan—who has an *absolute* advantage in nothing—has a *comparative advantage in berries*.

What happens when the two decide to produce more of the good in which they have a comparative advantage? The results are shown in Table 5. In the first row, we have Maryanne catching one more fish each day. This requires an additional hour, which she shifts out of picking berries. So Maryanne produces one more fish ($+1$) and one fewer cup of berries (-1). In the second row, we have Gilligan producing one fewer fish (-1). This frees up three hours. Since it takes Gilligan $1\frac{1}{2}$ hours to produce a cup of berries, he can use those three hours to produce two cups of berries ($+2$).

Now look at the last row. It shows what has happened to production of both goods on the island as a result of this little shift between the two. While fish

Even castaways do better when they specialize and exchange with each other, instead of trying to be self-sufficient.

TABLE 4		Opportunity Cost of:	
Opportunity Costs for Fish and Berries		**One More Fish**	**One More Cup of Berries**
	Maryanne	1 cup berries	1 fish
	Gilligan	2 cups berries	$\frac{1}{2}$ fish

	Change in Fish Production	Change in Berry Production	TABLE 5
			A Beneficial Change in Production
Maryanne	**+1**	**−1**	
Gilligan	**−1**	**+2**	
Total Island	**+0**	**+1**	

production remains unchanged, berry production has risen by one cup. And because total production has increased, so does total consumption. If the castaways can find some way of trading with each other, they can both come out ahead: consuming the same quantity of fish as before, but more berries.

As you can see in Table 5, when each castaway moves toward producing more of the good in which he or she has a *comparative advantage*, total production rises. Now, let's think about this. Because the castaways gain when they make this small shift toward their comparative advantage goods, why not make the change again? And again after that? In fact, why not keep repeating it until the opportunities for increasing total island production are exhausted, which occurs when one or both of them is devoting all of their time to producing just their comparative advantage good, and none of the other? In the end, the castaways enjoy a higher standard of living when they try to specialize and exchange goods with each other, compared to the level they'd enjoy under self-sufficiency.[8]

What is true for our shipwrecked island dwellers is also true for the entire economy:

> *Total production of every good or service will be greatest when individuals specialize according to their comparative advantage. This is another reason why specialization and exchange lead to higher living standards than does self-sufficiency.*

When we turn from our fictional island to the real world, is production, in fact, consistent with the principle of comparative advantage? Indeed, it is. A journalist may be able to paint her house more quickly than a house painter, giving her an *absolute* advantage in painting her home. Will she paint her own home? Except in unusual circumstances, no, because the journalist has a *comparative* advantage in writing news articles. Indeed, most journalists—like most college professors, attorneys, architects, and other professionals—hire house painters, leaving themselves more time to practice the professions in which they enjoy a comparative advantage.

Even comic book superheroes seem to behave consistently with comparative advantage. Superman can no doubt cook a meal, fix a car, chop wood, and do virtually *anything* faster than anyone else on the earth. Using our new vocabulary, we'd say that Superman has an absolute advantage in everything. But he has a clear *comparative* advantage in catching criminals and saving the universe from destruction, which is exactly what he spends his time doing.

---

[8] In this example, production of berries rises while fish production remains unchanged. But the castaways could instead choose to produce more fish and the same quantity of berries, or even more of both goods. Some end-of-chapter problems will guide you to these other outcomes.

Specialization in Perspective

The gains from specialization, whether they arise from developing expertise, minimizing downtime, or exploiting comparative advantage, can explain many features of our economy. For example, college students need to select a major and then, upon graduating, to decide on a specific career. Those who follow this path are often rewarded with higher incomes than those who dally. This is an encouragement to specialize. Society is better off if you specialize, since you will help the economy produce more, and society rewards you for this contribution with a higher income.

The gains from specialization can also explain why most of us end up working for business firms that employ dozens, or even hundreds or thousands, of other employees. Why do these business firms exist? Why isn't each of us a *self-employed* expert, exchanging our production with other self-employed experts? Part of the answer is that organizing production into business firms pushes the gains from specialization still further. Within a firm, some people can specialize in working with their hands, others in managing people, others in marketing, and still others in keeping the books. Each firm is a kind of minisociety within which specialization occurs. The result is greater production and a higher standard of living than we would achieve if we were all self-employed.

RESOURCE ALLOCATION

Ten thousand years ago, the Neolithic revolution began, and human society switched from hunting and gathering to farming and simple manufacturing. At the same time, human wants grew beyond mere food and shelter to the infinite variety of things that can be *made*. Ever since, all societies have been confronted with three important questions:

1. *Which* goods and services should be produced with society's resources?
2. *How* should they be produced?
3. *Who* should get them?

Resource allocation A method of determining which goods and services will be produced, how they will be produced, and who will get them.

Together, these three questions constitute the problem of **resource allocation**.

Let's first consider the *which* question. Should we produce more health care or more movies, more goods for consumers or more capital goods for businesses? Where on its production possibilities frontier should the economy operate? As you will see, there are different methods societies can use to answer these questions.

The *how* question is more complicated. Most goods and services can be produced in a variety of different ways, each method using more of some resources and less of others. For example, there are many ways to dig a ditch. We could use *no capital at all* and have dozens of workers digging with their bare hands. We could use *a small amount of capital* by giving each worker a shovel and thereby use less labor, since each worker would now be more productive. Or we could use *even more capital*—a power trencher—and dig the ditch with just one or two workers. In every economic system, there must always be some mechanism that determines how goods and services will be produced from the infinite variety of ways available.

Finally, the *who* question. Here is where economics interacts most strongly with politics. There are so many ways to divide ourselves into groups: men and women, rich and poor, skilled and unskilled, workers and owners, families and single people, young and old . . . the list is endless. How should the products of our economy be distributed among these different groups and among individuals within each group?

Determining *who* gets the economy's output is always the most controversial aspect of resource allocation. Over the last half-century, our society has become more sensitized to the way goods and services are distributed, and we increasingly ask whether that distribution is fair. For example, men get a disproportionately larger share of our national output than women do, whites get more than African-Americans and Hispanics, and middle-aged workers get more than the very old and the very young. As a society, we want to know *why* we observe these patterns (a positive economic question) and *what* we should do about them (a normative economic question).

The Three Methods of Resource Allocation

Throughout history, every society has relied primarily on one of three mechanisms for allocating resources. In a **traditional economy**, resources are allocated according to the long-lived practices of the past. Tradition was the dominant method of resource allocation for most of human history and remains strong in many tribal societies and small villages in parts of Africa, South America, Asia, and the Pacific. Typically, traditional methods of production are handed down by the village elders, and traditional principles of fairness govern the distribution of goods and services.

Traditional economy An economy in which resources are allocated according to long-lived practices from the past.

Economies in which resources are allocated mostly by tradition tend to be stable and predictable. But these economies have one serious drawback: They don't grow. With everyone locked into the traditional patterns of production, there is little room for innovation and technological change. Traditional economies are therefore likely to be stagnant economies.

In a **command economy**, resources are allocated mostly by explicit instructions from some higher authority. *Which* goods and services should we produce? The ones we're *ordered* to produce. *How* should we produce them? The way we're *told* to produce them. *Who* will get the goods and services? Whoever the authority *tells* us should get them.

Command or centrally planned economy An economic system in which resources are allocated according to explicit instructions from a central authority.

In a command economy, a government body *plans* how resources will be allocated. That is why command economies are also called **centrally planned economies**. But command economies are disappearing fast. Until about 20 years ago, examples would have included the former Soviet Union, Poland, Rumania, Bulgaria, Albania, China, and many others. Beginning in the late 1980s, all of these nations began abandoning central planning. The only examples left today are Cuba and North Korea, and even these economies—though still dominated by central planning—occasionally take steps away from it.

The third method of allocating resources—and the one with which you are no doubt most familiar—is "the market." In a **market economy**, neither long-held traditions nor commands from above guide most economic behavior. Instead, people are largely free to do what they want with the resources at their disposal. In the end, resources are allocated as a result of individual decision making. *Which* goods and services are produced? The ones that producers *choose* to produce. *How* are they produced? However producers *choose* to produce them. *Who* gets these goods and services? Anyone who *chooses* to buy them.

Market economy An economic system in which resources are allocated through individual decision making.

Of course, in a market system, freedom of choice is constrained by the resources one controls. And in this respect, we do not all start in the same place in the economic race. Some of us have inherited great intelligence, talent, or beauty; and some, such as the children of successful professionals, are born into a world of helpful personal contacts. Others, unfortunately, will inherit none of these advantages. In a market system, those who control more resources will have more choices available to them than those who control fewer resources. Nevertheless, given these different starting points, individual choice plays the major role in allocating resources in a market economy.

But wait . . . isn't there a problem here? People acting according to their own desires, without command or tradition to control them? This sounds like a recipe for chaos! How, in such a free-for-all, could resources possibly be *allocated*?

The answer is contained in two words: *markets* and *prices*.

The Nature of Markets

The market economy gets its name from something that nearly always happens when people are free to do what they want with the resources they possess. Inevitably, people decide to specialize in the production of one or a few things—often organizing themselves into business firms—and then sellers and buyers *come together to trade*. A **market** is a collection of buyers and sellers who have the potential to trade with one another.

Market A group of buyers and sellers with the potential to trade with each other.

In some cases, the market is *global*; that is, the market consists of buyers and sellers who are spread across the globe. The market for oil is an example of a global market, since buyers in any country can buy from sellers in any country. In other cases, the market is local. Markets for restaurant meals, haircuts, and taxi service are examples of local markets.

Markets play a major role in allocating resources by forcing individual decision makers to consider very carefully their decisions about buying and selling. They do so because of an important feature of every market: the *price* at which a good is bought and sold.

The Importance of Prices

Price The amount of money that must be paid to a seller to obtain a good or service.

A **price** is *the amount of money a buyer must pay to a seller for a good or service*. Price is not always the same as *cost*. In economics, as you've learned in this chapter, cost means *opportunity cost*—the *total* sacrifice needed to buy the good. While the price of a good is a *part* of its opportunity cost, it is not the only cost. For example, the price does not include the value of the time sacrificed to buy something. Buying a new jacket will require you to spend time traveling to and from the store, trying on different styles and sizes, and waiting in line at the cash register.

Still, in most cases, the price of a good is a significant part of its opportunity cost. For large purchases such as a home or automobile, the price will be *most* of the opportunity cost. And this is why prices are so important to the overall working of the economy: They confront individual decision makers with the costs of their choices.

Consider the example of purchasing a car. Because you must pay the price, you know that buying a new car will require you to cut back on purchases of other things. In this way, the opportunity cost to *society* of making another car is converted to an opportunity cost *for you*. If you value a new car more highly than the other things you must sacrifice for it, you will buy it. If not, you won't buy it.

Why is it so important that people face the opportunity costs of their actions? The following thought experiment can answer this question.

A Thought Experiment: Free Cars

Imagine that the government passes a new law: When anyone buys a new car, the government will reimburse that person for it immediately. The consequences would be easy to predict. First, on the day the law was passed, everyone would rush out to buy new cars. Why not, if cars are free? The entire stock of existing automobiles would be gone within days—maybe even hours. Many people who didn't value cars much at all, and who hardly ever used them, would find themselves owning several—one for each day of the week or to match the different colors in their wardrobe. Others who weren't able to act in time—including some who desperately needed a new car for their work or to run their households—would be unable to find one at all.

Over time, automobile companies would drastically increase production to meet the surge in demand for cars. So much of our available labor, capital, land, and entrepreneurial talent would be diverted to the automobile industry that we'd have to sacrifice huge quantities of all other goods and services. Thus, we'd end up *paying* for those additional cars in the end, by making do with less education, less medical care, perhaps even less food—all to support the widespread, frivolous use of cars. Almost everyone would conclude that society had been made worse off with the new "free-car" policy. By eliminating a price for automobiles, and severing the connection between the opportunity cost of producing a car and the individual's decision to get one, we would have created quite a mess for ourselves.

> *When resources are allocated by the market, and people must* pay *for their purchases, they are forced to consider the opportunity cost to society of their individual actions. In this way, markets are able to create a sensible allocation of resources.*

Resource Allocation in the United States

The United States has always been considered the leading example of a market economy. Each day, millions of distinct items are produced and sold in markets. Our grocery stores are always stocked with broccoli and tomato soup, and the drugstore always has Kleenex and aspirin—all due to the choices of individual producers and consumers. The goods that are traded, the way they are traded, and the price at which they trade are determined by the traders themselves. No direction from above is needed to keep markets working.

But even in the United States, there are numerous cases of resource allocation *outside* the market. For example, families are important institutions in the United States, and many economic decisions are made within them. Families tend to operate like traditional villages, not like market economies. For example, few parents make their children pay for goods and services provided inside the home.

Our economy also allocates some resources by command. Various levels of government collect, in total, about one-third of our incomes as taxes. We are *told* how much tax we must pay, and those who don't comply suffer serious penalties, including imprisonment. Government—rather than individual decision makers—spends the tax revenue. In this way, the government plays a major role in allocating resources—especially in determining which goods are produced and who gets them.

There are also other ways, aside from strict commands, that the government limits our market freedoms. Regulations designed to protect the environment, maintain safe workplaces, and ensure the safety of our food supply are just a few examples of government-imposed constraints on our individual choice.

What are we to make, then, of resource allocation in the United States? Markets are, indeed, constrained. But for each example we can find where resources are allocated by tradition or command, or where government restrictions seriously limit some market freedom, we can find hundreds of examples where individuals make choices according to their own desires. The things we buy, the jobs at which we work, the homes in which we live—in almost all cases, these result from market choices. The market, though not pure, is certainly the dominant method of resource allocation in the United States.

RESOURCE OWNERSHIP

So far, we've been concerned with how resources are allocated. Another important feature of an economic system is how resources are *owned*. The owner of a resource—a parcel of land, a factory, or one's own labor time—determines how it can be used and receives income when others use it. And there have been three primary modes of resource ownership in human history.

Under *communal* ownership, resources are owned by everyone—or by no one, depending on your point of view. They are simply there for the taking; no person or organization imposes any restrictions on their use or charges any fees.

Communism A type of economic system in which most resources are owned in common.

It is hard to find economies with significant communal ownership of resources. Karl Marx believed that, in time, all economies would evolve toward communal ownership, and he named this predicted system **communism**. In fact, none of the economies that called themselves communist (such as the former Soviet Union) ever achieved Marx's vision. This is not surprising: Communal ownership on a broad scale can work only when individuals have no conflicts over how resources are used. Therefore, communism requires the end of *scarcity*—an unlikely prospect in the foreseeable future.

Nevertheless, there are examples of communal ownership on a smaller scale. Traditional villages maintain communal ownership of land and sometimes cattle. Closer to home, most families operate on the principle of communal ownership. The house, television, telephone, and food in the refrigerator are treated as if owned jointly. More broadly, who "owns" our sidewalks, streets, and public beaches? No one does, really. In practice, all citizens are free to use them as much and as often as they would like. This is essentially communal ownership.

Socialism A type of economic system in which most resources are owned by the state.

Under **socialism**, the *state* owns most of the resources. The prime example is the former Soviet Union, where the state owned all of the land and capital equipment in the country. In many ways, it also owned the labor of individual households, since it was virtually the only employer in the nation and unemployment was considered a crime.

State ownership also occurs in nonsocialist economies. In the United States, national parks, state highway systems, military bases, public colleges and universities, and government buildings are all state-owned resources. Over a third of the land in the country is owned by the federal government. The military, even under our current volunteer system, is an example in which the state owns the labor of soldiers—albeit for a limited period of time.

Capitalism A type of economic system in which most resources are owned privately.

Finally, the third system. When most resources are owned *privately*—as in the United States—we have **capitalism**. Take the book you are reading right now. If you turn to the title page, you will see the imprint of the company that published this book. This is a corporation owned by thousands of individual stockholders. These individuals own the buildings, the land under them, the office furniture and computer equipment, and even the reputation of the company. When these facilities are used to produce and sell a book, the company's profits belong to these stockholders.

Similarly, the employees of the company are private individuals. They are selling a resource they own—their labor time—to the company, and they receive income—wages and salaries—in return.

The United States is one of the most capitalistic countries in the world. True, there are examples of state and communal ownership, as we've seen. But the dominant mode of resource ownership in the United States is *private* ownership. Resource owners keep most of the income they earn from supplying their resources, and they have broad freedom in deciding how their resources are used.

TYPES OF ECONOMIC SYSTEMS

We've used the phrase *economic system* a few times already in this book. But now it's time for a formal definition.

> An **economic system** is composed of two features: a mechanism for allocating resources and a mode of resource ownership.

Economic system A system of resource allocation and resource ownership.

Let's leave aside the rare economies in which communal ownership is dominant and those in which resources are allocated primarily by tradition. That leaves us with four basic types of economic systems, indicated by the four quadrants in Figure 6. In the upper left quadrant, we have *market capitalism*. In this system, resources are *allocated* primarily by the market and *owned* primarily by private individuals. Today, most nations have market capitalist economies, including all of the countries of North America and Western Europe, and most of those in Asia, Latin America, and Africa.

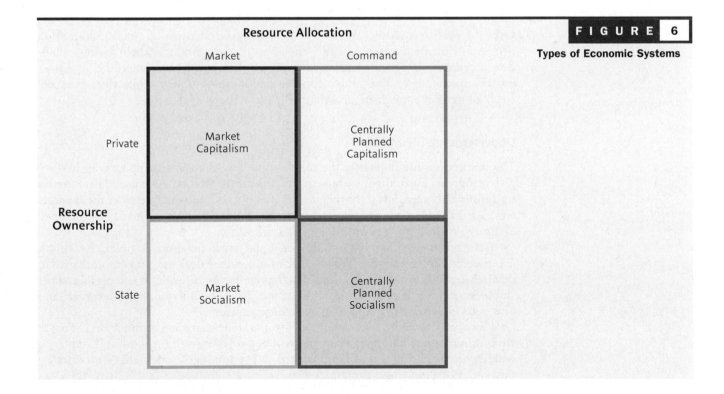

Resource Allocation

FIGURE 6

Types of Economic Systems

	Market	Command
Private	Market Capitalism	Centrally Planned Capitalism
State	Market Socialism	Centrally Planned Socialism

Resource Ownership

In the lower right quadrant is *centrally planned socialism*, under which resources are mostly allocated by command and mostly owned by the state. This *was* the system in the former Soviet Union and the nations of Eastern Europe until the late 1980s. But since then, these countries' economies have gone through cataclysmic change by moving from the lower right quadrant to the upper left. That is, these nations have simultaneously changed both their method of resource allocation and their systems of resource ownership.

Although market capitalism and centrally planned socialism have been the two paramount economic systems in modern history, there have been others. The upper right quadrant represents a system of *centrally planned capitalism*, in which resources are owned by private individuals yet allocated by command. In the recent past, countries such as Sweden and Japan—where the government has been more heavily involved in allocating resources than in the United States—have flirted with this type of system. Nations at war—like the United States during World War II—also move in this direction, as governments find it necessary to direct resources by command in order to ensure sufficient military production.

Finally, in the lower left quadrant is *market socialism*, in which resources are owned by the state yet allocated by the market mechanism. The possibility of market socialism has fascinated many social scientists, who believed it promised the best of both worlds: the freedom and efficiency of the market mechanism and the fairness and equity of socialism. There are, however, serious problems—many would say "unresolvable contradictions"—in trying to mix the two. The chief examples of market socialism in modern history were short-lived experiments—in Hungary and the former Yugoslavia in the 1950s and 1960s—in which the results were mixed at best.

Economic Systems and This Book

Over the past two decades, the world has changed dramatically: About 300 million people in Europe have come under the sway of the market as their nations abandoned centrally planned socialism; more than a billion have been added as China has changed course. The study of modern economies is now, more than ever, the study of market capitalism, and that will be the focus of our text.

Understanding the Market

The market is simultaneously the most simple and the most complex way to allocate resources. For individual buyers and sellers, the market is simple. There are no traditions or commands to be memorized and obeyed. Instead, we enter the markets we *wish* to trade in, and we respond to prices there as we *wish* to, unconcerned about the overall process of resource allocation.

But from the economist's point of view, the market is quite complex. Resources are allocated indirectly, as a *by-product* of individual decision making, rather than through easily identified traditions or commands. As a result, it often takes some skillful economic detective work to determine just how individuals are behaving and how resources are being allocated as a consequence.

How can we make sense of all of this apparent chaos and complexity? That is what economics is all about. And you will begin your detective work in Chapter 3, where you will learn about the most widely used model in the field of economics: the model of supply and demand.

USING THE THEORY

Are We Saving Lives Efficiently?

Earlier in this chapter, you learned that instances of gross productive inefficiency are not as easy to find in our economy as one might imagine. But many economists argue that our allocation of resources to lifesaving efforts is a glaring exception. In this section, we'll use some of the tools and concepts you've learned in this chapter to ask whether we are saving lives efficiently.

We can view "saving lives" as the output—a service—produced by the "lifesaving industry." This industry consists of private firms (such as medical practices and hospitals), as well as government agencies (such as the Department of Health and Human Services or the Environmental Protection Agency). In a productively efficient economy, we must pay an opportunity cost whenever we choose to save additional lives. That's because any lifesaving action we might take—building another emergency surgery center, running an advertising campaign to encourage healthier living, or requiring the substitution of costly but safe materials for less costly but toxic ones—would require us to use additional land, labor, capital, and entrepreneurship. And these resources could be used to produce other goods and services that we value.

© PHOTODISC/GETTY IMAGES

Figure 7 illustrates this opportunity cost with a production possibilities frontier. The number of lives saved per year is measured along the horizontal axis, and the quantity of all other goods (lumped together into a single category) is measured on the vertical axis. A productively efficient economy would be *on* the frontier, producing the maximum quantity of all other goods for any given number of lives saved. Equivalently, productive efficiency would mean saving the maximum possible number of lives for any given quantity of other goods

---

FIGURE 7

Efficiency and Inefficiency in Saving Lives

This PPF shows society's choice between saving lives (measured along the horizontal axis) and all other production (on the vertical axis). Operating on the curve (at a point like A) would be productively efficient. But if the life-saving industry is not efficient, then society is operating inside the PPF (at a point like B). Eliminating the inefficiency would enable us to save more lives, or have more of other goods, or both.

Quantity of All Other Goods per Year

Q_2 ···· B   A

Q_1 Number of Lives Saved per Year

produced. Point *A* on the PPF is one such productively efficient point, where we would save Q_1 lives per year, and produce the quantity Q_2 of all other goods. Once we are on the frontier, we can only save more lives by pulling resources away from producing other goods, and paying an opportunity cost in other goods foregone.

But what if there is productive *in*efficiency in the economy? And what if the source of the inefficiency is in the lifesaving industry itself? More specifically, what if more lives could be saved with the current quantity of resources used by the industry simply by reallocating those resources among different types of lifesaving activities? In that case, the economy would be operating at a point like *B*, *inside* the PPF. By eliminating the inefficiency, we could move *to* the frontier. For example, we could save more lives with no sacrifice of other goods (a move from point *B* to point *A*) or have more of other goods while saving the same number of lives (a move vertically upward from point *B* to a new, unmarked point on the PPF) or have more of both (upward and rightward from point *B*).

Economists argue that the United States and most other countries do, in fact, operate at a point like *B* because of productive inefficiency in saving lives. How have they come to such a conclusion?

The first step in the analysis is to remember that, in a market economy, resources sell at a price. This allows us to use the dollar cost of a lifesaving method to measure the value of the resources used up by that method.

Moreover, we can compare the "cost per year of life saved" of different methods. For example, in the United States we currently spend about $253 million on heart transplants each year and thereby add about 1,600 years to the lives of heart patients. Thus, the cost per year of life saved from heart transplants is $253,000,000/1,600 = $158,000 (rounded to the nearest thousand).

Table 6 lists several of the methods we currently use to save lives in the United States. Some of these methods reflect legal or regulatory decisions (such as the ban on asbestos) and others reflect standard medical practices (such as annual mammograms for women over 50). Other methods effectively save lives only sporadically (such as seat belts in school buses). You can see that the cost per life saved ranges widely—from $150 per year of life saved for a physician warning a patient to quit smoking, to over $66,000,000 per year of life saved from the ban on asbestos in automatic transmissions.

The table indicates that some lifesaving methods are highly cost effective. For example, our society probably exhausts the potential to save lives from brief physician antismoking intervention. Most doctors *do* warn their smoking patients to quit.

But the table also indicates some serious productive *in*efficiency in lifesaving. For example, screening and treating African-American newborns for sickle cell anemia is one of the least costly ways of saving a year of life in the United States—only $236 per year of life saved. Nevertheless, 20 percent of African-American newborns do *not* get this screening at all. Similarly, intensive intervention to discourage smoking is far from universal in the U.S. health care system, even though it has the relatively low cost of $2,587 per year of life saved.

Why is the less than universal use of these lower cost methods *productively inefficient*? To answer, let's do some thought experiments. First, let's imagine that we shift resources from heart transplants to *intensive* antismoking efforts. Then for each year of life we decided *not* to save with heart transplants, we would free up $157,821 in medical resources. If we applied those resources toward intensive antismoking efforts, at a cost of $2,587 per year of life saved, we could then save an additional $157,821/$2,587 = 61 life-years. In other words, we could increase the

	Cost per Life-Year Saved		TABLE 6
Method			**The Cost of Saving Lives**
Brief physician antismoking intervention:			
Single personal warning from physician to stop smoking	$150		
Sickle cell screening and treatment for African-American newborns	$236		
Replacing ambulances with helicopters for medical emergencies	$2,454		
Intensive physician antismoking intervention:			
Physician identification of smokers among their patients;			
three physician counseling sessions; two further sessions with			
smoking-cessation specialists; and materials—nicotine			
patch or nicotine gum	$2,587		
Mammograms: Once every three years, for ages 50–64	$2,700		
Chlorination of water supply	$4,000		
Next step after suspicious lung X-ray:			
PET Scan	$3,742		
Exploratory Surgery	$4,895		
Needle Biopsy	$7,116		
Vaccination of all infants against strep infections	$80,000		
Mammograms: Annually, for ages 50–64	$108,401		
Exercise electrocardiograms as screening test:			
For 40-year-old males	$124,374		
Heart transplants	$157,821		
Mammograms: Annually, for age 40–49	$186,635		
Exercise electrocardiograms as screening test:			
For 40-year-old females	$335,217		
Seat belts on school buses	$2,760,197		
Asbestos ban in automatic transmissions	$66,402,402		

Sources: Compiled from various publications. Individual sources available from authors upon request.

number of life-years saved without any increase in resources flowing to the health care sector, and therefore, without any sacrifice in other goods and services. If you look back at the definition of productive inefficiency given earlier in this chapter, you'll see why this is an example of it.

But why pick on heart transplants? Our ban on asbestos in automobile transmissions—which requires the purchase of more costly materials with greater quantities of scarce resources—costs us about $66 million for each life-year saved. Suppose these funds were spent instead to buy the resources needed to provide women aged 40 to 49 with annual mammograms (currently *not* part of most physicians' recommendations). Then for each life-year lost to asbestos, we'd save $66 million/186,635 = 354 life-years from earlier detection of breast cancer.

Of course, allocating lifesaving resources is much more complicated than our discussion so far has implied. For one thing, the benefits of lifesaving efforts are not fully captured by "life-years saved" (or even by an alternative measure, which accounts for improvement in *quality* of life). The cost per life-year saved from mandating seat belts on school buses is extremely high—almost $3 million. This is mostly because very few children die in school bus accidents—about 11 per year in the entire United States—and, according to the National Traffic Safety Board, few of these deaths would have been prevented with seat belts. But mandatory seat belts—rightly or wrongly—might decrease the anxiety of millions of parents as they send their children off to school. How should we value such a reduction in anxiety? Hard to say. But it's not unreasonable to include it as a benefit—at least in some way—when deciding about resources.

Another difficulty in allocating our lifesaving resources efficiently—which has become profoundly more serious in the last few years—is uncertainty. Consider, for example, our efforts to prevent a terrorist attack via hijacked airliners. What is the cost per life-year saved? We cannot know. An earlier study of antiterrorist efforts in the mid-1990s had estimated the cost at $8,000,000 per life-year saved, which seems productively inefficient.[9] But this study made two critical assumptions to arrive at that number. First, it assumed that without the new procedures 37 people would perish each year from airline-related terrorist incidents—equal to the rate we had had in the late 1980s and early 1990s. Second, the study assumed that the safety procedures being evaluated would be 100 percent effective in eliminating attacks. Clearly, trying to gauge and improve our productive efficiency in saving lives—which was never an exact science—has become even *less* exact in the post-9/11 era.

Summary

One of the most fundamental concepts in economics is *opportunity cost*. The opportunity cost of any choice is what we give up when we make that choice. At the individual level, opportunity cost arises from the scarcity of time or money; for society as a whole, it arises from the scarcity of resources—land, labor, capital, and entrepreneurship. To produce and enjoy more of one thing, we must shift resources away from producing something else. The correct measure of cost is not just the money price we pay, but the opportunity cost: what we must give up when we make a choice. The *law of increasing opportunity cost* tells us that the more of something we produce, the greater the opportunity cost of producing still more.

In a world of scarce resources, each society must have an economic system—its way of organizing economic activity. All *economic systems* feature *specialization*, where each person and firm concentrates on a limited number of productive activities, and *exchange*, through which we obtain most of what we desire by trading with others. Specialization and exchange enable us to enjoy higher living standards than would be possible under self-sufficiency. One way that specialization increases living standards is by allowing each of us to concentrate on tasks in which we have a comparative advantage.

Every economic system determines how resources are owned and how they are allocated. In a market capitalist economy, resources are owned primarily by private individuals and allocated primarily through markets. Prices play an important role in markets by forcing decision makers to take account of society's opportunity cost when they make choices.

Problem Set   *Answers to even-numbered Questions and Problems can be found on the text Web site at www.thomsonedu.com/economics/hall.*

1. Redraw Figure 2, but this time identify a different set of points along the frontier. Starting at point *F* (5,000 tanks, zero production of wheat), have each point you select show equal increments in the quantity of wheat produced. For example, a new point *H* should correspond to 200,000 bushels of wheat, point *J* to 400,000 bushels, point *K* to 600,000 bushels, and so on. Now observe what happens to the opportunity cost of "200,000 more bushels of wheat"

[9] "The Cost of Anti-terrorist Rhetoric," The Cato Review of Business and Government, Dec. 17, 1996, and authors' calculations to convert "per life saved" to "per year of life saved."

as you move leftward and upward along this PPF. Does the law of increasing opportunity cost apply to the production of wheat? Explain briefly.

2. Suppose that you are considering what to do with an upcoming weekend. Here are your options, from least to most preferred: (1) Study for upcoming midterms; (2) fly to Colorado for a quick ski trip; (3) go into seclusion in your dorm room and try to improve your score on a computer game. What is the opportunity cost of a decision to play the computer game all weekend?

3. How would a technological innovation in lifesaving—say, the discovery of a cure for cancer—affect the PPF in Figure 7?

4. How would a technological innovation in the production of *other* goods—say, the invention of a new kind of robot that speeds up assembly-line manufacturing—affect the PPF in Figure 7?

5. Suppose that one day, Gilligan (the castaway) eats a magical island plant that turns him into an expert at everything. In particular, it now takes him just half an hour to pick a quart of berries, and 15 minutes to catch a fish.
   a. Redo Table 3 in the chapter.
   b. Who—Gilligan or Maryanne—has a comparative advantage in picking berries? In fishing? When the castaways discover each other, which of the two should specialize in which task?
   c. Can *both* castaways benefit from Gilligan's new abilities? How?

6. Suppose that two different castaways, Mr. and Mrs. Howell, end up on a different island. Mr. Howell can pick 1 pineapple per hour, or 1 coconut. Mrs. Howell can pick 2 pineapples per hour, but it takes her two hours to pick a coconut.
   a. Construct a table like Table 3 showing Mr. and Mrs. Howell's labor requirements.
   b. Who—Mr. or Mrs. Howell—has a comparative advantage in picking pineapples? In picking coconuts? Which of the two should specialize in which tasks?
   c. Assume that Mr. and Mrs. Howell had originally washed ashore on different parts of the island, and that they originally each spent 12 hours per day working, spending 6 hours picking pineapples and 6 hours picking coconuts. How will their total production change if they find each other and begin to specialize?

7. You and a friend have decided to work jointly on a course project. Frankly, your friend is a less than ideal partner. His skills as a researcher are such that he can review and outline only two articles a day. Moreover, his hunt-and-peck style limits him to only 10 pages of typing a day. On the other hand, in a day you can produce six outlines or type 20 pages.
   a. Who has an absolute advantage in outlining, you or your friend? What about typing?

   b. Who has a comparative advantage in outlining? In typing?
   c. According to the principle of comparative advantage, who should specialize in which task?

8. One might think that performing a mammogram once each year—as opposed to once every three years—would triple the cost per life saved. But according to Table 6, peforming the exam annually raises the cost per life-year saved by about 40 times. Does this make sense? Explain.

9. Use the information in Table 1 as well as the assumption about foregone income made in the chapter to calculate the average opportunity cost of a year in college for a student at a four-year private institution under each the following assumptions:
   a. The student receives free room and board at home at no opportunity cost to the parents.
   b. The student receives an academic scholarship covering all tuition and fees (in the form of a grant, not a loan or a work study aid).
   c. The student works half time while at school at no additional emotional cost.

10. Use the information in Table 1 as well as the assumption about foregone income made in the chapter to compare the opportunity cost of attending a year of college for a student at a two-year public college under each of the following assumptions:
    a. The student receives free room and board at home at no opportunity cost to the parents.
    b. The student receives an academic scholarship covering all tuition and fees (in the form of a grant, not a loan or a work study aid).
    c. The student works half time while at school at no additional emotional cost.

11. Consider Kylie, who has been awarded academic scholarships covering all tuition and fees at three different colleges. College #1 is a two-year public college. College #2 is a four-year public college, and College #3 is a four-year private college. Explain why, if the decision is based solely on opportunity cost, Kylie will turn down her largest scholarship offers. (Use Table 1 in the chapter.)

12. Suppose the Internet enables more production of other goods *and* helps to save lives (for simplicity, assume proportional increases).
    a. Show how the PPF in Figure 7 would be affected.
    b. Does this affect any of the general conclusions about economic growth?

13. Suppose that an economy's PPF is a straight line, rather than a bowed out, concave curve. What would this say about the nature of opportunity cost as production is shifted from one good to the other?

Supply and Demand

Father Guido Sarducci, a character on the early *Saturday Night Live* shows, once observed that the average person remembers only about five minutes worth of material from college. He therefore proposed the "Five Minute University," where you'd learn only the five minutes of material you'd actually remember and dispense with the rest. The economics course would last only 10 seconds, just enough time for students to learn to recite three words: "supply and demand."

Of course, there is much more to economics than these three words. But many people *do* regard the phrase "supply and demand" as synonymous with economics and the concept is often misused. But surprisingly few people actually understand what the phrase means. In a debate about health care, poverty, recent events in the stock market, or the high price of housing, you might hear someone say, "Well, it's just a matter of supply and demand," as a way of dismissing the issue entirely. Others use the phrase with an exaggerated reverence, as if supply and demand were an inviolable physical law, like gravity, about which nothing can be done. So what does this oft-repeated phrase really mean?

First, supply and demand is just an economic model—nothing more and nothing less. It's a model designed to explain *how prices are determined in certain types of markets*.

Why has this model taken on such an exalted role in the field of economics? Because prices themselves play such an exalted role in the economy. In a market system, once the price of something has been determined, only those willing to pay that price will get it. Thus, prices determine which households will get which goods and services and which firms will get which resources. If you want to know why the cell phone industry is expanding while the video rental industry is shrinking, or why homelessness is a more pervasive problem in the United States than hunger, you need to understand how prices are determined. In this chapter, you will learn how the model of supply and demand works and how to use it. You will also learn about the strengths and limitations of the model. It will take more time than Guido Sarducci's 10-second economics course, but in the end you will know much more than just those three words.

MARKETS

Put any compound in front of a chemist, ask him what it is and what it can be used for, and he will immediately think of the basic elements—carbon, hydrogen, oxygen, and so on. Ask an economist almost any question about the economy, and he will immediately think about *markets*.

In ordinary language, a market is a specific location where buying and selling take place: a supermarket, a flea market, and so on. In economics, a market is not a place, but rather a collection of *traders*. More specifically,

> *a market is a group of buyers and sellers with the potential to trade with each other.*

Economists think of the economy as a collection of markets. In each of these markets, the collection of buyers and sellers will be different, depending on what is being traded. There is a market for oranges, another for automobiles, another for real estate, and still others for corporate stocks, labor services, land, euros, and anything else that is bought and sold.

However, unlike chemistry—in which the set of basic elements is always the same—in economics, we can define a market in *different* ways, depending on our purpose. In fact, in almost any economic analysis, the first step is to define and characterize the market or collection of markets to analyze.

HOW BROADLY SHOULD WE DEFINE THE MARKET?

Suppose we want to study the personal computer industry in the United States. Should we define the market very broadly ("the market for computers"), or very narrowly ("the market for ultra-light laptops"), or something in between ("the market for laptops")? The right choice depends on the problem we're trying to analyze.

For example, if we're interested in why computers *in general* have come down in price over the past decade, there would be no reason to divide computers into desktops and laptops. Such a distinction would only get in the way. Thus, we'd treat all types of computers as if they were the same good. Economists call this process **aggregation**—combining a group of distinct things into a single whole.

Aggregation The process of combining distinct things into a single whole.

But suppose we're asking a different question: Why do laptops always cost more than desktops with similar computing power? Then we'd aggregate all laptops together as one good, and all desktops as another, and look at each of these more narrowly defined markets.

The same general principle applies to the *geographic* breadth of the market. If we want to predict how instability in the Persian Gulf will affect gasoline prices around the world, we'd use the "global market for oil," in which the major oil producers in about 20 countries sell to buyers around the globe. But if we want to explain why gasoline is cheaper in the United States than in most of the rest of the world, we'd want to look at the "U.S. market for oil." In this market, global sellers choose how much oil to sell to U.S. buyers.

> *In economics, **markets** can be defined broadly or narrowly, depending on our purpose.*

How broadly or narrowly markets are defined is one of the most important differences between *macro*economics and *micro*economics. In macroeconomics, goods and services are aggregated to the highest levels. Macro models even lump all consumer goods—breakfast cereals, cell phones, blue jeans, and so forth—into the single category "consumption goods" and view them as if they are traded in a single, broadly defined market, "the market for consumption goods." Similarly, instead of recognizing different markets for shovels, bulldozers, computers, and factory buildings, macro models analyze the market for "capital goods." Defining markets this broadly allows macroeconomists to take an overall view of the economy without getting bogged down in the details.

In microeconomics, by contrast, markets are defined more narrowly. Instead of asking how much we'll spend on *consumer goods*, a microeconomist might ask how much we'll spend on *health care* or *video games*. Although microeconomics always involves some aggregation, the process stops before it reaches the highest level of generality.

PRODUCT AND RESOURCE MARKETS

Circular flow A simple model that shows how goods, resources, and dollar payments flow between households and firms.

Figure 1 displays the **circular flow** model of the economy, which helps us organize our thinking about markets. It shows how we can divide markets into two major categories, and how each category fits into the big picture.

The upper half of the diagram shows **product markets,** where goods and services such as soft drinks, word-processing software, gasoline, DVDs, college educational services, medical services, and more are bought and sold. The outer arrows represent the flow of *goods and services* from business firms (the sellers) to households (the buyers). The inner arrows show the associated flow of funds, where household payments for goods and services ($ Expenditures) become the receipts of businesses ($ Revenue).

Product markets Markets in which firms sell goods and services to households

Resource markets Markets in which households that own resources sell them to firms.

The lower half of the diagram depicts another type of market: **resource markets**, where labor, land, capital, and entrepreneurship are bought and sold. In these markets, as shown by the outer arrows, households (the ultimate owners of resources) act as sellers. Business firms, which use resources to make goods and services, are the buyers. The inner arrows in the lower half of the diagram show us that when businesses pay for the resources they use ($ Resource Payments), the funds flow to households ($ Income).

There is, of course, much more to the economy than this simple model captures. For example, we've left out the government, which buys many goods and services, and also produces some for the general public. And we've left out some markets entirely, such as markets where borrowing and lending takes place, or markets where foreign currencies are traded.

But for many problems, the simple circular flow model can help us understand and identify the participants and the type of market we are discussing. In this chapter, for example, our focus is on *product markets*, so we'll view households as buyers and business firms as sellers. Later in this book (in both microeconomics and macroeconomics), you'll encounter resource markets where these roles are reversed.

COMPETITION IN MARKETS

A final issue in defining a market is how individual buyers and sellers view the price of the product. In many cases, individual buyers or sellers have an important influence over the price. For example, in the national market for cornflakes, Kellogg's—an individual *seller*—simply sets its price every few months. It can raise the price and sell fewer boxes of cereal or lower the price and sell more. In a small-town, a major buyer of antiques may be able to negotiate special discount prices with the local antique shops. These are examples of *imperfectly competitive* markets.

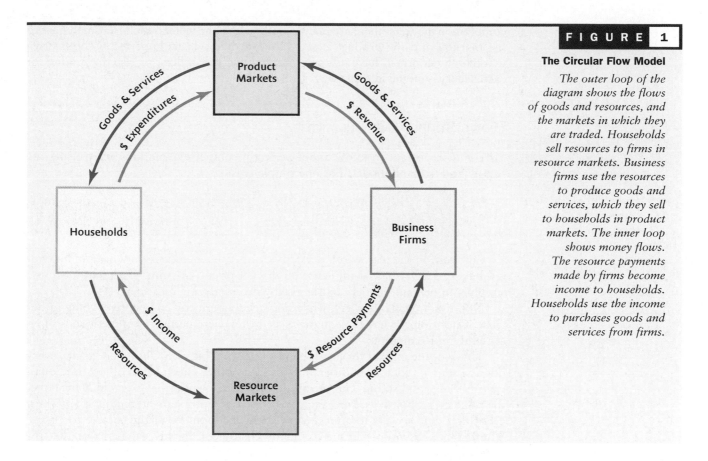

FIGURE 1

The Circular Flow Model

The outer loop of the diagram shows the flows of goods and resources, and the markets in which they are traded. Households sell resources to firms in resource markets. Business firms use the resources to produce goods and services, which they sell to households in product markets. The inner loop shows money flows. The resource payments made by firms become income to households. Households use the income to purchases goods and services from firms.

---

*In **imperfectly competitive markets**, individual buyers or sellers can influence the price of the product.*

Imperfectly competitive market A market in which a single buyer or seller has the power to influence the price of the product.

But now think about the national market for wheat. Can an individual seller have any impact on the market price? Not really. On any given day there is a going price for wheat—say, $5.80 per bushel. If a farmer tries to charge more than that—say, $5.85 per bushel—he won't sell any wheat at all! His customers will instead go to one of his many competitors and buy the identical product from them for less. Each wheat farmer must take the price of wheat as a "given."

The same is true of a single wheat *buyer:* If he tries to negotiate a lower price from a seller, he'd be laughed off the farm. "Why should I sell my wheat to you for $5.75 per bushel, when there are others who will pay me $5.80?" Accordingly, each buyer must take the market price as a given.

The market for wheat is an example of a *perfectly competitive market.*

---

*In **perfectly competitive markets** (or just **competitive markets**), each buyer and seller takes the market price as a given.*

Perfectly competitive market A market in which no buyer or seller has the power to influence the price.

What makes some markets imperfectly competitive and others perfectly competitive? You'll learn the complete answer, along with more formal definitions, when you are further into your study of *microeconomics*. But here's a hint: In perfectly competitive markets, there are many small buyers and sellers, each is a small part of the market, and the product is standardized, like wheat. Imperfectly competitive markets, by contrast, have just a few large buyers or sellers, or else the product of each seller is unique in some way.

USING SUPPLY AND DEMAND

Why is it important to know about perfectly competitive markets when using the supply and demand model? For one simple reason:

> *The supply and demand model is designed to explain how prices are determined in perfectly competitive markets.*

But wait. In the real world, perfectly competitive markets—in which an individual buyer or seller has *no* influence on market price—are rare. Does that mean the supply and demand model can't be used when analyzing most markets?

Not at all. Many markets, while not *strictly* perfectly competitive, come rather close. Choosing to view these markets as if they were perfectly competitive is often a useful approximation.

Think of the market for fast-food hot dogs in a big city. On the one hand, every hot dog stand is somewhat different from every other one in terms of location, quality of service, and so on. This means an individual vendor has *some* influence over the price of his hot dogs. For example, if his competitors are all charging $1.50 for a hot dog, but he sells in a more convenient location, he might be able to charge $1.60 or $1.70 without losing too many customers. In this sense, the market for sidewalk hot dogs does not seem perfectly competitive.

On the other hand, there are rather narrow limits to an individual seller's freedom to change his price. With so many vendors in a big city, who are not *that* different from one another, one who charged $2.00 or $2.25 might soon find that he's lost all of his customers to the other vendors who are charging the market price of $1.50. Since no single seller can deviate *too* much from the market price, we could—if we wanted to—view the market as more or less perfectly competitive.

How, then, do we decide whether to consider a market, such as the market for big-city hot dogs, as perfectly or imperfectly competitive? You won't be surprised to hear that it depends on the question we want to answer. If we want to explain why there are occasional price wars among hot dog vendors, or why some of them routinely charge higher prices than others, viewing the market as perfectly competitive would not work well—it would hide, rather than reveal, the answer. For these questions, we'd choose a *different* model—one designed for a type of *im*perfectly competitive market. (If your current course is *micro*economics, you will soon learn about these models and how to use them.)

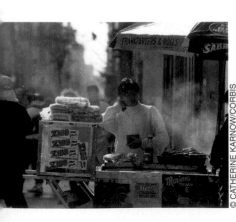

But if we want to know why hot dogs are cheaper than most other types of fast foods, the simplest approach is to view the market for hot dogs as perfectly competitive. True, each hot dog vendor does have *some* influence over the price. But that influence is so small, and the prices of different sellers are so similar, that our assumption of perfect competition works pretty well.

Perfect competition then, is a matter of degree, rather than an all-or-nothing characteristic. While there are very few markets in which sellers and buyers take the price as completely given, there are many markets in which a *narrow range* of prices is treated as a given (as in the market for hot dogs). In these markets, supply and demand often provides a good approximation to what is going on. This is why it has proven to be the most versatile and widely used model in the economist's tool kit. Neither laptop computers nor orange juice is traded in a perfectly competitive market. But ask an economist to tell you why the price of laptops decreases every year, or why the price of orange juice rises after a freeze in Florida, and he or she will invariably reach for supply and demand to find the answer.

Supply and demand are like two blades of a scissors: To analyze a market, we need both of them. In this and the next section, we will be sharpening those blades, learning separately about supply and demand. Then, we'll put them together and put them to use. Let's start with demand.

DEMAND

It's tempting to think of the "demand" for a product as just a psychological phenomenon, a pure "want" or "desire." But that notion can lead us astray. For example, you *want* all kinds of things: a bigger apartment, a better car, nicer clothes, more and better vacations. The list is endless. But you don't always *buy* them. Why not?

Because in addition to your wants—which you'd very much like to satisfy—you also face *constraints*. First, you have to *pay*. Second, you have limited funds with which to buy things, so every decision to buy one thing is also a decision *not* to buy something else (or a decision to save less, and have less buying power in the future). As a result, every purchase confronts you with an opportunity cost. Your "wants," together with the real-world constraints that you face, determine what you will choose to buy in any market. Hence, the following definition:

> The **quantity demanded** of a good or service is the number of units that all buyers in a market would choose to buy over a given time period, given the constraints that they face.

Quantity Demanded The amount of a good that all buyers in a market would choose to buy during a period of time, given their constraints.

Since this definition plays a key role in any supply and demand analysis, it's worth taking a closer look at it.

Quantity Demanded Implies a Choice. Quantity demanded doesn't tell us the amount of a good that households feel they "need" or "desire" in order to be happy. Instead, it tells us how much households would choose to buy *when they take into account the opportunity cost* of their decisions. The opportunity cost arises from the constraints households face, such as having to pay a given price for the good, limits on spendable funds, and so on.

Quantity Demanded Is Hypothetical. Will households actually be *able* to purchase the amount they want to purchase? As you'll soon see, usually yes. But there are special situations—analyzed in microeconomics—in which households are frustrated in buying all that they would like to buy. Quantity demanded makes no assumptions about the availability of the good. Instead, it's the answer to a hypothetical question: How much would households buy, given the constraints that they face, if the units they wanted to buy were available.

Quantity Demanded Depends on **Price.** The price of the good is just one variable among many that influences quantity demanded. But because one of our main purposes in building a supply and demand model is to explain how prices are determined, we try to keep that variable front-and-center in our thinking. This is why for the next few pages we'll assume that all other influences on demand are held constant, so we can explore the relationship between price and quantity demanded.

THE LAW OF DEMAND

How does a change in price affect quantity demanded? You probably know the answer to this already: When something is more expensive, people tend to buy less of it. This common observation applies to air travel, magazines, guitars, and virtually everything else that people buy. For all of these goods and services, price and quantity are *negatively related*: that is, when price rises, quantity demanded falls; when price falls, quantity demanded rises. This negative relationship is observed so regularly in markets that economists call it the *law of demand*.

Law of demand As the price of a good increases, the quantity demanded decreases.

> The **law of demand** states that when the price of a good rises and everything else remains the same, the quantity of the good demanded will fall.

Read that definition again, and notice the very important words, "everything else remains the same." The law of demand tells us what would happen *if* all the other influences on buyers' choices remained unchanged, and only one influence—the price of the good—changed.

This is an example of a common practice in economics. In the real world, many variables change *simultaneously*. But to understand changes in the economy, we must first understand the effect of each variable *separately*. So we conduct a series of mental experiments in which we ask: "What would happen if this one influence—and only this one—were to change?" The law of demand is the result of one such mental experiment, in which we imagine that the price of the good changes, but all other influences on quantity demanded remain constant.

Ceteris paribus Latin for "all else remaining the same."

Mental experiments like this are used so often in economics that we sometimes use a shorthand Latin expression to remind us that we are holding all but one influence constant: *ceteris paribus* (formally pronounced KAY-ter-is PAR-ih-bus, although it's acceptable to pronounce the first word as SEH-ter-is). This is Latin for "all else the same," or "all else remaining unchanged." Even when it is not explicitly stated, the *ceteris paribus* assumption is virtually always implied. The exceptions are cases where we consider two or more influences on a variable that change simultaneously, as we will do toward the end of this chapter.

THE DEMAND SCHEDULE AND THE DEMAND CURVE

To make our discussion more concrete, let's look at a specific market: the market for real maple syrup in the United States. In this market, we'll view the buyers as U.S. households, whereas the sellers (to be considered later) are maple syrup producers in the United States or Canada.

Demand schedule A list showing the quantities of a good that consumers would choose to purchase at different prices, with all other variables held constant.

Table 1 shows a hypothetical **demand schedule** for maple syrup in this market. This is *a list of different quantities demanded at different prices, with all other variables that affect the demand decision assumed constant*. For example, the demand schedule tells us that when the price of maple syrup is $2.00 per bottle, the quantity demanded will be 60,000 bottles per month. Notice that the demand schedule obeys

Price (per bottle)	Quantity Demanded (bottles per month)	**TABLE 1**
		Demand Schedule for Maple Syrup in the United States
$1.00	75,000	
$2.00	60,000	
$3.00	50,000	
$4.00	40,000	
$5.00	35,000	

the law of demand: As the price of maple syrup increases, *ceteris paribus*, the quantity demanded falls.

Now look at Figure 2. It shows a diagram that will appear again and again in your study of economics. In the figure, each price-and-quantity combination in Table 1 is represented by a point. For example, point *A* represents the price $4.00 and quantity 40,000, while point *B* represents the pair $2.00 and 60,000. When we connect all of these points with a line, we obtain the famous *demand curve*, labeled with a *D* in the figure.

> The **demand curve** *shows the relationship between the price of a good and the quantity demanded in the market, holding constant all other variables that influence demand. Each point on the curve shows the total quantity that buyers would choose to buy at a specific price.*

Demand curve The graphical depiction of a demand schedule; a curve showing the quantity of a good or service demanded at various prices, with all other variables held constant.

Notice that the demand curve in Figure 2—like virtually all demand curves—*slopes downward*. This is just a graphical representation of the law of demand.

SHIFTS VERSUS MOVEMENTS ALONG THE DEMAND CURVE

Markets are affected by a variety of events. Some events will cause us to *move along* the demand curve; others will cause the entire demand curve to *shift*. It is crucial to distinguish between these two very different types of effects.

Let's go back to Figure 2. There, you can see that when the price of maple syrup rises from $2.00 to $4.00 per bottle, the number of bottles demanded falls from 60,000 to 40,000. This is a movement *along* the demand curve, from point *B* to point *A*. In general,

> *a change in the price of a good causes a movement* along *the demand curve.*

In Figure 2, a *fall* in price would cause us to move *rightward* along the demand curve (from point *A* to point *B*), and a *rise* in price would cause us to move *leftward* along the demand curve (from *B* to *A*).

Remember, though, that when we draw a demand curve, we assume all other variables that might influence demand are *held constant* at some particular value. For example, the demand curve in Figure 2 might have been drawn to give us quantity demanded at each price when average household income in the United States remains constant at, say, $40,000 per year.

But suppose average income increases to $50,000? With more income, we'd expect households to buy more of *most* things, including maple syrup. This is illus-

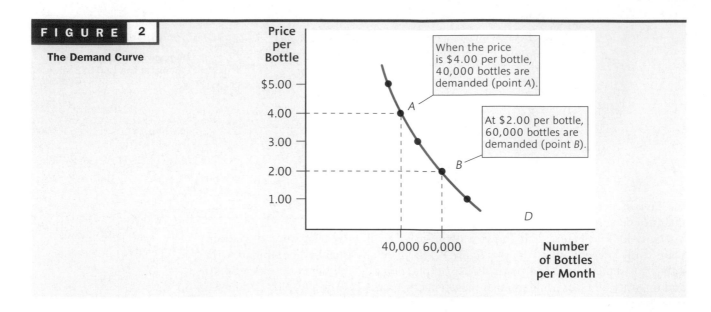

FIGURE 2

The Demand Curve

Price per Bottle

When the price is $4.00 per bottle, 40,000 bottles are demanded (point *A*).

At $2.00 per bottle, 60,000 bottles are demanded (point *B*).

$5.00

4.00 —— *A*

3.00

2.00 —— *B*

1.00

D

40,000 60,000

Number of Bottles per Month

trated in Table 2. At the original income level, households would choose to buy 60,000 bottles of maple syrup at $2.00 per bottle. But after income rises, they would choose to buy more at that price—80,000 bottles, according to Table 2. A similar change would occur at any other price for maple syrup: After income rises, households would choose to buy more than before. In other words, the rise in income *changes the entire relationship between price and quantity demanded.* We now have a *new* demand curve.

Figure 3 plots the new demand curve from the quantities in the third column of Table 2. The new demand curve lies to the *right* of the old curve. For example, at a price of $2.00, quantity demanded increases from 60,000 bottles on the old curve (point *B*) to 80,000 bottles on the *new* demand curve (point *C*). As you can see, the rise in household income has *shifted* the demand curve to the right.

More generally,

> *a change in any variable that affects demand—except for the good's price— causes the demand curve to shift.*

When buyers would choose to buy a greater quantity at any price, the demand curve shifts *rightward*. If they would decide to buy a smaller quantity at any price, the demand curve shifts *leftward*.

"CHANGE IN QUANTITY DEMANDED" VERSUS "CHANGE IN DEMAND"

Language is important when discussing demand. The term *quantity demanded* means a *particular amount* that buyers would choose to buy at a specific price, represented by a single point on a demand curve. *Demand*, by contrast, means the *entire relationship* between price and quantity demanded, represented by the entire demand curve.

For this reason, when a change in the price of a good moves us *along* a demand curve, we call it a **change in quantity demanded**. For example, in Figure 2, the movement from point *A* to point *B* is an *increase* in quantity demanded. This is a change from one number (40,000 bottles) to another (60,000 bottles).

Change in quantity demanded A movement along a demand curve in response to a change in price.

Price (per bottle)	Original Quantity Demanded (bottles per month)	New Quantity Demanded After Increase in Income (bottles per month)		
			TABLE	**2**
			Increase in Demand for Maple Syrup in the United States	
$1.00	75,000	95,000		
$2.00	60,000	80,000		
$3.00	50,000	70,000		
$4.00	40,000	60,000		
$5.00	35,000	55,000		

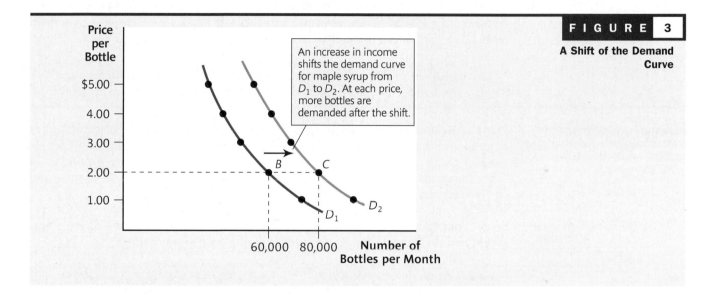

FIGURE **3**

A Shift of the Demand Curve

An increase in income shifts the demand curve for maple syrup from D_1 to D_2. At each price, more bottles are demanded after the shift.

When something *other* than the price changes, causing the entire demand curve to shift, we call it a **change in demand**. In Figure 3, for example, the shift in the curve would be called an *increase in demand*.

Change in demand A shift of a demand curve in response to a change in some variable other than price.

FACTORS THAT SHIFT THE DEMAND CURVE

Let's take a closer look at what might cause a change in demand (a shift of the demand curve). Keep in mind that for now, we're exploring *one factor at a time*, always keeping *all other determinants of demand constant*.

Income. In Figure 3, an increase in **income** shifted the demand for maple syrup to the right. In fact, a rise in income has the same effect on the demand for *most* goods. We call these **normal goods**. Housing, automobiles, health club memberships, and real maple syrup are all examples of normal goods.

But not all goods are normal. For some goods—called **inferior goods**—a rise in income would *decrease* demand—shifting the demand curve *leftward*. Regular-grade ground chuck is a good example. It's a cheap source of protein, but not as high in quality as sirloin. With higher income, households could more easily afford better types of meat—ground sirloin or steak, for example. As a result, higher

Income The amount that a person or firm earns over a particular period.

Normal good A good that people demand more of as their income rises.

Inferior good A good that people demand less of as their income rises.

incomes for buyers might cause the demand for ground chuck to *decrease*. For similar reasons, we might expect that Greyhound bus tickets (in contrast to airline tickets) and single-ply paper towels (in contrast to two-ply) are inferior goods.

> *A rise in income will* increase *the demand for a* normal *good, and* decrease *the demand for an* inferior *good*.

Wealth The total value of everything a person or firm owns, at a point in time, minus the total value of everything owed.

Wealth. Your **wealth** at any point in time is the total value of everything you *own* (cash, bank accounts, stocks, bonds, real estate or any other valuable property) minus the total dollar amount you *owe* (home mortgage, credit card debt, auto loan, student loan, and so on). Although income and wealth are different, (see the nearby Dangerous Curves box), they have similar effects on demand. Increases in wealth among buyers—because of an increase in the value of their stocks or bonds, for example—gives them more funds with which to purchase goods and services. As you might expect,

> *an increase in wealth will* increase *demand (shift the curve rightward) for a normal good, and* decrease *demand (shift the curve leftward) for an inferior good*.

Substitute A good that can be used in place of some other good and that fulfills more or less the same purpose.

Prices of Related Goods. A **substitute** is a good that can be used in place of another good and that fulfills more or less the same purpose. For example, many people use real maple syrup to sweeten their pancakes, but they could use a number of other things instead: honey, sugar, jam, or *artificial* maple syrup. Each of these can be considered a substitute for real maple syrup.

When the price of a substitute rises, people will choose to buy *more* maple syrup. For example, when the price of jam rises, some jam users will switch to maple syrup, and the demand for maple syrup will increase. In general,

> *a rise in the price of a substitute increases the demand for a good, shifting the demand curve to the right*.

DANGEROUS CURVES

Income versus Wealth It's easy to confuse *income* with *wealth*, because both are measured in dollars and both are sources of funds that can be spent on goods and services. But they are not the same thing. Your income is how much you earn *per period of time* (such as, $20 *per hour*, $3,500 *per month*, or $40,000 *per year*). Your wealth, by contrast, is the value of what you *own* minus the value of what you *owe* at a particular *moment in time*. (Such as, on December 31, 2005, the value of what you own is $12,000, but the value of what you owe is $9,000, so you have $3,000 in wealth.)

To help you see the difference: suppose you get a good job after you graduate, but you have very little in the bank, and you still have large, unpaid student loans. Then you'd have a moderate-to-high *income* (what you earn at your job each period), but your wealth would be negative (since what you would *owe* is greater than what you *own*).

Of course, if the price of a substitute falls, we have the opposite result: Demand for the original good decreases, shifting its demand curve to the left.

There are countless examples in which a change in a substitute's price affects demand for a good. A drop in the rental price of DVDs, *ceteris paribus*, would decrease the demand for movies at theaters. A rise in the price of beef, *ceteris paribus*, would increase the demand for chicken.

Complement A good that is used *together with* some other good.

A **complement** is the opposite of a substitute: It's used *together with* the good we are interested in. Pancake mix is a complement to maple syrup, since these two goods are used frequently in combination. If the price of pancake mix rises, some consumers will switch to other breakfasts—bacon and eggs, for example—that *don't* include maple syrup. The demand for maple syrup will decrease.

> *A rise in the price of a complement decreases the demand for a good, shifting the demand curve to the left.*

For this reason, we'd expect a higher price for automobiles to decrease the demand for gasoline. (To test yourself: How would a lower price for milk affect the demand for breakfast cereal?)

Population. As the population increases in an area, the number of buyers will ordinarily increase as well, and the demand for a good will increase. The growth of the U.S. population over the last 50 years has been an important reason (but not the only reason) for rightward shifts in the demand curves for food, housing, automobiles, and many other goods and services.

Expected Price. If buyers expect the price of maple syrup to rise next month, they may choose to purchase more *now* to stock up before the price hike. If people expect the price to drop, they may postpone buying, hoping to take advantage of the lower price later.

> *In many markets, an expectation that price will rise in the future shifts the* current *demand curve rightward, while an expectation that price will fall shifts the current demand curve leftward.*

Expected price changes are especially important in the markets for financial assets such as stocks and bonds and in the market for real estate. People want to buy more stocks, bonds, and real estate when they think their prices will rise in the near future. This shifts the demand curves for these items to the right.

Tastes. Suppose we know the number of buyers in the United States, their expectations about the future price of maple syrup, the prices of all related goods, and the average levels of income and wealth. Do we have all the information we need to draw the demand curve for maple syrup? Not really. Because we have not yet considered the psychological component—the habits and tastes that determine the basic desire people have for maple syrup. How many Americans eat breakfast every day? Of these, how many eat pancakes or waffles? How often? How many of them *like* maple syrup, and how much do they like it? And what about all of the other goods and services competing for consumers' dollars: How do buyers feel about *them*?

The questions could go on and on, pinpointing various characteristics about buyers that influence their attitudes toward maple syrup. The approach of economics is to lump all of these characteristics of buyers together and call them, simply, *tastes* or *preferences*. Economists are sometimes interested in where these tastes come from or what makes them change. But for the most part, economics deals with the *consequences* of a change in tastes, whatever the reason for its occurrence.

When tastes change *toward* a good (people favor it more), demand increases, and the demand curve shifts to the right. When tastes change *away* from a good, demand decreases, and the demand curve shifts to the left. An example of this is the change in tastes away from cigarettes over the past several decades. The cause may have been an aging population, a greater concern about health among people of *all* ages, or successful antismoking advertising. But regardless of the cause, the effect has been to decrease the demand for cigarettes, shifting the demand curve to the left.

FIGURE 4

**The Demand Curve—
A Summary**

price↓ ⟹ move rightward along curve

price↑ ⟹ move leftward along curve

- income or wealth↑
- price of substitute↑
- price of complement↓
- population↑
- expected price↑
- Tastes shift
  toward good

⟹ demand curve shifts rightward

- income or wealth↓
- price of substitute↓
- price of complement↑
- population↓
- expected price↓
- Tastes shift
  away from good

⟹ demand curve shifts leftward

DEMAND: A SUMMARY

Figure 4 summarizes the variables we've discussed that affect the demand side of the market and how their effects are represented with a demand curve. Notice the important distinction between movements *along* the demand curve and *shifts* of the entire curve.

Keep in mind that other variables, besides those listed in Figure 4, can influence demand. For example, government subsidies such as Federal Pell Grants for college shift the demand curve for higher education rightward. Expectations other than future price

Does Supply Affect Demand? A troubling thought may have occurred to you. Among the variables that shift the demand curve in Figure 3, shouldn't we include the amount of syrup available? Or to put the question another way, doesn't supply influence demand?

No—at least not directly. The demand curve by asking people a series of hypothetical questions about how much they *would like* to buy at each different price. A change in the amount available would not affect the answers to these questions, and so doesn't affect the curve itself. As you'll see later, a change in supply *will* change the *price* of the good, but this causes a movement along—not a shift of—the demand curve.

matter too. If buyers expect a recession and fear their incomes may fall in the future, their demand for many goods may decrease *now*, even though current income remains unchanged. Some of these other *shift-variables* for demand curves will be discussed in future chapters, as they become relevant in each case. But we'll always use the same logic we used here: If an event makes buyers want to purchase more or less of a good *at any price*, it causes the demand curve to shift.

SUPPLY

When most people hear the word *supply*, their first thought is that it's the amount of something "available," as if this amount were fixed in stone. For example, someone might say, "We can only drill so much oil from the ground," or "There are only so many apartments for rent in this town." And yet, the world's known oil reserves—as well as yearly production of oil—have increased dramatically over the last half century, as oil companies have found it worth their while to look harder for oil. Similarly, in most towns and cities, short buildings have been replaced with tall ones, and the number of apartments has increased. Supply, like demand, can change, and the amount of a good supplied in a market depends on the *choices* made by those who produce it.

What governs these choices? We assume that business firms' managers have a goal: to earn the highest profit possible. But they also face constraints. First, in a competitive market, the price they can charge for their product is a *given*—the market price. Second, firms have to pay the *costs* of producing and selling their product. These costs will depend on the production process they use, the prices they must pay for their inputs, and more. Business firms' desire for profit, together with the real-world constraints that they face, determines how much they will choose to sell in any market. Hence, the following definition:

Quantity supplied The specific amount of a good that *all* sellers in the market would choose to sell over some time period, given (1) a particular price for the good; (2) all other constraints on firms.

> *Quantity supplied is the number of units of a good that* all *sellers in the market would choose to sell over some time period, given the constraints that they face.*

Let's briefly go over the notion of quantity supplied to clarify what it means and doesn't mean.

Quantity Supplied Implies a Choice. We assume that the managers of business firms have a simple goal—to earn the highest possible profit. But they also face constraints: the specific price they can charge for the good, the cost of any inputs used, and so on. Quantity supplied doesn't tell us the amount of, say, maple syrup that sellers would like to sell *if* they could charge a thousand dollars for each bottle, and *if* they could produce it at zero cost. Instead, it's the quantity that firms *choose* to sell—the quantity that gives them the highest profit given the constraints they face.

Quantity Supplied Is Hypothetical. Will firms actually be *able* to sell the amount they want to sell at the going price? You'll soon see that they usually can. But the definition of quantity supplied makes no assumptions about firms' *ability* to sell the good. Quantity supplied answers the hypothetical question: How much *would* firms' managers sell, given the constraints they face, if they were able to sell all that they wanted.

Quantity Supplied Depends on **Price.** The price of the good is just one variable among many that influences quantity supplied. But—as with demand—we want to keep that variable foremost in our thinking. This is why for the next couple of pages we'll assume that all other influences on supply are held constant, so we can explore the relationship between price and quantity supplied.

THE LAW OF SUPPLY

How does a change in price affect quantity supplied? When a seller can get a higher price for a good, producing and selling it become more profitable. Producers will devote more resources toward its production—perhaps even pulling resources from other goods they produce—so they can sell more of the good in question. For example, a rise in the price of laptop computers will encourage computer makers to shift resources out of the production of other things (such as desktop computers) and toward the production of laptops.

In general, price and quantity supplied are *positively related:* When the price of a good rises, the quantity supplied will rise as well. This relationship between price and quantity supplied is called the law of supply, the counterpart to the law of demand we discussed earlier.

Law of supply As the price of a good increases, the quantity supplied increases.

> The **law of supply** states that when the price of a good rises, and everything else remains the same, the quantity of the good supplied will rise.

Once again, notice the very important words "everything else remains the same—*ceteris paribus.*" Although many other variables influence the quantity of a good supplied, the law of supply tells us what would happen if all of them remained unchanged and only one—the price of the good—changed.

THE SUPPLY SCHEDULE AND THE SUPPLY CURVE

Let's continue with our example of the market for maple syrup in the United States. Who are the suppliers in this market? Maple syrup producers are located mostly in the forests of Vermont, upstate New York, and Canada. The market quantity supplied is the amount of syrup all of these producers together would offer for sale at each price for maple syrup in the United States.

Supply schedule A list showing the quantities of a good or service that firms would choose to produce and sell at different prices, with all other variables held constant.

Table 3 shows the **supply schedule** for maple syrup—a *list of different quantities supplied at different prices, with all other variables held constant.* As you can see, the supply schedule obeys the law of supply: As the price of maple syrup rises, the quantity supplied rises along with it. But how can this be? After all, maple trees must be about 40 years old before they can be tapped for syrup, so any rise in quantity supplied now or in the near future cannot come from an increase in planting. What, then, causes quantity supplied to rise as price rises?

Many things. First, with higher prices, firms will find it profitable to tap existing trees more intensively. Second, evaporating and bottling can be done more carefully, so that less maple syrup is spilled and more is available for shipping. Finally, the product can be diverted from other areas and shipped to the United States instead. For example, if the price of maple syrup rises in the United States but not in Canada, producers would shift deliveries away from Canada so they could sell more in the United States.

Price (per bottle)	Quantity Supplied (bottles per month)	TABLE 3
		Supply Schedule for Maple Syrup in the United States
$1.00	25,000	
$2.00	40,000	
$3.00	50,000	
$4.00	60,000	
$5.00	65,000	

Now look at Figure 5, which shows a very important curve—the counterpart to the demand curve we drew earlier. In Figure 5, each point represents a price-quantity pair taken from Table 3. For example, point *F* in the figure corresponds to a price of $2.00 per bottle and a quantity of 40,000 bottles per month, while point *G* represents the price-quantity pair $4.00 and 60,000 bottles. Connecting all of these points with a solid line gives us the *supply curve* for maple syrup, labeled with an *S* in the figure.

> The **supply curve** shows the relationship between the price of a good and the quantity supplied in the market, holding constant the values of all other variables that affect supply. Each point on the curve shows the quantity that sellers would choose to sell at a specific price.

Supply curve A graphical depiction of a supply schedule; a curve showing the quantity of a good or service supplied at various prices, with all other variables held constant.

Notice that the supply curve in Figure 5—like all supply curves for goods and services—is *upward sloping*. This is the graphical representation of the law of supply.

SHIFTS VERSUS MOVEMENTS ALONG THE SUPPLY CURVE

As with the demand curve, it's important to distinguish those events that will cause us to *move along* a given supply curve for the good, and those that will cause the entire supply curve to *shift*.

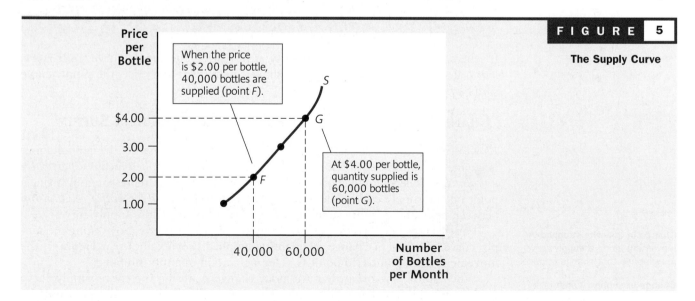

FIGURE 5

The Supply Curve

When the price is $2.00 per bottle, 40,000 bottles are supplied (point *F*).

At $4.00 per bottle, quantity supplied is 60,000 bottles (point *G*).

If you look once again at Figure 5, you'll see that if the price of maple syrup rises from $2.00 to $4.00 per bottle, the number of bottles supplied rises from 40,000 to 60,000. This is a movement *along* the supply curve, from point *F* to point *G*. In general,

> *a change in the price of a good causes a movement* along *the supply curve.*

In the figure, a *rise* in price would cause us to move *rightward* along the supply curve (from point *F* to point *G*) and a *fall* in price would move us *leftward* along the curve (from point *G* to point *F*).

But remember that when we draw a supply curve, we assume that all other variables that might influence supply are *held constant* at some particular values. For example, the supply curve in Figure 5 might tell us the quantity supplied at each price when the cost of an important input—transportation from the farm to the point of sale—remains constant.

But suppose the cost of transportation drops. Then, at any given price for maple syrup, firms would find it more profitable to produce and sell it. This is illustrated in Table 4. With the original transportation cost, and a selling price of $4.00 per bottle, firms would choose to sell 60,000 bottles. But after transportation cost falls, they would choose to produce and sell more—80,000 bottles in our example—assuming they could still charge $4.00 per bottle. A similar change would occur for any other price of maple syrup we might imagine: After transportation costs fall, firms would choose to sell more than before. In other words, *the entire relationship between price and quantity supplied has changed*, so we have a *new* supply curve.

Figure 6 plots the new supply curve from the quantities in the third column of Table 4. The new supply curve lies to the *right* of the old one. For example, at a price of $4.00, quantity supplied increases from 60,000 bottles on the old curve (point *G*) to 80,000 bottles on the *new* supply curve (point *J*). The drop in the transportation costs has *shifted* the supply curve to the right.

In general,

> *a change in any variable that affects supply—except for the good's price— causes the supply curve to shift.*

If sellers want to sell a greater quantity at any price, the supply curve shifts *rightward*. If sellers would prefer to sell a smaller quantity at any price, the supply curve shifts *leftward*.

"CHANGE IN QUANTITY SUPPLIED" VERSUS "CHANGE IN SUPPLY"

As we stressed in our discussion of the demand side of the market, be careful about language when thinking about supply. The term *quantity supplied* means a *particular amount* that sellers would choose to sell at a *particular* price, represented by a single point on the supply curve. The term *supply*, however, means the *entire relationship* between price and quantity supplied, as represented by the entire supply curve.

Change in quantity supplied A movement along a supply curve in response to a change in price.

For this reason, when the price of the good changes, and we move *along* the supply curve, we have a **change in quantity supplied**. For example, in Figure 5, the movement from point *F* to point *G* is an *increase* in quantity supplied.

Change in supply A shift of a supply curve in response to some variable other than price.

When something *other* than the price changes, causing the entire supply curve to shift, we call it a **change in supply**. The shift in Figure 6, for example, would be called an *increase in supply*.

Price (per bottle)	Original Quantity Supplied (bottles/month)	Quantity Supplied After Decrease in Transportation Cost	TABLE 4
			Increase in Supply of Maple Syrup in the United States
$1.00	25,000	45,000	
$2.00	40,000	60,000	
$3.00	50,000	70,000	
$4.00	60,000	80,000	
$5.00	65,000	90,000	

FACTORS THAT SHIFT THE SUPPLY CURVE

Let's take a closer look at some of the *causes* of a change in supply (a shift of the supply curve). As always, we're considering *one* variable at a time, keeping all other determinants of supply constant.

Input Prices. In Figure 6, we saw that a drop in transportation costs shifted the supply curve for maple syrup to the right. But producers of maple syrup use a variety of other inputs besides transportation: land, maple trees, evaporators, sap pans, labor, glass bottles, bottling machinery, and more. A lower price for any of these means a lower cost of producing and selling maple syrup, making it more profitable. As a result, we would expect producers to shift resources into maple syrup production, causing an increase in supply.

In general,

> *a fall in the price of an input causes an increase in supply, shifting the supply curve to the right.*

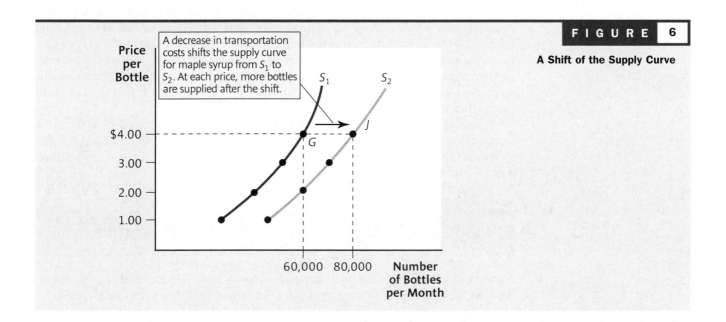

FIGURE 6

A Shift of the Supply Curve

A decrease in transportation costs shifts the supply curve for maple syrup from S_1 to S_2. At each price, more bottles are supplied after the shift.

Similarly, a rise in the price of an input causes a decrease in supply, shifting the supply curve to the left. If, for example, the wages of maple syrup workers rose, the supply curve in Figure 6 would shift to the left.

Price of Alternatives. Many firms can switch their production rather easily among several different goods or services, all of which require more or less the same inputs. For example, a dermatology practice can rather easily switch its specialty from acne treatments for the young to wrinkle treatments for the elderly. An automobile producer can—without too much adjustment—switch to producing light trucks. And a maple syrup producer could dry its maple syrup and produce maple *sugar* instead. Or it could even cut down its maple trees and sell maple wood as lumber. These other goods that firms *could* produce are called **alternate goods** and their prices influence the supply curve.

Alternate goods Other goods that a firm could produce, using some of the same types of inputs as the good in question.

For example, if the price of maple *sugar* rose, then at any given price for maple *syrup*, producers would choose to shift some production from syrup to sugar. This would be a decrease in the supply of maple syrup. If firms already are producing maple sugar, and its price *falls*, the supply of syrup would increase.

Alternate market A market other than the one being analyzed in which the same good could be sold.

Another alternative for the firm is to sell the *same* good in a *different* market, which we'll call an **alternate market**. For example, since we are considering the market for maple syrup in the United States, the maple syrup market in Canada is an alternate market for producers. For any given price in the United States, a rise in the price of maple syrup in Canada will cause producers to shift some sales from the United States to Canada. In the U.S. market, this will cause the supply curve to shift leftward.

> *When the price for an alternative rises—either an alternate good or the same good in an alternate market—the supply curve shifts leftward.*

Similarly, a decrease in the price of an alternate good (or a lower price in an alternate market) will shift the supply curve rightward.

Technology. A *technological advance* in production occurs whenever a firm can produce a given level of output in a new and cheaper way than before. For example, the discovery of a surgical procedure called Lasik—in which a laser is used to reshape the interior of the cornea rather than the outer surface—has enabled eye surgeons to correct their patients' vision with fewer follow-up visits and smaller quantities of medication than were used with previous procedures. This example is a technological advance because it enables firms to produce the same output (eye surgery) more cheaply than before.

In maple syrup production, a technological advance might be a new, more efficient tap that draws more maple syrup from each tree, or a new bottling method that reduces spillage. Advances like these would reduce the cost of producing maple syrup, making it more profitable, and producers would want to make and sell more of it at any price.

In general,

> *cost-saving technological advances increase the supply of a good, shifting the supply curve to the right.*

Number of Firms. A change in the number of firms in a market will change the quantity that all sellers together would want to sell at any given price. For example, if—over time—more people decided to open up maple syrup farms because it was a profitable business, the supply of maple syrup would increase. And if maple syrup farms began closing down, their number would be reduced and supply would decrease.

> *An increase in the number of sellers—with no other change—shifts the supply curve rightward.*

Expected Price. Imagine you're the president of Sticky's Maple Syrup, Inc., and you expect that the market price of maple syrup—over which you, as an individual seller, have no influence—to rise next month. What would you do? You'd certainly want to postpone selling your maple syrup until the price is higher and your profit greater. Therefore, at any given price *now*, you might slow down production, or just slow down sales by warehousing more of what you produce. If other firms have similar expectations of a price hike, they'll do the same. Thus, an expectation of a *future* price hike will decrease supply *in the present.*

Suppose instead you expect the market price to *drop* next month. Then—at any given price—you'd want to sell more *now*, by stepping up production and even selling out of your inventories. So an expected future drop in the price would cause an increase in supply in the present.

Does Demand Affect Supply? In the list of variables that shift the supply curve in Figure 7 we've left out the amount that buyers would like to buy. Is this a mistake? Doesn't demand affect supply?

The answer is no—at least, not directly. The supply curve tells us how much sellers would like to sell at each different price. Buyers' behavior doesn't affect this hypothetical quantity, so buyers cannot cause the supply curve to shift. As you'll soon see, buyers *can* affect the price of the good, which in turn affects quantity supplied. But this causes a movement *along* the supply curve—not a shift.

DANGEROUS CURVES

> *In many markets, an expectation of a* future price rise *shifts the current supply curve* leftward. *Similarly, an expectation of a* future price drop *shifts the current supply curve* rightward.

Changes in Weather and Other Natural Events. Weather conditions are an especially important determinant of the supply of agricultural goods.

> Favorable weather *increases crop yields, and causes a* rightward *shift of the supply curve for that crop.* Unfavorable weather *destroys crops and shrinks yields, and shifts the supply curve* leftward.

In addition to bad weather, natural disasters such as fires, hurricanes, and earthquakes can destroy or disrupt the productive capacity of *all* firms in a region. If many sellers of a particular good are located in the affected area, the supply curve for that good will shift leftward. For example, after Hurricanes Katrina and Rita struck the U.S. Gulf Coast in August and September of 2005, 20 percent of the nation's oil refining capacity was taken out for several weeks, causing a sizable leftward shift of the supply curve for gasoline.

SUPPLY—A SUMMARY

Figure 7 summarizes the various factors we've discussed that affect the supply side of the market, and how we illustrate them using a supply curve. But the short list

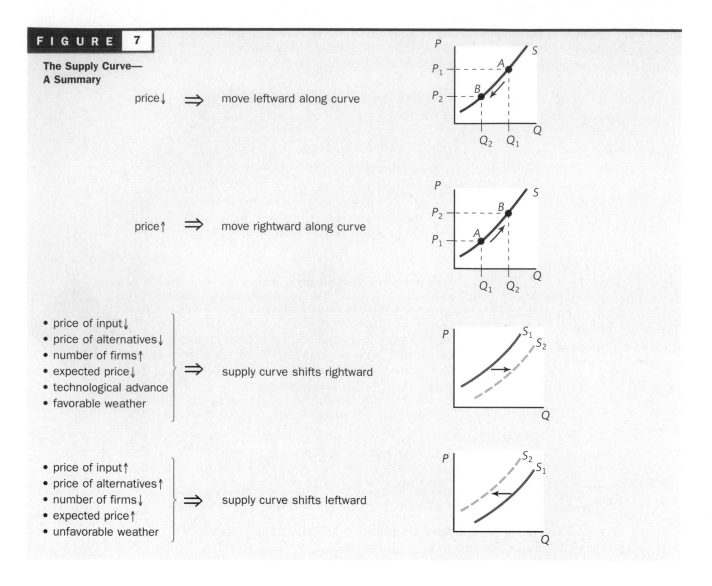

FIGURE 7

**The Supply Curve—
A Summary**

price↓ ⇒ move leftward along curve

price↑ ⇒ move rightward along curve

- price of input↓
- price of alternatives↓
- number of firms↑
- expected price↓
- technological advance
- favorable weather

⇒ supply curve shifts rightward

- price of input↑
- price of alternatives↑
- number of firms↓
- expected price↑
- unfavorable weather

⇒ supply curve shifts leftward

of *shift-variables* for supply is far from exhaustive. For example, a government tax on a good—or a government subsidy paid to producers—will shift the supply curve. So can other government policies, such as environmental and safety regulations.

Some of the other shift-variables for supply curves will be discussed as they become relevant in future chapters. The basic principle, however, is always the same: Anything that makes sellers want to sell more or less of a good *at any given price* will shift the supply curve.

PUTTING SUPPLY AND DEMAND TOGETHER

What happens when buyers and sellers, each having the desire and the ability to trade, come together in a market? The two sides of the market certainly have different agendas. Buyers would like to pay the lowest possible price, while sellers would like to charge the highest possible price. Is there chaos when they meet, with buyers and sellers endlessly chasing after each other or endlessly bargaining for advantage, so that trade never takes place? A casual look at the real world suggests not. In most markets, most of the time, there is order and stability in the encounters between buyers and sellers. In most cases, prices do not fluctuate wildly from moment to moment but seem to hover around a stable value. Even when this stability is short-lived—lasting only a day, an hour, or even a minute in some markets—for this short-time the market seems to be at rest. Whenever we study a market, therefore, we look for this state of rest—a price and quantity at which the market will settle, at least for a while.

Economists use the word *equilibrium* when referring to a state of rest. When a market is in equilibrium, both the price of the good and the quantity bought and sold have settled into a state of rest. More formally,

> the **equilibrium price** and **equilibrium quantity** are values for price and quantity in the market that, once achieved, will remain constant—unless and until the supply curve or the demand curve shifts.

Equilibrium price The market price that, once achieved, remains constant until either the demand curve or supply curve shifts.

Equilibrium quantity The market quantity bought and sold per period that, once achieved, remains constant until either the demand curve or supply curve shifts.

What is the *equilibrium* price of maple syrup in our example, and what is the *equilibrium* quantity that will be bought and sold? These are precisely the questions that the supply and demand model is designed to answer.

Look at Table 5, which combines the supply and demand schedules for maple syrup from Tables 1 and 3. We'll use Table 5 to find the equilibrium price in this market through the process of elimination.

Let's first ask what would happen if the price were $1.00 per bottle. At this price, Table 5 tells us that buyers would want to buy 75,000 bottles each month, while sellers would offer to sell only 25,000. There would be an **excess demand** of 50,000 bottles. What would happen? Buyers would compete with each other to get more maple syrup than was available, and would offer to pay a higher price rather than do without. The price would then rise. The same would occur if the price were $2.00, or any other price below $3.00.

Excess demand At a given price, the amount by which quantity demanded exceeds quantity supplied.

We conclude that any price less than $3.00 cannot be an equilibrium price. If the price starts below $3.00, it would start rising—*not* because the supply curve or the demand curve had shifted, but from natural forces within the market itself. This directly contradicts our definition of equilibrium price.

Figure 8 illustrates the same process by putting the supply and demand curves together on the same graph. As you can see, at a price of $1.00, quantity supplied

Price (per bottle)	Quantity Demanded (bottles per month)	Quantity Supplied (bottles per month)	Excess Demand or Supply?	Consequence
$1.00	75,000	25,000	Excess Demand	Price will Rise
$2.00	60,000	40,000	Excess Demand	Price will Rise
$3.00	**50,000**	**50,000**	**Neither**	**No Change in price**
$4.00	40,000	60,000	Excess Supply	Price will Fall
$5.00	35,000	65,000	Excess Supply	Price will Fall

T A B L E   5

Finding the Market Equilibrium

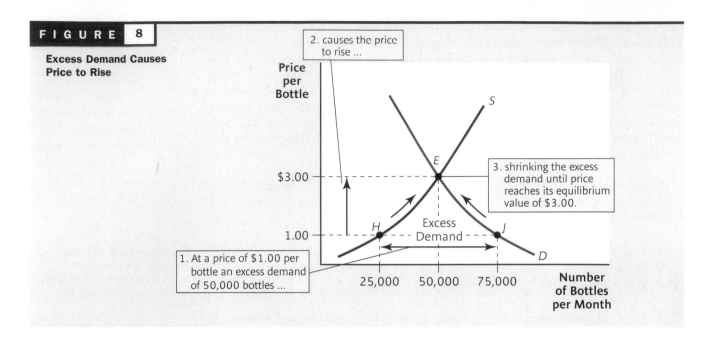

FIGURE 8

**Excess Demand Causes
Price to Rise**

2. causes the price
to rise ...

*Price
per
Bottle*

S

E

3. shrinking the excess
demand until price
reaches its equilibrium
value of $3.00.

$3.00

H Excess J
1.00   Demand

1. At a price of $1.00 per
bottle an excess demand
of 50,000 bottles ...

25,000   50,000   75,000   **Number
of Bottles
per Month**

D

of 25,000 bottles is found at point *H* on the supply curve, while quantity demanded is at point *J* on the demand curve. The horizontal difference between the two curves at $1.00 is a graphical representation of the excess demand at that price.

At this point, we should ask another question: If the price were initially $1.00, would it ever *stop* rising? Yes. Since excess demand is the reason for the price to rise, the process will stop when the excess demand is gone. And as you can see in Figure 8, the rise in price *shrinks* the excess demand in two ways. First, as price rises, buyers demand a smaller quantity—a leftward movement along the demand curve. Second, sellers increase supply to a larger quantity—a rightward movement along the supply curve. Finally, when the price reaches $3.00 per bottle, the excess demand is gone and the price stops rising.

This logic tells us that $3.00 is an *equilibrium* price in this market—a value that won't change as long as the supply and demand curves stay put. But is it the *only* equilibrium price? We've shown that any price *below* $3.00 is not an equilibrium, but what about a price *greater* than $3.00? Let's see.

Suppose the price of maple syrup was, say, $5.00 per bottle. Look again at Table 5 and you'll find that, at this price, quantity supplied would be 65,000 bottles per month, while quantity demanded would be only 35,000 bottles. There is an **excess supply** of 30,000 bottles. Sellers would compete with each other to sell more maple syrup than buyers wanted to buy, and the price would fall. Thus, $5.00 cannot be the equilibrium price.

Figure 9 provides a graphical view of the market in this situation. With a price of $5.00, the excess supply is the horizontal distance between points *K* (on the demand curve) and *L* (on the supply curve). In the figure, the resulting drop in price would move us along both the supply curve (leftward) and the demand curve (rightward). As these movements continued, the excess supply of maple syrup would shrink until it disappeared, once again, at a price of $3.00 per bottle. Our conclusion: If the price happens to be above $3.00, it will fall to $3.00 and then stop changing.

You can see that $3.00 is the equilibrium price—and the *only* equilibrium price—in this market. Moreover, at this price, sellers would want to sell 50,000 bottles—the

Excess supply At a given price, the amount by which quantity supplied exceeds quantity demanded.

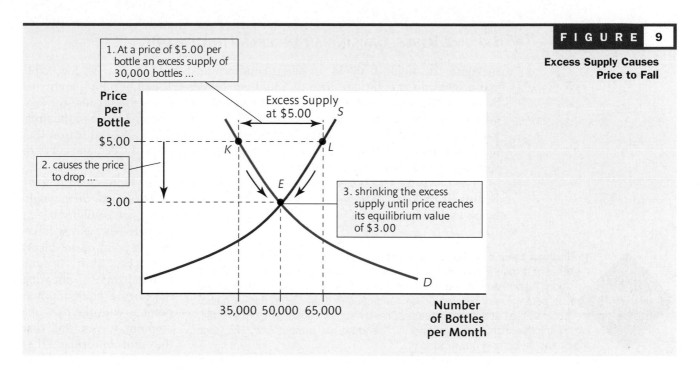

FIGURE 9

Excess Supply Causes
Price to Fall

same quantity that households would want to buy. So, when price comes to rest at $3.00, quantity comes to rest at 50,000 per month—the *equilibrium quantity*.

No doubt, you have noticed that $3.00 happens to be the price at which the supply and demand curves cross. This leads us to an easy, graphical technique for locating our equilibrium:

> *To find the equilibrium price and quantity in a competitive market, draw the supply and demand curves. The equilibrium price and equilibrium quantity can then be found on the vertical and horizontal axes, respectively, where the two curves cross.*

Notice that in equilibrium, the market is operating on *both* the supply curve *and* the demand curve so that—at a price of $3.00—quantity demanded and quantity supplied are equal. There are no dissatisfied buyers unable to find goods they want to purchase, nor are there any frustrated sellers unable to sell goods they want to sell. Indeed, this is why $3.00 is the equilibrium price. It's the only price that creates consistency between what buyers choose to buy and sellers choose to sell.

But we don't expect a market to stay at any particular equilibrium forever, as you're about to see.

WHAT HAPPENS WHEN THINGS CHANGE?

Remember that in order to draw the supply and demand curves in the first place, we had to assume particular values for all the other variables—besides price—that affect demand and supply. If one of these variables changes, then either the supply curve or the demand curve will shift, and our equilibrium will change as well. Let's look at some examples.

INCOME RISES, CAUSING AN INCREASE IN DEMAND

In Figure 10, point *E* shows an initial equilibrium in the U.S. market for maple syrup, with an equilibrium price of $3.00 per bottle, and equilibrium quantity of 50,000 bottles per month. Suppose that the incomes of buyers rise because the U.S. economy recovers rapidly from a recession. We know that income is one of the shift-variables in the demand curve (but not the supply curve). We also can reason that maple syrup is a *normal good*, so the rise in income will cause the demand curve to shift rightward. What happens then?

The old price—$3.00—is no longer the equilibrium price. How do we know? Because if the price *did* remain at $3.00 after the demand curve shifts, there would be an excess demand that would drive the price upward. The new equilibrium—at point *E'*—is the new intersection point of the curves *after* the shift in the demand curve. Comparing the original equilibrium at point *E* with the new one at point *E'*, we find that the shift in demand has caused the equilibrium price to rise (from $3.00 to $4.00) and the equilibrium quantity to rise as well (from 50,000 to 60,000 bottles per month).

DANGEROUS CURVES

The Endless Loop of Erroneous Logic In trying to work out what happens after, say, a rise in income, you might find yourself caught in an endless loop. It goes something like this: "A rise in income causes an increase in demand. An increase in demand causes the price to rise. A higher price causes supply to increase. Greater supply causes the price to fall. A lower price increases demand . . ." and so on, without end. The price keeps bobbing up and down, forever.

What's the mistake here? The first two statements ("a rise in income causes an increase in demand" and "an increase in demand causes price to rise") are entirely correct. But the next statement ("a higher price causes an increase in supply") is flat wrong, and so is everything that follows. A higher price does *not* cause an "increase in supply" (a shift of the supply curve). It causes an increase in *quantity supplied* (a movement *along* the supply curve).

Here's the correct sequence of events: "A rise in income causes an increase in demand. An increase in demand causes price to rise. A higher price causes an increase in *quantity supplied*, moving us along the supply curve until we reach the new equilibrium, with a higher price and greater quantity." End of story.

Notice, too, that in moving from point *E* to point *E'*, we move *along* the supply curve. That is, a shift of the demand curve has caused a movement along the supply curve. Why is this? The demand shift causes the *price* to rise, and a rise in price always causes a movement *along* the supply curve. But the supply curve itself does not shift because none of the variables that affect sellers—other than the price of the good—has changed.

In this example, the equilibrium price and quantity changed because income rose. But *any* event that shifted the demand curve rightward would have the same effect. For example, if tastes changed in favor of maple syrup, or a substitute good like jam rose in price, or a complementary good like pancake mix became cheaper, the demand curve for maple syrup would shift rightward, just as it did in Figure 10. So, we can summarize our findings as follows:

> *A rightward shift in the demand curve causes a rightward movement* along *the supply curve. Equilibrium price and equilibrium quantity both rise.*

BAD WEATHER CAUSES A DECREASE IN SUPPLY

Bad weather can affect supply for most agricultural goods, including maple syrup. An example occurred in January 1998, when New England and Quebec were struck

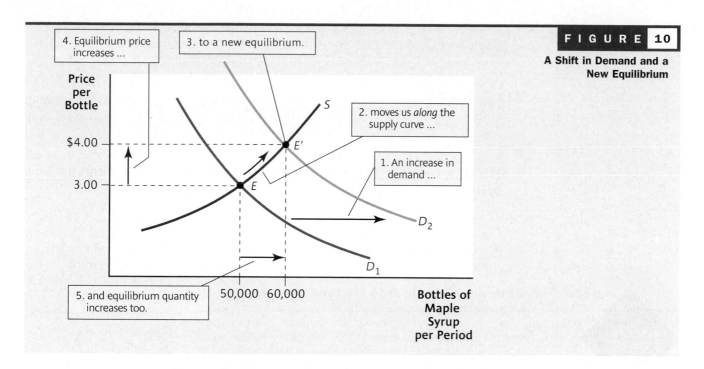

FIGURE 10

A Shift in Demand and a New Equilibrium

4. Equilibrium price increases ...

3. to a new equilibrium.

2. moves us *along* the supply curve ...

1. An increase in demand ...

5. and equilibrium quantity increases too.

by a severe ice storm. Hundreds of thousands of maple trees were downed, and many more were damaged. In Vermont alone, 10 percent of the maple trees were destroyed. How did this affect the market for maple syrup?

As you've learned, weather can be shift-variable for the supply curve. Look at Figure 11. Initially, the supply curve for maple syrup is S_1, with the market in equilibrium at Point E. When had weather hits, the supply curve shifts leftward— say, to S_2. The result: a rise in the equilibrium price of maple syrup (from $3.00 to $5.00 in the figure) and a fall in the equilibrium quantity (from 50,000 to 35,000 bottles).

In this case, it is bad weather that shifts the supply curve leftward. But suppose, instead, that the wages of maple syrup workers increase, or that evaporators become more expensive, or that some maple syrup producers go out of business and sell their

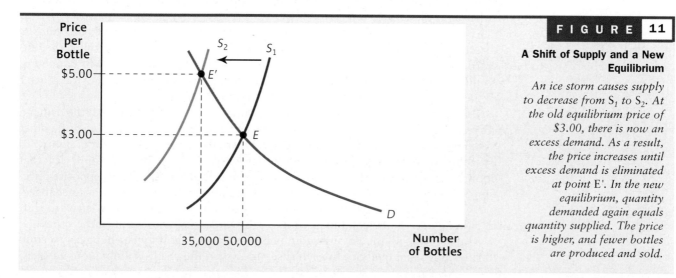

FIGURE 11

A Shift of Supply and a New Equilibrium

An ice storm causes supply to decrease from S_1 to S_2. At the old equilibrium price of $3.00, there is now an excess demand. As a result, the price increases until excess demand is eliminated at point E'. In the new equilibrium, quantity demanded again equals quantity supplied. The price is higher, and fewer bottles are produced and sold.

farms to housing developers. Any of these changes would shift the supply curve for maple syrup leftward, increasing the equilibrium price and decreasing the equilibrium quantity.

More generally,

> *A leftward shift of the supply curve causes a leftward movement* along *the demand curve. Equilibrium price rises, but equilibrium quantity falls.*

HIGHER INCOME AND BAD WEATHER TOGETHER: BOTH CURVES SHIFT

So far, we've considered examples in which just one curve shifts due to a change in a single variable that influences *either* demand or supply. But what would happen if two changes affected the market simultaneously? Then both curves would shift.

Do Curves Shift Up and Down? Or Right and Left? When describing an increase in demand or supply, it's tempting to substitute "upward" for "rightward," and to substitute "downward" for "leftward" when describing a decrease in demand or supply. But be careful! While this interchangeable language works for the demand curve, it does *not* work for the supply curve. To prove this to yourself, look at Figure 6. There you can see that a rightward shift of the supply curve (an increase in supply) is also a *downward* shift of the curve. In later chapters, it will sometimes make sense to describe shifts as upward or downward. For now, it's best to avoid these terms and stick with *rightward* and *leftward*.

Figure 12 shows what happens when we take the two factors we've just explored separately (a rise in income and bad weather) and combine them together. The rise in income causes the demand curve to shift rightward, from D_1 to D_2. The bad weather causes the supply curve to shift leftward, from S_1 to S_2. The result of all this is a change in equilibrium from point E to point E', where the new demand curve D_2 intersects the new supply curve S_2.

Notice that the equilibrium price rises from \$3.00 to \$6.00 in our example. This should come as no surprise. A rightward shift in the demand curve, with no other change, causes price to rise. And a leftward shift in the supply curve, with no other change, causes price to rise. So when we combine the two shifts together, the price must rise. In fact, the increase in the price will be greater than would be caused by either shift alone.

But what about equilibrium quantity? Here, the two shifts work in *opposite* directions. The rightward shift in demand works to increase quantity, while the leftward shift in supply works to decrease quantity. We can't say what will happen to equilibrium quantity until we know which shift is greater and thus has the greater influence. Quantity could rise, fall, or remain unchanged.

In Figure 12, it just so happens that the supply curve shifts more than the demand curve, so equilibrium quantity falls. But you can easily prove to yourself that the other outcomes are possible. First, draw a graph where the demand curves shifts rightward by more than the supply curve shifts leftward. In your graph, you'll see that equilibrium quantity rises. Then, draw one where both curves shift (in opposite directions) by equal amounts, and you'll see that equilibrium quantity remains unchanged.

We can also imagine other combinations of shifts. A rightward or leftward shift in either curve can be combined with a rightward or leftward shift in the other.

Table 6 lists all the possible combinations. It also shows what happens to equilibrium price and quantity in each case, and when the result is ambiguous (a ques-

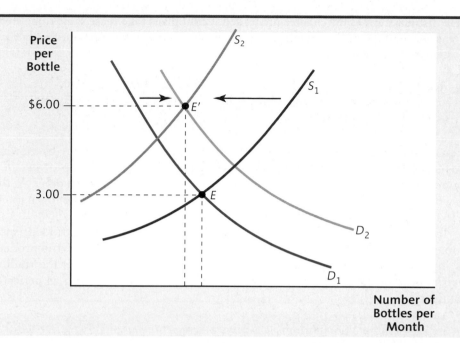

FIGURE 12

A Shift in Both Curves and a New Equilibrium

An increase in income shifts the demand curve rightward from D_1 to D_2. At the same time, bad weather shifts the supply curve leftward from S_1 to S_2. The equilibrium moves from point E to point E'. While the price must rise after these shifts, quantity could rise or fall or remain the same, depending on the relative sizes of the shifts. In the figure, quantity happens to fall.

tion mark). For example, the top left entry tells us that when both the supply and demand curves shift rightward, the equilibrium *quantity* will always rise, but the equilibrium price could rise, fall, or remain unchanged, depending on the relative *size* of the shifts.

Do *not* try to memorize the entries in Table 6. Instead, remember the advice in Chapter 1: to study economics actively, rather than passively. This would be a good time to put down the book, pick up a pencil and paper, and see whether you can draw a graph to illustrate each of the nine possible results in the table. When you see a question mark (?) for an ambiguous result, determine which shift would have to be greater for the variable to rise or to fall.

THE THREE-STEP PROCESS

In this chapter, we built a model—a supply and demand model—and then used it to analyze price changes in several markets. You may not have noticed it, but we took

	Increase in Demand (Rightward Shift)	No Change in Demand	Decrease in Demand (Leftward Shift)	TABLE 6
• **Increase in Supply** (Rightward Shift)	$P? \; Q\uparrow$	$P\downarrow \; Q\uparrow$	$P\downarrow \; Q?$	**Effect of Supply and Demand Shifts on Equilibrium Price (P) and Quantity (Q)**
• **No Change in Supply**	$P\uparrow \; Q\uparrow$	No change in P or Q	$P\downarrow \; Q\downarrow$	
• **Decrease in Supply** (Leftward Shift)	$P\uparrow \; Q?$	$P\uparrow \; Q\downarrow$	$P? \; Q\downarrow$	

three distinct steps as the chapter proceeded. Economists take these same three steps to answer many questions about the economy, as you'll see throughout this book.

Let's review these steps:

> **Step 1—Characterize the Market:** *Decide which market or markets best suit the problem being analyzed, and identify the decision makers (buyers and sellers) who interact there.*

In economics, we make sense of the very complex, real-world economy by viewing it as a collection of *markets*. Each of these markets involves a group of *decision makers*—buyers and sellers—who have the potential to trade with each other. At the very beginning of any economic analysis, we must decide which market or markets to look at and how these markets should be *defined*.

To define a market, we decide how to view (a) the thing being traded (such as maple syrup); (b) the decision makers in the market (such as maple syrup producers in New England and Canada selling to U.S. households); and (c) the trading environment (in this chapter, we viewed the market for maple syrup as perfectly competitive).

> **Step 2—Find the Equilibrium:** *Describe the conditions necessary for equilibrium in the market, and a method for determining that equilibrium.*

Once we've defined a market, and put buyers and sellers together, we look for the point at which the market will come to rest—the equilibrium. In this chapter, we used supply and demand to find the equilibrium price and quantity in a perfectly competitive market, but this is just one example of how economists apply Step 2.

> **Step 3—*What Happens When Things Change:*** *Explore how events or government policies change the market equilibrium.*

Once you've found the equilibrium, the next step is to ask how different events will *change* it. In this chapter, for example, we explored how rising income or bad weather (or both together) would affect the equilibrium price and quantity for maple syrup.

Economists follow this same three-step procedure to analyze important *microeconomic* questions. Why does government intervention to lower the price of a good (such as apartment rents) often backfire and sometimes harm the very people it was designed to help? Why do some people earn salaries that are hundreds of times higher than others? What would happen to the price of oil in world markets if supplies from the Persian Gulf were suddenly cut off? If you're studying *microeconomics*, you'll soon see how the three-step process helps us answer all of those questions.

Economists also use the procedure to address important *macroeconomic* questions. What caused the recession that began in early 2001, and what can we do to help avoid recessions in the future? Why has the United States experienced such low inflation in recent years, and how long can we expect our recent good fortune to continue? Why has the U.S. economy been growing so much more rapidly than the economies of continental Europe? In *macro*economics, the three steps help us answer once again.

In this book, we'll be taking these three steps again and again, and we'll often call them to your attention.

USING THE THEORY

© ASSOCIATED PRESS

Explaining Changes in Price and Quantity: Avian Flu in Early 2006

In 2005 and early 2006, the avian influenza virus was spreading rapidly among chicken flocks in Asia and Europe. More than a hundred million chickens in the affected countries had either died from the virus or been destroyed in an unsuccessful effort to slow its spread. But in early 2006, the virus had *not* yet struck flocks in the United States.

The spread of the avian flu virus raised many important questions for economists, health care professionals, medical researchers, and government agencies. But here we focus on a narrower topic: something that was happening in markets for chicken meat.

Here are two relevant facts about these markets toward the end of 2005 and into early 2006.[1]

- In Europe, people were buying substantially *less* chicken. (For example, over a period of a few months in early 2006, chicken consumption dropped by 20 percent in France, and a whopping 70 percent in Italy.)
- In the United States, people were buying *more* chicken.

At first glance (and especially to someone who has not studied supply and demand), the explanation might seem obvious. It would go something like this: "Since chickens were dying or being killed off in Europe, the Europeans had to make do with less chicken. But in the United States, where chicken flocks were unaffected, there was no such problem. And since in most years, the U.S. population rises and income goes up, American chicken consumption probably rose just like it usually does."

That sounds sensible. But an economist, hearing this explanation, would hesitate. There is an easy way to test this explanation: find out what happened to the *price* of chicken in Europe and the United States.

If the first-glance explanation is correct, then chicken prices should have risen in both Europe and the United States. The explanation for Europe (fewer chickens available) implies that the *supply* curve for chicken shifted *leftward*, raising equilibrium price. (Look back, for example, at Figure 11.) The explanation for the United States (the usual increases in income and population) implies that the *demand* curve for chicken shifted *rightward*, once again, raising the price of chicken. (Look back, for example, at Figure 10).

So what happened to chicken prices in Europe and the United States?

They fell in both markets. In fact, they plummeted. From June 2005 to March 2006, the price of chicken in both Europe and the United States dropped by about 70 percent.

So, what really happened? As you're about to see, the three-step process just discussed will help us find the answer.

---

[1] Scott Kilman and Jane Zhang, "Avian-Flu Concerns Overseas Damp U.S. Chicken Exports," *The Wall Street Journal*, March 11–12, 2006, p. A5. Other data on chicken markets comes from the Food and Agriculture Organization, "Poultry Trade Prospects for 2006 Jeopardized by Escalating AI Outbreaks," at www.fao.org, accessed on 3/16/06.

FIGURE 13

The European Market for Chicken

The Avian flu led to the destruction of a relatively small fraction of the world's chicken supply. In the market for dark-meat chicken in Europe, this caused a relatively small leftward shift in the supply curve, from S_{2005} to S_{2006}. At the same time, fear of Avian flu among Europeans caused a larger leftward shift in the demand curve, from D_{2005} to D_{2006}. The market equilibrium moved from point A to point B, with a decrease in equilibrium quantity from Q_1 to Q_2. Because the demand shift was greater than the supply shift, the market price fell, from $0.42 to $0.14 per pound.

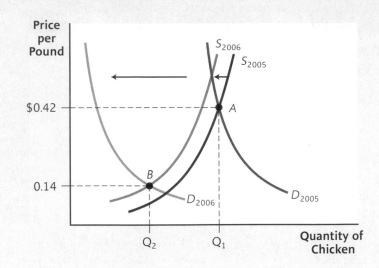

First, let's *characterize the market*. We are interested in explaining why things were *different* in Europe and the United States, so it makes sense to look at two geographic markets for chicken: one in Europe, and the other in the United States.

In Figure 13, we first illustrate the market in Europe. Because chicken (especially when frozen) is easily shipped from country to country, the supply side of this market consists of chicken producers around the world. These producers sell some portion of their chicken to buyers in Europe—the demand side of this market.

Now the second step: *Find the equilibrium*. Our starting point will be the summer of 2005, with demand curve D_{2005} and supply curve S_{2005}. The equilibrium occurs at the intersection of the two curves (point A), with quantity Q_1 and price equal to the dollar equivalent of about $0.42 per pound. (In this analysis, we're using the approximate wholesale price of dark-meat chicken. But other chicken-related prices behaved similarly during this period.)

Finally, the third step: *What happens when things change?* From 2005 to 2006, millions of chickens around the world died or were destroyed, so at any given price, suppliers would choose to sell fewer chickens in *any* market, including the European market. In Figure 13, the supply curve shifts leftward, to S_{2006}. But notice that this shift is depicted as rather small. That's because the millions of birds eliminated were only a tiny percentage of total world supply. (According to the Food and Agriculture Organization, the total number of chickens in the world is about 16 *trillion*, a significant fraction of which are brought to market each year.) Still, if this had been the only change in the market (as in the "first glance" explanation), chicken prices in Europe would have risen.

Since chicken prices actually *fell*, we know something else must have changed in this market. And indeed it did. As the avian influenza virus spread from Asia to Europe, consumers in Europe were gripped by a chicken panic. Even though there

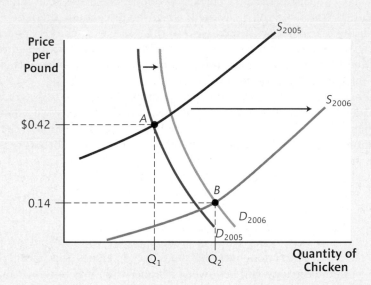

The U.S. Market for Chicken

As chicken prices declined in Europe (an alternate market for U.S. producers), the supply curve in the U.S. market shifted rightward, from S_{2005} to S_{2006}. At the same time, normal increases in income and population caused a (smaller) rightward shift in demand, from D_{2005} to D_{2006}. The market equilibrium moved from point A to point B with an increase in equilibrium quantity from Q_1 to Q_2. Because the supply shift was greater, the market price fell, from $0.42 to $0.14 per pound.

was no danger from eating infected chickens (cooking kills the virus), millions of consumers in Europe decided to take no chances. They simply stopped eating chicken. This is represented by the sizable *leftward shift in the demand curve*, to D_{2006} in Figure 13. The equilibrium price of dark meat chicken fell from about $0.42 per pound to about $0.14 per pound.

We know the leftward shift in the demand curve was greater than the leftward shift in the supply curve, because that is the only way to explain the drop in price that actually occurred. So, although a decrease in supply played *some* role in explaining the drop in European consumption (as in the first-glance explanation), a more important reason for the drop in consumption was a decrease in demand.

Now let's consider the *U.S.* market. The demand side of the market is chicken buyers in the United States. And once again, the supply side of the market consists of chicken producers around the world who have the potential to sell their chicken to Americans. However, in practice, the supply side of the market is limited to American chicken farmers. This is because the United States is a chicken *exporter*: it produces all the chickens demanded in the home market, and then some. This fact will turn out to be important.

Figure 14 depicts the U.S. chicken market. The initial equilibrium in June 2005 was at point *A*, with the price at about $0.42, the same price as in Europe.

Now let's look at what changed. In early 2006, there was no "chicken panic" in the United States since the virus had not yet affected U.S. chicken flocks. (Remember: The chicken in U.S. supermarkets was American-produced chicken.) And it is true that the United States was experiencing a healthy rate of income and population growth, so the demand for chicken—a normal good—rose. In Figure 14, we've shifted the demand curve rightward a bit, to D_{2006}. If this had been the only change, U.S. chicken prices would have risen somewhat.

But remember that chicken prices actually *fell*, so something else was going on. Here's what happened: For U.S. chicken producers, Europe is an *alternate market* to the United States. As you've learned, when the price in an alternate market falls, supply in the original market increases. In this case, with chicken prices in Europe falling, U.S. producers shifted sales back to the home market. In Figure 14, this is represented by a *rightward shift* in the supply curve to S_{2006}—more chicken offered in the United States at any given price.

We know that the rightward shift in the supply curve had to be greater than the rightward shift in the demand curve, because that is the only way the price could have fallen.[2] So, while rising demand played *some* role in explaining the rise in U.S. consumption (as in the first-glance explanation), a more important reason was the increase in supply.

Why should we worry about the proper explanation for this event, which happened in the past? Because, as you'll see in later chapters, the tools we've just used to analyze this past event can help us make proper predictions about the future as well. And they can be applied to *any* competitive market.

For example, some observers have predicted there will be rapid growth in solar-power electricity-generation over the next decade. Does this mean the price of solar-generated electricity will be lower or higher than it is now? Or in the market for health care, the price of many services, such as visits to the doctor or hospital stays, is likely to rise over the next decade. Will this be accompanied by an *increase* in the quantity of these services supplied? Or a decrease?

As you probably suspect, the answer to these questions, and hundreds more like them, depends on which force—demand or supply—is the dominant change in the market. You'll be asked to look at a few cases similar to these in the end-of-chapter problems.

Summary

In a market economy, prices are determined through the interaction of buyers and sellers in *markets*. *Perfectly competitive* markets have many buyers and sellers, and none of them individually can affect the market price. If an individual, buyer, or seller has the power to influence the price of a product, the market is *imperfectly competitive*.

The model of *supply and demand* explains how prices are determined in perfectly competitive markets. The *quantity demanded* of any good is the total amount buyers would choose to purchase given the constraints that they face. The *law of demand* states that quantity demanded is negatively related to price; it tells us that the *demand curve* slopes downward. The demand curve is drawn for given levels of income, wealth, tastes, prices of substitute and complementary goods, population, and expected future price. If any of those factors changes, the demand curve will shift.

The *quantity supplied* of a good is the total amount sellers would choose to produce and sell given the constraints that they face. According to the *law of supply*, supply curves slope upward. The supply curve will shift if there is a change in the price of an input, the price of an alternate good, the price in an alternate market, the number of firms, expectations of future prices, or (for some goods) a change in weather.

Equilibrium price and quantity in a market are found where the supply and demand curves intersect. If either of these curves shifts, price and quantity will change as the market moves to a new equilibrium.

Economists frequently use a three-step process to answer questions about the economy. The three steps—taken several times in this chapter—are to (1) characterize the market or markets involved in the question; (2) find the equilibrium in the market; and (3) ask what happens when something changes. This three-step process will be used throughout the textbook.

---

[2] In the figure, you'll notice that the supply curve shifts just enough to bring the price down to $0.14 per pound—the same as the new price in Europe. The U.S. price has to drop to about the same level as the price in Europe, because if not, U.S. producers would continue shifting sales away from Europe and into the United States, causing further price declines in the United States.

Problem Set   *Answers to even-numbered Questions and Problems can be found on the text Web site at www.thomsonedu.com/economics/hall.*

1. Consider the following statement: "In 2005 and 2006, as at many other times, new home building in most American cities slowed, and the price of housing came down. Therefore, one way for a city to bring down home prices is to use zoning regulations that slow down new home building." True or false? Explain.

2. In the late 1990s and through 2000, the British public became increasingly concerned about "Mad Cow Disease," which could be deadly to humans if they ate beef from these cattle. Fearing the disease, many consumers switched to other meats, like chicken, pork, or lamb. At the same time, the British government ordered the destruction of thousands of head of cattle. Illustrate the effects of these events on the equilibrium price and quantity in the market for British beef. Can we determine with certainty the direction of change for the quantity? For the price? Explain briefly.

3. Discuss, and illustrate with a graph, how each of the following events will affect the market for coffee:
   a. A blight on coffee plants kills off much of the Brazilian crop.
   b. The price of tea declines.
   c. Coffee workers organize themselves into a union and gain higher wages.
   d. Coffee is shown to cause cancer in laboratory rats.
   e. Coffee prices are expected to rise rapidly in the near future.

4. The following table gives hypothetical data for the quantity of two-bedroom rental apartments demanded and supplied in Peoria, Illinois:

Monthly Rent	Quantity Demanded (thousands)	Quantity Supplied (thousands)
$ 800	30	10
$1,000	25	14
$1,200	22	17
$1,400	19	19
$1,600	17	21
$1,800	15	22

   a. Graph the demand and supply curves.
   b. Find the equilibrium price and quantity.
   c. Explain briefly why a rent of $1,000 cannot be the equilibrium in this market.
   d. Suppose a tornado destroys a significant number of apartment buildings in Peoria, but doesn't affect people's desire to live there. Illustrate on your graph the effects on equilibrium price and quantity.

5. The following table gives hypothetical data for the quantity of alarm clocks demanded and supplied per month.

Price per Alarm Clock	Quantity Demanded	Quantity Supplied
$ 5	3,500	700
$10	3,000	900
$15	2,500	1,100
$20	2,000	1,300
$25	1,500	1,500
$30	1,000	1,700
$35	500	1,900

   a. Graph the demand and supply curves.
   b. Find the equilibrium price and quantity.
   c. Illustrate on your graph how a decrease in the price of telephone wake-up services would affect the market for alarm clocks.
   d. What would happen if there was a decrease in the price of wake-up services at the same time that the price of the plastic used to manufacture alarm clocks rose?

6. The following table gives hypothetical data for the quantity of electric scooters demanded and supplied per month.

Price per Electric Scooter	Quantity Demanded	Quantity Supplied
$150	500	250
$175	475	350
$200	450	450
$225	425	550
$250	400	650
$275	375	750

   a. Graph the demand and supply curves.
   b. Find the equilibrium price and quantity.
   c. Illustrate on your graph how an increase in the wage rate paid to scooter assemblers would affect the market for electric scooters.
   d. What would happen if there was an increase in the wage rate paid to scooter assemblers at the same time that tastes for electric scooters increased?

7. The following table gives hypothetical data for the quantity of gasoline demanded and supplied in Los Angeles per month.

Price per Gallon	Quantity Demanded (millions of gallons)	Quantity Supplied (millions of gallons)
$1.20	170	80
$1.30	156	105
$1.40	140	140
$1.50	123	175
$1.60	100	210
$1.70	95	238

a. Graph the demand and supply curves.
b. Find the equilibrium price and quantity.
c. Illustrate on your graph how a rise in the price of automobiles would affect the gasoline market.

8. How would each of the following affect the market for blue jeans in the United States? Illustrate each answer with a supply and demand diagram.
   a. The price of denim cloth increases.
   b. An economic slowdown in the United States causes household incomes to decrease.

9. Indicate which curve shifted—and in which direction—for each of the following. Assume that only one curve shifts.
   a. The price of furniture rises as the quantity bought and sold falls.
   b. Apartment vacancy rates increase while average monthly rent on apartments declines.
   c. The price of personal computers continues to decline as sales skyrocket.

10. Consider the following forecast: "In 2008, we predict that the demand curve for solar panels will continue its shift rightward, which will tend to raise price and quantity. However, with a higher price, supply will increase as well, shifting the supply curve rightward. A rightward shift of the supply curve will tend to lower price and raise quantity. We conclude that as 2008 proceeds, quantity will increase but the price of solar panels may either rise or fall." There is a serious mistake of logic in this forecast. Can you find it? Explain.

11. A couple of months after Hurricane Katrina, an article in *The New York Times* contained the following passage: "Gasoline prices—the national average is now $2.15, according to the Energy Information Administration—have fallen because higher prices held down demand and Gulf Coast supplies have been slowly restored."[3] The statement about supply is entirely correct and explains why gas prices came down. But the statement about demand confuses two concepts you learned about in this chapter.
    a. What two concepts does the statement about demand seem to confuse? Explain briefly.
    b. On a supply and demand diagram, show what most likely caused gasoline prices to rise when Hurricane Katrina shut down gasoline refineries on the Gulf Coast.
    c. On another supply and demand diagram, show what most likely happened in the market for gasoline as Gulf Coast refineries were repaired—and began operating again—after the Hurricane.

d. What role did the *demand* side of the market play in explaining the rise and fall of gas prices?

12. Draw supply and demand diagrams for market A for each of the following. Then use your diagrams to illustrate the impact of the following events. In each case, determine what happens to price and quantity in each market.
    a. A and B are substitutes, and the price of good B rises.
    b. A and B satisfy the same kinds of desires, and there is a shift in tastes away from A and toward B.
    c. A is a normal good, and incomes in the community increase.
    d. There is a technological advance in the production of good A.
    e. B is an input used to produce good A, and the price of B rises.

More Challenging

13. Suppose that demand is given by the equation $Q^D = 500 - 50P$, where Q^D is quantity demanded, and P is the price of the good. Supply is described by the equation $Q^S = 50 + 25P$, where Q^S is quantity supplied. What is the equilibrium price and quantity? (See Appendix.)

14. While crime rates have fallen across the country over the past few years, they have fallen especially rapidly in Manhattan. At the same time, there are some neighborhoods in the New York metropolitan area in which the crime rate has remained constant. Using supply and demand diagrams for rental housing, explain how a falling crime rate in Manhattan could make the residents in *other* neighborhoods *worse off*. (Hint: As people from around the country move to Manhattan, what happens to rents there? If people cannot afford to pay higher rent in Manhattan, what might they do?)

15. A Wall Street analyst observes the following equilibrium price-quantity combinations in the market for restaurant meals in a city over a four-year period:

Year	P	Q (thousands of meals per month)
1	$12	20
2	$15	30
3	$17	40
4	$20	50

She concludes that the market defies the law of demand. Is she correct? Why or why not?

[3] "Economic Memo: Upbeat Signs Hold Cautions for the Future," *New York Times*, November 30, 2005.

Solving for Equilibrium Algebraically

In the body of this chapter, notice that the supply and demand curves for maple syrup were *not* graphed as straight lines. This is because the data they were based on (as shown in the tables) were not consistent with a straight-line graph. You can verify this if you look back at Table 1: When the price rises from $1.00 to $2.00, quantity demanded drops by 15,000 (from 75,000 to 60,000). But when the price rises from $2.00 to $3.00, quantity demanded drops by 10,000 (from 60,000 to 50,000). Since the change in the independent variable (price) is $1.00 in both cases, but the change in the dependent variable (quantity demanded) is different, we know that when the relationship between quantity demanded and price is graphed, it will not be a straight line.

We have no reason to expect demand or supply curves in the real world to be straight lines (to be *linear*). However, it's often useful to approximate a curve with a straight line that is reasonably close to the original curve. One advantage of doing this is that we can then express both supply and demand as simple equations, and solve for the equilibrium using basic algebra.

For example, suppose the demand for take-out pizzas in a modest-size city is represented by the following equation:

$$Q^D = 64,000 - 3,000\,P$$

where Q^D stands for the quantity of pizzas demanded per week. This equation tells us that every time the price of pizza rises by $1.00, the number of pizzas demanded each week *falls* by 3,000. As we'd expect, there is a negative relationship between price and quantity demanded. Moreover, since quantity demanded always falls at the same rate (3,000 fewer pizzas for every $1.00 rise in price), the equation is linear.[1]

Now we'll add an equation for the supply curve:

$$Q^S = -20,000 + 4,000\,P$$

where Q^s stands for the quantity of pizzas supplied per week. This equation tells us that when the price of pizza rises by $1.00, the number of pizzas supplied per week *rises* by 4,000—the positive relationship we expect of a supply curve.[2] And like the demand curve, it's linear: Quantity supplied continues to rise at the same rate (4,000 more pizzas for every $1.00 increase in price).

We know that if this market is in equilibrium, quantity demanded (Q^D) will equal quantity supplied (Q^s). So let's *impose* that condition on these curves. That is, let's require $Q^D = Q^s$. This allows us to use the definitions for Q^D and Q^s that have price as a variable, and set those equal to each other in equilibrium:

$$64,000 - 3,000\,P = -20,000 + 4,000\,P$$

This is one equation with a single unknown—P—so we can use the rules of algebra to isolate P on one side of the equation. We do this by adding 3,000 P to both sides, which isolates P on the right, and adding 20,000 to both sides, which moves everything that *doesn't* involve P to the left, giving us:

$$84,000 = 7,000\,P$$

Finally, dividing both sides by 7,000 gives us

$$84,000/7,000 = P$$

or

$$P = 12$$

---

[1] If you try to graph the demand curve, don't forget that supply and demand graphs reverse the usual custom of where the independent and dependent variables are plotted. Quantity demanded is the dependent variable (it *depends* on price), and yet it's graphed on the *horizontal* axis.

[2] Don't be troubled by the negative sign ($-20,000$) in this equation. It helps determine a minimum price that suppliers must get in order to supply any pizza at all. Using the entire equation, we find that if price were $5.00, quantity supplied would be zero, and that price has to rise *above* $5.00 for any pizzas to be supplied in this market. But since a "negative supply" doesn't make sense, this equation is valid only for prices of $5.00 or greater.

We've found our equilibrium price: $12.

What about equilibrium quantity? In equilibrium, we know quantity demanded and quantity supplied are equal, so we can *either* solve for Q^D using the demand equation, or solve for Q^S using the supply equation, and we should get the same answer. For example, using the demand equation, and using the equilibrium price of $12:

$$Q^D = 64,000 - 3,000 \,(12)$$

or

$$Q^D = 28,000$$

To confirm that we didn't make any errors, we can also use the supply equation.

$$Q^S = -20,000 + 4,000 \,(12)$$

or

$$Q^S = 28,000$$

We've now confirmed that the equilibrium quantity is 28,000.

Working with Supply and Demand

In Chapter 3, you learned that supply and demand explain how prices are determined in competitive markets. You also learned how prices and quantities in markets can change. But this versatile model can do even more. We can use it to see what happens when governments intervene in markets to influence prices. We can add details to the model—such as measurements of buyers' and sellers' sensitivity to price changes—that will deepen our understanding of how markets work. And we can use it to gain insights into social policy issues, ranging from the war against illegal drugs to the problem of rising college tuition. This chapter is all about *working with* supply and demand, and applying it in the real world.

GOVERNMENT INTERVENTION IN MARKETS

The forces of supply and demand deserve some credit. They force the market price to adjust until something remarkable happens: The quantity that sellers want to sell is also the quantity that buyers want to buy. Thus, no buyer or seller should have trouble turning his intentions into actual market trades.

So, three cheers for supply and demand! Or better make that *two* cheers. Because while everyone agrees that having prices is necessary for the smooth functioning of our economy, not everyone is happy with the prices that supply and demand give us. Apartment dwellers often complain that their rent is too high, and farmers complain that the price of their crops is too low.

Responding to this dissatisfaction, governments will sometimes intervene to *change* the price in a market. In this section, we'll look at two methods governments use to prevent a market price from reaching its equilibrium value.

PRICE CEILINGS

Figure 1 shows our familiar market for maple syrup, with an equilibrium price of $3.00 per bottle. Suppose that maple syrup buyers complain to the government that this price is too high. And suppose the government responds by imposing a **price ceiling** in this market—a regulation preventing the price from rising above, say, $2.00 per bottle.

Price ceiling A government-imposed maximum price in a market.

If the ceiling is enforced, then producers will no longer be able to charge $3.00 for maple syrup but will have to content themselves with $2.00 instead. In Figure 1, we will move down along the supply curve, from point *E* to point *R*, decreasing quantity supplied from 50,000 bottles to 40,000. At the same time, the decrease in

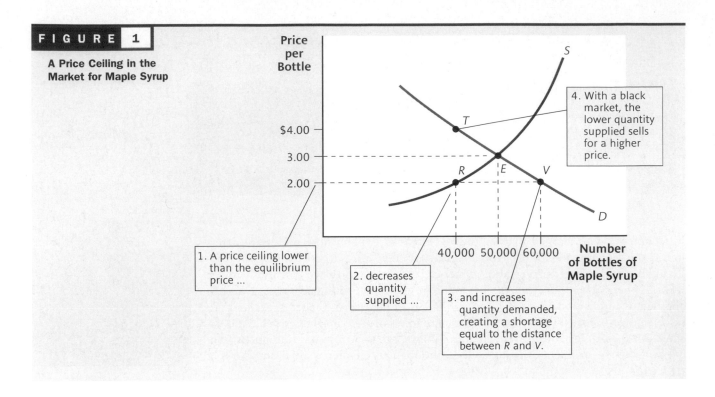

FIGURE 1

A Price Ceiling in the Market for Maple Syrup

Price per Bottle

$4.00

3.00

2.00

4. With a black market, the lower quantity supplied sells for a higher price.

1. A price ceiling lower than the equilibrium price ...

2. decreases quantity supplied ...

3. and increases quantity demanded, creating a shortage equal to the distance between *R* and *V*.

40,000 50,000 60,000

Number of Bottles of Maple Syrup

price will move us along the demand curve, from point *E* to point *V*, increasing quantity demanded from 50,000 to 60,000. These changes in quantities supplied and demanded together create an *excess demand* for maple syrup of 60,000 − 40,000 = 20,000 bottles each month. Ordinarily, the excess demand would force the price back up to $3.00. But now the price ceiling prevents this from occurring. What will happen?

There is a practical observation about markets that helps us arrive at an answer:

> *When quantity supplied and quantity demanded differ, the **short side of the market**—whichever of the two quantities is smaller—will prevail.*

Short side of the market The smaller of quantity supplied and quantity demanded at a particular price.

This simple rule follows from the voluntary nature of exchange in a market system: No one can be forced to buy or sell more than they want to. With an excess demand, *sellers* are the short side of the market. Since we cannot force them to sell any more than they want to (40,000 units) the result is a **shortage** of maple syrup—not enough available to satisfy demand at the going price.

Shortage An excess demand not eliminated by a rise in price, so that quantity demanded continues to exceed quantity supplied.

But this is not the end of the story. Because of the shortage, all 40,000 bottles produced each month will quickly disappear from store shelves, and many buyers will be disappointed. The next time people hear that maple syrup has become available, everyone will try to get there first, and we can expect long lines at stores. Those who really crave maple syrup may have to go from store to store, searching for that rare bottle. When we include the *opportunity cost* of the time spent waiting in line or shopping around, the ultimate effect of the price ceiling may be a *higher* cost of maple syrup for many consumers.

> *A price ceiling creates a shortage and increases the time and trouble required to buy the good. While the price decreases, the opportunity cost may rise.*

And there is still more. The government may be able to prevent maple syrup *producers* from selling above the price ceiling. But it may not be able to prevent a **black market**, where goods are sold illegally at prices higher than the legal ceiling.

Ironically, the black market price will typically exceed the original, freely determined equilibrium price—$3.00 per bottle in our example. To see why, look again at Figure 1. With a price ceiling of $2.00, sellers supply 40,000 bottles per month. Suppose all of this is bought by people—maple syrup scalpers, if you will—who then sell it at the highest price they can get. What price can they charge? We can use the demand curve to find out. At $4.00 per bottle (point *T*), the scalpers would just be able to sell all 40,000 bottles. They have no reason, therefore, to charge any less than this.

The unintended consequences of price ceilings—long lines, black markets, and, often, higher prices—explain why they are generally a poor way to bring down prices. Experience with price ceilings has generally confirmed this judgment. Many states do have laws to limit price hikes during declared emergencies, thereby creating temporary price ceilings. But permanent or semipermanent price ceilings are exceedingly rare.

There is, however, one type of market in which several cities have imposed long-lasting price ceilings: the market for apartment rentals.

Black market A market in which goods are sold illegally at a price above the legal ceiling.

Rent Controls

A price ceiling imposed in a rental housing market is called **rent control**. Most states have laws *prohibiting* rent control. But more than a dozen states do allow it. And in four of these states (New York, California, Maryland, and New Jersey), as well as in Washington D.C., some form of rent control has existed in several cities and towns for decades.

In theory, rent control is designed to keep housing affordable, especially for those with low incomes. But for this purpose, it's a very blunt instrument because it doesn't target those with low incomes. Rather, *anyone* who was lucky enough to be living in one of the affected units when rent control was first imposed or extended gets to pay less than market rent, as long as he or she continues to hold the lease on the unit. Many renters in cities such as New York and Santa Monica have higher incomes and living standards than do the owners from whom they rent.

Second, rent control causes the same sorts of problems as did our hypothetical price ceiling on maple syrup. It creates a persistent excess demand for rental units, so renters must spend more time and trouble finding an apartment. Typically, something akin to the "black market" develops: Real estate brokers quickly "snap up" the rent-controlled apartments (either because of their superior knowledge of the market, or their ability to negotiate exclusive contracts with the owners). Apartment seekers, who don't want to spend months searching on their own, will hire one of these brokers. Alternatively, one can sublet from a leaseholder, who will then charge market rent for the sublet and pocket the difference. Either way, many renters end up paying a higher cost for their apartment than the rent-controlled price.

Finally, rent controls cause a decrease in the quantity of apartments supplied (a movement along the supply curve). This is because lower rents reduce the incentives

Rent controls Government-imposed maximum rents on apartments and homes.

for owners to maintain existing apartments in rentable condition, and also reduce incentives to build new ones.[1]

In our example of the market for maple syrup, the decrease in quantity supplied—combined with a black market—caused the average buyer to end up paying a higher price than before the ceiling was imposed (see point T in Figure 1). The same thing can happen in the apartment rental market. As supply decreases, the total price of renting an apartment for a few years can rise above the market equilibrium price—if we include real estate commissions or the unofficial, higher rents paid by those who sublet.

PRICE FLOORS

Price floor A government-imposed minimum price in a market.

Sometimes, governments try to help sellers of a good by establishing a **price floor**—a minimum amount below which the price is not permitted to fall. The most common use of price floors around the world has been to raise prices (or prevent prices from falling) in agricultural markets. Price floors for agricultural goods are commonly called *price support programs.*

In the United States, price support programs began during the Great Depression, after farm prices fell by more than 50 percent between 1929 and 1932. The Agricultural Adjustment Act of 1933, and an amendment in 1935, gave the president the authority to intervene in markets for a variety of agricultural goods. Over the next 60 years, the United States Department of Agriculture (USDA) put in place programs to maintain high prices for cotton, wheat, rice, corn, tobacco, honey, milk, cheese, butter, and many other farm goods. Although some of these supports were removed over the last decade, many remain. For example, government policy still maintains price floors for peanuts, sugar, and dairy products.

To see how price floors work, let's look at the market for nonfat dry milk—a market in which the USDA has been supporting prices continually since 1933. Figure 2 shows that—before any price floor is imposed—the market is in equilibrium at point A, with an equilibrium price of 65 cents per pound and an equilibrium quantity of 200 million pounds per month.

Now let's examine the impact of the price floor recently set at $0.80 per pound. At this price, producers want to sell 220 million pounds, while consumers want to purchase only 180 million pounds. There is an excess supply of 220 million − 180 million = 40 million pounds. Our short-side rule tells us that buyers determine the amount actually traded. They purchase 180 million of the 220 million pounds produced, and producers are unable to sell the remainder. The excess supply of 40 million pounds would ordinarily push the market price down to its equilibrium value: $0.65. But now the price floor prevents this from happening. The result is a **surplus**—continuing extra production of nonfat dry milk that no one wants to buy at the going price.

Surplus An excess supply not eliminated by a fall in price, so that quantity supplied continues to exceed quantity demanded.

---

[1] Strong evidence to support this idea comes from Cambridge, Massachusetts. The town had strict rent controls on most apartments, until the law was struck down in a statewide initiative in 1994. As market rents rose to their equilibrium values, investment in the housing sector rose significantly more than would have been expected had rent controls still been in place, causing both the quantity and quality of apartments to increase. (Henry O. Pollakowski, "Rent Control and Housing Investment: Evidence from Deregulation in Cambridge, Massachusetts," *Civic Report*, No. 36, May 2003, Center for Civic Innovation, The Manhattan Institute.)

For another cost of rent control, see Edward Glaeser and E. F. P. Luttmer, "The Misallocation of Housing under Rent Control," *American Economic Review*, Vol. 93, No. 4, 2003, pp. 1027–1046.

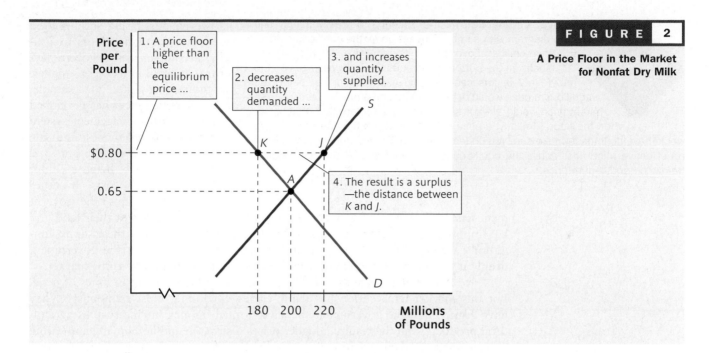

FIGURE 2

A Price Floor in the Market for Nonfat Dry Milk

If the government merely *declared* a price floor of $0.80 per pound, many farmers who are unable to sell all of their product would be tempted to sell some illegally at a price below the floor. This would take sales away from other farmers trying to sell at the higher price, so they, too, would feel pressure to violate the floor. Soon, the price floor would collapse.

To prevent this, governments around the world have developed a variety of policies designed to prevent surplus goods from forcing down the price. One method, frequently used in the United States, is for the government to promise to buy any unsold product at a guaranteed price. In the market for nonfat dry milk, for example, the government agrees to buy any unsold supplies from sellers at a price of $0.80 per pound. With this policy, no supplier would ever sell at any price *below* $0.80, since it could always sell to the government instead. With the price effectively stuck at $0.80, private buyers buy 180 million pounds—point *K* on the demand curve in Figure 2. But since quantity supplied is 220 million, at point *J*, the government must buy the excess supply of 40 million pounds each year. In other words, the government maintains the price floor by *buying up* the entire excess supply. This prevents the excess supply from doing what it would ordinarily do: drive the price down to its equilibrium value.

In 2003, for example, the USDA had to purchase 636 million pounds of surplus nonfat dry milk at a cost of about $500 million. By the end of that year, the government owned more than 1 billion pounds of nonfat dry milk—purchases that it had made in previous years and still held.

A price floor creates a surplus of a good. In order to maintain the price floor, the government must prevent the surplus from driving down the market price. In practice, the government often accomplishes this goal by purchasing the surplus itself.

DANGEROUS CURVES

Floor Above, Ceiling Below! It's tempting to draw a supply and demand diagram with a price floor set *under* the equilibrium price, or a price ceiling *above* the equilibrium price. After all, a floor is usually on the bottom of something, and a ceiling is on the top. Right? In this case, wrong! A price floor set *below* the equilibrium price would have no impact on a market, because the market price would *already* satisfy the requirement that it be higher than the floor. Similarly, a price ceiling set *above* the equilibrium price would have no impact (make sure you understand why). So remember: Always draw an effective price floor *above* the equilibrium price and an effective price ceiling *below* the equilibrium price.

However, purchasing surplus food is expensive, so price floors are usually accompanied by government efforts to *limit* any excess supplies. In the dairy market, for example, the U.S. government has developed a complicated management system to control the production and sale of milk to manufacturers and processors, which helps to limit the government's costs. In other agricultural markets, the government has ordered or paid farmers *not* to grow crops on portions of their land and has imposed strict limits on imports of food from abroad. Many of these supply limitations are still in place. As you can see, price floors often get the government deeply involved in production decisions, rather than leaving them to the market.

Price floors have certainly benefited farmers and helped them in times of need. But this market intervention has many critics—including most economists. They have argued that the government spends too much money buying surplus agricultural products, and the resulting higher prices distort the public's buying and eating habits—often to their nutritional detriment. For example, the General Accounting Office has estimated that from 1986 to 2001, price supports for dairy products have cost American consumers $10.4 billion in higher prices. And this does not include the cost of the health effects—such as calcium and protein deficiencies among poor children—due to decreased milk consumption. The irony is that many of the farmers who benefit from price floors are wealthy individuals or large, powerful corporations that do not need the assistance. Economists argue that assistance to farmers would be more cost-effective if given directly to those truly in need, rather than supporting all farmers with artificially high prices.

PRICE ELASTICITY OF DEMAND

Imagine that you are the mayor of one of America's large cities. Every day, the headlines blare about local problems—poverty, crime in the streets, the sorry state of public education, roads and bridges that are falling apart, traffic congestion—and you, as mayor, are held accountable for all of them. Of course, you could help alleviate these problems, if only you had more money to spend on them. You've already raised taxes as much as you can so, where to get the money?

One day, an aide bounds into your office. "I've got the perfect solution," he says, beaming. "We raise mass transit fares." He shows you a sheet of paper on which he's done the calculation: Each year, city residents take 100 million trips on public transportation. If fares are raised by 50 cents, the transit system will take in an additional $50 million—enough to make a dent in some of the city's problems.

You stroke your chin and think about it. So many issues to balance: fairness, practicality, the political impact. But then another thought occurs to you: Your aide has made a serious mistake! Public transportation—like virtually everything else that people buy—obeys the law of demand. A rise in price—with no other change—will cause a decrease in quantity demanded. If you raise fares, each *trip* will bring in more revenue, but there will be *fewer trips* taken. Mass transit revenue might rise or it might fall. How can you determine which will happen?

To answer that question, you would need one more piece of information: *price elasticity of demand*, which is a measure of how *sensitive* quantity demanded is to a change in price. But how to measure it?

THE PROBLEM WITH RATE OF CHANGE

You might think that the *slope* of the demand curve would be a good measure of price sensitivity. But using slope would create some serious problems. One problem is that slope arbitrarily depends on the units of measurement that we happen to choose. For example, suppose we use *tons* as our unit of measurement for tomatoes. And suppose that each time the price per ton drops by $100, quantity demanded rises by 1 ton. Using tons, the slope of the demand curve would be $-100/1 = -100$.

Now let's describe this same demand behavior using *pounds* instead of *tons*. When price per ton drops by $100, that's the same as price per *pound* dropping by $0.05. And when demand rises by 1 ton, it rises by 2,000 pounds. So, using pounds, when price drops by $0.05, quantity demanded rises by 2,000. Now, the slope of the demand curve is $-0.05/2,000 = -0.000025$. So even though buyers' sensitivity to price is the same in both cases, the slopes are very different.

A second problem is that the slope of the demand curve doesn't tell us anything about the *significance* of a change in price or quantity—whether it is a relatively small or a relatively large change. A price drop of $0.05, for example, is a tiny, hardly noticeable change for a good with a current price of $500. But it's a relatively huge change if the current price is $0.08. Our measure of price sensitivity should take account of this.

THE ELASTICITY APPROACH

The elasticity approach solves both of these problems by comparing the *percentage change* in quantity demanded with the *percentage change* in price.

More specifically:

> The **price elasticity of demand** (E_D) *for a good is the percentage change in quantity demanded divided by the percentage change in price:*
>
> $$E_D = \frac{\% \text{ Change in Quantity Demanded}}{\% \text{ Change in Price}}$$

Price elasticity of demand The sensitivity of quantity demanded to price; the percentage change in quantity demanded caused by a 1 percent change in price.

For example, if the price of newspapers falls by 2 percent, and this causes the quantity demanded to rise by 6 percent, then $E_D = 6\%/2\% = 3.0$. We would say "the price elasticity of demand for newspapers is 3.0."

Of course, when price *falls* by 2 percent, that's a change of *negative* 2 percent, while quantity demanded changes by +6 percent. So technically speaking, elasticity should be viewed as a negative number. In this book, we'll follow the common convention of dropping the minus sign. That way, when we compare elasticities and say that one is larger, we'll be comparing absolute values.

In our example, elasticity has the value 3.0. But what, exactly, does that number mean? Here is a straightforward way to interpret the number:

> *The price elasticity of demand* (E_D) *tells us the percentage change in quantity demanded for each 1 percent change in price.*

In our example, with $E_D = 3.0$, each 1 percent drop in price causes quantity demanded to rise by 3 percent.

Given this interpretation, it's clear that an elasticity value of 3.0 implies greater price sensitivity than an elasticity value of 2.0, or one of 0.7. More generally,

> *The greater the elasticity value, the more sensitive quantity demanded is to price.*

CALCULATING PRICE ELASTICITY OF DEMAND

When we calculate price elasticity of demand, we imagine that *only price* is changing, while we hold constant all other influences on quantity demanded, such as buyers' incomes, the prices of other goods, and so on. Thus, we measure elasticity for a movement *along* an unchanging demand curve.

Mistakes in Observing Elasticities It's tempting to calculate an elasticity from simple observation: looking at what actually happened to buyers' purchases after some price changed. But this often leads to serious errors. Elasticity of demand tells us the effect a price change would have on quantity demanded *if* all other influences on demand remain unchanged. But in the real world, it is unlikely that other influences will remain unchanged in the months or years after a price change.
Consider what happened in Baltimore in March 1996, when the city increased mass transit fares by 8 percent. Over the next six months, ridership *increased* by 4.5 percent. Does this mean that the elasticity of demand for mass transit in Baltimore is positive? Does mass transit violate the law of demand? Not at all. Around the time of the fare hike, the city also made improvements in service and advertised them heavily. This helped to change tastes in favor of mass transit, shifting the demand curve rightward. If all other influences on demand had remained unchanged—so that we moved along a stable demand curve—ridership would have fallen when the price rose. Economists and statisticians have developed tools to isolate the effect of price changes on quantity demanded, enabling them to estimate elasticities from actual data.

Figure 3, for example, shows a hypothetical demand curve in the market for avocados in a city. Suppose we want to measure elasticity along this demand curve between points A and B. As our first step, we'll calculate the percentage change in price.

Let's suppose we move from point A to point B. Price falls by $0.50. Since our starting price at point A was $1.50, this would be a 33 percent drop in price.

But wait . . . suppose we go in the reverse direction, from point B to A. Now our starting price would be $1.00, so the $0.50 price hike would be a 50 percent rise. As you can see, the percentage change in price (33 or 50 percent) depends on the direction we are moving. And the same will be true of quantity. Therefore, our elasticity value will also depend on which direction we move.

This presents us with a problem. Ideally, we'd like our measure of price sensitivity to be the same whether we go from A to B or from B to A, since each is simply the mirror image of the other. To accomplish this goal, elasticity calculations often use a special convention to get percentage changes: Instead of dividing the change in a variable by its *starting* value, we divide the change by the *average* of its starting and ending values. This is often called the "midpoint formula," because we are dividing the change by the midpoint between the old and new values.

> *When determining elasticities, we calculate the percentage change in a variable using the midpoint formula: the change in the variable divided by the average of the old and new values.*

FIGURE 3

Using the Midpoint Formula
for Elasticity

Price per Avocado

$1.50 — A

3. Elasticity of demand for the move from A to B is 20% / 40% = 0.5

1.00 — B

D

1. Using the midpoint formula, the percentage drop in price is $0.50/$1.25 = 0.40 or 40% ...

4,500   5,500

Quantity of Avocados per Week

2. and the percentage rise in quantity is 1,000 / 5,000 = 0.2 or 20%.

For example, in Figure 3, between points *A* and *B* the average of the old and new price is ($1.50 + $1.00)/2 = $1.25. Using this average price as our base, the percentage change in price is $0.50/$1.25 = 0.40 or 40 percent. With the midpoint formula, the percentage change in price is the same whether we move from *A* to *B*, or from *B* to *A*.

More generally, when price changes from any value P_0 to any other value P_1, we define the percentage change in price as

$$\% \text{ Change in Price} = \frac{(P_1 - P_0)}{\left[\dfrac{(P_1 + P_0)}{2}\right]}$$

The term in the numerator is the change in price; the term in the denominator is the average of the two prices.

The percentage change in quantity demanded is calculated in a similar way. When quantity demanded changes from Q_0 to Q_1, the percentage change is calculated as

$$\% \text{ Change in Quantity Demanded} = \frac{(Q_1 - Q_0)}{\left[\dfrac{(Q_1 + Q_0)}{2}\right]}$$

Once again, we are using the average of the initial and the new quantity demanded as our base quantity.

The midpoint formula is an approximation to the actual percentage change in a variable, but it has the advantage of giving us consistent elasticity values when we reverse directions. We will use the midpoint formula only when *calculating elasticity values from data on prices and quantities*. For all other purposes, we calculate percentage changes in the normal way, using the starting value as the base.

An Example

Let's calculate the price elasticity of demand for avocados along a part of the demand curve in Figure 3. As price falls from \$1.50 to \$1.00, quantity demanded rises from 4,500 to 5,500. Using the midpoint formula (and dropping negative signs):

$$\text{\% Change in Quantity Demanded} = \frac{[5,500-4,500]}{\left[\dfrac{(5,500 + 4,500)}{2}\right]} = \frac{1,000}{5,000} = 0.20 \text{ or } 20\%.$$

$$\text{\% Change in Price} = \frac{[\$1.00-\$1.50]}{\left[\dfrac{(\$1.00 + \$1.50)}{2}\right]} = \frac{\$0.50}{\$1.25} = 0.40 \text{ or } 40\%.$$

Finally, we use these numbers to calculate the price elasticity of demand:

$$E_D = \frac{\text{\% Change in Quantity Demanded}}{\text{\% Change in Price}} = \frac{20\%}{40\%} = 0.5.$$

Or, in simple English, a 1 percent change in price causes a $\frac{1}{2}$ percent change in quantity demanded.

TYPES OF DEMAND CURVES

Economists have found it useful to divide demand curves (or parts of demand curves) into categories, based on their elasticity values. These categories are illustrated in Figure 4.

Perfectly inelastic demand A price elasticity of demand equal to 0.

Panel (a) shows an extreme case, called **perfectly inelastic demand**, where the elasticity has a value of zero. A perfectly inelastic demand curve is vertical, so a change in price causes *no* change in quantity demanded. In the figure, when price rises from \$9 to \$11 (20 percent using the midpoint formula), our formula for price elasticity of demand (E_D) gives us $E_D = 0\%/20\% = 0$.

Panel (b) shows a case where quantity demanded has *some* sensitivity to price, but not much. Here, the same 20 percent price increase causes quantity demand to fall from 105 to 95 (a 10 percent decrease using the midpoint formula). In this case, $E_D = 10\%/20\% = 0.5$. This is an example **inelastic demand**, which occurs whenever $E_D < 1$ (quantity changes by a smaller percentage than price).

Inelastic demand A price elasticity of demand between 0 and 1.

Panel (c) shows a demand curve with more price sensitivity: the 20 percent rise in price causes quantity demanded to drop by 30 percent. Our elasticity calculation is $E_D = 30\%/20\% = 1.5$. This is an example of **elastic demand**, which occurs whenever $E_D > 1$ (quantity changes by a larger percentage than price changes).

Elastic demand A price elasticity of demand greater than 1.

Perfectly (infinitely) elastic demand A price elasticity of demand approaching infinity.

Finally, panel (d) shows another extreme case, called **perfectly elastic demand**, where the demand curve is horizontal. As long as the price stays at one particular value (where the demand curve touches the vertical axis), *any* quantity might be demanded. But even the tiniest price rise would cause quantity demanded to fall to zero. In this case, $E_D = \infty$ (elasticity is infinite) because no matter how small we make the percentage change in price (in the denominator), the percentage change in quantity (in the numerator) will always be infinitely larger.

Unit elastic demand A price elasticity of demand equal to 1.

What about the special case when elasticity of demand is *exactly* equal to 1.0? If you check the definitions, you'll see that demand is neither elastic nor inelastic, but lies between these categories. We call this case **unit elastic**. Take a moment to

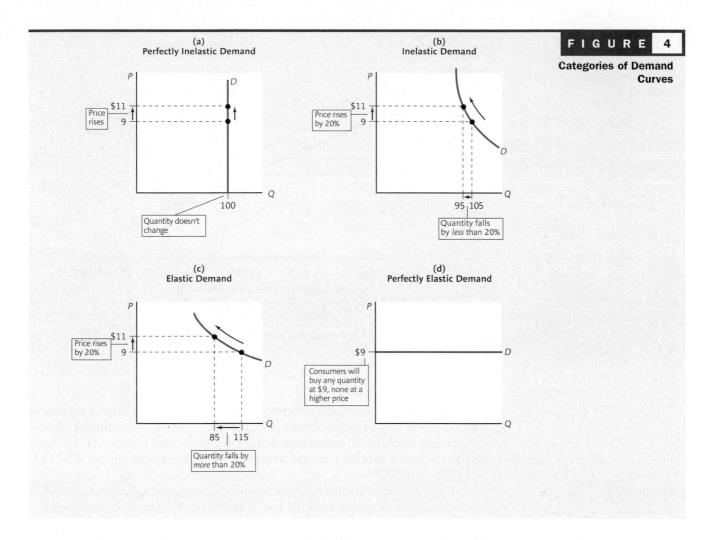

FIGURE 4

Categories of Demand Curves

(a)
Perfectly Inelastic Demand

(b)
Inelastic Demand

(c)
Elastic Demand

(d)
Perfectly Elastic Demand

draw a demand curve that is unit elastic for a price change from $9 to $11, choosing your numbers for quantity carefully.

ELASTICITY AND STRAIGHT-LINE DEMAND CURVES

Figure 5 shows a linear (straight-line) demand curve for laptop computers. Each time price drops by $500, the quantity of laptops demanded rises by 10,000. Because this behavior remains constant all along the curve, is the price elasticity of demand also constant?

Actually, no. Elasticity is the ratio of *percentage* changes; what remains constant along a linear demand curve is the ratio of *absolute* or *unit* changes.

In fact, we can show that as we move downward along a linear demand curve, the elasticity always increases. For example, let's calculate the elasticity between points *A* and *B*. Price falls from $2,000 to $1,500, a 28.6 percent drop using the midpoint formula. Quantity rises from 15,000 to 25,000, which is a 50 percent rise using the midpoint formula. Taking the ratio, elasticity for a move from point *A* to *B* is 50%/28.6% = 1.75.

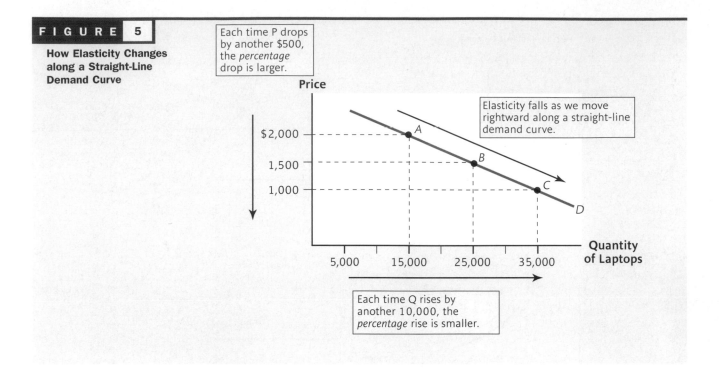

FIGURE 5

How Elasticity Changes along a Straight-Line Demand Curve

Each time P drops by another $500, the *percentage* drop is larger.

Elasticity falls as we move rightward along a straight-line demand curve.

Each time Q rises by another 10,000, the *percentage* rise is smaller.

Now let's calculate the elasticity between points *B* and *C*, where price falls from $1,500 to $1,000, and quantity rises from 25,000 to 35,000. For this change (as you can verify), price falls by 40 percent while quantity demanded rises by 33.3 percent (using the midpoint formula). So the elasticity for a move from point *B* to *C* is 40% / 33.3% = 1.20.

Notice what's happened: as we've moved downward and rightward along this straight-line demand curve, elasticity has fallen from 1.75 to 1.2. Demand has become *less elastic*.

There is a good reason for this. As we travel down the demand curve, the average quantity we use as the base for figuring percentage changes keeps increasing. So a constant 10,000 increase in quantity becomes a smaller and smaller *percentage* increase. The opposite also happens with price: It keeps getting smaller, so the same $500 decrease in price becomes a growing *percentage* decrease. Thus, as we travel down a linear demand curve, with $\%\Delta Q^D$ shrinking and $\%\Delta P$ growing, the ratio $\%\Delta Q^D / \%\Delta P$ decreases.

> *Elasticity of demand varies along a straight-line demand curve. More specifically, demand becomes less elastic (E_D gets smaller) as we move downward and rightward.*

This is a special conclusion about *linear* demand curves only. For *non*linear demand curves, moving down the curve can cause elasticity to rise, fall, or remain constant, depending on the shape of the curve.

ELASTICITY AND TOTAL REVENUE

When the price of a good increases, what happens to the total revenue of sellers in that market? Let's see. On the one hand, each unit sold can be sold for more, tending to increase revenue. On the other hand, fewer units will be sold, which works to decrease revenue. Which one will dominate?

The answer depends on the price elasticity of demand for the good. To see why, note that the total revenue of sellers in a market (*TR*) is the price per unit (*P*) times the quantity that people buy (*Q*):

$$TR = P \times Q.$$

When we raise price, *P* goes up, but *Q* goes down. What happens to the product depends on which one changes by a larger percentage.

Suppose that demand is *inelastic* (E_D < 1). Then a 1 percent rise in price will cause quantity demanded to fall by *less* than 1 percent. So the greater amount sellers get on each unit outweighs the impact of the drop in quantity, and total revenue will *rise*.

The behavior of total revenue can be seen very clearly on a graph, once you learn how to interpret it. Look at the left panel of Figure 6, which duplicates the inelastic demand curve introduced earlier. On this demand curve, let's start at a price of $9, and look at the rectangle with a corner at point A. The height of the rectangle is the price of $9, and the width is quantity of 105, so its *area* (height × width = *P* × *Q* = $9 × 105 = $945) is total revenue when price is $9.

More generally,

> *At any point on a demand curve, sellers' total revenue is the area of a rectangle with height equal to price and width equal to quantity demanded.*

Now let's raise the price to $11. The total revenue rectangle becomes the larger one, with a corner at point B. The area of this rectangle is *TR* = $11 × 95 = $1,045. The rise in price has *increased* total revenue.

(a) Inelastic Demand

(b) Elastic Demand

FIGURE 6

Elasticity and Total Revenue

In panel (a), demand is inelastic, so a rise in price causes total revenue to increase. Specifically, at a price of $9 (point A), total revenue is $9 × 105 = $945. When price rises to $11 (point B), total revenue increases to $11 × 95 = $1,045. In panel (b), demand is elastic, so a rise in price causes total revenue to decrease. Specifically, at a price of $9 (point A), total revenue is $9 × 115 = $1,035. When price rises to $11 (point B), total revenue falls to $11 × 85 = $935.

TABLE 1	Where Demand Is:	A Price Increase Will:	A Price Decrease Will:
Effects of Price Changes on Revenue	inelastic ($E_D < 1$)	increase revenue	decrease revenue
	unit elastic ($E_D = 1$)	cause no change in revenue	cause no change in revenue
	elastic ($E_D > 1$)	decrease revenue	increase revenue

Now suppose that demand is *elastic* ($E_D > 1$). Once again, a 1 percent rise in price causes quantity demanded to fall, but this time it falls by *more* than 1 percent. So the fact that sellers get more on each unit is outweighed by the drop in the quantity they sell, and total revenue *falls*.

This is shown in the right panel of Figure 6, using the example of elastic demand from a few pages earlier. When price is $9, *TR* is the area of the rectangle with a corner at point *A*, equal to $9 $\times$ 115 = $1,035. When price rises to $11, *TR* becomes the area of the taller rectangle with corner at point *B*. This area is $11 $\times$ 85 = $935. Because demand is elastic, the rise in price *decreases* total revenue.

We can conclude that:

> *An increase in price raises total revenue when demand is inelastic, and shrinks total revenue when demand is elastic.*

What if price fell instead of rose? Then, in Figure 6 we'd be making the reverse move: from point *B* to point *A* on each curve. And logic tells us that if demand is inelastic, total revenue must fall. If demand is elastic, the drop in price will cause total revenue to rise.

> *A decrease in price shrinks total revenue when demand is inelastic, and raises total revenue when demand is elastic.*

What happens if demand is unit elastic? You can probably guess. This would mean that a 1 percent change in price causes a 1 percent change in quantity, but in the opposite direction. The two effects on total revenue would cancel each other out, so total revenue would remain unchanged.

Table 1 summarizes these results about elasticity and total revenue. Don't try to memorize the table, but *do* use it to test yourself: Try to explain the logic for each entry.

DETERMINANTS OF ELASTICITY

Table 2 lists the price elasticity of demand for a variety of goods and services. You can see that the calculated elasticities vary widely. Why is the demand for Tide Detergent, Pepsi, and Coke highly elastic, while the demand for gasoline and eggs is so inelastic?

Availability of Substitutes

When close substitutes are available for a good, demand for it will be more elastic. Example: When the price of ground beef rises, with all other prices held constant,

Specific Brands		Narrow Categories		Broad Categories		TABLE 2
Tide Detergent	2.79	Transatlantic Air Travel	1.30	Recreation	1.09	**Some Short-Run Price Elasticities of Demand**
		Tourism in Thailand	1.20			
Pepsi	2.08	Ground Beef	1.02	Clothing	0.89	
Coke	1.71	Pork	0.78	Food	0.67	
		Milk	0.54	Imports	0.58	
		Cigarettes	0.45	Transportation	0.56	
		Electricity	0.40 to 0.50			
		Beer	0.26			
		Eggs	0.26			
		Gasoline	0.26			
		Oil	0.15			

Sources: Michael G. Vogt and Chutima Wittayakorn, "Determinants of the Demand for Thailand's Exports of Tourism," *Applied Economics*, Vol. 30, Issue 6, pp. 711–715. Sachin Gupta et al., "Do Household Scanner Data Provide Representative Inferences from Brand Choices? A Comparison with Store Data," *Journal of Marketing Research*, Fall 1996, pp. 383ff. F. Gasmi, J. J. Laffont, and Q. Vuong, "Econometric Analysis of Collusive Behavior in a Soft-Drink Market," *Journal of Economics and Management Strategy*, Summer 1992, pp. 277–311. Richard Blundell, Panos Pashardes, and Guglielmo Weber, "What Do We Learn about Consumer Demand Patterns from Micro Data?" *American Economic Review*, June 1993, pp. 570–597. Michael T. Maloney and Robert E. McCormick, "Setting the Record Straight: The Consumer Wins the Competition," *Citizens for a Sound Economy Foundation*, Issue Analysis No. 46, January 30, 1997. J. L. Sweeney, "The Response of Energy Demand to Higher Prices: What Have We Learned?" *American Economic Review*, May 1984, pp. 31–37. F. Chaloupka, "Rational Addictive Behavior and Cigarette Smoking," *Journal of Political Economy*, August 1991, pp. 722–742. J. M. Cigliano, "Price and Income Elasticities for Airline Travel," *Business Economics*, September 1980, pp. 17–21. M. D. Chinn, "Beware of Econometricians Bearing Estimates," *Journal of Policy Analysis and Management*, Fall 1991, pp. 546–557. M. R. Baye, D. W. Jansen, and Jae-Woo Lee, "Advertising Effects in Complete Demand Systems," *Applied Economics*, October 1992, pp. 1087–1096. Dale M. Heien, "The Structure of Food Demand: Interrelatedness and Duality," *American Journal of Agricultural Economics*, May 1982, pp. 213–221. Gary W. Brester and Michael K. Wohlgenant, "Estimating Interrelated Demands for Meats Using New Measures for Ground and Table Cut Beef," *American Journal of Agricultural Economics*, November 1991, pp. 1182–1194. David R. Henderson, "Do We Need to Go to War for Oil?" *Cato Foreign Policy Briefing*, No. 4, October 24, 1990. *Reducing Gasoline consumption*: Three Policy Options, A CBO Study, Congressional Budget Office, November 2002, p. 17.

consumers can easily switch to other forms of beef, or even chicken or pork. But when the price of gasoline rises, the substitutes that are available (using mass transit, carpooling, biking, or even not going places) are not as close. Thus, it is not surprising that the demand for ground beef is more elastic than the demand for gasoline.

> *When close substitutes are available for a product, demand tends to be more elastic.*

One factor that determines the closeness of substitutes is how narrowly or broadly we define the market we are analyzing. Demand in the market for beverages as a whole will be less elastic than demand in the market for soft drinks. And demand for soft drinks will be less elastic than the demand for Pepsi. This is because whenever we look at elasticity of demand in a market, we are holding constant all prices outside of the market. So in determining the elasticity for Pepsi, we ask what happens to quantity demanded when the price of Pepsi rises but the price of Coke remains constant. Since it is so easy to switch to Coke, demand is highly elastic. But in determining the elasticity for soft drinks, we ask what happens when the price of *all* soft drinks rise together, holding constant only the prices of things that are *not* soft drinks. Demand is therefore less elastic.

Some of the entries in Table 2 confirm this influence on elasticity. For example, the demand for transportation, a very broad category, is less elastic than the demand for transatlantic air travel. But other entries seem to contradict it. (Can you find one?) Remember, though, that there are other determinants of elasticity besides the narrowness or broadness of the market.

Necessities versus Luxuries

Goods that we think of as necessary for our survival or general well-being, and for which there are no close substitutes, are often referred to as "necessities." Most people would include the broad categories "food," "housing," and "medical care" in this category. When we regard something as a necessity, demand for it will tend to be less elastic. This is another reason why the elasticity of demand for gasoline is so small: Many people regard gasoline as a necessity.

But don't make the common mistake of thinking that people *must* buy a constant quantity of goods they regard as necessities, and cannot make do with any less. That would imply *perfectly inelastic* demand. Studies routinely show that demand for "necessities" is inelastic, but not perfectly inelastic. People do find ways to cut back on them when the price rises.

By contrast, goods that we can more easily do without—such as entertainment or vacation travel—are often referred to as "luxuries." Demand for these goods will tend to be more elastic, since people will cut back their purchases more when price rises.

> *Goods we regard as necessities tend to have less elastic demand than goods we regard as luxuries.*

In Table 2, for example, among the broad categories, the demands for food and clothing are less elastic than the demand for recreation. Remember, though, that how broadly or narrowly we define the market makes an important difference. We may regard broadly defined "medical care" as a necessity. But "Medical Care from Dr. Hacker" might be an easy-to-substitute for luxury, with a highly elastic demand.

Importance in Buyers' Budgets

When a good takes up a large part of your budget, a rise in price has a large impact on how much income you will have left to buy other things. All else equal, this will tend to make demand more elastic. For example, a vacation trip to Thailand would take a big bite out of most peoples' budgets. If the price of the vacation rises by, say, 20 percent, many people will start to consider other alternatives, since not doing so would mean a considerable sacrifice of other purchases.

Now consider the other extreme: ordinary table salt. A family with an income of $50,000 per year would spend less than 0.005 percent of its income on this good, so the price of salt could double or triple and have no significant impact on the ability to buy other goods. We would therefore expect the demand for table salt to be inelastic.

This insight helps us to explain some seemingly anomalous results in Table 2. Demand for food is more elastic than the demand for eggs. Based on the narrowness of definition, we would expect the reverse. But eggs make up a rather small fraction of the typical family's budget, and certainly smaller than food as a whole. This tends to reduce the elasticity of demand for eggs.

When spending on a good makes up a larger proportion of families' budgets, demand tends to be more elastic.

Time Horizon

How much time we wait after a price change can have an important impact on the elasticity of demand. The elasticities of demand in Table 2 are all **short-run elasticities**: the quantity response is measured for just a short time (usually a year or less) after the price change. A **long-run elasticity** measures the quantity response after more time has elapsed—typically a few years or more. In study after study, we find that demand is almost always more elastic in the long run than in the short run.

Why? Because the longer we wait after a sustained price change, the more time consumers have to make adjustments in their lives that affect their quantity demanded.

Short-run elasticity An elasticity measured just a short time after a price change.

Long-run elasticity An elasticity measured a year or more after a price change.

In general, the longer we wait after a price change to measure the quantity response, the more elastic is demand.

For example, while the short-run elasticity for gasoline is 0.26, most studies find that the long-run elasticity (after a few years) is at least three times as large. Table 3 illustrates why. It lists some of the ways people can adjust to a significant rise in the price of gasoline over the short run and the long run. Remember that the adjustments in the long-run column are *additional* adjustments people can make if given enough time. While some of them may seem extreme, thousands of families made these changes during the latter half of the 1970s, after the OPEC nations reduced oil supplies and the price of gasoline roughly quadrupled.

Short Run (a few months or less)	Long Run (a year or more)
Use public transit more often	Buy a more fuel-efficient car
Arrange a car pool	Move closer to your job
Get a tune-up	Switch to a job closer to home
Drive more slowly on the highway	Move to a city where less driving is required
Eliminate unnecessary trips (use mail order instead of driving to stores; locate goods by phone instead of driving around; shop for food less often and buy more each time)	
If there are two cars, use the more fuel-efficient one	

TABLE 3

Adjustments After a Rise in the Price of Gasoline

Two Practical Examples

Knowing the price elasticity of demand for a good or service can be highly useful to economists in practical work. In many cases, an economic analysis will center on the connection between price, quantity demanded, and total revenue. In this section, we provide two examples.

Elasticity and Mass Transit

Earlier in this chapter, you were asked to imagine that you were a mayor trying to determine whether raising mass transit fares would increase or decrease city revenues. Now you know that the answer depends on the price elasticity of demand for mass transit.

Several studies[2] have shown that the demand for mass transit services is *inelastic*. In the short run (the first year after the price change), the elasticity of demand ranges from 0.2 to 0.5. Over the long run (five to ten years), elasticity values are 0.6 to 0.9. Notice that although elasticity is greater in the long run than the short run, demand remains inelastic even in the long run. This means that a rise in fares would likely raise mass-transit revenue for a city, even in the long run.

Let's do an example. Suppose New York City raised subway and bus fares from the current $2.00 to $2.50, a 25 percent increase.[3] What would happen to revenue?

In the long run, elasticity is between 0.5 and 0.9, so let's choose an estimate in the middle of that range: 0.7. Using this elasticity, each 1 percent increase in fares would cause a 0.7 percent decrease in ridership. So our 25 percent fare hike would decrease ridership by $25 \times 0.7 = 17.5$ percent. New Yorkers take about 2 billion trips each year, so a 17.5 percent decrease would bring trips down by 350 million, to 1.65 billion per year.

Now let's calculate revenue, before and after the price hike. At the current price of $2, total revenue is 2 billion trips × $2 per trip = $4 billion. After the price hike, total revenue would be 1.65 billion trips × $2.50 per trip = $4.125 billion. We conclude that raising the fare would increase mass transit revenue by about $125 million per year in the long run.

Why, then, doesn't New York City raise the fare to $2.50? In fact, why doesn't it go further, to $3? Or $5? Or even $10?

For two reasons. First, elasticity estimates come from *past* data on the response to a price changes. When we ask what would happen if we raise the price, we are extrapolating from these past responses. For small price changes, the extrapolation is likely to be fairly accurate. But large price changes move us into unknown territory, and elasticity may change. Demand could be *elastic* for a very large price hike, and then total revenue would fall. This puts a limit on fares, even if a city's goal is the maximum possible revenue.

A second (and more important) reason is that generating revenue is only *one* consideration in setting mass transit fares. City governments are also concerned with providing affordable transportation to city residents, reducing traffic congestion on

---

[2] These studies are nicely summarized in Todd Litman, "Transit Price Elasticities and Cross-Elasticities," *Journal of Public Transportation*, Vol. 7, No. 2, 2004, pp. 37–58.

[3] Notice that we're calculating percentage changes the conventional way, rather than with the midpoint formula. Here, we are not trying to calculate an elasticity value. Instead, we're using one that has already been determined for us. While we could continue to use the midpoint formula, it would be cumbersome—especially when trying to determine the new quantity after the fare hike.

city streets, and limiting pollution. A fare increase, even if it would raise total revenue, would work against these other goals. This is why most cities keep the price of mass transit below the revenue-maximizing price.

Elasticity and an Oil Crisis

For the past five decades, the Persian Gulf has been a geopolitical hot spot. And the stakes for the rest of the world are high, because the region produces about one-fourth of the world's oil supply. That is why economists in government and industry are constantly asking "what if" questions about the world market for oil. One central question is this: If an event in the Persian Gulf were to disrupt oil supplies, what would happen to the price of oil on world markets? Not surprisingly, elasticity plays a crucial role in answering this question.

As you can see in Table 2, the short-run elasticity of demand for oil is about 0.15. This estimate is for the United States, but in our analysis, we'll use it as the price elasticity of demand for oil in the global market as well. Since a political or military crisis is usually a short-run phenomenon, the short-run elasticity is what we are interested in. But for this problem, we need to use elasticity in a new way. Remember that elasticity tells us the percentage decrease in quantity demanded for a 1 percent increase in price. But suppose we flip the elasticity fraction upside down, to get

$$\frac{1}{E_D} = \frac{\% \text{ Change in Price}}{\% \text{ Change in Quantity Demanded}}.$$

This number—the inverse of elasticity—tells us the percentage rise in price that would bring about each 1 percent decrease in quantity demanded. For oil, this number is $1/0.15 = 6.67$. What does this number mean? It tells us that to bring about each 1 percent decrease in world oil demand, oil prices would have to rise by 6.67 percent.

Now we can make reasonable forecasts about the impact of various events on oil prices. Imagine, for example, an event that temporarily removed half of the Persian Gulf's oil from world markets. And let's assume a worst-case scenario: No other nation increases its production during the time frame being considered. What would happen to world oil prices?

Since the Gulf produces about 25 percent of the world's oil, a reduction by half would decrease world oil supplies by $12\frac{1}{2}$ percent. It would then require a price increase of $12\frac{1}{2} \times 6.67 = 83.4$ percent to restore equilibrium to the market. If oil were initially selling at $60 per barrel, we could forecast the price to rise by $60 \times 0.834 = $50 per barrel, for a final price of about $110.

Why is it so important to forecast the price of oil that might result from a crisis? If you were a heavy industrial user of oil, you would know the answer. But the forecast is also of immense value to government economists, who would use it to help answer *other* questions. These would include macroeconomic questions, such as, how would such a rise in the price of oil affect the U.S. inflation rate? And microeconomic questions, such as, how would this rise in the price of oil affect the number of flights offered by U.S. airlines, and the prices they'd charge for them?

OTHER ELASTICITIES

The concept of *elasticity* is a very general one. It can be used to measure the sensitivity of virtually *any* variable to any other variable. All types of elasticity measures, however, share one thing in common: They tell us the percentage change in one variable caused by a 1 percent change in the other. Let's look briefly at three additional elasticity measures, and what each of them tells us.

INCOME ELASTICITY OF DEMAND

Income elasticity of demand The percentage change in quantity demanded caused by a 1 percent change in income.

You learned in Chapter 3 that household income is one of the variables that influences demand. The *income elasticity of demand* tells us how *sensitive* quantity demanded is to changes in buyers' incomes. The **income elasticity of demand** E_Y is the percentage change in quantity demanded divided by the percentage change in income, with all other influences on demand—including the price of the good—remaining constant:

$$\text{Income Elasticity} = \frac{\text{\% Change in Quantity Demanded}}{\text{\% Change in Income}}$$

Keep in mind that while a price elasticity measures the sensitivity of demand to price as we *move along the demand curve* from one point to another, an income elasticity tells us the relative *shift* in the demand curve—the percentage increase in quantity demanded *at a given price.*

An accurate knowledge of income elasticity can be crucial in predicting the growth in demand for a good as income grows over time. For example, economists know that different types of countries have different income elasticities of demand for oil. (In less-developed countries undergoing rapid industrialization, the income elasticity of demand for oil is typically twice as large as in developed countries.) These income elasticities, along with forecasts of income growth in different developing and developed countries, are used to predict global demand for oil and forecast future oil prices.

CROSS-PRICE ELASTICITY OF DEMAND

Cross-price elasticity of demand The percentage change in the quantity demanded of one good caused by a 1 percent change in the price of another good.

A cross-price elasticity relates the percentage change in quantity demanded for one good to the percentage change in the price of another good. More formally, we define the **cross-price elasticity of demand** between good X and good Z as:

$$\frac{\text{\% Change in Quantity Demanded of } X}{\text{\% Change in Price of } Z}$$

In words, a cross-price elasticity of demand tells us the percentage change in quantity demanded of a good for each 1 percent increase in the price of some other good, while all other influences on demand remain unchanged.

With a cross-price elasticity, the sign matters. A *positive* cross price elasticity means that the two goods are *substitutes*: A rise in the price of one good increases demand for the other good. For example, Coke and Pepsi are clearly substitutes, and the cross-price elasticity of Pepsi with Coke has, in one study, been estimated at 0.8.[4] This means that a 1 percent rise in the price of Coke, holding constant the price of Pepsi, causes a 0.8 percent *rise* in the quantity of Pepsi demanded.

[4] F. Gasmi, J. J. Laffont and Q. Vuong, "Econometric Analysis of Collusive Behavior in a Soft Drink Market," *Journal of Economics and Management Strategy*, Summer, 1992, pp. 277–311.

A *negative* cross-price elasticity means that the goods are *complements*: A rise in the price of one good decreases demand for the other. Since maple syrup and pancake mix are complements, we would expect a rise in the price of pancake mix to *decrease* the demand for maple syrup.

PRICE ELASTICITY OF SUPPLY

The **price elasticity of supply** is the percentage change in the quantity of a good supplied that is caused by a 1 percent change in the price of the good, with all other influences on supply held constant.

$$\text{Price Elasticity of Supply} = \frac{\%\text{ Change in Quantity Supplied}}{\%\text{ Change in Price}}$$

The price elasticity of supply measures the sensitivity of quantity supplied to price changes as we move *along* the supply curve. A large value for the price elasticity of supply means that quantity supplied is very sensitive to price changes. For example, an elasticity value of 5 would imply that if price increased by 1 percent, quantity supplied would rise by 5 percent.

A major determinant of supply elasticity is the ease with which suppliers can find profitable activities that are *alternatives* to producing the good in question. In general, supply will tend to be more elastic when suppliers can switch to producing alternate goods more easily.

When can we expect suppliers to have easy alternatives? First, the nature of the good itself plays a role. All else equal, the supply of envelopes should be more elastic than the supply of microprocessor chips. This is because envelope producers can more easily modify their production lines to produce alternative paper products. Microprocessor suppliers, however, would be hard-pressed to produce anything other than computer chips.

The narrowness of the market definition matters too—especially *geographic* narrowness. For example, the market for oranges in Illinois should be more supply-elastic than the market for oranges in the United States. In the Illinois market, a decrease in price would imply we are holding constant the price of oranges in *all other states*. This gives suppliers an easy alternative: They could sell their oranges in other states! Similarly, the supply of oranges to Chicago would be even more elastic than the supply of oranges to Illinois.

Finally, the *time horizon* is important. The longer we wait after a price change, the greater the supply response to a price change. As we will see when we discuss the theory of the firm, there usually is *some* response to a price change right away. Existing firms simply speed up or slow down production with their current facilities. But further responses come about as firms have time to change their plant and equipment, and new firms have time to enter or leave an industry.

TAXES AND MARKET EQUILIBRIUM

In the United States and most other countries, governments tax household income, corporate profits, real estate holdings, inheritances, imports, goods and services in general, and specific goods and services. Taxes provide revenue to all levels of government, enabling them to provide public services. But there are other motives for taxes as well. For example, income and inheritance taxes are often viewed as a means to correct inequities in the distribution of income and wealth. Taxes are also

Price elasticity of supply The percentage change in quantity supplied of a good or service caused by a 1 percent change in its price.

Excise tax A tax on a specific good or service.

©RF/ALAMY

levied on particular goods in order to raise their price and discourage their use. And these motives can overlap.

For example, state and local taxes on cigarettes are partly designed to discourage smoking, but many states and cities have become dependent on these taxes as a major source of revenue. Similarly, the gasoline tax originated to fund the building and maintaining of the national highway system. But in recent years, some have wanted to increase this tax to discourage the use of gasoline and thereby lessen U.S. dependence on foreign oil.

A tax on a specific good or service is called an **excise tax**. One market affected by a variety of federal and local excise taxes is the market for air travel. On a $300 round-trip ticket, with one stopover each way, the federal government charges $44.50 in taxes (to help pay for air traffic control and security operations), and another $18 for local governments (to help pay for various airport projects). This brings the total tax to $62.50—and it could rise to triple that amount if the flight crosses an international border.

The tax is *collected* from the airlines—they are the ones who send the checks to the government. But who really *pays* this tax? As you'll see, that depends on how the tax changes the *equilibrium* price in the market.

AN EXCISE TAX ON SELLERS

As stated above, the air travel excise tax is collected from the airlines themselves—the selling side of the market. Although the payments are actually made by periodic check payments, we can imagine that a government tax collector is standing next to the ticket agent, holding out his hand for a $60 payment each time a ticket is sold.

How does this affect the market for airline travel?

Suppose that before the tax is imposed, the supply curve for short-distance roundtrip flights is S_1 in Figure 7. (Ignore the curve above it for now). Point A on this curve tells us that 10 million tickets will be supplied by the airlines each year if

---

FIGURE 7

A Tax on Sellers Shifts the Supply Curve Upward

Before the tax, supply curve S_1 tells us the price the airlines must get in order to supply any given number of tickets. For example, in order to supply 10 million tickets, they must get $300 per ticket (point A). The supply curve $S_{After\ Tax}$ shows us that, with a $60 tax, the airlines must get $60 more than before to supply any given number of tickets. For example, to supply the same 10 million tickets, they must now get $360 (point A').

the price is $300. Let's rephrase this another way: *In order for the airlines to supply 10 million tickets, they must get $300 per ticket.*

What happens when our tax collector gets $60 for each ticket sold? What price must the airlines charge now to supply the same 10 million tickets? The answer is $360, at point A'. Only by charging $60 more to each passenger could they continue to get the amount ($300) that makes it just worth their while to supply 10 million tickets. The same is true at any other quantity we might imagine: The price would have to be $60 more than before to get the airlines to supply that same quantity. So imposing a $60 tax on the airlines shifts the entire supply curve *upward* by $60, to $S_{\text{After Tax}}$.

> *A tax collected from sellers shifts the supply curve upward by the amount of the tax.*

Now look at Figure 8, which shows the market for these flights. Before the tax is imposed, with supply curve S_1 and demand curve D_1, the equilibrium is at point A, with price at $300 and quantity at 10 million. After the $60 tax is imposed and the supply curve shifts up to $S_{\text{After Tax}}$, the new equilibrium price is $340, with 7.5 million tickets sold.

Who is paying this tax? Let's take a step back and think about it. Although the tax is collected from the airlines, who really *pays*—that is, who sacrifices funds they would otherwise have if not for the tax—is an entirely different question. Economists call the distribution of this sacrifice the **tax incidence**.

In our example, buyers paid $300 for each ticket before the tax, and $340 after. So buyers are really paying $40 of this tax each time they buy a ticket, in the form of a higher price.

Tax Incidence The division of a tax payment between buyers and sellers, determined by comparing the new (after tax) and old (pretax) market equilibriums.

FIGURE 8

The Effect of an Excise Tax Imposed on Sellers

Before the tax, the supply curve is S_1. With the market equilibrium at point A, 10 million tickets are sold for $300 each. A $60 tax imposed on sellers shifts the supply curve upward by $60, to $S_{\text{After Tax}}$. In the new equilibrium at point B, 7.5 million tickets are sold for $340 each. Buyers pay $340, which is $40 more than before. Thus, buyers pay $40 of the tax per ticket. Sellers (after deducting the $60 tax they must pay) are left with $280 per ticket, which is $20 less than before. Thus, sellers pay $20 of the tax per ticket.

Tax shifting The process by which some or all of a tax imposed on one side of a market ends up being paid by the other side of the market.

What about sellers? Before the tax, they got $300 for each ticket. After the tax, they collect $340 from passengers, but $60 of that goes to the government. If we want to know how much sellers get after taxes, we have to go back to the old supply curve S_1, which lies below the new supply curve by exactly $60. In effect, the old supply curve deducts the tax and shows us what the airlines really receive. When the airlines charge $340, the original supply curve S_1 shows us that they receive only $280. This is $20 less than they received before, so sellers end up paying $20 of the tax.

In general,

> The incidence of a tax that is collected from sellers falls on both sides of the market. Buyers pay more, and sellers receive less, for each unit sold.

AN EXCISE TAX ON BUYERS

Suppose that, instead of collecting the $60 tax from the airlines, the tax was collected directly from passengers. Before the tax is imposed, the demand curve for flights is D_1 in Figure 9. Point A on this curve tells us that 10 million tickets will be demanded by passengers each year if the price they have to pay is $300. Or, rephrased, *in order for passengers to demand 10 million tickets, the tickets must cost them $300 each*. If the cost per ticket is any more than that, passengers will not buy all 10 million tickets. Before the tax, the cost of each ticket to passengers is the same as the price they pay to the airlines.

Now let's impose the $60 tax on passengers. (Imagine a government tax collector standing at the ticketing booth, requiring each passenger to hand over $60 when they purchase their ticket.) What price will passengers now be willing to pay the airlines and still buy all 10 million tickets? The answer is $240, at point A'. We know this because only if they pay $240 to the airlines will the tickets continue to cost them the

F I G U R E   9

A Tax on Buyers Shifts the Demand Curve Downward

Before the tax, demand curve D_1 *tells us the price that buyers can be charged in order for them to demand any given number of tickets. For example, in order to demand 10 million tickets, they must be charged $300 per ticket (point A). The demand curve* $D_{After\ Tax}$ *shows us that, with a $60 tax imposed on buyers, they must be charged $60 less than before to demand any given number of tickets. For example, to demand the same 10 million tickets, they must now be charged $240 (point A').*

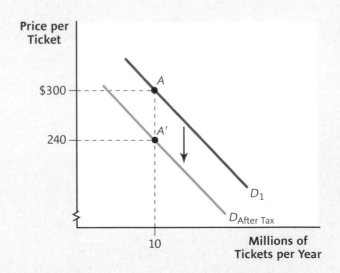

$300 each, which makes it just worth their while to demand all 10 million tickets. The same is true at any other quantity we might imagine: The price would have to be $60 less than before to induce passengers to demand that same quantity. So imposing a $60 tax on passengers shifts the entire demand curve *downward* by $60, to $D_{\text{After Tax}}$.

> *A tax collected from buyers shifts the demand curve downward by the amount of the tax.*

Figure 10 shows the impact on the market. Before the tax is imposed, with demand curve D_1 and supply curve S, the equilibrium is at point A, with price at $300 and quantity at 10 million. After the $60 tax is imposed, and the demand curve shifts down to $D_{\text{After Tax}}$, the new equilibrium price is $280, with 7.5 million tickets sold. With the tax imposed on buyers this time, the supply curve is not affected.

What is the incidence of this tax? Let's see . . . Buyers paid $300 for each ticket before the tax, and $280 after. But they also have to pay $60 to the government. If we want to know how much buyers pay *including* the tax, we have to go back to the old demand curve D_1, which lies above the new demand curve by exactly $60. As you can see, when buyers pay $280 to the airlines, they pay a total of $340. This is $40 more than they paid in total before, so buyers end up paying $40 of the tax.

What about sellers? Sellers received $300 for each ticket before the tax, and $280 after. So sellers are really paying $20 of this tax, in the form of a lower price.

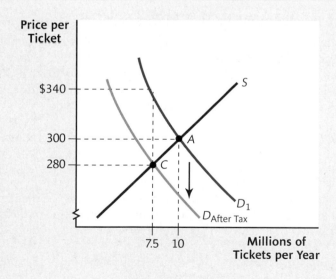

FIGURE 10

The Effect of an Excise Tax Imposed on Buyers

Before the tax, the demand curve is D_1. With the market equilibrium at point A, 10 million tickets are sold for $300 each. A $60 tax imposed on buyers shifts the demand curve downward by $60, to $D_{\text{After Tax}}$. In the new equilibrium at point C, 7.5 million tickets are sold for $280 each. Sellers get $280, which is $20 less than before. Thus, sellers pay $20 of the tax per ticket. Buyers (after adding the $60 tax they must pay) pay $340 per ticket, which is $40 more than before. Thus, buyers pay $40 of the tax per ticket. The part of the tax paid by each side of the market is the same whether the tax is imposed on buyers (this figure) or imposed on sellers (Figure 8).

> *The incidence of a tax that is collected from buyers falls on both sides of the market. Buyers pay more, and sellers receive less, for each unit sold.*

TAX INCIDENCE VERSUS TAX COLLECTION

The incidence of a tax depends on the shapes of the supply and demand curves, and is different in different types of markets. But you may have noticed that the incidence in our example is the same whether the tax is collected from buyers or sellers. In both cases, buyers pay $40 of the tax per ticket, and sellers pay $20. If you'll excuse the rhyme, this identical incidence is not a coincidence.

> *The incidence of a tax (the distribution of the burden between buyers and sellers) is the same whether the tax is collected from buyers or sellers.*

Why? Because the two methods of collecting taxes are not really different in any important economic sense. Whether the tax collector takes the $60 from the ticket agent when the ticket is sold, or takes $60 from the passenger when the ticket is sold, or takes it from both of them (at the exact instant that both sides have their hands on the money), one fact remains: Passengers will pay $60 more than the airlines receive. The market finds a new equilibrium reflecting this. In our example, this new equilibrium occurs where each ticket costs passengers $340 in total, and the airlines receive $280 of this, because that is the only incidence at which quantity demanded and supplied are equal.[5]

© DAN LAMONT/CORBIS

USING THE THEORY

Government Involvement in Two Markets

This chapter delved deeper into supply and demand. We discussed the impact of government interventions (price floors, price ceilings, and excise taxes) and some important uses of elasticity measures. In this last section, we'll use supply and demand analysis to look at government policy in two markets, and see how economists use some of the tools you've learned in this chapter.

THE WAR ON DRUGS: SHOULD WE FIGHT SUPPLY OR DEMAND?

Every year, the U.S. government spends about $20 billion intervening in the market for illegal drugs like cocaine, heroin, and marijuana. Most of this money is spent on efforts to restrict the *supply* of drugs. But many economists argue that society would be better off if antidrug efforts were shifted from the supply side to the demand side of the market. Why? The answer hinges on the price elasticity of demand for illegal drugs.

Look at Figure 11(a), which shows the market for heroin if there were no government intervention. The equilibrium would be at point *A*, with price P_1 and quan-

---

[5] In this chapter, we've considered only one type of burden caused by the tax: changes in *price*. But another burden of the tax is a decrease in *quantity*: fewer flights enjoyed by passengers, fewer flights generating revenue for the airlines. In Chapter 14, you'll learn a more comprehensive method of measuring the burden of a tax that takes into account changes in both price and quantity.

tity Q_1. Total revenue of sellers—and total spending by buyers—would be the area of the shaded rectangle, $P_1 \times Q_1$.

Figure 11(b) shows the impact of a policy to restrict supply through any one of several methods, including vigilant customs inspections, arrest and stiff penalties for drug dealers, or efforts to reduce drug traffic from producing countries like Colombia, North Korea, and Thailand. The decrease in supply is represented by a leftward shift of the supply curve, establishing a new equilibrium at price P_2 and quantity Q_2. As you can see, supply restrictions, if they successfully reduce the equilibrium quantity of heroin, will also raise its equilibrium price.

But now let's consider the impact of this policy on the users' total *expenditure* on drugs. Although the research is difficult, a number of studies have concluded that the demand for addictive drugs such as heroin and cocaine is very price *inelastic*. This is not surprising, given their addictive properties. As you've learned, when demand is inelastic, a rise in price will *increase* the revenue of sellers, which is the same as the total expenditure of buyers. This means that a policy of restricting the supply of illegal drugs, if successful, will also increase the total expenditure of drug users on their habit. In panel (b), total expenditure rises from the area of the shorter rectangle to the area of the taller one.

The change in total expenditure has serious consequences for our society. Many drug users support their habit through crime. If the total expenditure needed to support a drug habit rises, they may commit more crimes—and more serious ones. And don't forget that the total expenditure of drug users is also the total *revenue* of the illegal drug industry. The large revenues—and the associated larger profits to be made—attract organized as well as unorganized crime and lead to frequent and very violent turf wars.

The same logic, based on the inelastic demand for illegal drugs, has led many economists to advocate the controlled legalization of most currently illegal drugs. Others advocate a shift of emphasis in the war from decreasing supply to decreasing demand. Policies that might decrease the demand for illegal drugs and shift the demand curve leftward include stiffer penalties on drug *users*, heavier advertising against drug use, and greater availability of treatment centers for addicts. In addition, more of the effort against drug sellers could be directed at retailers rather than

FIGURE 11

The War on Drugs

Panel (a) shows the market for heroin in the absence of government intervention. Total expenditures—and total receipts of drug dealers—are given by the area of the shaded rectangle. Panel (b) shows the effect of a government effort to restrict supply: Price rises, but total expenditure increases. Panel (c) shows a policy of reducing demand: Price falls, and so does total expenditure.

those higher up the chain of supply. It is the retailers who promote drugs to future users and thus increase demand.

Figure 11(c) illustrates the impact these policies, if successful, would have on the market for heroin. As the demand curve shifts leftward, price *falls* from P_1 to P_3, and quantity demanded falls from Q_1 to Q_3. Now, we cannot say whether the drop in quantity will be greater under a demand shift than a supply shift (it depends on the relative sizes of the shifts). But we *can* be sure that a demand-focused policy will have a very different impact on equilibrium price, moving it down instead of up. Moreover, the demand shift will decrease total expenditure on drugs—to the *inner* shaded rectangle—since both price and quantity decrease. This can contribute to a lower crime rate by drug users and make the drug industry less attractive to potential dealers and producers.

HOW SCHOLARSHIPS INCREASE COLLEGE TUITION

Every year in the United States, federal and state governments provide more than $100 billion in subsidies—scholarships and other assistance—to help students pay the cost of a college education. The reasons for these policies are clear: We want to encourage more people to get college degrees. A college education gives substantial benefits to the degree-holders themselves, in the form of higher future incomes. And a more educated population creates benefits for society as a whole. There are also important equity considerations: Financial assistance increases the number of students from poor households, many of whom might otherwise have to forgo the benefits of college.

Over the past several decades, the cost of a college education has risen rapidly, and so have the government subsidies designed to help students pay. But many economists point out that rising subsidies, in addition to helping students cope with higher costs, also *contribute* to those higher costs.

To see why, look at Figure 12, which shows the market for attending college. Initially, without any government involvement, demand curve D_1 intersects supply curve S at point A. Four million students attend college each year, with each paying a total of $25,000 in tuition.

Now, let's introduce financial assistance: a subsidy of $10,000 per year for each student. First, note that a subsidy works just like a tax, only in the opposite direction. With a tax, the government takes a certain number of dollars from the buyer or seller each time a unit is sold. A subsidy *gives* dollars to the buyer or seller when a unit is sold. As with a tax, the results for buyers and sellers are the same whether the subsidy is actually paid out to buyers or to sellers.

In the figure, we assume that the subsidy is paid out to buyers—college students—to help them pay tuition. (In an end-of-chapter problem, you'll be asked to draw the graph when the subsidy is instead given to colleges.)

The subsidy shifts the demand curve *upward* by $10,000, to $D_{\text{After Subsidy}}$. Why? The old demand curve told us that if the price were $25,000, 4 million students would attend college. After a subsidy, the same 4 million students would choose to attend only if what they paid *from their own pockets* is still $25,000. A price of $35,000, with $10,000 kicked in from the government, would give us the same attendance of 4 million.

However, the subsidy *changes* the market equilibrium from point A to point B. Now, 4.8 million students decide to attend college. But notice that the price is higher as well: Colleges are now charging $31,000 per year.

FIGURE 12

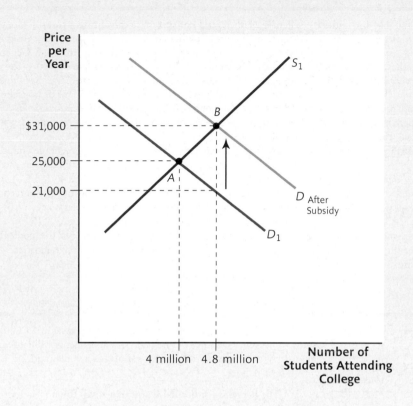

A Subsidy for Students Attending College

Before any subsidy, the demand curve for attending college is D_1. With the market equilibrium at point A, 4 million students attend, and each pays $25,000 per year in tuition. A $10,000 per year subsidy paid to buyers (students) shifts the demand curve upward by $10,000, to $D_{After\ Subsidy}$. In the new equilibrium at point B, 4.8 million students are attending and paying $31,000 per year. Colleges get $31,000, which is $6,000 more than before. Students (after deducting the $10,000 subsidy) pay $21,000, which is $4,000 less than before. Importantly, the cost to students goes down, but by less than the subsidy, because the subsidy leads to higher tuition as well.

Who benefits from the subsidy? Colleges benefit: They get more for each student who attends ($31,000 instead of $25,000). Students benefit as well: They pay $31,000 to the colleges, but the government pays $10,000 of that, so the cost to students has dropped to $21,000. However, notice that the $10,000 subsidy has *not* reduced the cost of college by a full $10,000. In our example, only $4,000 of the subsidy ends up as a direct benefit to the student, while the other $6,000 goes to the college.

This does not mean that subsidies for college are a bad thing. Since most colleges are nonprofit organizations, some of the additional $6,000 per student will pay for better classrooms, better faculty, or scholarships paid by the colleges themselves. Thus, one could argue that students ultimately get more than just $4,000 in benefits.

But the main point of this analysis is to show the role subsidies play in explaining high (and rising) tuition. You already knew that higher tuition leads to a call for greater subsidies. Our supply and demand analysis shows that greater subsidies lead to higher tuition as well.

Summary

The model of supply and demand is a powerful tool for understanding all sorts of economic events. For example, governments often intervene in markets—either by creating *price ceilings* or *price floors,* or by imposing taxes or subsidies. Supply and demand enables us to predict how these interventions affect the price of a good and the quantity exchanged.

The analysis shows that price ceilings and price floors are typically ineffective ways to help buyers or sellers of a good, and often create additional problems. It also shows that taxes and subsidies have the same economic impact regardless of whether the tax is imposed on buyers or sellers.

Another useful tool is the *price elasticity of demand,* defined as the percentage change in quantity demanded divided by the percentage change in price that caused it. In general, price elasticity of demand varies along a demand curve. In the special case of a straight-line demand curve, demand becomes more and more elastic as we move upward and leftward along the curve. Along an elastic portion of any demand curve, a rise in price causes

sellers' revenues (and consumers' expenditures) to fall. Along an *inelastic* portion of any demand curve, a rise in price causes sellers' revenues and consumers' expenditures to increase. Generally speaking, demand for a good tends to be more elastic: The less "necessary" the good is to our well-being, the easier it is to find substitutes for the good, and the greater the share of households' budgets that is spent on the good. And *long-run elasticities* are almost always larger—in absolute value—than *short-run elasticities.*

The *income elasticity of demand* is the percentage change in quantity demanded divided by the percentage change in income that causes it.

The *cross-price elasticity of demand* measures the percentage change in the quantity demanded of one good as a result of a 1 percent increase in the price of some other good.

And the *price elasticity of supply* measures the percentage change in quantity supplied for a 1 percent change in price.

Problem Set   *Answers to even-numbered Questions and Problems can be found on the text Web site at www.thomsonedu.com/economics/hall.*

1. The market for rice has the following supply and demand schedules:

P (per ton)	Q^D (tons)	Q^S (tons)
$10	100	0
$20	80	30
$30	60	40
$40	50	50
$50	40	60

To support rice producers, the government imposes a price floor of $50 per ton.
   a. What quantity will be traded in the market? Why?
   b. What steps might the government have to take to enforce the price floor?

2. The market for one-bedroom apartments in a city has the following supply and demand schedules:

Monthly Rent	Q^D (thousands)	Q^S (thousands)
$1,000	800	300
$1,200	600	350
$1,400	400	400
$1,600	200	450
$1,800	100	500

The government imposes a price ceiling (rent control) of $1,200.
   a. With the price ceiling, is there an excess demand, excess supply, or neither? If there is an excess demand or excess supply, state which and give the numerical value.
   b. What quantity of one-bedroom apartments will actually be rented?

   c. Suppose, instead, that the price ceiling is set at $1,600. What quantity of one-bedroom apartments will be rented now? Is there an excess supply, excess demand, or neither?

3. The demand for bottled water in a small town is as follows:

P (per bottle)	Q_d (bottles per week)
$1.00	500
$1.50	400
$2.00	300
$2.50	200
$3.00	100

   a. Is this a straight-line demand curve? How do you know?
   b. Calculate the price elasticity of demand for bottled water for a price rise from $1.00 to $1.50. Is demand elastic or inelastic for this price change?
   c. Calculate the price elasticity of demand for a price rise from $2.50 to $3.00. Is demand elastic or inelastic for this price change?
   d. According to the chapter, demand should become less and less elastic as we move downward and rightward along a straight-line demand curve. Use your answers in *b.* and *c.* to confirm this relationship.
   e. Create another column for total revenue on bottled water at each price.
   f. According to the chapter, a rise in price should *increase* total revenue on bottled water when demand is inelastic, and *decrease* total revenue when demand is elastic. Use your answers in *b.* and *c.*, and the new total revenue column you created, to confirm this.

4. In Figure 8, prove that the incidence of a $60 tax imposed on sellers could not be split equally between buyers and sellers, given the supply and demand curves as drawn. Hint: What price would the airline have to charge after the tax for an even split? What would happen in the market if the airlines charge this price?

5. Sketch a demand curve that is unit elastic for a price change between $9 and $11. Assume that the quantity demanded is 110 when price is $9. You'll have to determine the quantity demanded when price is $11.

6. In the chapter, you learned that one way the government enforces agricultural price floors is to buy up the excess supply itself. If the government wanted to follow a similar kind of policy to enforce a price *ceiling* (such as rent control), and thereby prevent black-market-type activity, what would it have to do? Is this a sensible solution for enforcing rent control? Briefly, why or why not?

7. In the chapter, we calculated the likely long-run change in revenue if New York City were to raise mass transit fares from $2.00 to $2.50. Use the same procedure to calculate the *short-run* impact of this fare hike. This time, you'll be choosing an elasticity in the middle of the range of short-run estimates (from 0.2 to 0.5).

8. In the chapter, using an estimate of the short-run elasticity of demand for oil (0.15), we found that a crisis that eliminated half of Persian Gulf oil supplies would cause the world price to rise from $60 to $110 per barrel in the short run. In the long run, the elasticity of demand for oil is considerably greater. Using a long-run elasticity value of 0.4, and a starting price of $60 per barrel, forecast the new long-run price after a crisis that wipes out half of Persian Gulf oil for a prolonged period.

9. Figure 12 shows the impact of a $10,000 subsidy on the market for college education when the subsidy is paid to college students. Starting with the same initial supply and demand curves, show what happens when the same $10,000 subsidy per student is paid to the *colleges* they attend. Suggestion: Trace the relevant curves from the figure on your own sheet of paper. (Hint: If a subsidy is paid directly to the colleges, which curve will shift? In what direction?)

10. The demand for rosebushes in a market is as follows:

Price (per rosebush)	Quantity Demanded (rosebushes per week)
$3	230
$4	150
$5	90
$6	40

a. Is this a straight-line demand curve? How do you know?

b. Calculate the price elasticity of demand for roses for a price increase from $3 to $4. Is demand elastic or inelastic for this price change?

c. Calculate the price elasticity of demand for roses for a price increase from $4 to $5. Is demand elastic or inelastic for this price change?

d. Use what you've learned about the determinants of price elasticity of demand to explain why this demand curve might exhibit the elasticity shown in parts *b.* and *c.*

11. Refer to Table 2 in this chapter and answer the following questions:
a. Which is more elastically demanded: cigarettes or pork? Does this make sense to you? Explain briefly.
b. If the price of milk rises by 5 percent, what will happen to the quantity demanded? (Be specific.)

12. Once again, refer to Table 2 in this chapter and answer the following questions:
a. Is the demand for recreation more or less elastic than the demand for clothing?
b. If 10,000 two-liter bottles of Pepsi are currently being demanded in your community each month, and the price increases from $0.90 to $1.00 per bottle, what will happen to quantity demanded? Be specific.
c. By how much would the price of ground beef have to increase (in percentage terms) in order to reduce quantity demanded by 5 percent?

13. Three Guys Named Al, a moving company, is contemplating a price hike. Currently, they charge $20 per hour, but Al thinks they could get $30. Al disagrees, saying it will hurt the business. Al, the brains of the outfit, has calculated the price elasticity of demand for their moving services in the range from $20 to $30 and found it to be 0.5.
a. Should they do as Al suggests and raise the price? Why or why not?
b. Currently, Three Guys is the only moving company in town. Al reads in the paper that several new movers are planning to set up shop there within the next year. Twelve months from now, is the demand for Three Guys' services likely to be more elastic, less elastic, or the same? Why?

More Challenging

14. In February, 2003, Germany's patent office proposed a solution to reimburse copyright holders for illegal digital file sharing: charging personal computer manufacturers a fee of $13 per computer that would go into a special fund to reimburse the copyright holders. Two computer makers—Fujitsu-Siemens and Hewlett-Packard—claimed that imposing the fee would do great injury to them because they would be *unable to pass any of the fee onto consumers.* Under what assumptions about the demand curve would the computer-makers' claim be true? Is this assumption realistic?

CHAPTER 5

Consumer Choice

You are constantly making economic decisions. Some of them are rather trivial. (Have coffee at Starbucks or more cheaply at home?) Others can have a profound impact on your life. (Live with your parents a while longer or get your own place?) The economic nature of all these decisions is rather obvious, since they all involve *spending*.

But in other cases, the economic nature of your decisions may be less obvious. Did you get up early today in order to get things done, or did you sleep in? Which leisure activities—movies, concerts, sports, hobbies—do you engage in, and how often do you decline an opportunity to have fun for lack of time? At this very moment, what have you decided *not* to do in order to make time to read this chapter? All of these are economic choices, too, because they require you to allocate a scarce resource—your *time*—among different alternatives.

To understand the economic choices that individuals make, we must know what they are trying to achieve (their goals) and the limitations they face in achieving them (their constraints).

But wait. How can we identify the goals and constraints of *consumers* when we are all so *different* from each other?

Indeed, we *are* different from one another . . . when it comes to *specific* goals and *specific* constraints. But at the highest level of generality, we are all very much alike. All of us, for example, would like to maximize our overall level of *satisfaction*. And all of us, as we attempt to satisfy our desires, come up against the same constraints: too little income or wealth to buy everything we might enjoy, and too little time to enjoy it all.

We'll start our analysis of individual choice with constraints, and then move on to goals. In most of the chapter, we will focus on choices about *spending:* how people decide what to buy. This is why the theory of individual decision making is often called "consumer theory." Later, in the Using the Theory section, we'll see how the theory can be broadened to include decisions about allocating scarce *time* among different activities.

THE BUDGET CONSTRAINT

Virtually all individuals must face two facts of economic life: (1) They have to pay prices for the goods and services they buy, and (2) they have limited funds to spend. These two facts are summarized by the consumer's *budget constraint:*

> *A consumer's **budget constraint** identifies which combinations of goods and services the consumer can afford with a limited budget, at given prices.*

Budget constraint The different combinations of goods a consumer can afford with a limited budget, at given prices.

Consider Max, a devoted fan of both movies and the local music scene, who has a total entertainment budget of $150 each month. Each movie costs Max $10, while the average ticket price for local rock concerts is $30. If Max were to spend all of his $150 budget on concerts at $30 each, he could see at most five each month. If he were to spend it all on movies at $10 each, he could see 15 of them.

But Max could also choose to spend *part* of his budget on concerts and *part* on movies. In this case, for each number of concerts, there is some *maximum* number of movies that he could see. For example, if he goes to one concert per month, it will cost him $30 of his $150 budget, leaving $120 available for movies. Thus, if Max were to choose one concert, the *maximum* number of films he could choose would be $120/$10 = 12.

Figure 1 lists, for each number of concerts, the maximum number of movies that Max could see. Each combination of goods in the table is affordable for Max, since each will cost him exactly $150. Combination *A,* at one extreme, represents no concerts and 15 movies. Combination *F,* the other extreme, represents 5 concerts and no movies. In each of the combinations between *A* and *F,* Max attends both concerts and movies.

The graph in Figure 1 plots the number of movies along the vertical axis and the number of concerts along the horizontal. Each of the points *A* through *F* corresponds to one of the combinations in the table. If we connect all of these points with a straight line, we have a graphical representation of Max's budget constraint, which we call Max's **budget line.**

Budget line The graphical representation of a budget constraint, showing the maximum affordable quantity of one good for given amounts of another good.

Note that any point below or to the left of the budget line is affordable. For example, two concerts and six movies—indicated by point *G*—would cost only $60 + $60 = $120. Max could certainly afford this combination. On the other hand, he *cannot* afford any combination *above* and to the right of this line. Point *H,* representing 3 concerts and 8 movies, would cost $90 + $80 = $170, which is beyond Max's budget. The budget line therefore serves as a *border* between those combinations that are affordable and those that arc not.

Let's look at Max's budget line more closely. The *vertical intercept* is 15, the number of movies Max could see if he attended zero concerts. Starting at the vertical intercept (point *A*), notice that each time Max increases one unit along the horizontal axis (attends one more concert), he must decrease 3 units along the vertical (see three fewer movies). Thus, the slope of the budget line is equal to −3. The slope tells us Max's *opportunity cost* of one more concert. That is, the opportunity cost of one more concert is 3 movies foregone.

There is an important relationship between the *prices* of two goods and the opportunity cost of having more of one or the other. The prices Max faces tell us how many dollars he must give up to get another unit of each good. If, however, we divide one money price by another money price, we get what is called a **relative price**, the price of one good *relative* to the other. Let's use the symbol P_c for the price of a concert and P_m for the price of a movie. Since P_c = $30 and P_m = $10, the *relative price of a concert* is the ratio P_c/P_m = $30/$10 = 3. Notice that 3 is the opportunity cost of another concert in terms of movies; and, except for the minus sign, it is also the slope of the budget line. That is, *the relative price of a*

Relative price The price of one good relative to the price of another.

FIGURE 1

The Budget Constraint

With $150 per month, Max can afford 15 movies and no concerts, ...

12 movies and 1 concert or any other combination *on* the budget line.

Points *below* the line are also affordable.

But *not* points *above* the line.

Max's Consumption Possibilities with Income of $150				
	Concerts at $30 each		**Movies at $10 each**	
	Quantity	**Total Expenditure on Concerts**	**Quantity**	**Total Expenditure on Movies**
A	0	$ 0	15	$150
B	1	$ 30	12	$120
C	2	$ 60	9	$ 90
D	3	$ 90	6	$ 60
E	4	$120	3	$ 30
F	5	$150	0	$ 0

concert, *the opportunity cost of another concert, and the slope of the budget line* have the same absolute value. This is one example of a general relationship:

> *The slope of the budget line indicates the spending tradeoff between one good and another—the amount of one good that must be sacrificed in order to buy more of another good. If P_y is the price of the good on the vertical axis and P_x is the price of the good on the horizontal axis, then the slope of the budget line is $-P_x/P_y$.*

CHANGES IN THE BUDGET LINE

To draw the budget line in Figure 1, we have assumed given prices for movies and concerts, and a given income that Max can spend on them. These "givens"—the prices of the goods and the consumer's income—are always *assumed constant* as we move along a budget line; if any one of them changes, the budget line will change as well. Let's see how.

Changes in Income

If Max's available income increases from $150 to $300 per month, then he can afford to see more movies, more concerts, or more of both, as shown by the change in his budget line in Figure 2(a). If Max were to devote *all* of his income to movies, he could now see 30 of them each month, instead of the 15 he was able to see before. Devoting his entire income to concerts would enable him to attend 10, rather than 5. Moreover, for any number of concerts, he will be able to see more movies than before. For example, before, when his budget was only $150, choosing 2 concerts would allow Max to see only 9 movies. Now, with a budget of $300, he can have 2 concerts and *24* movies.

The Budget Line's Slope It's tempting to think that the slope of the budget line should be $-P_y/P_x$, with the price of the vertical axis good y in the numerator. But notice that the slope is the other way around, $-P_x/P_y$, with P_x in the numerator. We've given some intuition for this in our example with Max, but if you'd like a formal proof, see the footnote.[1]

DANGEROUS CURVES

Notice that the old and new budget lines in Figure 2(a) are parallel; that is, they have the same slope of -3. This is because we changed Max's income but *not* prices. Since the ratio P_c/P_m has not changed, the spending tradeoff between movies and concerts remains the same. Thus,

> *an increase in income will shift the budget line upward (and rightward). A decrease in income will shift the budget line downward (and leftward). These shifts are parallel: Changes in income do not affect the budget line's slope.*

Changes in Price

Now let's go back to Max's original budget of $150 and explore what happens to the budget line when a price changes. Suppose the price of a movie falls from $10 to $5. The graph in Figure 2(b) shows Max's old and new budget lines. When the price of a movie falls, the budget line rotates outward; that is, the vertical intercept moves higher. The reason is this: When a movie costs $10, Max could spend his entire $150 on them and see 15; now that they cost $5, he can see a maximum of 30. The horizontal intercept—representing how many concerts Max could see with his entire income—doesn't change at all, since there has been no change in the price of a concert. Notice that the new budget line is also *steeper* than the original one, with slope equal to $-P_c/P_m = -\$30/\$5 = -6$. Now, with movies costing $5, the trade-off between movies and concerts is 6 to 1, instead of 3 to 1.

---

[1] To prove that the slope of the budget line is $= -P_x/P_y$, let Q_x and Q_y represent the quantities of good x and good y, respectively. Then the total amount a consumer spends on good y is P_yQ_y, and the total amount spent on good x is P_xQ_x. All along the budget line, the total amount spent on these two goods is equal to the total budget (B), so it must be that $P_xQ_x + P_yQ_y = B$. This is the equation for the budget line. Since the budget line graph has good y on the vertical axis, we can solve this equation for Q_y by rearranging terms: $Q_y = (B - P_xQ_x)/P_y$, which can be rewritten as $Q_y = (B/P_y) + (-P_x/P_y) Q_x$. This is the equation for a straight line. The first term in parentheses (B/P_y) is the vertical intercept, and the second term in parentheses $(-P_x/P_y)$ is the slope. (See the mathematical appendix to Chapter 1 if you need to review slopes and intercepts.)

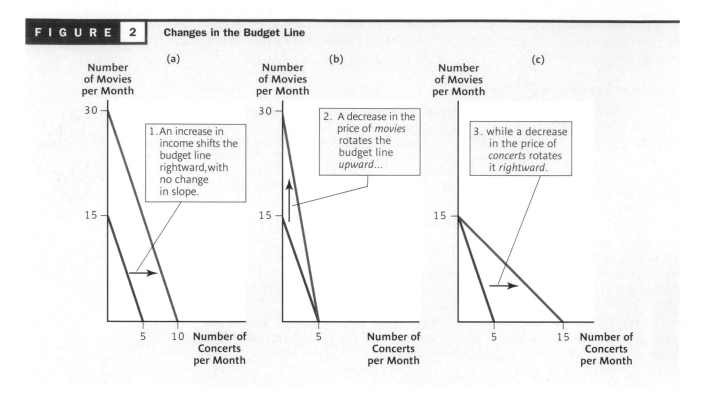

FIGURE 2   **Changes in the Budget Line**

Panel (c) of Figure 2 illustrates another price change. This time, it's a fall in the price of a *concert* from $30 to $10. Once again, the budget line rotates, but now it is the horizontal intercept (concerts) that changes and the vertical intercept (movies) that remains fixed.

We could draw similar diagrams illustrating a *rise* in the price of a movie or a concert, but you should try to do this on your own. In each case, one of the budget line's intercepts will change, as well as its slope:

> *When the price of a good changes, the budget line rotates: Both its slope and one of its intercepts will change.*

The budget constraint, as illustrated by the budget line, is one side of the story of consumer choice. It indicates the tradeoff consumers *are able to* make between one good and another. But just as important is the tradeoff that consumers *want to* make between one good and another, and this depends on consumers' *preferences,* the subject of the next section.

PREFERENCES

How can we possibly speak systematically about people's preferences? After all, people are different. They like different things. American teens delight in having a Coke with dinner, while the very idea makes a French person shudder. What would satisfy a Buddhist monk would hardly satisfy the typical American.

And even among "typical Americans," there is little consensus about tastes. Some read Jane Austen, while others pick John Grisham. Some like to spend their vacations traveling, whereas others would prefer to stay home and sleep in every day. Even those who like Häagen-Dazs ice cream can't agree on which is the best flavor—the company notices consistent, regional differences in consumption. In Los Angeles, chocolate chip is the clear favorite, while on most of the East Coast, it's butter pecan—except in New York City, where coffee wins hands down. (And economics instructors have different preferences about teaching consumer theory. More on this in a few pages.)

In spite of such wide differences in preferences, we can find some important common denominators—things that seem to be true for a wide variety of people. In our theory of consumer choice, we will focus on these common denominators.

RATIONALITY

One common denominator—and a critical assumption behind consumer theory—is that people *have* preferences. More specifically, we assume that you can look at two alternatives and state either that you prefer one to the other or that you are entirely indifferent between the two—you value them equally.

Another common denominator is that preferences are *logically consistent*, or *transitive*. If, for example, you prefer a sports car to a jeep, and a jeep to a motorcycle, then we assume that you will also prefer a sports car to a motorcycle. When a consumer can make choices, and is logically consistent, we say that she has **rational preferences**.

Notice that rationality is a matter of how you make your choices, and not what choices you make. You can be rational and like apples better than oranges, or oranges better than apples. You can be rational even if you like anchovies or brussels sprouts! What matters is that you make logically consistent choices, and most of us usually do.

Rational preferences Preferences that satisfy two conditions: (1) Any two alternatives can be compared, and one is preferred or else the two are valued equally, and (2) the comparisons are logically consistent or transitive.

MORE IS BETTER

Another feature of preferences that virtually all of us share is this: We generally feel that *more is better*. Specifically, if we get more of some good or service, and nothing else is taken away from us, we will generally feel better off.

This condition seems to be satisfied for the vast majority of goods we all consume. Of course, there are exceptions. If you hate eggplant, then the more of it you have, the worse off you are. Similarly, a dieter who says, "Don't bring any ice cream into the house. I don't want to be tempted," also violates the assumption. The model of consumer choice in this chapter is designed for preferences that satisfy the "more is better" condition, and it would have to be modified to take account of exceptions like these.

So far, our characterization of consumer preferences has been rather minimal. We've assumed only that consumers are rational and that they prefer more rather than less of every good we're considering. But even this limited information allows us to say the following:

The consumer will always choose a point on the budget line, rather than a point below it.

To see why this is so, look again at Figure 1. Max would never choose point *G,* representing 2 concerts and 6 movies, since there are affordable points—on the budget line—that we know make him better off. For example, point *C* has the same number of concerts, but more movies, while point *D* has the same number of movies, but more concerts. "More is better" tells us that Max will prefer *C* or *D* to *G,* so we know *G* won't be chosen. Indeed, if we look at any point below the budget line, we can always find at least one point on the budget line that is preferred, as long as more is better.

Knowing what Max will not do—knowing he *will not* choose a point inside his budget line—is helpful. It tells us that we can narrow our search for the point he *will* choose to just the ones along the budget line *AF.* But how can Max find the one point along the budget line that gives him a higher utility than all the others?

This is where your *instructor's* preferences come in. There are two theories of consumer decision making, and they share much in common. First, both assume that preferences are rational. Second, both assume that the consumer would be better off with more of any good we're considering. This means the consumer will always choose a combination of goods *on,* rather than below, his budget line. Finally, both theories come to the same general conclusions about consumer behavior. However, to *arrive* at those conclusions, each theory takes a different road.

The next section presents the "Marginal Utility" approach to consumer decision making. If, however, your instructor prefers the "Indifference Curve" approach, you can skip the next section and go straight to the appendix. Then, come back to the section titled "Income and Substitution Effects," which is where our two roads converge once again.

One warning, though. Both approaches to consumer theory are *models.* They use graphs and calculations to explain how consumers make choices. While the models are logical, they may appear unrealistic to you. And in one sense, they *are* unrealistic: Few consumers in the real world are aware of the techniques we'll discuss, yet they make choices all the time.

Economists don't imagine that, when making choices, households or consumers actually *use* these techniques. Rather, the assumption is that people mostly behave *as if* they use them. Indeed, most of the time, in most markets, household behavior has proven to be consistent with the model of consumer choice. When our goal is to describe and predict how consumers are likely to behave in markets—rather than describe what actually goes on in their minds—our theories of consumer decision making can be very useful.

CONSUMER DECISIONS: THE MARGINAL UTILITY APPROACH

Utility A quantitative measure of pleasure or satisfaction obtained from consuming goods and services.

Economists assume that *any* decision maker—a consumer, the manager of a business firm, or officials in a government agency—tries to make the *best* out of any situation. Marginal utility theory treats consumers as striving to maximize their **utility**—an actual *quantitative* measure of well-being or satisfaction. Anything that makes the consumer better off is assumed to raise his utility. Anything that makes the consumer worse off will decrease his utility.

UTILITY AND MARGINAL UTILITY

Figure 3 provides a graphical view of utility—in this case, the utility of a consumer named Lisa who likes ice cream cones. Look first at panel (a). On the horizontal axis, we'll measure the number of ice cream cones Lisa consumes each week. On the vertical axis, we'll measure the utility she derives from consuming each of them. If Lisa values ice cream cones, her utility will increase as she acquires more of them, as it does in the figure. There we see that when she has one cone, she enjoys total utility of 30 "utils," and when she has two cones, her total utility grows to 50 utils, and so on. Throughout the figure, the total utility Lisa derives from consuming ice cream cones keeps rising as she gets to consume more and more of them.

But notice something interesting, and important: Although Lisa's utility increases every time she consumes more ice cream, the *additional* utility she derives from each *successive* cone gets smaller and smaller as she gets more cones. We call the *change in utility* derived from consuming an *additional unit* of a good the *marginal utility* of that additional unit.

> *Marginal utility is the change in utility an individual enjoys from consuming an additional unit of a good.*

Marginal utility The change in total utility an individual obtains from consuming an additional unit of a good or service.

What we've observed about Lisa's utility can be restated this way: As she eats more and more ice cream cones in a given week, her *marginal utility* from another cone

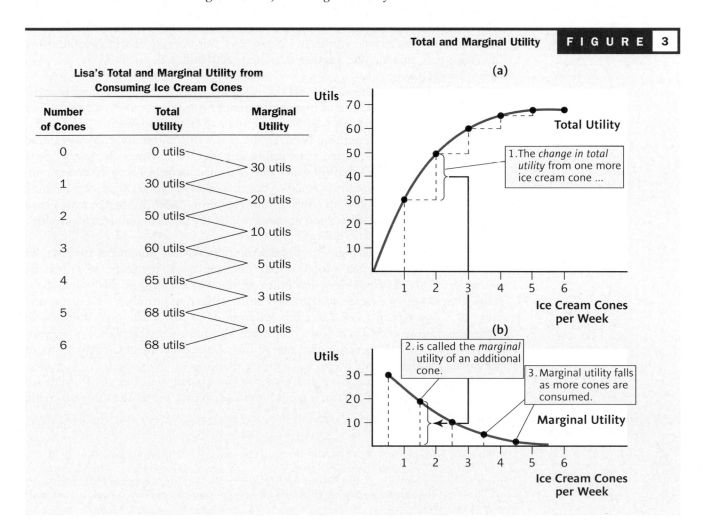

Total and Marginal Utility   FIGURE 3

Lisa's Total and Marginal Utility from Consuming Ice Cream Cones

Number of Cones	Total Utility	Marginal Utility
0	0 utils	
		30 utils
1	30 utils	
		20 utils
2	50 utils	
		10 utils
3	60 utils	
		5 utils
4	65 utils	
		3 utils
5	68 utils	
		0 utils
6	68 utils	

(a)

1. The *change in total utility* from one more ice cream cone ...

Total Utility

(b)

2. is called the *marginal utility* of an additional cone.

3. Marginal utility falls as more cones are consumed.

Marginal Utility

Law of diminishing marginal utility
As consumption of a good or service increases, marginal utility decreases.

declines. We call this the **law of diminishing marginal utility**, which the great economist Alfred Marshall (1842–1924) defined this way:

> *The marginal utility of a thing to anyone diminishes with every increase in the amount of it he already has.*[2]

According to the law of diminishing marginal utility, when you consume your first unit of some good, like an ice cream cone, you derive some amount of utility. When you get your second cone that week, you enjoy greater satisfaction than when you only had one, but the extra satisfaction you derive from the second is likely to be smaller than the satisfaction you derived from the first. Adding the third cone to your weekly consumption will no doubt increase your utility further, but again the marginal utility you derive from that third cone is likely to be less than the marginal utility you derived from the second.

Figure 3 will again help us see what's going on. The table summarizes the information in the total utility graph. The first two columns show, respectively, the quantity of cones Lisa consumes each week and the total utility she receives each week from consuming them. The third column shows the *marginal* utility she receives from each successive cone she consumes per week. As you can see in the table, Lisa's total utility keeps increasing (marginal utility is always positive) as she consumes more cones (up to five per week), but the rate at which total utility increases gets smaller and smaller (her marginal utility diminishes) as her consumption increases.

Marginal utility is shown in panel (b) of Figure 3. Because marginal utility is the change in utility caused by a change in consumption from one level to another, we plot each marginal utility entry between the old and new consumption levels.

Notice the close relationship between the graph of total utility in panel (a) and the corresponding graph of marginal utility in panel (b). If you look closely at the two graphs, you will see that for every one-unit increment in Lisa's ice cream consumption her marginal utility is equal to the change in her total utility. Diminishing marginal utility is seen in both panels of the figure: in panel (b), by the downward sloping marginal utility curve, and in panel (a), by the positive but decreasing slope (flattening out) of the total utility curve.

One last thing about Figure 3: Because marginal utility diminishes for Lisa, by the time she has consumed a total of five cones per week, the marginal utility she derives from an additional cone has fallen all the way to zero. At this point, she is fully satiated with ice cream and gets no extra satisfaction or utility from eating any more of it in a typical week. Once this satiation point is reached, even if ice cream were free, Lisa would turn it down ("Yechhh! Not more ice cream!!"). But remember from our earlier discussion that one of the assumptions we always make about preferences is that people prefer *more* rather than less of any good we're considering. So when we use marginal utility theory, we assume that marginal utility for every good is positive. For Lisa, it would mean she hasn't yet reached five ice cream cones per week.

---

[2] *Principles of Economics*, Book III, Ch. III, Appendix notes 1 & 2. Macmillan & Co., 1930. The term "marginal" is one that you'll encounter often in economics. The margin of a sheet of notebook paper is the area on the edge, just *beyond* the writing area. By analogy, a *marginal value* in economics measures what happens when we go a little bit *beyond* where we are now, by adding one more unit of something.

COMBINING THE BUDGET CONSTRAINT AND PREFERENCES

The marginal utility someone gets from consuming more of a good tells us about his *preferences*. His budget constraint, by contrast, tells us only which combinations of goods he can *afford*. If we combine information about preferences (marginal utility values) with information about what is affordable (the budget constraint), we can develop a useful rule to guide us to an individual's utility-maximizing choice.

To develop this rule, let's go back to Max and his choice between movies and concerts. Figure 4 reproduces Max's budget constraint from Figure 1. But now, we've added information about Max's preferences, in the table below the graph.

Each row of the table corresponds to a different point on Max's budget line. For example, the row labeled C corresponds to point C on the budget line. The second entry in each row tells us the number of concerts that Max attends each month, and the third entry tells us the marginal utility he gets from consuming the last concert. For example, at point C, Max attends two concerts, and the second one gives him an additional 1,200 utils beyond the first. Notice that as we move down along the budget line, from point A to B to C and so on, the number of concerts increases and the marginal utility numbers in the table get smaller, consistent with the law of diminishing marginal utility.

The fourth entry in each row shows something new: the marginal utility *per dollar* spent on concerts, obtained by dividing the marginal utility of the last concert (MU_c) by the price of a concert, giving us MU_c/P_c. This tells us the gain in utility Max gets *for each dollar he spends* on the last concert. For example, at point C, Max gains 1,200 utils from his second concert during the month, so his marginal utility *per dollar* spent on that concert is 1,200 utils/\$30 = 40 utils per dollar. Marginal utility per dollar, like marginal utility itself, declines as Max attends more concerts. After all, marginal utility itself decreases, and the price of a concert isn't changing, so the ratio of marginal utility to price must decrease as he sees more concerts.

The last three entries in each row give us similar information for movies: the number of movies attended, the marginal utility derived from the last movie (MU_m), and the marginal utility per dollar spent on the last movie (MU_m/P_m). As we travel *up* this column, Max attends more movies, and both marginal utility and marginal utility per dollar decline—once again, consistent with the law of diminishing marginal utility.

Now, Max's goal is to find the affordable combination of movies and concerts—the point on his budget line—that gives him the highest possible utility. As you are about to see, this will be the point at which *the marginal utility per dollar is the same for both goods.*

To see why, imagine that Max is searching along his budget line for the utility-maximizing point, and he's currently considering point B, which represents 1 concert and 12 movies. Is he maximizing his utility? Let's see. Comparing the fourth and seventh entries in row B of the table, we see that Max's marginal utility per dollar spent on concerts is 50 utils, while his marginal utility per dollar spent on movies is only 10 utils. Since he gains more additional utility from each dollar spent on concerts than from each dollar spent on movies, he will have a net gain in utility if he shifts some of his dollars from movies to concerts. To do this, he must travel farther down his budget line.

Next suppose that, after shifting his spending from movies to concerts, Max arrives at point C on his budget line. What should he do then? At point C, Max's *MU* per dollar spent on concerts is 40 utils, while his *MU* per dollar spent on movies

F I G U R E 4   **Consumer Decision Making**

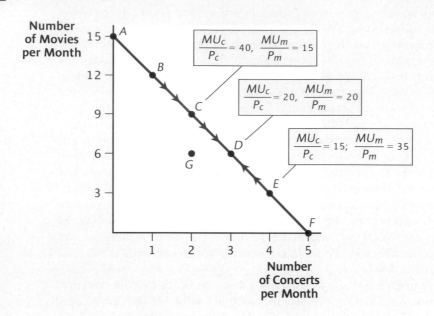

Income = $150 per month

	CONCERTS at $30 each				MOVIES at $10 each	
(1) Point on Budget Line	**(2)** Number of Concerts per Month	**(3)** Marginal Utility from Last Concert (MU_c)	**(4)** Marginal Utility per Dollar Spent on Last Concert $\left(\dfrac{MU_c}{P_c}\right)$	**(5)** Number of Movies per Month	**(6)** Marginal Utility from Last Movie (MU_m)	**(7)** Marginal Utility per Dollar Spent on Last Movie $\left(\dfrac{MU_m}{P_m}\right)$
A	0	—	—	15	50	5
B	1	1,500	50	12	100	10
C	2	1,200	40	9	150	15
D	**3**	**600**	**20**	**6**	**200**	**20**
E	4	450	15	3	350	35
F	5	360	12	0	—	

The budget line shows the maximum number of movies Max could attend for each number of concerts he attends. He would never choose an interior point like G because there are affordable points—on the line—that make him better off. Max will choose the point on the budget line at which the marginal utilities per dollar spent on movies and concerts are equal. From the table, this occurs at point D.

is 15 utils. Once again, he would gain utility by shifting from movies to concerts, traveling down his budget line once again.

Now suppose that Max arrives at point D. At this point, the MU per dollar spent on both movies and concerts is the same: 20 utils. There is no further gain from shifting spending from movies to concerts. At point D, Max has exploited all opportunities to make himself better off by moving down the budget line. He has maximized his utility.

But wait . . . what if Max had started at a point on his budget line *below* point D? Would he still end up at the same place? Yes, he would. Suppose Max finds himself at point E, with 4 concerts and 3 movies. Here, marginal utilities per dollar are 15 utils for concerts and 35 utils for movies. Now, Max could make himself better off by shifting spending away from concerts and toward movies. He will travel *up* the budget line, once again arriving at point D, where no further move will improve his well-being.

As you can see, it doesn't matter whether Max begins at a point on his budget line that's above point D or below it. Either way, if he keeps shifting spending toward the good with greater marginal utility per dollar, he will always end up at point D. And because marginal utility per dollar is the same for both goods at point D, there is nothing to gain by shifting spending in either direction.

What is true for Max and his choice between movies and concerts is true for *any* consumer and *any* two goods. We can generalize our result this way: For any two goods x and y, with prices P_x and P_y, whenever $MU_x/P_x > MU_y/P_y$, a consumer is made better off shifting spending away from y and toward x. When $MU_y/P_y > MU_x/P_x$, a consumer is made better off by shifting spending away from x and toward y. This leads us to an important conclusion:

> *A utility-maximizing consumer will choose the point on the budget line where marginal utility per dollar is the same for both goods ($MU_x/P_x = MU_y/P_y$). At that point, there is no further gain from reallocating expenditures in either direction.*

We can generalize even further. Suppose there are more than two goods an individual can buy. For example, we could imagine that Max wants to divide his entertainment budget among movies, concerts, football games, and what have you. Or we can think of a consumer who must allocate her entire income among thousands of different goods and services each month: different types of food, clothing, entertainment, transportation, and so on. Does our description of the optimal choice for the consumer still hold? Indeed, it does. No matter how many goods there are to choose from, when the consumer is doing as well as possible, it must be true that $MU_x/P_x = MU_y/P_y$ for *any* pair of

Why Use Marginal Utility *per Dollar*? In finding the utility-maximizing combination of goods for a consumer, why do we use marginal utility *per dollar* instead of just marginal utility? Shouldn't the consumer always shift spending wherever *marginal utility* is greater? The answer is no. The following thought experiment will help you see why. Imagine that you like to ski and you like going out for dinner. Currently, your marginal utility for one more skiing trip is 2,000 utils, and your marginal utility for an additional dinner is 1,000 utils. Should you shift your spending from dining out to skiing? It might seem so, since skiing has the higher marginal utility.

But what if skiing costs $200 per trip, while a dinner out costs only $20? Then, while it's true that another ski trip will give you twice as much utility as another dinner out, it's also true that *skiing costs 10 times as much.* You would have to sacrifice 10 dinners out for 1 ski trip, and that would make you *worse* off.

Instead, you should shift your spending in the other direction: from skiing to dining out. Money spent on additional ski trips will give you 2,000 utils/$200 = 10 utils per dollar, while money spent on additional dinners will give you 1,000 utils/$20 = 50 utils per dollar. Dining out clearly gives you "more bang for the buck" than skiing. The lesson: When trying to find the utility-maximizing combination of goods, compare marginal utilities *per dollar,* not marginal utilities of the two goods.

DANGEROUS CURVES

goods x and y. If this condition is *not* satisfied, the consumer will be better off consuming more of one and less of the other good in the pair.[3]

WHAT HAPPENS WHEN THINGS CHANGE?

If every one of our decisions had to be made only once, life would be much easier. But that's not how life is. Just when you think you've figured out what to do, things change. In a market economy, as you've learned, prices can change for any number of reasons. (See Chapter 3.) A consumer's income can change as well. He may lose a job or find a new one; she may get a raise or a cut in pay. Changes in our incomes or the prices we face cause us to rethink our spending decisions: What maximized utility before the change is unlikely to maximize it afterward. The result is a change in our behavior.

Changes in Income

Figure 5 illustrates how an increase in income might affect Max's choice between movies and concerts. As before, we assume that movies cost $10 each, that concerts cost $30 each, and that these prices are not changing. Initially, Max has $150 in income to spend on the two goods, so his budget line is the line from point A to point F. As we've already seen, under these conditions, Max would choose point D (three concerts and six movies) to maximize utility.

Now suppose Max's income increases to $300. Then his budget line will shift upward and outward in the figure. How will he respond? As always, he will search along his budget line until he finds the point where the marginal utility per dollar spent on both goods is the same. But where will this point be? There are several possibilities, and they depend on Max's preferences, as reflected in his marginal utility values for movies and concerts. Now that his income has increased, the points along Max's budget line have more movies for any number of concerts, or more concerts for any number of movies. Thus, we'll have to specify Max's preferences among these *new* combinations he can afford.

Let's start out with a simple assumption: that for Max, the marginal utility of any given movie depends only on the total number of movies per month, and *not* on the number of concerts. For example, the marginal utility of the *12th* movie per month would be 100 utils, regardless of whether that movie is enjoyed along with 1 concert per month (point B), or with 6 concerts (point H). Similarly, suppose that the marginal utility of any *concert* depends on only total concerts, and not on the number of movies that go with them. Then we can bring the marginal utility values for different numbers of movies and concerts from Figure 4 over to Figure 5. With our assumption that marginal utilities for one good are independent of amounts of the other, these marginal utility values will still apply to Max's new set of choices. Figure 5 also includes some additional marginal utility values for combinations that weren't affordable before, but are now. For example, the *sixth*

---

[3] There is one exception to this statement: Sometimes the optimal choice is to buy *none* of some good. For example, suppose that $MU_y/P_y > MU_x/P_x$ no matter how small a quantity of good x a person consumes. Then the consumer should always reduce consumption of good x further, until its quantity is zero. Economists call this a "corner solution" because when there are only two goods being considered, the individual will locate at one of the end points of the budget line in a corner of the diagram.

Effects of an Increase in Income   **F I G U R E** **5**

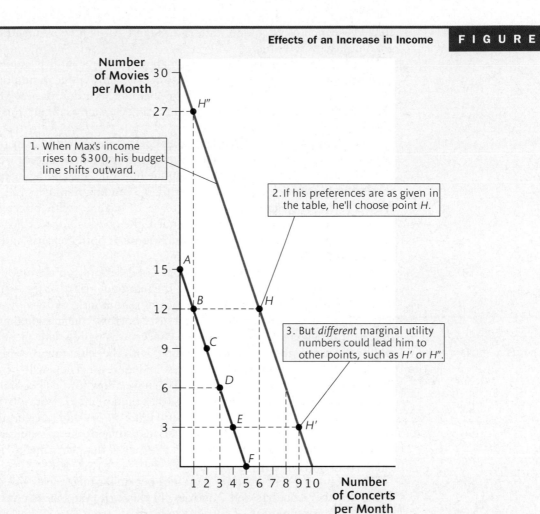

1. When Max's income rises to $300, his budget line shifts outward.

2. If his preferences are as given in the table, he'll choose point *H*.

3. But *different* marginal utility numbers could lead him to other points, such as *H'* or *H"*.

Income = $300 per month

	Concerts at $30 each			Movies at $10 each	
Number of Concerts per Month	Marginal Utility from Last Concert (MU_c)	Marginal Utility per Dollar Spent on Last Concert $\left(\dfrac{MU_c}{P_c}\right)$	Number of Movies per Month	Marginal Utility from Last Movie (MU_m)	Marginal Utility per Dollar Spent on Last Movie $\left(\dfrac{MU_m}{P_m}\right)$
3	600	20	21	20	2
4	450	15	18	30	3
5	360	12	15	50	5
6	**300**	**10**	**12**	**100**	**10**
7	180	6	9	150	15

concert—which Max couldn't afford in Figure 4—is now assumed to have a marginal utility of 300 utils.

With the preferences described by these marginal utility numbers, Max will search along his budget line for the best choice. This will lead him directly to point H, enjoying 6 concerts and 12 movies per month. For this choice, MU/P is 10 utils per dollar for both goods, so total utility can't be increased any further by shifting dollars from one good to the other.

Now let's take a step back from these calculations and look at the figure itself. We see that an increase in income has changed Max's best choice from point D on the old budget constraint to point H on the new one. In moving from D to H, Max chooses to buy more concerts (6 rather than 3) and more movies (12 rather than 6). As discussed in Chapter 3, if an increase in income (with prices held constant) increases the quantity of a good demanded, the good is *normal*. For Max, with the marginal utility values we've assumed in Figure 5, both concerts and movies would be normal goods.

But what if Max's feeling toward one good depends on the amount of the *other* good he's also enjoying? For example, the marginal utility of the 4th concert might *depend on* whether he's also seeing 3 movies that month, or 18 movies. In that case, when Max's income increases, we can't just "borrow" the marginal utility of the 4th concert from Figure 4, because the 4th concert was paired with the 3rd movie there, while in Figure 5, the 4th concert is paired with the 18th movie. And this will apply to *all* of the marginal utility numbers in Figure 5: They will be different than the numbers we've listed in the figure. When we allow for this possibility, Max's best choice in Figure 5 may be some point other than point H. Without more information—provided in a table like the one in Figure 5—we can't be certain which point will satisfy this condition. But we can discuss some of the possibilities.

Figure 5 illustrates two alternatives to point H that Max might choose, depending on his marginal utility values.

For example, Max's marginal utilities per dollar might now be equal at a point like H', with 9 concerts and 3 movies. In this case, the increase in income would cause Max's consumption of concerts to increase (from 3 to 9), but his consumption of movies to *fall* (from 6 to 3). If so, movies would be an *inferior good* for Max—one for which demand decreases when income increases—while concerts would be a *normal* good.

Finally, let's consider another possible outcome for Max: point H''. At this point, he attends more movies and fewer concerts compared to point D. If point H'' is where Max's marginal utilities per dollar are equal after the increase in income, then *concerts* would be the inferior good, and movies would be normal. An end-of-chapter problem will provide some supporting details for these alternatives—examples of preferences (marginal utility numbers) that would induce Max to choose point H' or H'', instead of H. But the fact that any of these outcomes are possible leads us to this general conclusion:

DANGEROUS CURVES

The Special Meaning of "Inferior" in Economics It's tempting to think that *inferior* goods are of lower quality than *normal* goods. But economists don't define normal or inferior based on the intrinsic properties of a good, but rather by the choices people make when their incomes increase. For example, Max may think that both movies and concerts are high-quality goods. When his income is low, he may see movies on most weekends because, being cheaper, they enable him to spread his budget further. But if his income increases, he can afford to switch from movies to concerts on some nights. If Max attends fewer movies with a higher income, then his *behavior* tells us that movies are inferior for him. If instead he chose to see fewer *concerts* when his income increased, then concerts would be the inferior good.

A rise in income—with no change in prices—leads to a new quantity demanded for each good. Whether a particular good is normal (quantity demanded increases) or inferior (quantity demanded decreases) depends on the individual's preferences, as represented by the marginal utilities for each good, at each point along his budget line.

Changes in Price

Let's explore what happens to Max when the price of a concert decreases from $30 to $10, while his income and the price of a movie remain unchanged. The drop in the price of concerts rotates Max's budget line rightward, pivoting around its vertical intercept, as illustrated in the upper panel of Figure 6. What will Max do after his budget line rotates in this way? Again, he will select the combination of movies and concerts on his budget line that makes him as well off as possible. This will be the combination at which the marginal utility per dollar spent on both goods is the same.

Once again, we've taken some of Max's marginal utility values from Figure 4 and added some additional numbers to construct the table in Figure 6. This table extends what we already knew about Max's preferences to cover the new, expanded possibilities. As we did earlier, we've made an assumption in borrowing the numbers for Figure 6 from our earlier table: that for Max, the marginal utility for one good is independent of the amount of the other good.

With the preferences represented by these marginal utility numbers, Max will search along his budget line for the best choice. This will lead him directly to point *J*, where his quantities demanded are 7 concerts and 8 movies. Note that with each concert costing only $10 now, Max can afford this combination. Moreover, it satisfies our utility-maximizing rule: Marginal utility per dollar is 18 for both goods.

What if we dropped the price of concerts again—this time—to $5? Then Max's budget line rotates further rightward, and he will once again find the utility-maximizing point. In the figure, Max is shown choosing point *K*, attending 10 concerts and 10 movies. (The table in the figure cannot be used to find point *K*, because the table assumes the price of concerts is $10.)

THE INDIVIDUAL'S DEMAND CURVE

You've just seen that each time the price of concerts changes, so does the quantity of concerts Max will want to see. The lower panel of Figure 6 highlights this relationship by plotting the quantity of concerts demanded on the horizontal axis and the price of concerts on the vertical axis. For example, in both the upper and lower panels, point *D* tells us that when the price of concerts is $30, Max will see three of them. When we connect points like *D*, *J*, and *K* in the lower panel, we get Max's **individual demand curve**, which shows *the quantity of a good he demands at each different price.* Notice that Max's demand curve for concerts slopes downward—a fall in the price of concerts increases the quantity demanded—showing that Max's responses to price changes obey the law of demand.

Individual demand curve A curve showing the quantity of a good or service demanded by a particular individual at each different price.

FIGURE 6 | Deriving the Demand Curve

(a)

1. When the price of concerts is $30, point D is best for Max.

2. If the price falls to $10, Max's budget line rotates rightward, and he chooses point J.

3. And if the price drops to $5, he chooses point K.

(b)

4. The demand curve shows the quantity Max chooses at each price.

Income = $150 per month

	Concerts at $10 each			Movies at $10 each	
Number of Concerts per Month	Marginal Utility from Last Concert (MU_c)	Marginal Utility per Dollar Spent on Last Concert $\left(\dfrac{MU_c}{P_c}\right)$	Number of Movies per Month	Marginal Utility from Last Movie (MU_m)	Marginal Utility per Dollar Spent on Last Movie $\left(\dfrac{MU_m}{P_m}\right)$
3	600	60	12	100	10
4	450	45	11	120	12
5	360	36	10	135	13.5
6	300	30	9	150	15
7	**180**	**18**	**8**	**180**	**18**
8	150	15	7	190	19
9	100	10	6	200	20
10	67.5	6.75	5	210	21

But if Max's preferences—and his marginal utility values—had been different, could his response to a price change have *violated* the law of demand? The answer is yes . . . and no. Yes, it is theoretically possible. (As a challenge, try identifying points on the three budget lines that would give Max an *upward-sloping* demand curve.) But no, it does not seem to happen in practice.

To understand why and to gain other insights, the next section takes a deeper look into the effects of a price change on quantity demanded.

INCOME AND SUBSTITUTION EFFECTS

Whether you've studied about the marginal utility approach (the previous section) or the indifference curve approach (appendix), you've learned a logical process that leads directly to an individual's demand curve. But the demand curve actually summarizes the impact of *two* separate effects of a price change on quantity demanded. As you are about to see, these two effects sometimes work together, and sometimes oppose each other.

THE SUBSTITUTION EFFECT

Suppose the price of a good falls. Then it becomes less expensive *relative to* other goods whose prices have not fallen. Some of these other goods are *substitutes* for the now cheaper good—they are different goods, but they are used to satisfy the same general desire. When *one* of the ways of satisfying a desire becomes relatively cheaper, consumers tend to purchase more of it (and tend to purchase less of the substitute goods).

In Max's case, concerts and movies, while different, both satisfy his desire to be entertained. When the price of concerts falls, so does its relative price (relative to movies). Max can now get more entertainment from his budget by substituting concerts in place of movies, so he will demand more concerts.

This impact of a price decrease is called a **substitution effect**: the consumer substitutes *toward* the good whose price has decreased, and away from other goods whose prices have remained unchanged.

> The **substitution effect** of a price change arises from a change in the relative price of a good, and it always moves quantity demanded in the **opposite direction** to the price change. When price decreases, the substitution effect works to increase quantity demanded; when price increases, the substitution effect works to decrease quantity demanded.

The substitution effect is a powerful force in the marketplace. For example, while the price of cellular phone calls has fallen in recent years, the price of pay phone calls has remained more or less the same. This fall in the relative price of cell phone calls has caused consumers to substitute toward them and away from using regular pay phones. As a result, many private providers of pay phones are having financial difficulty.

The substitution effect is also important from a theoretical perspective: It is the main factor responsible for the law of demand. Indeed, if the substitution effect were the *only* effect of a price change, the law of demand would be more than a law; it would be a logical necessity. But as we are about to see, a price change has another effect as well.

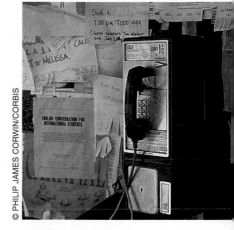

© PHILIP JAMES CORWIN/CORBIS

Cheaper cell phone calls, and the substitution effect, may soon drive pay phones out of the market.

Substitution effect As the price of a good falls, the consumer substitutes that good in place of other goods whose prices have not changed.

THE INCOME EFFECT

In Figure 6 (or Appendix Figure A.5), when the price of concerts drops from $30 to $10, Max's budget line rotates rightward. Max now has a wider range of options than before: He can consume more concerts, more movies, or *more of both*. The price decline of *one* good increases his total purchasing power over *both* goods.

A price cut gives the consumer a gift, which is rather like an increase in *income*. Indeed, in an important sense, it *is* an increase in *available* income: Point D (3 concerts and 6 movies) originally cost Max $150, but after the decrease in the price of concerts, the same combination would cost him just $(6 \times \$10) + (3 \times \$10) = \$90$, leaving him with $60 in *available income* to spend on more movies or concerts or both. This leads to the second effect of a change in price:

Income effect As the price of a good decreases, the consumer's purchasing power increases, causing a change in quantity demanded for the good.

> *The **income effect** of a price change arises from a change in purchasing power over both goods. A drop in price increases purchasing power, while a rise in price decreases purchasing power.*

How will a change in purchasing power influence the quantity of a good demanded? That depends. Recall that an increase in income will increase the demand for normal goods and decrease the demand for inferior goods. The same is true for the *income effect* of a price cut: It can work to either *increase* or *decrease* the quantity of a good demanded, depending on whether the good is normal or inferior. For example, if concerts are a normal good for Max, then the income effect of a price cut will lead him to consume more of them; if concerts are inferior, the income effect will lead him to consume fewer.

COMBINING SUBSTITUTION AND INCOME EFFECTS

Now let's look again at the impact of a price change, considering the substitution and income effects together. A change in the price of a good changes both the relative price of the good (the substitution effect) and the overall purchasing power of the consumer (the income effect). The ultimate impact of the price change on quantity demanded will depend on *both* of these effects. For normal goods, these two effects work together to push quantity demanded in the same direction. But for inferior goods, the two effects oppose each other. Let's see why.

Normal Goods. When the price of a normal good falls, the substitution effect *increases* quantity demanded. The price drop will also increase the consumer's purchasing power—and for a normal good—*increase* quantity demanded even further. The opposite occurs when price increases: The substitution effect decreases quantity demanded, and the decline in purchasing power further decreases it. Figure 7 summarizes how the substitution and income effects combine to make the price and quantity of a normal good move in opposite directions:

> *For normal goods, the substitution and income effects work together, causing quantity demanded to move in the opposite direction of the price. Normal goods, therefore, must always obey the law of demand.*

Inferior Goods. Now let's see how a price change affects the demand for *inferior* goods. As an example, consider intercity bus service. For many consumers, this is an

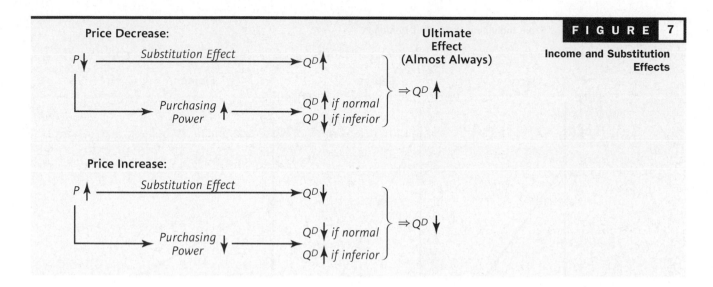

FIGURE 7

Income and Substitution Effects

inferior good: with a higher income, these consumers would choose quicker and more comfortable alternatives (such as air or train travel), and therefore demand *less* bus service. Now, if the price of bus service falls, the substitution effect would work, as always, to *increase* quantity demanded. The price cut will also, as always, increase the consumer's purchasing power. But if bus service is inferior, the rise in purchasing power will *decrease* quantity demanded. Thus, we have two opposing effects: the substitution effect, increasing quantity demanded, and the income effect, decreasing quantity demanded. In theory, either of these effects could dominate the other, so the quantity demanded could move in either direction.

In practice, however, the substitution effect almost always dominates for inferior goods.

Why? Because we consume such a wide variety of goods and services that a price cut in any one of them changes our purchasing power by only a small amount. For example, suppose you have an income of $20,000 per year, and you spend $500 per year on bus tickets. If the price of bus travel falls by, say, 20 percent, this would save you $100—like a gift of $100 in income. But $100 is only ½ percent of your income. Thus, a 20 percent fall in the price of bus travel would cause only a ½ percent rise in your purchasing power. Even if bus travel is, for you, an inferior good, we would expect only a tiny decrease in your quantity demanded when your purchasing power changes by such a small amount. Thus, the income effect should be very small. On the other hand, the *substitution* effect should be rather large: With bus travel now 20 percent cheaper, you will likely substitute away from other purchases and buy more bus travel.

> *For inferior goods, the substitution and income effects of a price change work against each other. The substitution effect moves quantity demanded in the opposite direction of the price, while the income effect moves it in the same direction as the price. But since the substitution effect virtually always dominates, consumption of inferior goods—like normal goods—will virtually always obey the law of demand.*

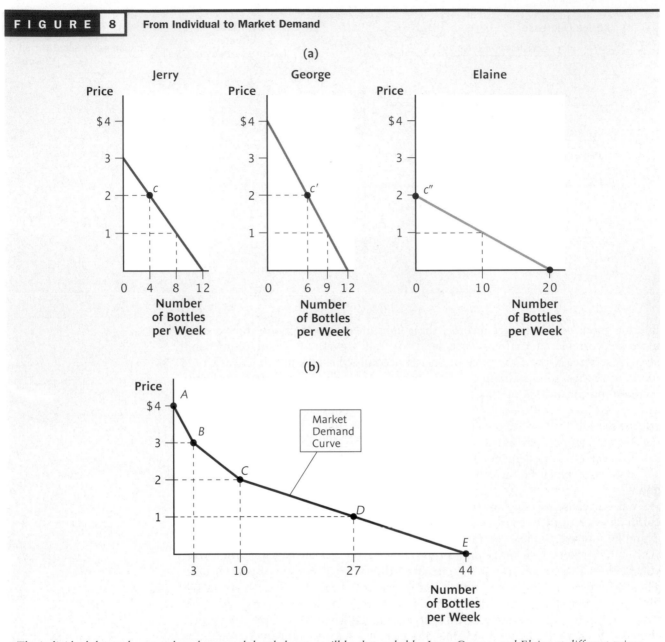

FIGURE 8   **From Individual to Market Demand**

The individual demand curves show how much bottled water will be demanded by Jerry, George, and Elaine at different prices. As the price falls, each demands more. The market demand curve in panel (b) is obtained by adding up the total quantity demanded by all market participants at different prices.

CONSUMERS IN MARKETS

Since the market demand curve tells us the quantity of a good demanded by *all* consumers in a market, it makes sense that we can derive it by adding up the individual demand curves of every consumer in that market.

Figure 8 illustrates how this can be done in a small local market for bottled water, where, for simplicity, we assume that there are only three consumers—Jerry, George, and Elaine. The first three diagrams show their individual demand curves.

If the market price were, say, $2 per bottle, Jerry would buy 4 bottles each week (point *c*), George would buy 6 (point *c'*), and Elaine would buy zero (point *c"*). Thus, the market quantity demanded at a price of $2 would be 4 + 6 + 0 = 10, which is point *C* on the market demand curve. To obtain the entire market demand curve, we repeat this procedure at each different price, adding up the quantities demanded by each individual to obtain the total quantity demanded in the market. (Verify on your own that points *A, B, D,* and *E* have been obtained in the same way.) In effect, we obtain the market demand curve by summing horizontally across each of the individual demand curves:

> *The market demand curve is found by horizontally summing the individual demand curves of every consumer in the market.*

Notice that as long as each individual's demand curve is downward sloping (and this will virtually always be the case), then the market demand curve will also be downward sloping. More directly, if a rise in price makes each consumer buy fewer units, then it will reduce the quantity bought by *all* consumers as well. Indeed, the market demand curve can still obey the law of demand even when *some* individuals violate it. Thus, although we are already quite confident about the law of demand at the individual level, we can be even *more* confident at the market level. This is why we always draw market demand curves with a downward slope.

CONSUMER THEORY IN PERSPECTIVE

Our model of consumer theory—whether using marginal utility or indifference curves—may strike you as rather simple. Indeed, it was *purposely* kept simple, to bring out the "big ideas" more clearly. But can it explain and predict behavior in more complicated, real-world situations? In many cases, yes—with appropriate modification. In other cases, . . . no.

EXTENSIONS OF THE MODEL

One problem our simple model ignores is *uncertainty*. In our model, the consumer knows with certainty the outcome of any choice—so many movies and concerts—and knows with certainty how much income is available for spending. But in many real-world situations, you make your choice and you take your chances. When you buy a car, it might be a lemon; when you pay for some types of surgery, there is a substantial risk that it will be unsuccessful; and when you buy a house, you cannot be sure of its condition or how much you will like the neighborhood. Income, too, is often uncertain. Employees risk being laid off, and self-employed lawyers, doctors, and small-business owners might have a good year or a bad year. When uncertainty is an important aspect of consumer choice, economists use other, more complex models. But even these models are based on the one you have learned in this chapter.

Another problem is *imperfect information*. In our model, consumers are assumed to *know* exactly what goods they are buying and the prices at which they can buy them. But in the real world, we must sometimes spend time and money to get this information. Prices can be different in different stores and on different days, depending on whether there is a sale, so we might have to make phone calls or shop around. To be sure of the quality of our purchases, we may have to subscribe to

Consumer Reports magazine or spend time inspecting goods or getting advice from others. Over the past few decades, economists have been intensely interested in imperfect information and its consequences for decision-making behavior. And our simple model—when modified to take account of the *cost* of acquiring information—has proven very useful.

A third problem is that people can spend more than their incomes in any given year, by borrowing funds or spending out of savings. Or they may spend less than their incomes because they choose to save or pay back debts. This, too, is easily handled by our model of consumer choice, for example, by defining one of the goods as "future consumption."

Finally, you might think that consumer theory always regards people as relentlessly selfish, concerned only about their own consumption. In fact, when people trade in impersonal markets this is mostly true: People *do* try to allocate their spending among different goods to achieve the greatest possible satisfaction. But in many areas of economic life, people act unselfishly. This, too, has been incorporated into the traditional model of consumer theory.

For example, Max's *own* utility might depend on the utility enjoyed by someone else—either a member of his own family, or others in his neighborhood or community, or even the average level of utility in the world. In fact, the "utility of others" can be treated as "another good" in the model. Useful analyses of charitable giving, bequests, and voting behavior have been based on this modification of the model.

CHALLENGES TO THE MODEL

From our discussion, you can see that the model of consumer choice is quite versatile, capable of adapting to more aspects of economic behavior than one might think. But economists have long observed that certain types of behavior do not fit the model at all. For example, people will sometimes *judge quality by price*. Diamonds, designer dresses, men's suits, doctors' services, and even automobiles are sometimes perceived as being better if their prices are higher. This means that the consumer cannot choose among different combinations of goods by themselves; she must first know their prices. And when prices change, so will her preferences—violating our description of rational preferences.

Behavioral Economics

Behavioral economics A subfield of economics focusing on behavior that deviates from the standard assumptions of economic models.

In recent years, a broader challenge has emerged from a new subfield of economics known as **behavioral economics**. Behavioral economists try to incorporate facts about actual human behavior—often pointed out by psychologists—that deviate from the standard assumptions of economic models. While economists—dating back to Adam Smith—have often reached outside the field for broader insights, behavioral economists do so in a more systematic and formal way. And while their models incorporate some of the traditional tools of economic analysis, others are conspicuously left out. Behavioral economists are represented on the faculties of the most prestigious universities, win major professional awards, and are the subject of much attention in the media.[4]

---

[4] A brief summary of behavioral economics, and some of the controversy surrounding it, is in Roger Lowenstein's "Exuberance Is Rational," *New York Times Magazine*, February 11, 2001. A more recent and informal discussion is in Craig Lambert, "The Marketplace of Perceptions," *Harvard Magazine*, March–April 2006.

To understand what's different about behavioral economics, let's take a broad look at the more standard approach of economics. As a rule, economists view decision makers as striving to achieve a well-defined goal: typically, the goal of *maximizing some quantity*. In this chapter, for example, consumers are viewed as trying to maximize their utility or well-being. In later chapters, business firms are striving to *maximize profit*. Even when households or firms are recognized as *groups* of individuals with different agendas, economists typically assume that maximization is involved. For example, while a firm's owners might want the firm to maximize profits, the managers might want to consider their own incomes, power, prestige, or job security. When the goals conflict, the behavior of the firm will depend on how the conflict is resolved. Still, each individual or group within the firm is depicted as trying to maximize something. Economists have often disagreed over *what* is being maximized, but have usually accepted the idea that *something* is.

Behavioral economists, however, point out that some human behavior is not consistent with *any* type of maximization. For example, stock market investors will often hold on to shares when the price has fallen, refusing to sell until the price rises enough to prevent any loss. They do so even if they know that selling the stock now and using the money for other purposes—such as buying a new car—would make them better off. Their desire to avoid regret over a past loss seems to get in the way of maximizing their current utility.

Another example: Dieters will often refuse to have ice cream in the house, to help them avoid temptation. This might seem innocuous, but it's inconsistent with our notion of the rational, utility-maximizing consumer. After all, if a consumer can select the utility-maximizing choice among all available options, he should never try to limit the options available. Or—more simply—a rational consumer should be able to say no, and not be harmed by the option of saying yes.

Indeed, there are many examples where emotion seems to trump narrowly defined rationality: procrastination, drug addiction, and even honesty—especially when telling the truth is costly and a lie would not be discovered. And how can it be rational to spend $3 on gas and wear and tear on your car just to drive to a slightly less-expensive supermarket, where you'll save only $2 at checkout? Moreover, why would someone make this drive for groceries, but not to save $3 on a $1,000 personal computer?

Behavioral economists have offered explanations for these and other examples of economic behavior that wholly or partially abandon the idea of maximization. Instead, they incorporate notions about people's *actual thinking process* in making decisions. And they point out that such behavior by large groups of people can alter a market's equilibrium, or how we view the equilibrium.

This can have important policy implications. For example, in Chapter 4, you learned that at least part of an excise tax will be shifted to buyers, raising their price and therefore harming them. But if buying cigarettes is an irrational addictive behavior rather than a choice, then a cigarette tax—if it encourages people to quit—can make them *better* off.[5]

However, before you start wondering why you've bothered to learn about the utility-maximizing consumer, or why you should go on to read about the profit-maximizing firm, a little perspective is in order. While we do, indeed, observe many cases where behavior is *not* rational, we observe far many more cases where it *is*.

[5] Jonathan Gruber and Botond Koszegi, "A Theory of Government Regulation of Addictive Bads: Optimal Tax Levels and Tax Incidence for Cigarette Excise Taxation," National Bureau of Economic Research Working Paper 8777, February 2002.

While the questions raised by behaviorists are fascinating, and their insights valuable, even its strongest proponents would *not* use behavioral models to explain why gasoline prices rise and fall, or how bad weather might affect Florida orange growers. In fact, they wouldn't use behavioral models to explain most of what happens in the vast majority of markets around the world, because the standard economic models work so much better for this purpose.

So while behavioral economics is often portrayed in the media as an "alternative" or even a "replacement" for traditional economic theory, few if any economists see it that way. Instead, behavioral economics is more commonly viewed as an addition to the existing body of economic theory—an extra limb that extends the theory's reach to some anomalous behavior.

USING THE THEORY

Improving Education

© SUSAN VAN ELTEN

So far in this chapter, we've considered the problem of a consumer trying to maximize utility by selecting the best combination of goods and services. But consumer theory can be extended to consider almost *any* decision between two alternatives, including activities that cost us time rather than dollars. In this section, we apply the model of consumer choice to an important issue: the quality of education.[6]

Each year, various agencies within the U.S. Department of Education spend hundreds of millions of dollars on research to assess and implement new educational techniques. For example, suppose it is thought that computer-assisted instruction might help students learn better or more quickly. A typical research project to test this hypothesis would be a *controlled experiment* in which one group of students would be taught with the computer-assisted instruction and the other group would be taught without it. Then students in both groups would be tested. If the first group scores significantly higher, computer-assisted instruction will be deemed successful; if not, it will be deemed unsuccessful. To the disappointment of education researchers, most promising new techniques are found to be unsuccessful: Students seem to score about the same, no matter which techniques are tried.

Economists find these studies highly suspect, since the experiments treat students as passive responders to stimuli. Presented with a stimulus (the new technique), students are assumed to give a simple response (scoring higher on the exam). Where in this model, economists ask, are students treated as *decision makers,* who must make *choices* about allocating their scarce time?

Let's apply our model of consumer choice to a student's time allocation problem. To keep things simple, we'll assume a bleak world in which there are only two activities: studying economics and studying French. Instead of costing money, each of these activities costs *time,* and there is only so much time available. And instead of buying quantities of two goods, students "buy" points on their exams with hours spent studying.

[6] This section is based on ideas originally published in Richard B. McKenzie and Gordon Tullock, *The New World of Economics*, 3d ed. (Burr Ridge, IL: Irwin, 1981).

FIGURE 9

Time Allocation

Panel (a) shows combinations of French and economics test scores that can be obtained for a given amount of study time. The slope of −2 indicates that each additional point in French requires a sacrifice of 2 points in economics. The student chooses point C. Panel (b) shows that computer-assisted French instruction causes the budget line to rotate outward; French points are now less expensive. The student might move to point D, attaining a higher French score. Or she might choose F, using all of the time freed up in French to study economics. Or she might choose an intermediate point such as E.

Panel (a) of Figure 9 shows how we can represent the time allocation problem graphically. The economics test score is measured on the vertical axis and the French score on the horizontal axis. The straight line in the figure is the student's budget line, showing the tradeoff between economics and French scores. Our student can achieve any combination of scores on this budget line with her scarce time.

A few things are worth noting about the budget line in the figure. First, the more study time you devote to a subject, the better you will do on the test. But that means *less* study time for the other subject and a lower test score there. Thus, the opportunity cost of scoring better in French is scoring lower in economics, and vice versa. This is why the budget line has a negative slope: The higher the score in French, the lower the score in economics. As our student moves downward along the budget line, she is shifting hours away from studying economics and toward studying French.

Second, notice that the vertical and horizontal axes both start at 70 rather than 0. This is to keep our example from becoming too depressing. If our student devotes *all* her study time to economics and none to French, she would score 90 in economics but still be able to score 70 (rather than zero) in French, just by attending class and paying attention. If she devotes all her time to French, she would score 80 in French and 70 in economics. (*Warning:* Do not try to use this example to convince your economics instructor you deserve at least a 70 on your next exam.)

Finally, the budget line in our example is drawn as a straight line with a slope of −2. So each additional point in French requires our student to sacrifice two points in economics. This assumption helps make the analysis more concrete. But none of our conclusions would be different if the budget line had a different slope, or even if it were curved so that the tradeoff would change as we moved along it. But let's take a moment to understand what our example implies.

As you've learned, the slope of any budget line is $-P_x/P_y$, where x is the good measured on the horizontal axis and y is the good measured on the vertical axis. We'll let P_F be the price of one point in French, and P_E be the price of one point in economics. Then, in our example, $-P_x/P_y$ translates into $-P_F/P_E$. But what is the "price" of a test point in French or economics? Unlike the case of Max, who had to allocate his scarce *funds* between concerts and movies, our student must allocate her scarce *time* between the two "goods" she desires: test points in French and test points in economics. The *price* of a test point is therefore not a money price, but rather a *time price:* the number of study hours needed to achieve an additional point. For example, it might take an additional two hours of studying to achieve another point in French ($P_F = 2$) but just one hour to get another point in economics ($P_E = 1$). This would give us a budget line with a slope of $-P_F/P_E = -2/1 = -2$, which is the slope used in Figure 9 (a).

Now let's turn our attention to student decision making. Our student derives satisfaction of utility from both her economics score and her French score—the greater either score, the better off she is. But among all those combinations of scores on her budget line, which is the best choice? That depends on the student's preferences, whether characterized by the marginal utility approach or the indifference curve approach. Suppose that initially, this student's best choice is at point C, where she scores 80 in economics and 75 in French.

Now, let's introduce a new computer-assisted technique in the French class, one that is, in fact, remarkably effective: It enables students to learn more French with the same study time or to study less and learn the same amount. This is a *decrease* in the price of French points—it now takes fewer hours to earn a point in French—so the budget line will rotate outward, as shown in panel (b) of Figure 9. On the new budget line, if our student devotes all of her time to French, she can score higher than before—90 instead of 80—so the horizontal intercept moves rightward. But since nothing has changed in her economics course, the vertical intercept remains unaffected. Notice, too, that the budget line's slope has changed to -1. Now, the opportunity cost of an additional point in French is one point in economics rather than two.

After the new technique is introduced in the French course, our *decision-making* student will locate at a point on her new budget line based once again on her preferences. Panel (b) illustrates some alternative possibilities. At point D, her performance in French would improve, but her economics performance would remain the same. This seems to be the kind of result education researchers have in mind when they design their experiments: If a successful technique is introduced in the French course, we should be able to measure the impact with a French test.

Point F illustrates a different choice: *Only* the economics performance improves, while the French score remains unchanged. Here, even though the technique in French is successful (it does, indeed, shift the budget line), none of its success shows up in higher French scores.

But wait: How can a new technique in the French course improve performance in economics but not at all in French? The answer is found by breaking down the impact of the new technique into our familiar income and substitution effects. The new technique lowers the student's time cost of getting additional points in French. The substitution effect (French points are relatively cheaper) will tend to improve her score in French, as she substitutes her time away from economics and toward French. But there is also an *"income"* effect: The "purchasing power" of her time has increased, since now she could use her fixed allotment of study time to "buy" higher scores in *both* courses. If performance in French is a normal good, this increase in "purchasing power" will work to increase her French score, but if it is an inferior good, it could work to *decrease* her French score. Point *F* could come about because French performance is *such* an inferior good that the negative income effect exactly cancels out the positive substitution effect. In this case, the education researchers will incorrectly judge the new technique a complete failure—it does not affect French scores at all.

Could this actually happen? Perhaps. It is easy to imagine a student deciding that 75 in French is good enough and using any study time freed up from better French instruction to improve her performance in some other course. More commonly, we expect a student to choose a point such as *E,* somewhere between points *D* and *F,* with performance improving in *both* courses. But even in this case, the higher French score measures just a *part* of the impact of the technique; the remaining effect is seen in a higher economics score.

This leads us to a general conclusion: When we recognize that students make *choices,* we expect only *some* of the impact of a better technique to show up in the course in which it is used. In the real world, college students typically take several courses at once and have other competing interests for their time as well (cultural events, parties, movies, exercising, and so on). Any time saved due to better teaching in a single course might well be "spent" on *all* of these alternatives, with only a little devoted to that single course. Thus, we cannot fully measure the impact of a new technique by looking at the score in one course alone. This suggests why educational research is conducted as it is: A more accurate assessment would require a thorough accounting for all of a student's time, which is both expensive and difficult to achieve. Nevertheless, we remain justified in treating this research with some skepticism.

Summary

Graphically, the budget constraint is represented by the *budget line.* Only combinations on or below the budget line are affordable. An increase in income shifts the budget line outward. A change in the price of a good causes the budget line to rotate. Whenever the budget line shifts or rotates, the consumer moves to a point on the *new* budget line. The consumer will always choose the point that provides the greatest level of satisfaction or *utility,* and this will depend on the consumer's unique preferences.

There are two alternative ways to represent consumer preferences, which lead to two different approaches to consumer decision making. The *marginal utility approach* is presented in the body of the chapter. In this approach, a utility-maximizing consumer chooses the combination of goods along her budget line at which the marginal utility per dollar spent is the same for all goods. When income or price changes, the consumer once again equates the marginal utility per dollar of both goods, resulting in a choice along the *new* budget line.

In the *indifference curve approach,* presented in the appendix, a consumer's preferences are represented by a collection of her *indifference curves,* called her *indifference map.* The highest level of utility or satisfaction is achieved at the point on the budget line that is also on the highest possible indifference curve. When income or price changes, the consumer moves to the point on the *new* budget line that is on the highest possible indifference curve.

Using either of the two approaches, we can trace the quantity of a good chosen at different prices for that good, and generate a downward sloping *demand* curve for that good. The downward slope reflects the interaction of the *substitution effect* and the *income effect.* For a normal good, both effects contribute to the downward slope of the demand curve. For an inferior good, we can have confidence that the substitution effect dominates the income effect, so—once again—the demand curve will slope downward.

Problem Set *Answers to even-numbered Questions and Problems can be found on the text Web site at www.thomsonedu.com/economics/hall.*

1. Parvez, a pharmacology student, has allocated $120 per month to spend on paperback novels and used CDs. Novels cost $8 each; CDs cost $6 each. Draw his budget line.
    a. Draw and label a second budget line that shows what happens when the price of a CD rises to $10.

    b. Draw and label a third budget line that shows what happens when the price of a CD rises to $10 *and* Parvez's income rises to $240.

2. [Uses the Marginal Utility Approach] Now go back to the original assumptions of problem 1 (novels cost $8, CDs cost $6,

and income is \$120). Suppose that Parvez is spending \$120 monthly on paperback novels and used CDs. For novels, $MU/P = 5$; for CDs, $MU/P = 4$. Is he maximizing his utility? If not, should he consume (1) more novels and fewer CDs or (2) more CDs and fewer novels? Explain briefly.

3. [Uses the Marginal Utility Approach] Anita consumes both pizza and Pepsi. The following tables show the amount of utility she obtains from different amounts of these two goods:

Pizza		Pepsi	
Quantity	Utility	Quantity	Utility
4 slices	115	5 cans	63
5 slices	135	6 cans	75
6 slices	154	7 cans	86
7 slices	171	8 cans	96

Suppose Pepsi costs \$0.50 per can, pizza costs \$1 per slice, and Anita has \$9 to spend on food and drink. What combination of pizza and Pepsi will maximize her utility?

4. Three people have the following individual demand schedules for Count Chocula cereal that show how many boxes each would purchase monthly at different prices:

Price	Person 1	Person 2	Person 3
\$5.00	0	1	2
\$4.50	0	2	3
\$4.00	0	3	4
\$3.50	1	3	5

a. What is the market demand schedule for this cereal? (Assume that these three people are the only buyers.) Draw the market demand curve.

b. Why might the three people have different demand schedules?

5. Suppose that 1,000 people in a market *each* have the same monthly demand curve for bottled water, given by the equation $Q^D = 100 - 25P$, where P is the price for a 12-ounce bottle in dollars.

a. How many bottles would be demanded in the entire market if the price is \$1?

b. How many bottles would be demanded in the entire market if the price is \$2?

c. Provide an equation for the *market* demand curve, showing how the market quantity demanded by all 1,000 consumers depends on the price.

6. What would happen to the market demand curve for polyester suits, an inferior good, if consumers' incomes rose?

7. Larsen E. Pulp, head of Pulp Fiction Publishing Co., just got some bad news: The price of paper, the company's most important input, has increased.

a. On a supply/demand diagram, show what will happen to the price of Pulp's output (novels).

b. Explain the resulting substitution and income effects for a typical Pulp customer. For each effect, will the customer's quantity demanded increase or decrease? Be sure to state any assumptions you are making.

8. "If a good is inferior, a rise in its price will cause people to buy more of it, thus violating the law of demand." True or false? Explain.

9. Which of the following descriptions of consumer behavior violates the assumption of *rational preferences*? Explain briefly.

a. Joseph is confused: He doesn't know whether he'd prefer to take a job now or go to college full-time.

b. Brenda likes mustard on her pasta, in spite of the fact that pasta is not meant to be eaten with mustard.

c. Brewster says, "I'd rather see an action movie than a romantic comedy, and I'd rather see a romantic comedy than a foreign film. But given the choice, I think I'd rather see a foreign film than an action movie."

10. [Uses the Indifference Curve Approach] Howard spends all of his income on magazines and novels. Illustrate each of the following situations on a graph, with the quantity of magazines on the vertical axis and the quantity of novels on the horizontal axis. Use two budget lines and two indifference curves on each graph.

a. When the price of magazines rises, Howard buys fewer magazines and more novels.

b. When Howard's income rises, he buys more magazines *and* more novels.

c. When Howard's income rises, he buys more magazines but *fewer* novels.

11. [Uses the Marginal Utility Approach] In Figure 5, we assumed that when Max's income rose, his marginal utility values for any given number of movies or concerts remained the same. But now suppose that when Max's income rises, and he can consume more movies and concerts, *an additional movie has less value* to Max than before. In particular, assume that Max's marginal utility values are as in the below table. Fill in the blanks for the missing values, and find Max's utility maximizing combination of concerts and movies. In Figure 5 in the chapter, at what point does Max end up?

Income = \$300 per month

Concerts at \$30 each			Movies at \$10 each		
(1) Number of Concerts per Month	(2) Marginal Utility from Last Concert	(3) Marginal Utility per Dollar Spent on Last Concert	(4) Number of Movies per Month	(5) Marginal Utility from Last Movie	(6) Marginal Utility per Dollar Spent on Last Movie
3	600		21	4	
4	450		18	6	
5	360		15	10	
6	300		12	20	
7	180		9	30	
8	150		6	35	
9	120		3	40	

12. [Uses the Marginal Utility Approach] In Figure 5, we assumed that when Max's income rose, his marginal utility values for any given number of movies or concerts remained the same. But now suppose that when Max's income rises, having the ability to enjoy more concerts or movies makes the *last movie* and the *last concert* *less valuable* to him, so all the marginal utility numbers shrink. In particular, assume that Max's marginal utility values are as in the following table. Fill in the blanks for the missing values, and find Max's utility-maximizing combination of concerts and movies. In Figure 5 in the chapter, at what point does Max end up?

Income = $300 per month

Concerts at $30 each			Movies at $10 each		
(1) Number of Concerts per Month	(2) Marginal Utility from Last Concert	(3) Marginal Utility per Dollar Spent on Last Concert	(4) Number of Movies per Month	(5) Marginal Utility from Last Movie	(6) Marginal Utility per Dollar Spent on Last Movie
1	450		27	150	
2	390		24	175	
3	300		21	200	
4	225		18	225	
5	180		15	250	
6	150		12	275	
7	90		9	300	
8	75		6	325	
9	60		3	350	

13. [Uses the Indifference Curve Approach]
    a. Draw a budget line for Cameron, who has a monthly income of $100. Assume that he buys steak and potatoes, and that steak costs $10 per pound and potatoes cost $2 per pound. Add an indifference curve for Cameron that is tangent to his budget line at the combination of 5 pounds of steak and 25 pounds of potatoes.
    b. Draw a new budget line for Cameron, if his monthly income falls to $80. Assume that potatoes are an inferior good to Cameron. Draw a new indifference curve tangent to his new budget constraint that reflects this inferiority. What will happen to Cameron's potato consumption? What will happen to his steak consumption?

14. [Uses the Indifference Curve Approach]
    a. Draw a budget line for Rafaella, who has a weekly income of $30. Assume that she buys chicken and eggs, and that chicken costs $5 per pound while eggs cost $1 each. Add an indifference curve for Rafaella that is tangent to her budget line at the combination of 4 pounds of chicken and 10 eggs.
    b. Draw a new budget line for Rafaella, if the price of chicken falls to $3 per pound. Assume that Rafaella

views chicken and eggs as substitutes. What will happen to her chicken consumption? What will happen to her egg consumption?

15. [Uses the Indifference Curve Approach]
    a. Draw a budget line for Lynne, who has a weekly income of $225. Assume that she buys food and clothes, and that food costs $15 per bag while clothes cost $25 per item. Add an indifference curve for Lynne that is tangent to her budget line at the combination of 3 items of clothing and 10 bags of food.
    b. Draw a new indifference curve for Lynne, showing what will happen if her tastes change, so that she gets more satisfaction from an extra item of clothing, and less satisfaction from an extra bag of food.
    c. Returning to the original tangency, what will happen if Lynne decides to join a nudist colony?

16. Use the numbers in the marginal utility columns of Figure 6 to figure out that point *K* is optimal after the price of concerts falls from $10 to $5.

More Challenging

17. The Smiths are a low-income family with $10,000 available annually to spend on food and shelter. Food costs $2 per unit, and shelter costs $1 per square foot per year. The Smiths are currently dividing the $10,000 equally between food and shelter. Use either the Marginal Utility Approach or Indifference Curve Approach.
    a. Draw their budget constraint on a diagram with food on the vertical axis and shelter on the horizontal axis. Label their current consumption choice. How much do they spend on food? On shelter?
    b. Suppose the price of shelter rises to $2 per square foot. Draw the new budget line. Can the Smiths continue to consume the same amounts of food and shelter as previously?
    c. In response to the increased price of shelter, the government makes available a special income supplement. The Smiths receive a cash grant of $5,000 that must be spent on food and shelter. Draw their new budget line and compare it to the line you derived in part *a*. *Could* the Smiths consume the same combination of food and shelter as in part *a*?
    d. With the cash grant and with shelter priced at $2 per square foot, *will* the family consume the same combination as in part *a*? Why, or why not?

18. When an economy is experiencing inflation, the prices of most goods and services are rising but at different rates. Imagine a simpler inflationary situation in which *all* prices, and all wages and incomes, are rising at the same rate, say 5 percent per year. What would happen to consumer choices in such a situation? (Hint: Think about what would happen to the budget line.)

19. [Uses the Indifference Curve Approach] With the quantity of popcorn on the vertical axis and the quantity of ice cream on the horizontal axis, draw indifference maps to illustrate

each of the following situations. (Hint: Each will look different from the indifference maps in the appendix, because each violates one of the assumptions we made there.)

a. Larry's marginal rate of substitution between ice cream and popcorn remains constant, no matter how much of each good he consumes.

b. Heather loves ice cream but hates popcorn.

c. When Andy eats ice cream, he tends to get addicted: The more he has, the more he wants still more, and he's willing to give up more and more popcorn to get the same amount of additional ice cream.

20. [Uses the Indifference Curve Approach] The appendix to this chapter states that when a consumer is buying the optimal combination of two goods x and y, then $MRS_{y,x} = P_x / P_y$. Draw a graph, with an indifference curve and a budget line, and with the quantity of y on the vertical axis, to illustrate the case where the consumer is buying a combination on his budget line for which $MRS_{y,x} > P_x / P_y$.

The Indifference Curve Approach

This appendix presents an alternative approach to consumer decision making, which comes to the same conclusions as the approach in the body of the chapter. The appendix can be read in place of the section titled, "Consumer Decisions: The Marginal Utility Approach." We're naming it the "Indifference Curve Approach" after a graph that you will soon encounter.

Let's start by reviewing what we've already discussed about preferences. We assume that an individual (1) can compare any two options and decide which is best, or that both are equally attractive, (2) makes choices that are logically consistent, and (3) prefers more of every good to less. The first two assumptions are summarized as rational preferences; the third tells us that a consumer will always choose to be *on* her budget line, rather than below it.

But now, we'll go a bit further.

AN INDIFFERENCE CURVE

In Figure A.1, look at point G, which represents 20 movies and 1 concert per month. Suppose we get Max to look at this figure with us, and ask him to imagine how satisfied he would be to have the combination at point G. Max thinks about it for a minute, then says, "Okay, I know how satisfied I would be." Next, we say to Max, "Suppose you are at point G and we give you *another* concert each month, for a total of 2. That would make you even *more* satisfied, right?" Since Max likes concerts, he nods his head. But then we ask, "After giving you this additional concert, how many movies could we *take away* from you and leave you no better or worse off than you were originally, at point G?" Obliging fellow that he is, Max thinks about it and answers, "Well, if I'm starting at point G, and you give me another concert, I suppose you could take away 9 movies and I'd be just as happy as I was at G."

Max has essentially told us that he is *indifferent between* point G on the one hand and point H on the other. We know this because starting at point G, adding 1 more concert and taking away 9 movies puts us at point H.

But let's keep going. Now we get Max to imagine that he's at point H, and we ask him the same question, and this time he answers, "I could trade 5 movies for 1 more concert and be equally well off." Now Max is telling us that he is indifferent between point H and J, since J gives him 1 more concert and 5 fewer movies than point H.

So far, we know Max is indifferent between point G and point H, and between point H and point J. So long as he is rational, he must be entirely indifferent among all three points—G, H, and J—since all three give him the same level of satisfaction. By continuing in this way, we can trace out a set of points that—as far as Max is concerned—are equally satisfying. When we connect these points with a curved line, we get one of Max's *indifference curves*.

> An **indifference curve**[7] represents all combinations of two goods that make the consumer equally well off.

Notice two things about the indifference curve in Figure A.1. First, it slopes downward. This follows from our assumption about preferences that "more is better." Every time we give Max another concert, we make him better off. In order to find another point on his indifference curve, we must make him worse off by the same amount, *taking away* some movies.

Second, notice the *curvature* of the indifference curve. As we move downward and rightward along it, the curve becomes flatter (the absolute value of its slope decreases). Why is this?

THE MARGINAL RATE OF SUBSTITUTION

We can better understand the shape of the indifference curve if we first think a bit more about what its slope

---

[7] Bolded terms in this appendix are defined at the end of the appendix and in the glossary.

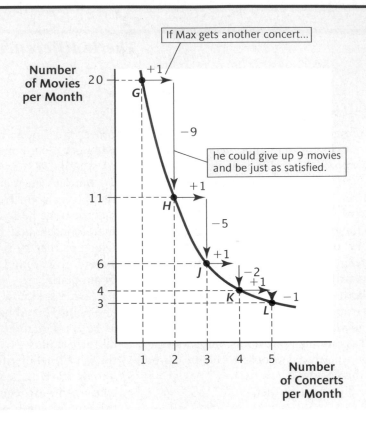

FIGURE A.1

An Indifference Curve

means. Think of the slope (without the minus sign) as the maximum number of movies that Max would *willingly trade* for one more concert. For example, going from point *G* to point *H*, Max gives up 9 movies for 1 concert and remains indifferent. Therefore, from point *G*, if he gave up *10* movies for 1 concert, he'd be *worse off*, and he would not willingly make that trade. Thus, at point *G*, the *greatest* number of movies he'd sacrifice for another concert would be 9.

This notion of "willingness to trade," as you'll soon see, has an important role to play in our model of consumer decision making. And there's a technical term for it: the *marginal rate of substitution of movies for concerts.*[8] More generally, when the quantity of good *y* is measured on the vertical axis, and the quantity of good *x* is measured on the horizontal axis,

> *the marginal rate of substitution of good y for good x (MRS$_{y,x}$) along any segment of an*

> *indifference curve is the absolute value of the slope along that segment. The MRS tells us the maximum amount of good y a consumer would willingly trade for one more unit of good x.*

This gives us another way of describing the shape of the indifference curve: As we move downward along the curve, the *MRS* (the number of movies Max would willing trade for another concert) gets smaller and smaller. To see why the *MRS* behaves this way, consider point *G*, high on Max's indifference curve. At this point, Max is seeing a lot of movies and relatively few concerts compared to points lower down, such as *J, K,* or *L*. With so few concerts, he'd value another one very highly. And with so many movies, each one he gives up doesn't harm him much. So, at a point like *G*, he'd be willing to trade a large number of movies for even one more concert. Using "*m*" for movies and "*c*" for concerts, his *MRS$_{m,c}$* is relatively large, and since the *MRS* is the absolute

[8] The term "marginal" is one that you'll encounter often in economics. The margin of a sheet of notebook paper is the area on the edge, just *beyond* the writing area. By analogy, a *marginal* value in economics measures what happens when we go a little bit *beyond* where we are now, by adding one or more unit of something.

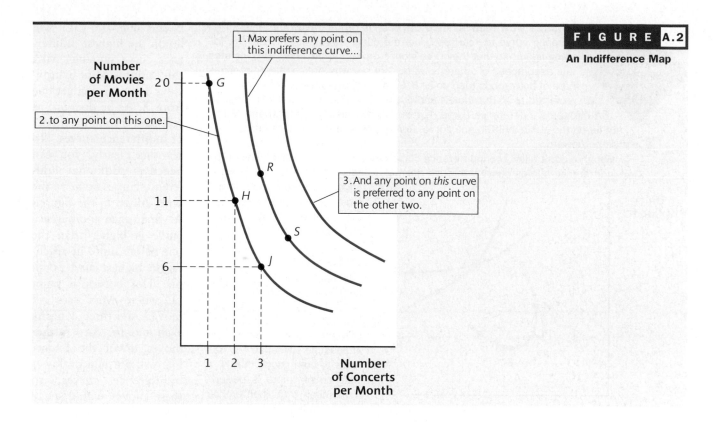

1. Max prefers any point on this indifference curve...

2. to any point on this one.

3. And any point on *this* curve is preferred to any point on the other two.

value of the indifference curve's slope, the curve is relatively steep at point G.

But as we continue traveling down his indifference curve, from G to H to J and so on, movies become scarcer for Max, so each one given up hurts him a bit more. At the same time, he's attending more and more concerts, so adding another one doesn't benefit him as much as before. At a point like K, then, Max is more reluctant to trade movies for concerts. To get another concert, he'd willingly trade fewer movies at point K than at point G. So at point K, the MRS is relatively small and the curve is relatively flat.

THE INDIFFERENCE MAP

To trace out the indifference curve in Figure A.1, we began at a specific point—point G. Figure A.2 reproduces that same indifference curve through G, H, and J. But now consider the new point R, which involves more movies *and* more concerts than at point H. We know that point R is preferred to point H ("more is better"), so it is not on the indifference curve that goes through H. However, we can use the same

procedure we used earlier to find a *new* indifference curve, connecting all points indifferent to point R. Indeed, we can repeat this procedure for any initial starting point we might choose, tracing out dozens or even hundreds of Max's indifference curves, as many as we'd like.

The result would be an **indifference map**, a set of indifference curves that describe Max's preferences, like the three curves in Figure A.2. We know that Max would always prefer any point on a higher indifference curve to any point on a lower one. For example, consider the points H and S. S represents more concerts but fewer movies than H. How can we know if Max prefers S to H, or H to S? Max's indifference map tells us that he *must* prefer S to H. Why? We know that he prefers R to H, since R has more of both goods. We also know that Max is indifferent between R and S, since they are on the same indifference curve. Since he is indifferent between S and R, but prefers R to H, then he must also prefer S to H.

The same technique could be used to show that

any point on a higher indifference curve is preferred to any point on a lower one.

Two Mistakes with Indifference Curves First, don't allow the ends of an indifference curve to "curl up," like the curve through point *B* in the following figure, so that the curve slopes upward at the ends. This violates our assumption of "more is better." To see why, notice that point *A* has more of both goods than point *B*. So as long as "more is better," *A* must be preferred to *B*. But then *A* and *B* are not indifferent, so they cannot lie on the same indifference curve. For the same reason, points *M* and *N* cannot lie on the same indifference curve. Remember that indifference curves cannot slope upward.

DANGEROUS CURVES

Second, don't allow two indifference curves to cross. For example, look at the two indifference curves passing through point *V*. *T* and *V* are on the same indifference curve, so the consumer must be indifferent between them. But *V* and *S* are also on the same indifference curve, so the consumer is indifferent between them, too. Since rationality requires the consumer's preferences to be consistent, the consumer must then also be indifferent between *T* and *S*, but this is impossible because *S* has more of both goods than *T*, a violation of "more is better." Remember that indifference curves cannot cross.

Units of Good Y

Units of Good X

budget line; and (2) it will lie on the highest indifference curve possible. Max can find this point by traveling down his budget line from *A*. As he does so, he will pass through a variety of indifference curves. (To see this clearly, you can pencil in additional indifference curves *between* the ones drawn in the figure.) At first, each indifference curve is higher than the one before, until he reachest the highest curve possible. This occurs at point *D*, where Max sees six movies and three concerts each month. Any further moves down the budget line will put him on lower indifference curves, so these moves would make him worse off. Point *D* is Max's optimal choice.

Notice something interesting about point *D*. First, it occurs where the indifference curve and the budget line are tangent—where they touch but don't cross. As you can see in the diagram, when an indifference curve actually crosses the budget line, we can always find some other point on the budget line that lies on a higher indifference curve.

Second, at point *D*, the slope of the indifference curve is the same as the slope of the budget line. Does this make sense? Yes, when you think about it this way: The absolute value of the indifference curve's slope—the *MRS*—tells us the rate at which Max would *willingly* trade movies for concerts. The slope of the budget line, by contrast, tells us the rate at which Max is *actually able* to trade movies for concerts. If there's any difference between the rate at which Max is *willing* to trade one good for another and the rate at which he is *able* to trade, he can always make himself better off by moving to another point on the budget line.

For example, suppose Max were at point *B* in Figure A.3. The indifference there is steeper than his budget line. In fact, the indifference curve appears to have a slope of about −6, so Max's MRS there is about 6; he'd

Thus, Max's indifference map tells us how he ranks all alternatives imaginable. This is why we say that an indifference map gives us a complete characterization of someone's preferences: It allows us to look at any two points and—just by seeing which indifference curves they are on—immediately know which, if either, is preferred.

CONSUMER DECISION MAKING

Now we can combine everything you've learned about budget lines in the chapter, and what you've learned about indifference curves in this appendix, to determine the combination of movies and concerts that Max should choose. Figure A.3 adds Max's budget line to his indifference map. In drawing the budget line, we assume that Max has a monthly entertainment budget of $150, and that a concert costs $30 and a movie costs $10.

We assume that Max—like any consumer—wants to make himself as well off as possible (to "maximize his utility"). Max's optimal combination of movies and concerts will satisfy two criteria: (1) it will be a point on his

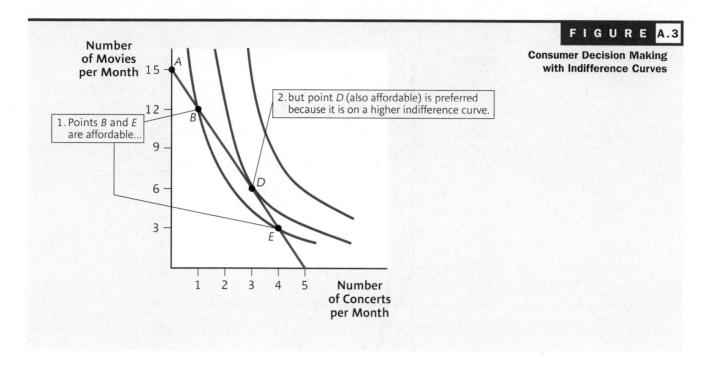

FIGURE A.3

Consumer Decision Making with Indifference Curves

willingly give up 6 movies for 1 more concert. But his budget line—as you learned earlier in the chapter—has a slope of −3. Thus, at point *B*, Max would be *willing* to trade about 6 movies for one concert. But according to his budget line, he is *able* to trade just 3 movies for each concert. If trading 6 movies for a concert would leave him indifferent, then trading just 3 movies for a concert must make him better off. We conclude that when Max's indifference curve is steeper than his budget line, he should spend more on concerts and less on movies.

Using similar reasoning, convince yourself that Max should make the opposite move—spending less on concerts and more on movies—if his indifference curve is *flatter* than his budget line, as it is at point *E*. Only when the indifference curve and the budget line have the same slope—when they touch but do not cross—is Max as well off as possible. This is the point where the indifference curve is *tangent* to the budget line. When Max, or any other consumer, strives to be as well off as possible, he will follow this rule:

> *The optimal combination of goods for a consumer is the point on the budget line where an indifference curve is tangent to the budget line.*

We can also express this decision-making rule in terms of the *MRS* and the prices of two goods. Recall that the slope of the budget line is $= -P_x/P_y$, so the absolute value of the budget line's slope is P_x/P_y. As you've just learned, the absolute value of the slope of an indifference curve is $MRS_{y,x}$. This allows us to state the decision-making rule as follows:

> *The optimal combination of two goods x and y is that combination on the budget line for which $MRS_{y,x} = P_x/P_y$.*

If this condition is not met, there will be a difference between the rate at which a consumer is *willing* to trade good *y* for good *x*, and the rate at which he is *able* to trade them. This will always give the consumer an opportunity to make himself better off.

WHAT HAPPENS WHEN THINGS CHANGE?

So far, as we've examined Max's search for the best combination of movies and concerts, we've assumed that Max's income, and the prices of each good, have remained unchanged. But in the real world, an individual's income, and the prices of the things they buy, *can* change. How would these changes affect a consumer's choice?

An Increase in Income

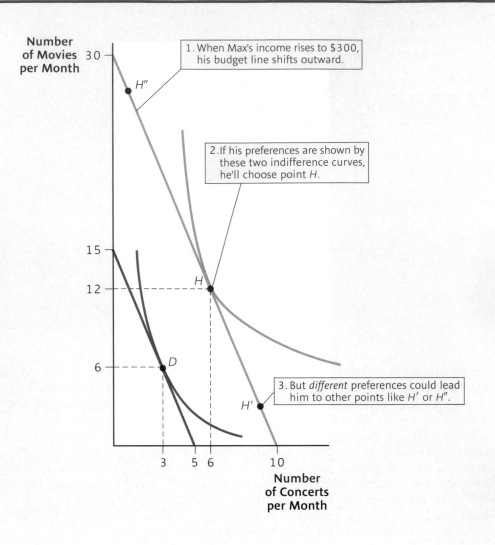

CHANGES IN INCOME

Figure A.4 illustrates how an increase in income might affect Max's choice between movies and concerts. We assume that movies cost $10 each, concerts cost $30 each, and that these prices are not changing. Initially, Max has $150 to spend on the two goods, so his budget line is the lower line through point *D*. As we've already seen, under these conditions, the optimal combination for Max is point *D* (3 concerts and 6 movies).

Now suppose Max's income increases to $300. Then his budget line will shift upward and rightward in the figure. How will he respond? As always, he will search along his budget line until he arrives at the highest possible indifference curve, which will be tangent to the budget line at that point.

But where will this point be? There are several possibilities, and they depend on Max's preferences, as reflected in his indifference map. In the figure, we've used an indifference map for Max that leads him to point *H*, enjoying 6 concerts and 12 movies per month. As you can see in the figure, at this point, he has reached the highest possible indifference curve that his budget allows. It's also the point at which $MRS_{m,c} = P_c / P_m = 3$.

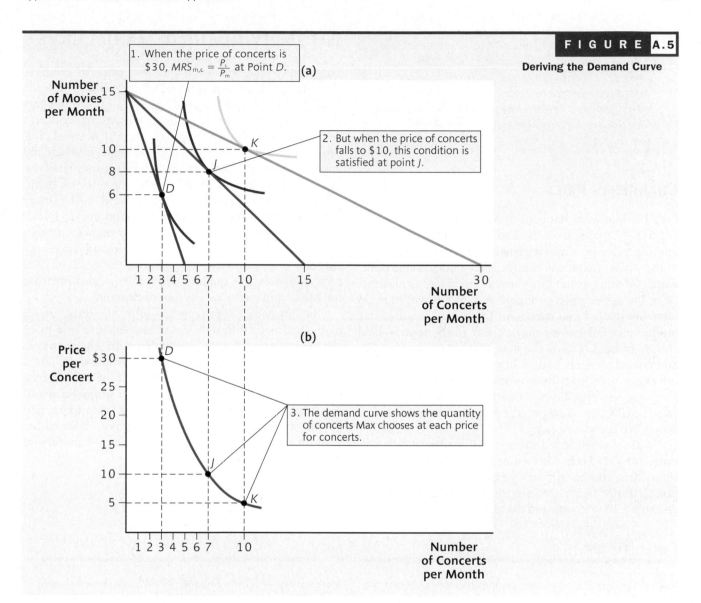

FIGURE A.5

Deriving the Demand Curve

1. When the price of concerts is $30, $MRS_{m,c} = \frac{P_c}{P_m}$ at Point D. **(a)**

2. But when the price of concerts falls to $10, this condition is satisfied at point J.

3. The demand curve shows the quantity of concerts Max chooses at each price for concerts.

Notice that, in moving from D to H, Max chooses to buy more concerts (6 rather than 3) and more movies (12 rather than 6). As discussed in Chapter 3, if an increase in income (with prices held constant) increases the quantity of a good demanded, the good is *normal*. For Max, with the indifference map we've assumed in Figure A.4, both concerts and movies would be normal goods.

But what if Max's preferences, and his indifference map, had been different from the one in the figure? For example, suppose that after income increased, the tangency between his budget line and the highest

indifference curve he could reach occurred at a point like H', with 9 concerts and 3 movies. In this case, the increase in income would cause Max's consumption of concerts to increase (from 3 to 9), but his consumption of movies to *fall* (from 6 to 3). If so, movies would be an *inferior good* for Max, one for which demand decreases when income increases, while concerts would be a normal good.

It's also possible for Max to have preferences that lead him to point H"—with more movies and fewer concerts compared to point D. In this case, *concerts* would be the inferior good and movies would be normal.

> *A rise in income, with no change in prices, leads to a new quantity demanded for each good. Whether a particular good is normal (quantity demanded increases) or inferior (quantity demanded decreases) depends on the individual's preferences, as represented by his indifference map.*

CHANGES IN PRICE

Let's explore what happens to Max when the price of a concert decreases from $30 to $10, while his income and the price of a movie remain unchanged. The drop in the price of concerts rotates Max's budget line rightward, pivoting around its vertical intercept, as illustrated in the upper panel of Figure A.5. What will Max do after his budget line rotates in this way? Based on his indifference curves—as they appear in the figure—he'd choose point *J*. This is the new combination of movies and concerts on his budget line that makes him as well off as possible (puts him on the highest possible indifference curve that he can afford). It's also the point at which $MRS_{m,c} = P_c/P_m = 1$, since movies and concerts now have the same price.

What if we dropped the price of concerts again, this time, to $5? Then Max's budget line rotates further rightward, and he will once again find the best possible point. In the figure, Max is shown choosing point *K*, attending 10 concerts and 10 movies.

THE INDIVIDUAL'S DEMAND CURVE

You've just seen that each time the price of concerts changes, so does the quantity of concerts Max will want to attend. The lower panel of Figure A.5 illustrates this relationship by plotting the quantity of concerts demanded on the horizontal axis and the *price* of concerts on the vertical axis. For example, in both the upper and lower panels, point *D* tells us that when the price of concerts is $30, Max will see three of them. When we connect points like *D, J,* and *K* in the lower panel, we get Max's **individual demand curve**, which shows the quantity of a good he demands at each different price. Notice that Max's demand curve for concerts slopes downward—a fall in the price of concerts increases the quantity demanded—showing that for Max, concerts obey the law of demand.

But if Max's preferences—and his indifference map—had been different, could his response to a price change have *violated* the law of demand? The answer is yes . . . and no. Yes, it is theoretically possible. (As a challenge, try penciling in a new set of indifference curves that would give Max an *upward-sloping* demand curve in the figure.) But no, it does not seem to happen in practice. To find out why, it's time to go back to the body of the chapter, to the section titled, "Income and Substitution Effects."

Definitions

Indifference curve A curve representing all combinations of two goods that make the consumer equally well off.

Indifference map A set of indifference curves that represent an individual's preferences.

Individual demand curve A curve showing the quantity of a good or service demanded by a particular individual at each different price.

Marginal rate of substitution ($MRS_{y,x}$) The maximum amount of good *y* a consumer would willingly trade for one more unit of good *x*. Also, the slope of a segment of an indifference curve.

Production and Cost

During the first few months of 2006, Home Depot announced that it would purchase Hughes Supply Company for $3.5 billion. The Walt Disney Company announced it would buy Pixar Animation Studios for $7.4 billion. And AT&T announced its intention to acquire BellSouth for $67 billion. There were dozens of other major acquisitions announced during those months as well.

Events like these are not unusual. In a typical year, more than a thousand U.S. corporations—with a total value of close to $1 trillion—are acquired by other corporations. Thousands more companies are acquired each year in Europe and Asia. The stockholders who own the firms being combined usually end up favoring these deals because they believe that a larger, combined firm will perform better in the marketplace than would two separate firms. In most cases, a major reason for this belief is the predicted impact the merger will have on *costs*.

This focus on costs is not surprising. A firm's managers strive to earn the highest possible **profit**—the difference between a firm's revenue and its costs. And controlling costs is one way to increase profit.

> **Profit** Total revenue minus total cost.

We'll have more to say about the firm's goal of maximizing profit, and the other important side of the profit calculation—revenue—in the next chapter. In this chapter, we'll be analyzing cost: how to think about it, how to measure it, and how decisions about production cause cost to change. But an understanding of cost first requires us to look more closely at the main activity of business firms: *production*.

PRODUCTION

Home Depot, Disney, and AT&T are all examples of **business firms**: organizations owned and operated by private individuals that specialize in production.

> **Business firm** An organization, owned and operated by private individuals, that specializes in production.

Your first image when you hear the word *production* may be a busy, noisy factory where goods are assembled, piece by piece, and then carted off to a warehouse for eventual sale to the public. Large manufacturers may come to mind—General Motors, Boeing, or even Ben & Jerry's. All of these companies produce things, but the word *production* encompasses more than just manufacturing.

> *Production is the process of combining inputs to make goods and services.*

Notice that the definition refers to goods *and* services. Some production does indeed create physical *goods,* like automobiles, aircraft, or ice cream. But production also creates *services*. Indeed, many of America's largest corporations are service providers, including Citicorp (banking and investment services), American Airlines (transportation services), Verizon (telecommunications services), and Wal-Mart (retailing services).

What about the inputs that are used to produce things? These include the four resources (land, labor, capital, and entrepreneurship), as well as other things. For example, to make the book you are reading now, a business firm (Thomson South-Western) used *labor* (the work of the authors, editors, art designers, and others), *capital* (buildings, office furniture, computers), and *land* (under the buildings). But the company also used *other* inputs that were produced by other firms, including raw materials like paper and ink, transportation and telecommunications services, and more.

TECHNOLOGY AND THE PRODUCTION FUNCTION

Technology A method by which inputs are combined to produce a good or service.

Which inputs will the firm need to produce its output? And in what amounts? These questions are answered by the firm's **technology**—the methods available for turning inputs into outputs. Technology is always changing. Scientific discoveries and new inventions result in entirely new inputs (such as the Internet), and firms often discover new ways of combining existing inputs. At any point in time, however, a firm's technology can be regarded as a *given*—a constraint on its production. This constraint is spelled out by the firm's *production function:*

Production function A function that indicates the maximum amount of output a firm can produce over some period of time from each combination of inputs.

> *For each different combination of inputs, a firm's **production function** tells us the maximum quantity of output it can produce over some period of time.*

The idea behind a production function is illustrated in Figure 1. Quantities of each input are plugged into the box representing the production function, and the maximum quantity of goods or services produced pops out. The production function itself—the box—is a mathematical function relating inputs and outputs.

When a firm uses many different inputs, production functions can be quite complicated. This is true even of small firms. For example, the production function for a video and DVD rental store would tell us how many movies it could rent per day with different combinations of floor space, shelving, salesclerks, cash registers, movies in stock, lighting, air conditioning, and so on.

In this chapter, to keep things simple, we'll spell out the production function for a mythical firm that uses only two inputs: capital and labor. Our firm is Spotless Car Wash, whose output is a service: washing cars. The firm's capital consists of automated car-washing lines, and its labor is full-time workers who drive the cars onto the line, drive them out, towel them down at the end, and deal with customers.[1] Spotless Car Wash, like any other firm, has a production function. When we plug in various quantities of labor (workers) and capital (automated lines), the production function tells us Spotless's output—the number of cars it washes per day.

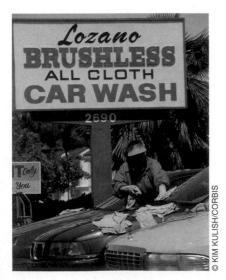

---

[1] Of course, a car wash would use other inputs besides just capital and labor: water, washrags, soap, electricity, and so on. But the costs of these inputs would be minor when compared to the costs of labor and capital. To keep our example simple, we ignore these other inputs.

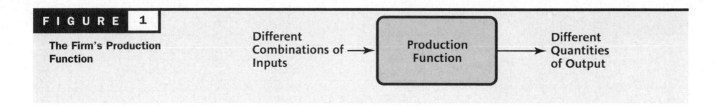

FIGURE 1

The Firm's Production Function

Different Combinations of Inputs → Production Function → Different Quantities of Output

SHORT-RUN VERSUS LONG-RUN DECISIONS

When a firm changes its level of production, it will want to adjust the amounts of inputs it uses. But these adjustments depend on the *time horizon* the firm's managers are thinking about. Some inputs can be adjusted relatively quickly. Most firms, for example, can hire more labor and purchase more raw materials within a few weeks or less. But at many firms, there are some inputs that can be adjusted only after a long time interval. It may take a year or longer before an automobile firm can purchase and install new, fully equipped assembly lines, or acquire additional factory space. And legal obligations, like leases or rental agreements, can delay efforts to downsize operations, because the firm will have to continue paying for equipment and buildings whether it uses them or not.

Thus, when we ask, "What will happen to the quantities of inputs the firm uses if it increases its production?" the answer will depend on whether we are asking about *next month* or *next year*. If it's next month, a firm may be stuck with the factory and equipment it currently has, so it can only increase quantities of labor and raw materials. If we're asking about next year, there is more flexibility—enough time to adjust capital equipment as well.

These considerations make it useful to divide the different time horizons firms can use into two broad categories: the *long run* and the *short run*.

> The **long run** is a time period long enough for a firm to change the quantity of all of its inputs.

Long run A time horizon long enough for a firm to vary all of its inputs.

Another way to say this is that, over the long run, all the inputs the firm uses are viewed as **variable inputs**—inputs that can be adjusted up or down as the quantity of output changes.

Variable input An input whose usage can change as the level of output changes.

At Spotless Car Wash, we'll imagine it takes one year to acquire and install a new automated line, or one year to sell the lines it already has. Thus, for Spotless the long run is a time horizon of one year or longer. When its managers make long-run decisions, they regard all inputs (labor and capital in this case) as variable inputs.

Good managers are concerned about the long run. But they also must make decisions about shorter time horizons, during which the company may be stuck with the current quantities of some inputs. We call these **fixed inputs**—inputs that, over the time period we're considering, cannot be adjusted as output changes. Using this terminology, we can define the short run as follows:

Fixed input An input whose quantity must remain constant, regardless of how much output is produced.

> The **short run** is a time period during which at least one of the firm's inputs is fixed.

Short run A time horizon during which at least one of the firm's inputs cannot be varied.

TABLE 1	Quantity of Capital	Quantity of Labor	Total Product (Cars Washed per Day)
Short-Run Production at Spotless Car Wash	1	0	0
	1	1	30
	1	2	90
	1	3	130
	1	4	160
	1	5	184
	1	6	196

For Spotless Car Wash, the short run is any time period less than a year, because that is how long it is stuck with its current quantity of automated lines. Over the short run, Spotless's labor is a variable input, but its capital is a fixed input.

PRODUCTION IN THE SHORT RUN

When firms make decisions over the short run, there is nothing they can do about their fixed inputs: They are stuck with whatever quantity they have. They can, however, make choices about their variable inputs. Indeed, we see examples of such short-run decisions all the time. Levi Strauss might decide to increase production of blue jeans over the next quarter by obtaining additional workers, cotton cloth, and sewing machines, yet continue to make do with the same factories because there isn't time to expand them or acquire new ones. Here, workers, cloth, and sewing machines are all variable over the quarter, while the factory buildings are fixed.

At Spotless Car Wash, over the short run, labor is the only variable input, and capital is the only fixed input. The three columns in Table 1 describe Spotless's production choices in the short run. Column 1 shows the quantity of the fixed input, capital (K); column 2 the quantity of the variable input, labor (L). Note that in the short run, Spotless is stuck with one unit of capital—one automated line—but it can take on as many or as few workers as it wishes. Column 3 shows the firm's *total product* (Q).

Total product The maximum quantity of output that can be produced from a given combination of inputs.

> *Total product is the maximum quantity of output that can be produced from a given combination of inputs.*

For example, the table shows us that with one automated line but no labor, total product is zero. With one line and six workers, total product is 196 cars washed per day.

Figure 2 shows Spotless's *total product curve*. The horizontal axis represents the number of workers, while the vertical axis measures total product. (The amount of capital—which is held fixed at one automated line—is not shown on the graph.) Notice that each time the firm hires another worker, output increases, so the total product curve slopes upward. The vertical arrows in the figure show precisely *how much* output increases with each one-unit rise in employment. We call this rise in output the *marginal product of labor*.

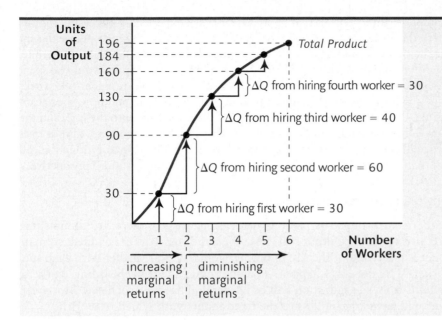

Total And Marginal Product

The total product curve shows the total amount of output that can be produced using various numbers of workers. The marginal product of labor (MPL) is the change in total product when another worker is hired. The MPL for each change in employment is indicated by the length of the vertical arrows.

Using the Greek letter Δ ("delta") to stand for "change in," we can define marginal product this way:

> *The **marginal product of labor** (MPL) is the change in total product (ΔQ) divided by the change in the number of workers employed (ΔL):*
>
> $$MPL = \frac{\Delta Q}{\Delta L}$$
>
> *The MPL tells us the rise in output produced when one more worker is hired.*

Marginal product of labor The additional output produced when one more worker is hired.

For example, if employment rises from 2 to 3 workers, total product rises from 90 to 130, so the marginal product of labor for *that* change in employment is calculated as $(130 - 90)/1 = 40$ units of output.

MARGINAL RETURNS TO LABOR

Look at the vertical arrows in Figure 2, which measure the marginal product of labor, and you may notice something interesting. As more and more workers are hired, the *MPL* first increases (the vertical arrows get longer) and then decreases (the arrows get shorter). This pattern is believed to be typical at many types of firms, so it's worth exploring.

Increasing Marginal Returns to Labor

When the marginal product of labor rises as more workers are hired, there are **increasing marginal returns to labor**. Each time a worker is hired, total output rises by more than it did when the previous worker was hired. Why might this happen? Additional workers may allow production to become more specialized.

Increasing marginal returns to labor The marginal product of labor increases as more labor is hired.

For example, Figure 2 tells us that Spotless Car Wash experiences increasing returns to labor up to the hiring of the second worker. While one worker *could* operate the car wash alone, he or she would have to do everything: drive the cars on and off the line, towel them down, and deal with customers. Much of this worker's time would be spent switching from one task to another. The result, as we see in Table 1, is that one worker can wash only 30 cars each day. Add a second worker, though, and now specialization is possible. One worker can collect money and drive the cars onto the line, and the other can drive them off and towel them down. Thus, with two workers, output rises all the way to 90 car washes per day; the second worker adds more to production (60 car washes) than the first (30 car washes) by making *both* workers more productive.

Diminishing Marginal Returns to Labor

Diminishing marginal returns to labor The marginal product of labor decreases as more labor is hired.

When the marginal product of labor is decreasing, we say there are **diminishing marginal returns to labor**. Output still rises when another worker is added, so marginal product is positive. But the rise in output is smaller and smaller with each successive worker. Why does this happen? For one thing, as we keep adding workers, additional gains from specialization will be harder and harder to achieve. Moreover, each worker will have less and less of the fixed inputs with which to work.

This last point is worth stressing. It applies not just to labor but to any variable input. In all kinds of production, if we keep increasing the quantity of any one input, while holding the others fixed, diminishing marginal returns will eventually set in. For example, if a farmer keeps adding additional pounds of fertilizer to a fixed amount of land, the yield may continue to increase, but eventually the *size* of the increase—the marginal product of fertilizer—will begin to come down. This tendency is so pervasive and widespread that it has been deemed a law, and economists have given that law a name:

Law of diminishing marginal returns As more and more of any input is added to a fixed amount of other inputs, its marginal product will eventually decline.

> The **law of diminishing (marginal) returns** states that as we continue to add more of any one input (holding the other inputs constant), its marginal product will eventually decline.

The law of diminishing returns is a physical law, not an economic one. It is based on the nature of production—on the physical relationship between inputs and outputs with a given technology.

Figure 2 tells us that at Spotless diminishing returns set in after two workers have been hired. Beyond this point, the firm is crowding more and more workers into a car wash with just one automated line. Output continues to increase, since there is usually *something* an additional worker can do to move the cars through the line more quickly, but the increase is less dramatic each time.

This section has been concerned with *production*—the *physical* relationship between inputs and outputs. But a more critical concern for a firm is: What will it *cost* to produce any level of output? Cost is measured in dollars and cents, not in physical units of inputs or outputs. But as you are about to see, what you've learned about production will help you understand the behavior of costs.

THINKING ABOUT COSTS

Talk to people who own or manage businesses, and it won't be long before the word *cost* comes up. People in business worry about measuring costs, controlling costs, and—most of all—reducing costs. This is not surprising: Owners want their firms to earn the highest possible profit, and costs must be subtracted from a firm's revenue to determine its profit.

Let's begin our thinking about cost by revisiting a familiar notion. In Chapter 2 you learned that economists always think of cost as *opportunity cost*—what we must give up in order to do something. This concept applies to the firm as well:

> *A firm's total cost of producing a given level of output is the opportunity cost of the owners—everything they must give up in order to produce that amount of output.*

This notion—that the cost of production is its opportunity cost—is at the core of economists' thinking about costs. It can help us understand which costs matter—and which don't—when making business decisions.

THE IRRELEVANCE OF SUNK COSTS

Suppose that last year, Acme Pharmaceutical Company spent $10 million developing a new drug to treat acne that, if successful, would have generated annual sales revenue many times that amount. At first, it seemed that the drug worked as intended. But then, just before launching production, management discovered that the new drug didn't cure acne at all—but is remarkably effective in treating a rare underarm fungus. In this smaller, less lucrative market, annual sales revenue would be just $30,000. Now management must decide: Should they sell the drug as an antifungus remedy?

When confronted with a problem like this, some people will answer something like this: "Acme should *not* sell the drug. You don't sell something for $30,000 a year when it cost you $10 million to make it." Others will respond this way: "Of course Acme should sell the drug. If they don't, they'd be wasting that huge investment of $10 million." But to an economist, neither approach to answering this question is correct, because both use the $10 million development cost to reach a conclusion—and that cost is completely *irrelevant* to the decision.

The $10 million already spent on developing the drug is an example of a *sunk cost*. More generally,

> *a sunk cost is one that already has been paid, or must be paid*, regardless of *any future action being considered.*

Sunk cost A cost that has been paid or must be paid, regardless of any future action being considered.

In the case of Acme, the development cost has been paid already, and the firm will not get this money back, whether it chooses to sell the drug in this new smaller market, or *not* to sell the drug there. Since it's not part of the opportunity cost of either choice—something that would have to be sacrificed *for* that choice—it should have no bearing on the decision. For Acme, as for any business,

> *Sunk costs should not be considered when making decisions.*

What *should* be considered are the costs that *do* depend on the decision about producing the drug, namely, the cost of actually manufacturing it and marketing it for the smaller market. If these costs are less than the $30,000 Acme could earn in annual revenue, Acme should produce the drug. Otherwise, it should not.

Look again at the definition of sunk cost and you'll see that even a *future* payment can be sunk, if an *unavoidable commitment to pay it has already been made.* Suppose, for example, Acme Pharmaceuticals has signed an employment contract with a research scientist, legally binding the firm to pay her annual salary for three years even if she is laid off. Although some or all of the payments haven't yet been made, all three years of salary are sunk costs for Acme because they *must* be made no matter what Acme does. As sunk costs, they are irrelevant to Acme's decisions.

Our insight about the irrelevance of sunk costs applies beyond the business sector, to decisions in general. For example, suppose that after completing two years of medical school, you've decided that you've made a mistake: You'd rather be a lawyer than a doctor. You might be tempted to stay in medical school because of the money and time you've already spent there. But you can't get your time back. And since you can't sell your two years of medical training to someone else, you can't get your money back either. Thus, the costs of your first two years in medical school have either *been* paid or the *commitment* to pay them has already been made (say, future payments on a student loan). They are sunk costs and should have no influence on your career decision. Only the costs that *depend* on your decision are relevant. If you choose to stay in medical school, you'll have to spend time, effort, and expense for your *remaining* years there. If you switch to law school, you'll spend the time, effort, and expense of three years *there*. These are the costs you should consider (along with the benefits) for each choice.

EXPLICIT VERSUS IMPLICIT COSTS

In Chapter 2, in discussing the opportunity cost of education, you learned that there are two types of costs: *explicit* (involving actual payments) and *implicit* (no money changes hands). The same distinction applies to costs for a business firm.

Suppose you've opened a restaurant in a building that you already owned. You don't pay any rent, so there's no explicit rental cost. Does this mean that using the building is free?

To an accountant—who focuses on actual money payments—the answer is yes. But to an economist—who thinks of opportunity cost—the answer is *absolutely not*. By using your own building for your restaurant, you are sacrificing the opportunity to rent it to someone else. This *foregone rent* is an *implicit cost,* and it is as much a cost of production as the rent you would pay if you rented the building from someone else. In both cases, something is given up to produce your output.

Now suppose that instead of borrowing money to set up your restaurant, you used $100,000 of your own money. Therefore, you aren't paying any interest. But there is an opportunity cost: your $100,000 *could* have been put in the bank or lent to someone else, where it would be earning interest for you. If the going interest rate is 5 percent, then each year that you run your restaurant, you are giving up $5,000 in interest you could have had instead. This *foregone interest* is another implicit cost of your business.

Finally, suppose you decided to manage your restaurant yourself. Have you escaped the costs of hiring a manager? Not really, because you are still bearing an opportunity cost: You *could* do something else with your time. We measure the value of your time as the income you *could* earn by devoting your labor to your next-best income-earning activity. This *foregone labor income*—the wage or salary you could be earning elsewhere—is an implicit cost of your business, and therefore part of its opportunity cost.

	TABLE 2
Explicit Costs	**Implicit Costs**
	A Firm's Costs
Rent paid out	Opportunity cost of:
Interest on loans	Owner's land and buildings (rent foregone)
Managers' salaries	Owner's money (investment income
Hourly workers' wages	foregone)
Cost of raw materials	Owner's time (labor income foregone)

Table 2 summarizes our discussion by listing some common categories of costs that business firms face, both explicit (on the left) and implicit (on the right).

COSTS IN THE SHORT RUN

Managers must answer questions about costs over different time horizons. One question might be, "How much will it cost us to produce a given level of output *this year*?" Another might be, "How much will it cost us to produce a given level of output *three years from now and beyond*?" In this section, we'll explore managers' view of costs over a short-run time horizon—a time period during which *at least one* of the firm's inputs is fixed. That is, we'll be looking at costs with a *short-run* planning horizon.

Remember that no matter how much output is produced, the quantity of a fixed input *must* remain the same. Other inputs, by contrast, can be varied as output changes. Because the firm has these two different types of inputs in the short run, it will also face two different types of costs.

The costs of a firm's fixed inputs are called, not surprisingly, **fixed costs**. Like the fixed inputs themselves, fixed costs must remain the same no matter what the level of output. Typically, we treat rent and interest—whether explicit or implicit—as fixed costs, since producing more or less output in the short run will not cause any of these costs to change. Managers typically refer to fixed costs as their *overhead costs,* or simply, *overhead.*

The costs of obtaining the firm's variable inputs are its **variable costs**. These costs, like the usage of variable inputs themselves, will rise as output increases. Most businesses treat the wages of hourly employees and the costs of raw materials as variable costs because quantities of both labor and raw materials can usually be adjusted rather rapidly.

Foregone Interest Can Be Tricky! Here are two common mistakes in calculating the implicit cost of funds you invest in your own business, such as the $100,000 in our restaurant example.

First, you might count the entire $100,000 as a cost, rather than just the foregone interest on that sum. Remember that a firm's costs are the *ongoing, yearly costs* for the owner. (That's what we'll eventually compare to the ongoing, annual revenue.) The $100,000 initial investment is only paid out once, not every year. If you sell the business, you will presumably get that sum back. But as long as you continue to own the business, the interest that *could* be earned on that $100,000 ($5,000 per year in our example) is an ongoing, yearly cost.

A second mistake is not realizing that, if conditions change, some of the foregone interest on your initial investment can become a *sunk cost.* For example, suppose you invest $100,000 to open a restaurant, and then the restaurant industry falls out of favor. If you sell now, you will only get $40,000. Then the ongoing cost of owning the business has just dropped to $2,000 per year—the interest foregone on $40,000 at 5 percent. That's the only part you could recover if you sold the restaurant, rather than continuing to own it. The interest you could have earned on the other $60,000 you invested no longer matters. It's a sunk cost because, regardless of any decision you make now or in the future, you will *not* get that $60,000 back, so you can *not* earn that interest.

DANGEROUS CURVES

Fixed costs Costs of fixed inputs, which remain constant as output changes.

Variable costs Costs of variable inputs, which change with output.

MEASURING SHORT-RUN COSTS

In Table 3, we return to our example—Spotless Car Wash—and ask: What happens to costs as output changes in the short run? The first three columns of the table tell us the inputs Spotless will use for each output level, just as in Table 1 a few pages earlier. But there is one slight difference: In Table 3, we've reversed the order of the columns, putting total output first. We are changing our perspective slightly: Now we want to observe how a change in the quantity of *output* causes the firm's *inputs*—and therefore its *costs*—to change.

We also need to know one more thing before we can analyze Spotless's costs: what it must *pay* for its inputs. In Table 3, the price of labor is set at $60 per worker per day, and the price of each automated car-washing line at $75 per day.

How do Spotless's short-run costs change as its output changes? Get ready, because there are a surprising number of different ways to answer that question, as illustrated in the remaining columns of Table 3.

Total Costs

Columns 4, 5, and 6 in the table show three different types of total costs. In column 4, we have Spotless's **total fixed cost** (TFC), the cost of all inputs that are fixed in the short run. Like the quantity of fixed inputs themselves, fixed costs remain the same no matter what the level of output.

Total fixed cost The cost of all inputs that are fixed in the short run.

For Spotless Car Wash, the daily cost of renting or owning one automated line is $75, so total fixed cost is $75. Running down the column, you can see that this cost—because it is fixed—remains the same no matter how many cars are washed each day.

TABLE 3										
Short-Run Costs for Spotless Car Wash		Labor cost = $60 per day				Capital cost = $75 per day				
	(1) Output (per Day)	**(2) Capital**	**(3) Labor**	**(4) TFC**	**(5) TVC**	**(6) TC**	**(7) MC**	**(8) AFC**	**(9) AVC**	**(10) ATC**
	0	1	0	$75	$ 0	$ 75		—	—	—
							$2.00			
	30	1	1	$75	$ 60	$135		$2.50	$2.00	$4.50
							$1.00			
	90	1	2	$75	$120	$195		$0.83	$1.33	$2.17
							$1.50			
	130	1	3	$75	$180	$255		$0.58	$1.38	$1.96
							$2.00			
	160	1	4	$75	$240	$315		$0.47	$1.50	$1.97
							$2.50			
	184	1	5	$75	$300	$375		$0.41	$1.63	$2.04
							$5.00			
	196	1	6	$75	$360	$435		$0.38	$1.84	$2.22

Column 5 shows **total variable cost** (*TVC*), the cost of all variable inputs. For Spotless, labor is the only variable input. As output increases, more labor will be needed, so *TVC* will rise. For example, to wash 90 cars each day requires 2 workers, and each worker must be paid $60 per day, so *TVC* will be 2 × $60 = $120. But to wash 130 cars requires 3 workers, so *TVC* will rise to 3 × $60 = $180.

Finally, column 6 shows us that

> *total cost* (**TC**) *is the sum of all fixed and variable costs:*
>
> $$TC = TFC + TVC.$$

For example, at 90 units of output, *TFC* = $75 and *TVC* = $120, so *TC* = $75 + $120 = $195. Because total variable cost rises with output, total cost rises as well.

Now look at Figure 3, where we've graphed all three total cost curves for Spotless Car Wash. Both the *TC* and *TVC* curves slope upward, since these costs increase along with output. *TFC* is represented in two ways in the graph. One is the *TFC* curve, which is a horizontal line, since *TFC* has the same value at any level of output. The other is the *vertical distance* between the rising *TVC* and *TC* curves, since *TFC* is always the *difference* between *TVC* and *TC*. In the graph, this vertical distance must remain the same, at $75, no matter what the level of output.

Average Costs

While total costs are important, sometimes it is more useful to track a firm's costs *per unit* of output, which we call its *average cost*. There are three different types of average cost, each obtained from one of the total cost concepts just discussed.

Total variable cost The cost of all variable inputs used in producing a particular level of output.

Total cost The costs of all inputs—fixed and variable.

FIGURE 3

The Firm's Total Cost Curves
At any level of output, total cost (TC) *is the sum of total fixed cost* (TFC) *and total variable cost* (TVC).

Average fixed cost Total fixed cost divided by the quantity of output produced.

> *The firm's average fixed cost* (AFC) *is its total fixed cost divided by the quantity* (Q) *of output:*
>
> $$AFC = \frac{TFC}{Q}.$$

No matter what kind of production or what kind of firm, *AFC* will always fall as output rises. Why? Because *TFC* remains constant, so a rise in *Q must* cause the ratio *TFC/Q* to fall. Business managers often refer to this decline in *AFC* as "spreading their overhead" over more output. For example, a restaurant has overhead costs for its buildings, furniture, and cooking equipment. The more meals it serves, the lower will be its overhead cost per meal.

For Spotless Car Wash, look at column 8 of the table. When output is 30 units, *AFC* is $75/30 = $2.50. But at 90 units of output, *AFC* drops to $75/90 = $0.83. And *AFC* keeps declining as we continue down the column. The more output produced, the lower is fixed cost per unit of output.

Average variable cost Total variable cost divided by the quantity of output produced.

> *Average variable cost* (AVC) *is the cost of the variable inputs per unit of output:*
>
> $$AVC = \frac{TVC}{Q}.$$

AVC is shown in column 9 of the table. For example, at 30 units of output, *TVC* = $60, so *AVC = TVC/Q* = $60/30 = $2.00.

What happens to *AVC* as output rises? If you run your finger down the *AVC* column in Table 3, you'll see a pattern: The *AVC* numbers first decrease and then increase. Economists believe that this pattern of decreasing and then increasing average variable cost is typical at many firms. When plotted in Figure 4, this pattern causes the *AVC* curve to have a U shape. We'll discuss the reason for this characteristic U shape a bit later.

Average total cost Total cost divided by the quantity of output produced.

> *Average total cost* (ATC) *is the total cost per unit of output:*
>
> $$ATC = \frac{TC}{Q}.$$

Values for *ATC* are listed in column 10 of Table 3. For example, at 90 units of output, *TC* = $195, so *ATC = TC/Q* = $195/90 = $2.17. And a quick look at column 10 shows that as output rises, *ATC* first falls and then rises. So the *ATC* curve—like the *AVC* curve—is U-shaped. However—as you can see in Figure 4—it is not identical to the *AVC* curve. At each level of output, the vertical distance between the two curves is equal to average *fixed* cost (*AFC*). Since *AFC* declines as output increases, the *ATC* curve and the *AVC* curve must get closer and closer together as we move rightward.

Marginal Cost

The total and average costs we've considered so far tell us about the firm's cost at a particular *level* of output. For many purposes, however, we are more interested in how cost *changes* when output *changes*. This information is provided by another cost concept:

> *Marginal cost* (MC) *is the change in total cost* (ΔTC) *divided by the change in output* (ΔQ):
>
> $$MC = \frac{\Delta TC}{\Delta Q}.$$
>
> *It tells us how much cost rises per unit increase in output.*

Marginal cost The increase in total cost from producing one more unit of output.

For Spotless Car Wash, marginal cost is entered in column 7 of Table 3 and graphed in Figure 4. Since marginal cost tells us what happens to total cost when output *changes*, the entries in the table are placed *between* one output level and another. For example, when output rises from 0 to 30, total cost rises from $75 to $135. For this change in output, we have $\Delta TC = \$135 - \$75 = \$60$, while $\Delta Q = 30$, so $MC = \$60/30 = \$2.00$. This entry is listed *between* the output levels 0 and 30 in the table.

EXPLAINING THE SHAPE OF THE MARGINAL COST CURVE

In Figure 4 marginal cost is graphed. (For now, ignore the other two cost curves.) As in the table, each value of marginal cost is plotted *between* output levels. For example, the marginal cost of increasing output from 0 to 30 is $2, and this is plotted at output level 15—midway between 0 and 30. Similarly, when going from 30 to 90 units of output, the *MC* is plotted midway between 30 and 90. If you look carefully at the *MC* curve in Figure 4, you'll see that *MC* first declines and then rises. Why is this? Here, we can use what we learned earlier about marginal returns to labor.

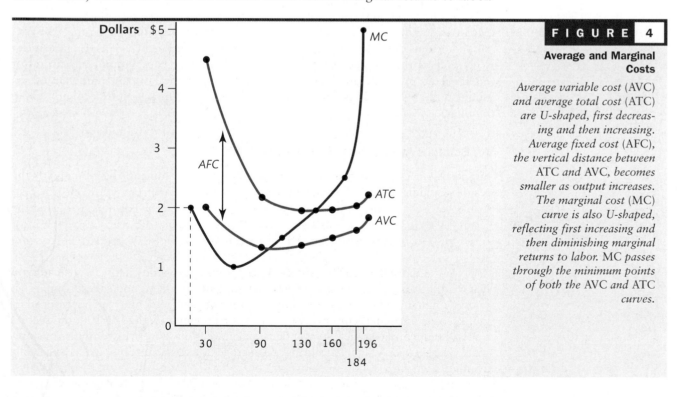

FIGURE 4

Average and Marginal Costs

Average variable cost (AVC) and average total cost (ATC) are U-shaped, first decreasing and then increasing. Average fixed cost (AFC), the vertical distance between ATC and AVC, becomes smaller as output increases. The marginal cost (MC) curve is also U-shaped, reflecting first increasing and then diminishing marginal returns to labor. MC passes through the minimum points of both the AVC and ATC curves.

At low levels of employment and output, there are increasing marginal returns to labor: $MPL = \Delta Q/\Delta L$ is rising. That is, each worker hired adds more to production than the worker before. But that means that *fewer additional workers are needed to produce an additional unit of output*. Now, since additional labor is this firm's only cost of increasing production, the cost of an additional unit of output (MC) must be falling. Thus, as long as MPL is rising, MC must be falling.

For Spotless, since MPL rises when employment increases from zero to one and again from one to two workers, MC must fall as the firm's output rises from zero to 30 units (produced by one worker) and then from 30 to 90 units (produced by two workers).

At higher levels of output, we have the opposite situation: Diminishing marginal returns set in and the marginal product of labor ($\Delta Q/\Delta L$) falls. Therefore, additional units of output require *more* and *more* additional labor. As a result, each additional unit of output costs more and more to produce. Thus, as long as MPL is falling, MC must be rising.

For Spotless, diminishing marginal returns to labor occur for all workers beyond the second, so MC rises for all increases in output beyond the change from 30 to 90.

To sum up:

> *When the marginal product of labor (MPL) rises, marginal cost (MC) falls. When MPL falls, MC rises. Since MPL ordinarily rises and then falls, MC will do the opposite: It will fall and then rise. Thus, the MC curve is U-shaped.*

THE RELATIONSHIP BETWEEN AVERAGE AND MARGINAL COSTS

Although marginal cost and average cost are not the same, there is an important relationship between them. Look again at Figure 4 and notice that all three curves—MC, AVC, and ATC—first fall and then rise, but not all at the same time. The MC curve bottoms out before either the AVC or ATC curve. Further, the MC curve intersects each of the average curves *at their lowest points*. These graphical features of Figure 4 are no accident; indeed, they follow from the laws of mathematics. To understand this, let's consider a related example with which you are probably more familiar.

An Example: Average and Marginal Test Scores

Suppose you take five tests in your economics course during the term, with the results listed in Table 4. To your immense pleasure, you score 100 on your first test. Your total score—the total number of points you have received thus far during the term—is 100. Your marginal score—the *change* in your total caused by the most recent test—will also be 100, since your total rose from 0 to 100. Your average score so far is 100 as well.

Now suppose that, for the second test, you forget to study actively. Instead, you just read the text while simultaneously watching music videos and eavesdropping on your roommate's phone conversations. As a result, you get a 50, which is your marginal score. Since this score is lower than your previous average of 100, the second test will pull your average down. Indeed, whenever you score is lower than your previous average, you will always bring the average down. In the table, we see that your average after the second test falls to 75.

Now you start to worry, so you turn off the TV while studying, and your performance improves a bit: You get a 60. Does the improvement in your score—from

50 to 60—increase your *average* score? No . . . your average will decrease once again, because your *marginal* score of 60 is *still* lower than your previous average of 75. As we know, when you score lower than your average, it pulls the average down, even if you're improving. In the table, we see that your average now falls to 70.

For your fourth exam, you study a bit harder and score a 70. This time, since your score is precisely *equal* to your previous average, the average remains unchanged at 70.

Finally, on your fifth and last test, your score improves once again, this time to 80. This time, you've scored *higher* than your previous average, pulling your average up from 70 to 72.

This example may be easy to understand because you are used to figuring out your average score in a course as you take additional exams. But the relationship between marginal and average spelled out here is universal: It is the same for grade point averages, batting averages—*and* costs.

Average and Marginal Cost

Now let's apply these insights to a firm's cost curves. We'll start with the relationship between the *MC* and *AVC* curves, because both curves reflect changes in the costs of variable inputs only. We already know that marginal cost first decreases and then increases (based on first increasing and then diminishing marginal returns to labor). At low levels of output, as marginal cost decreases, it is *lower* than average variable cost, so it will pull the average down: *AVC* decreases. But as marginal cost rises due to diminishing returns to labor, it eventually rises above *AVC*, pulling the average up: *AVC* rises. Because *AVC* first decreases and then rises, the *AVC* curve is U-shaped.

> *The U-shape of the* AVC *curve results from the U-shape of the* MC *curve, which in turn is based on increasing and then diminishing marginal returns to labor.*

There is a similar relationship between *MC* and *ATC*, except for one additional complication. *ATC* is the sum of *AVC* and *AFC*. *AFC always* falls as output rises.

Number of Tests Taken	Total Score	Marginal Score	Average Score
0	0		—
		100	
1	100		100
		50	
2	150		75
		60	
3	210		70
		70	
4	280		70
		80	
5	360		72

TABLE 4

Average and Marginal Test Scores

So at low levels of output, when both *AVC* and *AFC* are falling, *ATC* decreases—even more rapidly than AVC does. When *AVC* starts to rise, the effect of higher *AVC* and falling *AFC* compete with each other. But eventually, the rise in *AVC* wins out, and *ATC* begins to rise as well. This explains why the *ATC* curve is U-shaped.

> *The U shape of the* ATC *curve results from the behavior of both* AVC *and* AFC. *At low levels of output,* AVC *and* AFC *are both falling, so the* ATC *curve slopes downward. At higher levels of output, rising* AVC *overcomes falling* AFC, *and the* ATC *curve slopes upward.*

The relationships between *MC* and *AVC* and *MC* and *ATC* also tell us something important about the crossing point between the *MC* curve and the *AVC* curve in Figure 4. Whenever the *MC* curve is below one of the average curves, the average curve slopes downward. Whenever the *MC* curve is above the average curve, the average curve slopes upward. Therefore, when *MC* goes from below the average to above the average—that is, where the *MC* curve *crosses* the average curve—the average curve must be at its very *minimum* (where it changes from a downward slope to an upward slope).

> *The* MC *curve crosses both the* AVC *curve and the* ATC *curve at their respective minimum points.*

If you look at Table 3, you'll see that when Spotless's output rises from 30 to 90, *MC* is below *AVC*, and *AVC* falls. When output rises from 90 to 130, *MC* is above *AVC*, and *AVC* rises. As a result, in Figure 4, the *MC* curve crosses the *AVC* curve where *AVC* bottoms out. The same relationship holds for the *MC* and *ATC* curves. But because of the competing affects of *AFC* and *AVC* on *ATC*, it takes longer for the *ATC* curve to hit bottom than the *AVC* curve. That's why minimum *ATC* occurs at a higher output than does minimum *AVC*.

Time to Take a Break. By now, your mind may be swimming with concepts and terms: total, average, and marginal cost curves; fixed and variable costs; explicit and implicit costs. . . . We are covering a lot of ground here and still have a bit more to cover: production and cost in the *long run*.

As difficult as it may seem to keep these concepts straight, they will become increasingly easy to handle as you use them in the chapters to come. But it's best not to overload your brain with too much new material at one time. So if this is your first trip through this chapter, now is a good time for a break. Then, when you're fresh, come back and review the material you've read so far. When the terms and concepts start to feel familiar, you are ready to move on to the long run.

PRODUCTION AND COST IN THE LONG RUN

Most of the business firms you have contact with—such as your supermarket, the stores where you buy new clothes, your telephone company, and your Internet service provider—plan to be around for quite some time. They have a long-term planning horizon, as well as a short-term one. But so far, we've considered the behavior of costs only in the short run.

In the long run, costs behave differently, because the firm can adjust *all* of its inputs in any way it wants:

> *In the long run, there are no fixed inputs or fixed costs; all inputs and all costs are variable. The firm must decide what combination of inputs to use in producing any level of output.*

How will the firm choose? Its goal is to earn the highest possible profit, and to do this, it must follow the *least cost rule:*

> *To produce any given level of output, the firm will choose the input mix with the lowest cost.*

Let's apply the least cost rule to Spotless Car Wash. Suppose we want to know the cost of washing 196 cars per day. In the short run, of course, Spotless does not have to worry about how it would produce this level of output: It is stuck with one automated line, and the only way to wash 196 cars is to hire six workers (see Table 3). Total cost in the short run will be 6 × $60 + $75 = $435.

The Least Cost Rule When you read the *least cost rule* of production, you might think that the firm's long-run goal is to have the *least possible cost*. But that's not what the rule says. After all, in the long run, the least possible cost would be zero, and this could be achieved by not using any inputs and producing nothing!

The least cost rule says something different: that any *given* level of output should be produced at the lowest possible cost for *that* output level.

DANGEROUS CURVES

In the long run, however, Spotless can vary the number of automated lines as well as the number of workers. Spotless's production function will determine the different combinations of *both* inputs that can be used to produce any output level. Suppose, based on its production function, Spotless can use four different input combinations to wash 196 cars per day. These are listed in Table 5. Combination *A* uses the least capital and the most labor—no automated lines at all and nine workers washing the cars by hand. Combination *D* uses the most capital and the least labor—three automated lines with only three workers. Since each automated line costs $75 per day and each worker costs $60 per day, it is easy to calculate the cost of each production method. Spotless will choose the one with the lowest cost: combination *C*, with two automated lines and four workers, for a total cost of $390 per day.

Retracing our steps, we have found that if Spotless wants to wash 196 cars per day, it will examine the different methods of doing so and select the one with the

Method	Quantity of Capital	Quantity of Labor	Cost
A	0	9	$540
B	1	6	$435
C	2	4	$390
D	3	3	$405

TABLE 5

Four Ways to Wash 196 Cars per Day

TABLE 6	Output	LRTC	LRATC
Long-Run Costs for Spotless Car Wash	0	$ 0	—
	30	$ 100	$3.33
	90	$ 195	$2.17
	130	$ 255	$1.96
	160	$ 304	$1.90
	184	$ 360	$1.96
	196	$ 390	$1.99
	250	$ 650	$2.60
	300	$1,200	$4.00

Long-run total cost The cost of producing each quantity of output when all inputs are variable and the least-cost input mix is chosen.

least cost. Once it has determined the cheapest production method, the other, more expensive methods can be ignored.[2]

Table 6 shows the results of going through this procedure for several different levels of output. The second column, **long-run total cost** (**LRTC**), tells us the cost of producing each quantity of output *when the least-cost input mix is chosen*. For each output level, different production methods are examined, the cheapest one is chosen, and the others are ignored. Notice that the *LRTC* of zero units of output is $0. This will always be true for any firm. In the long run, all inputs can be adjusted as the firm wishes, and the cheapest way to produce zero output is to use *no* inputs at all. (For comparison, what is the *short*-run total cost of producing zero units? Why can it never be $0?)

Long-run average total cost The cost per unit of producing each quantity of output in the long run, when all inputs are variable.

The third column in Table 6 gives the **long-run average total cost** (**LRATC**), the cost per unit of output in the long run:

$$LRATC = \frac{LRTC}{Q}$$

Long-run average total cost is similar to average total cost, which was defined earlier. Both are obtained by dividing total cost by the level of output. There is one important difference, however: To calculate *ATC*, we used total cost (*TC*), which pertains to the short run, in the numerator. In calculating *LRATC*, we use *long-run* total cost (*LRTC*) in the numerator. Thus, *LRATC* tells us the cost per unit when the firm can vary *all* of its inputs and always chooses the cheapest input mix possible. *ATC*, however, tells us the cost per unit when the firm is stuck with some collection of fixed inputs and is able only to vary its remaining inputs, such as labor.

THE RELATIONSHIP BETWEEN LONG-RUN AND SHORT-RUN COSTS

If you compare Table 6 (long run) with Table 3 (short run), you will see something important: For some output levels, *LRTC* is smaller than *TC*. For example, Spotless can wash 196 cars for an *LRTC* of $390. But earlier, we saw that in the short run, the *TC* of washing these same 196 cars was $435. There is a reason

---

[2] The appendix to this chapter presents, in more detail, how firms choose the least-cost input mix when there is more than one variable input.

for this difference. Look back at Table 5, which lists the four different ways of washing 196 cars per day. In the short run, the firm is stuck with just one automated line, so its only option is method *B*. In the long run, however, the firm can change the number of automated lines, so it can choose any of the four methods of production, including method *C*, which is cheapest. The freedom to choose among different production methods usually enables the firm to select a cheaper input mix in the long run than it can in the short run. Thus, in the long run, the firm may be able to save money.

But not always. At some output levels, the freedom to adjust all inputs doesn't save the firm a dime. In our example, the long-run cost of washing 130 cars is $255—the same as the short-run cost (compare Tables 6 and 3). For this output level, it just so happens that the least-cost output mix uses one automated line, which is what Spotless is stuck with in the short run. So if Spotless wants to wash 130 cars, it cannot do so any more cheaply in the long run than in the short run.

More generally,

> *the long-run total cost of producing a given level of output can be less than or equal to, but not greater than, the short-run total cost* (LRTC ≤ TC).

We can also state this relationship in terms of *average* costs. That is, we can divide both sides of the inequality by Q and obtain $LRTC/Q \le TC/Q$. Using our definitions, this translates to $LRATC \le ATC$.

> *The long-run average cost of producing a given level of output can be less than or equal to, but not greater than, the short-run average total cost* (LRATC ≤ ATC).

Average Cost and Plant Size

Often, economists refer to the collection of inputs that are fixed in the short run as the firm's **plant**. For example, the plant of a computer manufacturer such as Dell might include its factory buildings and the assembly lines inside them. The plant of the Hertz car-rental company would include all of its automobiles and rental offices. For Spotless Car Wash, we've assumed that the plant is simply the company's capital equipment—the automated lines for washing cars. If Spotless were to add to its capital, then each time it acquired another automated line, it would have a different, and larger, plant. Viewed in this way, we can distinguish between the long run and the short run as follows: *In the long run, the firm can change the size of its plant; in the short run, it is stuck with its current plant.*

Now think about the *ATC* curve, which tells us the firm's average total cost in the short run. This curve is always drawn for a specific plant. That is, the *ATC* curve tells us how average cost behaves in the short run, *when the firm uses a plant of a given size*. If the firm had a different-size plant, it would be moving along a different *ATC* curve. In fact, there is a different *ATC* curve for each different plant the firm could have. In the long run, then, the firm can choose to operate on *any* of these *ATC* curves. To produce any level of output, it will always choose that *ATC* curve—among all of the *ATC* curves available—that enables it to produce at lowest possible average total cost. This insight tells us something about the relationship between the firm's *ATC* curves and its *LRATC* curve.

Plant The collection of fixed inputs at a firm's disposal.

FIGURE 5

Long-Run Average Total Cost

Average-total cost curves ATC$_0$, ATC$_1$, ATC$_2$, and ATC$_3$ show average costs when the firm has zero, one, two, and three automated lines, respectively. The LRATC curve combines portions of all the firm's ATC curves. In the long run, the firm will choose the lowest-cost ATC curve for each level of output.

Graphing the *LRATC* Curve

Look at Figure 5, which shows several different *ATC* curves for Spotless Car Wash. There is a lot going on in this figure, so let's take it one step at a time. First, find the curve labeled *ATC*$_1$. This is our familiar *ATC* curve—the same one shown in Figure 4—which we used to find Spotless's average total cost in the short run, when it was stuck with one automated line.

The other *ATC* curves refer to *different* plants that Spotless *might* have had instead. For example, the curve labeled *ATC*$_0$ shows how average total cost would behave if Spotless had a plant with *zero* automated lines washing all cars manually. *ATC*$_2$ shows average total cost with *two* automated lines, and so on. Since, in the long run, the firm can choose which size plant to operate, it can also choose on which of these *ATC* curves it wants to operate. And, as we know, in the long run, it will always choose the plant with the lowest possible average total cost for any output level it produces.

Let's take a specific example. Suppose that Spotless thinks that it might wash 130 cars per day. In the long run, what size plant should it choose? Scanning the different *ATC* curves in Figure 5, we see that the lowest possible per-unit cost—$1.96 per car—is at point *A* along *ATC*$_1$. The best plant for washing 130 cars per day, therefore, will have just one automated line. For this output level, Spotless would never choose a plant with zero lines, because it would then have to operate on *ATC*$_0$ at point *B*. Since point *B* is higher than point *A*, we know that point *B* represents a larger per-unit cost. Nor would the firm choose a plant with two lines—operating on *ATC*$_2$ at point *C*—for this would mean a still larger per-unit cost. Of all the possibilities for producing 130 units in the long run, Spotless would choose to operate at point *A* on *ATC*$_1$. So point *A* represents the *LRATC* of 130 units.

Now, suppose instead that Spotless wanted to produce 184 units of output in the long run. A plant with one automated line is no longer the best choice. Instead, the firm would choose a plant with *two* automated lines. How do we know? For an output of 184, the firm could choose point D on ATC_1, or point E on ATC_2. Since point E is lower, it is the better choice. At this point, average total cost would be $1.96, so this would be the *LRATC* of 184 units.

Continuing in this way, we could find the *LRATC* for *every* output level Spotless might produce. To produce any given level of output, the firm will always operate on the *lowest ATC* curve available. As output increases, it will move along an *ATC* curve until another, lower *ATC* curve becomes available—one with lower costs. At that point, the firm will increase its plant size, so it can move to the lower *ATC* curve. In the graph, as Spotless increases its output level from 90 to 175 units of output, it will continue to use a plant with one automated line and move along ATC_1. But if it wants to produce *more* than 175 units in the long run, it will increase its plant to *two* automated lines and begin moving along ATC_2.

Thus, we can trace out Spotless's *LRATC* curve by combining just the lowest portions of all the *ATC* curves from which the firm can choose. In Figure 5, this is the thick, scallop-shaped curve.

A firm's *LRATC* curve combines portions of each *ATC* curve available to the firm in the long run. For each output level, the firm will always choose to operate on the *ATC* curve with the lowest possible cost.

Figure 5 also gives us a view of the different options facing the firm in the short run and the long run. Once Spotless builds a plant with one automated line, its options in the short run are limited: It can only move along ATC_1. If it wants to increase its output from 130 to 184 units, it must move from point A to point D. But in the long run, it can move along its *LRATC* curve—from point A to point E— by changing the size of its plant.

More generally,

> *in the short run, a firm can only move along its current* ATC *curve. In the long run, however, it can move from one* ATC *curve to another by varying the size of its plant. As it does so, it will also be moving along its* LRATC *curve.*

Explaining the Shape of the *LRATC* Curve

In Figure 5, the *LRATC* curve has a scalloped look because the firm can only choose among four different plants. But many firms—especially large ones—can choose among hundreds or even thousands of different plant sizes. Each different plant size would be represented by a different *ATC* curve, so there would be hundreds of *ATC* curves crowded into the figure. As a result, the scallops would disappear, and the *LRATC* curve would appear as a smooth curve.

Figure 6 shows what the *LRATC* curve might look like for Mike's Pizza Restaurant. The horizontal axis measures the number of pizzas served per day. The vertical axis measures cost per pizza. Note that as we move along this curve, we are looking at *long-run* average total cost, which means that as output rises, not only can Mike's use more cooks, ingredients, and wait-staff, it can also adjust the size of its "plant"—its restaurant facility.

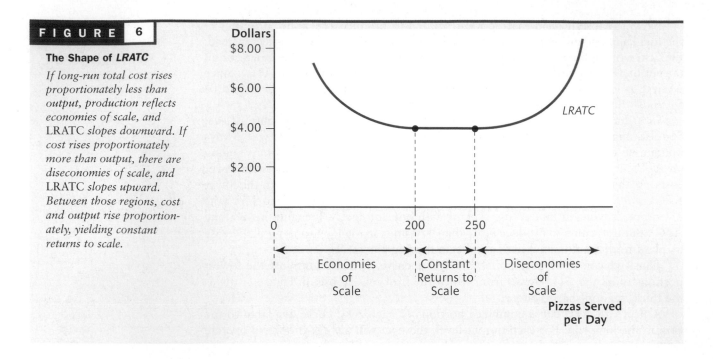

FIGURE 6

The Shape of *LRATC*

If long-run total cost rises proportionately less than output, production reflects economies of scale, and LRATC slopes downward. If cost rises proportionately more than output, there are diseconomies of scale, and LRATC slopes upward. Between those regions, cost and output rise proportionately, yielding constant returns to scale.

The *LRATC* curve for Mike's Pizza is U-shaped—much like the *AVC* and *ATC* curves you learned about earlier. That is, as output increases, long-run average costs first decline, then remain constant, and finally rise. Although there is no law or rule of logic that requires an *LRATC* curve to have all three of these phases, in many industries this seems to be the case. Let's see why, by considering each of the three phases in turn.

Economies of Scale

Economies of scale Long-run average total cost decreases as output increases.

When an increase in output causes *LRATC* to decrease, we say that the firm is enjoying **economies of scale:** The more output produced, the lower the cost per unit. Mike's Pizza has economies of scale for all output levels up to 200.

On a purely mathematical level, economies of scale means that long-run total cost is rising by a smaller proportion than output. For example, if a doubling of output (Q) can be accomplished with less than a doubling of costs, then the ratio $LRTC/Q = LRATC$ will decline, and—voilà!—economies of scale.

> *When long-run total cost rises proportionately less than output, production is characterized by economies of scale, and the* LRATC *curve slopes downward.*

So much for the mathematics. But in the real world, *why* should total costs ever increase by a smaller proportion than output? Why should a firm experience economies of scale?

Gains from Specialization. One reason for economies of scale is gains from specialization. At very low levels of output, workers may have to perform a greater variety of tasks, slowing them down and making them less productive. But as output increases and workers are added, more possibilities for specialization are created. For example, at low levels of output, Mike's Pizza might have a very small facility with just one employee. This one worker would do everything himself: cook the pizzas, take orders, clean the tables, accept payments, order ingredients, and so on. But as output expands, Mike can run a larger operation with more workers, each specializing in one of these tasks. Since each worker is more productive, output will increase by a greater proportion than costs.

The greatest opportunities for increased specialization occur when a firm is starting at a relatively low level of output, with a relatively small plant and small workforce. Thus, economies of scale are more likely to occur at lower levels of output.

Lumpy input An input whose quantity cannot be increased gradually as output increases, but must instead be adjusted in large jumps.

Spreading Costs of Lumpy Inputs. Another explanation for economies of scale involves the "lumpy" nature of many types of plant and equipment. **Lumpy inputs** are inputs that cannot be increased in tiny increments, but rather must be increased in large jumps.

A medical practice, for example, needs the use of an X-ray machine in order to serve patients. But it must buy one or more *whole* machines, not a half or a fifth of an X-ray machine. The more patients the practice serves, the lower will be the cost of the machine per patient.

We see this phenomenon in many types of businesses: Plant and equipment must be purchased in large lumps, and a low cost per unit is achieved only at high levels of output. Other inputs besides equipment can also be lumpy in this way. An answering service must have a receptionist on duty at all times, even if only a few calls come in each day. A theater must have at least one ticket seller and one projectionist, regardless of how many people come to see the show. In all of these cases, an increase in output allows the firm to spread the cost of lumpy inputs over greater amounts of output, lowering the cost *per unit of output*.

Making more efficient use of lumpy inputs will have more impact on *LRATC* at low levels of output when these inputs make up a greater proportion of the firm's total costs. At higher levels of output, the impact is smaller. For example, suppose Mike's restaurant must pay a yearly license fee of $3,650, which amounts to $10 per day. If output doubles from 10 to 20 pizzas per day, license costs per meal served will fall from $1 to $0.50. But if output doubles from 200 to 400, license costs per meal drop from $0.05 to $0.025—a hardly noticeable difference. Thus, spreading lumpy inputs across more output—like the gains from specialization—is more likely to create economies of scale at relatively low levels of output. This is another reason why the typical *LRATC* curve—as illustrated in Figure 6—slopes downward at relatively low levels of output.

Diseconomies of Scale

As output continues to increase, most firms will reach a point where bigness begins to cause problems. Large firms may require more layers of management, so communication and decision making become more time consuming and costly. Huge corporations like IBM, General Motors, and Verizon each have several hundred high-level managers, and thousands more at lower levels. Large firms may also have a harder time screening out misfits among new hires and monitoring those already working at the firm, so there is an increase in mistakes, shirking of responsibilities, and even theft from the firm. If Mike expands his facility so he can serve hundreds of pizzas per day, with dozens of employees, some of them might start sneaking pizzas home at the end of the day, others might take extra long breaks without anyone noticing, and so on. As output continues to rise and the firm has exhausted the cost-saving opportunities from increasing its scale of operations, these sorts of problems will eventually dominate, causing *LRATC* to rise. More generally,

Diseconomies of scale Long-run average total cost increases as output increases.

> *when long-run total cost rises more than in proportion to output, there are* **diseconomies of scale,** *and the* LRATC *curve slopes upward.*

While economies of scale are more likely at low levels of output, *dis*economies of scale are more likely at higher output levels. In Figure 6, you can see that Mike's Pizza does not experience diseconomies of scale until it is serving more than 250 pizzas per day.

Constant Returns to Scale

In Figure 6, for output levels between 200 and 250, the smoothed-out *LRATC* curve is roughly flat. Over this range of output, *LRATC* remains approximately constant as output increases. Here, output and *LRTC* rise by roughly the same proportion:

Constant returns to scale Long-run average total cost is unchanged as output increases.

> *When both output and long-run total cost rise by the same proportion, production is characterized by* **constant returns to scale,** *and the* LRATC *curve is flat.*

Why would a firm experience constant returns to scale? We have seen that as output increases, cost savings from specialization and spreading the costs of lumpy inputs will eventually be exhausted. But production may still have room to expand before the costly problems of "bigness" kick in. The firm will then have a range of output over which average cost neither rises nor falls as production increases—constant returns to scale. Notice that constant returns to scale, if present at all, are most likely to occur at some *intermediate* range of output.

In sum, when we look at the behavior of *LRATC*, we often expect a pattern like the following: economies of scale (decreasing *LRATC*) at relatively low levels of output, constant returns to scale (constant *LRATC*) at some intermediate levels of output, and diseconomies of scale (increasing *LRATC*) at relatively high levels of output. This is why *LRATC* curves are typically U-shaped.

Of course, even U-shaped *LRATC* curves will have different appearances for firms in different industries. And as you're about to see, these differences in *LRATC* curves have much to tell us about the economy.

COST: A SUMMARY

This chapter has presented a number of new terms and concepts. As you first learn them, it's easy to get them confused. Table 7 provides a useful summary, which you can use both as a reference and a self-test.

TABLE 7			
Types of Costs	**Term**	**Symbol and/or Formula**	**Definition**
	Explicit cost		A cost where an actual payment is made
	Implicit cost		An opportunity cost, but no actual payment is made
	Sunk cost		An irrelevant cost because it cannot be affected by any current or future decision
	Lumpy input cost		The cost of an input that can only be adjusted in large, indivisible amounts
	Short-run costs		
	Total fixed cost	*TFC*	The cost of all inputs that are fixed (cannot be adjusted) in the short run
	Total variable cost	*TVC*	The cost of all inputs that are variable (can be adjusted) in the short run
	Total cost	*TC* = *TFC* + *TVC*	The cost of all inputs in the short run
	Average fixed cost	*AFC* = *TFC/Q*	The cost of all fixed inputs per unit of output
	Average variable cost	*AVC* = *TVC/Q*	The cost of all variable inputs per unit of output
	Average total cost	*ATC* = *TC/Q*	The cost of all inputs per unit of output
	Marginal cost	*MC* = $\Delta TC/\Delta Q$	The change in total cost for each one-unit rise in output
	Long-run costs		
	Long-run total cost	*LRTC*	The cost of all inputs in the long run, using the least-cost method of producing any given output level
	Long-run average	*LRATC* = *LRTC/Q*	Cost per unit in the long run, using the least-cost method of producing any given output level

USING THE THEORY

The Urge to Merge

At the beginning of this chapter, we noted several large corporate mergers announced at the beginning of 2006. Although there are many reasons for mergers like these, economies of scale often plays an important role.

To see why, look at Figure 7, which shows a hypothetical *LRATC* curve for a firm. Notice that this *LRATC* curve exhibits economies of scale (slopes downward) up to an output level of 20,000 units per month, and then diseconomies of scale set in (the curve slopes upward). The output level at which an *LRATC* curve like this first hits bottom is known as the **minimum efficient scale (MES)** for the firm—the lowest output level that allows it to achieve minimum cost per unit in the long run. At the MES, the gains from greater specialization and spreading

© JAMES LEYNSE/CORBIS

Minimum efficient scale The lowest output level at which the firm's *LRATC* curve hits bottom.

FIGURE 7

LRATC for a Typical Firm in a Merger-Prone Industry

With market quantity demanded fixed at 60,000, and six firms of equal market share, each operates at point A, producing 10,000 units at $200 per unit. But any one firm can cut price slightly, increase market share, and operate with lower cost per unit, such as at the MES (point B). Other firms must match the first-mover's price; otherwise they lose market share and end up at a point like C, with higher cost per unit than originally. The result is a price war, with each firm ending up back at point A, only now—due to the lower price—they suffer losses. A series of mergers to create three large firms would enable each to operate at its MES (point B), with less likelihood of price wars and losses.

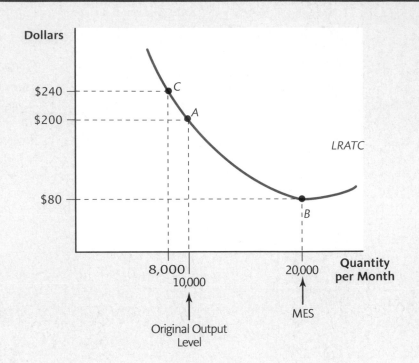

the costs of lumpy inputs have been largely exhausted, but the problems of bigness haven't yet taken over. In the figure, if this firm were producing at its MES of 20,000 units, its long-run cost per unit would be $80, at point *B*. This is the lowest possible cost per unit this firm could achieve.

Now let's suppose that there are *six* firms selling in this market. We'll assume these firms are identical. Since each uses the same technology, and all pay the same prices for their inputs, they each have an *LRATC* curve just like the one in the figure. Finally, we'll suppose that the output of the entire industry—at current prices—is 60,000 units per month, with each firm selling to one-sixth of this market. Thus, each firm operates at 10,000 units per month.

As you can see in the figure, with each firm producing 10,000 units (*less* than its MES), each is at point *A* on its *LRATC* curve. Cost per unit is $200—substantially above what cost per unit would be at the MES. There are unexploited economies of scale. We know that if this has been going on for a while, each firm must be charging *at least* $200; otherwise, it would not be able to cover its costs and would soon be out of business.

Let's suppose (arbitrarily) that each of the six firms is charging a price of $220 per unit. (In coming chapters, you'll learn how the price is determined in different types of markets.) Since cost per unit is $200, each firm's total profit is $20 × 10,000 = $200,000 per month. All the firms are earning a profit, so you might think this situation could continue indefinitely.

But it likely won't. A market like this is ripe for mergers. Why? To keep our story as simple as possible, let's suppose for now that the total market demand for the output of these six firms is a constant 60,000 units per month, no matter what happens to the price. In this market, it won't be long before one of the firms in this industry gets a brilliant idea: to lower its price below that of its competitors, so it can take some of the market away from them. The first firm to do so can lower its price *below* $200 because, by doing so, it will increase the quantity it sells. As a result, it will slide down its *LRATC* curve and operate at a cost per unit under $200, and less than the cost per unit of its competitors.

Let's suppose that this first mover lowers the price to $190, which is just enough to increase its sales to the MES of 20,000 units. Cost per unit falls to $80 (point *B*), so profit per unit rises to $190 − $80 = $110. With 20,000 units sold, the first mover's total profit rises to $110 × 20,000 = $2,200,000. Not a bad move!

Of course, this will not make the other firms in the industry happy. Because we assume that total sales are fixed at 60,000 units per month, the gain in sales by the first mover come at the expense of its competitors, who (we assume for now) have not yet lowered their own prices. As a result of the first mover *gaining* 10,000 units in sales, each of the remaining five firms has *lost* 2,000 in sales—declining to 8,000. These firms therefore move *leftward* and *upward* along their own *LRATC* curves, to point *C*. Cost per unit for each of them is now $240.

These five slow-moving firms now have some unpleasant choices. If they *raise* their price above $240 to try to cover their costs on each unit, they will lose further sales, and slide further up their *LRATC* curve, with still higher cost. If they *lower* prices to get some of their sales back from the first mover, the result may be a price war, which could take the price down to $80, as the first mover tries to defend its market share so it can continue operating at its MES. (We'll have more to say about price wars and how they erupt in Chapter 10.)

But remember: It is impossible for *all* six firms to operate at their MES of 20,000 because we're assuming that the total demand for this product is fixed at 60,000. So if the price war leads all firms to charge a price of $80, with each firm having one-sixth of the market, then each firm, including the first mover, is once again producing 10,000 units, at a cost of $200 per unit. Only now, with a lower price, each will suffer a loss.

We could continue this story, with all six firms deciding to raise their prices back to $220, until a price war breaks out again. But you can see that this market, with six firms, is very unstable. There are too many firms for each to satisfy the market demand of 60,000 while simultaneously operating at their MES. Price wars are likely to break out periodically, with periodic losses by all firms. If they try to make an illegal agreement not to lower their prices, in most countries (including the United States) they risk jail terms and huge fines.

Is there any way out of this mess? The title of this section gives the answer. If three of the six firms each combine with one of the others, the result will be three larger firms splitting the market among them. Each could then fully exploit its economies of scale, raising its output to the MES of 20,000, without overshooting the market's total demand of 60,000. While these firms *may* still compete for market share, the fact that each is operating at its MES means that each continues to operate at the lowest possible cost per unit merely by *maintaining* its proportional market share.

Of course, our story made several simplifications. Firms in an industry aren't really identical. And we assumed that demand was fixed at 60,000 units. In reality, we know that market demand curves have some elasticity, and that changes in price lead to changes in total market demand. We could incorporate more realistic assumptions, but they would complicate the analysis without changing its central point:

Economies of scale play an important role in determining the number of firms that survive in an industry. When there are significant, unexploited economies of scale (because the market has too many firms for each to operate near its minimum efficient scale), mergers often follow.

Economies of scale play a large role in explaining mergers in industries with high-cost lumpy inputs, such as large expenses for physical infrastructure, R&D, design, or marketing. By merging with other firms, these lumpy costs can be spread over more units of output, substantially lowering the new, larger firm's cost per unit. When AT&T purchased Bell South, for example, AT&Ts managers predicted cost savings of $2 billion per year, mostly from spreading the huge lumpy input costs of their physical telecommunications infrastructures, as well as the costs of their marketing, research and development, and billing departments, over more customers.[3]

On a smaller scale, in early 2006 two independent videogame developers (Collective, Inc., and Backbone Entertainment) announced they would merge to form a new firm: Foundation 9 Entertainment. The reason? The increasing sophistication of game systems had increased development costs (a lumpy input cost) for a new game to as much as $20 million for some titles.[4]

We'll have more to say about mergers and the behavior of large firms in future chapters (especially Chapters 9, 10, and 14). As you'll see, there are other motives for mergers that have nothing to do with economies of scale or costs. And even when a merger does bring down costs, it does not necessarily lead to lower prices for consumers. Indeed, economists become concerned when the number of firms in a market shrinks to just a few. This can mean less competition—and prices that are even higher than when the market had a larger number of higher cost firms.

Summary

Business firms combine inputs to produce outputs. A firm's *production function* describes the maximum output it can produce using different quantities of inputs. In the *short run,* at least one of the firm's inputs is fixed. In the *long run,* all inputs can be varied.

A firm's *cost of production* is the opportunity cost of its owners—everything they must give up in order to produce output. In the short run, some costs are *fixed* and independent of the level of production. Other costs—*variable costs*—change as production changes. *Marginal cost* is the change in total cost from producing one more unit of output. The *marginal cost curve* has a U shape, reflecting the underlying marginal product of labor. A variety of average cost curves can be defined. The *average variable cost curve* and the *average total cost curve* are each U-shaped, reflecting the relationship between average and marginal cost.

In the long run, all costs are variable. The firm's *long-run total cost curve* indicates the cost of producing each quantity of output with the least-cost input mix. The related *long-run average total cost (LRATC) curve* is formed by combining portions of different *ATC* curves, each portion representing a different plant size. The shape of the *LRATC* curve reflects the nature of returns to scale. It slopes downward when there are economies of scale, slopes upward when there are diseconomies of scale, and is flat when there are constant returns to scale. Economies of scale can play a role in explaining mergers and acquisitions, especially when there are too many firms for each to operate at its *minimum efficient scale.*

---

[3] Ken Belson, "AT&T Aims to Become All Things to All Customers," *New York Times*, March 7, 2006.
[4] Nick Wingfield, "Two Developers of Videogames Decide to Merge," *Wall Street Journal*, March 30, 2006.

Problem Set   *Answers to even-numbered Questions and Problems can be found on the text Web site at www.thomsonedu.com/economics/hall.*

1. The following table shows total output (in tax returns completed per day) of the accounting firm of Hoodwink and Finagle:

Number of Accountants	Number of Returns per Day
0	0
1	5
2	12
3	17
4	20
5	22

Assuming the quantity of capital (computers, adding machines, desks, etc.) remains constant at all output levels:

a. Calculate the marginal product of each accountant.
b. Over what range of employment do you see increasing returns to labor? Diminishing returns?
c. Explain why *MPL* might behave this way in the context of an accounting firm.

2. Down On Our Luck Studios has spent $100 million producing an awful film, *A Depressing Story About a Miserable Person*. If the studio releases the film, the most cost-effective marketing plan would cost an additional $5 million, bringing the total amount spent to $105 million. Box office sales under this plan are predicted to be $12 million, which would be split evenly between the theaters and the studio. Additional studio revenue from video and DVD sales would be about $2 million. Should the studio release the film? If no, briefly explain why not. If yes, explain how it could make sense to release a film that cost $105 million but earns only $12 million.

3. The following table gives the short-run and long-run total costs for various levels of output of Consolidated National Acme, Inc.:

Q	TC_1	TC_2
0	0	350
1	300	400
2	400	435
3	465	465
4	495	505
5	560	560
6	600	635
7	700	735

a. Which column, TC_1 or TC_2, gives long-run total cost, and which gives short-run total cost? How do you know?
b. For each level of output, find short-run *TFC*, *TVC*, *AFC*, *AVC*, and *MC*.
c. At what output level would the firm's short-run and long-run input mixes be the same?

d. Starting from producing two units, Consolidated's managers decide to double production to four units. So they simply double all of their inputs in the long run. Comment on their managerial skills.
e. Over what range of output do you see economies of scale? Diseconomies of scale? Constant returns to scale?

4. In a recent year, a long, hard winter gave rise to stronger-than-normal demand for heating oil. The following summer was characterized by strong demand for gasoline by vacationers. Show what these two events might have done to the short-run *MC*, *AVC*, and *ATC* curves of Continental Airlines. (Hint: How would these events affect the price of oil?)

5. Ludmilla's House of Schnitzel is currently producing 10 schnitzels a day at point *A* on the following diagram. Ludmilla's business partner, Hans (an impatient sort), wants her to double production immediately.

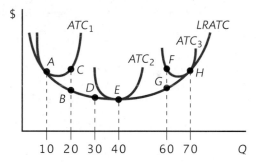

a. What point will likely illustrate Ludmilla's cost situation for the near future? Why?
b. If Ludmilla wants to keep producing 20 schnitzels, at what point does she want to be eventually? How can she get there?
c. Eventually, Ludmilla and company do very well, expanding until they find themselves making 70 schnitzels a day. But after a few years, Ludmilla discovers that profit was greater when she produced 20 schnitzels per day. She wants to scale back production to 20 schnitzels per day, laying off workers, selling off equipment, renting less space, and producing fewer schnitzels. Hans wants to reduce output by just cutting back on flour and milk and laying off workers. Who's right? Discuss the situation with reference to the relevant points on the diagram.
d. Does the figure tell us what output Ludmilla should aim for? Why or why not?

6. Clean 'n' Shine is a competitor to Spotless Car Wash. Like Spotless, it must pay $75 per day for each automated line it uses. But Clean 'n' Shine has been able to tap into a lower-cost pool of labor, paying its workers only $50 per day. Clean 'n' Shine's production technology is given in the following table. To determine its short-run cost structure, fill in the blanks in the table.

Short-Run Costs for Clean 'n' Shine Car Wash

(1) Output (per Day)	(2) Capital	(3) Labor	(4) TFC	(5) TVC	(6) TC	(7) MC	(8) AFC	(9) AVC	(10) ATC
0	1	0	$__	$__	$__		—	—	—
						$__			
30	1	1	$__	$__	$__		$__	$__	$__
						$__			
70	1	2	$__	$__	$__		$__	$__	$__
						$__			
120	1	3	$__	$__	$__		$__	$__	$__
						$__			
160	1	4	$__	$__	$__		$__	$__	$__
						$__			
190	1	5	$__	$__	$__		$__	$__	$__
						$__			
210	1	6	$__	$__	$__		$__	$__	$__

a. Over what range of output does Clean 'n' Shine experience increasing marginal returns to labor? Over what range does it experience diminishing marginal returns to labor?

b. As output increases, do average fixed costs behave as described in the text? Explain.

c. As output increases, do marginal cost, average variable cost, and average total cost behave as described in the text? Explain.

d. Looking at the numbers in the table, but without drawing any curves, is the relationship between MC and AVC as described in the text? What about the relationship between MC and ATC?

7. In Table 3, when output rises from 90 to 130 units, marginal cost is $1.50. For this change in output, marginal cost is greater than the previous AVC ($1.33) but less than the previous ATC ($2.17). According to the relationship between marginals and averages you learned in this chapter:

a. What should happen to AVC due to this change in output? Does it happen?

b. What should happen to ATC due to this change in output? Does it happen?

8. A soft drink manufacturer that uses just labor (variable) and capital (fixed) paid a consulting firm thousands of dollars to calculate short-run costs at various output levels. But after the cost table (see below) was handed over to the president of the soft drink company, he spilled Dr Pepper on it, making some of the entries illegible. The consulting firm, playing tough, is demanding another payment to provide a duplicate table.

Output per day	Units of Capital	Number of Workers	TFC	TVC	TC	MC	AFC	AVC	ATC
0	10	0	$1,000	?	?		?	?	?
						?			
20,000	10	100	?	$9,000	?		?	?	?
						?			
40,000	10	?	?	?	?		?	?	$0.325
						?			
60,000	10	225	?	?	?		?	?	?
						?			
80,000	10	?	?	?	$30,000		?	?	?

a. Should the soft drink president pay up? Or can he fill in the rest of the entries on his own? Fill in as many entries as you can to determine your answer. (Hint: First, determine the price of labor.)

b. Do *MC*, *AVC*, and *ATC* have the relationship to each other that you learned in this chapter? Explain.

9. "If a firm has diminishing returns to labor over some range of output, it cannot have economies of scale over that range." True or false? Explain briefly.

More Challenging

10. Draw the long-run total cost and long-run average cost curves for a firm that experiences:
    a. Constant returns to scale over all output levels.
    b. Diseconomies of scale over low levels of output, constant returns to scale over intermediate levels of output, and economies of scale over high output levels. Does this pattern of costs make sense? Why or why not?

11. A firm has the strange *ATC* curve drawn in the following figure. Sketch in the marginal cost curve this firm must have. (Hint: Use what you know about the marginal-average relationship. Note that this *MC* curve does *not* have a standard shape.)

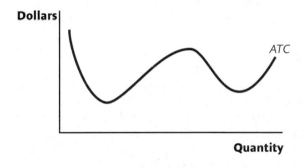

12. The following curve shows the *marginal* product of labor for a firm at different levels of output.
    a. Show what the corresponding total product curve would look like.
    b. Do the total and marginal product curves for this firm ever exhibit diminishing marginal returns to labor? Increasing marginal returns to labor?

APPENDIX

Isoquant Analysis: Finding the Least-Cost Input Mix

When a firm can vary more than one input, it can usually choose to produce any given output level in different ways. For example, in the long run, a car wash can vary both its labor and the number of automatic car-washing machines it uses. If it acquires more machines, it can wash the same number of cars with less labor. Even in the short run, a firm can often vary more than one input. A farmer might be able to achieve the same total yield using less fertilizer if he hires more labor to care for and harvest the crop.

How does a manager choose among different methods of production when she can vary more than one input? She will choose to produce any given level of output in the cheapest way possible. This appendix presents a graphical technique to help you understand how a firm with two variable inputs finds the lowest-cost production methods. The technique can be used over any time horizon—short run or long run—as long as there are two inputs whose quantities can be varied within that horizon. Finally, at the end of this appendix, the technique will be generalized to the case of *more than two* variable inputs.

ISOQUANTS

Imagine that you own an artichoke farm, and you are free to vary two inputs: labor and land. Your output is measured in "boxes of artichokes per month." Your farm's production function tells us the maximum possible number of boxes you could produce in a given month using different combinations of labor and land.

Alternatively, it tells us all the different input mixes that could be used to produce any given quantity of output.

Table A.1 lists some of the information we could obtain from your production function. Notice that, to produce each of the three output levels included in the table, there are many different combinations of inputs you could use. For example, the table tells us that your farm could produce 4,000 boxes of artichokes using 2 hectares of land and 18 workers, or 3 hectares and 11 workers, or 5 hectares and 5 workers, and so on.

(Note: If it seems to you that no artichoke farm would ever use some of these combinations—such as 14 hectares of land and 2 workers—you are right. But that is because of the relative *costs* of labor and land, which we haven't discussed yet. Table A.1 simply tells us what is *possible* for the firm, not what is sensible.)

The information in the table can also be illustrated with a graph. In Figure A.1, the quantity of land is plotted along the horizontal axis, and the number of workers on the vertical axis. Each combination of the two inputs is represented by a point. For example, the combination 3 *hectares, 11 workers* is represented by the point labeled *B*, while the combination 5 *hectares, 12 workers* is represented by point *F*.

Now let's focus on a single output level: 4,000 boxes per month. Table A.1 lists 5 of the different input combinations that can be used to produce this output level, each represented by a point in Figure A.1. When we connect all 5 points with a smooth line we get the

TABLE A.1	2,000 Boxes of Artichokes per Month		4,000 Boxes of Artichokes per Month		6,000 Boxes of Artichokes per Month	
	Hectares of Land	Number of Workers	Hectares of Land	Number of Workers	Hectares of Land	Number of Workers
	1	15	2	18	4	23
	2	7	3	11	5	12
	3	4	5	5	7	6
	6	2	7	3	11	4
	12	1	14	2	17	3

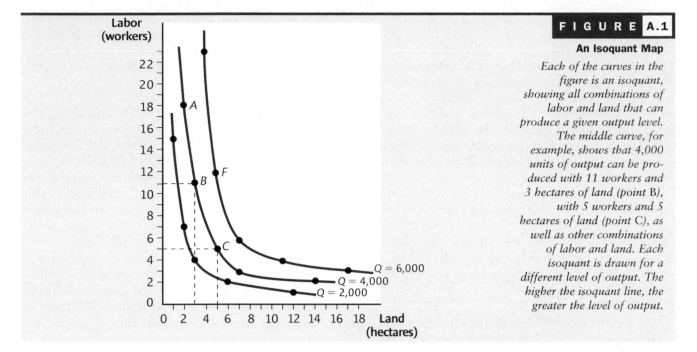

FIGURE A.1

An Isoquant Map

Each of the curves in the figure is an isoquant, showing all combinations of labor and land that can produce a given output level. The middle curve, for example, shows that 4,000 units of output can be produced with 11 workers and 3 hectares of land (point B), with 5 workers and 5 hectares of land (point C), as well as other combinations of labor and land. Each isoquant is drawn for a different level of output. The higher the isoquant line, the greater the level of output.

curve labeled "$Q = 4,000$" in Figure A.1. This curve is called an **isoquant**[5] ("iso" means "same," and "quant" stands for "quantity of output").

> *Every point on an isoquant represents an input mix that produces the same quantity of output.*[6]

Figure A.1 also shows two additional isoquants. The higher one is drawn for the output level $Q = 6,000$, and the lower one for the output level $Q = 2,000$. When these curves are shown together on a graph, we have an **isoquant map** for the firm.

THINGS TO KNOW ABOUT ISOQUANTS

As we move along any isoquant, the quantity of output remains the same, but the combination of inputs changes. More specifically, as we move along an isoquant, we are *substituting one input for another*. For example, as we move from point B to point C along the isoquant labeled $Q = 4,000$, the quantity of land rises from 3 to 5 hectares, while the number of workers falls from 11 to 5. You are substituting land for labor, while

[5] Bolded terms in this appendix are defined in the glossary.
[6] If you've read the appendix to Chapter 5, you will recognize that isoquants are similar to indifference curves. But while an indifference curve represents different combinations of two *goods* that give same level of *consumer satisfaction*, an isoquant represents different combinations of two *inputs* that give the same level of *firm output*.

maintaining the same level of output. Since each of the two inputs contributes to production, every time you increase one input, you must decrease the other in order to maintain the same level of output.

> *An increase in one input requires a decrease in the other input to keep total production unchanged. This is why isoquants always slope downward.*

What happens as we move from isoquant to isoquant? Whenever we move to a higher *isoquant* (moving northeasterly in Figure A.1), the quantity of output increases. Moving directly northward means you are using more labor with the same amount of land, and moving directly eastward means you are using more land with the same amount of labor. When you move both north and east simultaneously (as in the move from point B to point F), you are using more of *both* inputs. For all of these movements, output increases. For the same reason, if we move southwestward, output decreases.

> *Higher isoquants represent greater levels of output than lower isoquants.*

Finally, notice something else about Figure A.1: As we move rightward along any given isoquant, it becomes flatter. To understand why, we must take a closer look at an isoquant's slope.

THE MARGINAL RATE OF TECHNICAL SUBSTITUTION

The (absolute value of the) slope of an isoquant is called the **marginal rate of technical substitution (MRTS)**. As the name suggests, it measures the rate at which a firm can substitute one input for another while keeping output constant. In our example, the MRTS tells us how many *fewer* workers you can employ each time you use *one more hectare of land*, and still maintain the same level of output.

For example, if you move from point A to point B along isoquant Q = 4,000, you use 1 more hectare and 7 fewer workers, so the MRTS = 7/1 = 7 for that move. Going from point B to point C, you use 2 more hectares of land, and 6 fewer workers, so the MRTS = 6/2 = 3.

Using this new term, the changing slope of an isoquant can be expressed this way:

> *as we move rightward along any given isoquant, the marginal rate of technical substituation decreases.*

But why does the MRTS decrease? To answer this question, it helps to understand the relationship between the MRTS and the *marginal products* of land and labor. You've already learned that the marginal product of labor (MPL) is a firm's additional output when one more worker is hired and all other inputs

remain constant. The marginal product of land (MPN, using "N" for land) is defined in a similar way: It's the additional output a firm can produce with one additional unit of land (one more hectare, in our example), holding all other inputs constant.

Suppose that, starting from a given input mix, you discover that your MPN is 21 boxes of artichokes, and your MPL is 7 boxes. Then conduct the following mental experiment: Add one hectare of land, with no change in labor, and your output *increases* by 21 boxes. Then, give up 3 workers, with no change in land, and your output *decreases* by 3 × 7 = 21 boxes. In this case, adding 1 hectare of land, and hiring 3 fewer workers leaves your output unchanged. The slope of the isoquant for a move like this would be $\Delta L/\Delta N = -3/1 = -3$.

More generally, each time we change the amount of labor (L), the firm's output will change by $\Delta L \times MPL$. Each time we change the firm's land (N), the change in output will be $\Delta N \times MPN$. If we want the net result to be zero change in output, we must have

$$\Delta L \times MPL + \Delta N \times MPN = 0 \text{ or}$$
$$\Delta L \times MPL = -\Delta N \times MPN.$$

Rearranging this equation gives us:

$$\Delta L/\Delta N = -MPN/MPL.$$

The left-hand side is the ratio of the change in labor to the change in land needed to keep output unchanged, that is, *the slope of the isoquant*. The right-hand side

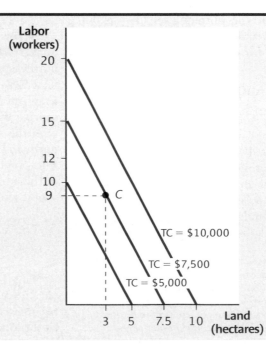

FIGURE A.2

Isocost Lines

Each of the lines in the figure is an isocost line, showing all combinations of labor and land that have the same total cost. The middle line, for example, shows that total cost will be $7,500 if 9 workers and 3 hectares of land are used (point C). All other combinations of land and labor on the middle line have the same total cost of $7,500. Each isocost line is drawn for a different value of total cost. The higher the isocost line, the greater is total cost.

tells us that this slope is equal to the ratio of the marginal products of land and labor, except for the sign, which is negative. That is,

> *at each point along an isoquant with land measured horizontally, and labor measured vertically, the (absolute value of the) slope of the isoquant, which we call the* MRTS, *is the ratio of the marginal products,* MPN/MPL.

Now, what does this have to do with the shape of the isoquant? As we move rightward and downward along an isoquant, the firm is acquiring more and more land, and using less and less labor. The marginal product of land will decrease—since land is becoming more plentiful—and the marginal product of labor will increase—since labor is becoming more and more scarce. Taken together, these changes tell us that the ratio *MPN/MPL* must fall and so must the slope of the isoquant.

> *An isoquant becomes flatter as we move rightward because the* **MPN** *decreases, while the* MPL *increases, so the ratio—MPN/MPL— decreases.*

ISOCOST LINES

An isoquant map shows us the different input mixes capable of producing different amounts of output. But how should the firm *choose* among all of these input mixes? In order to answer that question, we must know something about input *prices*. After all, if you own an artichoke farm, you must *pay* for your land and labor.

To keep the math simple, let's use round numbers. We'll suppose that the price of labor—the wage—is $500 per month ($P_L$ = $500), and the price of land— what you must pay in rent to its owner, or your implicit cost if you own the land yourself—is $1,000 per hectare per month (P_N = $1,000). An **isocost line** ("same cost" line) tells us all combinations of the two inputs that would require the same total outlay for the firm. It is very much like the *budget line* you learned about in Chapter 5, which showed all combinations of two *goods* that resulted in the same cost for the consumer. The difference is that an isocost line represents total cost to a *firm* rather than a consumer, and is based on paying for *inputs* rather than goods.

Figure A.2 shows three isocost lines for your artichoke farm. The middle line (labeled *TC* = $7,500) tells us all combinations of land and labor that would cost $7,500 per month. For example, point G represents the combination *3 hectares, 9 workers*, for a total cost of $3 \times \$1,000 + 9 \times \$500 = \$7,500$.

THINGS TO KNOW ABOUT ISOCOST LINES

Notice that all three isocost lines in Figure A.2 *slope downward*. Why is this? As you move rightward in the figure, you are using more land. If you continued to use an unchanged amount of labor, your cost would therefore increase. But an isocost line shows us input combinations with the *same* cost. Thus, to keep your cost unchanged as you use more land (move rightward), you must also employ *fewer* workers (move downward).

> *If you use more of one input, you must use less of the other input in order to keep your total cost unchanged. This is why isocost lines always slope downward.*

Notice, though, that the *slope* of the isocost line remains *constant* as we move along it. That is, isocost lines are *straight lines*. Why? Let's find an expression for the slope of the isocost line. Each time you change the number of workers by ΔL, your total cost will change by $P_L \times \Delta L$. Each time you change the amount of land you use by ΔN, your total cost will change by $P_N \times \Delta N$. In order for your total cost to remain the same as you change the amounts of both land and labor, the changes must satisfy the equation:

$$P_L \times \Delta L + P_N \times \Delta N = 0,$$

or

$$P_L \times \Delta L = -P_N \times \Delta N$$

which can be rearranged to

$$\Delta L / \Delta N = -P_N / P_L.$$

The term on the left is the change in labor divided by the change in land that leaves total cost unchanged—the slope of the isocost line. The term on the right is the (negative of the) ratio of the inputs' prices. In our example, with P_N = $1,000 and P_L = $500, the slope of the isocost line is $-\$1,000/\$500 = -2$.

Now you can see why the isocost line is a straight line: As long as the firm can continue to buy its inputs at unchanged prices, the ratio $-P_N/P_L$ will remain constant. Therefore, the slope of the isocost line will remain constant as well.

> *The slope of an isocost line with land (N) on the horizontal axis and labor (L) on the vertical axis is* $-P_N / P_L$. *This slope remains constant as we move along the line.*

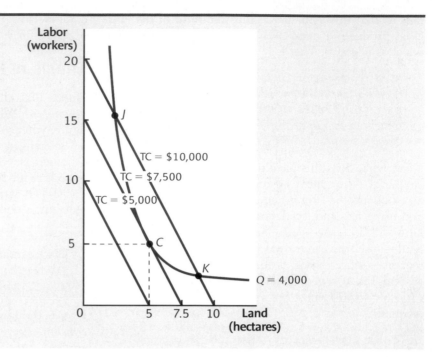

FIGURE A.3

The Least-Cost Input Combination for a Given Output Level

To produce any given level of output at the least possible cost, the firm should use the input combination where the isoquant for that output level is tangent to an isocost line. In the figure, the input combinations at points J, C, and K can all be used to produce 4,000 units of output. But the combination at point C (5 workers and 5 hectares of land), where the isoquant is tangent to the isocost line, is the least expensive input combination for that output level.

Finally, there is one more thing to note about isocost lines. As you move in a northeasterly direction in Figure A.2, to higher isocost lines, you are paying for greater amounts of land and labor, so your total cost must rise. For the same reason, as you move in a southwesterly direction, you are paying for smaller amounts of land and labor, so your total costs fall.

> *Higher isocost lines represent greater total costs for the firm than lower isocost lines.*

In Figure A.2, the highest line represents all inputs combinations with a total cost of $10,000, and the lowest line represents all combinations with a total cost of $5,000.

THE LEAST-COST INPUT COMBINATION

Now we are ready to combine what we know about a firm's production—represented by its isoquants—with our knowledge of the firm's costs—represented by its isocost lines. Together, these will allow us to find the least-cost input combination for producing any level of output a firm might choose to produce.

Suppose you want to know what is the best way to produce 4,000 boxes of artichokes per month. Figure A.3 reproduces the isoquant labeled Q = 4,000 from

Figure A.1, along with the three isocost lines from Figure A.2. You would like to find the input combination that is *capable* of producing 4,000 boxes (an input combination *on the isoquant Q = 4,000*), with the lowest possible cost (an input combination on the lowest possible isocost line). As you can see in the diagram, there is only one input combination that satisfies both requirements: point C. At this point, the firm uses 5 hectares of land, and 5 workers, for a total cost of 5 × $1,000 + 5 × $500 = $7,500. As you can see, while there are other input combinations that can also produce 4,000 boxes, such as point J or point K, each of these lie on a higher isocost line (TC = $10,000) and will require a greater total outlay than the least-cost combination at point C.

The least-cost combination will always be found where the isocost line is *tangent* to the isoquant. This is where the two lines touch each other at a single point, and both lines *have the same slope*.

> *The least-cost input combination for producing any level of output is found at the point where an isocost line is tangent to the isoquant for that output level.*

This result will prove very useful. We already know that the slope of the isoquant at any point is equal to −MPN/MPL. And we know that the slope of the isocost line is equal to $-P_N/P_L$. Putting the two together, we know that when you have found the least-cost input combination for any output level,

$$-MPN/MPL = -P_N/P_L$$

or

$$MPN/MPL = P_N/P_L.$$

The term on the left-hand side is just the *MRTS* between land and labor. We conclude that:

> *When a firm is using the least-cost combination of land and labor for a particular output level, the firm's* MRTS *between the two inputs* (MPN/MPL) *will equal the ratio of input prices* (P_N/P_L).

In our example, $P_N/P_L = \$1{,}000/\$500 = 2$. This tells us that, at point *C*, the ratio $MPN/MPL = 2$ as well.

Finally, we can rearrange the equation $MPN/MPL = P_N/P_L$ to get:

$$MPN/P_N = MPL/P_L.$$

This form of the equation gives us another insight. It says that when you have found the least-cost input mix for any output level, the marginal product of land divided by the price of land will be equal to the marginal product of labor divided by the price of labor.

How can we interpret the marginal product of an input divided by its price? It gives us the additional output from spending one more *dollar* on the input. For example, if the (monthly) price of a hectare of land is $\$1{,}000$, and using one more hectare increases your output by 21 boxes $(MPN = 21)$, then an additional *dollar* spent on land will give you $1/1{,}000$ of a hectare, which, in turn, will increase your output by $(1/1{,}000) \times 21 = 21/1{,}000$ or $.021$ boxes. So, $MPN/P_N = 21/1{,}000$ is the additional output from one more dollar spent on land. As a kind of shorthand, we'll call MPN/P_N the "marginal product per dollar" of land.

Using this language, we can state our result this way:

> *When a firm is using the least-cost combination of land and labor for any output level, the marginal product per dollar of land* (MPN/P_N) *must equal the marginal product per dollar of labor* (MPL/P_L).

In the next section, where this result is stated more generally, you will learn the intuition behind it.

GENERALIZING TO THE CASE OF MORE THAN TWO INPUTS

When a firm can vary three or more inputs, we cannot illustrate isoquants and isocost lines on a two-dimensional graph. Nevertheless, the conclusions we reached for the two-input case can be generalized to any number of inputs.

Suppose a firm has several variable inputs, which we can label *A*, *B*, *C*, . . . , with marginal products *MPA*, *MPB*, *MPC*, . . . and input prices P_A, P_B, P_C, ... Then for any level of output, the least-cost combination of all of these inputs will always satisfy:

$$MPA/P_A = MPB/P_B = MPC/P_C = \dots$$

That is,

> *when a firm with many variable inputs has found its least-cost input mix, the marginal product per dollar of any input will be equal to the marginal product per dollar of any other input.*

How do we know this must always be true? First, remember that MPA/P_A tells us the additional output the firm will produce *per additional dollar spent on input A*. Next, suppose we have two inputs, *A* and *B*, for which MPA/P_A is *not* equal to MPB/P_B. Then we can show that the firm can always shift its spending from one input to another, lowering its cost while leaving its output unchanged.

Let's take a specific example. Suppose that $MPA/P_A = 2$, and $MPB/P_B = 3$. Then the firm can easily save money by shifting dollars away from input *A* toward input *B*. Each dollar shifted away from *A* causes output to decrease by 2 units, while each dollar shifted toward input *B* causes output to rise by 3 units. Thus, the firm could shift dollars away from input *A*, and use only *some* of those dollars to increase the amount of input *B*, and still keep its production unchanged.

The same holds for any other two inputs we might compare: Whenever the marginal product per dollar is different for any two inputs, the firm can always shift its spending from the input with the lower marginal product per dollar to the input with the higher marginal product per dollar, achieving lower total cost with no change in output.

How Firms Make Decisions: Profit Maximization

In March, 2005, Sony released its new hand-held game player: the Sony PSP. It packed remarkable screen resolution, player controllability and wireless internet connectivity into a 10-ounce unit slightly smaller than a video tape. Sony knew it would be a top seller.

But long before the product was launched, the company had to answer several important questions. Where should the new product be produced: Japan, the United States, or perhaps Hong Kong? How much should the company spend on advertising, and in which types of media? How many games should be available for the unit when it is released, and who should develop them? And finally, what price should the company charge for each unit, and what rate of production should it plan for?

These last decisions—what price to charge and how much to produce—are the focus of this chapter. In the end, Sony decided to charge $249.99 for each unit and planned to produce about 15 million of them for the first year. But why didn't it charge a lower price that would allow it to sell even more units? Or a higher price that would give it more profit on each unit sold?

Although this chapter concentrates on firms' decisions about price and output level, the tools you will learn apply to many other firm decisions. How much should MasterCard spend on advertising? How late should Starbucks keep its coffee shops open? How many copies should *Newsweek* give away free to potential subscribers? Should movie theaters offer Wednesday afternoon showings that only a few people attend? This chapter will help you understand how firms answer these sorts of questions.

THE GOAL OF PROFIT MAXIMIZATION

To analyze decision making at the firm, let's start with a very basic question: What is the firm trying to maximize?

Economists have given this question a lot of thought. Some firms—especially large ones—are complex institutions in which many different groups of people work together. A firm's owners will usually want the firm to earn as much profit as possible. But the workers and managers who actually run the firm may have other agendas. They may try to divert the firm away from profit maximization in order to benefit themselves. For now, let's assume that workers and managers are faithful servants of the firm's owners. That is,

> *we will view the firm as a single economic decision maker whose goal is to maximize its owners' profit.*

Why do we make this assumption? Because it has proven so *useful* in understanding how firms behave. True, this assumption leaves out the details of these other agendas that often are present in real-world firms. But remember that every economic model *abstracts* from reality. To stay simple and comprehensible, it leaves out many real-world details and includes only what is relevant for the purpose at hand. If the purpose is to explain conflict within the firm or deviations from profit-maximizing behavior, or even fraudulent accounting practices by management (such as the 2002 corporate scandals at Enron, WorldCom, and other firms), then the differing goals of managers and owners should be a central element of the model.

But when the purpose is to explain how firms decide what price to charge and how much to produce, or whether to temporarily shut down the firm or continue operating, or whether to enter a new market or permanently leave a current one, the assumption of profit maximization has proven to be sufficient. It explains what firms actually do with reasonable—and sometimes remarkable—accuracy.

Why? Part of the reason is that managers who deviate *too* much from profit maximizing for *too* long are typically replaced. The managers may be sacked either by the current dissatisfied owners or by other firms that acquire the underperforming firm.

Another reason is that so many managers are well trained in the tools of profit maximization. This is in contrast to our model of consumer behavior, in which we asserted that consumers act *as if* they are using the model's graphs and calculations—although we recognize that most consumers never actually do. The basic economic model of the firm's behavior, however, is well understood *and used* by most managers, who have often taken several economics courses as part of their management education. In fact, economists' thinking about firm behavior has so permeated the language and culture of modern business that it's sometimes hard to distinguish where theory ends and practice begins.

UNDERSTANDING PROFIT

Profit is defined as the firm's *sales revenue* minus its *costs of production*. There is widespread agreement over how to measure the firm's revenue—the flow of money into the firm. But there are two different conceptions of the firm's costs, and each of them leads to a different definition of profit.

TWO DEFINITIONS OF PROFIT

One conception of costs is the one used by accountants. With a few exceptions, accountants consider only *explicit* costs, where money is actually paid out.[1] If we deduct only the costs recognized by accountants, we get one definition of profit:

$$\textbf{Accounting profit} = \text{Total revenue} - \text{Accounting costs.}$$

Accounting profit Total revenue minus accounting costs.

But economics, as you have learned, has a much broader view of cost—*opportunity cost*. For the firm's owners, opportunity cost is the total value of *everything* sacrificed to produce output. This includes not only the explicit costs recognized by accountants—such as wages and salaries and outlays on raw materials—but also *implicit costs*, when something is given up but no money changes hands. For example, if an owner contributes his own time or money to the firm, there will be

---

[1] One exception is *depreciation*, a charge for the gradual wearing out of the firm's plant and equipment. Accountants include this as a cost even though no money is actually paid out.

foregone wages or foregone investment income—both implicit costs for the firm.

This broader conception of costs leads to a second definition of profit:

Economic profit = Total revenue − *All* costs of production

= Total revenue − (Explicit costs + Implicit costs)

Economic profit Total revenue minus all costs of production, explicit and implicit.

The difference between economic profit and accounting profit is an important one; when they are confused, some serious (and costly) mistakes can result. An example might help make the difference clear.

Suppose you own a firm that produces T-shirts and you want to calculate your profit over the year. Your bookkeeper provides you with the following information:

Total Revenue from Selling T-shirts		**$300,000**
Cost of raw materials	$ 80,000	
Wages and salaries	150,000	
Electricity and phone	20,000	
Advertising cost	40,000	
Total Explicit Cost		**290,000**
Accounting Profit		**$ 10,000**

From the looks of things, your firm is earning a profit, so you might feel pretty good. Indeed, if you look only at money coming in and money going out, you have indeed earned a profit: $10,000 for the year . . . an accounting profit.

But suppose that in order to start your business you invested $100,000 of your own money—money that *could* be earning $6,000 in interest if you sold the business and got it back. Also, you are using two extra rooms in your own house as a factory—rooms that *could* be rented out for $4,000 per year. Finally, you are managing the business full-time, without receiving a separate salary, and you could instead be working at a job earning $40,000 per year. All of these costs—the interest, rent, and salary you *could* have earned—are implicit costs that have not been taken into account by your bookkeeper. They are part of the opportunity cost of your firm because they are sacrifices you made to operate your business.

Now let's look at this business from the economist's perspective and calculate your *economic* profit.

Total Revenue from Selling T-shirts		**$300,000**
Cost of raw materials	$ 80,000	
Wages and salaries	150,000	
Electricity and phone	20,000	
Advertising cost	40,000	
Total Explicit Costs	**$290,000**	
Investment income foregone	$ 6,000	
Rent foregone	4,000	
Salary foregone	40,000	
Total Implicit Costs	**$ 50,000**	
Total Costs		**$340,000**
Economic Profit		**−$ 40,000**

From an economic point of view, your business is not profitable at all, but is actually losing $40,000 per year! But wait—how can we say that your firm is suffering a loss when it takes in more money than it pays out? Because, as we've seen, your *opportunity cost*—the value of what you are giving up to produce your output—includes more than just money costs. When *all* costs are considered—implicit as well as explicit—your total revenue is not sufficient to cover what you have sacrificed to run your business. You would do better by shifting your time, your money, and your spare room to some alternative use.

Which of the two definitions of profit is the correct one? Either one of them, depending on the reason for measuring it. For tax purposes, the government is interested in profits as measured by accountants. The government cares only about the money you've earned, not what you *could* have earned had you done something else with your money or your time.

However, for our purposes—understanding the behavior of firms—economic profit is clearly better. Should your T-shirt factory stay in business? Should it expand or contract in the long run? Will other firms be attracted to the T-shirt industry? It is economic profit that will help us answer these questions, because it is economic profit that you and other owners care about.

> *The proper measure of profit for understanding and predicting the behavior of firms is* economic profit. *Unlike accounting profit, economic profit recognizes all the opportunity costs of production—both explicit costs and implicit costs.*

WHY ARE THERE PROFITS?

When you look at the income received by households in the economy, you see a variety of payments. Those who provide firms with land receive *rent*—the payment for land. Those who provide labor receive a wage or salary. And those who lend firms money so they can purchase capital equipment receive interest. The firm's profit goes to its owners. But what do the owners of the firm provide that earns them this payment?

Economists view profit as a payment for two contributions of entrepreneurs, which are just as necessary for production as are land, labor, or machinery. These two contributions are *risk taking* and *innovation*.

Consider a restaurant that happens to be earning profit for its owner. The land, labor, and capital the restaurant uses to produce its meals did not simply come together magically. Someone—the owner—had to be willing to take the initiative to set up the business, and this individual assumed the risk that the business might fail and the initial investment be lost. Because the consequences of loss are so severe, the reward for success must be large in order to induce an entrepreneur to establish a business.

On a larger scale, Ted Turner risked hundreds of millions of dollars in the late 1970s when he created Cable News Network (CNN). Now that CNN has turned out to be so successful, it is easy to forget how risky the venture was at the outset. At the time, many respected financial analysts forecast that the project would fail and Turner would be driven into bankruptcy.

Profits are also a reward for *innovation*. Ted Turner was the first to create a 24-hour global news network, just as Pierre Omidyar—when he founded eBay in 1995—was the first to establish a commercially viable online auction market. These are obvious innovations.

But innovations can also be more subtle, and they are more common than you might think. When you pass by a successful laundromat, you may not give it a second thought. But someone, at some time, had to be the first one to realize, "I bet a laundromat in this neighborhood would do well"—an innovation. There can also be innovations in the production process, such as the improvement in mass production that made the disposable contact lens possible.

In almost any business, if you look closely, you will find that some sort of innovation was needed to get things started. Innovation, like taking on the risk of losing substantial wealth, makes an essential contribution to production. Profit is, in part, a reward to those who innovate.

THE FIRM'S CONSTRAINTS

If the firm were free to earn whatever level of profit it wanted, it would earn virtually infinite profit. This would make the owners very happy. Unfortunately for owners, though, the firm is not free to do this; it faces *constraints* on both its revenue and its costs.

THE DEMAND CONSTRAINT

The constraint on the firm's revenue arises from a familiar concept: the demand curve. This curve always tells us the quantity of a good buyers wish to buy at different prices. But which buyers? And from which firms are they buying? Depending on how we answer these questions, we might be talking about different types of demand curves.

Market demand curves—like the ones you studied in Chapters 3 and 4—tell us the quantity demanded by *all* consumers from *all* firms in a market. In this chapter, we look at another kind of demand curve:

Demand curve facing the firm A curve that indicates, for different prices, the quantity of output that customers will purchase from a particular firm.

> The **demand curve facing the firm** tells us, for different prices, the quantity of output that customers will choose to purchase from that firm.

Notice that this new demand curve—the demand curve facing the firm—refers to only *one* firm, and to *all buyers* who are potential customers of that firm.

Let's consider the demand curve faced by Ned, the owner and manager of Ned's Beds, a manufacturer of bed frames. Figure 1 lists the different prices that Ned could charge for each bed frame and the number of them (per day) he can sell at each price. The figure also shows a graph of the demand curve facing Ned's firm. For each price (on the vertical axis), it shows us the quantity of output the firm can sell (on the horizontal axis). Notice that, like the other types of demand curves we have studied, the demand curve facing the firm slopes downward. In order to sell more bed frames, Ned must lower his price.[2]

The definition of the demand curve facing the firm suggests that once it selects a price, the firm has also determined how much output it will sell. But, as you saw a few chapters ago, we can also flip the demand relationship around: Once the firm

---

[2] The downward-sloping demand curve tells us that Ned's Beds sells its output in an *imperfectly competitive market*, a market where the firm can *set* its price. Most firms operate in this type of market. If a manager thinks, "I'd like to sell more output, but then I'd have to lower my price, so let's see if it's worth it," we know he operates in an imperfectly competitive market. In a *perfectly competitive market*, by contrast, the firm would have to accept the market price as given. We assumed that markets were perfectly competitive in Chapter 3. In the next chapter, we'll examine perfect competition in more detail.

has selected an output level, it has also determined the maximum price it can charge. This leads to an alternative definition:

> *The demand curve facing the firm shows us the maximum price the firm can charge to sell any given amount of output.*

Looking at Figure 1 from this perspective, we see that the horizontal axis shows alternative levels of output and the vertical axis shows the price Ned should charge if he wishes to sell each quantity of output.

These two different ways of defining the firm's demand curve show us that it is, indeed, a constraint for the firm. The firm can freely determine *either* its price *or* its level of output. But once it makes the choice, the other variable is automatically determined by the firm's demand curve. Thus, the firm has only *one* choice to make. Selecting a particular price *implies* a level of output, and selecting an output level *implies* a particular price. Economists typically focus on the choice of output level, with the price implied as a consequence. We will follow that convention in this textbook.

Demand and Total Revenue

A firm's **total revenue** is the total inflow of receipts from selling output. Each time the firm chooses a level of output, it also determines its total revenue. Why? Because once we know the level of output, we also know the highest price the firm can charge. Total revenue, which is the number of units of output times the price per unit, follows automatically.

The third column in Figure 1 lists the total revenue of Ned's Beds. Each entry is calculated by multiplying the quantity of output (column 2) by the price per unit (column 1). For example, if Ned's firm produces 2 bed frames per day, he can charge

© PHILIP GOULD/CORBIS

Like many other firms, a furniture manufacturer must determine either its price for its products, or its level of output; once it chooses price, its level of output is determined, and vice versa.

Total revenue The total inflow of receipts from selling a given amount of output.

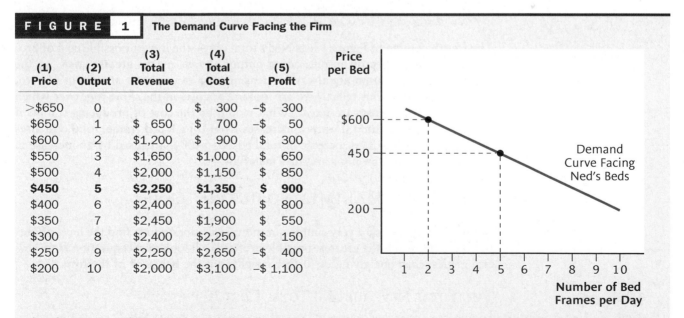

| **F I G U R E   1** | **The Demand Curve Facing the Firm** |

(1) Price	(2) Output	(3) Total Revenue	(4) Total Cost	(5) Profit
>$650	0	0	$ 300	−$ 300
$650	1	$ 650	$ 700	−$ 50
$600	2	$1,200	$ 900	$ 300
$550	3	$1,650	$1,000	$ 650
$500	4	$2,000	$1,150	$ 850
$450	**5**	**$2,250**	**$1,350**	**$ 900**
$400	6	$2,400	$1,600	$ 800
$350	7	$2,450	$1,900	$ 550
$300	8	$2,400	$2,250	$ 150
$250	9	$2,250	$2,650	−$ 400
$200	10	$2,000	$3,100	−$ 1,100

The table presents information about Ned's Beds. Data from the first two columns are plotted in the figure to show the demand curve facing the firm. At any point along that demand curve, the product of price and quantity equals total revenue, which is given in the third column of the table.

$600 for each of them, so total revenue will be 2 × $600 = $1,200. If Ned increases output to 3 units, he must lower the price to $550, earning a total revenue of 3 × $550 = $1,650. Because the firm's demand curve slopes downward, Ned must lower his price each time his output increases, or else he will not be able to sell all he produces. With more units of output, but each one selling at a lower price, total revenue could rise or fall. Scanning the total revenue column, we see that for this firm, total revenue first rises and then begins to fall. This will be discussed in greater detail later on.

THE COST CONSTRAINT

Every firm struggles to reduce costs, but there is a limit to how low costs can go. These limits impose a second constraint on the firm. Where do the limits come from? They come from concepts that you learned about in Chapter 6. Let's review them briefly.

First, the firm has a given production function, which is determined by its production technology. The production function tells us all the different ways in which the firm can produce any given level of output. In the long run, when all inputs are variable, the firm can use *any* method in its production function. In the short run, it is even more constrained: It can use only *some* of the methods in that production function, because one or more of its inputs are *fixed*.

Second, the firm must pay *prices* for each of the inputs that it uses, and we assume there is nothing the firm can do about those prices. Together, the production function and the prices of the inputs determine what it will cost to produce any given level of output. And once the firm chooses the *least cost* method available, it has driven the cost of producing that output level as low as it can go.

> *The firm uses its production function, and the prices it must pay for its inputs, to determine the least cost method of producing any given output level. Therefore, for any level of output the firm might want to produce, it must pay the cost of the "least cost method" of production.*

The fourth column of Figure 1 lists Ned's total cost—the lowest possible cost of producing each quantity of output. More output always means greater costs, so the numbers in this column are always increasing. For example, at an output of zero, total cost is $300. This tells us we are looking at costs in the short run, over which some of the firm's costs are *fixed*. (What would be the cost of producing 0 units if this were the long run?) If output increases from 0 to 1 bed frame, total cost rises from $300 to $700. This increase in total costs—$400—is caused by an increase in *variable* costs, such as labor and raw materials.

THE PROFIT-MAXIMIZING OUTPUT LEVEL

In this section, we ask a very simple question: How does a firm find the level of output that will earn it the greatest possible profit? We'll look at this question from several angles, each one giving us further insight into the behavior of the firm.

THE TOTAL REVENUE AND TOTAL COST APPROACH

At any given output level, the data in Figure 1 tell us (1) how much revenue the firm will earn and (2) its cost of production. We can then easily see how much profit the firm earns at each output level, which is the difference between total revenue (*TR*) and total cost (*TC*).

> *In the total revenue and total cost approach, we see the firm's profit as the difference between* TC *and* TR *at each output level. The firm chooses the output level where profit is greatest.*

Let's see how this works for Ned's Beds. Column 5 of Figure 1 lists total profit at each output level. If the firm were to produce no bed frames at all, total revenue (*TR*) would be 0, while total cost (*TC*) would be $300. Total profit would be $TR - TC = 0 - \$300 = -\$300$. We would say that the firm earns a profit of negative $300 or a **loss** of $300 per day. Producing one bed frame would raise total revenue to $650 and total cost to $700, for a loss of $50. Not until the firm produces 2 bed frames does total revenue rise above total cost and the firm begin to make a profit. At 2 bed frames per day, *TR* is $1,200 and *TC* is $900, so the firm earns a profit of $300. Remember that as long as we have been careful to include *all* costs in *TC*—implicit as well as explicit—the profits and losses we are calculating are *economic* profits and losses.

Loss The difference between total cost (*TC*) and total revenue (*TR*), when *TC* > *TR*.

In the total revenue and total cost approach, locating the profit-maximizing output level is straightforward: We just scan the numbers in the profit column until we find the largest value, $900, and the output level at which it is achieved, 5 units per day. We conclude that the profit-maximizing output for Ned's Beds is 5 units per day.

THE MARGINAL REVENUE AND MARGINAL COST APPROACH

There is another way to find the profit-maximizing level of output. This approach, which uses *marginal* concepts, gives us some powerful insights into the firm's decision-making process. It is also closer to the trial-and-error procedure at some firms, in which small experimental changes are made to determine the impact on profit.

Recall that *marginal* cost is the *change* in total cost per unit increase in output. Now, let's consider a similar concept for revenue.

> *Marginal revenue* (MR) *is the change in the firm's total revenue* (ΔTR) *divided by the change in its output* (ΔQ):
>
> $$MR = \Delta TR / \Delta Q$$
>
> MR *tells us how much revenue rises per unit increase in output.*

Marginal revenue The change in total revenue from producing one more unit of output.

Table 1 reproduces the *TR* and *TC* columns from Figure 1, but adds columns for marginal revenue and marginal cost. (In the table, output is always changing by one unit, so we can use Δ*TR* alone as our measure of marginal revenue.) For example, when output changes from 2 to 3 units, total revenue rises from $1,200 to $1,650. For this output change, *MR* = $450. As usual, marginals are placed *between* different output levels

Maximize Profit, Not Revenue You may be tempted to forget about profit and think that the firm should produce where its total revenue is maximized. As you can see in Figure 1 (column 3), total revenue is greatest when the firm produces 7 units per day, but at this output level, profit is not as high as it could be. The firm does better by producing only 5 units. True, revenue is lower at 5 units, but so are costs. It is the difference between revenue and cost that matters, not revenue alone.

DANGEROUS CURVES

TABLE 1	Output	Total Revenue	Marginal Revenue	Total Cost	Marginal Cost	Profit
More Data for Ned's Beds	0	0		$ 300		−$300
			$650		$400	
	1	$ 650		$ 700		−$ 50
			$550		$200	
	2	$1,200		$ 900		$300
			$450		$100	
	3	$1,650		$1,000		$650
			$350		$150	
	4	$2,000		$1,150		$850
			$250		$200	
	5	$2,250		$1,350		$900
			$150		$250	
	6	$2,400		$1,600		$800
			$ 50		$300	
	7	$2,450		$1,900		$550
			−$ 50		$350	
	8	$2,400		$2,250		$150
			−$150		$400	
	9	$2,250		$2,650		−$400
			−$250		$450	
	10	$2,000		$3,100		−$1,100

because they tell us what happens as output *changes* from one level to another.

There are two important things to notice about marginal revenue. First, when *MR* is *positive,* an increase in output causes total revenue to *rise.* In the table, *MR* is positive for all increases in output from 0 to 7 units. When *MR* is *negative,* an increase in output causes total revenue to *fall,* as occurs for all increases beyond 7 units.

The second thing to notice about *MR* is a bit more complicated: Each time output increases, *MR* is *smaller* than the price the firm charges at the new output level. For example, when output increases from 2 to 3 units, the firm's total revenue rises by $450—even though it sells the third unit for a price of $550. This may seem strange to you. After all, if the firm increases output from 2 to 3 units, and it gets $550 for the third unit of output, why doesn't its total revenue rise by $550?

The answer is found in the firm's downward-sloping demand curve, which tells us that to sell more output, the firm must cut its price. Look back at Figure 1 of this chapter. When output increases from 2 to 3 units, the firm must lower its price from $600 to $550. Moreover, the new price of $550 will apply to *all three* units the firm sells.[3] This means it *gains* some revenue—$550—by selling that third unit. But it also *loses* some revenue—$100—by having to lower the price by $50 on each of the two units of output it could have otherwise sold at $600. Marginal revenue will always equal the *difference* between this gain and loss in revenue—in this case, $550 − $100 = $450.

---

[3] Some firms can charge two or more different prices for the same product. We'll explore some examples in Chapter 9.

> *When a firm faces a downward-sloping demand curve, each increase in output causes a revenue gain, from selling additional output at the new price, and a revenue loss, from having to lower the price on all previous units of output. Marginal revenue is therefore less than the price of the last unit of output.[4]*

Using *MR* and *MC* to Maximize Profits

Now we'll see how marginal revenue, together with marginal cost, can be used to find the profit-maximizing output level. The logic behind the *MC* and *MR* approach is this:

> *An increase in output will always raise profit as long as marginal revenue is greater than marginal cost (MR > MC).*

Notice the word *always*. Let's see why this rather sweeping statement must be true. Table 1 tells us that when output rises from 2 to 3 units, *MR* is $450, while *MC* is $100. This change in output causes both total revenue and total cost to rise, but it causes revenue to rise by *more* than cost ($450 > $100). As a result, profit must increase. Indeed, looking at the profit column, we see that increasing output from 2 to 3 units *does* cause profit to increase, from $300 to $650.[5]

The converse of this statement is also true:

> *An increase in output will always lower profit whenever marginal revenue is less than marginal cost (MR < MC).*

For example, when output rises from 5 to 6 units, *MR* is $150, while *MC* is $250. For this change in output, both total revenue and total cost rise, but cost rises *more*, so profit must go down. In Table 1, you can see that this change in output does indeed cause profit to decline, from $900 to $800.

These insights about *MR* and *MC* lead us to the following simple guideline the firm should use to find its profit-maximizing level of output:

> *To find the profit-maximizing output level, the firm should increase output whenever* MR > MC, *and decrease output when* MR < MC.

Let's apply this rule to Ned's Beds. In Table 1 we see that when moving from 0 to 1 unit of output, *MR* is $650, while *MC* is only $400. Since *MR* is larger than *MC*, making this move will increase profit. Thus, if the firm is producing 0 beds, it should always increase to 1 bed. Should it stop there? Let's see. If it moves from 1

---

[4] There is a connection between the behavior of total revenue, marginal revenue, and the price elasticity of demand you learned about in Chapter 4. When demand is elastic, a fall in price—and the associated rise in quantity—causes total revenue to rise. In Table 1, total revenue rises (marginal revenue is positive) for all changes in output between 0 and 7 units. Therefore, we know that demand is elastic along the interval of the demand curve between 0 and 7 units. Similarly, demand is *inelastic* along the interval of the demand curve between 7 and 10 units.

[5] You may have noticed that the rise in profit ($350) is equal to the difference between *MR* and *MC* in this example. This is no accident. *MR* tells us the *rise* in revenue; *MC* tells us the *rise* in cost. The difference between them will always be the *rise* in profit.

to 2 beds, *MR* is $550, while *MC* is only $200. Once again, *MR > MC,* so the firm should increase to 2 beds. You can verify from the table that if the firm finds itself producing 0, 1, 2, 3, or 4 beds, *MR > MC* for an increase of 1 unit, so it will always make greater profit by increasing production.

Until, that is, output reaches 5 beds. At this point, the picture changes: From 5 to 6 beds, *MR* is $150, while *MC* is $250. For this move, *MR < MC,* so profits would decrease. Thus, if the firm is producing 5 beds, it should *not* increase to 6. The same is true at every other output level beyond 5 units: The firm should *not* raise its output, since *MR < MC* for each increase. We conclude that Ned maximizes his profit by producing 5 beds per day—the same answer we got using the *TR* and *TC* approach earlier.[6]

PROFIT MAXIMIZATION USING GRAPHS

Both approaches to maximizing profit (using totals or using marginals) can be seen even more clearly when we use graphs. In Figure 2(a) and (b), the data from Table 1 have been plotted—the *TC* and *TR* curves in the upper panel, and the *MC* and *MR* curves in the lower one.

The marginal revenue curve has an important relationship to the total revenue curve. As you can see in Figure 2(a), total revenue (*TR*) is plotted on the vertical axis, and quantity (*Q*) on the horizontal axis, so the slope along any interval is just $\Delta TR / \Delta Q$. But this is exactly the definition of marginal revenue.

> *The marginal revenue for any change in output is equal to the* slope *of the total revenue curve along that interval.*

Thus, as long as the *MR* curve lies above the horizontal axis (*MR > 0*), *TR* must be increasing and the *TR* curve must slope upward. In the figure, *MR > 0*, and the *TR* curve slopes upward from zero to 7 units. When the *MR* curve dips below the horizontal axis (*MR < 0*), *TR* is decreasing, so the *TR* curve begins to slope downward. In the figure, this occurs beyond 7 units of output. As output increases in Figure 2, *MR* is first positive and then turns negative, so the *TR* curve will first *rise* and then *fall.*

The *TR* and *TC* Approach Using Graphs

Now let's see how we can use the *TC* and *TR* curves to guide the firm to its profit-maximizing output level. We know that the firm earns a profit at any output level where *TR > TC*—where the *TR* curve lies *above* the *TC* curve. In Figure 2(a), you can see that all output levels from 2 through 8 units are profitable for the firm. The *amount* of profit is simply the *vertical distance* between the *TR* and *TC* curves, whenever the *TR* curve lies above the *TC* curve. Since the firm cannot sell part of a bed frame, it must choose whole numbers for its output, so the profit-maximizing output level is simply the whole-number quantity at which this vertical distance is greatest—5 units of output. Of course, the *TR* and *TC* curves in Figure 2 were plotted from the data in Table 1, so we should not be surprised to find the same profit-maximizing output level—5 units—that we found before when using the table.

---

[6] It sometimes happens that *MR* is precisely equal to *MC* for some change in output, although this does not occur in Table 1. In this case, increasing output would cause *both* cost and revenue to rise by equal amounts, so there would be *no* change in profit. The firm should not care whether it makes this change in output or not.

(a)

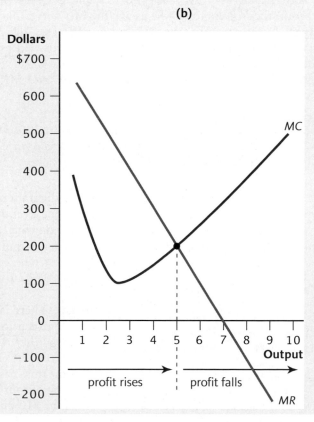

(b)

FIGURE 2

Profit Maximization

Panel (a) shows the firm's total revenue (TR) and total cost (TC) curves. Profit is the vertical distance between the two curves at any level of output. Profit is maximized when that vertical distance is greatest—at 5 units of output. Panel (b) shows the firm's marginal revenue (MR) and marginal cost (MC) curves. (As long as MR lies above the horizontal axis, the TR curve slopes upward.) Profit is maximized at the level of output closest to where the two curves cross—at 5 units of output.

We can sum up our graphical rule for using the *TR* and *TC* curves this way:

> *To maximize profit, the firm should produce the quantity of output where the vertical distance between the* TR *and* TC *curves is greatest and the* TR *curve lies above the* TC *curve.*

The *MR* and *MC* Approach Using Graphs

Figure 2 also illustrates the *MR* and *MC* approach to maximizing profits. As usual, the marginal data in panel (b) are plotted *between* output levels, since they tell us what happens as output changes from one level to another.

In the diagram, as long as output is less than 5 units, the *MR* curve lies above the *MC* curve (*MR* > *MC*), so the firm should produce more. For example, if we consider the move from 4 to 5 units, we compare the *MR* and *MC* curves at the midpoint between 4 and 5. Here, the *MR* curve lies above the *MC* curve, so increasing output from 4 to 5 will increase profit.

But now suppose the firm is producing 5 units and considering a move to 6. At the midpoint between 5 and 6 units, the *MR* curve has already crossed the *MC* curve, and now it lies *below* the *MC* curve. For this move, *MR* < *MC*, so raising output would *decrease* the firm's profit. The same is true for every increase in output beyond 5 units: The *MR* curve always lies below the *MC* curve, so the firm will decrease its profits by increasing output. Once again, we find that the profit-maximizing output level for the firm is 5 units.

Notice that the profit-maximizing output level—5 units—is the level closest to where the *MC* and *MR* curves cross. This is no accident. For each change in output that *increases* profit, the *MR* curve will lie above the *MC* curve. The first time that an output change *decreases* profit, the *MR* curve will cross the *MC* curve and dip below it. Thus, the *MC* and *MR* curves will always cross closest to the profit-maximizing output level.

With this graphical insight, we can summarize the *MC* and *MR* approach this way:

> *To maximize profit, the firm should produce the quantity of output closest to the point where* MC = MR—*that is, the quantity of output at which the* MC *and* MR *curves intersect.*

This rule is very useful, since it allows us to look at a diagram of *MC* and *MR* curves and *immediately* identify the profit-maximizing output level. In this text, you will often see this rule. When you read, "The profit-maximizing output level is where *MC* equals *MR*," translate to "The profit-maximizing output level is closest to the point where the *MC* curve crosses the *MR* curve."

A Proviso. There is, however, one important exception to this rule. Sometimes the *MC* and *MR* curves cross at two different points. In this case, the profit-maximizing output level is the one at which the *MC* curve crosses the *MR* curve *from below*.

DANGEROUS CURVES

Misusing the Gap Between *MR* and *MC* A common error is to think a firm should produce the level of output at which the difference between *MR* and *MC* is as large as possible, like 2 or 3 units of output in Figure 2. Let's see why this is wrong. If the firm produces 2 or 3 units, it would leave many profitable increases in output unexploited—increases where *MR* > *MC*. As long as *MR* is even a tiny bit larger than *MC*, it pays to increase output, since doing so will add more to revenue than to cost. The firm should be satisfied only when the difference between *MR* and *MC* is as *small* as possible, not as *large* as possible.

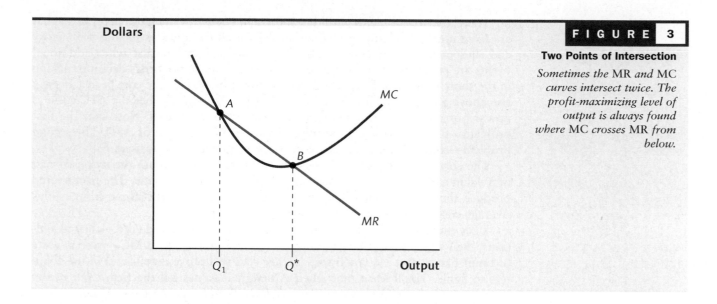

FIGURE 3

Two Points of Intersection

Sometimes the MR *and* MC *curves intersect twice. The profit-maximizing level of output is always found where* MC *crosses* MR *from below.*

Figure 3 shows why. At point *A*, the *MC* curve crosses the *MR* curve from *above*. Our rule tells us that the output level at this point, Q_1, is *not* profit maximizing. Why not? Because at output levels lower than Q_1, $MC > MR$, so profit *falls* as output increases toward Q_1. Also, profit *rises* as output increases *beyond* Q_1, since $MR > MC$ for these moves. Since it never pays to increase *to* Q_1, and profit rises when increasing *from* Q_1, we know that Q_1 cannot possibly maximize the firm's profit.

But now look at point *B*, where the *MC* curve crosses the *MR* curve from below. You can see that when we are at an output level lower than Q^*, it always pays to increase output, since $MR > MC$ for these moves. You can also see that, once we have arrived at Q^*, further increases will reduce profit, since $MC > MR$. Q^* is thus the profit-maximizing output level for this firm—the output level at which the *MC* curve crosses the *MR* curve *from below*.

WHAT ABOUT AVERAGE COSTS?

You may have noticed that this chapter has discussed *most* of the cost concepts introduced in Chapter 6. But it has not yet referred to *average* cost. There is a good reason for this. We have been concerned about how much the firm should produce if it wishes to earn the greatest possible level of profit. To achieve this goal, the firm should produce more output whenever doing so *increases* profit, and it needs to know only *marginal* cost and *marginal* revenue for this purpose. The different types of average cost (*ATC, AVC,* and *AFC*) are simply irrelevant. Indeed, a common error—sometimes made even by business managers—is to use *average* cost in place of *marginal* cost in making decisions.

For example, suppose a yacht maker wants to know how much his total cost will rise in the short run if he produces another unit of output. It is tempting—*but wrong*—for the yacht maker to reason this way: "My cost per unit (*ATC*) is currently $50,000 per yacht. Therefore, if I increase production by 1 unit, my total cost will rise by $50,000; if I increase production by 2 units, my total cost will rise by $100,000, and so on."

There are two problems with this approach. First, *ATC* includes many costs that are *fixed* in the short run—including the cost of all fixed inputs such as the factory and equipment and the design staff. These costs will *not* increase when additional yachts are produced, and they are therefore irrelevant to the firm's decision making in the short run. Second, *ATC changes* as output increases. The cost per yacht may rise above $50,000 or fall below $50,000, depending on whether the *ATC* curve is upward or downward sloping at the current production level. Note that the first problem—fixed costs—could be solved by using *AVC* instead of *ATC*. The second problem—changes in average cost—remains even when *AVC* is used.

The correct approach, as we've seen in this chapter, is to use the *marginal cost* of a yacht and to consider increases in output one unit at a time. The firm should produce the output level where its *MC* curve crosses its *MR* curve from below. Average cost doesn't help at all; it only confuses the issue.

Does this mean that all of your efforts to master *ATC* and *AVC*—their definitions, their relationship to each other, and their relationship to *MC*—were a waste of time? Far from it. As you'll see, average cost will prove *very* useful in the chapters to come. You'll learn that whereas marginal values tell the firm *what* to do, averages can tell the firm *how well* it has done. But average cost should *not* be used in place of marginal cost as a basis for decisions.

THE MARGINAL APPROACH TO PROFIT

The *MC* and *MR* approach for finding the profit-maximizing output level is actually a very specific application of a more general principle:

> The **marginal approach to profit** states that a firm should take any action that adds more to its revenue than to its costs.

Marginal approach to profit
A firm maximizes its profit by taking any action that adds more to its revenue than to its cost.

In this chapter, the action being considered is whether to increase output by 1 unit. We've learned that the firm should take this action whenever *MR* > *MC*.

But the same logic can be applied to *any other decision* facing the firm. Should a restaurant owner take out an ad in the local newspaper? Should a convenience store that currently closes at midnight stay open 24 hours instead? Should a private kindergarten hire another teacher? Should an inventor pay to produce an infomercial for her new gizmo? Should a bank install another ATM? The answer to all of these questions is yes—*if* the action would add more to revenue than to costs. In future chapters, we'll be using the marginal approach to profit to analyze some other types of firm decisions.

DEALING WITH LOSSES

So far, we have dealt only with the pleasant case of profitable firms and how they select their profit-maximizing output level. But what about a firm that cannot earn a positive profit at *any* output level? What should it do? The answer depends on what time horizon we are looking at.

THE SHORT RUN AND THE SHUTDOWN RULE

In the short run, the firm must pay for its fixed inputs, because there is not enough time to sell them or get out of lease and rental agreements. But the firm can *still* make decisions about production. And one of its options is to *shut down*—to stop producing output, at least temporarily.

At first glance, you might think that a loss-making firm should always shut down its operation in the short run. After all, why keep producing if you are not making any profit? In fact, it makes sense for some unprofitable firms to continue operating.

Imagine a firm with the *TC* and *TR* curves shown in the upper panel of Figure 4 (ignore the *TVC* curve for now). No matter what output level the firm produces, the *TC* curve lies above the *TR* curve, so it will suffer a loss—a negative profit. For this firm, the goal is still profit maximization. But now, the highest profit will be the one with the *least negative value*. In other words, profit maximization becomes *loss minimization*.

If the firm keeps producing, then the smallest possible loss is at an output level of Q^*, where the distance between the *TC* and *TR* curves is smallest. Q^* is also the output level we would find by using our marginal approach to profit (increasing output whenever that adds more to revenue than to costs). This is why, in the lower panel of Figure 4, the *MC* and *MR* curves must intersect at (or very close to) Q^*.

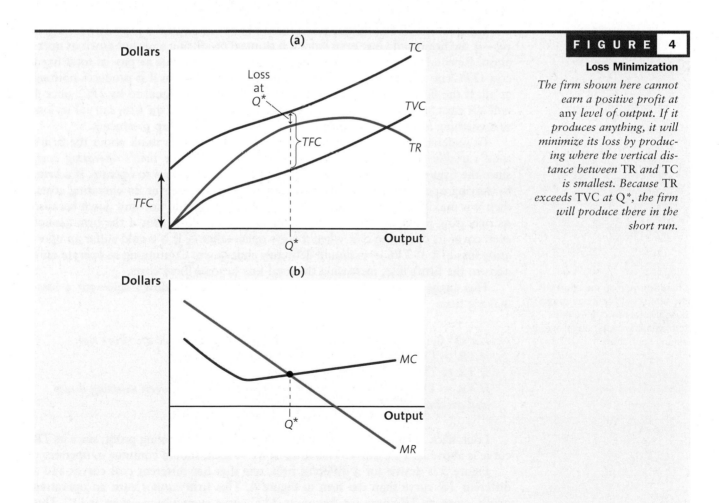

FIGURE 4

Loss Minimization

The firm shown here cannot earn a positive profit at any level of output. If it produces anything, it will minimize its loss by producing where the vertical distance between TR *and* TC *is smallest. Because* TR *exceeds* TVC *at* Q^**, the firm will produce there in the short run.*

FIGURE 5

Shut Down

At Q*, this firm's total variable cost exceeds its total revenue. The best policy is to shut down, produce nothing, and suffer a loss equal to TFC in the short run.

The question is: Should this firm produce at Q^* and suffer a loss? The answer is yes—*if* the firm would lose even *more* if it stopped producing and shut down its operation. Remember that, in the short run, a firm must continue to pay its total fixed cost (*TFC*) no matter what level of output it produces—even if it produces nothing at all. If the firm shuts down, it will therefore have a loss equal to its *TFC*, since it will not earn any revenue. But if, by producing some output, the firm can cut its loss to something *less* than *TFC*, then it should stay open and keep producing.

To understand the shutdown decision more clearly, let's think about the firm's total variable costs. Business managers often call *TVC* the firm's *operating cost*, since the firm only pays these variable costs when it continues to operate. If a firm, by staying open, can earn *more* than enough revenue to cover its operating costs, then it is making an *operating profit* (*TR > TVC*). It should not shut down because its operating profit can be used to help pay its fixed costs. But if the firm cannot even cover its operating cost when it stays open—that is, if it would suffer an *operating loss* (*TR < TVC*)—it should definitely shut down. Continuing to operate only *adds* to the firm's loss, increasing the total loss beyond fixed costs.

This suggests the following guideline—called the **shutdown rule**—for a loss-making firm:

Shutdown rule In the short run, the firm should continue to produce if total revenue exceeds total variable costs; otherwise, it should shut down.

> *Let Q^* be the output level at which* MR = MC. *Then, in the short run:*
> *If* TR > TVC *at Q^*, the firm should keep producing.*
> *If* TR < TVC *at Q^*, the firm should shut down.*
> *If* TR = TVC *at Q^*, the firm should be indifferent between shutting down and producing.*

Look back at Figure 4. At Q^*, the firm is making an operating profit, since its *TR* curve is above its *TVC* curve. This firm, as we've seen, should continue to operate.

Figure 5 is drawn for a different firm, one that has different cost curves and a different *TR* curve than the firm in Figure 4. This firm *cannot* earn an operating profit, since its *TR* curve lies below its *TVC* curve everywhere—even at Q^*. This firm should shut down.

The shutdown rule is a powerful predictor of firms' decisions to stay open or cease production in the short run. It tells us, for example, why some seasonal businesses—such as ice cream shops in summer resort areas—shut down in the winter, when *TR* drops so low that it becomes smaller than *TVC*. And it tells us why producers of steel, automobiles, agricultural goods, and television sets will often keep producing output for some time even when they are losing money.

THE LONG RUN: THE EXIT DECISION

The shutdown rule applies only in the short run, a time horizon too short for the firm to escape its commitments to pay for fixed inputs such as plant and equipment. In fact, we only use the term *shut down* when referring to the short run.

But a firm can also decide to stop producing in the long run. In that case, we say the firm has decided to **exit** the industry.

The long-run decision to exit is different than the short-run decision to shut down. That's because in the long run, there *are* no fixed costs, since all inputs can be varied. Therefore, a firm that exits, by reducing all of its inputs to zero, will have *zero* costs (an option not available in the short run). And since exit also means zero revenue, a firm that exits will earn zero profit. When would a firm decide to exit and earn zero profit? When its only other alternative is to earn *negative* profit.

Exit A permanent cessation of production when a firm leaves an industry.

> *A firm should exit the industry in the long run when—at its best possible output level—it has any loss at all.*

We will look more closely at the exit decision and other long-run considerations in the next chapter.

© GEORGE HALL/CORBIS

USING THE THEORY

Getting It Wrong and Getting It Right

Today, almost all managers have a good grasp of the concepts you've learned in this chapter, largely because microeconomics has become an important part of every business school curriculum. But if we go back a few decades—to when fewer managers had business degrees—we can find two examples of how management's failure to understand the basic theory of the firm led to serious errors. In one case, ignorance of the theory caused a large bank to go bankrupt; in the other, an airline was able to outperform its competitors because *they* remained ignorant of the theory. Even though these examples are old ones, they are classic.

GETTING IT WRONG: THE FAILURE OF FRANKLIN NATIONAL BANK

In the mid-1970s, Franklin National Bank—one of the largest banks in the United States—went bankrupt. The bank's management had made several errors, but we will focus on the most serious one.

First, a little background. A bank is very much like any other business firm: It produces output (in this case a service, making loans) using a variety of inputs (including the funds it lends out). The price of the bank's output is the interest rate it charges to borrowers. For example, with a 5 percent interest rate, the price of each dollar in loans is 5 cents per year.

Unfortunately for banks, they must also *pay* for the money they lend out. The largest source of funds is customer deposits, for which the bank must pay interest. If a bank wants to lend out *more* than its customers have deposited, it can obtain funds from a second source, the *federal funds market,* where banks lend money to one another. To borrow money in this market, the bank will usually have to pay a higher interest rate than it pays on customer deposits.

In mid-1974, John Sadlik, Franklin's chief financial officer, asked his staff to compute the average cost to the bank of a dollar in loanable funds. At the time, Franklin's funds came from three sources, each with its own associated interest cost:

Source	Interest Cost
Checking Accounts	2.25 percent
Savings Accounts	4 percent
Borrowed Funds	9–11 percent

What do these numbers tell us? First, each dollar deposited in a Franklin *checking* account cost the bank 2.25 cents per year,[7] while each dollar in a *savings* account cost Franklin 4 cents. Also, Franklin, like other banks at the time, had to pay between 9 and 11 cents on each dollar borrowed in the federal funds market. When Franklin's accountants were asked to figure out the average cost of a dollar in loans, they divided the total cost of funds by the number of dollars they had lent out. The number they came up with was 7 cents.

This average cost of 7 cents per dollar is an interesting number, but, as we know, it should have *no relevance to a profit-maximizing firm's decisions*. And this is where Franklin went wrong. At the time, all banks, including Franklin, were charging interest rates of 9 to 9.5 percent to their best customers. But Sadlik decided that since money was costing an *average* of 7 cents per dollar, the bank could make a tidy profit by lending money at 8 percent—earning 8 cents per dollar. Accordingly, he ordered his loan officers to approve any loan that could be made to a reputable borrower at 8 percent interest. Needless to say, with other banks continuing to charge 9 percent or more, Franklin National Bank became a very popular place from which to borrow money.

But where did Franklin get the additional funds it was lending out? That was a problem for the managers in *another* department at Franklin, who were responsible for *obtaining* funds. It was not easy to attract additional checking and savings account deposits, since, in the 1970s, the interest rate banks could pay was regulated by the government. That left only one alternative: the federal funds market. And this is exactly where Franklin went to obtain the funds pouring out of its lending department. Of course, these funds were borrowed not at 7 percent, the average cost of funds, but at 9 to 11 percent, the cost of borrowing in the federal funds market.

To understand Franklin's error, let's look again at the average cost figure it was using. This figure included an irrelevant cost: the cost of funds obtained from customer deposits. This cost was irrelevant to the bank's lending decisions, since *additional* loans

---

[7] This cost was not actually a direct interest payment to depositors, since in the 1970s banks generally did not pay interest on checking accounts. But banks *did* provide free services such as check clearing, monthly statements, free coffee, and even gifts to their checking account depositors, and the cost of these freebies was computed to be 2.25 cents per dollar of deposits.

would not come from these deposits, but rather from the more expensive federal funds market. Further, this average figure was doomed to rise as Franklin expanded its loans. How do we know this? The *marginal* cost of an additional dollar of loans—9 to 11 cents per dollar—was greater than the *average* cost—7 cents. As you know, whenever the marginal is greater than the average, it pulls the average up. Thus, Franklin was basing its decisions on an average cost figure that not only included irrelevant sunk costs but was bound to increase as its lending expanded.

More directly, we can see Franklin's error through the lens of the marginal approach. The *marginal revenue* of each additional dollar lent out at 8 percent was 8 cents, while the *marginal cost* of each additional dollar—since it came from the federal funds market—was 9 to 11 cents. *MC* was greater than *MR*, so Franklin was actually losing money each time its loan officers approved another loan! Not surprisingly, these loans—which never should have been made—caused Franklin's profits to *decrease*, and within a year the bank had lost hundreds of millions of dollars. This, together with other management errors, caused the bank to fail.

GETTING IT RIGHT: CONTINENTAL AIRLINES

In the early 1960s, Continental Airlines was doing something that seemed like a horrible mistake. All other airlines at the time were following a simple rule: They would offer a flight only if, on average, 65 percent of the seats could be filled with paying passengers, since only then could the flight break even. Continental, however, was flying jets filled to just 50 percent of capacity and was actually expanding flights on many routes. When word of Continental's policy leaked out, its stockholders were angry, and managers at competing airlines smiled knowingly, waiting for Continental to fail. Yet Continental's profits—already higher than the industry average—continued to grow. What was going on?

There *was*, indeed, a serious mistake being made, but by the *other* airlines, not Continental. This mistake should by now be familiar to you: using average cost instead of marginal cost to make decisions. The "65 percent of capacity" rule used throughout the industry was derived more or less as follows: The total cost of the airline for the year (*TC*) was divided by the number of flights during the year (*Q*) to obtain the average cost of a flight (*TC/Q = ATC*). For the typical flight, this came to about $4,000. Since a jet had to be 65 percent full in order to earn ticket sales of $4,000, the industry regarded any flight that repeatedly took off with less than 65 percent as a money loser and canceled it.

As usual, there are two problems with using *ATC* in this way. First, an airline's average cost per flight includes many costs that are irrelevant to the decision to add or subtract a flight. These *sunk costs* include the cost of running the reservations system, paying interest on the firm's debt, and fixed fees for landing rights at airports—none of which would change if the firm added or subtracted a flight. Also, average cost ordinarily *changes* as output changes, so it is wrong to assume it is constant in decisions about *changing* output.

Continental's management, led by its vice-president of operations, had decided to try the marginal approach to profit. Whenever a new flight was being considered, every department within the company was asked to determine the *additional* cost they would have to bear. Of course, the only additional costs were for additional *variable* inputs, such as additional flight attendants, ground crew personnel, in-flight meals, and jet fuel. These additional costs came to only about $2,000 per flight. Thus, the *marginal* cost of an additional flight—$2,000—was significantly less than the marginal revenue of a flight filled to 65 percent of capacity—$4,000. The marginal approach to profits tells us that when $MR > MC$, output should be increased, which is just what Continental was doing. Indeed, Continental correctly drew the conclusion that the marginal revenue of a flight filled at even 50 percent of capacity—$3,000—was *still* greater than its marginal cost, and so offering the flight would increase profit. This is why Continental was expanding routes even when it could fill only 50 percent of its seats.

In the early 1960s, Continental was able to outperform its competitors by using a secret—the marginal approach to profits. Today, of course, the secret is out, and all airlines use the marginal approach when deciding which flights to offer.[8]

Summary

In economics, we view the firm as a single economic decision maker with the goal of maximizing the owners' profit. Economic profit is total revenue minus *all* costs of production, explicit and implicit. In their pursuit of maximum profit, firms face two constraints. One is embodied in the demand curve the firm faces; it indicates the maximum price the firm can charge to sell any amount of output. This constraint determines the firm's revenue at each level of production. The other constraint is imposed by costs: More output always means greater costs. In choosing the profit-maximizing output, the firm must consider both revenues and costs.

One approach to choosing the optimal level of output is to measure profit as the difference between total revenue and total cost at each level of output, and then select the output level at which profit is greatest. An alternate approach uses *marginal revenue* (MR), the change in total revenue from producing one more unit of output, and *marginal cost* (MC), the change in total cost from producing one more unit. The firm should increase output whenever $MR > MC$, and lower output when $MR < MC$. The profit-maximizing output level is the one closest to the point where $MR = MC$.

If profit is negative, but total revenue exceeds total variable cost, the firm should continue producing in the short run. Otherwise, it should shut down and suffer a loss equal to its fixed cost. A firm with negative profit in the long run should exit the market.

Problem Set   *Answers to even-numbered Questions and Problems can be found on the text Web site at www.thomsonedu.com/economics/hall.*

1. You have a part-time work/study job at the library that pays $10 per hour, 3 hours per day on Saturdays and Sundays. Some friends want you to join them on a weekend ski trip leaving Friday night and returning Monday morning. They estimate your share of the gas, motel, lift tickets, and other expenses to be around $30. What is your total cost (considering both explicit and implicit costs) for the trip?

2. Until recently, you worked for a software development firm at a yearly salary of $35,000. Now, you decide to open your own business. You quit your job, cash in a $10,000 savings account (which pays 5 percent interest), and use the money to buy computer hardware to use in your business. You also convert a basement apartment in your house, which you have been renting for $250 a month, into a

workspace for your new software firm.

You lease some office equipment for $3,600 a year and hire two part-time programmers, whose combined salary is $25,000 a year. You also figure it costs around $50 a month to provide heat and light for your new office.

a. What are the total annual explicit costs of your new business?

b. What are the total annual implicit costs?

c. At the end of your first year, your accountant cheerily informs you that your total sales for the year amounted to $55,000. She congratulates you on a profitable year. Are her congratulations warranted? Why or why not?

3. The following data are price/quantity/cost combinations for Titan Industry's mainframe computer division:

---

[8] For more information about Continental's strategy, see "Airline Takes the Marginal Bone," *Business Week*, April 20, 1963, pp. 111–114.

Quantity	Price per Unit	Total Cost of Production
0	above $225,000	$200,000
1	$225,000	$250,000
2	$175,000	$275,000
3	$150,000	$325,000
4	$125,000	$400,000
5	$90,000	$500,000

a. What is the marginal revenue if output rises from 2 to 3 units? (Hint: Calculate total revenue at each output level first.) What is the marginal cost if output rises from 4 to 5 units?

b. What quantity should Titan produce to maximize total revenue? Total profit?

c. What is Titan's fixed cost? How do Titan's marginal costs behave as output increases?

4. Each entry in this table shows marginal revenue and marginal cost when a firm increases output to the given quantity:

Quantity	MR	MC
10		
	30	25
11		
	29	23
12		
	27	22
13		
	25	25
14		
	23	27
15		
	21	29
16		
	19	31
17		

What is the profit-maximizing level of output?

5. The following tables give information about demand and total cost for two firms. In the short run, how much should each produce?

Firm A

Quantity	Price	Total Cost
0	above $125	$250
1	$125	$400
2	$100	$500
3	$75	$550
4	$50	$600
5	$25	$700

Firm B

Quantity	Price	Total Cost
0	above $500	$ 500
1	$500	$ 700
2	$400	$ 900
3	$300	$1,100
4	$200	$1,300
5	$100	$1,500

6. At its best possible output level, a firm has total revenue of $3,500 per day and total cost of $7,000 per day. What should this firm do in the short run if:
a. the firm has total *fixed* costs of $3,000 per day?
b. the firm has total *variable* costs of $3,000 per day?

7. Suppose you own a restaurant that serves only dinner. You are trying to decide whether or not to rent out your dining room and kitchen during mornings to another firm, The Breakfast Club, Inc., that will serve only breakfast. Your restaurant currently has the following monthly costs:

Rent on building:	$2,000
Electricity:	$1,000
Wages and salaries:	$15,000
Advertising:	$2,000
Purchases of food and supplies:	$8,000
Your foregone labor income:	$4,000
Your foregone interest:	$1,000

a. Which of your current costs are implicit, and which are explicit?

b. Suppose The Breakfast Club, Inc., offers to pay $800 per month to use the building. They promise to use only their own food, and also to leave the place spotless when they leave each day. If you believe them, should you rent out your restaurant to them? Or does it depend? Explain.

8. Suppose that, due to a dramatic rise in real estate taxes, Ned's Beds' total fixed cost rises from $300 to $1,300 per day. Use the data of Table 1 to answer the following:
a. What does the tax hike do to Ned's *MC* and *MR* curves?
b. In the short run, how many beds should Ned produce after the rise in taxes?
c. In the long run, how many beds should Ned produce after the rise in taxes?

9. Suppose Ned's Beds does *not* have to lower the price in order to sell more beds. Specifically, suppose Ned can sell all the beds he wants at a price of $275 per bed.
a. What will Ned's *MR* curve look like? (Hint: How much will his revenue rise for each additional bed he sells?)
b. In Table 1, how would you change the numbers in the marginal revenue column to reflect the constant price for beds?
c. Using the marginal cost and *new* marginal revenue numbers in Table 1, find the number of beds Ned should sell.

More Challenging

10. A firm's *marginal profit* can be defined as the change in its profit when output increases by one unit.
    a.   Compute the marginal profit for each change in Ned's Beds' output in Table 1.
    b.   State a complete rule for finding the profit-maximizing output level in terms of marginal profit.
11. Howell Industries specializes in precision plastics. Their latest invention promises to revolutionize the electronics industry, and they have already made and sold 75 of the miracle devices. They have estimated average costs as given in the following table:

Unit	ATC
74	$10,000
75	$12,000
76	$14,000

Backus Electronics has just offered Howell $150,000 if it will produce the 76th unit. Should Howell accept the offer and manufacture the additional device?

Perfect Competition

When we observe buyers and sellers in action, we see that different goods and services are sold in vastly different ways. Consider advertising. Every day, we are inundated with sales pitches on television, radio, newspapers, and the Internet for a long list of products: toothpaste, perfume, automobiles, cat food, banking services, and more. But have you ever seen a farmer on television, trying to convince you to buy *his* wheat, rather than the wheat of other farmers? Do shareholders of major corporations like General Motors sell their stock by advertising in the newspaper? Why, in a world in which virtually *everything* seems to be advertised, do we not see ads for wheat, shares of stock, corn, crude oil, copper, or foreign currency?

Or consider profits. Anyone starting a business hopes to make as much profit as possible. Yet some companies—Microsoft, Quaker Oats, and PepsiCo, for example—earn sizable profits for their owners year after year, while at other companies, such as Delta Air Lines, General Motors, and most small businesses, economic profit may fluctuate from year to year, but on average it is very low.

When economists turn their attention to these observed differences in trading, they think immediately about *market structure*, the subject of this and the next two chapters. We've used this term informally before, but now it's time for a formal definition:

> By **market structure**, we mean all the characteristics of a market that influence the behavior of buyers and sellers when they come together to trade.

Market structure The characteristics of a market that influence how trading takes place.

To determine the structure of any particular market, we begin by asking three simple questions:

1. *How many* buyers and sellers are there in the market?
2. Is each seller offering a *standardized product,* more or less indistinguishable from that offered by other sellers, or are there significant differences among the products of different firms?
3. Are there any *barriers to entry or exit,* or can outsiders easily enter and leave this market?

The answers to these questions help us to classify a market into one of four basic types: *perfect competition, monopoly, monopolistic competition,* or *oligopoly.* The subject of this chapter is perfect competition. In the next two chapters, we'll look carefully at the other market structures.

WHAT IS PERFECT COMPETITION?

The phrase "perfect competition" should sound familiar, because you encountered it earlier, in Chapter 3. There you learned (briefly) that the famous supply and demand model explains how prices are determined in *perfectly competitive markets.* Now we're going to take a much deeper and more comprehensive look at perfectly competitive markets. By the end of this chapter, you will understand very clearly how perfect competition and the supply and demand model are related.

Let's start with the word *competition* itself. When you hear that word, you may think of an intense, personal rivalry, like that between two boxers competing in a ring or two students competing for the best grade in a small class. But there are other, less personal forms of competition. If you took the SAT exam to get into college, you were competing with thousands of other test takers in rooms just like yours, all across the country. But the competition was *impersonal:* You were trying to do the best that you could do, trying to outperform others in general, but not competing with any one individual in the room. In economics, the term "competition" is used in the latter sense. It describes a situation of diffuse, impersonal competition in a highly populated environment. The market structure you will learn about in this chapter—perfect competition—is an example of this notion.

THE THREE REQUIREMENTS OF PERFECT COMPETITION

Perfect competition A market structure in which there are many buyers and sellers, the product is standardized, and sellers can easily enter or exit the market.

> *Perfect competition is a market structure with three important characteristics:*
>
> 1. *There are large numbers of buyers and sellers, and each buys or sells only a tiny fraction of the total quantity in the market.*
> 2. *Sellers offer a standardized product.*
> 3. *Sellers can easily enter into or exit from the market.*

These three conditions probably raise more questions than they answer, so let's see what each one really means.

A Large Number of Buyers and Sellers

In perfect competition, there must be many buyers and sellers. How many? It would be nice if we could specify a number—like 1,000—for this requirement. Unfortunately, we cannot, since what constitutes a large number of buyers and sellers can be different under different conditions. What is important is this:

> *In a perfectly competitive market, the number of buyers and sellers is so large that no individual decision maker can significantly affect the price of the product by changing the quantity it buys or sells.*

Think of the world market for wheat. On the selling side, there are hundreds of thousands of individual wheat farmers—more than 250,000 in the United States alone. Each of these farmers produces only a tiny fraction of the total market quantity. If any one of them were to double, triple, or even quadruple production, the impact on total market quantity and market price would be negligible. The same is true on the buying side: There are so many small buyers that no one of them can affect the market price by increasing or decreasing its quantity demanded. Most agricultural markets conform to the large-number-of-small-firms requirement, as do markets for many commodities, such as gold or silver.

Now think about the market for athletic shoes. In 2005, three large firms—Nike, Adidas (including Reebok), and New Balance—accounted for about 75 percent of worldwide sales in this market. If any one of these producers decided to change its output by even 10 percent, the impact on total quantity supplied—and market price—would be *very* noticeable. The market for athletic shoes fails the large-number-of-small-firms requirement, so it is not an example of perfect competition.

A Standardized Product Offered by Sellers

In a perfectly competitive market, buyers do not perceive differences between the products of one seller and another. For example, buyers of wheat will ordinarily have no preference for one farmer's wheat over another's, so wheat would surely pass the standardized product test. The same is true of many other agricultural products—for example, corn syrup and soybeans. It is also true of commodities like crude oil or pork bellies, precious metals like gold or silver, and financial instruments such as the stocks and bonds of a particular firm. (One share of eBay stock is indistinguishable from another.)

When buyers *do* notice significant differences in the outputs of different sellers, the market is not perfectly competitive. For example, most consumers perceive differences among the various brands of coffee on the supermarket shelf and may have strong preferences for one particular brand. Coffee, therefore, fails the standardized product test of perfect competition. Other goods and services that would fail this test include personal computers, automobiles, houses, colleges, and medical care.

Easy Entry into and Exit from the Market

Entry into a market is rarely free; a new seller must always incur *some* costs to set up shop, begin production, and establish contacts with customers. But a perfectly competitive market has no *significant* barriers to discourage new entrants: Any firm wishing to enter can do business on the same terms as firms that are already there. For example, anyone who wants to start a wheat farm can do so, facing the same costs for land, farm equipment, seeds, fertilizer, and hired labor as existing farms. The same is true of anyone wishing to open up a dry cleaning shop, restaurant, or dog-walking service. Each of these examples would pass the easy-entry test of perfect competition.

In many markets, however, there are significant barriers to entry. These are often *legal barriers*. An example: For more than 70 years, the number of taxicabs licensed to operate in New York City was fixed, with occasional small changes, at around 12,000. From 2004 to 2006, the city expanded the number to around 13,000. But as long as there is a fixed number, true entry into this market is impossible—licenses may change hands, but the number of legally operated taxis cannot increase. Another example of legal barriers to entry is *zoning laws*. These place strict limits on how many businesses—movie theaters, supermarkets, hotels—can operate in a local area.

Aside from laws, significant barriers to entry can arise simply because existing sellers have an important advantage that new entrants cannot duplicate. The brand loyalty enjoyed by existing producers of breakfast cereals, instant coffee, and soft drinks would require a new entrant to wrest customers away from existing firms—a very costly undertaking. We will discuss these and other barriers to entry in more detail in later chapters.

In addition to easy entry, perfect competition is characterized by easy *exit:* A firm suffering a long-run loss must be able to sell off its plant and equipment and leave the industry for good, without obstacles. Some markets satisfy this requirement, and some do not. Plant-closing laws or union agreements can require lengthy advance notice and high severance pay when workers are laid off. Or capital equipment may be so highly specialized—like an assembly line designed to produce just one type of automobile—that it cannot be sold off if the firm decides to exit the market. These and other barriers to exit do not conform to the assumptions of perfect competition.

Toward the end of this chapter, you'll see that easy entry and exit have important implications for competitive markets in the long run.

IS PERFECT COMPETITION REALISTIC?

The three assumptions a market must satisfy to be perfectly competitive (or just "competitive," for short) are rather restrictive. Do any markets satisfy all these requirements? How broadly can we apply the model of perfect competition when we think about the real world?

In some cases, the model fits remarkably well. We have seen that the market for wheat, for example, passes all three tests for a competitive market: many buyers and sellers, standardized output, and easy entry and exit. Indeed, most agricultural markets satisfy the strict requirements of perfect competition quite closely, as do many financial markets and some markets for consumer goods and services.

But in the vast majority of markets, one or more of the assumptions of perfect competition will, in a strict sense, be violated. This might suggest that the model can be applied only in a few limited cases. Yet when economists look at real-world markets, they use the perfect competition model more than any other market model. Why is this?

First, the model of perfect competition is powerful. Using simple techniques, it leads to important predictions about a market's response to changes in consumer tastes, technology, and government policies. While other types of market structure models also yield valuable predictions, they are often more cumbersome and their predictions less definitive. Second, many markets, while not strictly perfectly competitive, come *reasonably* close. The more closely a real-world market fits the model, the more accurate our predictions will be when we use it.

We can even, with some caution, use the model to analyze markets that violate all three assumptions. Take the worldwide market for television sets. There are about a dozen major sellers in this market. Each of them knows that its output decisions will have *some* effect on the market price, but no one of them can have a *major* impact on price. Consumers do recognize the difference between one brand and another, but their preferences are not very strong, and most recognize that quality has become so standardized that all brands are actually close substitutes for each other. And there are indeed barriers to entry—existing firms have supply and distribution networks that would be difficult for new entrants to replicate—but these barriers are not *so* great that they would keep out new entrants if they saw the potential for high profit. Thus, although the market for televisions does not strictly satisfy any of the requirements of perfect competition, it is not *too* far off on any one of them. The model will not perform as accurately for televisions as it does for wheat, but, depending on how much accuracy we need, it may do just fine.

In sum, perfect competition can approximate conditions and yield accurate-enough predictions in a wide variety of markets. This is why you will often find economists using the model to analyze the markets for crude oil, consumer electronic goods, fast-food meals, medical care, and higher education, even though in each of these cases one or more of the requirements may not be strictly satisfied.

THE PERFECTLY COMPETITIVE FIRM

A market is a collection of individual decision makers, much as a human body is a collection of individual cells. In a perfectly competitive market, the individual cells (firms and consumers) and the overall body (the market) affect each other through a variety of feedback mechanisms. This is why, in learning about perfect competition, we must understand both the competitive firm and the competitive market in which it operates.

Figure 1(a) applies the tools you have already learned—supply and demand—to the competitive market for gold. The market demand curve slopes downward: As price falls, buyers will want to purchase more. The supply curve slopes upward: As price rises, the total quantity supplied by firms in the market will rise. The intersection of the supply and demand curves determines the equilibrium price of gold, which, in the figure, is $400 per troy ounce.[1] This is all familiar territory, which you learned in Chapter 3. But now, let's turn our attention to one of the many sellers in this market: Small Time Gold Mines, a small mining company.

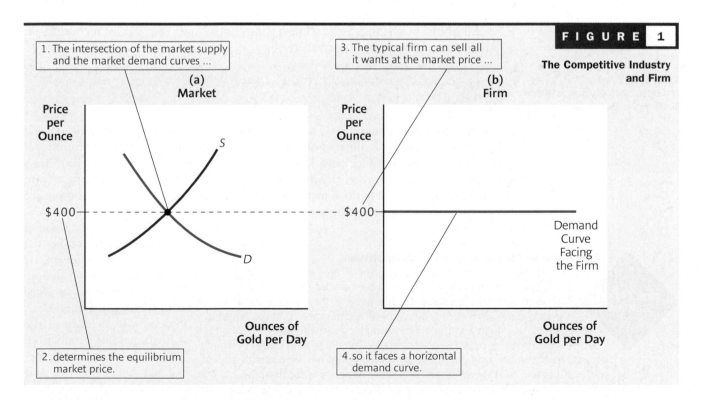

FIGURE 1

The Competitive Industry and Firm

1. The intersection of the market supply and the market demand curves …

**(a)
Market**

2. determines the equilibrium market price.

3. The typical firm can sell all it wants at the market price …

**(b)
Firm**

4. so it faces a horizontal demand curve.

[1] Gold is sold by the troy ounce, which is about 10 percent heavier than a regular ounce.

In addition to a cost constraint, Small Time Gold Mines faces a demand constraint, as does any firm. But there is something different about the demand constraint for a perfectly competitive firm like Small Time.

THE COMPETITIVE FIRM'S DEMAND CURVE

Panel (b) of Figure 1 shows the demand curve facing Small Time Gold Mines. Notice the special shape of this curve: It is horizontal, or perfectly price elastic. This tells us that no matter how much gold Small Time produces, it will always sell it at the same price—$400 per troy ounce.

> *A perfectly competitive firm faces a demand curve that is horizontal (perfectly elastic) at the market price.*

Why should this be?

First, in perfect competition, output is standardized—buyers do not distinguish the gold of one mine from that of another. If Small Time were to charge a price even a tiny bit higher than other producers, it would lose all of its customers; they would simply buy from Small Time's competitors. The horizontal demand curve captures this effect. It tells us that if Small Time raises its price above $400, it will not just sell *less* output, it will sell *no* output.

Second, Small Time is only a tiny producer relative to the entire gold market. No matter how much it produces and sells, it cannot make a noticeable difference in market quantity supplied, and so it cannot affect the market price. Once again, the horizontal demand curve describes this effect very well: The firm can increase its production without having to lower its price.

All of this means that Small Time has no control over the price of its output—it simply accepts the market price as given.

Price taker Any firm that treats the price of its product as given and beyond its control.

> *In perfect competition, the firm is a **price taker**: It treats the price of its output as given.*

The horizontal demand curve facing the firm and the corresponding price-taking behavior of firms are hallmarks of perfect competition. When a manager thinks, "If we produce more output, we will have to lower our price in order to sell it" then the firm faces a *downward sloping* demand curve and it is *not* a competitive firm. The manager of a competitive firm will always think, "We can sell all the output we want at the going price, so how much should we produce?"

Notice that, since a competitive firm takes the market price as given, its only decision is *how much output to produce and sell*. And that decision will determine the firm's cost of production, as well as its total revenue. Let's see how this works in practice with Small Time Gold Mines.

DANGEROUS CURVES

Two Demand Curves in Perfect Competition
In the model of perfect competition, there are *two different* demand curves, as shown in Figure 1. One is the familiar *market demand curve* (labeled with an uppercase *D*). The other is the *demand curve facing the individual firm* (typically labeled with a lowercase *d*). If you forget the distinction, you'll get confused. For example, you might start thinking that perfectly competitive markets are for special products with perfectly elastic demand. True, the demand curve facing the individual firm is perfectly elastic, but this has nothing to do with buyers' elasticity of demand for the product. The elasticity of demand for the product is given by the (downward sloping) *market* demand curve.

COST AND REVENUE DATA FOR A COMPETITIVE FIRM

Table 1 shows cost and revenue data for Small Time. In the first two columns are different quantities of gold that Small Time could produce each day and the selling price per ounce. Because Small Time is a competitive firm (a price taker), the price remains constant at $400 per ounce, no matter *how* much gold it produces.

Run your finger down the total revenue and marginal revenue columns. Since price is always $400, each time the firm produces another ounce of gold, total revenue rises by $400. This is why marginal revenue—the additional revenue from selling one more ounce of gold—remains constant at $400.

Figure 2 plots Small Time's total revenue and marginal revenue. Notice that the total revenue (TR) curve in the upper panel is a *straight line* that slopes upward; each time output increases by one unit, TR rises by the same $400. That is, the slope of the TR curve is equal to the price of output.

The marginal revenue (MR) curve in the lower panel is a *horizontal* line at the market price. In fact, the MR curve is the same horizontal line as the demand curve facing the firm. Why? Remember that marginal revenue is the additional revenue the firm earns from selling an additional unit of output. For a price-taking competitive firm, that additional revenue will always be the unchanging price it gets for each unit—in this case, $400.

TABLE 1

Cost and Revenue Data for Small Time Gold Mines

(1) Output (Troy Ounces of Gold per Day)	(2) Price (per Troy Ounce)	(3) Total Revenue	(4) Marginal Revenue	(5) Total Cost	(6) Marginal Cost	(7) Profit
0	$400	$ 0		$ 550		−$550
			$400		$450	
1	$400	$ 400		$1,000		−$600
			$400		$200	
2	$400	$ 800		$1,200		−$400
			$400		$ 50	
3	$400	$1,200		$1,250		−$ 50
			$400		$100	
4	$400	$1,600		$1,350		$250
			$400		$150	
5	$400	$2,000		$1,500		$500
			$400		$250	
6	$400	$2,400		$1,750		$650
			$400		$350	
7	**$400**	**$2,800**		**$2,100**		**$700**
			$400		$450	
8	$400	$3,200		$2,550		$650
			$400		$550	
9	$400	$3,600		$3,100		$500
			$400		$650	
10	$400	$4,000		$3,750		$250

> *For a competitive firm, marginal revenue is the same as the market price. For this reason, the marginal revenue curve and the demand curve facing the firm are the same: a horizontal line at the market price.*

In panel (b), we have labeled the horizontal line "*d = MR*," since this line is both the firm's demand curve (*d*) *and* its marginal revenue curve (*MR*).

Columns 5 and 6 of Table 1 show total cost and marginal cost for Small Time. There is nothing special about cost data for a competitive firm. In Figure 2, you can see that marginal cost (*MC*)—as usual—first falls and then rises. Total cost, therefore,

FIGURE **2**	

Profit Maximization in Perfect Competition

Panel (a) shows a competitive firm's total revenue (TR) and total cost (TC) curves. TR is a straight line with slope equal to the market price. Profit is maximized at 7 ounces per day, where the vertical distance between TR and TC is greatest. Panel (b) shows that profit is maximized where the marginal cost (MC) curve intersects the marginal revenue (MR) curve, which is also the firm's demand curve.

(a)

(b)

rises first at a decreasing rate and then at an increasing rate. (You may want to look at Chapter 6 to review why this cost behavior is so common.)

FINDING THE PROFIT-MAXIMIZING OUTPUT LEVEL

A competitive firm—like any other firm—wants to earn the highest possible profit, and to do so, it should use the principles you learned in Chapter 7. Although the diagrams look a bit different for competitive firms, the ideas behind them are the same. We can use either Table 1 or Figure 2 to find the profit-maximizing output level. And we can use the techniques you have already learned: the total revenue and total cost approach, or the marginal revenue and marginal cost approach.

The Total Revenue and Total Cost Approach

The TR and TC approach is the most direct way of viewing the firm's search for the profit-maximizing output level. Quite simply, at each output level, subtract total cost from total revenue to get total profit:

$$\text{Total Profit} = TR - TC$$

Then we just scan the different output levels to see which one gives the highest number for profit.

In Table 1, total profit is shown in the last column. A simple scan of that column tells us that $700 is the highest daily profit that Small Time Gold Mines can earn. To earn this profit, the first column tells us that Small Time must produce 7 ounces per day, its profit-maximizing output level.

The same approach to maximizing profit can be seen graphically, in the upper panel of Figure 2. There, total profit at any output level is the distance between the TR and TC curves. As you can see, this distance is greatest when the firm produces 7 units, verifying what we found in the table.

This approach is simple and straightforward, but it hides the interesting part of the story: the way that *changes* in output cause total revenue and total cost to change. The other approach to finding the profit-maximizing output level focuses on these changes.

The Marginal Revenue and Marginal Cost Approach

In the MR and MC approach, the firm should continue to increase output as long as marginal revenue is greater than marginal cost. You can verify, using Table 1, that if the firm is initially producing 1, 2, 3, 4, 5, or 6 units, it will find that $MR > MC$ when it raises output by one unit, so producing more will raise profit. Once the firm is producing 7 units, however, $MR < MC$, so further increases in output will reduce profit.

Alternatively, using the graph in panel (b) of Figure 2, we look for the output level at which $MR = MC$. As the graph shows, there are two output levels at which the MR and MC curves intersect. However, we can rule out the first crossing point because there, the MC curve crosses the MR curve from above. Remember that the profit-maximizing output is found where the MC curve crosses the MR curve from *below*, at 7 units of output.

You can see that finding the profit-maximizing output level for a competitive firm requires no new concepts or techniques; you have already learned everything you need to know in Chapter 7. In fact, the only difference is one of appearance.

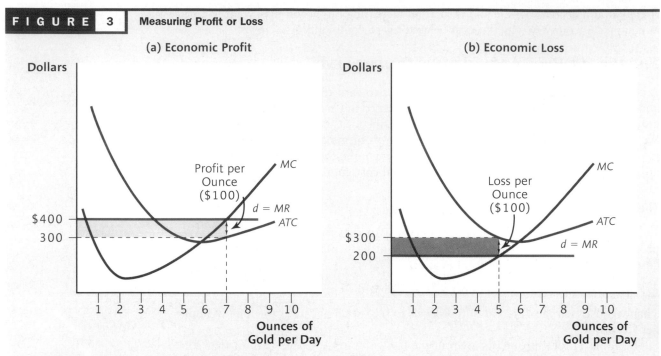

FIGURE 3 Measuring Profit or Loss

The competitive firm in panel (a) produces where marginal cost equals marginal revenue, or 7 units of output per day. Profit per unit at that output level is equal to revenue per unit ($400) minus cost per unit ($300), or $100 per unit. Total profit (indicated by the blue-shaded rectangle) is equal to profit per unit times the number of units sold, $100 × 7 = $700. In panel (b), we assume that the market price is lower, at $200 per ounce. The best the firm can do is to produce 5 ounces per day and suffer a loss shown by the red area. It loses $100 per ounce on each of those 5 ounces produced, so the total loss is $500—the area of the red-shaded rectangle.

Ned's Beds—our firm in Chapter 7—did *not* operate under perfect competition. As a result, both its demand curve and its marginal revenue curve sloped *downward*. Small Time, however, operates under perfect competition, so its demand and *MR* curves are the same horizontal line.

MEASURING TOTAL PROFIT

You have already seen one way to measure a firm's total profit on a graph: the vertical distance between the *TR* and *TC* curves. In this section, you will learn another graphical way to measure profit.

To do this, we start with the firm's *profit per unit*, which is the revenue it gets on each unit minus the cost per unit. Revenue per unit is just the price (*P*) of the firm's output, and cost per unit is our familiar average total cost, so we can write:

$$\text{Profit per unit} = P - ATC.$$

In Figure 3(a), Small Time's *ATC* curve has been plotted (calculated from the data in Table 1). When the firm is producing at the profit-maximizing output level, 7 units, its *ATC* is *TC/Q* = $2,100/7 = $300. Since the price of output is $400, profit *per unit* = *P* − *ATC* = $400 − $300 = $100. Graphically, this is the vertical distance between the firm's demand curve and its *ATC* curve at the profit-maximizing output level.

Once we know Small Time's profit per unit, it is easy to calculate its *total* profit: Just multiply profit per unit by the number of units sold. Small Time is earning $100 profit on each ounce of gold, and it sells 7 ounces in all, so total profit is $100 \times 7 = $700.

Now look at the blue-shaded rectangle in Figure 3(a). The height of this rectangle is profit per unit, and the width is the number of units produced. The *area* of the rectangle—height $\times$ width—equals Small Time's profit:

> *A firm earns a profit whenever* P > ATC. *Its total profit at the best output level equals the area of a rectangle with height equal to the distance between* P *and* ATC, *and width equal to the quantity of output.*

In the figure, Small Time is fortunate: At a price of $400, there are several output levels at which it can earn a profit. Its problem is to select the one that makes its profit as large as possible. (We should all wish for such problems.)

Misusing Profit per Unit It is tempting—but *wrong*—to think that the firm should produce where profit *per unit* (P − ATC) is greatest. The firm's goal is to maximize *total* profit, not profit per unit. Using Table 1 or Figure 3(a), you can verify that while Small Time's profit *per unit* is greatest at 6 units of output, its *total* profit is greatest at 7 units.

DANGEROUS CURVES

But what if the price had been lower than $400—so low, in fact, that Small Time could not make a profit at *any* output level? Then the best it can do is to choose the smallest possible loss. Just as we did in the case of profit, we can measure the firm's total loss using the *ATC* curve.

Panel (b) of Figure 3 reproduces Small Time's *ATC* and *MC* curves from panel (a). This time, however, we have assumed a lower price for gold—$200—so the firm's $d = MR$ curve is the horizontal line at $200. Since this line lies everywhere below the *ATC* curve, profit per unit (P − ATC) is always negative: Small Time cannot make a positive profit at *any* output level.

With a price of $200, the *MC* curve crosses the *MR* curve from below at 5 units of output. Unless Small Time decides to shut down (we'll discuss shutting down for competitive firms later), it should produce 5 units. At that level of output, *ATC* is $300, and profit per unit is P − ATC = $200 − $300 = −$100, a *loss* of $100 per unit. The total loss is loss per unit (negative profit per unit) times the number of units produced, or −$100 \times 5 = −$500. This is the area of the red-shaded rectangle in Figure 3(b), with height of $100 and width of 5 units:

> *A firm suffers a loss whenever* P < ATC *at the best level of output. Its total loss equals the area of a rectangle with height equal to the distance between* P *and* ATC, *and width equal to the quantity of output.*

The Firm's Short-Run Supply Curve

A competitive firm is a price taker: It takes the market price as given and then decides how much output it will produce at that price. If the market price changes for any reason, the price taken as given by the firm will change as well. The firm will then have to find a new profit-maximizing output level. Let's see how the firm's profit-maximizing output changes as the market price rises or falls.

Figure 4(a) shows *ATC*, *AVC*, and *MC* curves for a competitive producer of wheat. The figure also shows five hypothetical demand curves the firm might face,

FIGURE 4 Short-Run Supply Under Perfect Competition

Panel (a) shows a typical competitive firm facing various market prices. For prices between $1 and $3.50 per bushel, the profit-maximizing quantity is found by sliding along the MC curve. Below $1 per bushel, the firm is better off shutting down, because P < AVC, Panel (b) shows that the firm's supply curve consists of two segments. Above the shutdown price of $1 per bushel it follows the MC curve; below that price, it is coincident with the vertical axis.

each corresponding to a different market price for wheat. If the market price were $3.50 per bushel, the firm would face demand curve d_1, and its profit-maximizing output level—where MC and MR intersect—would be 7,000 bushels per year. If the price dropped to $2.50 per bushel, the firm would face demand curve d_2, and its profit-maximizing output level would drop to 5,000 bushels. You can see that the profit-maximizing output level is always found by traveling from the price, across to the firm's MC curve, and then down to the horizontal axis. In other words,

> *as the price of output changes, the firm will slide along its* MC *curve in deciding how much to produce.*

But there is one problem with this: If the firm is suffering a loss—a loss large enough to justify shutting down—then it will *not* produce along its MC curve; it will produce zero units instead. Thus, in order to know for certain how much output the firm will produce, we must bring in the shutdown rule.

The Shutdown Price

In Chapter 7, you learned that a firm should shut down in the short run if, at its best positive output level, it finds that $TR < TVC$. (In words, if the firm cannot even cover its operating costs, it should not continue to operate.) If $TR > TVC$, the firm should continue to operate.

But when we use a graph such as Figure 4(a), which has different prices *per unit* on the vertical axis and has curves showing cost *per unit*, it will be helpful to express this shutdown rule in "per unit" terms. Let's start with the rule from Chapter 7:

Shut down if $TR < TVC$

Next, with lowercase q representing the individual firm's output level, we divide both sides of the inequality by q:

Shut down if $(TR/q) < (TVC/q)$

Finally, we recognize that TR/q is just revenue per unit, or the price (P), and TVC/q is the firm's average variable cost (AVC), giving us

Shut down if $P < AVC$

Now let's apply the shutdown rule to the firms in Figure 4(a). Suppose the price drops down to $2 per bushel. At this price, the best output level is 4,000 bushels, and the firm suffers a loss, since $P < ATC$. Should the firm shut down? Let's see. At 4,000 bushels, it is also true that $P > AVC$, since the demand curve lies above the AVC curve at this output level. Thus, at a price of $2, the firm will stay open and produce 4,000 units of output.

Now, suppose the price drops all the way down to $0.50 per bushel. At this price, $MR = MC$ at 1,000 bushels. But notice that here $P < AVC$. Therefore, at a price of $0.50, this firm will shut down and produce *zero* units of output.

Finally, let's consider a price of $1. At this price, $MR = MC$ at 2,000 bushels, and here we have $P = AVC$. At $1, therefore, the firm will be indifferent between staying open and shutting down. We call this price the firm's **shut-down price**, since it will shut down at any price lower and stay open at any price higher.

Note that the shutdown price is found at the *minimum* of the AVC curve. Why? As the price decreases, the best output level is found by sliding along the MC curve, until MC and AVC cross. At that point, the firm will shut down. But—as you learned in Chapter 6—MC will always cross AVC at its minimum point.

Now let's recapitulate what we've found about the firm's output decision. For all prices above the minimum point on the AVC curve, the firm will stay open and will produce the level of output at which $MR = MC$. For these prices, the firm slides along its MC curve in deciding how much output to produce. But for any price below the minimum AVC, the firm will shut down and produce zero units. We can summarize all of this information in a single curve—the **firm's supply curve**—which tells us how much output the firm will produce at any price:

Shutdown price The price at which a firm is indifferent between producing and shutting down.

Firm's supply curve A curve that shows the quantity of output a competitive firm will produce at different prices.

> *A competitive firm's supply curve is its* MC *curve for all prices above* AVC, *and a vertical line at zero units for all prices below* AVC.

In panel (b) of Figure 4, we have drawn the supply curve for our hypothetical wheat farmer. As price declines from $3.50 to $1, output is determined by the firm's MC curve. For all prices *below* $1—the shutdown price—output is zero and the supply curve coincides with the vertical axis.

COMPETITIVE MARKETS IN THE SHORT RUN

Recall that the short run is a time period too short for the firm to vary its fixed inputs. Therefore, logically, the short run is also insufficient time for a *new* firm to acquire those fixed inputs and *enter* the market. Similarly, it is too short a period for firms to reduce their fixed inputs to zero and *exit* the market. We conclude that

F I G U R E 5   Deriving the Market Supply Curve

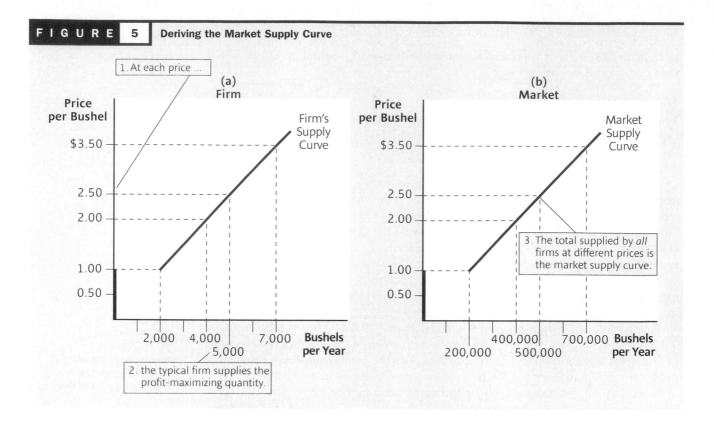

in the short run, the number of firms in the industry is fixed.

THE MARKET SUPPLY CURVE

Once we know how many firms there are in a market, and we know each firm's supply curve, we can easily determine the *market supply curve.*

*To obtain the **market supply curve,** we add up the quantities of output supplied by all firms in the market at each price.*

Market supply curve A curve indicating the quantity of output that all sellers in a market will produce at different prices in the short run.

To keep things simple, suppose there are 100 identical wheat farms and that each one has the supply curve shown in Figure 5(a). (This is the same supply curve we derived earlier, in Figure 4.) If the price is $3.50, each firm produces 7,000 bushels. With 100 such firms, the market quantity supplied is 7,000 × 100 = 700,000 bushels. If the price is $2.50, each firm supplies 5,000 bushels, so market supply is 500,000. Continuing in this way, we can trace out the market supply curve shown in panel (b) of Figure 5. Notice that once the price drops below $1—the shutdown price for each firm—the market supply curve jumps to zero.

The market supply curve in the figure is a *short-run* market supply curve, since it gives us the combined output level of just those firms *already* in the industry. As we move along this curve, we are assuming that two things are constant: (1) the fixed inputs of each firm and (2) the number of firms in the market.

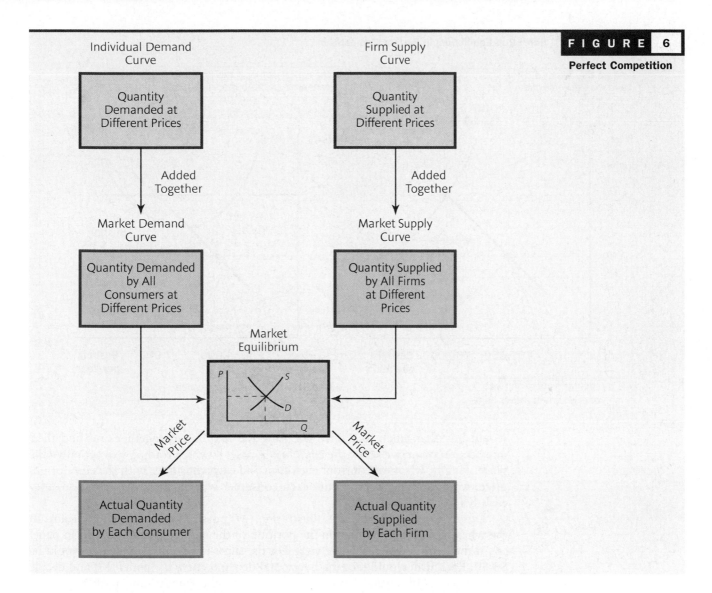

FIGURE 6

Perfect Competition

SHORT-RUN EQUILIBRIUM

How does a perfectly competitive market achieve equilibrium? We've already addressed this question in Chapter 3, in our study of supply and demand. But now we'll take a much closer look, paying attention to the individual firm and individual consumer as well as the market.

Figure 6 puts together the pieces we've discussed so far, including those from Chapter 5 on consumer choice. It paints a complete picture of how a competitive market arrives at its short-run equilibrium. On the right side, we add up the quantities supplied by all firms to obtain the market supply curve. On the left side, we add up the quantities demanded by all consumers to obtain the market demand curve.

At this stage, the market supply and demand curves show if/then relationships: *If* the price were such and such, *then* firms would supply this much and consumers

FIGURE 7 | Short-Run Equilibrium in Perfect Competition

1. When the demand curve is D_1 and market equilibrium is here ...

2. the typical firm operates here, earning economic profit in the short run.

(a) Market

(b) Firm

3. If the demand curve shifts to D_2 the market equilibrium moves here ...

4. and the typical firm operates here, suffering a short-run loss.

would buy that much. But once we bring the two curves together and find their intersection point, we know the *equilibrium* price at which trading will actually take place. Finally, when we confront each firm and each consumer with the equilibrium price, we find the actual quantity each consumer will buy and the actual quantity each firm will produce.

Figure 7 gets more specific, illustrating two possible short-run equilibriums in the wheat market, depending on the position of the market demand curve. In panel (a), if the market demand curve were D_1, the short-run equilibrium price would be $3.50. Each firm would face the horizontal demand curve d_1 [panel (b)] and decide to produce 7,000 bushels. With 100 such firms, the equilibrium market quantity would be 700,000 bushels. Notice that, at a price of $3.50, each firm is enjoying an economic profit, since $P > ATC$.

If the market demand curve were D_2 instead, the equilibrium price would be $2. Each firm would face demand curve d_2 and produce 4,000 bushels. With 100 firms, the equilibrium market quantity would be 400,000. Here, each firm is suffering an economic loss, since $P < ATC$. These two examples show us that

> *in short-run equilibrium, competitive firms can earn an economic profit or suffer an economic loss.*

We are about to leave the short run and turn our attention to what happens in a competitive market over the long run. But before we do, let's look once more at how a short-run equilibrium is established. One part of this process—combining supply and demand curves to find the market equilibrium—has been familiar to you all along. But now you can better appreciate how much information is contained within each of these curves and what an impressive job the market does coordinating millions of decisions made by people who may never even meet each other.

Think about it: So many individual consumers and firms, each with its own agenda, trading in the market. Not one of them has any power to decide or even influence the market price. Rather, the price is determined by *all* of them, adjusting until *total* quantity supplied is equal to *total* quantity demanded. Then, facing this equilibrium price, each consumer buys the quantity he or she wants, each firm produces the output level that it wants, and we can be confident that all of them will be able to realize their plans. Each buyer can find willing sellers, and each seller can find willing buyers.

> *In perfect competition, the market sums up the buying and selling preferences of individual consumers and producers, and determines the market price. Each buyer and seller then takes the market price as given, and each is able to buy or sell the desired quantity.*

This process is, from a certain perspective, a thing of beauty, and it happens each day in markets all across the world—markets for wheat, corn, barley, soybeans, apples, oranges, gold, silver, copper, and more. And something quite similar happens in other markets that do not strictly satisfy our requirements for perfect competition—markets for television sets, books, air conditioners, fast-food meals, oil, natural gas, bottled water, blue jeans . . . . The list is virtually endless.

COMPETITIVE MARKETS IN THE LONG RUN

The long run is a time horizon sufficiently long for firms to vary *all* of their inputs. This includes inputs that were treated as fixed in the short run, such as plant and equipment. Logically, then, the long run must be enough time for *new* firms to acquire those inputs and enter the market as new suppliers. And it is also long enough for existing firms to sell all such inputs and exit the market.

> *In the long run, new firms can enter a competitive market, and existing firms can exit the market.*

But what makes firms want to enter or exit a market? The driving force behind entry is economic profit, and the force behind exit is economic loss.

PROFIT AND LOSS AND THE LONG RUN

Recall that economic profit is the amount by which total revenue exceeds *all* costs of doing business. The costs we deduct include implicit costs like foregone investment income or foregone wages for an owner who devotes money or time to the business. Thus, when a firm earns positive economic profit, we know the owners are earning *more* than they could by devoting their money and time to some other activity.

A temporary episode of positive economic profit will not have much impact on a competitive industry, other than the temporary pleasure it gives the owners of competitive firms. But when positive profit reflects basic conditions in the industry

Long run exit from a market can occur in different ways. An example is when a firm (such as this retailer) goes entirely out of business.

and is expected to continue, major changes are in the works. Outsiders, hungry for profit themselves, will want to enter the market and—since *there are no barriers to entry*—they can do so.

On the other hand, if firms already in the industry are suffering economic losses, they are not earning enough revenue to cover all their costs. There must be other opportunities that would more adequately compensate the owners for their money or time. If this situation is expected to continue over the firm's long-run planning horizon—a period long enough to vary *all* inputs—there is only one thing for the firm to do: exit the industry by selling off its plant and equipment, thereby reducing its loss to zero.

> In a competitive market, economic profit and loss are the forces driving long-run change. The expectation of continued economic profit causes outsiders to enter the market; the expectation of continued economic losses causes firms in the market to exit.

In the real world of business, entry and exit occur in a variety of different ways. Sometimes it involves the formation of an entirely new firm, such as jetBlue, an airline formed in 2000. Entry can also occur when an existing firm adds a new product line, as Verizon and AT&T did when they entered the market for Internet telephone calls in 2004. Or, in a local market, entry can occur when an existing firm creates a new branch, such as when Wal-Mart or Starbucks builds a new store. In all of these cases, the number of sellers in the market increases.

Exit, too, can occur in different ways. Sometimes, it involves a firm going entirely out of business. The restaurant industry is especially prone to this type of exit: A recent study[2] found that about 60 percent of new restaurants in Columbus, Ohio went out of business within three years of opening. But exit can also occur when a firm switches out of a particular product line, even as it continues to produce other things. For example, publishing companies often decide to abandon unsuccessful magazines, yet they continue to thrive by publishing other magazines and books.

LONG-RUN EQUILIBRIUM

Entry and exit—however they occur—are powerful forces in real-world competitive markets. They determine how these markets change over the long run, how much output will be available to consumers, and the prices they must pay. To explore these issues, let's see how entry and exit move a market to its long-run equilibrium from different starting points.

From Short-Run Profit to Long-Run Equilibrium

Suppose that the market for wheat is initially in a short-run equilibrium like point A in panel (a) of Figure 8, with market supply curve S_1. The initial equilibrium price is $4.50 per bushel. In panel (b), we see that a typical competitive firm—producing 9,000 bushels—is earning economic profit, since $P > ATC$ at that output level. As long as we remain in the short run, with no new firms entering the market, this situation will not change.

---

[2] *Research News*. The Ohio State University, September 3, 2003.

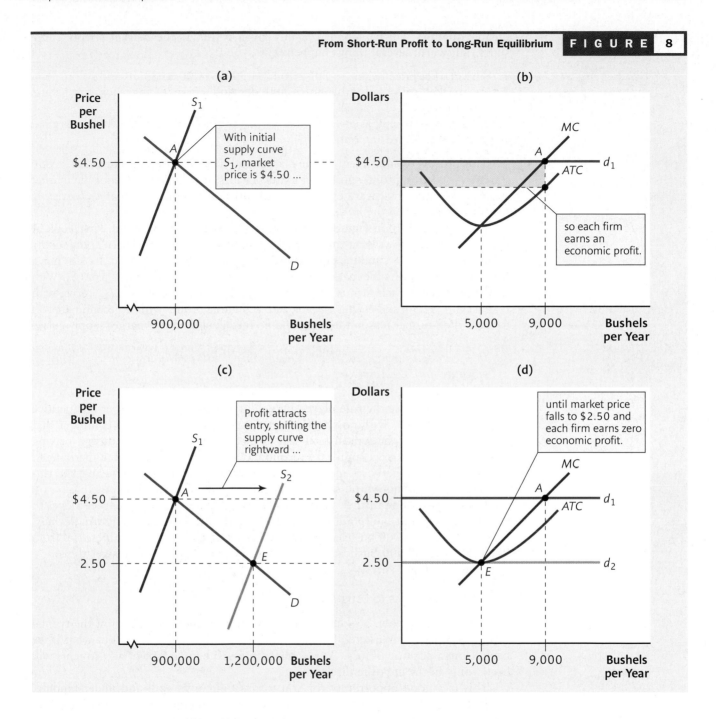

From Short-Run Profit to Long-Run Equilibrium FIGURE 8

(a)

Price per Bushel

$4.50

900,000 Bushels per Year

S_1

A

D

With initial supply curve S_1, market price is $4.50 ...

(b)

Dollars

$4.50

5,000 9,000 Bushels per Year

MC

A

d_1

ATC

so each firm earns an economic profit.

(c)

Price per Bushel

$4.50

2.50

900,000 1,200,000 Bushels per Year

S_1

S_2

A

E

D

Profit attracts entry, shifting the supply curve rightward ...

(d)

Dollars

$4.50

2.50

5,000 9,000 Bushels per Year

MC

A

d_1

ATC

E

d_2

until market price falls to $2.50 and each firm earns zero economic profit.

But as we enter the long run, much will change. First, economic profit will attract new entrants, increasing the number of firms in the market. Now remember (from Chapter 3) when we draw a market supply curve like S_1, we draw it for some *given* number of firms, and we hold that number constant. But in the long run, as the number of firms increases, the market supply curve will *shift rightward;* a greater quantity will be supplied at any given price. As the market supply curve shifts rightward, several things happen:

1. The market price begins to fall—from $4.50 to $4.00 to $3.50 and so on.
2. As market price falls, the horizontal demand curve facing each firm shifts downward.
3. Each firm—striving as always to maximize profit—will slide down its marginal cost curve, decreasing output.[3]

This process of adjustment, in the market and the firm, continues until the *reason for entry*—positive profit—no longer exists. That is, it will continue until the market supply curve shifts rightward enough, and the price falls enough, so that *each existing firm is earning zero economic profit.*

Panels (c) and (d) in Figure 8 show the final, long-run equilibrium. First, look at panel (c), which shows long-run market equilibrium at point E. The market supply curve has shifted to S_2, and the price has fallen to $2.50 per bushel. Next, look at panel (d), which tells us why the market supply curve stops shifting when it reaches S_2. With that supply curve, each firm is producing at the lowest point of its ATC curve, with $P = ATC = 2.50, and each is earning zero economic profit. With no economic profit, there is no further reason for entry, and no further shift in the market supply curve.

> *In a competitive market, positive economic profit continues to attract new entrants until economic profit is reduced to zero.*

Now you can see the role played by one of our assumptions about competitive markets: *easy entry*. With no significant barriers to entry, we can be confident that economic profit at the typical firm will attract new firms to the industry, driving down the market price until the economic profit disappears. If a permanent barrier—legal or otherwise—prevented new firms from coming into the market, this mechanism would not work, so long-run economic profit would be possible.

Before proceeding further, take a close look at Figure 8. As the market moves to its long-run equilibrium [point E in panels (c) and (d)], output at each firm *decreases* from 9,000 to 5,000 bushels. But in the market as a whole, output *increases* from 900,000 to 1,200,000 bushels. How can this be? (See if you can answer this question yourself. Hint: entry!)

From Short-Run Loss to Long-Run Equilibrium

We have just seen how, beginning from a position of short-run profit at the typical firm, a competitive market will adjust until the profit is eliminated. But what if we begin from a position of loss? As you might guess, the same type of adjustments will occur, only in the opposite direction.

This is a good opportunity for you to test your own skill and understanding. Study Figure 8 carefully. Then see if you can draw a similar diagram that illustrates the adjustment from short-run *loss* to long-run equilibrium. Use the same demand curve as in Figure 8, but draw in a new, appropriate market supply curve to create

---

[3] There is one other possible consequence that we ignore here: Entry into the industry, which changes the demand for the industry's inputs, may also change input prices. If this occurs, firms' cost curves can shift as well. We'll explore this possibility a few pages later.

an initial equilibrium price of $1.50. Then let the market work. Show what happens in the market, and at each firm, as economic loss causes some firms to exit. If you do this correctly, you'll end up once again at a market price of $2.50, with each firm earning zero economic profit. Your graph will illustrate the following conclusion:

> *In a competitive market, economic losses continue to cause exit until the losses are reduced to zero.*

Notice the role played by our assumption of *easy exit* in competitive markets. When there are no significant barriers to exit, we can be confident that economic loss will eventually drive firms from the industry, raising the market price until the typical firm breaks even again. Significant barriers to exit (such as a local law forbidding a plant from closing down) would prevent this mechanism from working, and economic losses could persist even in the long run.

THE NOTION OF ZERO PROFIT IN PERFECT COMPETITION

From the preceding discussion, you may wonder why anyone in his or her right mind would ever want to set up shop in a competitive industry or stay there for any length of time, since—in the long run—they can expect zero economic profit. Indeed, if you want to become a millionaire, you would be well advised not to buy a wheat farm. But most wheat farmers—like most other sellers in competitive markets—do not curse their fate. On the contrary, they are likely to be reasonably content with the performance of their businesses. How can this be?

Remember that zero *economic* profit is not the same as zero *accounting* profit. When a firm is making zero *economic* profit, it is still making some accounting profit. In fact, the accounting profit is just enough to cover all of the owner's implicit costs, including compensation for any foregone investment income or foregone salary. Suppose, for example, that a farmer paid $100,000 for land and works 40 hours per week. Suppose, too, that the $100,000 *could* be invested in some other way and earn $6,000 per year, and the farmer *could* work equally pleasantly elsewhere and earn $50,000 per year. Then the farm's implicit costs will be $56,000, and zero economic profit means that the farm is earning $56,000 in *accounting profit* each year. This won't make a farmer ecstatic, but it will make it worthwhile to keep working the farm. After all, if the farmer quits and takes up the next best alternative, he or she will do no better.

To emphasize that zero economic profit is not an unpleasant outcome, economists often replace it with the term **normal profit**, which is a synonym for "zero economic profit," or "just enough accounting profit to cover implicit costs." Using this language, we can summarize long-run conditions at the typical firm this way:

> *In the long run, the competitive firm will earn normal profit—that is, zero economic profit.*

Normal profit Another name for zero economic profit.

PERFECT COMPETITION AND PLANT SIZE

There is one more characteristic of competitive markets in the long run that we have not yet discussed: the plant size of the competitive firm. It turns out that the

FIGURE 9 Perfect Competition and Plant Size

1. With its current plant and *ATC* curve, this firm earns zero economic profit.

(a)

Dollars

LRATC

MC_1 ATC_1

P_1

$d_1 = MR_1$

2. But the firm *could* earn positive profit with a larger plant, producing here.

q_1

Output per Period

3. As *all* firms increase plant size and output, market price falls to its lowest possible level …

(b)

Dollars

LRATC

MC_2 ATC_2

E

P^*

$d_2 = MR_2$

4. and each earns zero economic profit, producing at minimum *LRATC*.

q^*

Output per Period

same forces—entry and exit—that cause all firms to earn zero economic profit *also* ensure that:

> *In long-run equilibrium, a competitive firm will select its plant size and output level to operate at the lowest possible long-run average cost.*

To see why, let's consider what would happen if this condition were violated. Figure 9(a) illustrates a firm in a perfectly competitive market. The firm faces a market price of P_1 and produces quantity q_1, where $MC_1 = MR_1$. With its current plant, the firm has average costs given by ATC_1. Note that the firm is earning zero profit, since average cost is equal to P_1 at the best output level.

But panel (a) does *not* show a true long-run equilibrium. How do we know this? First, in the long run, the typical firm will want to expand. Why? Because by increasing its plant size, it could slide down its *LRATC* curve and produce more output at a lower cost per unit. Since it is a perfectly competitive firm—a small participant in the market—it can expand in this way *without* worrying about affecting the market price. As a result, the firm, after expanding, could operate on a new, lower *ATC* curve, so that *ATC* is less than *P*. That is, by expanding, the firm could potentially earn an economic profit.

Second, this same opportunity to earn positive economic profit will attract new entrants that will establish larger plants from the outset.

Expansion by existing firms and entry by new ones increase market output and bring down the market price. (This would be illustrated by a rightward shift of the market supply curve, which is not shown in the figure.) The process will stop—and a long-run equilibrium will be established—only when there is no potential to earn positive economic profit with *any* plant size. As you can see in panel (b), this condition is satisfied only when each firm is operating at the minimum point on its *LRATC* curve, using the plant represented by ATC_2, and producing output of q^*. Entry and expansion must continue in this market until the price falls to P^* because only then will each firm—doing the best that it can do—earn zero economic profit. (*Question:* In the long run, what would happen to a firm if it refused to increase its plant size?)

A Summary of the Competitive Firm in the Long Run

Panel (b) of Figure 9 summarizes everything you have learned about the competitive firm in long-run equilibrium. The typical firm, taking the market price P^* as given, produces the profit-maximizing output level q^*, where $MR = MC$. Since this is the long run, each firm will be earning zero economic profit, so we also know that $P^* = ATC$. But since $P^* = MC$ and $P^* = ATC$, it must also be true that $MC = ATC$. As you learned in Chapter 6, *MC* and *ATC* are equal only at the minimum point of the *ATC* curve. Thus, we know that each firm must be operating at the lowest possible point on the *ATC* curve for the plant it is operating. Finally, each firm selects the plant that makes its *LRATC* as low as possible, so each operates at the minimum point on its *LRATC* curve.

As you can see, there is a lot going on in Figure 9(b). But we can put it all together with a very simple statement:

> *In long-run equilibrium, the competitive firm operates where* MC = *minimum* ATC = *minimum* LRATC = P.

In Figure 9(b), this equality is satisfied when the firm produces at point *E*, where its demand, marginal cost, *ATC*, and *LRATC* curves all intersect. This is a figure well worth remembering, since it summarizes so much information about competitive markets in a single picture. (Here is a useful self-test: Close the book, put away your notes, and draw a set of diagrams in which one curve at a time does *not* pass through the common intersection point of the other three. Then explain which principle of firm or market behavior is violated by your diagram. Do this separately for all four curves.)

Figure 9(b) also explains one of the important ways in which perfect competition benefits consumers: In the long run, each firm is driven to the plant size and output level at which its cost per unit is as low as possible. This lowest possible cost per unit is also the price per unit that consumers will pay. If price were any lower than P^*, it would not be worthwhile for firms to continue producing the good in the long run. Thus, given the *LRATC* curve faced by each firm in this industry—a curve that is determined by each firm's production technology and the prices of its inputs—P^* is the lowest possible price that will ensure the continued availability of the good. In perfect competition, consumers are getting the best deal they could possibly get.

WHAT HAPPENS WHEN THINGS CHANGE?

So far, you've learned how competitive firms make decisions, how these decisions lead to a short-run equilibrium in the market, and how the market moves from short- to long-run equilibrium through entry and exit. Now, it's time to ask: *What happens when things change?*

FIGURE 10   A Constant Cost Industry

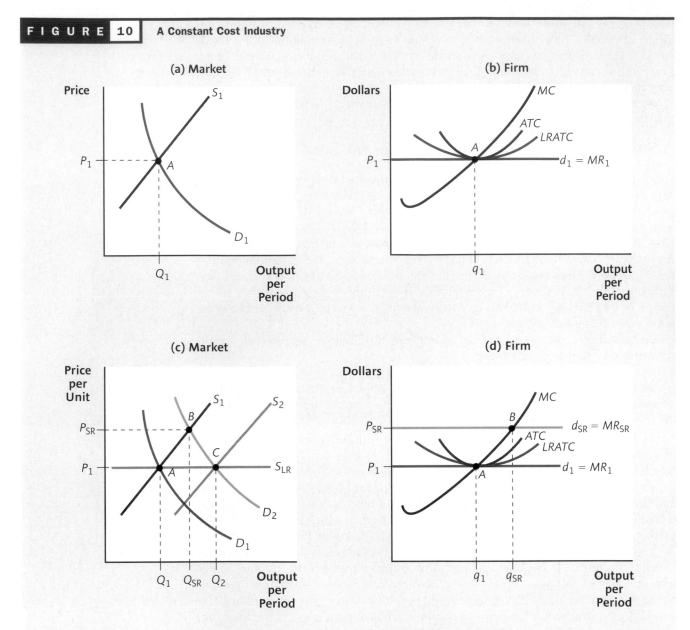

At point A in panel (a), the market is in long-run equilibrium. The typical firm in panel (b) operates at the minimum of its ATC and LRATC curves, and earns zero economic profit. The lower panels show what happens if demand increases. In the short run, the market reaches a new equilibrium at point B in panel (c), and the typical firm in panel (d) earns economic profit at the higher price P_{SR}. In the long run, profit attracts entry, increasing market supply and lowering price. Entry continues until economic profit at the typical firm in panel (d) is reduced to zero, which requires the price to drop to P_1, its original level. In panel (d), the typical firm returns to point A, and in panel (c), the new long-run market equilibrium is point C. The increase in demand raises output, but leaves price unchanged, as shown by the horizontal long-run supply curve connecting points A and C.

A CHANGE IN DEMAND

In Figure 10, panel (a) shows a competitive market that is initially in long-run equilibrium at point A, where the market demand curve D_1 and supply curve S_1 intersect. Panel (b) shows conditions at the firm, which faces demand curve d_1 and produces the profit-maximizing quantity q_1.

But now suppose that the market demand curve shifts rightward to D_2 and remains there. (This shift could be caused by any one of several factors. If you can't list some of them, turn back to Chapter 3.) Panels (c) and (d) show what happens. In the *short run*, the shift in demand moves the market equilibrium to point B, with market output Q_{SR} and price P_{SR}. At the same time, the demand curve facing each firm shifts upward, and each firm raises output to the new profit-maximizing level q_{SR}. At this output level, $P > ATC$, so each firm is earning economic profit. Thus, the short-run impact of an increase in demand is (1) a rise in market price, (2) a rise in market quantity, and (3) economic profits.

When we turn to the long run, we know that economic profit will attract the entry of new firms. And, as you learned a few pages ago, an increase in the number of firms shifts the market supply curve rightward, which drives down the price until the economic profit is eliminated. But how far must the price fall in order to bring this about? That is, how far can we expect the market supply curve to shift? That depends on whether or not the expansion of the industry causes each firm's cost curves to shift.

Do Demand Shifts Cause Supply Shifts? In Chapter 3, you learned that a rightward shift in demand does *not* cause a rightward shift in supply. Instead, it raises the price and causes *a movement along* the supply curve. But in Figure 10, the demand curve shifts rightward from D_1 to D_2, the price rises, and then . . . the supply curve shifts rightward! So, now you may be wondering whether demand shifts *do* cause supply shifts.

The answer is: They *don't*—in the short run. But demand shifts indirectly cause supply shifts in the long run. In the figure, you can see that the shift in demand first raises the price, moving us *along* the supply curve S_1 from point A to point B in the short run. This is just as you learned in Chapter 3, which only dealt with the short run. (In that chapter, we assumed the number of firms was constant.)

But now, we're extending our analysis further, into the long run. The rise in price causes new firms to enter by creating profit for firms already in the industry. An *increase in the number of firms* is a shift variable for the supply curve. This is why, in the long run, the supply curve shifts from S_1 to S_2.

DANGEROUS CURVES

A Constant Cost Industry

Let's assume, for now, that a change in industry output (such as when new firms enter) has no impact on the cost curves of the individual firm. This is called a **constant cost industry.** Then in panel (c), entry will continue—and the supply curve will continue shifting rightward—until the price returns to P_1, its original level. (At any higher price, each firm would still be earning economic profit, and new firms would still be entering.) Our new long-run equilibrium occurs at point C, with the supply curve S_2, price P_1, and market quantity Q_2. Panel (d) shows what happens at the typical firm: The price moves back to P_1, so the demand curve facing the firm shifts back to d_1, and the typical firm returns to its original level of output q_1.

There is a lot going on in Figure 10. But we can make the story simpler if we *skip over* the short-run equilibrium at point B, and just ask: What happens in the *long run* after the demand curve shifts rightward? The answer is: The market equilibrium will move from point A to point C. A line drawn through these two points tells us, in the long run, the market price we can expect for any quantity the market provides. In Figure 10, this is the thin line, which is called the *long-run supply curve* (S_{LR}).

> The **long-run supply curve** shows the relationship between market price and market quantity produced after all long-run adjustments have taken place.

Notice that, because we are dealing with a constant cost industry, the long-run supply curve is horizontal.

Constant cost industry An industry in which the long-run supply curve is horizontal because each firm's costs are unaffected by changes in industry output.

Long-run supply curve A curve indicating price and quantity combinations in an industry after all long-run adjustments have taken place.

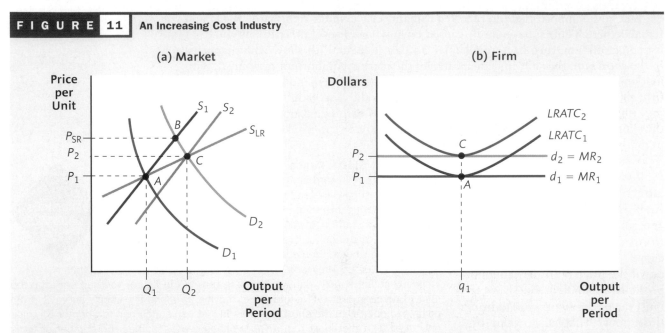

FIGURE 11 An Increasing Cost Industry

Point A *in both panels shows the initial long-run market equilibrium, with the typical firm earning zero economic profit. After demand increases, the market reaches a new short-run equilibrium at point B in panel (a). At the higher price, the typical firm earns economic profit (not shown). In the long run, profit attracts entry, supply increases and price begins to fall. But in an increasing cost industry, the rise in industry output also causes costs to rise, shifting up the LRATC curve. In the final, long-run market equilibrium (point C in both panels), price at P₂ is higher than originally, and the typical firm once again earns zero economic profit. The increase in demand raises both output and price, as shown [in panel (a)] by the upward-sloping long-run supply curve.*

> *In a constant cost industry, in which industry output has no effect on individual firms' cost curves, the long-run supply curve is horizontal. In the long-run, the industry will supply any amount of output demanded at an unchanged price.*

An Increasing Cost Industry

Increasing cost industry An industry in which the long-run supply curve slopes upward because each firm's *LRATC* curve shifts upward as industry output increases.

Our trip through Figure 10 illustrated the impact of an increase in demand for a constant cost industry, in which a rise in industry output had no impact on the cost curves of individual firms. But a constant cost industry is just one possible case.

In an **increasing cost industry**, a rise in industry output causes costs to *rise* at each firm in the long run. For example, wheat farming uses a great deal of land in the Midwestern United States. If the demand for wheat increased significantly, existing wheat farms would expand, and new farms would enter the industry. The long-run price of farmland would rise. Because *every* farm in the industry—the existing ones as well as new entrants—would have to pay more for farmland, their costs would rise.

Let's see how this changes the graphical analysis of an increase in demand. Panel (a) in Figure 11 shows a competitive market in an initial long-run equilibrium at point *A*. Panel (b) shows the situation of a single competitive firm in this market, facing demand curve d_1 and producing output level q_1. To keep the diagram simple, we've left out the *MC* and *ATC* curves for the firm and show the only cost curve that will matter to our analysis: the *LRATC* curve. Initially, the firm operates at the minimum point of $LRATC_1$.

Now suppose the demand curve shifts rightward to D_2 [panel (a)]. As a result, the short-run market equilibrium moves to point *B*, and price rises to P_{SR}. Because the typical firm enjoys economic profit (not shown), entry will occur in the long run, and the market supply curve shifts rightward. As usual, the supply curve will continue shifting rightward until economic profit is eliminated.

But this time, the rise in industry output causes the typical firm's *LRATC* curve to shift *upward* to $LRATC_2$. With higher long-run average cost, zero profit will occur at a price *higher* than the original price P_1. In Figure 11, the supply curve stops shifting when the price reaches P_2, with the new market equilibrium at point *C*. As panel (b) shows, once the price reaches P_2, the typical firm—facing the horizontal demand curve d_2—operates at the minimum point on $LRATC_2$, earning zero economic profit.

Let's now concentrate on just the long-run impact of the change in demand, which moves the equilibrium from point *A* to point *C*. Connecting these two equilibrium points gives us the long-run supply curve for this industry. As you can see, the curve slopes *upward*, telling us that the industry will supply greater output, but only with a higher price.

> *In an* increasing cost industry, *a rise in industry output shifts up each firm's* LRATC *curve, so that zero economic profit occurs at a higher price. The long-run supply curve slopes upward.*

The long-run supply curve tells us that an increasing cost industry will deliver more output, but only at a higher price. It also tells us that, if industry output decreases, the price will drop. This is because a decrease in output would cause each firm's *LRATC* curve to shift *downward* so that zero profit would be established at a *lower* price than initially.

A Decreasing Cost Industry

In a **decreasing cost industry,** a rise in industry output causes costs to *fall* at each firm in the long run. This might occur for a number of reasons. As an industry expands, there might be more workers in the area with the needed skills, making it easier and less expensive for each firm to find and recruit qualified employees. Or transportation costs might decrease.

For example, suppose that a modest size city has just a few sushi restaurants. Periodically, a partially loaded truck makes a special trip from a distant larger city to deliver raw fish, nori seaweed, wasabi, and other special ingredients to these few restaurants. Transportation costs—part of the price of the ingredients—will be rather high.

Now suppose that demand for sushi meals increases. Profits at the existing restaurants attract entry. With more restaurants ordering ingredients, the same delivery truck makes the same trip, but now it is fully loaded and the transportation costs are shared among more restaurants. As a result, transportation costs at *each* restaurant decrease—and each restaurant's *LRATC* curve shifts down. Competition among the restaurants then ensures that prices will drop to match the lower *LRATC*. As a result, the long-run effect of an increase in demand is a *lower* price for eating sushi at a restaurant—a downward sloping long-run supply curve.

Decreasing cost industry An industry in which the long-run supply curve slopes downward because each firm's *LRATC* curve shifts downward as industry output increases.

FIGURE 12 A Decreasing Cost Industry

Point A in both panels shows the initial long-run market equilibrium, with the typical firm earning zero economic profit. After demand increases, the market reaches a new short-run equilibrium at point B in panel (a). At the higher price, the typical firm earns economic profit (not shown). In the long run, profit attracts entry, supply increases and price begins to fall. But in a decreasing cost industry, the rise in industry output causes costs to fall, shifting down the LRATC curve. In the final, long-run market equilibrium (point C in both panels), price at P₂ is lower than originally, and the typical firm once again earns zero economic profit. The increase in demand raises output but lowers price, as shown [in panel (a)] by the downward-sloping long-run supply curve.

Similar-Sounding Terms, but Different Concepts You've learned a number of different terms having to do with rising costs. A direct comparison can help to prevent confusing them.

Diseconomies of scale (from Chapter 6) refers to a rise in long-run average cost due to an increase in a firm's *own* output. This is illustrated by a movement *along* the upward sloping portion of the firm's *LRATC* curve.

Increasing-cost industry (from this chapter) refers to a rise in a firm's long-run average cost at every output level, due to an increase in the *industry's* output. This is illustrated by an upward *shift* of the firm's *LRATC* curve.

Diminishing marginal returns (from Chapter 6) is most commonly applied as a short-run concept. It tells us that as a firm adds equal amounts of a single input, holding constant all other inputs, output will rise by smaller and smaller amounts. This explains *increasing marginal cost*—the upward-sloping portion of the firm's marginal cost curve.

Each of these terms has its opposite, having to do with *falling* costs: economies of scale, decreasing cost industry, and increasing marginal returns. You might want to test yourself by explaining how these three terms differ from one another.

Figure 12 illustrates how a decreasing cost industry behaves after an increase in demand. In panel (a), after the demand curve shifts rightward, the market equilibrium moves from *A* to *B* in the short run. The typical firm earns economic profit (not shown). In the long run, profit causes entry. But now, as the industry expands, the *LRATC* curve at each firm shifts *downward*. With lower cost per unit, zero economic profit occurs at a long-run equilibrium price *lower than the original price*. In the figure, the market reaches its new long-run equilibrium at point C, at the new, lower price P₂.

When we draw a line through the initial equilibrium at point A and the new long-run equilibrium at point C, we get the long-run supply curve for this industry.

As you can see, the curve slopes downward: In a decreasing cost industry, as industry output rises, the *price drops*.

> In a decreasing cost industry, *a rise in industry output shifts down each firm's LRATC curve, so that zero economic profit occurs at a lower price. The long-run supply curve slopes downward.*

The long-run supply curve tells us that in a decreasing cost industry, the more output produced, the lower the price. On the other hand, if industry output were to fall, the price would rise. This is because a decrease in output would cause each firm's *LRATC* curve to shift *upward*, so that zero profit would be established at a *higher* price than initially.

MARKET SIGNALS AND THE ECONOMY

The previous discussion of changes in demand included a lot of details, so let's take a moment to go over it in broad outline. You've seen that an *increase* in demand always leads to an *increase* in market output in the short run, as existing firms raise their output levels, and an even *greater* increase in output in the long run, as new firms enter the market.

We could have also analyzed what happens when demand *decreases*, but you'll be asked to do this on your own in the end-of-chapter problem set. If you do it correctly, you'll find that the leftward shift of the demand curve will cause a drop in output in the short run and an even greater drop in the long run. The effect on price will depend on the nature of the industry, (i.e., whether it is a constant, increasing, or decreasing cost industry).

But now let's step back from these details and see what they really tell us about the economy. We can start with a simple fact: In the real world, the demand curves for different goods and services are constantly shifting. For example, over the last decade, Americans have developed an increased taste for bottled water. The average American gulped down 8 gallons of the stuff in 1990, and almost three times that much—23 gallons—in 2004. As a consequence, the *production* of bottled water has increased dramatically. This seems like magic: Consumers want more bottled water and, presto!, the economy provides it. Our model of perfect competition shows us the workings behind this apparent magic, the logical sequence of events leading from our desire to consume more bottled water and its appearance on store shelves.

The secret—the trick up the magician's sleeve—is this: As demand increases or decreases in a market, *prices change*. And price changes act as *signals* for firms to enter or exit an industry. How do these signals work? As you've seen, when demand increases, the price tends to initially *overshoot* its long-run equilibrium value during the adjustment process, creating sizable temporary profits for existing firms. Similarly, when demand decreases, the price falls *below* its long-run equilibrium value, creating sizable losses for existing firms. These exaggerated, temporary movements in price, and the profits and losses they cause, are almost irresistible forces, pulling new firms into the market or driving existing firms out. In this way, the economy is driven to produce whatever collection of goods consumers prefer.

For example, as Americans shifted their tastes toward bottled water, the market demand curve for this good shifted rightward and the price rose. Initially, the price rose *above* its new long-run equilibrium value, leading to high profits at existing bottled water firms such as Poland Spring and Arrowhead. High profits, in turn, attracted entry—especially the entry of new brands from established firms not previously selling bottled water, such as Pepsi's Aquafina and Coke's Dasani. As a result, production expanded to match the increase in demand by consumers. More of our land, labor, capital, and entrepreneurial skills are now used to produce bottled water. Where did these resources come from?

In large part, they were freed up from those industries that experienced a *decline* in demand. In these industries, lower prices have caused exit, freeing up land, labor, capital, and entrepreneurship to be used in other, expanding industries, such as the bottled water industry.

Market signals Price changes that cause changes in production to match changes in consumer demand.

> *In a market economy, price changes act as **market signals**, ensuring that the pattern of production matches the pattern of consumer demands. When demand increases, a rise in price signals firms to enter the market, increasing industry output. When demand decreases, a fall in price signals firms to exit the market, decreasing industry output.*

Importantly, in a market economy, no single person or government agency directs this process. There is no central command post where information about consumer demand is assembled, and no one tells firms how to respond. Instead, existing firms and new entrants, in their *own* search for higher profits, respond to market signals and help move the overall market in the direction it needs to go. This is what Adam Smith meant when he suggested that individual decision makers act— as if guided by an *invisible hand*—for the overall benefit of society, even though, as individuals, they are merely trying to satisfy their own desires.

A Change in Technology

You've just learned how production in perfectly competitive markets responds to changes in consumer demand. Demand for a good increases, and production rises. Demand decreases; production falls.

But the service of competitive markets extends to other types of changes as well. In this section, we'll explore how competitive markets ensure that the benefits of technological advances are enjoyed by consumers.

One industry that has experienced especially rapid technological changes in the 1990s and 2000s is farming. By using genetically altered seeds, farmers are able to grow crops that are more resistant to insects and more tolerant of herbicides. This lowers the total—and average—cost of producing any given amount of the crop.

Figure 13 illustrates the market for corn, but it could just as well be the market for soybeans, cotton, or many other crops. In panel (a), the market begins at point *A*, where the price of corn is $3 per bushel. In panel (b), the typical farm produces 1,000 bushels per year and—with long-run average cost curve $LRATC_1$—earns zero economic profit.

Now let's see what happens when new, higher-yield corn seeds are made available. Suppose first that only one farm uses the new technology. This farm will enjoy a downward shift in its $LRATC$ curve from $LRATC_1$ to $LRATC_2$. Since it is so small relative to the market, it can produce all it wants and continue to sell at $3. Although we have not drawn in the farm's MC curve, you can see that the farm has several output levels from which to choose where price exceeds cost per unit and it can earn economic profit.

FIGURE 13 **Technological Change in Perfect Competition**

(a) Market

(b) Firm

Technological change may reduce LRATC. In panel (b), the first farms that adopt new technology will earn economic profit if they can sell at the old market price of $3 per bushel. That profit will lead its competitors to adopt the same technology and will also attract new entrants. As market supply increases, price falls until each farm is once again earning zero economic profit.

But not for long. In the long run, economic profit at this farm will cause two things to happen. First, all other farmers in the market will have a powerful incentive to adopt the new technology—to plant the new, genetically engineered seed themselves. Under perfect competition, they can do so; there are no barriers that prevent any farmer from using the same technology as any other. As these farms adopt the new seed technology, their *LRATC* curves, too, will drop down to $LRATC_2$.

Second, outsiders will have an incentive to enter this industry, using the new technology, shifting the market supply curve rightward (from S_1 to S_2) and driving down the market price. The process will stop only when the market price has reached the level at which *farms using the new technology* earn zero economic profit. In Figure 13, this occurs at a price of $2 per bushel.

From this example, we can draw two conclusions about technological change under perfect competition. First, what will happen to a farmer who is reluctant to change his technology? As *other* farms make the change, and the market price falls from $3 to $2, the reluctant farmer will find himself suffering an economic loss, since his average cost will remain at $3. His competitors will leave him to twist in the wind, and if he refuses to shape up, he will be forced to exit the industry. In the end, *all* farms in the market must use the new technology.

Second, who benefits from the new technology in the long run? Not the farmers who adopt it. *Some* farmers—the earliest adopters—may enjoy *short-run* profit before the price adjusts completely. But in the long run, all farmers will be right back where they started, earning zero economic profit. The gainers are *consumers* of corn, since they benefit from the lower price.

Although some of the data in this example are hypothetical, the story is not. The average American farmer today feeds 129 people, double the amount fed only a few years ago. And as our example suggests, powerful forces push farmers to adopt new productivity-enhancing technology. From 1995 to 2003, the fraction of U.S. corn acreage planted with genetically modified seeds increased from zero to 38 percent, and continues to grow rapidly. For soybeans, the comparable figures are zero to 80 percent.

More generally, we can summarize the impact of technological change as follows:

> *Under perfect competition, a technological advance leads to a rightward shift of the market supply curve, decreasing market price. In the short run, early adopters may enjoy economic profit, but in the long run, all adopters will earn zero economic profit. Firms that refuse to use the new technology will not survive.*

Technological advances in many competitive industries—mining, lumber, communication, entertainment, and others—have indeed spread quickly, shifting market supply curves rapidly and steadily rightward over the past 100 years. Competitive firms in these industries have had to continually adapt to new technologies in order to survive, leading to huge rewards for consumers.

© CHINCH GRYNIEWICZ/ ECONOSCENE/CORBIS

USING THE THEORY

Solar Power: An Increasing Cost Industry (for a While)

In the United States, solar power generates only a tiny fraction of total energy—about 0.1 percent. It generates an even lower fraction of the world's energy. The primary reason is cost: Even though sunshine is free, the cost of the solar panels needed to convert sunlight to electricity is relatively high. Technological advances have lowered the price of solar panels over the last couple of decades, but not by enough. When the cost and maintenance of the equipment is included, generating electricity from solar panels costs more than twice as much as generating the same energy from fossil fuels, at least at prices prevailing in the mid-2000s. As a result, in the absence of government involvement, only the most environmentally conscious households have decided to go solar.

Recently, various governments around the world decided it was time to get involved. In 2004, the German government promised to buy solar power from households at substantially above-market rates. Thousands of German households responded by installing solar panels on their roofs, transforming themselves from buyers to sellers of electricity. By 2006, Germany became the world's largest producer of solar energy.

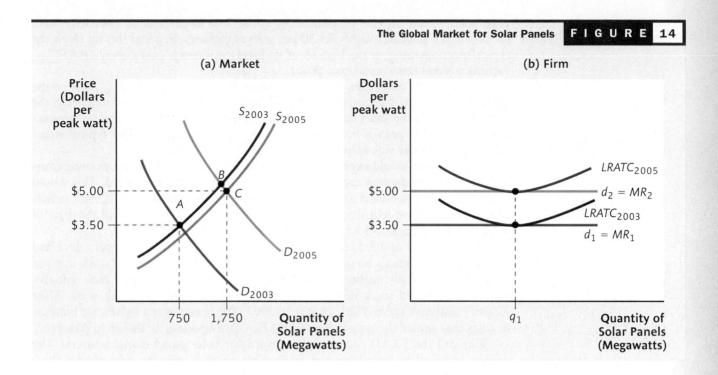

The Global Market for Solar Panels **FIGURE 14**

(a) Market

(b) Firm

The U.S. federal government followed with a more modest promise to cover up to $2,000 toward the roughly $25,000 cost of a typical home solar system. Individual states such as Washington, New Jersey, and New York added their own subsidies of several thousand dollars more. And in 2006, California vowed that it would have "a million solar roofs" in ten years. To get there, the state announced it would cover half of every household's cost of installing solar equipment.

It seemed as if solar energy was poised to take off. The dozen or so firms that made solar panels announced plans to step up production, and several new firms announced plans to enter the industry. In the United States, solar-generated electricity, which had typically grown by about 20 percent per year, began growing at twice that rate.

But the growth slowed dramatically in early 2006, even though the subsidies and incentives remained. What happened? It turned out that the solar panel industry was behaving as an *increasing cost industry*. And it is likely to continue behaving this way until around 2008 or 2009.

Figure 14 illustrates this situation.[4] Panel (a) shows the global market for solar panels. The horizontal axis measures the annual quantity of solar panels in megawatts of electricity-generating capacity. The vertical axis measures the price of the solar panels in dollars per watt of capacity. In 2003, with demand curve D_{2003} and supply curve S_{2003}, the market was in an initial long-run equilibrium at point A. That

---

[4] The information in this analysis comes from a variety of sources, including Eric Savitz, "A Place in the Sun," *Barron's*, September 19, 2005; John Carey, "What's Raining on Solar's Parade," *Business Week*, February 6, 2006; Jesse Pichel and Ming Yang, "Polysilicon Supply Constraint Limiting Industry Growth: 2005 Solar Year-end Review and 2006 Solar Industry Forecast," *Renewable Energy Access*, January 11, 2006; Jesse Pichel, "China's Solar Push More than Just Low-Cost," *Renewable Energy Access*, March 27, 2006.

year, solar panels capable of generating about 750 megawatts of electricity were produced at a price of roughly $3.50 per watt of capacity. In panel (b), we show the typical firm operating at the bottom of its long-run average cost curve, $LRATC_{2003}$ earning normal (zero) economic profit.

Over the next few years, the market demand curve shifted to D_{2005}, due to the subsidies offered by Germany, as well as by the federal and state governments in the United States. In the short run, the market moved to point B, with greater production and a higher price a bit above $5.00 per watt of capacity. The typical solar-panel manufacturer was earning economic profit (not shown).

Normally, we would expect profit to cause new firms to enter and existing firms to build more production capacity, moving the supply curve rightward. This would bring the price downward and cause a further expansion of output. If solar panels were a constant cost industry, we'd expect this process to continue until the price of solar panels fell back to $3.50 per watt.

But at the end of 2005, this adjustment process stopped. The supply curve had only shifted rightward a bit (to the curve S_{2005}), and the market seemed stuck at point C, with substantially higher prices and only slightly more output than initially. The price remained stuck near its short-run value of $5.00 per peak watt. Most industry analysts expected little change in 2007. The reason was a significant increase in costs that shifted the typical firm's $LRATC$ curve upward, as shown in panel (b).

Why did the $LRATC$ curve shift upward for solar panel manufacturers? The answer is found by switching our analysis to *another* industry. The photovoltaic cells that made up solar panels are made from *polysilicon*—one of the most abundant raw materials on the earth. But polysilicon has to be processed before it can be used by the solar panel industry.

Figure 15 shows the market for processed polysilicon. The demand curve, D_{2003}, shows the initial quantity demanded by the two industries that use polysilicon as an input: the semiconductor industry and the solar panel industry. Before the recent increase in demand for solar panels, the polysilicon industry had adjusted its manufacturing capacity to the demands of these two industries, reaching a long-run equilibrium at point E. The price for processed polysilicon was about $32 per kilogram.

As solar panel manufacturers began demanding more processed polysilicon, the demand curve for it shifted rightward, to D_{2005}. By this time, the world's polysilicon manufacturers were already operating at full capacity (the near-vertical portion of the supply curve), so further increases in demand resulted in higher prices, but little additional output (point F).[5]

Of course, with the price of polysilicon rising, the typical producer of *polysilicon* was earning economic profit (not shown). And since polysilicon processing is believed to be a *constant cost* industry, this should have caused expansion of the industry without any increase in price.

But during the mid-2000s, the polysilicon industry was not responding in this way. Existing firms were hesitant to increase their productive capacity, and potential new entrants stayed away. The reason was uncertainty. The new government subsidies that were driving the demand for solar panels could easily be reversed. Moreover, the semiconductor industry is notoriously cyclical; its demand for polysilicon could easily dry up. Firms did not want to take the risk of building new plants to manufacture polysilicon, increasing market supply, only to find that demand had decreased back to its original level. (With an increase in supply, and a return to the original market demand curve, the price of polysilicon would drop *below* its starting price of $32, and the typical polysilicon firm would experience a loss.) Because of this uncertainty, polysilicon

FIGURE 15

The Global Market for Polysilicon

Price per Kilogram

S_{2003}

$70 — — — — — — — — — ● F

32 — — — — — E

D_{2005}

D_{2003}

27

Quantity of Polysilicon (Millions of Kilograms per Year)

firms refused to expand their polysilicon capacity for several years, and the supply curve for polysilicon in Figure 15 stayed put.

Finally, in 2006, solar panel makers agreed to take on some of the risk themselves. They committed to buy polysilicon under long-term contracts, ensuring a future market for any greater output of the material. Given that assurance, the polysilicon industry began to build new manufacturing plants. Unfortunately, it takes two years or more for a new polysilicon processing plant to become operational. So the supply curve in Figure 15 will likely stay put, with prices remaining high, until some time in 2008.

Eventually, as the new manufacturing plants come on line, the supply curve in Figure 15 will shift rightward (not shown), returning the price of polysilicon to its original level of about $32 per kilogram. And this will cause the *LRATC* curve for the typical solar panel maker in Figure 14 to shift back down, resulting in economic profit, and further entry in the solar panel industry. The supply curve for solar panels will shift further rightward (not shown). And the solar panel industry—after spending several years as an increasing cost industry—will, in the end, behave as a constant cost industry.

---

[5] During the mid-2000s, other events, which complicate the analysis but don't change the conclusions, were occurring as well. Increased demand for polysilicon was coming not just from the solar industry, but also from the semiconductor industry, which was experiencing a cyclical upswing. This contributed to the rise in polysilicon prices, and contributed to an even greater upward shift in the *LRATC* curve in Figure 14. Also, by early 2006, virtually all of the polysilicon pouring out of processing plants had been bought earlier, under advanced-purchase contracts. So even if solar panel firms had been willing to pay a high price for the material, they would have been unable to obtain more than they had already committed to buy.

Summary

Perfect competition is a market structure in which (1) there are large numbers of buyers and sellers and each buys or sells only a tiny fraction of the total market quantity; (2) sellers offer a standardized product; and (3) sellers can easily enter or exit from the market. While few real markets satisfy these conditions precisely, the model is still useful in a wide variety of cases.

Each perfectly competitive firm faces a horizontal demand curve; it can sell as much as it wishes at the market price. The firm chooses its profit-maximizing output level by setting marginal cost equal to the market price. Its *short-run supply curve* is that part of its *MC* curve that lies above the average variable cost curve. Total profit is profit per unit ($P - ATC$) times the profit-maximizing quantity.

In the short run, market price is determined where the market supply curve—the horizontal sum of all firms' supply curves—crosses the market demand curve. In short-run equilibrium, existing firms can earn a profit (in which case new firms will enter) or suffer a loss (in which case existing firms will exit). Entry or exit will continue until, in the long run, each firm is earning zero economic profit. At each competitive firm in long-run equilibrium, price = marginal cost = minimum average total cost = minimum long-run average total cost.

When demand curves shift, prices change more in the short run than in the long run. The temporary, exaggerated price movements act as market signals, ensuring that output expands and contracts in each industry to match the pattern of consumer preferences.

In the long run, an increase in demand can result in a higher, lower, or unchanged market price, depending on whether the good is produced, respectively, in an *increasing cost industry*, *decreasing cost industry*, or *constant cost industry*. The long-run supply curve slopes upward in an increasing cost industry and slopes downward for a decreasing cost industry. In a constant cost industry, the long-run supply curve will be horizontal.

A technological advance in a perfectly competitive market causes the equilibrium price to fall and equilibrium quantity to rise. Each competitive firm must use the new technology in order to survive, but consumers reap all the benefits by paying a lower price.

Problem Set *Answers to even-numbered Questions and Problems can be found on the text Web site at www.thomsonedu.com/economics/hall.*

1. Assume that the market for cardboard is perfectly competitive (if not very exciting). In each of the following scenarios, should a typical firm continue to produce or should it shut down in the short run? Draw a diagram that illustrates the firm's situation in each case.
   a. Minimum $ATC = \$2.00$
      Minimum $AVC = \$1.50$
      Market price $= \$1.75$
   b. $MR = \$1.00$
      Minimum $AVC = \$1.50$
      Minimum $ATC = \$2.00$

2. Suppose that a perfectly competitive firm has the following total variable costs (*TVC*):

Quantity:	0	1	2	3	4	5	6
TVC:	$0	$6	$11	$15	$18	$22	$28

   It also has total fixed costs (*TFC*) of $6. If the market price is $5 per unit:
   a. Find the firm's profit-maximizing quantity using the marginal revenue and marginal cost approach.
   b. Check your results by re-solving the problem using the total revenue and total cost approach. Is the firm earning a positive profit, suffering a loss, or breaking even?

3. "*A profit-maximizing* competitive firm will produce the quantity of output at which price *exceeds* cost per unit by the greatest possible amount." True or false? Explain briefly. [Hint: See Figure 3(a).]

4. The following table gives quantity supplied and quantity demanded at various prices in the perfectly competitive meat-packing market:

Price (per lb.)	Q_S (in millions of lbs.)	Q_D (in millions of lbs.)
$1.00	10	100
$1.25	15	90
$1.50	25	75
$1.75	40	63
$2.00	55	55
$2.25	65	40

   Assume that each firm in the meat-packing industry faces the following cost structure:

Pounds	TC
60,000	$110,000
61,000	$111,000
62,000	$112,000
63,000	$115,000

   a. What is the profit-maximizing output level for the typical firm? (Hint: Calculate *MC* for each change in output, then find the equilibrium price, and calculate *MR* for each change in output.)
   b. Is this market in long-run equilibrium? Why or why not? (Hint: Calculate *ATC*.)

c. What do you expect to happen to the number of meat-packing firms over the long run? Why?

5. Assume that the kitty litter industry is perfectly competitive and is presently in long-run equilibrium:
   a. Draw diagrams for both the market and a typical firm, showing equilibrium price and quantity for the market, and *MC, ATC, AVC, MR,* and the demand curve for the firm.
   b. Your friend has always had a passion to get into the kitty litter business. If the market is in long-run equilibrium, will it be profitable for him to jump in headfirst (so to speak)? Why or why not?
   c. Suppose people begin to prefer dogs as pets, and cat ownership declines. Show on your diagrams from part (a) what happens in the industry and the firm in the long run, assuming that this is a constant cost industry.

6. In a perfectly competitive, increasing cost industry, is the long-run supply curve always flatter than the short-run market supply curve? Explain.

7. A student says, "My economics professor must be confused. First he tells us that in perfect competition, the demand curve is completely flat—horizontal. But then he draws a supply and demand diagram that has a downward-sloping demand curve. What gives?" Resolve this student's problem in a single sentence.

8. Assume that the firm shown in the following table produces output using one fixed input and one variable input.

Output	Price	Total Revenue	Marginal Revenue	Total Cost	Marginal Cost	Profit
0	$50	$0		$5		
					$35	
1	$50					
					$15	
2	$50					
					$35	
3	$50					
					$55	
4	$50					
					$65	

   a. Complete this table and use it to find this firm's short-run profit-maximizing quantity of output. How much profit will this firm earn?
   b. Redo the table and find the profit-maximizing quantity of output, if the price of the firm's fixed input rose from $5 to $10. How much profit will this firm earn now?
   c. Now redo the original table and find the profit-maximizing quantity of output, if the price of the firm's variable input rose so that *MC* increased by $20 at each level of output. How much profit will this firm earn in this case?

9. Assume that the firm shown in the following table produces output using one fixed input and one variable input.

   a. Complete this table and use it to find this firm's short-run profit-maximizing quantity of output. How much profit will this firm earn?
   b. Redo the table and find the profit-maximizing quantity of output, if the price of the firm's fixed input fell by half. How much profit will this firm earn now?
   c. Now redo the original table and find the profit-maximizing quantity of output, assuming the price of the variable input drops, and each *MC* value is 50% lower than before. How much profit will the firm earn in this case?

Output	Price	Total Revenue	Marginal Revenue	Total Cost	Marginal Cost	Profit
0	$3500	$0		$1000		
					$4000	
1	$3500					
					$3000	
2	$3500					
					$2000	
3	$3500					
					$1000	
4	$3500					
					$3000	
5	$3500					
					$4000	
6	$3500					
					$9000	
7	$3500					
					$36,000	
8	$3500					

10. Figure 11 shows the short-run and long-run adjustment process for an increasing cost industry responding to an increase in demand. Draw a similar two-panel diagram, illustrating the response of an increasing cost industry to a *decrease* in demand. Draw in the long-run supply curve. In the long run, will the price be higher or lower, compared to the initial price?

11. Figure 12 shows the short-run and long-run adjustment process for a decreasing cost industry responding to an increase in demand. Draw a similar two-panel diagram, illustrating the response of a decreasing cost industry to a *decrease* in demand. Draw in the long-run supply curve. In the long run, will the price be higher or lower, compared to the initial price?

More Challenging

12. Draw a diagram for a perfectly competitive firm in long run equilibrium. Include only the demand curve facing the firm and its *LRATC* curve. Then show the impact of an excise tax (some number of dollars per unit) imposed by the government *on this firm only* but not on any other firm in the market. Can we say what this firm will do in the long-run?

13. In Chapter 4, you learned that when an excise tax is imposed on buyers or sellers in a competitive market, the equilibrium price rises, and the tax payment is shared between buyers and sellers. To obtain that result, we used the (short-run) market supply curve. Now let's extend the analysis to the long run. Draw a two panel diagram: one panel for the market (demand and short-run supply curves only), the other panel for the typical firm (demand and *LRATC* curves only). Suppose an excise tax (some number of dollars per unit) is imposed on *all* sellers (firms) in this market.

a. Show what will happen in the *market* in the short run.

b. Show what will happen in *both* diagrams (market and typical firm) in the long run, assuming that this is a *constant cost industry*. [Hint: After the tax is imposed, will the typical firm earn a profit or suffer a loss? Will entry or exit occur?]

c. In the long run, do both buyers and sellers share in the payment of the excise tax? Explain briefly.

Monopoly

"Monopoly" is as close as economics comes to a dirty word. It is often associated with thoughts of extraordinary power, unfairly high prices, and exploitation. Even in the board game *Monopoly*, when you take over a neighborhood by buying up adjacent properties, you exploit other players by charging them higher rent.

The negative reputation of monopoly is in many ways deserved. A monopoly, as the only firm in its market, has the power to act in ways that a perfectly competitive firm cannot. Adam Smith's "invisible hand"—which channels the behavior of perfectly competitive firms into a socially beneficial outcome—doesn't poke, prod, or even lay a finger on a monopoly firm. Left unchecked, it will *not* create the best of all possible worlds for consumers. Indeed, when a monopoly "takes over" a previously competitive industry, great harm can be done to consumers and society in general. Monopolies, therefore, present a problem that nations around the world address with the very *visible* hand of government policy.

At the same time, a mythology has developed around monopolies. The media often portray their power as absolute and unlimited, and their behavior as capricious and unpredictable. As you are about to see, this characterization goes too far. A monopoly's power may be formidable, but it's far from unlimited. And monopoly behavior—far from capricious—is remarkably predictable.

This chapter will help you understand what monopolies are, how they arise, how they behave, and how they respond to changing market conditions. Our focus here will be on *understanding* monopolies and *predicting* their behavior. A fuller assessment of the monopoly problem and the policy options for dealing with it will be provided in Chapters 14 and 15.

WHAT IS A MONOPOLY?

In most of your purchases—a haircut, a meal at a restaurant, a car, a college education—more than one seller is competing for your dollars, and you can choose which one to buy from. But in some markets, you have no choice at all. If you want to mail a letter for normal delivery, you must use the U.S. Postal Service. In most American towns (at least for now), if you want cable television service, you must use the one cable television company in your neighborhood. Many cities have only a single local newspaper. And if you live in a very small town, you may have just one doctor, one gas station, or one movie theater to select from. These are all examples of *monopolies:*

Monopoly firm The only seller of a good or service that has no close substitutes.

Monopoly market The market in which a monopoly firm operates.

> A ***monopoly firm*** *is the only seller of a good or service with* no close substitutes. *The market in which the monopoly firm operates is called a* ***monopoly market.***

But applying it in the real world is not always so clear-cut. Whether we regard a market as having one seller, or many sellers, depends on how broadly we define that market. Or, to put it another way, it depends on how close the substitutes must be before we include them (and their sellers) as part of the market.

Suppose, for example, that you live in a city or town with just one daily newspaper. Is that newspaper a monopoly? It depends. If we view other news sources (such as television and Internet news) as "close substitutes" and include them in the market, then there are many competitors to the local newspaper. The newspaper market in the town would *not* be a monopoly. On the other hand, if we believe none of these sources are quite like the physical newspaper that appears at your doorstep each morning, we could choose to define the market narrowly to include only "physically delivered newspapers." In that case, the market is back to monopoly status.

It makes sense, then, to view monopoly as a spectrum rather than a strict category. On one end of this spectrum is *pure monopoly,* where there is just one seller of a good for which very few buyers could find a substitute. The only doctor, attorney, or food market in a small town comes very close to being a pure monopoly. Further along the spectrum, we reach firms that sell a good for which reasonable substitutes do exist, but they are not very *close* substitutes for most buyers or most purposes. The sole local cable company is an example of this middle ground because the currently available substitutes (satellite, broadcast, or Internet video) are too different to be considered close substitutes. So most economists would extend the label "monopoly" (without the "pure") to this part of the spectrum as well.

But as we go further along the spectrum, we find goods for which so many buyers can find close substitutes that the term *monopoly* no longer makes sense. For example, Gap Inc. is the only company that sells Gap jeans. But most people regard other brands of jeans as close substitutes for Gap jeans. Therefore, we would not say that Gap Inc. is a monopoly in the market for jeans because we would not define the market so narrowly as to include only "Gap jeans." In the market for jeans in general, there are many competitors.

HOW MONOPOLIES ARISE

The mere existence of a monopoly means that *something* is causing other firms to stay out of the market rather than enter and compete with the one firm already there. Broadly speaking, there must be some *barrier to entry.* The question, Why is the market a monopoly? then becomes, What *barrier* prevents other firms from entering the market? There are several possible answers.

ECONOMIES OF SCALE

One barrier to entry—and thus one explanation for a monopoly—is economies of scale. Recall from Chapter 6 that economies of scale in production causes a firm's

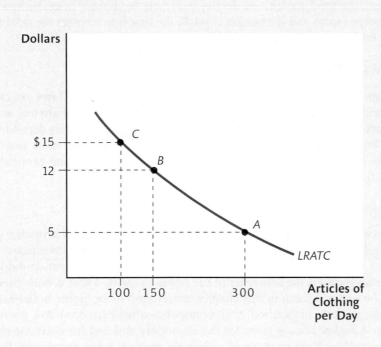

A Natural Monopoly

In the figure, the typical firm has an LRATC curve as shown, with economies of scale through an output level of 300, which is assumed to be the total market quantity. A single firm could serve the market at a cost of $5 per unit, operating at point A. Two firms splitting this market would each produce 150 units, with each operating at point B on its LRATC curve. Cost per unit would be $12, higher than with just one firm. Cost per unit would be even higher with three firms. Each would produce 100 units (point C), at a cost of $15 per unit. Since a single firm could produce at lower cost than two or more firms, this market tends naturally towards monopoly.

long-run average cost curve to slope downward. That is, the more output the firm produces, the lower will be its cost per unit. If economies of scale persists through a large-enough range of output, then a single firm can produce at lower cost than could two or more firms.

Figure 1 shows an example: the *LRATC* curve for a dry cleaner in a small town. We'll suppose the entire market for dry cleaning services in this town never exceeds 300 pieces of clothing per day. In the figure, the *LRATC* curve slopes downward, exhibiting economies of scale. Why might this be? A dry cleaning service uses a number of lumpy inputs: a parcel of land for the shop, a store clerk, a small dry cleaning machine if the clothes are cleaned on-site, or daily transportation to an off-site cleaning plant. The amounts of these inputs used, and their cost, would likely remain the same whether the service cleans 1 piece of clothing per day or 300. In the figure, we assume the costs of these lumpy inputs are large enough to cause cost *per unit* to decrease as they are spread among more units.

As a result, for all output levels the dry cleaning industry might produce in this small town (i.e., up to 300 pieces per day), one dry cleaner could achieve a lower cost per unit than could two or more dry cleaners. For example, the *LRATC* curve tells us that one firm could clean 300 pieces of clothing at a cost of $5 per piece (point *A*). But if two dry cleaners were to split this same output level (150 pieces of clothing each), each would have a higher cost per unit of $12 at point *B*. For three dry cleaners, cost per article cleaned would be $15 at point *C*, and so on. The first dry cleaner to locate in the town will have a cost advantage over any potential new entrants. This cost advantage will tend to keep newcomers out of the market.

Natural monopoly A monopoly that arises when, due to economies of scale, a single firm can produce for the entire market at lower cost per unit than could two or more firms.

A monopoly that arises because of economies of scale is called a **natural monopoly.** Local monopolies are often natural monopolies. In a very small town, there might be one gas station, one food market, one doctor, and so on. In all these cases, because there are sizable lumpy inputs and the market is small, the first firm to enter the market will likely be the last.

LEGAL BARRIERS

Many monopolies arise because of legal barriers. Of course, since laws are created by human beings, this immediately raises the question: Why would anyone want to create barriers that lead to monopoly? As you'll see, the answer varies depending on the type of barrier being erected. Here, we'll consider two of the most important legal barriers that give rise to monopolies: protection of intellectual property and government franchise.

Protection of Intellectual Property

The words you are reading right now are an example of *intellectual property,* which includes literary, artistic, and musical works, as well as scientific inventions. Most markets for a specific intellectual property are monopolies: One firm or individual owns the property and is the sole seller of the rights to use it. There is both good and bad in this. As you will learn in this chapter, prices tend to be higher under monopoly than under perfect competition, and monopolies often earn economic profit as a consequence. A higher price is good for the monopoly and bad for everyone else.

On the other hand, the promise of monopoly profit is what encourages the creation of original products and ideas, which benefits the rest of us. The Palm Pilot personal organizer, the Visex laser for reshaping the eye's cornea, and the Internet search engine Google were all launched by innovators who bore considerable costs and risks with an expectation of future economic profits. The same is true of every compact disc you listen to, every novel you read, and every movie you see.

In dealing with intellectual property, government strikes a compromise: It allows the creators of intellectual property to enjoy a monopoly and earn economic profit, *but only for a limited period of time.* Once the time is up, other sellers are allowed to enter the market, and it is hoped that competition among them will, in the end, bring down the price.

The two most important kinds of legal protection for intellectual property are *patents* and *copyrights.* New scientific discoveries and the products that result from them are protected by a **patent** obtained from the federal government. The patent prevents anyone else from selling the same discovery or product for about 20 years. If someone uses the discovery without obtaining (and paying for) permission from the patent owner, they can be sued. For example, the corporation that makes Blackberry email devices (Research in Motion) was sued by NTP, Inc., for unauthorized use of NTP's patented wireless email technology. In March 2006, Research in Motion agreed to settle the dispute by paying $613 million to NTP.

Patent A temporary grant of monopoly rights over a new product or scientific discovery.

Literary, musical, and artistic works are protected by a **copyright,** which grants exclusive rights over the material for at least 70 years and often longer. For example, the copyright on this book is owned by South-Western/Thomson Learning. No other company or individual can print copies and sell them to the public, and no one can quote from the book at length without obtaining South-Western's permission.

Copyright A grant of exclusive rights to sell a literary, musical, or artistic work.

Copyrights and patents are often sold to another person or firm, but this does not change the monopoly status of the market, since there is still just one seller. For example, the song "Happy Birthday" was originally written about a century ago, but first received copyright protection in 1935. Since then, the copyright has changed hands numerous times and is currently owned by Time Warner. Of course, you are free to sing this song at a private birthday party. But anyone who wants to sing it on radio or television—that is, anyone who wants to profit from the song— must obtain a license from Time Warner and pay a small royalty (at least until 2030, when the copyright expires).

Government Franchise

Some firms have their monopoly status guaranteed through **government franchise,** a grant of exclusive rights over a product. Here, the barrier to entry is quite simple: Any other firm that enters the market will be prosecuted!

Government franchise A government-granted right to be the sole seller of a product or service.

Governments usually grant franchises when they think the market is a *natural monopoly*. In this case, a single large firm enjoying economies of scale would have a lower cost per unit than multiple smaller firms, so government tries to serve the public interest by *ensuring* that there are no competitors. In exchange for its monopoly status, the seller must submit to either government ownership and control or government regulation over its prices and profits. (We'll have more to say about the regulation of monopoly in Chapter 15.)

This is the logic behind the monopoly status of the U.S. Postal Service. No matter how many letters it delivers, a postal firm must have enough letter carriers to reach every house every day. Two postal companies would need many more carriers to deliver the same total number of letters, raising costs and, ultimately, the price of mailing a letter. Thus, mail delivery is a natural monopoly, one that the federal government has chosen to own and control rather than merely regulate. Federal law prohibits any other firm from offering normal letter delivery service.

Local governments, too, create monopolies by granting exclusive franchises in a variety of industries believed to be natural monopolies. These include utility companies that provide electricity, gas, and water, as well as garbage collection services.

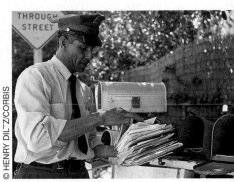

Since ordinary letter delivery is a natural monopoly, the U.S. Postal Service has been granted an exclusive government franchise to deliver the mail.

NETWORK EXTERNALITIES

Imagine that you have created a new, superior operating system for personal computers. Compared to Microsoft Windows, your operating system is less vulnerable to viruses, works 10 percent faster, and uses 10 percent less memory. It even allows the user to turn off the caps-lock key, which most people use only by mistake.

Now all you need is a few million dollars to launch your new product. You manage to get appointments with several venture capital firms, specialists in funding new projects. But every time you make your pitch, and the venture capital people realize what you're proposing, you get the same reaction: hysterical laughter. "But really," you say. "It works better than Windows. I can prove it." "We believe you," they always respond. And they do. And then . . . they start laughing again.

Why? Because you're trying to enter a market with significant *network externalities*.

> *Network externalities are the added benefits for all users of a good or service that arise because other people are using it too.*

Network externalities Additional benefits enjoyed by all users of a good or service because others use it as well.

When network externalities are present, joining a large network is more beneficial than joining a small network, even if the product in the larger network is somewhat inferior to the product in the smaller one. Once a network reaches a certain size, additional consumers will want to join just because so many others already have. And if joining the network requires you to buy a product produced by only one firm, that firm can rapidly become the leading supplier in the market.[1]

All of this applies to the market for computer operating systems. When you buy a Windows computer, you benefit from the existence of so many other Windows users in a variety of ways. First, you have access to a large number of other computers—owned by friends and coworkers—that you can easily operate. Second, you have access to more software programs (because software developers know they can reach a bigger market when they write programs for Windows). Finally, there are more people around who can help you when you have a problem, saving you the time and trouble of calling a help desk.

In addition to the advantages of *joining* a larger network, there is also an advantage in not leaving it once you've joined: avoiding *switching costs*. It takes time to learn to operate and get used to a new operating system. Although the time you've spent mastering Windows is a sunk cost, the time you'd have to spend mastering a new system can be avoided by staying in the network you're in.

Windows, the first operating system to be used by tens of millions of people, has clearly benefited from network externalities, as well as switching costs. And today, with the system installed on about 90 percent of all personal computers sold in the United States, Windows's leading position in personal computer operating systems would be difficult to overcome. For a new operating system to gain a foothold, the seller would have to incur substantial costs beyond just writing new code. It would have to create a new word processor and spreadsheet, or subsidize sellers of existing software to create versions for the new operating system. It would have to promote its product heavily. And it would have to endure a lengthy period of low prices in order to induce customers to switch.

The reason that venture capitalists would not be willing to bankroll your new operating system is that the costs of all these efforts—beyond your original creation of the operating system—would probably be greater than the revenue that your products would bring in. (If you had designed an operating system for servers instead of PCs, the venture capitalists might have taken you seriously. Network externalities are not nearly as strong for servers. As a result, Linux and other versions of Unix have gained a much larger foothold there.)

MONOPOLY BEHAVIOR

The goal of a monopoly, like that of any firm, is to earn the highest profit possible. And, like other firms, a monopolist faces constraints.

Reread that last sentence because it is important. It is tempting to think that a monopolist—because it faces no direct competitors in its market—is free of constraints

---

[1] The term *externality* will be defined formally in Chapter 15. But if you're curious, an externality is a by-product of a transaction that affects someone other than the buyer or seller (someone external to the transaction). In the case of network externalities, by paying to join the network (e.g., buying a Windows computer), you make the network larger, benefiting others (everyone else with a Windows computer) who weren't involved in your transaction.

or that its constraints are special ones, unlike those of any other firm. For example, many people think that the only force preventing a monopolist from charging outrageously high prices is public outrage. In this view, a monopoly cable company would charge $300, $500, or even $10,000 per month if only it could "get away with it."

But with a little reflection, it is easy to see that a monopolist faces purely *economic* constraints that limit its behavior—constraints that are in some ways similar to those faced by other, nonmonopoly firms. What are these constraints?

First, there is a constraint on the monopoly's *costs:* For any level of output the monopolist might produce, it must pay some total cost to produce it. This cost constraint is determined by the monopolist's production technology and by the prices it must pay for its inputs. In other words, the constraints on the monopolist's costs are the same as on any other type of firm, such as the perfectly competitive firm we studied in the previous chapter.

The monopolist also faces constraints on the price it can charge. This can be a bit confusing because a monopolist, unlike a competitive firm, is *not* a price taker: It does *not* take the market price as a given. Rather, it faces a given *demand curve*, which tells it how much output it can sell at any given price. Indeed, since a monopoly is the only firm in its market, the demand curve it faces is the *market* demand curve.

How, exactly, does the market demand curve constrain the monopoly?

That depends. As you'll see later in this chapter, some firms—including some monopolies—can charge different prices to different consumers, based on differences in the prices they are willing to pay. This kind of pricing is called *price discrimination*. Other firms—we'll call them *single-price firms*—must charge the same price for every unit they sell, regardless of any differences in willingness to pay among their customers. For the next several pages, we'll assume we are dealing with a single-price monopoly. (In general, when economists use the term "monopoly" without a modifier, it means "single-price monopoly.") We'll deal with price discrimination later in the chapter.

The constraint facing a single-price monopoly is very simple: It must choose one price among the different possible prices along its demand curve. Whatever price it selects will determine how much output it sells. Because the monopoly's demand curve slopes downward, choosing a higher price always means selling fewer units of output.

To sum up:

> *A (single-price) monopolist, like any other firm, strives to maximize profit— and like any other firm, it faces constraints. The cost constraint tells us what it will cost the monopoly to produce any level of output. The demand constraint tells us the highest price it can charge to sell any given level of output.*

MONOPOLY PRICE OR OUTPUT DECISION

Notice that the title of this section reads "price *or* output decision," not "price *and* output decision." The reason is that a monopoly does not make two separate decisions about price and quantity, but rather *one* decision. Once the firm determines its output level, it has also determined its price (the maximum price it can charge and still sell that output level). Similarly, once the firm determines its price, it has also determined its output level (the maximum output the firm can sell at that price).

How does a monopoly determine its profit-maximizing output level (and therefore its profit-maximizing price)? The same way as any other firm: It considers how a change in output would affect revenue on the one hand and cost on the other. We'll start by exploring the relationship between output and revenue.

Output and Revenue

Table 1 shows some data for Patty's Pool, a firm that owns and operates the only swimming pool in a small town—a local monopoly. Patty earns revenue by charging an admission fee for using her pool.

The first two columns show various output levels (swimmers per day) and the highest price (admission fee) Patty could charge for each output level. These two columns tell us that Patty faces a downward-sloping demand curve: The lower the fee, the greater the number of people who will pay to swim each day. This demand curve is graphed in Figure 2 (as the upper curve).

The demand curve should look familiar to you. In Chapter 7, Ned's Beds had to lower its price in order to sell more bed frames. The firm faced a downward-sloping demand curve much like the one shown here. Ned was not necessarily the only seller in his market, but as you'll see in the next chapter, monopolies are not the only firms that face downward-sloping demand curves.

The third column of the table shows Patty's total revenue per day (quantity times price) at each output level. For example, at an output level of 3, her daily revenue will be $3 \times \$10 = \$30$. And the last column shows Patty's marginal revenue (MR), which is the increase in her revenue for a one-unit rise in output. For example, when Patty's output rises from 3 to 4, her total revenue rises from $30 to $36, so her marginal revenue for this change is $36 - \$30 = \$6$.

TABLE 1				
Demand and Revenue at Patty's Pool	**Q (swimmers per day)**	**P (admission fee)**	**TR**	**MR**
	0	$13	$0	
				$12
	1	$12	$12	
				$10
	2	$11	$22	
				$8
	3	$10	$30	
				$6
	4	$9	$36	
				$4
	5	$8	$40	
				$2
	6	$7	$42	
				$0
	7	$6	$42	
				−$2
	8	$5	$40	
				−$4
	9	$4	$36	

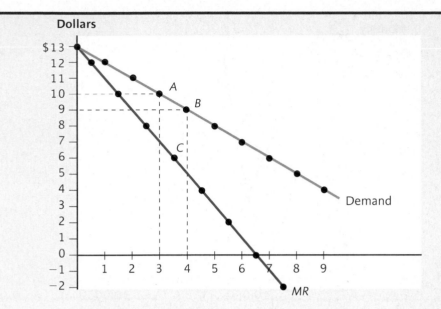

FIGURE 2

Demand and Marginal Revenue for Patty's Pool

When a firm faces a downward-sloping demand curve, marginal revenue (MR) is less than price, and the MR curve lies below the demand curve. For example, moving from point A to point B, output rises from 3 to 4 units, while price falls from $10 to $9. For this move, total revenue rises from $30 to $36, so marginal revenue (plotted at point C) is only $6—less than the new price of $9.

The marginal revenue column is graphed in Figure 2, *below* the demand curve. Why below? Mathematically, this is because when the firm's demand curve slopes downward, marginal revenue is less than the price for all increases in output (except the increase from zero to one unit). To see this, look at what happens when we move from point *A* to point *B* along the demand curve, and output rises from 3 to 4 units. The new price is $9, but the marginal revenue from producing the fourth unit is $6, which is less than the new price.

> *When any firm, including a monopoly, faces a downward-sloping demand curve, marginal revenue is less than the price of output. Therefore, the marginal revenue curve will lie below the demand curve.*

Why must marginal revenue be less than the price? Because when a firm faces a downward-sloping demand curve, it must lower the price in order to sell a greater quantity. But the lower price applies to *all* units it sells, including those it was *previously* selling at some higher price. For example, suppose Patty initially has 3 swimmers per day at $10 each. If she wants to move to 4 swimmers, Table 1 tells us that she must lower her price to $9. Patty would *gain* $9 in revenue by admitting one more swimmer at that price. But she would also *lose* some revenue, because each of the first three swimmers that she *used* to charge $10 will now be charged $9—a *loss* of $3 in revenue. If we add the $9 gained on the fourth swimmer and subtract the $3 lost from lowering the price to the other three, the net impact on revenue is an increase of $6—less than the $9 price she is now charging.

Notice, too, that for increases in output beyond 7, marginal revenue turns negative. For these changes in output, Patty loses more in revenue from dropping the price on previous units than she gains by selling one new unit. No firm would ever want to operate where marginal revenue is negative, because it could then increase its revenue *and* have lower costs by *decreasing* output.

FIGURE 3

Monopoly Price and Output Determination

Like any firm, the monopolist maximizes profit by producing where MC equals MR. Here, that quantity is 10,000 units. The price charged ($40) is read off the demand curve. It is the highest price at which the monopolist can sell the profit-maximizing level of output.

The Profit-Maximizing Output Level

Once you understand the relationship between output and revenue for a monopoly, the profit-maximizing output level can be found by applying our (now familiar) rule from Chapter 7, which tells us how *any* firm can find its profit-maximizing output level:

> *To maximize profit, a monopoly—like any firm—should produce the quantity where* MC = MR *and the* MC *curve crosses the* MR *curve from below.*

Let's apply this rule to a different firm, Zillion-Channel Cable, a monopoly that sells cable television service to the residents of a small city. We'll assume that Zillion-Channel is free from government regulation and is free to set the profit-maximizing price.

In Figure 3, we've plotted the firm's demand curve, showing the number of cable subscribers at each monthly price. As with Patty's Pool, Zillion-Channel's marginal revenue curve lies below its demand curve. The figure also shows Zillion-Channel's marginal cost curve.

The greatest profit possible occurs at an output level of 10,000, where the *MC* curve crosses the *MR* curve from below. In order to sell this level of output, the firm will charge a price of $40, located at point *E* on its demand curve. You can see that for a monopoly, *price and output are not independent decisions, but different ways of expressing the same decision.* Once Zillion-Channel determines its profit-maximizing output level (10,000 units), it has also determined its profit-maximizing price ($40), and vice versa.

MONOPOLY AND MARKET POWER

Market power The ability of a seller to raise price without losing all demand for the product being sold.

A monopoly is an example of a firm with **market power**—the ability to raise price without causing quantity demanded to go to zero. Any firm facing a downward-sloping demand curve has market power: As it raises its price, quantity demanded falls, but some customers who value the firm's product will continue to buy it at the higher price. Only perfectly competitive firms, which face horizontal demand curves, have no market power at all. For a competitive firm, raising price even a tiny bit above the market price reduces quantity demanded to zero. This is why in Chapter 8 we referred to a competitive firm as a *price taker:* It must accept the market price as a given, so there is no decision about price.

By contrast, when a firm has market power, it is a **price setter**—it makes a choice about what price to charge. The choice is limited by constraints (such as the demand curve itself), but it is still a choice. Monopolies are one example of price-setting firms, but they are not the only example. In the next chapter, you'll learn about other market structures besides monopoly in which firms have market power and are therefore price setters.

Price setter A firm (with market power) that selects its price, rather than accepting the market price as a given.

PROFIT AND LOSS

In Figure 3, we've illustrated Zillion-Channel's price and output level, but we cannot yet see whether the firm is making an economic profit or loss. This will require one more addition to the diagram—the average cost curve. Remember that

$$\text{Profit per Unit} = P - ATC.$$

At any output level, the price is read off the demand curve. Profit per unit, then, is just the vertical distance between the firm's demand curve and its *ATC* curve.

Figure 4(a) is just like Figure 3 but adds Zillion-Channel's *ATC* curve. As you can see, at the profit-maximizing output level of 10,000, price is $40 and average total cost is $32, so profit per unit is $8.

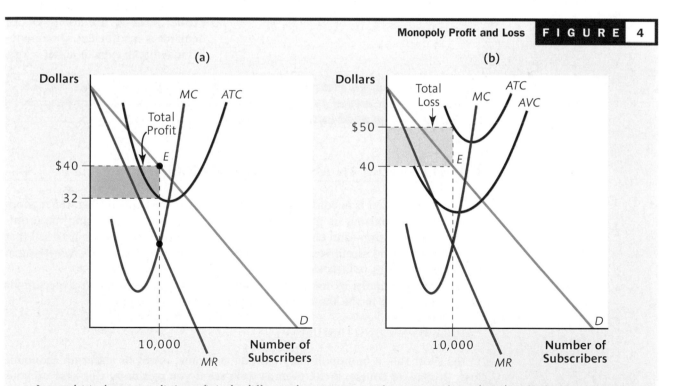

Monopoly Profit and Loss **FIGURE 4**

(a)

(b)

In panel (a), the monopolist's profit is the difference between price and average total cost (ATC) multiplied by the number of units sold. The blue area indicates a profit of $80,000. Panel (b) shows a monopolist suffering a loss. At the best level of output, ATC exceeds price. The pink rectangle shows a loss of $100,000.

Now look at the blue rectangle in the figure. The height of this rectangle is profit per unit ($8), and the width is the number of units produced (10,000). The *area* of the rectangle—height × width—equals Zillion-Channel's total profit, or $8 × 10,000 = $80,000.

> *A monopoly earns a profit whenever* P > ATC. *Its total profit at the best output level equals the area of a rectangle with height equal to the distance between* P *and* ATC *and width equal to the level of output.*

This should sound familiar: It is exactly how we represented the profit of a perfectly competitive firm (compare with Figure 3(a) in Chapter 8). The diagram looked different under perfect competition because the firm's demand curve was horizontal, whereas for a monopoly it is downward sloping.

Figure 4(b) illustrates the case of a monopoly suffering a loss. Here, costs are higher than in panel (a), and the *ATC* curve lies everywhere above the demand curve, so the firm will suffer a loss at any level of output. At the best output level—10,000—*ATC* is $50, so the loss per unit is $10. The total loss ($100,000) is the area of the pink rectangle, whose height is the loss per unit ($10) and width is the best output level (10,000).

A Monopoly Supply Curve? A question may have occurred to you: Where is the monopoly's *supply curve*? The answer is that *there is no supply curve for a monopoly*. A firm's supply curve tells us how much output a firm will want to produce and sell when it is *presented* with different prices. This makes sense for a perfectly competitive firm that takes the market price as given and responds by deciding how much output to produce. A monopoly, by contrast, is *not* a price taker; it *chooses* its price. Since the monopolist is free to choose any price it wants—and it will always choose the *profit-maximizing* price and no other—the notion of a supply curve does not apply to a monopoly.

DANGEROUS CURVES

As you can see, being a monopolist is no guarantee of profit. If costs are too high, or demand is insufficient, a monopolist may break even or suffer a loss.

> *A monopoly suffers a loss whenever* P < ATC. *Its total loss at the best output level equals the area of a rectangle with height equal to the distance between* ATC *and* P *and width equal to the level of output.*

EQUILIBRIUM IN MONOPOLY MARKETS

A monopoly market is in equilibrium when the only firm in the market, the monopoly firm, is maximizing its profit. After all, once the firm is producing the profit-maximizing quantity—and charging the highest price that will enable it to sell that quantity—it has no incentive to change either price or quantity, unless something in the market changes (which we'll explore later).

But for monopoly, as for perfect competition, we have different expectations about equilibrium in the short run and equilibrium in the long run.

SHORT-RUN EQUILIBRIUM

In the short run, a monopoly may earn an economic profit or suffer an economic loss. (It may, of course, break even as well; see if you can draw this case on your own.) A monopoly that is earning an economic profit will, of course, continue to operate in the short run, charging the price and producing the output level at which *MR = MC*, as in Figure 4(a).

But what if a monopoly suffers a loss in the short run? Then it will have to make the same decision as any other firm: to shut down or not to shut down. The rule you learned in Chapter 7—that a firm should shut down if $TR < TVC$ at the output level where marginal revenue and marginal cost are equal—applies to any firm, including a monopoly. And (as you learned in Chapter 8), the statement "$TR < TVC$" is equivalent to the statement "$P < AVC$." Therefore,

> *any firm—including a monopoly—should shut down if* P < AVC *at the output level where* MR = MC.

In Figure 4(b), Zillion-Channel is suffering a loss. But since $P = \$40$ and AVC is less than $40 at an output of 10,000, we have $P > AVC$: The firm should keep operating. On your own, draw in an alternative AVC curve in panel (b) that would cause Zillion-Channel to shut down. (Hint: It will be higher than the existing AVC curve.)

The shutdown rule should accurately predict the behavior of most privately owned and operated monopolies. But if a monopoly operates under a government franchise or regulation and produces a vital service such as transportation, mail delivery, or mass transit, the government may not allow it to shut down. If, for example, the monopoly suddenly finds that $P < AVC$ at every output level (perhaps because the cost of a variable input suddenly rises or because the demand curve suddenly shifts leftward), the government might order the firm to continue operating, and use tax revenue to cover the loss.

LONG-RUN EQUILIBRIUM

One of the most important insights of the previous chapter was that perfectly competitive firms *cannot* earn a profit in long-run equilibrium. Profit attracts new firms into the market, and market production increases. This, in turn, causes the market price to fall, eliminating any temporary profit earned by a competitive firm.

But there is no such process at work in a monopoly market, where barriers *prevent* the entry of other firms into the market. Outsiders will *want* to enter an industry when a monopoly is earning positive economic profit, but they will be *unable to do so.* Thus, the market provides no mechanism to eliminate monopoly profit.

> *Unlike perfectly competitive firms, monopolies may earn economic profit in the long run.*

What about economic loss? If a monopoly is franchised or regulated by the government, and it faces the prospect of long-run loss, the government may decide to subsidize it in order to keep it running. But if the monopoly is privately owned and controlled, it will not tolerate long-run losses. A monopoly suffering an economic loss that it expects to continue indefinitely should always exit the industry, just like any other firm.

> *A privately owned, unregulated monopoly suffering an economic loss in the long run will exit the industry, just as would any other business firm. In the long run, therefore, we should not find such monopolies suffering economic losses.*

COMPARING MONOPOLY TO PERFECT COMPETITION

We have already seen one important difference between monopoly and perfectly competitive markets: In perfect competition, economic profit is relentlessly reduced to zero by the entry of other firms; in monopoly, economic profit can continue indefinitely.

But monopoly also differs from perfect competition in another way:

> *All else equal, a monopoly market will have a higher price and lower output than a perfectly competitive market.*

To see why this is so, let's explore what would happen if a single firm took over a perfectly competitive market, changing the market to a monopoly. Panel (a) of Figure 5 illustrates a competitive market consisting of 100 identical firms. The market is in long-run equilibrium at point *E,* with a market price of $10 and market output of 100,000 units. In panel (b), the typical firm faces a horizontal demand curve at $10, produces output of 1,000 units, and earns zero economic profit.

Now, imagine that a single company buys all 100 firms, to form a monopoly. The new monopoly market is illustrated in panel (c). Under monopoly, the horizontal demand curve facing each firm becomes irrelevant. Now, the demand curve facing the monopoly is the downward-sloping *market* demand curve *D*—the same as the market demand curve in panel (a). Since the demand curve slopes downward, marginal revenue will be less than price, and the *MR* curve will lie everywhere below the demand curve. To maximize profit, the monopoly will want to find the output level at which *MC = MR*. But what is the new monopoly's *MC* curve?

We'll assume that the monopoly doesn't change the way output is produced. (This is part of the "all else equal" assumption in the highlighted statement above.) That is, each previously competitive firm will continue to produce its output with the same technology as before, only now it operates as one of 100 different plants that the monopoly controls. With this assumption, *the monopoly's marginal cost curve will be the same as the market supply curve in panel (a).* Why? First, remember that in a perfectly competitive industry the market supply curve is obtained by adding up each individual firm's supply curve, that is, each individual firm's marginal cost curve. Therefore, the market supply curve tells us the marginal cost—at each firm—of producing another unit of output for the market. When the monopoly takes over each of these individual firms, the market supply curve tells us how much it will cost the monopoly to produce another unit of output at each of its plants.

For example, point *E* on the market supply curve tells us that, when total supply is 100,000, with each plant producing 1,000 units, increasing output by one more unit will cost the monopoly $10 because that is the marginal cost at each of its plants. The same is true at every other point along the old competitive market supply curve: It will always tell us the new monopoly's cost of producing one more unit at each of the plants it now owns. In other words, the upward-sloping curve in panel (c), which is the market supply curve when the market is competitive, becomes the marginal cost curve for a single firm when the market is monopolized.

Now we have all the information we need to find the monopoly's choice of price and quantity. In panel (c), the monopoly's *MC* curve crosses the *MR* curve from

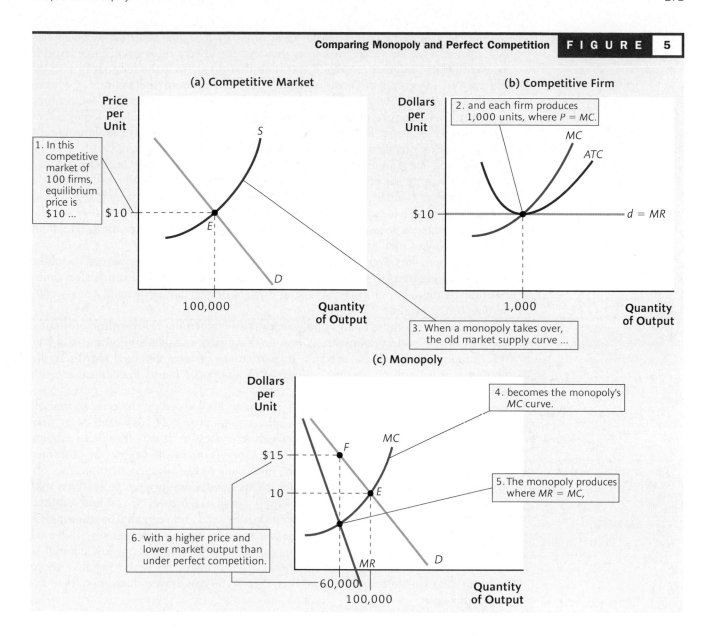

Comparing Monopoly and Perfect Competition FIGURE 5

(a) Competitive Market

Price per Unit

1. In this competitive market of 100 firms, equilibrium price is $10 ...

$10

S

E

D

100,000

Quantity of Output

(b) Competitive Firm

Dollars per Unit

2. and each firm produces 1,000 units, where $P = MC$.

MC

ATC

$10

$d = MR$

1,000

Quantity of Output

3. When a monopoly takes over, the old market supply curve ...

(c) Monopoly

Dollars per Unit

4. becomes the monopoly's MC curve.

MC

$15

F

5. The monopoly produces where $MR = MC$,

10

E

6. with a higher price and lower market output than under perfect competition.

MR

D

60,000

100,000

Quantity of Output

below at 60,000 units of output. This will be the monopoly's profit-maximizing output level. To sell this much output, the monopoly will charge $15 per unit—point *F* on its demand curve.

Notice what has happened in our example: After the monopoly takes over, the price rises from $10 to $15, and market quantity drops from 100,000 to 60,000. The monopoly, compared to a competitive market, *charges more and produces less.*

Why does this happen? When the market was perfectly competitive, each firm could sell all the output it wanted at the given market price of $10, and each firm knew it could earn an additional $10 in revenue for each additional unit it sold. The best option for the firm was to increase output until marginal cost rose to $10.

But the new monopoly does *not* treat price, or marginal revenue, as given values. Instead, it knows that raising its own output lowers the market price. And it knows that its marginal revenue is *less* than that price. So if the monopoly goes all the way to the competitive output level (100,000 units in the figure), it will be producing units for which *MR < MC* (all units beyond 60,000). This will reduce its profit. To maximize profit, the monopoly has to stop short of the competitive output—producing 60,000 rather than 100,000. Of course, since the monopoly sells a lower market quantity, it will charge a higher market price.

Now let's see who gains and who loses from the takeover. By raising price and restricting output, the new monopoly earns economic profit. We know this because if the firm were to charge $10—the old competitive price—each of its plants would break even, giving it zero economic profit. But we've just seen that $10 is *not* the profit-maximizing price—$15 is. So, the firm must make higher profit at $15 than at $10, or higher than zero economic profit.

Consumers, however, lose in two ways: They pay more for the output they buy, and, due to higher prices, they buy less output. The changeover from perfect competition to monopoly thus benefits the owners of the monopoly and harms consumers of the product.

Keep in mind, though, an important proviso concerning this result: Comparing monopoly and perfect competition, we see that price is higher and output is lower under monopoly *if all else is equal*. In particular, we have assumed that after the market is monopolized, the technology of production remains unchanged at each previously competitive firm.

But a monopoly may be able to *change* the technology of production, so that all else would *not* remain equal. For example, a monopoly may have each of its new plants *specialize* in some part of the production process, or it may be able to achieve efficiencies in product planning, employee supervision, bookkeeping, or customer relations. If these cost savings enable the monopoly to use a less costly input mix for any given output level, then the monopoly's marginal cost curve in panel (c) would be *lower* than the competitive market supply curve in panel (a). If you add another, lower *MC* curve to panel (c), you'll see that this tends to *decrease* the monopoly's price and *increase* its output level—exactly the reverse of the effects discussed earlier. If the cost savings are great enough, and the *MC* curve drops low enough, a profit-maximizing monopoly could even charge a lower price and produce more output than would a competitive market. (See if you can draw a diagram to demonstrate this case.)

The general conclusion is this:

> *The monopolization of a competitive industry leads to two opposing effects. First, for any given technology of production, monopolization leads to higher prices and lower output. Second,* changes *in the technology of production made possible under monopoly may lead to lower prices and higher output. The ultimate effect on price and quantity depends on which effect is stronger.*

GOVERNMENT AND MONOPOLY PROFIT

Monopolies, as you learned earlier, often exist with government permission. When we bring the government into our analysis, the monopoly's total profit may be less than that predicted by the analysis we've done so far. Government involvement reduces monopoly profit in two ways.

Government Regulation

As discussed earlier, in many cases of natural monopoly, a firm is granted a government franchise to be the sole seller in a market. This has been true of monopolies that provide water service, electricity, and natural gas. In exchange for its franchise, the monopoly must accept government regulation, often including the requirement that it submit its prices to a public commission for approval. The government will often want to keep prices high enough to keep the monopoly in business, but no higher. Since the monopoly will stay in business unless it suffers a long-run loss, the ideal pricing strategy for the regulatory commission would be to keep the monopoly's economic profit at zero.

Remember, though, that economic profit includes the opportunity cost of the funds invested by the monopoly's owners. If the public commission succeeds, the monopoly's *accounting* profit will be just enough to match what the owners could earn by investing their funds elsewhere—that is, the monopoly will earn zero economic profit. Government regulation of monopoly will be discussed further in Chapter 15.

Rent-Seeking Activity

Another factor that reduces a monopoly's profit comes from the interplay between politics and economics. As we've seen, many monopolies achieve and maintain their monopoly status due to legal barriers to entry. And many of these monopolies are completely unregulated. For example, a movie theater or miniature golf course may enjoy a monopoly in an area because zoning regulations prevent entry by competitors. Or, especially in less developed countries, a single firm may be granted the exclusive right to sell or produce a particular good even though it is not a natural monopoly. In all of these cases, the monopoly is left free to set its price as it wishes.

But legal barriers to entry—for example, zoning laws—are often controversial because, as you've learned, a monopoly may charge a higher price and produce less output than would a competitive market. Thus, government will be tempted to pull the plug on a monopoly's exclusive status and allow competitors into the market. The monopoly, in turn, will often take action to *preserve* legal barriers to entry. Economists call such actions *rent-seeking activity*.

> *Any costly action a firm undertakes to establish or maintain its monopoly status is called* **rent-seeking activity.**

Rent-seeking activity Any costly action a firm undertakes to establish or maintain its monopoly status.

In economics, the term *economic rent* refers to any earnings beyond the minimum needed in order for a good or service to be produced. For example, the minimum price to get *land* "produced" is zero, since it's a gift of nature. This is why all the earnings of landowners are called "rent." A monopoly's economic profit is another example of rent, since it represents earnings above the minimum needed in order for the monopoly to stay in business.

In countries with the most corrupt bureaucracies, rent-seeking activity typically takes the form of outright bribes to government officials. But rent seeking occurs in virtually all countries. It includes the time and money spent lobbying legislators and the public for favorable policies. The costs of such activities can reduce a monopoly's profit below what the simple monopoly model would suggest.

WHAT HAPPENS WHEN THINGS CHANGE?

Once a monopoly is maximizing profit, it has no incentive to change its price or its level of output . . . unless something that affects these decisions changes. In this section, we'll consider two such events: a change in demand for the monopolist's product, and a change in its costs.

A CHANGE IN DEMAND

Back in Chapter 8, we saw how a competitive market adjusted to a change in demand. In particular, we saw that an increase in demand caused an increase in both market price and market quantity.[2] Does the same general conclusion hold for a monopolist? Let's see.

Panel (a) of Figure 6 shows Zillion-Channel Cable earning a positive profit in the short run. As before, it is producing 10,000 units per month, charging $40 per unit, and earning a monthly profit of $80,000 (not shown). The fact that Zillion-Channel is a monopolist, however, does not mean that it is immune to shifts in demand.

What might cause a monopolist to experience a shift in demand? The list of possible causes is the same as for perfect competition. If you need a reminder of these causes, look back at Figure 4 in Chapter 3. For example, an increase in consumer tastes for the monopolist's good will shift its demand curve rightward, just as it shifts the market demand curve rightward in a competitive market.

Suppose that the demand for local cable service increases because a sitcom shown on one of Zillion-Channel's premium services attracts an enthusiastic following (an increase in tastes for cable services). In panel (b) of Figure 6, this is shown as a rightward shift of the demand curve from D_1 to D_2.

Notice that the marginal revenue curve shifts as well, from MR_1 to MR_2. Why is this? As you can see in the figure, a rightward shift in demand is also an *upward* shift in demand. At each quantity, the firm can charge a greater price than before. With a higher price, the rise in revenue (*MR*) for each increase in quantity will be greater as well. So the *MR* curve shifts upward (rightward), just like the demand curve. (If you want to demonstrate this with numbers, use Table 1. Cross out the price associated with each quantity and write in a price that's $2 greater instead. Then, recalculate the *TR* and *MR* columns. You'll see that marginal revenue for each increase in quantity is greater than before.)

With an unchanged cost structure, the new short-run equilibrium will occur where MR_2 intersects the unchanged *MC* curve. As you can see, the result is an increase in quantity from 10,000 to 11,000, and a higher price: $47 per month rather than the original $40. In this sense, monopoly markets behave very much like competitive markets (although the *extent* of the rise in price and quantity will generally *not* be the same as in a competitive market).

---

[2] One partial exception: in a *decreasing-cost* competitive industry, an increase in demand does raise both price and output in the short run. But in the long run, while output rises further, price drops below its initial value.

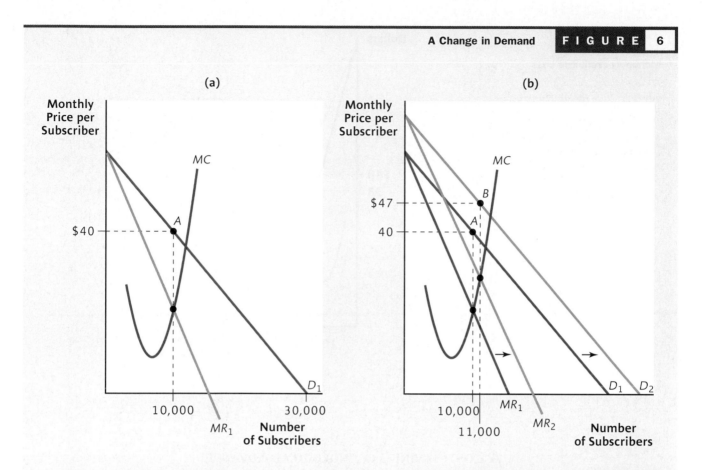

A Change in Demand   FIGURE 6

Panel (a) shows Zillion-Channel in equilibrium. It is providing 10,000 units of cable TV service at a price of $40 per month. Panel (b) shows the same firm following an increase in demand from D_1 to D_2. With the increased demand, MR is higher at each level of output. In the new equilibrium, Zillion-Channel is charging a higher price ($47), providing more TV service (11,000 units), and earning a larger profit.

What about the monopolist's profit, though? With both price and quantity now higher, total revenue has clearly increased. But total cost is higher as well. (Total cost always rises with greater output.) So it seems as if profit could either rise or fall.

It turns out, however, that profit *must* be higher in the new equilibrium at point B. We know that because Zillion-Channel has the option of continuing to sell its original quantity, 10,000, at a price higher than before. If, as we assume, it started out earning a profit at that output level, then the higher price would certainly give it an even *higher* profit. But the logic of *MR = MC* tells us that the greatest profit of all occurs at 11,000 units. So profit is certainly greater after the increase in demand.

We can conclude that:

A monopolist will react to an increase in demand by producing more output, charging a higher price, and earning a larger profit. It will react to a decrease in demand by reducing output, lowering price, and suffering a reduction in profit.

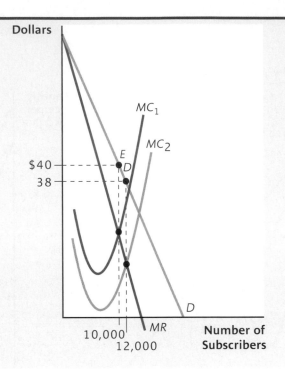

FIGURE 7

Monopoly Profit and Loss

A cost-saving technological advance shifts the monopolist's marginal cost curve down, from MC₁ to MC₂. Consumers gain because the price falls, but the drop in price is less than the drop in marginal cost. The monopoly gains because its profit is greater.

A COST-SAVING TECHNOLOGICAL ADVANCE

In Chapter 8, you learned that in a perfectly competitive market, all cost savings from a technological advance are passed along to consumers in the form of lower prices. Is the same true of monopoly? Let's see.

Suppose a new type of cable box becomes available that breaks down less often, requiring fewer service calls. When Zillion-Channel Cable begins using this equipment, it finds that it gets fewer service calls, so its labor costs decrease by $10 per customer.

Figure 7 shows the result. Before the new equipment is used, Zillion-Channel is charging $40 and producing output of 10,000, where its *MR* and *MC* curves cross. The technological advance, when it's distributed to all of Zillion's customers, will lower not only the monthly cost per *current* customer (shifting the *ATC* curve down by $10, which isn't shown), but also the monthly cost of servicing each *additional* subscriber. That is, Zillion's *marginal cost* curve will shift down by $10, from *MC*₁ to *MC*₂ (which *is* shown).

Zillion-Channel will now want to add subscribers. This is because, after the downward shift in the *MC* curve, *MR* exceeds *MC* at the original output of 10,000. An opportunity to raise profit by increasing output has been created. In the figure, the new intersection point between *MC* and *MR* occurs at an output level of 12,000, so that's Zillion-Channel's new profit-maximizing output level. The demand curve tells us that when output is 12,000, Zillion-Channel will charge a price of $38.

Furthermore, we know that Zillion-Channel's profits have increased. How? If Zillion-Channel had left its output unchanged, the downward shift in its *ATC* curve (not shown) would have raised its profit. Increasing output from 10,000 to 12,000 increased profit further (because $MR > MC$ for that move). Thus, profit must be higher.

Let's summarize what's happened: Zillion-Channel's cost per subscriber decreased by $10, but its price decreased by only $2 (from $40 to $38), and its profit increased. It appears that while consumers do get some benefit from the technological change, they don't get all the benefit. Zillion-Channel keeps a chunk of the benefits for itself (the biggest chunk, in our specific example).

We can summarize our results this way:

> *In general, a monopoly will pass to consumers only part of the benefits from a cost-saving technological change. After the change in technology, the monopoly's profits will be higher.*

This stands in sharp contrast to the impact of technological change in perfectly competitive markets, where—as stated earlier—all of the cost saving is passed along to consumers in the long run.

But there's a silver lining for consumers. Suppose that Zillion-Channel's monthly costs *increased* by $10 per subscriber, say, because of a rise in the wage rate needed to maintain its workforce. Figure 7 could be used to analyze this case as well. This time, the MC curve would shift *upward* by $10, so we'd view MC_2 as the initial curve and MC_1 as the new one. And while the price of cable service would rise, it would rise by *less* than the $10 increase in cost per unit (in our example, price would rise by only $2). Zillion-Channel would bear part of the burden of the increase in costs, and its profits would fall.

> *In general, a monopoly will pass only part of a cost increase on to consumers in the form of a higher price. After the cost increase, the monopoly's profits will be lower.*

PRICE DISCRIMINATION

So far, we've analyzed the decisions of a **single-price monopoly**—one that charges the same price on every unit that it sells. But not all monopolies operate this way. For example, local utilities typically charge different rates per kilowatt-hour, depending on whether the energy is used in a home or business. Telephone companies charge different rates for calls made by people on different calling plans. Nor is this multiprice policy limited to monopolies: Movie theaters charge lower prices to senior citizens, airlines charge lower prices to those who book their flights in advance, and supermarkets and food companies charge lower prices to customers who clip coupons from their local newspaper.

In some cases, the different prices are due to differences in the firm's costs of production. For example, it may be more expensive to deliver a product a great distance from the factory, so a firm may charge a higher price to customers in outlying areas. But in other cases, the different prices arise not from cost differences but from the firm's recognition that *some customers are willing to pay more than others:*

> *Price discrimination occurs when a firm charges different prices to different customers for reasons other than differences in costs.*

Single-price monopoly A monopoly firm that is limited to charging the same price for each unit of output sold.

Price discrimination Charging different prices to different customers for reasons other than differences in cost.

The term *discrimination* in this context requires some getting used to. In every-day language, *discrimination* carries a negative connotation: We think immediately of discrimination against someone because of his or her race, sex, or age. But a price-discriminating monopoly does not discriminate based on prejudice, stereo-types, or ill will toward any person or group; rather, it divides its customers into different categories based on their *willingness to pay* for the good—nothing more and nothing less. By doing so, a monopoly can squeeze even more profit out of the market. Why, then, doesn't *every* firm practice price discrimination?

REQUIREMENTS FOR PRICE DISCRIMINATION

Although every firm would *like* to practice price discrimination, not all of them can. To successfully price discriminate, three conditions must be satisfied:

1. *The firm must have market power.* That is, the firm must face a downward-sloping demand curve so that it behaves as a price setter. A monopoly will always satisfy this market power requirement.

    In contrast, a perfectly competitive firm faces a horizontal demand curve, and cannot price discriminate. If a perfectly competitive firm tries to charge some customers a higher price than others, the high-price customers would simply buy from other firms that are selling the same product at the market price.

2. *The firm must be able to identify consumers willing to pay more.* In order to determine which prices to charge to which customers, a firm must identify how much different groups of customers are willing to pay. But this is often difficult. Suppose your barber or hairstylist wanted to price discriminate. How would he determine how much you are willing to pay for a haircut? He could *ask* you, but . . . let's be real: You wouldn't tell him the truth, since you know he would only use the information to charge you more than you've been paying. Price-discriminating firms—in most cases—must be a bit sneaky, relying on more indirect methods to gauge their customers' willingness to pay.

    For example, airlines know that business travelers, who must get to their destination quickly, are willing to pay a higher price for air travel than are tourists or vacationers, who can more easily travel by train, bus, or car. Of course, if airlines merely *announced* a higher price for business travel, then no one would admit to being a business traveler when buying a ticket. So the airlines must find some way to identify business travelers without actually asking. Their method is crude but reasonably effective: Business travelers typically plan their trips at the last minute and don't stay over Saturday night, while tourists and vacationers generally plan long in advance and do stay over Saturday. Thus, the airlines give a discount to any customer who books a flight several weeks in advance and stays over, and they charge a higher price to those who book at the last minute and don't stay over.[3]

---

[3] It is sometimes argued that airlines' pricing behavior is based entirely on a cost difference to the airline. For example, it is probably more costly for an airline to keep seats available until the last minute because there is a risk that they will go unsold. The higher price for last-minute bookings would then compensate the airline for the unsold seats. (See, for example, the article by John R. Lott, Jr., and Russell D. Roberts in *Economic Inquiry*, January 1991.) But we know that cost differences are not the only reason for the price differential, or else the airlines would not have added the Saturday stayover requirement, which has nothing to do with their costs.

Catalog retailers—such as Victoria's Secret—have an easily available clue for determining who is willing to pay more: the customer's address. People who live in high-income zip codes are mailed catalogs with higher prices than people who live in lower-income areas. Some Internet retailers have even used software to track customers' past purchases to gauge whether each is a free spender or a careful shopper. Only the careful shoppers get the low prices.[4]

3. *The firm must be able to prevent low-price customers from reselling to high-price customers.* Preventing a product from being resold by low-price customers can be a vexing problem for a would-be discriminator. For example, when airlines began price discriminating, a resale market developed: Business travelers could buy tickets at the last minute from intermediaries, who had booked in advance at the lower price and then advertised their tickets for sale. To counter this, the airlines imposed the additional requirement of a Saturday stayover in order to buy at the lower price. By adding this restriction, the airlines were able to substantially reduce the reselling of low-price tickets to business travelers.

It is often easy to prevent resale of a *service* because of its personal nature. A hairstylist can charge different prices to different customers without fearing that one customer will sell her haircut to another. The same is true of the services provided by physicians, attorneys, and music teachers.

Resale of *goods,* however, is much harder to prevent, since goods can be easily transferred from person to person without losing their usefulness. A classic example of how far a company might have to go to prevent resale of a good is the case of Rohm and Haas, a chemical firm. In the 1940s, Rohm and Haas sold methyl methacrylate powder, used to make durable plastic, at two prices. Industrial users, who had many other options, paid 85 cents per pound; dental laboratories, which had no other choice of material for making dentures and were willing to pay more, were charged $22 per pound. In spite of Rohm and Haas's diligent efforts to prevent it, this price differential led to a flourishing resale market, in which industrial users were buying methyl methacrylate at 85 cents per pound and selling it for substantially more to dental laboratories. Internal memos at Rohm and Haas revealed that the company, desperate for a solution, considered (but did not finally adopt) a plan to put lead or even arsenic (!) in all powder sold at the lower price, so that dental laboratories would be unable to use it.[5]

EFFECTS OF PRICE DISCRIMINATION

Price discrimination always benefits the owners of a firm: When the firm can charge different prices to different consumers, it can use this ability to increase its profit. But the effects on consumers can vary. To understand how price discrimination affects the firm and the consumers of its product, let's take a simple example. Imagine that only one company—No-Choice Airlines—offers direct, small-plane flights between Omaha, Nebraska, and Salina, Kansas. (What barrier to entry might

[4] Anita Ramasastry, "Websites That Charge Different Customers Different Prices: Is Their 'Price Customization' Illegal? Should It Be?" *FindLaw Legal News and Commentary*, June 20, 2005. For a general discussion of Internet pricing, see Robert E. Hall, *Digital Dealing* (New York: W. W. Norton, 2002).
[5] From George W. Stocking and Myron W. Watkins, *Cartels in Action: Case Studies in International Business Diplomacy* (New York: The Twentieth Century Fund, 1946), p. 403.

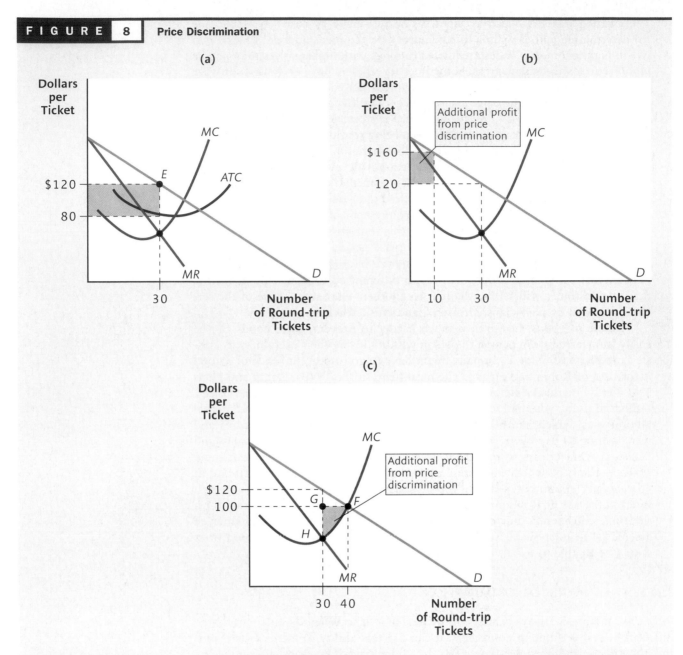

FIGURE 8 | **Price Discrimination**

Panel (a) shows a single-price monopoly airline selling 30 round-trip tickets per day at $120 each and earning a profit of $1,200 per day. Panel (b) shows the same airline if it can charge a higher price to its business travelers. The shaded rectangle shows the additional profit the airline earns by price discriminating; total profit is now $1,600. Panel (c) shows an alternative strategy. In addition to selling 30 regular tickets at $120 each, the airline attracts an additional 10 passengers at a lower student fare of $100. So profit rises by the area of the shaded region.

explain No-Choice's monopoly on this route? If you're stumped, look again at the section on the sources of monopoly in this chapter.)

Figure 8(a) illustrates what No-Choice would do if it could *not* price discriminate and had to operate as a single-price monopoly. Since $MR = MC$ at 30 round-trip tickets per day, No-Choice's profit-maximizing price would be $120 per ticket. The firm's average total cost for 30 round-trips is $80, so its profit per ticket would be $120 − $80 = $40. Total profit is $40 × 30 = $1,200, equal to the area of the shaded rectangle.

Price Discrimination That Harms Consumers

Now suppose that No-Choice discovers that on an average day, 10 of the 30 people buying tickets are business travelers who are willing to pay more, and it can identify them by their *un*willingness to book in advance and stay over on Saturday night. No-Choice could price discriminate by offering two prices: $120 for those who book in advance and stay over on Saturday, and $160 to all others. In effect, No-Choice is raising the price from $120 to $160 for its 10 business customers.

Let's calculate the impact on No-Choice's profit. Since it continues to sell the same 30 round-trip tickets, there is no impact on its costs. Its revenue, however, will rise: It charges $40 more than before on 10 of its round-trip tickets. Thus, No-Choice will earn an additional daily profit of $40 × 10 = $400. This *increase* in profit is identified as the shaded rectangle in Figure 8(b). Total profit is now the sum of two numbers: the profit No-Choice earned *before* price discrimination ($1,200, the area of the shaded rectangle in panel (a)) and the *increase* in profit due to price discrimination ($400, the area of the shaded rectangle in panel (b)). By price discriminating, No-Choice has raised its total profit from $1,200 to $1,600 per day.

What about consumers? Since 10 customers each pay $40 more than before, they lose 10 × $40 = $400 from paying the higher price. Other travelers, who continue to pay $120 for their tickets, are unaffected by the higher price.

Summing up, in this case the impact of price discrimination—compared to a single-price policy—is a direct transfer of funds from consumers to the firm. The increase in the firm's profit is equal to the additional payments by consumers. This conclusion applies more generally as well:

> *When price discrimination raises the price for some consumers above the price they would pay under a single-price policy, it harms consumers. The additional profit for the firm is equal to the monetary loss to consumers.*

Price Discrimination That Benefits Consumers

Let's go back to the initial situation facing No-Choice and suppose that, instead of charging a higher price to business travelers, it decides to price discriminate in a different way. No-Choice discovers that students who travel to college in Salina are going by train because it is cheaper. However, at a price of $100, the airline could sell an average of 10 round-trip tickets per day to the students. No-Choice's new policy is this: $120 for a round-trip ticket, but a special price of $100 for students who show their ID cards. The result is shown in panel (c). Although the decision to sell an additional 10 tickets pushes No-Choice beyond the output level at which $MC = MR$, this is no problem. The MR curve was drawn under the assumption that

No-Choice charges a single price and must lower the price on all tickets in order to sell more. But this is no longer the case. With price discrimination, the *MR* curve no longer tells us what will happen to No-Choice's revenue when output increases. As you are about to see, the firm will be able to increase its profit by selling the additional tickets.

The reasoning is as follows: No-Choice is now selling 10 *additional* round-trip tickets, so in this case both its cost and its revenue will change. Each additional ticket adds $100 to the firm's revenue; this is the new marginal revenue. Each additional ticket also adds an amount to costs given by the firm's *MC* curve. Thus, the distance between $100 and the *MC* curve gives the *additional profit* earned on each additional ticket, and the total additional profit is the shaded area *HGF* in panel (c) of Figure 8.

What about consumers? The original 30 consumers are unaffected, since their ticket price has not changed. But the new customers—the 10 students—come out ahead: Each is able to take the flight rather than the longer train trip. In this case, price discrimination benefits the monopoly at the same time as it benefits a group of consumers—the students who were not buying the service before, but who *will* buy it at a lower price and gain some benefits by doing so. Since no one's price is raised, no one is harmed by this policy:

> *When price discrimination lowers the price for some consumers below what they would pay under a single-price policy, it benefits consumers as well as the firm.*

Of course, it is possible for a firm to combine *both* types of price discrimination. That is, it could raise the price above what it would charge as a single-price monopoly for some consumers and lower it for others. This kind of price discrimination would increase the firm's profit, while benefiting some consumers and harming others. (For practice, draw a diagram showing the change in total profit if No-Choice were to charge three prices: a basic price of $120, a price of $160 for business travelers, and a price of $100 for students. Who would gain and who would lose?)

PERFECT PRICE DISCRIMINATION

Suppose a firm could somehow find out the maximum price customers would be willing to pay for *each* unit of output it sells. Then it could increase its profits even further by practicing *perfect price discrimination*:

Perfect price discrimination
Charging each customer the most he or she would be willing to pay for each unit purchased.

> *Under **perfect price discrimination**, a firm charges each customer the most the customer would be willing to pay for each unit he or she buys.*

Perfect price discrimination is very difficult to practice in the real world, since it would require the firm to read its customers' minds. However, many real-world situations come rather close to perfect price discrimination. Used-car dealers routinely post a sticker price far higher than the price they think they can actually get. They then size up each customer to determine the discount needed to complete the sale. The dealer may look at the customer's clothes and the car the customer is currently driving, inquire about the customer's job, and observe how sophisticated the customer is about cars. The aim is to determine the maximum price he or she would be

Perfect Price Discrimination

The single-price monopolist sells 30 dolls per day at $25 each. With a constant ATC of $10, she earns a profit of $450 per day, as shown by the blue rectangle. However, if she can charge each customer the maximum the customer is willing to pay, shown by the height of the demand curve, then her MR curve is the demand curve she faces. She should sell 60 dolls, where MC = P at point J. Her profit would increase to the area of triangle HBJ.

willing to pay. A similar sizing up takes place in flea markets, yard sales, and many other situations in which the final price is *negotiated* rather than fixed in advance.

To see how perfect price discrimination works, consider Nancy, who sells Elvis dolls at flea markets. To make our analysis simpler, we'll assume that Nancy has no fixed costs of doing business and that each doll costs her $10 to make, regardless of how many she produces. Thus, Nancy's cost per doll (*ATC*) is $10 at every output level. Further, since each *additional* doll costs $10 to make, her marginal cost (*MC*) is also $10 at any output level. This is why, in Figure 9, both the *MC* and *ATC* curves are the same horizontal line at $10.

Let's first suppose that Nancy is a single-price monopolist, charging a preannounced price on every doll she sells. The figure shows the demand curve she would face on a typical day: At a price of $30 she could sell 20 dolls, at a price of $25 she could sell 30, and so on. Nancy would earn maximum profit by charging $25 per doll and selling 30 dolls per day (why?). Her profit per unit would be $25 − $10 = $15— the vertical distance between the *ATC* curve and the demand curve at 30 units. Her total profit would be $15 × 30 dolls = $450 per day, which is equal to the area of the shaded rectangle.

Now, suppose that Nancy becomes especially good at sizing up her customers. She learns how to distinguish true Elvis fanatics (a white, sequined jumpsuit is a dead giveaway) from people who merely want the doll as a gag gift. Moreover, by observing the way people handle the doll and listening to their conversations with their companions, Nancy can discern the exact maximum price each customer would pay. In effect, she knows exactly where on the demand curve each customer would be located. With her new skills, Nancy can increase her profit by becoming a *perfect price discriminator:* For each unit along the horizontal axis, she will charge the price indicated by the vertical height of the demand curve.

How many dolls should Nancy sell now? To answer this question, we need to find the new output level at which $MR = MC$. But the MR curve in the figure is no longer valid: It was based on the assumption that Nancy had to lower the price on *all* units each time she wanted to sell another one. Now, as a perfect price discriminator, she needs to lower the price only on the *additional* unit she sells, and her revenue will rise by the price of that additional unit. For example, if she is currently selling 30 dolls and wants to sell 31, she would lower the price just on the additional doll by a tiny bit—say, to $24.50—and in that case, her revenue would rise by $24.50.

> *For a perfect price discriminator, marginal revenue is equal to the price of the additional unit sold. Thus, the firm's* MR *curve is the same as its demand curve.*

Now it is easy to see what Nancy should do: Since our requirement for profit maximization is that $MC = MR$, and for a perfect price discriminator, MR is the same as price (P), Nancy should produce where $MC = P$. In Figure 9, this occurs at point J, where the MC curve intersects the demand curve—at 60 units of output. At that point, the only way to increase sales would be to lower the price on an additional doll below $10, but since the marginal cost of a doll is always $10, we would have $P < MC$, and Nancy's profit would decline.

What is Nancy's profit-maximizing price? Think for a moment. Then see Footnote 6 for the answer.

What about Nancy's total profit? On each unit of output, she charges a price given by the demand curve and bears a cost of $10. Adding up the profit on *all* units gives us the area under the demand curve and above $10, or the area of triangle *HBJ* (not shaded).

Now we can determine who gains and who loses when Nancy transforms herself from a single-price monopolist to a perfect price discriminator. Nancy clearly gains: Her profit increases, from the shaded rectangle to the larger, unshaded triangle *HBJ*. Consumers of the product are the clear losers: Since they all pay the most they would willingly pay, no one gets to buy a doll at a price he or she would regard as a "good deal."

> A perfect price discriminator *increases profit at the expense of consumers, charging each customer the most he or she would willingly pay for the product.*

Price Discrimination in Everyday Life

Price discrimination is not limited to monopolies. It can be practiced by *any* firm that satisfies the three requirements discussed earlier. As a result, price discrimination is more prevalent than you might think.

Rebates on electronic goods are an example. If you've recently purchased a printer or computer, chances are your receipt included a coupon for a rebate from

---

[6] Sorry, that's a trick question: There *is* no profit-maximizing price. As a perfect price discriminator, Nancy earns the highest profit by charging *different* prices to different customers.

the store or the manufacturer—in effect, offering you a lower price. But to pay this lower price, you must go through the time and trouble to read all the directions, cut the UPC code from the box, mail it in, wait several weeks or months for your check to arrive, and then deposit the check.

Many people complain about all this time and trouble, and wonder why the manufacturer or store doesn't just lower the sticker price. The answer, in large part, is price discrimination. By adding time, trouble, and delay for the discount, the store can separate those who are very price sensitive (they will go through the trouble) from those who are not (they will forget about the rebate). In effect, each group is charged a different price.

Discount coupons for the supermarket or drugstore work much the same way. You only get the discount if you happen to have the coupon with you at the store. Only the most price-sensitive customers will go through the trouble of clipping, saving, and organizing their coupons so that they have them when they need them. Thus, the stores charge lower prices only to their most price-sensitive customers; everyone else pays the higher price.

When retailers put items "on sale" (for a reduced price) after a delay of weeks or months, it is in part an effort to price discriminate. Those who feel they must have the latest fashions, video games, or DVDs immediately after they arrive at the store, and have the income to buy them at higher prices, will make their purchases soon after the goods arrive. Weeks or months later, when the goods go on sale, everyone else pays a lower price.

Similarly, new books that come out first in hardcover at a high price, then in paperback at a much lower price, are another example of price discrimination. (The actual difference in manufacturing cost explains only a small part of the premium charged on a hardcover.) If reading the latest Stephen King novel is important to you and you are *willing* to pay a high price, you will buy it in hardcover soon after it arrives in the store. If you are more price sensitive, you'll wait for the paperback. In this way, the book company can charge a higher price only to some customers— those most willing to pay it.

Finally, colleges and universities are extensive practitioners of price discrimination. Because this example hits so close to home, we'll discuss it more extensively in our Using the Theory section.

USING THE THEORY

Price Discrimination at Colleges and Universities

Most colleges and universities give some kind of financial aid to a large proportion of their students. A typical aid package might include outright grants to help pay tuition and room and board, a low-interest loan, and a work-study job on campus. Colleges have many motives for this policy, such as having a more diverse student body and helping to create a better society by making educational services accessible to many who might not otherwise afford them. But increasingly, financial aid has been used as an effective method of price discrimination,

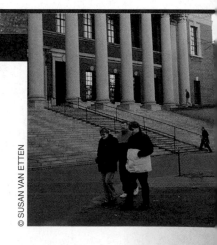
© SUSAN VAN ETTEN

TABLE 2		Quintile	Income Range	Actually Paid
Actual Payments for a Year at Williams (2001–2002)		Low	$ 0–$23,593	$ 1,683
		Lower-Middle	$ 23,594–$40,931	$ 5,186
		Middle	$ 40,932–$61,397	$ 7,199
		Upper-Middle	$ 61,398–$91,043	$13,764
		High	$91,044 and above	$22,013

Note: The official tuition was equal to $32,470.

designed to increase the revenue of the college. Although colleges are not strictly monopolies, we can use the tools of this chapter to analyze colleges' practice of price discrimination.

How does a college price discriminate? By offering different levels of assistance to different students, financial aid permits the college to charge different *prices* to each one. For example, if full tuition is $20,000 per year, then a student who receives a yearly $5,000 grant pays only $15,000 per year, a student who receives an $8,000 grant pays only $12,000 per year, and so on.

Colleges have long been in a good position to practice price discrimination because they satisfy all three requirements:

1. *Colleges have market power.* Although colleges are not monopolies (other, similar institutions are close substitutes), they do have market power. Each college is unique in some ways—location, reputation, living conditions, social life, and more. For this reason, colleges face downward-sloping demand curves for their services. A college can raise its price and lose only *some*, rather than all, of its enrollment applicants. Similarly, any college that wants to increase enrollment can do so by lowering its price and attracting more applications.

2. *Colleges are able to identify consumers willing to pay more.* Colleges have long been in an excellent position to discover how much their customers would be willing to pay for their product. Applicants for financial aid have had to submit data on their families' income and wealth. Admissions officials know that students from poor families are less likely to attend their institutions, unless they are offered a relatively low price, while students from wealthier families are more likely to attend even at higher prices. In recent years, however, colleges have gone even further in their attempts to identify willingness to pay. (See below.)

3. *Colleges are able to prevent low-price customers from reselling to high-price customers.* A college education is much like other personal services: Once you pay for it, you cannot resell it to another person.

---

[7] Catharine B. Bill and Gordon C. Winston, "Access: Net Prices, Affordability, and Equity at a Highly Selective College," December 2001, *Williams Project on the Economics of Higher Education*, Discussion Paper No. 62.

[8] Notice that none of the groups in the table paid the "full price" of $32,470. But students who were not in the sample (because they did not receive financial aid from Williams) may have paid this price.

The result is that colleges can (and do) charge vastly different prices for different students, highly correlated to their families' willingness to pay.

A recent study of price differentials at Williams College serves as a good example.[7] Table 2 is based on data for 827 students who received financial aid at Williams during the 2001–2002 academic year, when the "official price" was $32,470 (full tuition, room, board, and fees). The first column identifies the quintile in the U.S. population in which each student would be ranked, by family income. The second column identifies the income range associated with each quintile. The third provides the amount *actually* paid by the average student in each quintile: the official price for a year at Williams *minus* any financial aid provided in the form of outright grants. You can see that those with the highest incomes (and therefore, on average, the greatest willingness to pay) were charged an average of $22,013, while those in the lowest group paid only $1,683 for the year.[8]

Most colleges have been active price discriminators for decades, mostly using family income and wealth as their guide for "willingness to pay." But many stepped up their efforts in the 1990s when Congress changed the formula used to determine financial need, making most students eligible for assistance. This gave colleges more freedom to allocate financial aid dollars, and price discriminate even more extensively. Colleges began searching for new methods of identifying willingness to pay.

Several colleges hired specialized consultants, who used computer models to predict the likelihood that students would attend college at different prices. One consultant's pamphlet asked admissions officials, "Did you overspend to get students who would have matriculated with lesser aid? Did you underspend and lose students who would have come with more support?"[9]

As a result of practices like these, public and private colleges have shifted aid dollars toward top-ranked applicants, regardless of financial need, because those students have more options and are less likely to attend any college without financial aid. Drexel University in Philadelphia shifted aid toward those who applied as business majors after a computer model predicted that these students' enrollment decisions were more sensitive to price. Johns Hopkins University shifted aid dollars to humanities majors with SAT scores above 1200 and relatively low financial need, based on a similar model. Carnegie-Mellon went even further. It determined the effect on student "yield" (the percentage of students with certain characteristics who will actually enroll) of shifting aid dollars from one group to another. In addition, the school asked students who had been admitted to fax the school any better financial aid offers they received, so it could decide whether to match the offer from a special "reaction fund."

Many financial aid consultants have even recommended that colleges shift aid money away from students who come for on-campus interviews, since by doing so, those students reveal a strong desire to attend the college. There are rumors that some institutions have followed this advice, but no college has admitted to the practice.

[9] For this and other examples cited here, see "Colleges Manipulate Financial-Aid Offers, Shortchanging Many," *Wall Street Journal*, April 1, 1996, p. 1. See also "Price Wars on Campus," *Washington Post*, October 15, 2002, p. A1; "Testimony of Richard K. Vedder before the Committee on Education and the Workforce," U.S. House of Representatives, April 19, 2005; and Robert Tomsho, "Saying 'No' to the Ivy League," *Wall Street Journal*, April 20, 2006, p. D1.

More effective price discrimination at colleges and universities is certainly changing the traditional view of financial assistance as a program designed primarily to help those in need. And while it has benefited some groups of students, it has harmed others. Under the newer systems, those who can signal a lower willingness to pay have benefited from reduced prices, while those signaling greater willingness to pay have suffered a price increase.

But fully assessing the effects of price discrimination at colleges is complicated by one important fact: Most educational institutions are not private firms striving to maximize profits for their owners. Rather, they are *nonprofit* institutions, *without* private owners. Thus, any additional revenue they gain through price discrimination is likely to be used for educational purposes: to attract better faculty by raising salaries, to improve living conditions for students, to keep tuition from rising even faster, and even to provide increased aid for more students in the future. Each of these alternatives has value to the college and its students, suggesting that increased price discrimination at colleges, like so many other economic issues, is a matter of tradeoffs.

Summary

A *monopoly firm* is the only seller of a good or service with no close substitutes. Monopoly arises because of some barrier to entry: economies of scale, legal barriers, or network externalities. As the only seller, the monopoly faces the market demand curve and must decide what price (or prices) to charge in order to maximize profit.

Like other firms, a single-price monopolist will produce where $MR = MC$ and set the maximum price consumers are willing to pay for that quantity. Monopoly profit ($P - ATC$ multiplied by the quantity produced) can persist in the long run because of barriers to entry. However, government regulation and rent-seeking activity can reduce monopoly profit.

All else equal, a monopoly charges a higher price and produces less output than a perfectly competitive market. When demand for a monopoly's product increases, it will raise prices and increase production. When a monopoly's marginal costs decrease, it will pass only part of the cost savings on to consumers.

Some monopolies can practice *price discrimination* by charging different prices to different customers. Doing so requires the ability to identify customers who are willing to pay more and to prevent low-price customers from reselling to high-price customers. Price discrimination always benefits the monopolist (otherwise, it would charge a single price), but it may sometimes benefit some consumers as well.

Problem Set   *Answers to even-numbered Questions and Problems can be found on the text Web site at www.thomsonedu.com/economics/hall.*

1. In a certain large city, hot dog vendors are *perfectly competitive*, and face a market price of $1.00 per hot dog. Each hot dog vendor has the following total cost schedule:

Number of Hot Dogs per Day	Total Cost
0	$ 63
25	73
50	78
75	88
100	103
125	125
150	153
175	188
200	233

a. Add a *marginal cost* column to the right of the total cost column. (Hint: Don't forget to divide by the *change* in quantity when calculating MC.)

b. What is the profit-maximizing quantity of hot dogs for the typical vendor, and what profit (loss) will he earn (suffer)? Give your answer to the nearest 25 hot dogs.

One day, Zeke, a typical vendor, figures out that if he were the only seller in town, he would no longer have to sell his hot dogs at the market price of $1.00. Instead, he'd face the following demand schedule:

Price per Hot Dog	Number of Hot Dogs per Day
> $6.00	0
6.00	25
5.00	50
4.00	75
3.25	100
2.75	125
2.25	150
1.75	175
1.25	200

   c. Add *total revenue* and *marginal revenue* columns to the table above. (Hint: Once again, don't forget to divide by the *change* in quantity when calculating MR.)

   d. As a monopolist with the cost schedule given in the first table, how many hot dogs would Zeke choose to sell each day? What price would he charge?

   e. A lobbyist has approached Zeke, proposing to form a new organization called "Citizens to Eliminate Chaos in Hot Dog Sales." The organization will lobby the city council to grant Zeke the only hot dog license in town, and it is guaranteed to succeed. The only problem is, the lobbyist is asking for a payment that amounts to $200 per business day as long as Zeke stays in business. On purely economic grounds, should Zeke go for it? (Hint: If you're stumped, re-read the section on rent-seeking activity.)

2. Draw demand, *MR*, and *ATC* curves that show a monopoly that is just breaking even.

3. Below is demand and cost information for Warmfuzzy Press, which holds the copyright on the new best-seller, *Burping Your Inner Child*.

Q (No. of Copies)	P (per Book)	ATC (per Book)
100,000	$100	$20
200,000	$ 80	$15
300,000	$ 60	$16⅔
400,000	$ 40	$22½
500,000	$ 20	$31

   a. Determine what quantity of the book Warmfuzzy should print, and what price it should charge in order to maximize profit.

   b. What is Warmfuzzy's maximum profit?

   c. Prior to publication, the book's author renegotiates his contract with Warmfuzzy. He will receive a great big hug from the CEO, along with a one-time bonus of $1,000,000, payable when the book is published. This payment was not part of Warmfuzzy's original cost calculations. How many copies should Warmfuzzy publish now? Explain your reasoning.

4. Look at Figure 8(c). Clearly, *MR=MC* at point *H*. But when the airline sells discount tickets to college students, it is at point *F*, apparently violating the rule that *MR=MC*. Does this mean that for a price-discriminating monopoly, *MR=MC* doesn't hold? Explain.

5. A doctor in a rural area faces the following demand schedule:

Price per Office Visit	Number of Office Visits per Day
$200	2
$175	3
$150	5
$125	8
$100	12
$ 75	18
$ 50	23
$ 25	25

The doctor's marginal cost of seeing patients is a constant $50 per patient.

   a. If the doctor must charge all patients the same price, what price will she charge, and how many patients will she see each day?

   b. If the doctor can perfectly price discriminate, how many patients will she see each day?

6. You are thinking about tutoring students in economics, and your research has convinced you that you face the following demand curve for your services:

Price per Hour of Tutoring	Number of Students Tutored per Week
> $50	0
$40	1
$35	2
$27	3
$26	4
$20	5
$15	6
< $15	6

Each student who hires you gets one hour of tutoring per week. You have decided that your time and effort is worth $25 per hour and that you will not tutor anyone for less than that.

   a. Suppose you are wary that your students might talk to each other about the price you charge, so you decide to charge them all the same price. Determine (1) how many students you will tutor; (2) what price you will charge; and (3) your weekly earnings from tutoring.

   b. Now suppose you discover that your students don't know each other, and you decide to perfectly price discriminate. Once again, determine (1) how many students you will tutor; (2) what price you will charge; and (3) your weekly earnings from tutoring.

Now suppose that your city requires all tutors to get a license, at a cost of $1,300 per year ($25 per week).

c. Does it make sense for you to buy this license and be a tutor if you must charge each student the same price? Explain.

d. Does it make sense for you to buy the license and be a tutor if you can perfectly price discriminate? Explain.

7. Draw demand, *MR*, *MC*, *AVC*, and *ATC* curves that show a monopolist operating at a loss that would cause it to *stay open* in the short run, but *exit* the industry in the long run. Then, show how a technological advance that lowers *only* the monopolist's *fixed costs* could cause a change in its long-run exit decision.

8. Answer the following:
   a. Complete the following table and use it to find this monopolist's short-run profit-maximizing level of output. How much profit will this firm earn?
   b. Redo the table to show what will happen to the short-run profit-maximizing level of output if the monopolist's marginal costs rise by $1 at each level of output. How much profit will the firm earn now?
   c. Redo the original table to show what will happen to the short-run profit-maximizing level of output if the monopolist's marginal cost at each level of output is $0.40 less than before. How much profit would the firm earn in this case?

Output	Price	Total Revenue	Marginal Revenue	Total Cost	Marginal Cost	Profit
0	$5.60			$ 0.50		
1	$5.50			$ 3.50		
2	$5.40			$ 5.45		
3	$5.30			$ 6.45		
4	$5.20			$ 6.90		
5	$5.10			$ 8.90		
6	$5.05			$13.40		
7	$4.90			$20.40		

9. In the short run, a monopoly uses both fixed and variable inputs to produce its output. Draw a diagram illustrating a monopoly breaking even. Then alter your graph to show why, if the price of using a fixed input rises, there will be no change in the monopoly's short-run equilibrium price or quantity. (Hint: Which curves shift if the price of a fixed input rises?)

10. Suppose that Patty's Pool has the demand data given in Table 1 in the chapter. Further, suppose that Patty has just two types of costs: (1) rent of $25 per day and (2) towel service costs equal to 50 cents per swimmer. Over the short run, rent is a fixed cost (Patty has a lease she can't get out of), but towel service is a variable cost (it varies with the number of swimmers). Patty's marginal cost is therefore constant at 50 cents.
   a. Under these cost conditions, what are Patty's short-run profit-maximizing output and price? What is her profit or loss per day?
   b. Now suppose that, in addition to the costs just described, the town imposes a "swimming excise tax" on Patty's Pool equal to $2 per swimmer. What are Patty's new short-run profit-maximizing output and price? What is her new profit per day? (Hint: First decide whether or not the excise tax affects Patty's marginal cost.)
   c. In addition to the costs just described (including the swimming excise tax of $2 per swimmer), suppose the town imposes a "fixed swimming tax" requiring Patty to pay $2 per day for operating her pool, regardless of the number of swimmers. What are Patty's new short-run profit-maximizing output and price? What is her new profit per day? (Hint: First decide whether or not this new fixed swimming tax affects Patty's marginal cost.)
   d. Now suppose that costs are as in (c), except that the fixed swimming tax is $5 per day instead of $2 per day. What are Patty's new short-run profit-maximizing output and price? What is her new profit per day?
   e. With the $5 per day fixed swimming tax, what should Patty do in the short run? What should she do in the long run? (Hint: For the short run, think about the shutdown rule.)
   f. Based on your answers to *b, c, d,* and *e*, assess the following statement: "When an excise (variable) tax is imposed on a monopoly, it will pass part, but not all, of the tax on to consumers in the form of a higher price. But a fixed tax has no effect on monopoly behavior over any time horizon." Are both of these sentences true? Explain briefly.

More Challenging

11. Suppose that Patty's Pool has the demand data given in Table 1. Further, suppose that Patty has just two types of costs: (1) rent of $24 per day and (2) towel and other service costs equal to $5 per swimmer. Over the short run, rent is a fixed cost, but towel and other service costs are variable costs. Patty's marginal cost is therefore constant at $5.
   a. Under these cost conditions, and assuming first that Patty is a *single-price monopolist*, what are Patty's short-run profit-maximizing output and price? What is her profit or loss per day? (Hint: Be sure to check the shutdown rule if you determine that she is suffering a loss.) In the long run, should she stay in this business?
   b. Now suppose that Patty figures out a way to price discriminate by dividing her swimmers into two groups: those willing to pay the price in part *a* and those who would not be willing to pay that price but *would* swim if the price were $5. What is Patty's short-run

profit-maximizing output now? What is her profit or loss per day? In the long run, should she stay in this business? (Hint: Be sure to recalculate the *TR* and *MR* numbers to answer this question. Also, if Patty is indifferent between two output levels, choose the higher one.)

c. Let's say that Patty figures out a way to price discriminate by charging *three* different prices: a high price of $10 to those willing to pay that much to swim; a medium price equal to the price you found in part *a*; and a lower price of $5 to those who would not pay the price in part *a*, but would pay $5. What is Patty's short-run profit-maximizing output now? What is her profit or

loss per day? In the long run, should she stay in this business?

d. Now suppose that Patty figures out a way to *perfectly* price discriminate, still facing the same demand curve given in Table 1. What is Patty's short-run profit-maximizing output now? What is her profit or loss per day? In the long run, should she stay in this business?

12. Suppose a single-price monopoly's demand curve is given by $P = 20 - 4Q$, where P is price and Q is quantity demanded. Marginal revenue is $MR = 20 - 8Q$. Marginal cost is $MC = Q^2$. How much should this firm produce in order to maximize profit?

Monopolistic Competition and Oligopoly

On any given day, you are probably exposed to hundreds of advertisements. The morning newspaper announces special sales on clothes, computers, and paper towels. On the way to class, you might see numerous billboards competing for your attention, suggesting that you stay at the Holiday Inn, eat at Burger King, or buy the latest, lightest, thinnest iPod. You will likely spend more time watching television advertisements for breakfast cereals than you will spend eating them. And as you search for information on the Internet, ads for video cameras, credit cards, and vitamins flash before your eyes. No doubt about it: Advertising is everywhere in the economy.

Yet, so far in this book, not much has been said about advertising. There is a good reason for this: In the two market structures we have studied so far—perfect competition and monopoly—firms do little, if any, advertising. Indeed, perfectly competitive firms *never* advertise: Each firm produces the same product as any other, so what would they advertise? And, because each firm can sell all it wants at the market price, advertising would only raise costs without any benefit to the firm. Monopolists *sometimes* advertise, but—as the only seller of a good with no close substitutes—they are under no pressure to do so.

Where, then, is all the advertising coming from? To answer this question, we must look beyond the market structures we've studied so far and consider firms that are neither perfect competitors nor monopolists. That is what we will do in this chapter. While advertising is one interesting feature we will explore, there are many others as well.

THE CONCEPT OF IMPERFECT COMPETITION

When thinking of market structure, perfect competition and monopoly can be viewed as the two extremes. In perfect competition, there are so many firms producing the same product that each takes the market price as given. In monopoly, there is only one firm in the market, producing a product with no close substitutes, so the monopoly can set its price without worrying about other firms that are selling a similar product.

Most goods and services, however, are sold in markets that are neither perfectly competitive nor monopolies. Instead, they lie somewhere *between* these two extremes. In these markets, there is more than one firm, but each firm has some market power—some ability to set price.

Consider, for example, the market for wireless phone service in the United States. It is certainly not a monopoly because there is more than one firm. But there are not that many firms. In fact, three of them together (AT&T, Verizon Wireless, and Sprint) provide service to about 90 percent of the cell phone users in the United States. Moreover, the products they offer are different in ways that matter to consumers: quality and reliability of calls, remote area access, customer service, phones available with the service, and more. Thus, in terms of number of firms and the uniqueness of the product, the market for wireless phone service falls somewhere between the extremes of monopoly and perfect competition.

Or consider restaurants. Even a modest-size city such as Cincinnati has thousands of different restaurants. This is certainly a large number of competitors. But they are not *perfect* competitors, because each one sells a product that is differentiated in important ways—in the type of food served, the recipes used, the atmosphere, the location, and even the friendliness of the staff. The markets for wireless phone service and restaurant meals in most cities are examples of **imperfect competition.** Imperfectly competitive markets have more than one firm (so they are not monopolies), but they violate one or more of the requirements of perfect competition.[1]

In this chapter, we study two types of imperfectly competitive markets: *monopolistic competition* and *oligopoly.*

Imperfect competition A market structure in which there is more than one firm but one or more of the requirements of perfect competition is violated.

MONOPOLISTIC COMPETITION

Suppose you live in a midsize or large city, and you're embarking on a night out with some friends. As you head out in your car, you notice the gas tank is almost empty. You pass several gas stations, then find one that's not too expensive but doesn't have a line of cars waiting. After filling up, you pick up your friends, and a lively discussion ensues because everyone wants to go to a different pizza place. Finally, after some cajoling and compromising, you head across town to your group's choice. Over dinner, you all decide to see a movie. But that leads to another discussion: which multiplex to go to. One has the advantage of being closest, but the good movies there always sell out. A second has better popcorn, but it's impossible to park. And a third has great parking, but it's a 20-minute drive.

Although most people would have no reason to notice, all of your purchases that night would have something in common. The gas station, the restaurant, and the movie theater all sell their products under a market structure called **monopolistic competition.**

As the name suggests, monopolistic competition is a hybrid of perfect competition and monopoly, sharing some of the features of each. Specifically,

Monopolistic competition A market structure in which there are many firms selling products that are differentiated, and in which there is easy entry and exit.

a monopolistically competitive market has three fundamental characteristics:

1. *many buyers and sellers;*
2. *sellers offer a differentiated product; and*
3. *sellers can easily enter or exit the market.*

[1] Imperfect competition is sometimes defined as *any* market structure other than perfect competition, which would include monopoly.

If you compare this list of characteristics with the list for perfect competition (in Chapter 8), you'll notice that the first and last items are shared by both market structures. The second item is new, but it leads to a feature shared with monopoly. Let's examine each of these characteristics in turn.

Many Buyers and Sellers

In *perfect* competition, the existence of many buyers and sellers played an important role: ensuring that no individual buyer or seller could influence the market price. In monopolistic competition, the "many buyers and sellers" assumption plays the same role on the buying side: an individual *buyer* has no influence on the price he pays. But an individual seller, in spite of having many competitors, has market power and acts as a *price setter*.

Our assumption of many sellers, however, has another purpose: to ensure that no *strategic games* will be played among firms in the market. That is, when a firm under monopolistic competition makes a decision (about price, advertising, product guarantees, etc.), it assumes that its competitors will *not* react by changing *their* decisions. There are so many firms, each supplying such a small part of the market, that no one of them needs to worry that its actions will affect the others or generate a response.

Restaurants in most cities satisfy this requirement. With so many other restaurants, when one decides whether to offer an early-bird special or advertise in the local paper or put flyers under windshields, it usually doesn't worry how the other restaurants in the city will react.[2]

Sellers Offer a Differentiated Product

In perfect competition, sellers offer a standardized product. In *monopolistic competition,* by contrast, each seller produces a somewhat different product from the others. No two coffeehouses, photocopy shops, or food markets are exactly the same. For this reason, a monopolistic competitor can raise its price (up to a point) and lose only *some* of its customers. The others will stay with the firm because they like its product, even when it charges somewhat more than its competitors. Thus, a monopolistic competitor faces a *downward-sloping demand curve,* so it has market power. In this sense, it is more like a monopolist than a perfect competitor:

> *Because it produces a differentiated product, a monopolistic competitor faces a downward-sloping demand curve: When it raises its price a modest amount, quantity demanded will decline—but not all the way to zero.*

What makes a product differentiated? Sometimes, it is the *quality* of the product. By many objective standards—longevity, performance, frequency of repair—a Mercedes is a better car than a Hyundai. Similarly, based on room size and service, the Hilton has better hotel rooms than Motel 6. In other cases, the difference is a matter of taste rather than quality. In terms of measurable characteristics, Colgate

---

[2] Monopolistic competitors do replicate the successful practices of others in the market, as you'll see in a few pages. But a monopolistic competitor does not take into account the *potential* for imitation when making a decision. In the second half of this chapter, when we study oligopoly, we'll examine what happens when firms *do* take into account the potential reactions of their rivals.

toothpaste may be neither better nor worse than Crest, but each has its own flavor and texture, and each appeals to different people.

Another type of differentiation arises from differences in *location*. Two bookstores may be identical in every respect—range of selection, atmosphere, service—but you will often prefer the one closer to your home or office.

Ultimately, though, product differentiation is a subjective matter: A product is different whenever people *think* that it is, whether their perception is accurate or not. You may know, for example, that all bottles of bleach have identical ingredients—5.25 percent sodium hypochlorite and 94.75 percent water. But if *some* buyers think that Clorox bleach is different and would pay a bit more for it, then Clorox bleach is a differentiated product.

Because a monopolistic competitor faces a downward-sloping demand curve, the firm *chooses* its price. Like a monopoly, it is a price setter.

Easy Entry and Exit

This feature is shared by monopolistic competition and perfect competition, and—as you'll see—it plays the same role in both: ensuring that firms earn zero economic profit in the long run. Remember that "easy entry" does *not* mean that entry is effortless or inexpensive. Rather, it means that you can open up, say, a pizza place if you're willing to bear the same costs that existing pizza places must bear. There are no significant *barriers* to entry that keep out newcomers—no law, for example, that new pizza places must pay higher annual license fees than established ones.

In monopolistic competition, however, our assumption about easy entry goes further: Nothing stops a firm from copying the successful business practices of other firms. If one movie theater finds that offering lower prices for Wednesday-afternoon showings generates economic profit, any other movie theater can do the same. If Circuit City's four-year replacement plan for electronic goods brings it profit, then other electronic goods retailers can choose to offer the same plan. Although it may take time, success will eventually lead to imitation. You'll see that this extended view of entry—specific to monopolistic competition—plays a role in ensuring zero economic profit in the long run.

MONOPOLISTIC COMPETITION IN THE SHORT RUN

The individual monopolistic competitor behaves very much like a monopoly. Its constraints are its given production technology, the prices it must pay for its inputs, and the downward-sloping demand curve that it faces. And, like any other firm, its goal is to maximize profit by producing where $MR = MC$. The result may be economic profit or loss in the short run.

The key difference is this: While a monopoly is the *only* seller in its market, a monopolistic competitor is one of many sellers. When a *monopoly* raises its price, its customers must pay up or buy less of the product. When a *monopolistic competitor* raises its price, its customers have one additional option: They can buy a similar (though not identical) good from some other firm. Thus, all else equal, the demand curve facing a firm should be flatter under monopolistic competition than under monopoly. That is, since closer substitutes are available under monopolistic competition than under monopoly, a given rise in price should cause a greater fall in quantity demanded.

Figure 1 illustrates the situation of a monopolistic competitor, Kafka Exterminators. The figure shows the demand curve, d_1, that the firm faces, as well as the marginal

FIGURE 1

A Monopolistically Competitive Firm in the Short Run

Like any other firm, a monopolistic competitor maximizes profit by producing the level of output where its MR and MC curves intersect. Kafka Exterminators maximizes profit by servicing 250 homes per month. The profit-maximizing price ($70) is found on the demand curve at an output level of 250 (point A). Profit per unit of $40 is the difference between the price ($70) and average total cost ($30) at output of 250. Total profit is profit per unit times output ($40 × 250 = $10,000), equal to the area of the shaded rectangle.

revenue, marginal cost, and average total cost curves. As a monopolistic competitor, Kafka Exterminators competes with many other extermination services in its local area. Thus, if it raises its price, it will lose some of its customers to the competition. If Kafka had a *monopoly* on the local extermination business, we would expect the same rise in price to cause a smaller drop in quantity demanded, since customers would have to buy from Kafka or else get rid of their bugs on their own.

Like any other firm, Kafka Exterminators will produce where $MR = MC$. As you can see in Figure 1, when Kafka faces demand curve d_1 and the associated marginal revenue curve MR_1, its profit-maximizing output level is 250 homes serviced per month, and its profit-maximizing price is $70 per home. In the short run, the firm may earn an economic profit or an economic loss, or it may break even. In the figure, Kafka is earning an economic profit: Profit per unit is $P - ATC = \$70 - \$30 = \$40$, and total monthly profit—the area of the blue rectangle—is $\$40 \times 250 = \$10,000$.

MONOPOLISTIC COMPETITION IN THE LONG RUN

If Kafka Exterminators were a monopoly, Figure 1 might be the end of our story. The firm could continue to earn economic profit forever, since barriers to entry would keep out any potential competitors. But under monopolistic competition—in which there are no barriers to entry and exit—the firm will not enjoy its profit for long. New sellers will enter the market, attracted by the profits that can be earned there. And some of Kafka's customers will sign up with the new entrants. At any given price, Kafka will find itself servicing fewer homes than before, and the demand curve it faces will shift leftward. Entry will continue to occur, and the demand curve will

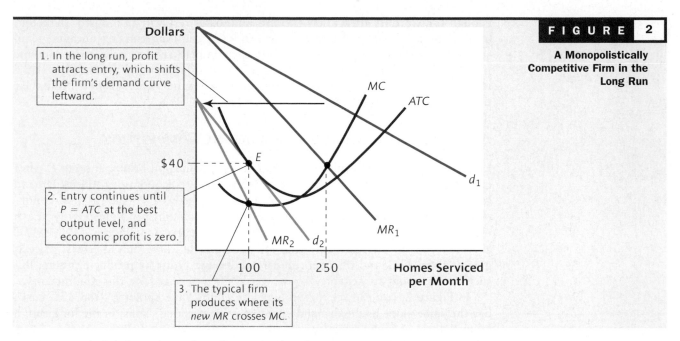

FIGURE 2

A Monopolistically Competitive Firm in the Long Run

1. In the long run, profit attracts entry, which shifts the firm's demand curve leftward.

2. Entry continues until P = ATC at the best output level, and economic profit is zero.

3. The typical firm produces where its *new MR* crosses *MC*.

Dollars

MC

ATC

$40

E

d_1

MR_2 d_2 MR_1

100   250   Homes Serviced per Month

continue to shift leftward, until Kafka and other firms are earning zero economic profit.

This process of adjustment is shown in Figure 2. The demand curve shifts leftward (from d_1 to d_2). The marginal revenue curve shifts left as well (from MR_1 to MR_2). Kafka's new profit-maximizing output level, 100, is found at the intersection point between its marginal cost curve and its *new* marginal revenue curve MR_2. Kafka's new price—found on its demand curve d_2 at 100 units—is $40. Finally, since *ATC* is also $40 at that output level, Kafka is earning zero economic profit— the best it can do in the long run.[3] In long-run equilibrium, the profit-maximizing price, $40, will always equal the average total cost of production.

We can also reverse these steps. If the typical firm is suffering an economic loss (draw this diagram on your own), *exit* will occur. With fewer competitors, those firms that remain in the market will gain customers, so their demand curves will shift *rightward*. Exit will cease only when the typical firm is earning zero economic profit, at point *E* in Figure 2. Thus, point *E* represents the long-run equilibrium of the typical firm whether we start from a position of economic profit or economic loss:

> *Under monopolistic competition, firms can earn positive or negative economic profit in the short run. But in the long run, free entry and exit will ensure that each firm earns zero economic profit, just as under perfect competition.*

Is this prediction of our model realistic? Indeed it is: In the real world, monopolistic competitors often earn economic profit or loss in the short run, but, given

---

[3] Other things may also happen as the industry expands. For example, the increased demand for inputs may raise or lower the typical firm's *ATC* and *MC* curves, depending on whether we are dealing with an increasing- or decreasing-cost industry. (See Chapter 8.) This does not change our main result, however: Entry into the market will continue until the typical firm earns zero economic profit, even if its *MC* and *ATC* curves have shifted.

enough time, profits attract new entrants and losses result in an industry shakeout, until firms are earning zero economic profit. In the long run, restaurants, retail stores, hair salons, and other monopolistically competitive firms earn zero economic profit for their owners. That is, there is just enough accounting profit to cover the implicit costs of doing business—just enough to keep the owners from shifting their time and money to some alternative enterprise.

EXCESS CAPACITY UNDER MONOPOLISTIC COMPETITION

Look again at Figure 2, which shows Kafka's long-run equilibrium, at point *E*, after entry has eliminated its profits. When Kafka earns zero economic profit, its demand curve touches, but does not cross, its *ATC* curve. This will be true for *any* monopolistic competitor in the long run. To see why, draw a diagram right now (you can use the margin of this page) that shows the demand curve actually *crossing* the *ATC* curve. If you do this correctly, you will find that at *some* output levels, price is greater than *ATC*, and the firm can earn economic profit by producing there. But such profit would attract entry, so we would not yet be in long-run equilibrium.

In Figure 2, you can see that in long-run equilibrium (point *E*), the *ATC* curve has the same slope as the demand curve, a *negative* slope. Thus, in the long run, a monopolistic competitor always produces on the *downward-sloping* portion of its *ATC* curve and therefore *never produces at minimum average cost*. Indeed, its output level is always *too small* to minimize cost per unit. The firm operates with *excess capacity*. (The output level at which cost per unit is minimized is often called capacity output.) In Figure 2, Kafka Exterminators *would* reach minimum cost per unit by servicing about 200 homes per month (the firm's capacity output), but in the long run, it will service only 100 homes per month.

> *In the long run, a monopolistic competitor will operate with excess capacity—that is, it will not sell enough output to achieve minimum cost per unit.*

To see why a monopolistic competitor *cannot* minimize average cost in the long run, imagine that Kafka Exterminators wanted to do so, by servicing 200 homes per month. With its current demand curve, it would suffer a loss, since *P* < *ATC* at that output level. It would quickly return to its profit-maximizing output of 100 homes, where at least it breaks even.

Excess capacity suggests that monopolistic competition is costly to consumers, and indeed it is. Recall that under perfect competition, *P* = minimum *ATC* in long-run equilibrium. (Look back at Figure 9 in Chapter 8.) But under monopolistic competition, *P* > minimum *ATC* in the long run. Thus, if the *ATC* curves were the same, price would always be greater under monopolistic competition.

This reasoning may tempt you to leap to a conclusion: Consumers are better off under perfect competition. But don't leap so fast. Remember that in order to get the beneficial results of perfect competition, all firms must produce identical output. It is precisely because monopolistic competitors produce *differentiated* output—and therefore have downward-sloping demand curves—that *P* > minimum *ATC* in the long run.

And consumers usually *benefit* from product differentiation. (If you don't think so, imagine how you would feel if every restaurant in your town served an identical menu, or if everyone had to wear the same type of clothing, or if every rock group in the country performed the same tunes in exactly the same way.) Seen in this light, we can regard the higher costs and prices under monopolistic competition as the price we pay for product variety. Some may argue that there is too much variety in a market economy—how many different brands of toothpaste do we really need?—but few would want to transform all monopolistically competitive industries into perfectly competitive ones.

NONPRICE COMPETITION

If a monopolistic competitor wants to increase its output, one way is to cut its price. That is, it can move *along* its demand curve. But a price cut is not the only way to increase output. Since the firm produces a differentiated product, it can sell more by convincing people that its own output is better than that of competing firms. Such efforts, if successful, will *shift* the firm's demand curve rightward.

> *Any action a firm takes to shift the demand curve for its output to the right is called **nonprice competition**.*

Nonprice competition Any action a firm takes to shift its demand curve rightward.

Better service, product guarantees, free home delivery, more attractive packaging, as well as advertising to inform customers about these things, are all examples of nonprice competition. Fast-food restaurants are notorious for nonprice competition. When Burger King says, "Have it your way," the company is saying, "Our hamburgers are better than those at McDonald's because *we* make them to order." When McDonald's responds with an attractive, fresh-faced young woman behind the counter, smiling broadly when you order a Happy Meal, it is saying, in effect, "So what if we don't make your burgers to order; our staff is better looking and more upbeat than Burger King's."

Nonprice competition is another reason why monopolistic competitors earn zero economic profit in the long run. If an innovative firm discovers a way to shift its demand curve rightward—say, by offering better service or more clever advertising—then in the *short run,* it may be able to earn a profit. This means that other, less innovative firms will experience a leftward shift in *their* demand curves, as they lose sales to their more innovative rival.

But not for long. Remember that in monopolistic competition, the "free entry" assumption includes the ability of new entrants, as well as existing firms, to replicate the successful business practices of others. If product guarantees are enabling some firms to earn economic profit, then *all* firms will offer product guarantees. If advertising is doing the trick, then *all* firms will start ad campaigns. In the long run, we can expect *all* monopolistic competitors to run advertisements, to be concerned about service, and to take whatever actions have proven profitable for other firms in the industry. All this nonprice competition is costly—one must *pay* for advertising, for product guarantees, for better staff training—and these costs must be included in each firm's *ATC* curve, shifting it upward. But none of this changes our conclusion that monopolistic competitors will earn zero economic profit in the long run.

Indeed, nonprice competition strengthens our conclusions. In the long run, the profitable firm will find its demand curve shifting leftward due to the entry of new firms, *or* the imitation of its successful nonprice competition, or both. In the end, each firm will find itself back in the situation depicted in Figure 2. Because of the costs of nonprice competition, each firm's *ATC* curve will be higher than it would otherwise be. However, it will still touch, but not cross, the demand curve, and the firm will still earn zero economic profit. We will take a closer look at one form of nonprice competition, advertising, in the Using the Theory section at the end of the chapter.

OLIGOPOLY

A monopolistic competitor enjoys a certain amount of independence. There are so many *other* firms selling in the market—each one such a small fish in such a large pond—that each of them can make decisions without worrying about how the others will react. For example, if a single pharmacy in a large city cuts its prices or begins advertising, it can safely assume that any other pharmacy that could benefit from price cutting or advertising has already done so, or will shortly do so, *regardless of its own actions*. Thus, there is no reason for the first pharmacy to take the reactions of other pharmacies into account when making its own decisions.

But in some markets, most of the output is sold by just a few firms. These markets are not monopolies (there is more than one seller), but they are not monopolistically competitive either. There are so few firms that the actions taken by any one will *very much* affect the others and will likely generate a direct response. For example, the market for DVD rentals by mail is dominated by three firms: Netflix, Wal-Mart, and Blockbuster. In late 2004, Netflix lowered the price of its basic plan (in which customers can have three movies out at one time) from $22 to $18 per month. In making this move, Netflix had to consider that it would attract business from its rivals, who might respond with their own price cuts. (Sure enough, within a week, Blockbuster cut the price of its own three-movie plan from $19 to $17.50.)

When just a few large firms dominate a market, so that the actions of each one have an important impact on the others, it would be foolish for any one firm to ignore its competitors' reactions. On the contrary, in such a market, each firm recognizes its *strategic interdependence* with the others. Before the management team makes a decision, it must reason as follows: "If we take action *A*, our competitors will do *B*, and then we would do *C*, and they would respond with *D*. . . ," and so on. This kind of thinking is the hallmark of the market structure we call *oligopoly:*

Oligopoly A market structure in which a small number of firms are strategically interdependent.

> An **oligopoly** *is a market dominated by a small number of strategically interdependent firms.*

There are many different types of oligopolies. The output may be more or less identical among firms, such as copper wire, or differentiated, such as laptop computers. An oligopoly market may be international, as in the market for automobile tires; mostly national, as in the U.S. market for breakfast cereals; or local, as in the market for some daily newspapers. There may be one dominant firm with a significantly larger share of the market than any of its rivals (such as Nike in the U.S. market for athletic shoes). Or there may be two or more large firms of roughly similar size, like Boeing and Airbus in the global market for large passenger aircraft. You can see that oligopoly markets can have different characteristics, but in all cases, *a small number of strategically interdependent firms produce the dominant share of output in the market.*

OLIGOPOLY IN THE REAL WORLD

While defining an oligopoly in theory is straightforward, *applying* the definition to real-world markets raises a host of problems. This is not just a matter of semantics. The extent to which a market follows the oligopoly model—with market dominance by a few firms—is at the heart of public policy toward market structure, a subject we'll examine more closely in Chapter 15.

What's so hard about identifying oligopoly in the real world?

Market Definition

In oligopoly, a few large firms dominate *the market*. But how should we define "the market"? With a narrow-enough definition, we can find oligopoly everywhere. For example, in a large city there will be thousands of restaurants, so we would properly consider the market for "restaurant meals" in that city to be monopolistically competitive. But if we define the market as "Thai restaurants within a half-mile from the civic center," there may be only two or three such firms, and voilá—we have an oligopoly!

Similarly, with a broad-enough definition, we can make any oligopoly disappear. In the U.S. market for breakfast cereal, just four firms control about 90 percent of the market—an oligopoly. But if we widen our market definition to include "all food," then these four firms compete with thousands of other firms. The market no longer satisfies the definition of oligopoly.

How, then, should we define a market in trying to identify oligopoly? The approach taken by economists (including those who work in government agencies that have the power to approve or prohibit mergers between large firms) is to define the market *just* broadly enough so that it includes all "reasonably close" substitutes. In many cases, common sense can guide us in applying this principle. Thus, we refer to the market for "breakfast cereals," because one breakfast cereal is a close substitute for another. The market for "food" would be too broad because it would include too many products that are not close substitutes. And the market for "corn-flakes" would be too narrow, because it would leave out other types of breakfast cereal, which are close substitutes.

But in some cases, common sense isn't definitive. Consider what happened in 2003, when Nestlé (whose product line includes Häagen-Dasz ice cream) announced that it planned to acquire Dreyer's (maker of several premium ice cream brands). In the market for "premium ice cream," Nestlé's acquisition would give it a 60 percent share—a level of dominance by one firm that should raise eyebrows. In the market for "all ice cream," however, Nestlé's share would be significantly smaller, barely enough to elicit a yawn. The question is: Are regular and premium ice cream "close enough" as substitutes that the market should include both? The government said no: It defined the market as "premium ice cream" only, and insisted that Dreyer's sell off some of its premium lines as a condition for approving the merger. But the government's view was not the only reasonable one.

Number of Firms

Oligopoly requires that a *few firms* dominate the market. Even if we can agree on a market's definition, what number qualifies as "a few"? Certainly 3 or 4. But is 7 firms too many? How about 12? In theory, we require a number small enough that each firm considers the reactions of its rivals when making decisions, that is, small enough to create strategic interdependence. A market with just 3 large firms will certainly display strong interdependence. As we consider markets with 5, or 10, or 15 firms, interdependence will diminish. At *some* point, the number of firms is so large, and interdependence so weak, that oligopoly becomes a poor description, and monopolistic competition would fit better. But there is no absolute number at which oligopoly ends and monopolistic competition begins.

Market Domination

Oligopoly requires that a few firms—whatever their number—*dominate* the market; that is, their combined share of the market is large. This is needed for strategic interdependence among firms. If, for example, the four largest firms together had a 15 percent share of the market, each would be too small to significantly affect the others. But if their combined market share were 90 percent, and all were roughly the same size, then decisions by any one would have huge impacts on the others; strategic interaction would be intense. But what if the combined market share were 70 percent? Or 50 percent? As the number shrinks, strategic interdependence becomes weaker.

You can see that oligopoly is a matter of degree, not an absolute classification. We can imagine a spectrum: At one end are industries in which a very small number of firms produce a large share of the output. In these industries, there is strong strategic interdependence among firms, so our ideas about oligopoly will fit very closely. As we proceed along the spectrum, market domination by the largest firms decreases, strategic interdependence declines, and oligopoly analysis has less to contribute to our understanding of firm and market behavior.

How Oligopolies Arise

Oligopoly firms do not always earn economic profit in the long run. But even when they do, entry into the market is limited, so that a few large firms continue to dominate the industry. Thus, our search for the origin of oligopolies is really a search for the specific *barriers to entry* that keep out competitors and maintain the dominance of just a few firms. What are these barriers?

Economies of Scale: Natural Oligopolies

In Chapter 6, you learned that economies of scale can limit the number of firms that can survive in a market. When the minimum efficient scale for a typical firm is a relatively large percentage of the market, a large firm, supplying a large share of the market, will have lower cost per unit than a small firm. Since small firms can't compete, only a few large firms survive, and the market becomes an oligopoly. Because this tends to happen on its own unless there is government intervention, such a market is often called a **natural oligopoly,** analogous to natural monopoly. Airlines, college textbook publishers, and passenger jet manufacturers are all examples of oligopolies in which economies of scale play a large role.

Natural oligopoly A market that tends naturally toward oligopoly because the minimum efficient scale of the typical firm is a large fraction of the market.

Reputation as a Barrier

A new entrant may suffer just from being new. Established oligopolists are likely to have favorable reputations. In many oligopolies—like the markets for soft drinks and breakfast cereals—heavy advertising expenditure has also helped to build and maintain brand loyalty. A new entrant might be able to catch up to those already in the industry, but this may require a substantial period of high advertising costs and low revenues.

In some cases, where the potential profits are great, investors may decide it is worth the risk and accept the initial losses in order to enter the industry. Ted Turner took such a risk and sustained several years of losses before his cable ventures (Cable News Network, Turner Network Television, and Turner Broadcasting System) earned a profit. But in other industries, the initial losses may be too great and the probability of success too low for investors to risk their money starting a new firm.

Strategic Barriers

Oligopoly firms often pursue strategies designed to keep out potential competitors. They can maintain excess production capacity as a signal to a potential entrant that, with little advance notice, they could easily saturate the market and leave the new entrant with little or no revenue. They can make special deals with distributors to receive the best shelf space in retail stores or make long-term arrangements with customers to ensure that their products are not displaced quickly by those of a new entrant. And they can spend large amounts on advertising to make it difficult for a new entrant to differentiate its product.

Legal Barriers

Patents and copyrights, which can be responsible for monopoly, can also create oligopolies. For example, all four government-approved drugs commonly prescribed to treat symptoms of Alzheimer's disease are still protected by patents. Until these patents expire, or several new drugs are developed, the market for Alzheimer's drugs will continue to be an oligopoly consisting of just four large pharmaceutical companies.

Like monopolies, oligopolies are not shy about lobbying the government to preserve their market domination. One of the easiest targets is foreign competition. U.S. steel companies are relentless in their efforts to limit the amount of foreign— especially Japanese—steel sold in the U.S. market. In the past, they have succeeded in getting special taxes on imported steel and financial penalties imposed upon successful foreign steel companies. Other U.S. industries, including automobiles, textiles, and lumber, have had similar successes.

Legal barriers can operate against *domestic* entrants, too. Zoning regulations may prohibit the building of a new supermarket, movie theater, or auto repair shop in a local market, thereby preserving the oligopoly status of the few firms already established there. Lobbying by established firms is often the source of these restrictive practices.

OLIGOPOLY VERSUS OTHER MARKET STRUCTURES

Of the market structures you have studied in this book, oligopoly presents the greatest challenge to economists. In the other types of markets—perfect competition, monopoly, and monopolistic competition—each firm acts independently, without worrying about the reactions of other firms. The firm's task is a simple one: to select an output level along its demand curve that gives it maximum profit.

But this approach doesn't describe an oligopolist. The essence of oligopoly, remember, is *strategic interdependence*, wherein each firm must anticipate the reactions of its rivals when making decisions. Thus, we cannot analyze one firm's decisions in isolation from other firms. In order to understand and predict behavior in oligopoly markets, economists have had to modify the tools used to analyze the other market structures and to develop entirely new tools as well.

Let's look at an example of strategic interdependence more closely and see why the tools we've used to analyze the other market structures will not work well for oligopoly. Remember Kafka Exterminators? Because it was a monopolistic competitor, it could raise or lower its price, and move along its demand curve, without having to worry that its decision would cause its competitors to change *their* prices. We could safely predict that Kafka would keep increasing its output until its marginal revenue and marginal cost were equal.

But what if Kafka had been an oligopolist—say, one of two exterminators in a small town? Then, whenever the other exterminator (selling a close substitute) changed its price, Kafka's demand curve would *shift*. (For example, if Kafka's rival dropped its price, then Kafka would service fewer households at any given price, so its demand curve would shift leftward.)

As a consequence, in oligopoly we cannot use the simple $MR = MC$ rule we used to explain a firm's behavior in other market structures. After all, if Kafka (as an oligopolist) increased its output and therefore lowered its price, and its rival responded by changing *its* price, then Kafka's demand curve would shift and so would its MR curve. The size of these shifts would depend on how much its rival changed its price in response. So there would be no stable MR curve that Kafka could move along in trying to follow the $MR = MC$ rule.

To predict what an oligopoly will do, we must explore the strategic interaction among firms. How do managers think their rivals will respond to their actions? How will they, in turn, react to these responses? And with all of this anticipation of actions and reactions, where will the market end up?

Game theory An approach to modeling the strategic interaction of oligopolists in terms of moves and countermoves.

You can see why oligopoly presents such a challenge, not only to the firms themselves, but also to economists studying them. However, one approach, called **game theory**, has yielded rich insights into oligopoly behavior.

THE GAME THEORY APPROACH

The word *game* applied to oligopoly decision making might seem out of place. Games—like poker, basketball, or chess—are usually played for fun, and even when money is at stake, the sums are usually small. What do games have in common with important business decisions, where hundreds of millions of dollars and thousands of jobs may be at stake?

In fact, quite a bit. In all games—except those of pure chance, such as roulette—a player's strategy must take account of the strategies followed by other players. This is precisely the situation of the oligopolist. Game theory analyzes oligopoly decisions as if they were games by looking at the rules players must follow, the payoffs they are trying to achieve, and the strategies they can use to achieve them.

The Prisoner's Dilemma

The easiest way to understand how game theory works is to start with a simple, noneconomic example—the prisoner's dilemma—that explains why a technique for obtaining confessions, commonly used by police, is so often successful. Imagine that two partners in crime (let's call them Rose and Colin) have committed a serious offense (say, murder) but have been arrested for a lesser offense (say, robbery). The police have enough evidence to ensure a robbery conviction, but their evidence for murder cannot be used in court. Their only hope for a murder conviction is to get one or both partners to incriminate the other.

The traditional strategy is to separate the partners and explain the following to each one: "Look, you're already facing a five-year sentence for robbery. But we'll offer you a deal: If you confess to the murder and implicate your partner, and your partner does *not* confess, we'll make sure that the D.A. goes easy on you. You'll get three years, tops. If you and your partner *both* confess, we'll send you each away for 20 years. But if your partner confesses, and you do *not*, we'll send *you* away for 30 years."

Payoff matrix A table showing the payoffs to each of two players for each pair of strategies they choose.

We can regard each partner in this situation as a *player* in a *game*. Figure 3 shows the **payoff matrix** for this game, a listing of the payoffs that each player will receive for each possible combination of strategies the two might select. The payoff matrix presents a lot of information at once, so let's take it step-by-step.

First, notice that each *column* represents a strategy that Colin might choose: confess or not confess. Second, each *row* represents a strategy that Rose might select: confess or not confess. Thus, each of the four boxes in the payoff matrix represents one of four possible strategy combinations that might be selected in this game:

1. Upper left box: Both Rose and Colin confess.
2. Lower left box: Colin confesses and Rose doesn't.
3. Upper right box: Rose confesses and Colin doesn't.
4. Lower right box: Neither Rose nor Colin confesses.

For centuries, police investigators have used the logic of the prisoner's dilemma game to outsmart partners in crime.

Let's now look at the game from Colin's point of view. The green-shaded entries in each box are Colin's possible *payoffs:* jail sentences. (Ignore the blue-shaded entries for now.) For example, the lower left square shows that when Colin confesses and Rose does not, Colin will receive just a three-year sentence.

Colin wants the best possible deal for himself, but he is not sure what his partner will do. (Remember, they are in separate rooms.) So Colin first asks himself which strategy would be best *if* his partner were to confess. The *top row* of the matrix guides us through his reasoning: "If Rose decides to confess, my best choice would be to confess, too, because then I'd get 20 years rather than 30." Next, Colin determines the best strategy if Rose does *not* confess. As the *bottom row* shows, he'll reason as follows: "If Rose does not confess, my best choice would be to confess, because then I'd get 3 years rather than 5."

Let's recap: If Rose confesses, Colin's best choice is to confess; if Rose does *not* confess, Colin's best choice is—once again—to confess. Thus, regardless of Rose's

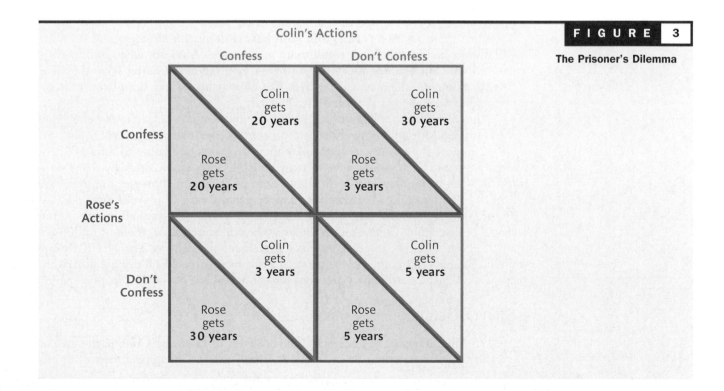

FIGURE 3

The Prisoner's Dilemma

Colin's Actions

	Confess	Don't Confess
Confess	Colin gets **20 years** / Rose gets **20 years**	Colin gets **30 years** / Rose gets **3 years**
Don't Confess	Colin gets **3 years** / Rose gets **30 years**	Colin gets **5 years** / Rose gets **5 years**

Rose's Actions

strategy, Colin's best choice is to confess. In this game, the strategy "confess" is an example of a *dominant strategy:*

Dominant strategy A strategy that is best for a player no matter what strategy the other player chooses.

> A *dominant strategy* is a strategy that is best for a player regardless of the strategy of the other player.

If a player has a dominant strategy in a game, we can safely assume that he will follow it.

What about Rose? In another room, she is presented with the *same* set of options and payoffs as her partner, as shown by the blue entries in the payoff matrix. When Rose looks down each *column,* she can see *her* possible payoffs for each strategy that Colin might follow. As you can see (and make sure that you can, by going through all the possibilities), Rose has the same dominant strategy as Colin: confess. We can now predict that *both* players will follow the strategy of confessing. The outcome of the game—the upper left-hand corner—is a confession from both partners, with each receiving a 20-year sentence.

The outcome of this game is an example of a *Nash equilibrium,* appropriately named after the mathematician John Nash, who originated the concept. (Nash won the Nobel Prize in economics in 1994, and was the subject of the film *A Beautiful Mind.*)

Nash equilibrium A situation in which every player of a game is taking the best action for themselves, given the actions taken by all other players.

> A *Nash equilibrium* is a combination of strategies in which each player is making the best choice for him- or herself, given the choices of all other players.

We use the term *equilibrium* for this situation because, once the players are in it, neither one would have an incentive to change his or her behavior. In a Nash equilibrium, if we took each player aside, and offered each one the opportunity to make a change, each would turn down the offer.

When there are two players and both have a dominant strategy, that outcome will always be the only Nash equilibrium in the game. After all, when both players have a dominant strategy, they *always* do best by using it, no matter what the other player is doing. And once each player has chosen his or her dominant strategy, neither would change it if offered the chance.

Note, however, that in Figure 3, both Rose and Colin could do even better than the Nash equilibrium if both choose *not* to confess (the lower right corner). But this would require the players to coordinate their decisions and come to an agreement not to confess. Each would have to trust that the other would stick by that agreement. When we think about Nash equilibrium or dominant strategies to predict the outcome of a game, however, we take a more narrow view of players' attitudes. We assume that each player acts in his or her own self-interest, always taking the option that is best for him or her. And in the prisoner's dilemma game, the best option for either player would be to break any such agreement and confess. This is why we end up in the upper left corner in the prisoner's dilemma game. We'll discuss other situations, in which coordinating decisions is a more realistic possibility, in a few pages.

SIMPLE OLIGOPOLY GAMES

The same method used to understand the behavior of Rose and Colin in the prisoner's dilemma can be applied to a simple oligopoly market. Imagine a town with just two gas stations: Gus's Gas and Filip's Fillup. This is an example of an oligopoly with just two firms, called a **duopoly**. We assume that Gus and Filip, like Rose and Colin in the prisoner's dilemma, must make their decisions independently, without knowing in advance what the other will do. We'll consider three types of situations these duopolists might face: (1) both players have dominant strategies, (2) only one player has a dominant strategy, and (3) neither player has a dominant strategy.

Duopoly An oligopoly market with only two sellers.

Both Players Have Dominant Strategies

Figure 4 shows an example of a payoff matrix in which (as you're about to see) both players have a dominant strategy. To keep it simple, we've limited each player to two possible actions: charging a high price or a low price for gas. The columns of the matrix represent Gus's possible strategies, while the rows represent Filip's strategies. Each square shows a possible payoff, yearly profit, for Gus (shaded purple) and Filip (shaded green). (Make sure you can see, for example, that if Gus sets a high price and Filip sets a low price, then Gus will suffer a loss of $10,000 while Filip will enjoy a profit of $75,000.)

The payoffs in the figure follow a logic that we find in many oligopoly markets: Each firm will make greater profit if all firms charge a higher price. But the best situation for any one firm is to have its rivals charge a high price, while *it alone* charges a low price and lures customers from the competition. The worst situation for any one firm is to charge a high price while its rivals charge a low one, for then it will lose much of its business to its rivals.

The entries in the payoff matrix in Figure 4 reflect this situation: Profits are higher ($50,000) for both Gus and Filip when they both charge a high price and

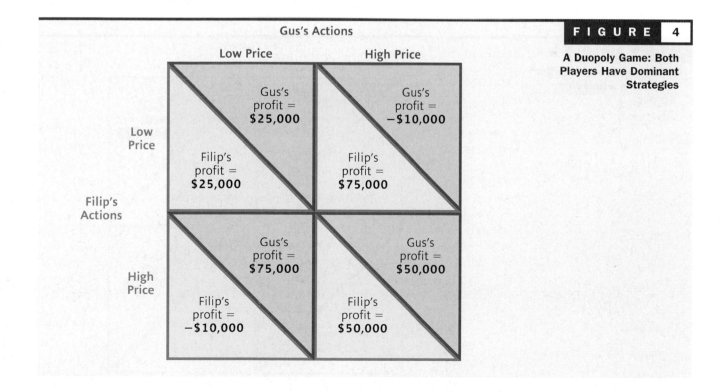

FIGURE 4

A Duopoly Game: Both Players Have Dominant Strategies

lower ($25,000) when they both charge a low price. But when the two follow different strategies, the low-price firm gets the best possible payoff ($75,000), while the high-price firm gets the worst possible payoff (−$10,000).

Let's look at the game from Gus's point of view, using the purple-shaded entries in the payoff matrix. If Filip chooses a low price (the top row), then Gus should choose a low price, too, since this will get him a $25,000 profit instead of a $10,000 loss. If Filip selects a high price (the bottom row), then, once again, Gus should choose a low price, since this will get him a profit of $75,000 rather than $50,000. Thus, no matter what Filip does, Gus's best move is to charge a low price—his *dominant* strategy.

A similar analysis from Filip's point of view, using the green-shaded entries, tells us that his dominant strategy is the same: a low price. Thus, the outcome of this game is the box in the upper left-hand corner, where both players charge a low price and each earns a profit of $25,000.

Notice that our outcome—like the outcome of the prisoner's dilemma—is a Nash equilibrium. Once Gus and Filip reach the upper left-hand corner, each is doing the best that he can do, given what the other is doing. Neither has any incentive to change.

Only One Player Has a Dominant Strategy

Figure 5 shows a payoff matrix that is exactly like the one in Figure 4 except for one alteration: Gus's payoff in the lower left-hand cell has been changed from $75,000 to $40,000. In this new game, Gus no longer has a dominant strategy. If Filip charges a low price, Gus should charge a low price; if Filip charges a high price, Gus should charge a high price. (Take a moment to verify this before reading on.) Thus, Gus's best choice depends on Filip's choice. However, since we haven't changed any of Filip's payoffs, he still has a dominant strategy: to charge a low price. Since Gus

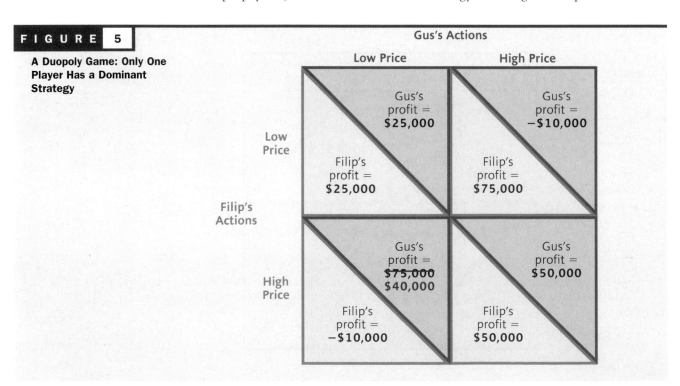

FIGURE 5

A Duopoly Game: Only One Player Has a Dominant Strategy

Gus's Actions

	Low Price	High Price
Low Price	Gus's profit = **$25,000** Filip's profit = **$25,000**	Gus's profit = **−$10,000** Filip's profit = **$75,000**
High Price	Gus's profit = **~~$75,000~~ $40,000** Filip's profit = **−$10,000**	Gus's profit = **$50,000** Filip's profit = **$50,000**

Filip's Actions

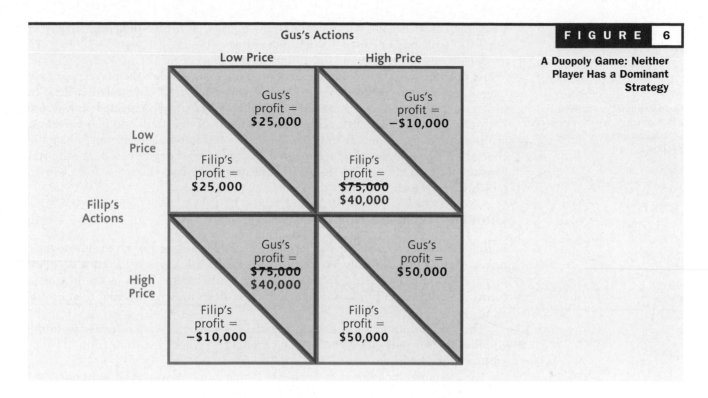

FIGURE 6

A Duopoly Game: Neither Player Has a Dominant Strategy

Gus's Actions

Low Price   High Price

Filip's Actions

Low Price

Gus's profit = $25,000

Filip's profit = $25,000

Gus's profit = −$10,000

Filip's profit = ~~$75,000~~ $40,000

High Price

Gus's profit = ~~$75,000~~ $40,000

Filip's profit = −$10,000

Gus's profit = $50,000

Filip's profit = $50,000

knows that Filip will select the low price, Gus will always select a low price too. We know, therefore, exactly where these two station owners will end up: both charging the low price.

No Player Has a Dominant Strategy

What happens in a game in which *neither* player has a dominant strategy? Figure 6 illustrates this situation. Now we've changed *Filip's* $75,000 payoff to $40,000, just as we did for Gus in our previous example. We've already shown in our previous example that Gus does not have a dominant strategy with his payoffs. You can easily prove to yourself that Filip has no dominant strategy either. In fact, in Figure 6, the best strategy for either player (low or high price) depends on the choice of the other. Therefore, it is more difficult to predict an outcome to this game.

Economists are very interested in situations like these, and have come up with some more advanced techniques to help predict how players are likely to behave in such situations. If you continue your study of microeconomics, you'll learn about some of these techniques.[4]

Repeated Play

While our simple example helps us understand the basic ideas of game theory, real-world oligopoly situations are seldom so simple. First, there will typically be more than two strategies from which to choose (for example, a variety of different prices or several different amounts to spend on *nonprice* competition such as advertising).

---

[4] For those interested, an excellent introduction to game theory, by Don Ross, is available online at *http://plato.stanford.edu/entries/game-theory/*.

Also, there will usually be more than two players, so a two-dimensional payoff matrix like the one in Figure 4 would not suffice.

Finally, in our examples, we've limited the players to *one* play of the game. While this might make sense in the prisoner's dilemma—where the players get only one chance to make a decision—it is not realistic for most oligopoly markets. In reality, for gas stations and almost all other oligopolies, there is **repeated play,** where both players select a strategy, observe the outcome of that trial, and play the game again and again, as long as they remain rivals. Repeated play can fundamentally change the way players view a game and lead to new strategies based on long-run considerations. One possible result of repeated trials is *cooperative behavior,* to which we now turn.

Repeated play A situation in which strategically interdependent sellers compete over many time periods.

COOPERATIVE BEHAVIOR IN OLIGOPOLY

In the real world, oligopolists will usually get more than one chance to choose their prices. Pepsi and Coca-Cola have been rivals in the soft drink market for decades, as have Kellogg, Post (Kraft Foods), Quaker, and General Mills in the breakfast cereal market. These firms can change their strategies after observing their rivals' strategies.

The equilibrium in a game with repeated plays may be very different from the equilibrium in a game played only once. Often, firms will evolve some form of *cooperation* in the long run.

For example, look again at Figure 4. If this game were played only once, we would expect each player to pursue its dominant strategy, select a low price, and end up with $25,000 in yearly profit. But there is a better outcome for both players. If each were to charge a high price, each would make a profit of $50,000 per year. If Gus and Filip remain competitors year after year, we might expect them to realize that by cooperating, they would both be better off. And there are many ways for the two to cooperate.

Explicit Collusion

Explicit collusion Cooperation involving direct communication between competing firms about setting prices.

The simplest form of cooperation is **explicit collusion,** in which managers meet face-to-face to decide how to set prices. These arrangements are commonly called price-fixing agreements. In our example, Gus and Filip might strike an agreement that each will charge a high price, moving the outcome of the game to the lower right-hand corner in Figure 4, where each earns $50,000 in yearly profit instead of $25,000.

Cartel A group of firms that selects a common price that maximizes total industry profits.

The most extreme form of explicit collusion is the creation of a **cartel**—a group of firms that tries to maximize the total profits of the group as a whole. To do this, the group of firms behaves as if it were a monopoly, treating the market demand curve as the "monopoly's" demand curve. Then, it finds the point on the demand curve—the price and quantity of output—that maximizes total profit. Each member is instructed to charge the agreed-upon price (cartels are often called *price-fixing* agreements), and each is allotted a share of the cartel's total output. This last step is crucial: If any member produces and sells more than its allotted portion, then the group's total *output* rises and the price will fall below the agreed-upon profit-maximizing price.

The most famous cartel in recent years has been OPEC—the Organization of Petroleum Exporting Countries—which meets periodically to influence the price of oil by setting the amount that each of its members can produce. In the mid-1970s, OPEC quadrupled its price per barrel in just two years, leading to a huge increase

Date of Fine	Company	Product	Fine	**T A B L E 1**
October 1996	Archer Daniels Midland Company	Lysine and citric acid	$100 million	**Some Recent U.S. Price-Fixing Cases**
April 1998	UCAR International	Graphite electrodes	$110 million	
May 1999	SGL Carbon	Graphite electrodes	$135 million	
May 1999	BASF AG	Vitamins	$225 million	
May 1999	F. Hoffmann-La Roche	Vitamins	$500 million	
May 2001	Mitsubishi Corp.	Graphite electrodes	$134 million	
September 2004	Infineon Technologies AG	DRAM processors	$160 million	
October 2005	Samsung	DRAM processors	$300 million	

in profits for the cartel's members. In the late 1990s, OPEC exerted its muscle once again, doubling the price of oil over a period of 18 months.

If explicit collusion to raise prices is such a good thing for oligopolists, why don't they all do it? A major reason is that it's usually *illegal*. OPEC was not considered illegal by any of the oil-producing nations, but cartels are against the law in the United States, the European Union, and most of the developed nations. In these countries, explicit collusion must be conducted with the utmost secrecy. And the penalties, if the oligopolists are caught, can be severe.

Interestingly, authorities in both the United States and Europe now use a strategy based on the prisoner's dilemma game to uncover price-fixing agreements: The first manager to confess is given automatic amnesty, while those who don't confess (or confess too late) are treated harshly. The U.S. Department of Justice has reported that since this policy went into effect in 1993, the number of corporate confessions and applications for amnesty has increased dramatically.[5] Table 1 lists some of the largest fines imposed by the U.S. government in recent years, after price-fixing arrangements were exposed and prosecuted.

The chances of getting caught, and the severe penalties at stake, often lead oligopolists to other forms of collusion that are harder to detect.

Tacit Collusion

Any time firms cooperate *without* an explicit agreement, they are engaging in **tacit collusion.** Typically, players adopt strategies along the following lines: "In general, I will set a high price. If my rival also sets a high price, I will go on setting a high price. If my rival sets a low price this time, I will punish him by setting a low price next time." You can see that if both players stick to this strategy, they will both likely set the high price. Each is waiting for the other to go first in setting a low price, so it may never happen.

This type of strategy is often called **tit-for-tat,** defined as doing to the other player what he has just done to you. In our gas station duopoly, for example, Gus will pick the high price whenever Filip has set the high price in the previous play,

Tacit collusion Any form of oligopolistic cooperation that does not involve an explicit agreement.

Tit-for-tat A game-theoretic strategy of doing to another player this period what he has done to you in the previous period.

[5] Speech by Scott Hammond, "An Update of the Antitrust Division's Criminal Enforcement Program," Department of Justice, November 16, 2005 (*http://www.usdoj.gov/atr/public/speeches/213247.htm*). This is also the source for Table 1.

and Gus will pick the low price if that is what Filip did in the previous play. With enough plays of the game, Filip may eventually catch on that he can get Gus to set the desired high price by setting the high price himself and that he should not exploit the situation by setting the low price, because that will cause Gus to set the low price next time. The result of every play will then be a *cooperative outcome:* The players move to the lower right-hand corner of Figure 4, with each firm earning the higher $50,000 in profit.

Tit-for-tat strategies are prominent in the airline industry. When one major airline announces special discounted fares, its rivals almost always announce identical fares the next day. The response from the rivals not only helps them remain competitive, but also provides a signal to the price-cutting airline that it will not be able to offer discounts that are unmatched by its rivals.

Another form of tacit collusion is **price leadership,** in which one firm, the *price leader,* sets its price, and other sellers copy that price. The leader may be the dominant firm in the industry (the one with the greatest market share, for example), or the position of leader may rotate from firm to firm. During the first half of the 20th century, U.S. Steel typically acted as the price leader in the steel industry: When it changed its prices, other firms would automatically follow. In recent decades, American Airlines has behaved as a price leader in many air-travel markets. American's price increases have often been matched within days by Delta, United, and other major airlines.

Price leadership A form of tacit collusion in which one firm sets a price that other firms copy.

With price leadership, there is no formal agreement. Rather, the choice of the leader, the criteria it uses to set its price, and the willingness of other firms to follow come about because the firms realize—without formal discussion—that the system benefits all of them. To keep the price-following firms from cheating—taking large amounts of business by setting a lower price than the price leader—the leader and the firms that choose to follow must be able to punish a cheater. They can do this by setting a low price as quickly as possible after anyone cheats. The expectation of that response may be enough to prevent the cheating in the first place.

The Limits to Collusion

It is tempting to think that collusion—whether explicit or tacit—gives oligopolies absolute power over their markets, leaving them free to jack up prices and exploit the public without limit. But oligopoly power, even with collusion, has its limits.

First, even colluding firms are constrained by the market demand curve: A rise in price will always reduce the quantity demanded from *all* firms together. There is one price—the cartel monopoly price—that maximizes the total profits of all firms in the market, and it will never serve the group's interest to charge any price higher than this.

Second, collusion, even when it is tacit, may be illegal. Although it may be difficult to prove, companies that even *appear* to be colluding may find themselves facing close government scrutiny. Indeed, hardly a month goes by without the announcement of one or more new investigations of collusion by the Justice Department.

Third, collusion is limited by powerful incentives to cheat on any agreement. As the next section shows, cheating is a problem among colluding oligopolists and often leads to the collapse of even the most formal agreements.

The Incentive to Cheat

Let's go back to Gus and Filip for a moment. After repeated plays of the game in Figure 4, with each play ending in the upper left-hand corner ($25,000 in profit for each player), our two gas station owners realize that they can do better with some form of collusion. One way or another—through a formal, explicit agreement, through tit-for-tat behavior, or through an understanding that one of the two will become the price leader—they arrive at the high-price cooperative solution. The outcome of the game then moves to the lower right-hand corner, where each firm earns $50,000 in profit. Will the market stay there?

Maybe. And maybe not. The problem is, each player may conclude that he can do even better by cheating. For example, once Gus commits to a high price, Filip can make even more profit ($75,000) by cheating and selling his gasoline at a lower price. This would reduce Gus's profit to −$10,000, so he, too, would likely switch to the low price, and the two players would be back to the noncooperative outcome based on their dominant strategies.

You might think that in a small-town duopoly of two gas stations such cheating would never occur, since each player can so easily observe what the other is doing, and neither party wants to return to the noncooperative equilibrium. But it may be in each player's interest to cheat *occasionally.* Filip, for example, might think he can enjoy a spell of high profit before Gus has a chance to react, and then—when Gus *does* react—Filip can revert to the cooperative scheme. Gus, by contrast, may try to discourage this with tit-for-tat moves, *punishing* Filip every time he cheats by matching Filip's price or going further and charging an even lower price (not shown on the payoff matrix). By doing so, he is telling Filip: Cheating is not in your interest. Filip, on the other hand, could then set his price still lower, informing Gus, "You better let me cheat occasionally, because punishing me is not in *your* interest."

As you can see, analyzing this sort of behavior requires some rather sophisticated game theory models, and economists are actively engaged in building them. Some of these models predict occasional price wars such as those observed in small-town markets for gasoline and fresh fruit or in national markets for air travel.

THE FUTURE OF OLIGOPOLY

Some people think that the United States and other Western economies are moving relentlessly toward oligopoly as the dominant market structure. Technological change is often cited as the reason. For example, in the early part of the 20th century, several dozen U.S. firms manufactured passenger cars. With the development of mass-production technology, the number soon fell to just a few. Stories like this suggest an economy in which markets are increasingly controlled and manipulated by a few players who, by colluding, exploit the public for their own gain. In 1932, two economists—Adolf Berle and Gardiner Means—noted the trend toward big business and predicted that, unless something were done to stop it, the 200 largest U.S. firms would control the nation's entire economy by 1970.

Berle and Means's prediction has not come true. Today, there are hundreds of thousands of ongoing businesses in the United States. But the prevalence of oligopoly in the national and world economies is anything but stable. Some forces in our society are helping to keep market dominance in check, while others encourage it. Let's consider some of the major forces affecting the future of oligopoly.

Antitrust Legislation and Enforcement

Antitrust policies in the United States and many other countries are designed to protect the interests of consumers by ensuring adequate competition in the marketplace. In practice, antitrust enforcement has focused on three types of actions: (1) preventing collusive agreements among firms, such as price-fixing agreements; (2) breaking up large firms or limiting their activities when market dominance harms consumers; and (3) preventing mergers that would lead to harmful market domination.

The impact of antitrust actions goes far beyond the specific companies called into the courtroom. Managers of firms even *considering* anticompetitive moves have to think long and hard about the consequences of acts that might violate the antitrust laws. For example, many economists believe that in the late 1940s and early 1950s, General Motors would have driven Ford and Chrysler out of business or bought them out were it not for fear of antitrust action.

Still, antitrust and other government policies toward business are a part of our *political* system. While the thrust of these policies is always to preserve competition, the type of competition preserved—and the zeal with which the policies are applied—can shift. Legislative changes in the 1990s, enabling banks to operate across state lines, led to a merger wave in the banking sector. While an economic force (economies of scale) propelled the mergers, a *political* change (new legislation) made it possible.

The Globalization of Markets

When the minimum efficient scale of the typical firm is large relative to the size of the market, a large firm has a cost advantage over a small one, and the result may be a natural oligopoly. But what if the *size of the market* increases? Then an unchanged MES becomes *relatively* smaller, when compared to the market. A larger number of firms could then survive. By enlarging markets from national ones to global ones, international trade can increase the number of firms in a market, thus decreasing market dominance by a few, and increasing competition.

Although oligopolists often try to prevent it, they face increasingly stiff competition from foreign producers. Some economists have argued, for example, that the U.S. market for automobiles now has so many foreign sellers that it resembles monopolistic competition more than oligopoly. Similar changes have occurred in the U.S. markets for color televisions, stereo equipment, computers, beer, and wine. At the same time, the entry of U.S. producers has helped to increase competition in foreign markets for movies, television shows, clothing, household cleaning products, and prepared foods.

Technological Change

One way that technological change works to *increase* competition is by creating new substitute goods. For example, email has provided a substitute for many types of hard copy: personal letters, bills, and some types of documents. The result is tough competition for one of our oldest monopolies—the U.S. Postal Service—as well as competition for a newer oligopoly—overnight package delivery services.

Technology can also reduce barriers to entry in much the same way that globalization does: by increasing the size of the market. A small town, for example, might be able to support only a few stores selling, say, luggage, file cabinets, or CDs, because the MES of a brick-and-mortar store is large relative to the small market there. But technology—the Internet—has enabled residents in many smaller towns to choose among a dozen or more online sellers of the same merchandise. By connecting the town's residents to the national market for retail services, the Internet has increased the size of the market in which they are buyers. In that larger, national market, several firms can compete.

However, technological change can also be seen as *encouraging* oligopoly. By extending the reach of large national retailers, the Internet enables them to become still larger. And if the small brick-and-mortar stores can't compete in this larger market, and go out of business, then the texture of retail service in the country changes. There are more firms competing for the business of residents in any town, but there are fewer of these firms nationwide, and they are larger. The result could be strategic interaction— and possibly collusion—among large national players.

Finally, some technologies actually *increase* the MES of the typical firm, thereby encouraging the formation of oligopolies. For example, producers of digital products—like entertainment, software, and information—have very high up-front costs (lumpy inputs) in creating their goods and services, but almost nonexistent costs of duplicating them to produce and sell another unit. The cost to a software firm of having another buyer download the program, for example, is almost nonexistent. For this reason, a firm in a digital market can continue to experience economies of scale until it serves a relatively large fraction of a national or even global market. Microsoft, Disney, and Time Warner are examples of companies for which new technology has led to a larger market share.

USING THE THEORY

© MEDIOIMAGES/GETTY IMAGES

Advertising in Monopolistic Competition and Oligopoly

We began this chapter by noting that perfect competitors never advertise and monopolies advertise relatively little. But advertising is almost always found under monopolistic competition and very often in oligopoly. Why? All monopolistic competitors, and many oligopolists, produce differentiated products. In these types of markets, the firm gains customers by convincing them that its product is different and better in some way than that of its competitors. Advertising, whether it merely informs customers about the product ("The new Toyota Corolla gets 45 miles per gallon on the highway") or attempts to influence them more subtly and psychologically ("Our exotic perfume will fill your life with mystery and intrigue"), is one way to sharply differentiate a product in the minds of consumers. Since other firms will take advantage of the opportunity to advertise, any firm that *doesn't* advertise will be lost in the shuffle. In this section, we use the tools we've learned in this chapter to look at some aspects of the economics of advertising.

ADVERTISING AND MARKET EQUILIBRIUM UNDER MONOPOLISTIC COMPETITION

A monopolistic competitor advertises for two reasons: to shift its demand curve rightward (greater quantity demanded at each price) and to make demand for its output *less* elastic (so it can raise price and suffer a smaller decrease in quantity demanded). Advertising costs money, so in addition to its impact on the demand curve, it will also affect the firm's *ATC* curve. What is the ultimate impact of advertising on the typical firm?

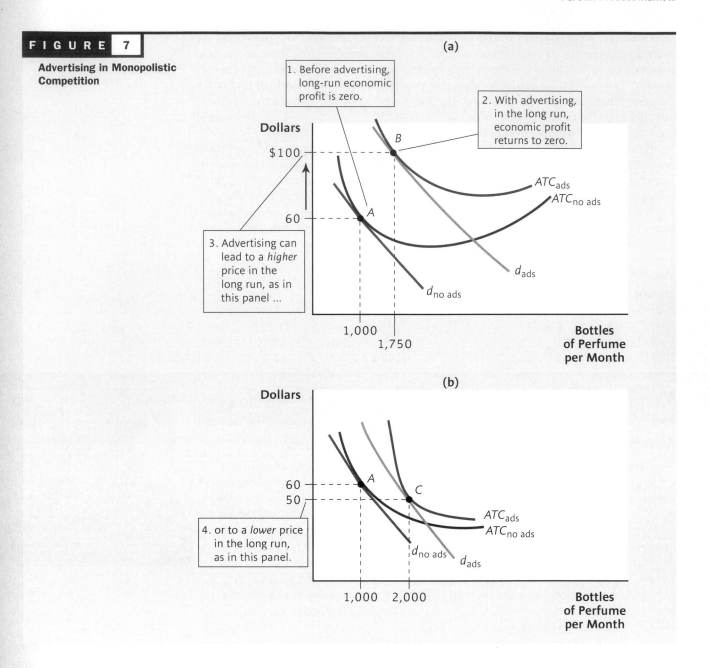

FIGURE 7

Advertising in Monopolistic Competition

(a)

1. Before advertising, long-run economic profit is zero.

2. With advertising, in the long run, economic profit returns to zero.

3. Advertising can lead to a *higher* price in the long run, as in this panel ...

(b)

4. or to a *lower* price in the long run, as in this panel.

Figure 7(a) shows demand and *ATC* curves for a company, Narcissus Fragrance, that manufactures and sells perfume. Initially, there is no advertising at all in the industry. Narcissus is in long-run equilibrium at point *A*, in panel (a), where its demand curve (*d*ₙₒ ₐds) and *ATC* curve (*ATC*ₙₒ ₐds) touch, so economic profit is zero. The firm charges $60 per bottle and sells at the profit-maximizing output level of 1,000 bottles per month. This is the output level where its marginal revenue and marginal cost curves (not shown) intersect.

Now suppose that we introduce advertising into this market. Initially, the first few firms that discover advertising may have a temporary advantage over firms that don't advertise. But remember that in monopolistic competition any successful form of nonprice competition will be automatically replicated by *all* firms (otherwise they would be at a competitive disadvantage). So let's skip over the temporary situation in which only some firms advertise, and examine our new long-run equilibrium when *all* firms advertise. In the long run, how will advertising change the situation of a typical monopolistic competitor in this market?

One change is that, with each firm paying additional costs for advertising, cost per unit will be greater at every output level. So the typical firm's *ATC* curve will shift upward. In panel (a), we show that Narcissus's *ATC* curve shifts upward to ATC_{ads}. Notice, however, that the upward shift is smaller at higher output levels, where the cost of any given ad campaign is spread over a larger number of units.

In addition to the shift in *ATC*, we can expect that with all firms advertising, the demand for the product *in general* will increase. (More people are aware of the product, or have had their appetites stimulated.) And this, in turn, means that *each* firm should be able to sell more units at any given price than before: The demand curve facing each firm shifts rightward.

How much will the typical firm's demand curve shift? We know that, in the long run, the combination of a rightward shift in demand and an upward shift in *ATC* must eventually lead to a new equilibrium in which economic profit is zero. To see why, remember that if advertising creates economic profit in the short run, entry will occur, and every firm's demand curve will then shift leftward. If advertising creates economic loss in the short run, exit will occur, and the remaining firms' demand curves will shift rightward. In the end, long-run equilibrium (a situation of neither entry nor exit) requires that the typical firm earn zero economic profit. And in monopolistic competition, as you've learned, this can only occur when the demand curve touches but does not cross the *ATC* curve, with $P = ATC$ at the profit-maximizing output level. In panel (a), the new long-run equilibrium for our typical firm, Narcissus, occurs at point *B*. Narcissus sells 1,750 bottles of perfume and charges consumers a higher price ($100) than before. But because it has to pay for advertising, it is breaking even, just as it was in the initial long-run equilibrium without advertising.

In panel (a), the impact of advertising is to *raise* prices for consumers. When consumers buy perfume, they are now paying for the advertising as well as all the inputs they paid for before. But you may be surprised that advertising can also have the opposite result: It can actually *lower* prices for consumers.

Panel (b) illustrates this case. As before, we begin in a long-run equilibrium with no advertising in the market, and Narcissus operating at point *A*. When we introduce advertising to all firms, each firm (including Narcissus) sees its *ATC* curve shift upward, to ATC_{ads}. But this time, when long-run equilibrium is restored with zero economic profit (point *C*), Narcissus is charging only $50—less than the initial $60. Advertising has brought down the price of perfume.

How can this be? By advertising, each firm is able to produce and sell more output. This remains true even when *all* firms advertise because total market demand has increased. Since the firm was originally on the downward-sloping portion of its *ATC* curve, we know that its *non*advertising costs per unit will decline as output expands. If this decline is great enough—as in panel (b)—then costs per unit will drop, even when the cost of advertising is included. In other words, because you and I and everyone else is buying more perfume, each producer can operate, with lower costs per unit. In the long run, entry will force each firm to pass the cost savings on to us.

Our analysis suggests the following conclusion:

> *Under monopolistic competition, advertising may increase the size of the market so that more units are sold. But in the long run, each firm earns zero economic profit, just as it would if no firm were advertising. The price to the consumer may either rise or fall.*

ADVERTISING AND COLLUSION IN OLIGOPOLY

In this chapter, you've learned that oligopolists have a strong incentive to engage in tacit collusion. But such collusion is difficult to detect. When one firm raises its prices and others follow, that may be evidence of price leadership, or it may be that costs in the industry have risen, and *all* firms—affected in the same way—have decided independently to raise their prices. But in some cases, such as strategic decisions about advertising, we can use a simple game theory model to show that collusion is almost certainly taking place.

Let's take the airline industry as an example. Polls have shown that passengers have been very concerned about airline safety. This was true before the infamous hijacking of four airliners on September 11, 2001, when thousands died. Since that incident, safety has weighed even more heavily on the minds of those considering flying. Any airline that could convince the public of its superior safety record would profit considerably.

In theory, *any* airline should be able to claim superior safety. After all, there are many different ways to interpret safety data. By searching hard enough, almost any airline could come up with a measure by which it would appear the "safest." And any airline that actually imposed special passenger and baggage screening procedures could tout the changes in its ads, taking business from other airlines. Yet no airline has ever run an advertisement with information about its security policies or attacked those of a competitor. Let's see why.

Figure 8 shows some hypothetical payoffs from this sort of advertising as seen by two firms, United Airlines and American Airlines, competing on a particular route. Focus first on the top, green-shaded entries, which show the payoffs for American. If neither firm ran safety ads, American would earn a level of profit we will call *medium,* as a benchmark. If American ran ads touting its own safety, but United did not, American's profit would certainly increase—to "high" in the payoff matrix. If both firms ran safety ads—especially negative ads that attacked their rival—the public's demand for airline tickets would certainly decline. Reminded of the dangers of flying, more consumers would choose to travel by train, bus, or car. American's profit in this case would be lower than if *neither* firm ran ads, so we have labeled it "low" in the payoff matrix. Finally, the worst possible result for American—"very low" in the figure—occurs when United touts its own safety record, but American does not.

Now consider American's possible strategies. If United decides to run the ads (the top row), American's best action is to run them as well. If United does not run the ads (bottom row), American's best action is still to run the ads. Thus, American has a dominant strategy: Regardless of what United does, it should run the safety ads.

As you can verify, United, whose payoffs are in the lower, red-shaded entries, faces an entirely symmetrical situation. It, too, has the same dominant strategy: Run the ads. Thus, when each airline acts independently, the outcome of this game is shown in the upper left-hand corner, where each airline runs ads and earns a low profit.

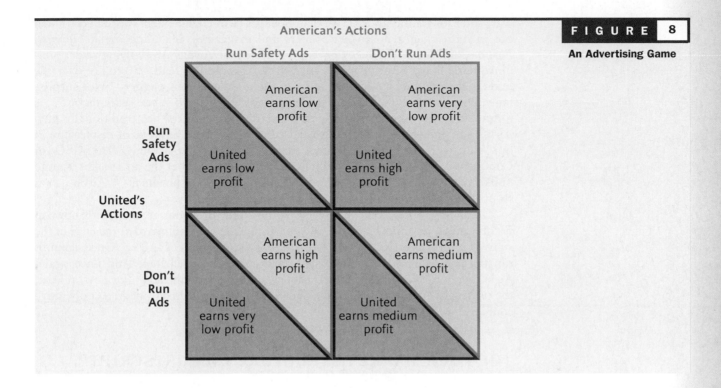

FIGURE 8

An Advertising Game

So why don't we observe that outcome?

The answer is that the airlines are playing against each other repeatedly and reach the kind of cooperative equilibrium we discussed earlier. Each airline can punish its rival next time if it fails to cooperate this time. In the cooperative outcome, each airline plays the strategy that it will *not* run the ads as long as its rival does not. The game's outcome moves to the lower right-hand corner. Here, neither firm runs ads, and each earns medium rather than low profit. This is the result we see in the airline industry.

Until the 1980s, a similar collusive understanding seemed to characterize the automobile industry. As long as the "Big Three" dominated auto sales in the United States, the word *safety* was never heard in their advertising. There seemed to be an understanding that all three would earn greater profits if consumers were *not* reminded of the dangers of driving.

Things changed in the 1980s, however, as foreign firms' share of the U.S. market rose dramatically. One of the new players, Volvo, decided that its safety features were so far superior to its competitors that it no longer paid to play by the rules. Volvo began running television advertisements that not only stressed its own safety features but implied that competing products were dangerous. (On a rainy night, a worried father stops his son at the door, hands him some keys, and says, "Here, son, take the Volvo.") Once Volvo began running ads like these, the other automakers had no choice but to reciprocate. Now, automobile ads routinely mention safety features like antilock brakes and air bags.

Something similar *almost* happened in the airline travel industry. But the "Volvo" in this case was not an airline, but an aircraft manufacturer. In November 1999, Airbus ran ads designed to convince the public that its four-engine A340 jets were safe for transatlantic travel than Boeing's twin-engine 777s. A print ad—taken out in more than a dozen newspapers and magazines, including the *Economist, Fortune,* and the *Wall Street Journal*—shows a lone Airbus A340 flying under ominous, dark skies, with a choppy sea below. The caption read, "If you're over the middle of the Pacific, you want to be in the middle of *four* engines." Not surprisingly, Boeing condemned the ad, declaring that "this not so subtle scare-tactic . . . is a dramatic departure from the high standards our industry has traditionally met. Airbus's actions have, rightfully so, raised a considerable amount of displeasure in our industry." The major airlines reacted even more strongly. The CEO of Continental Airlines, Gordon Bethune, informed Airbus that the ad "makes it more unlikely we would put our confidence in you or your products."[6] Airbus soon stopped running the ads.

Until July 2002, that is, when Airbus did it again at the Air Show in Farnborough, England. This time, Airbus installed a huge billboard at the edge of the runway with a new slogan: "A340—4 ENGINES 4 LONG HAUL." Once again, it ran full-page ads in daily newspapers and air show magazines. And once again, Airbus was attacked by the industry and eventually pulled the ads.[7] For now, at least, the passenger aircraft industry, like the airline industry, seems to be in a cooperative equilibrium.

THE FOUR MARKET STRUCTURES: A POSTSCRIPT

You have now been introduced to the four different market structures: perfect competition, monopoly, monopolistic competition, and oligopoly. Each has different characteristics, and each leads to different predictions about pricing, profit, nonprice competition, and firms' responses to changes in their environments.

Table 2 summarizes some of the assumptions and predictions associated with each of the four market structures. While the table is a useful review of the *models* we have studied, it is not a how-to guide for analyzing real-world markets: We cannot simply look at the array of markets we see around us and say, "This one is perfectly competitive," "That one is an oligopoly," and so on. Why not? Because markets in the real world will typically have characteristics of more than one kind of market structure. A particular barbecue restaurant, for example, may be viewed as a monopolistic competitor in the market for *restaurants* in Memphis, or an oligopolist in the market for *barbecue* restaurants in Memphis, or a monopolist in the market for barbecue restaurants *within walking distance of Graceland.*

But, as we've seen several times in this text, our choice of model is not really arbitrary. Rather, it depends on the *questions we are trying to answer.* Suppose we're interested in explaining why a *particular* barbecue restaurant with no nearby competitors earns economic profit year after year, or why it spends so much of its profit on rent-seeking activity (lobbying the local zoning board). Then, we would most

---

[6] "Competitor's 'Scare Tactic' Vexes Boeing," *Herald Net,* November 6, 1999 (*www.heraldnet.com*); "Airlines Blast New Ads from Airbus . . ." *Wall Street Journal,* November 22, 1999.
[7] Kathleen Hanser, "An Airbus Advertising Campaign at the Farnborough Air Show Stoked the Fires in the Debate Between . . . Two Engines & Four Engines," *Boeing Frontiers* (Vol. 1, Issue 5), September 2002.

	Perfect Competition	Monopolistic Competition	Oligopoly	Monopoly
ASSUMPTIONS:				
Number of firms	Very many	Many	Few	One
Output of different firms	Standardized	Differentiated	Standardized or differentiated	—
View of pricing	Price taker	Price setter	Price setter	Price setter
Barriers to entry or exit?	No	No	Yes	Yes
Strategic interdependence?	No	No	Yes	No
PREDICTIONS:				
Price and output decisions	$MC = MR$	$MC = MR$	Through strategic interdependence	$MC = MR$
Short-run profit	Positive, zero, or negative	Positive, zero, or negative	Positive, zero, or negative	Positive, zero, or negative
Long-run profit	Zero	Zero	Positive or zero	Positive or zero
Advertising?	Never	Almost always	Maybe, if differentiated product	Sometimes

A Summary of Market Structures   **TABLE 2**

likely use the monopoly model. If we want to explain why *most* barbecue restaurants do *not* earn much economic profit, or why they pay for advertisements in the yellow pages and the local newspapers, or why there is so much excess capacity (empty tables) in the industry, we would use the model of monopolistic competition. To explain a price war among the few restaurants in a neighborhood, or to explore the possibility of explicit or tacit collusion in pricing or advertising, we would use the oligopoly model. And if we're interested in barbecue restaurants as an example of *restaurants in general*, and we want general explanations about restaurant prices, or the expansion or contraction of the restaurant industry in a city or country, we would use the perfectly competitive model (supply and demand curves for restaurant meals). We would ignore the distinctions between different restaurants and any barriers to entry that might exist.

We will come back to the four market structures again (in Chapters 14 and 15) when we consider the operation of the microeconomy as a whole, the notion of economic efficiency, and the proper role of government in the economy.

Summary

Monopolistic competition is a market structure in which there are many small buyers and sellers, easy entry and exit, and firms sell differentiated products. As in monopoly, each firm faces a downward-sloping demand curve, chooses the profit-maximizing quantity where $MR = MC$, and charges the maximum price it can for that quantity. As in perfect competition, short-run profit attracts new entrants. As firms enter the industry, the demand curves facing existing firms shift leftward. Eventually, each firm earns zero economic profit and produces at greater than minimum average cost.

An *oligopoly* is a market structure dominated by a small number of strategically interdependent firms. New entry is deterred by economies of scale, reputational barriers, strategic barriers, and legal barriers to entry. Because each firm, when making decisions, must anticipate its rivals' reactions, oligopoly

behavior is hard to predict. However, one approach, *game theory*, has offered rich insights.

In game theory, a *payoff matrix* indicates the payoff to each firm for each combination of strategies adopted by that firm and its rivals. A *dominant strategy* is a strategy that is best for a particular firm regardless of what its rival does. If there is no cooperation among firms, any firm that has a dominant strategy will play it, and that helps predict the outcome of the game.

Sometimes oligopolists can cooperate to increase profits. *Explicit collusion*, in which managers meet to set prices, is illegal in the United States and many other countries. As a result, other forms of *tacit collusion* have evolved. Still, cheating is a constant threat to collusion. Government antitrust enforcement, market globalization, and technological change are forces that can encourage or discourage the formation of oligopolies.

Problem Set   *Answers to even-numbered Questions and Problems can be found on the text Web site at www.thomsonedu.com/economics/hall.*

1. Draw the relevant curves to show a monopolistic competitor suffering a loss in the short run. What will this firm do in the long run if the situation does not improve? How would this action affect *other* firms in this market?

2. Draw the relevant curves to show a monopolistic competitor earning an economic profit in the short run. Graphically show what this firm can expect to happen to this economic profit in the long run.

3. The owner of an optometry practice, in a city with more than a hundred other such practices, has the following demand and cost schedules for eye exams:

Price per Eye Exam	Eye Exams per Week	Total Cost per Week	Total Revenue per Week	Marginal Revenue	Marginal Cost
$100	100	$10,500			
$ 80	140	$10,800			
$ 60	200	$11,300			
$ 40	310	$12,290			
$ 20	550	$14,762			

   a. Fill in the columns for total revenue, marginal revenue, and marginal cost. (Remember to put *MR* and *MC* *between* output levels.)
   b. Briefly explain why an optometry practice (like this one) might face a downward-sloping demand curve, even if it is one out of more than a hundred. (Hint: What might make this market monopolistically competitive rather than perfectly competitive?)
   c. Use the data you filled in for the marginal revenue and

   marginal cost columns to find the profit-maximizing price and the profit-maximizing number of eye exams per week for this practice.

4. Tino owns a taco stand in Houston, Texas, where there are dozens of other taco stands. He faces the following demand and cost schedules for his taco plates (two tacos and a side of refried beans):

Price per Taco Plate	Taco Plates per Week	Total Cost per Week	Total Revenue per Week	Marginal Revenue	Marginal Cost
$5	50	$ 30			
$4	80	$ 50			
$3	150	$ 176			
$2	800	$1,476			
$1	1,100	$2,136			

   a. Fill in the columns for total revenue, marginal revenue, and marginal cost and use the table to find the profit-maximizing price and the profit-maximizing number of taco plates per week for Tino's Taco Stand. (Remember to put *MR* and *MC* *between* output levels.)
   b. Redo the table to show what will happen in the short run if Tino spends $100 on an advertising campaign that increases the quantity demanded at each output level by 20 percent. What will happen to his profit-maximizing price and profit-maximizing number of taco plates per week? Do you expect this outcome to persist? Explain.

5. Suppose that the cost data in problem 3 are for the short run, and that the owner of the practice suddenly realizes that she forgot to include her only fixed cost: her license fee of $2,600 per year (which is $50 per week). Should the practice shut down in the short run? Why or why not?

6. Assume that the plastics business is monopolistically competitive.
    a. Draw a graph showing the long-run equilibrium situation for a typical firm in the industry. Clearly label the demand, *MR*, *MC*, and *ATC* curves.
    b. One of the major inputs into plastics is oil. Draw a new graph illustrating the short-run position of a plastics company after an increase in oil prices. Again, show all relevant curves.
    c. If oil prices remain at the new, higher level, what will happen to get firms in the plastics industry back to a long-run equilibrium?

7. Draw a diagram, including demand, marginal revenue, marginal cost, and any other curves necessary, to illustrate each of the following two situations for a monopolistic competitor:
    a. The firm is suffering a loss, and should shut down in the short run.
    b. The firm is suffering a loss, but should stay open in the short run.

8. In a small Nevada town, Ptomaine Flats, there are only two restaurants, the Road Kill Cafe and, for Italian fare, Sal Monella's. Each restaurant has to decide whether to clean up its act or to continue to ignore health code violations.

    Each restaurant currently makes $7,000 a year in profit. If they both tidy up a bit, they will attract more patrons but must bear the (substantial) cost of the cleanup; so they will both be left with a profit of $5,000. However, if one cleans up and the other doesn't, the influx of diners to the cleaner joint will more than cover the costs of the scrubbing; the more hygienic place ends up with $12,000, and the grubbier establishment incurs a loss of $3,000.
    a. Write out the payoff matrix for this game, clearly labeling strategies and payoffs to each player.
    b. What is each player's dominant strategy?
    c. What will be the outcome of the game? Explain your answer.
    d. Suppose the two restaurants believe they will face the same decision repeatedly. How might the outcome differ? Why?
    e. Assume that if one cleans up and one stays dirty, the cleaner restaurant makes only $6,000 in profit. All other payoffs are the same as before. What will the outcome of the game be now without cooperation? With cooperation?

9. Professor Clemens has two students enrolled in his riverboat pilot course, Huck and Tom. The final exam counts as 100 percent of the course grade. If one student passes the exam and one student fails, Professor Clemens announces that he will assign the passer an A and the failer an F. If both students pass, he will give them both Bs. If both students fail, he will give them both Cs. Assume that if each student studies, he passes the exam; if he doesn't study, he fails. Finally, assume that although studying is hard, either student would prefer to study and get an A or a B than not study and get a C or lower.
    a. Write out the payoff matrix for Tom and Huck, clearly labeling strategies and identifying payoffs for each player for each combination of strategies (the payoffs will be letter grades).
    b. What is each player's dominant strategy?
    c. What will be the outcome of the game? Explain your answer.
    d. Could Huck and Tom benefit by cooperating (i.e., coordinating their strategies in this game)? Why or why not?
    e. Now suppose that Professor Clemens decides to penalize Huck for talking in class. He tells Huck that if he passes the exam and Tom does not, Huck will get a C instead of an A. All other payoffs will remain the same. What will be the likely outcome if the test is only offered once? What will be the likely outcome if the test is offered 50 times?

10. Assume that Nike and Adidas are the only sellers of athletic footwear in the United States. They are deciding how much to charge for similar shoes. The two choices are "High" (H) and "Outrageously High" (OH). Nike's payoffs are in the lower left of each cell in the payoff matrix below:
    a. Do both companies have dominant strategies? If so, what are they?
    b. What will be the outcome of the game?
    c. If Nike becomes the acknowledged price leader in the industry, what will be its dominant strategy? What will be the outcome of the game? Why?

More Challenging

11. Suppose that the government has decided to tax all the firms in a monopolistically competitive industry. Specifically, suppose it levies a fixed tax on each firm; that is, the amount of the tax is the same regardless of how much output the firm produces. In the short run, how would that tax affect the price, output level, and profit of the typical firm in that industry? What would be the effect in the long run?

12. To the right, you will find the payoff matrix for a two-player game, where each player has three possible strategies: A, B, and C. The payoff for player 1 is listed in the lower left portion of each cell. Assume there is no cooperation among players.

    a. Does either player have a dominant strategy? If so, which player or players, and what is the dominant strategy?

    b. Can we predict the outcome of this game from the payoff matrix using the methods you've learned in the chapter? Why or why not?

    c. Suppose that strategy C is no longer available to either player. Does either player have a dominant strategy now? Can you now predict the outcome of the game? Explain.

The Labor Market

If you plan to look for a job when you graduate from college, you'll have a lot of company: More than a million other new graduates will be seeking work. They will be offering their college-enhanced labor services to employers that are expanding their workforce or replacing retiring workers. In this environment, are you likely to find the kind of job that puts your college degree to good use?

According to the Bureau of Labor Statistics (BLS), the answer is: *very* likely. In a typical year, almost all of those new graduates will find jobs that either *require* a college degree, or at which new hires are increasingly expected to have one.[1]

And the job will most likely pay more than one requiring only a high school education. In early 2006, for example, the median high school graduate earned $592 per week, while the median college graduate (with a bachelor's or higher degree) earned $1,019.[2] The college—high school earnings differential has been widening for more than two decades, and few economists expect it to narrow significantly, if at all, in the coming decade.

These observations raise some interesting questions. For example, why do such a large fraction of college graduates, year after year, obtain the type of job they are looking for, that is, jobs that typically require a college degree? After all, *your* decision to become, say, a marketing manager trainee, computer systems analyst, or high school teacher is based on your *own* agenda. But those who hire college graduates have their own, entirely different agendas—in most cases, to earn the highest possible profit for their firms. How do these different agendas result in a reasonably good match of job seekers and job offers? Moreover, why do college graduates earn so much more than high school graduates? And why is this earnings differential growing larger, even as more and more workers with college degrees pour into the labor market?

Once you understand how labor markets work—the subject of this chapter— you'll know how to answer these questions.

FACTOR MARKETS IN GENERAL

So far in this book, we have analyzed a variety of markets—for maple syrup, chicken, cable TV service, household extermination services, gasoline, perfume, airline travel,

---

[1] Jill N. Lacey and Olivia Crosby, "Job Outlook for College Graduates," *Occupational Outlook Quarterly,* U.S. Bureau of Labor Statistics, Winter 2004–2005.

[2] "Usual Weekly Earnings of Wage and Salary Workers: First Quarter, 2006," *News*, Bureau of Labor Statistics, April 20, 2006, Table 4. Data are for full-time wage and salary workers over 25. The median weekly figure for those with a bachelor's but no higher degree was $933.

Product markets Markets in which firms sell goods and services to households or other firms.

Factor markets Markets in which resources—labor, capital, land and natural resources, and entrepreneurship—are sold to firms.

and more. All of these markets had one thing in common: They were **product markets,** in which firms sell goods and services to households or other firms. Of course, products aren't made out of thin air, but rather from the economy's *resources*—labor, capital, land, and entrepreneurship. The use of these resources must be purchased from those who own them. Since resources are sometimes called *factors of production,* the markets in which they are traded are called **factor markets.** Labor markets, for example, are a type of factor market.

In this and the next two chapters, we switch our focus from product markets to factor markets. But you will find much that is familiar in our approach. First, just as there are different *market structures* in which products can be traded, the same is true of factor markets. The model of perfectly competitive product markets, for example, has its counterpart in factor markets. Second, we'll be using familiar tools: profit maximization, marginal decision making, equilibrium, and more.

But factor markets also differ from product markets in important ways. Figure 1 illustrates one important difference. It shows another version of the *circular flow model* from Chapter 3. In this version, we've left out the money flows in order to highlight the roles of product and factor markets in the economy. As you can see, in product markets, households typically demand the products, and firms supply them. In factor markets, these roles are reversed: Firms demand resources such as labor, land, or capital, and they are supplied by the households who own these resources.

FIGURE 1

Product Markets and Factor Markets

In product markets, households demand goods and services, and firms supply them. In factor markets, the roles are reversed: Firms demand resources—such as labor, capital, land, or entrepreneurship. Households supply them.

The figure also illustrates how behavior in product and factor markets are connected. When people demand more of a good, and firms respond by increasing quantity supplied, firms will also demand more resources. For example, if households want to buy more cars and Ford Motor Company produces more of them, the company will need to hire more labor, use more machinery, and so on. It will also need more inputs from other firms—glass, steel, tires—and these firms, in turn, will demand more resources. Thus, the demand for resources in the economy arises from the demand for goods and services.

> *The demand for a resource—such as labor—is a **derived demand**. That is, it arises from, and will vary with, the demand for the firm's output.*

Derived demand The demand for a resource that arises from, and varies with, the demand for the product it helps to produce.

The phrase "will vary with" is important: A firm's demand for a resource will change whenever the demand for its product changes. Over the past few decades, as the demand for jeans has grown, the demand for labor and other resources by The Gap, Levi Strauss & Co., and Old Navy has grown as well. By contrast, as the demand for cigarettes has decreased, the demand for labor, farmland, and other resources by cigarette makers and their suppliers has fallen.

LABOR MARKETS IN PARTICULAR

The basic approach we will take in studying the labor market may initially strike you as a bit heartless: We will treat labor as a commodity—something that is bought and sold in the marketplace—and regard the wage rate as the price of that commodity. The wage rate can be defined as an hourly rate (e.g., $20 per hour), a daily rate ($160 per day), or a rate for any other time unit.

As a first approximation, we explain how a worker's wage rate is determined in the same way we'd explain the price of a bushel of wheat. That is, we look at how groups of economic decision makers come together in markets in order to trade. We then look for the equilibrium price determined in those markets and—eventually—explore how various changes affect that equilibrium price. We do this for one simple reason: It works.

Of course, labor *is* different from other things that are traded. First, sellers of wheat do not care who buys their product, as long as they get the market price. Sellers of labor, on the other hand, care about many things besides their wage rate when they look for a job: working conditions, friendly coworkers, commuting distance, possibilities for advancement, prestige, a sense of fulfillment, and more.

There is also a special meaning to the price in a labor market: the wage rate. Most of the income people earn over their lifetimes will come from their jobs, and their hourly, weekly, or yearly wage will determine how well they can feed, clothe, house, and otherwise provide for themselves and their families. This adds a special moral dimension to events in the labor market.

In this chapter, we apply the basic model of supply and demand to explain how wage rates and employment are determined and what causes them to change. Toward the end of the chapter, we'll also discuss some of the special features of the labor market and continue to explore them in the next chapter.

DEFINING A LABOR MARKET

When you begin searching for a job after college, you will become a seller in a labor market. But which labor market? As you've seen several times in this book,

> *how broadly or narrowly we define a market depends on the specific questions we wish to answer.*

For example, suppose we are interested in explaining why college graduates, on average, earn more than those with just high school diplomas. We would want to define two very broad labor markets: one for all college graduates in the United States and another for all high-school-only graduates. In the college labor market, buyers would be all the firms that employ college-educated labor, and sellers would be all those with college degrees who are working or looking for work. We'd use similar definitions for buyers and sellers in the high school labor market. Then, we'd explore why the equilibrium wage in each of these broadly defined labor markets differs.

On the other hand, we might be interested in finding out how salaries in some profession (say, medicine) are determined. For this purpose, we would use a narrower definition: the market for physicians in the United States. The sellers would be all individuals with medical degrees, and the buyers would be all the hospitals, universities, and private practices that hire them. Or, if we want to know why physicians in Boston are paid more than physicians elsewhere in the country, we'd define our labor market even more narrowly. In this chapter, we will be asking many different questions about labor markets, and will need to look at both broadly and narrowly defined markets to answer them.

COMPETITIVE LABOR MARKETS

In most of this chapter, we'll be viewing both product and labor markets that are *perfectly competitive*. So let's begin by defining perfect competition in a labor market.

Perfectly competitive labor market A labor market with many indistinguishable sellers of labor and many buyers, and with easy entry and exit of workers.

> *A **perfectly competitive labor market** has the following three characteristics:*
>
> 1. *There are large numbers of buyers (firms) and sellers (households), and each individual firm or household is only a tiny part of the labor market.*
> 2. *All workers in the labor market appear the same to firms.*
> 3. *Workers can easily enter into or exit from the labor market.*

Do these conditions sound familiar? They should, since they are almost identical to the features of perfect competition in a product market (Chapter 8). The only difference is that here it is labor, rather than a good or service, that is being traded.

Very few labor markets *strictly* satisfy all three of these requirements. But many markets come close enough to make the perfectly competitive model a useful approximation. The more closely a particular labor market satisfies the conditions, the more accurate our analysis will be.

For example, consider the requirement that all workers are the same. We know that no two workers are ever precisely the same, just as no two computers made by different companies are identical. But when we want to explain price changes for computers in general, we ignore the difference between one brand and another, and assume we are dealing with a standardized product. Similarly, when we want to explain changes in the wage rate for large groups of workers, it will often make sense to ignore the differences among workers, and assume that employers view all workers in a labor market as essentially the same. (We'll discuss the other requirements of perfect competition in labor markets as we use them.)

In most of this chapter, we'll be using the perfectly competitive model. That is, we'll assume that firms sell their *products* in a perfectly competitive product market and demand their *labor* in a perfectly competitive labor market. We do this because the perfectly competitive model is such a useful model for answering the types of questions we'll be asking. But we'll also look at some important departures from perfect competition in the appendices (at the end of this chapter and the next one).[3]

DEMAND FOR LABOR BY A SINGLE FIRM

A competitive labor market has two sides: buyers and sellers. In this section, we begin our exploration of the buying side of the market—labor demand—by looking at how a firm decides how much labor to employ. But before we get into the mechanics, let's step back a bit and consider the demand for *any* type of resource.

RESOURCE DEMAND: A GENERAL RULE

In Chapter 7 you learned a general rule for the firm called the *marginal approach to profit:*

> *The marginal approach to profit states that a firm should take any action that adds more to its revenue than it adds to its cost.*

In the last several chapters, you've seen this rule applied to one kind of action: increasing production. Our rule in this case translated to: Increase output by another unit whenever doing so adds more to revenue (*MR*) than it adds to cost (*MC*).

When we view the firm as a buyer in a factor market, we use the same principle of marginal decision making. Only this time the action under consideration is "increase employment of the resource by another unit." So our rule translates to: *Increase employment of any resource whenever doing so adds more to revenue than it adds to cost.*

To avoid confusion between decisions about resources and decisions about output, we don't use the terms *marginal revenue* and *marginal cost* when discussing factor markets. But we do use very similar terms.

To track changes on the revenue side, we use the term *marginal revenue product.*

---

[3] More specifically, the appendix to this chapter deals with an important departure from perfect competition called *monopsony,* in which a single firm is a large and important employer in its labor market. Chapter 12 will explore what happens in labor markets when there are *barriers to entry, differences in ability,* and *discrimination.*

Marginal revenue product (*MRP*)
The change in the firm's total revenue divided by the change in its employment of a resource.

*A firm's **marginal revenue product** (MRP) for any resource is the change in the firm's total revenue (ΔTR) divided by the change in its employment of the resource (Δ Quantity of resource):*

$$MRP = \frac{\Delta TR}{\Delta \text{ Quantity of resource}}$$

The MRP tells us the change in total revenue for a one-unit increase in the resource.

Why does hiring a resource change revenue? When the firm employs more of any resource, it will produce and sell more output, and this will affect its total revenue. To track changes on the cost side, we use the term marginal factor cost:

Marginal factor cost (*MFC*)
The change in the firm's total cost divided by the change in its employment of a resource.

*A firm's **marginal factor cost** (MFC) for any resource is the change in the firm's total cost (ΔTC) divided by the change in its employment of the resource (Δ Quantity of resource):*

$$MFC = \frac{\Delta TC}{\Delta \text{ Quantity of resource}}$$

The MFC tells us the rise in total cost for a one-unit increase in the resource.

Once you are familiar with this special terminology, the marginal approach to profit gives the firm a complete guide to its behavior in a factor market:

To maximize profit, the firm should increase its employment of any resource whenever MRP > MFC, but not when MRP < MFC. Thus, the profit-maximizing quantity of any resource is the quantity at which MRP = MFC.

The logic of this rule is straightforward: If *MRP > MFC*, employing another unit of the resource adds more to revenue than to cost, so profit will rise. When *MRP < MFC*, using another unit of the resource adds more to cost than to revenue, so profit falls. When the firm exploits every opportunity to increase profit—that is, adding another unit of the resource whenever *MRP > MFC*—it will arrive at the point at which *MRP = MFC*.

To see this rule in action, let's now apply it to the firm's decision about how much labor to hire. Until we get to the appendix, we'll analyze labor demand under conditions of *perfect competition*. That is, we'll assume the firm sells its output in a perfectly competitive *product* market and hires its workers in a perfectly competitive *labor* market. Moreover, to start simply, we'll initially look at a firm for which labor is the *only* variable input.

THE FIRM'S EMPLOYMENT DECISION

In Table 1, we return to a firm we first met in Chapter 6: Spotless Car Wash. The first two columns in the table are reproduced from Table 3 of that chapter and introduce nothing new. Column 1 shows different numbers of workers that Spotless can hire, column 2 the quantity of output produced each day.

Data for Spotless Car Wash (Perfectly Competitive Product and Labor Markets)					**T A B L E 1**	
(1) **Quantity** **of Labor**	**(2)** **Total** **Product** **(Cars Washed** **per Day)**	**(3)** **Marginal Product** **of Labor (MPL)**	**(4)** **Price per** **Car Wash**	**(5)** **Total** **Revenue**	**(6)** **Marginal Revenue** **Product (MRP)**	**(7)** **Wage (W)**
0	0		$4	$ 0		$60
		30			$120	
1	30		$4	$120		$60
		60			$240	
2	90		$4	$360		$60
		40			$160	
3	130		$4	$520		$60
		30			$120	
4	160		$4	$640		$60
		24			$ 96	
5	**184**		**$4**	**$736**		**$60**
		12			$ 48	
6	196		$4	$784		$60
		4			$ 16	
7	200		$4	$800		$60

Column 3 shows the marginal product of labor (*MPL*)—the additional output produced when *one more* worker is hired. For example, when the firm hires the third worker, output rises from 90 to 130, so the *MPL* for this change in employment is 40.

The marginal product of labor was discussed in Chapter 6, where it helped us understand the shape of the marginal cost curve. Recall that at very low levels of employment, the *MPL* tends to rise as employment rises, but as more and more workers are added, the *MPL* will eventually decrease. In Table 1, notice that the marginal product of labor *increases* as employment rises from 0 to 1 to 2 workers. Therefore, from 0 to 2 workers, Spotless has *increasing marginal returns to labor*. Beyond 2 workers, however, additional employment causes the marginal product of labor to *decrease,* and Spotless has *diminishing marginal returns to labor*. (See Chapter 6 if you need a refresher on returns to labor.)

Column 4 shows the price Spotless can charge for each car wash. The price remains constant at $4, no matter how much output is produced, telling us that Spotless is a competitive firm in its product market. It can wash all the cars it wants without decreasing the price. The fifth column lists the firm's total revenue for each number of workers, found by multiplying the quantity of output (column 2) by the price (column 4).

The Competitive Firm's *MRP*

Now look at column 6, which shows the marginal revenue product (*MRP*) of labor. For any change in employment, the *MRP* is the change in total revenue in column 5 divided by the change in employment in column 1. For example, when the firm increases employment from 2 to 3 workers (an increase of 1 worker), its daily revenue rises from $360 to $520, an increase of $160. For this change in employment,

$$MRP \text{ of labor} = \frac{\Delta TR}{\Delta \text{ Quantity of labor}} = \$160/1 = \$160$$

But we can also calculate Spotless's *MRP* of labor in another way. Since it sells its output (car washes) in a perfectly competitive market, Spotless can increase production without affecting the market price of $4. When Spotless employs one more worker, its output rises by the marginal product of labor (*MPL*), and each additional unit of output sells for $4. Therefore, revenue will rise by $4 × *MPL*. So now we have another way to calculate the *MRP*: Multiply the market price in column 4 by the *MPL* in column 3. For example, when moving from 2 to 3 workers, Spotless washes 40 more cars (*MPL* = 40), for which it gets $4 each. So its revenue rises by $4 × *MPL* = $4 × 40 = $160. This is the same value for the *MRP* of labor that we obtained above.

In general,

> *when output is sold in a competitive product market, the* MRP *for any change in employment will equal the price of output (P) times the marginal product of labor* (MPL):
>
> $$MRP = P \times MPL$$

This explains why the *MRP* values in the table first rise and then fall. As you learned in Chapter 6 (and were recently reminded), we expect increasing marginal returns to labor (rising *MPL*) at low levels of employment, and diminishing marginal returns (falling *MPL*) at higher levels of employment. Since *P* remains constant, the behavior of *MRP* = *P* × *MPL* mirrors that of *MPL*, first rising and then falling.[4]

The Competitive Firm's *MFC*

We've just looked at Spotless's *MRP*, which tells us how hiring an additional worker changes the firm's *revenue*. But how will it change the firm's costs? That is, what is Spotless's *MFC*?

In a competitive labor market, there are so many buyers and sellers of labor, and each is such a tiny part of the market that no buyer or seller can influence the market price of labor: the wage rate. This means that a firm in a competitive labor market is a **wage taker**: It takes the market wage as a given. In column 7 of the table, we assume that this market wage rate is $60 per day. So for Spotless, no matter what its current level of employment, its marginal factor cost of labor is always $60 per day:

$$MFC \text{ of labor} = \frac{\Delta TC}{\Delta \text{ Quantity of labor}} = \$60/1 = \$60$$

Wage taker A firm or worker that takes the market wage rate as a given when making employment decisions.

---

[4] *MRP* = *P* × *MPL* holds only when output is sold in a perfectly competitive market, in which the firm faces a horizontal demand curve for its product. If the firm faces a *downward-sloping* demand curve for its product, as in monopoly or monopolistic competition, there is a different relationship between *MRP* and *MPL*. Hiring another worker still increases output by the *MPL*, but now the firm must drop its price in order to sell the additional output. In this case, hiring another worker increases the firm's revenue by the additional output produced (*MPL*) times the increase in revenue per unit increase in output (*MR*). Thus, with a downward-sloping demand curve for its product, *MRP* = *MPL* × *MR*.

More generally,

> *When labor is hired in a competitive labor market, the* MFC *for any change in employment is the market wage rate* (W).

The Profit-Maximizing Employment Level

How does a firm that operates in competitive product and labor markets find the profit-maximizing level of employment? We can apply the general principle involving *MRP* and *MFC* developed earlier, recognizing that *MFC* in this case is the same as the wage rate, W. This suggests the following simple rule:

> *Hire another worker when* MRP > W, *but not when* MRP < W.

Let's apply the guideline to Spotless Car Wash. When going from 0 to 1 worker, revenue rises by \$120 (*MRP* = \$120) and costs rise by \$60 (*MFC* = *W* = \$60). Since revenue rises more than costs (*MRP* > *W*), hiring this first worker will add to the firm's profit. The same is true when the second, third, fourth, and fifth workers are hired. (Verify this on your own.) But in moving from the fifth to the sixth worker, *MRP* = \$48, while *W* = \$60. Since *MRP* < *W*, the firm should *not* hire the sixth worker; it should stop at the fifth. We have found the firm's profit-maximizing level of employment: five workers.

We can understand Spotless's employment decision even better by graphing the marginal data from Table 1, as we've done in Figure 2. As usual, marginal values are plotted *between* employment levels, since they tell us what happens as employment changes from one level to another. The value of *MRP* first rises and then falls as employment changes, so the *MRP curve* in the figure first slopes upward and then downward. The wage rate (the cost per day of hiring the additional worker) is always the same, as shown by the horizontal line at \$60.

Don't Take *MPL* Personally Remember that marginal productivity (as well as the marginal revenue product derived from it) is a characteristic of production, not a characteristic of an individual worker. The *MPL* tells us how much a firm's output will increase when one more worker is hired. It is easy to confuse this with an individual's *personal* productivity, which is based on skill and effort. To see the difference, consider this example: Suppose you can type 90 words a minute with no mistakes; your personal productivity as a typist is very high. If a word processing firm hires you, by how much will its output of finished manuscripts increase? That depends. Suppose the firm has just five computers. If you were, say, the fifth worker hired, you would get your own computer, and production would increase considerably. But if you were the twentieth worker hired, you would have to share a computer with perhaps three other workers, and much of your time would be spent waiting for a machine; output would not rise much at all. Even though your own skills are the same in both cases, the output you would *add* to the firm if hired—the marginal productivity of labor at the firm—would be quite different.

As long as employment is less than five workers, the *MRP* curve lies above the wage line (*MRP* > *W*), so the firm should hire another worker. But suppose the firm has hired five workers and is considering hiring a sixth. For this move, the *MRP* curve lies *below* the wage line. Since *MRP* < *W*, increasing employment would *decrease* the firm's profit. The same is true for every increase in employment beyond five workers. Using Figure 2, we see that the optimal employment level is five workers, just as we found earlier using Table 1.

The profit-maximizing number of workers, five, is the employment level closest to where *MRP* = *W*—that is, where the *MRP* curve crosses the wage line. The reason for this is straightforward: For each change in employment that *increases* profit, the *MRP* curve will lie above the wage line. The first time that hiring a worker *decreases* profit, the *MRP* curve will cross the wage line and dip below it.

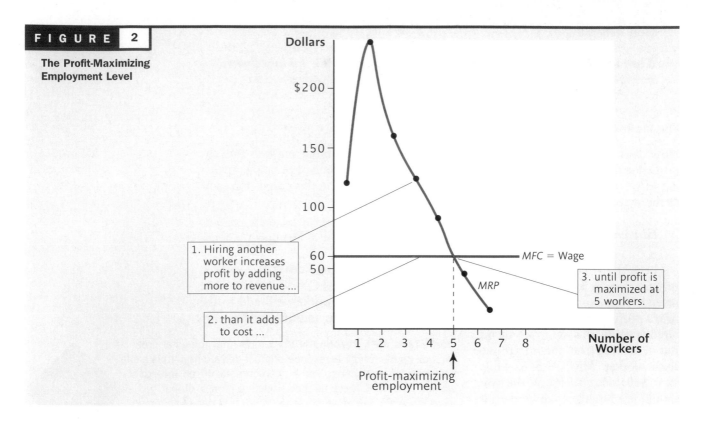

FIGURE 2

The Profit-Maximizing Employment Level

1. Hiring another worker increases profit by adding more to revenue ...

2. than it adds to cost ...

3. until profit is maximized at 5 workers.

MFC = Wage

MRP

Profit-maximizing employment

This observation allows us to state a simple rule for the firm's employment decision:

> To *maximize profit, the firm should hire the number of workers such that* MRP = W—*that is, where the* MRP *curve intersects the wage line.*[5]

TWO APPROACHES TO PROFIT MAXIMIZATION

Let's compare two different approaches that a firm can use to maximize its profit. In previous chapters, we used the *MR* and *MC* approach to find profit-maximizing *output*. In this chapter, we've used the *MRP* and *MFC* approach (or *MRP* and *W* approach, in a perfectly competitive labor market) to find profit-maximizing *employment*.

Can these two approaches lead to different decisions? In our example, the *MRP* and *MFC* approach tells Spotless to employ five workers, which (as you can see in Table 1) implies a total output of 184 car washes per day. Could the *MC* and *MR* approach guide Spotless to some *other* level of output, say, 196 car washes?

[5] There is one proviso, however: Profits are maximized only if the *MRP* curve crosses the wage line *from above*—that is, if we are on the *downward-sloping* portion of the *MRP* curve. To prove this to yourself, draw an example in which the upward-sloping portion of the *MRP* curve crosses the wage line from below. Notice that the *MRP* will always be greater than the wage to the right of the crossing point, so it will always pay for the firm to *increase* employment beyond the crossing point. From now on, the diagrams in this chapter will show only the downward-sloping part of the *MRP* curve, since this is the only part used by the firm to make its employment decision.

The answer is: No, because these two "different" approaches are actually the same method viewed in two different ways. To see this, remember that hiring another worker increases the firm's output and therefore changes both its revenue and its cost. For example, in Table 1, increasing employment from four to five workers raises output by 24 units (from 160 to 184 units), and also increases revenue by \$96 and cost by \$60. Since hiring the fifth worker increases revenue more than it raises cost (i.e., $MRP > W$), then it must be that increasing output by 24 units raises revenue by more than it raises cost (i.e., $MR > MC$ for that increase in output).

This applies more generally: Whenever $MRP > MFC$ for a change in employment, $MR > MC$ for the associated rise in output. Whenever $MRP < MFC$ for a change in employment, $MR < MC$ for the associated rise in output. And if $MRP = MFC$ for a change in employment, then it must be that $MR = MC$ for the associated change in output. (To help you see the connection between these two approaches even more clearly, add columns for MR and MC in Table 1 and find the profit-maximizing output level using the MR and MC approach. But when calculating MR and MC, don't forget to divide ΔTR and ΔTC by the change in *output*, which is *not* one unit in the table.)

THE FIRM'S LABOR DEMAND CURVE

In Table 1, the wage rate the firm had to pay was \$60 per day. But what if the wage had been different, say, \$45 per day? As you can verify on your own, at this lower wage rate, the firm would have hired six workers instead of five. The optimal level of employment will always depend on the wage rate.

Figure 3 shows what happens at the typical firm as the wage rate varies. For each wage rate, the optimal level of employment, where $MRP = W$, is found by traveling horizontally over to the MRP curve and then down to the horizontal axis. For example, with a wage rate of W_1, the firm will want to hire n_1 workers. If the wage drops to W_2, the optimal level of employment rises to n_2. As the wage rate drops, the firm moves along its MRP curve in deciding how many workers to hire.

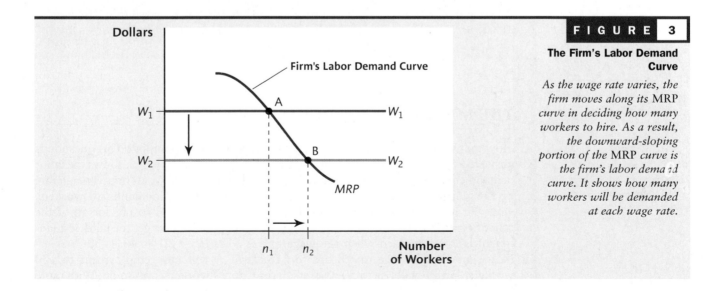

FIGURE 3

The Firm's Labor Demand Curve

As the wage rate varies, the firm moves along its MRP curve in deciding how many workers to hire. As a result, the downward-sloping portion of the MRP curve is the firm's labor demand curve. It shows how many workers will be demanded at each wage rate.

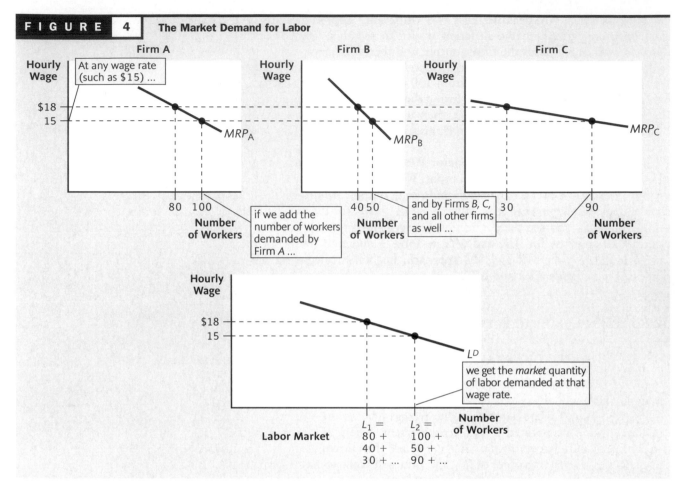

FIGURE 4 The Market Demand for Labor

This is why we call the downward-sloping portion of the *MRP* curve the *firm's labor demand curve:*

> *The downward-sloping portion of the* MRP *curve is the firm's labor demand curve, telling us how much labor the firm will want to employ at each wage rate.*

THE MARKET DEMAND FOR LABOR

How many workers will all firms in a labor market want to employ? This question is answered by the *market* labor demand curve. Look at Figure 4, which shows the labor demand curves for three of the many firms in a labor market. At an hourly wage rate of $18, Firm *A*'s labor demand curve, MRP_A, tells us that it demands 80 workers, while Firm *B* demands 40 workers, Firm *C* demands 30, and so on, for all of the other firms in this labor market. By adding up these numbers, we get the market quantity of labor demanded when the wage rate is $18: $L_1 = 80 + 40 + 30 + \cdots$. Now suppose the wage rate drops to $15. Firm *A* will raise employment to 100 workers, Firm *B* will rise to 50 workers, Firm *C* to 90 workers, and so on. With more

The Labor Demand Curve: A Movement Along versus a Shift | **FIGURE 5**

(a)

Hourly Wage

A change in the wage rate moves us *along* the labor demand curve.

$18
$15

A
B

L^D

1,000 1,500 | Number of Workers

(b)

Hourly Wage

A change in any *other* determinant of labor demand *shifts* the curve.

$18

L^D

400 1,000 1,600 | Number of Workers

workers demanded by each individual firm, the market quantity of labor demanded will rise to $L_2 = 100 + 50 + 90 + \cdots$

> The **market labor demand curve** tells us the total number of workers all firms in a labor market want to employ at each wage rate. It is found by horizontally summing across all firms' individual labor demand curves.

Market labor demand curve
Curve indicating the total number of workers all firms in a labor market want to employ at each wage rate.

Notice that the market labor demand curve slopes downward just like the labor demand curve of each firm. If a drop in the wage rate causes the quantity of labor demanded by each firm to rise, it will raise quantity demanded in the market as well.

SHIFTS IN THE MARKET LABOR DEMAND CURVE

A change in the wage rate causes a movement *along* a market labor demand curve, as in the move from point *A* to point *B* in Figure 5(a). But labor demand curves can also shift. Panel (b) of Figure 5 illustrates both a rightward and a leftward shift in the labor demand curve. This shift means that, *at any given wage rate,* more or less labor is demanded in this market than before. For example, after the rightward shift in the figure, the total quantity of labor demanded at a wage of $18 would rise from 1,000 to 1,600.

What causes a market labor demand curve to shift? In general,

> a change in any variable that affects the quantity of labor demanded—except for the wage rate—causes the labor demand curve to shift.

Let's consider some specific variables that can shift the labor demand curve.

A Change in the Price of the Product

When a competitive firm can sell at a higher price, it will produce more output, and therefore employ more labor. We can also see this by using the firm's demand for

Industrial robots are substitutable for less-skilled, assembly-line labor, but complementary with highly skilled labor that programs and repairs the robots.

Substitutable input An input whose use decreases the marginal product of another input.

Complementary input An input whose use increases the marginal product of another input.

labor based on *MRP*. Remember that the *MRP* at any level of employment is equal to the price of the firm's product times the marginal product of labor: $MRP = P \times MPL$. So a rise in *P*, with no other change affecting the firm, will raise *MRP* at each level of employment. Firms will want to hire *more* workers than before at any wage rate. (If you want to prove this to yourself, go back to Table 1 and change the price per car wash from $4 to $6, and change columns 4, 5, and 6 accordingly. You'll see that with an unchanged daily wage, Spotless Car Wash would want to increase employment from 5 to 6 workers.)

> *A rise in the price of a product, ceteris paribus, will increase the demand for labor used to produce that product. The labor demand curve shifts rightward.*

Of course, if we reverse the change, so the price of the product falls instead of rises, the labor demand curve will shift to the left.

A Change in the Price of Another Input

In Table 1 (Spotless Car Wash), and in our discussion so far, we've assumed that the firm has only one variable input: Labor. But in the long run, firms can vary *all* inputs. And even in the short run, more than one input may be variable. For example, a firm may employ several distinct types of labor, and we can regard each type as a separate variable input. Most firms use several types of raw materials, which can be varied in the short run as well.

When a firm can vary more than one input, a change in the price of some *other* input can affect its demand for labor. The nature of the effect depends on whether the other input is *complementary* or *substitutable* for the labor we are analyzing.

A **substitutable input** is one that *decreases* the marginal product of a particular type of labor. Usually, the input can be used *instead* of this type of labor.

For example, many factories use automated machinery to package goods with very little human involvement. The automated machinery is a *substitute* for less-skilled product packagers. Let's take a long-run view, regarding this machinery as a variable input, and imagine that its price drops. Then the least-cost input mix for producing any given level of output will change: Firms will want to use more of the now cheaper machines and fewer less-skilled packagers. As a result, the demand for less-skilled packagers will shift *leftward*.[6]

A **complementary input**, by contrast, is one that *increases* the marginal product of a particular type of labor. Usually, the input is used *by* this type of labor, making it *more* productive.

Those automatic packaging machines we just discussed, which are substitutable for less-skilled labor—are *complementary* with a different type of factory labor: the higher-skilled workers who program, maintain, and repair the machines. If packaging machines become cheaper, and more of them are used, the marginal productivity

---

[6] This effect on labor demand is an example of the *substitution effect* of a change in an input's price. But another effect works in the opposite direction: As packaging machines become cheaper, the firm's *marginal cost* curve shifts downward, thereby raising its profit-maximizing output level. When firms produce more, they tend to demand more of *all* inputs—perhaps even less-skilled packagers. This effect on labor demand is called the *output effect* of an input price change. In our discussions of substitutable input prices, we've focused only on the substitution effect.

of these higher-skilled workers rises. Firms will tend to employ more of them, shifting the demand curve for this type of labor to the right.

In general,

> *when the price of some other input decreases, the market labor demand curve may shift rightward or leftward. It will likely shift rightward if that other input is complementary with labor and leftward if the other input is substitutable for labor.*

Notice that the same input—automatic packaging machines—can be substitutable for one type of labor and complementary with another type of labor. So the impact on the labor demand curve will depend on which labor market we are analyzing.

A Change in Technology

Many changes in technology involve the discovery and use of an entirely new input to produce a good or service. For example, the development of the Internet in the mid- and late 1990s created a new input for producing many services (retail sales, information, banking, entertainment, and more). New medical diagnostic techniques, cell phones, and genetically modified seeds are other examples of entirely new inputs.

How does the introduction of a new input affect the market demand for labor? Not surprisingly, that depends on whether the new input is substitutable or complementary with the type of labor we are analyzing.

For example, the Internet is a *complementary* input for journalists, attorneys, doctors, scientific researchers, and many other professionals who frequently search for information as part of their jobs. Because the Internet speeds these searches, it has made this type of labor more productive. All else equal, we therefore expect the development of the Internet to *increase* the market demand for journalists, attorneys, doctors, scientific researchers, and other professionals.

Dangerous Curves: Robotophobia In the 1950s and 1960s, there was great concern about "automation"—the use of computers and industrial robots to perform tasks previously done by human beings. Many pundits argued that automation would cause a reduction in the demand for "workers" in general, and result in ever-rising unemployment until there were no jobs left. Even today, as computers become more sophisticated and do more tasks previously done by humans, it's easy to fall into the trap of imagining that one day there will be no jobs left.

This fear is based on a failure to distinguish between different types of labor. Remember that any given technological change (such as the Internet) will generally be substitutable for some types of labor but complementary with other types. Accordingly, while automation can lead to a lower equilibrium level of employment in some labor markets, it leads to *higher* equilibrium employment in other markets by making the labor there more productive.

To test yourself: If a robot were designed that could find defects in a pair of jeans as well as a human worker does now, which jobs would be threatened? Which jobs would expand? (Hint: Who designs the robots, creates and updates the software that runs them, markets them to manufacturers, and repairs them when they malfunction?)

But the Internet is *substitutable* for *other* types of labor. Let's discuss an example that, for undergraduates in college, might be a bit painful. Ten or fifteen years ago, one of your professors might very likely have hired you as an undergraduate research assistant to search for basic information at the library. This kind of research assistance was also common at newspapers, laboratories, and think tanks.

But now, using the Internet, a professor, journalist, or scientist can often retrieve the information herself in less time than it would take to explain to an untrained assistant what is being sought. The Internet, it turns out, is substitutable for the

TABLE 2	An Increase in	Will cause the market labor demand curve to
Shifts in the Labor Demand Curve	The price of the product	Shift rightward
	The price of a complementary input	Shift leftward
	The price of a substitutable input	Shift rightward
	The number of firms in the market	Shift rightward
	Technology*	Shift rightward if complementary with this labor, leftward if substitutable for this labor

*An "increase" in technology here means a technological advance.

labor of undergraduate research assistants: It decreases their marginal product of labor at any given level of employment, and therefore decreases the demand for their services at any given wage rate. (The Internet seems *not* to have had this effect on the demand for *graduate* student research assistants. Can you think of a reason why?)

> *All else equal, a technological change shifts the labor demand curve* right- ward *when it is* complementary *with the labor in that market, and* leftward *when it is* substitutable *for the labor in that market.*

A Change in the Number of Firms

Within the United States, firms are continually entering and leaving local labor mar- kets. The entry of new firms will shift the market labor demand curve rightward; exit will shift the curve to the left.

Sometimes, entry is due to the birth of an entirely new industry, as when new Internet firms like Amazon.com, eBay, and Google were created in the 1990s. These new firms caused the demand for many types of labor to shift rightward in several urban areas, especially the area around San Francisco. Other times, entry and exit occur when firms migrate from one local labor market to another. In the mid-1990s, firms in the computer chip industry began relocating to Oregon, shift- ing the demand for labor rightward in that state and leftward in the areas they abandoned.

Table 2 summarizes what you have learned about shifts in the market labor demand curve. Be careful as you look at the table; it shows only increases in each variable. A decrease in each variable would shift the labor demand curve in the opposite direction.

LABOR SUPPLY

So far, we've considered the demand side of the labor market and the behavior of firms that demand labor. Now we turn our attention to the *supply* side of the labor market and to the *households* that supply labor to firms. We begin with the indi- vidual's labor supply decision and then move on to discuss labor supply in the mar- ket as a whole.

INDIVIDUAL LABOR SUPPLY

Think of the last time you looked for a job—perhaps a summer job, or a part-time job while going to school. There may have been hundreds—perhaps even thousands—of others looking for similar jobs in your geographic area. Your own decision to sell your labor was a very small drop in a very large bucket: Your decision had no effect on the market wage.

This characteristic—so many sellers that no single one can affect the market wage—is one of our conditions for perfect competition, and it is satisfied in most labor markets.

> *In a competitive labor market, each seller is a wage taker; he or she takes the market wage rate as given.*

This is an important constraint on your job decision. You cannot choose your wage rate; it is determined by conditions in the market.

The Labor Supply Choice

The wage rate you can earn plays an important role in a tradeoff that we all face: The more time we spend enjoying leisure activities—talking with friends, going to the movies, reading, exercising, and so on—the less time we spend working and earning income. The wage rate determines the exact nature of this tradeoff. For example, if you can earn $20 per hour by working, then each additional hour of leisure time will cost you $20 in foregone income. In a sense, $20 is the *price* of an additional hour of leisure, since that is what you must give up, in money terms, to enjoy it.

Since different people are paid different wage rates, they will face different income–leisure tradeoffs. An hour of leisure is "more expensive" to someone who earns $100 per hour than to someone with a wage of $20 per hour.

But in addition to differences in wage rates, there is another way that the income–leisure tradeoff can differ among people: Some workers have considerable freedom to vary their weekly hours of work, and some do not.

For example, many self-employed professionals—doctors, lawyers, writers, and others—can adjust their work hours as they please, by increasing or decreasing the number of clients they serve. In addition, hourly workers can sometimes vary their hours of work by choosing to switch between part-time and full-time work or by accepting or refusing overtime. In these cases where hours can be varied, economists think about labor supply using a model of individual choice very similar to the one you learned for consumer theory in Chapter 5. However, instead of choosing the optimal combination of different *goods*, the individual chooses the optimal combination of *income* and *leisure*.

But in most labor markets, you will have relatively little freedom to vary your work hours because your employer will expect you to work a fixed number of hours—typically, eight hours a day, five days a week. In this case, your choice is not *how much* to work but rather *whether to offer your labor in a particular market*. Your choice of work hours in any labor market is constrained to 40 hours per week or zero hours per week. In this chapter, we'll focus on *fixed-hours* labor markets like this, since they are so common in the real world.

Reservation Wages

Reservation wage The lowest wage rate at which an individual would supply labor to a particular labor market.

One of the authors of this text, in his youth, spent six months working as an egg cleaner—cleaning the chicken droppings off fertilized eggs for eight hours a day, five days a week. It is not the most pleasant job, and chances are you are not currently planning to enter this line of work. But might you think again and decide that egg cleaning isn't all that bad if the job paid $50 per hour? $100 per hour? What about $200 per hour? Surely there is *some* wage rate that would induce you to take a job as an egg cleaner. Economists call the *lowest wage rate* that would convince you to offer your labor services in a market your **reservation wage** for that labor market. Until you reach this wage rate, you are reserving your time for other uses that give you more satisfaction—either not working at all or working in some other labor market. Whenever the wage rate in a market exceeds your reservation wage for that market, you will decide to work there. When the market wage rate is less than your reservation wage for that market, you will prefer not to work there.[7]

MARKET LABOR SUPPLY

When we speak of the quantity of labor supplied in a (fixed-hours) labor market, we mean the number of qualified people who want jobs there. As we've seen, an individual will want to work in a market whenever the wage rate there is greater than his or her reservation wage. But because workers have different preferences for different types of jobs, and different preferences for working at all, they will have different reservation wages for any particular labor market. For example, if you hate snakes, your reservation wage for a job as assistant snake trainer at a circus would be very high, perhaps $200 per hour or more. If you love snakes, you might jump at the chance to work with them even at a wage of only $10 per hour.

As the wage rate in a market rises, it will exceed more individuals' reservation wages, so more people will offer their labor in that market. Therefore, *ceteris paribus*,

> the higher the wage rate in a labor market, the greater the quantity of labor supplied in that market.

Labor supply curve A curve indicating the number of people who want jobs in a labor market at each wage rate.

Panel (a) of Figure 6 illustrates a **labor supply curve** in a hypothetical labor market, telling us the number of people who will want jobs there at each wage rate. In this market, the quantity of labor supplied at an hourly wage of $15 is 1,000 workers, so we know that 1,000 people have reservation wages of $15 per hour or less. At a wage of $18, the quantity of labor supplied is 1,200, so we know that another 200 people have reservation wages between $15 and $18 per hour.

---

[7] What happens if the market wage exceeds your reservation wage in more than one market at the same time? As long as preferences are *rational* (see Chapter 5), this cannot happen, for it would mean that you cannot decide which labor market is more attractive; you'd want to enter two labor markets simultaneously. For example, if you say your reservation wage for cleaning eggs is $25 per hour, and the market wage of egg cleaners is $26, then you will become an egg cleaner, giving up all other work opportunities. In other words, at a wage of $26, egg cleaning becomes your most preferred job. In that case, your reservation wage at all other jobs *must* be higher than the market wage in those jobs, or else you wouldn't have been willing to pass them up.

SHIFTS IN THE MARKET LABOR SUPPLY CURVE

A change in the wage rate causes a movement *along* a labor supply curve, as in the move from point C to point D in Figure 6(a). But labor supply curves can (and often do) *shift*. Panel (b) of Figure 6 illustrates both a rightward and a leftward shift in the labor supply curve. After the shift, *at any given wage rate,* either a greater or a smaller number of people want to work in this market than before. For example, after the rightward shift shown in the figure, the total quantity of labor supplied at a wage of $15 would rise from 1,000 to 1,800. After the leftward shift shown, the quantity of labor supplied at that wage falls to 400.

What makes a labor supply curve shift? At the most general level,

> *a market labor supply curve will shift when something other than a change in the wage rate causes a change in the number of people who want to work in a particular market.*

But let's be more specific. What, exactly, will cause a labor supply curve to shift?

A Change in the Market Wage Rate in Other Labor Markets

Imagine that you're a senior in college, with a double major in English and Economics. You're planning on looking for a job as a business journalist because it combines both of your interests: writing and economics. Based on your market research, you could expect a first-year salary of $40,000 for the types of jobs for which you're applying.

But one day, as you are sending out résumés, a friend calls you. "Guess what," he says. "I just heard that investment banks are looking for people who know some economics and can write clearly. They're paying $60,000 for entry-level positions." Upon hearing this news, you switch tactics and start applying for jobs in the investment banking industry.

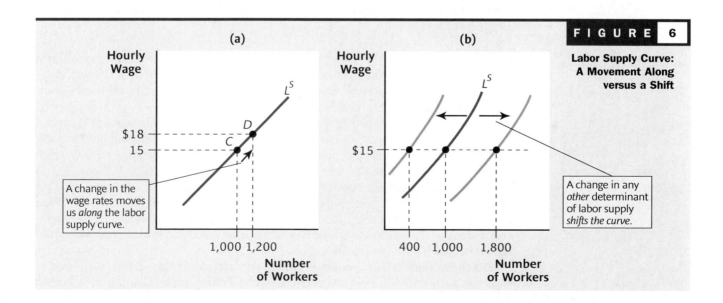

FIGURE 6

Labor Supply Curve: A Movement Along versus a Shift

Would your behavior in this story be plausible? Absolutely. Many people will pull out of one labor market and enter another because of a widening wage differential between them. In our example, your behavior—and the behavior of hundreds of others like you—would cause the labor supply curve in the market for business journalists to shift leftward.

The moral of the story is that labor supply behavior in *one* labor market may depend importantly on conditions in *other* labor markets. More specifically,

> *as long as some individuals can choose to supply their labor in two different markets, a rise in the wage rate in one market will cause a leftward shift in the labor supply curve in the other market.*

Changes in the Number of Qualified People

All else equal, a rise in the number of people qualified to work in a labor market will shift the labor supply curve rightward. By "qualified," we mean having the required skills or training, or living in the required area (for a geographically defined labor market).

What causes the number of qualified people to change?

Population Growth. The U.S. population grows by about 2.5 million people every year, because births exceed deaths by about 1.6 million, and because immigration exceeds emigration by about 900,000. This population growth continually increases the total labor supply in the country (in the broadly defined market for *labor in general*). It also tends to increase labor supply in most narrowly defined labor markets, by increasing the number of people qualified to enter those labor markets.

Changes in population growth, or growth in a subgroup of the population, can change the rate at which labor supply curves shift rightward. In recent years, immigration (because of a surge of undocumented workers from Mexico) has been predominantly low-skilled labor. As a result, labor supply curves have shifted rightward especially rapidly in the markets for domestic help, farm work, and restaurant and hotel work—the types of labor for which formal education or training are not usually required.

Human Capital Costs. For some jobs, the human capital requirements are significant and obvious. Highly paid professions come to mind, such as doctors, lawyers, engineers, architects, or business managers. But in most jobs you can think of—computer repair, plumbing, carpentry, language tutoring, and so on—a worker is expected to have specific skills before entering the labor market. Acquiring these skills can be costly—in time, money, or both. A change in the cost of acquiring human capital can affect the number of people who will decide to invest in training at any given wage rate, and therefore shift the labor supply curve.

For example, suppose business schools across the country raised their tuition for MBA degrees by 20 percent, and there were no other changes in the economy. What would happen in the market for business managers? Initially, nothing. The suppliers of labor in this market are those who already have MBA degrees, and they would be unaffected by the tuition hike.

But now think about people deciding on careers. At any given wage rate, a career in business will look less attractive than before, now that tuition is higher.

	Men	Married Men (Spouse Present)	Women	Married Women (Spouse Present)	TABLE 3
1960	83.3	89.2	37.7	31.9	Labor Force Participation Rates (Percent of Those Over 16 Working or Looking for Work)
1970	79.7	86.1	43.3	40.5	
1980	77.4	80.9	51.5	49.8	
1990	76.4	78.6	57.5	58.4	
2000	74.8	77.3	59.9	61.1	
2004	73.3	77.1	59.2	60.5	

Source: U.S. Census Bureau, *Statistical Abstract of the United States, 1999* (Tables 657 and 658), *2000* (Tables 645 and 651), and *2006* (Tables 578 and 584).

And at any given wage rate for MBA holders, fewer people would enroll in MBA programs. Within a few years—the time it takes to get through the program—the labor supply curve in the market for managers with MBA degrees would shift left-ward, as retiring managers would not be fully replaced with new entrants.

More generally,

an increase in the cost of acquiring human capital needed to enter a labor market will eventually shift the labor supply curve leftward; a decrease in the cost of acquiring human capital will eventually shift the labor supply curve rightward.

Changes in Tastes

In any population, there is a spectrum of tastes for different types of jobs. Some part of the population will like working with numbers and hate working with people; another part will prefer just the reverse. Some like danger and excitement, whereas others like safety and routine. A change in these tastes can change people's reservation wages in a labor market and therefore change the number of people who want to work in a labor market at any given wage rate. That is, a change in tastes can shift the market labor supply curve.

Tastes can also change for working in general. An example is illustrated in Table 3, which shows the change in women's labor force participation from 1960 to 2004. In 1960, only 38 percent of women over 16 were in the labor force (working or looking for work), compared to 83 percent of men. By 2004, women's labor force participation rate had increased to almost 60 percent. The change was even more dramatic for married women. In 1960, only 32 percent were in the labor force; by 2004, the proportion had almost doubled.

An important reason for this increase in labor supply appears to be a change in tastes. Many women changed their views of themselves and their economic role in society during this period and decided that they would prefer to work.

Changes in tastes occur in more narrowly defined markets as well. In the midst of the social turmoil of the late 1960s and early 1970s, many college graduates wanted jobs that made a direct, visible contribution to community well-being. Certain careers—teachers, social workers, community organizers—were especially

TABLE 4	An increase in	Will cause the market labor supply curve to
Shifts in the Labor Supply Curve	The wage rate in an alternative market	Shift leftward
	Numbers of qualified people	Shift rightward
	Tastes for work in a market	Shift rightward

popular. As a result, the labor supply curves in these markets shifted rightward. At the same time, traditionally higher paying careers in corporate finance, marketing, and sales became relatively less popular, shifting labor supply curves in these markets leftward.[8] Starting in the early 1980s, and continuing today, tastes have changed back: High-income jobs in business, law, and high-tech fields have become increasingly popular, reversing the labor supply shifts of the 1960s.

Table 4 summarizes the causes of shifts in the market labor supply curve. Compare it with Table 2 to make sure you know the difference between changes that shift the labor demand curve and those that shift the labor supply curve.

SHORT-RUN VERSUS LONG-RUN LABOR SUPPLY

The quantity of labor supplied to a market depends crucially on the period we are considering. In general, when we adopt a longer time horizon, the quantity of labor supplied will be more sensitive to changes in the wage rate; labor supply will be more *elastic*. Why is this? We know that higher wage rates will increase the quantity of labor supplied to a market. But it often *takes time* for people to acquire the skills needed to qualify in a labor market or to move from one labor market to another.

In some markets, the time needed to acquire skills can be considerable. To qualify as a lawyer requires three full years of postcollege training; a college professor generally needs four years or more; and a physician requires at least seven years, and more in many specialties. Other jobs, such as secretary or construction worker, may have shorter training requirements, but it may still take considerable time before the full response to a wage change occurs.

For example, suppose the wage rate of secretaries increases. Before the full labor supply response occurs, people deciding on careers must *learn* about the change, *decide* to become secretaries, acquire the needed word processing and other skills, prepare their résumés, find out which jobs are available, and, finally, begin looking. It is only at the last stage, where an individual begins *looking* for a job, that he or she becomes part of the total labor supply in a market. The full labor supply response to a wage rate change can take many months or even years, depending on the adjustments required.

When analyzing a *local* labor market, there is another reason to expect a delayed labor supply response: It often takes considerable time to move from one local labor market to another.

---

[8] Since the number of workers with college degrees rises every year, the labor supply curve in most professional markets shifts rightward each year. The change in tastes discussed here actually caused labor supply curves in high-income jobs to shift rightward *more slowly* than they otherwise would have.

To take account of these delays, it is convenient to define two periods for labor supply behavior. We define the *short run* as a period too short for people to move to a new locality or to acquire new skills. Thus, in the short run, the labor supply response to a change in the wage rate comes from those who *already have the skills and geographic location* needed to work in a market.

The *long run,* by contrast, is enough time to acquire new skills or to change location. In the long run, the labor supply response to a change in the wage rate includes those who will move into or out of the area and those who will acquire the skills needed to qualify in the labor market.

Figure 7 illustrates this distinction on a graph. When the wage rate is $15, 1,000 workers supply labor in the market shown. Now suppose the wage rises to $20. In the short run, the quantity of labor supplied will increase from 1,000 to 2,000 because more of those who *already* have the skills and who *already* live in the area will decide to work in this market at the higher wage rate. Thus, in the short run, we will move along the labor supply curve L_1^S, from point A to point B.

But as we proceed into the long run, the higher wage rate will attract new entrants into the labor market. These are people who were not able to work in this labor market before, but who have now acquired the needed skills or moved to the relevant geographic area. Remember that the number of qualified people in a labor market is a *shift variable* for the labor supply curve—something we hold constant in drawing the (short-run) labor supply curve L_1^S. But now—as new entrants raise the number of qualified people—the labor supply curve shifts rightward, and continues to shift rightward until the entry of new workers stops. In Figure 7, this occurs when the labor supply curve reaches L_2^S, at which point all those who want to enter this labor market at the wage of $20 have done so. In the long run, if the wage rate were to remain at $20, the quantity of labor supplied would rise all the way to 3,000.

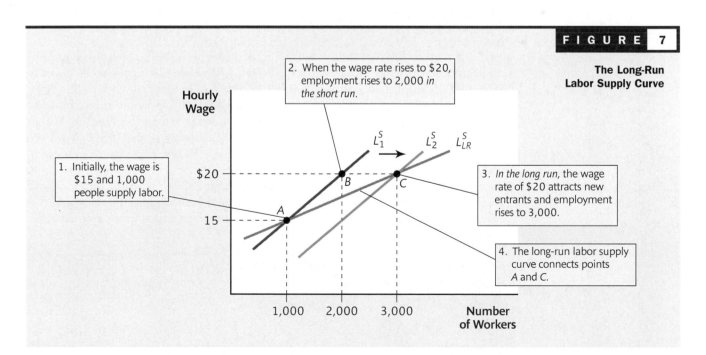

FIGURE 7

The Long-Run Labor Supply Curve

Hourly Wage

2. When the wage rate rises to $20, employment rises to 2,000 *in the short run*.

1. Initially, the wage is $15 and 1,000 people supply labor.

3. *In the long run*, the wage rate of $20 attracts new entrants and employment rises to 3,000.

4. The long-run labor supply curve connects points A and C.

L_1^S L_2^S L_{LR}^S

$20

15

A   B   C

1,000   2,000   3,000

Number of Workers

If we ask, "What is the *long-run* labor supply response if the wage rate rises from $15 to $20?" Our answer is "The amount of labor supplied increases from 1,000 to 3,000." In other words, in the long run, we move from point *A* to point *C* in the figure. If we connect these two points with a line, we have the *long-run labor supply curve* labeled L_{LR}^S:

Long-run labor supply curve
Curve indicating how many people will want to work in a labor market after full adjustment to a change in the wage rate.

> The **long-run labor supply curve** tells us how many people will want to work in a labor market at each wage rate, after all adjustments have taken place. That is, after all those who want to acquire new skills or who want to move to another location have done so.

Notice that the long-run labor supply curve (L_{LR}^S) is more *wage elastic* than the short-run labor supply curve (L_1^S). That is, when the wage rate increases by a given percentage, labor supply rises by a greater percentage in the long run than in the short run. This will always be the case. When the wage rate increases, the long-run labor supply response includes all those who will enter the labor market in the short run, *plus* the *additional* people who will enter the market in the long run. Thus,

> the long-run labor supply response is more wage elastic than the short-run labor supply response.

LABOR MARKET EQUILIBRIUM

Figure 8 illustrates the market for paralegals in the United States. (Paralegals are professionals with legal training, but no law degree, who assist lawyers.) The equilibrium in this market occurs where the supply and demand curves intersect at point *A*. The equilibrium wage is $20 per hour, and equilibrium employment is 250,000 paralegals.

How can we have confidence that the market will, indeed, reach this equilibrium? Suppose the wage rate is below $20—say, $12. Then law firms would want to hire 300,000 paralegals, but only 200,000 people would want to work in this labor market. Competing with each other to hire paralegals, firms would drive the wage rate up. Therefore, $12 cannot be the equilibrium wage rate in this market: At that value, it would automatically begin rising. Once the hourly wage hit $20, however, there would be no incentive for any firm to offer a higher wage, since every firm could hire all the paralegals it wanted at $20.

Similarly, if the hourly wage were *greater* than $20 (say, $28), more people would want to work as paralegals than firms would want to hire. Firms would discover that they can pay less and still hire all the paralegals they want, so the hourly wage would begin to drop—down to $20.

> The forces of supply and demand drive a competitive labor market to its equilibrium point—the point where the labor supply and labor demand curves intersect.

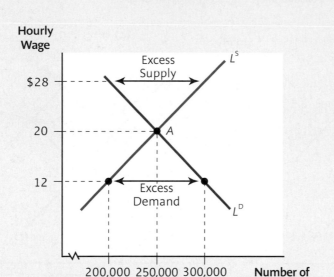

FIGURE 8

Equilibrium in a Labor Market

In the competitive labor market for paralegals, the equilibrium wage is $20 per hour, and equilibrium employment is 250,000 paralegals. If the hourly wage were lower, at $12, firms would want to hire 300,000 paralegals, but the number of qualified people who would want to work in this field would be only 200,000. The excess demand of 100,000 would drive the wage up. If the hourly wage were higher than equilibrium, e.g. $28, more people would want to work as paralegals than firms would want to employ. The excess supply would drive the wage down.

WHAT HAPPENS WHEN THINGS CHANGE?

Labor markets, like product markets, are in continual flux. A variety of events can cause the labor demand curve or the labor supply curve to shift. In this section, we explore how these shifts affect the equilibrium in a labor market.

A CHANGE IN LABOR DEMAND

In Figure 9(a), the labor market for paralegals is initially in equilibrium at point A, where the demand curve L_1^D intersects the short-run labor supply curve L_1^S. The equilibrium hourly wage is $20, and equilibrium employment is 250,000. We'll assume that this is a *long-run* equilibrium: Everyone who would like to supply labor in this market at the going wage has had enough time to acquire the qualifications and enter it.

Now suppose that there is an increase in demand for paralegals. (For a list of reasons this might occur, look back at Table 2.) What will happen in this labor market?

The Short-Run Impact

Figure 9(a) shows what happens in the short run—a period of time too short for people to acquire the qualifications to enter this labor market. The increase in labor demand creates an excess demand for paralegals at the old wage rate of $20. As the

FIGURE 9   **An Increase in Labor Demand: Short-Run and Long-Run Effects**

In panel (a), the market for paralegals begins in long-run equilibrium at point A. An increase in demand for paralegals shifts the labor demand curve rightward (to L_2^D) and drives the equilibrium hourly wage to $28 in the short run (point B). Employment rises from 250,000 to 300,000.

In the long run [panel (b)], the higher wage attracts additional workers to become qualified as paralegals, shifting the labor supply curve rightward (to L_2^S). The final long-run equilibrium is at point C. The wage, $23, is higher than initially, but lower than the short-run equilibrium wage at point B. Employment rises further in the long run, to 330,000.

The long-run labor supply curve through points A and C shows how many people would want to work as paralegals at any wage rate, after all long-run adjustments have taken place.

excess demand drives up the wage rate, the market moves along the labor supply curve L_1^S: The number of *already qualified* people who decide to work as paralegals (rather than do other things) will rise. The new, short-run equilibrium occurs at point *B*, with a market wage rate of $28 and employment of 300,000.

But this is not the end of our story.

The Long-Run Impact

With the new, higher wage rate of $28 (point *B*), being a paralegal has become more attractive than it was before. Over the long run, more people will acquire the qualifications to do this job, so the total number qualified will rise. In panel (b) of Figure 9, the entry of new qualified people shifts the labor supply curve rightward, causing us to move along labor demand curve L_2^D. Employment expands further, and the market wage rate gradually comes down.

When will this process cease? Only when entry into this labor market is no longer attractive. In the figure, this occurs at point *C*, when the labor supply curve reaches L_2^S, the wage settles at $23, and market employment rises to 330,000. Notice that entry stops *before* the wage rate falls back to its original value of $20. Why?

Largely because people have different tastes. In any labor market, those who want to be there the most—who have the lowest reservation wages—will be there already, in the initial equilibrium. In our example, when we were in our initial long-run equilibrium at point *A*, everyone who *wanted* to be a paralegal at a wage of $20 was already working as one. Everyone else had other, preferable options, given their tastes and the other opportunities available, and the $20 wage offered to paralegals. So in the long run, if we are to end up with a *greater* number of people working as paralegals than we started with, we must have a greater wage rate ($23 in this case) to attract and retain these additional workers.

As you can see, the consequences for wage rates are quite different in the short run than in the long run.[9] In the short run, there is a relatively large rise in the wage—from $20 to $28. Indeed, the wage rate actually *overshoots* its long-run equilibrium value. Over time, as more people are attracted into the market and the labor supply curve shifts rightward, the wage rate falls to its long-run equilibrium value.

> *Wage rates, like the prices of goods and services, act as market signals—leading workers to move to areas where their work is most valued. When the labor demand curve shifts, the wage rate will overshoot its long-run equilibrium value. But as the signal begins to work, the temporary overshooting of the wage rate subsides.*

A CHANGE IN LABOR SUPPLY

You've just seen that the labor supply curve will shift as part of the long-run adjustment process, after a shift change in labor demand. But a shift in the labor supply curve can also be the initial event that sets off changes in a labor market.

For the most part, changes in labor supply happen slowly. A look back at Table 4 shows why. While tastes for different jobs can and do change, the changes are usually very gradual. The cost of acquiring human capital can change more rapidly, but this will not shift a labor supply curve until some time later. For example, a drop in the price of going to medical school would shift the labor supply curve for doctors rightward *seven or more years later*—when those who enter medical school finally get their degrees and finish their internships and begin to enter the job market. Similarly, when the wage rate in some alternative labor market changes, such as the rate in another city, it takes time for people to move from one location to another and enter a new labor market.

Nevertheless, these shifts—as gradual as they may be—are important in understanding labor market changes, especially over the long run. Figure 10 illustrates an example. Once again we begin at point *A*, with 250,000 paralegals and an hourly wage of $20. We can imagine that, at point *A*, the number of new paralegals graduating from training schools is just enough to replace those who are retiring, so the market is in a long-run equilibrium.

Now suppose that several new, low-cost schools open up to train paralegals, and competition among schools causes a drop in tuition. What would happen in the market for paralegals?

---

[9] In our discussion of the long run, we've focused on adjustments on the supply side of the labor market. But there may also be long-run changes on the demand side. For example, after a rise in the wage rate, firms may want to substitute other inputs (such as capital) for the now-more-expensive labor. Incorporating these further adjustments in labor demand would not change any of our conclusions.

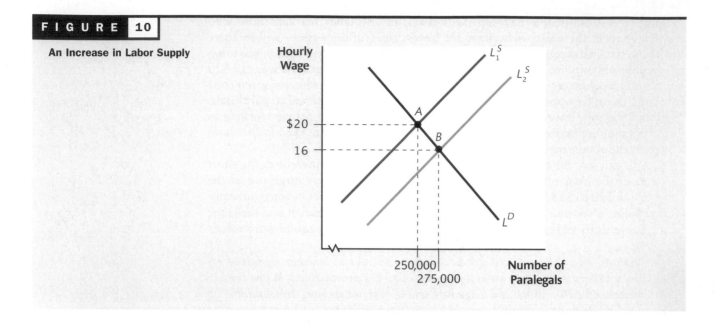

FIGURE 10

An Increase in Labor Supply

In the short-run, nothing. (Remember that the short run is, by definition, too short for people to acquire new qualifications.) Even if there were an immediate increase in enrollments in paralegal programs, there would be no impact on the labor market until the new enrollees graduate. It typically takes a year or longer to complete a certificate program in paralegal studies. So a reduction in tuition would take at least that long to affect labor supply.

After a year or longer, however, labor supply would increase, as the number of newly qualified people coming into the market would now exceed the number retiring. The new, long-run equilibrium occurs at point B, with employment rising to 275,000, and the wage rate falling to $16.

> *Changes in labor supply, on their own, cause changes in wage rates. All else equal, an increase in labor supply will cause the equilibrium wage to fall; a decrease in labor supply will cause the equilibrium wage to rise.*

A Change in Both Labor Supply and Labor Demand

What happens when both labor supply and labor demand change together? Let's look at an example: the market for business professors during the 1990s and early 2000s.

The typical qualification for regular business faculty is a PhD in business. But during the 1990s, salaries *outside* academia for those with business degrees (both PhDs and MBAs) rose dramatically. This affected the supply of business professors in two ways. First, among those who already had PhDs, the wage in an *alternative* labor market (firms outside of academia) rose. Second, the high salaries for new MBAs lured more of them directly into the job market, leaving fewer to continue in school to get PhDs. As PhDs retired, the total number of qualified people (PhDs in business) declined. Both of these factors—the increase in the wage in an alternative

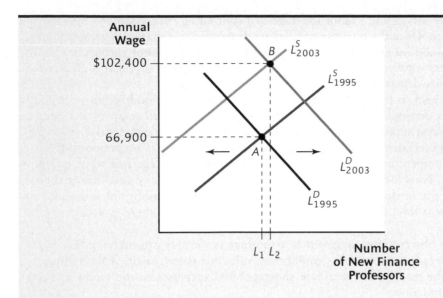

FIGURE 11

The Market for Finance Professors (1995–2003)

During the 1990s, the market supply of new finance professors fell, as shown by the leftward shift of the market supply curve. At the same time, increased demand for finance courses caused the demand curve to shift rightward. As a result, the equilibrium wage rose from $66,900 to $102,400.

labor market, and the decrease in the number of qualified people—contributed to a leftward shift of the supply curve for business professors.

There were also changes on the demand side of the market. Business was becoming an increasingly popular field to study—in large part due to the high salaries one could earn with an MBA. With the demand for business classes surging, business schools expanded enrollments, and they wanted to employ more business professors at any given wage. This caused the labor demand curve for business professors to shift rightward.

For an example of what happened, look at Figure 11. It shows a subset of the market for business school professors: *new professors of finance*. The suppliers in this market are those who have just earned their PhD in finance and are looking for an entry-level job as an assistant professor. The demanders are the business schools trying to hire new PhDs in finance. In 1995, with labor demand curve L^D_{1995} and labor supply curve L^S_{1995}, the average (equilibrium) salary of new finance professors was $66,900 (point A).

Over the next several years, due to the changes we've discussed, the labor supply curve shifted leftward (to L^S_{2003}), and the labor demand curve shifted rightward (to L^D_{2003}). The result was a huge rise in average salaries: By 2003, new finance professors were earning $102,400 in their first year on the job.[10] Notice that while the shifts in labor demand and labor supply had opposing effects on employment, both shifts contributed to the rise in salaries.

LABOR SHORTAGES AND SURPLUSES

You'll often hear about a shortage or a surplus of labor in some profession or trade. In the early 1990s there was a surplus of scientists, in the mid-1990s a shortage of software developers, and in the mid-2000s, the media frequently warned about a coming shortage of health care workers.

[10] "2003–2004 Salary Survey, Executive Summary," December 2003, Association to Advance Collegiate Schools of Business Web site. Figures are mean salary of *new* doctorates in finance taking first-year teaching positions.

Labor shortage The quantity of labor demanded exceeds the quantity supplied for some period of time.

Labor surplus The quantity of labor supplied exceeds the quantity demanded for some period of time.

Economists define a **labor shortage** as a continuing *excess demand* for labor—a situation in which the quantity of workers demanded in a market is greater than the quantity supplied at the prevailing wage rate. Similarly, a **labor surplus** is a continuing *excess supply* of workers, when the quantity of labor supplied is greater than the quantity demanded.

Look back at Figure 8. When the hourly wage is at its equilibrium value ($20), quantities demanded and supplied are equal—there is neither an excess demand nor an excess supply of paralegals. We've argued that, in a competitive labor market, any excess demand or supply would be self-correcting. Competition for scarce jobs or competition for scarce workers would drive the wage rate to its equilibrium value. Now look back at Figures 9, 10, and 11. There, we saw that changes in labor supply or demand or both cause changes in the equilibrium wage rate and employment level. But—as long as the wage can adjust—there is no shortage or surplus.

These observations suggest that a shortage or surplus can occur only when the wage rate *fails* to move to its equilibrium value for some reason. This is important because the media often attribute shortages and surpluses to the forces of supply and demand alone.

Shortages and surpluses in a labor market are not *the natural consequence of shifts in supply and demand curves. A labor shortage will occur only when the wage rate fails to rise to its equilibrium value. Similarly, a labor surplus will occur only when the wage rate fails to fall to its equilibrium value.*

Microeconomists are very interested in shortages and surpluses because they are costly for individuals, for firms, and for society as a whole. A shortage in a labor market makes it harder for firms to find workers and forces them to pay higher recruiting costs to fill job vacancies. In the end, some vacancies must remain unfilled—there are simply not enough workers to go around—which means that valuable output will not be produced.

Similarly, a surplus in a labor market makes it harder for workers to find jobs in that market. Time that could be spent earning income and producing output is instead devoted to sending out résumés, pounding the pavement, or waiting around for good fortune to strike.

Why would a wage rate sometimes fail to adjust to its equilibrium value? Toward the beginning of this chapter, it was pointed out that while the labor market is just like other markets in many respects, it also has some special features. First, the price of labor—the wage rate—is the chief source of most households' incomes. Most of us would not want to work for an employer who changed our wage rate every time there was a shift in labor demand or labor supply, because our income would change rather haphazardly. A firm that developed a reputation for frequent wage cutting would have difficulty attracting workers in the first place. It might have to pay higher wage rates, on average, than a firm with a reputation for paying more stable wages. By developing a reputation for wage stability, a firm has an easier time attracting labor and can earn higher profit in the long run.

Moreover, pay cuts can harm employee morale: Many qualified employees may quit, and those who remain may not work as hard. This makes firms reluctant to cut wages, even when the *equilibrium* wage in a labor market falls. But it can *also* create a reluctance to *raise* wages when the equilibrium wage rate rises. If the higher equilibrium is temporary, the firm will face an unpleasant choice later: to continue paying the high wages (even though the equilibrium wage has fallen), or to cut pay, with all the negative consequences we've discussed.

With this in mind, consider what happens when shifts in labor demand or supply (as in Figures 9 and 10) increase the equilibrium wage. At the original wage rate, there would be an excess demand for labor, which would ordinarily drive the wage rate up. But if firms resist pay hikes for some time, the result will be a labor shortage. Firms will not be able to hire all the workers they want at the going wage, and there will be unfilled jobs. However, if the change in the equilibrium wage is long-lasting (months? years?), we can eventually expect the market wage to catch up to the equilibrium wage.

The same logic applies for shifts that *decrease* the equilibrium wage. Firms may be slow to cut pay, creating a labor *surplus* in which qualified job applicants exceed the number of openings. Eventually, however, we expect the wage to move down to its new, lower equilibrium value.

© SUSAN VAN ETTEN

USING THE THEORY

Understanding the Market for College-Educated Labor

Students have many motives for attending college, but one of the most important motives is to invest in their own human capital. Put very simply, going to college will enable you to earn a higher income than you would otherwise be able to earn. How much higher? Economists answer this question by tracking the college *wage premium*, the percentage by which the average college graduate's income exceeds the average high school graduate's income. The wage premium was relatively stable in the 1960s and 1970s, at around 40 to 50 percent. But the premium began to rise sharply in the 1980s and continued its rise through the early 2000s. In 2004, the college wage premium was 74 percent for men and 95 percent for women.[11]

The tools you've learned in this chapter can help you understand why the wage premium has behaved this way. The first step is to realize that, each year, the labor markets for those with college degrees and those with high school diplomas experience changes like those shown in Figure 12. That is, each year, in each of these labor markets, both the labor supply curve and the labor demand curve shift rightward. The wage rate, however, may rise or fall in each market, depending on which curve shifts rightward *more*—the labor supply curve, or the labor demand curve.

Let's focus first on the market for those with college degrees during the past few decades. Each year, the labor supply curve in this market has shifted rightward for two reasons. First is a rising population. Even if the fraction of the population graduating from college had remained constant, a rising population means a greater *number* of people with college degrees in the labor market.

A second reason is an increase in the *proportion* of young people attending college. For example, the proportion of recent high school graduates enrolled in college

---

[11] U.S. Census Bureau, *Historical Income Tables*, Tables P-16 and P-17. Based on median earnings for age 25 years and over.

FIGURE 12

**The Market for
College-Educated Labor**

Note: Based on U.S. Census Bureau, *Historical Income Tables,* Tables P-16 and P-17, for workers with bachelor's degrees only (no further academic or professional education). Median earnings are author approximations: a weighted average of median earnings for men and median earnings for women, with weights equal to percentages of men and women with bachelor's degrees in each year.

rose from 49 percent in 1980 to 64 percent in 2003.[12] This, in turn, was partly caused by a change in tastes for college education and partly by a delayed, long-run response to the higher wage rates earned by college graduates in earlier years.

But labor *demand* has grown each year as well. In part, this is due to the normal growth in the economy. As firms grow larger, and new firms are born, more labor is demanded at any wage rate.

But another reason for increases in labor demand has been technological change. Over the last few decades, technological change has increased the skill requirements for many types of work. Routine jobs such as adding up numbers, handling simple requests for information over the phone, or connecting parts on an assembly line are increasingly being performed by computers and other machines. The jobs offered to *people,* meanwhile, have required greater skills than before. Instead of performing routine tasks, firms want to hire people who can write software, who can design and service computers and Web pages, and who know how to use high-tech equipment. As a result, many firms have shifted their hiring efforts toward college graduates, who are believed to have more skills and to be more capable of acquiring new skills.

Figure 12 illustrates the shifts in labor supply and demand that have occurred in the market for those with bachelor's (but no higher) degrees. As you can see, from 1978 to 2004, the labor demand curve has shifted by *more* than the labor supply curve. In other words, the expansion of the economy (more and larger firms) and technological change have caused the demand for college-educated labor to rise faster than the number of people with college degrees. The result has been a rise in

[12] *Statistical Abstract of the United States, 2006,* Table 263.

the median annual pay of college-educated workers over this period, from $37,404 (in 2004 dollars) to $41,218.[13]

Meanwhile, in the market for those with only high school diplomas, the picture has been rather bleak. An important reason is, once again, technological change. While the technological advances of the past few decades have speeded the growth in demand for college-educated labor, it has worked to *slow* the growth in demand for less-educated workers. For those with only a high school education, labor demand has grown more slowly than labor supply. As a result, from 1978 to 2004, their median annual earnings have dropped from $24,977 (in 2004 dollars) to $22,650.[14]

What will happen to the wages of college-educated workers, and their wage premium, in the future? That depends on the relative strengths of two competing trends.

One trend is a further rightward shift of the labor *supply* curve in this market, beyond the shift we would expect from normal population growth. Why? In large part, it's a continued response of young people to the high wage premium in previous years. In purely economic terms, college continues to be a very profitable investment (as we'll explore further in Chapter 13). As a result, each year, a greater proportion of young people decide to attend college. While expected increases in the *cost* of college work against this trend, they are not expected to reverse it.

The other trend is a further rightward shift in the labor *demand* curve, beyond the shift we'd expect from normal growth in the economy. And a major reason for the increase in labor demand is further technological change. Most of the technological changes over the next decade, as in past decades, are expected to be *complementary* with high-skilled (i.e., college-educated) labor, but substitutable for low-skilled labor (i.e., high school degree or less).

Note that rightward shifts in labor *supply*, by themselves, work to decrease the earnings of college-educated labor, while rightward shifts in labor *demand* work to increase earnings. But labor market economists predict that in the future, as in the past, the labor demand curve will shift rightward more rapidly than the labor supply curve. Thus, the pay of college graduates is expected to rise. In the market for high school graduates, however, shifts in the labor supply curve are expected to equal or outpace shifts in the demand curve, causing stagnant or falling wages. As a result, the wage *premium* for college students is expected to increase.

Interestingly, this wage premium for college graduates is one of the reasons behind a trend toward greater income inequality in the 1980s, 1990s, and early 2000s. But it is not the only reason. Studies have shown that inequality has increased even within groups: greater inequality *among* college graduates and *among* high school graduates. What explains this growing income inequality?

To answer that question, we must extend our analysis of labor markets, and also consider economic inequality more generally. We begin to do that in the next chapter.

---

[13] Why such a small rise in median real earnings over such a long period? In part, this reflects measurement problems: Over this period, there was a rise in the fraction of total employee compensation provided as benefits (especially health care), which is not included in earnings. Also, inaccuracies in measuring inflation generally lead to an underestimate in real (constant dollar) earnings growth. But another important reason for the slow growth in median earnings has been the increase in income inequality *among* college graduates. We'll discuss this further in the next chapter.

[14] For a further explanation of the behavior of wages for college and high school graduates over time, see David H. Autor, Lawrence F. Katz, and Melissa S. Kearney, "Trends in U.S. Wage Inequality: Re-Assessing the Revisionists," National Bureau of Economic Research Working Paper No. 11627, September 2005.

Summary

Firms need *resources*—land, labor, capital, and entrepreneurship—in order to produce output. These resources are traded in *factor markets* in which firms are demanders and households are suppliers. The *labor market* is a key factor market. A *perfectly competitive labor market* is one in which there are many buyers and sellers, all workers appear the same to firms, and there is easy entry and exit.

The demand for labor by a firm is a *derived demand*—derived from the demand for the product the firm produces. In a competitive labor market, each firm faces a market-determined wage rate. The firm hires up to the point at which the *marginal revenue product (MRP)* of labor—the change in total revenue from hiring one more worker—equals the wage rate. The firm's *labor demand curve* is the negatively sloped portion of its *MRP* curve. The *market demand for labor* is the horizontal sum of all firms' individual labor demand curves.

On the supply side, the upward-sloping *labor supply curve* reflects households' *reservation wages*. A higher wage rate will attract more labor to a particular market. The market labor supply and demand curves intersect to determine the market wage rate and employment for a given category of labor.

Labor market equilibrium can change for a variety of reasons. Shifts in either the labor demand or labor supply curve will lead to

a new equilibrium wage rate and employment combination. An increase in labor *demand* would result from an increase in the price of firms' output, a lower price for an input that is complementary with labor, a complementary technological change, or an increase in the number of firms hiring in that market. In each case, the market labor demand curve would shift rightward, increasing both the wage rate and the level of employment. Market labor *supply* can increase as a result of a decrease in the wage rate in other labor markets, an increase in the number of qualified people, or a change in tastes in favor of work in that market. Such increase in labor supply would decrease the wage rate while increasing the level of employment.

It is important to distinguish between a short-run and a long-run change in labor market equilibrium. In the short run, we assume a fixed number of qualified people who are located in the geographic area of the labor market. The long run, by contrast, is a period of time long enough for workers to acquire new job skills or to move to new geographic locations. That is, in the long run outsiders can enter the market and supply labor there. After a shift in labor demand, the wage rate will generally *overshoot* its ultimate value in the short run, and then gradually move toward its new long-run equilibrium value.

Problem Set   *Answers to even-numbered Questions and Problems can be found on the text Web site at www.thomsonedu.com/economics/hall.*

1. In the nation of Barronia, the market for construction workers is perfectly competitive. Explain what would happen to the equilibrium wage rate and equilibrium employment of construction workers under each of the following circumstances:

   a. Young adults in Barronia begin to develop a taste for living in their own homes and apartments, instead of living with their parents until marriage.

   b. Construction firms begin to use newly developed robots that perform many tasks formerly done by construction workers.

   c. Because of a war in neighboring Erronia, Erronian construction workers flee across the border to Barronia.

   d. There is an increased demand for automobiles in Barronia, and Barronian construction workers have the skills necessary to produce automobiles.

2. The following gives employment and daily output information for Your Mama, a perfectly competitive manufacturer of computer motherboards.

Number of Workers	Total Output
10	80
11	88
12	94
13	97
14	99

   A motherboard worker at Your Mama earns $80 a day, and motherboards sell for $27.50.

   a. How many workers will be employed? How do you know?

   b. Suppose the market wage for motherboard workers increases by $5 per day per worker, but the market price of motherboards remains unchanged. What will happen to employment at the firm? Why?

3. a. Complete the following table and determine how many workers this firm will employ, and how much output it will produce. (Remember to place *MFC* and *MRP* between the rows.)

Price	Output (per day)	Labor	Total Revenue	MRP	Daily Wage	Total Cost of Labor	MFC
$50	100	6			$400		
$50	200	8			$400		
$50	300	12			$400		
$50	400	18			$400		
$50	500	26			$400		
$50	600	36			$400		
$50	700	51			$400		
$50	800	80			$400		

   b. Redo the table in part (a) to show what will happen if the price of output falls to $25. Then determine the new levels of employment and output.

4. You are given the following information about a packaged lunch-meat company, By-products-R-Us:

Number of Workers	Packages per Week
1	100
2	250
3	450
4	600
5	700
6	750
7	775

   a. Over what range of output are there increasing returns to labor? . . . diminishing returns to labor?
   b. Suppose By-products sells its meat in a perfectly competitive market where the price is $6 per package. Create new columns for total revenue and marginal revenue product, and fill them in.
   c. Suppose By-products hires its labor in a perfectly competitive labor market, where the wage is $700 per week. How many workers should it hire, and how many packages should it produce each week?

5. Defense-related industries were a major employer of physicists throughout the cold war. When tensions ended after the fall of the Soviet Union, however, defense cutbacks ensued.
   a. Using graphs, illustrate the short-run impact of defense cutbacks on the market for physicists. Assuming the market adjusted to the new short-run equilibrium, what would have happened to their equilibrium wage rate and the number employed? Would the cutbacks have caused unemployment among physicists? Why or why not?
   b. In reality, many defense firms had long-term contracts with their professionals, locking them into specific salaries for years at a time. How does this fact alter your answer to (a)? Could it explain why unemployment occurred among physicists in the early 1990s? Explain.

6. Suppose that dehydrated meat is an inferior good. Discuss the short-run effects on the equilibrium wage rate and level of employment in the dehydrated meat industry of an increase in national income.

7. After September 2001, the United States began revamping federal agencies—such as the FBI and the CIA—to closely monitor extremist groups in the United States and abroad. At the same time, these agencies discovered that they had very few agents who could speak Middle Eastern and South Asian languages, and immediately began to correct the deficiency. Economists immediately made two predictions. Draw one or more diagrams to illustrate each of these predictions, and explain briefly.
   Prediction #1: Salaries for U.S. residents who knew these languages would rise dramatically over the next year or so.
   Prediction #2: Even though the government's need for these professionals would continue for at least a decade, their salaries would, after rising, eventually come down and begin to return toward (but not go all the way to) their pre-September 2001 levels.

8. Add MR and MC columns to Table 1 in the chapter and find the profit-maximizing output level using the MR and MC approach. When calculating MR and MC, don't forget to divide ΔTR and ΔTC by the change in output, which is not *one* unit in the table. Does the profit-maximizing output level differ from the one found in the chapter, using the MRP and MFC approach? Explain briefly.

More Challenging

9. Many people think that immigration into the United States, because it causes competition for jobs, will lower the wage rates of U.S. workers. Yet, even though the United States admits hundreds of thousands of immigrants each year, the average U.S. wage has continued to grow. Can you explain why? Are there any groups of workers within the economy for whom the fear of lower wages is justified? Explain.

10. Reread the section "The Two Approaches to Profit Maximization" in the chapter. Then, show that the MR = MC rule and the MRP = W rule give the same result for employment and output for the packaged meat firm, By-products-R-Us, in problem 4. (Hint: Create new columns for MR and MC from the information given.)

11. Suppose a firm sells its output in a market that is *not* perfectly competitive, and can produce five different daily output levels: 300, 400, 500, 600, or 700. The firm has the following daily demand schedule, along with indicated labor requirements for each output level:

P	Q	Labor
$10	300	5
$ 9	400	9
$ 8	500	15
$ 7	600	22
$ 6	700	30

   Suppose, too, that the firm hires its labor in a competitive labor market, where workers must be paid $65 per day. Use the MRP = W rule to find the firm's profit-maximizing employment level, price of output, and daily output level. (Hint: MRP is defined, as always, as $\Delta TR/\Delta L$, where L is the quantity of labor.)

12. [Appendix] Rework problem 11, only now assume that the firm is a monopsonist that faces the following labor supply curve.

Labor	Wage Rate
5	$45
9	$55
15	$65
22	$75
30	$85

APPENDIX

Monopsony

In the body of this chapter, we analyzed perfectly competitive labor markets, in which each firm is an insignificant buyer of labor that takes the market wage it must pay as a given. Perfect competition is a useful assumption in many cases, even when its requirements are not strictly satisfied. But sometimes the departures from the model are so glaring—or the questions we're asking have to do with those departures—that using the perfectly competitive model doesn't make sense. One such case is a labor market structure called *monopsony*.

> **A pure monopsony** *labor market is one in which a single firm is the only employer.*

While *pure* monopsony is extremely rare, we can use the term **monopsony** more loosely (without the "pure") for situations in which a single firm is such a *large* employer in a market that its employment decisions affect the market wage. For example, a town with one large hospital may not be the *only* employer of nurses in the area, but it will likely provide jobs to a significant portion of them. When the hospital hires more nurses, its own increase in labor demand can drive up the market wage for nurses. Similarly, staff cutbacks can cause the market wage to drop.

A large university in a small college town is another example. The faculty at the university are often mobile, so the university must compete for them in a national market in which it may be only a small buyer. But in the markets for administrative staff, maintenance workers, and security guards, workers are more often rooted in the community, with long-standing ties to family and friends. For these workers, the university may be the main option for employment. When the university expands its labor force, it can drive wage rates up in these markets, while contractions in university employment can push wage rates down.

A monopsony employer treats the wage rate as a decision variable, much like a monopolist treats the price of its product. For a monopsonist, each level of employment corresponds to a different wage rate. Therefore, deciding to employ a certain number of workers *implies* paying a certain wage, and vice versa.

The wage decision is just the flip side of the employment decision.

How does a monopsonist decide how much labor to employ (or what wage to pay)?

SPOTLESS CAR WASH AS A MONOPSONY

To explore monopsony decisions, let's go back to Spotless Car Wash. But this time, instead of assuming that Spotless hires its labor in a perfectly competitive market, we'll assume that it's a monopsonist.

Table A.1 illustrates the relevant data. Most of the columns are identical to the same numbered columns in Table 1 presented earlier in this chapter. (We've left out column 3—the *MPL*—to make room for some new columns.) Columns 1 and 2—reproduced from Table 1—show various quantities of labor and total product. These numbers come from Spotless's *production* function, and are unaffected by the structure of the labor market. The next three columns—listing the price of a car wash, total revenue, and marginal revenue product—add information about the *product* market (perfectly competitive), but, once again, these numbers have nothing to do with the labor market.

Where Spotless's monopsony status starts to matter is in column 7, which lists the wage at each employment level. When we assumed that Spotless hired labor in a perfectly competitive labor market, it took the wage as given, and paid $60 per day regardless of how many workers it chose to employ. It decided to hire five workers at that wage rate.

But now, with Spotless as a monopsonist, the more workers that it hires, the more it will have to pay them. After all, each worker has a different reservation wage for working. To convince someone who *wasn't* working before to start washing cars, Spotless must make the prospect worthwhile: It must offer a wage higher than that person's reservation wage. For example, if Spotless wants to employ three workers, it must pay a daily wage of $40. But to hire a fourth worker, it will have to increase the daily wage to $50.

	T A B L E	A.1
	Spotless Car Wash as a Monopsonist in the Labor Market	

(1) Quantity of Labor	(2) Total Product (Cars Washed per Day)	(4) Price per Car Wash	(5) Total Revenue	(6) Marginal Revenue Product (MRP)	(7) Daily Wage	(8) Total Labor Cost	(9) Marginal Factor Cost (MFC)
0	0	$4	$ 0		<$20	$ 0	
				$120			$ 20
1	30	$4	$120		$20	$ 20	
				$240			$ 40
2	90	$4	$360		$30	$ 60	
				$160			$ 60
3	130	$4	$520		$40	$120	
				$120			$ 80
4	160	$4	$640		$50	$200	
				$ 96			$100
5	184	$4	$736		$60	$300	
				$ 48			$120
6	196	$4	$784		$70	$420	
				$ 16			$140
7	200	$4	$800		$80	$560	

Now we'll make one additional assumption: Spotless must pay the same wage to *all* of its workers. It cannot "wage discriminate" by, for example, increasing employment from three to four workers with a secret offer of $50 to the fourth worker while continuing to pay the other three $40.

This assumption—that all workers are paid the same wage—is important as we move to column 8, which lists total labor cost for each level of employment. To employ one worker, the firm's total labor cost is just $20—the reservation wage of that worker. But to hire two workers, the firm must pay $30—the reservation wage of the second worker—to *both* workers. This would raise labor cost to 2 × $30 = $60.

The last column lists the *marginal factor cost* (MFC) of labor. As before, the MFC tells us the increase in cost when one more worker is hired. When the firm increases employment from, say, two to three workers, labor cost rises from $60 to $120, an increase of $60. So the MFC for this employment change is $60.

If you look down the MFC numbers in column 9, and compare them with the wage rate values in column 7, you'll notice something interesting: For any change in employment (other than hiring the first worker), the MFC is larger than the wage that Spotless pays.

For a monopsonist, MFC at any level of employment is greater than the wage rate.

As you're about to see, this will affect both the level of employment at Spotless, and the wage its workers will earn.

THE PROFIT-MAXIMIZING EMPLOYMENT LEVEL

The *general* guideline for profit-maximizing employment is no different for a monopsonist than for any other firm: Increase employment as long as MRP > MFC, and stop as soon as MRP < MFC, or the two are equal. In the table, the guideline tells us to compare the numbers in column 6 (MRP) and column 9 (MFC). For all workers up to the fourth, we find that MRP > MFC, so Spotless increases its profit by hiring them. For example, going from three to four workers, MRP = $120, while MFC = $80. Hiring the fourth worker adds more to revenue than to cost, so profit rises. But for the fifth worker, MRP = $96, while MFC = $100. This move would add more to Spotless's cost than to its revenue, reducing profit. Thus, Spotless should hire four workers, and no more.

Figure A.1 shows this same decision process graphically. The figure reproduces Spotless's MRP curve from Figure 2. The figure also shows the labor *supply* curve facing the firm. This curve tells us the wage Spotless must offer to attract different numbers of workers. A firm in a competitive labor market faces a *horizontal* supply curve for labor (it can hire all the workers it wants at the market wage rate), but a monopsonist faces an *upward*-sloping labor supply curve (to hire another worker, it must offer a higher wage). In fact, if Spotless is the *only* employer in town—a pure monopsony—then the labor supply curve it faces will be the same as the market labor supply curve in the town.

The final curve, labeled *MFC*, plots the *MFC* numbers from column 9. Notice that the *MFC* curve lies *above* the labor supply curve. This is a graphical representation of the point made earlier:

> *Since* MFC *for a monopsonist is greater than the wage rate, the* MFC *curve lies* above *the labor supply curve.*

In the figure, to maximize profit, Spotless should increase employment until *MRP* = *MFC* (at point *E*), which occurs at four workers. But what *wage* will it pay? The answer—$50—is found on the labor supply curve L_S at point *F*. After all, it's the labor supply curve, not the *MFC* curve, that tells us what Spotless must pay to attract four workers.

COMPARING MONOPSONY TO PERFECTLY COMPETITIVE LABOR MARKETS

When we compare Spotless as a perfect competitor (Figure 2) with Spotless as a monopsonist (Figure A.1), we come to some disturbing conclusions. First, let's note that nothing has changed from Figure 2 to Figure A.1 *other than* the switch from a perfectly competitive labor market to a monopsony. In both figures, Spotless is the same firm, producing its car washes with the same production function, having the same *MRP* curve, and selling its car washes for $4 each. Moreover, in both cases, Spotless *could* choose to hire five workers at $60 each, paying a total labor cost of $300 per day. In perfect competition, Spotless made just that choice, hiring all five workers and paying each one $60. As a monopsonist, although Spotless *could* make the same choice (the labor supply curve tells us that five people would work at the firm if they were paid $60 each), it chooses not to.

Why? Because as a monopsonist, if Spotless employs the fifth worker it must not only pay him or her $60 (which, by itself, would be profitable), but must *also* increase the wage of its *other* four workers from $50 to

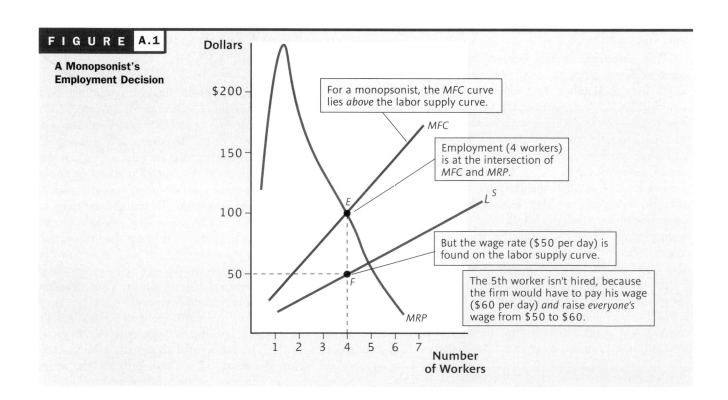

FIGURE A.1

A Monopsonist's Employment Decision

For a monopsonist, the *MFC* curve lies *above* the labor supply curve.

Employment (4 workers) is at the intersection of *MFC* and *MRP*.

But the wage rate ($50 per day) is found on the labor supply curve.

The 5th worker isn't hired, because the firm would have to pay his wage ($60 per day) *and* raise *everyone's* wage from $50 to $60.

$60. When this pay hike for the others is added to the cost of the fifth worker, Spotless would be sacrificing profit if it made the hire. So, as a monopsonist, Spotless employs less labor than it did as a perfect competitor.

Also note that, with four workers instead of five, Spotless washes fewer cars as a monopsonist (160 per day) than it did as a perfectly competitive firm (184 per day). Producing less output is the flip side of hiring fewer workers.

Finally, as a monopsonist, Spotless pays *all* of its workers a lower wage ($50) than it did as a perfect competitor. This, too, is a direct consequence of lower employment: The fewer workers the firm wants to employ, the lower the wage it needs to pay in order to attract them.

The results for Spotless hold more generally as well:

> *When all else is the same, firms in monopsony labor markets (1) employ fewer workers, (2) produce less output, and (3) pay lower wages than firms in perfectly competitive labor markets.*

As you can see, neither workers nor consumers are well served by monopsony. In this sense, monopsony resembles *monopoly* in a product market, and both market structures present a challenge for public policy. In the next chapter, we'll come back to monopsony when we explore the impact of unions and the minimum wage in a labor market.

CHAPTER 12

Economic Inequality

When we went to do the deals for Shrek 2, *they were made in one day. It was that fast and that easy. It was also probably the biggest payday in movie history. They were each paid $10 million for what is in effect 18 hours of work.*

Jeffrey Katzenberg, cofounder of DreamWorks SKG, referring to payments made to Eddie Murphy, Mike Myers, and Cameron Diaz for voiceovers.[1]

Imagine, for a pleasant moment, that you are Eddie Murphy, Mike Myers, or Cameron Diaz. Your typical workday begins in a limousine, escorting you to the site of the day's recording. There you are doted on by assistants whose sole job is to keep you happy, who look at you respectfully, even worshipfully. Finally, you perform the day's work: a few hours worth of reading from a script. If you make a mistake, everyone laughs good-naturedly, and you get another chance to get it right—as many chances as you need. And after doing this each day for a few weeks, you pick up a check for $10 million.

Now, switch gears and imagine that you have a less-rewarding job, say, as a short-order cook at a coffeehouse. You spend the day sweating over a hot grill, spinning a little metal wheel with an endless supply of orders. You cook several hundred meals that day, all the while suffering the short tempers of waiters and waitresses who want you to do it faster, who glare at you if you forget that a customer wanted french fries instead of home fries, and who call you everything but your proper name. For toiling in this way day after day, for an entire year, you earn $20,000.

And some people would consider you lucky: According to the U.S. Census Bureau, about 37 million people live in poverty, with even smaller incomes—too small to achieve a standard of living considered acceptable in our time.

We live in a country with extreme differences in wealth and income. One reason for this is a difference in wage rates. In economics, the concept of a *wage rate* is much broader than its official meaning as the rate of pay for people who are officially paid by the hour. In fact, an hourly wage rate can be calculated for *anyone* who works by dividing the earnings over a week, month, or year by the number of hours worked during that period. In this way, we can calculate the hourly wage rate for a sales representative paid on commission, or a movie star with a

---

[1] "Question and Answer: Movie Mogul Jeffrey Katzenberg," *Reel West* (Vol. 17, No. 4) July–August 2002.

three-picture deal, or a corporate executive earning a salary and a year-end bonus and other compensation.

The first part of this chapter focuses on differences in these broadly defined wage rates, and why they differ so widely among workers. As you'll see, we can explain much about wage differences, using the tools you learned in the previous chapter. But labor earnings are just one source of income. Those who own other resources—such as capital and land—earn income from them as well. In the second half of this chapter, we expand our analysis to the distribution of income from *all* sources, as well as the distribution of wealth.

WHY DO WAGES DIFFER?

At any time, some of the wage inequality we observe is *short-run* inequality. Because of delays in reaching long-run equilibrium, two labor markets that are heading toward equal wage rates might pay very different rates for some period of time. But there is also *long-run* wage inequality—differences in wages that persist after all long-run adjustments have taken place. Economists are generally more interested in these long-run differences in wages, since the short-run differences, by definition, will disappear with time.

As a starting point, consider Table 1, which shows hourly earnings in 2004 for full-time workers in selected occupations. Each row of the table lists not only the median wage rate (in bold) but also the wage rate at the 10th and 90th percentiles for the occupation. For example, the second row shows that 10 percent of full-time physicians earned $15.03 per hour or less, while 90 percent earned $108.92 or less (so the top 10 percent earned $108.92 or more). And the bolded middle column tells us that in 2004, half of physicians earned less than $60.91 per hour while the other half earned more.

Note the inequality in wage rates among *different* occupations. These sharp differences occur even for jobs in the same industry, in which the work is often similar. Compare, for example, the median hourly wage rate of a business professor ($36.77) and a political science professor ($30.55), or that of a physician ($60.91) and a registered nurse ($25.44).

But you can also see sharp differences in earnings *within* many occupations. For airline pilots, the wage rate at the 90th percentile is more than five times higher than at the 10th. Even in the lowest-paying occupations, wage rates at the 90th percentile are typically twice those at the 10th.

The table tells us that there is substantial wage inequality among and within occupations in the U.S. labor market. Moreover, wage inequality is *persistent*. The highest-paid and lowest-paid occupations have been so for decades. And year after year, the highest-paid workers within an occupation earn substantially more than the lowest.

Moreover, Table 1—and the Bureau of Labor Statistics data on which it is based—underestimates the full extent of wage inequality in the U.S. labor market. It does not include bonuses, fringe benefits, or other additional labor earnings that are substantially greater for the highest-paying occupations and the highest-paid workers within each job. It also leaves out those at the very top—such as chief executive officers of top corporations, sports celebrities, and movie stars. For example, Eddie Murphy's wage rate on most films is between $10,000 and $20,000 per hour. If the quote at the beginning of this chapter is accurate, he earned an

TABLE 1				
Hourly Earnings of Full-time Workers in Selected Occupations, 2004	**Occupation**	**10th Percentile**	**Median (50th Percentile)**	**90th Percentile**
	Airline pilots and navigators	$35.34	**$118.73**	$189.78
	Physicians	$15.03	**$ 60.91**	$108.92
	Pharmacists	$36.59	**$ 42.85**	$ 48.83
	Managers (marketing, advertising, and public relations)	$23.50	**$ 42.28**	$ 79.39
	College teachers, business	$23.31	**$ 36.77**	$ 68.35
	College teachers, political science	$24.58	**$ 30.55**	$ 52.55
	Elementary school teachers	$20.99	**$ 30.37**	$ 48.13
	Electric installers and repairers	$19.00	**$ 26.51**	$ 34.32
	Registered nurses	$18.60	**$ 25.44**	$ 36.30
	Lathe and turning machine operators	$10.87	**$ 16.55**	$ 23.90
	Cabinetmakers	$ 9.75	**$ 12.50**	$ 16.50
	Bank tellers	$ 8.25	**$ 10.41**	$ 14.04
	Cashiers	$ 6.50	**$ 8.75**	$ 13.10
	Kitchen workers, food preparation	$ 6.00	**$ 8.25**	$ 12.00

Source: Selected data from *National Compensation Survey: Occupational Wages in the United States, July 2004* (Supplemental Table 1.2), Bureau of Labor Statistics. The BLS data are based on surveys of about 18,000 business establishments employing about 86 million workers.

astounding $550,000 per hour on *Shrek 2*. Baseball star Alex Rodriguez earns $50,000 each time he steps to the plate.

How can an hour of human labor have such different values in the market?

AN IMAGINARY WORLD

To understand why wages differ in the real world, let's start by imagining an *unreal* world, with three features:

1. Except for differences in wages, all jobs are equally attractive to all workers.
2. All workers are equally able to do any job.
3. All labor markets are perfectly competitive.

In such a world, we would expect every worker to earn an identical wage in the long run. Let's see why.

Figure 1 shows two different labor markets that initially have different wage rates. Panel (a) shows a local market for elementary school teachers, with an initial equilibrium at point *A* and a wage of $30 per hour. Panel (b) shows the market for advertis-

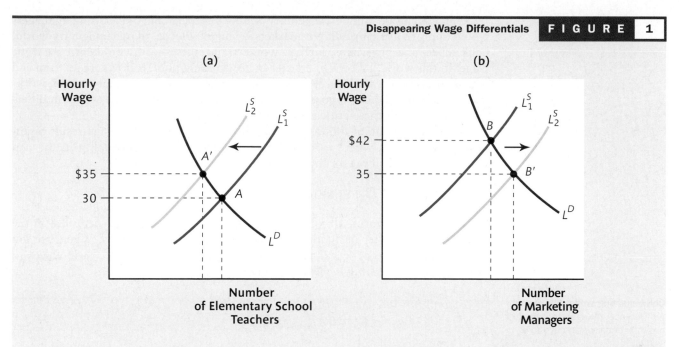

Disappearing Wage Differentials   **FIGURE 1**

Initially, the supply and demand for elementary school teachers in panel (a) determine an equilibrium wage of $30 per hour—
at point A. In panel (b), the equilibrium wage for advertising managers is initially $42 per hour. If these markets are competitive,
if the two jobs are equally attractive, and if all workers are equally able to do both jobs, this wage differential cannot persist.
Some elementary school teachers will give up that occupation, reducing supply in panel (a), and become advertising managers,
increasing supply in panel (b). This migration will continue until the wage in both markets is equal—at $35 in the figure.

ing account managers, who, at point *B*, earn $42 per hour. In our imaginary world, could this diagram describe the *long-run* equilibrium in these markets? Absolutely not.

Imagine that you are an elementary school teacher. By our first assumption, you would find being an advertising manager just as attractive as teaching school. But since advertising managers earn more, you would prefer to be one. By our second assumption, you are *qualified* to be an advertising manager, and by our third assumption, there are no barriers to prevent you from becoming one. Thus, you—and many of your fellow teachers—will begin looking for jobs as advertising managers. In panel (a) the labor supply curve will shift leftward (exit from the market for elementary school teachers), and in panel (b) the labor supply curve will shift rightward (entry into the market for advertising managers). As these shifts occur, the market wage rate of elementary school teachers will rise and that of advertising managers will fall.

When will the entry and exit stop? When there is no longer any reason for an elementary school teacher to want to be an advertising manager—that is, when both labor markets are paying the same wage rate ($35 in our example). In the long run, the market for elementary school teachers reaches equilibrium at point *A'* and the market for advertising managers at point *B'*.

Note that these long-run adjustments will occur even if no one actually *switches* jobs. If advertising managers are paid more, then *new* entrants into the labor force— choosing their occupation for the first time—will pick that job over elementary school teaching. As more teachers retire than enter, their number will shrink. Meanwhile, as more advertising managers enter than retire, their number will grow. These changes will continue until the long-run wage rate is equal in both markets.

Our conclusion about elementary school teachers and advertising managers would apply to *any* pair of labor markets we might choose. In our imaginary world, bank tellers and physicians, kitchen workers and nurses—all would earn the same wage. In this world, labor is like water in a swimming pool: It flows freely from end to end ensuring that the level is the same everywhere. In our imaginary world, workers will flow into labor markets with higher wages, evening out the wages in different jobs . . . *if* our three critical assumptions are satisfied.

But take any one of these assumptions away, and the equal-wage result disappears. This tells us where to look for the sources of wage inequality in the real world: a *violation* of one or more of our three assumptions.

COMPENSATING DIFFERENTIALS

In our imaginary world, all jobs were equally attractive to all workers. But in the real world, jobs differ in hundreds of ways that matter to workers. When one job is intrinsically more or less attractive than another, we can expect their wages to differ by a *compensating wage differential*:

Compensating wage differential
A difference in wages that makes two jobs equally attractive to a worker.

> *A compensating wage differential is the difference in wage rates that makes two jobs equally attractive to workers.*

To see how compensating wage differentials come about, let's consider some of the important ways in which jobs can differ.

Nonmonetary Job Characteristics

Suppose you clean offices in a skyscraper, and you could earn $1 more per hour washing the building's windows . . . from the *outside*. Would you "flow" to the window washer's labor market, like water in a pool? Probably not. The higher risk of death just wouldn't be worth it.

Nonmonetary job characteristic
Any aspect of a job—other than the wage—that matters to a potential or current employee.

Danger is an example of a **nonmonetary job characteristic**. It is an aspect of a job—good or bad—that is not easily measured in dollars. When you think about a career, whether you are aware of it or not, you are evaluating hundreds of nonmonetary job characteristics: the risk of death or injury, the cleanliness of the work environment, the prestige you can expect in your community, the amount of physical exertion required, the degree of intellectual stimulation, the potential for advancement . . . the list goes on and on.

What does all this suggest about differing wages in the long run? Remember that in long-run equilibrium, people must have no incentive to leave one labor market and enter another. But workers will be satisfied to stay in a job they consider less desirable only if it pays a compensating wage differential. The compensating differential will be just enough to keep workers from migrating from one labor market to another.

Let's see how compensating differentials figure into our example of elementary school teachers and advertising managers. Look back at Figure 1. Earlier, we saw that if both jobs were equally attractive, both would pay the same wage rate in the long run. But now let's make the opposite extreme assumption: that everyone in the population prefers to teach children rather than work in advertising. Further, suppose it takes a wage differential of $12 in favor of advertising to make the two jobs equally attractive. Then the long-run equilibrium would remain at the initial points *A* and *B*, with advertising managers earning a compensating wage differential of

$12 per hour to make up for the less desirable features of their job. Even with the higher wage rate for advertising managers, elementary school teachers would not want to switch jobs.

> *The nonmonetary characteristics of different jobs give rise to compensating wage differentials. Jobs considered intrinsically less attractive will tend to pay higher wages, other things being equal.*

What about unusually *attractive* jobs? Compared to the average job, these will generally pay *negative* compensating differentials. For example, many new college graduates are attracted to careers in the arts or the media. Since entry-level jobs in these industries are so desirable for nonmonetary reasons, they tend, on average, to pay lower wages than similar jobs in other industries.

Of course, different people have different tastes for working and living conditions. While some prefer a quiet, laid-back work environment like a library or laboratory, others like the commotion of a loading dock or a trading floor. While most people are extremely averse to risking their lives, some actually prefer to live dangerously, as in police work or rescue operations. Therefore, we cannot use our own preferences to declare a job as less attractive or more attractive, or to decide which jobs should pay a positive or negative compensating differential. Rather, when labor markets are perfectly competitive, the entry and exit of workers automatically determines the compensating wage differential in each labor market.

Compensating wage differentials are one reason most economists are skeptical about the idea of *comparable worth*, which holds that a government agency should determine the skills required to perform different jobs and mandate the wage differences needed between them. Although this policy could correct some inequities when labor markets are imperfectly competitive, it could also introduce serious inequities of its own, since no one can know how different workers would value the hundreds of characteristics of each job. Economists generally prefer policies to increase competition and eliminate discrimination, so that the market itself can determine comparable worth.

A Digression: It Pays to Be Unusual. One implication of compensating wage differentials is that workers with unusual tastes often have a monetary advantage in the labor market. For example, only a small fraction of workers *like* dangerous jobs, such as police work. As long as the labor market is competitive, and there is relatively high demand for workers in dangerous jobs, police officers will earn more than those in other, similar jobs that have a lower risk of death or injury. But if you are one of those unusual people who *like* danger, you will earn the same compensating wage differential as all other police officers, even though you would have chosen to be a police officer anyway.

Similarly, if you like the frigid winter weather in Alaska, if you like washing windows on the 90th floor, or if you think it would be fun to defend the cigarette industry in the media, you can earn a higher wage by putting your somewhat unusual tastes to work.

Cost-of-Living Differences

Many people would find living in Cleveland and living in Philadelphia about equally attractive. Yet wages in Philadelphia are about 10 percent higher than in Cleveland. Why? One major reason is that prices in Philadelphia are about

10 percent higher than in Cleveland. If wages were equal in the two cities, many people deciding where to live would prefer Cleveland, where their earnings would have greater purchasing power. The supply of labor in Philadelphia's labor markets would shrink, increasing the wage there, while the supply in Cleveland's labor markets would rise, driving down the wage in Cleveland. In the end, the wage difference would be sufficient to compensate Philadelphians for the higher cost of living in their city.

> *Differences in living costs can cause compensating wage differentials. Areas where living costs are higher than average will tend to have higher-than-average wages.*

Human Capital Requirements

All else equal, jobs that require more education and training will be less attractive. In order to attract workers, these jobs must offer higher pay than other jobs that are similar in other ways but require less training.

Let's go back to Figure 1, but this time imagine that we're comparing the market for elementary school teachers in the left panel with the market for *physicians* in the right panel, with an initial equilibrium wage of $61. Would we expect labor supply curves in these two markets to shift until wage rates were equal for both? No, because physicians must complete an additional three years of medical school after college, plus a residency and sometimes further training. If these jobs were equally attractive in all other ways, then in long-run equilibrium physicians will earn substantially more than elementary school teachers to compensate for the higher costs (such as tuition and foregone income) of becoming a doctor.

> *Differences in human capital requirements can give rise to compensating wage differentials. Jobs that require more costly training will tend to pay higher wages.*

Compensating differentials explain much of the wage differential between jobs requiring college degrees and those that require only a high school diploma. The relatively high earnings of doctors, attorneys, research scientists, and college professors reflect—at least in part—compensating differentials for the especially high human capital requirements—and human capital costs—of entering their professions.

The idea of compensating wage differentials dates back to Adam Smith, who first observed that unpleasant jobs seem to pay more than other jobs that require similar skills and qualifications. It is a powerful concept, and it can explain many of the differences we observe in wages . . . but not all of them.

DIFFERENCES IN ABILITY

In December 2000, at the age of 26, Alex Rodriguez signed a 10-year contract to play baseball for the Texas Rangers (later the New York Yankees) at an average salary of $25 million per year. Was this salary so high because of a compensating differential for the unpleasantness of playing professional baseball? Was the cost of living in Dallas hundreds of times greater than in other cities? Had Rodriguez, at the age of 26, spent more years honing his skills than the average attorney, doctor, architect, or engineer—or even more than the average baseball player?

The answer to all of these questions is no. We have overlooked the obvious explanation: Rodriguez is an *outstanding* baseball player, better than 99.999 percent of the population could ever hope to be. And this is largely due to Rodriguez's exceptional gifts—both physical (natural agility, coordination, and speed) and emotional (the temperament and character needed to train and exploit those gifts).

Even though Alex Rodriguez may be an extreme case, the principle applies across the board. Not everyone has the intelligence needed to be a research scientist, the steady hand to be a neurosurgeon, the quick-thinking ability to be a commodities trader, the well-organized mind to be a business manager, or the talent to be an artist or a ballet dancer. This violates our imaginary-world principle that all workers have equal ability to do any job—or at least equal ability to acquire the skills needed. And that explains much of the wage inequality we observe in the real world.

We can understand this in terms of Figure 1 of this chapter. A wage differential between two otherwise equal jobs could persist if those working for lower wages (point A in panel (a)) cannot enter the high-wage market (point B in panel (b)) because—regardless of how much human capital they acquire—they can never perform well enough. *All else equal, differences in intrinsic ability—including the ability to acquire sophisticated skills—can lead to persistently higher wage rates in jobs requiring those skills.*

Wage rate inequality, and income inequality more generally, increased during the 1990s and early 2000s (see the discussion later in this chapter). Part of the reason may be that differences in abilities have become more important in the labor market. Scientific discoveries and technological advances have increased the skill requirements of many jobs, and the abilities needed to *acquire* those skills. This can create persistent—and increasing—wage differences between high-skilled and low-skilled workers.

Differences in intrinsic ability help to explain persistent differences in pay *between* occupations (e.g., why the average advertising manager earns more than human capital costs alone can explain). But it also plays an important role in explaining pay differences *within* an occupation (e.g., why the very best advertising managers earn far more than the median). Suppose that two advertising managers have equal education and training, but manager A, being more talented, can design better ad campaigns and attract twice as many high-paying clients as can manager B. Then, in an otherwise competitive labor market, a firm will be willing to pay manager A twice as much as manager B.

> *In general, those with greater ability to do a job well—based on their talent, intelligence, motivation, or perseverance—will be more valuable to firms. As a result, firms will be willing to pay them a higher wage rate, beyond any compensating differential for their human capital investment.*

Differences in ability also help explain why workers' pay tends to rise with age and experience on the job. Experience not only adds to a worker's human capital but also provides a signal of ability to employers. Hiring a new, untested worker—even one who seems to have great talent—is always a bit risky, since the worker's basic ability hasn't yet been proven. By contrast, hiring or continuing to employ someone with a history of advancement and accomplishments reduces this risk. All else equal, firms will typically pay more for a worker with a proven track record. Not surprisingly, when wage rates within an occupation are broken down by age (not shown in Table 1), workers who are older—and have been in their occupation longer—dominate the higher percentiles, while younger and newer entrants are more prevalent in the lower percentiles.

Differences in ability, combined with mass media technologies that can reach ever-widening audiences, are especially important in explaining the remarkably high and growing earnings of "stars" in sports and entertainment, as we discuss in the next section.

The Economics of Superstars

© MITCHELL GERBER/CORBIS

Although Eddie Murphy's acting talent may not be a thousand times better than the average, he earns more than a thousand times the average actor's salary because he is at the top of his profession.

Alex Rodriguez is an example of a *superstar*—an individual widely viewed as among the top few in his or her profession. In recent years, superstars have included actors such as Mel Gibson, Eddie Murphy, and Julia Roberts; talk show hosts Jay Leno and David Letterman; news anchors Brian Williams and Katie Couric; novelists Stephen King and J. K. Rowling; and film directors Stephen Spielberg and Ridley Scott.

When we try to explain the extremely high wage rates of these superstars based on their exceptional abilities alone, we confront a puzzle. Clearly Alex Rodriguez has more athletic ability, and more skill in honing it, than almost anyone in the population, including other major-league baseball players. But can this explain a salary that is *25 times* that of the median major-league player? By any measure, is Rodriguez *25 times better*?

Or consider, *NBC Nightly News* anchor Brian Williams. He may deliver the evening news better than most local news anchors. But is he "better enough" to justify a salary estimated to be more than 100 times higher?[2] And most would agree that Eddie Murphy's voice work for *Shrek 2* was better than, say, the voiceovers on the Saturday morning cartoon shows. But Murphy's hourly pay was about 3,000 times greater than that of the typical cartoon voice actor.[3] Is he *that much better*? The very top writers, rock stars, comedians, talk show hosts, and movie directors all earn wage premiums that seem vastly out of proportion to their additional abilities. Why?

The explanation in all these cases *is* based on ability—and also the exaggerated rewards the market bestows on those deemed the best or one of the best in a field.[4] Say you like to read one mystery novel a month for entertainment. If you can choose between the best novel published that month or one that is almost—but not quite—as good, you will naturally choose the one you think is best. Only people who read *two* novels each month would choose the best *and* the second best, and only those who read three will choose the top three. If most people rank recent mystery novels in the same order, then the best will sell millions of copies,

---

[2] According to the Bureau of Labor Statistics, *Occupational Outlook Handbook, 2006–2007 Edition*, the median annual salary of broadcast news analysts (news anchors) in 2004 was $31,320. Brian Williams's annual salary is typically reported as $4 million. (See, for example, "Salary Guide: Who Makes How Much," *New York Magazine*, September 26, 2005.)

[3] Voice actors on Saturday morning cartoons are paid $636 for a four-hour session (not counting time spent rehearsing and auditioning). Patrick Goldstein, "The Big Picture: A Voice Actor Speaks for Herself," *Los Angeles Times*, December 18, 2001.

[4] The seminal article on this theory is Sherwin Rosen, "The Economics of Superstars," *American Economic Review*, American Economic Association, Vol. 71, No. 5, 1981, pp. 845–58. A less technical version is Sherwin Rosen, "The Economics of Superstars," *The American Scholar*, Vol. 52, No. 4, 1983. See also Robert H. Frank and Philip J. Cook, *The Winner Take All Society* (New York: The Free Press, 1995).

the second best might sell hundreds of thousands, and the third best might sell only thousands. Even though all three novels might be very close in quality, a publisher will earn *10 times* more revenue selling the best novel (compared to the second best), and 10 times more revenue selling the second best (compared to the third best), and so on. Accordingly, a publisher will be willing to pay the same multiples in advances and royalties when bidding for contracts with mystery novelists of different rankings. Even if the top author is viewed as only *slightly* better than the next one down, as long as the vast majority of readers agree on the ranking, she can end up earning 10 times as much.

The same thing happens in markets for athletes, rock concerts, action movies, and news broadcasts. In all these cases, where mass media technology enables a service to be sold to millions of people and where there is wide agreement about ranking the best, the differences in rewards can be vastly disproportionate to differences in ability. The owner of the Texas Rangers was willing to pay Alex Rodriguez $25 million each year because he believed that Rodriguez, as a superstar, would bring in *at least* that much additional revenue each year—from ticket sales, skybox rentals, TV and radio broadcasting fees, concession sales, parking fees, and more.

But the phenomenon applies beyond sports and entertainment markets. Suppose you have a net worth of $100 million, and you are being sued for all of it. And suppose the *best* attorney you could hire has a 90 percent chance of winning your case. The *second best,* who is very close in ability, has an 88 percent chance of success. How much more would you pay to hire the best one? And if the best isn't available, what premium would you pay for the second best, if the third best has an 85 percent chance of success?

With a little thought, you can apply the "economics of superstars" to many types of professions: physicians, political campaign strategists, even college professors. And in the Using the Theory section at the end of this chapter, you'll see that this theory plays some role (but *not* the only role) in explaining the high and growing salaries of top corporate managers.

BARRIERS TO ENTRY

In our imaginary world, which includes perfectly competitive labor markets, there are no barriers to entering any trade or profession. But in the real world, barriers keep would-be entrants out of some labor markets, enabling these markets to continue paying higher wages than otherwise.

For example, in Figure 1, what if all of our imaginary-world assumptions hold, except one: A barrier prevents school teachers from becoming advertising managers, even though the latter earn a higher wage. Going back to our analogy of water in a swimming pool, a barrier to entry is like a wall in the middle of the pool. It blocks the flow, allowing one end to have a higher water level than the other.

Since barriers to entry help maintain high wages for those protected by the barriers (those who already have jobs in the protected market), we should not be surprised to find that in almost all cases, it is those already employed who are responsible for erecting the barriers. But it is not enough to simply put up a sign, "Newcomers, stay out!" The pull of higher wages is a powerful force, and preventing entry requires a force at least as powerful. What keeps newcomers out of a market, thus maintaining a higher-than-competitive wage for those already working there?

Occupational Licensing

In many labor markets, occupational licensing laws keep out potential entrants. Highly paid professionals such as doctors, lawyers, and dentists, as well as those who practice a trade, like barbers, beauticians, and plumbers, cannot legally sell their services without first obtaining a license. In many states you cannot even sell the service of braiding hair without a license. In order to get the license, you must complete a long course in cosmetology and pass an exam. Typically, a licensing board is comprised of people already in the occupation, who are sometimes exempt from new educational requirements.

Barriers like these artificially raise the cost of acquiring human capital, and stop the flow of new workers into a profession before the wage can fall to that in other, similar labor markets. (For a complete list of jobs requiring licenses by state, see *http: www.acinet.org/acinet/licensedoccupations.*)

In some professions, the barrier goes beyond just adding requirements, and actually controls the number who are permitted to enter. For example, to become an attorney, you must pass the bar exam in your state. This is after you've completed law school. Some states, such as California, are suspected of tightly controlling the pass rate in order to restrict competition from new entrants, especially the entry of attorneys with licenses from other states. (California is one of several states with no reciprocity agreement that recognizes other state licenses.)

Union Wage Setting

A labor union represents the collective interests of its members. Unions have many functions, including pressing for better and safer working conditions, operating apprenticeship programs, and administering pension programs. But a major objective of a union is to raise its members' pay. Federal law prohibits a union from creating an overt barrier to entry. Instead, the union creates a barrier *indirectly,* by using its power to negotiate a higher-than-competitive wage that the firm must pay. As we know from the last chapter, at a higher wage, the firm will have a lower profit-maximizing employment level. Thus, many potential workers are kept out of union jobs because the firm will not hire them at the union wage.

Figure 2 illustrates how unions can create wage differences. We assume that jobs in two industries—long-haul trucking and short-haul trucking—are equally attractive in all respects other than the wage rate. With no labor union, these two markets would reach equilibrium at points A and B, respectively, where both pay the same wage, W_1.

Now suppose instead that long-haul truckers are organized into a union, which has negotiated a higher wage, W_2, with employers. At this wage, employment of long-haul truckers drops from 300,000 to 250,000, (point A'), while the number who would like to work in this market rises to 350,000. There is an excess supply of long-haul truckers equal to $350,000 - 250,000 = 100,000$. Ordinarily, we would expect an excess supply of labor to force the wage down, but the union wage agreement prevents this.

With fewer jobs available in the unionized sector, some former long-haul truckers will look for work as *nonunion,* short-haul truckers. Thus, in panel (b), the labor supply curve shifts rightward. In equilibrium, the number of short-haul truckers rises from 200,000 to 225,000, and the wage of short-haul truckers drops to W_3. The end result is a union–nonunion wage differential of $W_2 - W_3$. Notice that only *part* of the differential ($W_2 - W_1$) represents an increase in union wages; the other part ($W_1 - W_3$) comes from a decrease in *nonunion* wages.

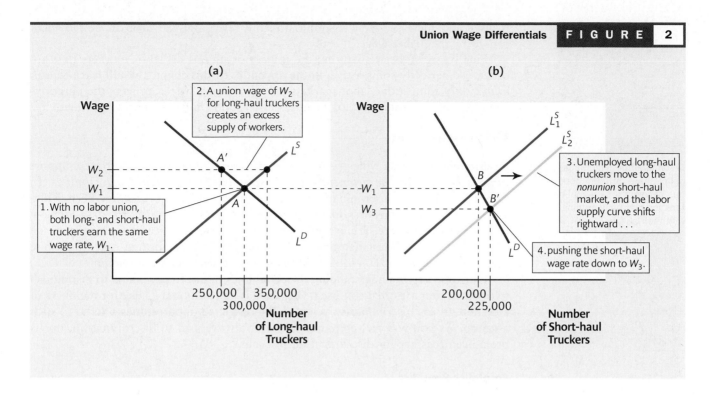

Union Wage Differentials | **FIGURE** | **2**

(a)

Wage

2. A union wage of W_2 for long-haul truckers creates an excess supply of workers.

L^S

A'

W_2

W_1

A

1. With no labor union, both long- and short-haul truckers earn the same wage rate, W_1.

L^D

250,000   350,000
300,000
Number of Long-haul Truckers

(b)

Wage

L^S_1

L^S_2

B

W_1

B'

W_3

3. Unemployed long-haul truckers move to the *nonunion* short-haul market, and the labor supply curve shifts rightward . . .

L^D

4. pushing the short-haul wage rate down to W_3.

200,000
225,000
Number of Short-haul Truckers

In a competitive labor market, a union—by raising the wage firms must pay—decreases total employment in the union sector. This, in turn, causes wages in the nonunion sector to drop. The combined result is a wage differential between union and nonunion wages.

Two decades ago, when unions were a more powerful force in U.S. labor markets, the union wage differential was an important subject of study. But in recent decades, unions' bargaining power has been significantly weakened. One reason is the economy's increasing openness to international trade in goods and capital. If a union wage rate is set too high, U.S. firms can shift (or threaten to shift) production overseas. (Union agreements specify the wage rate the firm must pay for American workers only.)

Second, union membership in the United States has dwindled. In the mid-1950s, about 25 percent of the total U.S. labor force was unionized. Today, the comparable figure is less than 11 percent. Nevertheless, unions still maintain a significant presence in many industries, such as automobiles, steel, coal, construction, mining, trucking, and the government sector. They have certainly been responsible for at least *some* of the higher wages earned in those industries.

Of course, we're viewing unions here from one perspective only: to explain how wage differences can arise. The full effect of unions on labor markets is much more complex. For example, many of the features of modern work that we take for granted today—such as paid vacations and overtime pay—originated in union struggles with management.

Moreover, through grievance procedures and other forms of communications with management, unions may raise worker morale and reduce labor turnover. If this results in a higher marginal product of labor, the demand for labor by unionized firms could increase, reducing (and possibly reversing) the drop in employment caused by the higher wage.

Finally, we've been analyzing the impact of unions on labor markets that are otherwise perfectly competitive. In the appendix to this chapter, you'll learn that in *imperfectly* competitive labor markets, a higher union wage can have the paradoxical effect of *increasing* employment—even with no change in worker productivity.

DISCRIMINATION

Discrimination When a group of people have different opportunities because of personal characteristics that have nothing to do with their abilities.

Discrimination occurs when *the members of a group of people have different opportunities because of characteristics that have nothing to do with their abilities.* In recent U.S. history, discrimination against women and minorities has been widespread in housing, business loans, consumer services, and jobs. The last arena—jobs—is our focus here. While tough laws and government incentive programs have lessened overt job discrimination—such as the help wanted ads that asked for white males as late as the 1950s—less obvious forms of discrimination remain.

Our first step in understanding the economics of discrimination is to distinguish two words that are often confused. *Prejudice* is an emotional dislike for members of a certain group; *discrimination* refers to the restricted opportunities offered to such a group. As you will see, prejudice does not always lead to discrimination, nor is prejudice necessary for discrimination to occur.

Employer Prejudice

When you think of job discrimination, your first image might be a manager who refuses to hire members of some group, such as African-Americans or women, because of pure prejudice. As a result, the victims of prejudice, prevented from working at high-paying jobs, must accept lower wages elsewhere. No doubt, many employers hire according to their personal prejudices. But it may surprise you to learn that economists generally consider employer prejudice one of the *least* important sources of labor market discrimination.

To see why, look at Figure 3, which shows the labor market divided into two broad sectors, A and B. To keep things simple, we'll assume that all workers have the same qualifications and that they find jobs in either sector equally attractive. Under these conditions, if there were *no* discrimination, both sectors would pay the same wage, W_1.

Now suppose the firms in sector A decide they no longer wish to employ members of some group—say, women. What would happen? Women would begin looking for jobs in the *nondiscriminating* sector B, and the labor supply curve there would shift rightward. The equilibrium would move from F to F', decreasing the wage to W_2. At the same time, with women no longer welcome in sector A, the labor supply curve there would shift leftward, moving the market from E to E' and driving the wage up to W_3. It appears that employer discrimination would create a gender wage differential equal to $W_3 - W_2$.

But the differential would be only temporary. Why? With the wage rate in sector B now lower, *men* would exit that market and seek jobs in the higher-paying sector A. These movements would reverse the changes in labor supply, and, in the end, both sectors would pay the same wage again. Employer prejudice against women might lead to a permanent change in the *composition* of labor in each sector—with only men working in sector A and both sexes working in sector B—but *no change in wage rates*.

But employer prejudice might not even change the composition of labor as described, because another force tends to eliminate this form of discrimination

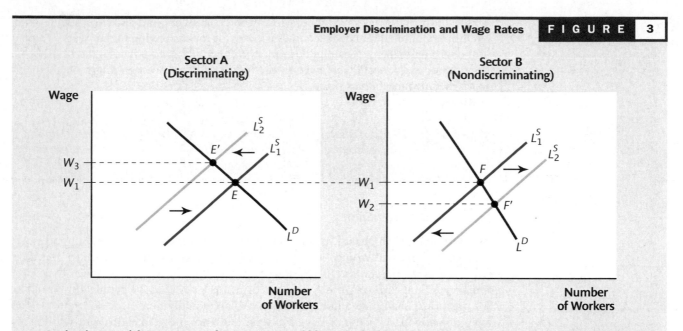

Employer Discrimination and Wage Rates   FIGURE 3

Sector A
(Discriminating)

Sector B
(Nondiscriminating)

In the absence of discrimination, the wage rate would be W_1 in both sector A and sector B. If firms in sector A discriminate against some group—such as women—the group would seek work in the nondiscriminating sector, B. The increased labor supply in sector B causes the wage there to fall to W_2, while the decreased supply in sector A causes the wage there to rise to W_3. But only temporarily if the discrimination results from employer prejudice. As men migrate from sector B to the now higher wage sector A, the labor supply changes in both sectors are reversed. The wage returns to W_1 in both sectors.

altogether: the product market. Since biased employers must initially pay higher wages to employ men, they will have higher average costs than unbiased employers. If biased firms sell their product in a competitive market, they will suffer losses and ultimately be forced to exit their industries. Over the long run, prejudiced employers should be replaced with unprejudiced ones. Even if the product market is imperfectly competitive, the firm will still have its stockholders or owners to contend with. Unless *their* prejudice is so strong that they are willing to forego profit, management will be under pressure to hire qualified women rather than pay a premium to hire men. In either case,

> *when prejudice originates with employers, competitive labor markets work to discourage discrimination and reduce or eliminate any wage gap between the favored and the unfavored group.*

Employee and Customer Prejudice

What if *workers*, rather than employers, are prejudiced? Then our conclusions can be very different. If, for example, a significant number of male assembly-line workers dislike supervision by women, then the nonprejudiced employer would face an unpleasant choice: (1) *Don't* hire female supervisors, (2) hire them in spite of prejudiced assembly-line workers, or (3) hire only *non*prejudiced assembly-line workers. Choices (2) and (3) could be costly for the firm, perhaps more costly than paying more to hire male supervisors. If so, a firm that makes choices (2) or (3) might be unable to compete with other firms in the industry that make choice (1). So in the case of employee prejudice, we cannot count on the market to solve the problem.

The same argument applies if the prejudice originates with the firm's *customers*. For example, if many automobile owners distrust female mechanics, then an auto repair shop that hires them would lose some customers and sacrifice profit. True, excluding qualified female mechanics is costly; it means paying higher wages to men and charging higher prices. But customers will be willing to *pay* a higher price, since they prefer male mechanics. Even in the long run, then, women might be excluded from the auto mechanics trade.

More generally,

> *when prejudice originates with the firm's employees or its customers, market forces may encourage, rather than discourage, discrimination and can lead to a permanent wage gap between the favored and unfavored groups.*

Statistical Discrimination

Suppose you are in charge of hiring 10 new employees at your firm. Suppose, too, that young, married women in your industry are twice as likely as men to quit their jobs within two years (say, because women are more likely to quit when they have children). Quits are very costly to your firm. Let's say that 20 people apply for the 10 positions—half men and half women. All are equally qualified, and you have no way of knowing which *individuals* among them are more likely to quit within two years. Whom will you hire?

If your sole goal is to maximize the firm's profit, you will hire the men. Notice that in this example, there was no mention of prejudice. Indeed, even if there isn't a trace of prejudice in you, in the firm's employees, or in its customers, profit maximization may still dictate hiring the men.

Statistical discrimination When individuals are excluded from an activity based on the statistical probability of behavior in their group, rather than their personal characteristics.

Statistical discrimination—so called because individuals are excluded based on the statistical probability of behavior in their group, rather than their own personal traits—is a case of discrimination without prejudice. It can lead an unbiased profit-maximizing employer to discriminate against an individual member of a group, even though that particular individual might never engage in the feared behavior.

But, as some observers have pointed out, statistical discrimination can also be a cover for prejudice. For example, consider statistical discrimination against women. True, women are more likely to leave work to care for their children. But men are more likely to develop alcohol and drug problems, which can lead to poor judgment and costly accidents on the job. If there were no prejudice, then the risks associated with hiring men would be thrown into the equation. According to critics of the statistical discrimination theory, the negative behavior of a favored group (such as men) is rarely considered by employers.

Discrimination and Wage Differentials

How much have the wages of victimized groups been reduced because of discrimination? As you are about to see, this is a very difficult question to answer.

A starting point—but *only* a starting point—is Table 2, which shows median earnings for different groups of full-time workers in the population. Notice the substantial earnings gap between men and women of either race and between whites and blacks of either sex. Doesn't this prove that the impact of discrimination on wages is substantial? Not necessarily.

Consider the black–white differential for men. In 2006, black men earned 25 percent less than white men, on average. But *some* of this difference is due to differences in education, job experience, job choice, and geographic location between whites and blacks. For example, while 18 percent of black adults have college

	Median Income	Percentage of White Male Income	TABLE 2
White Males	$818	100%	**Median Weekly Earnings, 2006 (Full-time Wage and Salary Workers Over Age 25)**
Black Males	$616	75%	
Hispanic Males	$535	65%	
White Females	$636	78%	
Black Females	$571	70%	
Hispanic Females	$465	57%	

Source: Bureau of Labor Statistics News Release, "*Usual Weekly Earnings,*" April 20, 2006. Data are for first quarter of 2006. (*Note:* Persons of Hispanic origin may be of any race.)

degrees, about 28 percent of white adults do. Even if all firms were completely color-blind in their hiring and wage payments, disproportionately fewer blacks would have higher-paying jobs requiring college degrees, and this would produce an earnings differential in favor of whites. The same would apply if blacks were more likely to live in low-wage areas or, on average, had fewer years of prior experience when applying for jobs.

Several studies suggest that if we limit comparisons to whites and blacks with the same educational background, geographic location, and, in some cases, the same ability (measured by a variety of different tests), 50 percent or more of the earnings difference disappears.[5]

Does this mean that discrimination accounts for half or less of the earnings differential? Not at all: Some of the observed differences in education, geographic location, and ability may be the *result* of job market discrimination.

Figure 4 illustrates this vicious cycle. Let's assume that job discrimination initially causes a wage differential between equally qualified whites and blacks. With a lower wage, blacks have less incentive to remain in the labor force or to invest in human capital, since they reap smaller rewards for these activities. The result is that blacks, on average, have less education and less job experience than whites, and even color-blind employers will hire disproportionately fewer blacks in high-paying jobs, perpetuating their lower wages.

In addition to job market discrimination, there may be *premarket* discrimination—unequal treatment in education and housing—that occurs *before* an individual enters the labor market. For example, regardless of black families' incomes, prior housing discrimination may have excluded them from neighborhoods with better public schools, resulting in fewer blacks being admitted to college. Discriminatory treatment by teachers within a school may contribute to lowered aspirations and diminished job-market expectations. All of these can contribute to the low-wage syndrome.

Similar reasoning applies to the earnings gap between women and men. On the one hand, we have a large earnings gap. In 2006, the earnings of white female workers were 78 percent of those of white men. On the other hand, studies suggest that almost all of this gap is due to differences in skills, experience, or the types of jobs chosen.[6] But differences can *result* from lower wages caused by discrimination. For

[5] See, for example, June O'Neill, "The Role of Human Capital in Earnings Differences between Black and White Men," *Journal of Economic Perspectives*, 1990, pp. 25–45; and Derek A. Neal and William R. Johnson, "The Role of Pre-Market Factors in Black-White Wage Differences," *Journal of Political Economy*, Vol. 104, No. 5, 1996, pp. 869–895.

[6] June O'Neill, "Catching Up: The Gender Gap in Wages, circa 2000," *American Economic Review*, Vol. 93, No. 2, 2003, pp. 309–314.

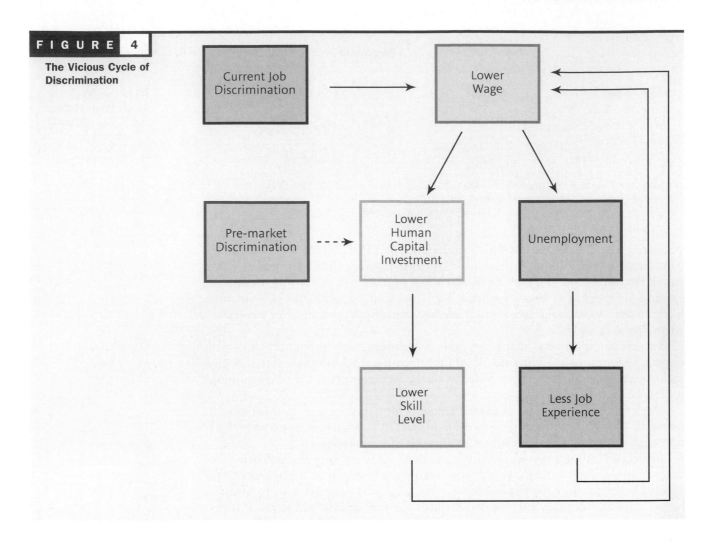

FIGURE 4

The Vicious Cycle of Discrimination

example, if women believe they will earn less than men, or have a harder time being hired in certain jobs, they may have less incentive to invest in human capital or enter certain labor markets.

In the end, we do not know nearly as much about the impact of discrimination on wages as we would like to know. But we do know this:

> *The simple wage gap between two groups tends to* overestimate *the impact of job-market discrimination on earnings, because it fails to account for differences in worker skill, experience, and job choice. However, controlling for these characteristics may* underestimate *the impact of discrimination, since they may in part* result *from discrimination.*

THE MINIMUM WAGE CONTROVERSY

A policy frequently advocated to reduce income inequality, at least at the lower end of the distribution, is an increase in the minimum wage. A minimum wage law makes it illegal to hire a worker for less than a specified wage, in any labor market covered by the law. Many countries have minimum wage laws. In the United States, about 90 percent of the labor force is covered by the federal minimum wage law. Forty-four states have their own minimum wage laws.

The federal minimum wage was first established in the United States in 1938 at 25 cents per hour. Congress has increased it twenty times, and in 2006 the minimum stood at $5.15 per hour. Of course, prices rose during this period. When adjusted for inflation, the purchasing power of the minimum wage reached its peak in 1968. Since then, its purchasing power has fallen more than 40 percent. The decline in purchasing power has led to frequent calls in Congress to raise the federal minimum by as much as 40 percent and caused several states to raise their own minimum wages. In 2006, the highest state minimums were in Washington State ($7.63), Oregon ($7.50), and Vermont ($7.25). San Francisco has its own minimum wage, indexed to inflation, which reached $8.82 in 2006.

To most people, the idea behind a higher minimum wage is simple: It increases the pay of those who earn the least, and therefore helps to reduce economic inequality. But economists—even those who favor raising the minimum wage—regularly point out that the story is *not* that simple.

Who Pays for a Higher Minimum Wage?

A higher minimum wage rate raises average and marginal costs in industries that employ minimum wage labor. The result is a rise in product prices, much as occurs with an excise tax (see Chapter 4). In the short run, the higher prices enable firms to shift some, but not all, of the higher labor costs onto their customers. Thus, in the short run, the cost of the higher minimum wage is paid by both firms and consumers.

In the long run, if product markets are competitive, firms return to zero economic profit—the same situation they were in before the minimum wage was raised. But prices remain higher, to match the higher long-run average costs. Thus, the long-run burden of the minimum wage in competitive industries falls entirely on consumers.

This already suggests something peculiar about using the minimum wage for income redistribution. Instead of redistributing income from the rich to the poor, a higher minimum wage redistributes it from *customers* of minimum-wage paying industries (who may be rich or poor) to minimum wage workers . . . who may or may not be poor, as we discuss in the next section.

Who Benefits from a Higher Minimum Wage?

Anyone trying to support a family with a minimum wage job is certainly poor. At $5.15 per hour, a full-time minimum wage job would pay just $10,712 per year. But economists point out that a higher minimum wage is a rather blunt instrument for helping the poor because it applies to *any* worker earning the minimum, regardless of their economic situation.

According to the Bureau of Labor Statistics,[7] out of 75 million hourly workers, about 1.9 million earn at or below the minimum wage. Of these, about a quarter are between the ages of 16 and 19, and another quarter are between the ages of 20 and 24. Many of these young people (especially teenagers) live at home with families that run the gamut from the poor to middle class to rich. Thus, many who will benefit from

[7] "Characteristics of Minimum Wage Workers: 2005," Bureau of Labor Statistics, *www.bls.gov*.

a higher minimum wage are economically better off than those who pay for it. This makes a higher minimum wage a rather blunt instrument for reducing inequality.

Labor Market Effects of the Minimum Wage

Another problem with raising the minimum wage is that it can harm some of the very workers it is designed to help. To see why, look at Figure 5, which shows three different labor markets:

- the market for unskilled labor that is effectively *covered* by the minimum wage law (the law applies and is followed)
- the market for unskilled labor that is *not* covered (the law doesn't apply[8] or is not effectively enforced, such as in some very small businesses)
- the market for skilled labor

Let's assume that initially, there is *no* minimum wage, and each labor market has reached its long-run equilibrium. The two unskilled labor markets in the first two panels operate at points *A* and *B*, respectively, with an hourly wage of $4. The wage is initially the same in both unskilled markets because, in the absence of a minimum wage law, workers would migrate to whichever market had the higher wage, eliminating any wage difference. In the skilled labor market in panel (c), the wage rate is considerably higher, at $20.

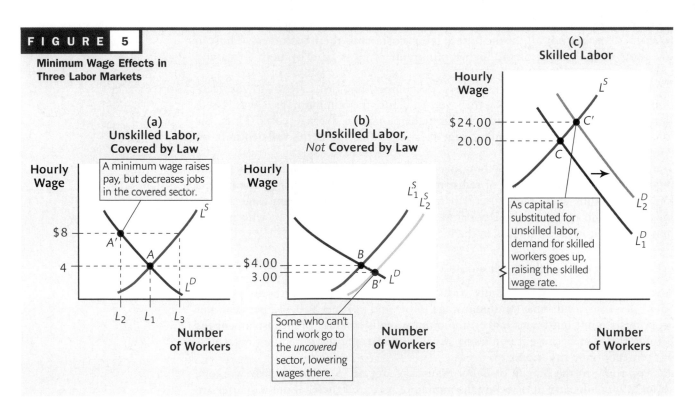

FIGURE 5

Minimum Wage Effects in Three Labor Markets

[8] Those not covered by the federal minimum wage law, or for whom a special, lower wage applies, include seasonal workers, many types of agricultural workers, baby-sitters, newspaper delivery workers, restaurant workers who receive tips, companions for the elderly, those with certain disabilities, and teenagers for the first 90 days on the job.

Now let's introduce a minimum wage of $8 for the *covered* unskilled market in panel (a). The minimum wage, just like any price floor, creates an excess supply in that market. Part of the excess supply comes from the decrease in the quantity of labor demanded (from L_1 to L_2). The other part arises from an increase in the quantity of labor supplied (from L_1 to L_3) because more people seek work in this market at the higher wage. Ordinarily, the excess supply of L_3-L_1 would bring the wage rate down, but the minimum wage law prevents this.

You can already see that the minimum wage benefits some low-skilled workers (those who keep their jobs and are paid more) but harms others (those who lose their jobs). The job losses in panel (a) can be especially harmful to young workers who are not college bound. A good performance at a first job—even a minimum wage job—can enable an unskilled worker to seek higher-wage employment later. This is somewhat analogous to the way college students use unpaid internships—which are not covered by minimum wage law—to beef up their résumés and improve their future employment prospects. By reducing employment for unskilled workers, some young people will be deprived of this chance to build a job history.

But this is not the end of the story.

Some who lose their jobs in the covered sector move to the only labor market where they can find work—the uncovered market in panel (b). There the labor supply curve shifts rightward, from L_1^S to L_2^S. As the new entrants compete for jobs with those already working there, the wage rate falls—to $3 in our example.

Are skilled workers in panel (c) affected by the minimum wage? You might think not because they already earn above the minimum. But remember: As the wage rises in panel (a), and employment falls, firms will be substituting other inputs, such as capital, for unskilled labor. For example, an unskilled product packager might be replaced by a high-tech packaging machine that is produced, operated, and maintained by skilled workers. Substitution like this shifts the labor demand curve in panel (c) rightward, from L_1^D to L_2^D. The skilled wage rate rises—to $24 in our example.

To summarize:

> *A higher minimum wage benefits those unskilled workers who maintain their jobs and are paid more. It also benefits skilled workers by raising their equilibrium wage. But it harms those unskilled workers who cannot find work, and those who work in the uncovered sector, where wages decrease.*

Because this policy is such a blunt instrument for helping low-income people at best, and because it harms some of those it is supposed to help, many economists oppose raising the minimum wage as a strategy to help low-income workers. Instead, they advocate a superior alternative.

The EITC Alternative

An alternative to the minimum wage, which has been very well regarded by economists, is the Earned Income Tax Credit (EITC). Begun in 1975 and expanded several times, the EITC supplements the incomes of low-income working people.

In 2006, the EITC for a low-income worker supporting two children could reach more than $4,000 from the federal government, and often another $1,000 or more from a state EITC. This is in addition to any income earned on the job. Many low-income workers are eligible to receive their EITC payments along with their regular paychecks, rather than waiting until the end of the year when they file their taxes. A series of studies have shown that the EITC has lifted millions of people out of poverty, both directly (through cash payments received), and indirectly (through greater labor force participation and greater labor earnings).[9]

The EITC has several advantages over the minimum wage:

- The minimum wage applies to any unskilled worker in the covered sector, regardless of family income or economic need. The EITC, by contrast, is only available to low-income households and provides greater benefits to those supporting children.
- The costs of the minimum wage are spread among households rather haphazardly, with no regard to income. The funds for the EITC come from a progressive federal tax system, making it genuinely redistributive from higher income to lower income households.
- The minimum wage is likely to reduce employment, but the EITC tends to increase employment.

Why the Controversy?

Given all the problems with the minimum wage and the existence of a superior alternative, you might think that economists overwhelmingly oppose any increase in the minimum wage. But that is generally not the case. Surveys of economists—including those specializing in labor markets—show majorities favor at least some increase in the minimum wage.[10] There are several reasons for this.

First, the employment effects of a small increase in the minimum wage are viewed by some as modest. Most of the employment effects would fall on teenagers, and the consensus view is that a 10 percent increase in the minimum wage (say, from $5.15 to $5.65) would cause total teenage employment to fall by about 2 percent. Some go even further, pointing to research by two prominent labor economists[11] that suggests a rise in the minimum wage causes *no* decrease in employment. The methods of this research have been hotly debated, and its conclusions have not been widely accepted by the profession.[12]

Another reason for supporting a higher minimum wage is political. Funds for expanding the EITC, which come out of general government revenues, are constrained by federal budget discipline. The costs of a higher minimum wage (higher prices for consumers and/or lower earnings for business owners) are nonbudgetary and more easily hidden from view. Thus, even those who would prefer an expanded EITC may believe it is easier to get public support for a higher minimum wage.

---

[9] See, for example, Nada Eissa and Jeffrey B. Liebman, "Labor Supply Response to the Earned Income Tax Credit," *Quarterly Journal of Economics*, Vol. 112, No. 2, 1996, pp. 605–637; and Bruce D. Meyer and Dan T. Rosenbaum, "Welfare, the Earned Income Tax Credit, and the Labor Supply of Single Mothers," *Quarterly Journal of Economics*, Vol. 116, No. 3, 2001, pp. 1063–2014.

[10] See, for example, Robert Whaples, "Is There Consensus Among American Labor Economists," *Journal of Labor Research*, Vol. XVII, No. 4, 1996, pp. 730–731; and Victor R. Fuchs, Alan B. Krueger, and James M. Porterba, "Economists' Views about Parameters, Values and Policies: Survey Results in Labor and Public Economics," *The Journal of Economic Literature*, Vol. 36, No. 3, 1998, pp. 1387–1425.

[11] David Card and Alan B. Krueger, *Myth and Measurement: The New Economics of the Minimum Wage* (Princeton, NJ: Princeton University Press, 1995).

[12] In a 2000 survey of members of the American Economic Association, 73.5 percent agreed (or agreed with provisos) with the following statement: "Minimum wages increase unemployment among young and unskilled workers." (Dan Fuller and Doris Geide-Stevenson, "Consensus Among Economists: Revisited," *Journal of Economic Education*, Vol. 34, 2003, pp. 369–387.)

INCOME INEQUALITY

Wage differentials among households are an important cause of income inequality, but not the only cause. Two people with identical *hourly* wage rates may have vastly different wage or salary *incomes* because one is unemployed more often than the other or because one works more hours each week than the other.

Moreover, wages and salaries are not the only source of income. Some households supply capital or entrepreneurship (earning interest income or profit) or land (earning rental income). These forms of income are often called *nonlabor income* or **property income,** to distinguish them from the wage and salary income derived from labor alone. Some of the largest incomes—such as Bill Gates's—are mostly property income. Many households also receive **transfer payments** from the government, such as Social Security, unemployment insurance, or welfare payments.

When we discuss income inequality, we are ultimately concerned about inequality in *total* income, regardless of source.

Property income Income derived from supplying capital, entrepreneurship, land, or natural resources.

Transfer payment Any payment that is not compensation for supplying goods, services, or resources.

MEASURING INCOME INEQUALITY

How much income inequality is there in the United States? Although there are many measures of income inequality, they all leave much to be desired. Here, we consider two commonly cited measures.

The Poverty Rate

The **poverty rate** tells us the percentage of families whose incomes fall below a certain minimum, called the **poverty line** or poverty threshold. The poverty line was first determined in 1964. That year, the government estimated the cost of feeding families of different types (number of children, rural versus urban, etc.). The government then assumed that a family needed at least twice its basic food budget to pay for *other* necessities like housing, clothing, and transportation. So the poverty threshold for each type of family was roughly triple its basic food budget.

For subsequent years the threshold has been increased by the rate of inflation. In 2005 the poverty threshold for a single person under 65 was an annual income of $10,160. For a family of two with no children, it was $13,145, and for a couple with two children, $19,971.

Finally, the poverty rate is then defined as the percentage of U.S. people who fall below their respective poverty lines, given their family status. In 2005 the official U.S. poverty rate was 12.6 percent, telling us that 126 out of every 1,000 people fell below the poverty line defined for their characteristics. During the past two decades, the poverty rate hovered around 13 percent until the late 1990s, when it fell rapidly toward 11 percent. It rose again in the early 2000s, partly due to the recession of 2001 and the slow recovery afterward.

Poverty rates are important because they keep policy makers and the public aware of conditions at the bottom of the economic ladder. Of particular concern is the unequal *distribution* of poverty among different groups in the population. As you can see in Table 3, the poverty rate for blacks and Hispanics has remained stubbornly above that for white families.

The poverty rate gives us important information about the poorest families and how poverty is distributed among different groups within society. As a measure of income inequality, however, the poverty rate suffers from some serious drawbacks.

Poverty rate The percentage of families whose incomes fall below a certain minimum—the poverty line.

Poverty line The income level below which a family is considered to be in poverty.

TABLE 3	Year	All People	White	Black	Hispanic
U.S. Poverty Rates for Different Groups	1980	13.0%	9.1%	32.5%	25.7%
	1990	13.5%	8.8%	31.9%	28.1%
	2000	11.3%	7.4%	22.5%	21.5%
	2001	11.7%	7.8%	22.7%	21.4%
	2002	12.1%	8.0%	23.9%	21.8%
	2003	12.5%	8.2%	24.3%	22.5%
	2004	12.7%	8.7%	24.7%	21.9%
	2005	12.6%	8.3%	24.7%	21.8%

Source: U.S. Census Bureau (*http://www.census.gov*), "Historical Poverty Tables" Table 2; and Poverty 2004, Table 1. Poverty rates are for individuals; data for white excludes Hispanic.

First, poverty is very sensitive to how income is defined. The official poverty rate ignores the income-lowering effect of taxes, including the Social Security taxes paid by many low-income working people. But it also ignores the income-raising effect of a variety of government benefits for the poor, such as food stamps, Medicaid, rent subsidies, and cash. The government publishes alternative measures of poverty that account for these and other factors, but they are somewhat controversial. Depending on the adjustment method used, the poverty rate in 2003—officially 12.5 percent—could instead have been as low as 7.4 percent or as high as 14.5 percent.[13]

A second problem is that *changes* in the poverty rate may not tell us what we think they do. When the poverty rate rises, we immediately imagine that a greater fraction of the population has *fallen* into poverty. And this may very well describe what is happening. But the poverty rate could also rise because more poor people have come into the country. Some economists believe that greater immigration—especially from Mexico—has played an important role in the rise in poverty during the 2000s. (Both legal and illegal immigrants are covered in the poverty survey.)

Finally, even if all the problems of definition and measurement were fixed, the poverty rate—as a measure of income inequality—has another problem: It ignores inequality among those *above* the poverty line. For a more comprehensive picture of inequality, we must turn to other measures, such as the one introduced in the next section.

The Lorenz Curve and the Gini Coefficient

Table 4 provides data that we can use to measure inequality across the entire spectrum of the income distribution. The table shows the percentage of total income earned by each fifth of the population, when households are arranged by their incomes from lowest to highest. For example, the row labeled 2004 shows us that in 2004, the 20 percent of households with the lowest incomes (the lowest fifth) earned only 3.4 percent of total income earned by all households. The last row of the table shows the household income range for each income group during 2004.

---

[13] The higher figure involves the fullest adjustment recommended by the National Academy of Sciences. See U.S. Census Bureau, "Alternative Measures of Poverty Estimates in the United States: 2003," June 2005, Tables 1 and 3.

Percent of Total Household Income Earned by Each Fifth of U.S. Households					TABLE 4
	Lowest Fifth	Second Fifth	Third Fifth	Fourth Fifth	Highest Fifth	Gini Coefficient
1970	4.1%	10.8%	17.4%	24.5%	43.3%	.394
1980	4.3%	10.3%	16.9%	24.9%	43.7%	.403
1990	3.9%	9.6%	15.9%	24.0%	46.6%	.428
2000	3.6%	8.9%	14.8%	23.0%	49.6%	.462
2004	3.4%	8.7%	14.7%	23.2%	50.1%	.466
Annual Income, 2004	$0 to $18,500	$18,501 to $34,738	$34,739 to $55,325	$55,326 to $88,029	>$88,029	

Source: U.S. Census Bureau Historical Income Tables, Households, Tables H1, H2 and H4 (*http://www.census.gov*). Significant definitional and methodological changes instituted in 1993 caused some of the rise in measured inequality between 1990 and 2000.

For example, a household that earned $50,000 in income in 2004 would be part of the *third* fifth, falling within the $34,739 to $55,325 range.

If all households had earned identical incomes in a year, then the bottom fifth, and every fifth, would have earned exactly 20 percent of the total income that year. The first five entries would each be 20 percent. But notice the high degree of *in*equality, especially at the high and low ends. The bottom fifth earn far less than 20 percent of the total, and the top fifth earn far more—greater than twice their population proportion.

Now look at Figure 6. The horizontal axis measures the cumulative percentages of total households, and the vertical axis measures the cumulative percentage of total income. For example, in 2004, the bottom 20 percent of households earned 3.4 percent of the total income, and the next 20 percent earned 8.7 percent, so the bottom 40 percent earned 3.4 percent + 8.7 percent = 12.1 percent of total income. Thus, one of the points in the figure is 40 percent on the horizontal axis and 12.1 percent on the vertical. The curve drawn through all the points obtained in this way is called the **Lorenz curve.**

If all households earned the same income, the Lorenz curve would be the thick straight line with a slope of 1 (marked "Line of Complete Equality"), since the bottom 20 percent would earn 20 percent of the total, the bottom 40 percent would earn 40 percent, and so on, until we reached 100 percent of all households, which—by definition—always earn 100 percent of the income. By contrast, the Lorenz curve in an economy with inequality will always be bowed out in the middle, although it will start and end at the same points as the line of complete equality. This gives us a visual representation of income inequality: The more bowed out the Lorenz curve—or the greater the area marked *A* in the figure—the greater will be the degree of inequality.

One numerical measure of income inequality, the **Gini coefficient,** is obtained from the Lorenz curve in a very simple way: We divide area *A* in Figure 6 by the total area underneath the diagonal (area *A* plus area *B*). The more unequal the income distribution, the larger will be area *A* relative to area *A* + *B*, and the larger will be the Gini coefficient. If there were complete income equality—where everyone earned the same income—then area *A* would equal zero, so the Gini coefficient, *A*/(*A* + *B*), would equal zero as well. The highest degree of inequality—where one person earned all the income, and the rest earned none—would give a Gini coefficient of 1.0. (Prove this to yourself by drawing the Lorenz curve for this case.)

Lorenz curve When households are arrayed according to their incomes, a line showing the cumulative percent of income received by each cumulative percent of households.

Gini coefficient A measure of income inequality; the ratio of the area above a Lorenz curve and under the complete equality line to the area under the diagonal.

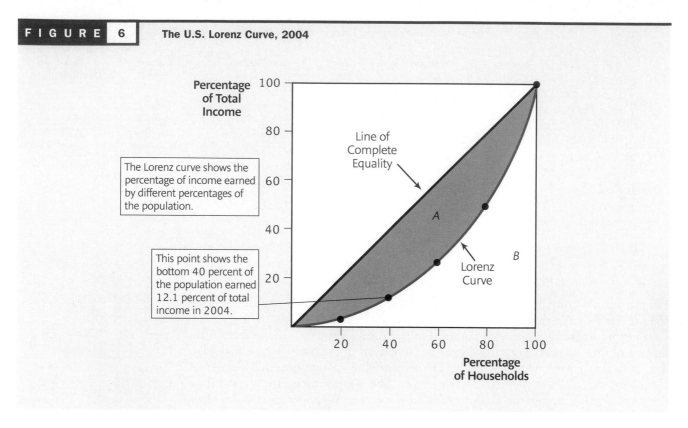

FIGURE 6   The U.S. Lorenz Curve, 2004

Percentage of Total Income

The Lorenz curve shows the percentage of income earned by different percentages of the population.

This point shows the bottom 40 percent of the population earned 12.1 percent of total income in 2004.

Line of Complete Equality

Lorenz Curve

Percentage of Households

In general:

> *The larger the Gini coefficient—up to a maximum of 1.0—the greater is the degree of income inequality.*

The last column in Table 4 shows Gini coefficients for different years. For example, in 2004, the Gini coefficient was 0.466.

Taxes and Inequality

The household incomes used to plot the Lorenz curve and obtain the Gini ratio are *pretax* incomes. Even though it is useful to measure inequality this way—to keep track of how the economy is distributing the rewards from economic activity—it is *after-tax* income that matters for economic well-being.

Progressive income tax A tax that collects a higher percentage of total income from higher income households.

How do taxes affect the distribution of income? That depends. A **progressive tax,** such as the U.S. federal income tax, collects a greater *percentage* of income from higher income households than from lower income households. In theory, such a tax helps to equalize the (after-tax) income distribution. While not all federal taxes are progressive, research has shown that the direct and indirect impact of *all* federal taxes, taken together, is indeed progressive. For example, in 2003, the federal tax system reduced the bottom quintile's income by 4.8 percent, but it reduced the top quintile's income by 25 percent.[14]

---

[14] "Historical Effective Tax Rates: 1979–2003," Congressional Budget Office, December 2005, Table 1A. The effect of the tax system on income quintiles is from the same source, Table 1C.

Even so, it turns out that federal taxes have little impact on the overall distribution of income and the Lorenz curve. For example, when we adjust for the impact of the federal tax system, it adds only about 1 percentage point to the shares of *each* of the lowest three quintiles. This difference would be hardly noticeable in Figure 6. Including the impact of state and local taxes would be more complicated, but it would not change our conclusion: The tax system, as a whole, has little impact on the overall picture of income inequality in the United States.

In many other developed countries—such as France, the United Kingdom, Germany, and Sweden—a greater share of income is taken in taxes, and the tax system is more progressive than in the United States.[15] For these countries, the after-tax Lorenz curve differs more sharply from the pretax Lorenz curve.

INCOME AND WEALTH

The first half of this chapter discussed one reason why income is distributed unequally: the vastly different wage rates paid to different workers for an hour of labor. But another cause of income inequality is *wealth* inequality.

A household's *wealth* or *net worth* is the total value of all the assets it owns—including real estate, stocks, bonds, and bank accounts—minus the value of its debts. A household that owns more than it owes has positive wealth, and will have negative wealth if it owes more than it owns.

Table 5 shows the percentage of total household net worth in the United States owned by various percentages of the population in four different years. Other than a rise in the share of wealth owned by the wealthiest 400 households, there are no strong trends in wealth inequality over time. But there is still something striking in the table: Wealth is distributed with an astonishing degree of inequality. In 2004, the bottom half of the population (0 to 50th percentile) held just 2.5 percent of total wealth, while the top 1 percent (99th to 100th percentile) held a third of the total.

This can be seen even more starkly in Figure 7, which plots a Lorenz curve for wealth in 2004 along with the Lorenz curve for income in that year. You can see that the Lorenz curve for wealth is substantially more bowed out than that for income, reflecting considerably more inequality in the distribution of wealth.

Wealth inequality is related to income inequality. First, greater wealth leads to greater income. If you own an apartment building, mini-mall, or office tower, you'll

	0 to 50th Percentile	50th to 90th Percentile	90th to 95th Percentile	95th to 99th Percentile	99th to 100th Percentile	Richest 400 People
1989	3.0%	29.9%	13.0%	24.1%	30.1%	1.5%
1995	3.6%	28.6%	11.9%	21.3%	34.6%	1.7%
2001	2.8%	27.4%	12.1%	25.0%	32.7%	2.2%
2004	2.5%	27.9%	12.0%	24.1%	33.4%	2.0%

TABLE 5

Percent of Total Household Net Worth Owned by Fractions of U.S. Households

Source: Arthur B. Kennickell, "Currents and Undercurrents: Changes in the Distribution of Wealth, 1989–2004," Survey of Consumer Finances, Federal Reserve Board, January 30, 2006.

[15] See, for example, Alberto Alesina, Edward L. Glaeser, and Bruce Sacerdote, "Why Doesn't the U.S. Have a European-Style Welfare State?" Working Paper No. 8524, National Bureau of Economic Research, October 2001.

FIGURE 7

U.S. Lorenz Curves for Income and Wealth, 2004
The Lorenz curve shows even greater inequality in wealth distribution than in income distribution.

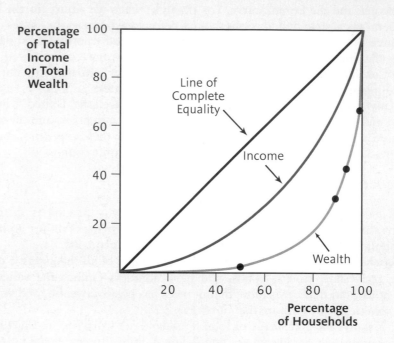

receive periodic income in the form of rent. If you own shares of stock in a corporation, you will receive a share of the firm's profit; if you own bonds, you will receive interest payments. Inequality in the distribution of wealth thus contributes to income inequality.

But the causation also runs the other way: Those with the lowest incomes are the least able to save, which is one way a family can build up its wealth. Thus, income inequality contributes to wealth inequality.

Wealth inequality is important for other reasons as well. Wealth provides financial and psychological security beyond its contribution to income. It allows one to pass economic advantage to one's heirs. And it can be a source of political influence—even a source of funds to run for president, as Steve Forbes did in 1996 and again in 2000. Therefore, wealth inequality raises issues that go far beyond income inequality.

GROWING INCOME INEQUALITY

Look at the last column of Table 4, which shows how the Gini coefficient for income has changed from 1970 to 2004. There is a clear trend upward, suggesting an increase in inequality. The other columns tell us where we should look to explain this trend. In each quintile (except the top one), the share of income has trended downward. But in the top quintile, there has been a noticeable rise.

But the full story is revealed in Table 6, which shows what has been happening *within* the highest quintile.[16] Look first at the column labeled "Top 10 Percent,"

---

[16] Table 6 is not strictly comparable to Table 4. The IRS data in Table 6 are based on tax-paying units, rather than households, with imputations for those who did not file returns. Also, Table 6 excludes capital gains and losses from income. (At the very top, capital gains and losses can be large, one-time events that would obscure the changing picture of regular earnings.)

	Top 10 Percent	Top 1 Percent	Top 0.1 Percent	Top 0.01 Percent	**TABLE 6**
					Income Shares at the Very Top, 1970–2004
1970	31.5%	7.8%	1.9%	0.5%	
1980	32.9%	8.2%	2.2%	0.7%	
1990	38.8%	13.0%	4.9%	1.8%	
2000	43.1%	16.5%	7.1%	2.8%	
2001	42.2%	15.4%	6.3%	2.4%	
2002	41.7%	14.6%	5.8%	2.2%	
2003	42.0%	14.9%	6.0%	2.4%	
2004	42.9%	16.2%	7.0%	2.9%	
Annual income, 2004	> $92,315	> $276,945	> $1,128,525	> $5,019,015	

Source: Emmanuel Saez, Professor of Economics at University of California at Berkeley (posted at *http://elsa.berkeley.edu/~saez/TabFig2004prel.xls*), Table A1.

which gives the share of total income earned by those in the top tenth of the income distribution. Over the last few decades, this group saw its share rise from 31.5 percent to 42.9 percent of the total—a rise of about 11 percentage points. The next column (the Top 1 Percent) shows us that most of the gains of the top 10 percent actually went to the top tenth of that group, whose share rose from 7.8 percent to 16.2 percent.

But let's keep going. More than half of the gains of the top 1 percent went to the top tenth within *that* group: the top 0.1 percent of earners. Finally, the last column shows that, within the top 0.1 percent, about half of the gains went to those at the very, very top: the top 0.01 percent (one-out-of-ten-thousand) whose earnings exceeded $5 million in 2004 (shown in the last row).

The picture being painted is this:

Virtually all of the rise in income inequality over the last several decades has occurred at the high end of the income distribution. And the higher one goes, the more disproportionate the gains in income.

Keep in mind that these are *shares* of total income. A rising share for those at the top does *not necessarily* mean a fall in any other group's income, as long as the total is growing as well. And the total *did* grow. Moreover, for most of this period (except the last few years), inflation-adjusted earnings grew for *every* quintile of households. But much of the total growth went to those at the very top, and growth for everyone else was very slow. Recent research by Ian Dew-Becker and Robert J. Gordon[17] describes this in a rather startling way: For the 35 years from 1966 to 2001, half of the total *gain* in U.S. total income went to those in the top 10 percent of the income distribution. And these trends became stronger in the 1990s and early 2000s.

Among other, similarly developed countries in the EU, there has been no such trend toward greater inequality. The one exception is the United Kingdom, where—although inequality is increasing—it has not approached U.S. levels.[18]

[17] Ian Dew-Becker and Robert J. Gordon, "Where Did the Productivity Growth Go? Inflation Dynamics and the Distribution of Income," NBER Working Paper No. 11842, December 2005.
[18] See the data posted by Emmanuel Saez at *http://elsa.berkeley.edu/~saez/TabFig2004prel.xls*), Figure 12. Also, John Weeks, "Inequality Trends in Some Developed OECD Countries," Department of Economic and Social Affairs Working Paper No. 6, United Nations, October 2005.

What is responsible for this dramatic increase in inequality in the United States?

Dew-Becker and Gordon consider, and reject, several possibilities. One is wealth. Although it is true that wealth inequality creates significant income inequality in any given year, it appears *not* to be the cause of any *growth* in inequality over the past few decades. In fact, the rise in inequality remains pretty much the same if we limit our view to income earned from labor.[19]

The authors argue that there are two primary causes for rising inequality at the top. One is the rapid growth in the pay of CEOs and other top managers of large corporations. We'll discuss this further in the Using the Theory section of this chapter.

The other cause for rising U.S. inequality at the top is an increase in the earning power of superstars, discussed earlier in this chapter. In particular, technological changes involving CDs, cable television, and downloadable files on the Internet have further widened the audiences for the best in sports and entertainment. This has increased the rewards to those at the very top, at the expense of those further down.

As for why this trend is stronger in the United States than other countries, we can only speculate. Is it because U.S. superstars have a wider home market to start with, and broader global reach, than their counterparts in other countries? Or are huge superstar incomes more culturally acceptable in the United States than in Europe, where egalitarian sentiment and the potential for envy seem to be stronger? Or something else? The answers will have to await further research.

EVALUATING ECONOMIC INEQUALITY

Is income inequality a bad thing? That depends. For most of this chapter, we've tried to be mostly descriptive, avoiding value judgments about the words *equality* and *inequality*. But ask yourself: As you've been reading, have you made the implicit judgment that inequality is bad, while equality is good? Many people (but few economists) automatically react in this way. They confuse *equality*, which means that everyone gets the same result, with *equity*, which implies fair and equal treatment.

But how could inequality ever be considered equitable?

THE ISSUE OF MOBILITY

Most of us would agree that to the extent that income inequality is a problem, it is *lifetime income inequality* that we should be concerned about. But all of our inequality measurements give us a snapshot of the income distribution, rather than a moving picture of income over a lifetime. These snapshots tell us that, year after year, the bottom 20 percent of households always have 3 to 4 percent of the total income. That means one thing if, year after year, the bottom is always the same households. But it means something else entirely if it's a different set of households each year.

The United States has a relatively mobile society: people switch careers, change jobs, and start new businesses more often than in most other countries. These changes, as well as pure chance, will give people good years and bad years. If many

---

[19] Another rejected explanation is the college wage premium in high-skilled jobs. This can explain a considerable part of any given year's income inequality, but not the recent *growth* in inequality. They also reject explanations that pertain to the very bottom—such as immigration of less skilled workers or decreases in the inflation-adjusted minimum wage.

of those at the bottom or top are there only temporarily, then over a longer time horizon, there is less inequality than our measures suggest.

Moreover, one's own income tends to change in a predictable pattern over one's lifetime. Most workers start out earning low incomes, which then rise as they acquire more skills and experience, and, finally, fall sharply in retirement. This, too, can distort our measures of income inequality.

To take an extreme example, imagine an economy that always has just five workers, each of whom passes through the same five phases of income over their lives: $40,000 per year in the first decade, $60,000 in the second decade, $80,000 in the third, $100,000 in the fourth, and then $20,000 in the decade of retirement. Suppose, too, that at any point in time, one worker is in each phase. Then total yearly income in the economy will be $20,000 + $40,000 + $60,000 + $80,000 + $100,000 = $300,000. Each year, the bottom fifth (the retired worker) would earn just $20,000/$300,000 = 0.066 of total income. The top fifth (the worker at the height of her earning power) would have $100,000/$300,000 = 0.333 of total income. Even though everyone would have an identical income profile over his or her lifetime—total equality of *lifetime earnings*—the Lorenz curve would show substantial inequality.

Economists are very interested in income mobility, and have done some research that tracks the same set of households over time, to see how their position changes. One typical study[20] found that about half of the households that were in the bottom fifth of the income distribution in 1988 had escaped to other, higher quintiles by 1998. And about half of the households that started in the top fifth in 1988 had moved down to other quintiles by 1998. This suggests a significant degree of U.S. income mobility, and that incomes are more equally distributed over lifetimes than they are in any given year.

On the other hand, with a slight rephrasing ("fully half of the households that started in the bottom or top fifth were still in the same quintile ten years later"), the same data suggest a significant degree of *im*mobility. While looking at a longer period reduces inequality, it doesn't make it go away.

Studies of income mobility suggest that our snapshot measures of income distribution exaggerate lifetime income inequality among the population. However, a significant fraction of the population seems to be rather immobile—stuck at the bottom or enjoying the benefits of the top, year after year.

Earlier, you saw that our snapshot measures show an increase in income inequality over recent decades. But has the income distribution also become less *mobile* over this time period? The evidence is mixed. Some studies suggest that, in recent decades, long-term income in the United States has become slightly less mobile and more unequally distributed,[21] while other studies show no such trend.[22]

---

[20] Katherine Bradbury and Jane Katz, "Are Lifetime Incomes Growing More Unequal?" *Regional Review,* Federal Reserve Bank of Boston, Fourth Quarter 2002.

[21] See, for example, Audra Bowlus and Jean-Marc Robin, "Twenty Years of Rising Inequality in U.S. Lifetime Labor Income Values," *Review of Economic Studies*, Vol. 71, No. 3, 2004, pp. 709–742.

[22] See, for example, Gary Solon and Chul-In Lee, "Trends in Intergenerational Income Mobility," University of Michigan mimeo, October 2004.

Economic Inequality and Fairness

Fairness is difficult to define, in large part because we all have such different ideas about what it is. Witness the conflicts—which often come to blows—among kids at play, where the accusation "That's not fair" is invariably answered with "Yes, it is." Or think about the conflicts over marital property in divorce proceedings, over business property in the dissolution of a partnership, or over the grades given by teachers. In all of these cases, highly emotional disputes center on entirely different definitions of fair.

Since the controversy over fairness is based on conflicting values, can economics contribute to this debate? To some degree, yes.

First, despite the controversy, there are *some* issues of fairness on which almost everyone agrees. By identifying the different causes of income inequality—as we've done in this chapter—we can at least pinpoint those types of inequality that almost all of us would regard as fair and those we would regard as unfair. This is no small accomplishment, and it can help us avoid policies that would, when properly understood, actually make the distribution of income more *unfair*.

For example, almost everyone would agree that income inequality due solely to compensating wage differentials is entirely fair. If one worker must put up with longer hours, a greater risk of death, more unpleasant weather, a greater risk of unemployment, or more years of schooling than another, it is only fair that he or she be paid more. Thus, eliminating compensating wage differentials, which would make incomes more *equal*, would also make them less *fair* to most of us.

The same holds for some of the inequality in property income. Remember the fable of the grasshopper, who fiddled all day, and the ant, who prepared for winter? Although many well-to-do Americans have inherited their wealth, many others have acquired theirs through years of working long hours, saving, or bearing risk. If some of us could have chosen to make these sacrifices, but did not, is it really fair for all of us to have the same wealth? Is it fair for the grasshopper to end up as wealthy as the ant? Most of us would say no.

These observations suggest some *limited* common ground:

> *Inequality that results from equal opportunity, but different choices, is generally regarded as fair.*

By showing how labor markets work, and by identifying sources of inequality, economics can help us identify inequality that results from different choices rather than from different opportunities. In this way, it can help resolve *some* issues of fairness.

Unfortunately, that doesn't take us very far. Much of the income inequality—especially at the extremes—seems to originate in different *opportunities*. And here, issues of fairness remain contentious. For example, even if we agree that labor market discrimination is unfair, there is disagreement about the solution. Some favor strong affirmative action programs in schools and workplaces; others believe that the government and courts should intervene only in cases where discrimination is clearly occurring.

There is even more disagreement about inherited wealth. We all know that it creates unequal opportunities—with those born into rich families able to make choices that are unavailable to others. But there are sharp divisions over the appropriate policy response. Some favor very high estate taxes, with most private wealth going to the government at death, in part to help create a more level playing field. Others believe that the freedom to use one's property as one wishes, including passing it on to one's heirs, is a fundamental human right.

Similar disagreements occur over inequality arising from inherited talent, intelligence, beauty, or physical strength that people exploit in superstar markets. Should we do something about their astronomical incomes? Or are these incomes *earned*, fair and square?

Even if we agree that a certain type of inequality should be reduced, there is still the question of how far to reduce it. Most methods of redistributing income come with a cost: a reduction in the total income generated by society as a whole.

Economist Arthur Okun used the metaphor of a "leaky bucket" to describe government programs to redistribute income: "The money must be carried from the rich to the poor in a leaky bucket. Some of it will simply disappear in transit, so the poor will not receive all the money that is taken from the rich."[23] The leakage is not just from the bureaucratic costs of government transfer programs, but also changes in incentives that shrink the total economic pie. For example, raising income tax rates on higher income households will, to some extent, reduce their incentive to work and create output. A higher tax rate on corporate profits will, to some extent, reduce the incentive to invest in new productive capital or form new corporations. Thus, even when we agree that reducing some types of inequality would be fair in theory—a tall order in itself—we have to ask how far we are willing to go. In general, the more equality we try to engineer, the greater the leakage.

One famous effort to form a consensus about fairness was made by John Rawls, a Harvard philosopher.[24] Rawls maintained that we could discover the rules of a fair and just society by imagining that we had to create them *before knowing* whether we'd be born into a wealthy family or a poor one, endowed with great talent, intelligence, or beauty, or with very little of these qualities.

Rawls argued that the rules we would create in this mental experiment should define our standard of justice. One of his most famous conclusions was that—because any of us might end up in the worst of all possible situations—we would all agree to create a society in which the least well-off person was made as well-off as possible. In this view, inequality is justified only when it raises the position of the person at the bottom.

Rawls's ideas were highly controversial. And issues of fairness in a democracy are ultimately decided in the voting booth, by people who *are* already born and already know their relative initial position. This is one reason why issues of economic fairness—such as our judgments about the growing economic inequality of the last few decades, and what should be done about it—will remain controversial. The Using the Theory section that follows looks at one of the biggest recent controversies relating to economic inequality.

[23] Arthur Okun, "Equality versus Efficiency: The Big Tradeoff," Washington, D.C., Brookings Institution, 1975.
[24] John Rawls, *A Theory of Justice* (Cambridge, MA: Harvard University Press, 1972).

USING THE THEORY

Soaring CEO Pay

During the 1990s and the early 2000s, payments to chief executive officers (CEOs) of major U.S. corporations rose dramatically. And they were very high to begin with. From 1980 to 2003 (in 2003 dollars), average annual compensation for a CEO in a top 100 corporation increased from under $4 million to about $20 million.[25] While average pay can be skewed by just a few CEOs with enormous compensation, other measures tell a similar story. For example, in 1995, among 350 large U.S. corporations, the median CEO earned $2.7 million, or about 95 times the pay of the median U.S. worker. By 2005, the median CEO in this group earned $6.8 million, about 179 times the median worker's pay.[26]

Explosive growth in management pay occurred further down the line as well—for CEOs in the top 500 firms, and for the top managers below CEO rank. But it was CEO pay, in particular, that received increasing media attention and fueled a virulent debate during the 1990s and 2000s.

Table 7 illustrates why the issue has caught the public's attention. It lists the 10 corporations with the highest paid CEOs in 2005 (among corporations for which full data was available). Look at the last column, which shows total compensation for the CEO of each company. Four of them earned more than $100 million in 2005, and even the *lowest* paid CEO in the group earned $56 million. In order to find a CEO that earned less than $10 million in 2005, we'd have to extend the list pretty far, to the 142nd highest paid CEO.

Now look at the other columns, which break total compensation into two categories. The numbers in the first category—salary and bonus—are generally high in themselves. But most of the earnings of these CEOs were in the form of *additional compensation*. And almost all of this additional compensation was in the form of *stock options* or *restricted stock grants*.

Stock options give the person who holds them the automatic right to buy shares in the company at a predetermined price, usually the market price of shares on the day the options are awarded. If the share price rises *above* that predetermined price, they can be purchased for less than their current value, giving the buyer an immediate gain in wealth.[27] Most of the additional CEO compensation in the table was in the form of stock options, used by CEOs to purchase stock after its price had risen.

[25] Information in this section on CEO and other executive pay is primarily from three sources: (1) "Special Report: CEO Compensation," *Forbes*, April 20, 2006; (2) Lucian Bebchuk and Yaniv Grinstein, "The Growth of Executive Pay," June 2005, NBER Working Paper No. 11443; and (3) data posted by Emmanuel Saez, Professor of Economics at University of California at Berkeley, at *http://elsa.berkeley.edu/~saez/TabFig2004prel.xls*, especially "Data for Figure 11" (readjusted by authors into 2003 dollars).

[26] "Research on CEO Pay for Business Roundtable," Frederick W. Cook & Co., June 29, 2006 (available at *www.businessroundtable.org*).

[27] If you're interested, you can see the options contract awarded to Meg Whitman, CEO of eBay, at *http://contracts.corporate.findlawe.com/agreements/ebay/whitman.html*. The options were awarded in February 1998, at the prevailing price at the time. Within six months, she used them to purchase eBay shares that had risen substantially in price, for a gain of $43.2 million.

TABLE 7	Corporation	CEO Salary and Bonus, 2005	Additional Compensation in 2005	Total Compensation in 2005
Corporations with Highest-Paid CEOs in 2005	Capital One Financial	$0	$249.4 million	**$249.4 million**
	Cendant	$15.6 million	$124.3 million	**$140.0 million**
	KB Home	$6.1 million	$129.4 million	**$135.5 million**
	Lehman Bros. Holdings	$14.5 million	$108.2 million	**$122.7 million**
	Occidental Petroleum	$4.9 million	$75.8 million	**$80.7 million**
	Oracle	$7.5 million	$67.9 million	**$75.3 million**
	Symantec	$2.5 million	$69.4 million	**$71.8 million**
	Caremark Rx	$4.8 million	$64.9 million	**$69.7 million**
	Cisco Systems	$1.7 million	$61.3 million	**$63.0 million**
	Ryland Group	$17.5 million	$39.0 million	**$56.5 million**

Source: "Special Report: CEO Compensation," Forbes, April 20, 2006. (Differs slightly from the Forbes top 10 list due to the deletion of two CEOs for whom only 2004 information was available.)

Restricted stock grants are actual gifts of shares of stock. The restriction is that the shares cannot be immediately sold. Rather, only a portion—typically 20 to 25 percent of the shares granted—can be sold in any one year that a manager is with the company.

Note that although the logic is more complicated, stock options and stock grants—just like a salary—are a *cost* to the corporation. In both cases, shares that the corporation *could* have sold at the higher market price are instead made available to the manager for a lower price (options) or free of charge (grants). So in the end, these are just other ways, but not costless ways, for a corporation to pay its CEO and other managers.

Which brings us to the central question: Why is CEO compensation, especially in these additional stock-based forms, so high? And why has it risen so rapidly over the past decade?

THE ABILITY EXPLANATION

Part of the explanation—but only part—can be found in the normal workings of the market for CEOs. Steering a major U.S. corporation is a difficult job. And the job has become even more difficult over the past decade, as corporations have grown larger and as globalization and rapid technological change have dramatically increased the stakes of strategic decision making. Very few people have the ability to do this job, and fewer still have *proven* ability by having successfully managed a large corporation in the past. With such a small number of qualified people, and an increasingly complex business environment, the demand for top candidates is high relative to supply. A major corporation that wants to hire a top CEO will find itself bidding with hundreds of other corporations for this scarce pool of labor.

Second, the market for CEOs shares some of the features of the *superstar* labor markets discussed earlier, like those for movie and sports stars. Suppose that an industry is going through changes, and the firm must make important strategic decisions that will set its course for several years. Then hiring the *slightly* better CEO, who is able to make slightly better decisions, could make a *huge* difference in total profits. It could even make the difference between survival and bankruptcy.

To get an idea of the numbers, suppose that Starbucks is in the market for a new CEO. There are two groups of candidates—A and B—which are very close in quality, but not identical. With a CEO from Group A, annual earnings are expected to be, say, 2 percent greater than for a CEO from Group B. How much *more* would Starbucks shareholders be willing to pay to hire a CEO from Group A, rather than one from group B?

Let's see. In 2005, Starbucks' total net income (profit) was $494.5 million. Two percent of that is $9.8 million. So that is the greatest *premium* shareholders would be willing to pay to hire a CEO from Group A, rather than from Group B. Will the shareholders actually *have* to pay that much? Yes, as long as there are many *other* firms of similar size bidding up the salaries of Group A candidates. With enough competition, any large firm that doesn't pay what a Group A candidate is worth will lose out to another firm that *does* pay. Of course, Group B candidates will also earn *their* own premium if they can perform slightly better than Group C candidates, and so on down the line. So even the average CEO will earn a substantial premium over the average worker.

In sum:

> *According to the ability explanation, top CEO salaries are so high because top CEOs can generate so many millions of dollars in additional profit for their shareholders, and because so many large companies are competing for their talents.*

The ability explanation is also consistent with the rapid *growth* of CEO salaries. As the largest companies get larger, a capable CEO's potential contribution to total profit rises as well. In fact, by almost any measure, the typical top-100 or top-500 U.S. corporation has grown about sixfold over the past 25 years. And during this period, CEO pay at these corporations has increased about sixfold as well.[28] Using this reasoning, we can also explain why, in Europe, CEO pay is lower and has risen more modestly. The top European companies are smaller. Therefore, a European CEO—even if equal in ability to his or her American counterpart—would not add as much value for shareholders.

If this scenario, based on ability, entirely explained high and rising CEO pay, there would be no reason for shareholders to be upset. Moreover, there would be little reason for the government to get involved, other than ensuring that the tax system takes a politically determined fair share of these high incomes, relative to the shares taken from other income groups.

But shareholders and the government *have* been upset about skyrocketing CEO pay—because there is more to the story.

THE MARKET FAILURE EXPLANATION

The market for CEOs seems to suffer from some serious *market failures*—a term that will be formally defined and discussed later, in Chapter 15. But the general idea

---

[28] Xavier Gabaiz and Augustin Landier, "Why Has CEO Pay Increased So Much?" MIT Department of Economics Working Paper No. 06-13, January 26, 2006. For a nontechnical summary, see Tyler Cowen, "A Contrarian Look at Whether U.S. Chief Executives Are Overpaid," *New York Times*, May 18, 2006.

is this: A market *fails* when its normal equilibrium does not allocate resources in the best interests of society.

How does the labor market for CEOs *fail*? One problem relates to the *principal–agent relationship* in this market. A *principal* is a person who has an interest at stake, and hires an *agent* to act on his behalf. The agent could be a baby-sitter hired by a parent, or an auto mechanic hired to fix your car, . . . or a CEO hired to maximize profit for a corporation's shareholders.

Principal–agent relationships are a natural consequence of specialization, in which most members of society find it advantageous to specialize in an occupation and perform work for others. The **principal–agent problem**, however, arises when an agent is able to maximize her *own* well-being instead of the well-being of the principal who hired her. And this, in turn, occurs when a principal cannot fully *monitor* an agent's performance (such as when you don't have the expertise to know whether your auto mechanic really performed all the work that's on the bill).

Principal–agent problem A situation in which an agent maximizes her own well-being at the expense of the principal who hired her

The CEO–shareholder relationship is a case in point. Here, shareholders are the principals, and they have neither the expertise nor the information needed to monitor management performance. As a result, shareholders would find it difficult to determine on their own whether high management salaries or generous fringe benefits are in their interests (i.e., necessary to retain top-level managers who are contributing even more than their compensation to the firm's profit) or merely an example of management pursuing its own interests (extracting excessive pay from shareholders).

Large, publicly held corporations use a variety of methods to help solve the principal–agent problem. One of these is a government regulation: The shareholders vote into office a *board of directors* to monitor the firm for them. Board members, who are paid for their work, are supposed to have the expertise, motivation, and power to ensure performance on behalf of the stockholders. Indeed, the board of directors hires, and can fire, the CEO.

Corporations also create incentives to align the interests of managers with those of the shareholders. In theory, stock options and restricted stock grants are examples. Options, for example, should benefit managers *only if* they take actions that raise the corporation's profits, make the stock more attractive to buyers, and thereby raise its price. Restricted stock grants, too, benefit managers more when the share price rises than when it falls. In both cases, management is given a stake in raising the price of the shares, and creating wealth for the corporation's owners.

That's all well in theory. But in the view of many economists, these very methods designed to *solve* the principal–agent problem have become part of the problem itself.

Let's first consider the behavior of boards of directors. CEOs control the flow of information to the board, so they can present a biased view of their decisions and outcomes—one that hides actions that are harming shareholders. Also, boards of directors create *another* principal–agent problem: Board members—the agents of the shareholders—may have their own interests, such as collecting their paychecks without doing the hard work of monitoring the firm's performance. Even worse, CEOs frequently sit on *each other's* boards, creating an "I'll scratch your back if you'll scratch mine" mentality. All of these problems can help CEOs extract greater salaries from their boards—and therefore, from their shareholders—than would be justified by their abilities.

Now let's again consider stock options and grants. Although designed to help *solve* the principal–agent problem, they can also worsen it. Because stock-based compensation seems to be a reward for good performance, it can become a less obvious way for CEOs to extract excessive pay from shareholders. Until 2006, companies did not have to report options as a full cost to the corporation. Thus, boards of directors could provide generous options grants to top executives without fully adjusting the firm's reported profit.

Critics have argued that options and stock grants cannot be justified as incentive pay, in theory or practice. They reward CEOs for *any* rise in the stock's price—even one caused by a general stock market boom to which the CEO contributed nothing. Indeed, during the 1990s, the general rise in share prices rewarded almost all CEOs, regardless of their performance. At the same time, when the market falls, CEOs have asked for, and received, new options with a lower exercise price, arguing that they should not be penalized for a general market drop. This protects CEOs (but not their shareholders) from the consequences of a falling market.

Moreover, the evidence suggests only a tenuous connection between amounts awarded and performance. For example, *Forbes* magazine has ranked the performance of 189 CEOs at top corporations who have been in office for several years. The ranking—which goes from 1 (best) to 189 (worst)—is based on the performance of the company relative to other firms in the same industry. Among the 10 highest paid CEOs in Table 7, seven were ranked below 100, and three ranked below 170.

Beyond stock-based compensation, there have been hefty raises, bonuses, and lavish fringe benefits awarded to CEOs who have been outperformed by the market in general, and by competitors in their industry. And boards of directors have agreed to contracts guaranteeing CEOs millions of dollars in severance pay, even if they are fired for *poor* performance.

All of this suggests that CEOs are being rewarded for reasons other than their benefit to shareholders, and that the principal–agent problem may be the culprit.

> *In the market failure explanation, the principal–agent problem has enabled top CEOs to increasingly exploit their positions within the firm, extracting more compensation than their shareholders would knowingly and willingly provide.*

In this view, CEO pay in Europe has been more modest because the principal–agent problem there is less severe. Shares of large corporations in Europe are concentrated among fewer owners. And shareholders with a larger stake have more incentive to monitor CEO behavior and detect mischief themselves, rather than leave it entirely to directors. Moreover, stock-based compensation is a much smaller fraction of CEO earnings in Europe, so it is easier for shareholders and the general public to observe and understand CEO pay.[29]

CEOs of U.S. corporations have been under increasing scrutiny in recent years. Hundreds of shareholders' resolutions have been introduced to limit their boards' flexibility in awarding options, stock grants, bonuses, salaries, severance pay, and more. The government has chimed in as well. Among other steps, it now requires companies to "expense" stock options, deducting their value from corporate earnings, so their cost will be more transparent to shareholders.

And the media have been watching as well. In March 2006, the *Wall Street Journal* reported something suspicious about the timing of options grants at many firms: They seemed especially likely to be awarded when the stock's price hit a

---

[29] Richard Posner has speculated that, because there is more direct monitoring of European CEOs, there may be less need for arms-length incentive formulas, such as stock options. Instead, the European CEO can be rewarded directly with raises and bonuses only when justified by actual performance. Richard Posner, "Are CEOs Overpaid?" Posted on *The Becker Posner Blog,* May 14, 2006, *http:// www.becker-posner-blog.com/index.html.*

temporary low, making the exercise price low as well.[30] (The lower the exercise price of the option, the greater the likelihood that the stock will eventually rise above that price, and the more value the option will have.) In one case, the odds that a series of grants to the CEO would have been so nicely timed by chance were less than one in 300 billion! Within two months of the *Journal*'s story, about 20 companies were under government investigation for illegal "backdating" of options awards, and 10 executives or board members had resigned.

Corporate scandals, such as the options backdating story, have become part of the background for discussions of CEO pay. But many economists believe that even in a well-functioning market, huge reductions in CEO pay are unlikely. Why? Because qualified CEOs are scarce, and the rewards to shareholders from hiring a better CEO are enormous. Shareholders thus still have an incentive to offer CEOs pay that is many times that of the average employee. A case in point occurred in March 2005. A small group of Morgan Stanley shareholders put forth a resolution to limit the CEO's pay to 100 times the average of nonmanagerial employees, unless the shareholders approved more. The resolution was resoundingly defeated by shareholders, receiving less than 15 percent of the votes cast.

Summary

In all nations, incomes vary markedly. Partly, that's because of differences in wages that can be traced to differences in the attractiveness of jobs, differences in ability, and imperfections in labor markets. When the attractiveness of two jobs differs, *compensating wage differentials* will emerge to offset those differences. When the ability of workers differs, the more able workers will earn higher wages. Because of the superstar nature of many professions, small differences in ability can create extremely large wage differentials. And in some cases, barriers to entry contribute to higher wages for protected workers.

Another reason for wage differentials is prejudice. When employer prejudice exists, market forces work to discourage discrimination and reduce wage gaps between groups. However, employee and customer prejudice encourage discrimination and can lead to permanent wage gaps.

One frequent proposal for reducing income inequality is an increase in the *minimum wage*. This is controversial because the costs and benefits of the minimum wage do not fall exclusively on high- and low-income households, respectively. A higher minimum wage is also believed to reduce employment among low-skilled workers, especially teenagers, and to reduce the wages of unskilled workers in industries not covered by the law. A more efficient redistributive policy is the *earned income tax credit* (EITC), which targets low-income working households. The *poverty rate* measures the fraction of the population whose income falls below an inflation-adjusted poverty line. It is sensitive to how income is defined and measured and doesn't tell us about inequality among those above the poverty line. The *Lorenz curve* and associated *Gini coefficient* give a more comprehensive measure of income inequality.

Over the past few decades, income inequality has grown. Most of this growth has been an increase in the share at the very top of the income distribution. The superstar phenomenon and the growth in the pay of CEOs and top managers are two explanations for this growth.

When evaluating income inequality, it is important to distinguish between lifetime inequality and inequality in any given year. Because of income mobility, inequality lessens as income is measured over longer time periods. It is also important to distinguish between different reasons for the income inequality. Some reasons would be regarded as fair by most people; others are more controversial. Finally, in designing policies to reduce inequality, it is important to consider the effects on total income.

Problem Set   *Answers to even-numbered Questions and Problems can be found on the text Web site at www.thomsonedu.com/economics/hall.*

1. The labor markets for factory workers and construction workers are in equilibrium: The wage in both is W_0, and the number employed is N_0. Assume that both labor markets are perfectly competitive, there are no barriers to entry or exit of workers, and workers are equally qualified to do both jobs and find them equally attractive.

    a. Unexpectedly, demand for factory output soars. Using graphs, show the short-run effect on the equilibrium wage and number employed in factories.
    b. Draw graphs that illustrate the long-run equilibrium position in the two industries.

[30] Charles Forelle and James Bandler, "The Perfect Payday," *Wall Street Journal*, March 18, 2006, p. A1.

2. The following table lists the annual income of the 10 citizens of the little town of Dismal Seepage.

Joe	$10,000	Dick	$18,000
Jim	$15,000	Ellen	$ 3,000
Sue	$ 4,000	Ann	$30,000
Jack	$25,000	Ralph	$ 8,000
Roy	$ 7,000	Bill	$50,000

a. Draw the Lorenz curve for this community.
b. Make a rough estimate of the Gini coefficient.
c. Assume that all the people in town live alone and that the yearly cost of food for a single person is $4,000. What is the official poverty rate in the town?

3. Refer to question 2.
a. Dismal Seepage decides to tax 5 percent of the income of each of the richest 20 percent of its citizens and divide this tax revenue equally between each of the poorest 40 percent of its citizens. Make a list showing each citizen's income after taxes and transfer payments and draw the city's new Lorenz curve. How does this Lorenz curve compare with the one found in 2(a)?
b. Citizens of Bleak Ooze, located 2 miles from Dismal Seepage, hear about Dismal Seepage's tax and transfer payment plan. What will happen to the average income for each of these two cities? What will happen to the Lorenz curve in Bleak Ooze?
c. Assume that low-income citizens are more geographically mobile than high-income ones (because they don't own homes or have stable employment, for instance). How will this change your results in part (b)?

4. Reports of what is happening to average CEO compensation often vary, even when they refer to the same group of CEOs, the same time period, and the same definition of compensation. That's because some reports use *average* (mean) compensation in the group, while others use *median* compensation. Using the group of ten highest-paid CEOs in Table 7:
a. What is the *average* (mean) total compensation of CEOs in the group?
b. What is the *median* total compensation of CEOs in the group? (Hint: To determine the median value in a group with an even number of members, use the average of the two closest to the middle.)
c. Suppose that the compensation of the best-paid CEO in this group rises by 20 perrcent, while that of the lowest-paid falls by 20 percent. What is the percentage change in average (mean) total compensation? What is the percentage change in median total compensation?

5. State how each of the following would affect the average wage of college professors relative to other professionals in the long run. In each case, illustrate with a supply and demand diagram.
a. Requirements to become a college professor are increased from one to two PhD degrees.

b. Urban colleges around the country relocate to rural areas.
c. The college-age population decreases.
d. The number of courses college professors have to teach each year is reduced by 25%. (Note: Be sure to state any assumptions you use to arrive at your answer.)

6. Draw the Lorenz curve for an economy in which one person earns all the income and the rest earn nothing. Then, calculate the Gini coefficient for this economy.

7. [Appendix required] Look again at Figure A.1. What would the minimum wage rate have to be to get this monopsonist to hire the number of workers and pay the same wage rate as a firm operating in a perfectly competitive labor market? Draw the firm's new *MFC* curve at this minimum wage rate.

More Challenging

8. Some advocates of the minimum wage argue that any decrease in the employment of the unskilled will be slight. They assert that an increase in the minimum wage will actually increase the total amount paid to unskilled workers (i.e., wage × number of unskilled workers employed). Discuss what assumptions they are making about the wage elasticity of labor demand.

9. [Appendix Required]
a. Redraw Figure A.1 Show what will happen when the union wage rate (the wage rate determined through wage bargaining) is set at the wage rate paid if this were a perfectly competitive labor market.
b. Now assume that the union wage rate is set above the wage rate paid if this were a perfectly competitive labor market, but below the *MRP* of the last worker hired by the monopsonist in the absence of a union. Redraw Figure A.1, drawing the new *MFC* curve, and labeling the union wage rate W* and the number of workers hired in this situation L*.
c. Redraw Figure A.1 again. Show an example of a union wage rate that will actually reduce employment below what the monopsonist would have chosen if it had not had to bargain with a union. Is it realistic to believe that a union would bargain for such a high wage rate?
d. Over what range can the union wage rate be set without reducing employment below the nonunion employment level?

10. Suppose the demand for unskilled labor were completely *inelastic* with respect to the wage rate. Using graphs similar to those in Figure 5, but modified to reflect this new assumption, explain how a minimum wage above the equilibrium wage for covered unskilled workers would affect employment and the wage rate among:
a. Covered, unskilled workers
b. Uncovered, unskilled workers
c. Skilled workers

The Minimum Wage and Union Bargaining Under Monopsony

The body of this chapter analyzed labor markets with specific departures from perfect competition, such as a specific barrier to entry or differences in ability among workers. In the appendix to Chapter 11, however, you learned about an entirely different structure for the labor market: monopsony. A *pure* monopsony (a labor market with only one employer) is extremely rare. But when an employer is large enough for its employment decisions to influence the market wage, we say that it has *monopsony power* because its behavior is similar to a pure monopsony. In this appendix, we'll see how monopsony power not only changes, but can actually reverse, our most important conclusions about the minimum wage and the impact of labor unions.

Let's first briefly review the employment decision of a monopsony firm, as illustrated in the left panel of Figure A.1. First, the firm faces the *upward-sloping labor* supply curve L^S; it must pay a higher wage each time it wants to hire an additional worker, given by the height of the curve L^S. But the higher wage must be paid not just to the newly hired worker, but to *all* employees, including those previously working for a lower wage. As a result, the monopsony's marginal factor cost (*MFC*)—the cost of hiring the additional worker—is greater than the wage paid to that worker. This is why, in the figure, the monopsony's *MFC* curve lies *above* the labor supply curve L^S.

In the absence of a minimum wage or a union, this firm's profit-maximizing employment is found at point *E,* where the marginal revenue product (*MRP*) and *MFC* curves intersect. The firm hires 100 workers and pays an hourly wage of $4 at point *F*—on the curve L^S.

MONOPSONY AND THE MINIMUM WAGE

How does a monopsony firm respond to a minimum wage law? Look at the right-hand panel of Figure A.1, in which a minimum wage of $6 per hour—higher than the equilibrium wage of $4—is imposed. Now the firm must immediately raise the wage of all *existing* employees to $6. Moreover, the labor supply curve L^S tells us that $6 per hour is high enough to attract 125 workers. For any employment level *up to* 125 workers, the firm can hire another worker without raising the pay of any of its existing employees, since they're *already* earning $6. So the added cost of a new worker is just $6 per hour.

What if the firm wants to hire a 126th worker? Then it will have to raise the wage *above* $6, not just for that new worker, but for *all* workers, just as it had to do when *no* minimum wage was in effect. So, for the 126th worker and beyond, the *MFC* is the same as it was before the minimum wage.

This analysis suggests that imposing a minimum wage on a monopsony labor market gives the firm a rather strange-looking *MFC* curve, which is shown with darker shading in the right panel. For all employment levels up to 125, the *MFC* curve is a horizontal line at $6. Then it jumps vertically upward to the original (pre–minimum wage) *MFC* curve for all rises in employment beyond 126.

How many workers should the firm employ now? The answer—as always—is given by the intersection of the *MFC* and *MRP* curves. But now this intersection occurs along the vertical part of the *MFC* curve. As you can see in the figure, for employment *up to* 125, *MRP* > *MFC,* so the firm should increase hiring. For employment *beyond* 125, *MFC* > *MRP,* so the firm should stop at 125 workers, at point *G.*

Looking at the figure, you can see that with *no* minimum wage the firm pays $4 per hour and employs 100 workers. But with a minimum wage, the firm pays $6 per hour and employs 125 workers. The minimum wage causes the firm to *pay a higher wage rate* and *increase employment.*

The firm loses profit because it must pay a higher wage rate. But once confronted with this requirement, the *highest profit it can earn* under the circumstances calls for an increase in hiring.

> For a firm with monopsony power, a minimum wage law can not only increase the wage rate a firm pays but also increase employment at the firm.

FIGURE A.1   **The Minimum Wage in a Monopsony Labor Market**

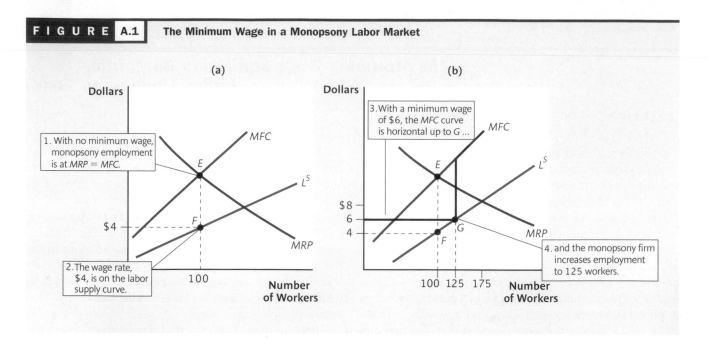

Note that this is very different from the minimum wage's effect in a competitive labor market, where a rise in the minimum increases pay for those still working but causes some to lose their jobs. Under monopsony, no one need be laid off, and employment can very well rise.

There are two provisos here. First, the kind of monopsony power likely to generate this result is not common in practice, outside of small towns with one or a few dominant firms in the labor market. Second, even under monopsony, there is a limit to how high the minimum wage can go without causing employment to fall. If you pencil in the horizontal section of the *MFC* curve for different minimum wages in the figure, you'll see that a minimum wage of $8 gives the maximum employment possible: 175 workers. For any minimum wage higher than $8, employment will be less than 175, and if it rises too high, employment could fall below 100 (the original employment level without a minimum wage).

MONOPSONY AND UNION BARGAINING

As you saw in the chapter, a union reduces employment by driving up the wage in a *perfectly competitive labor market*. The union will try to strike the right balance between higher wages and higher employment for its members (and potential members).

But when a union confronts a firm with *monopsony power*, the result can be very different. Figure A.1, once again, can be used to illustrate the situation. The left-hand panel can represent the market without a labor union, in which the firm pays a wage of $4 per hour and employs 100 workers.

Now suppose a union is empowered to negotiate the wage the firm must pay to all its workers. In effect, the union—because of its role in determining the wage the firm will pay—becomes the only *seller* of labor to the firm: a monopoly seller. The firm, however, has monopsony power as a large *buyer* of labor from the union. This situation, in which monopsony confronts monopoly, is often called *bilateral monopoly*. And the wage will be determined by negotiation between the firm and the union.

What tradeoff will the union face now? Surprisingly, over some range of wage rates the answer is: no tradeoff at all. Suppose, for example, that we're once again dealing with the firm in Figure A.1, which is initially employing 100 workers and paying a wage rate of $4. Then the union negotiates a wage of $6. As was the case in our minimum wage example, the firm will immediately have to raise all of its employees' wage rates to $6. It can then hire another worker at $6 per hour, and not have to raise its existing workers' pay any further—up to 125 workers. To go beyond 125 workers, the firm must offer higher pay to *all* workers, just as it did before there was a union. So—just as in the figure—the monopsony firm's *MFC* curve will be a horizontal line at $6 up to 125 workers, at which point it jumps up to the old *MFC* curve.

The firm reacts to the $6 union wage the same way it reacted to the $6 minimum wage: It raises employment from 100 to 125 workers. And an $8 union wage (not shown) would increase employment to 175. Clearly, in the situation depicted in the right panel of Figure A.1, the union would like *at least* an $8 wage, since it wins on both employment *and* pay. The union might even prefer a wage *greater* than $8, which involves some tradeoff between employment and pay. The *firm*, however, wants a union wage of only $4, since any higher wage rate reduces its profit.

The inevitable result is *wage bargaining*, with each side using the power at its disposal to move the outcome closer to its own goal.

The result of union bargaining—if the wage is not set too high—can be very different from the outcome in a competitive labor market:

> *In a monopsony labor market, a union that wins a higher wage rate for its members can not only increase their pay but may be able to increase employment at the firm.*

As with the minimum wage, a wage rate of $8 in the figure will maximize employment at 175. As the wage continues to rise beyond that limit, employment falls, eventually dropping below the original, nonunion level of 100.

CHAPTER
13

Capital and Financial Markets

If you are like most people reading this book, you have already decided to make a tradeoff: to give up some income now, so you can have more income in the future. You made the decision when you chose to attend college. You are either *not* earning income for now (if you're not working) or earning less than you could at a full-time job (if you work part-time). In return, after graduation, you can expect to earn more than you would without a college degree.

There are, of course, other reasons to attend college than just the boost in future income it will give you. But let's be narrow-minded for a moment, and think only about the money. Is the tradeoff worth it?

We'll discuss the answer at the end of this chapter. You'll see that the method we'll use helps us answer a variety of economic questions. The method is used by Starbucks when it must decide whether to open a new store in a particular location. And by Pfizer when it decides how much of the firm's yearly income to put into research and development on new drugs. It is also used by financial market analysts, when they are asked whether a share of Google stock is really worth its price of several hundred dollars. All of these decisions involve comparing future earnings with current costs; therefore, they require putting a value on money to be received *in the future*.

In this chapter, we'll be discussing how such decisions are made. We'll first look at decisions about investing in physical capital, such as factory buildings or machinery. Then we'll turn our attention to the value of financial assets, specifically stocks and bonds. Finally, in the Using the Theory section, we'll turn to the decision to invest in human capital—specifically, your decision to attend college.

PHYSICAL CAPITAL AND THE FIRM'S INVESTMENT DECISION

The concept of *capital* was introduced in the first chapter of this book. There, you learned that capital is one of society's *resources,* along with land, labor, and entrepreneurship. More specifically, capital is a produced long-lasting *tool* that is used, in turn, to produce goods and services. You also learned that we can classify capital into two categories: *physical capital,* such as the plant and equipment owned by business firms, and *human capital,* the skills and training of the labor force. In this section, we'll focus on firms' decisions about physical capital.

How does a business firm decide how much physical capital to use? In the same way that it makes any other decision. The firm's goal is to maximize its profit—not just this year, but over many years into the future. What guidelines should a firm use? First, we'll make some unrealistic assumptions that will allow us to use a simple and familiar approach. This will help you see what's special about capital, and why, in the end, we'll have to use a more complex method.

A FIRST, SIMPLE APPROACH

In this section, we'll assume that *one of two* special conditions holds: Either (1) *firms rent their capital at a constant price,* just as they rent their labor (by the hour, week, or year); or (2) *firms buy their capital, but it lasts forever.* In either case, as you'll see, we can analyze the firm's decision to use more capital just as we analyzed its decision to employ another worker.

Let's make this more concrete with an example. Imagine you are the fleet manager at Quicksilver Delivery Service. Your firm delivers packages for small retailers in the Chicago metropolitan area. We'll assume this market is close enough to perfectly competitive (there are many other, essentially identical firms), so Quicksilver must take the market price of package delivery as a given—$4 per package. You are responsible for determining the number of trucks the firm should use.

Your first step is to remember the *marginal approach to profit,* which you've encountered several times earlier in this book. For reinforcement, here it is again:

> *The marginal approach to profit states that a firm should take any action that adds more to its revenue than it adds to its cost.*

Here, we regard the action as "add another truck." Keep in mind that when we use this approach, revenue and cost are measured *per period,* such as revenue and cost per year. So, the marginal approach says that you should acquire the use of another truck if doing so will increase yearly revenue more than it increases yearly cost.

Using the language we developed in Chapter 11, we can define the *marginal revenue product (MRP)* of trucks as the additional yearly revenue you'd get from using one more truck. We can also define the *marginal factor cost (MFC)* of trucks as the additional yearly cost of using one more truck. Then the profit-maximizing rule translates to: Use another truck whenever its *MRP* is greater than its *MFC.*

Table 1 lists the relevant data for each truck you might use. Let's start with the *MRP* column and get some idea where these numbers might come from. If you had just one truck, you would use it in the Northern territory, one of two areas that is best for package delivery. Having this truck would enable your firm to deliver 2,500 additional packages each year, thereby generating $4 \times 2,500 = \$10,000$ in additional yearly revenue.[1] So the *marginal revenue product (MRP)* of that first truck is $10,000 per year, which is listed in the second column.

A second new truck would be used in a new Northeast territory. It turns out that this area is just as good for business, so that truck, too, would generate $10,000 in

---

[1] In this example, we are ignoring other costs besides rent associated with additional trucks, such as more gasoline, additional maintenance, and salaries for additional drivers. But they could easily be included. One way is to imagine that the MRP numbers in Table 1 have already accounted for these costs. That is, imagine that each MRP number represents *net* additional revenue, after deducting (from actual revenue) the annual cost of gasoline, maintenance, and driver. This net additional revenue is then compared to the cost of renting the truck.

TABLE 1	Trucks	Additional Annual Revenue (*MRP*)	Additional Annual Cost (*MFC*)
Additional Data for Quicksilver Delivery Service	First Truck	$10,000	$5,000
	Second Truck	$10,000	$5,000
	Third Truck	$ 8,000	$5,000
	Fourth Truck	$ 5,500	$5,000
	Fifth Truck	$ 2,000	$5,000

additional revenue each year. A third truck would be used in the Eastern territory where, in the course of a typical year, it would generate only $8,000 in additional revenue. A fourth truck could generate $5,500 in additional revenue on a new Southern route. And a fifth truck would be used for special deliveries when the other trucks are busy, generating only $2,000 in additional revenue.

Now let's assume you will *rent* your trucks (the first of our special assumptions). Specifically, each additional truck will cost you $5,000 per year in rent. Then the yearly *MFC* is $5,000, which is listed in the third column of Table 1. You should rent all trucks for which the yearly increase in revenue (*MRP*) is greater than the *MFC* of $5,000. As you can see in the table, this means you should rent the first four trucks, but not the fifth. For the fifth truck, the *MRP* of $2,000 is less than the *MFC* of $5,000.

Suppose instead that you must *buy* your trucks, at a cost of $50,000 each. Then, using our second special assumption that a truck will last forever, once you pay the $50,000 you are done making payments. Except for one thing: As long as you own the truck, you give up investment income. If we assume that each forever-lasting truck could, at any time, be sold for the same $50,000 it originally cost, then each year that you continue to own and use one (rather than sell it), you are sacrificing interest on that $50,000. This is a continuing, yearly cost for each truck. If the annual rate of return on alternative investments is 10 percent, then owning a truck costs you $0.10 \times \$50,000 = \$5,000$ per year, for as long as you own it. Remember that when maximizing economic profit, an implicit cost is treated just like an explicit cost. So, in this case too, your *MFC* is $5,000 for each additional truck. You should buy the first four trucks, but not the fifth.

> When firms rent capital, or the capital they buy lasts forever, we can apply the marginal approach to profits just as we apply it for the firm's labor decision: The firm should buy another unit of capital whenever its marginal revenue product is greater than its marginal factor cost.

Why the Simple Approach Usually Fails

The simple approach, unfortunately, will not help us understand investment decisions, because our special assumptions are problematic. First, our assumption that capital can be *rented*—while it may work for *some* firms—does not work for the economy in general. That's because every unit of capital in use is owned by someone or some firm. Even if Quicksilver Delivery Service rents its trucks, it will be renting them from a truck rental firm that purchased them. For any unit of capital employed in the economy, some firm—somewhere along the line—must have made the decision to purchase it. So if we want to understand decisions about capital investment in the economy, we must ultimately account for the decisions of firms that *purchase* the capital before it is used. For that reason, from this point on, we'll focus on the firms that *purchase* their capital.

Second, capital does *not* last forever. Why is this a problem? Imagine—to start with an extreme case—that a truck lasts only one year and then falls apart and becomes worthless. Then you wouldn't want to purchase even the first truck at $50,000, since (see Table 1) it would only generate $10,000 in revenue before it fell apart. Even if a truck lasted two years, or even three years, you would not want to buy one. Clearly, the length of time that capital lasts matters when deciding whether to buy it.

But what if a truck lasted 15 years? Then buying it *might* make sense. However, now you have a problem: You'd have to pay $50,000 for each truck *now*, but the revenue from the truck would be spread out over the next 15 years.

"That's easy," you might think. "I'll just add up the revenue each truck will earn in each of those 15 years. The first truck has an *MRP* of $10,000 per year, so over 15 years, the truck will earn 15 × $10,000 = $150,000 in revenue. If it only costs $50,000, I should buy it for the firm. Even the fourth truck, with an *MRP* of $6,000, would earn 15 × $6,000 = $90,000 over its life, so—at a price of $50,000—I should order that one too."

But if you reason this way, you are making a serious error: You're treating each year's revenue as equally valuable, regardless of *when* the revenue is earned. In reality, the value of a future payment depends on *when* that payment is received. To see why, we'll have to take a detour from Quicksilver Delivery and explore the issue of future payments more generally. We'll come back to Quicksilver and its trucks when we're done.

THE VALUE OF FUTURE DOLLARS

To see why the value of a future payment depends on *when* that payment is received, just run through the following thought experiment. Imagine that you are given the choice between receiving $1,000 now and $1,000 one year from now. Do you have to think hard before making up your mind? Regardless of when you will actually spend the money, it is always better to have the dollars earlier rather than later.

For example, say you don't plan to spend the money until next year. Then, if you get the $1,000 now, you could put it in the bank and earn interest for a year, giving you *more* than $1,000 when you finally spend it. On the other hand, say you need to spend the money right away. Then receiving it *now* rather than later saves you the interest you would have to pay to borrow the money for immediate use.

> *Because present dollars can earn interest, and because borrowing dollars requires payment of interest, it is always preferable to receive a given sum of money earlier rather than later. Therefore, a dollar received later has less value than a dollar received now.*

Knowing that dollars received in the future are worth less than dollars received today is an important insight. But *how much* less is a future dollar worth?

To answer that question, we use a concept called *present value*.

A truck, like most types of physical capital, will increase a firm's revenue for many years. As a result, the firm must calculate the present-dollar equivalent of future receipts.

Present value The value, in today's dollars, of a sum of money to be received or paid at a specific date in the future.

> The **present value** (PV) of a future payment is the value of that future payment in today's dollars. Alternatively, it is the most anyone would pay today for the right to receive the future payment.

To understand this concept better, let's work out a simple example: What is the present value of $1,000 to be received one year in the future? That is, what is the most you would pay *today* in order to receive $1,000 one year from today? The answer is certainly *not* $1,000. If you paid $1,000 today for a guaranteed $1,000 in one year, you would be giving up interest. If you lent the money, you'd end up with *more* than $1,000 one year later. So it never makes sense to pay $1,000 now for $1,000 to be received one year from now.

But would you pay $900 for the guaranteed future payment? Or $800? That depends on how much interest you *could* earn by lending funds to someone else for a year. In fact, the most you'd pay is the amount that, if you lent it out for interest, would get you *exactly* $1,000 in one year. That amount of money is the *present value* (PV) of $1,000 to be received in one year, since that is the most you would part with today in exchange for the future payment.

Suppose the interest rate at which you can lend funds is 10 percent per year. Then the present value of $1,000 to be received one year from today is an amount of money that, if lent out at 10 percent annual interest, would give you precisely $1,000 in one year. At 10 percent interest, each dollar you lend out will give you 1.10 dollars in one year, so the PV we seek will satisfy the following equation:

$$PV \times 1.10 = \$1,000.$$

Solving for PV, we get

$$PV = \frac{\$1,000}{1.10} = \$909.09$$

In words, if you lent out $909.09 at 10 percent interest, you would have $1,000 one year from today. Therefore, $909.09 is the most you would be willing to give up today for $1,000 in one year. Or, more formally, *$909.09 is the present value of $1,000 received one year from now.*

We can generalize this result by noting that, if the interest rate had been something other than 0.10—we'll call it r—or the amount of money had been something other than $1,000—say, Y dollars—then the present value would satisfy the equation

$$PV \times (1 + r) = Y$$

or

$$PV = \frac{Y}{(1 + r)}.$$

What if the payment of $Y were to be received *two* years from now instead of one? Then we can use the same logic to find the present value. In that case, each dollar lent out now would become $(1 + r)$ dollars after one year. Then, when the dollar plus the earned interest was lent out again for a second year, it would become $(1 + r)(1 + r) = (1 + r)^2$ dollars at the end of the second year. Thus, the PV will satisfy

$$PV \times (1 + r)^2 = Y$$

and solving for PV, we obtain

$$PV = \frac{Y}{(1 + r)^2}.$$

Finally, for payments to be received one, two, or any number of years n in the future, we can state that

the present value of $\$Y$ to be received n *years in the future is equal to*

$$PV = \frac{Y}{(1 + r)^n}.$$

For example, with an interest rate of 10 percent, the present value of $\$1,000$ to be received three years in the future would be

$$PV = \frac{\$1,000}{(1.10)^3} = \$751.31$$

The process of making dollars of different dates comparable is called **discounting**. The value of r used in this process is called the **discount rate**[2]. In simple calculations involving no risk, the discount rate is just the interest rate at which you can borrow and lend. When we introduce the issue of risk a bit later, you'll see that the discount rate is related to the interest rate but can differ from it. Table 2 shows the present value of a dollar to be received at different times in the future, at different discount rates (rounded to the nearest penny).

For example, what is the present value of $\$1$ to be received 10 years from today? If the interest rate is 10 percent, the present-day equivalent is $\$1$ *divided by* $(1.10)^{10}$, or $\$1.00/2.59 = \$0.39$. This tells us that, when the interest rate (discount rate) is 10 percent, anyone expecting to receive $\$1$ ten years from today might just as well accept $\$0.39$ now. After all, when loaned at 10 percent interest per year, 39 cents will get you $\$1$ in ten years.

From the logic of present-value calculations, and from the entries in Table 2, you can see that

the present value of a future payment is smaller if (1) the size of the payment is smaller, (2) the interest rate is larger, or (3) the payment is received later.

Once you remember that present value is what you'd pay today for a payment you'd receive in the future, it's rather obvious why a smaller future payment would have a smaller present value. The other two factors have to do with how much

Discounting The act of converting a future value into its present-day equivalent.

Discount rate The interest rate used in computing present values.

---

[2] In macroeconomics, the term *discount rate* has a completely different meaning: It's the interest rate that the Federal Reserve charges banks when it lends them reserves. There is no connection between the two different meanings of the term.

TABLE 2		Value of $1 to Be Received at Various Numbers of Years in the Future, at Different Discount Rates		
Present Values of $1 Future Payments	No. of Years in Future	5 Percent	10 Percent	15 Percent
	0	$1.00	$1.00	$1.00
	1	$0.95	$0.91	$0.87
	2	$0.91	$0.83	$0.76
	3	$0.86	$0.75	$0.66
	4	$0.82	$0.68	$0.57
	5	$0.78	$0.62	$0.50
	10	$0.61	$0.39	$0.25
	20	$0.38	$0.15	$0.06

DANGEROUS CURVES

Percentages and Decimals Be careful when working with interest rates: They can be expressed in either percentage form or decimal form. An interest rate of 5 percent (5%) can also be expressed in decimal form as 0.05.

In the expression $1+r$, r is always in decimal form. For example, $1+r$ is equal to 1.05 when the interest rate is 5 percent. Similarly, an interest rate of 0.5% (*one-half* of 1 percent) would translate to 0.005 in decimal form, and $1+r$ would then equal 1.005.

interest you sacrifice by waiting. A higher interest rate or a longer postponement of the payment means that each dollar you give up today *could* earn even more interest while you are waiting. So for any given future payment, you won't want to give up as many dollars today.

Finally, there is one more way in which we use the formula for present value calculations: to determine the value of a *stream* of future payments, with each individual payment to be received at a *different* time in the future. Consider the value, in today's dollars, of the following stream of future payments: $1,000 to be received one year from now, $900 to be received two years from now, and $600 to be received three years from now. To get the present value of this stream of payments, we first calculate the present value of each payment, and then we add those present values together:

$$PV = \frac{\$1,000}{(1+r)} + \frac{\$900}{(1+r)^2} + \frac{\$600}{(1+r)^3}$$

With an interest rate of 10 percent, the *total* present value of the entire stream of payments is equal to:

$$PV = \frac{\$1,000}{(1.10)} + \frac{\$900}{(1.10)^2} + \frac{\$600}{(1.10)^3}$$

$$= \$909.09 + \$743.80 + \$450.79$$

$$= \$2,103.68$$

The logic of present value shows us why anyone who expects to receive a stream of future payments must discount each of those payments before adding them together. The next section provides an example of how firms use present value to make decisions about investing in new capital.

THE FIRM'S DEMAND FOR CAPITAL

Let's return to your problem at Quicksilver Delivery Service. How many trucks should you buy? Table 3 shows the present value calculations you'd need to make, under the following conditions: (1) each truck's yearly *MRP* is the same as it was in Table 1, a few pages earlier; (2) each truck has an expected useful life of 15 years, so that Quicksilver can look forward to 15 years of additional revenue from each truck; and (3) the appropriate discount rate for Quicksilver's present value calculations is 10 percent.

When Are Future Payments Received? Businesses typically earn revenue every day they are in operation. However, in calculating present discounted value, it would be cumbersome to discount each day's revenue by the appropriate discount factor. As a useful approximation, we can treat each year's revenue as if it is all received in one lump sum at the *end* of the year. This is the convention followed in this book for all future payments. Thus, when we say that a firm or individual receives a payment of $10,000 "in the first year," we mean "at the end of the first year." (Can you see how we've used this assumption in Table 3?)

For example, the first truck gives Quicksilver $10,000 per year in additional revenue for 15 years. Since we're assuming for simplicity that each year's revenue is received at the *end* of each year (see the Dangerous Curves feature above), the present value of the first year's revenue is $10,000/(1.1); the present value of the second year's revenue is $10,000/(1.1)^2; and so on. When these present values are added together for all 15 years, we find that the first truck gives the firm $76,060.80 in total additional revenue in present value terms. Similarly, the *PV* of all the revenue from the *fourth* truck is $41,833.44.

Now that we know the total present value that you gain from each truck, do we know how many trucks you should buy? Almost, but not quite. There is still the matter of how much each truck *costs*. But now that we've translated *all* the additional revenue from each truck into a single, present value number, we know the benefits of each truck measured in *today's dollars*. That measure can be compared to the truck's cost, which must *also* be *paid* in today's dollars. If trucks cost

Truck	Additional Annual Revenue (*MRP*)	Total Present Value of Additional Revenue over 15 years
1	$10,000	$\frac{\$10,000}{(1.1)} + \frac{\$10,000}{(1.1)^2} + \cdots + \frac{\$10,000}{(1.1)^{15}} = \$76,060.80$
2	$10,000	$\frac{\$10,000}{(1.1)} + \frac{\$10,000}{(1.1)^2} + \cdots + \frac{\$10,000}{(1.1)^{15}} = \$76,060.80$
3	$ 8,000	$\frac{\$8,000}{(1.1)} + \frac{\$8,000}{(1.1)^2} + \cdots + \frac{\$8,000}{(1.1)^{15}} = \$60,848.64$
4	$ 5,500	$\frac{\$5,500}{(1.1)} + \frac{\$5,500}{(1.1)^2} + \cdots + \frac{\$5,500}{(1.1)^{15}} = \$41,833.44$
5	$ 2,000	$\frac{\$2,000}{(1.1)} + \frac{\$2,000}{(1.1)^2} + \cdots + \frac{\$2,000}{(1.1)^{15}} = \$15,212.16$

TABLE 3

The Present Value of Trucks at Quicksilver Delivery Service (with a Discount Rate of 10%)

$50,000, the firm gains more benefits (in future revenue) than costs for the first three trucks. But the purchase of the fourth truck, whose benefit to the firm is only $41,833.44 in today's dollars, does not make sense, since the cost in today's dollars is $50,000. Quicksilver should buy only three trucks.

Our examples have focused on a special type of capital—delivery trucks. But the same logic works for any other type of physical capital—automated assembly lines, desktop computers, filing cabinets, locomotives, and construction cranes. In each of these cases, the first step in making a decision about a capital purchase is to put a value on an additional unit of capital. This value is the total present value of the future revenue generated by the capital.

This first step—putting a value on physical capital—is so important and so widely applicable that we can refer to it as a general principle:

> The *principle of asset valuation* says that the value of any asset is the sum of the present values of all the future benefits it generates.

The principle of asset valuation tells us how to determine the marginal benefit from buying another unit of capital, such as another truck. Then, as we've done with Quicksilver, we compare this marginal benefit with the cost of the capital itself. As you've seen, the firm should then buy any unit of capital for which the marginal benefit (total present value of future revenue) is greater than the cost.

WHAT HAPPENS WHEN THINGS CHANGE: THE INVESTMENT CURVE

Investment is the term economists use to describe firms' purchases of new capital over some period of time. In the example above, if trucks cost $50,000 each, Quicksilver should buy three of them. If it bought all three trucks this year, its investment expenditures for the year would be $50,000 × 3 = $150,000.

But this conclusion about investment is based on the assumption that the interest rate, and Quicksilver's discount rate, is 10 percent. With a lower interest rate—say, 5 percent—each year's revenue would have a higher present value, so the total present value of each truck would be higher. Our conclusion about Quicksilver's investment spending might then change. Similarly, a rise in the interest rate—say, to 15 percent—would *lower* the present value of each year's revenue, and *decrease* the total present value of a truck.

Table 4 shows how our total present value calculations for each truck change as the interest rate changes. The table assumes that the other ingredients in the firm's decision making do not change. Each package delivered still generates revenue of $4, and the productivity of each truck is still what it was before. For instance, a truck used on the Northern route would still allow Quicksilver to deliver 2,500 additional packages each year.

The numbers in the last three columns are each calculated just as were the numbers we calculated in Table 3. The only difference is that, instead of always assuming a discount rate of 10 percent, Table 4 shows the total present value for each truck under three different interest rates. Notice what happens as we move from left to right in the table for any particular truck: The interest rate rises, from 5 percent to 10 percent to 15 percent, and the value of the truck to the firm falls.

Now, if trucks cost $50,000 each, how much will Quicksilver invest (spend on new trucks) at any given interest rate? Let's see. If the interest rate is 5 percent, Quicksilver should buy four trucks, because each of the first four trucks has a total

Truck	Additional Annual Revenue	Total Present Value with a Discount Rate of:			TABLE 4
		5%	10%	15%	Present Value Calculations for Various Interest Rates
1	$10,000	$103,797	$76,061	$58,474	
2	$10,000	$103,797	$76,061	$58,474	
3	$ 8,000	$ 83,037	$60,849	$46,779	
4	$ 5,500	$ 57,088	$41,833	$32,161	
5	$ 2,000	$ 20,759	$15,212	$11,695	

present value greater than $50,000 at that interest rate. The fifth truck, however, has a total present value of only $20,759, so the firm should not buy that one. Thus, if the interest rate is 5 percent, Quicksilver's investment spending will be $50,000 × 4 = $200,000.

If the interest rate rises to 10 percent, we are back to the conclusion we reached in Table 3, which assumed a 10 percent interest rate: Quicksilver should buy three trucks when the interest rate is 10 percent. (You can also verify this using the middle column of Table 3.) Quicksilver's total investment spending would *decrease* to $50,000 × 3 = $150,000. Finally, if the interest rate rises to 15 percent, Quicksilver should buy only two trucks, so its total investment spending is $50,000 × 2 = $100,000.

What is true for Quicksilver is true for every other truck-buying firm in the economy: The higher the interest rate, the fewer trucks delivery services and other truck-buying firms will want to purchase, and the smaller will be investment expenditures on trucks during the year.

Take a moment to think about why this happens. The trucks themselves are the same, and they are just as productive as before. But each truck is less valuable to firms in *present-dollar* terms. That's because—with a higher interest rate—the future additional revenue from each truck is worth *less* in today's dollars (delayed earnings impose a greater opportunity cost in lost interest). But the truck still costs the same in today's dollars, regardless of the interest (or discount) rate. So with a high interest rate, each firm will want fewer trucks at any given price.

The same logic applies to other capital purchases. At high interest rates, U.S. firms end up buying less of all different kinds of capital—not just delivery trucks, but also other durable goods such as computers, machine tools, combines, and printing presses. It should be no surprise, then, that we come to the following conclusion:

As the interest rate rises, each business firm in the economy—using the principle of asset valuation—will place a lower value on additional capital, and decide to purchase less of it. Therefore, in the economy as a whole, a rise in the interest rate causes a decrease in investment expenditures.

The relationship between the interest rate and investment expenditure is illustrated by the economy's investment curve, shown in Figure 1. The curve slopes downward, indicating that a drop in the interest rate causes investment spending to rise. When you study *macroeconomics*, you'll learn that the investment curve is important for the performance of the overall economy, for several reasons. But here's a hint as to one of them: When the interest rate falls, the increased investment in new capital means that the nation's *capital stock*—the total quantity of installed

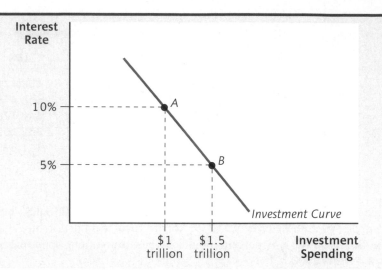

FIGURE 1

The Investment Curve

As the interest rate falls from 10 percent to 5 percent, each firm that buys a particular type of capital will buy more of it. As a result, the economy's total investment in physical capital rises from $1 trillion to $1.5 trillion. This is shown as the movement from point A to point B along the investment curve in the figure.

capital—will grow more rapidly than it otherwise would. With more capital, labor will be more productive, and our standard of living will be higher. This relationship between the interest rate, investment spending, and the ultimate size of our capital stock is one reason that policy makers pay so much attention to the overall level of interest rates in the economy.

To recap:

> *Lower interest rates increase firms' investment in physical capital, causing the capital stock to be larger, and our overall standard of living to be higher.*

FINANCIAL MARKETS

You may be wondering what financial markets, like the markets for stocks and bonds, have to do with the other subject of this chapter: markets for capital. After all, capital—like a machine or a factor—is something *real*; it enables a firm to produce real goods and services.

But in financial markets, the things being traded are just *pieces of paper*, which don't directly help anyone to produce anything. So what do these pieces of paper have to do with capital?

Actually, quite a bit. The pieces of paper being traded in financial markets are **financial assets**—promises to pay future income to their owners. Because capital lasts for many years, most firms fund their capital purchases by issuing and selling these financial assets. For example, the firm might issue and sell shares of stock in the company, obligating it to pay those who hold the shares part of the firm's future profits. Or it might sell bonds, which are promises to pay back a sum of money in the future, along with interest payments. This leaves the firm with long-lasting capital, but also a long-lasting obligation to make future payments. So there is a close *economic* connection between a firm's decision to demand capital equipment and its decision to supply financial assets.

But there is another connection between these two types of markets as well. Because a financial asset gives its holder a stream of future payments, the value of a

Financial asset A promise to pay future income in some form, such as future profits or future interest payments.

financial asset is calculated in the same way as the value of any other asset, such as a truck or a computer: We find the *total present value* of the future payments the asset will generate. Thus, the method of valuation is another connection between markets for capital and markets for financial assets.

> *The principle of asset valuation applies to financial assets as well as physical assets. In each case, the value of the asset is the sum of the present values of the future benefits.*

In the rest of this chapter, we'll explore two types of financial assets: bonds and stocks. We'll also analyze the very well-publicized markets in which these assets are traded.

THE BOND MARKET

If a firm wants to buy a new fleet of trucks, build a new factory, or upgrade its computer system, it must decide how to finance that purchase. One way to do this is to sell **bonds.** A bond is simply a promise to pay a certain amount of money, called the **principal** or **face value,** at some future date. Although $10,000 is the most common principal amount, you can also find bonds with face values of $100,000, $5,000, and other amounts.

A bond's **maturity date** is the date on which the principal will be paid to the bond's owner. If a bond has a maturity date 30 years after the date on which it was first sold, we'd call it a 30-year bond. Other bonds have shorter maturities—15 years, 10 years, 1 year, 6 months, or even 3 months.

Some bonds, including many of those sold by the U.S. federal government, are **pure discount bonds.** A discount bond is one that does not make any payments except for the principal it pays at maturity. For example, at some time in your life, you may have gotten a gift of a U.S. savings bond, issued by the federal government and sold at most banks. A $100 savings bond is a promise by the federal government to pay $100 to the bond's owner in, say, 20 years. If the savings bond sells for $38 and pays $100 at maturity, the total interest on the bond is $62, the difference between what the bond originally sold for and what the owner will receive at maturity.

Most bonds, however, promise—in addition to repayment of principal—a series of interim payments called **coupon payments.** For example, a 30-year, $10,000 bond might promise a coupon payment—say, $600—each year for the next 30 years, and then pay $10,000 at maturity.

A bond's **yield** is the effective annual interest rate that the bond earns for its owner. For example, if you buy a 20-year savings bond for $38 that will give you $100 in 20 years, your annual yield is 5 percent. That's because if you put $38 in the bank for 20 years at 5 percent interest, you'd end up with $100 after 20 years—the same as you get with the savings bond. The yield on a bond, as you will see later on, is closely related to the price that someone pays for the bond.

How Much Is a Bond Worth?

To determine the value of a bond, let's start with a simple example: a pure discount bond that promises to pay $10,000 when it matures in exactly one year. The $10,000 is a future payment, and our method of calculating its value should not surprise you: It involves *present value.* Let's suppose the interest rate at which you can

Bond A promise to pay back borrowed funds, issued by a corporation or government agency.

Principal (face value) The amount of money a bond promises to pay when it matures.

Maturity date The date at which a bond's principal amount will be paid to the bond's owner.

Pure discount bond A bond that promises no payments except for the principal it pays at maturity.

Coupon payments A series of periodic payments that a bond promises before maturity.

Yield The rate of return a bond earns for its owner.

borrow and lend funds is 10 percent. Then we can determine the present value of the bond with our discounting formula as:

$$PV = \frac{\$Y}{(1+r)} = \frac{\$10{,}000}{1.10} = \$9{,}091.$$

Since the present value of $10,000 to be received in one year is $9,091, that is the most you should pay for the bond. Assuming the bond's current owner can borrow and lend at the same 10 percent interest rate as you, then $9,091 is the lowest price at which she will sell the bond to you. We conclude that this bond will sell for $9,091, no more and no less.

The same principle applies to more complicated types of bonds, such as discount bonds that don't pay off for many years, or coupon bonds. For example, suppose a bond maturing in five years has a principal of $10,000, and also promises a coupon payment of $600 each year until maturity, with the first payment made one year from today. The total present value of this bond would be:

$$PV = \frac{\$600}{(1.10)} + \frac{\$600}{(1.10)^2} + \frac{\$600}{(1.10)^3} + \frac{\$600}{(1.10)^4}$$
$$+ \frac{\$600}{(1.10)^5} + \frac{\$10{,}000}{(1.10)^5} = \$8{,}484.$$

Once again, this total present value—$8,484—is what the bond is worth, and this is the price at which it will trade, as long as buyers and sellers use the same discount rate of 10 percent in their calculations.

Bond Prices and Bond Yields

There is an important relationship between the price of a bond and the yield or rate of return the bond earns for its owner. This is easiest to see with a pure discount bond, such as the bond that pays $10,000 in one year in our example above. Suppose you bought this bond for $8,000. Then, at the end of the year, you would earn interest of $10,000 − $8,000 = $2,000 on an asset that cost you $8,000. Your annual yield would be $2,000/$8,000 = 0.25 or 25 percent.

But now suppose you paid $9,000 for that same bond. Then your interest earnings would be $10,000 − $9,000 = $1,000, and your annual yield would be $1,000/$9,000 = 0.111 or 11.1 percent.

As you can see, the yield you earn on a bond depends on the price you pay for it. For each price, there is a different yield. And the greater the price of a bond, the lower the yield on that bond. This applies not only to simple discount bonds, but also to more complicated bonds with coupon payments. And the reasoning is the same in both cases: A bond promises to pay fixed amounts of dollars at fixed dates in the future. The more you end up paying for those promised future payments, the lower your rate of return.

More generally:

There is an inverse relationship between bond prices and bond yields. The higher the price of any given bond, the lower the yield on that bond.

What is true for a single bond is also true for bonds in general: When many bonds' prices are rising together, so that the average price of bonds rises, then the average yield on bonds must be falling.

Primary and Secondary Bond Markets

Every type of financial asset is traded in two different types of markets. The **primary market** is where newly issued financial assets are sold for the first time. But once a financial asset is sold in the primary market, the buyer is free to sell it to someone else. When a previously issued asset is sold again, the sale takes place in the **secondary market**. Most of the trading that takes place in financial markets on any given day is *secondary market trading*.

Applying this distinction to bonds, we would say that the *primary bond market* is where newly issued bonds are sold to their original buyers, while the *secondary bond market* is where previously issued bonds change hands.

It is only in the primary market that a firm actually obtains funds for its investment projects. Once a firm has issued and sold a bond, that bond can change hands many times in the secondary market, but the firm will not benefit directly from these sales. Secondary market trading is an exchange between private parties, and the original issuing firm or government agency is not involved.

Still, firms and government agencies follow secondary bond markets closely. Why? Because bond prices (and therefore bond yields) in the secondary and primary markets are closely related. In fact, otherwise similar bonds in these two markets are perfect substitutes for each other. For example, suppose that IBM wants to borrow funds by issuing 10-year, $10,000 bonds in the primary market. In order to attract buyers, it will have to sell these *new* bonds at the same price as any *old* $10,000 IBM bonds trading in the secondary market that still have 10 years left before maturity. After all, there is no reason for a bond buyer to prefer a new, 10-year bond to an old bond that has 10 years left to run—as long as both are issued by the same corporation and both have the same face value. Thus,

> *while bond issuers are not direct participants in secondary market trading, they are affected by what happens in the secondary market. More specifically, if a bond's price rises in the secondary market, the price one can charge for similar, newly issued bonds in the primary market will rise as well.*

Since there is such a close relationship between bond prices and bond yields, we can also express this idea in terms of yields.

> *If a bond's yield falls in the secondary market, the yield of similar, newly issued bonds in the primary market will fall as well.*

A bond's yield is the interest rate a firm ends up paying when it issues bonds and sells them in the primary market. So a firm would like its bond yield to be as small as possible (and its bond price to be as high as possible).

Why Do Bond Yields Differ?

Thousands of different kinds of bonds are traded in financial markets every day. There are corporate bonds of various maturities and bonds issued by local, state, and federal governments and government agencies. Bonds issued by foreign firms

Primary market The market in which newly issued financial assets are sold for the first time.

Secondary market The market in which previously issued financial assets are sold.

and governments are also traded in the United States. And each bond has its own unique yield. Why is this? Why don't all bonds give the same yield? That is, why doesn't each bond sell at a price that makes its yield identical to the yield on any other bond?

The answer is that bonds differ in important ways from one another. One difference is in their *default risk*. A bond is a promise to pay in the future, and there is always a danger that the promise won't be kept. Private firms do occasionally go bankrupt and default on their obligations; some recent examples include Enron and WorldCom. Bond buyers and sellers account for differences in default risk by adjusting the discount rate used to calculate the present value of a bond.

If you are *absolutely certain* that you will receive the promised future payment, then your discount rate should be the interest rate you *could* earn on *other*, absolutely certain investments. The promises made by the U.S. government are generally considered the most reliable, and the interest rate on U.S. government securities is often called the *riskless rate*. So, if you have the same faith in the bond you are considering buying as you would in U.S. government bonds, then you should use the interest rate on otherwise similar government bonds as your discount rate, and calculate the total *PV* accordingly.

When a bond has a higher likelihood of default, the opportunity cost of your funds to buy it is greater than just the interest foregone because you are also foregoing safety: You risk losing the entire value of the bond. Therefore, for riskier bonds, your discount rate should include the opportunity cost of foregone interest that you could have earned on U.S. government bonds, *plus* an extra premium reflecting the higher risk. And the riskier the bond, the higher the discount rate you should apply to it, and the lower will be its total present value.

> *To put a value on riskier bonds, market participants use a higher discount rate than on safe bonds. This leads to lower total present values and lower prices people are willing to pay for the riskier bonds. With lower prices, riskier bonds have higher yields.*

Table 5 shows that the market does value bonds in this way. In the table, bonds are listed in the order of increasing risk, according to Moody's Investor's Services, a private corporation that analyzes corporations and municipalities that issue bonds and estimates the likelihood that they will default. U.S. Treasury bonds top the list.

TABLE 5	Rating	Interest Rate
Interest Rates on 5-Year Bonds, August 25, 2006	U.S. Treasury bond	4.76 percent
	Aaa corporate bond	5.26 percent
	Aa corporate bond	5.37 percent
	A corporate bond	5.45 percent
	Baa corporate bond	6.19 percent
	Ba corporate bond	7.07 percent
	B corporate bond	8.70 percent

Source: http://bonds.yahoo.com/rates.html (accessed on August 26, 2006); bond rates below A rating are based on sample of individual bond quotes on the same date.

They are backed by the promise of the U.S. government and have virtually zero probability of default. Next is Aaa, considered "best quality," the highest rating given to the most credit-worthy corporations and municipalities. The ratings continue down through Aa (high quality), A (favorable), Baa (medium-grade), and so on. Notice how the yields diverged on August 25, 2006. For example, the difference between the riskless yield of 4.76 percent on U.S. Treasury bonds (which have virtually zero probability of default) and the more risky Baa yield was about 1.4 percentage points. That difference is the premium that compensates investors for the chance that a Baa bond will go into default in a given year.

Riskiness is just one reason that bond prices and bond yields differ. If you go on to study financial economics, you'll learn that two bonds with equal default risk can have different yields for a variety of reasons, including differences in their maturity dates, differences in their frequency of coupon payments, or because one bond is more widely traded (and therefore easier to sell on short notice) than another.

Explaining a Particular Bond's Price

Bond prices are determined by supply and demand. Figure 2 provides an example. It shows supply and demand curves for a General Motors (GM) bond that matures in exactly one year, with a face value of $10,000 and a coupon of $1,000. One year from today, the owner of this bond will receive $10,000 + $1,000 = $11,000 from General Motors. The number of these bonds is on the horizontal axis, and the price of each bond is on the vertical axis.

Notice that the supply curve, B^S, is vertical. Unlike most supply curves you've studied in this book—which tell you the quantity that suppliers want to *sell* over a given *period* of time—the supply curve in Figure 2 is somewhat different. It tells us the quantity of this particular bond *in existence* at a *given moment*. This quantity, 6,000, is the number of these bonds that General Motors has issued in the past, in the primary market. The supply curve also tells us the number of bonds that people are currently holding, since every bond in existence is being held by someone.

The supply curve is vertical because, on any given day, the number of these bonds will remain the same no matter what the price. The number changes only if

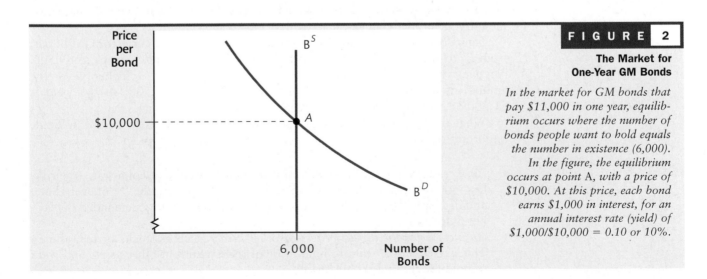

FIGURE 2

The Market for One-Year GM Bonds

In the market for GM bonds that pay $11,000 in one year, equilibrium occurs where the number of bonds people want to hold equals the number in existence (6,000). In the figure, the equilibrium occurs at point A, with a price of $10,000. At this price, each bond earns $1,000 in interest, for an annual interest rate (yield) of $1,000/$10,000 = 0.10 or 10%.

GM issues more of these bonds, or pays some off and doesn't issue new bonds to replace them. If GM issues more bonds, the supply curve shifts rightward. If it retires some bonds, the curve shifts to the left.

The demand curve, B^D, tells us the quantity of these bonds that people *want* to hold at a given moment, at different hypothetical prices. It slopes downward, telling us that the lower the price, the more of these bonds people will want to hold. As you've learned, the value of a bond is given by its present value, which is calculated based on a discount rate. The discount rate depends, in part, on the risk premium that individuals attach to the bond. But because people differ in their attitudes toward risk, and in their beliefs about the riskiness of a particular bond, they will apply different risk premiums in making their calculations. Therefore, they will each come up with different present values for a bond. As the price decreases, it drops below more and more individuals' present values, so more and more of them decide that holding the bond is a good deal.

You can see in the figure that at any price greater than $10,000, the quantity of bonds people *are* holding (given by the supply curve) exceeds the number that people *want* to hold (on the demand curve). There would be an excess supply of this bond, and people would try to sell it. This would drive the price down to $10,000, at which point people would be willing to hold all 6,000 bonds in existence. At any price lower than $10,000, people want to hold *more* of these bonds than they are holding, and they will drive the price up trying to acquire them.

When the market is in equilibrium at a price of $10,000, this one-year GM bond will pay interest of $11,000 − $10,000 = $1,000. Anyone who buys it will have a yield of $1,000/$10,000 = 0.10 or 10 percent.

Bond prices achieve their equilibrium value almost instantly. It takes just a few seconds for people to call in an offer to sell or buy bonds when there is an excess supply or demand. Only at the equilibrium price will every seller find a buyer and every buyer find a seller, so that every bond will be willingly held.

Changes in a Bond's Price

Most bonds' prices change every day, and even minute by minute. Because bonds virtually always trade at their equilibrium prices, and because the supply curve shifts only rarely (when new bonds are issued), it must be changes in demand that cause these frequent price changes.

Figure 3 shows an example: a leftward shift in the demand curve for GM bonds, from B_1^D to B_2^D. As a result of the shift, the new equilibrium price drops to $9,500. Anyone who buys the bond at this lower price will earn a higher yield: the annual interest payment is now $11,000 − $9,500 = $1,500, so the yield is $1,500/$9,500 = 0.158 or 15.8 percent.

What might cause the demand curve to shift leftward, as in Figure 3? Some important reasons are:

- *An increase in the (riskless) interest rate.* This raises the discount rate (the riskless interest rate plus the risk premium) used in calculating the PV of every bond and decreases their present values. At any price, the quantity demanded of *every* bond decreases.
- *An increase in the attractiveness of other assets* (such as stocks or real estate). This makes people want to hold more of their wealth in other assets and want to hold fewer bonds at any price.

FIGURE 3

A Decrease in Demand for GM Bonds

When the demand for one-year GM bonds decreases, the equilibrium moves from point A to point B, and the price drops to $9,500. Because the bonds still pay $11,000 in one year, anyone who buys at the new price earns interest of $1,500. The annual yield is now $1,500/$9,500 = 0.158 or 15.8%

- *An increase in the perceived riskiness of the bond.* This leads to a higher risk premium for *PV* calculations, a lower present value, and a decrease in quantity demanded at any price.
- *Expectations of any of the above.* If people expect any of the above events to occur in the future, they will expect the demand curve B^D to shift leftward as well, and the future price of the bond to drop. As a result, people will want to hold fewer bonds at any given price *now.*

A striking example of how an increase in the perceived riskiness of a bond can cause demand to decrease occurred on May 5, 2005. That day, Standard & Poor's (a bond-rating corporation that competes with Moody's) concluded it had doubts about the ability of two automobile companies—General Motors and Ford—to keep their financial promises. It announced that it was downgrading these corporations' bonds to a higher risk. Within minutes, bond traders—applying a higher discount rate—lowered the estimated present value of these bonds. The demand curves for GM and Ford bonds shifted leftward (as in Figure 3), and the price dropped sharply. In a single day, the price of GM bonds dropped by 5.7 percent, and the price of Ford bonds dropped by 7.2 percent.

THE STOCK MARKET

A **share of stock,** like a bond, is a financial asset that promises its owner future payments. But the nature of the promise is very different for these two types of assets. When a corporation issues a bond, it is *borrowing* funds and promising to pay them back. But when a corporation issues a share of stock, it brings in new ownership of the firm itself. In fact, a share of stock *is*, by definition, *a share of ownership* in the firm. Those who buy the shares provide the firm with funds, and, in return, they are entitled to a share of the firm's future profits.

When a firm wishes to raise money in the stock market, it gets in touch with an investment bank. Investment banks are firms that specialize in assessing the market potential of new stock issues. Together, the firm and its investment banker develop a prospectus that describes the offering—the nature of the firm's business, the number of shares that will be sold, and so on. The purpose of the prospectus is to inform potential investors of the risks involved. It must be reviewed by the *Securities and*

Share of stock A share of ownership in a corporation.

Exchange Commission, the principal regulatory agency that oversees financial markets. Once the prospectus is approved, the firm can sell shares to the public.

Primary and Secondary Stock Markets

When a corporation issues new shares, they are sold in the *primary stock market.* The only time a corporation receives any income from a trade in its stock is when the corporation itself sells the stock in the primary market. From then on, the stock is traded in the *secondary market*—the market in which previously issued shares are sold and resold.

As in the bond market, the issuing corporation has no *direct* relationship with the secondary market. But the secondary market is very important to firms that raise funds in the primary market, for two reasons. First, because of the secondary market, people who buy shares know they can easily sell them when they want. This makes people more willing to hold stock, including any new shares firms issue to raise funds.

Second, stock prices in the secondary market affect the price a firm can get when it sells shares in the primary market. In fact, when a firm's shares are already trading in the secondary market, a small offering of new shares will always sell at the secondary market price. That's because the shares trading in the secondary markets are perfect substitutes for the new shares.

Direct and Indirect Ownership of Stock

Many people own shares of stock directly. You or a family member may have purchased stock for your own account, by calling a broker or going online and ordering, say, 200 shares of Barnes and Noble stock. The stock is then held by your brokerage firm, and you are free to buy more or sell it any time you want, with a phone call or an online order.

Mutual fund A corporation that specializes in owning shares of stock in other corporations.

But you can also own stock *indirectly,* by purchasing shares of a **mutual fund**. A mutual fund is a corporation that, in turn, buys shares of stock in *other* corporations. There are mutual funds that specialize in Internet companies, in foreign companies located in specific regions like Europe or Asia, and in long-lived companies that have a reputation for stable, slow-growing profits. Most mutual funds advertise that, by doing careful research into companies and making professional predictions about the future, they can pick stocks within their specialty more wisely than a nonprofessional can. We'll discuss the accuracy of this claim later in this chapter.

Stock ownership in the United States is growing rapidly. Today, about half of all American households own shares of stock or mutual fund shares, up from about 20 percent of households in 1980.

Why Do People Hold Stock?

Why do so many individuals and fund managers choose to put their money into stocks? You already know part of the answer: When you own a share of stock, you own part of the corporation. Indeed, the fraction of the corporation that you own is equal to the fraction of the company's total stock that you own. For example, in June 2006, Starbucks Corporation had 764.7 million shares outstanding. If you owned 7,600 shares of Starbucks stock, then you owned 7,600/7,674,000 = .00001, or about one-thousandth of 1 percent of that firm. This means you are, in essence, entitled to a thousandth of a percent of the firm's after-tax profit.

In practice, however, most firms do not pay out *all* of their profit to shareholders. Instead, some of the profit is kept as *retained earnings,* for later use by the firm.

The part of profit that is distributed to shareholders is called **dividends.** A firm's dividend payments benefit stockholders in much the same way that interest payments benefit bondholders, providing a source of steady income. Of course, as a part owner of a firm, you are part owner of any retained earnings as well, even if you will not benefit from them until later.

> **Dividends** Part of a firm's current profit that is distributed to shareholders.

Aside from dividends, a second—and usually more important—reason that people hold stocks is that they hope to enjoy **capital gains:** the return someone gets when they sell an asset at a higher price than they paid for it. For example, if you buy shares of Hewlett Packard at $30 per share, and later sell them at $35 per share, your capital gain is $5 per share. This is in addition to any dividends the firm paid to you while you owned the stock.

> **Capital gain** The return someone gets by selling a financial asset at a price higher than they paid for it.

Some stocks pay no dividends at all, because the management believes that stockholders are best served by reinvesting all profits within the firm so that *future* profits will be even higher. The idea is to invest profits back into the corporation, enabling it to purchase new capital, develop new products, or purchase other profitable firms. If the firm uses this money well, then future profits (and future dividends) can be even greater. And in the meantime, higher profits raise the price of the stock so that shareholders can get capital gains when they sell it. Until 2003, Microsoft had never paid a dividend. But by plowing its profits back into the company, the firm's shares grew to a total value of almost $300 billion in mid-2003. The company's shareholders had great faith that they would eventually get cash from the firm, and in March 2003, it happened: Microsoft paid its first dividend.

Over the past century, corporate stocks have generally been a good investment. They were especially rewarding during the 1990s, enjoying (on average) a 15 percent annual return. That means that the average $1,000 invested in the stock market on January 1, 1990, would have increased in value to $3,860 by the middle of 2006. However, the stock market is volatile; over shorter periods of time, one cannot assume that stock prices will rise at all. For example, if you invested $1,000 in the market on January 1, 2000, your stocks would have been worth only about $864 by the middle of 2006.

Valuing a Share of Stock

The value of a share of stock, like any other asset, is the total present value of its future payments. For a share of stock, the future payments are all the profits that the share is expected to earn for its owner. But over what time horizon should stocks be valued? Unlike a bond, which has a maturity date, a share of stock is expected to remain an earning asset for whomever owns it for as long as the company exists. This is essentially forever, unless market participants anticipate the firm will go out of business at some future date.

Fortunately, there are formulas to measure the total present value of a firm's future profits under a variety of different assumptions. For example, the simplest formula tells us that

> *if a firm will earn a constant $Y in profit after taxes each year forever, then the total present value of these future profits is $Y/r, where r is the discount rate.*[3]

---

[3] There are other present value formulas for more complicated earnings forecasts, such as earnings that are expected to *grow* at a constant rate, or grow for some period and then stabilize, and more. If you go further in your study of economics or finance, you will learn some of them.

So, for example, if a firm is expected to earn $10 million in after-tax profit for its owners per year forever, and the discount rate is 10 percent, then—according to the formula—the total PV of those future profits is $10 million/0.10 = $100 million.

What about the value of a single *share* of this firm's stock? If there are 1 million shares of stock outstanding for this firm, then each share should be worth one one-millionth of the firm's total value. So each share's price should be $100 million/ 1 million = $100.

> *The value of a share of stock in a firm is equal to the total present value of the firm's after-tax profit divided by the number of shares outstanding.*

Note that we are valuing a share of stock by future profits, not by dividends. Remember that firms often plow some or all of their profits back into the firm in order to generate more growth. What counts is after-tax *profits*, because these belong to the firm's shareholders, whether they receive them as dividends or not.

Reading the Stock Pages

In the United States, financial markets are so important that stock and bond prices are monitored on a continuous basis. If you wish to know the value of a stock, you can find out instantly by checking with a broker or logging on to a Web site that reports such information. One such site is Yahoo Finance (*http://finance.yahoo.com*) but there are dozens of others. In addition, stock prices and other information are reported daily in local newspapers and in specialized financial publications such as the *Wall Street Journal*.

To some people, the pages that cover the stock market look as impenetrable as Egyptian hieroglyphics. But in fact, the information on the stock pages is very easy to understand, once you decide to learn it.

Figure 4 shows an excerpt from the New York Stock Exchange Composite Transactions reported in the August 2, 2006, *Wall Street Journal*. The data refer to the previous trading day: Tuesday, August 1, 2006.

Let's focus on the stock of FedEx Corporation (listed as FedExCp), the second stock listed. We'll go column by column and discuss each entry, using the column headings at the top of the *Wall Street Journal* clipping.

- **52-WEEK HI LO:** These two columns tell us the highest ($120.01) and lowest ($76.81) prices, respectively, for FedEx shares over the past year.
- **STOCK (DIV):** The letters in this column show the corporation's name, typically abbreviated, as in "FedExCp" for FedEx Corporation. The number next to the name is FedEx's current annual dividend payment, which is .36 or 36 cents per share. (Dividends are paid quarterly, so the actual payment would be 9 cents per share per quarter.) The letter *f* next to the number refers to a footnote (not shown here), stating that FedEx's dividend payment was recently increased.
- **YLD%:** This is FedEx's *dividend yield*—the annual dividend payment as a percentage of the stock's current price. For FedEx, the dividend yield was 0.3 percent. This means that if someone bought FedEx on August 1, 2006, the dividend of 36 cents over the year would earn them a 0.3 percent annual rate of return on their investment.
- **PE:** This stands for *price-earnings ratio*—the current stock price divided by the firm's after-tax profit per share during the previous twelve months. The PE ratio

FIGURE 4

Stock Market Table for Trading on August 1, 2006

Source: The Wall Street Journal
(August 2, 2006).

52-WEEK			YLD		VOL		NET
HI	LO	STOCK (DIV)	%	PE	100s	CLOSE	CHG
40.17	29.56	FedInv B .72	2.3	15	5975	30.72	−0.29
120.01	76.81	FedExCp .36f	.3	18	25631	103.21	−1.50
22.95	13.27	Felcor .50	2.3	dd	6260	21.98	−0.02
14.65	8.63	FldmnMallProp .91	8.3	dd	60	10.90	−0.08
22.50	20.18	Ferrellgas 2.00	8.8	13	1074	22.63	0.14
22.59	13.82	Ferro lf .58	3.6	30	2556	16	−0.15
15.06	7.90	Fiat ADS	...	...	158	14.18	0.02
45	33.70	FidNtlFnl s 1.00	2.6	12	10275	38.24	−0.11
41.50	30.20	FidelityNtlInfo .20a	.6	...	3572	35.20	−0.54
26	17.92	FidNtlTitle n 1.12e	5.9	...	5724	19.02	0.15
30.13	24.17	FnlFed s .40	1.5	17	1516	27.15	0.28
13.40	8.77	FstAcceptance	...	22	814	11.86	−0.18
49.50	35.80	FstAmCp .72	2.0	8	5209	36.73	−0.28
24.43	8.59	FstBcp lf .28	3.0	5	1687	9.33	−0.16
14.70	12.14	FstCmwlthFnl .68	5.4	18	1447	12.69	−0.30

gives the cost of the stock *per dollar* of the firm's yearly after-tax profits. For FedEx, the PE ratio of 18 tells us that if you bought this stock on that day, you would be paying $18 for each dollar of yearly profits.

Many people theorize that a stock with a low PE ratio is a better deal, since the cost per dollar of profit is lower. But PE ratios can be deceiving. Something unattractive about a firm's future can makes its PE ratio particularly low. And a firm with very good prospects that aren't yet reflected in current profits may have an unusually high PE ratio. Thus, the PE ratio alone is a poor guide to whether a stock is a good bargain.

- **VOL 100s:** the number of shares, in hundreds, traded on that particular day. The number 25,631 tells us that on August 1, 2006, the number of shares that traded hands was $25,631 \times 100 = 2,563,100$.
- **CLOSE:** The last price at which a share of FedEx stock was sold that day. On August 1, 2006, the last person who bought FedEx stock paid $103.21 for each share purchased.
- **NET CHG:** The net change in the stock's price. More specifically, this number shows how much the stock rose or fell from the previous day's close to this day's close. Since FedEx had a closing price of $103.21 on this trading day, and a net change of −$1.50, we know that its closing price the day before must have been $104.71.

In addition to reporting on individual stocks, the *Wall Street Journal* and other newspapers report on changes in different stock market averages or indexes. These are meant to represent movements in stock prices as a whole, or movements in particular types of stocks. The most popular average is the **Dow Jones Industrial Average,** which tracks the prices of 30 of the largest companies in the United States, including Boeing, Microsoft, and Wal-Mart. Another popular average is the much broader **Standard & Poor's 500,** which tracks stock prices of 500 large corporations.

Dow Jones Industrial Average An index of the prices of stocks of 30 large U.S. firms.

Standard & Poor's 500 An index of the prices of stocks of 500 large U.S. firms.

Explaining a Particular Stock's Price

Glancing at the newspaper clipping in Figure 4, you can see that most stocks experience a price change on any given day. Why? Like all prices, stock prices are determined by supply and demand. However, as with bonds, our supply and demand curves require careful interpretation.

Figure 5 presents a supply and demand diagram for the shares of FedEx. The supply curve tells us the quantity of FedEx shares *in existence* at any moment in time. This is the number of shares that people are *actually* holding.

On any given day, the number of FedEx shares in existence is just the number that FedEx has issued previously, up until that day. Therefore, no matter what happens to the price today, the number of shares remains unchanged. This is why the supply curve in the figure is a vertical line at 305 million, showing that there are 305 million shares in existence regardless of the price.

Now, just because 305 million shares of FedEx stock actually exist, that does not mean that this is the number of shares that people *want* to hold at any given price. The desire to hold FedEx shares is given by the downward-sloping demand curve. As you can see, the lower the price of the stock, the more shares of FedEx people will want to hold. Why is this?

As you've learned, the value of a share of stock to any owner is equal to the total present value of its future after-tax profits. However, individuals do not all calculate this total present value in the same way. Some may believe that FedEx's profits will continue to grow as rapidly as they have in the past, while others—more pessimistic—may believe that FedEx's best days are behind it, forecasting a much lower growth rate. Some investors may feel quite certain about their forecast, or else don't mind risk much at all. Others may be especially uncertain or risk averse, and use a higher discount rate that lowers the present value of each future year's profit.

Thus, at any given moment, there is an array of estimates of a stock's total present value. As the price of the stock comes down, it descends below more and more people's total present value estimates, and so more and more will find the stock to be a bargain and want to hold it. This is what the downward-sloping demand curve tells us.

In Figure 5, you can see that at any price other than $100 per share, the number of shares people *are* holding (on the supply curve) will differ from the number they

FIGURE 5

The Market for FedEx Shares

1. The supply curve is vertical at 305 million—the total number of shares FedEx has issued.

2. The downward-sloping demand curve shows how many shares the public *wants* to hold at each price.

3. The equilibrium is at point *A*, where people *want* to hold all the shares in existence.

Price per Share

$122

100

78

S

A

D

305 million

Shares of FedEx

want to hold (on the demand curve). For example, at a price of $78 per share, people would want to hold more shares than they are currently holding. Many would try to buy the stock, and the price would be bid up. At $122 per share, the opposite occurs: People find themselves holding more shares than they want to hold, and they will try to get rid of the excess by selling them. The sudden sales would cause the price to drop. Only at the equilibrium price of $100, where the supply and demand curves intersect, are people satisfied holding the number of shares they are *actually* holding.

As with bonds, stocks achieve their equilibrium prices almost instantly. Legions of stock traders—both individuals and professional fund managers—sit poised at their computers, ready to buy or sell a particular firm's shares the minute they feel they have an excess supply or a shortage of those shares. Thus, we can have confidence that the price of a share at any time is the equilibrium price.

Changes in a Stock's Price

Why do stock prices *change* so often? Or, since stocks sell at their equilibrium prices at almost every instant, we can ask: Why do shares' *equilibrium* prices change so often?

Since a supply curve, like that in Figure 5, only shifts when the firm issues new shares (an infrequent occurrence), the day-to-day changes in equilibrium prices cannot be caused by shifts in the supply curve. So they must be caused by shifts in *demand*. Figure 6 shows how a rightward shift in the demand curve for shares of FedEx could cause the price to rise to $125 per share. Indeed, on rare occasions, the demand curve for a firm's shares has shifted so far rightward in a single day that the share price doubled or even tripled.

But what causes these sudden shifts in demand for a share of stock? Here are some important examples, each causing the demand curve to shift rightward:

* *Release of new information suggesting greater profits than previously anticipated*. Expectations of higher future profits per share would increase the present value of a share—the amount that people think the share is worth. People will want to hold more shares at any current price.

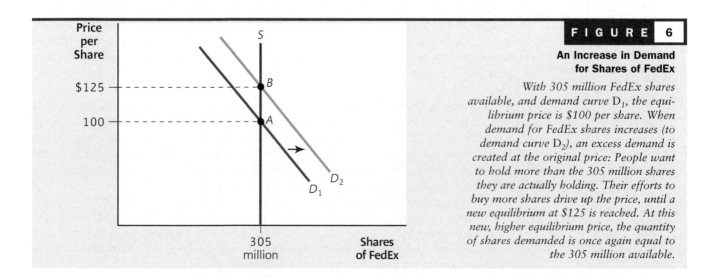

FIGURE 6

An Increase in Demand for Shares of FedEx

With 305 million FedEx shares available, and demand curve D₁, the equilibrium price is $100 per share. When demand for FedEx shares increases (to demand curve D₂), an excess demand is created at the original price: People want to hold more than the 305 million shares they are actually holding. Their efforts to buy more shares drive up the price, until a new equilibrium at $125 is reached. At this new, higher equilibrium price, the quantity of shares demanded is once again equal to the 305 million available.

- *A decrease in interest rates.* This lowers the discount rate (the riskless rate plus the risk premium) used in calculating the *PV* of every firm's stock, and increases their present values. At any price, the quantity demanded of *every* stock increases.
- *A decrease in the attractiveness of other assets.* All else equal, if other assets such as bonds, real estate, or commodities like gold and silver become less attractive, people will want to hold more of their wealth in stocks at any given price.
- *Expectations of any of the above.* If people *expect* any of these events to occur in the future, they will also expect the demand curve for shares to shift rightward, and the price of the stock to rise. As a result, anticipating the price rise, people will want to hold more shares at any given price *now*.

When stock prices make significant, sudden moves, it is usually because some new information has become available. For example, suppose that jet fuel prices decreased dramatically and were expected to stay low for some time. Since jet fuel is a major cost for FedEx, people would expect higher future profits for the company. Estimates of the present value of profits would rise, shifting the demand curve to the right. As in Figure 6, this would increase the price of the stock.

On the other hand, suppose that United Parcel Service, FedEx's chief competitor, announced a significant price cut for its overnight shipping service. In that case, people would expect UPS sales to increase at the expense of FedEx, or that FedEx would have to lower its own prices in order to keep its market share. Either way, a lower profit per share for FedEx would be forecasted, the demand curve for its shares would shift leftward, and the price would fall (not shown in the figure).

Efficient Markets Theory

Every day, financial news programs, such as *Wall Street Week* or CNBC's *Squawk Box,* offer stock market advice to millions of television viewers. The stock market analysts interviewed on these shows tell us that they have done some careful research, or that they have a secret formula, and that by following their advice, you'll earn more dividends and capital gains than you could hope to earn on your own. Of course, for the *really* good predictions, you'll have to pay a price and subscribe to their private newsletter or use them as your stockbroker.

Efficient market A market that instantaneously incorporates all available information relevant to a stock's price.

Economists believe that analysts can often explain stock price movements in the *past*. But they are extremely skeptical about anyone's ability to *predict* stock price changes in the future. This is because economists tend to take the **efficient markets** view of the stock market. According to this view, the stock market digests new information that might affect stock prices *efficiently,* that is, rapidly and thoroughly.

The implications of the efficient markets view are startling. First, it means that you cannot, on average, beat the market by doing research and finding and buying underpriced (or selling overpriced) stocks. You cannot do this because any research that *you* do will also be done by others and is therefore already incorporated into the stock's price. That means—if the goal is to outperform a broad stock market average like the Standard & Poor's 500—you are largely wasting your time.

For example, suppose that you spend a lot of time investigating the XYZ corporation, which is experimenting with a new, patented technology. If successful, it will generate enormous profits. Every day, you look at press clippings, search Web pages, and learn all about this new technology. You even do some complicated statistical work to estimate how much potential profits the technology could earn for XYZ, Inc.

One day, XYZ, Inc., reports that a very preliminary experiment was promising. Only very savvy people like you could read the details and come to the proper conclusion: The chances that the new technology will work have just doubled. Instantly, you go to the Web and look up the stock's price . . . only to find that it has already jumped higher. Why? Because there were hundreds of others just like you—some of them professionals managing billions of dollars of other people's wealth—who did the same research you did. They all have recognized the likelihood of greater future profit, and have attached a greater present value to this corporation's stock. By the time you go to buy shares, the demand curve has already shifted rightward.

But wait. *Someone* had to get there first. Surely *that* person benefited from their research, right? Actually, no. Assuming that the news was a surprise, only those lucky enough to be *already* holding the stock at the time of the announcement will benefit. They will immediately adjust their asking price upward, so no one will be able to buy at the lower, preannouncement price.

The same is true of strategies to profit from *patterns* in stock trading, often called *technical analysis*. In the efficient markets view, this is a waste of time as well. Imagine a very simple pattern: Because of exuberance or fatigue or superstition, people are more likely to buy stocks than to sell them on Friday, so on average, stock prices rise every Friday. Since everyone would anticipate this pattern, they would buy stocks on Thursday, hoping to profit from the Friday runup. But this would cause stocks to rise on Thursday, not Friday, so people would buy on Wednesday, and so on. Soon, there would be no patterns at all; every day would be like any other day. Even though this is a very simple example, the logic applies to *any* pattern an analyst might uncover.

> *According to efficient markets theory, any information that helps one predict the future price of a specific stock or the market in general is instantly incorporated into stock prices. The only ones who benefit are those who are lucky enough to be holding the stock before the information became available.*[4]

The theory of efficient markets is one of the most exhaustively tested theories in all of economics. Thousands of studies have confirmed the efficiency of stock prices with respect to all sorts of information. You can't beat the market by buying stocks only in companies whose presidents went to MIT (or anywhere else). You can't beat the market by buying stock only in companies in growing industries. You can't beat it by buying stocks that have risen. You can't beat the market by buying stocks that have collapsed. You can't beat the market, period!

Common Objections to Efficient Markets Theory

When students first learn about efficient markets theory, two objections often come to mind. Here is how economists often respond to them.

Efficient markets theory can't be true. Otherwise, why would financial institutions spend so much money doing research on particular stocks, or on the market in general? The cynical response to this objection is that many financial institutions earn

---

[4] One exception to this rule is *insiders*—those with connections to the firm and access to information *before* it becomes public. They can buy or sell stock early, before information is reflected in the price of the stock. Profiting from insider information is illegal. Those who do so, if they are caught, pay stiff fines and sometimes even go to jail. However, enforcement of insider trading laws is difficult, since it is often hard to detect.

their income from commissions when their clients buy and sell stocks. Frequent research reports on stocks—"what's hot and what's not"—help these institutions convince their clients to trade more frequently.

A less cynical response draws on what you've learned about perfectly competitive markets in Chapter 8. Because there are no artificial barriers to doing stock market research and trading for profit, efficient markets theory assumes individuals and firms will continue to enter the market until the profit is reduced to zero.

But remember: It is *economic* profit that is reduced to zero through entry. In long-run equilibrium, stock researchers would earn just enough *accounting* profit to compensate for the implicit costs of their activities, such as foregone income. If it takes some special talent or ability to do this kind of research, then annual accounting profit would drop to the salary that people with these special talents or abilities could earn elsewhere. Thus, there is room to justify a positive salary for those who analyze the market.

However, also remember that the equilibrium rate of return to researching the market is determined largely by the thousands of professionals who manage enormous amounts of other people's wealth. If they beat the market by only a tiny—almost imperceptible—fraction, they have justified their salary. For example, suppose a professional managing a portfolio of $3 billion in wealth can generate an annual rate of return that is 0.01 percent higher than the market average. That additional return would be $300,000 per year—enough to justify up to that much in salary. Now consider someone managing his or her own portfolio of, say, $100,000. Once entry by professionals has reduced the return to doing research down to 0.01 percent, the individual investor—doing his own, full-time research, or using the research of others—increases his earnings by only $10 per year.

Efficient markets theory can't be true. I just saw a money manager interviewed on CNBC, and he beat the market by more than 5 percentage points, three years in a row! Efficient markets theory does not rule out luck. With hundreds of thousands of people around the world trading stocks, we would expect some of them to be unusually lucky even if they operated by sheer guesswork. And we would expect some small number to do so many years in a row. An unusually good performance by a few—in a process involving many—does not prove any actual skill.

To prove this to yourself, imagine that 20,000 stock traders each picked their stocks by throwing darts at the stock page, and timed their buying and selling by flipping a coin every day. If we ignore trading commissions, this group would, on average, perform about as well as the stock market as a whole. But through luck alone, *some* would be very successful in any given year—beating the market by, say, 5 percentage points or more.

Let's suppose that by using this random process we can expect 10 percent of the group to be "very successful" in any given year. (An equivalent 10 percent would be "very unsuccessful.") At the end of the first year, 2,000 of the 20,000 random players would be very successful. Out of those 2,000 who were successful the first year, 200 would do it again the second year too. And out of those 200, 20 would do it the third year too. Those 20 people would fill plenty of interview slots on CNBC, bragging that they successfully beat the market three years in a row. But the fourth year, each of them would be no more likely to beat the market than would any other player, because they would still be selecting their stocks randomly.

Efficient Markets Theory and the Average Investor

Although the idea of efficient markets is sweeping and rules out a great many investment strategies as worthless, its implications for the investor who understands it can be quite valuable.

First, just because you can't outperform the market doesn't mean you shouldn't invest in the market at all. The average stock's price, over long periods of time, tends to rise. In fact, if dividends and capital gains are added together, stocks—over the long run—earn their holders a better yield than bonds. This is because stocks are more risky, and investors in the stock market must be compensated for bearing that risk.

Second, if someone asks you to pay for their stock-picking advice, *don't*. You can do just as well by picking stocks on your own, even if you pick them randomly. The stocks you pick will be as likely to rise or fall as stocks chosen by an expert.

Third, because you have to pay commissions when you trade stocks, you should trade as little as possible. By using a "buy and hold" strategy, you can participate in the long-run, higher-than-bonds rate of return at minimum expense.

Finally, choose a diversified portfolio with different stocks that tend not to rise and fall together. Such a portfolio will have less risk than an undiversified portfolio with the same expected rate of return. The investor who follows the implications of the efficient markets hypothesis will assemble a diversified set of stocks and then hold on to them, buying and selling only when new cash comes in or cash needs to be taken out.

THE ECONOMIC ROLE OF FINANCIAL MARKETS

Now that we've investigated some of the specific details regarding financial markets, it is worthwhile to back up and take a broader view. What functions do financial markets play? In this section, we will take an economist's viewpoint and try to pinpoint just exactly how financial markets make us all better off.

If there is a single word that resonates throughout this chapter, it is *time*. Markets for capital as well as financial markets reflect decisions made over time. When a firm purchases a capital asset, it makes an expenditure today in return for a machine or plant that generates benefits many years into the future. When an individual buys a financial asset, costs are incurred today in exchange for future benefits.

In the absence of markets for capital, we would all be constrained to live as if there were literally no tomorrow. We would have to forego the productivity advances embodied in new capital goods. Each of us—and society as a whole—would be much poorer.

We would also be poorer if there were no *financial* markets. Firms would be unable to become very large or grow very fast if they were constrained to fund their growth solely through their own retained earnings. Without financial markets, there would be no Verizon, no Amazon, and no Microsoft, and we would not be able to enjoy the goods and services these firms produce. All three of these firms—and indeed, most major corporations—turned to the stock and bond markets to obtain funds for their capital acquisitions.

Moreover, without financial markets, we would be constrained as individuals. We could save for retirement or for our children's education, but not very fruitfully, because we would not earn any interest or dividends on our savings. Without financial markets, banks would be little more than safe houses, storing our cash until we needed it and charging us a fee for the service instead of paying us interest.

All of the markets we have studied in this chapter enable us to save funds and earn a rate of return, and they enable firms to invest and grow. They help relax the economic constraints imposed by scarcity. And they certainly contribute to the high standard of living we enjoy. When savers and borrowers come together in financial markets, both sides benefit.

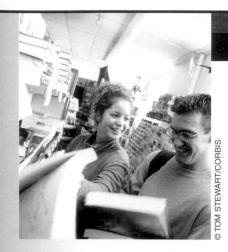

© TOM STEWART/CORBIS

USING THE THEORY

College as an Investment

Previously in this book, we've discussed some of the economic aspects of attending college. In Chapter 2, we analyzed the costs of college. In Chapter 11, we discussed one of the benefits of college: the *wage premium* that college graduates earn over high school graduates. Now, we'll compare these costs and benefits to ask: Is college a wise financial investment?

Traditionally, the answer has always been a resounding yes. But in recent years, tuition—one component of costs—has been growing rapidly. At the same time, the wage premium, which grew especially rapidly in the 1980s and 1990s, has grown more slowly in the 2000s. Has the answer changed?

The decision to attend college is remarkably similar to the other sorts of decisions we've discussed in this chapter. Getting a college education is an investment in *human capital*. It involves purchasing an asset—a college degree—that is expected to yield a stream of future benefits, in the form of a greater annual income. The benefits will accrue over your working life. But the costs have to be paid sooner—over just four years. As with any other problem involving benefits and costs over various future periods, the right answer is found by comparing the *present value* of these benefits and costs.

The Costs of College

To calculate the present value of the *costs* of college, let's use the most expensive choice: a private college, with no scholarship or grant aid. (A student loan will not ordinarily change the present value of the costs; it will just redistribute when they are actually paid.)

We'll use the data from Table 1 in Chapter 2, for the 2005–2006 academic year. Adding only the *additional* expenses for attending college (tuition, books, and other supplies), the *explicit* cost is $22,140 per year for four years. Assuming a student does not work during the nine months they are attending college (but works during the summer), there is also an important *implicit* cost: foregone income. As discussed in Chapter 2, average annual earnings for high school graduates who work full-time are about $22,000. A college student who sacrifices nine months of earnings at this rate will forego income of 9/12 × $22,000 = $16,500 per year. Adding explicit and implicit costs together, we get an annual cost of college of $22,140 + $16,500 = $38,640.

Since this cost is paid each year over four years, our next step is to compute the present value. We'll use a 5 percent discount rate (roughly equal to the riskless interest rate as this is written). And to make the problem simpler, we'll assume that each year's costs are paid at the end of each year (our rule for approximating present value), and that the costs of college remain constant over the period. (In the end-of-chapter problems, you'll be asked to re-do the calculations under different assumptions.)

Using our simplifying assumptions, the present value of the cost of four years of college is

$$PV \text{ of cost of private college}$$
$$= \frac{\$38,640}{1.05} + \frac{\$38,640}{(1.05)^2} + \frac{\$38,640}{(1.05)^3} + \frac{\$38,640}{(1.05)^4} = \$137,016$$

In words, with a 5 percent discount rate, the costs you will pay over the four years to attend college are equivalent to paying $137,016 today. Therefore, if the present value of your future benefits exceeds $137,016, you are getting a "good deal." That is, the return on your investment will be higher than for an alternative investment paying 5 percent per year (such as putting $137,016 into Treasury bills).

The Financial Benefits of College

Studies of income by age and education show that (1) earnings generally increase with age (and therefore experience) for all education groups; (2) earnings increase with education for all age groups (once the education is completed); and (3) earnings rise with age more sharply for those with more education.

Figure 7 illustrates all three of these observations. It shows the average earnings of full-time workers in different age groups in 2004, with each line corresponding to a different level of education.

As you can see in the figure, high school graduates (the lowest line) have the lowest earnings at *all* age groups. Within any age group, the greater the education, the greater the earnings. For example, in the 35–44 age group, the average high

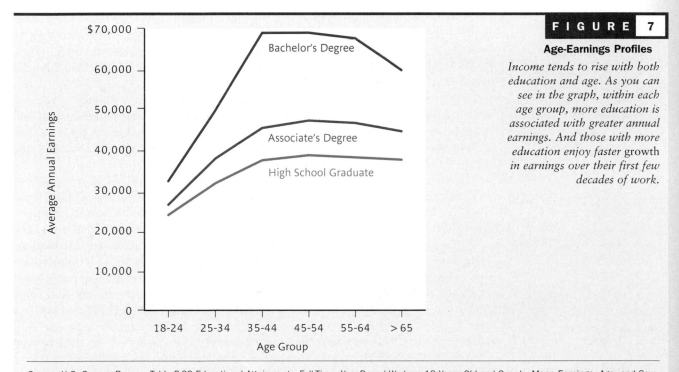

FIGURE 7

Age-Earnings Profiles

Income tends to rise with both education and age. As you can see in the graph, within each age group, more education is associated with greater annual earnings. And those with more education enjoy faster growth in earnings over their first few decades of work.

Source: U.S. Census Bureau, Table P-32 Educational Attainment—Full-Time, Year-Round Workers 18 Years Old and Over by Mean Earnings, Age, and Sex: 1991 to 2004. Weighted average of men and women was calculated by authors. Note that by restricting the earnings to full-time workers, the data do not reflect any decrease in earnings among those who retire, work part-time, or spend time unemployed.

school graduate who worked full-time earned about $37,014, while the average college graduate (with no higher degree) earned about $68,583. Those who went on to earn professional degrees (not shown in the diagram) do even better at each age. In the 35–44 age group, their average earnings are $129,227.

These earnings in 2004 don't necessarily predict what will happen to today's graduates. But the general relationship between earnings and age or education has been present for decades and is expected to continue into the future.

One frequently cited statistic is that today's college graduate can expect to earn at least $1 million more over their working lifetime than a high school graduate. But remember: Most of the additional earnings from college will be received far into the future, when they are worth substantially less in present value terms. For example, with a 5 percent discount rate, one dollar in additional earnings received 30 years from now has a present value of only 23 cents. To properly evaluate the benefits, we must use the present value of these additional earnings.

As you can see in Figure 7, the *additional* earnings from attending college grow with time, starting at about $8,000 after graduation, and rising to about $30,000 during the peak earnings years. Using these numbers, and a 5 percent discount rate, we find (through tedious calculations) that the *increase* in earnings from college, over a typical working life, has a present value of $326,738.

Comparing Costs and Benefits

We've seen that in present value terms, attending college gives expected benefits worth $326,738 today. For the private school option under the assumptions we've made, the *costs* of college have a present value of $137,016. Comparing the two, the benefits are substantially greater. College is a good investment.

How good? Interpreting these numbers in different ways can help us get some perspective. For example, we can ask: How much would college have to cost today to make it a poor investment? The answer is: more than $326,738. If college costs, say, $330,000 in present value terms, you would have a better lifetime financial result putting that amount into Treasury bills.

We can also ask: On purely financial grounds, what sum of money would we have to give you *today* to make you decide *not* to attend college? In this case, you would not have to pay any of the costs, but you'd be deprived of all benefits. The sum we would have to offer you would be $326,738 − $137,016 = $189,722—the net benefit, in present value terms, of college.

Finally, we can ask: What is the annual rate of return provided by an investment in a college degree? Or, to put it another way, what rate of return would have to be available on an alternative investment to make it financially equivalent to obtaining a college degree? To answer, we must find the discount rate that would make the PDV of the benefits of college equal to the PDV of its costs. Once again, the calculations are tedious, but the result for our example (a private institution with no financial aid and the typical age–earnings differentials shown in Figure 7) is an annual average rate of return of 9.6 percent.[5] Thus, on purely financial grounds, if you can find some other investment with a consistent annual rate of return greater than 9.6 percent over

---

[5] Separating by sex, the annual rate of return to a college degree is 10.4 percent for men, and 9.3 percent for women. For most students, the rates of return are even greater than in our example, because the cost of college is lower (due to scholarships or grants or attending a lower-tuition public institution).

Also, keep in mind that interest rates on alternative investments include compensation for inflation. But in our calculations, we've assumed that the earnings differentials in Figure 7 remain constant. If we allow for future increases in the differential due to inflation or other causes, college becomes an even more attractive investment when compared to the alternatives.

the next 40 or so years, with an equivalent degree of certainty, it would dominate an investment in a college degree. If you find such an investment, please let us know.

Some Provisos

We've made a number of assumptions in our example that make college look like a somewhat better deal than it is. For example, we've assumed that none of the costs of college will rise over the four years—neither tuition nor the salary you could earn with a high school degree. We've also used the riskless interest rate as the discount rate. In fact, one could argue that the future wage premium for college graduates is uncertain, so a higher discount rate including some risk premium would be more appropriate. Incorporating these changes into our example would change the numbers, but not by much.

On the other hand, some of our assumptions make college look substantially less attractive. In our example, a college student does not work at all (except during summers), chooses a high-tuition private college, and receives no grants or scholarships. Changing any of these could make college a substantially more attractive investment.

But there are other, more theoretical questions about our analysis. It is certainly true that college graduates earn more at every age (after graduation) than high school graduates. But why? Do they *learn* things in college that make them more productive, and therefore more valuable, to a future employer? Or by graduating from college, do they "signal" to employers that they have certain characteristics (ability, intelligence, perseverance, social skills, organizational skills—all needed to get the diploma) that make them worth a higher salary? In either case, college is still a good investment. The only way to get the benefits of greater income is to get the degree.

But there is another way to explain the data that could, in theory, seriously undermine college as an investment. What if some fraction of the population possesses some characteristic (let's called it I&I, for "intelligence and initiative") that enables them to earn more, *regardless* of their education. And what if people who possess I&I are also more likely than others to attend college because they have a *taste* for it—they like to learn, and like the challenge and intellectual environment that college provides. In that case, we would still observe the pattern of earnings in Figure 7. But college as an *investment* would not be the only reason. To some extent, those with higher earnings in the figure just *happened* to have more education because they like education; but they would have had those higher earnings with or without the education. (Bill Gates, who dropped out of Harvard in his freshman year, is a prime example.)

If this explained *all* of the higher earnings of college graduates, college would be a bad financial investment. You'd be paying a present value of perhaps $137,000 for future benefits of . . . zero (in strictly monetary terms). Labor economists have looked at this question in a variety of ways (including studies of identical twins).[6] The consensus is that only a small amount (10 percent in one study) of the higher earnings of college graduates can be attributed to causes other than attending college. So whether you are actually learning valuable skills in college, or just signaling to employers that you would be a productive employee, college remains a very good financial investment.

---

[6] For a good summary, see David Card, "The Causal Effect of Education on Earnings," in *Handbook of Labor Economics*, Vol. 3A (Orley C. Ashenfelter and David Card, editors.), pp. 1801–1863.

Summary

Capital and financial assets provide to their owners future benefits that can be obtained by purchasing the asset that generates them. The principle of asset valuation tells us how firms and individuals determine the value of any long-lived asset—the total present value of all the future income the asset will generate. If the future income is certain, then the *discount rate* used to calculate present value is the interest rate earned on alternative, riskless assets (such as U.S. government bonds). If the future income is less certain, a large discount rate, which includes a risk premium, is used.

If a firm's physical capital lasted forever, or could be rented indefinitely at a constant price per period, it would find the profit-maximizing quantity of capital just as it finds the profit-maximizing quantity of labor: increasing its use of capital until its marginal revenue product (*MRP*) per period equaled its marginal factor cost per period. However, because capital does not last forever, a different decision process must be used. The firm should buy any unit of capital for which the total present value of all future years' revenue is greater than the purchase price. This total present value will be smaller when interest rates are higher. Therefore, higher interest rates discourage investment in physical capital.

There are many types of financial markets, including those for bonds and corporate stock. The price of a bond will equal the total present value of its future payments. There is an inverse relationship between the price of a bond and its yield (rate of return). The price of any particular bond is determined by supply and demand. The supply curve is vertical, while the demand curve slopes downward, reflecting differences in beliefs about present value among potential bondholders.

The value of a share of corporate stock is the total present value of the future after-tax profits of the firm, divided by the number of shares outstanding. The price of a share, like the price of a bond, is determined by the intersection of a vertical supply curve and a downward-sloping demand curve.

Efficient markets theory suggests that at any moment, the price of a stock already incorporates all available information that would enable someone to predict its future price. Therefore, research to help pick individual stocks or to detect trading patterns is not worth an investor's time or money.

Problem Set   *Answers to even-numbered Questions and Problems can be found on the text Web site at www.thomsonedu.com/economics/hall.*

1. You are considering buying a new laser printer to use in your part-time desktop publishing business. The printer will cost $380, and you expect it to produce additional revenue of $100 per year for each of the next five years. At the end of the fifth year, it will be worthless. Answer the following questions:
   a. What is the value of the printer to you if the relevant discount rate is 10 percent? Is the purchase of the printer justified?
   b. Would your answer to part (a) change if the discount rate were 8 percent? Is the purchase justified in that case? Explain.
   c. Would your answer to part (a) change if the printer cost $350? Is the purchase justified in that case?
   d. Would your answer to part (a) change if the printer could be sold for $500 at the end of the fifth year? Is the purchase justified in that case? Explain.
   What lessons can you derive from your answers to these questions?

2. Your inventory manager has asked you to approve the purchase of a new inventory control software package. The software will cost $200,000 and will last for four years, after which it will become obsolete. If you do not approve this purchase, your company will have to hire two new inventory clerks, paying each $30,000 per year. Answer the following questions:
   a. Should you approve the purchase of the inventory control software if the relevant annual discount rate is 7 percent?

   b. Would your answer to part (a) change if the annual discount rate is 9 percent? Explain.
   c. Would your answer to part (a) change if the software cost $220,000? Explain.
   d. Would your answer to part (a) change if the software would not become obsolete until the last day of its sixth year?

3. Ice Age Ice is trying to decide how many $150,000 commercial ice makers to buy. Assume that each machine is expected to last for seven years. Complete the following table if the appropriate discount rate is 5 percent. How many ice makers should Ice Age Ice purchase? How low would the price per machine have to fall before the firm would buy four ice makers?

Ice Machines	Additional Annual Revenue	Total Present Value of Additional Revenue over Seven Years
1	$26,000	
2	$25,000	
3	$16,000	
4	$12,000	
5	$ 6,000	

4. Your firm is considering purchasing some computers. Each computer costs $2,600, and each has an annual marginal revenue product. Because you plan to use the computers for different purposes, you have ranked those purposes in descending order of annual additional revenue as follows:

Computer	Annual *MRP*
1	$3,000
2	$2,000
3	$1,000
4	$ 500

    a. Assume that each computer has a useful life of three years, and no value thereafter. If the relevant discount rate is 10 percent per year, how many computers should you purchase?

    b. If, before you purchased the computers, a drop in interest rates caused your discount rate to fall to 5 percent per year, how many computers would you purchase?

5. A drug manufacturer is considering how many of four new drugs to develop. Suppose it takes one year and $10 million to develop a new drug, with the entire cost being paid up front (immediately). The expected yearly profits from the new drugs will begin in the *second* year, and are given in the table below:

Drug	Annual Profit
A	$ 7 million
B	$ 5.5 million
C	$ 5 million
D	$ 4 million

These profits accrue *only* while the drug is protected by a patent; once the patent runs out, profit is zero.

    a. If the discount rate is 10 percent and patents are granted for just two years, which drugs should be developed?

    b. If the discount rate is 10 percent and patents are granted for three years, which drugs should be developed?

    c. Answer (a) and (b) again, this time assuming the discount rate is 5 percent.

    d. Based on your answers above, what is the relationship between new drug development and (1) the discount rate; (2) the duration of patent protection?

    e. Is there any downside to a change in patent duration designed to speed the development of new drugs? Explain briefly.

6. Good news! Gold has just been discovered in your backyard. Mining engineers tell you that you can expect to extract five ounces of gold per year forever. Gold is currently selling for $400 per ounce, and that price is not expected to change. If the discount rate is 5 percent per year, estimate the total value of your gold mine.

7. One year ago, you bought a two-year bond for $900. The bond has a face value of $1,000 and has one year left until maturity. It promises one additional interest payment of $50 at the maturity date. If the discount rate is 5 percent per year, what capital gain (or loss) can you expect if you sell the bond today?

8. Suppose a bond has a face value of $100,000 with a maturity date three years from now. The bond also gives coupon payments of $5,000 at the end of each of the next three years. What will this bond sell for if the discount rate is

    a. 5 percent?

    b. 10 percent?

9. Suppose a bond has a face value of $250,000 with a maturity date four years from now. The bond also gives coupon payments of $8,000 at the end of each of the next four years.

    a. What will this bond sell for if the discount rate is 4 percent?

    b. What will this bond sell for if the discount rate is 5 percent?

    c. What is the relationship between bond price and bond yield in this exercise?

10. Suppose that people are sure that a firm will earn annual profit of $10 per share forever. If the discount rate is 10 percent, how much will people pay for a share of this firm's stock? Suppose that people become uncertain about future profits, causing them to use a discount rate of 15 percent. How much will they pay now?

11. In the market for Amazon.com *bonds*, explain how each of the following events would affect (1) the price and (2) the yield?

    a. Moody's upgrades the bond from Aa to Aaa.

    b. The interest rate on U.S. government bonds decreases.

    c. People *expect* the interest rate on U.S. government bonds to decrease, but it hasn't yet happened.

    d. People suddenly believe that housing prices are about to drop.

12. In the market for Amazon.com *stock*, explain how each of the following events would affect the stock's price.

    a. The interest rate on U.S. government bonds rises.

    b. People *expect* the interest rate on U.S. government bonds to rise, but it hasn't yet risen.

    c. Google announces that it will soon start competing with Amazon in the market for books, DVDs, and everything else that Amazon sells.

    d. People begin to think that housing prices will rise dramatically over the next year.

13. Suppose that 1,000,000 people select which stocks to buy and hold for the year by throwing darts at the stock page. Suppose, too, that in any given year:

- The average stock price rises by 7 percent.
- In any given year, 50 percent of the dart throwers will have a return that is average or better.
- In any given year and by luck alone, 20 percent of the dart throwers will "beat the average" by 5 percentage points or more
- In any given year and by luck alone, 10 percent of the dart throwers will beat the average by 10 percentage points or more.

    a. After five years, how many people will honestly report that they've earned 7 percent or more on their stocks in *each* of the previous five years?

    b. After five years, how many people will honestly report that they've earned 12 percent or more on their stocks in *each* of the previous five years?

    c. After five years, how many people will honestly report

that they've earned 17 percent or more on their stocks in *each* of the previous five years?

14. State whether each of the following, with no other change, would *increase* or *decrease* the economic attractiveness of going to college, and give a brief explanation for each.
    a. A decrease in estimated working life.
    b. An increase in the earnings of the average high school student.
    c. Permanently higher interest rates in the economy.

15. In the Using the Theory section, we calculated the present value of attending a private college, under the assumption that the costs remain the same for each of the four years. Recalculate the present value of these costs under the assumption that while implicit costs remain the same, tuition and other *explicit* costs rise by 8 percent per year, starting with the second year's tuition and expenses. (Continue to assume that all costs are paid at the end of each year.)

16. In the Using the Theory section, we calculated the present value of attending a private college, under the assumption that each year's costs are paid at the *end* of the year. Recalculate the present value of these costs under the assumption that all costs are paid at the *beginning* of each year.

17. In the Using the Theory section, we calculated the present value of the costs of attending a private college, with no financial aid.
    a. Using Table 1 in Chapter 2, what would have been the present value of the cost of college if we had done the analysis for a four-year public institution, with no financial aid? (Hint: You won't use all the entries in the table, and you will use some numbers that are *not* in the table.)
    b. What is the percentage difference between the present value of costs at a private versus a public institution?
    c. Private college tuition is about four times higher than public college tuition. Explain briefly why the (present value) cost figures do not differ this widely.

More Challenging

18. The present value formula can be modified to account for variable interest (and discount) rates over time. For a three-year time horizon, the modified formula would be:

$$\text{Value} = \frac{Y_1}{(1 + r_1)} + \frac{Y_2}{(1 + r_1)(1 + r_2)}$$

$$+ \frac{Y_3}{(1 + r_1)(1 + r_2)(1 + r_3)}$$

where r_1, r_2, and r_3 are the discount rates in years 1, 2, and 3, respectively. Suppose a firm is considering two projects—A and B—with the following costs and revenues:

Project	Cost	Year 1 Revenue	Year 2 Revenue	Year 3 Revenue
A	50	20	20	20
B	33	20	30	40

Use this information to determine which of the projects should be undertaken if:
    a. The sequence of discount rates is $r_1 = 0.1$, $r_2 = 0.11$, $r_3 = 0.121$ (i.e., the discount rate grows by 10 percent per year starting from a discount rate of 10 percent).
    b. The sequence of discount rates is $r_1 = 0.1$, $r_2 = 0.09$, $r_3 = 0.081$ (i.e., the discount rate declines by 10 percent per year starting from a discount rate of 10 percent).
    c. What lesson can you derive from your answers in parts (a) and (b)?

Economic Efficiency and the Competitive Ideal

Throughout this book you've learned about the different types of markets in which products and resources are traded. Most of our discussion has been *descriptive*: For each type of market structure, we reached conclusions about price, quantity, firm profit, and how changes of various kinds affect the market equilibrium.

In this chapter, we will look at markets in a different way—*assessing* them in terms of their *economic efficiency*. As you'll soon see, there is more to the concept of efficiency than you might think.

We'll focus first on the idea of economic efficiency itself: what it is and what it is not. Next, you'll learn how economists measure the gains from trading, and use this measure to gauge whether or not a market is efficient. You'll see why perfectly competitive markets are considered economically efficient, and why other market structures fall short of this ideal. We'll also explore how some government actions can *prevent* a market from achieving an efficient outcome.

Of course, the market—left on its own—is sometimes *not* efficient, and government action can be an appropriate remedy. We'll take up these situations, and government's role in fostering efficiency, in the next chapter.

THE MEANING OF ECONOMIC EFFICIENCY

What, exactly, do we mean by the word *efficiency*? We all use this word, or its opposite, in our everyday conversation: "I wish I could organize my time more efficiently," "He's such an inefficient worker," "Our office is organized very efficiently," and so on. In each of these cases, we use the word *inefficient* to mean "wasteful" and *efficient* to mean "the absence of waste."

In economics, too, efficiency means the absence of waste, although a very specific kind of waste: *the waste of an opportunity to make someone better off without harming anyone else.* More specifically,

> economic efficiency *is achieved when we cannot rearrange the production or allocation of goods to make one person better off without making anybody else worse off.*

Notice that economic efficiency is a limited concept. Even though it is an important goal for a society, it is not the only goal. Most of us would list fairness as another important social goal. But an efficient economy is not necessarily a fair economy. For example, an economy could, in theory, be efficient even if 99 percent of its income went to a single person—a situation that almost everyone would regard as unfair.

Economists are concerned about both efficiency and fairness. But they generally spend more time and energy on efficiency. Why? Largely because it is so much easier for people to agree about efficiency. We all define fairness differently, depending on our different ethical and moral views. Issues of fairness must therefore be resolved politically.

But virtually all of us would agree that if we fail to take actions that would make some people in our society better off *without harming anyone*—that is, if we fail to achieve economic efficiency—we have wasted a valuable opportunity. Economics— by helping us understand the preconditions for economic efficiency and teaching us how we can bring about those preconditions—can make a major contribution to our material well-being.

PARETO IMPROVEMENTS

Imagine the following scenario: A boy and a girl are having lunch in elementary school. The boy frowns at a peanut butter and jelly sandwich, which, on this particular day, makes the girl's mouth water. She says, "Wanna trade?" The boy looks at her chicken sandwich, considers a moment, and says, "Okay."

This little scene, which is played out thousands of times every day in schools around the country, is an example of a trade that makes people better off without harming anyone. And as simple as it seems, such trading is at the core of the concept of economic efficiency. It is an example of a *Pareto* (pronounced puh-RAY-toe) *improvement*, named after the Italian economist, Vilfredo Pareto (1848–1923), who first systematically explored the issue of economic efficiency.

Pareto improvement An action that makes at least one person better off, and harms no one.

> A ***Pareto improvement*** *is any action that makes at least one person better off, and harms no one.*

In a market economy such as that in the United States, where trading is voluntary, literally hundreds of millions of Pareto improvements take place every day. Almost every purchase is an example of a Pareto improvement. If you pay $30 for a pair of jeans, then the jeans must be worth more to you than the $30 that you parted with or you wouldn't have bought them. Thus, you are better off after making the purchase. On the other side, the owner of the store must have valued your $30 more highly than he valued the jeans or he wouldn't have sold them to you. So he is better off, too. Your purchase of the jeans, like virtually every purchase made by every consumer every day, is an example of a Pareto improvement.

The notion of a Pareto improvement helps us arrive at a formal definition of economic efficiency:

> *Economic efficiency is achieved when every possible Pareto improvement is exploited.*

This definition can be applied to any part of the economy, or to the economy as a whole. For example, is the number of rental apartments in Chicago efficient? We would rephrase the question this way: Could an increase or decrease from the current number of apartments make at least one person better off without harming anyone? If the answer is yes, then some Pareto improvements have *not* yet been exploited, so the market quantity is *in*efficient. If the answer is no, then all Pareto-improving changes in quantity *have* been exploited, so the market has achieved the efficient quantity.

The definition can also be applied to the economy as a whole. Of course, no economy can exploit *every* Pareto improvement. But achieving something close to economic efficiency is an important goal. As you will see in this chapter, perfectly competitive markets tend to be economically efficient. And well-functioning market economies tend to generate outcomes that are reasonably close to efficient.

SIDE PAYMENTS AND PARETO IMPROVEMENTS

So far, the Pareto improvements we've considered are easily arranged transactions. Because both parties come out ahead, they have every incentive to find each other and trade.

But there are more complicated situations in which a Pareto improvement will come about only if one side makes a special kind of payment to the other, which we call a *side payment*. These are situations in which an action, without the side payment, would benefit one group and harm another.

Here's a simple example. The owner of an empty lot wants to build a movie theater on her property. Many people might gain from the theater: the owner of the lot, moviegoers, the theater's employees, and more. But the residents in the immediate vicinity might be harmed, because the theater will bring noise and traffic congestion.

Imagine that we can measure the gains and losses for each person in the town in dollars. When we sum them up, the total benefits to the gainers are valued at $100,000 while the total harm to the losers is valued at $70,000.

Building the theater—by itself—would *not* be a Pareto improvement, because even though some would benefit, others would be hurt. But suppose we can arrange for a *side payment*. Specifically, we collect $80,000 from those who benefit and pay it to those who are harmed. Those who make the payment will come out ahead: They initially gained $100,000 worth of benefits, so after paying $80,000, they are left with net benefits of $20,000. Those who initially didn't want the theater come out ahead as well: They suffer harm worth $70,000, but the $80,000 payment gives them a net benefit of $10,000.

If you experiment around a bit, you'll see that *any* side payment greater than $70,000 and less than $100,000 would make building the theater a Pareto improvement.

More generally,

> *if any action creates greater total gains for some than total losses to others, then a side payment exists which, if transferred from the gainers to the losers, would make the action a Pareto improvement.*

Any side payment with a value between the total benefits to the gainers and the total losses to the losers will do the trick.

This has an important implication for economic efficiency. If there is an action that benefits some more than it harms others, and *if an appropriate side payment can be easily arranged*, then *not* taking the action is a waste of an opportunity to make everyone better off. Economic efficiency requires that we find, and exploit, opportunities that—with side payments—would be Pareto improvements.

But reread the italicized words in the paragraph above. The appropriate side payment—as you'll see in the next chapter—is *not* always easy to arrange. In many instances, arranging a side payment to ensure that everyone benefits has high costs. It may be that, after deducting these costs, too little would be left to adequately compensate the losers while still leaving the gainers better off.

When a side payment *cannot* be made—or for any reason is *not* made—then even though the action might create greater gain than harm, it might not be considered fair. Achieving the efficient outcome then becomes *one* consideration, but not the only one. We'll come back to this important issue of side payments later in the chapter and see how it justifies, on efficiency grounds, many instances of government involvement.

COMPETITIVE MARKETS AND ECONOMIC EFFICIENCY

In a market system, firms and consumers are largely free to produce and consume as they wish, without anyone orchestrating the process from above. Can we expect such unsupervised trading to be economically efficient? That is, when the market reaches equilibrium, will we discover there are no remaining Pareto improvements, so we are not wasting opportunities to make people better off?

In this section, you'll see that the answer is usually yes . . . *if* trading takes place in perfectly competitive markets. To see this, we'll return to two familiar tools—the demand curve and the supply curve—but we'll be interpreting them in a new way.

REINTERPRETING THE DEMAND CURVE

Figure 1 shows a market demand curve for guitar lessons. It also indicates the specific person who would be taking each lesson along the curve. For example, at a price of $25, only Flo—who values guitar lessons the most—takes a lesson, so weekly quantity demanded is one. If the price drops to $23, Joe will take one lesson, so quantity demanded is two. At $21, Flo will decide to take a second lesson each week, so quantity demanded rises to three. This is the standard way of thinking about a market demand curve: It tells us quantity demanded at each price.

But we can also view the curve in a different way: It tells us the maximum price someone would be willing to pay for each unit. Therefore, it tells us how much that unit is *worth* to the person who buys it. In Figure 1, for example, the maximum value of the first lesson to some consumer in the market is just a tiny bit greater than $25. How do we know this? Because Flo, who values this lesson more highly than anyone else, will not buy it at any price greater than $25. But if the price falls to $25, she will buy it. When she decides to buy it, she must be getting at least a tiny bit more in value than the $25 she is giving up. So the value of that first lesson must be just a tiny bit more than $25. Ignoring for the moment the phrase "tiny bit more," we can say that the first lesson in the market is worth $25 to some consumer (Flo), the second is worth $23 to some consumer (Joe), and the third is worth $21 (Flo again).

Notice that each guitar lesson in the market has a different value. In part, this is because consumers differ in their incomes and tastes. (For example, based on differences in their incomes or tastes, Flo values one lesson per week more than does Joe.) But also, for each individual, the value of additional lessons declines as more lessons are taken. Flo, for example, values her first weekly lesson at $25, but her second at only $21.

Of course, in Figure 1, we've simplified by assuming there are very few consumers in the market for guitar lessons. This makes the graph easier to read. But the point is the same whether there are 5 consumers in the market, or 500, or 50,000. In general,

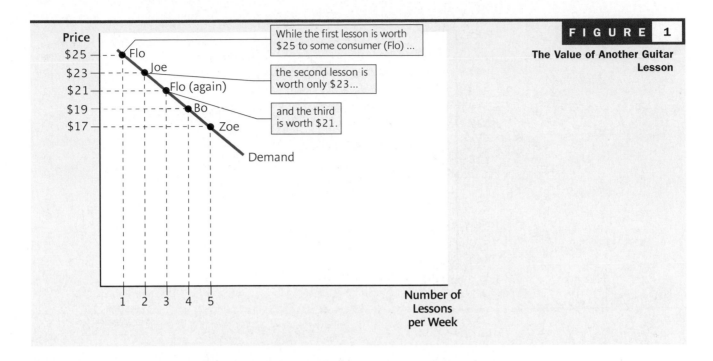

FIGURE 1

The Value of Another Guitar Lesson

> *the height of the market demand curve at any quantity shows us the value—to someone—of the last unit of the good consumed.*

REINTERPRETING THE SUPPLY CURVE

Now let's look at the other side of the market: those who *supply* guitar lessons. Figure 2 shows us a supply curve for guitar lessons. The figure also indicates who would be supplying each lesson. For example, at a price of $13, Martin would offer one lesson each week. If the price rose to $15, Martin would offer two lessons per week, and at $17, another teacher—Gibson—would enter the market and offer a third. This is the standard way to view the supply curve: It tells us the quantity supplied at each price.

But we can also interpret the supply curve this way: It tells us the minimum price a seller must get in order to supply that lesson. For example, for the first lesson, the price would have to be at least $13. At any price less than that, no one will offer it. However, when the price reaches $13, one supplier (Martin) will decide to offer it. Similarly, $15 is the minimum price it would take to get some producer in this market (Martin again) to supply the second lesson, and $17 is what it would take for the third lesson to be supplied (Gibson this time).

Why does it take higher prices to get more lessons? Because offering lessons is *costly* to guitar teachers. Not only do they have to rent studio space, but they must also use their time, which comes at an opportunity cost. In order to get someone to supply a guitar lesson, the price must *at least* cover the additional costs of giving that lesson. We can expect this additional cost to rise as more lessons are given. (For example, the opportunity cost of a guitar teacher's time will rise as he gives more lessons and has less free time to do other things.)

The minimum price that would convince Martin, Gibson, or any other teacher to supply a lesson will be the amount that just barely compensates for the additional

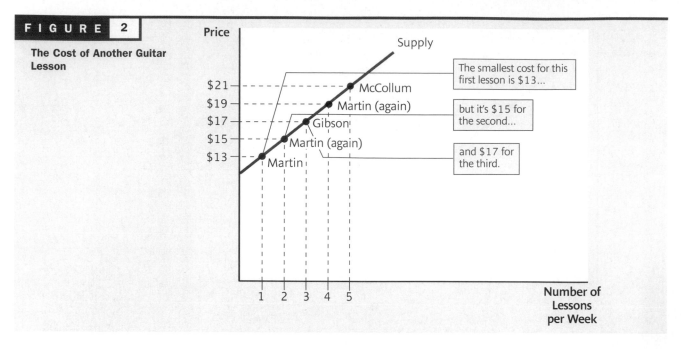

FIGURE 2

The Cost of Another Guitar Lesson

cost of that lesson—and a tiny bit more. Ignoring the phrase "a tiny bit more," we can say that

> *the height of the market supply curve at any quantity shows us the additional cost—to some producer—of each unit of the good supplied.*[1]

THE EFFICIENT QUANTITY OF A GOOD

Figure 3 combines the supply and demand curves for guitar lessons. Remember that the demand curve shows us the *value* of each lesson to some *consumer* and the supply curve shows us the additional *cost* of each lesson to some producer. We can then find the efficient quantity of weekly guitar lessons by using the following logical principle:

> *Whenever—at some quantity—the demand curve is* higher *than the supply curve, the value of one more unit to some consumer is greater than its additional cost to some producer.*

This means that when the demand curve lies above the supply curve, we can always find a price for one more unit that makes both the consumer and the producer better off.

Here's an example: Look at the *second* lesson in the figure. Tracing up vertically, we see that the demand curve (with a height of $23) lies above the supply curve (with a height of $15). That tells us that some consumer—Joe—values this lesson more than it would cost some teacher—Martin—to provide it. If Joe can *buy* the lesson at any price *less than $23*, he comes out ahead; if Martin can *sell* it for any price

---

[1] If you've been reading the chapters in order, you'll recognize *additional cost* as *marginal cost,* first introduced in Chapter 6 and discussed in later chapters. That is, the height of the supply curve tells us the lowest marginal cost at which each unit could be supplied in the market.

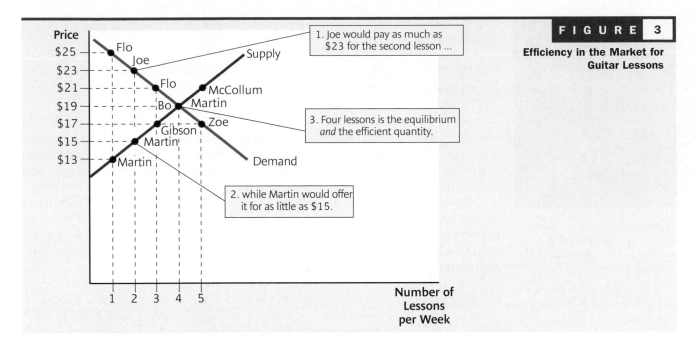

FIGURE 3

Efficiency in the Market for Guitar Lessons

1. Joe would pay as much as $23 for the second lesson ...

3. Four lessons is the equilibrium *and* the efficient quantity.

2. while Martin would offer it for as little as $15.

greater than $15, he comes out ahead. So, at any price *between $15 and $23,* both will come out ahead and no one is harmed: a Pareto improvement.

Continuing in this way, we find that the third lesson, and even the fourth, could be offered as Pareto improvements. (The fourth would be only a *slight* Pareto improvement, because its value is just a tiny bit greater than $19 and its cost a tiny bit less than $19.)

What about lessons for which the demand curve is *lower* than the supply curve—such as the fifth? Then there is *no* price at which both could come out ahead. To Zoe, the consumer who values the fifth weekly lesson the most, it's worth only $17. And for McCollum, the one who could provide it at the lowest additional cost, that cost would be $21. Producing this lesson could not be a Pareto improvement— no matter what the price—since the lowest cost of providing it is greater than its highest value to anyone in the market.

Let's recap: Whenever the demand curve lies *above* the supply curve, producing another lesson is a Pareto improvement. Whenever the demand curve lies *below* the supply curve, producing another lesson can*not* be a Pareto improvement. This tells us that the efficient quantity of guitar lessons—the quantity at which all Pareto improvements are exploited—is where the demand curve and supply curve intersect. At this quantity, the value of the last unit produced will be equal to (or possibly a tiny bit greater than) the cost of providing it.

> *The efficient quantity of a good is the quantity at which the market demand curve and market supply curve intersect.*

THE EFFICIENCY OF PERFECT COMPETITION

As you learned in Chapter 3 (and again in Chapter 8), when markets behave as the model of perfect competition predicts, the price adjusts until the market quantity reaches its *equilibrium:* where the market demand curve and market supply curve intersect. But we've just seen that this quantity is also the *economically efficient*

If the market for guitar lessons is perfectly competitive, the equilibrium quantity will be the efficient quantity.

quantity—the one that exploits all possible Pareto improvements. This gives us a very important and powerful result:

> A *well-functioning, perfectly competitive market will automatically achieve the* efficient *quantity.*

Let's consider this statement carefully. It tells us that, if we leave producers and consumers alone to trade with each other as they wish, then—as long as the market is working well and it's perfectly competitive—the market will exploit every opportunity to make someone better off that doesn't harm anyone else. No special side payments need to be arranged, because the price paid for the good *is itself* the side payment.

The notion that perfect competition—where many buyers and sellers each try to do the best for themselves—actually delivers efficient markets is one of the most important ideas in economics. The great British economist of the 18th century, Adam Smith, coined the term *invisible hand* to describe the force that leads a competitive economy toward economic efficiency:

> *[The individual] neither intends to promote the public interest, nor knows how much he is promoting it . . . he intends only his own gain, and he is in this, as in many other cases, led by an* invisible hand *to promote an end which was not part of his intention.*[2]

We can recognize the *end* promoted by the invisible hand as the economically efficient outcome.

MEASURING MARKET GAINS

When markets are *not* perfectly competitive, or when they fail to function in other ways, they are *in*efficient. By comparing the actual benefits a market delivers with the benefits it *could* provide if it were operating efficiently, we can estimate what we lose from the inefficiency. In this section, you'll learn how economists measure the benefits traders receive in a market—and the potential benefits not realized.

CONSUMER SURPLUS

Let's start with the benefits enjoyed by consumers in a market. Consumers rarely have to pay what a unit of a good is actually worth to them. Regardless of how much they value the good, they can buy all they choose at the market price. For example, in panel (a) of Figure 4, the equilibrium price of guitar lessons is $19. So Flo is able to buy her first lesson at $19, even though that lesson is *worth* $25 to her. By being able to purchase the lesson for less than its value to her, Flo gets a net benefit—called *consumer surplus*—on that lesson.

Consumer surplus The difference between the value of a unit of a good to the buyer and what the buyer actually pays for it.

> A buyer's **consumer surplus** *on a unit of a good is the difference between its value to the buyer and what the buyer* actually *pays for that unit.*

Flo's consumer surplus on the first lesson is equal to $25 − $19 = $6. It can be represented graphically by the *shaded area* of the first (leftmost) rectangle in the upper

[2] Adam Smith, *The Wealth of Nations* (Modern Library Classics edition, 2000), p. 423.

panel, which has a base of one unit and height of $6 (from $19 to $25).

Continuing down the demand curve, the consumer surplus on the *second* guitar lesson purchased in this market (by Joe) would be what that lesson is worth to him ($23) minus what he actually pays ($19), or $4. This is represented by the shaded area of the second, smaller rectangle. In similar fashion, the area of the third rectangle gives us a $2 consumer surplus on the third lesson (Flo again). The fourth lesson is purchased by Bo. Since the most he'd be willing to pay for that lesson is $19, its value to him is at most a tiny bit more than $19—say, $19.01. When the

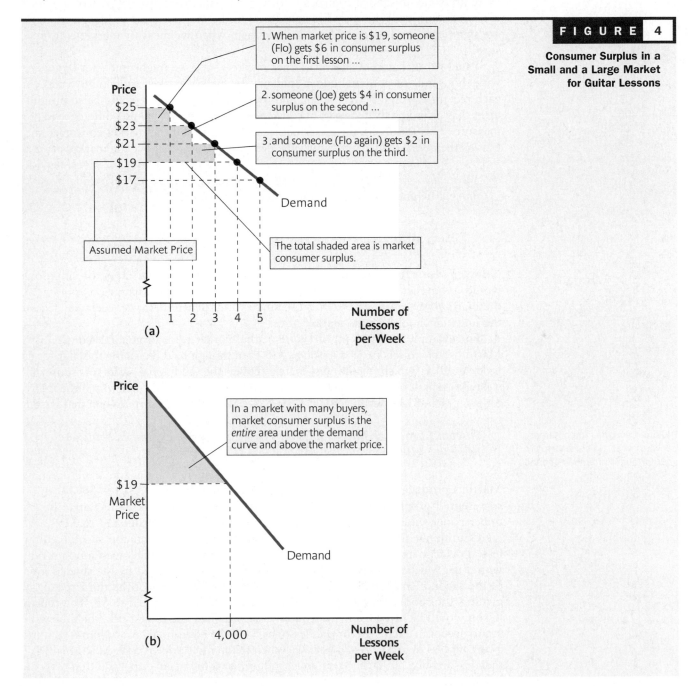

FIGURE 4

Consumer Surplus in a Small and a Large Market for Guitar Lessons

Market consumer surplus The total consumer surplus enjoyed by all consumers in a market.

market price is $19, Bo will buy the lesson, but he hardly gets any consumer surplus at all—so little that we can safely ignore it.

The total consumer surplus enjoyed by *all* consumers in a market is called **market consumer surplus,** the sum of the consumer surplus on all units (the areas of the shaded rectangles). In the figure, with the price of guitar lessons at $19, market consumer surplus is $6 + $4 + $2 = $12. Notice that this is *roughly* equal to the entire area under the demand curve and above the market price of $19. We say *roughly* because there are some unshaded triangles in the upper panel that are *not* part of anyone's consumer surplus. With only five consumers in the market, these unshaded triangles are significant, and we should not include them when we measure market consumer surplus.

Panel (b) of Figure 4 shows a larger market—one we might find in a large city, with thousands of potential guitar students. In such a market, a one-unit width for each rectangle would be very small, and the unshaded triangles would be so insignificant that including them as part of consumer surplus hardly makes a difference in our measure. This is why, in the lower panel, we've indicated the market consumer surplus as the *entire* shaded area under the demand curve and above the market price.

> We measure market consumer surplus, in dollars, as the total area under *the market demand curve and* above *the market price.*

PRODUCER SURPLUS

Now let's turn to the supply side of the market. Only in the rarest of situations would a supplier have to sell each unit at the lowest acceptable price. As long as there are *many* sellers and each is too small to influence the price, each can sell all the units he chooses at the market price.

For example, in panel (a) of Figure 5, the market price of guitar lessons is $19. Martin is able to sell the first lesson at $19 even though he'd be *willing* to sell it for as little as $13, which would just barely cover the additional costs of supplying it (studio rental, opportunity cost of time, and so on). By being able to sell the lesson for *more* than $13, Martin gets a net benefit—called *producer surplus*—on that lesson.

Producer surplus The difference between what the seller actually gets for a unit of a good and the cost of providing it.

> A seller's **producer surplus** on a unit of a good is the difference between the price the seller gets and the additional cost of providing it.

Martin's producer surplus on the first lesson is equal to $19 − $13 = $6. It can be represented graphically by the *shaded area* of the first (leftmost) rectangle in the upper panel, which has a base of one unit and height of $6 (from $13 to $19).

Continuing up the supply curve, the producer surplus on the *second* guitar lesson (Martin again) is the price for that lesson ($19) minus the lowest amount that would get Martin to supply it ($15), or $4. This is represented by the shaded area of the second, smaller rectangle. In similar fashion, the area of the third rectangle gives us the producer surplus on the third lesson (Gibson), equal to $2. The fourth lesson would be provided by Martin once again. Since the lowest price he'd be willing to accept in exchange for that lesson is $19, the additional cost to him is at most a tiny bit less than $19—say, $18.99. When the market price is $19, Martin will sell that lesson, but he hardly gets any producer surplus at all—so little that we can safely ignore it.

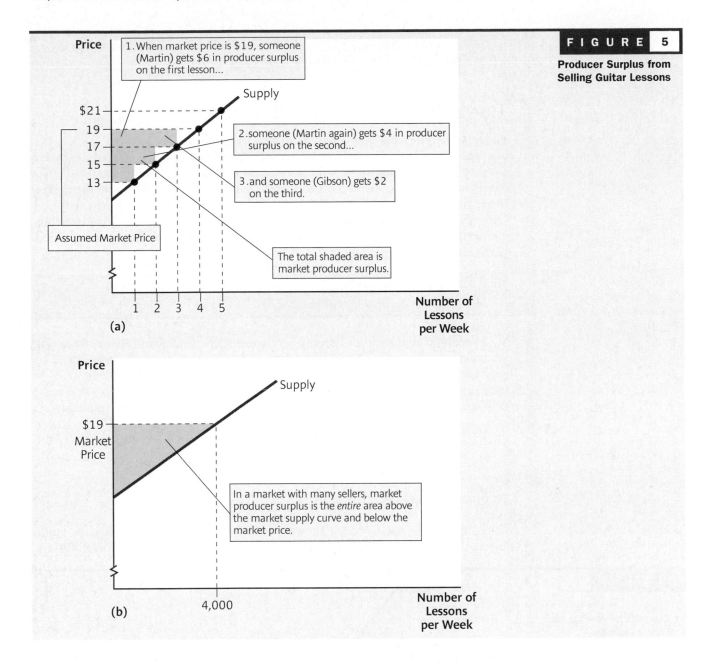

FIGURE 5

Producer Surplus from
Selling Guitar Lessons

(a)

1. When market price is $19, someone (Martin) gets $6 in producer surplus on the first lesson...

2. someone (Martin again) gets $4 in producer surplus on the second...

3. and someone (Gibson) gets $2 on the third.

The total shaded area is market producer surplus.

Assumed Market Price

Supply

Number of Lessons per Week

(b)

In a market with many sellers, market producer surplus is the *entire* area above the market supply curve and below the market price.

Supply

Number of Lessons per Week

The total producer surplus gained by *all* sellers in a market is called **market producer surplus,** found by adding up the shaded rectangles gained by *all* sellers in the market. In the figure, with the market price for guitar lessons at $19, market producer surplus is $6 + $4 + $2 = $12. Notice that this is *roughly* equal to the entire shaded area *above* the supply curve and *below* the market price of $19—except for the little unshaded triangles in panel (a).

Panel (b) of Figure 5 shows a larger market for guitar lessons, which might have hundreds of potential teachers, each capable of offering a dozen or more lessons every week. In such a market, the unshaded triangles are insignificant, so market producer surplus would essentially equal the *entire* shaded area above the supply curve and below the market price.

Market producer surplus The total producer surplus gained by all sellers in a market.

We measure market producer surplus, in dollars, as the total area above the market supply curve and below the market price.

TOTAL BENEFITS AND EFFICIENCY

Figure 6 combines the supply and demand curves for the large market in the previous figures. It shows consumer and producer surplus when this perfectly competitive market is in *equilibrium*, with price equal to $19 and quantity equal to 4,000. Market consumer surplus is the area under the demand curve and above the market price, or the blue-shaded area. Market producer surplus is the (red-shaded) area under the market price and above the supply curve. The total shaded area (both blue and red) represents the total benefits that consumers and producers receive from participating in this market.

*We measure the **total benefits** gained in a market as the sum of consumer and producer surplus in that market.*

There is an important relationship between efficiency and total benefits. Each time we make a Pareto improvement in a market (making at least one party better off and harming no one), total benefits increase. But efficiency means that all such Pareto improvements have been exploited. Therefore, efficiency means that we've exploited all opportunities to increase total benefits. Or, to put it more succinctly:

A market is efficient when total benefits—the sum of consumer and producer surplus—are maximized in that market.

PERFECT COMPETITION: THE TOTAL BENEFITS VIEW

Look again at Figure 6, which shows the perfectly competitive market for guitar lessons at the equilibrium price and quantity. When this market is in equilibrium,

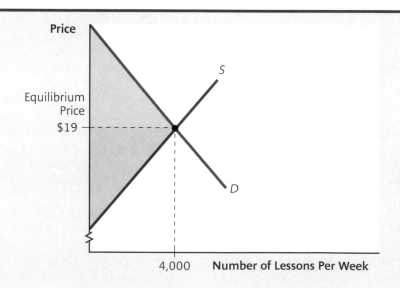

FIGURE 6

Total Benefits in a Competitive Market for Guitar Lessons

When a competitive market reaches equilibrium, the sum of market consumer surplus and market producer surplus is maximized. At any quantity less than 4,000 or greater than 4,000, total benefits will be smaller.

the total benefits—the sum of the blue- and red-shaded areas—are the maximum total benefits achievable in this market. How do we know this? Because any change in either the quantity or the price away from their equilibrium values will shrink the total benefits.

Total benefits The sum of consumer and producer surplus in a particular market.

Let's first see what would happen if we arbitrarily moved the *quantity* of guitar lessons to some value other than 4,000. Suppose the market were forced to supply *more* than 4,000—say, 5,000. For lessons 4,001 to 5,000, the supply curve lies above the demand curve, so their cost to the seller would be greater than their value to the buyer. Providing these additional lessons cannot add to total benefits in the market. In fact, no matter what price is charged for them, each additional lesson would *reduce* total benefits. For example, if a lesson has a cost of $21 but a value of $17, then producing that lesson *reduces* total benefits by $4, regardless of the price charged. (Charging $21 or more puts the entire loss on the buyer; charging $17 or less puts the entire loss on the seller.) Therefore, as we increase quantity above 4,000, total benefits fall.

What about a quantity *less* than 4,000—say, 3,000? For lessons 3,001 to 4,000, the demand curve lies above the supply curve, so their value to the buyer would be greater than their cost to the seller. These potential gains are lost when quantity is reduced to 3,000. Therefore, as we decrease quantity below 4,000, we reduce total benefits.

Because increasing the quantity above or below 4,000 *reduces* total benefits, we know that at 4,000, total benefits are maximized. More generally,

> *in a well-functioning, perfectly competitive market, the equilibrium quantity maximizes total benefits. This is another illustration that the equilibrium under perfect competition is efficient.*

INEFFICIENCY AND DEADWEIGHT LOSS

Our example of the perfectly competitive market for guitar lessons can be regarded as a benchmark (and ideal) case. The market, left to itself, exploits every possible Pareto improvement involving buyers and sellers.

But markets don't always achieve this efficient outcome. In some cases government intervention may be preventing efficiency. In other cases the nature of the market itself is responsible. In this section, we'll explore some examples of each of these cases of *in*efficiency.

A PRICE CEILING

What happens in an otherwise efficient market if we lower the price *below* its equilibrium value? How does a *price ceiling* affect total benefits?

If the quantity remained the same, the change in price would change the way benefits are allocated, but not their total. For example, consider a guitar lesson that is initially produced and sold for $19. If we force the price down to $17, and if that guitar lesson were *still* produced, the seller would enjoy $2 less in benefits, and the buyer would enjoy $2 more. By merely transferring benefits from one party to the other, we would not affect the total.

However, as you learned in Chapter 4, a price ceiling *does* change quantity. In a market economy we cannot force people to sell more than they want to. So a price ceiling that lowers the price will *reduce* the quantity sold.

Figure 7 shows the impact of a $15 price ceiling imposed on the market for guitar lessons. At that price, quantity supplied of 2,000 lessons per week is smaller than quantity demanded of 6,000. Since sellers are the short side of this market, and they can't be forced to offer more than 2,000 lessons, that will be the market quantity bought and sold.

The figure also shows how buyers' and sellers' market benefits are affected by the price ceiling, assuming no black market develops. (In the problem set, you'll be asked to analyze a price ceiling with a black market.) Producer surplus (shaded in red) is the area above the supply curve and below the new market price of $15, up to 2,000 units. Consumer surplus (in blue) is the area below the demand curve and above $15 also *up to 2,000 units.* Even though consumers would like to buy *more* than 2,000 units at a price of $15, we must stop at 2,000 when measuring their surplus: The lessons beyond 2,000 are no longer provided, so no consumer surplus is gained from them.

Comparing the market with the price ceiling (Figure 7) to the market *without* the price ceiling (Figure 6), it looks like the blue area measuring consumer surplus (marked B and C) has increased. (It won't always increase, but it does in our example.) But the price ceiling *decreases* the red area (marked A) measuring producer surplus. (An effective price ceiling will always reduce producer surplus.)

What has happened to the *total* of producer and consumer surplus? If you compare total benefits in Figure 6 with total benefits in Figure 7, you'll see that the price ceiling causes total benefits to fall. Specifically, in Figure 7, total benefits have been reduced by the area of the unshaded triangle. This area represents benefits that *could* be achieved in the market but are *not* achieved, because the market quantity drops from its efficient level of 4,000 to the inefficient level of 2,000.

The unshaded triangle is an example of what economists call a *deadweight loss* (sometimes also called a *welfare loss* or *excess burden*).

FIGURE 7

The Inefficiency of a Price Ceiling

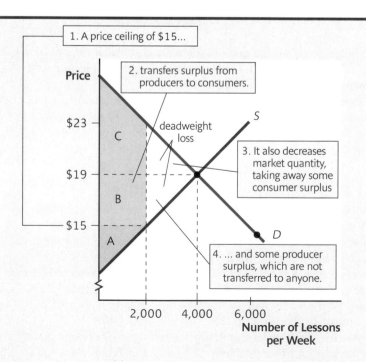

1. A price ceiling of $15...

2. transfers surplus from producers to consumers.

deadweight loss

3. It also decreases market quantity, taking away some consumer surplus

4. ... and some producer surplus, which are not transferred to anyone.

> *The **deadweight loss** in a market is the loss of potential benefits (measured in dollars) due to a deviation from the efficient outcome.*

Deadweight loss The dollar value of potential benefits not achieved due to inefficiency in a particular market.

As you can see in the figure, a price ceiling causes a deadweight loss because it moves the market quantity away from its efficient level.

Calculating the Deadweight Loss

To make this more concrete, let's calculate the *dollar value* of the deadweight loss caused by the price ceiling—the area of the unshaded triangle. From high school algebra, the area of any triangle is $\frac{1}{2} \times$ base $\times$ height. Imagine that our triangle has been tipped on its side, so that its *vertical* side is the *base*. This side goes from $15 to $23, so the base has a length of $23 - $15 = $8. The horizontal dashed line cutting through the middle of the triangle would be its *height*. This line goes from 2,000 to 4,000, so its length is 2,000. Applying the formula, we find that the loss $= \frac{1}{2} \times$ base $\times$ height $= \frac{1}{2} \times \$8 \times 2,000 = \$8,000$.

In words, when this market is delivering only 2,000 lessons per week instead of the efficient 4,000, guitar teachers and students together lose $8,000 in potential benefits—per *week*. If measured yearly, the deadweight loss would be 52 weeks $\times$ $8,000 per week = $416,000 per year.

A PRICE FLOOR

What happens in an otherwise efficient market if we raise the price *above* its equilibrium value? That is, how does a price *floor* affect total benefits? The analysis is very similar to that for a price ceiling.

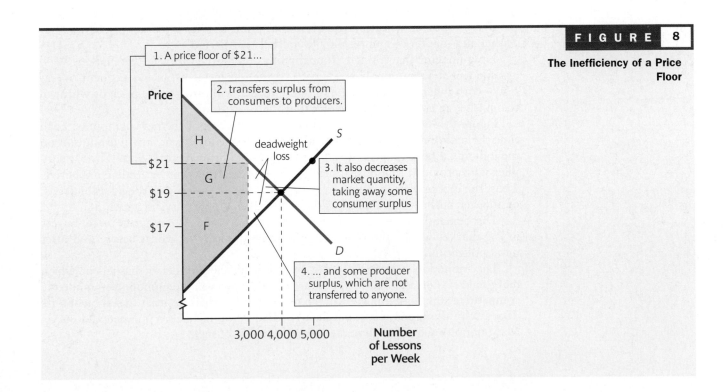

FIGURE 8

The Inefficiency of a Price Floor

1. A price floor of $21...

2. transfers surplus from consumers to producers.

deadweight loss

3. It also decreases market quantity, taking away some consumer surplus

4. ... and some producer surplus, which are not transferred to anyone.

Price

$21

$19

$17

H

G

F

S

D

3,000 4,000 5,000

Number of Lessons per Week

Figure 8 shows the impact of a price *floor* in our market, set at $21 per lesson. At that price, quantity demanded of 3,000 lessons per week is smaller than quantity supplied of 5,000. Now *buyers* are the short side of this market, so 3,000 will be the market quantity.

Producer surplus after the price floor is shaded in red and consumer surplus in blue. Notice that both surpluses are measured only up to 3,000 lessons—the quantity actually provided. Comparing the market with the price floor (Figure 8) to the market *without* the price floor (Figure 6), we find that the red area measuring producer surplus (marked F and G) has increased. (It won't necessarily increase, but it does in our example.) But the price floor *decreases* the blue area (marked H) measuring consumer surplus. (An effective price floor will always reduce consumer surplus.)

What has happened to the *total* of producer and consumer surplus? If you compare total benefits in Figure 6 with total benefits in Figure 8, you'll see that the price floor causes total benefits to fall. In Figure 8, the *deadweight loss* from the floor is equal to the area of the unshaded triangle. (In the problem set, you'll be asked to calculate the dollar value of this deadweight loss.)

MONOPOLY AND MARKET POWER

A firm has *market power* when it can influence the price that it charges for its product. Monopolists, oligopolists, and monopolistic competitors all have some degree of market power because they *set* their price in order to maximize profit, rather than take the price as given.

In monopolistic competition, the presence of many competitors generally limits market power and helps keep prices low. But when a market has just one seller, or a few oligopolists who collude, the price can be significantly higher than in an otherwise similar competitive market. With a higher price, a lower quantity will be produced and sold—a quantity that is *less* than the efficient quantity.

To see how this works, look at Figure 9(a). The left panel shows a perfectly competitive market for wheat, in equilibrium at point *E*, with a market price of $3 per bushel and market output of 500,000 bushels per period.

Now imagine that a single company buys up all the farms in this market. We'll assume this new monopoly treats each of the old farms as an independent operation—with one exception: The monopoly owner will now set the price of wheat in the market so as to maximize its total profit.

Figure 9(b) shows the market from the perspective of the new monopoly. Each time the monopoly wants to sell an additional bushel of wheat, it will produce it on the individual farm that can do so at the lowest additional cost—that is, by the supplier who provided that bushel before, when the market was perfectly competitive. Thus, the monopoly's marginal cost curve in panel (b)—showing the additional cost of another bushel—is the same as the old market supply curve in panel (a).

The demand curves in the two panels are the same: *At any given price*, buyers in the market would choose to buy the same quantity of wheat before and after monopolization.

The monopoly maximizes profit by choosing the number of bushels at which marginal revenue and marginal cost are equal. However, the monopoly—unlike the competitive suppliers—must drop the price on *all* bushels in order to sell one more. That's why the monopoly's marginal revenue curve lies below the demand curve: Marginal revenue is less than the price of the last bushel.

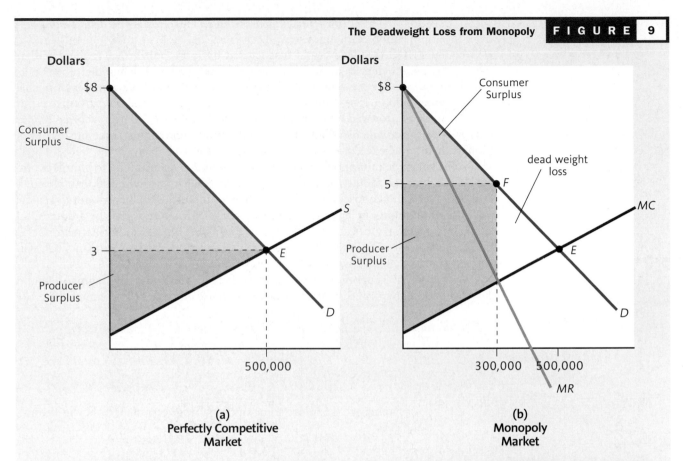

The Deadweight Loss from Monopoly   FIGURE 9

(a)
Perfectly Competitive Market

(b)
Monopoly Market

In panel (a), the market for wheat is perfectly competitive. Price is $3 per bushel, and output is 500,000 bushels per period. Total benefits are equal to the area of the two shaded triangles.

In panel (b), the market for wheat is monopolized. The competitive market supply curve becomes the monopoly's MC curve. The monopoly, at point F, supplies fewer bushels (300,000) at a higher price ($5). Potential benefits on bushels 300,001 to 500,000—for which the value to some buyer would be greater than the marginal cost—are not realized. The result is a deadweight loss equal to the area of the unshaded triangle.

In panel (b), you can see that the monopoly's profit-maximizing output level is 300,000 bushels, and it charges the highest price—$5—at which it can sell that quantity. Consumer surplus is the blue-shaded area—below the demand curve and above the market price of $5.

The monopoly's producer surplus is the purple-shaded area (above its new marginal cost curve and below the market price of $5). Why? Because producer surplus on each unit for the monopoly is the difference between the added cost of that unit (given by the MC curve) and what it actually gets for it ($5). When we sum up this surplus for all 300,000 units produced, the result is the purple-shaded area.

What has happened to the *total* of producer and consumer surplus? Compare total benefits in the perfectly competitive market (the shaded areas in panel (a)) with total benefits under monopoly (the shaded areas of panel (b)). You'll see that the monopoly takeover has caused total benefits to fall. Specifically, total benefits have been reduced by the area of the *unshaded triangle*. This area is the *deadweight loss* from monopolization of the industry.

To understand the deadweight loss caused by monopolization, remember that 500,000 is the efficient quantity—the quantity supplied and demanded under perfect competition. But the monopoly provides only 300,000. Providing each bushel from number 300,001 to number 500,000 would be a Pareto improvement, but none of these is provided. Why not? Because *the monopoly charges a price that is greater than marginal cost*. Thus, buyers will choose *not* to buy some bushels even though their value exceeds the cost of providing them.

Note that if the monopoly could *price discriminate*—continuing to charge $5 on bushels 1 through 300,000, and then charge $3 for bushels 300,001 through 500,000—it *would* choose to supply the efficient quantity. (You may want to review price discrimination in Chapter 9; in this case, the *MR* curve would be a horizontal line at $3 for all quantities from 300,001 to 500,000.) But as you've learned, not all firms can price discriminate. A *single-price* monopoly, like the one in panel (b), will be inefficient.

Our example generalizes to any firm facing a downward-sloping demand curve—that is, any firm with market power—that cannot price discriminate.

> Monopoly and imperfectly competitive markets—in which firms charge a single price on all units that is greater than marginal cost—are generally inefficient. Price is too high, and output is too low, to maximize the total benefits in the market.

In the next chapter, we'll explore some options for government policy in dealing with monopoly.

USING THE THEORY

Taxes and Deadweight Losses

The government needs revenue in order to function. And it obtains revenue by taxing income from several sources: wages and salaries, interest, profits, capital gains. There are also taxes on purchases in general (sales taxes) and taxes on specific goods (excise taxes), such as gasoline, cigarettes, alcoholic beverages, and airline travel.

In Chapter 4, you learned that imposing a tax on a competitive market will change the equilibrium quantity. Based on what you've learned in *this* chapter, you won't be surprised that imposing a tax on an otherwise efficient market creates a deadweight loss.

Figure 10 revisits the excise tax on airline tickets, first discussed in Chapter 4. The initial equilibrium is at point A, with 10 million tickets sold per year at a price of $300 per ticket. We impose a tax of $60 per ticket, collected from sellers. Now to supply any given number of tickets, a price is required that is $60 greater than before. As a result, the supply curve shifts upward by $60, to $S_{\text{After Tax}}$. The market

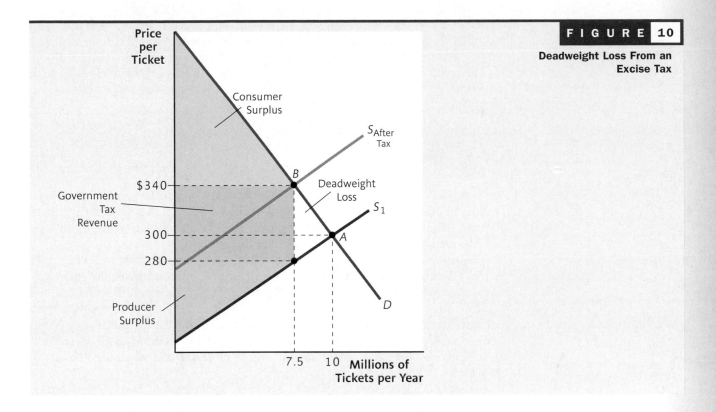

FIGURE 10

Deadweight Loss From an Excise Tax

equilibrium moves from point *A* to point *B*, with the new quantity equal to 7.5 million tickets per year. Buyers now pay $340 per ticket, and sellers receive $280 (after we deduct the $60 tax they must pay).

This was our familiar analysis from Chapter 4. But let's look at taxes in terms of consumer and producer surplus and total benefits. After the tax, consumer surplus (shaded blue) is the area under the demand curve and above the price of $340 that consumers pay. Producer surplus (shaded red) is the area above the supply curve and below the price of $280 that sellers now receive.

But there is one more benefit to consider: the government revenue from the tax. After all, this revenue can be used to reduce other taxes (a benefit to other taxpayers) or to provide government services (a benefit to those who receive them).

In the figure, the government's revenue is equal to the area of the green-shaded rectangle. To see why, note that the tax per ticket is $60, the height of the green rectangle. It is collected on each of 7.5 million tickets per year, the base of the rectangle. When we multiply the tax per ticket times the number of tickets, we get $60 × 7.5 million = $450 million, which is the area of the green rectangle.

If we now add together consumer surplus (blue), producer surplus (purple), and the government's tax revenue (green), we get the total benefits after tax in this market. Comparing this total to what benefits would be with *no* tax (all of the shaded areas together plus the unshaded triangle), we see that total benefits have been reduced by the area of the unshaded triangle—the deadweight loss from the tax.

As always, the deadweight loss occurs because quantity has changed. If the quantity had remained at the efficient level, the tax would have merely redistributed benefits from buyers and sellers to the government, with no change in the total. But the tax—by raising the price buyers pay and lowering the price sellers receive—

results in fewer tickets being sold. The "missing tickets" (from 7,500,001 to 10,000,000) previously provided benefits to both buyers and sellers, but now they provide benefits to no one—not even the government.

The result we obtained for an excise tax applies to other types of taxes as well. In general,

> *A tax imposed on an otherwise efficient market creates a deadweight loss: the loss in benefits to buyers and sellers is greater than the gain in revenue to the government.*

For example, the payroll tax on wages creates a deadweight loss in *labor* markets. The loss in benefits to those who buy labor (firms) and sell it (households) is greater than the gain in revenue to the government, so total benefits decrease. (You'll be asked to analyze a labor market tax in the problem set.)

The personal income tax, which is a tax on wage income together with other sources of income, has a similar effect. And taxes on interest, dividends, and capital gains create deadweight losses in otherwise efficient markets for capital.

How large are these deadweight losses from taxes? They can be substantial. Estimates of the deadweight loss from various taxes in the United States range from 20 to 60 cents on each dollar of revenue collected.[3] This would mean that each dollar collected by the government reduces total consumer and producer surplus by between $1.20 and $1.60.

In specific cases, the deadweight loss per dollar raised can be even larger. Consider the impact of an excise tax on high-speed Internet access—something that was being considered in 1998. One study[4] concluded that a $2 per month usage tax would have raised $36 million in government revenues per year. But annual consumer surplus would have decreased by $80 million, and producer surplus by another $20 million. This leaves a deadweight loss of $80 million + $20 million − $36 million = $64 million per year. Dividing by the $36 million in annual revenues, the loss is $1.80 for each dollar collected.

Does knowledge about deadweight losses help us? After all, doesn't the government need revenue? Doesn't it have to impose taxes? Indeed it does. But recognizing *why* a tax causes a deadweight loss can help us design more efficient tax policies. A deadweight loss arises because the *quantity* of the good or resource being traded decreases below the efficient quantity. And, in turn, the quantity falls because the tax changes the *price* paid by buyers and received by sellers. When demand or supply is very elastic (sensitive to price), even a small tax will result in a relatively large change in quantity, and deadweight losses will be relatively large. But the opposite applies as well: the more *inelastic* is demand or supply, the smaller will be the deadweight loss.

Therefore,

> *All else equal, taxes create smaller deadweight losses when they are imposed on markets in which demand or supply is relatively inelastic.*

---

[3] Congressional Budget Office, *Budget Options*, February 2001, p. 381.

[4] Austan Goolsbee, "The Value of Broadband and the Deadweight Loss of Taxing New Technology," *Working Paper No. 11994*, National Bureau of Economic Research, February 2006. This deadweight loss comes from a reduction in quantity among those who have access to broadband. Goolsbee estimates that if further effects of the tax were included—such as delays in providing broadband access to new areas of the country—the deadweight loss from the tax would more than double.

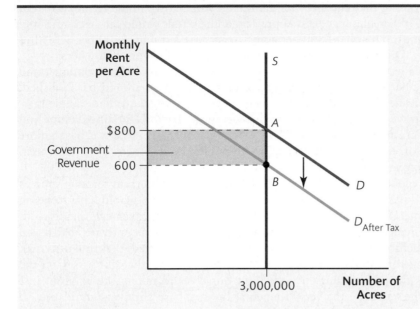

A Tax on Land

The market for land is initially in equilibrium at point A, with monthly rent equal to $800 per acre, and all 3 million acres rented. When a tax of $200 is imposed, the demand curve shifts downward to D$_{After\ Tax}$, and the new market equilibrium is at point B. Rent decreases from $800 to $600 (by the full amount of the tax), and the government's dollar revenue gain is equal to the dollar loss by landowners. Renters pay none of the tax. Since the equilibrium quantity of rented land remains unchanged, there is no deadweight loss.

In the extreme case, if supply or demand were *completely* inelastic, a tax would cause no change in quantity, and no deadweight loss at all.

A TAX ON LAND

Let's consider a tax on a market with a completely inelastic supply: the market for land. In Figure 11, we assume for simplicity that all land in this market is rented. The demand curve tells us the quantity of land people would want to rent at each price (each monthly rent). The supply curve tells us the quantity of land that owners make available to renters.

Notice that the supply curve for land is vertical. The price may rise or fall, but the same quantity (3 million acres) will always be available. Initially, the market is in equilibrium at point A, with rent of $800 per acre per month.

Now let's impose a tax of $200 per acre per month on land rentals. We'll first imagine that we impose the tax on the *renters*. In this case, the demand curve shifts downward to D$_{After\ Tax}$. Why? To get renters to choose any given quantity, they must be charged $200 less than before, because now they also have to pay the tax.

The tax moves the market equilibrium from *A* to *B*, and rent drops by the full amount of the tax, from $800 to $600. This tells us that renters neither gain nor lose: Including the tax, they still pay $800 per acre and still rent 3 million acres. *Landowners*, however, receive only $600 per acre, so they lose $200 per acre. They pay the entire tax. The total loss for landowners is $200 × 3 million = $600 million per month.

But notice that the landowners' loss is precisely equal to the government's gain in revenue, which is also $600 million (the area shaded green). The tax causes no deadweight loss at all; it has merely transferred dollars from landowners to the government.

What if the tax were imposed on *landowners* instead of renters? The result would be exactly the same. The owners might *try* to pass some or all of the tax on to renters by raising the rent they charge. But as you can see in the figure, any rent greater than $800 creates an excess supply of land, so rent would fall back to $800. Because rent must remain at $800 per acre, owners are left with $600 per acre after paying the tax. Once again, the entire burden of the tax falls on the owners.

Economists have long debated the idea of a land tax. In 1879, economist and social philosopher Henry George proposed that other taxes should be abolished, and that government should raise *all* of its revenue by taxing land. The "single-tax" movement that was formed to advocate this idea was very influential for a time and still has some prominent adherents. While Henry George's proposal was based more on concerns for equity than efficiency, there is clearly an efficiency argument in favor of shifting more of the tax burden to land.

But many economists see problems in a major shift from current revenue sources to a land tax. First, in order to avoid deadweight loss, the tax would have to be on the value of the *land only*—excluding the value of any improvements made to it. Such improvements include homes, factories, irrigation systems, private roads, and other infrastructure. If the value of such improvements is taxed, their quantity will fall in the long run, and we are back to the problem of deadweight losses on the improvements themselves. But once we limit ourselves to taxing the value of just land, minus the value of any improvements, the tax base shrinks significantly. It would be too small to substitute completely for other sources of revenue.

There are also equity considerations. By lowering rent, a shift to a land tax would decrease the benefits to owning land. This would occur *after* people had bought land at a price based on the current tax system. A rise in land taxes would thus force these people to either (1) suffer a lower-than-expected rate of return on their investment, or (2) suffer a capital loss if they try to sell their land. (Once rents fall, the price any new buyer would pay for land would drop as well.)

In spite of these objections, the idea of shifting *some* of the tax burden toward gifts of nature like land, as well as toward other resources with a completely inelastic supply (such as radio spectrum or airline corridors), is alive and well.[5]

One final word about taxes. If you've read this section carefully, you've seen that we've often used the phrase "otherwise efficient market" in discussing the deadweight loss from a tax. But in some cases, when a market is *not* otherwise efficient, imposing a tax can actually *make* it efficient. We'll explore these cases, as well as other situations in which government action can help to foster efficiency, in the next chapter.

Summary

A *Pareto improvement* is a change that makes at least one person better off, and harms no one. A market or an economy is *economically efficient* when all Pareto improvements have been exploited. When well-functioning, perfectly competitive markets are left free to reach equilibrium, they are economically efficient.

Economic efficiency can also be viewed as the outcome that maximizes *total benefits* in a market. In a market without taxes, total benefits are the sum of *consumer surplus* (the dollar value to consumers minus what they actually pay) and *producer surplus* (the dollar value producers receive minus the minimum payment necessary to get them to produce). Because it is effi-

[5] For a recent, well-argued defense of such a shift, see Fred Foldvary, "Geo-Rent: A Plea to Public Economists," *Econ Journal Watch*, April 2005, pp. 106–132.

cient, the equilibrium quantity in a perfectly competitive market maximizes total benefits.

When market quantity deviates from the efficient quantity, the result is a *deadweight loss*: the value of potential benefits not achieved due to inefficiency. A price *ceiling* or a price *floor* in an otherwise efficient market may or may not increase the surplus for one side of the market. But it changes the equilibrium quantity, and therefore decreases *total* benefits and creates a deadweight loss.

A deadweight loss also occurs when a competitive market is monopolized, or when a tax is imposed in an otherwise efficient market. The more elastic is demand or supply, the greater is the deadweight loss from any given tax.

Problem Set

Answers to even-numbered Questions and Problems can be found on the text Web site at www.thomsonedu.com/economics/hall.

1. In Figure 3, suppose that, initially, McCollum is providing the fifth guitar lesson to Zoe for a price of $16. Who would gain and who would lose from this lesson and how much?

2. Figure 8 shows a price floor of $21 in the market for guitar lessons. Calculate the dollar value of the deadweight loss caused by the price floor, using the numbers on the graph.

3. The following table shows the quantities of bottled water demanded and supplied per week at different prices in a particular city:

Price	Quantity Demanded	Quantity Supplied
$1.10	8,000	0
$1.15	7,000	1,000
$1.20	6,000	2,000
$1.25	5,000	3,000
$1.30	4,000	4,000
$1.35	3,000	5,000
$1.40	2,000	6,000
$1.45	1,000	7,000
$1.50	0	8,000

   a. Draw the supply and demand curves for this market, and identify the equilibrium price and quantity.
   b. Identify on your graph areas for market consumer surplus and market producer surplus when the market is in equilibrium.
   c. Using your graph, calculate the dollar value of market consumer surplus, market producer surplus, and the total net benefits in the market at equilibrium.

4. Suppose the government imposes a price *ceiling* of $1.20 in the market for bottled water in problem 3. Calculate the dollar value of each of the following:
   a. Market consumer surplus
   b. Market producer surplus
   c. Total net benefits in the market
   d. The deadweight loss from the price ceiling

5. Suppose the government imposes a price *floor* of $1.40 in the market for bottled water in problem 3. Calculate the dollar value of each of the following:
   a. Market consumer surplus
   b. Market producer surplus
   c. Total benefits in the market
   d. The deadweight loss from the price floor

6. Calculate the deadweight loss caused by the monopolization of the wheat industry in Figure 9. (Note: For marginal revenue at 300,000 bushels, use $2.00.)

7. Toward the end of the chapter, you learned that a tax on labor income can cause a deadweight loss, just like an excise tax on a good.
   a. Draw a diagram of a labor market in which the equilibrium wage is $20 per hour and total employment is 10,000 workers. On the graph, identify an area that represents total benefits to workers. (Hint: This area will be analogous to producer surplus in a goods market. Think about each point on the labor supply curve, and ask: What is the lowest wage at which this worker would supply labor, compared to the wage they are actually being paid?)
   b. On the same graph, identify an area that represents total benefits to firms from hiring labor. (Hint: This area will be analogous to consumer surplus in a goods market. Think about each point on the labor demand curve, and ask: What is the highest wage the firm would pay to hire *this* particular worker, compared to the wage it is actually paying?)
   c. Draw a second diagram showing the impact of a $10 per hour tax on labor income, collected from workers. On this diagram, identify areas that represent, after the tax, each of the following: (1) the total benefits to workers, (2) the total benefits to firms, (3) the government's tax revenue, and (4) the deadweight loss from the tax.

More Challenging

8. Figure 7 shows how a price ceiling affects consumer and producer surplus in the competitive market for guitar lessons. Suppose instead that Figure 7 (and all of the numbers in it) depicts the competitive market for tickets to rock concerts by local bands. Further, when the city imposes a $15 price ceiling, a black market develops in which ticket scalpers buy up all of the tickets available, and sell them all at the highest single price that the market will bear. Draw a graph and identify areas for each of the following after the price ceiling is imposed:

a. Consumer surplus
b. Producer surplus
c. Ticket scalpers' revenue.
d. Deadweight loss

9. Suppose the weekly quantity demanded (Q^D) for a good is given by the equation $Q^D = 10,000 - 80P$, and the weekly quantity supplied (Q^S) is given by $Q^S = 20P$, where P is the price per unit.
    a. What is the equilibrium price and quantity?

b. When the market is in equilibrium, what are the values of consumer surplus, producer surplus, and total benefits? (Hint: Sketch a rough graph first.)
c. Find the value of the deadweight loss (dollars per week) if a price ceiling of $80 is imposed on this market.
d. Find the value of the deadweight loss (dollars per week) if a price floor of $110 is imposed on this market.

Government's Role in Economic Efficiency

In nations around the world, virtually every disagreement about the economy ultimately leads to government. And some disagreements start there as well.

In the United States, for example, hardly a day goes by without a speech in Congress attacking or applauding the government's spending on defense, education, environmental programs, and more.

Underlying many of these speeches are sharp disagreements about the *role* that government should play in economic life. Should it help people send their children to private schools by giving them vouchers? Should it discourage the merger of two large airlines? Should local governments collect trash and run prisons, or should these services be contracted out to private firms? How far should the government go in regulating the activities of private businesses? Similar controversies exist in other developed market economies, such as the nations of the European Union or Japan.

But these disagreements tend to obscure a remarkable degree of *agreement* about the economy and the government's role in it. For example, in the United States and most other countries, the vast majority of goods and services you buy are provided by private firms. Almost everyone agrees that's how it should be. Hardly anyone proposes that the government should provide the economy's books, jeans, computers, entertainment, or soft drinks. At the same time, there is widespread agreement that certain goods and services should be provided by government alone, such as general police protection, the court system, and national defense. Much of this agreement is based on ideas about economic efficiency.

In the previous chapter, we looked at ways in which government intervention in an otherwise efficient market *reduced* total benefits and created *in*efficiency. In this chapter, by contrast, we'll be looking at how government intervention can *increase* total benefits in markets, and create efficiency where it would not otherwise exist.

We'll first consider government's provision of the broad framework that enables the market system to work. Then we'll turn our attention to the problems that can plague individual markets, and the role of government in solving these problems.

THE LEGAL AND REGULATORY INFRASTRUCTURE

One way that government contributes to efficiency is by providing the infrastructure that permits markets to function. The word *infrastructure* suggests roads, bridges, airports, waterways, and the like. Indeed, this sort of *physical* infrastructure, often provided by government, is vital for a well-functioning market system.

But equally important is the government-provided *institutional* infrastructure: the legal and regulatory framework without which markets could function only primitively, if at all.

THE LEGAL SYSTEM

Laws are important for noneconomic reasons. The law protects us from many kinds of physical and emotional harm, guarantees us freedom of speech and other vital civil liberties, and helps provide a sense of security and dignity in our lives. But people often overlook the purely *economic* role of law—ways in which it supports markets and helps us achieve economic efficiency.

Criminal law, for example, makes it illegal to engage in many types of involuntary exchange—such as robbery—in which one party is harmed. In this way, criminal law encourages people to channel their efforts into mutually beneficial, voluntary exchanges—that is, into Pareto improvements.

Property law enables society to assign ownership to assets (such as land, housing, capital equipment, or financial assets) and determine who is entitled to the rewards. This, in turn, encourages people to find the most productive uses for their property, rather than spend time trying to capture the property of others, or prevent others from taking the property they have.

Contract law enables parties to exchange promises involving future activities. It specifies what sorts of promises can be made, and establishes procedures for compensation if one party breaks the promise. Without well-enforced contract law, much productive activity would come to a halt, because people would be wary of fulfilling their side of a bargain first. For example, you would not be able to hire someone to fix your roof because the roofer would insist on payment first, and you would insist he do the work first. Similarly, you would not invest in a company, because you wouldn't trust that you'd receive your share of the future profits.

Tort law defines obligations among people who are *not* linked by contracts. It defines the types of harm for which someone can seek remedy, and the procedures for injured persons to collect reasonable compensation. Tort law helps protect consumers from unsafe products (such as automobiles with brakes that may fail). It also helps protect businesses from unreasonable liabilities (you can't sue Spalding if you trip on a tennis ball). U.S. tort law has become especially controversial in recent years, with one side claiming that costly, frivolous lawsuits are restraining beneficial production, and the other stressing that only the threat of lawsuits keeps a business's eye on consumer safety. But without some form of tort law, many Pareto improvements would never take place; virtually all production carries the risk of harm to someone.

Antitrust law is designed to prevent businesses from engaging in behavior that limits competition and harms consumers. For example, the *Sherman Act* of 1890 prohibits collusion to fix prices, as well as certain types of competitive behavior that can lead to a monopoly. The *Clayton Act* of 1914 gave the federal government the power to prevent mergers and acquisitions that would harm competition. Because (as you'll soon see) monopoly behavior is inefficient, antitrust enforcement that preserves competition is another way that government can contribute to economic efficiency.

REGULATION

Regulation is fundamentally different from legal procedures. The legal system imposes fines or other penalties when a business violates the law. But regulation goes further. It directs businesses to take some specific actions and prohibits other actions, often on a case-by-case basis. This can contribute to efficiency by protecting buyers, sellers, or third parties from some of the potential harm that market exchanges might otherwise cause.

For example, in the United States, the Food and Drug Administration (FDA) can prohibit a pharmaceutical company from selling a particular drug, or order that further research be done to prove its safety or effectiveness. The Environmental Protection Agency (EPA) has detailed control over what substances a business can release into the atmosphere or into the water. The Securities and Exchange Commission (SEC) can prohibit a company from issuing new shares of stock to the public, or require additional information before the shares are sold.

THE IMPORTANCE OF INFRASTRUCTURE

Almost every Pareto improvement we can think of relies on the legal and regulatory components of our institutional infrastructure. Recall the last time you bought a meal in a restaurant. If you paid cash, the criminal law against counterfeiting enabled the restaurant to more readily accept your paper currency. If you paid by credit card, contract law assured the restaurant that it would eventually be paid by the credit card company. The restaurant itself couldn't function without contracts with its suppliers, landlord, and employees. And you could be reasonably confident that the food was not contaminated, in part because of inspections by local regulatory agencies and also because tort law provides legal disincentives for harmful products.

Americans take their institutional infrastructure almost completely for granted. The best way to appreciate the infrastructure of the United States is to visit another country that has a poor one. In many countries, the police are more likely to steal from citizens than to protect them from thievery. In some nations, the people have no effective rights to their own property: Somebody can start building a shack on their land, and the government won't stop him. If a person is injured by a drunk driver, there may be no system for compensating her or punishing the driver. Many nations suffer from powerful mafias that extort protection money by threatening to shut down businesses or physically harm their owners.

For example, a study commissioned by the World Bank estimated that Russian households pay $3 billion in bribes each year, about half the amount they pay in income taxes. Most of the bribes paid by households went to education workers (including teachers!) and traffic police. Russian businesses pay even more in bribes: about $33 billion.[1]

Another World Bank study found that in Guatemala it would take about 4 years of legal procedures to collect on a sizeable debt, even when the collector is unambiguously in the right. In Indonesia there would be no point in trying to collect, because the administrative and legal costs would exceed the amount owed.[2]

Although these are extreme examples, all too many nations suffer from problems of this type. The result is serious economic inefficiency that reduces living standards.

---

[1] "A Russian Tilts at Graft," *New York Times*, February 10, 2003; and "Report: Russian Society Saturated by Corruption," *Helsingin Sanomat*, International Edition, August 13, 2002 (*http://www. helsinki-hs.net/archive.asp*).

[2] *Doing Business*, World Bank Report, 2006 (*http://www.doingbusiness.org/ExploreTopics/Enforcing Contracts/*).

FIGURE 1

Government Infrastructure and Output per Worker

Countries with low-quality infrastructures produced an average of only $3,000 per worker per year in 1988. These countries tend to have corrupt governments, poor enforcement of contracts, and weak property rights. Countries with higher quality infrastructures, including the United States, produced an average of $17,000 per worker per year.

Source: Robert E. Hall and Charles I. Jones, "The Productivity of Nations," National Bureau of Economic Research Working Paper 5812, November 1997.

Figure 1 shows that when countries are divided into three groups, according to the quality of their institutional infrastructure, there is a strong relation between infrastructure and output per worker. The countries on the left—the ones with the lowest quality infrastructures—were able to produce only about $3,000 in output per worker per year in 1988. These are the nations where property rights were weak, contracts were not enforced, and the government was more often predator than protector of economic activity. In the middle of the figure are countries with medium-quality infrastructures, averaging about $5,500 in output per worker per year. On the right are the best-organized countries, averaging $17,000 in output per worker. Within this group, nations with the very best infrastructures—such as the United States, Sweden, and Japan—achieved output levels more than double that average.

MARKET FAILURES

The legal and regulatory infrastructure we've been discussing largely helps to create fertile ground for markets to operate and generate Pareto improvements. But there is another vitally important role for government: to intervene in situations of *market failure*.

Market failure A market that fails to take advantage of every Pareto improvement.

> A *market failure* occurs when a market—even with the proper institutional support—is economically in*efficient*.

You've already encountered one specific example of a market failure: the *principal–agent problem* in the market for CEOs (see Chapter 12). Here, we'll focus on four general types of market failures to which economists have devoted a lot of attention: (1) monopoly markets; (2) externalities; (3) public goods; and (4) information asymmetry. As you'll see, government involvement can often help deal with, and even cure, a market failure. But government involvement has costs as well as benefits, and sometimes government policies create problems of their own. While economists and policy makers agree in theory on what causes a market failure, dealing with real-world market failures remains one of the most controversial aspects of government policy.

MONOPOLY

In Chapter 14, you learned that a monopoly market, or a market in which firms have significant market power, is inefficient. In such markets price is too high, and output is too low, to maximize the total benefits achievable: a market failure.

Is there a proper role for government to make such markets more efficient, and thus cure a market failure?

Antitrust Law as a Remedy

In Chapter 14 (Figure 9), we imagined that a perfectly competitive market for wheat was taken over by a monopoly, which then raised the price and reduced output. For this type of monopoly market, there may be a solution: Since the market would function very well under competitive conditions, the government could use *antitrust law* to break the monopoly into several competing firms. But breaking up a monopoly would *not* make sense in other cases where the market would perform even worse with more competition.

For example, monopolies that arise from patents and copyrights, as discussed in Chapter 9, provide an incentive for artistic creations and scientific discovery. Breaking up a monopoly in, say, a particular drug—by removing its patent before it expired—would lead to a greater and closer-to-efficient quantity of *that* drug. But it would also reduce incentives to develop *future* drugs. Over a long period of time, the benefits from the drug industry as a whole could be reduced. Drug prices are controversial: There are hot debates about the duration of drug patents and what should qualify as a patentable drug. But no one seriously proposes destroying temporary drug monopolies by eliminating patents and turning the market into anything resembling perfect competition.

Similarly, market power that arises from *network externalities*—discussed in Chapter 9—offers benefits that would be hard to achieve under more competitive conditions. Microsoft, for example, takes advantage of its market power in several ways. But the Windows network, which provides substantial benefits, is possible because a single firm produces the operating system used by most personal computers.

Finally, when a monopoly arises as a *natural monopoly*, using antitrust law to break it up or even to prevent its formation in the first place is a poor remedy. Because this type of monopoly presents special challenges, it's worth its own discussion.

The Special Case of Natural Monopoly

In Chapter 9, you learned that a *natural monopoly* exists when, due to economies of scale, one firm can produce for the entire market at a lower cost per unit than could two or more firms. If the government steps aside, such a market will naturally evolve toward monopoly.

Regulating a Natural Monopoly

Left unregulated, the cable monopoly would serve 50,000 households, where MC = MR. This is inefficient, because units 50,001 to 100,000 have value to some consumers greater than their marginal cost.

By mandating a price of $20, government regulators could achieve the efficient outcome—100,000 households—at point B. But with price less than LRATC, the monopoly would suffer a loss, so it would have to be subsidized or go out of business.

The alternative, which is typically chosen, is to set price at $38—the lowest achievable average cost in this market, which includes a "fair rate of return." At this price, the monopoly serves 85,000 households. This is not the efficient quantity of 100,000, but is closer to the efficient outcome than would be achieved without regulation.

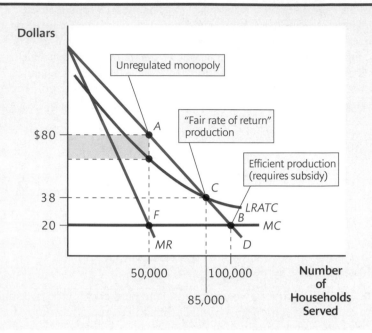

Figure 2 presents an example of a natural monopoly: a local cable company in a small city.

A cable company has important *lumpy inputs*—inputs needed in fixed amounts over a wide range of output. These include costly underground cable to neighborhoods, a legal department to negotiate contracts with entertainment providers, and more. Spreading these costs over more subscribers creates economies of scale. In the figure, these economies of scale continue until the entire market is served: The *LRATC* curve slopes ever downward.

To serve an *additional* household, however, is *not* very costly to a cable company: just the installation appointment, some additional above-ground cable, and handling the occasional customer complaint. Therefore, *marginal* cost for a cable company is relatively low. In Figure 2, we assume that marginal cost is a constant $20 per additional household—no matter how many households are served. Accordingly, the marginal cost curve is a horizontal line at $20.

If the market for cable service in the city is left to itself, one firm would become the sole supplier. In the absence of any government intervention, it would then sign up the profit-maximizing number of households, where marginal revenue (*MR*) and marginal cost (*MC*) are equal. In the figure, the *MR* and *MC* curves intersect at point *F*, and the cable monopoly will sign up 50,000 households. The price, at point *A* on the demand curve, is $80 per month. Profit is the area of the shaded rectangle.

But point *A*—with an output of 50,000—is *inefficient*. The 50,001st through the 100,000th households still value cable service more than the additional cost of providing it to them, so total net benefits in the market would rise if they acquired service. But when the monopoly is left at liberty to charge $80 for service, these households do not buy it. In fact, the efficient level of output is 100,000 households, at point *B*, where the *MC* curve crosses the demand curve. The monopoly—by failing to provide this quantity—is a market failure. What can the government do?

Using antitrust law to break this natural monopoly into several competing firms would not make sense. With several firms—each supplying to only a part of the market—each firm's cost per unit would be even higher than the monopoly's cost per unit. Therefore, the price in a more competitive market could never be $15 (the price needed to get us to the efficient point *B*). In fact, competition, by raising cost per unit, might result in an even *higher* price than under monopoly, reducing the total net benefits from the market.

But if breaking up a natural monopoly is not advisable, what *can* government do to bring us closer to economic efficiency? One option is public *ownership* and *operation* of cable service, as is done with the post office, another natural monopoly. Public takeover of private business is rare, except when certain conditions are present (to be discussed later in this chapter). That leaves one other option, and the one local governments actually choose for the cable industry: *regulation*.

Regulation of Natural Monopoly

At the beginning of this chapter, you learned that under regulation, a government agency digs deep into the operations of a business and takes some of the firm's decisions under its own control. In the case of a natural monopoly, regulators would tell the firm what price it can charge.

One option for regulators is **marginal cost pricing**: setting the price equal to the firm's marginal cost of production.[3] In the figure, where marginal cost is constant at $20, the regulators would set price equal to $20. This will automatically bring the market to the efficient level of output: At a price of $20 for service, 100,000 households will sign up.

Marginal cost pricing Setting a monopoly's regulated price equal to marginal cost where the marginal cost curve crosses the market demand curve.

But this creates a serious problem. If you look again at Figure 2, you'll notice that the *MC* curve lies everywhere *below* the *LRATC* curve. This must be the case for a natural monopoly, since economies of scale—the reason for the natural monopoly—means that the *LRATC* curve slopes downward, and this can occur only when marginal cost is less than average cost. (See Chapter 6 on the marginal–average relationship if you've forgotten why. Here, both marginal cost and average cost refer to the long run.)

Now you can see the problem for regulators: If they set the efficient price of $15 so that buyers demand the efficient quantity of 100,000, the firm's cost per unit is *greater* than $15. The firm would suffer a loss. In the long run, it would go out of business. Therefore, with marginal cost pricing, the government must also *subsidize* the natural monopoly—to cover its losses with government funds. This is often controversial because it requires taxpayers in general, rather than just the monopoly's customers, to help pay for the product.

Because of the problems with marginal cost pricing, regulators around the world more commonly choose an alternative, called **average cost pricing**. With this method, the price is set where the *LRATC* curve crosses the demand curve. In the figure, this occurs at a price of $38.

Average cost pricing Setting a monopoly's regulated price equal to long-run average cost where the *LRATC* curve crosses the market demand curve.

Average cost pricing is sometimes called *fair rate of return* pricing. Remember that average total cost incorporates *all* costs, including the opportunity cost of

---

[3] In the figure, marginal cost is constant. When marginal cost rises with output, efficiency requires the regulator to set price equal to the value of marginal cost *where the marginal cost curve crosses the demand curve*. At this price, every unit valued more than its marginal cost would be purchased.

owners' funds. Thus, a fair rate of return to owners is already built into the *LRATC* curve. When the firm charges $38 per unit, it is covering *all* of its production costs—including a fair rate of return for owners. Moreover, $38 is the lowest price the natural monopoly could charge without suffering a loss. (Confirm for yourself that if it charged any less, it would operate at a point on the demand curve *below* the *LRATC* curve, creating a loss.)

More generally,

> *with average cost pricing, regulators strive to set the price equal to cost per unit where the* LRATC *curve crosses the demand curve. The natural monopoly makes zero economic profit, which provides its owners with a fair rate of return and keeps the monopoly in business.*

Average cost pricing is not a perfect solution. For one thing, it does not quite make the market efficient. For example, notice that in Figure 2, only 85,000 units are produced, instead of the efficient quantity of 100,000. Nevertheless, compared to no regulation at all, average cost pricing lowers the price to consumers and increases the quantity they buy, bringing us closer to the efficient level.

Another problem with average cost pricing is that it provides little or no incentive for the natural monopoly to economize on capital. That is, the monopoly can grow larger and larger—taking in more and more new owners by issuing stock and using the proceeds to buy machinery, office buildings, and other forms of capital—confident that the regulators will always ensure that the price will be adjusted upward to ensure a fair rate of return. This can lead to rising costs for customers, and a further movement away from the efficient output level.

EXTERNALITIES

If you live in a dormitory, you have no doubt had the unpleasant experience of trying to study while the stereo in the next room is blasting through your walls—and usually not your choice of music. This may not sound like an economic problem, but it is one. The problem is that your neighbor, in deciding to listen to loud music, is considering only the private costs (the sacrifice of his own time) and private benefits (the enjoyment of music) of his action. He is not considering the harm it causes to you. Indeed, the harm you suffer might be greater than the benefit he gets from blasting his music.

When a private action has side effects that affect other people in important ways, we have the problem of externalities:

Externality A by-product of a good or activity that affects someone not immediately involved in the transaction.

> *An **externality** is a by-product of a good or activity that affects someone not immediately involved in the transaction.*

A *negative externality* is a by-product that causes harm to others not involved in the transaction. A *positive externality* is one that creates benefits for others. As you are about to see, the presence of either type of externality results in a market failure because the market, on its own, does not provide the efficient quantity.

The Private Solution to a Negative Externality

Under certain conditions, the inefficiency that would be caused by a negative externality will automatically be resolved by the parties themselves. Recall our example in Chapter 14 of the movie theater that would create $100,000 in benefits for some residents, but $70,000 in harm to others. Because the gains to the gainers are greater than the losses to the losers, the efficient outcome is to build the theater. Otherwise, we can identify a Pareto improvement that is not being exploited (namely, building the theater with a side payment sufficient to compensate those harmed).

In our example, *many* residents of the town were affected. But imagine instead that just *one* person stands to gain (let's call her Grace, the person who wants to build the theater in her empty lot) and just *one* person who would be harmed (let's call him Fernando, the person who lives next door to the lot and would suffer from the noise). In this situation, as long as *either* party has clear legal rights in the case, the outcome will be efficient: The theater will be built.

Let's suppose first that Grace has the legal right to build whatever she wants on her property. Then the case is open and shut: She will build the theater. Because Grace has the rights, she will not need to make any side payment to Fernando. Fernando will suffer, but the theater will be built.

Now suppose that Fernando has the right to block the theater from being built unless he approves. In this case, Grace will find it worth her while to pay Fernando for his approval. Because her potential gains are greater than Fernando's loss, she will still come out ahead, even after compensating Fernando. (A side payment of $80,000, for example, would make them both gainers.)

As you can see, regardless of who has the rights, the efficient outcome—building the theater—will be the result. No government intervention is required, other than the initial establishment of legal rights in the case.

What if building the theater were *not* the efficient outcome, because the losses would exceed the gains? Then it would *not* be built—regardless of who possesses the legal rights. (A problem at the end of this chapter will guide you through a specific example.)

Our conclusion—that building the theater depends only on whether it is efficient, and not on who holds the rights—is a rather surprising result. It is an example of the *Coase theorem,* named after economist Ronald Coase:

> The **Coase theorem** states that—*when side payments can be negotiated and arranged without cost—the private market will solve the externality problem on its own, always arriving at the efficient outcome. While the initial distribution of legal rights will determine the allocation of gains and losses among the parties, it will not affect the action taken.*

Coase theorem When a side payment can be arranged without cost, the market will solve an externality problem—and create the efficient outcome—on its own.

Note that the Coase theorem requires that side payments can be arranged *without cost*—or, in practice, that the cost is so low relative to the gains or losses at stake that it doesn't matter. This requirement is most likely to be satisfied when all three of the following conditions are present: (1) legal rights are clearly established; (2) legal rights can be easily transferred; and (3) the number of people involved is very small.

However, many real-world situations do not satisfy these conditions. Legal rights are often in dispute. If the rights are vaguely defined in our example, Grace and Fernando would very likely end up in court. Since courts are often more concerned about fairness or legal interpretation than efficiency, the outcome may not be the efficient one. (This is not necessarily bad; fairness, as we've stressed, is a concern as well as efficiency.)

Furthermore, once a court decides the issue, legal rights may not be transferable. For example, if Fernando wins the court case and blocks the theater, the court may not allow him to reverse his decision if Grace offers him a side payment.

But the biggest problem in applying the Coase theorem to many real-world externalities is the third condition: Often, a large number of people are involved. In Chapter 14, we assumed—more realistically—that building the movie theater would affect *many* people in the town, positively and negatively. It would be very costly to determine the gains and losses for each one, get them all together, and then come up with a solution that would please everyone. Moreover, when many people are involved, achieving efficiency with side payments is plagued by an often insoluble problem, to which we turn now.

The Free Rider Problem

Once again, suppose that the efficient outcome in our example is to build the theater. Suppose, too, that those who would be harmed have the legal right to prevent this outcome. Accordingly, a side payment has been negotiated by representatives of the gainers and the losers—one that makes everyone come out ahead. The total side payment is $80,000, with each of the gainers told to contribute, say, $500. Now, we face another problem: A gainer may try to get a *free ride,* refusing to pay. After all, his own part of the payment is so small—just a "drop in the bucket"—that the theater will be built regardless. He may claim that he doesn't receive benefits, or just laugh off anyone who comes to collect. (Remember, the government is not involved at this point.) If *many* of those who should contribute think this way and attempt to get a free ride, we have the *free rider problem.*

Free rider problem When the efficient outcome requires a side payment but individual gainers will not contribute.

> The **free rider problem** occurs when an efficient outcome requires a side payment but individual gainers—each obligated to pay a small share of the side payment—will not contribute.

The free rider problem, if extensive enough, can shrink the total side payment until it is too small to compensate those harmed. In that case, the private arrangement—based on voluntary participation rather than government coercion—will break down and the efficient outcome will not be achieved. Indeed, the free rider problem stands in the way of many Pareto improvements. And it is one of the main reasons we typically turn to government to deal with important externalities that affect many people.

Market Externalities and Government Solutions

A competitive market has, by definition, many buyers and sellers. So when a negative externality affects a *market*, the private (Coase theorem) solution may not work.

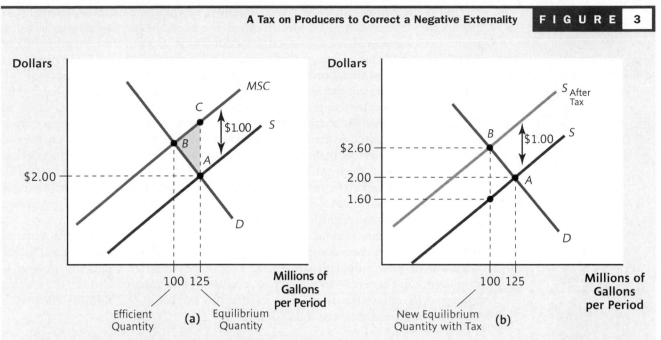

A Tax on Producers to Correct a Negative Externality   FIGURE 3

In the competitive market for gasoline in panel (a), the market equilibrium is at point A. But the supply curve includes only marginal costs to private suppliers, ignoring the negative externality of $1.00 per gallon. When the negative externality is added to other costs, the result is the marginal social cost curve (MSC). The efficient output level is at point B. Without government intervention, the units from 100 million to 125 million are produced, even though their full cost (given by the MSC curve) is greater than their value (on the demand curve). The result is a deadweight loss equal to the area of the shaded triangle.

In panel (b), the negative externality is corrected with a tax on suppliers. The tax-per-unit is $1.00—equal to the negative externality per unit. The supply curve shifts upward by the amount of the tax, moving the market equilibrium to the efficient point B. Only units valued at least as much as their full cost—the first 100 million units—are produced.

Many negative externalities in markets are caused by some form of *pollution.* Cities pollute rivers and lakes with sewage, and industries pollute them with chemicals. Cars and power plants pollute the atmosphere. As you are about to see, the market for a good that creates pollution—like markets with other negative externalities—is inefficient.

Panel (a) of Figure 3 illustrates an inefficiency in the market for gasoline, which pollutes the air with carbon monoxide and soot, dust, and other visible and microscopic solids. In the figure, we assume that the market is perfectly competitive. (Ignore the curve labeled MSC for now.) The supply curve S—like every market supply curve we've considered so far—reflects the costs of inputs used by *gasoline producers.* The height of the supply curve at any output level tells us the marginal cost (MC) of producing the last unit of output.

But the supply curve does *not* reflect any costs to the general public—such as the health and environmental damage caused by pollution—because (before government involvement) the firm does not have to pay them. The market reaches equilibrium at point A, where the supply curve S and the demand curve D intersect. The equilibrium quantity of gasoline is 125 million gallons per period, and the price is $2.00 per gallon.

Marginal social cost (MSC) The full cost of producing another unit of a good, including the marginal cost to the producer *and* any harm caused to third parties.

But if gasoline causes a negative externality, 125 million is *not* the efficient output level. We can see this by incorporating the negative externality into our diagram. Let's suppose that each gallon of gas imposes a cost to the general public of $1.00. Let's add this cost to the marginal cost already paid by gasoline producers to get the **marginal social cost** (*MSC*) of another unit of gasoline. *MSC* includes *all* costs of producing another unit of gas: the resources used up and paid for by the industry, *and* the costs imposed on third parties. This is why the *MSC* curve in Figure 3 lies *above* the market supply curve. Now let's find the efficient output level. Efficiency requires that the market provide only those units that are valued more highly by consumers than they cost to produce. The *MSC* curve tells us what it *really* costs to produce gas, when *all* costs are considered. For all units up to 100 million, the demand curve lies above the *MSC* curve, so those units are more highly valued than their costs. Total benefits in the market are increased by providing the first 100 million gallons.

But for all units *beyond* 100 million, the *MSC* curve lies above the demand curve. These units should *not* be produced, because they cost more—in the fullest sense—than their value to consumers. Each time a unit beyond 100 million is produced, total benefits—to producers, consumers, *and* society—shrink. The labeled triangle *ABC* shows the *deadweight loss* for this market in equilibrium—the loss in benefits from producing too much output.

> *A market with a negative externality associated with producing or consuming a good will produce* more *than the efficient quantity, creating a deadweight loss.*

How can we achieve the efficient result of 100 million gallons?

Taxing a Negative Externality

One way the government could move the gasoline market to the efficient quantity is a tax on producers. Panel (b) of Figure 3 shows the effect of a tax of $1.00 per gallon, which is the harm caused by each additional gallon of gas. In addition to paying for its other inputs, each firm would have to pay $1.00 per gallon to the government. As each firm's marginal cost rose by $1.00, the market supply curve would shift upward by $1.00, raising it to the position of the *MSC* curve. Once the tax is in place, the market would reach a new equilibrium at point *B*—producing the efficient quantity of 100 million gallons.

Notice that, in the new equilibrium, the price of gasoline to consumers rises from $2.00 to $2.60. Producers, meanwhile, keep only $1.60 of that $2.60 because they have to pay $1.00 to the government. Thus, the payment of the externality tax is shared between consumers and producers.

> *A tax on each unit of a good, equal to the external harm it causes, can correct a negative externality and bring the market to an efficient output level.*

In our example we imposed the tax on *suppliers* of gasoline. If the same tax were imposed on *buyers*, the graph would look different, but the result would be the same: The market would move to the efficient quantity. (You'll be asked to show this in an end-of-chapter problem.)

Taxes to correct negative externalities have been used in countries around the world: Sweden has imposed a tax on each kilogram of nitrogen oxide emitted by power plants. Denmark imposes taxes on businesses that produce, and households that consume, products that cause carbon dioxide emissions. Malaysia taxes harmful by-products of palm oil mills. And Vietnam has imposed a tax on coal production—largely because of the harm to tourism caused by unsightly coal mines.[4] In the United States, however, negative externalities are more often corrected by other methods.

Regulation and Tradable Permits

A tax is not the only way to correct a negative externality. Government can also use *regulation* to move a market closer to the efficient point. For example, in the gasoline market, regulators could tell car owners how much they could drive, or tell car producers how much pollution their vehicles are allowed to create. Indeed, this last regulation—state pollution restrictions on new automobiles—has been the method of choice for reducing pollution from automobiles in the United States.

But in the last two decades, the U.S. government has also relied increasingly on an innovative technique—called *tradable permits*—to reduce several types of pollution. This method is based on an understanding of Pareto improvements.

A **tradable permit** is a license that allows a company to release a unit of pollution into the environment over some period of time. By issuing a fixed number of permits, the government determines the total level of pollution that can be legally emitted each period. However, firms can sell their government-issued permits to other firms in an organized market.

Tradable permit A license that allows a company to release a unit of pollution into the environment over some period of time.

A firm whose technology would make it very costly to reduce pollution generally *buys* permits in the market. By buying a permit at a price lower than its cost of reducing pollution by another unit, the high-cost firm comes out ahead. At the same time, a firm whose technology enables it to reduce pollution rather cheaply will *sell* permits. By giving up permits, the low-cost firm takes on the obligation to reduce its pollution further. But by selling the permit at a price greater than its pollution-control cost, the low-cost firm gains as well.

The trading of permits shifts the costs of any given level of environmental improvement toward those firms that can do so more cheaply. The general public, however, is not affected by the trade because total pollution remains unchanged. Therefore, for any given level of pollution, allowing firms to buy and sell licenses generates Pareto improvements. Viewed another way, tradable permits—by making it cheaper to lower pollution—have enabled the U.S. government to impose stricter environmental standards with the same total burden on producers.

Tradable permits have been used since the early 1980s to reduce several types of pollution. Permits for adding lead to gasoline virtually eliminated leaded gasoline from the market within 5 years. And a system of tradable permits begun in 1990 for sulfur dioxide (the pollutant that causes acid rain) cut emissions in half within 5 years—well ahead of schedule and at much lower cost than anticipated. In 2005, the

---

[4] International Institute for Sustainable Development Web page (*http://iisd.ca/susprod/displaydetails. asp?id=74*).

European Union established a system of tradable permits for several greenhouse gases. Many countries also participate in a global system of credits that functions much like tradable permits. The Dutch government, for example, has constructed a modern refuse plant in Brazil to reduce methane emissions from more primitive trash dumps. In this way, the Dutch obtain credits for reducing emissions at a fraction of what it would cost to reduce them at home.

Dealing with a Positive Externality

For a positive externality, the by-product of a good or service *benefits* other parties rather than harms them. Once again, the market will not arrive at the economically efficient output level. But in this case, output will be *too low*.

Examples of positive externalities abound. Some of the benefits of your college degree are enjoyed by others (for example, more education makes you a more informed voter). A homeowner who plants flowers in the front yard or keeps her lawn neatly trimmed creates enjoyment for everyone who walks by, and helps to raise property values in the neighborhood.

A particularly interesting example of a positive externality is a specific kind of antitheft device for cars. Most antitheft measures—such as decals or flashing lights that warn of car alarms, or steering wheel locks such as The Club—involve no positive externality. The benefits from these devices—a reduction in the likelihood of theft—go only to the owner. In fact, these devices create a *negative* externality: When a thief spots one, he simply moves on to the next car. Thus, each person who buys The Club or a visible car alarm increases the likelihood of theft for everyone else.

But a device currently marketed as LoJack works differently.[5] There is no decal or any other sign that the car is protected. In fact, there is nothing to stop or discourage the thief from stealing the car. That's not the idea. LoJack is simply a hidden tracking device in the car. After the car is reported stolen, the police activate the device, which enables them to locate and recover it. The recovery rate for cars with LoJack is about 90 percent (compared to the average of 63 percent). This part of LoJack's benefit—the increased chance of getting the car back—goes to the owner and his insurance company.

But there is an even larger benefit, in the form of a positive externality: LoJack reduces the likelihood of car thefts for *everyone*, even those who do not have it. This externality comes about in two ways. First, when the police locate a car through LoJack, they have a high probability of catching the thieves (most of whom are repeat offenders) and locating the "chop shops" where stolen cars are recycled for sale. This is because the tracking device enables the car to be located quickly—usually within a couple of hours of being stolen. Every thief caught substantially reduces future car theft. Studies have shown that if even a tiny fraction of cars in an area have LoJack installed, a serial car thief will eventually take one, and will likely be caught.

Second, once a sufficient number of cars have LoJack, stealing cars becomes a much riskier business. The only way a thief can avoid stealing a LoJack-equipped car is to stop stealing cars.

---

[5] Ian Ayres and Steven D. Levitt, "Measuring Positive Externalities from Unobservable Victim Precaution: An Empirical Analysis of LoJack," *Quarterly Journal of Economics*, Vol. 113, No. 1, 1998, pp. 43–77. See also the less technical discussion by Ian Ayres and Barry Nalebuff, "Stop, Thief!" *Forbes*, January 10, 2005.

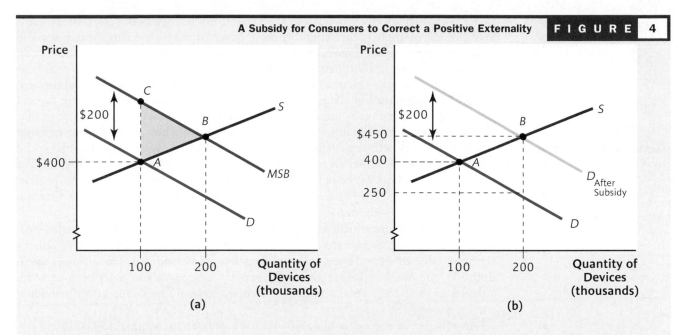

A Subsidy for Consumers to Correct a Positive Externality | **FIGURE 4**

In the market for car-tracking devices in panel (a), equilibrium is at point A. The demand curve depicts the benefits to buyers only, ignoring the positive externality of $200 per unit. When this positive externality is added to buyer's benefits, the result is the marginal social benefits (MSB). The efficient level of output is at point B. But without government intervention, the units from 100 thousand to 200 thousand are not produced, even though their full benefit (given by the MSB curve) exceeds their cost (given by the supply curve).

In panel (b), the positive externality is corrected with a subsidy paid to buyers. The subsidy per unit is $200—equal to the positive externality per unit. The demand curve shifts upward by the amount of the subsidy, moving the market equilibrium to the efficient outcome at point B.

Unfortunately, car owners do not take into account the benefits for others when they think about buying the device. Rather, they compare the cost (about $700) with the benefits to *themselves*. The device is not a good deal for most drivers—especially if they have theft insurance for their cars.

One might think that insurance companies would, on their own, give huge discounts to drivers who install LoJack in their cars. But it is not worth it to them to do so. Suppose an insurance company insures, say, 10 percent of the drivers in a city. Then 90 percent of the benefits of reduced theft would go to *other* insurance companies. As a result, the insurance companies, if left to themselves, would offer only small discounts, covering only a fraction of the cost of the device.

The result of this positive externality is an inefficient market. To see this more clearly, look at Figure 4. There, we assume that the market for car-tracking devices is competitive, with many suppliers. (This is somewhat anticipatory. As of mid-2006, LoJack corporation is the only maker. But other firms are planning to enter this market.[6] As the devices become more popular, we can expect a more competitive market to emerge.)

In the figure, the height of the supply curve S reflects the costs of providing another device. The height of the demand curve D measures the value of each device—to the person who buys it. But the demand curve does not reflect any of the

[6] "LoJack's Stronger Signal," *Business Week*, January 16, 2006.

benefits that the device provides to the general public. Without government intervention, the market reaches equilibrium at point A, where the supply and demand curves intersect. In the figure, we assume a competitive market would establish an equilibrium price of $400, with 100,000 devices sold per year.

But this is not the efficient output level. We can see this by incorporating the positive externality into our diagram. Let's suppose that each device gives the general public $200 in benefits, by reducing car theft in general. (Research has suggested that external benefits are usually much greater than this.) When we add these external benefits to the benefits enjoyed by the buyers themselves, we get the **marginal social benefit** (*MSB*) of another device. *MSB* includes *all* the benefits of putting another device in a car—both to the holder *and* to society at large. This is why the *MSB* curve in panel (a) of Figure 4 lies *above* the market demand curve. The distance between the curves is $200—the value of the positive externality from each device.

Marginal social benefit (MSB) The full benefit of producing another unit of a good, including the benefit to the consumer *and* any benefits enjoyed by third parties.

Now let's find the efficient output level. Efficiency requires that the market provide any unit with more value than the cost to produce it. The *MSB* curve tells us the true value of each device, when *all* benefits are considered. For all units up to 200,000, the *MSB* curve lies above the supply curve, so these units provide more value than their cost. Total benefits in the market would be increased by providing the units.

If you ignore the demand curve and look only at the supply and *MSB* curves, you can see that producing less than the efficient quantity creates a deadweight loss. This loss—the area of the triangle labeled *ABC*—tells us the potential benefits that are *not* achieved by the market.

> *A market with a positive externality associated with producing or consuming a good will produce less than the efficient quantity, creating a deadweight loss.*

How can we achieve the efficient quantity of 200,000 devices per year? One method would be a government *subsidy* paid to those who buy the device. In panel (b) of Figure 4, we show the effect of a subsidy of $200 per device, which is the benefit to others from each device purchased. With the subsidy, each car owner adds $200 to the personal value of buying the device. The demand curve shifts up by $200, because now that each driver will receive that sum from the government, each would be willing to pay that much more.

Notice that, in the new equilibrium, the price of a device rises—from $400 to $450. This is what causes producers to make more of them. But buyers, after accounting for the subsidy, pay only $450 − $200 = $250. This is what causes more people to buy it.

> *A subsidy on each unit of a good, equal to the external benefits it creates, can correct a positive externality and bring the market to an efficient output level.*

A subsidy for buyers is not the only way government could cure this market failure. If the same subsidy were given to *sellers,* the graph would look different, but the result would be the same: The market would move to the efficient quantity. (You'll be asked to show this in an end-of-chapter problem.) Still another solution is to require insurance companies to give substantially larger discounts to their policyholders who have the device. This would solve the free rider problem that currently prevents the insurance industry from taking meaningful action. By mid-2006, five states had come to the same conclusion: They have mandated substantial discounts on auto insurance for car owners who have installed LoJack.

PUBLIC GOODS

So far, all of our examples of market failures have been goods that are left to the market to provide. The market failure arises because some government manipulation of the price is needed (via a tax, subsidy, or regulation) to induce firms to move the quantity closer to the efficient level.

But some types of goods, by their nature, are especially difficult for the market to provide, or to provide even close to efficiently. Such goods require a more *direct* form of involvement, in which the government itself provides the goods. These are called *public goods*. (A more formal definition follows a bit later.)

To understand what makes a good public rather than private, let's begin by discussing two important features of *private goods*. First, a private good is characterized by **rivalry** in consumption—if one person consumes it, someone else cannot. If you rent an apartment, then someone else will *not* be able to rent that apartment. The same applies to most goods that you buy—food, computers, air travel, and so on. Rivalry also applies to privately provided services: the time you spend with your doctor, lawyer, or career counselor is time that someone else will *not* spend with that professional.

Rivalry A situation in which one person's consumption of a unit of a good or service means that no one else can consume that unit.

Most of the goods and services we've considered so far in this text are rival goods. By allowing the market to provide rival goods at a *price*, we ensure that people take account of the opportunity costs to society of their decisions to use these goods. If they were provided free of charge, people would tend to use them even if their value were less than the value of the resources used to produce them. Moreover, offering a rival good free of charge would enable some people who don't value it very highly to grab up all available supplies, depriving others who might value the goods even more. Thus, leaving such goods to the market—where a price reflecting marginal cost is charged—tends to promote economic efficiency.

A second feature of a private good is **excludability**, the ability to exclude those who do not pay for a good from enjoying it. Excludability is what makes it *possible* for a private business to provide a good. After all, without excludability people would never pay, so any private firm that tried to provide the good would quickly go out of business.

Excludability The ability to exclude those who do not pay for a good from consuming it.

Let's sum up the discussion so far: Excludability means that firms *can* provide a good. Rivalry means that a price *should* be charged for a good (something that private firms do automatically). If a good has both of these characteristics, it is called a *pure private good*.

> A good *that is both* rivalrous *and* excludable *is a **pure private good**. In the absence of any significant market failure, private firms will provide these goods at close to efficient levels.*

Pure private good A good that is both rivalrous and excludable.

But not all goods or services have these characteristics.

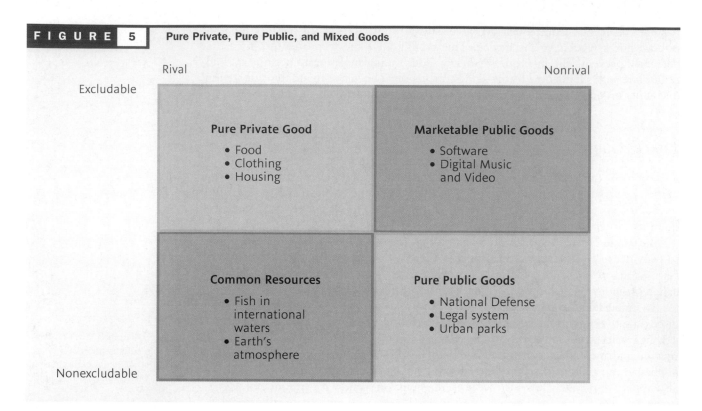

FIGURE 5   Pure Private, Pure Public, and Mixed Goods

Pure Public Goods

Consider a small, urban park whose chief benefit is that people find it nice to look at when they walk by. To provide and maintain the park is costly. But its benefits are *nonexcludable*—there is no practical way to limit enjoyment just to those who pay. (If you constructed a giant fence, then *no* passersby would see the park.) No one could earn revenue from such a park, so private firms would not provide it.

The walk-by park is also *nonrival*. One person's enjoyment while passing does not prevent or lessen the enjoyment of anyone else. Moreover, no more of society's resources are used up when another person views it. For this reason, even if a firm *could* figure out a way to charge for the park, charging would be inefficient. Each time an additional person sees the park, a Pareto improvement takes place: That person gains and no one loses. Thus, to be economically efficient, everyone who places *any value at all* on seeing the park should be able to see it. This can only happen if the price is *zero*.

Generalizing from this example: If a good is nonrival, the private market *should* not provide it, since efficiency requires a price of zero. And if the good is also nonexcludable, the private market is usually *unable* to provide it anyway. A good with both of these characteristics is called a *pure public good*.

Something you'll never see.

Pure public good A good that is both nonrival and nonexcludable.

> *A good that is both nonrival and nonexcludable is a **pure public good**. These goods are generally provided by government without charge, because the private market cannot supply them at all, or cannot supply them efficiently.*

Figure 5 illustrates the classification of goods into pure private and pure public, and provides some examples. (Ignore the other two categories for now.) Pure private goods are in the upper left corner. There is general agreement that private firms should provide such goods in the market and charge for them. While government may intervene in these markets, it does not generally provide the goods itself.

In the lower right corner are pure public goods. It is generally agreed that government should provide these goods without charge. A classic example is national defense. It would be virtually impossible to exclude those who did not pay from enjoying most of the benefits of national defense, as long as they remain in the country. And once a given quantity of national defense is provided, extending its benefits to an additional person requires no additional resources, nor does it lessen anyone else's defense.

Mixed Goods

Goods that appear in the other two corners of Figure 5 can be called *mixed goods* because they share features of both public and private goods. These goods are becoming increasingly important in our society.

Marketable Public Goods. In the upper right corner are goods that are excludable, but nonrival. We'll call these **marketable public goods**. Because their benefits are excludable, the market generally can, and generally does, provide them at a price. But because they are nonrival, the quantity is less than efficient. Some people decide not to pay the price and don't consume, even though their consumption would not use up resources or lessen anyone else's enjoyment.

Marketable public good An excludable and nonrival good. Generally provided by the market for a price, though efficiency would require a price of zero.

An example is a downloadable music file. Recent court cases and other efforts have largely eliminated unauthorized downloading at no charge. As a result, these files are now excludable: private firms (such as Apple and RealNetworks) offer them for sale, and only those who pay can download them. But they could provide an *additional* music file—or allow customers to share with anyone they wanted—without decreasing anyone else's enjoyment. The same is true of any other form of digital information or entertainment: software, movies, articles from restricted Web sites such as those of *Wall Street Journal* and *Atlantic Monthly,* and more. All are provided privately at less than efficient quantities.

In some cases, if firms can rely on advertising for their revenue, we can get closer to the efficient quantity. Broadcast television and Google searches are examples of marketable public goods that are offered privately, at no charge, because they are supported entirely by advertising.

But in most cases, a price is charged, and we accept the resulting inefficiency. Most economists would not even describe these goods as a market failure. It is true that, once such goods are created and we desire them, public provision at no charge would generate the efficient quantity. But having the government deeply involved in providing our music or software, and making decisions about which products to provide, would be unacceptable to most of us.

Public *Provision* versus Public *Production* Don't confuse public *provision* of a good with public *production*. The government must *provide* a pure public good in order to correct the market failure problem. But it can provide it by either producing the good itself (public production) or contracting production out to private firms (private production). Many local governments, for example, pay private firms to collect trash or run prisons. These services are privately produced, but purchased by government and *publicly provided* without charge to residents. Similarly, almost all of the *goods* that are used for national defense—tanks, radar equipment, laser-guided munitions—are produced by private firms and purchased by the federal government. However, the government chooses *public production* for the *service* of national defense itself: It hires, trains, and manages U.S. military personnel, rather than contracting this production out to private firms. But it's the government's *provision* of national defense without charge—not the government production—that cures the market failure.

DANGEROUS CURVES

Common Resource A nonexcludable and rival good.
Generally available free of
charge, though efficiency would
require a positive price.

Common Resources. In the lower left corner of Figure 5 is another category of mixed good: nonexcludable, but rivalrous. Crowded city streets and some important natural resources fall into this category. They are often called **common resources** because they are available to everyone in common—no one can be excluded from consuming them. But their consumption lessens the benefits available for others.

Economists use the term *tragedy of the commons* to describe the problem caused by many of these goods. In a traditional English village, the commons was an area freely available to all families for grazing their animals. Grazing rights are a rivalrous good: If one cow eats the grass, another can't. But the commons had no method of exclusion, so it was overgrazed, causing harm to *all* families.

Tragedy of the commons The
problem of overuse when a good
is rivalrous but nonexcludable.

> The **tragedy of the commons** *occurs when rivalrous but nonexcludable goods are overused, to the detriment of all.*

When common resources are used within a single country, that country's government can sometimes solve the market failure by passing laws or regulations to limit consumption. But when a nonexcludable resource is shared internationally, it is much harder to find a solution, and the tragedy of the commons often results.

An example is fishing in international waters. No one owns these areas of the ocean, and no single government can tell people not to fish in them. And since no one charges for the fish removed, fishing boats use huge nets that catch just about every source of protein (most of which is ground up to be used as cattle feed). These methods are also changing the ocean's ecosystem, threatening species of ocean life further down the food chain. Although scientists have recommended specific limits on national governments since 1987, virtually every country—concerned about the welfare of its *own* fishing industry—has chosen to ignore the recommendations. Each government is a free rider in the international community, reasoning that its own fish catch is just a "drop in the bucket," and that whatever other governments do, it is better off allowing its *own* crews to continue depleting the fish.

Another example of a common resource is the earth's atmosphere. The planet is warming. To the extent that this trend is exacerbated by emissions of carbon dioxide and other greenhouse gases, the world would have an interest in reducing this activity. But reducing emissions is costly. And it would benefit everyone on the planet, whether they helped pay these costs or not. Therefore, each country—and even each person—can be a free rider, with the result that nothing is done. This is the logic behind international efforts to assign quotas or tradable permits for emissions.

Some Important Provisos

Classifying goods into the four categories in Figure 5 is not always cut-and-dried. Consider a newspaper. It is mostly rival: The newspaper I buy at the newsstand and take home can't be bought and taken home by you. It is also largely excludable: You can't take it from the newsstand unless you pay.

But an important aspect of a newspaper is the *information inside it*. This information is largely nonrival (I can tell you what I've read without diminishing anyone else's knowledge) and largely nonexcludable (once I tell you the news, you've gotten it without having to pay the newspaper company).

Another complication is that the same good can be rival at some times and non-rival at others. Think about a highway. On a Sunday afternoon, with few cars on the road, it is nonrival: Another vehicle does not lessen anyone else's benefits. But when the highway is congested, it becomes rivalrous: Each additional driver subtracts benefits for everyone else on the road.

Finally, excludability is actually more a spectrum than a binary trait. At one end are goods that are easily excludable at very low cost. For example, alarm tags and a single security guard can make most items in a large store excludable at little cost. At the other extreme, the cost is so high as to be impractical. (Imagine trying to charge pedestrians for their use of the sidewalk.) A further complication is that technological progress can change the cost of excluding nonpayers. The Using the Theory section of this chapter provides an example: The streets of central London, which have always been a common resource, were recently made excludable by using previously unavailable technology.

For all these reasons, not all goods will fall cleanly into just one category in Figure 5, or remain in the same category over time. Nevertheless, the categories help us understand the role of rivalry and excludability in creating market failures and creating an efficiency role for government.

ASYMMETRIC INFORMATION

When we observe that a perfectly competitive market—without externalities—will provide the efficient quantity of a good, we make some implicit assumptions. For example, we assume that each party knows what it is getting and what it is giving up. We also assume that this information is costless. But this is not always the case.

Suppose you buy a bottle of sugar pills for $50 because you believe they will help you shed pounds without diet or exercise. The seller is better off, but you are worse off. Moreover, this transaction likely *decreases* total benefits. You lost $50 and also suffered the humiliation of being fooled; the seller gained *less* than $50 because he has to deduct from his revenue the time and expense of making and marketing the pills.

This transaction is an example of a problem known as **asymmetric information**—when one party to a transaction knows something about its value that the other party does not know. Asymmetric information can cause markets to fail in numerous ways, depending on the type of information involved

Asymmetric information A situation in which one party to a transaction has relevant information not known by the other party.

Adverse Selection

One type of asymmetric information concerns the *quality* of a good. The classic example is the used-car market. The owner of a car knows much more about its quality than anyone else. From general knowledge or life experience, buyers may know the quality of the *average* used car, but not the particular one being offered to them. The buyer's willingness to pay for any particular car will thus be based on the average quality of used cars.

In this sort of market, anyone who sells a "lemon"—an unusually poor car—stands to gain, because the car can be sold for more than its value. By contrast, anyone with a great used car would lose out in this market, because buyers could believe it to be of average quality. The result is a market with a disproportionate number of lemons.

Of course, as the market becomes awash in lemons, the average quality drops further, reducing used-car prices even more. Soon, the market is offering nothing but lemons. The good-quality cars have disappeared: Used-car prices are so low that the good cars are kept by their owners or sold only to friends.

In this example, asymmetric information about quality leads to the problem of **adverse selection**. The market acts as if it is "selecting" only the worst cars to offer for sale. Pareto improvements—in which people sell good used cars to strangers at mutually beneficial prices—remain unexploited.

Adverse selection occurs in many markets. In labor markets, employers are more likely to let go of their "lemons" and retain their highest-quality workers. In insurance markets, those with the poorest health—who get the best deal—are most likely to sign up for health insurance at any price. This can drive up the cost of insurance until people of average or good health are priced out of the market.

Adverse selection A situation in which asymmetric information about quality eliminates high-quality goods from a market.

Something you'll never see.

Moral Hazard

Another problem plaguing insurance markets arises from lack of information about someone's *future behavior*. It is called *moral hazard*—the tendency for people to change their behavior and act less responsibly when they are protected from the harmful consequences of their behavior. For example, suppose you are away from home and realize you may have forgotten to lock your front door. Without theft insurance, you would think about the full value of what you'd lose if you were robbed. You might then go to considerable trouble to return home and check the lock. But if you have theft insurance you might only consider *part* of the cost—the part that *you* would pay. The rest of the cost—covered by your insurance company—would not matter to you. You would be less likely to return home to check the lock. In this way, theft insurance leads to fewer locked doors, a greater incidence of theft, and higher insurance costs for everyone.

Moral hazard is a problem, to some degree, for every kind of insurance in which the insured has some influence over the likelihood or amount of their future loss. Insuring people for floods or earthquakes not only makes them more likely to live in areas prone to those natural disasters but reduces their incentive to make their homes less vulnerable to damage. And though few people would choose to become ill just because they have health insurance, there is still a moral hazard problem: The more of my costs that are covered by the insurance company, the less I care whether my doctor charges excessive fees or uses inefficient and costly procedures as part of my health care.

The Principal–Agent Problem

Finally, another potential market failure that arises from information asymmetry is the *principal–agent problem*. We introduced this briefly in our discussion of CEO pay in Chapter 12. A principal is someone who hires someone else—an agent—to act in the principal's interest. The problem arises when the principal does not have full information about the agent's performance. This enables the agent to act in his *own* interest, at the expense of the principal.

A classic example is when you hire someone to fix your car. Unless you stand and watch (and also have expertise in car repair), you won't know whether the mechanic has done all he promised, and done it well. Some of your payment may just be a transfer of benefits from you to the mechanic, leaving you worse off. Knowing this, you may not want to take your car to a mechanic at all, and may do so only when the car stops running.

Principal–agent problems plague transactions involving individual contractors (roofers, plumbers, and so forth) and also many labor market relationships. As discussed in Chapter 12, managers are hired to be agents of the stockholders. But managers have their own goals that may conflict with those of the stockholders (higher-than-competitive salaries for themselves, larger-than-efficient offices, padded expense accounts, and more). Similarly, the hourly workers (agents) are hired by managers (principals) on behalf of *their* principals—the stockholders. But hourly workers can find hidden ways of shirking that managers cannot monitor, such as emailing friends instead of working when the boss isn't looking.

Market and Government Solutions

Some of the inefficiency created by information asymmetries can be addressed by the market itself. The problem of adverse selection in the used-car market, for example, can be partly corrected through *reputation*. A used-car dealer can hire mechanics to carefully screen the cars it buys and develop a reputation for selling only high-quality used cars. It could also signal to buyers that its cars are above-average quality by offering a warranty. The business could then charge a premium—which consumers would be willing to pay—to cover the additional costs of the mechanics and the warranty.

Or consider the problem of moral hazard. In some insurance markets, an insurance company could determine which consumers are most likely to exhibit costly behavior (for example, those who have made more insurance claims in the past). These people can be charged higher rates. In this way, those who behave more responsibly will not be priced out of the market.

The principal–agent problem can be partly addressed by offering agents incentives for good performance. One example is a *contingent contract,* which spells out rewards and penalties based on the agent's future behavior. (If I hire you to fix my roof, the contract requires you to fix it again if it leaks within the next six months.) Within business firms, the goals of employees and owners can be more closely aligned by long-term employment contracts, profit-sharing, and bonuses, for example.

All of these market-based methods are often used by buyers and sellers to *reduce* the inefficiency caused by information asymmetry. But they cannot eliminate it. The market's corrective efforts always entail a cost—either to obtain the additional information or to deal with its absence. This additional cost is like a tax on the product. And, like a tax, it creates its own deadweight loss.

When the market failure is significant, and when government solutions have a lower cost than market solutions, the government's direct involvement can be justified on efficiency grounds.

Regulation—discussed earlier in this chapter—is one way that government attempts to correct problems of information asymmetry. For example, left to the market, pharmaceutical companies would know more about their drugs, and the nature of the research done on them, than those who buy or prescribe the drugs. The Food and Drug Administration, by imposing standards for research, safety, and effectiveness, helps to correct this asymmetry. Similarly, the Securities and Exchange Commission requires that corporations follow approved procedures in organizing and disclosing information relevant to shareholders. The Federal Trade Commission (FTC) and a variety of state agencies regulate a variety of markets, including the used-car market, to prevent misrepresentations and deceptive practices.

One of the major policy debates of the 2000s concerns the proper role for government in the market for health insurance—a market plagued by both moral hazard and adverse selection (see above), along with special ethical and humanitarian considerations. In many countries in Europe and elsewhere, the government has chosen to solve the adverse selection problem by providing its own, universal health insurance to all citizens. The government then deals with the moral hazard problem by regulating the fees that doctors and hospitals can charge, and rationing health care among competing demands. In the United States, government health insurance has been more controversial and is currently provided only to the elderly and the very poor. The rest of the population is either insured by private insurance companies (through their employer or on a policy purchased individually) or has no health insurance coverage at all.

EFFICIENCY AND GOVERNMENT IN PERSPECTIVE

In this chapter, you've seen that an economy with *well-functioning, perfectly competitive markets* tends to be economically efficient. But notice the italicized words. As you've seen in this chapter, many types of government involvement are needed to ensure that markets function well and to deal with market failures. The government helps markets to function by providing a legal and regulatory infrastructure. And the government frequently intervenes in markets directly, to correct market failures.

These cases of government involvement are not without controversy. In fact, most of the controversies that pit Democrats against Republicans in the United States (or Conservatives against Labourites in Britain, or Social Democrats against Christian Democrats in Germany) relate to when, and to what extent, the government should be involved in the economy. Debates about public education, Social Security, international trade, health care, and immigration all center on questions of the proper role for government.

Those who tend to be skeptical of government solutions point out several potential problems.

Government Failure.   Government itself can be plagued by the same types of problems that cause market failures in the private economy. One example is the principal–agent problem. Government officials are the agents of the general public and are supposed to serve the public interest. But these officials may have their own incentives, such as expanding the size of their departmental budgets. Although there are checks and balances for monitoring and limiting this type of behavior, they are not always effective.

Government officials can also be influenced by lobbies for special-interest groups. The benefits from a single, favorable government decision are highly concentrated on a specific firm or industry, but the *costs* of that one decision are widely dispersed among the population. Therefore, firms have great incentive to lobby for favorable policies, while the general public has little incentive to oppose them. For example, from 1997 to 2002, during a period of rapid changes in the health care system that were being shaped by legislation, the pharmaceutical industry spent an estimated $478 million directly lobbying Congress and an additional $172 million on federal campaign contributions, TV ads, and general efforts to sway public opinion.[7]

---

[7] "Drug Industry Sees Increase in Lobbying," *Wall Street Journal*, June 24, 2003.

Expenditures of this magnitude can tilt government decision making in favor of a specific industry—which may or may not be the most efficient policy decision.

Deadweight Loss from Taxes. In order for government to have the funds it needs to support markets and do other things, it must raise revenue through taxes. As you learned in Chapter 14, these taxes—when they are imposed on otherwise-efficient labor markets, product markets, or capital markets—introduce deadweight losses of their own. This cost of government activity should be considered along with the benefits in evaluating any government action.

Dissatisfaction with Public Goods. With a *private* good, each of us—facing the market price—buys whatever quantity we choose. We may feel frustrated about the size of our income or wealth, but given those constraints, each of us is free to purchase the quantity of each good that brings us the most satisfaction as individuals. If one person loves Italian food and another loves rock concerts, we'd expect to see them purchasing vastly different amounts of these two goods, based on their differing preferences.

But *public* goods, by their nature, are provided in a politically determined quantity, and *everyone* must consume the same amount. One person can't consume a strong national defense while another consumes a weak one. So, even if the political process is working *well,* about half the population will feel we are spending too much on a specific public good, and half the population will believe we are spending too little. This does not mean the government is acting inefficiently; but it does explain some of the controversy over government involvement in the economy.

Equity. Fostering efficiency—the focus of this chapter—is just one of the government's roles in the economy. We also want our government to be concerned with equity, fairness, justice, and more. These are not issues about which people easily agree.

In Chapter 12 we discussed some of the controversies surrounding government policies aimed directly at equity. But every government policy designed to improve efficiency also has consequences for equity. Taxing gasoline to correct an externality would hit the poor harder than the rich, while taxing airline travel would do the opposite. Eliminating price floors for agricultural goods might move the economy toward efficiency, but it would cause harm to many farmers and their families. Almost every change in the tax code designed to improve efficiency will raise a firestorm of protest because of the way it might affect equity. This limits the government's ability to focus on efficiency when dealing with market failures.

The controversies we've discussed can be so heated and so varied that it is easy to forget how much agreement there is about the role of government. Anyone studying the role of government in the economies of the United States, Canada, Mexico, France, Germany, Britain, Japan, and the vast majority of other developed economies, is struck by one glaring fact: Most economic activity is carried out among private individuals. In all of these countries, there is widespread agreement that although government intervention is often necessary, the most powerful forces that exploit Pareto improvements and drive the economy toward efficiency are the actions of individual producers and consumers. And among these countries, there is also substantial commonality in the relatively smaller list of goods and services provided by government.

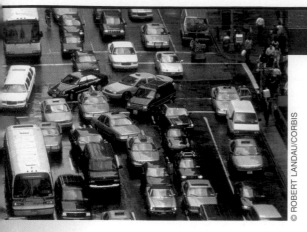

© ROBERT LANDAU/CORBIS

USING THE THEORY

Traffic as a Market Failure

Almost everyone in the United States has been caught in a traffic jam in some large town or city at some point in their lives. For many, it's a daily experience. Congested streets create even larger problems in some European and Asian cities, and in some developing countries, they can bring economic life to a halt for hours at a time. And the problem in most cities is getting worse.

Consider London. Traffic congestion has worsened dramatically in recent decades, especially in the historic inner city. By 2000, an average of 250,000 cars were entering this eight-square-mile area each day, and average traffic speeds had slowed to nine miles per hour—about the speed of a horse-coach a century earlier. In New York, about 250,000 cars enter central Manhattan, also about eight square miles, in just *3 hours* every morning, slowing traffic to an average speed of just seven miles per hour.[8] Urban traffic congestion relates to our use of a good: *city streets*. And we can view the traffic problem as a market failure in two different ways.

First, traffic is an externality problem. When you decide to take your car onto a city street, your decision is based on the costs and benefits to *you*. But if the road is already crowded, your decision creates a negative externality as well: By adding to the traffic, you increase the delay and frustration, gasoline costs, and risk of accident for *others*. Of course, you include the effects of traffic congestion *on yourself* in making your decision to get into your car; but you don't take into account these costs for *others*.

For example, let's suppose that when 1,000 additional cars enter central Manhattan during the morning rush hours, the result is 6 minutes (1/10 of an hour) of additional delay for all 250,000 cars that will be in the area for the next 3 hours. (Traffic congestion lasts longer than its original cause and spreads quickly beyond its point of origin by blocking cross traffic.) Assuming just one person in each car, the total hours of delay would be $250,000 \times \frac{1}{10} = 25,000$ hours. If this time is valued at just $10 per hour—less than the average hourly wage—the cost is $250,000. Therefore, if you are just *one* of those additional 1,000 entering the area, the cost you impose on others is $250,000/1,000 = $250.

Would you take your car into the city if you had to pay $250 or more? Or might you instead take the bus or subway? For most people entering the city, the answer would be bus or subway. But because they only bear their own direct costs—gas, wear and tear on their *own* car, and their *own* time—the result is inefficiency: People are consuming another unit of a good (the car trip) whose value to them is less than its marginal *social* cost. Total net benefits decrease.

Second, city streets can be viewed as a common resource in the lower left quadrant of Figure 5. At peak times, city streets are rivalrous: The space occupied by your car can't be occupied by anyone else's car. On the other hand, streets are not easily excludable. This is why, for the most part, governments *treat* city streets as if they are a pure public good: providing them free of charge to all who want to use them. The result—as in so many other cases of providing a rivalrous good free of charge—is a tragedy of the commons: Consumption increases until everyone is harmed.

[8] Randy Kennedy, "The Day the Traffic Disappeared," *New York Times Magazine*, April 20, 2003.

Can the government solve the problem? From the externality perspective, the solution would require drivers to pay for the externality they impose on others. From the rivalry perspective, the solution is similar: People must pay for a rivalrous good in order to avoid the tragedy of the commons. But is this feasible?

Some cities, such as New York, do charge tolls for cars that enter via bridges or tunnels. But entry tolls are problematic, and are rarely set high enough to solve the problem of congestion at peak travel times. One reason is the difficulty of efficiently targeting the entry tolls toward those causing the externality or consuming the rivalrous good. For example, those who live *inside* the city but still contribute to the traffic don't pay the toll at all. And those entering from outside, but who plan to drive to a noncongested (nonrivalrous) area must pay the same toll as people creating more of a problem. New electronic tracking technologies could perhaps solve this problem by imposing fees on each vehicle based on its contribution to congestion. The fees could vary by time of day and the actual locations through which a vehicle travels.

But there is a bigger problem: the political damage to any elected representative who would propose a fee high enough to be efficient on a good that has traditionally been free. Such fees can create resentment among the electorate in general, and also raise serious equity issues. After all, the fee cannot be trivial: It must be high enough to dissuade at least *some* people from driving at certain hours, which is high enough to create hardship for poorer families. True, they could be promised compensation or increased government services from the revenue the fee would provide. But people might not trust the government's promise, given other priorities for city funds.

All of this conventional political wisdom may have changed since early 2003, when Ken Livingstone—the mayor of London—decided to take a chance: His administration established a 5 pound (about $8) *per day* user fee on any automobile that appeared in the eight-square-mile boundary of London's inner city. The fee had to be paid in advance, by 10 P.M. the night before travel. This added to its opportunity cost (the time and trouble of paying the fee), especially for those who don't plan their travel well in advance. Any car that was seen parked in, driving through, or in any way appeared within the zone would be required to pay the fee. Violators faced fines of 80 pounds (about $130), and were almost certain to be caught: The city positioned more than 700 cameras throughout the zone to record license plate numbers and send the optical data to a central computer, which would instantly determine if the vehicle owner had paid the fee. Livingstone addressed the equity issue as well, using almost all of the additional city revenue for significant expansions in bus service.

The London experiment is widely viewed as a success. Comparing mid-2005 with the period before the fee, passenger car traffic was down by 30 percent, bus and bicycle transport were up, and congestion was down. The political opposition proved manageable: Livingstone—a far left socialist—was reelected in 2004 and announced plans to expand his market-based solution to other areas of London.

Charging tolls is not the only way to deal with traffic congestion. In Shanghai, the city government decides how many additional cars it will allow each month, and then auctions off just that number of license plates. If 5,000 license plates are available in a particular month, the top 5,000 bidders will get them—and no one else. In some months, the auction price of the license plate approaches half or more of the price of a new car.

Shanghai's approach has not caught on elsewhere. But London's approach has. It is being studied by city officials in Europe, Australia, and the United States. Some cities in these countries are already in the planning stages of a London-type system.

And the idea has been extended to deal with highway traffic as well. Texas, Florida, and Missouri have greatly expanded the use of toll booths on formerly free stretches of road. And in some areas (Orange County and San Diego in California and Toronto, Canada), drivers can use specially constructed highways or lanes for a fee that varies with miles traveled, time of day, and traffic conditions. New technologies for electronic monitoring and billing have made this possible, bringing excludability to highways and city streets.

Summary

Government contributes to economic efficiency in two general ways. First, it provides the legal and regulatory system that enables the market system to function. Second, it often steps in to correct specific *market failures*—situations in which a specific market, left to itself, is inefficient.

One solution for the market failure of monopoly or monopoly power (used when the market is not a natural monopoly) is antitrust action to create more competition. For a *natural monopoly*, a common solution is a regulated price that includes a fair rate of return for owners.

Externalities—unpriced by-products of economic transactions that affect outsiders—are not always market failures; the *Coase theorem* tells us that under certain conditions, the market can solve the externality problem with private action. When private action is not possible, externalities can be corrected through taxes, subsidies, regulation, or tradable permits.

Pure public goods—those that are nonrival and nonexcludable—are a market failure because private firms generally will not provide them, and the efficient price in any case is zero. These goods are typically provided by government at no charge.

Asymmetric information can create market failures when it leads to *adverse selection*, *moral hazard*, or the *principal–agent problem*. The market can address some of these problems itself, but government often uses regulation to help solve them.

Government solutions to market failures are often imperfect and can introduce their own inefficiencies. And virtually all government policies have implications for equity, which is another important issue for government. For this and other reasons, government solutions to market failures are often controversial.

Problem Set   *Answers to even-numbered Questions and Problems can be found on the text Web site at www.thomsonedu.com/economics/hall.*

1. Review the section of the chapter titled, "The Private Solution to a Negative Externality." Suppose that Grace gains $70,000 from building the theater, but the harm to Fernando is $100,000.
   a. Is it efficient to build the theater? Briefly, why or why not?
   b. If Fernando has the legal right to *prevent* the theater from being built, would you expect Grace to get his permission with a side payment? Why or why not?
   c. If Grace has the legal right to *build* the theater, would you expect the theater to be built? Why or why not?

2. Figure 3 shows the market for gasoline with a negative externality from pollution. Using the information in both panels, calculate the dollar value of the deadweight loss per period before any government intervention.

3. Figure 4 shows the market for car-tracking devices with a positive externality. Using the information in both panels, calculate the dollar value of the deadweight loss per period before any government intervention.

4. Last year, Pat and Chris occupied separate apartments. Each consumed 400 gallons of hot water monthly. This year, they are sharing an apartment. To their surprise, they find that they are using a total of 1,000 gallons per month between them. Why? What concept discussed in this chapter is illustrated by this example?

5. Some have argued that the music industry is by nature inefficient because once a piece of music is produced, the firm that owns it has a monopoly and charges the monopoly price. Yet, the marginal cost of making the music available to one more member of the public (via the Internet) is zero. Draw a diagram, similar to Figure 2, to represent this situation. Identify on your diagram:

a. The efficient level of production

b. The level of production a government-regulated music industry would earn if it were permitted to charge just enough for a "fair rate of return"

c. The level of production provided by the (currently unregulated) industry

6. In Figure 3(b), a negative externality was corrected with a $1.00 per gallon tax on gasoline producers. Draw a diagram to show that the total price paid by consumers, the total price received by firms, and the equilibrium quantity would have been exactly the same if the same tax had been imposed on gasoline consumers instead of producers.

7. In Figure 4(b), a positive externality was corrected with a $200 subsidy paid to buyers. Draw a diagram to show that the total price paid by buyers, the total price received by sellers, and the equilibrium quantity of devices would have been exactly the same if the $200 subsidy per device had been given to suppliers instead.

8. Each of the following is an example of (or would lead to) a particular type of market failure arising from information asymmetry. Identify the type of market failure and justify your answer briefly.

a. A woman in the "dating market" complains, "All the good ones are taken."

b. A college announces a new policy: Any senior with a GPA less than 2.0 will, upon graduation, have all grades of C− or lower retroactively raised to a grade of C.

c. A restaurant in New York hires workers to pass out fliers to pedestrians all over the city, and pays them based on how many fliers they get into people's hands.

More Challenging

9. The following table shows the quantities of car alarms demanded and supplied per year in a town:

Price	Quantity Demanded	Quantity Supplied
$ 75	800	0
$100	750	150
$125	700	300
$150	650	450
$175	600	600
$200	550	750
$225	500	900
$250	450	1,050

Without drawing a graph, determine the efficient quantity in this market under each of the following assumptions:

a. Each car alarm sold creates a negative externality (noise pollution) that causes $100 in harm to the public.

b. Each car alarm creates a *positive* externality (reduced law enforcement costs) that provides $100 in benefits to the public.

10. Suppose Douglas and Ziffel have properties that adjoin the farm of Mr. Haney. The current zoning law permits Haney to use the farm for any purpose. Haney has decided to raise pigs (the best use of the land). A pig farm will earn $50,000 per year, forever.

a. Assume the interest rate is 10 percent per year. What is Haney's pig farm worth? (Hint: Use a special formula from Chapter 13.)

b. Suppose the next best use of Haney's property is residential, where it could earn $20,000 per year. What is the minimum one-time payment Haney would accept to agree to restrict his land for residential use forever?

c. Suppose Douglas is willing to pay $200,000 for an end to pig farming on Haney's land, while Ziffel is willing to pay no more than $150,000. (For some reason, Ziffel does not mind pig farming as much as Douglas does.) If Douglas pays Haney $200,000 and Ziffel pays Haney $150,000, and Haney converts his land to residential use, is this a Pareto improvement? Who benefits, who loses, and by how much?

d. Suppose instead that Douglas pays $150,000 and Ziffel pays $150,000. Is this move a Pareto improvement? Who benefits, who loses, and by how much?

Comparative Advantage and the Gains from International Trade

Consumers love bargains. And the rest of the world offers U.S. consumers bargains galore: cars from Japan, computer memory chips from Korea, shoes and clothing from China, tomatoes from Mexico, lumber from Canada, and sugar from the Caribbean. But Americans' purchases of foreign-made goods have always been a controversial subject. Should we let these bargain goods into the country? Consumers certainly benefit when we do so. But don't cheap foreign goods threaten the jobs of American workers and the profits of American producers? How do we balance the interests of specific workers and producers on the one hand with the interests of consumers in general? These questions are important not just in the United States, but in every country of the world.

Over the post–World War II period, there has been a worldwide movement toward a policy of *free trade*—the unhindered movement of goods and services across national boundaries. An example of this movement was the creation—in 1995—of a new international body: the World Trade Organization (WTO). The WTO's goal is to help resolve trade disputes among its members and to reduce obstacles to free trade around the world.

And to some extent it has succeeded: Import taxes, import limitations, and all kinds of crafty regulations designed to keep out imports are gradually falling away. Today, almost one-third of the world's production is exported to other countries. One hundred forty-nine countries have joined the WTO, including the most recent member, Saudi Arabia. Some 26 other countries, including Russia and Vietnam, are eager to join the free trade group.

But even though many barriers have come down, others remain—and new ones have come up. As of 2006, the United States was still refusing to eliminate its long-standing quota on sugar imports as well as more recent barriers to importing shrimp from Vietnam, Brazil, Thailand, and several other countries. The European Union continued to restrict the sale of U.S. beef, high-tech equipment, and entertainment programming. China was trying to keep out American-made automobile parts.

Looking at the contradictory mix of trade policies that exist in the world, we are left to wonder: Is free international trade a good thing that makes us better off, or is it bad for us and something that should be kept in check? In this chapter, you'll learn to apply the tools of economics to issues surrounding international trade. Most important, you'll see how we can extend economic analysis to a global context, in which markets extend across international borders.

THE LOGIC OF FREE TRADE

Many of us like the idea of being self-reliant. A very few even prefer to live by themselves in a remote region of Alaska or the backcountry of Montana. But consider the defects of self-sufficiency: If you lived all by yourself, you would be poor. You could not *export* or sell to others any part of your own production, nor could you *import* or buy from others anything they have produced. You would be limited to consuming the goods and services that you produced. Undoubtedly, the food, clothing, and housing you would manage to produce by yourself would be small in quantity and poor in quality—nothing like the items you currently enjoy. And there would be many things you could not get at all—electricity, television, cars, airplane trips, or the penicillin that could save your life.

The defects of self-sufficiency explain why most people do not choose it. Rather, people prefer to specialize and trade with each other. In Chapter 2, you learned that specialization and exchange enable us to enjoy greater production and higher living standards than would otherwise be possible.

This principle applies not just to individuals, but also to *groups* of individuals, such as those living within the boundaries that define cities, counties, states, or nations. That is, just as we all benefit when *individuals* specialize and exchange with each other, so, too, we can benefit when *groups* of individuals specialize in producing different goods and services, and exchange them with other *groups*.

Imagine what would happen if the residents of your state switched from a policy of open trading with other states to one of self-sufficiency, refusing to import anything from "foreign states" or to export anything to them. Such an arrangement would be preferable to individual self-sufficiency; at least there would be specialization and trade *within* the state. But the elimination of trading between states would surely result in many sacrifices. Lacking the necessary inputs for their production, for instance, your state might have to do without bananas, cotton, or tires. And the goods that *were* made in your state would likely be produced inefficiently. For example, while residents of Vermont *could* drill for oil, and Texans *could* produce maple syrup, they could do so only at great cost of resources.

Thus, it would make no sense to insist on the economic self-sufficiency of each of the 50 states. And the founders of the United States knew this. They placed prohibitions against tariffs, quotas, and other barriers to interstate commerce right in the U.S. Constitution. The people of Vermont and Texas are vastly better off under free trade among the states than they would be if each state were self-sufficient.

What is true for states is also true for entire nations. The members of the WTO have carried the argument to its ultimate conclusion: National specialization and exchange can expand world living standards through free *international* trade. Such trade involves the movement of goods and services across national boundaries. Goods and services produced domestically, but sold abroad, are called **exports;** those produced abroad, but consumed domestically, are called **imports.** The long-term goal of the WTO is to remove all barriers to exports and imports in order to encourage among nations the specialization and trade that have been so successful within nations.

Exports Goods and services produced domestically, but sold abroad.

Imports Goods and services produced abroad, but consumed domestically.

THE THEORY OF COMPARATIVE ADVANTAGE

In Chapter 2, you learned about absolute and comparative advantage for trade between individuals. Now we'll apply these concepts to trade between nations.

Economists who first considered the benefits of international trade focused on a country's absolute advantage. Using the definition from Chapter 2, but applying it to nations rather than individuals, we say that

> *A country has an absolute advantage in a good when it can produce it using* fewer resources *than another country.*

As the early economists saw it, the citizens of every nation could improve their economic welfare by specializing in the production of goods in which they had an absolute advantage and exporting them to other countries. In turn, they would import goods from countries that had an absolute advantage in those goods.

In 1817, however, the British economist David Ricardo disagreed. Absolute advantage, he argued, was not a necessary ingredient for mutually beneficial international trade. The key was *comparative advantage:*

> *A nation has a comparative advantage in producing a good if it can produce it at a* lower opportunity cost *than some other country.*

Notice the difference between the definitions of absolute advantage and comparative advantage. While absolute advantage in a good is defined by the resources used to produce it, comparative advantage is based on the *opportunity cost* of producing it. The opportunity cost of producing something is the *other goods* that these resources *could* have produced instead.

Ricardo argued that a potential trading partner could be absolutely inferior in the production of every single good—requiring more resources per unit of each good than any other country—and still have a comparative advantage in some good. The comparative advantage would arise because the country was *less* inferior at producing some goods than others. Likewise, a country that had an absolute advantage in producing everything could—contrary to common opinion—still benefit from trade. It would have a comparative advantage only in some, but not all, goods.

DETERMINING COMPARATIVE ADVANTAGE

To illustrate Ricardo's insight, let's consider a hypothetical world that has only two countries: the United States and China. Both are producing only two goods: soybeans and T-shirts. And—to keep things as simple as possible—we'll imagine that these goods are being produced with just one resource: labor.

Table 1 shows the amount of labor, in hours, required to produce one bushel of soybeans or one T-shirt in each country. We assume that hours per unit remain *constant*, no matter how much of a good is produced. For example, the entry "5 hours" tells us that it takes 5 hours of labor to produce one bushel of soybeans in China. This will be true no matter how many bushels China produces.

In the table, we've given the United States an *absolute advantage* in producing both goods. That is, it takes fewer resources (less labor time) to produce either soybeans or T-shirts in the United States than in China. But—as you are about to see—China will still have a *comparative* advantage in one of these goods.

Labor Requirements per:	United States	China	TABLE 1
			Labor Requirements per Unit
Bushel of soybeans	$\frac{1}{2}$ hour	5 hours	
T-shirt	$\frac{1}{4}$ hour	1 hour	

To determine comparative advantage, we'll use the information in Table 1 to calculate opportunity costs. Let's first find the opportunity cost of one more bushel of soybeans in the United States. In order to produce this bushel, the United States would have to divert a half hour of labor from making T-shirts. Since each T-shirt requires a $\frac{1}{4}$ hour of labor, taking away $\frac{1}{2}$ hour would reduce production of T-shirts by 2. Thus, the opportunity cost of one more bushel of soybeans in the United States is 2 T-shirts. This opportunity cost is recorded in Table 2; check the table and make sure you can find the entry.

Now let's do the same for China. There, producing an additional bushel of soybeans requires 5 hours of labor, which would have to be diverted from the T-shirt industry. Since each T-shirt requires 1 hour of labor in China, taking away 5 hours would mean 5 fewer T-shirts. Thus, in China, the opportunity cost of one bushel of soybeans is 5 T-shirts, which can also be found in Table 2.

Summing up, we see that the opportunity cost of a bushel of soybeans is 2 T-shirts in the United States and 5 T-shirts in China. Therefore, the United States—with the lower opportunity cost—has a comparative advantage in producing soybeans.

Notice that in Table 2, we do similar calculations for the opportunity cost of T-shirts, measuring the opportunity cost in terms of bushels of soybeans *foregone*. These computations are summarized in the last row of the table. Make sure you can use these numbers to verify that China has a comparative advantage in producing T-shirts.

Now we can use our conclusions about comparative advantage to show how both countries can gain from trade. The explanation comes in two steps. First, we show that if China could be persuaded to produce more T-shirts and the United States more soybeans, the world's total production of both goods will increase. Second, we show how each country can come out ahead by trading with the other.

HOW SPECIALIZATION INCREASES WORLD PRODUCTION

Figure 1 shows production possibilities frontiers for the United States and China. In the left panel, we assume that the United States has 100 million hours of labor per year, which it must allocate between soybeans (on the horizontal axis) and T-shirts (on the vertical axis). To obtain the PPF for the United States, we first suppose that all 100 million hours of labor were allocated to T-shirts. The United States could then produce 400 million of them per year (because each one requires $\frac{1}{4}$ hour of

Opportunity Costs per:	United States	China	TABLE 2
			Opportunity Costs
Bushel of soybeans	2 T-shirts	5 T-shirts	
T-shirt	$\frac{1}{2}$ bushel of soybeans	$\frac{1}{5}$ bushel of soybeans	

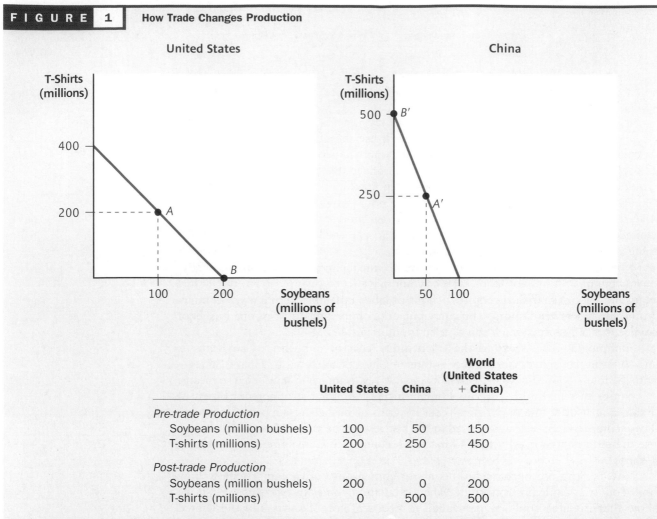

FIGURE 1 How Trade Changes Production

	United States	China	World (United States + China)
Pre-trade Production			
Soybeans (million bushels)	100	50	150
T-shirts (millions)	200	250	450
Post-trade Production			
Soybeans (million bushels)	200	0	200
T-shirts (millions)	0	500	500

Before international trade opens up in soybeans and T-shirts, the United States is assumed to produce in the middle of its linear PPF at point A, representing 100 million bushels of soybeans and 200 million T-shirts. Similarly, China is assumed to produce at point A', representing 50 million bushels of soybeans and 250 million T-shirts.

After trade, each country will completely specialize in its comparative advantage good. The United States will shift all resources into soybeans (200 million bushels) at point B, and China will put all resources into T-shirts (500 million) at point B'. The result is greater world production of both goods. World soybean production rises from 150 million to 200 million bushels, and world T-shirt production rises from 450 million to 500 million.

labor). Accordingly, the upper-most point on the PPF represents 400 million T-shirts and zero bushels of soybeans.

To get the rest of the points, remember that the opportunity cost of one more bushel of soybeans is 2 T-shirts. Therefore, each time we move rightward by one unit (one more bushel), we must move downward by 2 units (2 fewer T-shirts). Accordingly, the PPF for the United States will be a straight line, with a slope of -2. The PPF ends where the United States would be allocating all of its 100 million hours to soybeans, producing 200 million bushels.

Notice that this PPF is a straight line, unlike the curved PPFs in Chapter 2. A linear PPF follows from our assumption that hours per unit—and therefore opportunity costs—remain constant no matter how much of either good is produced. Essentially, to keep things simple, we are assuming *constant opportunity costs*, rather than increasing opportunity cost as in the PPFs drawn in Chapter 2. (We'll discuss the implications of this in a few pages.)

The right panel shows China's PPF, under the assumption that China has 500 million hours of labor per year. On your own, be sure you can see how the two endpoints of China's PPF are determined. Also, be sure you understand why the slope of China's PPF will be -5. (Hint: What is the opportunity cost of another bushel of soybeans in China?)

Before international trade occurs, we assume (arbitrarily) that both countries are operating in the middle of their respective PPFs. The United States is at point A, producing 100 million bushels of soybeans and 200 million T-shirts each year. This combination of goods is also U.S. *consumption* per year: Without trade, you can only consume what you produce. In the right panel, China is at point A', producing and consuming 50 million bushels of soybeans and 250 million T-shirts.

Now look at the table that accompanies the figure. The first two rows tell us the production of each good in each country before trade opens up, and also world production of each good. As you can see, with the United States producing at point A along its PPF and China producing at point A', the world (the United States and China combined) produces 150 million bushels of soybeans and 450 million T-shirts per year.

Let's now see what happens to world *production* when trade opens up. We'll have each country devote *all* of its resources to the good in which it has a comparative advantage. The United States, with a comparative advantage in soybeans, moves to point B on its PPF, producing 200 million bushels of soybeans and zero T-shirts. China moves to point B' on its PPF, producing 500 million T-shirts and zero soybeans. The new production levels for each country are entered in the last two rows of the table in Figure 1.

Finally, look at the last column of numbers in the table. For both goods, world production has increased. Soybean output is up from 150 million to 200 million bushels, and T-shirt production is up from 450 million to 500 million. This increase in world production has been accomplished without adding any resources to either country. The world's resources are simply being used more efficiently.

Although our example has just two countries and two goods, it illustrates a broader conclusion:

> *When countries specialize according to their comparative advantage, the world's resources are used more efficiently, enabling greater production of every good.*

How Each Nation Gains from International Trade

Now let's show that both countries can gain from trade. As you've seen, when the two countries specialize in their comparative advantage good, they produce more of that good but none of the other. For example, China produces more T-shirts but no soybeans. However, by trading some of its comparative advantage good for the other good, each country can *consume* more of both goods.

Table 3 illustrates this conclusion. The first row of numbers shows how specialization has changed production in each country, based on the movement along the PPF in Figure 1. To get from changes in production to changes in consumption, we have to consider what each country is exporting and importing. The second row in the table shows one possible example. We suppose that the United States will exchange 80 million bushels of soybeans for 240 million T-shirts from China.

TABLE 3		United States		China	
The Gains from Specialization and Trade		**Soybeans (million bushels)**	**T-Shirts (millions)**	**Soybeans (million bushels)**	**T-Shirts (millions)**
	Change in Production	+100	−200	−50	+250
	Exports (−) or Imports (+)	−80	+240	+80	−240
	Net Gain in Consumption	+20	+40	+30	+10

A country's exports are represented with a minus sign (they contribute negatively to consumption) and its imports with a plus sign (they add to consumption). The third row shows how consumption of each good changes after considering both production changes and international trade.

Let's first consider the United States. When it moved from point *A* to point *B* along its PPF, soybean production increased from 100 million to 200 million bushels—an increase of 100 million, hence the entry +100 in the first row. But it exported 80 million bushels (−80 in the second row), leaving the United States to consume 20 more bushels than it had before trade (+20 in the third row). Similarly, U.S. production of T-shirts decreased from 200 million to zero (−200), but the United States imports 240 million (+240), for a net gain of 40 million T-shirts (+40).

In China, soybean production has decreased by 50 million bushels (−50), but imports are 80 million. Therefore, China ends up with 30 million more bushels of soybeans. China has also increased production of T-shirts by 250 million, but exports 240 million of those, so it is left with 10 million more after trade.

These changes in consumption are illustrated Figure 2. Once again, we show the PPFs for the United States and China. But now we compare consumption in each country before trade with consumption *after* trade. The United States began with 100 million bushels of soybeans and 200 million T-shirts (point *A*). After specialization and trade, it moves to 120 million bushels of soybeans and 240 million T-shirts (point *C*). Similarly, China began by consuming 50 million bushels of soybeans and 250 million T-shirts (point *A'*). After specialization and trade, it consumes 80 million bushels of soybeans and 260 million T-shirts (point *C'*).

Notice that points *C* and *C'* lie *beyond* each country's PPF. While the PPF still shows possibilities for *production* of the two goods, *consumption* is no longer limited to what is produced. Instead, with trade, a country can consume more of both goods than it would be capable of producing and consuming on its own.

Let's take a step back and consider what we've discovered. First, look back at Table 1. Based on the required labor hours, the United States has an *absolute advantage* in both goods: It can produce both soybeans and T-shirts using fewer hours of labor than can China. But in Table 2, we saw that the United States has a *comparative advantage* in only *one* of these goods—soybeans—and China has a comparative advantage in the other—T-shirts. This is because the *opportunity costs* of each good differ in the two countries. Then, in Figure 1, we saw how world production of both goods increases when each country shifts its resources toward its comparative advantage good. Finally, in the last row of Table 3 and in Figure 2, we saw that *international trade* can enable *each* country to end up with more of *both* goods.

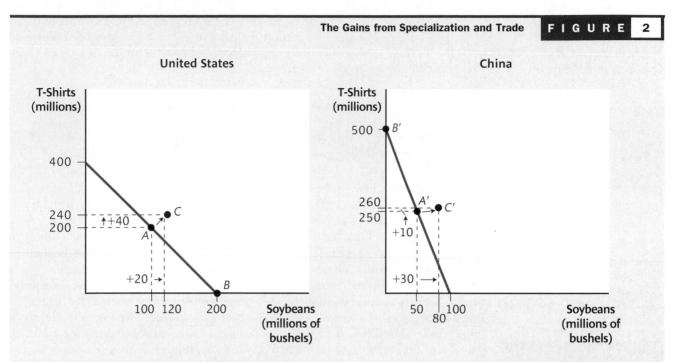

The Gains from Specialization and Trade   **FIGURE 2**

With international trade, the U.S. moves production from point A to point B, but consumes at point C—beyond its PPF. Soybean production increases from 100 million (at point A) to 200 million (at point B). After exporting 80 million bushels to China, the United States is left with 120 million (at point C), for a net gain of 20 million bushels. With terms of trade assumed to be 3 T-shirts for 1 bushel of soybeans, the United States trades its soybeans for 240 million T-shirts. United States T-shirt consumption rises from 200 million (point A) to 240 million (point C).

In China, production moves from point A' to point B', but consumption is at point C'. T-shirt production rises from 250 million (at point A') to 500 million (at point B'). After exporting 240 million T-shirts to the United States, China is left with 260 million (point C'), for a net gain of 10 million. China trades its T-shirts for 80 million bushels of soybeans from the United States, so China's soybean consumption rises from 50 million (at point A') to 80 million (at point C').

> *As long as opportunity costs differ, specialization and trade can be beneficial to all involved. This remains true whether the parties are different nations, different states, different counties, or different individuals. It remains true even if one party has an all-round absolute advantage or disadvantage.*

THE TERMS OF TRADE

In our ongoing example, China exports 240 million T-shirts in exchange for 80 million bushels of soybeans. This exchange ratio (240 million to 80 million, or 3 to 1) is knows as the **terms of trade**—the quantity of one good that is exchanged for one unit of the other.

The terms of trade determine how the gains from international trade are *distributed* among countries. Our particular choice of 3 to 1 apportioned the gains as shown in the last row of Table 3. But with different terms of trade, the gains would have been apportioned differently. In the problems at the end of this chapter, you will be asked to recalculate the gains for each country with different terms of trade. You'll see that with different terms of trade, both countries still gain, but the distribution of the gains between countries changes.

Terms of trade The ratio at which a country can trade domestically produced products for foreign-produced products.

But notice that the terms of trade were not even *used* in our example until we arrived at Table 3. The gains from trade for the *world as a whole* were demonstrated in Figure 1, and were based entirely on the increase in world production when countries specialize according to comparative advantage.

> *For the world as a whole, the gains from international trade are due to increased production as nations specialize according to comparative advantage.* How *those world gains are distributed among specific countries depends on the terms of trade.*

We won't consider here precisely *how* the terms of trade are determined (it's a matter of supply and demand). But we *will* establish the limits within which the terms of trade must fall.

Look again at Table 2. China would never give up *more* than 5 T-shirts to import 1 bushel of soybeans. Why not? Because it could always get a bushel for 5 T-shirts *domestically,* simply by shifting resources into soybean production.

Similarly, the United States would never export a bushel of soybeans for *fewer* than 2 T-shirts because it could get 2 T-shirts for a bushel domestically (again, by shifting resources). Therefore, when these two nations trade, we know the terms of trade will lie *somewhere between* 5 T-shirts for 1 bushel and 2 T-shirts for 1 bushel. Outside of that range, one of the two countries would refuse to trade. Note that in our example, we assume terms of trade of 3 T-shirts for 1 bushel—well within the acceptable range.

SOME PROVISOS ABOUT SPECIALIZATION

Our simple example seems to suggest that countries should specialize *completely,* producing *only* the goods in which they have a comparative advantage. That is, it seems that China should get out of soybean production *entirely,* and the United States should get out of T-shirt production *entirely.*

The real world, however, is more complicated than our simplified example might suggest. Despite divergent opportunity costs, sometimes it does *not* make sense for two countries to trade with each other, or it might make sense to trade, but *not* completely specialize. Following are some real-world considerations that can lead to reduced trade or incomplete specialization.

Countries can gain when they shift production toward their comparative advantage goods (such as textiles in China), and trade them for other goods from other countries.

Costs of Trading

If there are high transportation costs or high costs of making deals across national boundaries, trade may be reduced and even become prohibitively expensive. High transportation costs are especially important for perishable goods, such as ice cream, which must be shipped frozen, and most personal services, such as haircuts, eye exams, and restaurant meals. These goods are less subject to trade according to comparative advantage. (Imagine the travel cost for a U.S. resident to see an optometrist in China, where eye exams are less expensive.)

The costs of making deals are generally higher for international trade than for trade within domestic borders. For one thing, different laws must be dealt with and different business and marketing customs must be mastered. In addition, international trade involves the exchange of one country's currency for another. This can introduce additional costs and risks that don't exist for domestic trade, because exchange rates can change before a contract is settled with payment. High transportation costs and high costs of making deals help explain why nations continue to produce some goods in which they do not have a comparative advantage and why there is less than complete specialization in the world.

Sizes of Countries

Our earlier example featured two large economies capable of fully satisfying each other's demands. But sometimes a very large country, such as the United States, trades with a very small one, such as the Pacific island nation of Tonga. If the smaller country specialized completely, its output would be insufficient to fully meet the demand of the larger one. While the smaller country would specialize *completely,* the larger country would not. Instead, the larger country would continue to produce both goods. This helps to explain why the United States continues to produce bananas, even though we do so at a much higher opportunity cost than many small Latin American nations.

Increasing Opportunity Cost

In all of our tables, we have assumed that opportunity cost remains constant as production changes. For example, in Table 2, the opportunity cost of a bushel of soybeans remains at 2 T-shirts for the United States, regardless of how many bushels it produces. But more typically, the opportunity cost of a good rises as more of it is produced. (Why? You may want to review the law of increasing opportunity cost in Chapter 2.) In that case, each step on the road to specialization would change the opportunity cost. A point might be reached—before complete specialization—in which opportunity costs became *equal* in the two countries, and there would be no further mutual gains from trading. (Remember: Opportunity costs must *differ* between the two countries in order for trade to be mutually beneficial.) In the end, while trading will occur, there will not be complete specialization. Instead, each country will produce both goods, just as China and the United States each produce T-shirts *and* soybeans in the real world.

Government Barriers to Trade

Governments can enact barriers to trading. In some cases, these barriers increase trading costs; in other cases, they make trade impossible. Since this is such an important topic, we'll consider government-imposed barriers to trade in a separate section, later in the chapter.

THE SOURCES OF COMPARATIVE ADVANTAGE

We've just seen how nations can benefit from specialization and trade when they have comparative advantages. But what determines comparative advantage in the first place?

In many cases, the answer is the *resources* a country has at its disposal.

> *A country that has relatively large amounts of a particular resource at its disposal will tend to have a comparative advantage in goods that make heavy use of that resource.*

This is most easy to see when the relevant resources are *gifts of nature*, such as a specific natural resource or a climate especially suited to a particular product.

TABLE 4		
Examples of National Specialties in International Trade	**Country**	**Specialization Resulting from Natural Resources or Climate**
	Saudi Arabia	Oil
	Canada	Timber
	United States	Grain
	Spain	Olive oil
	Mexico	Tomatoes
	Jamaica	Aluminum ore
	Italy	Wine
	Israel	Citrus fruit
	Niger	Uranium
	Country	**Specialization *Not* Based on Natural Resources or Climate**
	Japan	Cars, consumer electronics
	United States	Software, movies, music, aircraft
	Switzerland	Watches
	Korea	Cars, steel, ships
	China	Textiles, toys, shoes
	Great Britain	Financial services
	Pakistan	Textiles

The top part of Table 4 contains some examples. Saudi Arabia has a comparative advantage in the production of oil because it has oil fields with billions of barrels of oil that can be extracted at low cost. The United States' comparative advantage in crops such as wheat and soybeans is partly explained by its abundant farmland. Canada is a major exporter of timber because its climate and geography make its land more suitable for growing trees than other crops. Canada is a good example of comparative advantage without absolute advantage: It grows a lot of timber, not because it can do so using fewer resources than other countries, but because its land is even more poorly suited to growing other things.

But now look at the bottom half of Table 4. It shows examples of international specialization that arise from some cause *other* than natural resources. Japan has a strong comparative advantage in making automobiles. Yet none of the *natural* resources needed to make cars are available in Japan; the iron ore, coal, and oil needed to produce cars are all imported.

What explains the cases of comparative advantage in the bottom half of Table 4? In part, it is due to resources *other* than natural resources or climate. The United States is rich in both physical capital and human capital. As a result, the United States tends to have a comparative advantage in goods and services that make heavy use of computers, tractors, and satellite technology, as well as goods that require highly skilled labor. This, in part, explains the U.S. comparative advantage in the design and production of aircraft, a good that makes heavy use of physical capital (such as computer-based design systems) and human capital (highly trained engineers).

In less developed countries, by contrast, capital and skilled labor are relatively scarce, but less-skilled labor is plentiful. Accordingly, these countries tend to have a comparative advantage in products that make heavy use of less-skilled labor, such as textiles and light manufacturing. Note, however, that as a country develops—and acquires more physical and human capital—its pattern of comparative advantage can change. Japan, Korea, and Singapore, after a few decades of very rapid development, acquired a comparative advantage in several goods that, at one time, were specialties of the United States and Europe—including automobiles, steel, and sophisticated consumer electronics.

But another aspect of the bottom half of Table 4 is harder to explain: Why do specific countries develop a *particular* specialty? For example, if you think you know why Japan dominates the world market for VCRs and other consumer electronics—say, some unique capacity to mass-produce precision products—be sure you can explain why Japan is a distant second in computer printers. The company that dominates the market for printers—Hewlett Packard—is a U.S. firm.

Similarly, we take the worldwide dominance of American movies for granted. But if you try to explain it based on the availability of resources like physical capital or highly skilled labor, or cultural traditions that encouraged artists, writers, or actors, then why not Britain or France? At the time the film industry developed in the United States, these two countries had similar endowments of physical and human capital, and much older and stronger theatrical traditions than the United States. Yet their film industries—in spite of massive government subsidies—are a very distant second and third compared to that of the United States.

In even the most remote corner of the world, the cars, cameras, and VCRs will be Japanese, the movies and music American, the clothing from Hong Kong or China, and the bankers from Britain. These specialties are certainly *consistent* with the capital and other resources each nation has at its disposal, but explaining why each *specific* case of comparative advantage arose in the first place is not easy.

We can, however, explain why a country *retains* its comparative advantage once it gets started. Japan today enjoys a huge comparative advantage in cars and consumer electronics in large part because it has accumulated a capital stock—both physical capital and human capital—well suited to producing those goods. The physical capital stock includes the many manufacturing plants and design facilities that the Japanese have built over the years.

But Japan's human capital is no less important. Japanese managers know how to anticipate the features that tomorrow's buyers of cars and electronic products will want around the world. And Japanese workers have developed skills adapted for producing these products. The stocks of physical and human capital in Japan sustain its comparative advantage just as stocks of natural resources lead to comparative advantages in other countries. More likely than not, Japan will continue to have a comparative advantage in cars and electronics, just as the United States will continue to have a comparative advantage in making movies.

> *Countries often develop strong comparative advantages in the goods they have produced in the past, regardless of why they began producing those goods in the first place.*

WHY SOME PEOPLE OBJECT TO FREE TRADE

Given the clear benefits that nations can derive by specializing and trading, why would anyone ever *object* to free international trade? Why do the same governments that join the WTO turn around and create roadblocks to unhindered trade? The answer is not too difficult to find: Despite the benefit to the nation as a whole, some groups within the country, in the short run, are likely to lose from free trade, even while others gain a great deal more. Unfortunately, instead of finding ways to compensate the losers—to make them better off as well—we often allow them to block free trade policies. The simple model of supply and demand helps illustrate this story.

Figure 3 shows the market for shrimp in the United States. Both the supply and demand curve in the figure represent the *domestic* market only. That is, the supply curve tells us the quantity supplied at each price by U.S. producers; the demand curve tells us quantity demanded at each price by U.S. consumers. With no international trade in shrimp, the U.S. market would achieve equilibrium at point *A*, at a price of $7 per pound. This relatively high price reflects the relatively high opportunity cost of producing shrimp in the United States. Both production and consumption would be 400 million pounds per year.

The United States does not have a comparative advantage in shrimp. Other countries that *do* have a comparative advantage (such as Vietnam, Thailand, and Brazil) would like to sell it to us. Moreover, because their opportunity cost of producing shrimp is less than in the United States, their price tends to be lower as well. Let's suppose that the *world price* of shrimp—the price at which other countries offer to sell it to Americans—is $3 per pound. To keep our example simple, we'll also assume this price remains constant, no matter how much shrimp Americans buy from the rest of the world. (In effect, we're assuming that under international trade, the United States would be a relatively small buyer in a much larger world market.)

Now let's open up free trade in shrimp. Because Americans can buy unlimited quantities of imported shrimp at $3, domestic producers will have to lower their price to $3 as well in order to sell any. So the price of *all* shrimp in the U.S. market falls to $3 per pound—the same as the world price.

As the price drops, two things happen. On the one hand, we move along the demand curve from point *A* to point *C*: U.S. consumers buy more shrimp (900 million pounds) because it is cheaper. On the other hand, we move along the supply curve from point *A* to point *B*: U.S. producers decrease their quantity supplied (to

FIGURE 3

The Impact of Trade

With no international trade, equilibrium in the U.S. market for shrimp is at point A, where domestic quantity supplied equals domestic quantity demanded. Price is $7 per pound, and 400 million pounds are consumed each year.

When U.S. consumers can import shrimp at the lower world price of $3.00 per pound, quantity supplied falls to 100 million pounds, while quantity demanded rises to 900 million. The difference—800 million pounds—is imports from the world market.

Consumers of shrimp gain from trade—they enjoy a greater quantity at a lower price. But producers lose—they sell less at a lower price.

100 million pounds). The difference between domestic supply of 100 million and domestic demand of 900 million is the amount of shrimp the United States imports each year: 800 million pounds.

You've already learned (in the last section) that international trade according to comparative advantage makes a country better off: It increases total world production and enables consumers to enjoy greater quantities of goods and services. But not *everyone* is better off. It is easy to figure out who will be happy and who will be unhappy in the United States. American consumers are delighted: They are buying more shrimp at a lower price. American producers are miserable: They are selling less shrimp at a lower price.

> *International trade makes each country, as a whole, better off. But not everyone gains, because cheap imports from abroad—while beneficial to domestic consumers—are harmful to domestic producers.*

THE ANTITRADE BIAS AND SOME ANTIDOTES

Imagine that a bill comes before Congress to prohibit or restrict the sale of cheap shrimp from abroad, so that its U.S. price can rise above $3.00. Domestic producers would favor the bill. Domestic consumers would oppose it. But not with equally loud voices. After all, the harm to consumers from this restriction of trade would be spread widely among *all* U.S. consumers. The loss to any individual would be very small. For example, if the total loss to U.S. consumers were $200 million per year, the total harm to any single consumer would be less than a dollar. As a result, no individual consumer of shrimp has a strong incentive to lobby Congress, or to join a dues-paying organization that would act on behalf of shrimp consumers to oppose this antitrade bill.

By contrast, the benefits from this restriction of trade would be highly concentrated on a much smaller group of people: those who work in or own firms in the domestic shrimp industry. They have a powerful incentive to lobby against free trade in shrimp. Not surprisingly, when it comes to trade policy, the voices raised *against imports* are loud and clear, while those *for imports* are often nonexistent. Since a country has the power to restrict imports from other countries, the lobbying can—and often does—lead to a restriction on free trade. The United States, for example, continues to restrict imports of shrimp from low-cost producers, largely due to powerful lobbying by the U.S. shrimp industry.

A similar process works against U.S. *exports* to other countries. In this case, the foreign producers who would have to compete with U.S. goods will complain loudest, while foreign consumers who stand to gain will be mostly silent. The U.S. exporters—who are not constituents of these foreign governments—will have little influence in the debate. Thus, just as there is a policy bias against U.S. imports in the United States, there is a policy bias against U.S. exports in other countries.

> *The distribution of gains and losses creates a policy bias against free trade. Consumers who benefit from buying a specific product have little incentive to lobby for imports of that product. But domestic producers harmed by the imports have a powerful incentive to lobby against them.*

There are, however, three antidotes to this policy bias.

All or Nothing Trade Agreements

In a bilateral or multilateral trade agreement, two or more countries agree to trade freely in many goods—or even all goods—simultaneously. These agreements are typically negotiated by government officials and then presented to legislatures as "all-or-nothing" deals: The agreement must be approved or rejected as a whole, without any amendments that make exceptions for specific industries.

Such agreements can bring in another constituent to lobby for free trade: *exporters* in both countries. Ordinarily, exporters have no ability to influence the debate because their ability to export is decided in the *importing* country, where they have little influence. But in an all-or-nothing free trade deal, they can lobby their *own* country to allow imports as a way of enabling them to sell their exports. In this way, a balance of forces is created. Domestic producers threatened by imports will lobby against trade agreements in each country. But potential exporters will lobby just as strongly *for* the agreement.

An example was the North American Free Trade Agreement (NAFTA) between the United States, Canada, and Mexico, which went into effect in 1994, and has eliminated barriers on most products produced by the three nations. NAFTA was hotly opposed in all three countries by many producers and some labor unions who stood to lose from imports, but was just as hotly favored by producers and workers who stood to gain from exports. (The biggest gainers—consumers in the three countries—were hardly involved in the debate, for reasons we've discussed.)

More recently, a similar conflict arose over the Dominican Republic–Central American Free Trade Agreement (DR-CAFTA). In each country (including the U.S.) producers who would have to compete with imports lobbied against the bill, while exporters in each country lobbied for it. In mid-2005, the U.S. Congress narrowly approved the agreement; by mid-2006, most of the other countries involved had given their approval as well.

The World Trade Organization

Another antidote to antitrade bias is the World Trade Organization. By setting standards for acceptable and unacceptable trade restrictions and making rulings in specific cases, the WTO has some power to influence nations' trade policies. But its influence is limited because the WTO has no enforcement power. For example, the WTO has ruled several times against European trade barriers against U.S. beef, with little effect. Still, a negative WTO ruling puts public relations pressure on a country, and allows a nation harmed by restrictions on its exports to retaliate, in good conscience, with its own trade barriers.

Industries as Consumers

Whenever we use the word *consumer*, we naturally think of a household buying products for its own enjoyment. But the term can apply to any buyer of a product, including a firm that uses it as an input. If these firms are among the "consumers" who benefit from cheaper imports, and if the good is an important part of these firms' costs, they have an incentive to lobby for free trade in the good. For example, in late 2004, the textile industry lobbied the Bush administration to slow the rise in clothing imports from China. But U.S. clothing retailers and importers—for whom clothing is an input—lobbied strongly *against* any trade barriers. While the retailers and importers ultimately lost the battle in May 2005, their opposition delayed the restrictions for months and influenced the final policy adopted.

HOW FREE TRADE IS RESTRICTED

So far in this chapter, you've learned that specialization and trade according to comparative advantage can dramatically improve the well-being of entire nations. This is why governments generally favor free trade. Yet international trade can, in the short run, hurt particular groups of people. These groups often lobby their government to restrict free trade.

When governments decide to accommodate the opponents of free trade, they are apt to use one of two devices to restrict trade: tariffs or quotas.

TARIFFS

A **tariff** is a tax on imported goods. It can be a fixed dollar amount per physical unit, or it can be a percentage of the good's value. In either case, the effect in the tariff-imposing country is similar.

Tariff A tax on imports.

Figure 4 illustrates the effect of a U.S. tariff of $2 per pound on imported shrimp. Before the tariff is imposed, the price of shrimp under free trade is the world price: $3 per pound. The U.S. imports 800 million pounds per year (the distance *BC*). When the tariff is imposed, U.S. importers must still pay the same $3 per pound to their foreign suppliers. But now they must also pay $2 per pound to the U.S. government. Thus, the price of imported shrimp will rise from $3 to $5 per pound to cover the additional cost of the tariff.[1]

The higher price for imported shrimp allows U.S. producers to charge $5 for their domestic shrimp as well. As the price of shrimp rises, domestic quantity supplied

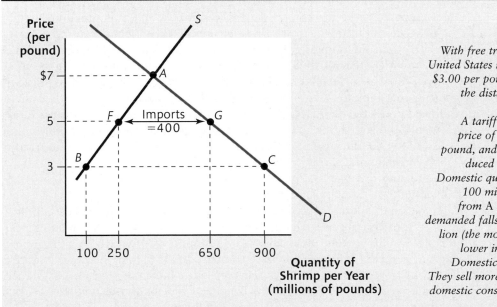

Price (per pound)

Quantity of Shrimp per Year (millions of pounds)

FIGURE 4

The Effects of a Tariff

With free trade in shrimp, the price in the United States is the same as the world price: $3.00 per pound. U.S. imports are equal to the distance from B to C, 800 million pounds per year.

A tariff of $2.00 per pound raises the price of imported shrimp to $5.00 per pound, and the price of domestically produced shrimp rises to the same level. Domestic quantity supplied increases from 100 million to 250 million (the move from A to B), while domestic quantity demanded falls from 900 million to 650 million (the move from C to G). The result is lower imports of 400 million pounds. Domestic suppliers gain from the tariff: They sell more shrimp at a higher price. But domestic consumers lose: They pay a higher price and consume less.

[1] If the United States is a large buyer in the world market for shrimp, the reduction in imports caused by the tariff would cause the world price to fall. This would change the quantitative results in our example. However, the price in the United States would still rise above $3.00, and all of our conclusions about the impact of tariffs would still hold.

increases (a movement along the supply curve from point *B* to point *F*). At the same time, domestic quantity demanded *decreases* (a movement along the demand curve from point *C* to point *G*). The final result is a reduction in imports, from 800 million before the tariff to 400 million after the tariff.

As you can see, American consumers are worse off: They pay more for shrimp and enjoy less of it. But U.S. producers are better off: They sell more shrimp at a higher price.

But we also know this: Since the volume of trade has decreased, the gains from trade according to comparative advantage have been reduced as well. The United States, as a whole, is worse off as a result of the tariff.

> *Tariffs reduce the volume of trade and raise the domestic prices of imported goods. In the country that imposes the tariff, producers gain, but consumers lose. The country as a whole loses, because tariffs decrease the volume of trade and therefore decrease the gains from trade.*

Quotas

Quota A limit on the physical volume of imports.

A **quota** is a government decree that limits the imports of a good to a specified maximum physical quantity, such as 400 million pounds of shrimp per year. Because the goal is to restrict imports, a quota is set below the level of imports that would occur under free trade. Its general effects are very similar to the effects of a tariff.

Figure 4, which we used to illustrate tariffs, can also be used to analyze the impact of a quota. In the figure, we start with our free trade price of $3. Consumers are buying 900 million pounds, and domestic producers are selling 100 million pounds per year. The difference of 800 million pounds is satisfied by imports.

Now suppose the United States imposes a quota of 400 million pounds (equal to the distance *FG* in the figure). At $3 per pound, the gap between the domestic supply curve and the domestic demand curve would still be 900 million pounds, which is more than the 400 million pounds of foreign shrimp allowed into the country. There is an excess demand for shrimp, which drives up the price. The price will keep rising until the gap between the supply and demand curves shrinks to the quantity allowed under the quota. As you can see in the figure, only when the price rises to $5 would the gap shrink to 400 million pounds. Thus, a quota of 400 million gives us exactly the same result as did a tariff of $2: In both cases, the price rises to $5, and yearly imports shrink to 400 million pounds.

The previous discussion seems to suggest that tariffs and quotas are pretty much the same. But even though the price and level of imports may end up being the same, there is one important difference between these two trade-restricting policies. A tariff, after all, is a *tax* on imported goods. Therefore, when a government imposes a tariff, it collects some revenue every time a good is imported. Even though the country loses from a tariff, it loses a bit less (compared to a quota) because at least it collects some revenue from the tariff. This revenue can be used to fund government programs or reduce other taxes, to the benefit of the country as a whole. When a government imposes a quota, however, it typically gains no revenue at all.

> *Quotas have effects similar to tariffs: They reduce the quantity of imports and raise domestic prices. While both measures help domestic producers, they reduce the benefits of trade to the nation as a whole. However, a tariff has one saving grace: increased government revenue.*

Economists, who generally oppose measures such as quotas and tariffs to restrict trade, argue that, if one of these devices must be used, tariffs are the better choice. While both policies reduce the gains that countries can enjoy from specializing and trading with each other, the tariff provides some compensation in the form of additional government revenue.

PROTECTIONISM

This chapter has outlined the *gains* that arise from international trade, but it has also outlined some of the *pain* trade can cause to different groups within a country. While the country as a whole benefits, those who own or work in firms that have to compete with cheap imports will be harmed. The groups who suffer from trade with other nations have developed a number of arguments against free trade. Together, these arguments form a position known as **protectionism**—the belief that a nation's industries should be *protected* from free trade with other nations.

Protectionism The belief that a nation's industries should be protected from foreign competition.

PROTECTIONIST MYTHS

Some protectionist arguments are rather sophisticated and require careful consideration. We'll consider some of these a bit later. But antitrade groups have also promulgated a number of myths to support their protectionist beliefs. Let's consider some of these myths.

Myth #1 "A HIGH-WAGE COUNTRY CANNOT AFFORD FREE TRADE WITH A LOW-WAGE COUNTRY. THE HIGH-WAGE COUNTRY WILL EITHER BE UNDERSOLD IN EVERYTHING AND LOSE ALL OF ITS INDUSTRIES, OR ELSE ITS WORKERS WILL HAVE TO ACCEPT EQUALLY LOW WAGES AND EQUALLY LOW LIVING STANDARDS."
It's true that some countries have much higher wages than others. Here are 2004 figures for average hourly wages of manufacturing workers, including benefits such as holiday pay and health insurance: Germany, $32.53; United States, $23.17; Japan, $21.90; Italy, $20.48; Korea, $11.52; Singapore, $7.45; Brazil, $3.03; Mexico, $2.50; and less than a dollar in China, India, and Bangladesh. This leads to the fear that the poorer countries will be able to charge lower prices for their goods, putting American workers out of jobs unless they, too, agree to work for low wages.

But this argument is incorrect, for two reasons. First, it is true that American workers are paid more than Chinese workers, but this is because the average American worker is more *productive* than his or her Chinese counterpart. After all, the American workforce is more highly educated, and American firms provide their workers with more sophisticated machinery than do Chinese firms. If an American can produce more output than a Chinese worker in an hour, then even though wage rates in the United States may be greater, cost *per unit* produced can still be lower in the United States.

But suppose the cost per unit *were* lower in China. Then there is still another, more basic argument against the fear of a general job loss or falling wages in the United States: comparative advantage. Let's take an extreme case. Suppose that labor productivity were the same in the United States and China, so that China— with lower wages—could produce *everything* more cheaply than the United States could. Both countries would still gain if China specialized in products in which its cost advantage was relatively large and the United States specialized in goods in which China's cost advantage was relatively small. That is, the United States would still have a comparative advantage in some things and there would be mutual gains from trade.

Myth #2 "A low-productivity country cannot afford free trade with a high-productivity country. The former will be clobbered by the latter and lose all of its industries."

This argument is the flip side of the first myth. Here, it is the poorer, less-developed country that is supposedly harmed by trade with a richer country. But this myth confuses absolute advantage with comparative advantage. Suppose the high-productivity country (say, the United States) could produce *every* good with fewer resources than the low-productivity country (say, China). Once again, the low-productivity country would *still* have a comparative advantage in *some* goods. It would then gain by producing those goods and trading with the high-productivity country. This is the case in our hypothetical example that began with Table 1. In that example, the United States has an absolute advantage in both goods, yet—as we've seen—trade still benefits both countries.

To make the point even clearer, let's bring it closer to home. Suppose there is a small, poor town in the United States where workers are relatively uneducated and work with little capital equipment, so their productivity is very low. Would the residents of this town be better off sealing their borders and not trading with the rest of the United States, which has higher productivity? Before you answer, think what this would mean: The residents of the poor town would have to produce everything on their own: grow their own food, make their own cars and television sets, and even provide their own entertainment. Clearly, they would be worse off in isolation. And what is true *within* a country is also true *between* different countries: Closing off trade will make a nation, as a whole, worse off, regardless of its level of wages or productivity. Even a low-productivity country is made better off by trading with other nations.

Myth #3 International trade decreases the total number of jobs in a country. It is true that a sudden opening up of trade temporarily disrupts markets. There can even be a temporary drop in employment as jobs are lost in some sectors before they are created in other sectors. But neither logic nor observation supports the view that international trade causes any long-lasting drop in total employment. In the United States, for example, as international trade has expanded rapidly in recent decades, total employment has risen steadily. And the U.S. unemployment rate has trended downward, not upward.

This myth about losses in total employment comes from looking at only one side of the international trade coin: imports. It is true that international trade destroys jobs in those industries that now have to compete with cheaper imports from abroad. But trade also creates *new* jobs in the export sector. When trade is balanced—exports and imports are equal—there is no reason to expect the jobs lost in the import-competing sector to exceed the jobs gained in the export sector.

What about when trade is unbalanced, as when a country runs a *trade deficit* (the value of imports exceeds the value of exports)? Even in this case, there is no reason for total employment to decrease. The United States has run a trade deficit every year for decades: We spend more dollars buying imports from other countries than they return to us by buying our products. As a result, producers in these other countries start to pile up dollar balances. But they don't just hold onto these dollar balances, which pay no interest or other return. Instead, they invest these dollars in U.S. financial markets, purchasing stocks and bonds and making bank deposits. The funds are then lent out to U.S. firms and households who, in turn, spend them—on new capital equipment, new housing construction, or other things. In this way, while some jobs are lost when Americans spend their dollars on imports rather than U.S. goods, other jobs are created when the dollars flow back into the U.S. through the financial markets. A trade deficit can cause other problems for a country (as you will learn when you study macroeconomics), but it does not reduce total employment.

Myth #4 "IN RECENT TIMES, THE DECLINING WAGES OF AMERICA'S UNSKILLED WORKERS ARE DUE TO EVER-EXPANDING TRADE BETWEEN THE UNITED STATES AND OTHER COUNTRIES."
True enough, unskilled workers have lost ground over the past 25 years. College graduates have enjoyed growing purchasing power from their earnings, while those with only a high school education or less have lost purchasing power. Rising trade with low-wage countries has been blamed for this adverse trend.

But before we jump to conclusions, let's take a closer look. Our discussion earlier in this chapter tells us where to look for effects that come through trade. If the opening of trade has harmed low-skilled workers in the United States, it would have done so by lowering the prices of products that employ large numbers of those workers. A study taking this approach found almost no change in the relative prices of products in the United States that employ large numbers of unskilled workers. Studies that take other approaches have found only modest effects. In general, economists who have looked at the impact of trade on U.S. labor markets have concluded that foreign trade is a small contributor to the depressed earnings of low-wage workers. A much more important factor is technological change, and the greater skills needed to work with new technologies.[2]

SOPHISTICATED ARGUMENTS FOR PROTECTION

While most of the protectionist arguments we read in the media are based on a misunderstanding of comparative advantage, some more recent arguments for protecting domestic industries are based on a more sophisticated understanding of how markets work. These arguments have become collectively known as *strategic trade policy*. According to its proponents, a nation can gain in some circumstances by assisting certain *strategic industries* that benefit society as a whole, but that may not thrive in an environment of free trade.

Strategic trade policy is most effective in situations where a market is dominated by a few large firms. With few firms, the forces of competition—which ordinarily reduce profits in an industry to very low levels—will not operate. Therefore, each firm in the industry may earn high profits. These profits benefit not only the owners of the firm but also the nation more generally, since the government will be able to capture some of the profit with the corporate profits tax. When a government helps an industry compete internationally, it increases the likelihood that high profits—and the resulting general benefits—will be shifted from a foreign country to its own country. Thus, interfering with free trade—through quotas, tariffs, or even a direct subsidy to domestic firms—might actually benefit the country.

An argument related to strategic trade policy is the **infant industry argument.** This argument begins with a simple observation: In order to enjoy the full benefits of trade, markets must allocate resources toward those goods in which a nation has a comparative advantage. This includes not only markets for resources such as labor

Infant industry argument The argument that a new industry in which a country has a comparative advantage might need protection from foreign competition in order to flourish.

[2] See, for example, Gary Burtless, Robert Lawrence, Robert Litan, and Robert Shapiro, *Globaphobia: Confronting Fears About Free Trade* (Washington, DC: The Brookings Institution Press, 1998). See also the recent survey by Bernard Hoekman and L. Alan Winters, "Trade and Employment: Stylized Facts and Research Findings," mimeo, World Bank Development Research Group, March 2005.

and land, but also *financial markets*, where firms obtain funds for new products. But in some countries—especially developing countries—financial markets do not work very well. Poor legal systems or incomplete information about firms and products may prevent a new industry from obtaining financing, even though the country would have a comparative advantage in that industry once it was formed. In this case, protecting the infant industry from foreign competition may be warranted until the industry can stand on its own feet.

Strategic trade policy and support for infant industries are controversial. Opponents of these ideas stress three problems:

1. Once the principle of government assistance to an industry is accepted, special-interest groups of all kinds will lobby to get the assistance, whether it benefits the general public or not.
2. When one country provides assistance to an industry by keeping out foreign goods, other nations may respond in kind. If they respond with tariffs and quotas of their own, the result is a shrinking volume of world trade and falling living standards. If subsidies are used to support a strategic industry, and another country responds with its own subsidies, then both governments lose revenue, and neither gains the sought-after profits.
3. Strategic trade policy assumes that the government has the information to determine which industries, infant or otherwise, are truly strategic and which are not.

Still, the arguments related to strategic trade policy suggest that government protection or assistance *may* be warranted in some circumstances, even if putting this support into practice proves difficult. Moreover, the arguments help to remind us of the conditions under which free trade is most beneficial to a nation:

> *Production is most likely to reflect the principle of comparative advantage when firms can obtain funds for investment projects and when they can freely enter industries that are profitable. Thus, free trade, without government intervention, works best when markets are working well.*

This may explain, in part, why the United States, where markets function relatively well, has for decades been among the strongest supporters of the free trade ideal.

PROTECTIONISM IN THE UNITED STATES

Americans can enjoy the benefits of importing many of the products listed in Table 4: olive oil from Spain, watches from Switzerland, tomatoes from Mexico, cars and VCRs from Japan. But on the other side of the ledger, U.S. consumers have suffered and U.S. producers have gained from some persistent barriers to trade. Table 5 lists some examples of American protectionism—through tariffs, quotas, or similar policies—that have continued for years.

As you can see, protection is costly. Quotas and tariffs on apparel and textiles, the most costly U.S. trade barrier, force American consumers to pay $33.6 billion more for clothes each year. And while protection saves an estimated 168,786 workers in this industry from having to make the painful adjustment of finding other work, it does so at an annual cost of $199,241 per worker. Both workers and consumers could be made better off if textile workers were paid any amount up to $199,241 *not* to work and consumers were allowed to buy inexpensive textiles from abroad.

Protected Industry	Annual Cost to Consumers	Number of Jobs Saved	Annual Cost per Job Saved	TABLE 5
				Some Examples of U.S. Protectionism
Apparel and Textiles	$33,629 million	168,786	$ 199,241	
Maritime Services	$ 2,522 million	4,411	$ 571,668	
Sugar	$ 1,868 million	2,261	$ 826,104	
Dairy Products	$ 1,630 million	2,378	$ 685,323	
Softwood Lumber	$ 632 million	605	$1,044,271	
Women's Nonathletic Footwear	$ 518 million	3,702	$ 139,800	
Glassware	$ 366 million	1,477	$ 247,889	
Luggage	$ 290 million	226	$1,285,078	
Peanuts	$ 74 million	397	$ 187,223	

Source: *The Fruits of Free Trade*, Federal Reserve Bank of Dallas, Annual Report, 2002, Exhibit 11.

In some cases, the cost per job saved is staggering. The table shows that trade barriers preventing Americans from buying inexpensive luggage save just a couple of hundred jobs, at a yearly cost of more than $1 million each. Trade barriers on sugar are almost as bad: While 2,261 jobs are saved, the annual cost per job is $826,104.

In addition to the dozens of industries in the United States permanently protected from foreign competition, dozens more each year are granted temporary protection when the U.S. government finds a foreign producer or industry guilty of *dumping*— selling their products in the United States at "unfairly" low prices that harm a U.S. industry. Most economists believe that these low prices are most often the result of comparative advantage, and that the United States as a whole would gain from importing the good. Vietnam, for example, has a clear comparative advantage in producing shrimp. But in 2005, based on a complaint by the Southern Shrimp Alliance, the U.S. government imposed tariffs of up to 26 percent on Vietnamese shrimp.

In the Using the Theory section that follows, we take a closer look at one of the longest-running examples of protectionism in the United States.

USING THE THEORY

The U.S. Sugar Quota[3]

The United States has protected U.S. sugar producers from foreign competition since the 1930s. Since the 1980s, the protection has been provided in the form of a price guarantee. Essentially, the government has promised U.S. sugar beet and sugar cane producers and processors that they can sell their sugar at a predetermined price—22 cents a pound— regardless of the world price of sugar.

© RICHARD LORD/PHOTOEDIT, INC.

[3] Information in this section is based on: Mark A. Groombridge, "America's Bittersweet Sugar Policy," *Trade Briefing Paper No. 13*, Cato Institute, December 4, 2001; Lance Gay, "Soured on Sugar Prices, Candy Makers Leave the U.S.," *Scripps Howard News Service*, June 18, 2003; "Closing the 'Stuffed Molasses' Loophole," *White Paper*, United States Sugar Corporation (*http://www.ussugar.com/pressroom/white_papers/stuffed_molasses.html*); and Remy Jurenas, "Sugar Policy Issues," *CRS Issue Brief for Congress*, Congressional Research Service, February 16, 2006.

This may not sound like a high price for sugar. But in the rest of the world, people and businesses can buy sugar for a lot less. From 2000 to 2005, the world price of sugar has averaged about 9 cents a pound, while Americans have continued to pay 22 cents. Even in 1985, when the world price of sugar plunged to just 4 cents a pound—a bonanza for sugar buyers around the world—American buyers were not invited to the party: The United States price remained at 22 cents.

Because the world price of sugar is so consistently below the U.S. price, the government cannot keep its promise to support sugar prices while simultaneously allowing free trade in sugar. With free trade, the price of sugar in the United States would plummet. The government's solution is a sugar quota. More accurately, the government decides how much foreign sugar it will allow into the United States each year, free of any tariff; all sugar beyond the allowed amount is hit with a heavy tariff of about 16 cents a pound. Since the tariff is so high, no one in the United States imports sugar beyond the allowed amount. So, in effect, the United States has a sugar quota.

The *primary* effects of the sugar quota are on sugar producers and sugar consumers. As you've learned, an import quota raises the domestic price of sugar (the quota's purpose). Sugar producers benefit. But sugar consumers are hurt even more.

And the harm is substantial. Table 5 shows that American consumers pay almost $2 billion more each year for sugar and products containing sugar due to the sugar quota. But spread widely over the U.S. population, this amounts to less than $15 per person per year. This probably explains why you haven't bothered to lobby for free trade in sugar.

But the costs of the sugar quota go beyond ordinary consumers. Industrial sugar users—such as the ice cream industry—are affected by the higher price too, not all of which can be passed on to consumers. So they try to avoid the quota's harm in other ways. One way is to waste resources buying sugar abroad disguised as other products. In the late 1990s and early 2000s, U.S. firms bought about 125,000 tons of sugar each year mixed with molasses, which was not restricted by the sugar quota. The sugar was then separated from the molasses. Even with these additional (and wasteful) processing costs, it was still a better deal to buy the disguised sugar abroad than to buy it through regular channels in the United States.

And sometimes a firm decides it's just not worth it anymore. In June 2003, Lifesavers was added to the list of other candy and baked-goods manufacturers who simply gave up trying to buy sugar in the United States, and moved their production facilities to Canada. In Canada, which doesn't have a quota, sugar can be purchased at the lower, world price.

Taxpayers, too, pay a cost for the sugar quota because as part of its price support program, the U.S. government must occasionally buy excess sugar from producers. In 2005, the U.S. government was storing about 759,000 tons of sugar at a cost of more than $1 million per month. The government must also hire special agents to detect and prevent sugar from entering the country illegally.

A final cost of the sugar quota is one that we have not yet considered in our discussion of international trade. In Figure 4, when a U.S. tariff or quota caused imports to shrink, we assumed that the world price of the good remained unchanged. But when a country is a very large buyer in the world market, a reduction in its purchases can cause the world price to drop. Essentially, the quota—by keeping sugar out—causes greater quantities of sugar to be dumped onto the world market, depressing its price. This hurts the poorest countries in the world that rely on sugar as an important source of export revenue. The sugar quota's harm to these countries has been estimated at about $1.5 billion per year.

Why do we bear all of these costs? Because of lobbying by groups who enjoy highly concentrated benefits. There are about 13,000 sugar farms in the United States. When the $2 billion in additional spending by U.S. consumers is spread among this small number of farms, the additional revenue averages out to more than $150,000 per farm per year. Those benefits are sizable enough to mobilize sugar producers each time their protection is threatened.

And mobilize they do. In 2004, the United States negotiated a free trade agreement with Australia that eliminated barriers on almost every good or service . . . except sugar. In 2005, the United States approved DR-CAFTA—a free trade agreement with five Central American countries and the Dominican Republic. Once again, sugar was an exception: Additional sugar imports from all six countries combined were restricted to less than 2 percent of the U.S. market.

There is another group that receives concentrated benefits from the sugar quota: producers of high-fructose corn syrup, the closest substitute for sugar. Because of the sugar quota, high-fructose corn syrup can be sold at a substantially higher price.

Not surprisingly, the largest producer of high-fructose corn syrup in the U.S. market—the Archer Daniels Midland (ADM) company—has funded organizations that lobby Congress and try to sway public opinion in the United States. Occasionally, you may see a full-page newspaper advertisement paid for by one of these groups, arguing that sugar in the United States is cheap. And it is . . . until you find out what the country next door is paying.

Summary

A country has a *comparative advantage* in a good when it can produce it at a lower opportunity cost than another country. When countries specialize in the production of their comparative advantage goods, world production rises. Both countries benefit as consumption rises in each country. The distribution of the benefits between countries depends on the *terms of trade*—the rate at which the imported goods are traded for the exported goods.

Despite the benefits to each nation as a whole, those who supply goods that must compete with cheaper imports are harmed. Because the gains from trade are spread widely while the harm is concentrated among a smaller number of people, the latter have an incentive to lobby against free trade. Those harmed often encourage government to block or reduce trade through the use of *tariffs* (taxes on imported goods) and *quotas* (limits on the volume of imports).

A variety of arguments have been proposed in support of protectionism. Some are clearly invalid and fail to recognize the principle that both sides gain when countries trade according to their comparative advantage. More sophisticated arguments for restricting trade may have merit in certain circumstances. These include strategic trade policy—the notion that governments should assist certain strategic industries—and the idea of protecting infant industries when financial markets are imperfect.

Problem Set   *Answers to even-numbered Questions and Problems can be found on the text Web site at www.thomsonedu.com/economics/hall.*

1. Suppose that the costs of production of winter hats and wheat in two countries are as follows:

	United States	Russia
Per winter hat	$10	5,000 rubles
Per bushel of wheat	$1	2,500 rubles

a. What is the opportunity cost of producing one more winter hat in the United States? In Russia?

b. What is the opportunity cost of producing one more bushel of wheat in the United States? In Russia?

c. Which country has a comparative advantage in winter hats? In wheat?

2. Suppose that the Marshall Islands does not trade with the outside world. It has a competitive domestic market for

VCRs. The market supply and demand curves are reflected in this table:

Price ($/VCR)	Quantity Demanded	Quantity Supplied
500	0	500
400	100	400
300	200	300
200	300	200
100	400	100
0	500	0

a. Plot the supply and demand curves and determine the domestic equilibrium price and quantity.

b. Suddenly, the islanders discover the virtues of free exchange and begin trading with the outside world. The Marshall Islands is a very small country, and so its trading has no effect on the price established in the world market. It can import as many VCRs as it wishes at the world price of $100 per VCR. In this situation, how many VCRs will be purchased in the Marshall Islands? How many will be produced there? How many will be imported?

c. After protests from domestic producers, the government decides to impose a tariff of $100 per imported VCR. Now how many VCRs will be purchased in the Marshall Islands? How many will be produced there? How many will be imported?

d. What is the government's revenue from the tariff described in part (c)?

e. Compare the effect of the tariff described in part (c) with a quota that limits imports to 100 VCRs per year.

3. The following table gives information about the supply and demand for beef in the European Union. The prices are in euros, and quantities are millions of pounds of beef per month. (You may wish to draw the supply and demand curves to help you visualize what is happening.)

Price	Quantity Supplied	Quantity Demanded
0	0	160
2	20	140
4	40	120
6	60	100
8	80	80
10	100	60
12	120	40

a. In the absence of international trade, what is the equilibrium price and quantity of beef?

b. If trade opens up, and the world price of beef is (and remains) 2 euros per pound of beef, how much beef will EU producers supply? How much beef will EU consumers demand? How much beef will be imported?

c. Within the EU, who gains and who loses when trade opens up?

4. Using the data on supply and demand in problem 3, suppose the EU imposed a tariff of 2 euros on each pound of beef.

a. How much beef would EU producers supply?

b. How much beef would EU consumers demand?

c. How much beef would the EU import?

d. How much total revenue would EU government authorities collect from the tariff?

5. Using the data on supply and demand in problem 3, suppose the EU imposed a quota on imports of beef equal to 40 million pounds of beef per month.

a. What would be the price of beef in the EU?

b. How much beef would EU producers supply?

c. How much beef would EU consumers demand?

6. Refer to Table 3 in the chapter. Suppose the terms of trade are *two and a half* T-shirts for each bushel of soybeans (instead of three for one as in the chapter). As in the chapter, assume the United States increases soybean production by 100 million bushels and exports 80 million of them to China, and that China decreases its own soybean production by 50 million bushels. Some of the remaining numbers in the table will have to change to be consistent with these new specifications. Then, answer each of the following questions.

a. Does China still gain from trade? Explain briefly.

b. Does the United States still gain from trade? Explain briefly.

c. Compare the effects of trade for China under the new and old terms of trade. In which case does China fare better? Explain briefly.

d. Compare the effects of trade for the United States under the new and old terms of trade. In which case does the United States fare better? Explain briefly.

7. Refer to Table 3 in the chapter. Suppose the terms of trade are *four* T-shirts for each bushel of soybeans (instead of three for one as in the chapter). Assume the United States increases soybean production by 100 million bushels and exports 60 million to China. China increases its T-shirt production by 250 million. Some of the remaining numbers in the table will have to change, to be consistent with these new specifications. Then, answer each of the following

questions.

a. Does China still gain from trade? Explain briefly.

b. Does the United States still gain from trade? Explain briefly.

c. Compare the effects of trade for China under the new and old terms of trade. In which case does China fare better? Explain briefly.

d. Compare the effects of trade for the United States under the new and old terms of trade. In which case does the United States fare better? Explain briefly.

8. Redraw the PPFs for the United States and China from Figure 2 in the chapter. Assume that the initial production and consumption points (A and A') and the new production points (B and B') are the same as in that figure. Plot the new consumption points (C and C') that correspond to your results from the previous problem (7).

9. The following table shows the hypothetical labor requirements per ton of wool and per hand-knotted rug, for New Zealand and for India.

Labor Requirements per Unit

	New Zealand	India
Per ton of wool	10 hours	40 hours
Per hand-knotted rug	60 hours	80 hours

a. Which country has an absolute advantage in each product?

b. Calculate the opportunity cost in each country for each of the two products. Which country has a comparative advantage in each product?

c. If India produces one more rug and exports it to New Zealand, what is the lowest price (measured in tons of wool) that it would accept? What is the highest price that New Zealand would pay? Within what range will the equilibrium terms of trade lie?

10. Using the data from problem 9, suppose that New Zealand has 300 million hours of labor per period, while India has 800 million hours.

a. Draw PPFs for both countries for the two goods (put quantity of wool on the vertical axis).

b. Suppose that, before trade, each country uses half of its labor to produce wool and half to produce rugs. Locate each country's production point on its PPF (label it A for New Zealand, and A' for India).

c. After trade opens up and each country specializes in its comparative advantage good, locate each country's production point on its PPF (label it B for New Zealand, and B' for India).

More Challenging

11. This problem uses the data from problem 9, and the graphs you drew in problem 10. Suppose that the terms of trade end up at 4 tons of wool for 1 hand-knotted rug. Suppose, too, that New Zealand decides to export 12 million tons of wool to India.

a. How many rugs will New Zealand import from India?

b. What will be New Zealand's consumption of each good after trade?

c. What will be India's consumption of each good after trade?

d. On the PPFs you drew for problem 10, plot each country's consumption point after trade. Label it C for New Zealand, and C' for India.

12. In Figures 3 and 4, we assumed that the world price of a good was fixed, and not affected by the quantity of imports a country chooses. But if a country is large relative to the world market, its imports can influence the world price.

Suppose the market for good X involves only two large countries (A and B), with supply and demand schedules as shown below:

Country A			Country B		
Price per Unit of Good X (measured in dollars)	Quantity Demanded of Good X	Quantity Supplied of Good X	Price per Unit of Good X (measured in dollars)	Quantity Demanded of Good X	Quantity Supplied of Good X
$10	1	25	$10	5	11
9	2	22	9	6	10
8	3	19	8	7	9
7	4	16	7	8	8
6	5	13	6	9	7
5	6	10	5	10	6
4	7	7	4	11	5
3	8	4	3	12	4

a. Plot the supply and demand curves for each country.

b. Before international trade, what is the equilibrium price and quantity in each country?

For the remaining questions, assume that the two countries can trade in good X.

c. Which country will export good X?

d. What will be the equilibrium world price? (Hint: This will be the price at which the quantity of exports from one country equals the quantity of imports to the other.)

e. What will happen to production and consumption in Country A?

f. What will happen to production and consumption in Country B?

g. What quantity will be exported (and also imported) in equilibrium?

h. On your graph, label the new levels of production and consumption in each country, as well as distances representing exports and imports.

What Macroeconomics Tries to Explain

You have no doubt seen photographs of the earth taken from satellites thousands of miles away. Viewed from that great distance, the world's vast oceans look like puddles, and its mountain ranges like wrinkles on a bedspread. In contrast to our customary view from the earth's surface—of a car, a tree, a building—this is a view of the big picture.

These two different ways of viewing the earth—from up close or from thousands of miles away—are analogous to two different ways of viewing the economy. When we look through the *microeconomic lens—from up close—we see the behavior of individual decision makers and individual markets.* When we look through the macroeconomic lens—from a distance—these smaller features fade away, and we see only the broad outlines of the economy.

Which view is better? That depends on what we're trying to do. If we want to know why computers are getting better and cheaper each year, or why the earnings of business professors are rising so rapidly, we need the close-up view of microeconomics. But to answer questions about the *overall* economy—about the overall level of economic activity, our standard of living, or the percentage of our potential workforce that is unemployed—we need the more comprehensive view of *macroeconomics.*

MACROECONOMIC GOALS

While there is some disagreement among economists about *how* to make the macroeconomy perform well, there is widespread agreement about the goals we are trying to achieve:

> *Economists—and society at large—agree on three important macroeconomic goals: economic growth, full employment, and stable prices.*

Why is there such universal agreement on these three goals? Because achieving them gives us the opportunity to make *all* of our citizens better off. Let's take a closer look at each of these goals and see why they are so important.

ECONOMIC GROWTH

Imagine that you were a typical American worker living at the beginning of the 20th century. You would work about 60 hours every week, and your yearly salary—about $450—would buy a bit less than $9,000 would buy today. You could expect to die at the age of 47. If you fell seriously ill before then, your doctor wouldn't be able to help much: There were no X-ray machines or blood tests, and little effective medicine for the few diseases that could be diagnosed. You would probably never hear the sounds produced by the best musicians of the day, or see the performances of the best actors, dancers, or singers. And the most exotic travel you'd enjoy would likely be a trip to a nearby state.

Today, the typical worker has it considerably better. He or she works about 35 hours per week and is paid about $40,000 per year, not to mention fringe benefits such as health insurance, retirement benefits, and paid vacation. Thanks to advances in medicine, nutrition, and hygiene, the average worker can expect to live into his or her late 70s. And more of a worker's free time today is really free: There are machines to do laundry and dishes, cars to get to and from work, telephones for quick communication, and personal computers to keep track of finances, appointments, and correspondence. Finally, during their lifetimes, most Americans will have traveled—for enjoyment—to many locations in the United States or abroad.

Economic growth The increase in our production of goods and services that occurs over long periods of time.

What is responsible for these dramatic changes in economic well-being? The answer is: **economic growth**—the increase in our production of goods and services that occurs over long periods of time. In the United States, as in most developed economies, the annual output of goods and services has risen over time, and risen faster than the population. As a result, the average person can consume much more today—more food, clothing, housing, medical care, entertainment, and travel—than in the year 1900.

Economists monitor economic growth by keeping track of *real gross domestic product* (*real GDP*): the total quantity of goods and services produced in a country over a year. When real GDP rises faster than the population, output per person rises, and so does the average standard of living.

Figure 1 shows real GDP in the United States from 1929 to the first half of 2006, measured in dollars of output at 2000 prices. As you can see, real GDP has increased dramatically. Part of the reason for the rise is an increase in population: More workers can produce more goods and services. But real GDP has actually increased *faster* than the population: During this period, while the U.S. population did not quite triple, annual production of goods and services has increased more than tenfold. Hence, the remarkable rise in the average American's living standard.

But when we look more closely at the data, we discover something important: Although output has grown, the *rate* of growth has varied over the decades. From 1959 to 1973, real GDP grew, on average, by 4.2 percent per year. But from 1973 to 1991, average annual growth slowed to 2.7 percent. Then, from 1991 to 2006, growth picked up again, averaging 3.3 percent per year. These may seem like slight differences. But over long periods of time, such small differences in growth rates can cause huge differences in living standards. For example, suppose that in each of the 20 years between 1986 and 2006, real GDP had grown by just one percentage point more than its actual rate. Then, over that entire period, the United States would have produced about $20 trillion *more* in goods and services than we *actually* produced (valuing these goods and services at 2000 prices). That amounts to more than $65,000 for each person in the population.

Growth increases the size of the economic pie, so it becomes possible—at least in principle—for every citizen to have a larger slice. But in practice, growth does *not* benefit everyone. Living standards will always rise more rapidly for some groups than for others, and some may even find their slice of the pie shrinking.

For example, since the late 1970s, economic growth has improved the living standards of the highly skilled, while less-skilled workers have benefited very little.

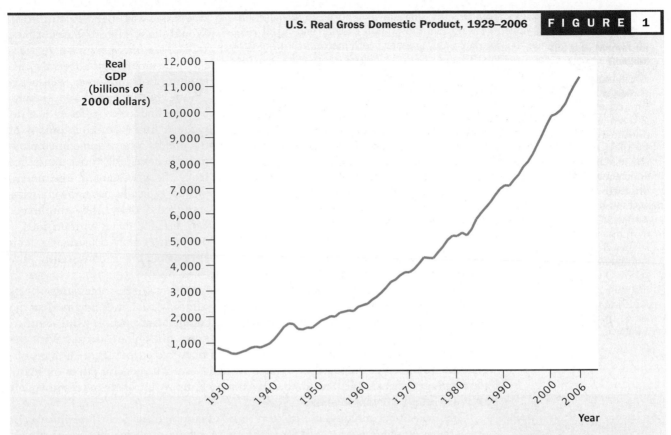

U.S. Real Gross Domestic Product, 1929–2006 · **FIGURE 1**

Real GDP has increased dramatically over the past 75 years. In the figure, real GDP is measured in dollars of output valued at 2000 prices. (The measurement of real GDP will be discussed in more detail in the next two chapters.)

Partly, this is due to improvements in technology that have lowered the earnings of workers whose roles can be taken by computers and machines. But very few economists would advocate a halt to growth as a solution to the problems of unskilled workers. Some believe that, in the long run, everyone will indeed benefit from growth. Others see a role for the government in taxing successful people and providing benefits to those left behind by growth. But in either case, economic growth, by increasing the size of the overall pie, is seen as an important part of the solution.

Macroeconomics helps us understand a number of issues surrounding economic growth. What makes real GDP grow in the first place? Why does it grow more rapidly in some decades than in others? Why do some countries experience very rapid growth—some much faster than the United States—while others seem unable to grow at all? Can government policy do anything to alter the growth rate? And are there any downsides to such policies?

High Employment (or Low Unemployment)

Economic growth is one of our most important goals, but not the only one. Suppose our real GDP were growing at, say, a 3 percent annual rate, but 10 percent of the

Growth Rates from Graphs In Figure 1, it looks like real GDP has not only been growing, but growing at a faster and faster rate, since the line becomes steeper over time. But the real GDP line would get steeper even if the growth rate were *constant* over the entire period. That's because as real GDP rises from an increasingly higher and higher level, the same *percentage* growth rate is a greater and greater *absolute* increase in GDP.

For example, when real GDP is $5 trillion, 3 percent growth would be a rise of $5 trillion × 0.03 = $0.15 trillion that year. But when real GDP is $10 trillion, the same 3 percent growth would be $10 trillion × 0.03 = $0.30 trillion. Since the slope of the line depends on the *absolute* rise rather than the *percentage* rise, the line gets steeper when the growth rate remains constant.

In fact, the line can become steeper even if the percentage growth rate *decreases* over time. As you've read, real GDP actually grew faster from 1959 to 1973 (where the line is flatter) than during any subsequent period (where the line is steeper). In subsequent chapters, you'll see other graphs that make it easier to see changes in the growth rate of real GDP.

workforce was unable to find work. Would the economy be performing well? Not really, for two reasons. First, unemployment affects the distribution of economic well-being among our citizens. People who cannot find jobs suffer a loss of income. And even though many of the jobless receive some unemployment benefits and other assistance from the government, the unemployed typically have lower living standards than the employed. Concern for those without jobs is one reason that consistently high employment—or consistently low *unemployment*—is an important macroeconomic goal.

But in addition to the impact on the unemployed themselves, joblessness affects *all* of us—even those who *have* jobs. A high unemployment rate means that the economy is not achieving its full economic potential: Many people who *want* to work and produce additional goods and services are not able to do so. With the same number of people—but fewer goods and services to distribute among that population—the average standard of living will be lower. This general effect on living standards gives us another reason to strive for consistently high rates of employment and low rates of unemployment.

One measure economists use to keep track of employment is the *unemployment rate*—the percentage of the workforce that is searching for a job but hasn't found one. Figure 2 shows the average unemployment rate during each of the past 86 years. Notice that the unemployment rate is never zero; there are always *some* people looking for work, even when the economy is doing well. But in some years, unemployment is unusually high. The worst example occurred during the Great Depression of the 1930s, when millions of workers lost their jobs and the unemployment rate reached 25 percent. One in four potential workers could not find a job. More recently, in 1982 and 1983, the unemployment rate averaged almost 10 percent.

The nation's commitment to high employment has twice been written into law. With the memory of the Great Depression still fresh, Congress passed the *Employment Act of 1946*, which required the federal government to "promote maximum employment, production, and purchasing power." It did not, however, dictate a target rate of unemployment the government should aim for. A numerical target was added in 1978, when Congress passed the *Full Employment and Balanced Growth Act*, which called for an unemployment rate of 4 percent.

A glance at Figure 2 shows how seldom we have hit this target over the last few decades. In fact, we did not hit it at all through the 1970s and 1980s. But in the 1990s, we came closer and closer and finally, in December 1999, we reached the 4 percent target for the first time since the 1960s. But it did not stay there long. In the early 2000s, the average unemployment rate has fluctuated, ranging from a high of 6.0 percent in 2003 to a low of 4.6 percent for most of 2006.

Why has the unemployment rate been above its target so often? Why were we able to reach 4 percent unemployment at the end of the 1990s, but not maintain it through the early 2000s? And what causes the average unemployment rate to

© TONY FREEMAN/PHOTOEDIT

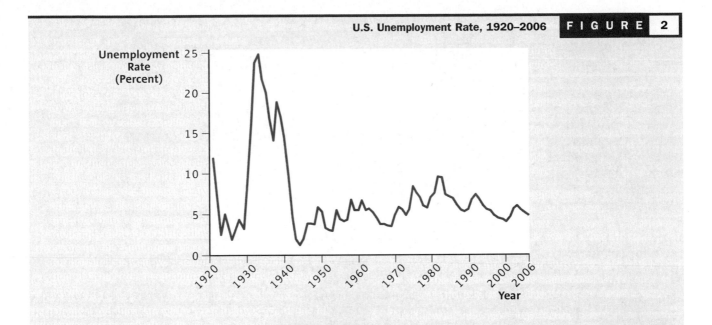

U.S. Unemployment Rate, 1920–2006   **FIGURE 2**

The unemployment rate fluctuates over time. During the Great Depression of the 1930s, unemployment was extremely high, reaching 25 percent in 1933. In the early 1980s, the rate averaged 10 percent. And during the 1990s, it fell rapidly, reaching 4 percent before turning up in the early 2000s.

fluctuate from year to year, as shown in Figure 2? These are all questions that your study of macroeconomics will help you answer.

Employment and the Business Cycle

When firms produce more output, they hire more workers; when they produce less output, they tend to lay off workers. We would thus expect real GDP and employment to be closely related, and indeed they are. In recent years, each 1 percent drop in output has been associated with the loss of more than half a million jobs. Consistently high employment, then, requires a high, stable level of output.

Unfortunately, output has *not* been very stable. If you look back at Figure 1, you will see that while real GDP has climbed upward over time, it has been a bumpy ride. The periodic fluctuations in GDP—the bumps in the figure—are called **business cycles.**

Figure 3 shows a close-up view of a hypothetical business cycle. First, notice the thin upward-sloping line. This shows the long-run upward trend of real GDP, which we refer to as *economic growth*. The thicker line shows the business cycle that occurs *around* the long-run trend. When output rises, we are in the **expansion** phase of the cycle; when output falls, we are in the *contraction* or **recession** phase. (Officially, a recession is a contraction considered significant in terms of depth, breadth, and duration.)

Of course, real-world business cycles never look quite like the smooth, symmetrical cycle in Figure 3, but rather like the jagged, irregular cycles of Figure 1. Recessions can be severe or mild, and they can last several years or less than a single year. When a recession is particularly severe and long lasting, it is called a **depression.** In the 20th century, the United States experienced just one decline in output serious enough to be considered a depression—the worldwide *Great Depression* of the

Business cycles Fluctuations in real GDP around its long-term growth trend.

Expansion A period of increasing real GDP.
Recession A period of significant decline in real GDP.

Depression An unusually severe recession.

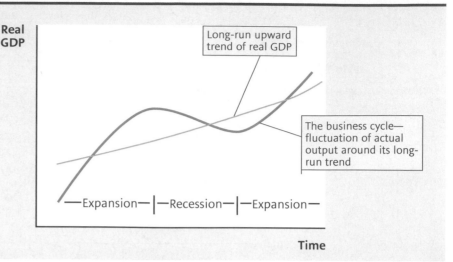

FIGURE 3

The Business Cycle

Over time, real GDP fluctuates around an overall upward trend. Such fluctuations are called business cycles. *When output rises, we are in the* expansion *phase of the cycle; when output falls, we are in a* recession.

Expansion versus Economic Growth Although the terms *expansion* and *economic growth* both refer to increases in real GDP, they are not the same. *Economic growth* refers to the long-run upward trend in output over a long period of time, usually more than a decade. It is measured as the *average* annual change in output over the entire period. An *expansion* refers to a usually shorter period of time during which output increases quarter by quarter or year by year.

Here's an example of the difference: From 1973 to 1991, output increased at an *average rate* of 2.7 percent per year over the entire period. This was the rate of economic growth during the period. But during a *part* of this long period—the early 1980s—output *fell* for several quarters. This was a contraction. During another part of this long period—the mid- and late 1980s—output rose every quarter. This was an expansion.

1930s. From 1929 to 1933, the first four years of the Great Depression, U.S. output dropped by more than 25 percent.

But even during more normal times, the economy has gone through many recessions. Since 1959, we have suffered through two severe recessions (in 1974–75 and 1981–82) and several more mild ones, such as the recession from March to November of 2001.

Why are there business cycles? Is there anything we can do to prevent recessions from occurring, or at least make them milder and shorter? And why—even after a period of severe depression as in the 1930s—does the economy eventually move back toward its long-run growth trend? These are all questions that macroeconomics helps us answer.

STABLE PRICES

Figure 4 shows the annual inflation rate—the percentage increase in the average level of prices—from 1922 to the first half of 2006.[1] With very few exceptions, the inflation rate has been positive: On average, prices have risen in each of those years. But notice the wide variations in inflation. In 1979 and 1980, we had double-digit inflation: Prices rose by more than 12 percent in both years. During that time, polls showed that people were more concerned about inflation than any other national problem—more than unemployment, crime, poverty, pollution, or anything else. During the 1990s, the inflation rate averaged less than 3 percent per year, and it has

[1] Figure 4 is based on the Consumer Price Index, the most popular measure of the price level, as well as historical estimates of what this index *would* have been in the early part of the 20th century, before the index existed. We'll discuss the Consumer Price Index and other measures of inflation in more detail in later chapters.

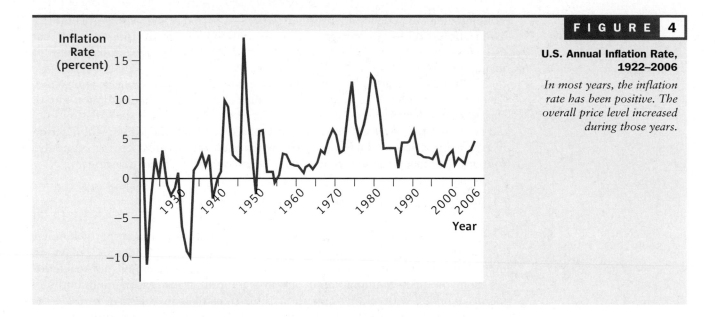

FIGURE   4

**U.S. Annual Inflation Rate,
1922–2006**

*In most years, the inflation
rate has been positive. The
overall price level increased
during those years.*

averaged about 2.8 percent during the 2000s (through mid-2006). As a result, we hardly seem to notice it at all. Pollsters no longer include "rising prices" as a category when asking about the most important problems facing the country.

Other countries have not been so lucky. In the 1980s, several Latin American nations experienced inflation rates of thousands of percent per year. In the early 1990s, some of the newly emerging nations of Central Europe and the former Soviet Union suffered annual inflation rates in the triple digits.

An extreme case was the new nation of Serbia, where prices rose by 1,880 percent in the single month of August 1993. If prices had continued to rise at that rate all year, the annual inflation rate would have been 363,000,000,000,000,000 percent. A more recent example is Zimbabwe. The annual inflation rate has been consistently above 200 percent since 2003, and it reached 1,000 percent in mid-2006.

Why are stable prices—a low inflation rate—an important macroeconomic goal? Because inflation is *costly* to society. With annual inflation rates in the thousands of percent, the costs are easy to see: The purchasing power of the currency declines so rapidly that people are no longer willing to hold it. This breakdown of the monetary system forces people to waste valuable time and resources bartering with each other—for example, trading plumbing services for dentistry services. With so much time spent trying to find trading partners, there is little time left for producing goods and services. As a result, the average standard of living falls.

With inflation rates of 12 or 13 percent—such as the United States experienced in the late 1970s—the costs to society are less obvious and less severe. But they are still significant. And when it comes time to bring down the inflation rate, painful corrective actions by government are sometimes required. These actions can cause output to decline and unemployment to rise. For example, in order to bring the inflation rate down from the high levels of the late 1970s (see Figure 4), government policy purposely caused a severe recession in 1981–82, reducing output and increasing unemployment.

Economists regard *some* inflation as good for the economy. In fact, in 2001 and 2002, policy makers worried that the inflation rate might fall *too low,* and that the economy might experience a harmful *deflation*—a period of *decreasing* prices. Price stabilization requires not only preventing the inflation rate from rising too high, but also preventing it from falling too *low*, where it would be dangerously close to turning negative.

The previous paragraphs may have raised a number of questions in your mind. What causes inflation or deflation? How would a *moderately* high inflation rate of 7 or 8 percent harm society? How does a recession bring down the inflation rate, and how does the government actually *create* a recession? And why might a period of decreasing prices—which sounds so wonderful—be a threat to the economy? Your study of macroeconomics will help you answer all of these questions.

THE MACROECONOMIC APPROACH

If you have already studied microeconomics, you will notice much that is familiar in macroeconomics. The *three-step process* introduced in Chapter 3 plays an important role in both branches of the field. But the macroeconomic approach differs from the microeconomic approach in significant ways. Most importantly, in *microeconomics*, we typically apply our three steps to *one market at a time*—the market for soybeans, for neurosurgeons, or for car washes. In *macroeconomics*, by contrast, we want to understand how the entire economy behaves. Thus, we apply the steps to *all markets simultaneously*. This includes not only markets for goods and services, but also markets for labor and for financial assets like stocks and bonds.

How can we possibly hope to deal with all of these markets at the same time? One way would be to build a gigantic model that included every individual market in the economy. The model would have tens of thousands of supply and demand curves, which could be used to determine tens of thousands of prices and quantities. With today's fast, powerful computers, we could, in principle, build this kind of model.

But it would not be easy. We would need to gather data on every good and service in the economy, every type of labor, every type of financial asset, and so on. As you might guess, this would be a formidable task, requiring thousands of workers just to gather the data alone. And in the end, the model would not prove very useful. We would not learn much about the economy from it: With so many individual trees, we could not see the forest.

Moreover, the model's predictions would be highly suspect: With so much information and so many moving parts, high standards of accuracy would be difficult to maintain. Even the government of the former Soviet Union, which directed production throughout the economy until the 1990s, was unable to keep track of all the markets under its control. In a market economy, where production decisions are made by individual firms, the task would be even harder.

What, then, is a macroeconomist to do? The answer is a word that you will become very familiar with in the chapters to come: *aggregation*.

AGGREGATION IN MACROECONOMICS

Aggregation The process of combining different things into a single category.

Aggregation is the process of combining different things into a single category, and treating them as a whole. It is a basic tool of reasoning, one that you often use without being aware of it. If you say, "I applied for five jobs last month," you are aggregating five very different workplaces into the single category, *jobs*. Whenever you say, "I'm going out with my friends," you are combining several different people into a single category: people you consider *friends*.

Aggregation plays a key role in both micro- and macroeconomics. Microeconomists will speak of the market for automobiles, lumping Toyotas, Fords, BMWs, and other types of cars into a single category. But in macroeconomics, we take aggregation to the extreme. Because we want to consider the entire economy at once, and yet keep our model as simple as possible, we must aggregate all markets into the broadest possible categories. For example, we lump together all the goods and services that households buy—newspapers, pizza, couches, and haircuts—into the single category *consumption goods*. We combine all the different types of capital purchased by business firms—forklifts, factory buildings, office computers, and trucks—into the single category *investment goods*. Often we go even further, lumping consumption, investment, and all other types of goods into the single category *output* or *real GDP*. And in macroeconomics, we typically combine the thousands of different types of workers in the economy—doctors, construction workers, plumbers, college professors—into the category, *labor*. By aggregating in this way, we can create workable and reasonably accurate models that teach us a great deal about how the overall economy operates.

"Micro" versus "Macro" In many English words, the prefix *macro* means "large" and *micro* means "small." As a result, you might think that in microeconomics, we study economic units in which small sums of money are involved, while in macroeconomics we study units involving greater sums. But this is not correct: The annual output of General Motors is considerably greater than the total annual output of many small countries, such as Estonia or Guatemala. Yet when we study the behavior of General Motors, we are practicing *microeconomics,* and when we study changes in output in Estonia, we are practicing *macroeconomics*. Why? Microeconomics is concerned with the behavior and interaction of *individual* firms and markets, even if they are very large; macroeconomics is concerned with the behavior of *entire economies*, even if they are very small.

DANGEROUS CURVES

MACROECONOMIC CONTROVERSIES

Macroeconomics is full of disputes and disagreements. Indeed, modern macroeconomics, which began with the publication of *The General Theory of Employment, Interest, and Money* by British economist John Maynard Keynes in 1936, originated in controversy. Keynes was taking on the conventional wisdom of his time, *classical economics,* which held that the macroeconomy worked very well on its own, and the best policy for the government to follow was *laissez-faire*—"leave it alone." As he was working on *The General Theory,* Keynes wrote to his friend, the playwright George Bernard Shaw, "I believe myself to be writing a book on economic theory which will largely revolutionize—not, I suppose, at once but in the course of the next ten years—the way the world thinks about economic problems."

Keynes's prediction was on the money. After the publication of his book, economists argued about its merits, but 10 years later, the majority of the profession had been won over: They had become Keynesians. This new school of thought held that the economy does *not* do well on its own (one needed only to look at the Great Depression for evidence) and requires continual guidance from an activist and well-intentioned government.

From the late 1940s until the early 1960s, events seemed to prove the Keynesians correct. Then, beginning in the 1960s, several distinguished economists began to challenge Keynesian ideas. Their counterrevolutionary views, which in many ways mirrored those of the classical economists, were strengthened by events in the 1970s, when the economy's behavior began to contradict some Keynesian ideas. Today, much of this disagreement has been resolved and a modern consensus—incorporating both Keynesian and classical ideas—has emerged. But there are still controversies.

Consider, for example, the controversy over the Bush administration's $350 billion 10-year tax cut. In May 2003, the tax cut was approved by 231 to 200 in the House of Representatives, and passed the Senate only when Vice President Cheney cast his vote to break a 50–50 tie. Within hours of passage, the following appeared on CNN's Web site:

> *"This is a great victory for the American people," said Senate Majority Leader Bill Frist, R-Tennessee. "The wonderful thing is it really boils down to greater job security for people."*

> *"This is a policy of debt, deficits, and decline," said Sen. Kent Conrad, D-North Dakota, adding, "This is a scandal in the making. We're going to read there are perverse results as a result of this tax policy."*[2]

Similar opposing views were expressed by economists associated with the Bush administration on the one hand, and those associated with the Democratic Party on the other. What are we to make of macroeconomic policy controversies like these, which occur so often on the political scene?

Remember the distinction between *positive (what is)* and *normative (what should be)*? Some of these disagreements are *positive* in nature. While economists and policy makers often agree on the broad outlines of how the macroeconomy works, they may disagree on some of the details. For example, they may disagree about the economy's current direction or momentum, or the relative effectiveness of different policies in altering the economy's course. Indeed, the two opposing senators quoted above were expressing at least in part a positive disagreement: a disagreement about the *impact* that tax cuts would have on the economy.

But disagreements that *sound* positive often have *normative* origins. For example in 2003, Democrats in Congress criticized the Bush tax cut as unfair, because it gave the biggest tax reduction to those with the highest incomes. Republicans in Congress countered that the tax cut was fair, because taxpayers with the highest incomes paid higher taxes to begin with. In the competitive and confrontational arena of politics—with each side trying to muster all the arguments it can—positive economics is often enlisted. In 2003, Republicans who began with the view that the Bush tax cut was fair invariably *also* argued that it was the most effective policy to spur the economy into a healthy expansion phase (see Figure 3). And they found a number of economists—who may have had similar normative views—to support that argument. Democrats who began with the view that the tax cut was *un*fair invariably *also* argued that it would cause great harm to the economy. And they found a number of economists—who may have had similar normative views—to support *that* argument.

Because of such political battles, people who follow the news often think that there is little agreement among economists about how the macroeconomy works. In fact, the profession has come to a consensus on many basic principles, and we will stress these as we go. And even when there are disagreements, there is surprising consensus on the approach that should be taken to resolve them.

You won't find this consensus expressed in a hot political debate. But you *will* find it in academic journals and conferences, and in reports issued by certain non-partisan research organizations or government agencies. And—we hope—you will find it in the chapters to come.

[2] "Congress Approves Tax-Cut Package," CNN.com/Inside Politics, May 23, 2002.

AS YOU STUDY MACROECONOMICS...

Macroeconomics is a fascinating and wide-ranging subject. You will find that each piece of the macroeconomic puzzle connects to all of the other pieces in many different ways. Each time one of your questions is answered, ten more will spring up in your mind, each demanding immediate attention. This presents a problem for textbook writers, and for your instructor as well: What is the best order in which to present the principles of macroeconomics? One way is to follow the order of questions as they would occur to a curious reader. For example, learning about unemployment raises questions about international trade, so we could then skip to that topic. But it also raises questions about government spending, economic growth, wages, banking, and much, much more. And each of these topics raises questions about still others. Organizing the material in this way would make you feel like a ball in a pinball machine, bouncing from bumper to bumper. This pinball approach—bouncing from topic to topic—is the one taken by the media when reporting on the economy. If you have ever tried to learn economics from a newspaper, you know how frustrating this approach can be.

In our study of macroeconomics, we will follow a different approach: presenting material as it is *needed* for what follows. In this way, what you learn in one chapter will form the foundation for the material in the next, and your understanding of macroeconomics will deepen as you go.

But be forewarned: This approach requires considerable patience on your part. Many of the questions that will pop into your head will have to be postponed until the proper foundations for answering them have been established. It might help, though, to give you a *brief* indication of what is to come.

In the next two chapters, we will discuss three of the most important aggregates in macroeconomics: output, employment, and the price level. You will see why each of these is important to our economic well-being, how we keep track of them with government statistics, and how to interpret these statistics with a critical eye.

Then, in the remainder of the book, we study how the macroeconomy operates. We'll start with the long run: What makes an economy grow over long periods of time, and which government policies are likely to help or hinder that growth.

Then, we turn our attention to the short run. You will learn why the economy behaves differently in the short run than in the long run, why we have business cycles, and how these cycles may be affected by government policies. We'll also expand our analysis to include the banking system and the money supply, and the special challenges they pose for government policy makers.

Finally, we'll turn our attention to the special problems of a global economy. You'll learn how trade with other nations constrains and expands our macro policy options at home and how economic events abroad influence our own economy. You will also learn why the United States has run persistent trade deficits with the rest of the world and what that means for our citizens.

This sounds like quite a lot of ground to cover, and, indeed, it is. But it's not as daunting as it might sound. Remember that the study of macroeconomics—like the macroeconomy itself—is not a series of separate units, but an integrated whole. As you go from chapter to chapter, each principle you learn is a stepping-stone to the next one. Little by little, your knowledge and understanding will accumulate and deepen. Most students are genuinely surprised at how well they understand the macroeconomy after a single introductory course, and find the reward well worth the effort.

Summary

Macroeconomics is the study of the economy as a whole. It deals with issues such as economic growth, unemployment, inflation, and government policies that might influence the overall level of economic activity.

Economists generally agree about the importance of three main macroeconomic goals. The first of these is economic growth. If output, real gross domestic product, grows faster than population, the average person can enjoy an improved standard of living.

High employment is another important goal. When employment is low (unemployment is high), it harms not only the unemployed themselves, but also society in general: Society loses output that could have been produced.

The third macroeconomic goal is stable prices. This goal is important because inflation—especially very high inflation—imposes costs on society and can lower living standards.

Because an economy like that of the United States is so large and complex, the models we use to analyze the economy must be highly aggregated. For example, we lump together millions of different goods to create an aggregate called "output." We combine all their prices into a single "price index."

Macroeconomics is often controversial. It may seem that macroeconomists agree on very little, but there is actually broad consensus on many positive economic issues. The roots of most macroeconomic controversies are normative.

Problem Set   *Answers to even-numbered Questions and Problems can be found on the text Web site at www.thomsonedu.com/economics/hall.*

1. In 1973, real GDP (at 2000 prices) was $4,342 billion. In 2000, it was $9,817 billion. During the same period, the U.S. population rose from 212 million to 281 million.
   a. What was the total percentage increase in real GDP from 1973 to 2000?
   b. What was the total percentage increase in the U.S. population during this period?
   c. Calculate real GDP per person in 1973 and in 2000. By what percentage did output per person grow over this period?

2. Suppose that real GDP had grown by 8 percent per year from 1973 to 2000. Using the data from problem 1:
   a. What would real GDP have been in 2000?
   b. How much would output *per person* in 2000 have increased (compared to its actual value in 2000) if annual growth in real GDP over this period had been 8 percent?

3. a. The average growth rate for real GDP in the United States was 3.7 percent from 1991 to 2000. Use the information in the following table (which gives the actual GDP numbers measured in 2000 dollars) to calculate how much more we would have produced in 2000 if real GDP had grown by 4.7 percent per year over that period.

Year	Real GDP (Billions of 2000 dollars)
1991	$7,100.5
1992	$7,336.6
1993	$7,532.7
1994	$7,835.5
1995	$8,031.7
1996	$8,328.9
1997	$8,703.5
1998	$9,066.9
1999	$9,470.3
2000	$9,817.0

   b. Calculate, for a 2000 population of 281 million people, how much higher the average output per person would have been in 2000 if the growth rate had been 4.7 percent per year over this period.

4. Assume that the country of Ziponia produced real GDP equal to $5,000 (in billions) in the year 2000.
   a. Calculate Ziponia's output from 2000 to 2006, assuming that it experienced a constant growth rate of 6 percent per year over this period. Use your answers to construct a graph similar to the one in Figure 1. Is the slope of this graph constant? Explain.
   b. Calculate Ziponia's output from 2000 to 2006, assuming that its growth rate was 6 percent from 2000 to 2001, and then the growth rate fell by 1 percentage point each year. Plot these points onto your graph from part (a). Is the slope of this graph constant? Explain.

Production, Income, and Employment

On the first Friday of every month, at 8:00 A.M., dozens of journalists mill about in a room in the Department of Labor. They are waiting for the arrival of the press officer from the government's Bureau of Labor Statistics. When he enters the room, carrying a stack of papers, the buzz of conversation stops. The papers contain the monthly report on the experience of the American workforce. They summarize everything the government knows about hiring and firing at businesses across the country; about the number of people working, the hours they worked, and the incomes they earned; and about the number of people *not* working and what they did instead. But one number looms large in the journalists' minds as they scan the report and compose their stories: the percentage of the labor force that could not find jobs, or the nation's *unemployment rate.*

Every three months, a similar scene takes place at the Department of Commerce. In this case, the reporters are there for the quarterly report on the nation's output of goods and services and the incomes we have earned from producing it. Once again, there is tremendous detail. Output is broken down by the industry that produced it and by the sector that purchased it. Income is broken down into different types of earners. And once again, the reporters' eyes will focus on a single number, a number that will dominate their stories and create headlines in newspapers across the country: the nation's *gross domestic product.*

The government knows that its reports on employment and production will have a major impact on the American political scene, and on financial markets in the United States and around the world. So it takes great pains to ensure fair and equal access to the information. For example, the Bureau of Labor Statistics allows journalists to look at the employment report at 8:00 A.M. on the day of the release (the first Friday of every month). But they must stay inside a room—appropriately called the lockup room—and cannot contact the outside world until the official release time of 8:30 A.M. At 8:29 A.M., the reporters are permitted to hook up their laptop modems, and then a countdown begins. At precisely 8:30 A.M., the reporters are permitted to transmit their stories. At the same instant, the Bureau posts its report on an Internet Web site (*http://www.bls.gov*).

And the world reacts. Within seconds, wire-service headlines appear on computer screens: "Unemployment Rate Up Two-Tenths of a Percent" or "Nation's Production Steady." Within minutes, financial traders, for whom these news flashes provide clues about the economy's future, make snap decisions to buy or sell, moving stock and bond prices. And throughout the day, politicians and pundits will respond with sound bites, attacking or defending the administration's economic policies.

In this chapter, we will take our first look at production and employment in the economy, focusing on two key variables: *gross domestic product* and the *unemployment rate*. The purpose here is not to explain what causes these variables to rise or fall. That will come a few chapters later, when we begin to study macroeconomic models. Here, we focus on the reality behind the numbers: what the statistics tell us about the economy, how the government obtains them, and how they are sometimes misused.

PRODUCTION AND GROSS DOMESTIC PRODUCT

You have probably heard the phrase *gross domestic product*—or its more familiar abbreviation, GDP—many times. It is one of those economic terms that is frequently used by the media and by politicians. In the first half of this chapter, we take a close look at GDP.

GDP: A DEFINITION

The U.S. government has been measuring the nation's total production since the 1930s. You might think that this is an easy number to calculate, at least in theory: Simply add up the output of every firm in the country during the year. Unfortunately, measuring total production is not so straightforward, and there are many conceptual traps and pitfalls. This is why economists have come up with a very precise definition of GDP.

Gross domestic product (GDP)
The total value of all final goods and services produced for the marketplace during a given year, within the nation's borders.

> The nation's **gross domestic product (GDP)** is the total value of all final goods and services produced for the marketplace during a given period, within the nation's borders.

Quite a mouthful. But every part of this definition is absolutely necessary. To see why, let's break the definition down into pieces and look more closely at each one.

The total value . . .

An old expression tells us that "you can't add apples and oranges." But that is just what government statisticians must do when they measure our total output. In a typical day, American firms produce millions of *loaves* of bread, thousands of *pounds* of peanut butter, hundreds of *hours* of television programming, and so on. These are different products, and each is measured in its own type of units. Yet, somehow, we must combine all of them into a single number. But how?

The approach of GDP is to add up the *dollar value* of every good or service—the number of dollars each product is sold for. As a result, GDP is measured in dollar units. For example, in 2005, the GDP of the United States was about $12,456,000,000,000—give or take a few billion dollars. (That's about $12.5 trillion.)

Using dollar values to calculate GDP has two important advantages. First, it gives us a common unit of measurement for very different things, thus allowing us to add up "apples and oranges." Second, it ensures that a good that uses more resources to produce (a computer chip) will count more in GDP than a good that uses fewer resources (a tortilla chip).

However, using the dollar prices at which goods and services actually sell also creates a problem: If prices rise, then GDP will rise, even if we are not actually *producing* more. For this reason, when tracking changes in production over time, GDP must be adjusted to take away the effects of inflation. We'll come back to this issue again a bit later in the chapter.

... of all final ...

When measuring production, we do not count *every* good or service produced in the economy, but only those that are sold to their *final users*. An example will illustrate why.

Figure 1 shows a simplified version of the stages of production for a ream (500 sheets) of notebook paper: A lumber company cuts down trees and produces $1.00 worth of wood chips. These are sold to a paper mill for $1.00. The mill cooks, bleaches, and refines the wood chips, turning them into paper rolls. These are sold to an office supplies manufacturer for $1.50. This manufacturer cuts the paper, prints lines and margins on it, and sells it to a wholesaler for $2.25. The wholesaler sells it to a retail store for $3.50, and then, finally, it is sold to a consumer—perhaps you—for $5.00.

Should we add the value of *all* this production, and include $1.00 + $1.50 + $2.25 + $3.50 + $5.00 = $13.25 in GDP each time a ream of notebook paper is produced? No, this would clearly be a mistake because all of this production ends up creating a good worth only $5 in the end. In fact, the $5 you pay for this good already *includes* the value of all the other production in the process.

In our example, the goods sold by the lumber company, paper mill, office supplies manufacturer, and wholesaler are all **intermediate goods**—goods used up in the process of producing something else. But the retailer (say, your local stationery store) sells a **final good**—a product sold to its *final user* (you). If we separately added in the production of intermediate goods when calculating GDP, we would be counting them more than once, since they are already included in the value of the final good.

> *To avoid overcounting intermediate products when measuring GDP, we add up the value of final goods and services only. The value of all intermediate products is automatically included in the value of the final products they are used to create.*

... goods and services ...

We all know a good when we see one: We can look at it, feel it, weigh it, and, in some cases, eat it, strum it, or swing a bat at it. Not so with a service: When you

Intermediate goods Goods used up in producing final goods.

Final good A good sold to its final user.

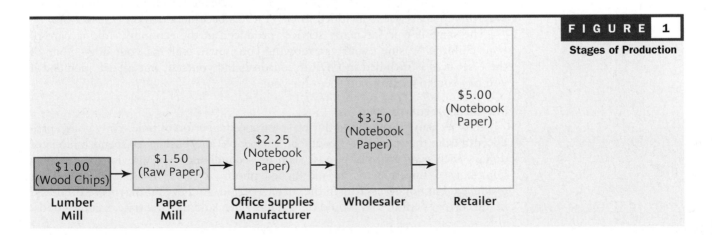

FIGURE 1

Stages of Production

get a medical checkup, a haircut, or a car wash, the *effects* of the service may linger, but the service itself is used up the moment it is produced. Nonetheless, final services count in GDP in the same way as final goods.

Services have become an increasingly important part of our total output in recent decades. The service sector has grown from about a third of U.S. output in 1950 to well over half of our output in 2006. These include the services produced by Internet providers, the health care industry, the banking industry, the educational system, and the entertainment industry.

. . . produced . . .

GDP counts only things that are *produced*. This may sound obvious, but it is easy to forget. Every day, Americans buy billions of dollars worth of things that are *not* produced, or at least not produced during the period being considered. These are not counted in that period's GDP. For example, people may buy land, or they may buy financial assets such as stocks or bonds. While these things cost money, they are not counted in GDP because they are not "goods and services *produced.*" Land, for example, is not produced at all. Stocks and bonds represent a claim to ownership or to receive future payments, but they are not themselves produced goods or services.

The Services of Dealers, Brokers, and Other Sellers You've learned that GDP excludes the value of many things that are bought and sold—such as land, financial assets, and used goods—because they are not *currently produced goods and services.* But all of this buying and selling *can* contribute to GDP indirectly. How? If a dealer or broker is involved in the transaction, then that dealer or broker is producing a current service: bringing buyer and seller together. The value of this service is part of current GDP.

For example, suppose you bought a secondhand book at your college bookstore for $50. Suppose, too, that the store had bought the book from another student for $30. Then the purchase of the used book will contribute $20 to this year's GDP. Why? Because $20 is the value of the bookstore's services; it's the premium you pay to buy the book in the store, rather than going through the trouble to find the original seller yourself. The remainder of your purchase—$30—represents the value of the used book itself, and is *not* counted in GDP. The book was already counted when it was newly produced, in this or a previous year.

. . . for the marketplace . . .

GDP does not include *all* final goods and services produced in the economy. Rather, it includes only the ones produced for the marketplace, that is, with the intention of being *sold.* Because of this restriction, we exclude many important goods and services from our measure. For example, when you clean your own home, you have produced a final service—housecleaning—but it is *not* counted in GDP because you are doing it for yourself, not for the marketplace. If you hire a housecleaner to clean your home, however, this final service *is* included in GDP; it has become a market transaction.

The same is true for many services produced in the economy. Taking care of your children, washing your car, mowing your lawn, walking your dog—none of these services is included in GDP if you do it for yourself, but all *are* included if you pay someone else to do them for you.

. . . during a given period . . .

GDP measures production during some specific period of time. Only goods produced during that period are counted. But people and businesses spend billions of dollars each year on *used* goods, such as secondhand cars, previously occupied homes, used furniture, or an old signed photo of Elvis. These goods were all *produced*, but not necessarily in the current period. And even if they *were* produced in the current period, they would only count when sold the *first* time, as new goods.

If we counted them again each time they were resold, we would overestimate total production for the period.

What duration of time should we use for GDP? In theory, we could use any duration. In 2005, for example, the United States produced an average of $34 billion worth of output each day, $1 trillion each month, and $12.5 trillion for the year as a whole. Thus, we could measure daily GDP, monthly GDP, and so on. In practice, however, GDP is measured for *each quarter* and then reported as an *annual rate* for that quarter.

To understand this, look at Table 1, which shows how GDP was actually reported by the government during the course of 2005. A few months

TABLE 1
Quarterly and Annual GDP in 2005

	GDP ($ billions)
Quarters	
2005—I	$12,173.2
2005—II	$12,346.1
2005—III	$12,573.5
2005—IV	$12,730.5
Year	
2005	$12,455.8

Source: Bureau of Economic Analysis (*www.bea.gov*), August 30, 2006 revision.

after the end of each quarter, the government releases its estimates for GDP for that quarter, and then revises the estimates periodically as new information is obtained. Look at the row for 2005—I, the first quarter (January through March of 2005). During that quarter the U.S. economy *actually* produced about $3,043 billion in final goods and services. But you won't see that number in the table. What you *will* see is how much we *would* have produced during an entire year if we produced at that quarter's rate for *four* full quarters (4 × $3,043.3 billion = $12,173.2 billion).[1] Once the fourth-quarter figures are in, the government also reports the official GDP figure for the entire year—what we *actually* produced during the entire year. For 2005, that was $12,445.8 billion.

. . . within the nation's borders.

U.S. GDP measures output produced *within U.S. borders,* regardless of whether it was produced by Americans. This means we *include* output produced by foreign-owned resources and foreign citizens located in the United States, and we *exclude* output produced by Americans located in other countries. For example, when the rock band U2, whose members reside in Ireland, gives a concert tour in the United States, the value of their services is counted in U.S. GDP but not in Ireland's GDP. Similarly, the services of an American nurse working in an Ethiopian hospital are part of Ethiopian GDP and not U.S. GDP.

THE EXPENDITURE APPROACH TO GDP

The Commerce Department's Bureau of Economic Analysis (BEA), the agency responsible for measuring the nation's production, calculates GDP in several different ways. The most important of these is the *expenditure approach.* Because this method of measuring GDP tells us so much about the structure of our economy, we'll spend the next several pages on it.

In the expenditure approach, we divide output into four categories according to which group in the economy purchases it as the final user. The four categories are:

---

[1] There is one other twist to the government's reporting: Before multiplying by 4, each quarter's production is *seasonally adjusted*—raised or lowered to eliminate any changes that usually occur during that time of year.

1. *Consumption goods and services (C)*, purchased by households;
2. *Private investment goods and services (I)*, purchased by businesses;
3. *Government goods and services (G)*, purchased by government agencies;
4. *Net exports (NX)*, purchased by foreigners.

This is an exhaustive list: Everyone who purchases a good or service included in U.S. GDP must be either a U.S. household, U.S. business, or U.S. government agency (including state and local government); otherwise, they are part of the foreign sector. Thus, when we add up the purchases of all four groups, we must get GDP:

Expenditure approach Measuring GDP by adding the value of goods and services purchased by each type of final user.

> *In the **expenditure approach** to measuring GDP, we add up the value of the goods and services purchased by each type of final user:*
>
> $$GDP = C + I + G + NX$$

Table 2 shows the part of GDP purchased by each sector during the entire year 2005. Ignore the finer details for now and just concentrate on the last number in each column. Applying the expenditure approach to GDP in 2005 gives us GDP = $C + I + G + NX = \$8,742 + \$2,057 + \$2,373 + (-\$716) = \$12,456$ billion.

Now let's take a closer look at each of the four components of GDP.

Consumption Spending

Consumption (C) is the largest component of GDP—making up about 70 percent of total production in recent years—and the easiest to understand:

Consumption (C) The part of GDP purchased by households as final users.

> ***Consumption** is the part of GDP purchased by households as final users.*

TABLE   2   GDP in 2005: The Expenditure Approach

Consumption Purchases ($ billion)		Private Investment Purchases ($ billion)		Government Purchases ($ billion)		Net Exports ($ billion)	
Services	$5,170	Plant, Equipment, and Software	$1,266	Government Consumption	$1,976	Exports	$1,303
Nondurable Goods	$2,539	New-Home Construction	$ 770	Government Investment	$ 397	Imports	$2,019
Durable Goods	$1,033	Changes in Business Inventories	$ 21				
Consumption =	**$8,742**	**Private Investment =**	**$2,057**	**Government Purchases =**	**$2,373**	**Net Exports =**	**−$ 716**

GDP = *C + I + G + NX*

   = $8,742 + $2,057 + $2,373 + (−$716)

   = $12,456 billion

Source: Bureau of Economic Analysis, "National Income and Product Account Tables" (*www.bea.gov*).

Almost everything that households buy during the year—restaurant meals, gasoline, new clothes, doctors' visits, movies, electricity, and more—is included as part of consumption spending when we calculate GDP.

But notice the word *almost*.

Some of the things that households buy are *not* part of consumption in GDP. First, used goods that households buy are excluded. As discussed earlier, these were already counted when they were originally sold as new goods.

Second, households buy assets—like stocks, bonds, and land—that are *not* goods and services. These are excluded from consumption, as well as from GDP.

Third, *newly constructed homes*—even though part of GDP and usually purchased directly by households—are included as investment, rather than consumption. We'll discuss the reasons for this in the next section.

Finally, there are two things included in consumption even though households don't actually buy them: (1) the total value of food products produced on farms that are consumed by the farmers and their families themselves; and (2) the total value of housing services provided by owner-occupied homes. The government estimates how much the food consumed on farms *could* have been sold for, and how much owner-occupied homes *could* have been rented for. These estimates are included as part of consumption spending, and therefore included in GDP as well.

Private Investment

In Chapter 2, you learned that one of the four resources is capital, a long-lasting tool used in production, and which is *itself* produced. Examples are oil drilling rigs, cash registers, office telephone equipment, and wireless phone towers. When we sum the value of all capital goods like these in the country, we get our *capital stock*.

Understanding the concept of capital stock helps us understand and define the concept of investment. A rough definition of **private investment** is *capital formation*— the *increase* in the nation's capital stock during the year.

More specifically,

> *private investment has three components: (1) business purchases of plant, equipment, and software; (2) new-home construction; and (3) changes in business firms' inventory stocks (changes in stocks of unsold goods).*

Private investment (*I*) The sum of business plant, equipment, and software purchases, new-home construction, and inventory changes; often referred to as just *investment*.

Each of these components requires some explanation.

Business Purchases of Plant, Equipment, and Software. This category might seem confusing at first glance. Why aren't plant, equipment, and software considered intermediate goods? After all, business firms buy these things in order to produce other things. Doesn't the value of their final goods include the value of their plant, equipment, and software as well?

Actually, no, and if you go back to the definition of intermediate goods, you will see why. Intermediate goods are *used up* in producing the current year's GDP. But a firm's plant, equipment, and software are intended to last for many years; only a small part of them is used up to make the current year's output. Thus, we regard new plant, equipment, and software as final goods, and we regard the firms that buy them as the final users of those goods.

For example, suppose our paper mill—the firm that turns wood chips into raw paper—builds a new factory building that is expected to last for 50 years. Then only a small fraction of that factory building—one-fiftieth—is used up in any one year's production of raw paper, and only this small part of the factory building's value will be reflected in the value of the firm's paper production. But since the entire factory is produced during the year, we must include its full value *somewhere* in our measure of production. We therefore count the whole factory building as investment in GDP.

Plant, equipment, and software purchases are always the largest component of private investment. And 2005 was no exception, as you can see in the second column of Table 2. That year, businesses purchased and installed $1,266 billion worth of plant, equipment, and software, which was almost two-thirds of total private investment.

New-Home Construction. As you can see in Table 2, new-home construction made up a significant part of total private investment in 2005. But it may strike you as odd that this category is part of investment spending at all, since most new homes are purchased by households and could reasonably be considered consumption spending instead. Why is new-home construction counted as investment spending in GDP?

Largely because residential housing is an important part of the nation's *capital stock*. Just as an oil-drilling rig will continue to provide oil-drilling services for many years, so, too, a home will continue to provide housing services into the future. Because we want our measure of private investment to roughly correspond to the increase in the nation's capital stock, we include this important category of capital formation as part of private investment.

Unsold goods, like those pictured in this warehouse, are considered inventories. The change *in these inventories is included as investment when calculating GDP.*

Changes in Inventories. Inventories are goods that have been produced but not yet sold. They include goods on store shelves, goods making their way through the production process in factories, and raw materials waiting to be used. We count the *change* in firms' inventories as part of investment in measuring GDP. Why? When goods are produced but not sold during the year, they end up in some firm's inventory stocks. If we did *not* count changes in inventories, we would be missing this important part of current production. Remember that GDP is designed to measure total *production,* not just the part of production that is sold during the year.

To understand this more clearly, suppose that in some year, the automobile industry produced $100 billion worth of automobiles, and that $80 billion worth was sold to consumers. Then the other $20 billion remained unsold and was added to the auto companies' inventories. If we counted consumption spending alone ($80 billion), we would underestimate automobile production in GDP. To ensure a proper measure, we must include not only the $80 billion in cars sold (consumption), but also the $20 billion *change* in inventories (private investment). In the end, the contribution to GDP is $80 billion (consumption) + $20 billion (private investment) = $100 billion, which is, indeed, the total value of automobile production during the year.

What if inventory stocks *decline* during the year, so that the change in inventories is negative? Our rule still holds: We include the change in inventories in our measure of GDP. But in this case, we add a *negative* number. For example, if the automobile industry produced $100 billion worth of cars this year, but consumers bought $120 billion, then $20 billion worth must have come from inventory stocks. This $20 billion worth of cars was produced (and counted) in previous years, so it should not be counted in this year's GDP. In this case, the consumption spending of $120 billion *overestimates* automobile production during the year, so subtracting $20 billion corrects for this overcount. In the end, GDP would rise by $120 billion (consumption) + [−$20 billion (private investment)] = $100 billion.

But why are inventory changes included in investment, rather than some other component of GDP? Because unsold goods are part of the nation's capital stock. They will provide services in the future, when they are finally sold and used. An increase in inventories represents capital formation. A decrease in inventories—negative investment—is a decrease in the nation's capital.

Inventory changes are generally the smallest component of private investment, but the most highly volatile in percentage terms. In 2005, for example, inventories rose by $21 billion; one year earlier, they rose by $55 billion—almost three times as much. Part of the reason for this volatility is that, while some inventory investment is intended, much of it is *unintended*. As the economy begins to slow, for example, businesses may be unable to sell all of the goods they have produced and had planned to sell. The unsold output is added to inventory stocks—an unintended increase in inventories. During rapid expansions, the opposite may happen: Businesses find themselves selling more than they produced—an unintended (though welcome) decrease in inventories.

Private Investment and the Capital Stock: Some Provisos.   A few pages ago, it was pointed out that private investment corresponds only *roughly* to the increase in the nation's capital stock. Why this cautious language? Because changes in the nation's capital stock are somewhat more complicated than we are able to capture with private investment alone.

First, private investment *excludes* some production that adds to the nation's capital stock. Specifically, private investment does not include:

- *Government investment.* An important part of the nation's capital stock is owned and operated not by businesses, but by government—federal, state, and local. Courthouses, police cars, fire stations, schools, weather satellites, military aircraft, highways, and bridges are all examples of government capital. If you look at the third column of Table 2, for example, you'll see that the BEA estimated government investment to be $397 billion in 2005; that was the part of government spending that was devoted to capital formation in 2005.
- *Consumer durables.* Goods such as furniture, automobiles, washing machines, and personal computers for home use can be considered capital goods because they will continue to provide services for many years. In 2005, households purchased $1,033 billion worth of consumer durables (see Table 2, first column).
- *Human capital.* Think about a surgeon's skills in performing a heart bypass operation, or a police detective's ability to find clues and solve a murder, or a Web page designer's mastery of HTML and Java. These types of knowledge will continue to provide valuable services well into the future, just like plant and equipment or new housing. To measure the increase in the capital stock most broadly, then, we *should* include the additional skills and training acquired by the workforce during the year.

In addition to excluding some types of capital formation, private investment also errs in the other direction: It ignores *depreciation*—the capital that is used up during the year. Fortunately, the BEA estimates depreciation of the private and public capital stock, allowing us to calculate **net investment** (total investment minus depreciation) for these sectors. For example, for 2005, the BEA estimates that $1,353 billion of the private capital stock depreciated during the year (not shown in Table 2). So net private investment that year was only $2,057 billion − $1,353 billion = $704 billion.

Net investment Investment minus depreciation.

Similarly, the BEA estimates that $252 billion in government capital depreciated in 2005, so net government investment that year was $397 billion − $252 billion = $145 billion.

Government Purchases

Government purchases (G)
Spending by federal, state, and local governments on goods and services.

In 2005, the government bought $2,373 billion worth of goods and services that were part of GDP—almost a fifth of the total. This component of GDP is called **government purchases,** although in recent years the Department of Commerce has begun to use the phrase *government consumption and investment purchases.* Government *investment,* as discussed earlier, refers to capital goods purchased by government agencies. The rest of government purchases is considered government *consumption:* spending on goods and services that are used up during the period. This includes the salaries of government workers and military personnel, and raw materials such as computer paper for government offices, gasoline for government vehicles, and the electricity used in government buildings.

There are a few things to keep in mind about government purchases in GDP. First, we include purchases by state and local governments as well as the federal government. In macroeconomics, it makes little difference whether the purchases are made by a local government agency like the parks department of Kalamazoo, Michigan, or a huge federal agency such as the U.S. Department of Defense.

DANGEROUS CURVES

Investment: Economics versus Ordinary English Be *extremely* careful when using the term *investment* in your economics course. In economics, investment refers to capital formation, such as the building of a new factory, home, or hospital, or the production and installation of new capital equipment, or the accumulation of inventories by business firms. In everyday language, however, *investment* has a very different meaning: a place to put your wealth. Thus, in ordinary English, you invest whenever you buy stocks or bonds or certificates of deposit or when you lend money to a friend who is starting up a business. But in the language of economics, you have not invested but merely changed the form in which you are holding your wealth (say, from checking account balances to stocks or bonds). To avoid confusion, remember that investment takes place when there is new production of capital goods— that is, when there is *capital formation.*

Second, government purchases include *goods*—like fighter jets, police cars, school buildings, and spy satellites—and *services*—such as those performed by police, legislators, and military personnel.

The government is considered to be the final purchaser of these things even if it uses them to make other goods or services. For example, if you are taking economics at a public college or university that produces educational services, then your professor is selling teaching services to a state or city government. His or her salary enters into GDP as part of government purchases.

Transfer payment Any payment that is not compensation for supplying goods, services, or resources.

Finally, it's important to distinguish between government *purchases*—which are counted in GDP—and government *outlays* as measured by local, state, and federal budgets and reported in the media. What's the difference? In addition to their purchases of goods and services, government agencies also disburse money for **transfer payments.** These funds are *given* to people or organizations—*not* to buy goods or services from them, but rather to fulfill some social obligation or goal. For example, Social Security payments by the federal government, unemployment insurance and welfare payments by state governments, and money disbursed to homeless shelters and soup kitchens by city governments are all examples of transfer payments. They are not included in government purchases, because the government itself has not actually purchased any goods and services with these funds.

The important thing to remember about transfer payments is this:

> *Transfer payments represent money redistributed from one group of citizens (taxpayers) to another (the poor, the unemployed, the elderly). While transfers are included in government budgets as outlays, they are not included in the government purchases component of GDP.*

Net Exports

There is one more category of buyers of output produced in the United States: *the foreign sector.* Looking back at Table 2, the fourth column tells us that in 2005, purchasers *outside* the nation bought approximately $1,303 billion of U.S. goods and services—about 10 percent of our GDP. These exports are part of U.S. production of goods and services and so are included in GDP.

However, in recognizing dealings with the rest of the world, we must correct an inaccuracy in our measure of GDP the way we've reported it so far. Americans buy many goods and services every year that were produced *outside* the United States (Chinese shoes, Japanese cars, Mexican beer, Costa Rican coffee). When we add up the final purchases of households, businesses, and government agencies, we *overcount* U.S. production because we include goods and services produced abroad. But these are *not* part of U.S. output. To correct for this overcount, we deduct all U.S. *imports* during the year, leaving us with just the output produced in the United States. In 2005, these imports amounted to $2,019 billion, an amount equal to about 16 percent of our GDP.

Let's recap: To obtain an accurate measure of GDP, we must include U.S. production that is purchased by foreigners: total exports. But to correct for including goods produced abroad, we must subtract Americans' purchases of goods produced outside of the United States: total imports. In practice, we take both of these steps together by adding **net exports** (**NX**), which are total exports minus total imports.

Net exports (NX) Total exports minus total imports.

> *To properly account for output sold to, and bought from, foreigners, we must include net exports—the difference between exports and imports—as part of expenditure in GDP.*

In 2005, when total exports were $1,303 billion and total imports were $2,019 billion, net exports (as you can see in Table 2) were $1,303 - $2,019 = -$716 billion. The negative number indicates that the imports we're subtracting from GDP are greater than the exports we're adding.

OTHER APPROACHES TO GDP

In addition to the expenditure approach, in which we calculate GDP as $C + I + G + NX$, there are other ways of measuring GDP. You may be wondering: Why bother? Why not just use one method—whichever is best—and stick to it?

Actually, there are two good reasons for measuring GDP in different ways. The first is practical. Each method of measuring GDP is subject to measurement errors. By calculating total output in several different ways and then trying to resolve the differences, the BEA gets a more accurate measure than would be possible with one method alone.

The second reason is that the different ways of measuring total output give us different insights into the structure of our economy. Let's take a look at two more ways of measuring—and thinking about—GDP.

The Value-Added Approach

In the expenditure approach, we record goods and services only when they are sold to their final users—at the end of the production process. But we can also measure GDP by adding up each *firm's* contribution to the product *as it is produced*.

A firm's contribution to a product is called its *value added*. More formally,

Value added The revenue a firm receives minus the cost of the intermediate goods it buys.

> *a firm's **value added** is the revenue it receives for its output, minus the cost of all the intermediate goods that it buys.*

Look back at Figure 1, which traces the production of a ream of notebook paper. The paper mill, for example, buys $1.00 worth of wood chips (an intermediate good) from the lumber company. It turns wood chips into raw paper, which it sells for $1.50. The value added by the paper mill is $1.50 − $1.00 = $0.50. Similarly, the office supplies maker buys $1.50 worth of paper (an intermediate good) from the paper mill and sells it for $2.25. Its value added is $2.25 − $1.50 = $0.75. If we total the value added by each firm, we should get the final value of the notebook paper, as shown in Table 3. (Notice that we assume the first producer in this process—the lumber company—uses no intermediate goods.)

The total value added is $1.00 + $0.50 + $0.75 + $1.25 + $1.50 = $5.00, which is equal to the final sales price of the ream of paper. For any good or service, it will always be the case that the sum of the values added by all firms equals the final sales price. This leads to our second method of measuring GDP:

Value-added approach Measuring GDP by summing the values added by all firms in the economy.

> *In the **value-added approach**, GDP is the sum of the values added by all firms in the economy.*

The Factor Payments Approach

If a bakery sells $200,000 worth of bread during the year and buys $25,000 in intermediate goods (flour, eggs, yeast), then its value added is $200,000 − $25,000 = $175,000. This is also the sum that will be *left over* from its revenue after the bakery pays for its intermediate goods.

TABLE 3				
Value Added at Different Stages of Production	**Firm**	**Cost of Intermediate Goods**	**Revenue**	**Value Added**
	Lumber Company	$ 0	$1.00	$1.00
	Paper Mill	$1.00	$1.50	$0.50
	Office Supplies Manufacturer	$1.50	$2.25	$0.75
	Wholesaler	$2.25	$3.50	$1.25
	Retailer	$3.50	$5.00	$1.50
				Total: $5.00

Where does this $175,000 go? Since we've already deducted the payment for intermediate goods, the rest must go to pay for the *resources* used by the bakery during the year: the land, labor, capital, and entrepreneurship that it used to add value to its intermediate goods.

Payments to owners of resources are called **factor payments**, because resources are also called the factors of production. Owners of capital (such as those who lend funds to the firm so that *it* can buy its buildings and machinery) receive *interest payments*. Owners of land and natural resources receive *rent*. And those who provide labor to the firm receive *wages and salaries*.

Factor payments Payments to the owners of resources that are used in production.

Finally, there is one additional resource used by the firm: *entrepreneurship*. In every capitalist economy, the entrepreneurs are those who visualize society's needs, mobilize and coordinate the other resources so that production can take place, and gamble that the enterprise will succeed. The people who provide this entrepreneurship (often the owners of the firms) receive a fourth type of factor payment: *profit*.

Now let's go back to our bakery, which received $200,000 in revenue during the year. We've seen that $25,000 of this went to pay for intermediate goods, leaving $175,000 in value added earned by the factors of production. Let's suppose that $110,000 went to pay the wages of the bakery's employees, $10,000 was paid out as interest on loans, and $15,000 was paid in rent for the land under the bakery. That leaves $175,000 − $110,000 − $10,000 − $15,000 = $40,000. This last sum—since it doesn't go to anyone else—goes to the owners of the bakery. It, too, is a factor payment—profit—for the entrepreneurship they provide. Thus, when all of the factor payments, including profit, are added together, the total will be $110,000 + $10,000 + $15,000 + $40,000 = $175,000—precisely equal to the value added at the bakery. More generally,

in any year, the value added by a firm is equal to the total factor payments made by that firm.

Earlier, we learned that GDP equals the sum of all firms' value added; now we've learned that each firm's value added is equal to its factor payments. Thus, GDP must equal the total factor payments made by all firms in the economy. Since all of these factor payments are received by households in the form of wages and salaries, rent, interest, or profit, we have our *third* method of measuring GDP:

*In the **factor payments approach**, GDP is measured by adding up all of the income—wages and salaries, rent, interest, and profit—earned by all households in the economy.[2]*

Factor payments approach Measuring GDP by summing the factor payments earned by all households in the economy.

At first glance, the factor payments approach seems the same as the value-added approach. Each firm's value added is also its factor payments. But the difference is in the way the numbers are added up. In the value-added approach, we go firm by firm and add each one's value added. In the factor payments approach, we go household by household and add up the various types of factor payments earned by each one. Then we get subtotals for each type of factor payment—total wages and

---

[2] Actually, this is just an approximation. Before a firm pays its factors of production, it first deducts a small amount for depreciation of its plant and equipment, and another small amount for the sales taxes it must pay to the government. Thus, GDP and total factor payments are slightly different. We ignore this difference in the text.

salaries earned by all households, total interest, total rent, and total profit. Finally, we add these subtotals together to get total factor payments.

As stated earlier, having alternative methods to get GDP helps deal with measurement errors. But the factor payments approach, in particular, also gives us a key insight about the macroeconomy. On the one hand, total factor payments are just another way of measuring GDP. On the other hand, total factor payments are equal to total household income. Therefore,

> *the total output of the economy (GDP) is equal to the total income earned in the economy.*

This simple idea—output equals income—follows directly from the factor payments approach to GDP. It explains why macroeconomists use the terms *output* and *income* interchangeably: They are one and the same. If output rises, income rises by the same amount; if output falls, income falls by an equal amount. We'll be using this very important insight in several chapters to come.

MEASURING GDP: A SUMMARY

You've now learned three different ways to calculate GDP:

Expenditure Approach: GDP = C + I + G + NX

Value-Added Approach: GDP = Sum of value added by all firms

Factor Payments Approach: GDP = Sum of factor payments earned by all households

= Wages and salaries + interest

+ rent + profit

= Total household income

We will use these three approaches to GDP again and again as we study what makes the economy tick. But for now, make sure you understand why each one of them should, in theory, give us the same number for GDP.

REAL VERSUS NOMINAL GDP

Since GDP is measured in dollars, we have a serious problem when we want to track the change in output over time. The problem is that the value of the dollar—its purchasing power—is itself changing. As prices have risen over the years, the value of the dollar has steadily fallen. Trying to keep track of GDP using dollars in different years is like trying to keep track of a child's height using a ruler whose length changes each year. If we find that the child is three rulers tall in one year and four rulers tall in the next, we cannot know how much the child has grown, if at all, until we adjust for the effects of a changing ruler. The same is true for GDP and for any other economic variable measured in dollars: We usually need to adjust our measurements to reflect changes in the value of the dollar.

> *When a variable is measured in dollars, with no adjustment for the dollar's changing value, it is called a **nominal variable**. When a variable is adjusted for the dollar's changing value, it is called a **real variable**.*

Nominal variable A variable measured without adjustment for the dollar's changing value.

Real variable A variable adjusted for changes in the dollar's value.

Most government statistics are reported in both nominal and real terms, but economists focus almost exclusively on real variables. This is because changes in nominal variables don't really tell us much. For example, from the second to the third quarter of 2001 (not shown in earlier tables), nominal GDP increased from $10,050 billion to $10,098 billion, an increase of one-half of 1 percent. But production as measured by *real GDP* actually *decreased* over that period. The increase in nominal GDP was due entirely to a rise in prices. Real GDP corrects for this rise in prices by recognizing that the dollar's value (its purchasing power) declined, and by measuring production in adjusted dollars.

The distinction between nominal and real values is crucial in macroeconomics. The public, the media, and sometimes even government officials have been confused by a failure to make this distinction. Whenever we want to track significant changes in key macroeconomic variables—such as the average wage rate, wealth, income, and GDP or any of its components—we always use *real* variables.

> *When comparing variables measured in dollars over time, it is important to translate nominal values (which are measured in current dollars) to real values (which adjust for the dollar's changing value).*

In the next chapter, you'll learn how economists translate some important nominal variables into real variables.

How GDP Is Used

We've come a long way since 1931. In that year—as the United States plummeted into the worst depression in its history—Congress summoned economists from government agencies, from academia, and from the private sector to testify about the state of the economy. They were asked the most basic questions: How much output was the nation producing, and how much had production fallen since 1929? How much income were Americans earning, and how much were they spending? How much profit were businesses earning, and what were they doing with their profits? To the surprise of the members of Congress, no one could answer any of these questions, because *no one was keeping track of our national income and output!* The most recent measurement, which was rather incomplete, had been made in 1929.

Thus began the U.S. system of national income accounts, a system whose value was instantly recognized around the world and rapidly copied by other countries. Today, the government's reports on GDP are used to steer the economy over both the short run and the long run.

In the short run, sudden changes in real GDP can alert us to the onset of a recession or a too-rapid expansion that can overheat the economy. Many (but not all) economists believe that, if alerted in time, policies can be designed to help keep the economy on a more balanced course.

GDP is also used to measure the long-run growth rate of the economy's output. Indeed, we typically define the average *standard of living* as *output per capita*: real GDP divided by the population. In order for output per capita to rise, real GDP must grow faster than the population. Since the U.S. population tends to grow by

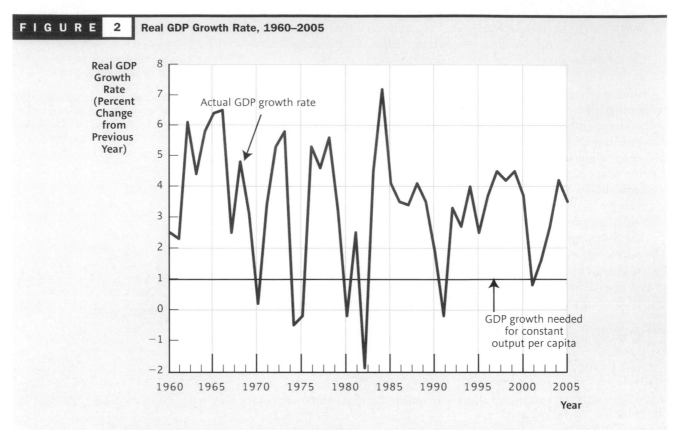

FIGURE 2 Real GDP Growth Rate, 1960–2005

Although the growth rate of real GDP has fluctuated over time, it has on average exceeded the 1 percent rate needed to maintain output per capita.

Source: Bureau of Economic Analysis, *National Economic Accounts*, Table 1.1.1.

about 1 percent per year, a real GDP growth rate of 1 percent per year is needed just to *maintain* our output per capita; higher growth rates are needed to increase it.

Look at Figure 2, which shows the annual percentage change in real GDP from 1960 through 2005. The lower horizontal line indicates the 1 percent growth needed to just maintain output per capita. You can see that, on average, real GDP has grown by more than this. This tells us that output per capita has steadily increased over time.

But growth in real GDP is also important for another reason: to ensure that the economy generates sufficient new *jobs* for a workforce that is not only growing in number, but also becoming more productive. Each year, the average worker is capable of producing more output, due to advances in technology, increases in the capital stock, and the greater skills of workers themselves. But if each worker can produce more output, then output must increase even *faster* than the population to create enough jobs for everyone who wants to work. If not, the unemployment rate will rise. For example, suppose that output per worker doubled over some period of time. If *total* output doubled as well, the number of *jobs* would remain constant. But unemployment would rise because the workforce would be growing, while the number of jobs would not.

Over the period shown in Figure 2, real GDP needed to grow by an average of about 3.3 percent per year to prevent the unemployment rate from rising. And although growth fluctuated widely, the average annual growth rate of the period was, in fact, about 3.3 percent. Most economists are confident that, over the long run, real GDP will rise fast enough to generate the jobs needed by a growing and more productive workforce, just as it has in the past. Later, you'll learn the reasons for this confidence.

To sum up: We use GDP to guide the economy in two ways. In the short run, it alerts us to recessions and give us a chance to stabilize the economy. And over long periods it tells us whether our economy is growing fast enough to raise output per capita and our standard of living, and fast enough to generate sufficient jobs for a growing population.

PROBLEMS WITH GDP

You have seen that GDP is an extremely useful concept. But the measurement of GDP is plagued by some serious problems.

Quality Changes

Suppose a new ballpoint pen comes out that lasts four times as long as previous versions. What *should* happen to GDP? Ideally, each new pen should count the same as four old pens, since one new pen offers the same *writing services* as four old ones. But the analysts at the Bureau of Economic Analysis would most likely treat this new pen the same as an old pen and record an increase in GDP only if the total number of pens increased. Why? Because the BEA has a limited budget. While it does include the impact of quality changes for many goods and services (such as automobiles and computers), the BEA simply does not have the resources to estimate quality changes for millions of different goods and services. These include many consumer goods (such as razor blades that shave closer and last longer), medical services (increased surgery success rates and shorter recovery periods), and retail services (faster checkout times due to optical scanners). Ignoring these quality improvements causes GDP to understate the true growth in output from year to year.

The Underground Economy

Some production is hidden from government authorities, either because it is illegal (drugs, prostitution, most gambling) or because those engaged in it are avoiding taxes. Production in these hidden markets, which comprise the *underground economy,* cannot be measured accurately, so the BEA must estimate it. Many economists believe that the BEA's estimates are too low. As a result, GDP may understate total output. However, because the *relative* importance of the underground economy does not change rapidly, the BEA's estimates of *changes* in GDP from year to year should not be seriously affected.

Nonmarket Production

With a few exceptions, GDP does not include **nonmarket production:** goods and services that are produced but not sold in the marketplace. All of the housecleaning, typing, sewing, lawn mowing, and child rearing that people do themselves, rather than hiring someone else, are excluded from GDP. Whenever a nonmarket transaction (say, cleaning your apartment) becomes a market transaction (hiring a housecleaner to do it for you), GDP will rise, even though total production (cleaning one apartment) has remained the same.

Nonmarket production Goods and services that are produced but not sold in a market.

Over the last half-century, much production has shifted away from the home and to the market. Parenting, which was not counted in past years' GDP, has become day care, which *does* count—currently contributing several billion dollars annually to GDP. Similarly, home-cooked food has been replaced by takeout, talking to a friend has been replaced by therapy, and the neighbor who watches your house while you're away has been replaced by a store-bought alarm system or an increase in police protection. In all of these cases, real GDP increases, even though production has not. This can exaggerate the growth in GDP over long periods of time.

Other Aspects of Economic Well-Being

Earlier we mentioned that output per capita (real GDP divided by the population) is often referred to as a country's standard of living. And for good reason: Our economic well-being depends to a large extent on the quantity of goods and services available per person. Food, clothing, transportation, and health care are all examples of things that contribute to our economic satisfaction, and all are included in our measure of GDP.

But output per capita is an imperfect measure of living standards. First, many things that contribute to our economic welfare are not captured by GDP at all: leisure time, an equitable distribution of income, a sense of community, and more. GDP also ignores economic "bads"—crime, pollution, traffic congestion, and more—which make us worse off.

Finally, GDP does not distinguish between production that makes us better off and production that only prevents us from becoming worse off. For example, every year hundreds of thousands of automobile accidents result in billions of dollars spent on car repair, medical expenses, insurance, and legal services—production that counts in GDP as much as any other production. But we'd be better off if the same total output of goods and services was devoted to doing things that we enjoy, rather than to coping with things that harm us.

USING GDP PROPERLY

The previous discussion suggests that, for certain purposes, GDP must be used with caution. One example is interpreting changes in GDP growth over the long run. Suppose, for example, that over the next 10 or 15 years, growth in real GDP per capita slows down a bit. It might mean that something is going wrong, and we should change course. But it *could* be partly a measurement problem: the underground economy or unrecorded quality changes may be becoming more important. Or it could be a willing tradeoff: less output growth in exchange for more leisure time. Similarly, if GDP growth gradually accelerates, it could mean faster growth in our economic welfare. But some of the improvement might come from economic activity shifting out of the home and into the market even more rapidly than in the past.

Caution is also required for some comparisons of economic well-being across countries. Everyone agrees that economic welfare is substantially greater in the United States than in Pakistan or Cambodia. Output per capita—which is almost 20 times greater in the United States—captures most of this difference.

But what about the United States versus, say, Germany? Output per capita is about 40 percent greater in the United States. But a greater fraction of Americans work, and the average American worker spends about 30 percent more hours on the job each year than the average German. So Americans have more goods, but Germans have more leisure. Who is economically better off? And by how much?

There is no objective answer, but using output per capita as the sole criterion would be misleading.

GDP works very well, however, as a guide to the short-run performance of the economy. Look back at the list of problems with GDP. The distortion in GDP measurement caused by each problem is likely to remain fairly constant from quarter to quarter. If GDP suddenly drops, it is extremely unlikely that the underground economy has suddenly become more important, or that there has been a sudden shift from market to nonmarket activities, or that we are suddenly missing more quality changes than usual. Rather, we can be reasonably certain that output and economic activity are slowing down.

> *Short-term changes in real GDP are fairly accurate reflections of the state of the economy. A significant quarter-to-quarter change in real GDP indicates a change in actual production, rather than a measurement problem.*

This is why policy makers, businesspeople, and the media pay such close attention to GDP as a guide to the economy from quarter to quarter.

EMPLOYMENT AND UNEMPLOYMENT

When you think of unemployment, you may have an image in your mind that goes something like this: As the economy slides into recession, an anxious employee is called into an office and handed a pink slip by a grim-faced manager. "Sorry," the manager says, "I wish there were some other way. . . ." The worker spends the next few months checking the classified ads, pounding the pavement, and sending out résumés in a desperate search for work. And perhaps, after months of trying, the laid-off worker gives up, spending days at the neighborhood bar, drinking away the shame and frustration, and sinking lower and lower into despair and inertia.

For some people, joblessness begins and ends very much like this—a human tragedy, and a needless one. On one side, we have people who want to work and support themselves by producing something; on the other side is the rest of society, which could certainly use more goods and services. Yet somehow, the system isn't working, and the jobless cannot find work. The result is often hardship for the unemployed and their families, and a loss to society in general.

But this is just one face of unemployment, and there are others. Some instances of unemployment, for example, have little to do with macroeconomic conditions. And frequently, unemployment causes a lot less suffering than in our grim story.

TYPES OF UNEMPLOYMENT

In the United States, people are considered unemployed if they are: (1) not working and (2) actively seeking a job. But unemployment can arise for a variety of reasons, each with its own policy implications. This is why economists have found it useful to classify unemployment into four different categories, each arising from a different cause and each having different consequences.

Frictional Unemployment

Short-term joblessness experienced by people who are between jobs or who are entering the labor market for the first time or after an absence is called **frictional**

Frictional unemployment
Joblessness experienced by people who are between jobs or who are just entering or reentering the labor market.

unemployment. In the real world, it takes time to find a job—time to prepare your résumé, to decide where to send it, to wait for responses, and then to investigate job offers so you can make a wise choice. It also takes time for different employers to consider your skills and qualifications and to decide whether you are right for their firms. If you are not working during that time, you will be unemployed: searching for work but not working.

Because frictional unemployment is, by definition, short term, it causes little hardship to those affected by it. In most cases, people have enough savings to support themselves through a short spell of joblessness, or else they can borrow on their credit cards or from friends or family to tide them over. Moreover, this kind of unemployment has important benefits: By spending time searching rather than jumping at the first opening that comes their way, people find jobs for which they are better suited and in which they will ultimately be more productive. As a result, workers earn higher incomes, firms have more productive employees, and society has more goods and services.

Seasonal Unemployment

Seasonal unemployment
Joblessness related to changes in weather, tourist patterns, or other seasonal factors.

Joblessness related to changes in weather, tourist patterns, or other seasonal factors is called **seasonal unemployment.** For example, most ski instructors lose their jobs every April or May, and many construction workers are laid off each winter.

Seasonal unemployment, like frictional unemployment, is rather benign: It is short term and, because it is entirely predictable, workers are often compensated in advance for the unemployment they experience in the off-season. Construction workers, for example, are paid higher-than-average hourly wages, in part to compensate them for their high probability of joblessness in the winter.

However, seasonal unemployment complicates the interpretation of unemployment data. Seasonal factors push the unemployment rate up in certain months of the year and pull it down in others, even when overall conditions in the economy remain unchanged. For example, each June, unemployment rises as millions of high school and college students—who do not want to work during the school year—begin looking for summer jobs. If the government reported the actual rise in unemployment in June, it would *seem* as if labor market conditions were deteriorating. In fact, the rise is just a predictable and temporary seasonal change. To prevent any misunderstandings, the government usually reports the *seasonally adjusted* rate of unemployment, a rate that reflects only those changes beyond normal for the month. For example, if the unemployment rate in June is typically one percentage point higher than during the rest of the year, then the seasonally adjusted rate for June will be the actual rate minus one percentage point.

Structural Unemployment

Sometimes, there are jobs available and workers who would be delighted to have them, but job seekers and employers are mismatched in some way. For example, in 2005, there were plenty of job openings for business professors; for nurses and nurse practitioners; for translators of strategic languages like Arabic, Persian, and Urdu; and in many other professions. Many of the unemployed, however, had been laid off from the airline, automobile, and textile industries and did not have the skills and training to work where the jobs were going begging. This is a *skill* mismatch.

The mismatch can also be *geographic,* as when construction jobs go begging in Northern California, Oregon, and Washington, but unemployed construction workers live in other states.

Unemployment that results from these kinds of mismatches is called **structural unemployment,** because it arises from *structural change* in the economy: when old, dying industries are replaced with new ones that require different skills and are located in different areas of the country. Structural unemployment is generally a stubborn, *long-term* problem, often lasting several years or more. Why? Because it can take considerable time for the structurally unemployed to find jobs—time to relocate to another part of the country or time to acquire new skills. To make matters worse, the structurally unemployed—who could benefit from financial assistance for job training or relocation—usually cannot get loans because they don't have jobs.

In recent decades, structural unemployment has been a much bigger problem in other countries, especially in Europe, than it is in the United States. Table 4 shows average unemployment rates in the United States and several European countries from 1995 to 2005 as well as in early 2006. Unemployment rates were consistently higher in continental Europe than in the United States during this decade and, in most of these countries, were still high in early 2006. And the unemployed remain jobless longer in Europe (where more than a third of all the unemployed have been so for more than a year) than in the United States (where only one in ten has been jobless for more than a year).

Within the United States, some areas have higher structural unemployment than others. For example, in early 2006 when the U.S. unemployment rate was 4.7 percent, the rate in Ohio was 5.5 percent; in South Carolina, 6.6 percent; and in Michigan, 7.2 percent.

The types of unemployment we've considered so far—frictional, structural, and seasonal—arise largely from *microeconomic* causes; that is, they are attributable to changes in specific industries and specific labor markets, rather than to the overall level of production in the country. This kind of unemployment cannot be entirely eliminated, as people will always spend some time searching for new jobs, there will always be seasonal industries in the economy, and structural changes will, from time to time, require workers to move to new locations or gain new job skills. Some amount of microeconomic unemployment is a sign of a dynamic economy. It allows

Structural unemployment
Joblessness arising from mismatches between workers' skills and employers' requirements or between workers' locations and employers' locations.

TABLE 4

Average Unemployment Rates in Several Countries, 1995–2005 and early 2006

Country	Average Unemployment Rate, 1995–2005	Unemployment Rate, early 2006
France	10.2 %	9.3 %
Italy	9.9 %	7.8 %
Canada	7.2 %	5.6 %
United Kingdom	6.2 %	5.2 %
Germany	8.9 %	8.8 %
Sweden	7.2 %	6.3 %
United States	5.2 %	4.7 %

Source: "Comparative Unemployment Rates in Nine Countries, 1995–2006," available online at Bureau of Labor Statistics, Foreign Labor Statistics page (*www.bls.gov/fls/home.htm*). European rates have been adjusted by the BLS for comparability to U.S. rates. Ten-year averages were calculated by authors from the BLS data. Early 2006 unemployment rates are for March 2006 except for Italy (4th quarter, 2005), the United Kingdom (February 2006), and Sweden (1st quarter, 2005).

workers to sort themselves into the best possible jobs, enables us to enjoy seasonal goods and services like winter skiing and summers at the beach, and permits the economy to go through structural changes when needed.

But frictional, structural, and seasonal unemployment rates are not fixed in stone, and government policy may be able to influence them. In the United States, many economists believe that we can continue to enjoy the benefits of a fast-changing and flexible economy with a lower unemployment rate. To achieve this goal, they advocate programs to help match the unemployed with employers and to help the jobless relocate and learn new skills.

In Europe, by contrast, most economists believe that government labor and regulatory policies have been a *cause* of the structural unemployment problem. For example, government regulations make it costly or impossible for many European firms to lay off workers once they are hired. That encourages firms to retain any *currently* employed workers. But it also discourages new hiring, because firms regard any newly hired worker as a permanent obligation, even if future production turns down and the new worker is no longer needed.

France, in particular, has been plagued by this problem. The unemployment rate among the young (under age 26) is 23 percent, and rises to around 40 percent in the mostly minority suburbs around Paris. In early 2006, the French government announced a new policy: For the first two years at a new job, young workers could be fired by their employers without the usual costly and time-consuming bureaucratic procedures. But when the proposal led to street riots in Paris, the government backed down.

European unemployment benefits may also play a role in high structural unemployment. Benefits in Europe are more generous than in the United States, and the benefits are given for longer durations with a greater fraction of the potential labor force eligible to receive them. While this certainly helps the unemployed deal with the hardship of job loss, it also means that European workers have less incentive to seek new work once they lose a job.

Note, however, that in both Europe and the United States, the proposed solutions for high seasonal, frictional, or structural unemployment are changes in labor or regulatory policies, rather than changes in macroeconomic policy.

Our fourth and last type of unemployment, however, has an entirely *macroeconomic* cause and requires macroeconomic solutions.

Cyclical Unemployment

Cyclical unemployment
Joblessness arising from changes in production over the business cycle.

When the economy goes into a recession and total output falls, the unemployment rate rises. Many previously employed workers lose their jobs and have difficulty finding new ones. At the same time, there are fewer openings, so new entrants to the labor force must spend more than the usual time searching before they are hired. This type of unemployment—because it is caused by the business cycle—is called **cyclical unemployment.**

Look at Figure 3, which shows the unemployment rate in the United States for each quarter from 1960 to mid-2006, and notice the rises that occurred during periods of recession (shaded). For example, in the recessions of the early 1980s, the unemployment rate rose from about 6 percent to more than 10 percent. And during the more recent recession from March to November of 2001, the unemployment rate rose from 4.2 percent to 5.6 percent. These were rises in cyclical unemployment.

Since it arises from conditions in the overall economy, cyclical unemployment is a problem for *macroeconomic* policy. This is why macroeconomists focus almost

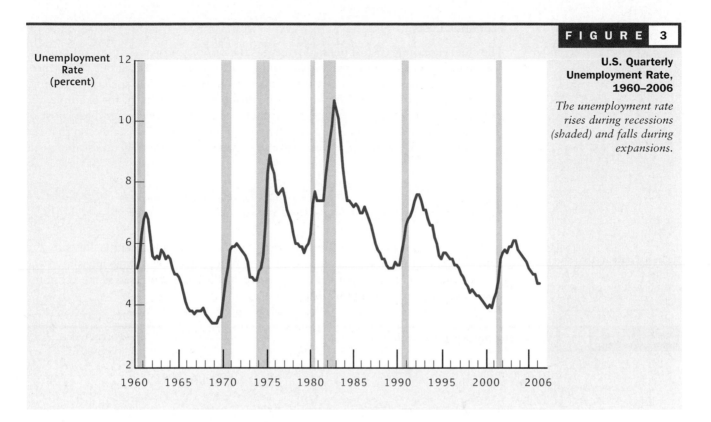

FIGURE 3

U.S. Quarterly Unemployment Rate, 1960–2006

The unemployment rate rises during recessions (shaded) and falls during expansions.

exclusively on cyclical unemployment, rather than the other types of joblessness. Reflecting this emphasis, macroeconomists say we have reached **full employment** when *cyclical unemployment is reduced to zero*, even though substantial amounts of frictional, seasonal, and structural unemployment may remain:

> *In macroeconomics, full employment means zero cyclical unemployment. But the overall unemployment rate at full employment is greater than zero because there are still positive levels of frictional, seasonal, and structural unemployment.*

How do we tell how much of our unemployment is cyclical? Many economists believe that today, normal amounts of frictional, seasonal, and structural unemployment account for an unemployment rate of between 4.5 and 5.0 percent in the United States. Therefore, any unemployment beyond this is considered cyclical unemployment. For example, when the actual unemployment rate was 5.6 percent in November 2001, we would say that 0.6 to 1.1 percent of the labor force was cyclically unemployed.

Full employment A situation in which there is no cyclical unemployment.

THE COSTS OF UNEMPLOYMENT

Why are we so concerned about achieving a low rate of unemployment? What are the *costs* of unemployment to our society? We can identify two different types of costs: economic costs (those that can be readily measured in dollar terms) and broader costs (which are difficult to measure in dollars, but still affect us in important ways).

Economic Costs

The chief economic cost of unemployment is the *opportunity cost* of lost output: the goods and services the jobless *would* produce if they were working but do not produce because they cannot find work. This cost is borne by our society in general, although the burden may fall more on one group than another. If, for example, the unemployed were simply left to fend for themselves, then *they* would bear most of the cost. In fact, the unemployed are often given government assistance, so that the costs are spread somewhat among citizens in general. But there is no escaping this central fact:

> *When there is cyclical unemployment, the nation produces less output, and therefore some group or groups within society must consume less output.*

Potential output The level of output the economy could produce if operating at full employment.

One way of viewing the economic cost of cyclical unemployment is illustrated in Figure 4. The green line shows real GDP over time, while the orange line shows the path of our **potential output**—the output we *could* have produced if the economy were operating at full employment.

FIGURE 4   **Actual and Potential Real GDP, 1960–2005**

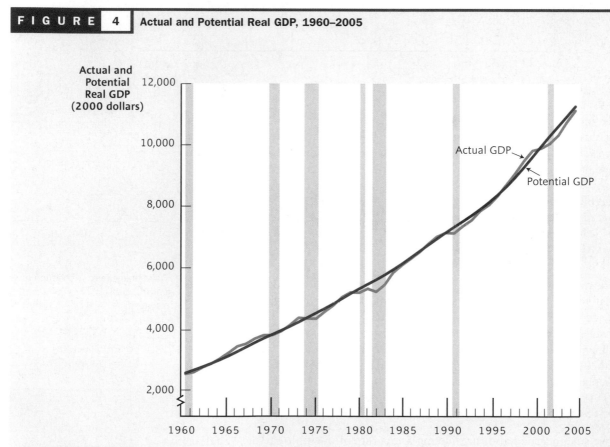

Actual and Potential Real GDP (2000 dollars)

Actual GDP

Potential GDP

Measured in 2000 dollars.

Sources: Real GDP from Bureau of Economic Analysis, "National Economic Accounts," Table 1.1.6 (*www.bea.gov*); Potential Real GDP from Congressional Budget Office, "Data Underlying Table 2-2: Key Assumptions in CBO's Projection of Potential Output" (By calendar year), The Budget and Economic Outlook: Fiscal Years 2006–2016, January 2006 (*www.cbo.gov*).

Notice that actual output is sometimes *above* potential output. At these times, unemployment is *below* the full-employment rate. For example, during the expansion in the late 1960s, cyclical unemployment was eliminated, and the sum of frictional, seasonal, and structural unemployment dropped below 4.5 percent, its normal level for those years. At other times, real GDP is *below* potential output, most often during and following a recession. At these times, unemployment rises above the full-employment rate. During the 2001 recession, the unemployment rate rose from 4.2 percent to 5.6 percent, then hovered near or above 6 percent for the next two years.

In the figure, you can see that we have spent more of the last 40 years operating *below* our potential than above it. That is, the cyclical ups and downs of the economy have, on balance, led to lower living standards than we would have had if the economy had always operated just at potential output.

Broader Costs

There are also costs of unemployment that go beyond lost output. Unemployment—especially when it lasts for many months or years—can have serious psychological and physical effects. Some studies have found that increases in unemployment cause noticeable rises in the number of heart attack deaths, suicides, and admissions to state prisons and psychiatric hospitals. The jobless are more likely to suffer a variety of health problems, including high blood pressure, heart disorders, troubled sleep, and back pain. There may be other problems—such as domestic violence, depression, and alcoholism—that are more difficult to document. And, tragically, most of those who lose their job and remain unemployed for long periods also lose their health insurance, increasing the likelihood that these problems will have serious consequences.

Unemployment also causes setbacks in achieving important social goals. For example, most of us want a fair and just society where all people have an equal chance to better themselves. But our citizens do not bear the burden of unemployment equally. In a recession, we do not all suffer a reduction in our work hours; instead, some people are laid off entirely, while others continue to work roughly the same hours.

Moreover, the burden of unemployment is not shared equally among different groups in the population, but tends to fall most heavily on minorities, especially minority youth. As a rough rule of thumb, the unemployment rate for blacks is twice that for whites; and the rate for *teenage* blacks is triple the rate for blacks overall. Table 5 shows that the unemployment rates for May 2006 are roughly consistent with this general experience. Notice the extremely high unemployment rate for black teenagers: 25 percent. This contributes to a vicious cycle of poverty and discrimination: When minority youths are deprived of that all-important first job, they remain at a disadvantage in the labor market for years to come.

HOW UNEMPLOYMENT IS MEASURED

In May 2006, about 155 million Americans were not employed, according to official government statistics. Were all of these people

TABLE 5

Unemployment Rates for Various Groups, May 2006

Group	Unemployment Rate
Whites	4.1%
Hispanics	5.0%
Blacks	8.9%
White Teenagers	12.7%
Black Teenagers	25.0%

Source: The Employment Situation: May 2006, Bureau of Labor Statistics (seasonally adjusted data).

unemployed? Absolutely not. In theory, the unemployed are those who are *willing and able* to work but do not have jobs. Most of the 155 million nonworking Americans were either *unable* or *unwilling* to work. For example, the very old, the very young, and the very ill were unable to work, as were those serving prison terms. Others were able to work, but preferred not to, including millions of college students, homemakers, and retired people. Still others were in the military and are counted in the population, but not counted when calculating civilian employment statistics.

But how, in practice, can we determine who is willing and able? This is a thorny problem, and there is no perfect solution to it. In the United States, we determine whether a person is willing and able to work by his or her *behavior*. More specifically, to be counted as unemployed, you must have recently *searched* for work. But how can we tell who has, and who has not, recently searched for work?

The Census Bureau's Household Survey

Every month, thousands of interviewers from the United States Census Bureau—acting on behalf of the U.S. Bureau of Labor Statistics—conduct a survey of 60,000 households across America. This sample of households is carefully selected to give information about the entire population. Household members who are under 16, in the military, or currently residing in an institution like a prison or hospital are excluded from the survey. The interviewer will then ask questions about the remaining household members' activities during the *previous week*.

Figure 5 shows roughly how this works. First, the interviewer asks whether the household member has worked one or more hours for pay or profit. If the answer is yes, the person is considered employed; if no, another question is asked: Has she been *temporarily* laid off from a job from which she is waiting to be recalled? A yes means the person is unemployed whether or not the person searched for a new job; a no leads to one more question: Did the person actively *search* for work during the previous four weeks. If yes, the person is unemployed; if no, she is not in the labor force.

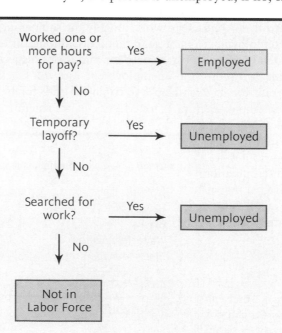

FIGURE 5

How the BLS Measures Employment Status

BLS interviewers ask a series of questions to determine whether an individual is employed, unemployed, or not in the labor force.

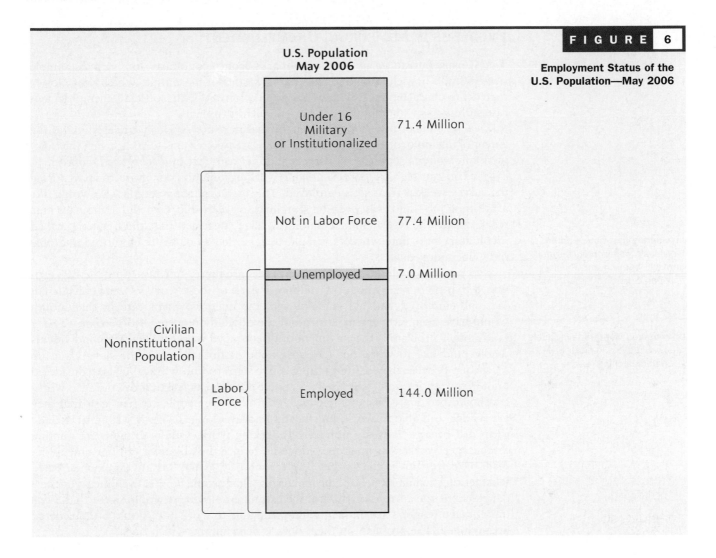

FIGURE 6

**Employment Status of the
U.S. Population—May 2006**

**U.S. Population
May 2006**

Under 16
Military
or Institutionalized — 71.4 Million

Not in Labor Force — 77.4 Million

Unemployed — 7.0 Million

Civilian
Noninstitutional
Population

Labor
Force

Employed — 144.0 Million

Figure 6 illustrates how the BLS, extrapolating from its 60,000-household sample, classified the U.S. population in May 2006. First, note that about 71 million people were ruled out from consideration because they were under 16 years of age, living in institutions, or in the military. The remaining 228 million people made up the civilian, noninstitutional population, and of these, 144.0 million were employed and 7.0 million were unemployed. Adding the employed and unemployed together gives us the **labor force**, equal to 144.0 million + 7.0 million = 151.0 million.

Finally, we come to the official **unemployment rate**, which is defined as the percentage of the labor force that is unemployed:

$$\text{Unemployment rate} = \frac{\text{Unemployed}}{\text{Labor force}} = \frac{\text{Unemployed}}{(\text{Unemployed} + \text{Employed})}$$

Using the numbers in Figure 6, the U.S. unemployment rate in May 2006 was calculated as 7.0/(7.0 + 144.0) = .046 or 4.6 percent. This was the number released to journalists at 8:00 A.M. on the first Friday of June 2006, and the number that made headlines in your local newspaper the next day.

Labor force Those people who have a job or who are looking for one.

Unemployment rate The fraction of the labor force that is without a job.

PROBLEMS IN MEASURING UNEMPLOYMENT

The Census Bureau earns very high marks from economists for both its sample size—60,000 households—and the characteristics of its sample, which very closely match the characteristics of the U.S. population. Still, the official unemployment rate suffers from some important measurement problems.

Many economists believe that our official measure seriously underestimates the extent of unemployment in our society. There are two reasons for this belief: the treatment of *involuntary part-time workers* and the treatment of *discouraged workers*.

As you can see in Figure 5, anyone working one hour or more for pay during the survey week is treated as employed. This includes many people who would like a full-time job—and may even be searching for one—but who did some part-time work during the week. Some economists have suggested that these people, called **involuntary part-time workers,** should be regarded as partially employed and partially unemployed.

How many involuntary part-time workers are there? In May 2006, the BLS estimated that there were about 4.0 million. If each of these workers were considered, say, half-employed and half-unemployed, the unemployment rate in that month would have been 6.0 percent, instead of the officially reported 4.6 percent.

Another problem is the treatment of **discouraged workers**. These are individuals who would like to work but feel little hope of finding a job and have given up searching. Because they are not taking active steps to find work, they are considered "not in the labor force" (see Figure 5). Some economists feel that discouraged workers should be counted as unemployed. After all, these people are telling us that they are willing and able to work, but they are not working. It seems wrong to exclude them just because they are not actively seeking work. Others argue that counting discouraged workers as unemployed would reduce the objectivity of our unemployment measure. Talk is cheap, they believe, and people may *say* anything when asked whether they would like a job; the real test is what people *do*. Yet even the staunchest defenders of the current method of measuring employment would agree that *some* discouraged workers are, in fact, willing and able to work and should be considered unemployed. The problem, in their view, is determining which ones.

How many discouraged workers are there? No one knows for sure. The BLS tries to count them, but defining who is genuinely discouraged is yet another thorny problem. Using the BLS's rather strict criteria, there were 323,000 discouraged workers in May 2006. But with a looser, unofficial definition of "discouraged worker"—people who are not working but say they want a job—the count rises to 5.2 million. Including some or all of these people among the unemployed could raise the unemployment rate significantly.

Still, the unemployment rate, as currently measured, tells us something important: the number of people who are *searching* for jobs, but have not yet found them. It is not exactly the same as the percentage of those willing and able to work that is jobless. But if we could obtain a perfect measure of the latter, the unemployment rate, as currently measured, would be highly correlated with it.

Moreover, the unemployment rate tells us something unique about conditions in the macroeconomy. When the unemployment rate is relatively low—so that few people are actively seeking work—a firm that wants to hire more workers may be forced to lure them from other firms, by offering a higher wage rate. This puts upward pressure on wages and can lead to future inflation. A high unemployment rate, by contrast, tells us that firms can more easily expand by hiring those who are

Involuntary part-time workers Individuals who would like a full-time job, but who are working only part time.

Discouraged workers Individuals who would like a job, but have given up searching for one.

actively seeking work, without having to lure new workers from another firm and without having to offer higher wages. This suggests little inflationary danger. Later in the book, we will discuss the connection between unemployment and inflation more fully.

USING THE THEORY

© 2005 GETTY IMAGES

SUDDEN DISASTERS AND GDP

People are sometimes surprised that some horrific national disasters—man-made and natural—have had relatively little impact on U.S. GDP. Such events may cause thousands of deaths, devastate a city or region, disrupt economic activity on a wide scale, and hold the national attention for months. Yet when we look back at the behavior of the nation's real GDP, the effects are almost imperceptible.

For example, look at Figure 7, which shows quarterly GDP from 1998 through early 2006. Two major disasters occurred within this period. The first was the terrorist attack of September 2001, which killed more than 3,000 people, destroyed one of the largest office complexes in the United States, and led to major disruptions of production in lower Manhattan for weeks. If you search for the impact in Figure 7, you may think you've found it in the widening gap between actual and potential real GDP around that time. But look closely: GDP began to flatten in mid-2000, more than a year *before* the attack, due to a slowdown from other causes. Even though the attack no doubt worsened and prolonged that slowdown, a separate impact on production is hardly discernible.

Now consider Hurricanes Katrina and Rita, which hit the Gulf Coast in August and September of 2005. The hurricanes devastated huge areas of Louisiana and Mississippi, destroyed hundreds of thousands of homes, and left most of the city of New Orleans uninhabitable for months. About 250,000 people in the area lost their jobs—many of them for a few months or longer. But once again, the impact on GDP appears to be slight: a barely noticeable slowdown in growth from the third to the fourth quarter of 2005, and then the effect seems to disappear. And if you look for an effect on *yearly* GDP in Figure 4, it is not apparent at all.

Why is GDP so stubbornly unmoved by such cataclysmic events? Disasters such as the terrorist attack of 2001 or the hurricanes of 2005 generally have two types of effects on real GDP. One is the *direct* impact of the event itself. The other is the *indirect* effects that follow as economic decision makers respond to the event. Let's consider each of these types of effects in turn for the hurricanes of 2005.

DIRECT EFFECTS: DESTRUCTION AND DISRUPTION

Table 6 shows a range of estimates for the physical destruction caused by Hurricanes Katrina and Rita in 2005. The total loss—between $69 billion and $130 billion—included about 287,000 homes destroyed or damaged (about half of them in New Orleans), as well as severe damage to oil and natural gas platforms and pipelines. Even though much of this property destruction was insured, the insurance merely redistributes the financial burden; it does not affect the total value of the loss.

FIGURE 7

Quarterly GDP During Two Recent Disasters

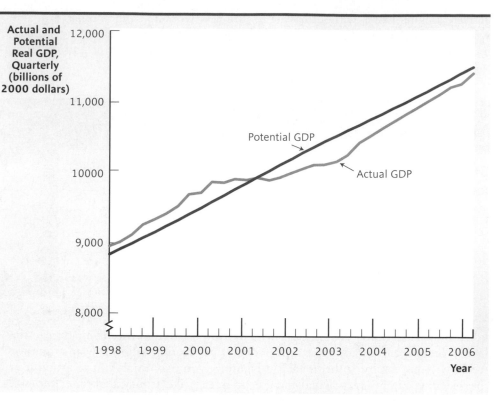

TABLE 6

Property Destruction from Hurricanes Katrina and Rita, 2005

Type of Property	Estimated Loss
Residential housing	$17 billion to $33 billion
Consumer durables (autos, furniture, appliances)	$5 billion to $9 billion
Energy infrastructure	$18 billion to $31 billion
Nonenergy business property	$16 billion to $32 billion
Public infrastructure	$13 billion to $25 billion
Total	**$69 billion to $130 billion**

Source: Based on Douglas Holtz-Eakin, "The Macroeconomic and Budgetary Effects of Hurricanes Katrina and Rita," *CBO Testimony before the Committee on the Budget, U.S. House of Representatives,* October 6, 2005.

How does all this destruction affect GDP? Not nearly as much as you might think. A disaster destroys part of the nation's *capital stock*. But remember that GDP does *not* measure the resources at our disposal, but rather the production we get *from* those resources.[3] The impact on GDP is therefore limited to the loss of output that the destroyed resources would otherwise have enabled us to produce. Destroyed

---

[3] Destruction of capital does, however, directly affect *net national product*, which is defined as GDP minus depreciation of the capital stock during the period. Destruction of capital from a disaster is considered depreciation, and is therefore deducted when calculating net national product.

factory buildings, oil rigs, and office buildings mean less production of manufactured goods, energy, and services. And every destroyed home is one that is no longer producing housing services (which are also part of GDP). This is how physical destruction has a direct impact on GDP.

How much *production* did we lose from the loss of these resources? Table 7 shows how the U.S. Congressional Budget Office (CBO) answered this question. The first three rows of numbers refer to the direct impact of the destruction and disruption of economic activity from the hurricanes. Notice that the CBO uses the value-added approach to estimate this impact. That is, the effects on GDP are categorized by the sector that produces it—energy, agricultural, or housing services—rather than by the final user that buys the production. This is for practical reasons. When productive capital is destroyed, it is easier to identify the decrease in production at its source. For example, after the destruction of energy infrastructure, it is relatively easy to estimate the total decrease in energy production (value added by the oil and gas industries). It would be much more difficult to determine which final users would have bought goods and services produced with this energy (consumers, businesses, government, or foreigners).

If you subtotal the decrease in value added by these three sectors for the second half of 2005, you'll find that the direct impact of the hurricanes was a decrease in production of between $20 billion and $32 billion.[4] While this is a large number, it is very small compared to the size of the economy. In the second half of 2005, GDP was running at an annual rate of $12.6 trillion. Thus, the direct impact on production was at most 0.25 percent (a quarter of 1 percent) of GDP during that period.[5]

	Second Half, 2005	First Half, 2006	Second Half, 2006	
				TABLE 7
Direct effects				**Estimated and Projected Effects of Hurricanes Katrina and Rita on GDP (billions of 2005 dollars at annual rates)**
Energy production	−18 to −28	−8 to −10	−5 to −7	
Housing services	−1 to −2	−2 to −4	−1 to −3	
Agricultural production	−1 to −2	0	0	
Indirect effects				
Reduced consumption spending (beyond direct effects)	−14 to −22	−7 to −11	−3 to −8	
Replacement investment	+6 to +12	+16 to +34	+16 to +35	
Increased government spending on goods and services	+6 to +10	+12 to +18	+14 to +20	
Total impact on real GDP	**−22 to −32**	**+11 to +27**	**+21 to +37**	

Source: Based on Douglas Holtz-Eakin, "The Macroeconomic and Budgetary Effects of Hurricanes Katrina and Rita," *CBO Testimony before the Committee on the Budget, U.S. House of Representatives*, October 6, 2005.

[4] Remember that GDP figures for periods shorter than a year are always reported at an annual rate—how much the production *would* be if it continued at that rate for a year. So the actual direct loss in production for the second half of 2005 was between $10 billion and $16 billion.

[5] Another way to understand why the effect is relatively small is to compare the total destruction of capital in Table 6—$69 billion to $130 billion—to the nation's total physical capital stock in 2005, which was $38 trillion. Thus, the hurricanes destroyed at most 0.34 percent of the nation's capital.

INDIRECT EFFECTS: GOVERNMENT AND PRIVATE RESPONSES

We've seen that the direct effect of the hurricanes on GDP was relatively small. (And the direct effects of September 11 were even smaller.) But what about the indirect effects—those that result from decisions made afterward? These have the *potential* to be more harmful and long-lasting. But in fact, any indirect decreases in production are usually smaller than the direct decrease—and very short-lived. One reason is changes in macroeconomic policy that are designed to counteract the decrease in production. (You will learn about these efforts and how they work in subsequent chapters.) But another reason is that the indirect effects themselves work in both directions: Some tend to decrease production, while others work to increase it. Within a short time, the forces that increase production come to dominate.

The indirect effects of the hurricanes are reported in the second three rows of numbers in Table 7. Notice that these effects are estimated using the expenditure approach to GDP. This too is for practical reasons. The indirect effects come from decisions about *spending* by different sectors of the economy—households, businesses, and government agencies. Thus, the effects are most easily estimated by looking at each type of final user whose spending is likely to change.

Of the three indirect effects, only one is negative: the decrease in consumption spending. For the hurricanes, this decrease came about for two reasons. First (as happens in *any* regional disaster), those who lived in the affected region and lost jobs and property saw significant reductions in their income and wealth. As a result, they reduced their spending on goods and services produced by firms across the country. These firms responded by producing less.

But there was also a special impact on consumption, because the hurricanes knocked out large chunks of the nation's energy infrastructure, including pipelines and refineries. This caused a spike in energy prices—for gasoline, natural gas, and electricity. Nationwide, as consumers spent more on energy-related products, they cut back on their purchases of other goods and services.

Working against these negative effects was spending to rebuild and repair damage, and government purchases of food, housing, and medical care to distribute to those in need. If you subtotal the effects of these spending changes, you'll see that even in the second half of 2005, the net impact was only slightly negative. By the first half of 2006, the impact turns positive.

THE TOTAL IMPACT ON GDP

The last row of Table 7 traces the total impact of the hurricanes on GDP over time. In the second half of 2005, the direct impact of the destruction and the further decrease in consumption spending dominate. But notice that even in this early period, they are substantially mitigated by the positive effects of reconstruction and government assistance. The total impact in the second half of 2005 is a reduction in the annual rate of GDP by $22 billion to $32 billion—a reduction of 0.25 percent.

But by the first half of 2006, the impact of the hurricanes on GDP turns *positive* and remains positive for the second half as well. That is, production is greater throughout 2006 than it would have been if there had been no hurricane. As you can see, this happens because the negative effects on production gradually weaken, while the positive effects of replacement investment and government assistance gradually grow and ultimately dominate.

DRAWING CONCLUSIONS

One conclusion we can draw from this analysis is that *local* disasters generally have relatively small effects on the nation's GDP. This is especially true when the locality affected produces only a small fraction of the country's total output. In the case of the hurricanes, Louisiana and Mississippi—the two states most affected—together produce only about 2 percent of the nation's GDP. And Manhattan—the area most profoundly affected by the attacks of September 11—produces about 1.5 percent of our GDP.[6] And although the response of consumers can cause further decreases in production, the need to replace destroyed capital and government assistance help to counter these effects.

However, there are two mistakes to avoid in analyzing the economic impacts of disasters. One mistake is to think that, because a disaster actually increases production (as it did in 2006), we end up economically better off for it. Actually, we do not. Aside from the human tragedy of lives lost and communities destroyed, we must remember that much of the additional production after a disaster is used to bring our capital stock back to where it was beforehand. Although the disaster causes us to produce more, it does not enable us to *enjoy* more goods and services than we would if the disaster had not occurred. This is one of those cases we discussed in the chapter, in which GDP—which measures only production, rather than its purpose— provides an imperfect measure of economic well-being.

The second mistake is to extrapolate too broadly from past disasters to future ones. The direct effects of recent disasters—such as the attack of 2001 or the hurricanes of 2005—affected specific cities or a region of the country, leaving the rest unaffected. But disasters can occur on a larger scale. A flu pandemic, for example, would impact the entire country within a short period of time, creating a human tragedy of larger magnitude than any of our recent disasters. The purely economic effect would be much greater as well. The Congressional Budget Office has estimated that even a mild pandemic would reduce real GDP by about 1.5 percent. And a more serious pandemic caused by a more virulent strain of flu virus could reduce real GDP by as much as 5 percent—an impact 20 times greater than that of the hurricanes of 2005.[7]

---

[6] This assumes that Manhattan's share of GDP is equal to its share of personal income, as estimated by the Bureau of Economic Analysis.

[7] *A Potential Influenza Pandemic: An Update on Possible Macroeconomic Effects and Policy Issues*, Congressional Budget Office, May 22, 2006.

Summary

This chapter discusses how two key macroeconomic aggregates are measured and reported. One is *gross domestic product*—the total value of all final goods and services produced for the marketplace during a given period, within a nation's borders. GDP is a measure of an economy's total production.

In the *expenditure approach*, GDP is calculated as the sum of spending by households, businesses, government agencies, and foreigners on domestically produced goods and services. The *value-added approach* computes GDP by adding up each firm's contributions to the total product as it is being produced. Value added at each stage of production is the revenue a firm receives minus the cost of the intermediate inputs it uses. The *factor payments approach* sums the wages and salaries, rent, interest, and profit earned by all households. The three approaches reflect three different ways of viewing and measuring GDP.

Since nominal GDP is measured in current dollars, it changes when either production or prices change. *Real GDP* is nominal GDP adjusted for price changes; it rises only when production rises.

Real GDP is most useful in the short run, for giving warnings about impending recessions. For other uses, it is plagued by important inaccuracies. It does not fully reflect quality changes or production in the underground economy, and it does not include many types of nonmarket production. GDP is only a very rough measure of economic welfare because it excludes many aspects of the economy that add to or detract from economic well-being.

When real GDP grows, employment tends to rise and—if real GDP grows fast enough—the unemployment rate falls. In the United States, a person is considered unemployed if he or she does not have a job but is actively seeking one. Economists have found it useful to classify unemployment into four different categories. *Frictional unemployment* is short-term unemployment experienced by people between jobs or by those who are just entering the job market. *Seasonal unemployment* is related to changes in the weather, tourist patterns, or other predictable seasonal changes. *Structural unemployment* results from mismatches, in skills or location, between jobs and workers. Finally, *cyclical unemployment* occurs because of the business cycle. Seasonal and frictional unemployment can be beneficial to the economy. Structural and cyclical unemployment, however, create harm to the individuals involved, and the economy as a whole suffers the loss of output that the unemployed could have produced. From a macroeconomic perspective, we say the economy is at *full employment* when there is no cyclical unemployment, even though normal amounts of frictional, seasonal, and structural unemployment remain.

Problem Set   *Answers to even-numbered Questions and Problems can be found on the text Web site at www.thomsonedu.com/economics/hall.*

1. Using the expenditure approach, which of the following would be directly counted as part of U.S. GDP? For those that count, state whether the action causes an increase in *C*, *I*, *G*, or *NX*. (If you need to make any special assumptions, state them.)
   a. A new personal computer produced by IBM, which remained unsold at the year's end
   b. A physician's services to a household
   c. Produce bought by a restaurant to serve to customers
   d. The purchase of 1,000 shares of Disney stock
   e. The sale of 50 acres of commercial property
   f. A real estate agent's commission from the sale of property
   g. A transaction in which you clean your roommate's apartment in exchange for his working on your car
   h. An Apple iMac computer produced in the United States and purchased by a French citizen
   i. The government's Social Security payments to retired people

2. Calculate the total change in a year's GDP for each of the following scenarios:
   a. A family sells a home, without using a broker, for $150,000. They could have rented it on the open market for $700 per month. They buy a 10-year-old condominium for $200,000; the broker's fee on the transaction is 6 percent of the selling price. The condo's owner was formerly renting the unit at $500 per month.
   b. General Electric uses $10 million worth of steel, glass, and plastic to produce its dishwashers. Wages and salaries in the dishwasher division are $40 million; the division's only other expense is $15 million in interest that it pays on its bonds. The division's revenue for the year is $75 million.
   c. On March 31, you decide to stop throwing away $50 a month on convenience store nachos. You buy $200 worth of equipment, cornmeal, and cheese and make your own nachos for the rest of the year.
   d. You win $25,000 in your state's lottery. Ever the entrepreneur, you decide to open a Ping-Pong ball washing service, buying $15,000 worth of equipment from SpiffyBall Ltd. of Hong Kong and $10,000 from Ball-B-Kleen of Toledo, Ohio.
   e. Tone-Deaf Artists, Inc., produces 100,000 new CDs that it prices at $15 apiece. Ten thousand CDs are sold abroad, but, alas, the rest remain unsold on warehouse shelves.

3. The country of Freedonia uses the same method to calculate the unemployment rate as the U.S. Bureau of Labor Statistics uses. From the following data, compute Freedonia's unemployment rate.

Population	10,000,000
Under 16	3,000,000
Over 16	
In military service	500,000
In hospitals	200,000
In prison	100,000
Worked one hour or more in previous week	4,000,000
Searched for work during previous four weeks	1,000,000

4. Toward the end of this chapter, it was stated that if half of the 4.0 million involuntary part-time workers in May 2006 were counted as unemployed, then the unemployment rate that month would have been 6.0 percent instead of 4.6 percent. Do the necessary calculations to confirm this statement, using the information in Figure 6. (Hint: The labor force will not be affected.)

5. In December 2005, the BLS estimated there were 7.4 million unemployed, 142.8 million employed, 451,000 discouraged workers, and 4.8 million people (including discouraged workers) who were not working but said they wanted a job. What would the unemployment rate have been in December 2005 if it had included among the unemployed:
   a. All officially discouraged workers?
   b. All those who were not working but said they wanted a job? (Hint: Don't forget about how these inclusions would affect the labor force.)

6. Ginny asks, "If I buy a sweater that was produced in Malaysia, why is its purchase price subtracted from GDP?" How should you answer her question? (You may assume, for simplicity, that there was no value added to the sweater in the United States.)

7. Suppose that in one year household consumption falls by $20 billion (compared to the year before), but business firms continue to produce consumer goods at an unchanged rate. If there is no other change affecting real GDP that year, what will happen to total real GDP? What will happen to each of its components?

8. a. The country of Ziponia uses the same method to calculate the unemployment rate as the U.S. Bureau of Labor Statistics uses. From the data below, compute Ziponia's unemployment rate.

Population	60,000
Under 16	9,000
Over 16	
In military service	600
In hospitals	60
In prison	200
Worked one hour or more in previous week	46,000
Searched for work during previous four weeks	2,140
Did not work in previous week but would have taken a job if one were offered	200

b. How large is Ziponia's labor force?
c. How many discouraged workers (loosely defined) live in Ziponia?
d. Not all of Ziponia's citizens are accounted for in part (a). How are the missing citizens classified? Give some examples of what they may be doing.
e. How many of Ziponia's citizens are not in the labor force?

9. Refer to question 8. The 2,140 Ziponians who searched for work during the previous four weeks included: 54 ski resort employees who lost their winter jobs but expect to get them back in late fall; 200 recent high school graduates; 258 former textile workers who lost their jobs when their employers moved their operations overseas; 143 mothers and 19 fathers who had stayed at home to raise their children but who recently decided to reenter the work force; 394 high school and college students who want summer jobs; 127 people who live in West Ziponia and lost their jobs when their employers moved operations to East Ziponia, but who are not qualified for the remaining jobs in the west; 110 recent college graduates; and 32 retirees who decided to return to the workforce. The remaining job seekers lost their jobs due to a recession. Use this information to:
   a. Classify the job seekers by their type of unemployment, and calculate how many fell into each category.
   b. Find the frictional, seasonal, structural, and cyclical unemployment rates.

10. The following table shows an estimate of the destruction caused by the terrorist attacks of September 11:

Type of Property	Estimated Loss
World Trade Center Complex buildings	$ 6.7 billion
Contents of Buildings in World Trade Center Complex	$ 5.2 billion
Buildings nearby	$ 4.5 billion
Public infrastructure (subway, commuter rail, and utilities)	$ 3.7 billion
Total	**$20.1 billion**

Source: Modified from Jason Bram, James Orr, and Carol Rapaport, "Measuring the Effects of the September 11 Attack on New York City," *Federal Reserve Bank of New York Policy Review*, November 2002.

Use the following two facts (from the Bureau of Economic Analysis) as needed to answer the questions below:
   Fact #1: GDP in 2001 was $10 trillion.
   Fact #2: Manhattan produces 1.5 percent of the nation's GDP.
   a. Assume that each dollar of destroyed property reduces annual production by 10 cents (a rough estimate of the general impact of capital destruction on GDP), and that none of the destroyed property was replaced over the next 12 months. Estimate the percentage impact on

GDP during the 12 months after the attacks due to the physical destruction alone.

b. Suppose that, in addition to the property destruction, the attack created disruption of economic activity, and that Manhattan's production was cut in half for 2 weeks. Estimate the percentage impact on GDP for the *quarter* due to this disruption alone.

c. Again, suppose Manhattan's production was cut in half for 2 weeks. Estimate the percentage impact on GDP for the *year* due to this disruption alone.

More Challenging

11. Suppose, in a given year, someone buys a General Motors automobile for $30,000. That same year, GM produced the car in Michigan, using $10,000 in parts imported from Japan. However, the parts imported from Japan themselves contained $3,000 in components produced in the United States.

a. By how much does U.S. GDP rise?

b. Using the expenditure approach, what is the change in each component (*C, I, G,* and *NX*) of U.S. GDP?

c. What is the change in Japan's GDP and each of its components?

12. After the attacks of September 11, 2001, U.S. businesses began to spend more on security, and continue to do so today. For example, airlines and package delivery services run more background checks on their employees, and office buildings hire more security guards than they did before the attack. What impact have these decisions had on real GDP? (Hint: Is the new spending considered to be purchases of final goods?)

The Price Level and Inflation

About a hundred years ago, you could buy a pound of coffee for 15 cents, see a Broadway play for 40 cents, buy a new suit for $6, and attend a private college for $200 in yearly tuition.[1] Needless to say, the price of each of these items has gone up considerably since then. Microeconomic causes—changes in individual markets—can explain only a tiny fraction of these price changes. For the most part, these price rises came about because of a continually rising **price level**—the average level of prices in the economy.

When the price level rises, the value of the dollar—its purchasing power—falls. And this presents a problem. We measure many economic variables—such as income, production, or the wage rate—in dollars. But over time, how can we keep track of them when our unit of measurement—the dollar—has a changing value? It would be like trying to monitor a child's height over the years with a yardstick whose length changes every year. To make sensible comparisons of variables measured in dollars, we must know how the dollar's purchasing power changes from period to period. And this requires us to know how the price level is changing.

In this chapter, we'll discuss how the price level and its rate of change are measured, and some of the difficulties and controversies involved. We'll postpone until later chapters the question of *why* prices change from year to year.

Price level The average level of prices in the economy.

MEASURING THE PRICE LEVEL AND INFLATION

Economists use several different measures of the price level, depending on their purpose. But all of them have one thing in common: They are all calculated and reported as *index numbers*. Because index numbers have some special features, it's worth discussing them more generally before we look specifically at price indexes.

INDEX NUMBERS IN GENERAL

Most measures of the price level are reported in the form of an **index**—a series of numbers, each one representing a different period. Index numbers are meaningful only in a *relative* sense: We compare one period's index number with that of another period and can quickly see which one is larger and by what percentage. But the actual value of an index number for a particular period has no meaning in and of itself.

Index A series of numbers used to track a variable's rise or fall over time.

---

[1] Scott Derks, ed., *The Value of the Dollar: Prices and Incomes in the United States: 1860–1989* (Detroit, MI: Gale Research Inc., 1994), various pages.

In general, an index number for any measure is calculated as

$$\frac{\text{Value of measure in current period}}{\text{Value of measure in base period}} \times 100.$$

Let's see how index numbers work with a simple example. Suppose we want to measure how violence on TV has changed over time, and we have data on the number of violent acts shown in each of several years. We could then construct a TV-violence index. Our first step would be to choose a *base period*—a period to be used as a benchmark. Let's choose 2000 as our base period, and suppose that there were 10,433 violent acts on television in that year. Then our violence index in any current year would be calculated as

$$\frac{\text{Number of violent acts in current year}}{10,433} \times 100.$$

In 2000, the base year, the index will have the value $(10,433/10,433) \times 100 = 100$. Look again at the general formula for index numbers, and you will see that this is always true: *An index will always equal 100 in the base period.*

Now let's calculate the value of our index in another year. If there were 14,534 violent acts in 2005, then the index that year would have the value

$$\frac{14,534}{10,433} \times 100 = 139.3.$$

Index numbers compress and simplify information so that we can see how things are changing at a glance. Our media violence index, for example, tells us at a glance that the number of violent acts in 2005 was 139.3 percent of the number in 2000. Or, more simply, TV violence grew by 39.3 percent between 2000 and 2005.

THE CONSUMER PRICE INDEX

Consumer Price Index An index of the cost, through time, of a fixed market basket of goods purchased by a typical household in some base period.

The most widely used measure of the price level in the United States is the **Consumer Price Index (CPI)**. This index, which is designed to track the prices paid by the typical consumer, is compiled and reported by the Bureau of Labor Statistics.

Measuring the prices paid by the typical consumer is not easy. The BLS must solve a number of conceptual problems before it begins (such as deciding which items to include and what weight to give to each item). Then there are a host of practical problems. Let's discuss how all these problems are dealt with in the CPI.

Which Items to Include?

The goal of the CPI is to track the prices paid by *consumers*, and no one else. So, as a start, the CPI includes the part of GDP that consumers purchase as final users (new clothes, new furniture, new cars, haircuts, or restaurant meals). But it also includes two types of goods and services that consumers buy, even though they are *not* part of GDP: (1) household purchases of used goods such as used cars or used computers and (2) household purchases of imports from other countries—French cheese, Japanese cars, and Mexican tomatoes.

The CPI does *not* include goods and services purchased by anyone other than consumers. It leaves out purchases by businesses (for capital equipment, raw materials, or wholesale goods). It leaves out goods and services purchased by government agencies (military equipment and the services of police officers and public school teachers). And it leaves out goods and services that are purchased by foreigners (U.S. exports).

Finally, remember that the CPI tracks the prices of goods and services only. Consumers also buy assets, such as stocks, bonds, and homes. The prices paid for these assets are *not* included in the CPI. For housing, the CPI (like GDP) includes the price of housing *services* rather than the value of the home or apartment itself. So for rental units, the CPI tracks the average rent people pay; for owner-occupied units, the CPI uses the rent that owners *would* pay if they had to rent their homes instead of owning them.

How Much Weight for Each Item?

In any given month, different prices will change by different amounts. The average price of doctors' visits might rise by 1 percent, the price of blue jeans might rise by a tenth of a percent, the price of milk might fall by half a percent, and so on. When prices change at different rates, and when some are rising while others are falling, how can we track the change in the *average* price level? It would be a mistake to use a simple average of all prices, adding them up and dividing by the number of goods. A proper measure must recognize that we spend very little of our incomes on some goods—such as Tabasco sauce—and much more on others—like gasoline or rent.

The CPI's approach is to track the cost of the *CPI market basket*—the collection of goods and services that the typical consumer buys. If the market basket's cost rises by 10 percent over some period, then the price level, as reported by the CPI, will rise by 10 percent. This way, goods and services that are relatively unimportant in the typical consumer's budget will have little weight in the CPI. Tabasco sauce could triple in price and have no noticeable impact on the cost of the complete market basket. Goods that are more important—such as gas or rent—will have more weight.

To determine the CPI market basket, the BLS surveys thousands of families every couple of years, and records their spending in detail. It uses these spending patterns to construct a market basket containing thousands of different goods and services, with each one weighted according to its relative importance in the average family's budget.[2]

Figure 1 shows the broadest categories of the CPI market basket, and the proportion of total spending on each one in December 2005. For example, all the items in the category "food and beverages" together made up 15.0 percent of the typical consumer's spending, while all of the items included in "housing" amounted to 42.4 percent. The communication category—amounting to 3.1 percent—includes phone and Internet service, as well as computer hardware and software.

Tracking and Reporting the Price Level

Each month, hundreds of BLS employees visit thousands of stores, gas stations, medical offices, and apartments across the country. Their job is to record the prices of specific goods and services in the market basket—about 80,000 price quotes in all. All this information is fed into a central database, and used to determine the new cost of the CPI market basket for that month.

---

[2] More specifically, the Bureau of Labor Statistics compiles two different types of market baskets to reflect the spending habits of two different types of people: (1) "All Urban Workers," resulting in the CPI-U; and (2) "Urban Wage Earners and Clerical Workers," resulting in the CPI-W. The CPI-U is the index most commonly reported and followed in the media, and it is used throughout this chapter.

FIGURE 1

Broad Categories and Relative Importance in the CPI, December 2005

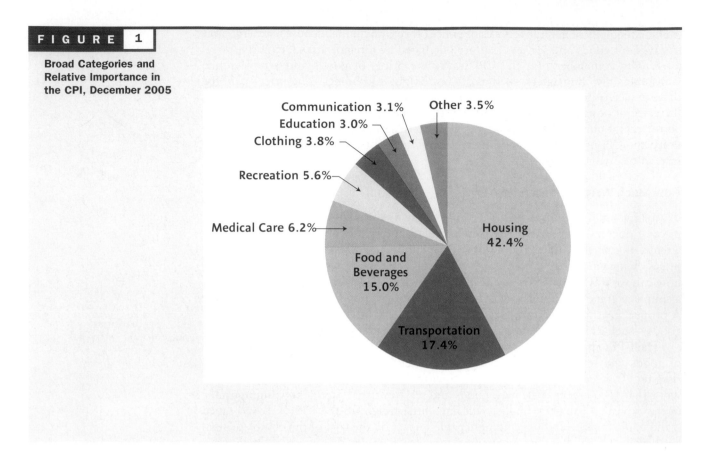

In recent years, the base period for the CPI has been July 1983. Following our general formula for price indexes, the CPI is calculated as follows:

$$\text{CPI} = \frac{\text{Cost of market basket in current period}}{\text{Cost of market basket in July 1983}} \times 100.$$

This simple formula shows us what the CPI tracks: the changing cost of a basket of goods.[3] In July 1983, the value of the CPI is 100. In any month in which the basket cost more than July 1983, the CPI's value is greater than 100. For periods (before July 1983) in which the basket's cost was lower, the CPI is less than 100. The appendix to this chapter provides a more detailed example of how the CPI is calculated.

Table 1 shows the actual value of the CPI for December of selected years. Because it is reported in index number form, we can easily see how much the price level has changed over different time intervals. In December 2005, for example, the CPI had a value of 196.8, telling us that the typical market basket in that year cost 96.8 percent more than it would have cost in the July 1983 base period. In December 1970, the CPI was 39.8, so the cost of the market basket in that year was only 39.8 percent of its cost in July 1983.

---

[3] The formula, however, ignores another feature of the CPI: the periodic updating of items and their relative importance in the CPI market basket. Each time the market basket is updated, the BLS splices a new CPI series onto the old one. But it retains July 1983 as the base period for index number calculation.

FROM PRICE INDEX TO INFLATION RATE

The Consumer Price Index is a measure of the price *level* in the economy. The **inflation rate** measures how fast the price level is changing. More specifically, it tells us the percentage change in the price level from one period to the next. For example, let's calculate the inflation rate for the year 2005. Table 1 tells us that, from December 2004 to December 2005, the CPI rose from 190.3 to 196.8. Therefore, the annual inflation rate over the year 2005 was (196.8−190.3) / 190.3 = 0.034, or 3.4 percent.

The CPI is reported monthly, but the reported rate is virtually always seasonally adjusted and reported as an annual rate. For example, from April 2006 to May 2006, the seasonally adjusted CPI rose from 201.0 to 201.9. Therefore, the percentage increase in the CPI for May was (201.9 − 201.0)/201.0 = 0.0045 or 0.45 percent. But the media reported inflation for May as 5.5 percent. That's because inflation of 0.45 percent per month for 12 months would, over a year, result in annual inflation of 5.5 percent.

Figure 2 shows the annual rate of inflation, as measured by the CPI, since 1950. For each year, the inflation rate is calculated as the percentage change in the CPI from December of the previous year to December of that year. For example, the CPI in December 2004 was 190.3, and in December 2005 it was 196.8. The inflation rate for 2005 was therefore (196.8 − 190.3)/190.3 = 0.034 or 3.4 percent.

Whenever the price level rises, as it usually does, the inflation rate will be positive. When the price level falls, as it did during the Great Depression (not shown) and in 1954 (shown in Figure 2), we have negative inflation, which is called **deflation**. As you can see in the figure, the U.S. inflation rate was low in the 1950s, began to creep up in the 1960s, then spiked upward in the 1970s and early 1980s, and has been low ever since. In later chapters, you will learn what causes the inflation rate to rise and fall, and some of the reasons it has behaved as it has over the past several decades.

	TABLE	1

Consumer Price Index, December, Selected Years, 1970–2005

Year	Consumer Price Index (December)
1970	39.8
1980	86.3
1990	133.8
2000	174.0
2001	176.7
2002	180.9
2003	184.3
2004	190.3
2005	196.8

Source: Bureau of Labor Statistics, Consumer Price Index—All Urban Consumers (*www.bls.gov*).

Inflation rate The percentage change in the price level from one period to the next.

Deflation A *decrease* in the price level from one period to the next.

HOW THE CPI IS USED

The CPI is the most important and widely used measure of prices in the United States. It is used in three ways:

As a Policy Target. In the introductory macroeconomics chapter, we saw that price stability—or a low inflation rate—is one of the nation's important macroeconomic goals. One of the measures used to gauge our success in achieving low inflation is the CPI.

To Index Payments. An **indexed payment** is one that is periodically adjusted so that it rises and falls by the same percentage as a price index. Indexing a payment makes up for any loss of purchasing power caused by inflation. Ideally, indexing would adjust a nominal payment by just enough to keep its purchasing power unchanged. In the United States, more than 50 million Social Security recipients

Indexed payment A payment that is periodically adjusted in proportion with a price index.

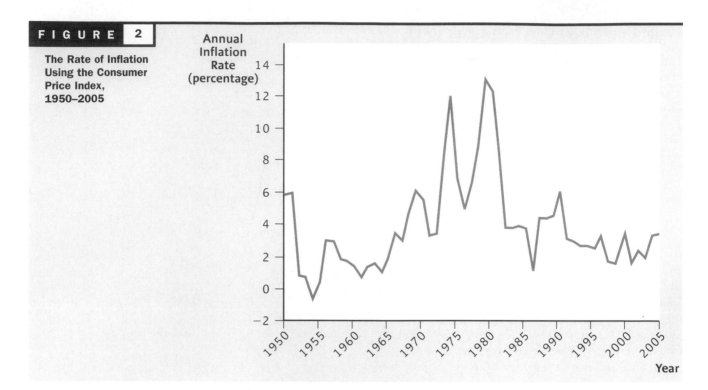

FIGURE 2

The Rate of Inflation Using the Consumer Price Index, 1950–2005

and government retirees have their benefit payments indexed to the CPI. More than 2 million workers have labor contracts that index their wages to the CPI. The U.S. income tax is indexed as well: The threshold income levels—at which people move into higher tax brackets—rise along with the CPI. And the government sells bonds that are indexed to the CPI. The owner of an indexed bond receives a payment each year to make up for the loss of purchasing power when the CPI rises.

To Translate from Nominal to Real Values. In order to compare economic values from different periods, we must translate *nominal variables*, measured in the number of dollars, into *real variables,* which are adjusted for the change in the dollar's purchasing power. The CPI is often used for this translation. Since calculating real variables is one of the most important uses of the CPI, let's discuss this in more detail.

REAL VARIABLES AND ADJUSTMENT FOR INFLATION

Suppose that from December 2007 to December 2012, your nominal wage—what you are paid in dollars—rises from $15 to $30 per hour. Will you be better off? That depends. You will be earning twice as many dollars. But you should care not about how many green pieces of paper you earn, but how many goods and services you can buy with that paper. How, then, can we tell what happens to your purchasing power?

Rising Prices versus Rising Inflation People often confuse the statement "prices are rising" with the statement "inflation is rising," but they do not mean the same thing. Remember that the inflation rate is the *rate of change* of the price level. To have rising inflation, the price level must be rising by a greater and greater percentage each period. But we can also have rising prices and *falling* inflation. For example, from 1996 to 1998, the CPI rose each year: "Prices were rising." But they rose by a smaller percentage each year than the year before, so "inflation was falling"—from 3.4 percent in 1996 to 1.7 percent in 1997 and to 1.6 percent in 1998.

DANGEROUS CURVES

By focusing not on the *nominal wage* (the number of *dollars* you earn) but on the *real wage* (the *purchasing power* of your wage). To track your real wage, we need to look at the number of dollars you earn *relative to the price level*.

Since the "typical worker" and the "typical consumer" are pretty much the same, the CPI is usually the price index used to calculate the real wage. The real-wage formula is as follows:

$$\text{Real wage in any year} = \frac{\text{Nominal wage in that year}}{\text{CPI in that year}} \times 100.$$

To see that this formula makes sense, let's go back to our fictional example: From 2007 to 2012, your nominal wage doubles from $15 to $30 per hour. Now, suppose the price of everything that you buy doubles at the same time. It is easy to see that in this case, your purchasing power would remain unchanged. And that is just what our formula tells us: If prices double, the CPI doubles as well. With 2007 as our base year, the CPI would increase from 100 in 2007, to 200 in the year 2012. The *real* wage would be ($15/100) × 100 = $15 in 2007, and ($30/200) × 100 = $15 in 2012. The real wage would remain unchanged.

Now suppose that prices doubled over this period but your nominal wage remains unchanged at $15. In this case, your purchasing power would be cut in half. You'd have the same number of dollars, but each one would buy half as much as it did before. Our formula gives us a real wage of ($15/100) × 100 = $15 in 2007 and ($15/200) × 100 = $7.50 in 2012. The real wage falls by half.

Now look at Table 2, which shows the average hourly earnings of wage earners (people who are paid by the hour) over the past three decades. In the first two columns, you can see that the average American wage earner was paid $4.87 per hour in December 1975, and more than triple that—$16.37—in December 2005. Does this mean the average hourly worker was paid more in 2005 than in 1975? In *dollars*, the answer is clearly yes. But what about in *purchasing power*? Or, using the new terminology you've learned: What happened to the *real wage* over this period?

Let's see. We know that the *nominal wage* rose from $4.87 in 1975 to $16.37 in 2005. But, according to the table, the CPI rose from 55.5 to 196.8 over the same period. Using our formula, we find that:

Year	Nominal Wage (dollars per hour)	CPI	Real Wage (1983 dollars per hour)
1975	4.87	55.5	8.77
1980	7.12	86.3	8.25
1985	8.86	109.3	8.11
1990	10.35	133.8	7.74
1995	11.79	153.5	7.68
2000	14.29	174.0	8.21
2005	16.37	196.8	8.32

TABLE 2

Nominal and Real Wages (in December of Each Year)

Source: Bureau of Labor Statistics, Statistical Tables, *http://www.bls.gov*. Wage and CPI data for December of each year. Nominal wage: average hourly earnings of production or nonsupervisory workers in nonfarm private sector; CPI: CPI-All Urban Consumers.

$$\text{Real wage in 1975} = \frac{\$4.87}{55.5} \times 100 = \$8.77$$

$$\text{Real wage in 2005} = \frac{\$16.37}{196.8} \times 100 = \$8.32.$$

Thus, although the average worker earned more *dollars* in 2005 than in 1975, when we use the CPI as our measure of prices, her purchasing power seems to have fallen over those years.

Important Provisos About Wage Data

It is tempting to come to a sweeping conclusion from information such as that in Table 2 and our previous discussion: that nonsupervisory workers were economically worse off in 2005 than in 1975. This would be a mistake, for several reasons. Here, we'll highlight just two of them.

First, over the past three decades, an increasing share of worker compensation has been nonwage benefits, such as employer contributions to retirement accounts and health insurance. By 2005, these benefits reached more than a quarter of total compensation for hourly workers, but they are not included in the hourly wage in Table 2. If benefits were included, real hourly pay would be greater in 2005 than in 1975.

Second, as we'll discuss later in this chapter, changes in the CPI overestimate inflation somewhat. Over a long time period such as three decades, this can make a big difference. A more accurate measure of the price level would show a rise in the hourly wage (even excluding benefits) over this period.

Still, while the adjustment for inflation in Table 2 is imperfect, no one would argue that we would get a clearer picture of worker pay by leaving the adjustment out. Using the nominal wage, we would conclude that worker pay (excluding benefits) more than tripled during this period. This is *not* a meaningful description of what happened. The important point to remember here is that

> when comparing dollar values over time, we care not about the number of dollars, but about their purchasing power. Thus, we translate nominal values into real values using the formula
>
> $$\text{Real value} = \frac{\text{Nominal value}}{\text{Price index}} \times 100.$$

This formula, usually using the CPI as the price index, is how most real values in the economy are calculated. But there is one important exception: To calculate real GDP, the government uses a different procedure, to which we now turn.

THE GDP PRICE INDEX AND REAL GDP

In the previous chapter, we discussed the difference between nominal GDP and real GDP. After reading this chapter, you might think that real GDP is calculated just like the real wage: dividing nominal GDP by the Consumer Price Index. But the Consumer Price Index is *not* used to calculate real GDP. Instead, a special price index—which we can call the **GDP price index**—is used.

GDP price index An index of the price level for all final goods and services included in GDP.

The most important differences between the CPI and the GDP price index are in the types of goods and services covered by each index. First, the GDP price index *includes* some prices that the CPI ignores. In particular, while the CPI tracks only the prices of goods bought by American *consumers*, the GDP price index must also include the prices of goods purchased by the government, investment goods purchased by businesses, and exports, which are purchased by foreigners.

Second, the GDP price index *excludes* some prices that are part of the CPI. In particular, the GDP price index leaves out used goods and imports, both of which are included in the CPI. This makes sense, because while used goods and imports are part of the typical consumer's market basket, they do not contribute to current U.S. GDP.

We can summarize the chief difference between the CPI and the GDP price index this way:

> *The GDP price index measures the prices of all goods and services that are included in U.S. GDP, while the CPI measures the prices of all goods and services bought by U.S. households.*[4]

THE COSTS OF INFLATION

A high rate of inflation—whether it is measured by the CPI or the GDP price index—is never welcome news. What's so bad about inflation? As we've seen, it certainly makes your task as an economics student more difficult: Rather than taking nominal variables at face value, you must do those troublesome calculations to convert them into real variables.

But inflation causes much more trouble than this. It can impose costs on society and on each of us individually. Yet when most people are asked *what* the cost of inflation is, they come up with an incorrect answer.

THE INFLATION MYTH

Most people think that inflation, merely by making goods and services more expensive, erodes the average purchasing power of income in the economy. The reason for this belief is easy to see: The higher the price level, the fewer goods and services a given number of dollars will buy. It stands to reason, then, that inflation—which raises prices—must be destroying the purchasing power of our incomes. Right?

Actually, this statement is mostly wrong.

To see why, remember that every market transaction involves *two* parties—a buyer and a seller. When a price rises, buyers of that good must pay more, but sellers get more revenue when they sell it. The loss in buyers' real income is matched by the rise in sellers' real income. Inflation may *redistribute* purchasing power, but it does not change the *average* purchasing power, when we include both buyers and sellers in the average.

In fact, most people in the economy participate on both sides of the market. On the one hand, they are consumers—as when they shop for food or clothing or furniture. On the other hand, they work in business firms that *sell* products and may benefit (in the form of higher wages or higher profits) when their firms' revenues rise. Thus, when prices rise, a particular person may find that her purchasing power has either risen or fallen, depending on whether she is affected more as a seller or as a

---

[4] The technical name for the GDP price index is the *chain-type annual weights GDP price index*. It differs from the CPI not only in goods covered, but also in its mathematical formula.

buyer. But regardless of the outcome for individuals, our conclusion remains the same:

> *Inflation can redistribute purchasing power from one group to another, but it does not directly decrease the average real income in the economy.*

Why, then, do people continue to believe that inflation robs the average citizen of real income? Largely because real incomes sometimes do decline—for *other* reasons. Inflation—while not the *cause* of the decline—will often be the *mechanism* that brings it about. Just as we often blame the messenger for bringing bad news, so too we often blame inflation for lowering our purchasing power when the real cause lies elsewhere.

Let's consider an example. In Table 2, notice the decline in real wages during the late 1970s. The real wage (excluding benefits) fell from $8.77 in 1975 to $8.25 in 1980, a decline of about 6 percent. Other data show that during this period, not only wage earners but also salaried workers, small-business owners, and corporate shareholders all suffered stagnant or declining real incomes. What was the cause?

There were several reasons, but one of the most important was the dramatic rise in the price of imported oil—from $3 per barrel in 1973 to $34 in 1981, an increase of more than 1,000 percent. The higher price for oil meant that oil-exporting countries, like Saudi Arabia, Kuwait, and Iraq, got more goods and services for each barrel of oil they supplied to the rest of the world, including the United States. But with these countries claiming more of America's output, less remained for the typical American. That is, the typical American family had to suffer a decline in real income. As always, a rise in price shifted income from buyers to sellers. But in this case, the sellers were *foreigners*, while the buyers were Americans. Thus, the rise in the price of foreign oil caused average purchasing power in the United States to decline.

But what was the mechanism that brought about the decline? Since real income is equal to (Nominal income/Price index) × 100, it can decrease in one of two ways: a fall in the numerator (nominal income) or a rise in the denominator (the price index). The decline in real income in the 1970s came entirely from an increase in the denominator.

Look back at Figure 2. You can see that this period of declining real income in the United States was also a period of unusually high inflation; at its peak in 1979, the inflation rate exceeded 13 percent. As a result, most people blamed *inflation* for their loss of purchasing power. But inflation was not the cause; it was just the *mechanism*. The cause was a change in the terms of trade between the United States and the oil-exporting countries—a change that resulted in higher oil prices.

To summarize, the common idea that inflation imposes a cost on society by directly decreasing average real income in the economy is incorrect. But inflation *does* impose costs on society, as the next section shows.

THE REDISTRIBUTIVE COST OF INFLATION

One cost of inflation is that it often redistributes purchasing power *within* society. But because the winners and losers are chosen haphazardly—rather than by conscious social policy—the redistribution of purchasing power is not generally desirable. In some cases, the shift in purchasing power is downright perverse—harming the needy and helping those who are already well off.

How does inflation sometimes redistribute real income? An increase in the price level reduces the purchasing power of any payment that is specified in *nominal* terms. For example, some workers have contracts that set their nominal wage for two or three years, regardless of any future inflation. The nationally set minimum wage, too, is set for several years and specified in nominal dollars. Under these circumstances, inflation can harm ordinary workers, since it erodes the purchasing power of their prespecified nominal wage. Real income is redistributed from these workers to their employers, who benefit by paying a lower real wage.

But the effect can also work the other way: benefiting ordinary households and harming businesses. For example, many homeowners sign fixed-dollar mortgage agreements with a bank. These are promises to pay the bank the same nominal sum each month. Inflation can reduce the *real* value of these payments, thus redistributing purchasing power away from the bank and toward the average homeowner.

In general,

> *inflation can shift purchasing power away from those who are awaiting future payments specified in dollars, and toward those who are obligated to make such payments.*

But does inflation *always* redistribute income from one party in a contract to another? Actually, no; if the inflation is *expected* by both parties, it should not redistribute income. The next section explains why.

Accurately Expected Inflation Does *Not* Shift Purchasing Power

Suppose a labor union is negotiating a 3-year contract with an employer, and both sides agree that each year, workers should get a 3 percent increase in their *real wage*. Labor contracts, like most other contracts, are usually specified in nominal terms: The firm will agree to give workers so many additional *dollars per hour* each year. If neither side anticipates any inflation, they should simply negotiate a 3 percent *nominal* wage hike. With an unchanged price level, the *real* wage would then also rise by the desired 3 percent.

But suppose instead that both sides anticipate 10 percent inflation each year for the next three years. Then, they must agree to *more* than a 3 percent nominal wage increase in order to raise the real wage by 3 percent. How much more?

We can answer this question with a simple mathematical rule:

> *Over any period, the percentage change in a real value (%ΔReal) is approximately equal to the percentage change in the associated nominal value (%ΔNominal) minus the percentage change in the price level (%ΔP):*
>
> $$\%\Delta Real = \%\Delta Nominal - \%\Delta P$$

Over each year, if the inflation rate is 10 percent and the real wage is to rise by 3 percent, then the change in the nominal wage must (approximately) satisfy the equation

$$3 \text{ percent} = \% \Delta \text{Nominal} - 10 \text{ percent}$$

$$\% \Delta \text{Nominal} = 13 \text{ percent.}$$

The required nominal wage hike is 13 percent.

You can see that as long as both sides correctly anticipate the inflation, and no one stops them from negotiating a 13 percent nominal wage hike, inflation will *not* affect either party in real terms:

> *If inflation is correctly anticipated, and if both parties take it into account, then inflation will not redistribute purchasing power.*

We come to a similar conclusion about contracts between lenders and borrowers. When you lend someone money, you receive a reward—an interest payment—for letting that person use your money instead of spending it yourself. The annual *interest rate* is the interest payment divided by the amount of money you have lent. For example, if you lend someone $1,000 and receive back $1,040 one year later, then your interest is $40, and the interest *rate* on the loan is $40/$1,000 = 0.04, or 4 percent.

Nominal interest rate The annual percent increase in a lender's dollars from making a loan.

Real interest rate The annual percent increase in a lender's purchasing power from making a loan.

But there are actually *two* interest rates associated with every loan. One is the **nominal interest rate**—the percentage increase in the lender's *dollars* each year from making the loan. The other is the **real interest rate**—the percentage increase in the lender's *purchasing power* each year from making the loan. It is the *real* rate—the change in purchasing power—that lenders and borrowers should care about.

In the absence of inflation, real and nominal interest rates would always be equal. A 4 percent increase in the lender's *dollars* would always imply a 4 percent increase in her purchasing power. But if there is inflation, it will reduce the purchasing power of the money paid back. Does this mean that inflation redistributes purchasing power? Not if the inflation is correctly anticipated, and if there are no restrictions on making loan contracts.

For example, suppose both parties anticipate annual inflation of 5 percent and want to arrange a contract whereby the lender will be paid a 4 percent *real* interest rate each year. What *nominal* interest rate should they choose? Since the annual interest rate is the *percentage change* in the lender's funds over the year, we can use our approximation rule,

$$\%\Delta\,\text{Real} = \%\Delta\,\text{Nominal} - \%\Delta\,P.$$

For each year of the loan, this becomes

%Δ in lender's purchasing power = %Δ in lender's dollars − Rate of inflation

or

Real interest rate = Nominal interest rate − Rate of inflation.

In our example, where we want the real interest rate to equal 4 percent per year when the inflation rate is 5 percent per year, we must have

4 percent = Nominal interest rate − 5 percent

or

Nominal interest rate = 9 percent.

Once again, we see that as long as both parties correctly anticipate the inflation rate, and face no restrictions on contracts (that is, they are free to set the nominal interest rate at 9 percent), then no one gains or loses.

When inflation is *not* correctly anticipated, however, our conclusion is very different.

Unexpected Inflation *Does* Shift Purchasing Power

Suppose that, expecting no inflation, you agree to lend money at a 4 percent nominal interest rate for one year. You and the borrower think that this will translate into a 4 percent real rate. But it turns out you are both wrong: The price level actually rises by 3 percent, so the *real* interest rate ends up being 4 percent − 3 percent = 1 percent. As a lender, you have given up the use of your money for the year, expecting to be rewarded with a 4 percent increase in purchasing power. But you get only a 1 percent increase. Your borrower was willing to pay 4 percent in purchasing power, but ends up paying only 1 percent. *Unexpected* inflation has led to a better deal for your borrower and a worse deal for you, the lender.

That will not make you happy. But it could be even worse. Suppose the inflation rate is higher—say, 6 percent. Then your real interest rate ends up at 4 percent − 6 percent = −2 percent, a negative real interest rate. You get back *less* in purchasing power than you lend out. You are *paying* (in purchasing power) for the privilege of lending out your money. The borrower is *rewarded* (in purchasing power) for borrowing!

Negative real interest rates like this are not just a theoretical possibility. In the late 1970s, when inflation was higher than expected for several years in a row, many borrowers ending up "paying" negative real interest rates to lenders.

Now, let's consider one more possibility: Expected inflation is 6 percent, so you negotiate a 10 percent nominal rate, thinking this will translate to a 4 percent real rate. But the actual inflation rate turns out to be zero, so the real interest rate is 10 percent − 0 percent = 10 percent. In this case, inflation turns out to be *less* than expected, so the *real* interest rate is higher than either of you anticipated. The borrower is harmed and you (the lender) benefit.

These examples apply, more generally, to any agreement on future payments: to a worker waiting for a wage payment and the employer who has promised to pay it; to a doctor who has sent out a bill and the patient who has not yet paid it; or to a supplier who has delivered goods and his customer who hasn't yet paid for them.

> *When inflationary expectations are inaccurate, purchasing power is shifted between those obliged to make future payments and those waiting to be paid. An inflation rate higher than expected harms those awaiting payment and benefits the payers; an inflation rate lower than expected harms the payers and benefits those awaiting payment.*

THE RESOURCE COST OF INFLATION

In addition to its possible redistribution of income, inflation imposes another cost upon society. To cope with inflation, we are forced to use up time and other resources as we go about our daily economic activities (shopping, selling, saving) that we could otherwise have devoted to productive activities. Thus, inflation imposes an *opportunity cost* on society as a whole and on each of its members:

> *When people must spend time and other resources coping with inflation, they pay an opportunity cost—they sacrifice the goods and services those resources could have produced instead.*

Let's first consider the resources used up by *consumers* to cope with inflation. Suppose you shop for clothes twice a year. You've discovered that both The Gap and Banana Republic sell clothing of similar quality and have similar service, and you naturally want to shop at the one with the lower prices. If there is no inflation, your task is easy: You shop first at The Gap and then at Banana Republic; thereafter, you rely on your memory to determine which is less expensive.

With inflation, however, things are more difficult. Suppose you find that prices at Banana Republic are higher than you remember them to be at The Gap. It may be that Banana Republic is the more expensive store, or it may be that prices have risen at *both* stores. How can you tell? Only a trip back to The Gap will answer the question—a trip that will cost you extra time and trouble. If prices are rising very rapidly, you may have to visit both stores on the same day to be sure which one is cheaper. Now, multiply this time and trouble by all the different types of shopping you must do on a regular or occasional basis—for groceries, an apartment, a car, concert tickets, compact discs, restaurant meals, and more. Inflation can make you use up valuable time—time you could have spent earning income or enjoying leisure activities. True, if you shop for some of these items on the Internet, you can compare prices in less time, but not zero time. And most shopping is *not* done over the Internet.

Inflation also forces *sellers* to use up resources. First, remember that sellers of goods and services are also buyers of resources and intermediate goods. They, too, must do comparison shopping when there is inflation, which uses up hired labor time. Second, each time sellers raise prices, labor is needed to put new price tags on merchandise, to enter new prices into a computer scanning system, to update the HTML code on a Web page, or to change the prices on advertising brochures or menus.

Finally, inflation makes us all use up resources managing our financial affairs. When the inflation rate is high, we'll try to keep our funds in accounts that pay high nominal interest rates, in order to preserve our purchasing power. And we'll try to keep as little as possible in cash or in low-interest checking accounts. Of course, this means more frequent trips to the bank or the automatic teller machine, to transfer money into our checking accounts or get cash each time we need it.

All of these additional activities—inspecting prices at several stores or Web sites, changing price tags or price entries, going back and forth to the automatic teller machine—use up time and other resources. From society's point of view, these resources could have been used to produce *other* goods and services that we'd enjoy.

You may not have thought much about the resource cost of inflation because in recent years, U.S. inflation has been so low—averaging about 3 percent during the 1990s, and about 2.75 percent from 2000 to mid-2006. Such a low rate of inflation is often called *creeping inflation;* from week to week or month to month, the price level creeps up so slowly that we hardly notice the change. The cost of coping with creeping inflation is negligible. And (as you'll see in a later chapter) low, creeping inflation may actually be good for the economy.

But it has not always been this way. Three times during the last 50 years, we have had double-digit inflation: about 14 percent during 1947–48, 12 percent in 1974, and 13 percent during 1979 and 1980. Going back farther, the annual inflation rate reached almost 20 percent during World War I and rose above 25 percent during the Civil War.

And as serious as these episodes of American inflation have been, they pale in comparison to the experiences of other countries. In the 1980s, several South American countries experienced inflation greater than 1,000 percent per year, and in mid-2006, Zimbabwe's inflation rate approached that level as well. In Germany during the 1920s, the inflation rate reached thousands of percent per *month*. And even worse was the Yugoslavian inflation of 1993–94. In one month alone—January 1994—the price level rose by 313 million percent.

When inflation reaches extremely high rates like these, normal economic life breaks down. No one wants to hold the national currency—or even accept it as payment—because it loses its value so rapidly. For some transactions, people will use a foreign currency, such as the U.S. dollar. But because there are insufficient quantities of foreign currency available in the country, most people are forced to barter—trading goods for goods rather than goods for money. Buying and selling becomes so inefficient and time consuming that production and living standards plummet.

IS THE CPI ACCURATE?

The Bureau of Labor Statistics spends millions of dollars gathering data to ensure that its measure of inflation is accurate. To determine the market basket of the typical consumer, the BLS analyzes the spending habits of thousands of households. Every month, the bureau's shoppers visit 23,000 retail stores and about 50,000 housing units (rental apartments and owner-occupied homes) to record 80,000 different prices.

The BLS is a highly professional agency. Billions of dollars are at stake for each 1 percent change in the CPI, and the BLS deserves high praise for keeping its measurement honest and free of political manipulation. Nevertheless, conceptual problems and resource limitations make the CPI fall short of the ideal measure of inflation. Economists—even those who work in the BLS—widely agree that the CPI overstates the U.S. inflation rate. By how much?

According to a report by an advisory committee of economists in 1996, the overall bias was at least 1.1 percent during the 1980s and early 1990s.[5] That is, in a typical year, the reported rise in the CPI was about 1 percentage point greater than the true rise in the price level. The BLS has been working hard to reduce this upward bias and—especially in the late 1990s—it made some progress. But significant bias remains.

SOURCES OF BIAS IN THE CPI

There are several reasons for the upward bias in the CPI.

Substitution Bias

Until recently, the CPI almost completely ignored a general principle of consumer behavior: People tend to *substitute* goods that have become relatively cheaper in place of goods that have become relatively more expensive. For example, in the seven years from 1973 to 1980, the retail price of oil-related products—like gasoline and home heating oil—increased by more than 300 percent, while the prices of most other goods and services rose by less than 100 percent. As a result, people found ways to conserve on oil products. They joined carpools, used public transportation, insulated their homes, and in many cases moved closer to their workplaces to shorten their commute. Yet throughout this period, the CPI basket—based on a survey of buying patterns in 1972–73—assumed that consumers were buying unchanged quantities of oil products.

[5] See *Toward a More Accurate Measure of the Cost of Living*, Report to the Senate Finance Committee from the Advisory Commission to Study the Consumer Price Index, December 1996.

The treatment of oil products is an example of a more general problem that has plagued the CPI for decades. Until recently, the CPI used fixed *quantities* to determine the relative importance of each item. That is, it assumed that households continued to buy each good or service in the same quantities in which they bought it during the most recent household survey—until the next household survey. Compounding the problem, the survey to determine spending patterns—and to update the market basket—was taken only about once every 10 years or so. So by the end of each 10-year period, the CPI's assumptions about spending habits could be far off the mark, as they were in the case of oil in the 1970s.

The BLS has *partially* fixed this problem, in two ways.[6] First, beginning in 2002, it began updating the market basket with a household survey every 2 years instead of every 10 years. This is widely considered an important improvement in CPI measurement.

Second, since January 1999, the CPI has no longer assumed that the typical consumer continues to buy the same *quantity* of each good that he bought in the last household "market basket" survey. Instead, the CPI now assumes that when a good's relative price rises by 10 percent, consumers buy 10 percent less of it, and switch their purchases to other goods whose prices are rising more slowly.

However, this is only a partial fix. The CPI still only recognizes the possibility of such substitution *within* categories of goods and *not among* them. For example, if the price of steak rises relative to the price of hamburger meat, the CPI now assumes that consumers will substitute away from steak and toward hamburger meat, since both are in the same category: *beef.* However, if the price of all beef products rises relative to chicken and pork, the CPI assumes that there is *no* substitution at all from beef toward chicken and pork. As a result, beef products still would be overweighted in the CPI until the next survey.

> *Although the BLS has partially fixed the problem, the CPI still suffers from substitution bias. That is, categories of goods whose prices are rising most rapidly are overweighted in the CPI market basket and categories of goods whose prices are rising most slowly are underweighted.*

New Technologies

New technologies are another source of upward bias in the CPI. One problem is that goods using new technologies are introduced into the BLS market basket only after a lag. These goods often drop rapidly in price after they are introduced, helping to balance out price rises in other goods. By excluding a category of goods whose prices are dropping, the CPI overstates the rate of inflation. For example, even though many consumers were buying and using cellular phones throughout the 1990s, they were not included in the BLS basket of goods until 1998. As a result, the CPI missed the rapid decline in the price of cell phones. Now that the market basket of the typical consumer is updated every 2 years instead of every 10, this source of bias has been reduced but not completely eliminated.

But there is another issue with new technologies: They often offer consumers a lower cost alternative for obtaining the same service. For example, the introduction

---

[6] For a discussion of these and other recent changes in the CPI, see Robert J. Gordon, "The Boskin Commission Report: A Retrospective One Decade Later," *International Productivity Monitor*, Spring 2006.

of cable television lowered the cost of entertainment significantly by offering a new, cheaper alternative to going out to see movies. This should have registered as a drop in the price of "seeing movies." But the CPI does not have any good way to measure this reduction in the cost of living. Instead, it treats cable television as an entirely separate service.

> *The CPI excludes new products that tend to drop in price when they first come on the market. When those products are included, the CPI regards them as entirely separate from existing goods and services, instead of recognizing that they lower the cost of achieving a given level of service.*

Changes in Quality

Many products are improving over time. Cars are much more reliable than they used to be and require much less routine maintenance. They have features like air bags and antilock brakes that were unknown in the early 1980s. The BLS struggles to deal with these changes. As far back as 1967, it has recognized that when the price of a car rises, some of that price hike is not really inflation, but instead the result of charging more because the consumer is *getting* more. In recent years, the BLS has adopted some routine statistical procedures to automatically adjust price changes for quality improvements for certain goods, such as personal computers and televisions. And in 1997, it introduced a major change in its treatment of health care costs. Before then, the CPI would track the price of individual health care components, such as "a night in the hospital" or "a post-surgery checkup." But after 1997, it began tracking the overall cost of treating specific diseases or conditions. Thus, the introduction of a new type of heart surgery that requires fewer days of hospitalization (and no change in other inputs) would be recorded as a *decrease* in the price of heart surgery.

But most goods and services do not get this special treatment. There is no explicit recognition that home appliances are more reliable, that audio equipment has better sound, that many medical treatments are more *effective* at prolonging life and health (aside from reducing hospital stays or doctor visits), that home power tools are safer, and so on.[7]

Take the Internet. Every year, it offers more information and entertainment content, a greater number of retailers from which to buy things, and faster and more intelligent search engines to help you find it all. Yet, the Internet—which was introduced into the CPI in 1998—has been treated as a service whose quality has not changed. If the price of Internet service rises, the CPI considers it inflation rather than paying more to *get* more. And if the price stays the same, the CPI ignores the *decrease* in the cost per unit of available content and treats the price as unchanged.

> *The CPI fails to fully account for quality improvements in the goods and services in its market basket and, therefore, overestimates how fast the price of the basket is rising.*

---

[7] There is, however, some implicit adjusting for quality. When a new model of a good is introduced at a higher price, the BLS assumes that the entire price increase is due to quality improvement rather than inflation. But the BLS does *not* recognize the possibility of more "bang for the buck"—that the value of the new model's higher quality might exceed any rise in its price.

Growth in Discounting

When a Wal-Mart opens up, many people begin to shop there. And for good reason: Prices at Wal-Mart are substantially lower than at other stores. For example, identical food items cost between 15 and 25 percent less at a Wal-Mart than at the typical supermarket (unless the supermarket has to compete with a nearby Wal-Mart).[8]

The BLS recognizes that people shop at Wal-Mart, and tracks changes in the prices of items sold there. But it fails to register a drop in prices when a new Wal-Mart first opens and people can suddenly buy the same goods for less. Wal-Mart and other discount chains have expanded rapidly in recent years, and continue to do so; the CPI systematically misses the price drop from the shift to these discounters.

> *The CPI does not recognize that a new discount outlet lowers the prices on many items for the people who begin shopping there. As a result, as discount outlets expand into new areas, the CPI overstates the inflation rate for food, electronic appliances, clothing, and other items sold there.*

THE OVERALL BIAS AND ITS CONSEQUENCES

While the BLS has fixed some of the problems with the CPI, economists are in general agreement that it continues to overestimate inflation. By how much? That depends on what we mean by "inflation." If we mean the rate of price increase for the typical consumer's market basket, then the overestimate—after the improvements made in the late 1990s—is probably a bit less than one percentage point per year. But if we define inflation the way it is often interpreted—as the percentage change in the *cost of living*—then the CPI's overestimate of annual inflation is unknown, but much greater. This is largely because of how the CPI responds to technological change.

When a new good comes to market, it is dropped into the CPI market basket at some point, and the CPI tracks changes in its price from that time forward. But the increase in economic well-being made possible by *introducing* the good in the first place—and from its continued availability—is never accounted for. Even if the BLS was able to incorporate the good as soon as it came to market, and even if it accurately adjusted for subsequent quality improvements, it would still be missing the most important factor: the rise in living standards made possible by the new good's availability.

For example, we've already discussed the CPI's failure to account for quality improvements in the Internet after it was dropped into the basket in 1998. But beyond this problem, the CPI has *never* recognized how the Internet has lowered the cost of achieving any given level of economic satisfaction (think of email, news, online entertainment, online purchases, online dating, blogs, and more). The same is true for new medical procedures or prescription drugs that can treat or cure formerly untreatable diseases: The CPI ignores the longer and healthier lives that the new treatments often make possible. In this way, the CPI misses a highly relevant

---

[8] Hausman, J. and E. Leibtag, "CPI Bias from Supercenters: Does the BLS Know that Wal-Mart Exists?" NBER Working Paper No. 10712, National Bureau of Economic Research, Inc., Cambridge, MA, August 2004.

fact: New goods raise the living standard we can achieve at any given dollar cost. Or, equivalently, they lower the dollar cost of achieving any given living standard.

How serious is this problem? No one knows for sure. But many economists believe that the error from ignoring the effect of new goods on living standards could be substantial—much larger than the combined effects of the other biases in the CPI discussed in this chapter.[9]

> *The upward bias in the CPI depends on what we are trying to measure. If the target is the cost of the typical consumer's market basket, then the current upward bias is probably less than one percentage point per year. If the target is the cost of achieving a given standard of living, the upward bias is substantially greater.*

What are the implications of this bias in the CPI? That depends on our purpose in using it. If we are trying to measure inflationary tendencies in the economy, to help guide macroeconomic policy, then the CPI's failure to track the cost of achieving a given living standard is irrelevant. The policy goal is to avoid the costs to society when the price level—however it is interpreted—changes rapidly. The CPI is one of several useful tools to help achieve this goal.

But there are other purposes for which the measurement errors in the CPI matter a great deal. One such purpose is to determine the behavior of real wages over long periods of time. Look back at Table 2, which shows the behavior of the real hourly wage (not including benefits) over the past 40 years. It tells us that the real hourly wage was lower in 2005 than in 1975. Can we have faith in that result? Not really. Aside from the problem discussed earlier (the exclusion of increasingly important non-wage benefits), we have the problem of CPI bias. With the errors in each year's CPI accumulating over time, the overstatement of the price level after 40 years is huge. (An end-of-chapter problem will help you see this.) Moreover, the CPI is never revised retroactively, so any improvements in measurement made in later years—which reduce the bias—leave the historical record unchanged.[10]

Another purpose for which measurement errors matter is indexing. Millions of people have their retirement benefits, wages, interest payments, or federal tax brackets adjusted for inflation as determined by the CPI. Thus, any errors have important implications for the government budget, as well as the economy. In the Using the Theory section, we look at one example of this issue: the controversy over indexing Social Security benefits to the CPI.

Still, as imperfect as the CPI is for some purposes, no one would argue that we get a clearer picture of economic values by not adjusting for inflation at all. As long as the measurement errors are relatively small, even an imperfect adjustment for inflation will come closer to the truth than no adjustment at all.

---

[9] See, for example, the suggestions of Jerry Hausman, "Sources of Bias and Solutions to Bias in the CPI," *Journal of Economic Perspectives*, Vol. 17, No. 1, Winter 2003.

[10] The Bureau of Labor Statistics has published experimental price indexes, which correct some of its earlier errors and are revised retroactively. And, since 1999, it has been publishing an improved index that largely solves the substitution bias, called the Chained Consumer Price Index for All Urban Consumers. But these other price indexes are not widely reported in the media and are not used for indexing.

USING THE THEORY

THE CONTROVERSY OVER INDEXING SOCIAL SECURITY BENEFITS

In recent years, the Social Security system—which provides benefits to almost 50 million retired workers in the United States—has become embroiled in controversy. On the one hand, it has been of immense benefit to millions of people. For most of them, it provides an important supplement to other sources of retirement income. For about 10 million retirees, Social Security is the *only* source of income. This has made the program immensely popular.

On the other hand, Social Security is one of the largest and most expensive of all federal government programs, paying out more than $500 billion in 2005. And as the baby-boom generation begins to retire over the next several years, the costs of the system will balloon, adding to the government's projected budget deficits. This has led to calls to reduce the budgetary costs by changing the way that benefits are determined.

Let's consider how Social Security benefits are determined. First, the benefits of each year's *new* retirees are tied to the average wage rate in the economy at the time of retirement. As living standards and wages rise over time, each new group of retirees is granted a higher real benefit payment when they first retire. This part is not controversial.

But once a retiree's initial benefit is assigned, his payments in future years are indexed to the CPI. That is, his nominal (dollar) benefit automatically increases at the same percentage rate as the CPI. This is the controversial part.

The justification for indexing is to preserve the purchasing power of the benefit payment for all retirees for as long as they live. But because changes in the CPI *overstate* inflation, benefits are *over*indexed. That is, the nominal payment rises by more than the actual rise in the price level. As a result, the real benefit payment rises over time.

Table 3 illustrates how this works, with a hypothetical example. We assume that someone retires in 2006 with an initial promise of $25,000 per year in benefits (about the maximum initial benefit payable that year). The benefit payment is then indexed to the CPI for the next 20 years. We also assume that an accurate price index would rise at 2 percent per year (that is, we assume the inflation rate is actually 2 percent per year). Column (1) shows the value of this accurate price index in each year, using 2006 as our base year.

In columns (2) and (3), we assume that the CPI—to which benefits are indexed—is accurate. Accordingly, column (2) shows nominal benefits starting at $25,000 and then growing by 2 percent per year with the CPI. For example, in the second year, benefits rise to $25,000 × 1.02 = $25,500. In the third year, they rise by another 2 percent, to $25,500 × 1.02 = $26,010. Continuing in this way, the nominal payment in the twentieth year would reach $25,000 × $(1.02)^{20}$ = $37,149.

Column (3) shows the real benefit payment in each year. It is obtained using our formula:

$$\text{Real value} = \frac{\text{Nominal value}}{\text{Price index}} \times 100.$$

TABLE 3

Indexing and "Overindexing" Social Security Benefits

Year	(1) Accurate Price Index (2006 = 100)	Benefits Indexed to Accurate CPI (rising at 2%)		Benefits Indexed to Overstated CPI (rising at 3%)	
		(2) Nominal Annual Benefit (indexed at 2% per year)	(3) Real Annual Benefit, [(2) ÷ (1)] × 100	(4) Nominal Annual Benefit (indexed at 3% per year)	(5) Real Annual Benefit, [(4) ÷ (1)] × 100
2006	100.00	$25,000	$25,000	$25,000	$25,000
2007	102.00	$25,500	$25,000	$25,750	$25,245
2008	104.04	$26,010	$25,000	$26,523	$25,493
2009	106.12	$26,532	$25,000	$27,318	$25,742
. . .	. . .	. . .	. . .	. . .	. . .
2026	148.59	$37,149	$25,000	$45,153	$30,388

In our example, each value in column (2) is divided by the accurate price index in column (1) to obtain the real payment in column (3). For example, in the second year, with the price index equal to 102, the real payment is

$$\text{Real payment} = \frac{\$25,500}{102} \times 100 = \$25,000.$$

As you can see, when the benefit payment is indexed to an accurate CPI, the real payment remains unchanged at $25,000 (in 2006 dollars). This is not surprising. The purpose of indexing is to keep a real payment constant. With no inaccuracy in the CPI, this is exactly what indexing does.

Now, let's see what happens when benefits are indexed to a CPI that *overesti-mates* inflation by one percentage point each year. That is, we'll continue to assume that inflation is actually 2 percent per year, but nominal benefit payments will now rise with the (erroneous) CPI at 3 percent per year. In column (4), nominal benefits start at $25,000. In the second year, benefits are $25,000 × 1.03 = $25,750; in the third year, they rise to $25,750 × 1.03 = $26,523, and so on.

Finally, we calculate the real benefit payment each year. But remember: The real benefit is its *actual* purchasing power. In this scenario, although the CPI reports inflation of 3 percent, prices are *actually* rising at only 2 percent per year. So, to determine the real benefit in any year, we must divide the overindexed nominal payment in column (4) by the actual price level in column (1). In the second year, the real payment is

$$\text{Real payment} = \frac{\$25,750}{102} \times 100 = \$25,245.$$

In the third year, the real payment is

$$\text{Real payment} = \frac{\$26,523}{104.04} \times 100 = \$25,493.$$

As you can see, rather than just maintaining the real benefit over time, indexing to an upward-biased CPI results in a *continually increasing real benefit payment*. By the last year of retirement, the real benefit payment rises to $30,388—an increase of more than 21 percent.

This will suit Social Security recipients just fine. And it may suit the rest of us too—when the economy is growing at a rapid pace. After all, why shouldn't retirees get a larger slice of the economic pie when the pie itself is growing rapidly and everyone else's slice is growing as well? But note that the increase in real benefits happens *automatically,* due to overindexing, *regardless* of the rate of economic growth. If real GDP growth slows down or disappears, the average Social Security recipient will *still* get a growing slice of the pie each year, even if everyone else's slice is shrinking. (Because Social Security is financed by tax payments from the rest of society, any increase in real benefits shrinks the after-tax real income of nonretirees.)

More generally,

> *when a payment is indexed and the price index overstates inflation, the real payment increases over time. Purchasing power is automatically shifted toward those who are indexed and away from the rest of society.*

This general principle applies whether the economy is growing rapidly or slowly, and it applies to anyone who is indexed: Social Security recipients, government pensioners, union workers with indexed wage contracts, or anyone else.

Because it is widely recognized that the CPI overstates inflation, there have been calls to adjust the indexing formula for Social Security. One proposal is to index to the CPI minus one-half of a percentage point, to correct for at least some of measurement error. Other proposals are to more aggressively fix the problems of the CPI itself, which might decrease the reported annual inflation rate by a half percentage point or more.

But some economists have argued that the system should be left alone. For one thing, the elderly consume a different market basket than the "typical consumer." They spend a greater fraction of their income on health care (for which prices are rising rapidly) and much less on new technology goods like laptop computers or cell phones (for which prices are falling). According to this argument, any overstatement of inflation by the CPI helps to compensate for the higher inflation faced by the elderly.

The Bureau of Labor Statistics has been compiling an experimental index, the CPI-E ("E" for elderly), based on a market basket more representative for those receiving benefits. From 1982 to 2005, the CPI-E has risen faster than the version of the CPI used for indexing Social Security,[11] by about 0.4 percentage points each year. But this tells us that reasonable estimates of the upward bias of the CPI have *more* than compensated for the higher inflation faced by the elderly, suggesting that some change to indexing may still be needed.

Another argument used by advocates of the current system is that it helps to reduce a source of inequity among retirees.[12] Remember that each group's initial benefit is determined by the average wage at their time of retirement. Thus, those who retired in earlier years were awarded a lower initial real benefit than those who retired in later years. Overindexing for inflation thus helps to reduce the difference in real benefits among retirees, because the longer someone has been retired, the more they have gained from the upward bias in the CPI.

---

[11] Social Security benefits are indexed to the CPI-W, which is based on the typical market basket of urban wage earners and clerical workers. Over the past few decades, it has risen slightly more slowly than the CPI-U, which covers all urban workers.

[12] This point has been made by Martin Neil Baily, "Policy Implications of the Boskin Commission Report," *International Productivity Monitor,* Spring 2006.

Summary

The value of a dollar is its purchasing power, and this changes as the prices of the things we buy change. The overall trend of prices is measured using a price index. Like any index number, a price index is calculated as: (Value in current period/Value in base period) × 100. The most widely used price index in the United States is the *Consumer Price Index (CPI)*, which tracks the prices paid for a typical consumer's "market basket." The percentage change in the CPI is the inflation rate.

The most common uses of the CPI are for indexing payments, as a policy target, and to translate from nominal to real variables. Many nominal variables, such as the nominal wage, can be corrected for price changes by dividing by the CPI and then multiplying by 100. The result is a real variable, such as the real wage, that rises and falls only when its purchasing power rises and falls. Another price index in common use is the GDP price index. It tracks prices of all final goods and services included in GDP.

Inflation, a rise over time in a price index, is costly to our society. One of inflation's costs is an arbitrary redistribution of purchasing power. Unanticipated inflation shifts purchasing power away from those awaiting future dollar payments and toward those obligated to make such payments. Another cost of inflation is the resource cost: People use valuable time and other resources trying to cope with inflation.

It is widely agreed that the CPI has overstated inflation in recent decades. As a result, the official statistics on real variables may contain errors, and people whose incomes are indexed to the CPI may be overindexed, enjoying an increase in real income that is paid for by the rest of society. The Bureau of Labor Statistics has been trying to eliminate the upward bias in the CPI. Much progress has been made, but some upward bias remains. The CPI is especially inaccurate as an index of the cost of achieving a given standard of living.

Problem Set   *Answers to even-numbered Questions and Problems can be found on the text Web site at www.thomsonedu.com/economics/hall.*

1. Calculate each of the following from the data in Table 1 in this chapter.
   a. The inflation rate for the year 2005
   b. *Total* inflation (the total percentage change in the price level) from December 1970 to December 2005
2. Using the data in Table 2, calculate the following for the period 2000–2005:
   a. The total percentage change in the nominal wage
   b. The total percentage change in the price level
3. Use your answers from problems 2(a) and 2(b) to obtain the total percentage change in the real wage (excluding benefits) from 2000 to 2005. (Hint: Use the rule given earlier in the chapter for obtaining the percentage change in a real variable from the percentage change in the nominal variable and the percentage change in the price level.)
4. Calculate the total percentage change in the real wage (excluding benefits) from 2000 to 2005 using the last column of Table 2. Compare your answer to the answer in problem 3. Which is the more accurate answer?
5. In Table 2, you can see that the CPI rose from 55.5 in December 1975 to 196.8 in December 2005. The *average* annual inflation rate from 1975 to 2005 was 4.31 percent. That is, $55.5 \times (1.0431)^{30} = 196.8$. Suppose that this average annual rate of inflation overstates the actual annual inflation rate by one percentage point.
   a. What would be the value of an accurate CPI in December 2005?
   b. What would be an accurate value for the real wage (excluding benefits) in December 2005? (Use information in Table 2.)
   c. Determine the total percentage change in the real wage (excluding benefits) from December 1975 to December 2005 using your answer in (b).

6. Given the following *year-end* data, calculate both the inflation rate and the real wage for years 2, 3, and 4.

Year	CPI	Inflation Rate	Nominal Wage	Real Wage
1	100		$10.00	—
2	110	—	$12.00	—
3	120	—	$13.00	—
4	115	—	$12.75	—

7. If there is 5 percent inflation each year for 8 years, what is the *total* amount of inflation (i.e., the total percentage rise in the price level) over the entire 8-year period? (Hint: The answer is *not* 40 percent.)
8. Given the following data, calculate the approximate real interest rate for years 2, 3, and 4. (Assume that each CPI number tells us the price level at the *end* of each year.)

End of Year	CPI	Nominal Interest Rate	Real Interest Rate
1	100		
2	110	15%	—
3	120	13%	—
4	115	8%	—

If you lent $200 to a friend at the beginning of year 2 at the prevailing nominal interest rate of 15 percent, and your friend returned the money, with the interest, at the end of year 2, did you benefit from the deal?

9. (Requires appendix) An economy has only two goods, whose prices and typical consumption quantities are as follows:

	Dec. 2005		Dec. 2006	
	Price	Quantity	Price	Quantity
Fruit (lbs)	$1.00	100	$1.00	150
Nuts (lbs)	$3.00	50	$4.00	25

a. Using December 2005 as the base period for calculations and also as the year for measuring the typical consumer's market basket, calculate the CPI in December 2005 and December 2006.
b. What is the annual inflation rate for 2006?
c. Do you think your answer in (b) would understate the actual inflation rate in 2006? Briefly, why or why not?

10. Complete the following table. (CPI numbers are for the end of each year.)

Year	CPI	Inflation Rate	Nominal Wage	Real Wage
1	37	—	$ 5.60	
2	48		$ 7	
3		10%	$11.26	
4		19%		$25
5	60		$15	

11. a. Jodie earned $25,000 at the end of year 1, when the CPI was 460. If the CPI at the end of year 2 is 504, what would Jodie have to earn at the end of year 2 to maintain a constant real wage?
    b. What would she have to earn in year 2 to obtain a 5 percent increase in her real wage? What percentage increase in the nominal wage is this?

12. During the late 19th and early 20th centuries, many U.S. farmers favored inflationary government policies. Why might this have been the case? (Hint: Do farmers typically pay for their land in full at the time of purchase?)

13. As in Table 3, consider someone who retires in 2006 with $25,000 in initial Social Security benefits per year, and that the actual inflation rate is 2 percent per year over the next 20 years. But now, suppose that the CPI overstates inflation as 4 percent per year (i.e., an overstatement of 2 full percentage points).
    a. What would the *real* benefit payment be in 2026?
    b. What would be the *total percentage increase* in the real benefit payment from 2006 to 2026?

More Challenging

14. Suppose we want to change the base period of the CPI from July 1983 to December 2000. Recalculate December's CPI for each of the years in Table 1, so that the table gives the same information about inflation, but the CPI in December 2000 now has the value 100 instead of 174.0.

15. Inflation is sometimes said to be a tax on nominal money holdings. If you hold $100 and the price level increases by 10 percent, the purchasing power of that $100 falls by about 10 percent. Who benefits from this inflation tax?

APPENDIX

Calculating the Consumer Price Index

The Consumer Price Index (CPI) is the government's most popular measure of inflation. It tracks the cost of the collection of goods, called the *CPI market basket,* bought by a typical consumer in some *base period*. This appendix demonstrates how the Bureau of Labor Statistics calculates the CPI. To help you follow the steps clearly, we'll do the calculations for a very simple economy with just two goods: hamburger meat and oranges (not a pleasant world, but a manageable one). Table A.1 shows prices for each good, and the quantities produced and consumed, in two different periods: December 2004 (the base period) and December 2005. The market basket (measured in the base period) is given in the third column of the table: In December 2004, the typical consumer buys 30 pounds of hamburger and 50 pounds of oranges. Our formula for the CPI in any period t is

CPI in period t

$$= \frac{\text{Cost of market basket at prices in period } t}{\text{Cost of market basket at 2004 prices}} \times 100$$

where each year's prices are measured in December of that year.

Table A.2 shows the calculations we must do to determine the CPI in December 2004 and December 2005. In the table, you can see that the cost of the 2004 market basket at 2004 prices is $200. The cost of the *same* market basket at 2005's higher prices is $235.

To determine the CPI in December 2004—the base period—we use the formula with period t equal to 2004, giving us

CPI in 2004

$$= \frac{\text{Cost of 2004 basket at 2004 prices}}{\text{Cost of 2004 basket at 2004 prices}} \times 100$$

$$= \frac{\$200}{\$200} \times 100 = 100.$$

That is, the CPI in December 2004—the base period—is equal to 100. (The formula, as you can see, is set up so that the CPI will always equal 100 in the base period, regardless of which base period we choose.)

TABLE A.1

Prices and Weekly Quantities in a Two-Good Economy

	December 2004		December 2005	
	Price (per lb)	Quantity (lbs)	Price (per lb)	Quantity (lbs)
Hamburger Meat	$5.00	30	$6.00	10
Oranges	$1.00	50	$1.10	100

TABLE A.2

Calculations for the CPI

	At December 2004 Prices	At December 2005 Prices
Cost of 30 lbs of Hamburger	$5.00 × 30 = $150	$6.00 × 30 = $180
Cost of 50 lbs of Oranges	$1.00 × 50 = $50	$1.10 × 50 = $55
Cost of Entire Market Basket	$150 + $50 = $200	$180 + $55 = $235

Now let's apply the formula again, to get the value of the CPI in December 2005:

CPI in 2005

$$= \frac{\text{Cost of 2004 basket at 2005 prices}}{\text{Cost of 2004 basket at 2004 prices}} \times 100$$

$$= \frac{\$235}{\$200} \times 100 = 117.5.$$

From December 2004 to December 2005, the CPI rises from 100 to 117.5. The rate of inflation over the year 2005 is therefore 17.5 percent.

Notice that the CPI gives more weight to price changes of goods that are more important in the consumer's budget. In our example, the percentage rise in the CPI (17.5 percent) is closer to the percentage rise in the price of hamburger (20 percent) than it is to the percentage price rise of oranges (10 percent). This is because a greater percentage of the budget is *spent* on hamburger than on oranges, so hamburger carries more weight in the CPI.

But one of the CPI's problems, discussed in the body of the chapter, is *substitution bias*. The CPI recognizes that consumers substitute *within* categories of goods. For example, if we had a third good, steak, the CPI would recognize that consumers will buy more steak if the price of hamburger rises faster than the price of steak. But the CPI assumes there is no substitution *among* categories—between beef products and fruit, for example. No matter how much the relative price of beef products like hamburger rises, the CPI assumes that people will continue to buy the same quantity of it, rather than substitute goods in other categories like oranges. Therefore, as the price of hamburger rises, the CPI assumes that we spend a greater and greater percentage of our budgets on it; hamburger gets *increasing weight* in the CPI. In our example, spending on hamburger is assumed to rise from \$150/\$200 = 0.75, or 75 percent of the typical weekly budget, to \$180/\$235 = 0.766, or 76.6 percent. In fact, however, the rapid rise in price would cause people to substitute *away* from hamburger toward other goods whose prices are rising more slowly.

This is what occurs in our two-good example, as you can see in the last column of Table A.1. In 2005, the quantity of hamburger purchased drops to 10, and the quantity of oranges rises to 100. In an ideal measure, the decrease in the quantity of hamburger would reduce its weight in determining the overall rate of inflation. But the CPI ignores the information in the last column of Table A.1, which shows the new quantities purchased in 2005. This failure to correct for substitution bias across categories of goods is one of the reasons the CPI overstates inflation.

The Classical Long-Run Model

Economists often disagree with each other. In news interviews, class lectures, and editorials, they give differing opinions about even the simplest matters. To the casual observer, it might seem that economics is little more than guesswork, where anyone's opinion is as good as anyone else's. But there is actually much more agreement among economists than there appears to be.

Take the following typical example: At a time when the economy is performing well, two distinguished economists appear on *CNN NewsNight*. In a somber tone, the anchor asks each of them what should be done to maintain the health of the economy. "We need to reduce the government's budget deficit by cutting government spending or raising taxes," replies the first economist. "This will enable private businesses to borrow more, so they can purchase new capital and the economy can grow faster." (Don't worry if this chain of logic isn't clear to you yet; it will be by the end of the next chapter.)

"No, no, no," the second economist might interrupt. "Cutting the deficit is the *worst* thing we could do right now. The economy appears to be slowing, and if we raise taxes or cut government spending, we'd reduce the take-home pay of households, causing them to cut their own spending. We'd push the economy toward a recession—one that the U.S. Federal Reserve might not be able to prevent." (You'll begin learning what's behind this argument a few chapters later.)

Which of these economists would be right? Surprisingly, it's entirely possible for *both* of them to be correct. But how can this be? Aren't the two responses contradictory? Not necessarily, because each economist might be hearing—and answering—a different question. The first economist is addressing the likely *long-run* impact of a cut in the government's budget deficit: the impact we might expect after several years have elapsed. The second economist, by contrast, is focusing on a possible *short-run* impact: the effects we might see over the next year.

Once the distinction between the long run and the short run becomes clear, many apparent disagreements among macroeconomists dissolve. If the news anchor had asked our two economists about the *long-run* impact of cutting the deficit, both may well have agreed that it would lead to more investment by business firms and faster economic growth. If asked about the *short-run* impact, both may have agreed about the potential danger of recession. If no time horizon is specified, however, an economist is likely to focus on the horizon he or she feels is most important—something about which economists sometimes *do* disagree. The real dispute, though, is less over how the economy *works* and more about what our priorities should be in guiding it.

Ideally, we would like our economy to do well in both the long run and the short run. Unfortunately, there is often a tradeoff between these two goals: Doing better in the short run can require some sacrifice of long-run goals, and vice versa. The problem for policy makers is much like that of the captain of a ship sailing through the North Atlantic. On the one hand, he wants to reach his destination (his long-run goal); on the other hand, he must avoid icebergs along the way (his short-run goal). As you might imagine, avoiding icebergs may require the captain to deviate from an ideal long-run course. At the same time, reaching port might require risking the occasional iceberg.

The same is true of the macroeconomy. If you flip back two chapters and look at Figure 4, you will see that there are two types of movements in total output. The long-run trajectory shows the growth of potential output. The short-run movements around that trajectory we call economic fluctuations or business cycles. Macroeconomists are concerned with both types of movements. But, as you will see, policies that can help us smooth out economic fluctuations may prove harmful to growth in the long run, while policies that promise a high rate of growth might require us to put up with more severe fluctuations in the short run.

MACROECONOMIC MODELS: CLASSICAL VERSUS KEYNESIAN

Classical model A macro-economic model that explains the long-run behavior of the economy.

The **classical model**, developed by economists in the 19th and early 20th centuries, was an attempt to explain a key observation about the economy: Over periods of several years or longer, the economy performs rather well. That is, if we step back from current conditions and view the economy over a long stretch of time, we see that it operates reasonably close to its potential output. And even when it deviates, it does not do so for very long. Business cycles may come and go, but the economy eventually returns to full employment. Indeed, if we think in terms of decades rather than years or quarters, the business cycle fades in significance much like the waves in a choppy sea disappear when viewed from a jet plane.

In the classical view, this behavior is no accident: Powerful forces are at work that drive the economy toward full employment. Many of the classical economists went even further, arguing that these forces operated within a reasonably short period of time. And even today, an important group of macroeconomists continues to believe that the classical model is useful even in the shorter run.

Until the Great Depression of the 1930s, there was little reason to question these classical ideas. True, output fluctuated around its trend, and from time to time there were serious recessions, but output always returned to its potential, full-employment level within a few years or less, just as the classical economists predicted. But during the Great Depression, output was stuck far below its potential for many years. For some reason, the economy wasn't working the way the classical model said it should.

In 1936, in the midst of the Great Depression, the British economist John Maynard Keynes offered an explanation for the economy's poor performance. His new model of the economy—soon dubbed the *Keynesian model*—changed many economists' thinking.[1] Keynes and his followers argued that, while the classical model might

---

[1] Keynes's attack on the classical model was presented in his book *The General Theory of Employment, Interest and Money* (1936). Unfortunately, it's a very difficult book to read, though you may want to try. Keynes's assumptions were not always clear, and some of his text is open to multiple interpretations. As a result, economists have been arguing for decades about what Keynes really meant.

explain the economy's operation in the long run, the long run could be a very long time in arriving. In the meantime, production could be stuck below its potential, as it seemed to be during the Great Depression.

Keynesian ideas became increasingly popular in universities and government agencies during the 1940s and 1950s. By the mid-1960s, the entire profession had been won over: Macroeconomics *was* Keynesian economics, and the classical model was removed from virtually all introductory economics textbooks. You might be wondering, then, why we are bothering with the classical model here. After all, it's an older model of the economy, one that was largely discredited and replaced, just as the Ptolemaic view that the sun circled the earth was supplanted by the more modern, Copernican view. Right?

Not really. The classical model is still important, for two reasons. First, in recent decades, there has been an active counterrevolution against Keynes's approach to understanding the macroeconomy. Many of the counterrevolutionary new theories are based largely on classical ideas. In some cases, the new theories are just classical economics in modern clothing, but in other cases significant new ideas have been added. By studying classical macroeconomics, you will be better prepared to understand the controversies centering on these newer schools of thought.

The second—and more important—reason for us to study the classical model is its usefulness in understanding the economy over the long run. Even the many economists who find the classical model inadequate for understanding the economy in the short run find it extremely useful in analyzing the economy in the long run.

> *Keynes's ideas and their further development help us understand economic fluctuations—movements in output around its long-run trend. But the classical model has proven more useful in explaining the long-run trend itself.*

This is why we will use the terms "classical view" and "long-run view" interchangeably in the rest of the book; in either case, we mean "the ideas of the classical model used to explain the economy's long-run behavior."

ASSUMPTIONS OF THE CLASSICAL MODEL

Remember from Chapter 1 that all models begin with *assumptions* about the world. The classical model is no exception. Many of its assumptions are *simplifying;* they make the model more manageable, enabling us to see the broad outlines of economic behavior without getting lost in the details. Typically, these assumptions involve aggregation. We combine the many different interest rates in the economy and refer to a single interest rate. We combine the many different types of labor in the economy into a single aggregate labor market. These simplifications are usually harmless: Adding more detail would make our work more difficult, but it would not add much insight; nor would it change any of the central conclusions of the classical view.

There is, however, one assumption in the classical model that goes beyond mere simplification. This is an assumption about how the world works, and it is critical to the conclusions we will reach in this and the next chapter. We can state it in two words: *Markets clear.*

> *A critical assumption in the classical model is that **markets clear**: The price in every market will adjust until quantity supplied and quantity demanded are equal.*

Market clearing Adjustment of prices until quantities supplied and demanded are equal.

Does the market-clearing assumption sound familiar? It should: It was the basic idea behind our study of supply and demand. When we look at the economy through the classical lens, we assume that the forces of supply and demand work fairly well throughout the economy and that markets do reach equilibrium. An excess supply of anything traded will lead to a fall in its price; an excess demand will drive the price up.

The market-clearing assumption, which permeates classical thinking about the economy, provides an early hint about why the classical model does a better job over longer time periods (several years or more) than shorter ones. In some markets, prices might not fully adjust to their equilibrium values for many months or even years after some change in the economy. An excess supply or excess demand might persist for some time. Still, if we wait long enough, an excess supply in a market will eventually force the price down, and an excess demand will eventually drive the price up. That is, *eventually*, the market will clear. Therefore, when we are trying to explain the economy's behavior over the long run, market clearing seems to be a reasonable assumption.

In the remainder of the chapter, we'll use the classical model to answer a variety of important questions about the economy in the long run, such as:

- How is total employment determined?
- How much output will we produce?
- What role does total spending play in the economy?
- What happens when things change?

Keep in mind that, in our discussion of the classical model, we will focus on *real* variables: real GDP, the real wage, real saving, and so on. These variables are typically measured in the dollars of some base year, and their numerical values change only when their *purchasing power* changes. Even though our *actual* measures of the price level are imperfect, you can think of a real variable as one that reflects *true* purchasing power—the value we'd obtain if we used a perfectly accurate price index.

HOW MUCH OUTPUT WILL WE PRODUCE?

Over the last decade, on average, the U.S. economy produced about $10 trillion worth of goods and services per year (valued in 2000 dollars). How was this average level of output determined? Why didn't we produce $14 trillion per year? Or just $2 trillion? There are so many things to consider when answering this question, variables you constantly hear about in the news: wages, interest rates, investment spending, government spending, taxes, and more. Each of these concepts plays an important role in determining total output, and our task in this chapter is to show how they all fit together.

But what a task! How can we disentangle the web of economic interactions we see around us? Our starting point will be the first step of our *three-step process*, introduced toward the end of Chapter 3. To review, that first step was to *characterize the market*—to decide which market or markets best suit the problem being analyzed, which means identifying the buyers and sellers and the type of environment in which they trade.

But which market should we start with?

The classical approach is to start at the beginning, with the *reason* for all this production in the first place: our desire for goods and services, and our need for income in order to buy them. In a market economy, people get their income from supplying labor and other resources to firms. Firms, in turn, use these resources to make the goods and services that people demand. Thus, a logical place to start our analysis is the markets for resources: labor, land, capital, and entrepreneurship.

For now we'll concentrate our attention on just one type of resource: labor. We'll assume that firms are already using the available quantities of the other resources. Moreover, because we are building a *macroeconomic* model, we'll aggregate all the different types of labor—office workers, construction workers, factory workers, teachers, waiters, writers, and more—into a single variable, simply called *labor.*

Our question is: How many workers will be employed in the economy?

THE LABOR MARKET

The classical labor market is illustrated in Figure 1. The number of workers is measured on the horizontal axis, and the real hourly wage rate is measured on the vertical axis. Remember that the *real wage*—which is measured in the dollars of some base year—tells us the amount of goods that workers can buy with an hour's earnings.

Now look at the two curves in the figure. These are supply and demand curves, similar to the supply and demand curves for maple syrup, but there is one key difference: For a *good* such as maple syrup, households are the demanders and firms the suppliers. But for labor, the roles are reversed: Households supply labor and firms demand it.

The curve labeled L^S is the **labor supply curve** in this market; it tells us how many people will want to work at each wage. The upward slope tells us that the greater the real wage, the greater the number of people who will want to work. Why does the labor supply curve slope upward?

Labor supply curve Indicates how many people will want to work at various real wage rates.

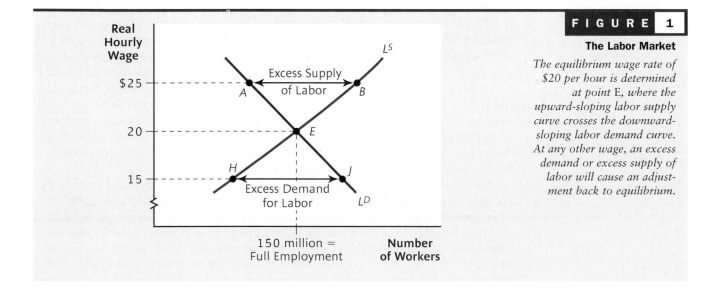

F I G U R E 1

The Labor Market

The equilibrium wage rate of $20 per hour is determined at point E, where the upward-sloping labor supply curve crosses the downward-sloping labor demand curve. At any other wage, an excess demand or excess supply of labor will cause an adjustment back to equilibrium.

To earn income, you must go to work and give up other activities such as school, parenting, or leisure. Thus, each of us will want to work only if the income we will earn *at least* compensates us for the other activities that we will give up.

Of course, people value their time differently. But for each of us, there is some critical wage rate above which we would decide that we're better off working. Below that wage, we would be better off not working. In Figure 1,

> *the labor supply curve slopes upward because, as the wage rate increases, more and more individuals are better off working than not working. Thus, a rise in the wage rate increases the number of people in the economy who want to work—to supply their labor.*

Labor demand curve Indicates how many workers firms will want to hire at various real wage rates.

The curve labeled L^D is the **labor demand curve,** which shows the number of workers firms will want to hire at any real wage. Why does this curve slope downward?

In deciding how much labor to hire, a firm's goal is to earn the greatest possible profit: the difference between sales revenue and costs. A firm will want to keep hiring additional workers as long as the output produced by those workers adds more to the firm's revenue than it adds to costs.

Now think about what happens as the wage rate rises. Some workers that added more to revenue than to cost at the lower wage will now cost more than they add in revenue. Accordingly, the firm will not want to employ these workers at the higher wage.

> *As the wage rate increases, each firm in the economy will find that, to maximize profit, it should employ fewer workers than before. When all firms behave this way together, a rise in the wage rate will decrease the quantity of labor demanded in the economy.*

Remember that in the classical view, *all markets clear,* and that includes the market for labor. Specifically, the real wage adjusts until the quantities of labor supplied and demanded are equal. In the labor market in Figure 1, the market-clearing wage is $20 per hour because that is where the labor supply and labor demand curves intersect. While every worker would prefer to earn $25 rather than $20, at $25 there would be an excess supply of labor equal to the distance *AB*. With not enough jobs to go around, competition among workers would drive the wage downward. Similarly, firms might prefer to pay their workers $15 rather than $20, but at $15, the excess demand for labor (equal to the distance *HJ*) would drive the wage upward. When the wage is $20, however, there is neither an excess demand nor an excess supply of labor, so the wage will neither increase nor decrease. Thus, $20 is the equilibrium wage in the economy. Reading along the horizontal axis, we see that at this wage, 150 million people will be working.

Notice that, in the figure, labor is fully employed; that is, the number of workers that firms want to hire is equal to the number of people who want jobs. Therefore, everyone who wants a job at the market wage of $20 should be able to find one. Small amounts of frictional unemployment might exist, since it takes some time for new workers or job switchers to find jobs. And there might be structural unemployment, due to some mismatch between those who want jobs in the market and the types of jobs available. But there is no *cyclical* unemployment of the type we discussed two chapters ago.

Full employment of the labor force is an important feature of the classical model. As long as we can count on markets (including the labor market) to clear, government action is not needed to ensure full employment; it happens automatically:

In the classical view, the economy achieves full employment on its own.

Automatic full employment may strike you as odd, since it contradicts the cyclical unemployment we sometimes see around us. For example, in the recession of 2001, millions of workers around the country, in all kinds of professions and labor markets, were unable to find jobs for many months. Remember, though, that the classical model takes the long-run view, and over long periods of time, full employment is a fairly accurate description of the U.S. labor market. Cyclical unemployment, by definition, lasts only as long as the current business cycle itself; it is not a permanent, long-run problem.

DETERMINING THE ECONOMY'S OUTPUT

So far, we've focused on the labor market to determine the economy's level of employment. In our example, 150 million people will have jobs. Now we ask: How much output (real GDP) will these 150 million workers produce? The answer depends on two things: (1) the amount of other resources available for labor to use; and (2) the state of *technology*, which determines how much output we can produce with those resources.

In this chapter, remember that we're focusing on only one resource—labor—and we're treating the quantities of all other resources firms use as fixed during the period we're analyzing. Now we'll go even further: We'll assume that technology does not change.

Why do we make these assumptions? After all, in the real world technology *does* change, the capital stock *does* grow, new natural resources *can* be discovered, and the number and quality of entrepreneurs *can* change. Isn't it unrealistic to hold all of these things constant?

Yes, but our assumption is only temporary. The most effective way to master a macroeconomic model is "divide and conquer": Start with a part of the model, understand it well, and then add in other parts. Accordingly, our classical analysis of the economy is divided into two separate questions: (1) What would be the long-run equilibrium of the economy *if* there were a constant state of technology and *if* quantities of all resources besides labor were fixed? And (2) What happens to this long-run equilibrium when technology and the quantities of other resources change? In this chapter, we focus on the first question. In the next chapter on economic growth, we'll address the second question.

The Production Function

With a constant technology, and given quantities of all resources other than labor, only one variable can affect total output: the quantity of labor. So it's time to explore the relationship between total employment and total production in the economy. This relationship is given by the economy's *aggregate production function*.

*The **aggregate production function** (or just **production function**) shows the total output the economy can produce with different quantities of labor, given constant amounts of other resources and the current state of technology.*

Aggregate production function
The relationship showing how much total output can be produced with different quantities of labor, with quantities of all other resources held constant.

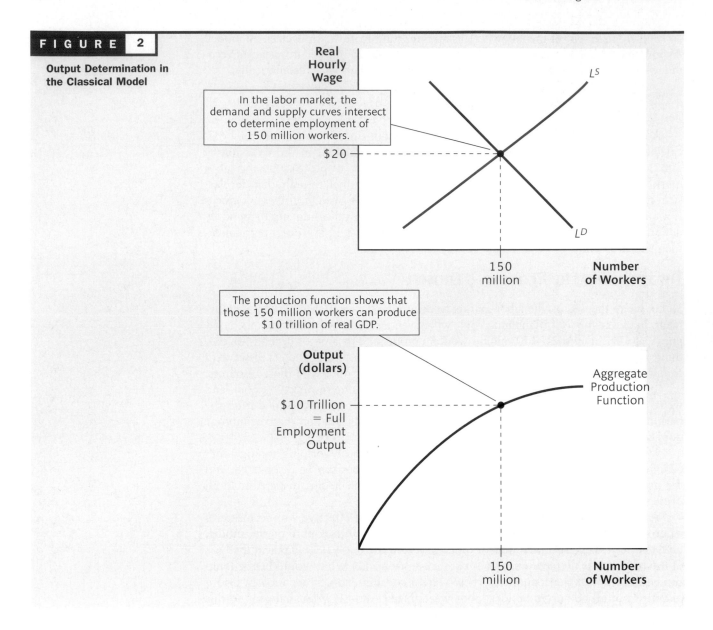

FIGURE 2

Output Determination in the Classical Model

In the labor market, the demand and supply curves intersect to determine employment of 150 million workers.

The production function shows that those 150 million workers can produce $10 trillion of real GDP.

The bottom panel of Figure 2 shows what a nation's aggregate production function might look like. The upward slope tells us that an increase in the number of people working will increase the quantity of output produced. But notice the shape of the production function: It flattens out as we move rightward along it.

The declining slope of the aggregate production function is the result of *diminishing returns to labor:* Output rises when another worker is added, but the rise is smaller and smaller with each successive worker.

Why does this happen? For one thing, as we keep adding workers, gains from specialization are harder and harder to come by. Moreover, as we continue to add workers, each one will have less and less of the other resources to work with. For example, each time more agricultural workers are added to a fixed amount of farmland, output might rise. But as we continue to add workers and there are more and more workers per acre, output will rise by less and less with each new worker. The same is true when more factory workers are added to a fixed amount of factory floor space and machinery, or more professors are added to a fixed number of classrooms: Output continues to rise, but by less and less with each added worker.

Figure 2 also illustrates how the aggregate production function, together with the labor market, determines the economy's total output or real GDP. In our example, the labor market (upper panel) automatically generates full employment of 150 million workers, and the production function (lower panel) tells us that 150 million workers—together with the available amounts of other resources and the current state of technology—can produce $10 trillion worth of output. Since $10 trillion is the output produced by a fully employed labor force, it is also the economy's potential output level.

> *In the classical, long-run view, the economy reaches its potential output automatically.*

This last statement is an important conclusion of the classical model and an important characteristic of the economy in the long run: Output tends toward its potential, full-employment level *on its own,* with no need for government to steer the economy toward it. And we have arrived at this conclusion merely by assuming that the labor market clears and observing the relationship between employment and output.

THE ROLE OF SPENDING

Something may be bothering you about the classical view of output determination, a potential problem we have so far carefully avoided: What if business firms are unable to sell all the output produced by a fully employed labor force? Then business firms will not continue to employ workers who produce output that is not being sold, and the economy will not remain at full employment for very long. Thus, if we are asserting that potential output is the economy's equilibrium, we had better be sure that *total spending* on output is equal to *total production* during any given year. But can we be sure of this?

In the classical view, the answer is, absolutely yes! We'll demonstrate this in two stages: first, in a very simple (but very unrealistic) economy, and then, under more realistic conditions.

TOTAL SPENDING IN A VERY SIMPLE ECONOMY

Imagine a world much simpler than our own, a world with just two types of economic units: households and business firms. In this world, households spend all of their income on goods and services. They do not save any of their income, nor do they pay taxes, nor do they buy any products from abroad. Such an economy is illustrated in Figure 3.

Let's assume that $10 trillion worth of goods and services are produced in this economy during the year. As you learned two chapters ago, the value of the total

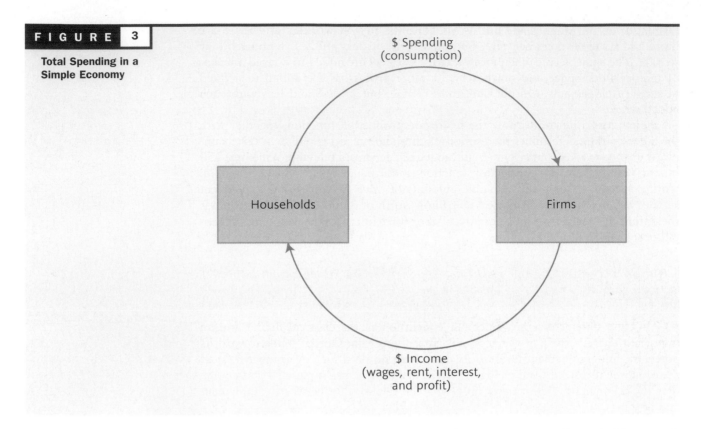

FIGURE 3

Total Spending in a Simple Economy

output of firms is equal to the total income (factor payments) of households. So with firms producing $10 trillion in output, they also pay out $10 trillion to households in the form of wages, rent, interest, and profit. What happens to this $10 trillion in household income? In this simple economy, with no saving, no taxes, and no goods purchased from abroad, the $10 trillion has nowhere to go except to be spent on domestically produced output. Thus, household consumption spending will equal $10 trillion—the same as the value of output that firms are producing.

In general,

> *in a simple economy with just households and firms, in which households spend all of their income on domestic output, total spending must be equal to total output.*

Say's law The idea that total spending will be sufficient to purchase the total output produced.

This simple proposition is called **Say's law,** after the early 19th-century economist Jean Baptiste Say, who popularized the idea. Say noted that each time a good or service is produced, an equal amount of income is created. This income is spent, so it comes back to the business sector to purchase its goods and services. In Say's own words:

> A product *is no sooner created than it, from that instant, affords a market for other products to the full extent of its own value. . . . Thus, the mere circumstance of the creation of one product immediately opens a vent for other products.*[2]

---

[2] J. B. Say, *A Treatise on Political Economy,* 4th ed. (London: Longman, 1821), Vol. I, p. 167.

For example, each time a shirt manufacturer produces a $25 shirt, it creates $25 in factor payments to households. (Forgot why? Go back two chapters and refresh your memory about the factor payments approach to GDP.) But in the simple economy we're analyzing, that $25 in factor payments will lead to $25 in total spending—just enough to buy the very shirt produced. Of course, the households who receive the $25 in factor payments won't necessarily buy a shirt with it; the shirt manufacturer must still worry about selling its own specific output. But in the *aggregate*, we needn't worry about there being sufficient demand for the total output produced. Business firms—by producing output—also create a demand for goods and services equal to the value of that output.

> *Say's law states that by producing goods and services, firms create a total demand for goods and services equal to what they have produced. Or, more simply, supply creates its own demand.*

Say's law is crucial to the classical view of the economy. Why? Remember that because the labor market is assumed to clear, firms will hire all the workers who want jobs and produce our *potential* or *full-employment* output level. But firms will only *continue* to produce this level of output if they can *sell* it all. In the simple economy of Figure 3, Say's law assures us that, in the aggregate, spending will be just high enough for firms to sell all the output that a fully employed labor force can produce. As a result, full employment can be maintained.

But the economy in Figure 3 leaves out some important details of economies in the real world. Does Say's law also apply in a more realistic economy? Let's see.

TOTAL SPENDING IN A MORE REALISTIC ECONOMY

The real-world economy is more complicated than the imaginary one we've just considered. One complication is trade with the rest of the world. We'll deal with international trade in the appendix to this chapter. For now, we'll continue to assume that we're in a *closed economy*—one that does not have any economic dealings with the rest of the world. But here we'll add some features that we ignored before.

In the real world:

- Households don't spend *all* their income. Rather, some of their income is saved or goes to pay taxes.
- Households are not the only spenders in the economy. Rather, businesses and the government also buy final goods and services.

With these added details,will Say's law still apply?

Let's consider the economy of Classica, a fictional economy that behaves according to the classical model, but more realistically than the economy of Figure 3. Data on Classica's economy in 2006 are given in Table 1. Notice that total output and total income are both equal to $10 trillion in 2006, which is assumed to be Classica's full-employment or potential output level.

Next come three entries that refer to spending by the final users who purchase Classica's GDP. Note that, unlike the households in Figure 3, Classica's households spend only *part* of their income, $7 trillion, on consumption goods (C). Skipping down to government purchases (G), we find that Classica's government sector—combining its national, regional, and local government agencies—purchases $2 trillion in goods and services.

TABLE 1		
Flows in the Economy of Classica, 2006	Total Output (GDP)	$10 trillion
	Total Income	$10 trillion
	Consumption Spending (C)	$7 trillion
	Planned Investment Spending (I^p)	$1 trillion
	Government Purchases (G)	$2 trillion
	Net Taxes (T)	$1.25 trillion
	Household Saving (S)	$1.75 trillion

Some New Macroeconomic Variables

In addition to consumption and government purchases—with which you are already familiar—Table 1 includes some new variables. Since these will be used throughout the rest of this book, it's worth defining and discussing them here.

Planned Investment Spending (I^p). Two chapters ago, you learned that total investment spending—the component labeled I in the expenditure approach to GDP—includes not only business spending on new capital but also *changes in firms' inventories* over a period of time. Inventory changes occur when firms produce more than they sell (an increase in inventories) or sell more than they produce (a decrease in inventories).

Our ultimate goal is to find out if Say's law works in Classica—if total spending exactly matches Classica's total output. Therefore, it would be a mistake to include inventory changes—which represent the mismatch between sales and production—as part of investment spending. When we exclude inventory changes from investment spending, we're left with *planned investment spending*.

Planned investment spending
Business purchases of plant and equipment.

> *Planned investment spending* (I^p) *over a period of time is total investment spending* (I) *minus the change in inventories over the period:*
>
> $$I^p = I - \Delta \text{ inventories}.$$

Here, we're using the Greek letter Δ ("delta") to indicate a change in a variable.

Why do we call this new variable *planned* investment? In the real world, some inventory changes are, in fact, planned by firms. But they can also come as a surprise. For example, suppose Calvin Klein produces $40 million in clothing during a quarter, planning to sell all of it. But during the quarter, it actually ships and sells only $35 million. Then $5 million in unsold output would be an *unplanned increase in inventories*—a surprise, rather than a planned result. On the other hand, if Calvin Klein sold $43 million, then $3 million in sales would come out of inventories. This would be an *unplanned decrease in inventories*—a surprise in the other direction.

Changes in inventories are generally the only component of spending in GDP that is not planned. A firm does not "discover" at the end of a quarter that it has purchased a new factory. This type of investment is intended and planned in advance. And—other than Homer in *The Simpsons*—a consumer doesn't "discover" that he has purchased a new car or a lifetime supply of slurpies; consumption spending is intentional.

In this and future chapters, to keep our discussions simple we'll regard *all* inventory changes as unplanned surprises. This is why, after deducting inventory changes from total investment, we call what is left *planned investment*. In Table 1, you can see that Classica's planned investment spending—which excludes any changes in inventories—is $1 trillion.

Net Tax Revenue (T). Recall (from two chapters ago) that *transfer payments* are government outlays that are *not* spent on goods and services. These transfers—which include unemployment insurance, welfare payments, and Social Security benefits—are just *given* to people, either out of social concern (welfare payments), to keep a promise (Social Security payments), or elements of both (unemployment insurance).

In the macroeconomy, government transfer payments are like negative taxes: They represent the part of tax revenue that the government takes from one set of households (taxpayers) but gives right back to another set of households (such as Social Security recipients), and are not available for government purchases. Because transfer payments stay *within* the household sector, we can treat them as if they were never paid to the government at all. We do this by focusing on *net taxes:*

> *Net taxes* (T) *are total government tax revenue minus government transfer payments:*
>
> $$T = \textit{Total tax revenue} - \textit{Transfers}.$$

Net taxes Government tax revenues minus transfer payments.

For example, in 2006 net taxes in Classica are $1.25 trillion. This number might result from total tax revenue of $2 trillion and $0.75 trillion in government transfer payments. It could also result from $3 trillion in tax revenue and $1.75 trillion in transfers. From the macroeconomic perspective, net taxes—what the government has available for purchases—are $1.25 trillion in either case.

Household Saving (S). We'll define household saving in two steps. First, we determine how much income the household sector has left after payment of net taxes. This is the household sector's **disposable income**:

$$\textit{Disposable income} = \textit{Total income} - \textit{Net taxes}.$$

Disposable income Household income minus net taxes, which is either spent or saved.

The household sector can *dispose* of this disposable (after-tax) income in only two ways: either by spending it (C) or by *not* spending it. The part that is *not* spent is defined as (**household**) saving (S):

$$S = \textit{Disposable income} - C.$$

(Household) saving The portion of after-tax income that households do not spend on consumption.

The last entry in Table 1 tells us that in Classica, household saving is $1.75 trillion. Let's check this using disposable income. From the table, total income is $7 trillion and net taxes are $1.25 trillion, so disposable income (not shown in the table) is $10 trillion − $1.25 trillion = $8.75 trillion. Consumption spending is $7 trillion, so:

$$S = \textit{Disposable income} - C = \$8.75 \text{ trillion} - \$7 \text{ trillion} = \$1.75 \text{ trillion}$$

Total Spending in Classica

In Classica, total spending is the sum of the purchases made by the household sector (C), the business sector (I^P), and the government sector (G):

$$\text{Total spending} = C + I^P + G.$$

Or, using the numbers in Table 1:

$$\text{Total spending} = \$7 \text{ trillion} + \$1 \text{ trillion} + \$2 \text{ trillion} = \$10 \text{ trillion}.$$

This may strike you as suspiciously convenient: Total spending is exactly equal to total output, just as we'd like it to be if we want Classica to continue producing its potential output of $10 trillion. And just what we needed to illustrate Say's law in this more realistic economy.

But we haven't yet proven anything; we've just cooked up an example that made the numbers come out this way. The question is, do we have any reason to *expect* the economy to give us numbers like these automatically, with total spending precisely equal to total output?

The rectangles in Figure 4 provide some perspective on this question and suggest the way to an answer. Total output (represented by the first rectangle) is, by definition, always equal in value to total income (the second rectangle). As we've seen in Figure 3, if households *spent* all of this income, then consumption spending would equal total output.

But in Classica, households do *not* spend all of their income. Some income goes to pay net taxes ($1.25 trillion), and some is saved ($1.75 trillion). We can think of

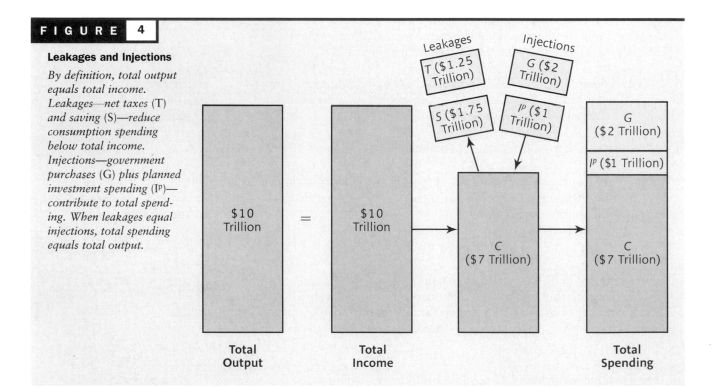

FIGURE 4

Leakages and Injections

By definition, total output equals total income. Leakages—net taxes (T) and saving (S)—reduce consumption spending below total income. Injections—government purchases (G) plus planned investment spending (I^P)—contribute to total spending. When leakages equal injections, total spending equals total output.

Leakages: T ($1.25 Trillion), S ($1.75 Trillion)

Injections: G ($2 Trillion), I^P ($1 Trillion)

$10 Trillion = $10 Trillion

C ($7 Trillion)

G ($2 Trillion)
I^P ($1 Trillion)
C ($7 Trillion)

Total Output   Total Income   Total Spending

saving and net taxes as **leakages** out of spending: income that households receive, but do not spend. Leakages reduce consumption spending below total income, as you can see in the third, lower rectangle. In Classica, total leakages = $1.75 trillion + $1.25 trillion = $3 trillion, and this must be subtracted from income of $10 trillion to get consumption spending of $7 trillion. Thus, if consumption spending were the only spending in the economy, business firms would be unable to sell their entire potential output of $10 trillion.

Fortunately, in addition to leakages, there are **injections**—spending from sources *other* than households. Injections boost total spending and enable firms to produce and sell a level of output greater than just consumption spending.

There are two types of injections in the economy. First is the government's purchases of goods and services. When government agencies—federal, state, or local—buy aircraft, cleaning supplies, cellular phones, or computers, they are buying a part of the economy's output.

The other injection is planned investment spending (I^p). When business firms purchase new computers, trucks, or machinery, or they build new factories or office buildings, they are buying a part of the GDP along with consumers and the government.

Take another look at the rectangles in Figure 4. Notice that in going from total output to total spending, leakages are subtracted and injections are added. Clearly, total output and total spending will be equal only if leakages and injections are equal as well.

> *Total spending will equal total output if and only if total leakages in the economy are equal to total injections—that is, only if the sum of saving and net taxes is equal to the sum of planned investment spending and government purchases.*

And here is a surprising result: In the classical model, this condition will automatically be satisfied. To see why, we must first take a detour through another important market. Then we'll come back to the equality of leakages and injections.

THE LOANABLE FUNDS MARKET

The **loanable funds market** is where households make their saving available to those who need additional funds. When you save—that is, when you have income left over after paying taxes and buying consumption goods—you can put your surplus funds in a bank, buy a bond or a share of stock, or use the funds to buy a variety of other assets. In each of these cases, you would be a supplier in the loanable funds market.

Households supply funds because they receive a reward for doing so. But the reward comes in different forms. When the suppliers *lend* out funds, the reward is *interest payments*. When the funds are provided through the stock market, the suppliers become part owners of the firm and their payment is called *dividends*. To keep our discussion simple, we'll assume that all funds made available by households are *loaned* and that the payment is simply *interest*.

> *The total supply of loanable funds is equal to household saving. The funds supplied are loaned out, and households receive interest payments on these funds.*

Leakages Income earned, but not spent, by households during a given year.

Injections Spending from sources other than households.

Loanable funds market The market in which households make their saving available to borrowers.

On the other side of the market are those who want to obtain funds—demanders in this market. Business firms are one set of demanders of funds. When Avis wants to add cars to its automobile rental fleet, when McDonald's wants to build a new beef-processing plant, or when the local dry cleaner wants to buy new dry cleaning machines, it will likely raise the funds in the loanable funds market. It may take out a bank loan, sell bonds, or sell new shares of stock. In each of these cases, a firm's planned investment spending would be equal to the funds it obtains from the loanable funds market. To keep the discussion simple, we'll assume that business firms *borrow* the funds they obtain in the loanable funds market.

> *Businesses' demand for loanable funds is equal to their planned investment spending. The funds obtained are borrowed, and firms* pay interest *on their loans.*

Aside from households and business firms, the other major player in the loanable funds market is the government sector. Government participates in the market whenever it runs a budget deficit or a budget surplus.

Budget deficit The excess of government purchases over net taxes.

When government purchases of goods and services (G) are greater than net taxes (T), the government runs a **budget deficit** equal to $G - T$. When government purchases of goods and services (G) are less than net taxes (T), the government runs a **budget surplus** equal to $T - G$.

Budget surplus The excess of net taxes over government purchases.

In our example in Table 1, Classica's government is running a budget deficit: Government purchases are $2 trillion, while net taxes are $1.25 trillion, giving us a deficit of $2 trillion − $1.25 trillion = $0.75 trillion. This deficit is financed by borrowing in the loanable funds market. In any year, the government's demand for funds is equal to its deficit.

> *When the government runs a budget deficit, its demand for loanable funds is equal to its deficit. The funds are borrowed, and the government* pays interest *on its loans.*

(What if Classica's government were running a surplus? You'll be asked to consider that in the end-of-chapter problems.)

We can summarize our view of the loanable funds market so far with these two points:

- The supply of funds is household saving.
- The demand for funds is the sum of the business sector's planned investment spending and the government sector's budget deficit, if any.

Now let's take a closer look at the behavior of each of the key players—households, business firms, and the government—in the market for loanable funds.

THE SUPPLY OF FUNDS CURVE

Since interest is the reward for saving and supplying funds to the financial market, a rise in the interest rate *increases* the quantity of funds supplied (household saving), while a drop in the interest rate decreases it. This relationship is illustrated by Classica's upward-sloping **supply of funds curve** in Figure 5. If the interest rate is 3 percent, households save $1.5 trillion, and if the interest rate rises to 5 percent, people save more and the quantity of funds supplied rises to $1.75 trillion.

Supply of funds curve Indicates the level of household saving at various interest rates.

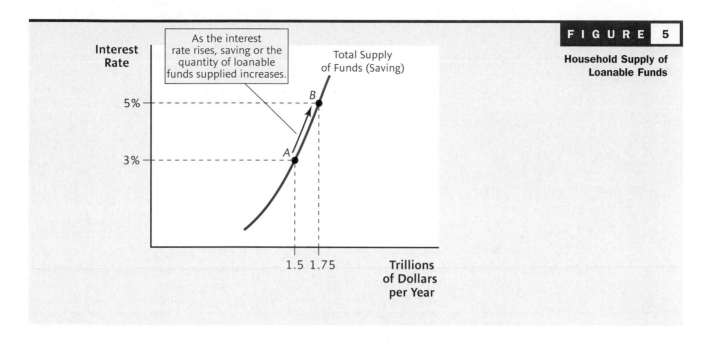

FIGURE 5

Household Supply of
Loanable Funds

> *The quantity of funds supplied to the financial market depends positively on the interest rate. This is why the saving or supply of funds curve slopes upward.*

Of course, other things can affect saving besides the interest rate: tax rates, expectations about the future, and the general willingness of households to postpone consumption, to name a few. In drawing the supply of funds curve, we assume each of these variables is constant. In the next chapter, we'll explore what happens when some of these variables change.

The Demand for Funds Curve

Businesses buy plant and equipment when the expected benefits exceed the costs. Since businesses obtain the funds for their investment spending from the loanable funds market, a key cost of any investment project is the interest rate that must be paid on borrowed funds. As the interest rate rises and investment costs increase, fewer projects will look attractive, and planned investment spending will decline. This is the logic of the downward-sloping **business demand for funds curve** in Figure 6. At a 5 percent interest rate, firms would borrow $1 trillion and spend it on capital equipment; at an interest rate of 3 percent, business borrowing and investment spending would rise to $1.5 trillion.

Business demand for funds curve Indicates the level of investment spending firms plan at various interest rates.

> *When the interest rate falls, investment spending and the business borrowing needed to finance it rise.*

What about the government's demand for funds? Will it, too, be influenced by the interest rate? Probably not very much. Government seems to be cushioned from the cost–benefit considerations that haunt business decisions. Any company president who ignored interest rates in deciding how much to borrow would be quickly out of a job. U.S. presidents and legislators have often done so with little political cost.

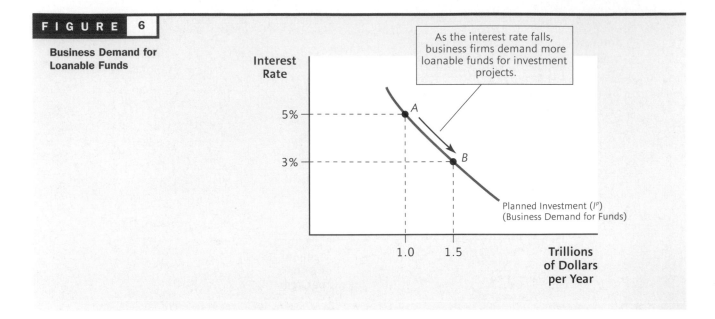

FIGURE 6

Business Demand for Loanable Funds

As the interest rate falls, business firms demand more loanable funds for investment projects.

Planned Investment (I^p)
(Business Demand for Funds)

For this reason, when government is running a budget deficit, our classical model treats government borrowing as independent of the interest rate: No matter what the interest rate, the government sector's deficit—and its borrowing—is the same. This is why we have graphed the **government's demand for funds curve** as a vertical line in panel (b) of Figure 7.

Government demand for funds curve Indicates the amount of government borrowing at various interest rates.

> *The government sector's deficit and, therefore, its demand for funds are independent of the interest rate.*

In the figure, the government deficit—and hence the government's demand for funds—is equal to $0.75 trillion at any interest rate.

Figure 7 also shows that the **total demand for funds curve** is found by horizontally summing the business demand curve [panel (a)] and the government demand curve [panel (b)]. For example, if the interest rate is 5 percent, firms demand $1 trillion in funds and the government demands $0.75 trillion, so that the total quantity of loanable funds demanded is $1.75 trillion. A drop in the interest rate—to 3 percent—increases business borrowing to $1.5 trillion while the government's borrowing remains at $0.75 trillion, so the total quantity of funds demanded rises to $2.25 trillion.

Total demand for funds curve Indicates the total amount of borrowing at various interest rates.

> *As the interest rate decreases, the quantity of funds demanded by business firms increases, while the quantity demanded by the government remains unchanged. Therefore, the total quantity of funds demanded rises.*

EQUILIBRIUM IN THE LOANABLE FUNDS MARKET

In the classical view, the loanable funds market—like all other markets—is assumed to clear: The interest rate will rise or fall until the quantities of funds supplied and demanded are equal. Figure 8 illustrates the loanable funds market of Classica, our

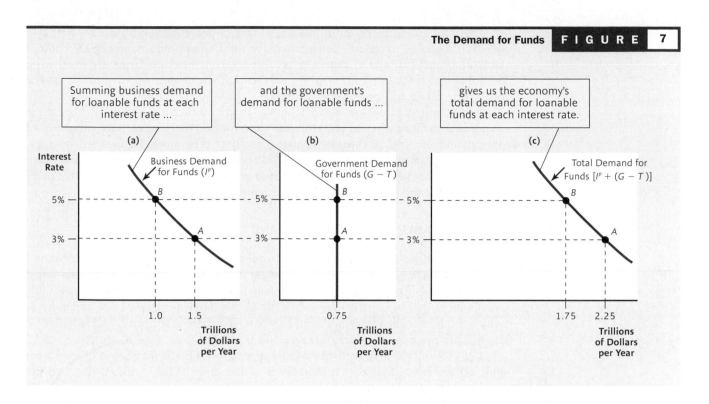

The Demand for Funds FIGURE 7

Summing business demand for loanable funds at each interest rate ...

and the government's demand for loanable funds ...

gives us the economy's total demand for loanable funds at each interest rate.

(a)

(b)

(c)

Interest Rate

Business Demand for Funds (I^P)

Government Demand for Funds ($G - T$)

Total Demand for Funds [$I^P + (G - T)$]

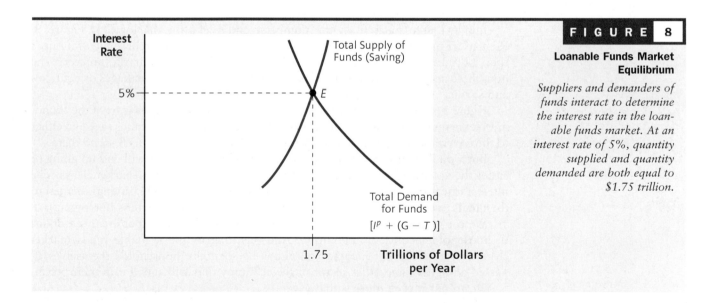

FIGURE 8

Loanable Funds Market Equilibrium

Suppliers and demanders of funds interact to determine the interest rate in the loanable funds market. At an interest rate of 5%, quantity supplied and quantity demanded are both equal to $1.75 trillion.

Interest Rate

Total Supply of Funds (Saving)

Total Demand for Funds

[$I^P + (G - T)$]

fictional economy. Equilibrium occurs at point *E*, with an interest rate of 5 percent and total saving equal to $1.75 trillion. (To convince yourself that 5 percent is the equilibrium interest rate, mark an interest rate of 4 percent on the graph. Would there be an excess demand or an excess supply of loanable funds at this rate? How would the interest rate change? Then do the same for an interest rate of 6 percent.)

Once we know the equilibrium interest rate (5 percent), we can use the first two panels of Figure 7 to tell us exactly where the total household saving of $1.75 billion ends up. Panel (a) tells us that at 5 percent interest, business firms are borrowing $1 trillion of the total, and panel (b) tells us that the government is borrowing the remaining $0.75 trillion to cover its deficit.

So far, our exploration of the loanable funds market has shown us how three important variables in the economy are determined: the interest rate, the level of saving, and the level of investment. But it really tells us more. Remember the question that sent us on this detour into the loanable funds market in the first place: Can we be sure that all of the output produced at full employment will be purchased? We now have the tools to answer this question.

THE LOANABLE FUNDS MARKET AND SAY'S LAW

In Figure 4 of this chapter, you saw that total spending will equal total output if and only if *total leakages* in the economy (saving plus net taxes) are equal to *total injections* (planned investment plus government purchases). Now we can see why this requirement will be satisfied automatically in the classical model. Look at Figure 9, which duplicates the rectangles from Figure 4. But there is something added: arrows to indicate the flows between leakages and injections.

Let's follow the arrows to see what happens to all the leakages out of spending. One arrow shows that the entire leakage of net taxes ($1.25 trillion) flows to the government, which spends it.

Now look at the other two arrows that show us what happens to the $1.75 trillion leakage of household saving. $0.75 trillion of this saving is borrowed by the government, while the rest—$1 trillion—is borrowed by business firms.

But let's step back from the numbers, and focus on the logic of Figure 9. Remember our question: Will total spending be sufficient to purchase the economy's total output? And remember what created some doubt about the answer: The household sector spends only *part* of its income, because of the leakages of net taxes and saving.

Figure 9 shows us that net taxes and savings don't just disappear from the economy. Net taxes go to the government, which *spends them*. And any funds saved go either to the government—which spends them—or to business firms—which spend them.

But wait . . . how do we know that *all* funds that are saved will end up going to either the government or businesses? Because the loanable funds market clears: The interest rate adjusts until the quantity of loanable funds supplied (saving) is equal to the quantity of loanable funds demanded (government and business borrowing).

We can put all this together as follows: Every dollar of output creates a dollar of household income, by definition. And—as long as the loanable funds market clears—every dollar of income will either be spent by households themselves or passed along to some *other* sector of the economy that will spend it in their place.

Or, to put it even more simply,

> *as long as the loanable funds market clears, Say's law holds: Total spending equals total output. This is true even in a more realistic economy with saving, taxes, investment, and a government deficit.*

Here's another way to see the same result, in terms of a simple equation. Because the loanable funds market clears, we know that the interest rate—the price in this

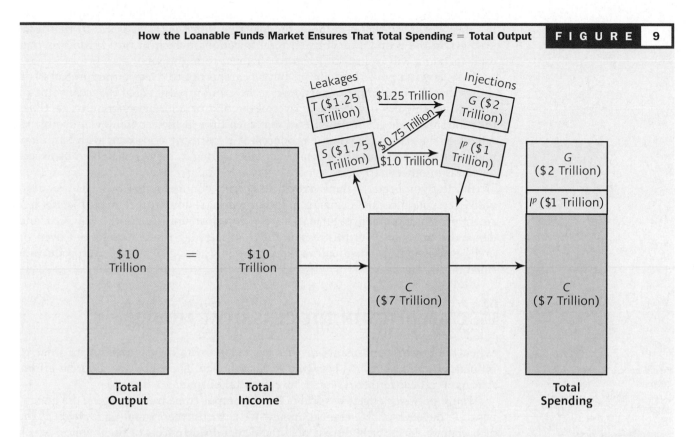

How the Loanable Funds Market Ensures That Total Spending = Total Output FIGURE 9

Because the loanable funds market clears, we know that total leakages will automatically equal total injections. The leakage of net taxes goes to the government and is spent on government purchases. If the government is running a budget deficit, it will also borrow part of the leakage of household saving and spend that too. Any household saving left over will be borrowed by business firms and spent on capital. Thus, every dollar of leakages turns into spending by either government or private business firms.

market—will rise or fall until the quantity of funds supplied (savings, S) is equal to the quantity of funds demanded (planned investment plus the deficit, or $I^p + (G - T)$):

Loanable funds market clears $\Rightarrow$ $\underbrace{S}_{\text{Quantity of funds supplied}}$ = $\underbrace{I^p + (G - T)}_{\text{Quantity of funds demanded}}$

Rearranging this equation by moving T to the left side, we have:

Loanable funds market clears $\Rightarrow$ $\underbrace{S + T}_{\text{Leakages}}$ = $\underbrace{I^p + G}_{\text{Injections}}$

Finally, remember that

Leakages = Injections $\Rightarrow$ Total spending = Total output

In other words, market clearing in the loanable funds market *assures us* that total leakages in the economy will equal total injections, which in turn *assures us* that total spending will be just sufficient to purchase total output.

Say's law is a powerful concept. But be careful not to overinterpret it. Say's law shows that the *total* value of spending in the economy will equal the *total* value of output, which rules out a *general* overproduction or underproduction of goods in the economy. It does not promise us that each firm in the economy will be able to sell all of the particular good it produces. It is perfectly consistent with Say's law that there be excess supplies in some markets, as long as they are balanced by excess demands in other markets.

But lest you begin to think that the classical economy might be a chaotic mess, with excess supplies and demands in lots of markets, don't forget about the *market-clearing* assumption. In each market, prices adjust until quantities supplied and demanded are equal. For this reason, the classical, long-run view rules out over- or underproduction in individual markets, as well as the generalized overproduction ruled out by Say's law.

FISCAL POLICY IN THE CLASSICAL MODEL

Fiscal policy A change in government purchases or net taxes designed to change total output.

Demand-side effects Macroeconomic policy effects on total output that work through changes in total spending.

When the government changes either net taxes or its own purchases in order to influence total output, it is engaging in **fiscal policy**. There are two different effects that fiscal policy, in theory, could have on total output.

The *supply-side* effects of fiscal policy on output come from changing the quantities of resources available in the economy. We'll discuss these supply-side effects in the next chapter. Here, we'll discuss only the **demand-side effects** of fiscal policy, which are entirely different. These effects arise from fiscal policy's impact on total spending.

At first glance, using fiscal policy to change total spending and thereby change the economy's real GDP seems workable. For example, if the government cuts taxes or increases transfer payments, households would have more income, so their consumption spending would increase. Or the government itself could purchase more goods and services. In either case, if total spending rises, and business firms *sell* more output, they should want to hire more workers and *produce* more output as well. The economy's real GDP would rise.

It sounds reasonable. Does it work?

Not if the economy behaves according to the classical model. As you are about to see, in the classical model *fiscal policy has no demand-side effects at all*.

AN INCREASE IN GOVERNMENT PURCHASES

Let's first see what would happen if the government of Classica attempted to increase employment and output by increasing government purchases. More specifically, suppose the government raised its spending by $0.5 trillion, hiring people to fix roads and bridges, or hiring more teachers, or increasing its spending on goods and services for homeland security. What would happen?

To answer this, we must first answer another question: Where will Classica's government get the additional $0.5 trillion it spends? If net taxes are unchanged (as we are assuming), then the government deficit will rise, so the government must dip into the loanable funds market to *borrow* the additional funds.

FIGURE 10

Crowding Out from an Increase in Government Purchases

Beginning from equilibrium at point A, an increase in the budget deficit caused by additional government purchases shifts the demand for funds curve from $I^p + G_1 - T$ to $I^p + G_2 - T$. At point H, the quantity of funds demanded exceeds the quantity supplied, so the interest rate begins to rise. As it rises, households are led to save more, and business firms invest less. In the new equilibrium at point B, both consumption and investment spending have been completely crowded out by the increased government spending.

Figure 10 illustrates the effects. Initially, with government purchases equal to $2 trillion, the demand for funds curve is $I^p + G_1 - T$, where G_1 represents the initial level of government purchases. The equilibrium occurs at point *A* with the interest rate equal to 5 percent. If government purchases increase by $0.5 trillion, with no change in taxes, the budget deficit increases by $0.5 trillion and so does the government's demand for funds. The demand for funds curve shifts rightward by $0.5 trillion to $I^p + G_2 - T$, where G_2 represents an amount $0.5 trillion greater than G_1. After the shift, there would be an excess demand for funds at the original interest rate of 5 percent. The total quantity of funds demanded would be $2.25 trillion (point *H*), while the quantity supplied would continue to be $1.75 trillion (point *A*). Thus, the excess demand for funds would be equal to the distance *AH* in the figure, or $0.5 trillion. This excess demand drives up the interest rate to 7 percent. As the interest rate rises, two things happen.

First, a higher interest rate chokes off some investment spending, as business firms decide that certain investment projects no longer make sense. For example, the local dry cleaner might wish to borrow funds for a new machine at an interest rate of 5 percent, but not at 7 percent. In the figure, we move along the new demand for funds curve from point *H* to point *B*. Planned investment drops by $0.2 trillion (because the total demand for funds falls from $2.25 trillion to $2.05 trillion). (Question: How do we know that only business borrowing, and not also government borrowing, adjusts as we move from point *H* to point *B*?) Thus, one consequence of the rise in government purchases is a *decrease in planned investment spending.*

But that's not all: The rise in the interest rate also causes saving to increase. Of course, when people save more of their incomes, they spend less, so another consequence of the rise in government purchases is a *decrease in consumption spending.* In the figure, we move from point *A* to point *B* along the saving

G and T Are Separate Variables It is common to think that a rise in government purchases (*G*) implies an equal rise in net taxes (*T*) to pay for it. But as you've seen in our discussion, economists treat *G* and *T* as two separate variables. Unless stated otherwise, we use the *ceteris paribus* assumption: When we change *G*, we assume *T* remains constant, and when we change *T*, we assume *G* remains constant. It is the budget deficit (or surplus) that changes when *T* or *G* changes.

DANGEROUS CURVES

curve. As saving increases from $1.75 trillion to $2.05 trillion—a rise of $0.3 trillion—consumption falls by $0.3 trillion.

Let's recap: As a result of the increase in government purchases, both planned investment spending and consumption spending decline. We say that the government's purchases have *crowded out* the spending of households (C) and businesses (I^p).

Crowding out A decline in one sector's spending caused by an increase in some other sector's spending.

> *Crowding out is a decline in one sector's spending caused by an increase in some other sector's spending.*

But we are not quite finished. If we sum the drop in C and the drop in I^p, we find that total private sector spending has fallen by $0.3 trillion + $0.2 trillion = $0.5 trillion. That is, the drop in private sector spending is *precisely equal* to the rise in government purchases, G. Not only is there crowding out, there is **complete crowding out:** Each dollar of government purchases causes private sector spending to decline by a full dollar. The net effect is that total spending ($C + I^p + G$) does not change at all!

Complete crowding out A dollar-for-dollar decline in one sector's spending caused by an increase in some other sector's spending.

> *In the classical model, a rise in government purchases completely crowds out private sector spending, so total spending remains unchanged.*

A closer look at Figure 10 shows that this conclusion always holds, regardless of the particular numbers used or the shapes of the curves. When G increases, the demand for funds curve shifts rightward by the same amount that G rises, or the distance from point A to point H. Then the interest rate rises, moving us along the supply of funds curve from point A to point B. As a result, saving rises (and consumption falls) by the distance AF. But the rise in the interest rate *also* causes a movement along the demand for funds curve, from point H to point B. As a result, investment spending falls by the amount FH.

The final impact can be summarized as follows:

- $G\uparrow = AH$

- $C\downarrow = AF$

- $I^p\downarrow = FH$

And since $AF + FH = AH$, we know that the combined decrease in C and I^p is precisely equal to the increase in G.

Because there is complete crowding out in the classical model, a rise in government purchases cannot change total spending. And the logic behind this result is straightforward. Each additional dollar the government spends is obtained from the loanable funds market, where *it would have been spent by someone else* if the government hadn't borrowed it. How do we know this? Because the loanable funds market funnels every dollar of household saving—no more and no less—to either the government or business firms. If the government borrows more, it just removes funds that would have been spent by businesses (the drop in I^p) or by consumers (the drop in C).

Remember that the goal of this increase in government purchases was to increase output and employment *by increasing total spending*. But now we see that the policy fails to increase spending at all. Therefore, *in the classical model, an increase in government purchases has no demand-side effects on total output or total employment.*

Of course, the opposite sequence of events would happen if government purchases *decreased*: The drop in G would *shrink* the deficit. The interest rate would decline, and private sector spending (C and I^p) would rise by the same amount that government purchases had fallen. (See if you can draw the graphs to prove this to yourself.) Once again, total spending and total output would remain unchanged.

A Decrease in Net Taxes

Suppose that the government, instead of increasing its own purchases by $0.5 trillion, tried to increase total spending through a $0.5 trillion cut in net taxes. For example, the government could decrease income tax collections by $0.5 trillion, or increase transfer payments such as unemployment benefits by that amount. What would happen?

In general, households respond to a cut in net taxes by spending some of it and saving the rest. But let's give this policy every chance of working by making an extreme assumption in its favor: We'll assume that households *spend the entire $0.5 trillion tax cut* on consumption goods; they save none of it.

Figure 11 shows what will happen in the market for loanable funds. Initially, the demand for funds curve is $I^p + G - T_1$, where T_1 is the initial level of net taxes. The equilibrium is at point A, with an interest rate of 5 percent. If we cut net taxes (T) by $0.5 trillion, while holding government purchases constant, the budget deficit increases by $0.5 trillion, and so does the government's demand for funds. The demand for funds curve shifts rightward to $I^p + G - T_2$, where T_2 is an amount $0.5 trillion less than T_1.

The increase in the demand for funds drives the interest rate up to 7 percent, until we reach a new equilibrium at point B. As the interest rate rises, two things happen.

First, a higher interest rate will encourage more saving, which means a decrease in consumption spending. This is a movement along the supply of funds curve, from point A to point B, with saving rising (and consumption falling) by $0.3 trillion.

Second, a higher interest rate will decrease investment spending. This is shown by the movement from H to B along the new demand for funds curve. Planned investment decreases by $0.2 trillion.

What has happened to *total* spending? Only two components of spending have changed in this case: C and I^p. Let's first consider what's happened to consumption (C). First, we had a $0.5 trillion *rise* in consumption from the tax cut (remember: we assumed the entire tax cut was spent). This is equal to the horizontal distance AH. Then, because the interest rate rose, we had a $0.3 billion *decrease* in consumption. This decrease is equal to the horizontal distance AF. Taking both effects together, the net effect is a rise of $0.5 trillion − $0.3 trillion = $0.2 trillion. This net rise in consumption is shown by the distance FH.

Now remember what has happened to planned investment spending: It fell by $0.2 billion (the distance FH)—the same amount that consumption spending rose. In other words, the tax cut increases consumption but decreases planned investment by the same amount. We can say that higher consumption spending *completely crowds out* planned investment spending, leaving total spending unchanged.

FIGURE 11 Crowding Out from a Tax Cut

Beginning from equilibrium at point A, *an increase in the budget deficit caused by a tax cut shifts the demand for funds curve from* $I^p + G - T_1$ *to* $I^p + G - T_2$. *If the tax cut is entirely spent, consumption initially rises by the distance* AH.

At the original interest rate of 5 percent, the quantity of funds demanded now exceeds the quantity supplied. This causes the interest rate to rise.

As the interest rate rises, we move from A *to* B *along the supply of funds curve. Saving rises (and consumption falls) by the distance* AF. *The final rise in consumption is* FH. *We also move along the demand for funds curve from* H *to* B, *so investment falls by the distance* FH. *In the new equilibrium at point* B, *consumption (which has risen by* FH) *has completely crowded out investment (which has dropped by* FH).

> *In the classical model, a cut in net taxes raises consumption, which completely crowds out planned investment. Total spending remains unchanged, so the tax cut has no demand-side effects on total output or employment.*

THE CLASSICAL MODEL: A SUMMARY

You've just completed a first tour of the classical model, our framework for understanding the economy in the long run. In the (optional) appendix, we extend this model to the global economy. And in the next chapter, we'll be using the classical model to understand economic growth. But before we do, let's review what we've done, and what we've concluded.

We began with a critical assumption: All markets clear. We then applied the three-step process to organize our thinking of the economy. First, we focused on an important market—the labor market. We identified the buyers and sellers in that market (Step 1), and then found equilibrium employment (Step 2) by assuming that the labor market cleared. We went through a similar process with the loanable funds market, identifying the suppliers and demanders (Step 1) and finding the equilibrium in that market as well (Step 2). We then showed that total spending will be just sufficient to purchase our potential output, reinforcing our confidence in the full-employment equilibrium we found. Finally, we explored what happens when things change (Step 3). In particular, we saw that fiscal policy changes have no demand-side effects on total output and total employment.

Our explorations have considered just some of the possible scenarios under which the economy might operate. For example, we've assumed that the government runs a budget deficit. But we could also explore what happens when the government starts out with a budget *surplus*, collecting more in net taxes than it spends on its purchases. We also assumed that any tax cut was entirely spent by households on consumption goods. But we could also ask what happens when some or all of a tax cut is saved.

You'll be asked to explore some of these other scenarios in the end-of-chapter problems. When you do, you'll see that the graphs may look different, but the important conclusions still hold. These general conclusions are:

- In the classical model, the government needn't worry about employment. The economy will achieve full employment on its own.
- In the classical model, the government needn't worry about total spending. The economy will generate just enough spending on its own to buy the output that a fully employed labor force produces.
- In the classical model, fiscal policy has no *demand-side effects* on output or employment.

Using the Theory

This chapter does not end with the usual Using the Theory section. Instead, we will spend the next entire chapter using the classical model to explore a topic for which the model is very well-suited: Economic Growth.

Summary

The classical model is an attempt to explain the behavior of the economy over long time periods. Its most critical assumption is that markets clear—that prices adjust in every market to equate quantities demanded and supplied. The labor market is the starting point of the classical model. When the labor market clears, we have full employment and the economy produces the potential level of output.

The economy's production function shows the total output that can be produced with different quantities of labor and for given amounts of other resources and a given state of technology. When the labor market is at full employment, the production function can be used to determine the economy's potential level of output.

According to Say's law, total spending in the economy will always be just sufficient to purchase the amount of total output produced. By producing and selling goods and services, firms create a total demand equal to what they have produced. Taxes are channeled to the government, which spends them. If households

do not spend their entire after-tax incomes, the excess is channeled, as saving, into the loanable funds market, where it is borrowed and spent by businesses and government.

In the loanable funds market, the quantity of funds supplied equals household saving, which depends positively on the interest rate. The quantity of funds demanded equals planned investment, which depends negatively on the interest rate, and any government budget deficit, if there is one. The interest rate adjusts so that the quantity of funds supplied always equals the quantity demanded. Equivalently, it adjusts so that saving (S) equals the sum of planned investment spending (I^p) and the government budget deficit ($G - T$).

Fiscal policy has no demand-side effects on output in the classical model. An increase in government purchases results in complete crowding out of planned investment and consumption spending. A tax cut causes greater consumption spending to completely crowd out investment spending. In both cases, fiscal policy leaves total spending unchanged.

Problem Set
Answers to even-numbered Questions and Problems can be found on the text Web site at www.thomsonedu.com/economics/hall.

1. Use a diagram similar to Figure 2 to illustrate the effect, on aggregate output and the real hourly wage, of (a) an increase in labor demand and (b) an increase in labor supply.

2. Draw a diagram (similar to Figure 10 in this chapter) illustrating the impact of a *decrease* in government purchases. Assume the government is running a budget deficit both before and after the change in government purchases. On your diagram, identify distances that represent:
   a. The decrease in government purchases
   b. The increase in consumption spending
   c. The increase in planned investment spending

3. Consider the following statement: "In the classical model, just as an *increase* in government purchases causes complete crowding *out,* so a *decrease* in government purchases causes complete crowding *in.*"
   a. In this statement, explain what is meant by "crowding in" and "complete crowding in."
   b. Is the statement true? (Hint: Look at the diagram you drew in problem 2.)

4. The following data ($ millions) are for the island nation of Pacifica.

Total output	$10
Total income	$10
Consumption	$ 6
Government spending	$ 3
Total tax revenue	$ 2.5
Transfer payments	$ 0.5

   a. Use this information to find Pacifica's net taxes, disposable income, and savings.
   b. Determine whether the government is running a budget surplus, budget deficit, or balanced budget.
   c. Find planned investment by calculating how much is available in the loanable funds market after the government has borrowed what it might need.
   d. Does total output equal total spending?
   e. Show your answers on a diagram similar to the one in Figure 9 in the chapter.

5. Return to problem 4. What will happen if consumption spending starts to rise? Assume no change in net taxes. Show the effect on the loanable funds market, and explain what will happen to C, I^p, and G. (Note: You won't be able to find specific numbers.)

6. As the baby boomers retire, spending on Social Security benefits is expected to rise dramatically. Show the impact on a diagram of the loanable funds market, assuming that the government is initially running a budget deficit, and that all the additional Social Security benefits are *spent.* If there is no other change in policy, what would you expect to be the total impact on consumption spending? On planned investment spending?

7. The following data give a complete picture of the household, business, and government sectors for 2006 in the small nation of Sylvania. (All dollar figures are in billions.)

Consumption spending	$ 50
Capital stock (end of 2005)	$100
Capital stock (end of 2006)	$103
Change in inventories	$ 0
Government welfare payments	$ 5
Government unemployment insurance payments	$ 2
Government payroll	$ 3
Government outlays for materials	$ 2
Depreciation	$ 7
Interest rate	6%

   Assuming the government budget for 2006 was in balance, (G = T), calculate each of the following (in order):
   a. Government purchases
   b. Net taxes
   c. Total planned investment
   d. Real GDP
   e. Total saving
   f. Total leakages
   g. Total injections

8. For the economy in problem 7, suppose that the government had purchased $2 billion more in goods and services than you found in that problem, with no change in taxes.
   a. Explain how each of the variables you calculated in problem 7 would be affected (i.e., state whether it would increase or decrease).
   b. Draw a graph illustrating the impact of the $2 billion increase in government purchases on the loanable funds market. Clearly label the equilibrium interest rate, saving, and total quantity of funds demanded at both the original and the new level of government purchases. (Note: You won't be able to find specific numbers.)

9. When the government runs a budget surplus (T > G), it deposits any unspent tax revenue into the banking system, thus adding to the supply of loanable funds. In this case, the supply of loanable funds is household saving plus the budget surplus [S + (T − G)], while the demand for funds is just planned investment (I^p).
   a. Draw a diagram of the loanable funds market with a budget surplus, showing the equilibrium interest rate and quantity of funds demanded and supplied.
   b. Prove that when the loanable funds market is in equilibrium, total leakages (S + T) are equal to total injections (I^p + G). (Hint: Use the same method as used in the chapter for the case of a budget deficit.)
   c. Show (on your graph) what happens when government purchases increase, identifying any decrease in consumption and planned investment on the graph (similar to what was done in Figure 10).
   d. When the government is running a budget surplus, does

an increase in government purchases cause complete crowding out? Explain briefly.

More Challenging

10. Figure 11 shows the impact of a tax cut on the loanable funds market when the entire tax cut is spent. What if, instead, the entire tax cut had been *saved*?
    a. Draw a diagram of the loanable funds market showing the impact of a tax cut that is entirely saved. (Assume the government is already running a budget deficit.)
    b. What happens to the interest rate after the tax cut? Explain briefly.
    c. In Figure 11, the tax cut caused consumption spending to crowd out planned investment spending. How does a tax cut that is entirely saved affect the components of total spending?

11. [Requires appendix] Suppose that the government budget is balanced ($G = T$), and household saving is $1 trillion.
    a. If this is a closed economy, what is the value of planned investment (I^P)?
    b. If this is an open economy with balanced trade ($IM = X$), will investment have the same value as you found in (a)? Briefly, why or why not?

c. If this is an open economy with a trade deficit ($IM > X$), will planned investment have the same value as you found in (a)? Briefly, why or why not?

12. [Requires appendix] Suppose that Classica has international trade, but it is running a trade surplus ($X > IM$) rather than a trade deficit as in the appendix. Suppose, too, that Classica's government is running a budget deficit.
    a. Draw a diagram for Classica's loanable funds market, being careful to include the trade surplus in the label for one of the curves. (Hint: When Classica runs a trade surplus equal to $X - IM$, foreigners spend more dollars on Classica's goods than they get by selling their goods to Classica. From where do you think foreigners get these dollars?)
    b. Label the initial equilibrium point A.
    c. Give an equation showing that, in equilibrium, the quantity of loanable funds demanded (on one side) is equal to the quantity of loanable funds supplied (on the other side).
    d. Rearrange your equation to show that, even when Classica runs a trade surplus, its leakages and injections are equal.

APPENDIX

The Classical Model in an Open Economy

So far in this chapter, we've been working with a *closed economy*—one that has no trade with other nations. What is different in an *open economy* with imports and exports of goods and services? The most general answer is: not much. All of the conclusions of the classical model still hold. But there are a few added complications in showing that Say's law holds—that total spending equals total output.

Let's suppose that in Classica (the economy used in the chapter), households, business firms, and government agencies spend $1.5 trillion on *imports* from other countries. This $1.5 trillion is income received by households, but *not* spent on Classica's output. It is an additional *leakage* in the economy. Total leakages are now imports (*IM*) along with the other leakages of saving (*S*) and taxes (*T*).

But once we recognize international trade, we must add foreign spending on Classica's *exports* as an *injection* into Classica's spending. Total injections are now exports (*X*) along with planned investment (*I^p*) and government purchases (*G*).

Finally, total spending on Classica's output must be modified. When we add together the spending of Classica's households, business firms, and government, we've included some imports in each category. We've thus *over*estimated total spending on Classica's output. To correct for this error, we must subtract imports (*IM*) from $C + I^p + G$ to get total spending by Classicans on their own country's output. Then we must add exports (*X*) to get the total spending from *all* sources on Classica's output. These modifications give us

$$\text{Total spending} = C + I^p + G + (X - IM)$$

Will this new expression for total spending be equal to total output? We'll explore this under two different scenarios.

BALANCED TRADE: EXPORTS = IMPORTS

With *balanced* trade, exports (*X*) and imports (*IM*) are equal, so the last term added in total spending (*X − IM*) is zero. In this case, total spending in Classica will be $C + I^p + G$, just as it was in a closed economy.

Will total spending of $C + I^p + G$ be equal to total output, even though there are exports and imports? The answer is yes, as we can see by thinking about leakages and injections. In the case of balanced trade, the $1.5 trillion that leaks out of Classica's spending to buy imports (*IM*) is equal to the $1.5 billion that comes back to Classica to buy its exports (*X*). Because total leakages and total injections were equal in the closed economy (before we included imports and exports), they must be equal now as well.

But what happens if trade is *not* balanced?

In the next section, we'll consider what happens to spending when a country imports more than it exports. You'll be invited to analyze the opposite case (exports exceed imports) in an end-of-chapter problem.

UNBALANCED TRADE: IMPORTS > EXPORTS

Suppose, as before, that Classica's households import $1.5 trillion in goods produced in other countries. But now, residents of these other countries want to purchase only $1 trillion in goods from Classica. Classica will then be running a *trade deficit* equal to the excess of its imports (*IM*) over its exports (*X*):

$$\text{Trade deficit} = IM - X = \$1.5 \text{ trillion} - \$1 \text{ trillion}$$
$$= \$0.5 \text{ trillion.}$$

Now, it seems we have a problem. With imports greater than exports, won't Classica's leakages (*S + T +*

IM) be greater than injections ($I^p + G + X$)? And won't total spending therefore be less than total output?

The answer is no.

To see why, let's assume (as we've done all along in the chapter) that Classica's currency is the dollar. The 1.5 trillion in dollars that Classica's households spend on imports during the year does not just disappear. Rather, the dollars are passed along to the foreign countries producing the goods that Classica imports. In our current example, the residents of these foreign countries return $1 trillion of the $1.5 trillion back to Classica as spending on Classica's exports. But what about the other $0.5 trillion? If foreigners are rational, they will not want to just keep this money, because dollars by themselves pay no interest or other return. Foreigners will, instead, want to purchase Classica's stocks or bonds, or even just deposit funds in a bank in Classica. If they do any of these things, they *supply funds to Classica's loanable funds market* and make them available to Classica's borrowers.[3]

> When a country runs a trade deficit (imports exceed exports), foreigners will supply loanable funds to that country equal to its trade deficit.

With a trade deficit, the supply of funds in Classica becomes household saving (*S*) *plus* the flow of funds coming from foreigners (*IM − X*):

$$\text{Total supply of funds} = S + (IM - X)$$

The total demand for funds is still business borrowing (I^p) plus the government's budget deficit ($G - T$):

$$\text{Total demand for funds} = I^p + (G - T)$$

Figure A.1 shows the loanable funds market in Classica, where we've added Classica's trade deficit to its supply of loanable funds. Equilibrium occurs at point *E*, with an interest rate of 5 percent and $2.25 trillion in loanable funds supplied and demanded. Of this $2.25 trillion, we know that foreigners are supplying $0.5 trillion of the total, so households must be supplying (saving) the other $1.75 trillion.

In equilibrium, the quantity of funds supplied and demanded are equal:

Loanable funds market clears ⇒

$$\underbrace{S + (IM - X)}_{\substack{\text{Quantity of} \\ \text{funds supplied}}} = \underbrace{I^p + (G - T)}_{\substack{\text{Quantity of} \\ \text{funds demanded}}}$$

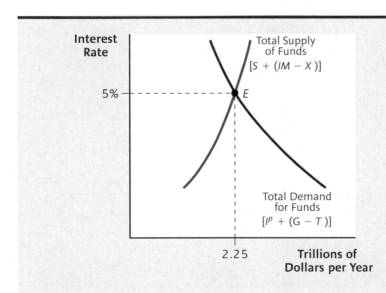

When Classica runs a trade deficit (its imports exceed its exports), foreigners earn more dollars (Classica's currency) selling goods to Classica than they spend on goods from Classica. The excess dollars are returned to Classica's loanable funds market, where they become part of the supply of loanable funds. When the loanable funds market clears, we have S + IM − X = I^p + G − T. *This, in turn, means that total leakages (S + T + IM) equal total injections (I^p + G + X).*

[3] There is another part of the story we are leaving out here: the foreign exchange market. When Classica's households import goods, they may pay in dollars, but the foreign firms are paid in their own local currencies. Someone must exchange Classica's dollars for foreign currency— a bank or a foreign government. It is these banks or foreign governments that, in turn, supply the excess dollars to Classica's loanable funds market. We'll deal more explicitly with foreign exchange markets in the last chapter of this book.

Let's now rearrange this equation by moving T over to the left and X over to the right:

Loanable funds market clears $\Rightarrow$

$$\underbrace{S + T + IM}_{\text{Leakages}} = \underbrace{I^p + G + X}_{\text{Injections}}$$

This last equation shows us that total leakages and total injections are equal in Classica, even when it runs a trade deficit. But if leakages and injections are equal, then total spending must equal total output. Even with a trade deficit, Say's law still holds.

Let's take a step back and understand the reasoning behind this result about spending. Even though Classica is running a trade deficit, every dollar of the $10 trillion that households earn will still be spent on Classica's production—either by households themselves or by some other sector that spends it in their place. The dollars spent on imports are either spent on Classica's exports or put into its loanable funds market, where they are borrowed and spent by business firms or the government. And, as before, taxes and saving are also spent by either the government or business firms.

CHAPTER 21

Economic Growth and Rising Living Standards

Economist Thomas Malthus, writing in 1798, came to a striking conclusion: "Population, when unchecked, goes on doubling itself every twenty-five years, or increases in a geometrical ratio. . . . The means of subsistence . . . could not possibly be made to increase faster than in an arithmetic ratio."[1] From this simple logic, Malthus forecast a horrible fate for the human race. There would be repeated famines and wars to keep the rapidly growing population in balance with the more slowly growing supply of food and other necessities.

But history has proven Malthus wrong . . . at least in part. In the industrialized nations, living standards have increased beyond the wildest dreams of anyone alive in Malthus's time. Economists today are optimistic about these nations' long-run material prospects. At the same time, living standards in many of the less developed countries have remained stubbornly close to survival level and, in some cases, have fallen below it.

What are we to make of this? Why have living standards steadily increased in some nations but not in others? And what, if anything, can governments do to speed the rise in living standards? These are questions about economic growth—the long-run increase in an economy's output of goods and services.

In this chapter, you will learn what makes economies grow. Our approach will make use of the classical model, focusing on Step 3 of the three-step process: What Happens When Things Change? As you'll see, growth arises from *shifts* of the curves of the classical model. And by the end of this chapter, you will know why increasing the rate of economic growth is not easy. Even though nations can take measures to speed growth, each measure carries an opportunity cost. More specifically,

achieving a higher rate of growth in the long run generally requires some sacrifice in the short run.

THE IMPORTANCE OF GROWTH

Why should we be concerned about economic growth? For one simple reason:

When output grows faster than the population, GDP per capita, our measure of the ***average standard of living****, will rise. When output grows more slowly than the population, the average standard of living will fall.*

Average standard of living Total output (real GDP) per person.

[1] Thomas Robert Malthus, *An Essay on the Principle of Population*, 1798.

Measuring the standard of living by GDP per capita may seem limiting. After all, as we saw three chapters ago, many important aspects of our quality of life are not captured in GDP. Leisure time, workplace safety, good health, a clean environment—we care about all of these. Yet they are not considered in GDP.

Still, many aspects of our quality of life *are* counted in GDP: food, housing, medical care, education, transportation services, and movies, to name a few. It is not surprising, then, that economic growth—measured by increases in GDP—remains a vital concern in every nation.

Economic growth is especially important in countries with income levels far below those of Europe, Japan, and the United States. The average standard of living in some third-world nations is so low that many families can barely acquire the basic necessities of life, and many others perish from disease or starvation.

Table 1 lists GDP per capita, infant mortality rates, life expectancies, and adult literacy rates for some of the richest and poorest countries. The statistics for the poor countries are grim enough, but even they capture only part of the story. Unsafe and unclean workplaces, inadequate housing, and other sources of misery are part of daily life for most people in these countries. Other than emigration, economic growth is their only hope.

Growth is a high priority in prosperous nations, too. As we know, resources are scarce, and we cannot produce enough of everything to satisfy all of our desires simultaneously. We want more and better medical care, education, vacations, entertainment . . . the list is endless. When output per capita is growing, it's at least *possible* for everyone to enjoy an increase in material well-being without anyone having to cut back. We can also accomplish important social goals—helping the

TABLE 1				
Some Indicators of Economic Well-Being in Rich and Poor Countries, 2003				
Country	**Real GDP per Capita**	**Infant Mortality Rate (per 1,000 Live Births)**	**Life Expectancy at Birth**	**Adult Literacy Rate**
Rich Countries				
United States	$37,562	7	77.4	Greater than 99%
Japan	$27,967	3	82.0	Greater than 99%
Germany	$27,756	4	78.7	Greater than 99%
France	$27,677	4	79.5	Greater than 99%
United Kingdom	$27,147	5	78.4	Greater than 99%
Italy	$27,119	4	80.1	98.5%
Poor Countries				
Azerbaijan	$3,617	75	66.9	98.8%
Ghana	$2,238	59	56.8	54.1%
Pakistan	$2,097	81	63.0	48.7%
Cambodia	$2,078	97	56.2	73.6%
Zambia	$ 877	102	37.5	67.9%
Sierra Leone	$ 548	166	40.8	29.6%

Sources: United Nations Development Programme, *Human Development Report,* 2005, pp. 219–222 and 250–253.

poor, improving education, cleaning up the environment—by asking those who are doing well to sacrifice part of the rise in their material well-being, rather than suffer a drop.

But when output per capita stagnates, material gains become a fight over a fixed pie: The more purchasing power my neighbor has, the less is left for me. With everyone struggling for a larger piece of this fixed pie, conflict replaces cooperation. Efforts to help the less fortunate, wipe out illiteracy, reduce air pollution—all are seen as threats, rather than opportunities.

In the 1950s and 1960s, economic growth in the wealthier nations seemed to be taking care of itself. Economists and policy makers focused their attention on short-run movements around full-employment output, rather than on the growth of full-employment output itself. The real payoff for government seemed to be in preventing recessions and depressions—in keeping the economy operating as close to its potential as possible.

All of that changed starting in the 1970s, and economic growth became a national and international preoccupation. Like most changes in perception and thought, this one was driven by experience. Table 2 tells the story. It gives the average yearly growth rates of real GDP per capita for the United States and some of our key trading partners.

Over most of the postwar period, output in the more prosperous industrialized countries (such as the United States, the United Kingdom, and Canada) grew by 2 or 3 percent per year, while output in the less wealthy ones—those with some catching up to do—grew even faster. But beginning in the mid-1970s, all of these nations saw their growth rates slip.

In the late 1990s and early 2000s, only the United States and the United Kingdom returned to their previous high rates of growth, while the other industrialized countries continued to grow more slowly than their historical averages.

Looking at the table, you might think that this slowing in growth was rather insignificant. Do the tiny differences between the pre-1972 and the post-1972 growth rates really matter? Indeed, they do. Recall our example a few chapters ago in which an increase in the U.S. growth rate of around one percentage point over the past 20 years would mean $20 trillion in additional output over the entire period. Seemingly small differences in growth rates matter a great deal.

Country	1948–1972	1972–1988	1988–1995	1995–2004	TABLE 2
United States	2.2%	1.7%	1.0%	2.3%	**Average Annual Growth Rate of Real GDP per Capita**
United Kingdom	2.4	2.1	0.9	2.5	
Canada	2.9	2.6	0.6	2.4	
France	4.3	2.1	1.2	1.8	
Italy	4.9	2.8	1.6	1.3	
West Germany	5.7	2.2	1.3	1.2	
Japan	8.2	3.3	2.1	1.3	

Sources: Angus Maddison, *Phases of Capitalist Development* (Oxford: Oxford University Press, 1982); U.S. Census Bureau IDB Summary Demographic Data (*http://www.census.gov/ipc/www/idbsum.html*); *Economic Report of the President*, 2002, 2005, Table B-112; and various OECD publications. *Note:* Data for Germany includes West Germany only through 1995, and all of Germany after 1995.

WHAT MAKES ECONOMIES GROW?

A useful way to start thinking about long-run growth is to look at what determines our potential GDP in any given period. Starting this process is very simple: We can say that real GDP depends on

- The amount of output the average worker can produce in an hour
- The number of hours the average worker spends at the job
- The fraction of the population that is working
- The size of the population

If you spend a moment considering each of these variables, you'll see that—all else equal—if any one of them increases, real GDP rises.

Before we start working with these determinants of growth, let's briefly discuss how the first three are measured. The amount of output the average worker produces in an hour is called **labor productivity**, or just **productivity**. It is measured by taking the total output (real GDP) of the economy over a period of time and dividing by the total number of hours that *everyone* worked during that period.

Labor productivity The output produced by the average worker in an hour.

$$\text{Productivity} = \text{Output per hour} = \frac{\text{Total output}}{\text{Total hours worked}}$$

For example, if during a given year all workers in the United States spent a total of 300 billion hours at their jobs and produced $12 trillion worth of output, then on average, labor productivity would be $12 trillion/300 billion hours = $40 per hour. Or in words, the average worker would produce $40 worth of output in an hour. As you'll see later in this chapter, increases in productivity are one of the most important contributors to economic growth.

Next, the hours of the average worker can be found by dividing the total hours worked over a period by total employment (the *number* of people who worked during the period).

$$\text{Average hours} = \frac{\text{Total hours}}{\text{Total employment}}$$

For example, if total employment is 150 million people and they work a total of 300 billion hours per year, then average annual hours would be 300 billion hours/150 million workers = 2,000 hours.

Now let's turn to the fraction of the population that is working. This is called the **employment–population ratio (EPR)** and is found by dividing total employment by the population:[2]

Employment–population ratio (EPR) The percentage of the population that is working.

$$\text{EPR} = \frac{\text{Total employment}}{\text{Population}}$$

Now that we understand how these variables are measured, let's multiply them together and cancel out the like terms:

$$\frac{\text{Total output}}{\text{Total hours}} \times \frac{\text{Total hours}}{\text{Total employment}} \times \frac{\text{Total employment}}{\text{Population}} \times \text{Population}$$

$$= \text{Total output.}$$

---

[2] In actual practice in the United States and many other countries, the population base for the EPR is more limited. In the United States, for example, the EPR is technically the fraction of the *civilian, noninstitutional population over the age of 16* that is employed. We'll ignore this technical definition in our analysis and consider the EPR to be the fraction of the entire population that is working.

where the last inequality follows after canceling terms that appear in both a numerator and a denominator. Thus, we can write our equation for total output as:

Total output = Productivity × Average hours × EPR × Population.

Now we'll borrow a rule from mathematics that states that if two variables A and B are multiplied together, then the percentage change in their product is approximately equal to the sum of their percentage changes. In symbols:

$$\%\Delta (A \times B) \approx \%\Delta A + \%\Delta B.$$

Applying this rule to all four variables in the right side of our equation, as well as to total output on the left, we find that the growth rate of total output over any period of time is

$$\%\Delta \text{ Total output} \approx \%\Delta \text{ Productivity} + \%\Delta \text{ Average hours} +$$

$$\%\Delta \text{ EPR} + \%\Delta \text{ Population}.$$

This last equation, which we'll call the economy's **growth equation**, shows how four different variables contribute to the growth rate of real GDP.

Now look at Table 3, which shows how each of these variables has contributed to output growth during different periods of recent U.S. history, as well as a six-year future projection. For example, the first column tells us that from 1953 to 1973, real GDP grew, on average, by 3.6 percent per year. Of that growth, 1.6 percentage points were due to a growing population, and 0.1 percentage points were due to a rise in the employment–population ratio. Average hours—which decreased during the period—contributed negatively to growth, reducing it by a third of a percentage point. Finally, growth in labor productivity contributed 2.2 percent during this period.

Going across the rows and moving from period to period, you can see that almost all of the growth in real GDP over the last 50 years (and projected for the near future) has come from two factors: population growth and productivity growth. Increases in the employment–population ratio have contributed somewhat in the past, and average hours have decreased slightly, slowing growth in real GDP.

Growth equation An equation showing the percentage growth rate of output as the sum of the growth rates of productivity, average hours, the employment–population ratio, and population.

Annual Percentage Growth in Real GDP Due to:	1953 to 1973	1973 to 1995	1995 to 2005	2005 to 2010 (projected)
Population	1.6	1.4	1.2	1.1
EPR	0.1	0.4	0.0	−0.1
Average Hours	−0.3	−0.3	−0.2	−0.1
Productivity	2.2	1.3	2.3	2.3
Total	3.6	2.8	3.3	3.2

T A B L E   3

Factors Contributing to Growth in U.S. Real GDP

Source: Economic Report of the President, 2006, Table 1–2, p. 44, and author calculations. (The *Economic Report* lists nonfarm business productivity only. In this table, annual productivity growth has been reduced by 0.2 to 0.5 percentage points in each period to account for slightly slower output growth in the government and farm sectors.)

ECONOMIC GROWTH AND LIVING STANDARDS

Ultimately, growth in real GDP—by itself—does not guarantee a rising standard of living. Imagine, for example, that real GDP grew by 10 percent over some period while the population doubled. With 10 percent more output divided among twice as many people, the average standard of living would clearly decrease even though real output was growing. What matters for the standard of living is *real GDP per capita*—our total output of goods and services *per person*. Over the long run, since real GDP tends to hover near *potential* output, living standards will depend on *potential* output per person.

To see more clearly what causes potential output per person to rise, let's go back to our basic growth equation:

$$\text{Total output} = \text{Productivity} \times \text{Average hours} \times \text{EPR} \times \text{Population.}$$

If we divide both sides of this equation by the population, we get:

$$\frac{\text{Total output}}{\text{Population}} = \text{Productivity} \times \text{Average hours} \times \text{EPR.}$$

And, in terms of percentage growth rates:

$$\%\Delta \text{ Total output per person} \approx \%\Delta \text{ Productivity} +$$

$$\%\Delta \text{ Average hours} + \%\Delta \text{ EPR.}$$

Notice that population drops out of the equation. This tells us that the only way to raise the average standard of living is to increase productivity, increase average hours, or increase the percentage of the population that is working.

But as we saw in Table 3, average hours in the United States have decreased over the past several decades and are projected to remain constant for several years. In continental Europe, the decrease in average hours has been even greater. This is why we'll focus our discussion on the remaining two factors in our equation: the EPR and productivity.

> To explain growth in output per person and living standards in the United States and other developed nations, economists look at two factors: increases in the employment–population ratio and growth in productivity.

Now it's time to look more closely at *how* these two factors raise the average standard of living. And the classical model that you learned in the last chapter is very well suited to helping us understand this. We'll start by considering increases in the labor force participation rate.

GROWTH IN THE EMPLOYMENT–POPULATION RATIO (EPR)

Over the long run, the employment–population ratio rises only when total employment increases at a faster rate than the population. For example, if total employment is

50 million out of a population of 100 million, then the EPR is 50 million/100 million = 0.5. If both total employment and population grow by 10 percent, then the EPR will be 55 million/110 million = 0.5, the same as before. With population growth of 10 percent, total employment would have to grow by *more* than 10 percent in order for the EPR to rise and thereby contribute to growth in living standards. And if total employment were to grow by *less* than 10 percent, the EPR would fall, contributing to a drop in living standards.

If we treat the rate of population growth as a given, then the growth rate of total employment will determine what happens to the EPR. More specifically,

> *for a given growth rate of the population, the greater the growth of total employment, the greater will be the rise (or the smaller will be the drop) in the EPR.*

But what causes employment to grow? The classical model can help us answer this question.

One possibility is an increase in labor *supply:* a rise in the number of people who would like to work at any given wage. This is illustrated in Figure 1 by a rightward shift in the labor supply curve. We'll discuss *why* the labor supply curve might shift later; here, we'll concentrate on the consequences of the shift.

Before the shift, the labor supply curve is L_1^S, the market clears at a wage of $20 per hour, and the fully employed labor force is 150 million workers. The aggregate production function tells us that, with the given amounts of other resources in the economy, and the given state of technology, 150 million workers can produce $10 trillion in goods and services—the initial value of full-employment output. When the labor supply curve shifts to L_2^S, the market-clearing wage drops to $16. Business firms, finding labor cheaper to hire, increase the number of workers employed along the labor demand curve, from point A to point B. The labor force increases to 180 million workers, and full-employment output rises to $11.5 trillion.

But growth in employment can also arise from an increase in labor demand: a rise in the number of workers that firms would like to hire at any given wage. Once again, we'll consider the *causes* of labor demand changes momentarily; here, we focus on the *consequences*.

Graphically, an increase in labor demand is represented by a rightward shift in the labor demand curve, as in Figure 2. As the wage rate rises from $20 to its new equilibrium of $22, we move along the labor supply curve from point A to point B. More people decide they want to work as the wage rises. Equilibrium employment once again rises from 150 million to 180 million workers, so full-employment output will rise. Thus,

> *growth in employment can arise from an increase in labor supply (a rightward shift in the labor supply curve) or an increase in labor demand (a rightward shift of the labor demand curve).*

You may have noticed one very important difference between the labor market outcomes in Figures 1 and 2: When labor *supply* increases, the wage rate falls (from $20 to $16 in Figure 1); when labor *demand* increases, the wage rate rises (from $20 to $22 in Figure 2). Which of the figures describes the actual experience of the U.S. labor market?

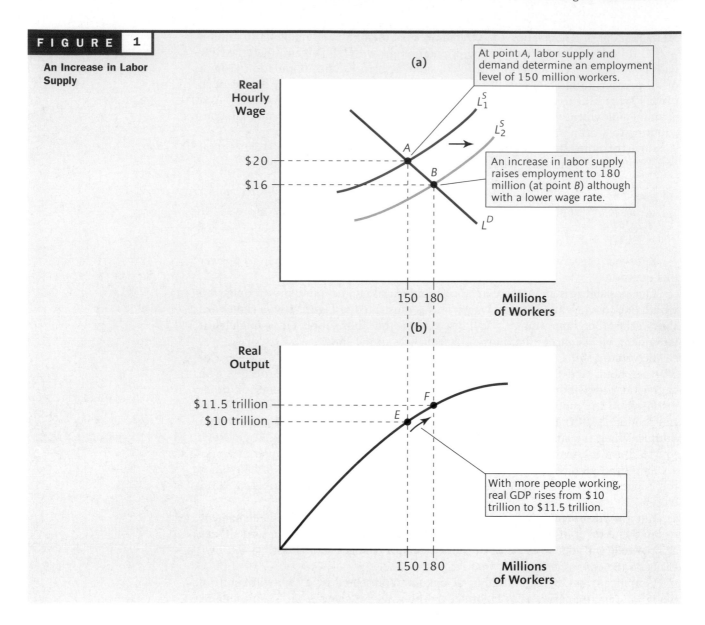

FIGURE 1

An Increase in Labor Supply

(a)

Real Hourly Wage

At point *A*, labor supply and demand determine an employment level of 150 million workers.

L_1^S

L_2^S

$20

$16

A

B

An increase in labor supply raises employment to 180 million (at point *B*) although with a lower wage rate.

L^D

150 180   **Millions of Workers**

(b)

Real Output

$11.5 trillion

$10 trillion

F

E

With more people working, real GDP rises from $10 trillion to $11.5 trillion.

150 180   **Millions of Workers**

Actually, a combination of both. Over most of the past century, the U.S. labor supply curve shifted steadily rightward, sometimes slowly, sometimes more rapidly. Why the shift in labor supply? In part, the reason was steady population growth: The more people there are, the more will want to work at any wage. But another reason was an important change in tastes: an increase in the desire of women (especially married women) to work.

But as the labor supply curve shifted rightward, the labor demand curve shifted rightward as well. Firms acquired more and better capital equipment for their employees to use. Managers and accountants began keeping track of inventories and other important accounts with lightning-fast computer software instead of account ledgers. Supermarket clerks began using electronic scanners instead of hand-entry cash registers. And college professors or their research assistants began gathering

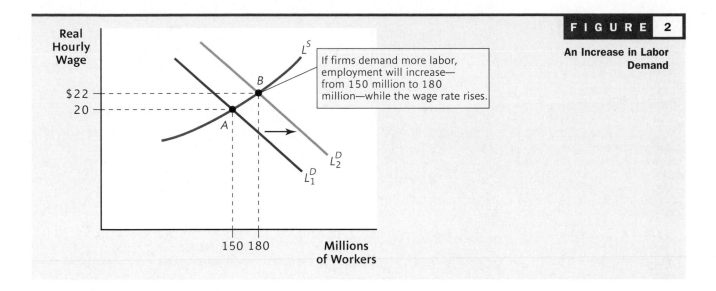

FIGURE 2

An Increase in Labor Demand

If firms demand more labor, employment will increase—from 150 million to 180 million—while the wage rate rises.

data by searching for a few minutes on the Web instead of a few hours in the library. At the same time, workers became better educated and better trained. These changes increased the amount of output a worker could produce in any given period, so firms wanted to hire more of them at any wage.[3]

In fact, over the past century, increases in labor demand outpaced increases in labor supply, so that, on balance, the average wage rate rose and employment increased. This is illustrated in Figure 3, which shows a shift in the labor supply curve from L_1^S to L_2^S, and an even greater shift in the labor demand curve from L_1^D to L_2^D.

The impact of these changes on total employment has been dramatic. Between 1948 and 2006, employment rose from 56 million to about 145 million. But what about the employment–population ratio? It, too, rose: from 57 percent of the (adult) population to about 63 percent. This tells us that employment grew *faster* than the population during this period. And as you've learned, such an increase in the EPR causes not just real GDP, but real GDP *per capita*, to grow. However, most of the rise in the EPR was due to a special factor that is unlikely to be repeated: the greater labor force participation rate of women—especially married women—during the 1960s, 1970s, and 1980s. In the 1990s—as the female EPR stabilized—this source of growth disappeared.

Currently, the U.S. Bureau of Labor Statistics predicts employment growth of 1 percent per year until the year 2010—about the same as the growth rate of the population. Thus, the employment–population ratio is not expected to grow at all. Employment growth—while it will raise real GDP—will not increase real GDP per capita, and so will not contribute to a rise in living standards.

Could we do anything about this? Could we speed up the rightward shifts in the labor demand and labor supply curves over the next few years, so that employment grows faster than the 1 percent annual growth rate of the population? Yes, we could.

---

[3] These changes in physical and human capital have also shifted the economy's production function, but we'll consider that in the next section.

FIGURE 3

**The U.S. Labor Market
Over a Century**

*Over the past century,
increases in labor demand
have outpaced increases in
supply. As a result, both
the level of employment
and the average wage have
risen.*

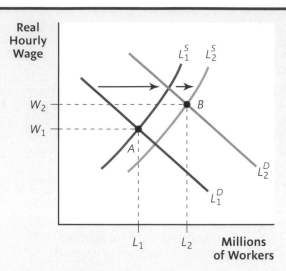

But as you read on, keep in mind that these measures to increase employment are not necessarily socially desirable. They would, most likely, accomplish the goal, but they would also have costs—costs that Americans may or may not be willing to pay. Later, we'll discuss these costs.

HOW TO INCREASE EMPLOYMENT AND THE EPR

One set of policies to speed the rise in employment focuses on changing labor supply. And an often-proposed example of this type of policy is a decrease in income tax rates. Imagine that you have a professional degree in accounting, physical therapy, or some other field, and you are considering whether to take a job. Suppose the going rate for your professional services is $30 per hour. If your average tax rate is 33 percent, then one-third of your income will be taxed away, so your take-home pay would be only $20 per hour. But if your tax rate were cut to 20 percent, you would take home $24 per hour. Since you care about your take-home pay, you will respond to a tax cut in the same way you would respond to a wage increase—even if the wage your potential employer pays does not change at all. If you would be willing to take a job that offers a take-home pay of $24, but not one that offers $20, then the tax cut would be just what was needed to get you to seek work.

When we extend your reaction to the population as a whole, we can see that a cut in the income tax rate can convince more people to seek jobs at any given wage, shifting the labor supply curve rightward. This is why economists and politicians who focus on the economy's long-run growth often recommend lower taxes on labor income to encourage more rapid growth in employment. They point out that many American workers must pay combined federal, state, and local taxes of more than 40 cents out of each additional dollar they earn, and that this may be discouraging labor market participation in the United States.

Indeed, this was an important part of the logic behind the two tax cuts engineered by President Bush early in his administration. For example, the first tax cut, which Congress passed after much debate in June 2001, called for gradually reduced tax rates over 10 years. It reduced the cumulative tax burden on households by about $1.35 trillion over that period.

In addition to tax rate changes, some economists have advocated changes in government transfer programs to speed the growth in employment. They argue that the current structure of many government programs creates disincentives to work. For example, families receiving welfare payments, food stamps, unemployment benefits, and Social Security retirement payments all face steep losses in their benefits if they go to work or increase their work effort. Redesigning these programs might therefore stimulate growth in labor supply.

This reasoning was an important motive behind the sweeping reforms in the U.S. welfare system passed by Congress, and signed by President Clinton, in August 1996. Among other things, the reforms reduced the number of people who were eligible for benefits, cut the benefit amount for many of those still eligible, and set a maximum coverage period of five years for most welfare recipients. Later in this chapter, we'll discuss some of the *costs* of potentially growth-enhancing measures like these. Here, we only point out that changes in benefit programs have the potential to change labor supply.

> *A cut in tax rates increases the reward for working, while a cut in benefits to the needy increases the hardship of not working. Either policy can speed the rightward shifts in the labor supply curve and speed the growth in employment, raising the EPR and output per person.*

Government policies can also affect the labor *demand* curve. In recent decades, subsidies for education and training, such as government-guaranteed loans for college students or special training programs for the unemployed, have helped to increase the skills of the labor force and made workers more valuable to potential employers. Government also subsidizes employment more directly—by contributing part of the wage when certain categories of workers are hired—the disabled, college work-study participants, and, in some experimental programs, inner-city youth. By enlarging these programs, government could increase the number of workers hired at any given wage and thus shift the labor demand curve to the right:

> *Government policies that help increase the skills of the workforce or that subsidize employment more directly speed the rightward shift in the labor demand curve, increasing the EPR and output per person.*

Efforts to create growth in the employment–population ratio are sometimes controversial. In recent decades, those who prefer an activist government have favored policies to increase labor *demand* through government-sponsored training programs, more aid to college students, employment subsidies to firms, and similar programs. Those who prefer a more *laissez-faire* approach have generally favored policies to increase the labor *supply* by *decreasing* government involvement—lower taxes or a less generous social safety net.

In any case, the employment–population ratio is unlikely to contribute to growth in the near future. For one thing, the retirement of the baby boomers is expected to *decrease* the EPR over the next few decades. And the sorts of employment policies we've discussed here would, at best, lead to a one-time rise in the EPR, rather than a continually rising EPR that would contribute to sustained economic growth.

GROWTH IN PRODUCTIVITY

If you look back at Table 3, you'll see that growth in productivity has been responsible for most of the growth in real GDP over the last 50 years. (The period from 1973 to 1995, when population growth led slightly, is the exception.) And as you've learned, population growth—while it can raise real GDP—cannot raise real GDP *per capita*. If we restrict ourselves to the three factors in Table 3 that *can* raise real GDP per capita, we see that

> *over the past several decades, and into the near future, virtually all growth in the average standard of living can be attributed to growth in productivity.*

Not surprisingly, when economists analyze rising living standards, they think first and foremost about growth in productivity.

Table 3 shows that productivity is expected to grow at about 2.3 percent over the next several years. Can we make it grow even faster?

GROWTH IN THE CAPITAL STOCK

One key to productivity growth is the nation's capital stock or, more precisely, the amount of capital available for the average worker in the economy. You can dig more ditches with a shovel than with your hands, and even more with a backhoe. And the economy can produce more automobiles, medical services, and education when the average employee in these industries has more machinery, technical equipment, and computers to work with.

Capital per worker The total capital stock divided by total employment.

A rise in **capital per worker**—the total capital stock divided by the labor force—results in greater productivity. Figure 4 shows this from the perspective of the

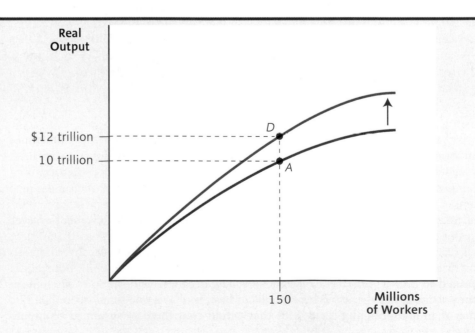

FIGURE 4

Capital Accumulation and the Production Function

An increase in the capital stock shifts the production function upward. At point A, 150 million workers could produce $10 trillion of real GDP. With more capital, those same workers could produce $12 trillion of real GDP.

classical model. Initially, the economy operates at point *A* on the lower aggregate production function, where 150 million workers produce $10 trillion in output. An increase in the capital stock shifts the production function upward, since any given number of workers can produce more output if there is more capital to work with. Assuming that the labor force remains at 150 million, there will be more capital per worker, greater productivity, and the economy will move to point *D*. At this point, 150 million workers produce $12 trillion in output.

However, in the real world, as the capital stock grows, so does the labor force. While any increase in capital will shift up the production function as in the figure, productivity will rise only if capital *per worker* increases—that is, only if the nation's total capital stock grows *faster* than the labor force.

> *All else equal, if the capital stock grows faster than the labor force, then capital per worker will rise, and labor productivity will increase along with it. But if the capital stock grows more slowly than the labor force, then capital per worker will fall, and labor productivity will fall as well.*

As business firms acquire more machinery and other capital equipment, the economy's production function shifts upward.

In the United States and most other developed countries, the capital stock has grown more rapidly than the labor force. This is one reason that labor productivity has risen over time. But in some developing countries, the capital stock has grown at about the same rate as, or even more slowly than, the labor force, and labor productivity has remained stagnant or fallen. We will return to this problem in the Using the Theory section of this chapter.

INVESTMENT AND THE CAPITAL STOCK

What determines how fast the capital stock rises, and whether it will rise faster than the labor force? The answer is: the rate of *planned investment spending* in the economy. Investment spending and the capital stock are related to each other, but they are different *kinds* of variables. Specifically, capital is a *stock* variable while investment spending is a *flow* variable.

> A **stock variable** *measures a quantity at a moment in time.* A **flow variable** *measures a process over a period of time.*

Stock variable A variable measuring a quantity at a moment in time.

Flow variable A variable measuring a *process* over some period of time.

To use an analogy, think of a bathtub being filled with water. The water *in* the tub is a stock variable—so many gallons at any given moment. The water *flowing into* the tub is a flow variable—so many gallons *per minute* or *per hour*. You can always identify a flow variable by the addition of "per period" in its definition. Even when not explicitly stated, some period of time is always implied in a flow variable.

The capital stock—the total amount of plant and equipment that exists in the economy—is like the quantity of water *in* the tub. It can be measured at any given moment. Investment spending—the amount of *new* capital being installed over some time interval—is like the water flowing *into* the tub. Investment spending is defined *per period*—such as *per quarter* or *per year*. In the simplest terms, investment spending *adds* to the capital stock over time.

But there is one more flow involved in the capital–investment relationship: *depreciation*. Each period, some of the capital stock is used up. If a computer is expected to last only three years, for example, then each year the computer depreciates by about a third of its initial value. Depreciation tends to *reduce* the capital stock over time. (In our tub analogy, depreciation is like the flow of water draining *out* each period.) *As long as investment is greater than depreciation* (more water flows into the tub than drains out), *the capital stock will rise*. Moreover, for any rate of depreciation, the greater the flow of investment spending, the faster the rise in the capital stock.

Pulling all of this together leads us to an important conclusion about investment spending and the capital stock:

> *For a given rate of depreciation and a given growth rate of employment, a higher rate of investment spending causes faster growth in capital per worker and productivity, and faster growth in the average standard of living.*

This is why when economists think about raising productivity via the capital stock, they focus on raising the rate of investment spending.

How to Increase Investment

A government seeking to spur investment has more than one weapon in its arsenal. It can direct its efforts toward businesses themselves, toward the household sector, or toward its own budget.

Targeting Businesses: Increasing the Incentive to Invest

One kind of policy to increase investment targets the business sector itself, with the goal of increasing planned investment spending. Figure 5 shows how this works. The figure shows a simplified view of the loanable funds market where—to focus on investment—we assume that there is no budget deficit, so there is no government demand for funds. The initial equilibrium in the market is at point *A*, where household saving (the supply of funds) and investment (the demand for funds) are both equal to $1.5 trillion and the interest rate is 3 percent. Now suppose that the government takes steps to make investment more profitable so that—at any interest rate—firms will want to purchase $0.75 trillion more in capital equipment than

FIGURE 5

An Increase in Investment Spending

Government policies that make investment more profitable will increase investment spending at each interest rate. The resulting rightward shift of the investment demand curve (by the distance AF) leads to a higher level of investment spending, at point B.

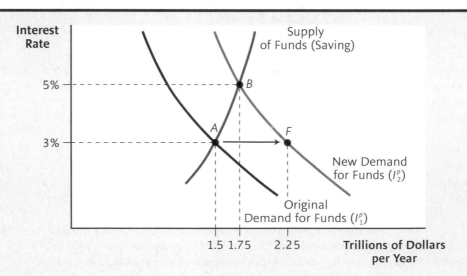

before. Then the investment curve would shift rightward by $0.75 trillion and the interest rate would rise from 3 percent to 5 percent. Note that, as the interest rate rises, some—but not all—of the original increase in planned investment is choked off. In the end, investment rises from $1.5 trillion to $1.75 trillion, and so each year $0.25 trillion more is added to the capital stock than would otherwise be added.

These are the mechanics of a rightward shift in the investment curve. But what government measures would *cause* such a shift in the first place? That is, how could the government help to make investment spending more profitable for firms?

One such measure would be a reduction in the **corporate profits tax**, which would allow firms and their owners to keep more of the profits they earn from investment projects. Another, even more direct, policy is an **investment tax credit**, which subsidizes corporate investment in new capital equipment.

Corporate profits tax A tax on the profits earned by corporations.

Investment tax credit A reduction in taxes for firms that invest in new capital.

> *Reducing business taxes or providing specific investment incentives can shift the investment curve rightward, thereby creating faster growth in physical capital. This leads to faster growth in productivity and output per capita.*

Of course, the same reasoning applies in reverse: An *increase* in the corporate profits tax or the *elimination* of an investment tax credit would shift the investment curve to the left, slowing the rate of investment, the growth of the capital stock, and the rise in living standards.

Targeting Households: Increasing the Incentive to Save

An increase in investment spending can also originate in the household sector, through an increase in the desire to save. This is illustrated in Figure 6. If households decide to save more of their incomes at any given interest rate, the supply of funds curve will shift rightward. The increase in saving drives down the interest rate, from 5 percent to 3 percent, which, in turn, causes investment to increase. With a lower interest rate, NBC might decide to borrow funds to build another production studio, or the corner grocery store may finally decide to borrow the funds it needs for a new electronic scanner at the checkout stand. In this way, an increase in the desire to save is translated, via the loanable funds market, into an increase in investment and faster growth in the capital stock.

What might cause households to increase their saving? The answer is found in the reasons people save in the first place. And to understand these reasons, you needn't look farther than yourself or your own family. You might currently be saving for a large purchase (a car, a house, a vacation, college tuition) or to build a financial cushion in case of hard times ahead. You might even be saving to support yourself during retirement, though this is a distant thought for most college students.

Given these motives, what would make you save *more*? Several things: greater uncertainty about your economic future, an increase in your life expectancy, anticipation of an earlier retirement, a change in tastes toward big-ticket items, or even just a change in your attitude about saving. Any of these changes—if they occurred in many households simultaneously—would shift the saving curve (the supply of funds curve) to the right, as in Figure 6.

But government policy can increase household saving as well. One way is to decrease the **capital gains tax**. A capital gain is the profit you earn when you sell an

Capital gains tax A tax on profits earned when a financial asset is sold at more than its acquisition price.

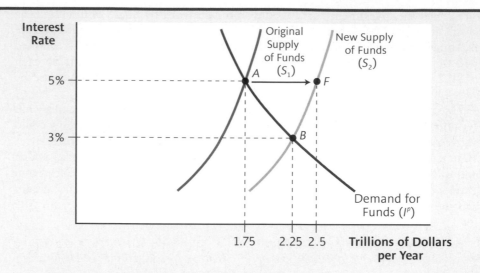

FIGURE 6

An Increase in Saving

If households decide to save more of their incomes, the supply of funds curve will shift rightward (by the distance AF). With more funds available, the interest rate will fall. Businesses will respond by increasing their borrowing, and investment will increase from $1.75 trillion to $2.25 trillion.

asset, such as a share of stock or a bond, at a higher price than you paid for it. By lowering the special tax rate for capital gains, households would be able to keep more of the capital gains they earn. As a result, stocks and bonds would become more rewarding to own, and you might decide to reduce your current spending in order to buy them. If other households react in the same way, total saving would rise, and the supply of funds to the loanable funds market would increase.

This was the logic behind a key component of the Bush administration's second tax cut, signed into law in May 2003. The tax cut included a reduction in the capital gains tax, from 20 percent to 15 percent for higher income households, and from 10 percent to 5 percent (and down to 0 percent in 2008) for lower income households. The lower tax rates applied only to *long-term* capital gains—gains on assets held for a year or longer—to encourage people to put their funds into stocks and other assets and keep them there, rather than engage in short-term speculation.

The 2003 tax cut on capital gains was controversial for two reasons. First, there was an equity issue: Because most of the capital gains in the economy are earned by higher income households, high-income households benefited more than low-income households. Second, the government was already running a substantial budget deficit in 2003, and the tax cuts threatened to raise it further. As you'll see in the next section, higher budget deficits can work *against* economic growth.

Consumption tax A tax on the part of their income that households spend.

Another frequently proposed measure is to switch from the current U.S. income tax—which taxes all income whether it is spent or saved—to a **consumption tax**, which would tax only the income that households spend. A consumption tax could work just like the current income tax, except that you would deduct your saving from your income and pay taxes on the remainder. This would increase the reward for saving. By saving, you would earn additional interest on the part of your income that would have been taxed away under an income tax. Currently, individual retirement accounts (IRAs) and employer-sponsored 401(k) plans allow households to deduct limited amounts of saving from their incomes before paying taxes. A general consumption tax would go much further and allow *all* saving to be deducted.

Another change that would increase household saving—if we were to choose this route—would be to modify the government programs that form our social safety net. Social Security payments to the elderly, unemployment insurance payments for those who lose their jobs, and Medicaid for those too poor to afford health care—all help to guarantee a basic floor for living standards. But by reducing the fear and anxiety of possible adverse economic outcomes, these government transfer programs also reduce households' incentive to save as a precaution.

> *Government can alter the tax and transfer system to increase incentives for saving. This would make more funds available for investment, speed growth in the capital stock, and speed the rise in living standards.*

(Do any of these methods of increasing saving disturb you? Remember, we are not advocating any measures here; rather, we are merely noting that such measures would increase saving and promote economic growth. We'll discuss the *costs* of growth-promoting measures later.)

Shrinking the Budget Deficit

A final pro-investment measure is directed at the government sector itself. The previous chapter showed that an increase in government purchases, financed by borrowing in the financial market, completely crowds out consumption and investment. A *decrease* in government purchases has the opposite effect: raising consumption and investment.

Figure 7 reintroduces the government to the loanable funds market to show how this works. Initially, the budget deficit is $0.75 trillion, equal to the distance *EA*. The total demand for funds is the sum of investment and the government's budget deficit, given by the curve labeled $I^p + (G - T)$. The demand for funds curve intersects the supply of funds curve at point *A*, creating an equilibrium interest rate of 5 percent and equilibrium saving of $1.75 trillion. At this interest rate, investment spending is only $1 trillion. The part of saving not going to finance investment

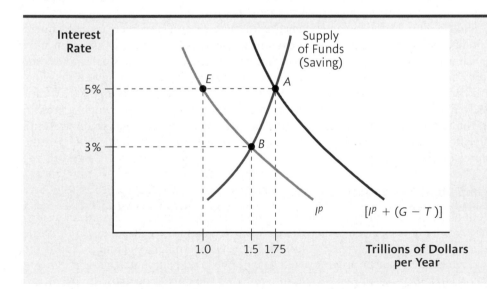

FIGURE 7

Deficit Reduction and Investment Spending

Eliminating the government's budget deficit will reduce government borrowing in the loanable funds market. As a result, the total demand for funds will fall, as will the interest rate. At a lower interest rate, businesses will increase their investment spending from $1.0 trillion (point E) to $1.5 trillion (point B).

spending ($1.75 trillion − $1 trillion = $0.75 trillion) is being used to finance the budget deficit.

Now consider what happens if the government eliminates the deficit—say, by reducing its purchases by $0.75 trillion. The demand for funds would consist of investment spending only. Since there would be no other borrowing, the new equilibrium would be point *B*, with an interest rate of 3 percent and investment equal to $1.5 trillion—greater than before. By balancing its budget, the government no longer needs to borrow in the loanable funds market, which frees up funds to flow to the business sector instead.

The link between the government budget, the interest rate, and investment spending is the major reason the U.S. government, and governments around the world, try to reduce and, if possible, eliminate budget deficits. They have learned that

> *a shrinking deficit or a rising surplus tends to reduce interest rates and increase investment, thus speeding the growth in the capital stock.*

In the 1990s, Congress set strict limits on the growth of government spending, and the budget deficit began shrinking. The restraints on spending, and rapid economic growth during the 1990s, finally turned the federal budget from deficit to surplus in 1998, and continued surpluses were projected for more than a decade. These surpluses were viewed as positive for economic growth: They would help keep the interest rate low, which in turn would lead to greater business investment spending.

When President George W. Bush took office in 2001, the direction of growth policy shifted away from preserving budget surpluses and toward lower tax rates. The first Bush tax cut in 2001(a total of $1.35 trillion over 10 years) purposely cut into potential future surpluses in order to reduce the tax burden on American households. Shortly afterward, a series of events pushed the budget into deficit. These included a continuing recession that had begun in March 2001 and the attacks of September 11, which resulted in large increases in military and homeland security spending. And a second tax cut in 2003—amounting to $350 billion over 10 years—increased current and projected deficits further.

The tax cuts included some elements (discussed earlier) to increase investment spending, such as a lower tax rate for capital gains and tax incentives for investment by small businesses. Also, you've learned that cutting income tax rates can have some effect on the labor force participation rate by shifting the labor supply curve rightward. But the tax cuts—by raising current and future budget deficits—would ultimately drive the interest rate higher than it would otherwise be, which works in opposition to the growth benefits of the tax cut. We'll discuss budget deficits and their effects on the economy more thoroughly toward the end of this book, in the chapter on fiscal policy.

An Important Proviso about the Budget Deficit

A reduction in the deficit or an increase in the surplus—even if they stimulate private investment—are not *necessarily* pro-growth measures. It depends on *how* the budget changes. By an increase in taxes? A cut in government spending? And if the latter, which government programs will be cut? Welfare? National defense? Highway repair? The answers can make a big difference to the impact on growth.

For example, in our discussions of the capital stock so far, we've ignored government capital—roads, communication lines, bridges, and dams. To understand the importance of government capital, just imagine what life would be like without it. How would factories obtain their raw materials or distribute their goods if no one repaired the roads? How would contracts between buyers and sellers be enforced if there were no public buildings to house courts and police departments? It is clear that

government investment in new capital and the maintenance of existing capital make important contributions to economic growth.

This important observation complicates our view of deficit reduction. It is still true that a decrease in government spending will lower the interest rate and increase private investment. But if the budget cutting falls largely on government investment, the negative effect of smaller *public* investment will offset some of the positive impact of greater *private* investment. Shrinking the deficit will then alter the *mix* of capital—more private and less public—and the effect on growth could go either way. A society rife with lawlessness, deteriorating roads and bridges, or an unreliable communications network might benefit from a shift toward public capital. For example, a study of public budgets in African nations—which have poor road conditions—found that each one-dollar-per-year cut in the road-maintenance budget increased vehicle operating costs by between $2 and $3 per year, and, in one case, by as much as $22 per year.[4] This is an example of a cut in government spending that, even if it reduces the deficit, probably hinders growth. By contrast, in Sweden—a country with a fully developed and well-maintained public infrastructure—recent governments have decided to shift the mix away from public and toward private capital, in part because they believed this would speed growth.

The impact of deficit reduction on economic growth depends on which government programs are cut. Shrinking the deficit by cutting government investment will not stimulate growth as much as would cutting other types of government spending.

HUMAN CAPITAL AND ECONOMIC GROWTH

So far, the only type of capital we've discussed is physical capital—the plant and equipment workers use to produce output. But when we think of the capital stock most broadly, we include *human capital* as well. Human capital—the skills and knowledge possessed by workers—is as central to economic growth as is physical capital. After all, most types of physical capital—computers, CAT scanners, and even shovels—will contribute little to output unless workers know how to use them. And when more workers gain skills or improve their existing skills, output rises just as it does when workers have more physical capital:

An increase in human capital works like an increase in physical capital to increase output: It causes the production function to shift upward, raises productivity, and increases the average standard of living.

[4] This World Bank study was cited in *The Economist,* June 10, 1995, p. 72.

There is another similarity between human and physical capital: Both are *stocks* that are increased by *flows* of investment. The stock of human capital increases whenever investment in new skills during some period, through education and training, exceeds the depreciation of existing skills over the same period, through retirement, death, or disuse. Therefore, greater investment in human capital will speed the growth of the human capital stock, increasing the growth rate of productivity and living standards.

Human capital investments are made by business firms (when they help to train their employees), by government (through public education and subsidized training), and by households (when they pay for general education or professional training). Human capital investments have played an important role in recent U.S. economic growth. Can we do anything to increase our rate of investment in human capital?

In part, we've already answered this question: Some of the same policies that increase investment in *physical* capital also work to raise investment in human capital. For example, a decrease in the budget deficit would lower the interest rate and make it cheaper for households to borrow for college loans and training programs. A change in the tax system that increases the incentive to save would have the same impact, since this, too, would lower interest rates. And an easing of the tax burden on business firms could increase the profitability of *their* human capital investments, leading to more and better worker training programs.

But there is more: Human capital, unlike physical capital, cannot be separated from the person who provides it. If you own a building, you can rent it out to one firm and sell your labor to another. But if you have training as a doctor, your labor and your human capital must be sold together, as a package. Moreover, your wage or salary will be payment for both your labor and your human capital. This means that income tax reductions—which we discussed earlier as a means of increasing labor supply—can also increase the profitability of human capital to households, and increase their rate of investment in their own skills and training.

For example, suppose an accountant is considering whether to attend a course in corporate financial reporting, which would increase her professional skills. The course costs \$4,000 and will increase the accountant's income by \$1,000 per year for the rest of her career. With a tax rate of 40 percent, her take-home pay would increase by \$600 per year, so her annual rate of return on her investment would be \$600/\$4,000 = 15 percent. But with a lower tax rate—say, 20 percent—her take-home pay would rise by \$800 per year, so her rate of return would be \$800/\$4,000 = 20 percent. The lower the tax rate, the greater is the rate of return on the accountant's human capital investment, and the more likely she will be to acquire new skills. Thus,

> *many of the pro-growth policies discussed earlier—policies that increase employment or increase investment in physical capital—are also effective in promoting investment in human capital.*

TECHNOLOGICAL CHANGE

Technological change The invention or discovery of new inputs, new outputs, or new production methods.

So far, we've discussed how productivity growth is increased by greater investment in physical or human capital. But another important source of growth is **technological change**—the invention or discovery of new inputs, new outputs, or new methods of production. Indeed, it is largely because of technological change that Malthus's horrible prediction (cited at the beginning of this chapter) has not come true. In the last 60 years, for example, the inventions of synthetic fertilizers, hybrid corn, and chemical pesticides have enabled world food production to increase faster than population.

New technology affects the economy in much the same way as do increases in the capital stock. Flip back to Figure 4 of this chapter. There, you saw that an increase in the capital stock would shift the production function upward and increase output. New technology, too, shifts the production function upward because it enables any given number of workers to produce more output.

It follows that

> *the faster the rate of technological change, the greater the growth rate of productivity, and the faster the rise in living standards.*

It might seem that technological change is one of those things that just happens. Thomas Edison invents electricity, or Steve Jobs and Steve Wozniak develop the first practical personal computer in their garage. But the pace of technological change is not as haphazard as it seems. The transistor was invented as part of a massive research and development effort by AT&T to improve the performance of communications electronics. Similarly, the next developments in computer technology, transportation, and more will depend in part on how much money is spent on research and development (R&D) by the leading technology firms:

> *The rate of technological change in the economy depends largely on firms' total spending on R&D. Policies that increase R&D spending will increase the pace of technological change.*

What can the government do to increase spending on R&D? First, it can increase its own direct support for R&D by carrying out more research in its own laboratories or increasing funding for universities and tax incentives to private research labs.

Second, the government can enhance **patent protection**, which increases rewards for those who create new technology by giving them exclusive rights to use it or sell it. Hundreds of thousands of new patents are issued every year in the United States: to pharmaceutical companies for new prescription drugs, to telecommunications companies for new cellular technologies, and to the producers of a variety of household goods ranging from can openers to microwave ovens.

Patent protection A government grant of exclusive rights to use or sell a new technology.

Because patent protection increases the rewards that developers can expect from new inventions, it encourages them to spend more on R&D. By broadening patent protection—issuing patents on a wider variety of discoveries—or by lengthening patent protection—increasing the number of years during which the developer has exclusive rights to market the invention—the government could increase the expected profits from new technologies. That would increase total spending on R&D and increase the pace of technological change.

Finally, R&D spending is in many ways just like other types of investment spending: The funds are drawn from the loanable funds market, and R&D programs require firms to buy something now (laboratories, the services of research scientists, materials for prototypes) for the uncertain prospect of profits in the future. Therefore, almost any policy that stimulates investment spending in general will also increase spending on R&D. Cutting the tax rate on capital gains or on corporate profits, or lowering interest rates by encouraging greater saving or by reducing the budget deficit, can each help to increase spending on R&D and increase the rate of technological change.

GROWTH POLICIES: A SUMMARY

In this chapter, you've learned about the forces that affect economic growth, as well as a host of government policies that can make the economy grow faster. If you are having trouble keeping it all straight, Table 4—which summarizes all of this information—might help.

As you look at the table, you'll notice that many of the policies that affect economic growth are *fiscal policies*—changes in government purchases or net taxes designed to affect total output. In the previous chapter, you learned that fiscal policy has no *demand-side* effects on output. But in this chapter, you've seen that fiscal policy *can* affect output in a different way—by changing the resources available in the economy. For example, tax rates influence the number of people who want to work and change the quantity of labor employed. Fiscal changes can also change the rate of investment spending and therefore influence the capital stock firms will have in the future. These effects of fiscal policy—changing total output by changing the resources available in the economy—are called **supply-side effects**.

Supply-side effects
Macroeconomic policy effects on total output that work by changing the quantities of resources available.

> *In the long run, while fiscal policy cannot influence total output by changing total spending (demand-side effects), it* can *influence output by changing the quantity of resources available for production (supply-side effects).*

Table 4 also shows that some pro-growth policies can work through multiple channels. For example, a less-generous social safety net would have three separate impacts on growth: (1) an increase in labor supply (by making alternatives to working more draconian); (2) an increase in the incentive to save (because people would worry more about their future); and (3) a reduction in the budget deficit (through lower transfer payments). The first effect raises the EPR, and the other two raise investment and productivity.

Finally, the table shows that some policies that *increase* economic growth through one channel can simultaneously work *against* growth through another channel. For example, in the first row of the table, you can see that a *decrease* in income tax rates contributes to growth by increasing employment. But farther down, you'll see that an *increase* in taxes can aid growth by shrinking a budget deficit (implying that a *decrease* in taxes would have the opposite effect and harm growth). Thus, a decrease in tax rates simultaneously helps growth through one channel and harms growth through another.

The fact that a single policy can have two competing effects on the economy helps us understand one reason for controversy in macroeconomic policy. When we cut income taxes, for example, the ultimate effect on economic growth will depend on which of the two effects is stronger, something over which economists can and do disagree. The Bush tax cut in 2001 was seen by some economists as a growth-enhancing measure (those who stressed the impact on employment) and by others as harmful to

	Factors That Influence Growth in Output per Capita		**TABLE 4**
Examples of Pro-Growth Policies	**Method of Impact**	**Immediate Goal**	**Effect on Growth Equation**
• Decrease income or payroll tax rates • Less-generous social safety net	Increase in labor supply	Employment ↑	EPR growth rate ↑
• Specific employment subsidies • Any policy that raises labor productivity (e.g., all policies below)	Increase in labor demand		
• Investment tax credit • Decrease corporate profits tax rate • Greater subsidies for student loans	Direct impact on investment	Greater investment in: • Human capital • Physical capital • R&D	Productivity growth rate ↑
• Tax incentives for saving [IRAs, 401(k)s] • Decrease capital gains tax rate • Less-generous social safety net	Increase in saving $\Rightarrow$ $r\downarrow \Rightarrow l^p \uparrow$		
• Decrease in government purchases • Increase in taxes • Decrease in transfer payments	Decrease in budget deficit $\Rightarrow r\downarrow \Rightarrow l^p \uparrow$		

economic growth (those who stressed the effect on the government's budget, and the consequences for interest rates and investment).

The biggest controversies regarding growth policies, however, are not about their effectiveness but about their *costs*.

THE COSTS OF ECONOMIC GROWTH

So far in this chapter, we've discussed a variety of policies that could increase the rate of economic growth and speed the rise in living standards. Why don't all nations pursue these policies and push their rates of economic growth to the maximum? For example, why did the U.S. standard of living (output per capita) grow by 2.1 percent per year between 1995 and 2005? Why not 4 percent per year? Or 6 percent? Or even more?

In this section, you will see that

> *promoting economic growth involves unavoidable tradeoffs: It requires some groups, or the nation as a whole, to give up something else that is valued.*

Economics is famous for making the public aware of policy tradeoffs. One of the most important things you will learn in your introductory economics course is that there are no costless solutions to society's problems. Just as individuals face an opportunity cost when they take an action (they must give up something else that they value), so, too, policy makers face an opportunity cost whenever they pursue a policy: They must compromise on achieving some other social goal.

What are the costs of growth?

BUDGETARY COSTS

If you look again at Table 4, you'll see that many of the pro-growth policies we've analyzed involve some kind of tax cut. Cutting the income tax rate may increase the labor force participation rate. Cutting taxes on capital gains or corporate profits will increase investment directly. And cutting taxes on saving will increase household saving, lower interest rates, and thus increase investment spending indirectly. Unfortunately, implementing any of these tax cuts would force the government to choose among three unpleasant alternatives: increase some other tax to regain the lost revenue, cut government spending, or permit the budget deficit to rise.

Who will bear the burden of this budgetary cost? That depends on which alternative is chosen. Under the first option—increasing some other tax—the burden falls on those who pay the other tax. For example, if income taxes are cut, real estate taxes might be increased. A family might pay lower income taxes, but higher property taxes. Whether it comes out ahead or behind will depend on how much income the family earns relative to how much property it owns.

The second option, cutting government spending, imposes the burden on those who currently benefit from government programs. This includes those who directly benefit from specific programs—like welfare recipients or farmers. It also includes those who benefit from government spending more indirectly. Even though you may earn your income in the private sector, if government spending is cut, you may suffer from a deterioration of public roads, decreased police protection, or poorer schools for your children.

The third option—a larger budget deficit or a smaller budget surplus—is more complicated. Suppose a tax cut causes the government to end up with a larger deficit. Then greater government borrowing will increase the total amount of government debt outstanding—called the *national debt*. This means greater interest payments by future generations and higher taxes.

But that is not all. From the previous chapter, we know that a rise in the budget deficit (by increasing the demand for funds) drives up the interest rate. The higher interest rate will reduce investment in physical capital and R&D by businesses, as well as investment in human capital by households, and both effects will work to decrease economic growth. It is even possible that so much private investment will be crowded out that the tax cut, originally designed to boost economic growth, ends up slowing growth instead. At best, the growth-enhancing effects of the tax cut will be weakened. This is why advocates of high growth rates usually propose one of the other options—a rise in some other tax or a cut in government spending—as part of a pro-growth tax cut.

In sum,

> *even though properly targeted tax cuts can increase the rate of economic growth, they will generally force us to either redistribute the tax burden or cut government programs.*

CONSUMPTION COSTS

Any pro-growth policy that works by increasing investment—in physical capital, human capital, or R&D—requires a sacrifice of current consumption spending. We use *resources* to construct new oil rigs or factory buildings, or to build and staff new training facilities and research laboratories. These resources could have been used instead to produce clothing, automobiles, video games, and other consumer goods. In other words, we face a tradeoff: The more capital goods we produce in any given year, the fewer consumption goods we can enjoy in that year.

The role of this tradeoff in economic growth can be clearly seen with a familiar tool from Chapter 2: the production possibilities frontier (PPF). Figure 8 shows the PPF for a nation with some given amount of land, labor, capital, and entrepreneurship that must be allocated to the production of two types of output: capital goods and consumption goods. At point *K*, the nation is using all of its resources to produce capital goods and none to produce consumption goods. Point C represents the opposite extreme: all resources used to produce consumption goods and none for capital goods. Ordinarily, a nation will operate at an intermediate point such as *A*, where it is producing both capital and consumption goods.

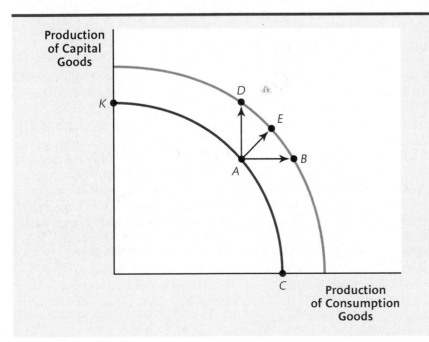

FIGURE 8

Consumption, Investment, and Economic Growth

In the current period, a nation can choose to produce only consumer goods (point C), or it can produce some capital goods by sacrificing some current consumption, as at point A. If investment at point A exceeds capital depreciation, the capital stock will grow, and the production possibilities frontier will shift outward. After it does, the nation can produce more consumption goods (point B), more capital goods (point D), or more of both (point E).

Now, as long as capital production at point A is greater than the depreciation of existing capital, the capital stock will grow. In future periods, the economy—with more capital—can produce more output, as shown by the outward shift of the PPF in the figure. If a nation can produce more output, then it can produce more consumption goods and the same quantity of capital goods (moving from point A to point B), or more capital goods and the same quantity of consumption goods (from point A to point D) or more of both (from point A to point E).

Let's take a closer look at how this sacrifice of current consumption goods might come about. Suppose that some change in government policy—an investment tax credit or a lengthening of the patent period for new inventions—successfully increases investment. (Go back to Figure 5.) What will happen? Businesses—demanding more loanable funds—will drive up the interest rate, and households all over the country will find that saving has become more attractive. As families increase their saving, we move rightward along the economy's supply of funds curve. In this way, firms get the funds they need to purchase new capital. But a decision to *save more* is also a decision to *spend less*. As current saving rises, current consumption spending necessarily falls. By driving up the interest rate, *the increase in investment spending causes a voluntary decrease in consumption spending by households*. Resources are freed from producing consumption goods and diverted to producing capital goods instead.

Although this decrease in consumption spending is voluntary, it is still a cost that we pay. And in some cases, a painful cost: Some of the increase in the household sector's net saving results from a decrease in borrowing by households that—at higher interest rates—can no longer afford to finance purchases of homes, cars, or furniture. In sum,

> *greater investment in physical capital, human capital, or R&D will lead to faster economic growth and higher living standards in the future, but we will have fewer consumer goods to enjoy in the present.*

OPPORTUNITY COSTS OF WORKERS' TIME

An increase in the employment–population ratio or average hours will increase living standards, as measured by output per capita. There will be more output to divide among a given population. But this increase in output per capita comes at a cost: a decrease in time spent in nonmarket activities. For example, with a greater fraction of the population working, a smaller fraction is spending time at home. This might mean that more students have summer jobs, more elderly workers are postponing their retirement, or more previously nonworking spouses are entering the labor force. Similarly, an increase in average working hours would mean that the average worker will have less time for other activities—less time to watch television, read novels, garden, fix up the house, teach his or her children, or do volunteer work.

Thus, when economic growth comes about from increases in the EPR or in average hours, we face a tradeoff: On the one hand, we can enjoy higher incomes and more goods and services; on the other hand, we will have less time to do things other than work in the market. In a market economy, where choices are voluntary, the value of the income gained must be greater than the value of the time given up. No one forces us to reenter the labor force or to increase working hours. So anyone who takes either of these actions must be better off for doing so. Still, we must recognize that *something* of value is always given up when employment or hours increase:

> *An increase in the employment–population ratio or a rise in average hours will increase living standards as measured by output per capita, but also require us to sacrifice time previously spent in nonmarket activities.*

SACRIFICE OF OTHER SOCIAL GOALS

Rapid economic growth is an important social goal, but it's not the only one. Some of the policies that quicken the pace of growth require us to sacrifice other goals that we care about. For example, you've seen that restructuring and even reducing government transfer payments could increase saving, leading to more investment and faster growth. But such a move would cut the incomes of those who benefit from the current system and force some citizens into levels of poverty that society may find unacceptable. You've learned that extending patent protection would increase incentives for research and development. But it would also extend the monopoly power exercised by patent holders and force consumers to pay higher prices for drugs, electronic equipment, and even packaged foods in the present.

Of course, the argument cuts both ways: Just as government policies to stimulate investment require us to sacrifice other goals, so, too, can the pursuit of other goals impede investment spending and economic growth. Most of us would like to see a cleaner environment and safer workplaces. But safety and environmental regulations can reduce the rate of profit on new capital and shrink investment spending.

Does this mean that business taxes and government regulations should be reduced to the absolute minimum? Not at all. As in most matters of economic policy, we face a tradeoff:

> *Achieving greater worker safety, a cleaner environment, and other social goals requires the sacrifice of some economic growth along the way. Alternatively, achieving greater economic growth may require some compromise on other things we care about.*

When values differ, people will disagree on just how much we should sacrifice for economic growth or how much growth we should sacrifice for other goals.

USING THE THEORY

Economic Growth in the Less-Developed Countries

In most countries, Malthus's dire predictions (cited at the beginning of this chapter) have not come true. One reason is that increases in the capital stock have raised productivity and increased the average standard of living. Increases in the capital stock are even more important in the less-developed countries (LDCs), which have relatively little capital to begin with. In these countries, even small increases in capital formation can have dramatic effects on living standards.

© RAFIQUR RAHMAN/REUTERS/CORBIS

But how does a nation go about increasing its capital stock? As you've learned, there are a variety of measures, all designed to accomplish the same goal: shifting resources away from consumer-goods production toward the production of physical and human capital. A very simple formula.

Some countries that were once LDCs—like Hong Kong, Singapore, South Korea, and India—have applied the formula very effectively. Output per capita in these countries has grown by an average of 4 or 5 percent per year for the past two decades. China's output per capita has grown even faster over this period, with an average annual increase of 8 percent. All these countries were able to shift resources from consumption goods into capital goods in part by pursuing many of the growth-enhancing measures discussed in this chapter: large subsidies for human and physical capital investments, pro-growth tax cuts to encourage saving and investment, and the willingness to sacrifice other social goals—especially a clean environment—for growth.[5] These economies gave up large amounts of potential consumption during a period of intensive capital formation.

But other LDCs have had great difficulty raising living standards. Table 5 shows growth rates for several of them, over the periods 1975–1990 and 1990–2003. In some cases, such as Bangladesh, Ghana, and Benin, there is at least some cause for optimism: Stagnating or declining living standards in the earlier period have given way to slow but consistent growth. In other cases—such as Kenya—living standards have barely budged over the past few decades. In still other cases—for example, Haiti and Sierra Leone—output per capita has been falling ever more rapidly. Why do some LDCs have such difficulty achieving economic growth?

Much of the explanation for the low growth rates of many LDCs lies with three characteristics that they share:

1. *Very low current output per capita.* Living standards are so low in some LDCs that they cannot take advantage of the tradeoff between producing consumption goods and producing capital goods. In these countries, pulling resources out of consumption would threaten the survival of many families.

TABLE 5		
Economic Growth in Selected Poor Countries	**Average Annual Growth Rate of Output per Capita**	
Country	**1975–1990**	**1990–2003**
Bangladesh	0.9	3.1
Ghana	−0.8	1.8
Benin	−0.6	2.2
Kenya	0.9	−0.6
Haiti	−1.9	−2.8
Sierra Leone	−1.5	−5.3

Source: United Nations Development Programme, *Human Development Report 2005*, pp. 266–269, and author calculations.

[5] Some of these countries also had some special advantages—such as a high level of human capital to start with.

At the household level, the problem is an inability to save: Incomes are so low that households must spend all they earn on consumption.

2. *High population growth rates.* Low living standards and high population growth rates are linked together in a cruel circle of logic. On the one hand, rapid population growth by itself tends to reduce living standards. On the other hand, a low standard of living tends to increase population growth. Why? First, the poor are often uneducated in matters of family planning. Second, high mortality rates among infants and children encourage families to have many offspring, to ensure the survival of at least a few to care for parents in their old age. As a result, while the average woman in the United States will have fewer than two children in her lifetime, the average woman in Haiti will have four children; in Kenya, five children; and in Sierra Leone, more than six.

3. *Poor infrastructure.* Political instability, poor law enforcement, corruption, and adverse government regulations make many LDCs unprofitable places to invest. Low rates of investment mean a smaller capital stock and lower productivity. Infrastructure problems also harm worker productivity in another way: Citizens must spend time guarding against thievery and trying to induce the government to let them operate businesses—time they could otherwise spend producing output.

These three characteristics—low current production, high population growth, and poor infrastructure—interact to create a vicious circle of continuing poverty, which we can understand with the help of the familiar PPF between capital goods and consumption goods. Look back at Figure 8, and now imagine that it applies to a poor, developing country. In this case, an outward shift of the PPF does not, in itself, guarantee an increase in the standard of living. In the LDCs, the population growth rate is often very high, and employment grows at the same rate as the population. If employment grows more rapidly than the capital stock, then even though the PPF is shifting outward, capital per worker will decline. Unless some other factor—such as technological change—is raising productivity, then living standards will fall.

> *In order to have rising capital per worker—an important source of growth in productivity and living standards—a nation's stock of capital must not only grow but grow faster than its population.*

Point N in Figure 9 shows the minimum amount of investment needed to maintain capital per worker, and therefore labor productivity and living standards, for a given rate of population growth. For example, if the population is growing at 4 percent per year, then point N indicates the annual investment needed to increase the total capital stock by 4 percent per year. If investment is just equal to N, then capital per worker—and living standards—remains constant. If investment exceeds N, then capital per worker—and living standards—will rise. Of course, the greater the growth in population, the higher point N will be on the vertical axis, since greater investment will be needed just to keep up with population growth. (We assume throughout this discussion that the labor force and employment are both rising at the same rate as the population.)

The PPF in Figure 9 has an added feature: Point S shows the minimum acceptable level of consumption, the amount of consumer goods the economy *must* produce

FIGURE 9

LDC Growth and Living Standards

In order to increase capital per worker when population is growing, yearly investment spending must exceed some minimum level N. In any year, there is a minimum level of consumption, S, needed to support the population. If output is currently at point H, capital per worker and living standards are stagnant. But movement to a point like J would require an unacceptably low level of consumption.

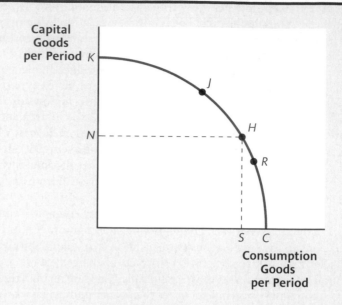

in a year. For example, *S* might represent the consumption goods needed to prevent starvation among the least well off, or to prevent unacceptable social consequences, such as violent revolution.

Now we can see the problem faced by some less-developed economies. Output is currently at a point like *H* in Figure 9, with annual investment just equal to *N*. The capital stock is not growing fast enough to increase capital per worker, and so labor productivity and living standards are stagnant. In this situation, the PPF shifts outward each year, but not quickly enough to improve people's lives. In the most desperate countries, the situation is worse: They operate at a point like *R*, with investment *below* N. Even though the capital stock is growing, it does not grow fast enough, so capital per worker and living standards decline.

The solution to this problem appears to be an increase in capital production beyond point *N*—a movement *along* the PPF from point *H* to a point such as *J*. As investment rises above *N*, capital per worker rises, and the PPF shifts outward rapidly enough over time to raise living standards. In a wealthy country, like the United States, such a move could be engineered by changes in taxes or other government policies. But in the LDCs depicted here, such a move would be intolerable: At point *H*, consumption is already equal to *S*, the lowest acceptable level. Moving to point *J* would require reducing consumption *below S*.

> *The poorest LDCs are too poor to take advantage of the tradeoff between consumption and capital production in order to increase their living standards. Since they cannot reduce consumption below current levels, they cannot produce enough capital to keep up with their rising populations.*

In recent history, a variety of methods have been attempted to break out of this vicious circle of poverty.

- *Brute force.* The most tragic way to break out of the cycle is to simply force the economy from a point like *H* to a point like *J*, even though consumption falls below the minimally acceptable level *S*.

    An example occurred during the 1930s, when the dictator Joseph Stalin moved the Soviet economy in this way by ordering farmers into the city to produce capital equipment rather than food. With fewer people working on farms, agricultural production declined and there was not enough food to go around. Stalin's solution was to confiscate food from the remaining farmers and give it to the urban workforce. Of course, this meant starvation for millions of farmers. Millions more who complained too loudly, or who otherwise represented a political threat, were rounded up and executed.

- *Target the wealthy.* In this method, the economy moves from point *H* to point *J* while limiting the sacrifice of consumption to the wealthy. Figure 10(a) shows this graphically. The minimally acceptable level of consumption moves leftward, from *S* to *S′*, because total consumption can be reduced to a lower level than before without threatening the survival of the poor. The drop in consumption to point *J* (which is now acceptable) frees up resources for investment. However, this method is not often practical because the wealthy have the most influence with government in LDCs. Being more mobile, they can easily relocate to other countries, taking their savings with them. This is why efforts to shift the sacrifice to the wealthy are often combined with restrictions on personal liberties, such as the freedom to travel or to invest abroad. These moves often backfire in the long run, since restrictions on personal and economic freedom are remembered long after they are removed and make the public—especially foreigners—hesitant to invest in that country.

- *Decrease population growth.* Consider a nation producing at point *H* in Figure 10(b). Capital production is just sufficient to keep up with a rising population. The PPF shifts outward each year, but because capital per worker remains constant, living standards remain constant. If this nation can reduce its population growth rate, however, the level of capital production needed to just maintain capital per worker moves downward, from *N* to *N′*. The economy can then continue to operate at point *H*, but now—with the population growing more slowly than the capital stock—capital per worker and living standards rise.

    Reducing population growth was an important part of China's growth strategy, bringing the number of births per woman down from six in 1970 to less than two in 1980 (and to 1.7 in 2000). But it has involved severe restrictions on the rights of individual families to have children, including heavy fines and, in many cases, forced abortions and sterilizations. Although restrictions and enforcement have been loosened considerably, China's government continues to regulate childbearing as part of its effort to raise living standards, and announced in 2006 that it would continue to do so through at least 2010.

- *Foreign assistance.* Since the 1940s, assistance from wealthier countries—either individually or through international organizations such as the World Bank or the International Monetary Fund—has been viewed as the most humane way for LDCs to break out of poverty. Providing capital goods to an LDC allows its capital stock to grow faster with no decrease in consumption goods. This is illustrated in Figure 10(c), where the additional capital allows the country to operate *beyond* its PPF, moving from point *H* to point *F*. The LDC still *produces* at point *H*. But point *F* shows the new combination of consumption goods and capital goods the country obtains over the year.

FIGURE **10** Some Growth Options for LDCs

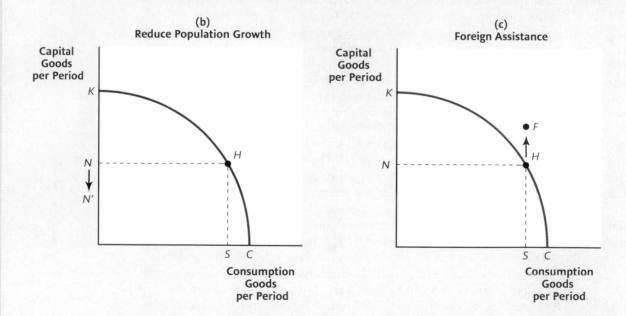

In all three panels, an LDC is initially producing at point H, where consumption is just equal to the amount needed for survival (S), and capital production is just equal to the amount needed to keep up with a rising population (N).

In panel (a), resources are shifted from producing capital goods to producing consumer goods. But because any decrease in consumption is limited to the wealthy, the minimum-survival level of consumption decreases from S to S'. At point J, the LDC can produce more capital and raise living standards over time while still meeting survival needs for consumption.

In panel (b), the LDC reduces the population growth rate, so that capital production needed to keep up with a rising population decreases from N to N'. Although production remains at point H, capital per worker now rises, raising living standards over time.

In panel (c), capital goods are obtained externally, through foreign investment or foreign assistance. The economy continues to produce at point H, but with the total amount of capital added each period greater than N (at point F), capital per worker and living standards rise over time.

Alternatively, foreign assistance could provide consumption goods, allowing the country to free up its own resources for capital production while maintaining minimal levels of consumption. In Figure 10(c), the country would move leftward along the PPF (not shown), but the combination of consumption and capital goods would once again be at point *F*. Either form of assistance could enable the capital stock to grow faster than the population for some time, setting the stage for sustained growth in living standards.

At least, that's the theory. But the failure of so many poor countries to gain traction, despite trillions of dollars in foreign assistance over the past half century, has made many economists skeptical. They put much of the blame on one of the features of LDCs discussed earlier: poor institutional infrastructure. When corrupt or undeveloped legal systems fail to protect property rights or enforce contracts, savers will not lend to domestic borrowers, and entrepreneurs will not start productive businesses. When corrupt governments siphon off most of the foreign aid dollars toward military spending or lavish lifestyles for the politically connected, little is left for improving the health and education of the population or increasing the stock of productive capital.

Although most economists believe that foreign assistance is still important, they are paying increasing attention to the institutional infrastructure of the recipient countries. This was the thinking behind the *Millennium Challenge Account* established by the Bush administration in 2004. It provides significantly increased amounts of foreign aid . . . with a catch: Countries must meet guidelines for reducing corruption, improving the environment for entrepreneurship, and working to improve the health and human capital of their citizens. The program has been given high marks for its design, but it is still too early to judge its ultimate effectiveness.

Summary

The growth rate of real GDP is a key determinant of economic well-being. If output grows faster than the population, then output per person—and the average standard of living—will rise. But in order for output per person to rise, either average working hours, the *employment–population ratio (EPR)*, or productivity must increase. In developed countries, average hours have been decreasing and are unlikely to rise in the future. Growth in the EPR has been responsible for considerable past growth in the United States and several other countries. It can be increased by policy changes that increase labor supply (such as tax cuts) or labor demand (such as subsidized job training or employment subsidies). But in the future, continual rises in the EPR are unlikely. This leaves increases in *productivity*—a major contributor to growth in the past—as the main source of growth in the future.

Productivity increases when capital per worker rises or there are advances in technology. When the flow of investment spending is greater than the flow of depreciation over some period of time, the capital stock will rise. An increase in the capital stock shifts the production function upward, enabling any given number of workers to produce more output. If the capital stock rises at a faster rate than the labor force, then *capital per worker* rises, and so does productivity.

Investment can be encouraged by government policies. It can be stimulated directly through reductions in the corporate profits tax rate or through subsidies. Or investment can be increased indirectly through government policies that bring about lower interest rates, such as changes in tax policy to encourage more saving or reductions in the government's budget deficit.

Technological change—the application of new inputs or new methods of production—also raises productivity. The rate of technological change depends partly on spending on research and development, either by government or private firms. Almost any government policy that increases investment spending in general will also increase spending on research and development, and therefore increase the pace of technological change. In addition, patent protection can specifically influence research and development of new, patentable products and technologies.

Economic growth is not costless. Tax cuts that stimulate employment, capital formation, or technological progress require increases in other taxes, cuts in spending programs, or an increase in the national debt. Any increase in employment from a given population requires a sacrifice of leisure time and other nonmarket activities. More broadly, any increase in investment requires the sacrifice of consumption today.

Problem Set   *Answers to even-numbered Questions and Problems can be found on the text Web site at www.thomsonedu.com/economics/hall.*

1. For each of the following, (1) determine the impact on full-employment output and (2) illustrate the immediate and long-run impact using the classical model (labor market, production function, or loanable funds market).
   a. Increased immigration
   b. An aging of the population with an increasing proportion of retirees
   c. A decline in the tax rate on corporate profits
   d. A reduction of unemployment benefits
   e. The development of the Internet

2. Below are GDP and growth data for the United States and four other countries:

	1950 Real GDP per Capita (in 1990 dollars)	1990 Real GDP per Capita (in 1990 dollars)	Average Yearly Growth Rate
United States	$9,573	$21,558	2.0%
France	$5,221	$17,959	3.0%
Japan	$1,873	$19,425	5.7%
Kenya	$ 609	$ 1,055	1.3%
India	$ 597	$ 1,348	2.0%

Source: Angus Maddison, *Monitoring the World Economy, 1820–1992* (Paris: OECD, 1995).

   a. For both years, calculate each country's per capita GDP as a percentage of U.S. per capita GDP. Which countries appeared to be catching up to the United States, and which were lagging behind?
   b. If all these countries had continued to grow (from 1990 onward) at the average growth rates given, in what year would France have caught up to the United States? In what years (respectively) would India and Kenya have caught up to the United States?

3. Below are hypothetical data for the country of Barrovia:

	Population (millions)	Employment (millions)	Average Yearly Hours	Labor Productivity (output per hour)	Total Yearly Output
2002	100	50	2,000	$4.75	—
2003	104	51	2,000	$4.75	—
2004	107	53	1,950	$5.00	—
2005	108	57	1,950	$5.00	—
2006	110	57	2,000	$5.00	—

   a. Fill in the entries for total output in each of the five years.
   b. Calculate the following for each year (except 2002):
      (1) Population growth rate (from previous year)
      (2) Growth rate of output (from previous year)
      (3) Growth rate of per capita output (from previous year)

4. In addition to shifting the production function upward, an increase in the capital stock will ordinarily make workers more productive and shift the labor demand curve rightward. Graphically illustrate the full impact of an increase in the nation's capital stock under this assumption.

5. Show what would happen to the production function if the capital stock decreased. Suppose, too, that the decrease in the capital stock—because it made workers less productive to firms—shifted the labor demand curve leftward. Graphically illustrate the full impact of a decrease in the nation's capital stock under this assumption. What government policies could cause a decrease in the capital stock?

6. State whether each of the following statements is true or false, and explain your reasoning briefly.
   a. "A permanent increase in employment from a lower to a higher level will cause an increase in real GDP, but not continued growth in real GDP."
   b. "A permanent increase in the nation's capital stock to a new, higher level will cause an increase in real GDP, but not continued growth in real GDP."
   c. "With constant population, work hours, and technology, as long as planned investment spending continues to be greater than depreciation, real GDP will continue to grow year after year."
   d. "All else equal, a permanent increase in an economy's rate of planned investment spending will cause real GDP to grow faster each year than it would at the old, lower level of investment spending."

7. On a diagram, draw an economy's production function. On the same diagram, add curves to illustrate where the production function would be in five years under each of the following assumptions. (Label your additional curves a, b, and c, and assume nothing else affecting economic growth changes.)
   a. Planned investment remains constant at its current level, which exceeds depreciation.
   b. Planned investment remains constant at its current level, which is less than depreciation.
   c. Planned investment rises above its current level, which exceeds depreciation.

8. Complete the table on page 661, then find the growth rate of output from Year 1 to Year 2, from Year 2 to Year 3, and from Year 3 to Year 4, in terms of the percentage change in each of its components.

9. Redraw Figure 9 from the chapter, adding the new PPF the country would face in Year 2 if it produces at point *H* in Year 1. Explain your drawing. (Hint: Does a shifting PPF always mean a change in living standards?)

10. For each of the following scenarios, calculate (1) the percentage change in real GDP; (2) the percentage change in real GDP per capita.
   a. Average hours are constant; EPR, productivity, and population each increase by 2%.

	Year 1	Year 2	Year 3	Year 4
Total hours worked	192 million	200 million	285 million	368 million
Employment	1,200,000	1,400,000	1,900,000	2,100,000
Population	2,000,000	2,500,000	2,900,000	3,200,000
Productivity	$50 per hour	$52.50 per hour	$58 per hour	$60 per hour
Average hours per worker				
EPR				
Total output				

Table for Problem 8

b. Average hours and EPR are constant; productivity and population each increase by 2%.

c. Average hours, productivity, and population each increase by 2%; EPR is constant.

d. Average hours and EPR each decrease by 2%; productivity and population each increase by 2%.

11. Evaluate the following statement: "Continual population growth, with no other change affecting economic growth, leads to continual growth in real GDP, but a continual drop in living standards." Briefly explain why you believe the statement is true or false.

More Challenging

12. Assume that average work hours and the employment–population ratio remain constant in a less developed country. The country initially has $100 billion in capital. For each of the following scenarios, describe what will happen over time to the LDC's (1) production possibilities frontier for capital and consumption goods; (2) capital per worker; and (3) average living standard.

a. Population grows by 2% per year, depreciation of capital stock is 2% per year, and investment (new capital production) each year is equal to 4% of capital stock at the beginning of the year.

b. Population grows by 1% per year, depreciation of capital stock is 2% per year, and investment (new capital production) each year is equal to 4% of capital stock at the beginning of the year.

c. Population is constant, depreciation of capital stock is 2% per year, and investment (new capital production) each year is equal to 1% of capital stock at the beginning of the year.

13. Economist Amartya Sen has argued that famines in underdeveloped countries are not simply the result of crop failures or natural disasters. Instead, he suggests that wars, especially civil wars, are linked to most famine episodes in recent history. Using a framework similar to Figure 10, discuss the probable effect of war on a country's PPF. Explain what would happen if the country were initially operating at or near a point like S, the minimum acceptable level of consumption.

Economic Fluctuations

If you are like most college students, you will be looking for a job when you graduate, or you will already have one and want to keep it for a while. In either case, your fate is not entirely in your own hands. Your job prospects will depend, at least in part, on the overall level of economic activity in the country.

If the classical model of the previous two chapters described the economy at every point in time, you'd have nothing to worry about. Full employment would be achieved automatically, so you could be confident of getting a job at the going wage for someone with your skills and characteristics. Unfortunately, this is not always how the world works: Neither output nor employment grows as smoothly and steadily as the classical model predicts. Instead, as far back as we have data, the United States and similar countries have experienced *economic fluctuations*.

Look at panel (a) of Figure 1. The orange line shows estimated full-employment or potential output since 1960—the level of real GDP predicted by the classical model. As a result of economic growth, full-employment output rises steadily.

But now look at the green line, which shows *actual* output each quarter (at an annual rate). You can see that actual GDP fluctuates above and below the classical model's predictions. During *recessions*, which are shaded in the figure, output declines, occasionally sharply. During *expansions* (the unshaded periods) output rises quickly, usually faster than potential output is rising. Indeed, in the later stages of an expansion, output often *exceeds* potential output—a situation that economists call a **boom**.

Boom A period of time during which real GDP is above potential GDP.

Panel (b) shows another characteristic of expansions and recessions: fluctuations in employment. During expansions, such as the period from 1983 to 1990, employment grows rapidly. During recessions (shaded), such as 1990–91, employment declines.

Figure 1 shows us that employment and output move very closely together. But the figure doesn't tell us anything about the *causal* relationship between them. However, as you'll see in this chapter, we have good reason to conclude that over the business cycle, it is changes in output that cause firms to change their employment levels. For example, in a recession, many business firms lay off workers. If asked why, they would answer that they are reducing employment *because* they are producing less output.

Finally, look at Figure 2, which presents the unemployment rate over the same period as in Figure 1. Figure 2 shows a critical aspect of fluctuations—the bulge of unemployment that occurs during each recession. When GDP falls, the unemployment rate increases. In recent decades, the worst bulge in unemployment occurred in 1982, when more than 10 percent of the labor force was looking for work. In expansions, on the other hand, the unemployment rate falls. During the long expansion of the 1990s, for example, the unemployment rate fell from 7.8 percent to 4.2 percent.

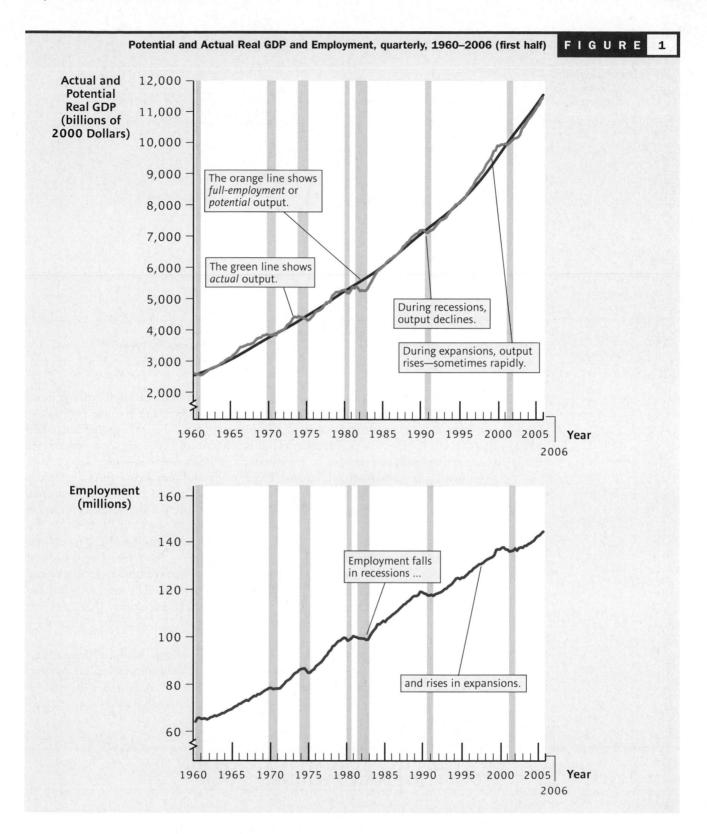

Potential and Actual Real GDP and Employment, quarterly, 1960–2006 (first half) FIGURE 1

Actual and Potential Real GDP (billions of 2000 Dollars)

The orange line shows *full-employment* or *potential* output.

The green line shows *actual* output.

During recessions, output declines.

During expansions, output rises—sometimes rapidly.

Employment (millions)

Employment falls in recessions ...

and rises in expansions.

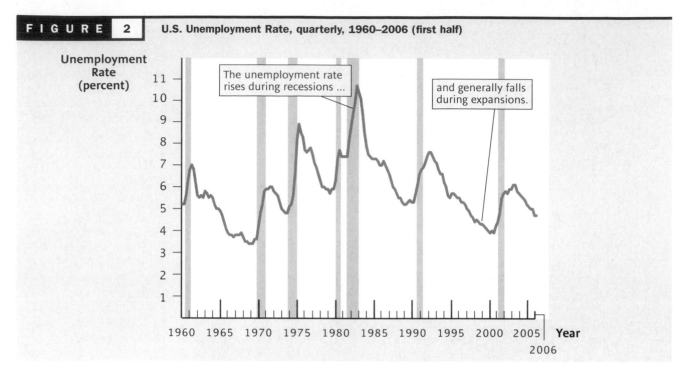

FIGURE 2   U.S. Unemployment Rate, quarterly, 1960–2006 (first half)

In our most recent expansion (2002–?), the unemployment rate fell from around 6 percent down to 4.6 percent (in June 2006). In some expansions, the unemployment rate can drop even lower than the full-employment level. In the sustained expansion of the late 1960s, for example, it reached a low of just over 3 percent. At the same time, output exceeded its potential, as you can verify in Figure 1.

Figure 1 also shows something else: Expansions and recessions don't last forever. Indeed, sometimes they are rather brief. The recession of 1990–91, for example, ended within a year. And the recession that began in March 2001 officially ended in November of that year.

But if you look carefully at the figure, you'll see that the back-to-back recessions of the early 1980s extended over 3 full years. And during the Great Depression of the 1930s (not shown), it took more than a decade for the economy to return to full employment. Expansions too can last for extended periods. The expansion of the 1980s lasted about 7 years, from 1983 to 1990. And the expansion that began in March 1991 turned out to be the longest expansion in U.S. economic history—a duration of 10 years.

The next several chapters deal with economic fluctuations. We have three things to explain: (1) *why* they occur in the first place, (2) why they sometimes last so long, and (3) why they do not last forever. But our first step is to ask whether the macroeconomic model you've already studied—the classical, long-run model—can explain why economic fluctuations occur.

CAN THE CLASSICAL MODEL EXPLAIN ECONOMIC FLUCTUATIONS?

The classical model does a good job of explaining why the economy tends to operate near its potential output level, on average, over long periods of time. But can it help us understand the facts of economic fluctuations, as shown in Figures 1 and 2? More specifically, can the classical model explain why GDP and employment typically fall *below* potential during a recession and often rise above it in an expansion? Let's see.

SHIFTS IN LABOR DEMAND

One idea, studied by a number of economists, is that a recession might be caused by a leftward shift of the labor demand curve. This possibility is illustrated in Figure 3, in which a leftward shift in the labor demand curve would move us down and to the left along the labor supply curve. In the diagram, the labor market equilibrium would move from point *E* to point *F*, employment would fall, and so would the real wage rate. Is this a reasonable explanation for recessions? Most economists feel that the answer is no, and for a very good reason.

The labor demand curve tells us the number of workers the nation's firms want to employ at each real wage rate. A leftward shift of this curve would mean that firms want to hire *fewer* workers at any given wage than they wanted to hire before. What could make them come to such a decision? One possibility is that firms are suddenly unable to sell all the output they produce. Therefore, the story would go, they must cut back production and hire fewer workers at any wage.

But as you've learned, in the classical model, total spending is *never* deficient. On the contrary, from the classical viewpoint, total spending is automatically equal to whatever level of output firms decide to produce. As you learned two chapters ago when we analyzed fiscal policy, a decrease in spending by one sector of the economy (such as the government) would cause an equal *increase* in spending by other sectors, with no change in total spending. While it is true that a decrease in output would cause total spending to decrease along with it (because Say's law tells us total spending is always equal to total output), the causation cannot go the other way in the classical model. In that model, changes in total spending cannot arise on their own. Therefore, if we want to explain a leftward shift in the labor demand curve using the classical model, we must look for some explanation other than a sudden change in spending.

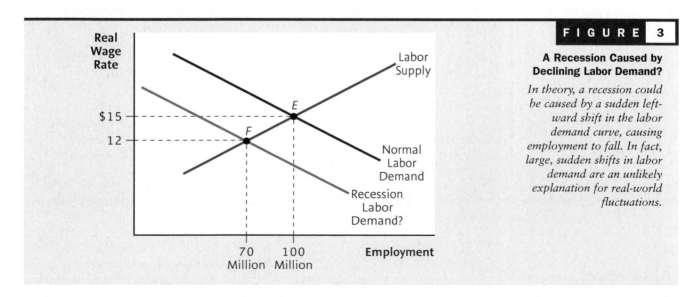

FIGURE 3

A Recession Caused by Declining Labor Demand?

In theory, a recession could be caused by a sudden leftward shift in the labor demand curve, causing employment to fall. In fact, large, sudden shifts in labor demand are an unlikely explanation for real-world fluctuations.

Another possibility is that the labor demand curve shifts leftward because workers have become less *productive* and therefore less valuable to firms. This might happen if there were a sudden decrease in the capital stock, so that each worker had less equipment to work with. Or it might happen if workers suddenly forgot how to do things—how to operate a computer or use a screwdriver or fix an oil rig. Short of a major war that destroys plant and equipment, or an epidemic of amnesia, it is highly unlikely that workers would become less productive so suddenly. Thus, a leftward shift of the labor demand curve is an unlikely explanation for recessions.

What about booms? Could a *rightward* shift of the labor demand curve (not shown in Figure 3) explain them? Once again, a change in total spending cannot be the answer. In the classical model, as discussed a few paragraphs ago, changes in spending are caused by changes in employment and output, not the other way around. Nor can we explain a boom by arguing that workers have suddenly become more productive. Even though it is true that the capital stock grows over time and workers continually gain new skills—and that both of these movements shift the labor demand curve to the right—such shifts take place at a glacial pace. Compared to the amount of machinery already in place, and to the knowledge and skills that the labor force already has, annual increments in physical capital or knowledge are simply too small to have much of an impact on labor demand. Thus, a sudden rightward shift of the labor demand curve is an unlikely explanation for an expansion that pushes us beyond potential output.

> Because shifts in the labor demand curve are not very large from year to year, the classical model cannot explain real-world economic fluctuations through shifts in labor demand.

SHIFTS IN LABOR SUPPLY

A second way the classical model might explain a recession is through a shift in the labor supply curve. Figure 4 shows how this would work. If the labor supply curve

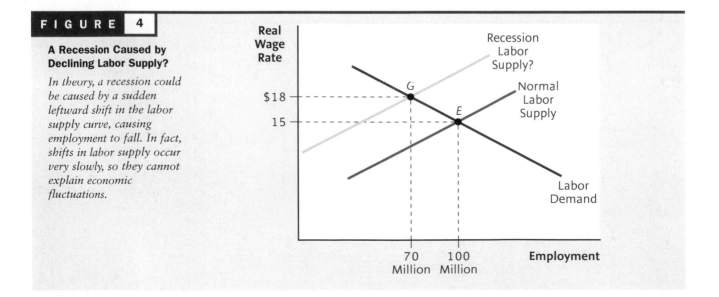

FIGURE 4

A Recession Caused by Declining Labor Supply?

In theory, a recession could be caused by a sudden leftward shift in the labor supply curve, causing employment to fall. In fact, shifts in labor supply occur very slowly, so they cannot explain economic fluctuations.

shifted to the left, the equilibrium would move up and to the left along the labor demand curve, from point E to point G. The level of employment would fall, and output would fall with it.

This explanation of recessions has almost no support among economists. First, remember that the labor supply schedule tells us, at each real wage rate, the number of people who *would like to* work. This number reflects millions of families' preferences about working in the market rather than pursuing other activities, such as taking care of children, going to school, or enjoying leisure time. A leftward shift in labor supply would mean that fewer people want to work at any given wage—that preferences have changed toward these other, nonwork activities. But in reality, preferences tend to change very slowly, and certainly not rapidly enough to explain recessions.

Second, even if such a shift in preferences did occur, it could not explain the facts of real-world downturns. Recessions are times when unusually large numbers of people are looking for work (see Figure 2). It would be hard to square that fact with a shift in preferences away from working.

The same arguments could be made about expansions: To explain them with labor supply shifts, we would have to believe that preferences suddenly change *toward* market work and away from other activities—an unlikely occurrence. And, in any case, expansions are periods when the unemployment rate typically falls to unusually low levels; *fewer*—not more—people are seeking work.

> Because sudden shifts of the labor supply curve are unlikely to occur, and because they could not accurately describe the facts of the economic cycle, the classical model cannot explain fluctuations through shifts in the supply of labor.

VERDICT: THE CLASSICAL MODEL CANNOT EXPLAIN ECONOMIC FLUCTUATIONS

In earlier chapters, we stressed that the classical model works well in explaining the movements of the economy in the longer run. Now we see that it does a rather poor job of explaining the economy in the short run. Why is this? Largely because the classical model involves assumptions about the economy that make sense in the longer run, but not in the short run. Chief among these is the assumption that the labor market clears—that is, that the labor market operates at the point of intersection of the labor supply and labor demand curves. As long as this assumption holds, a boom or recession would have to arise from a sudden, significant *movement* in that intersection point, caused by a sudden and significant *shift* in either the labor demand curve or the labor supply curve.

But now, we've seen that such sudden shifts are very unlikely. Moreover, even if they did occur, they could not explain the changes in job-seeking activity that we observe in real-world recessions. And this, in a nutshell, is why we must reject the classical model when we turn our attention to the short run.

> We cannot explain the facts of short-run economic fluctuations with a model in which the labor market always clears. This is why the classical model, which assumes that the market always clears, does a poor job of explaining the economy in the short run.

WHAT TRIGGERS ECONOMIC FLUCTUATIONS?

Recessions that bring output below potential and expansions that drive output above potential are periods during which the economy is going a bit haywire. In a recession, millions of qualified people *want* to work at the going wage rate, but firms won't hire them. Managers would *like* to hire them, but they aren't selling enough output—in part because so many people are unemployed. The macroeconomy seems to be preventing opportunities for mutual gain.

In a boom, the economy is going haywire in a different way. The unemployment rate is so low the normal job-search activity—which accounts for frictional unemployment—is short-circuited. Firms, desperate to hire workers because production is so high, are less careful about whom they hire. The result is a poorer-than-normal match between workers and their jobs. Moreover, the overheating of the economy that occurs in a boom can lead to inflation. We'll discuss how this happens a few chapters from now. But the basic outline is this: Because qualified workers are so scarce, firms must compete fiercely with each other to hire them. This drives up wage rates in the economy, raises production costs for firms, and ultimately causes firms to raise their prices.

Booms and recessions are periods during which the economy deviates from the normal, full-employment equilibrium of the classical model. The question is: Why do such deviations occur? Let's start to answer this question by looking at a world that is much simpler than our own.

A VERY SIMPLE ECONOMY

Imagine an economy with just two people: Yasmin and Pepe. Yasmin is especially good at making popcorn, but she eats only yogurt. Pepe, by contrast, is very good at making yogurt, but he eats only popcorn. If things are going well, Yasmin and Pepe will make suitable amounts of popcorn and yogurt and trade with each other. Because of the gains from specialization, their trade will make them both better off than if they tried to function without trading. And under ordinary circumstances, Yasmin and Pepe will take advantage of all mutually beneficial opportunities for trading. Our two-person economy will thus operate at full employment, since both individuals will be fully engaged in making products for the other. You can think of their trading equilibrium as being like the labor market equilibrium in the classical model.

Now, suppose there is a breakdown in communication. For example, Yasmin may get the impression that Pepe is not going to want as much popcorn as before. She would then decide to *make* less popcorn for Pepe. At their next trading session, Pepe will be offered less popcorn, so he will decide to produce less yogurt. The result: Total production in the economy declines, and our two traders will lose some of the benefits of trading. This corresponds to a recession.

Alternatively, suppose Yasmin thinks that Pepe will want *more* popcorn than before. This might lead her to *increase* her production, working more than she normally prefers to work so she can get more yogurt from Pepe before his demand for popcorn returns to normal. Yasmin's production of popcorn—and therefore, total output in the economy—rises even if Yasmin's expectations turn out to be wrong and Pepe does *not* want more popcorn. Temporarily, we are in a boom.

In reading the previous paragraph, you might be thinking, "Wait a minute. If either Yasmin or Pepe got the impression that the other might want less or more of the other's product, wouldn't a simple conversation between them straighten things out?" If these are your thoughts, you are absolutely right. A breakdown in communication and a sudden change in production would be extremely unlikely . . . *in a simple economy with just two people.* And therein lies the problem: The real-world economy is much more complex than the world of Yasmin and Pepe.

THE REAL-WORLD ECONOMY

Think about the U.S. economy, with its millions of businesses producing goods and services for hundreds of millions of people. In many cases, production must be planned long before goods are actually sold. For example, from inception to final production, it takes nearly a year to build a house and two years to develop a new automobile model or produce a Hollywood film. If one firm—say, General Motors—believes that consumers will buy fewer of its cars next year, it cannot simply call a meeting of all potential customers and find out whether its fears are justified. Nor can it convince people, as Yasmin can convince Pepe, that their own jobs depend on their buying a GM car. Most potential car buyers do *not* work for General Motors and don't perceive any connection between buying a car and keeping their own jobs. Under the circumstances, it may be entirely logical for General Motors to plan for a lower production level and lay off some of its workers.

Of course, this would not be the end of the story. By decreasing its workforce, GM would create further problems for the economy. The workers it has laid off, who will earn less income or none at all, will cut back on *their* spending for a variety of consumer goods—restaurant meals, movies, vacation travel—and they will certainly postpone any large purchases they'd been planning, such as a new large-screen television or that family trip to Disney World. This will cause other firms—the firms producing these consumer goods and services—to cut back on *their* production, laying off *their* workers, and so on. In other words, what began as a perceived decrease in spending in one sector of the economy can work its way through other sectors, causing a full-blown recession.

This example illustrates a theme that we will revisit in the next chapter: the interdependence between production and income. When people spend their incomes, they give firms the revenue they need to hire workers and pay them income! If any link in this chain is broken, output and income may both decline. In our example, the link was broken because of incorrect expectations by firms in one sector of the economy. But there are other causes of recessions as well, also centering on the interdependence between production and income, and a failure to coordinate the decisions of millions of firms and households.

The classical model, however, waves these potential problems aside. It assumes that workers and firms, with the aid of markets, can work things out—like Yasmin and Pepe—and enjoy the benefits of producing and trading. And the classical model is right: People *will* work things out . . . eventually. But in the short run, we need to look carefully at the problems of coordinating production, trade, and consumption in an economy with millions of people and businesses.

A boom can arise in much the same way as a recession. It might start because of an increase in production in one sector of the economy, say, the housing sector. With more production and more workers earning higher incomes, spending increases in other sectors as well, until output rises above the classical, full-employment level.

EXAMPLES OF RECESSIONS AND EXPANSIONS

In the preceding discussion, General Motors decided to cut back on its production of cars because its managers believed, rightly or wrongly, that the demand for GM cars had decreased. Often, many firms will face a real or predicted drop in spending at the same time. The resulting changes in production ultimately work their way through the entire economy, and often cause full-fledged macroeconomic fluctuations.

Table 1 lists some of the recessions and notable expansions of the last 50 years, along with the events and spending changes that are thought to have caused them or at least contributed heavily. You can see that each of these events first affected spending and output in one or more sectors of the economy. For example, several recessions have been set off by increases in oil prices. The initial impact of higher oil prices is often felt most strongly on energy-using goods and services, such as new

TABLE 1 Recent Expansions and Recessions				
Period			**Event**	**Major Spending Changes**
Early 1950s	Expansion		Korean War	Defense spending ↑
1953	Recession		End of Korean War	Defense spending ↓
Late 1960s	Expansion		Vietnam War	Defense spending ↑
1970	Recession		Change in Federal Reserve policy	Spending on new homes ↓
1974	Recession		Dramatic increase in oil prices	Spending on cars and other energy-using products ↓
1980	Recession		Dramatic increase in oil prices	Spending on cars and other energy-using products ↓
1981–82	Recession		Change in Federal Reserve policy	Spending on new homes, cars, and business investment ↓
Early 1980s	Expansion		Military buildup	Defense spending ↑
Late 1980s	Expansion		Dramatic decline in oil prices	Spending on energy-using products ↑
1990	Recession		Large increase in oil prices; collapse of Soviet Union	Spending on cars and other energy-using products ↓; Defense spending ↓
1991–2000	Expansion		Technological advances in computers; development of the Internet; high wealth creation	Spending on capital equipment ↑; Consumption spending ↑
2001	Recession		Investment in new technology slows; technology-fueled bubble of optimism bursts; wealth destruction	Spending on capital equipment ↓
2002–?	Expansion		Changes in fiscal and Federal Reserve policies; rapid rise in housing wealth	Consumption spending ↑

cars and trucks, or vacation travel. Also, because consumers spend more on expensive gasoline and other products made from oil, they have less income left over to spend on a variety of other goods and services. Other recessions were precipitated by military cutbacks. Still others came about when the Federal Reserve caused sudden increases in interest rates that led to decreased spending on new homes and other goods. (You'll learn about the Federal Reserve and its policies a few chapters from now.)

Strong expansions, on the other hand, have been caused by military buildups, by falling oil prices that stimulated consumption spending, and by bursts of planned investment spending. The long expansion of the mid- and late 1990s, for example, began when the development of the Internet, and improvements in computers more generally, led to an increase in investment spending. Once the economy began expanding, it was further spurred by other factors, such as a rise in stock prices and consumer optimism, both of which led to an increase in consumption spending.

When a decrease in spending causes production cutbacks in one or more sectors of the economy, firms will lay off workers. The laid-off workers, suffering decreases in their incomes, cut back their own spending on other products, causing further layoffs in other sectors. The economy can continue sliding downward, and remain below potential output, for a year or longer. The same process works in reverse during an expansion: Higher spending leads to greater production, higher employment, and still greater spending, possibly leading to a boom in which the economy remains overheated for some time.

Booms and recessions do not last forever, however. The economy eventually adjusts back to full-employment output. Often, a change in government macroeconomic policy helps the adjustment process along, speeding the return to full employment. Other times, a policy mistake thwarts the adjustment process, prolonging or deepening a costly recession, or exacerbating a boom and overheating the economy even more.

How does this adjustment process work? This is a question we'll be coming back to a few chapters from now, after you've learned some new tools for analyzing the economy's behavior over the short run.

Half of our recessions since the early 1950s have been caused, at least in part, by rapid rises in oil prices.

WHERE DO WE GO FROM HERE?

The classical model that you've learned in previous chapters is certainly useful: It helps us understand economic growth over time, and how economic events and economic policies affect the economy over the long run. But in trying to understand expansions and recessions—where they come from, and why they can last for one or more years—we've had to depart from the strict framework of the classical model.

One theme of our discussion has been the central role of spending in understanding economic fluctuations. In the classical model, spending could be safely ignored. First, Say's law assured us that total spending would always be sufficient to buy the output produced at full employment. Second, a change in spending—for example, a decrease in military spending by the government—would cause other categories of spending to rise by just the right amount to make up for the lower spending of the government. In the long run, we can have faith in the classical perspective on spending.

But in the short run, we've seen that changes in spending affect production, often in one or more specific sectors. When employment changes in those sectors, the spending of workers *there* will change as well, affecting demand in still other sectors. Clearly, if we want to understand fluctuations, we need to take a close look at spending. This is what we will do in the next chapter, when we study the *short-run macro model.*

Summary

The classical model does not always do a good job of describing the economy over short time periods. Over periods of a few years, national economies experience economic fluctuations in which output rises above or falls below its long-term growth path. Significant periods of falling output are called recessions, while periods of rapidly rising output are expansions. If an expansion causes output to rise above potential (or full-employment) output, it is called a boom. When real GDP fluctuates, it causes the level of employment and the unemployment rate to fluctuate as well.

The classical model cannot explain economic fluctuations because it assumes that the labor market always clears; that is, it always operates at the point where the labor supply and demand curves intersect. Evidence suggests that this market-clearing assumption is not always valid over short time periods. And when we try to explain economic fluctuations using the classical model, we come up short. Neither shifts in the labor demand curve, nor shifts in the labor supply curve, offer a realistic explanation for what happens during a recession or a boom.

In a simple, two-person economy, decisions about spending and production could be easily coordinated, so economic fluctuations would be easy to avoid. But in a market economy with millions of people and firms, decisions about spending and production cannot be coordinated, making the economy vulnerable to changes in production that are harmful to everyone involved.

Deviations from the full-employment level of output are often caused by changes in spending that initially affect one or more sectors and then work their way through the entire economy. Decreases in spending can cause recessions, while increases in spending can cause expansions that lead to booms. Eventually, output will return to its long-run equilibrium level, but it does not do so immediately. The origins of economic fluctuations can be understood more fully with the short-run macro model, which we will study in the next chapter.

Problem Set   *Answers to even-numbered Questions and Problems can be found on the text Web site at www.thomsonedu.com/economics/hall.*

1. Using the upper panel of Figure 1, identify two time spans during which the U.S. economy was enjoying an expansion but *not* a boom. (Hint: Reread the first page of this chapter.)
2. This chapter explains how a decrease in spending—such as investment spending—could cause a recession. But in the classical model, a decrease in investment spending could *not* cause a recession. Why not? (Hint: Use the loanable funds market diagram.)
3. "Every U.S. recession over the last 6 decades has been caused by an increase in oil prices." True or false? Explain briefly.
4. "Immediately after a recession ends, the unemployment rate begins dropping." Evaluate this statement, based on the historical record in Figure 2.

The Short-Run Macro Model

Every December, newspapers and television news broadcasts focus their attention on spending. You might see a reporter standing in front of a Circuit City outlet, warning that unless holiday shoppers loosen their wallets and spend big on computers, DVD players, vacation trips, toys, and new cars, the economy is in for trouble.

Of course, spending matters during the rest of the year, too. But holiday spending attracts our attention because the normal forces at work during the rest of the year become more concentrated in late November and December. Factories churn out merchandise, and stores stock up at higher than normal rates. If consumers are in Scrooge-like moods, unsold goods will pile up in stores. In the months that follow, these stores will cut back on their orders for new goods. Factories will decrease production and lay off workers.

And the story will not end there. The laid-off workers—even those who collect some unemployment benefits—will see their incomes decline. As a consequence, they will spend less on a variety of consumer goods. This will cause other firms—the ones that produce those consumer goods—to cut back on *their* production.

This hypothetical example reinforces a conclusion we reached in the last chapter: Spending is very important in the short run. And it points out an interesting circularity: The more income households earn, the more they will spend. That is, *spending depends on income*. But the more households spend, the more output firms will produce—and the more income they will pay out to households that supply labor and other resources. Thus, *income depends on spending*.

> *In the short run, spending depends on income, and income depends on spending.*

In this chapter, we will explore this circular connection between spending and income. We will do so with a very simple macroeconomic model, which we'll call the **short-run macro model**. Many of the ideas behind the model were originally developed by the economist John Maynard Keynes in the 1930s. The model's perspective on the economy is in many ways opposite to that of the classical model. When we take the short-run view, total spending determines the level of production, and changes in spending play the central role in explaining economic fluctuations.

To keep the model as simple as possible, we will—for the time being—ignore all influences on production *besides* spending. As a result, the short-run model may appear strange to you at first, like a drive along an unfamiliar highway. You may wonder: Where is all the scenery you are used to seeing along the classical road? Where are the labor market, the production function, the loanable funds market,

Short-run macro model A macroeconomic model that explains how changes in spending can affect real GDP in the short run.

673

and the market-clearing assumption? Rest assured that many of these concepts are still with us, lurking in the background and waiting to be exposed, and we will come back to them in later chapters. But in this chapter, we assume that spending—and *only* spending—determines how much output the economy will produce.

As we proceed, remember that we are more interested in explaining real variables (adjusted for changes in the price level) than nominal variables (measured in current dollars). Therefore, whenever we discuss any dollar-denominated variable (such as consumption spending, income, or GDP) we will always mean the *real* variable—even when the word "real" is not included.

CONSUMPTION SPENDING

A natural place for us to begin our look at spending is with its largest component: *consumption spending.* In all, household spending on consumer goods—groceries, rent, car repairs, movies, telephone calls, and furniture—is more than two-thirds of total spending in the economy. What determines the total amount of consumption spending?

One way to answer is to start by thinking about yourself or your family. What determines your spending in any given month, quarter, or year?

Disposable Income. The first thing that comes to mind is your income: The more you earn, the more you spend. But in macroeconomics, small differences in language can be crucial. It's not exactly your *income* per period—what you are paid by your employer—that determines your spending, but rather what you get to *keep* from that income after deducting any taxes you have to pay. Moreover, some people receive a flow of transfer payments from the government—such as unemployment insurance benefits or Social Security payments—which they can spend in addition to any income received from an employer. If we start with the income households earn, deduct all tax payments, and then add in any transfer received, we get *disposable income*—a term introduced with the classical model. This is the income households are free to spend or save as they wish.

Disposable income = Income − Tax payments + Transfers received.

This can be rewritten as:

Disposable income = Income − (Taxes − Transfers).

Finally, remember that the term in parentheses, Taxes − Transfers, is defined as *net taxes.* So the easiest way to think of disposable income is:

Disposable income = Income − Net taxes.

All else equal, you'd certainly spend more on consumer goods with a disposable income of $50,000 per year than with $20,000 per year. And in the economy as a whole, *a rise in disposable income—with no other change—causes a rise in consumption spending.*

Wealth. Consumption spending is also influenced by *wealth*—the total value of household assets (home, stocks, bonds, bank accounts, and the like) minus outstanding liabilities (student loans, mortgage loans, credit card debt, and so on). Even if your disposable income stayed the same, an increase in your wealth—say, because you own stocks or bonds that have risen in value—would probably induce you to spend more. In general, *a rise in wealth, with no other change, causes a rise in consumption spending.*

The Interest Rate. The interest rate is the reward people get for saving, or what they have to pay when they borrow. You would probably save more each year if the interest rate was 10 percent than if it was 2 percent. But when you save more of your disposable income, you spend less. Even households with a negative net worth—who are not "savers" in the common sense of the term—are influenced by the interest rate. For example, people with credit card or other debts must decide each month how much of their debt balance to pay down. The higher the interest rate, the greater the incentive to pay back debt, and the less will be spent on consumption goods. *All else equal, a rise in the interest rate causes a decrease in consumption spending.*

Expectations. Expectations about the future can affect spending as well. If you become more optimistic about your job security or expect a big raise, you might spend more of your income *now.* Similarly, if you become more pessimistic—worried about losing your job or taking a pay cut—you'd probably spend less now. *All else equal, optimism about future income causes an increase in consumption spending.*

Other variables, too, can influence your consumption spending, including inheritances you expect to receive over your lifetime, and even how long you expect to live. But disposable income, wealth, the interest rate, and expectations are the key variables we'll be coming back to again and again in the short-run macroeconomic model. And just as these variables influence the consumption spending of each individual household, they also influence the consumption spending of the household sector as a whole.

Unless we're focusing on an individual household to make a point (as in the preceding paragraphs), in macroeconomics, we use phrases like "disposable income," "wealth," or "consumption spending" to mean the *total* disposable income, *total* wealth, and *total* consumption spending of all households in the economy combined. So we can state our conclusions this way:

> *All else equal, consumption spending increases when:*
>
> - *Disposable income rises*
> - *Wealth rises*
> - *The interest rate falls*
> - *Households become more optimistic about the future*

CONSUMPTION AND DISPOSABLE INCOME

Of all the factors that influence consumption spending, the most important and stable determinant is disposable income. Figure 1 shows the relationship between (real) consumption spending and (real) disposable income in the United States from 1985 to 2005. Each point in the diagram represents a different year. For example, the point labeled "2005" represents a disposable income in that year of $8,112 billion and consumption spending of $7,857 billion. Notice that as disposable income rises, consumption spending rises as well. Indeed, almost all of the variation in consumption spending from year to year can be explained by variations in disposable income.

FIGURE 1   **U.S. Consumption and Disposable Income, 1985–2005**

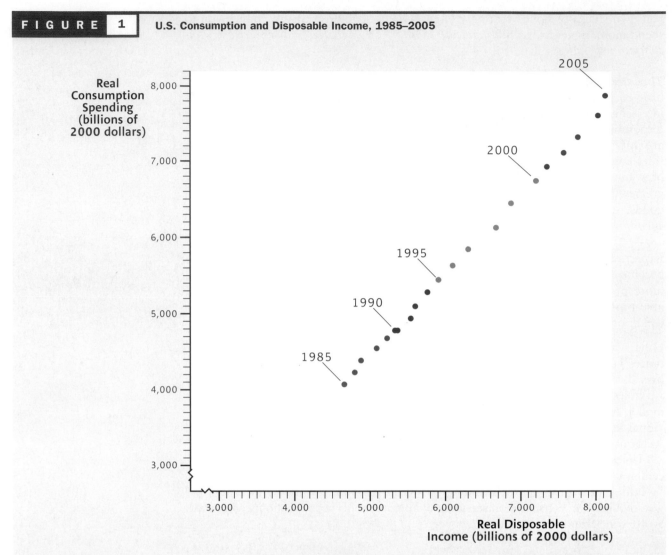

When real consumption expenditure is plotted against real disposable income, the resulting relationship is almost perfectly linear: As real disposable income rises, so does real consumption spending.

Source: Bureau of Economic Analysis, National Income and Product Accounts Tables, Tables 2.1 and 1.1.6.

Although the other factors we've discussed do affect consumption spending, their impact appears to be relatively minor.

There is something even more interesting about Figure 1: The relationship between consumption and disposable income is almost perfectly *linear;* the points lie remarkably close to a straight line. This almost-linear relationship between consumption and disposable income has been observed in a wide variety of historical periods and a wide variety of nations. This is why, when we represent the relationship between disposable income and consumption with a diagram or an equation, we use a straight line.

Real Disposable Income (billions of dollars per year)	Real Consumption Spending (billions of dollars per year)
0	2,000
1,000	2,600
2,000	3,200
3,000	3,800
4,000	4,400
5,000	5,000
6,000	5,600
7,000	6,200
8,000	6,800

TABLE 1

Hypothetical Data on Disposable Income and Consumption

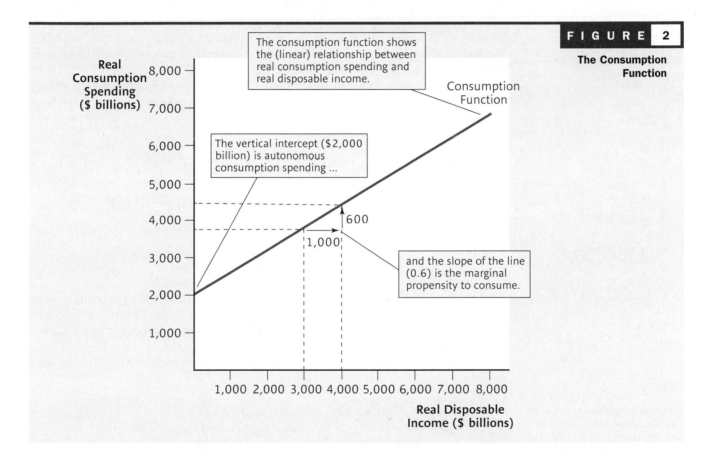

FIGURE 2

The Consumption Function

The consumption function shows the (linear) relationship between real consumption spending and real disposable income.

Consumption Function

The vertical intercept ($2,000 billion) is autonomous consumption spending ...

and the slope of the line (0.6) is the marginal propensity to consume.

Our discussion will be clearer if we move from the actual data in Figure 1 to the hypothetical example in Table 1. Each row in the table represents a combination of (real) disposable income and (real) consumption we might observe in an economy. For example, the table shows us that if disposable income were equal to $7,000 billion in some year, consumption spending would equal $6,200 billion in that year. When we plot these data on a graph, we obtain the straight line in Figure 2. This line is

Consumption function A positively sloped relationship between real consumption spending and real disposable income.

called the **consumption function** because it illustrates the functional relationship between consumption and disposable income.

Like every straight line, the consumption function in Figure 2 has two main features: a vertical intercept and a slope. Mathematically, the intercept—in this case, $2,000 billion—tells us how much consumption spending there would be in the economy if disposable income were zero. However, the real purpose of the vertical intercept is not to identify what would actually happen at zero disposable income, but rather to help us identify the particular line that represents consumption spending in the diagram. After all, we could draw many lines that have the same slope as the one in the figure. But only one of them has a vertical intercept of $2,000.

The vertical intercept in the figure also has a name: **autonomous consumption spending.** It represents the influence on consumption spending of everything *other than* disposable income. For example, if household wealth were to increase, consumption would be greater at any level of disposable income. In that case, the entire consumption function in the figure would shift upward, so its vertical intercept would increase. We would call this *an increase in autonomous consumption spending.* Similarly, a decrease in wealth would cause a *decrease in autonomous consumption spending*, and shift the consumption function downward.

Autonomous consumption spending The part of consumption spending that is independent of income; also the vertical intercept of the consumption function.

The second important feature of Figure 2 is the slope, which shows the change along the vertical axis divided by the change along the horizontal axis as we go from one point to another on the line:

$$\text{Slope} = \frac{\Delta \text{Consumption}}{\Delta \text{Disposable income}}$$

As you can see in the table, each time disposable income rises by $1,000 billion, consumption spending rises by $600 billion, so that the slope is

$$\frac{\$600 \text{ billion}}{\$1,000 \text{ billion}} = 0.6$$

The slope in Figure 2 is an important feature not just of the consumption function itself, but also of the macroeconomic analysis we will build from it. This is why economists have given this slope a special name, the *marginal propensity to consume,* abbreviated *MPC*. In our example, the *MPC* is 0.6.

We can think of the *MPC* in three different ways, but each of them has the same meaning:

Marginal propensity to consume The amount by which consumption spending rises when disposable income rises by one dollar.

> *The **marginal propensity to consume** (MPC) is (1) the slope of the consumption function; (2) the change in consumption divided by the change in disposable income; or (3) the amount by which consumption spending rises when disposable income rises by one dollar.*

Logic suggests that the *MPC* should be larger than zero (when income rises, consumption spending will *rise*), but less than one (the rise in consumption will be *smaller* than the rise in disposable income). This is certainly true in our example where *MPC* is 0.6 and each one-dollar rise in disposable income causes spending to rise by 60 cents. An *MPC* between zero and one is also observed in economies throughout the world. Accordingly, we will always assume that $0 < MPC < 1$.

Representing Consumption with an Equation

Sometimes, we'll want to use an equation to represent the straight-line consumption function. The most general form of the equation is

$$C = a + b \times (\text{Disposable income})$$

where C is consumption spending. The term a is the vertical intercept of the consumption function. It represents the theoretical level of consumption spending at disposable income = 0, which you've learned is called *autonomous consumption spending*. In the equation, you can see clearly that autonomous consumption (a) is the part of consumption that does *not* depend on disposable income. In our example in Figure 2, a is equal to $2,000 billion.

The other term, b, is the slope of the consumption function. This is our familiar marginal propensity to consume (MPC), telling us how much consumption *increases* each time disposable income rises by a dollar. In our example in Figure 2, b is equal to 0.6.

CONSUMPTION AND INCOME

The consumption function is an important building block of our analysis. Consumption is the largest component of spending, and disposable income is the most important determinant of consumption. But there is one limitation of the line as we've drawn it in Figure 2: It shows us the value of consumption at each level of *disposable* income, whereas we will need to know the value of consumption spending at each level of *income*. Disposable income, you remember, is the income that the household sector has left after deducting net taxes. How can we convert the line in Figure 2 into a relationship between consumption and income?

Table 2 illustrates the consumption–income relationship when the household sector pays net taxes. In the table, we treat net taxes as a fixed amount—in this case, $2,000 billion. Some taxes are, indeed, fixed in this way, such as the taxes assessed on real estate by local governments. Other taxes, like the personal income tax and the sales tax, rise and fall with income in the economy. Still, treating net taxes as if they are independent of income, as in Table 2, will simplify our discussion without changing our results in any important way.

Notice that the last two columns of the table are identical to the columns in Table 1: In both tables, we assume that the relationship between consumption spending and *disposable* income is the same. For example, both tables show us that, when disposable income is $7,000 billion, consumption spending is $6,200 billion. But in Table 2, we see that disposable income of $7,000 billion is associated with *income* of $9,000 billion. Thus, when income is $9,000 billion, consumption spending is $6,200 billion. By comparing the first and last columns of Table 2, we can trace out the relationship between consumption and income. This relationship—which we call the **consumption–income line**—is graphed in Figure 3.

If you compare the consumption–income line in Figure 3 with the line in Figure 2, you will notice that both have the same slope of 0.6, but the consumption–income line is lower by $1,200 billion. Net taxes have lowered the consumption–income line. Why? Because at any level of income, taxes reduce disposable income and therefore reduce consumption spending.

But why is the consumption–income line lower by precisely $1,200 billion? We can reason it out as follows: Any increase in net taxes (T) will cause consumption

Consumption–income line A line showing aggregate consumption spending at each level of income or GDP.

	Income or GDP (billions of dollars per year)	Tax Collections (billions of dollars per year)	Disposable Income (billions of dollars per year)	Consumption Spending (billions of dollars per year)
	2,000	2,000	0	2,000
	3,000	2,000	1,000	2,600
	4,000	2,000	2,000	3,200
	5,000	2,000	3,000	3,800
	6,000	2,000	4,000	4,400
	7,000	2,000	5,000	5,000
	8,000	2,000	6,000	5,600
	9,000	2,000	7,000	6,200
	10,000	2,000	8,000	6,800

TABLE 2

The Relationship Between Consumption and Income

FIGURE 3 The Consumption–Income Line

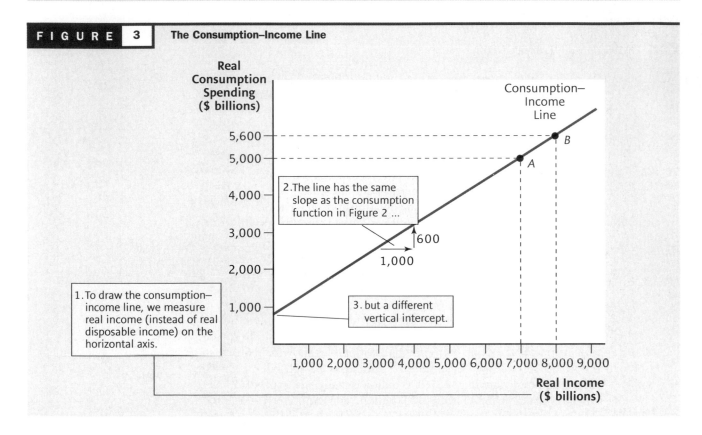

spending to fall by $MPC \times \Delta T$. In our example, when we impose taxes of $2,000 billion on the population, disposable income will drop by $2,000 billion at any level of income. With an MPC of 0.6, consumption at any level of income falls by $0.6 \times \$2,000$ billion = $1,200 billion.

Finally, we noted earlier that the *slope* of the consumption–income line is unaffected by net taxes. This is because with net taxes held at a fixed amount, disposable income rises dollar-for-dollar with income. With an MPC of 0.6, consumption spending will rise by 60 cents each time income rises by a dollar, just as it rises by 60 cents each time *disposable* income rises by a dollar. You can see this in Table 2: Each time income rises by $1,000 billion, consumption spending rises by $600 billion, giving the consumption–income line a slope of $600 billion/$1,000 billion = 0.6, just as in the case with no taxes. More generally,

> *when the government collects a fixed amount of taxes from households, the line representing the relationship between consumption and income is shifted downward by the amount of the tax times the marginal propensity to consume (MPC). The slope of this line is unaffected by taxes and is equal to the MPC.*

Shifts in the Consumption–Income Line

As you've learned, consumption spending depends positively on income: If income increases and net taxes remain unchanged, disposable income will rise, and consumption spending will rise along with it. The chain of causation can be represented this way:

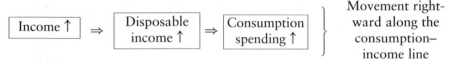

In Figure 3, this change in consumption spending would be represented by a *movement along* the consumption–income line. For example, a rise in income from $7,000 billion to $8,000 billion would cause consumption spending to increase from $5,000 billion to $5,600 billion, moving us from point A to point B along the consumption–income line.

But consumption spending can also change for reasons other than a change in income, causing the consumption–income line itself to shift. For example, a decrease in net taxes will increase *disposable* income at each level of income. Consumption spending will then increase at any income level, shifting the entire line upward. The mechanism works like this:

In Figure 4, a decrease in taxes from $2,000 billion to $500 billion increases spending income at each income level by $1,500 billion, and causes consumption at each income level to increase by 0.6 × $1,500 billion = $900 billion. This means that the consumption line shifts upward, to the upper line in the figure.

In addition to net taxes, all the other influences on consumption spending, other than income, shift the consumption–income line as well. But these other shift-variables work by changing the value of *autonomous consumption,* the vertical intercept of the consumption function in Figure 2. For example, an increase in household wealth would increase autonomous consumption, and shift the consumption–income line upward, as in Figure 4. Increases in autonomous consumption could also occur

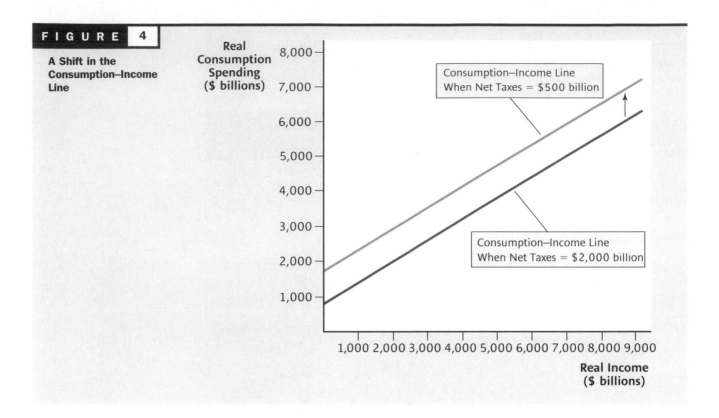

FIGURE 4

A Shift in the Consumption–Income Line

if the interest rate decreased, or if households became more optimistic about the future. In general, increases in autonomous consumption work this way:

We can summarize our discussion of changes in consumption spending as follows:

> *When a change in income causes consumption spending to change, we move along the consumption–income line. When a change in anything else besides income causes consumption spending to change, the line will shift.*

Table 3 provides a more specific summary of the various changes that cause the consumption–income line to shift.

GETTING TO TOTAL SPENDING

In addition to household consumption spending, there are three other types of spending on goods and services produced by American firms: investment, government

	Consumption–Income Line Shifts Upward When:	Consumption–Income Line Shifts Downward When:	TABLE 3

Shifts in the Consumption–Income Line

Net taxes ↓ { Transfers ↑ / Taxes ↓ }   Net Taxes ↑ { Transfers ↓ / Taxes ↑ }

Autonomous consumption (a) ↑ { Household wealth ↑ / Interest rate ↓ / Greater optimism }   Autonomous Consumption (a) ↓ { Household wealth ↓ / Interest rate ↑ / Greater pessimism }

purchases, and purchases by foreigners. Let's consider each of these types of spending in turn.

INVESTMENT SPENDING

Remember that in the definition of GDP, the word *investment* by itself (represented by the letter *I* by itself) consists of three components: (1) business spending on plant and equipment; (2) purchases of new homes; and (3) accumulation of unsold inventories. In this chapter, as we did when we studied the classical model, we focus not on investment, but on *planned investment* or *investment spending* (we'll use these two terms interchangeably).

Planned investment (I^p) is business purchases of plant and equipment and construction of new homes.

Why do we focus on planned investment and leave out inventory accumulation? When we look at how spending influences the economy, we are interested in the purchases households, firms, and the government *want* to make. But some inventory changes, as you learned a few chapters ago, are *unplanned* and *undesired* occurrences that firms try to avoid. While firms want to have *some* inventories on hand, sudden *changes* in inventories are typically not desirable. To keep the model simple, we treat *all* inventory changes as temporary, unplanned occurrences for the firm, and we exclude them when we measure spending in the economy.

> In the short-run macro model, (planned) investment spending (I^p) is plant and equipment purchases by business firms and new home construction. Inventory investment is treated as unintentional and undesired, and is therefore excluded from our definition of investment spending.

What determines the level of investment spending in a given year? In this chapter, we will regard investment spending as a *fixed value*, determined by forces outside of our analysis. We will explore what happens when that fixed value happens to change. But we'll postpone for a couple of chapters any formal treatment of the determinants of investment spending.

> For now, we regard investment spending (I^p) as a given value, determined by forces outside of our model.

GOVERNMENT PURCHASES

Government purchases include all of the goods and services that government agencies—federal, state, and local—buy during the year. We treat government purchases in the same way as investment spending: as a given value, determined by forces outside of our analysis. Why?

The relationship between government purchases and other macroeconomic variables is rather weak. In recent decades, the biggest changes in government purchases have involved military spending. These changes have been based on world politics rather than macroeconomic conditions. So assuming that government spending is a given value, independent of the other variables in our model, is realistic.

> *In the short-run macro model, government purchases are treated as a given value, determined by forces outside of the model.*

As with investment spending, we'll be exploring what happens when the "given value" of government purchases changes. But we will not try to explain what causes it to change.

NET EXPORTS

If we want to measure total spending on U.S. output, we must also consider the international sector. About 11 percent of U.S.-produced goods are sold to *foreign* consumers, *foreign* businesses, and *foreign* governments. These U.S. *exports* are as much a part of total spending on U.S. output as the other types of spending we've discussed so far. Thus, exports must be included in our measure of total spending.

International trade in goods and services also requires us to make an adjustment to the other components of spending. A portion (about 16 percent) of the output bought by *American* consumers, firms, and government agencies was produced abroad. From the U.S. point of view, these are *imports*: spending on foreign, rather than U.S., output. These imports are included in our measures of consumption, investment, and government spending, giving us an exaggerated measure of spending on *American* output. But we can easily correct for this overcount by simply deducting imported consumption goods from our measure of consumption, deducting imported investment goods from our measure of investment spending, and deducting imported government purchases from our measure of government purchases. Or, combining all these deductions together, we simply deduct *total* imports to correct our exaggerated measure of *total* spending.

In sum, to incorporate the international sector into our measure of total spending, we must add U.S. exports and subtract U.S. imports. These two adjustments can be made together by simply including *net exports* (NX) as the foreign sector's contribution to total spending.

$$\text{Net exports} = \text{Total exports} - \text{Total imports.}$$

Net exports can change for a variety of reasons: changes in tastes toward or away from a particular country's goods, changes in the price of foreign currency on world foreign exchange markets, and more. In the last chapter of this book, we'll discuss in more detail how and why net exports change. But in this chapter, to keep things simple, we assume that net exports—like investment spending and government purchases—are some given amount. We'll explore what happens when that amount changes, but we will not, in this chapter, try to explain what causes net exports to change.

> *For now, we regard net exports as a given value, determined by forces outside of our model.*

It is important to remember that net exports can be *negative;* and in the United States, they have been negative since 1982. Negative net exports means that our imports are greater than our exports. Or, equivalently, Americans are buying more foreign goods and services than foreigners are buying of ours. In that case, net exports contribute *negatively* to total spending on U.S. output.

SUMMING UP: AGGREGATE EXPENDITURE

Now that we've discussed all of the components of spending in the economy, we can be more precise about measuring total spending. First, we'll use the phrase *aggregate expenditure* to mean total spending on U.S. output over some period of time. More formally,

> ***aggregate expenditure*** *is the sum of spending by households, businesses, the government, and the foreign sector on final goods and services produced in the United States.*

Aggregate expenditure (AE) The sum of spending by households, business firms, the government, and foreigners on final goods and services produced in the United States.

Remembering that C stands for household consumption spending, I^p for investment spending, G for government purchases, and NX for net exports, we have

$$\text{Aggregate expenditure} = C + I^p + G + NX.$$

Aggregate expenditure plays a key role in explaining economic fluctuations, as you'll soon see.

INCOME AND AGGREGATE EXPENDITURE

As we discussed earlier, the relationship between income and spending is circular: Spending depends on income, and income depends on spending. In Table 4, we take up the first part of that circle: how total spending depends on income. In the table, column 1 lists some possible income levels, and column 2 shows the level of consumption spending we can expect at each income level. These two columns are just the consumption–income relationship we introduced earlier, in Table 2.

Column 3 shows that business firms in this economy are assumed to buy $800 billion per year in plant and equipment, regardless of the level of income. Government purchases are also fixed in value, as shown by column 4: At every

GDP versus Aggregate Expenditure The definition of aggregate expenditure looks very similar to the definition of GDP presented in the chapter entitled "Production, Income, and Employment." Does this mean that aggregate expenditure and total output are always the same number? Not at all. There is a slight—but important—difference in the definitions. GDP is defined as $C + I + G + NX$. Aggregate expenditure, by contrast, is defined as $C + I^p + G + NX$. The difference is that GDP adds actual investment (I), which includes business firms' inventory investment. Aggregate expenditure adds just planned investment (I^p), which *excludes* inventory investment. The two numbers will not be equal unless inventory investment is zero. (We'll use this fact to help us find the equilibrium GDP in the next section.)

DANGEROUS CURVES

TABLE	4	The Relationship Between Income and Aggregate Expenditure					
(1) Income or GDP (billions of dollars per year)	(2) Consumption Spending (billions of dollars per year)	(3) Investment Spending (billions of dollars per year)	(4) Government Purchases (billions of dollars per year)	(5) Net Exports (billions of dollars per year)	(6) Aggregate Expenditure (AE) (billions of dollars per year)	(7) Change in Inventories (billions of dollars per year)
4,000	3,200	800	1,000	600	5,600	−1,600
5,000	3,800	800	1,000	600	6,200	−1,200
6,000	4,400	800	1,000	600	6,800	−800
7,000	5,000	800	1,000	600	7,400	−400
8,000	**5,600**	**800**	**1,000**	**600**	**8,000**	**0**
9,000	6,200	800	1,000	600	8,600	400
10,000	6,800	800	1,000	600	9,200	800
11,000	7,400	800	1,000	600	9,800	1,200
12,000	8,000	800	1,000	600	10,400	1,600

level of income, the government buys $1,000 billion in goods and services. And net exports, in column 5, are assumed to be $600 billion at each level of income. Finally, if we add together the entries in columns 2, 3, 4, and 5, we get $C + I^p + G + NX$, or aggregate expenditure, shown in column 6. (For now, ignore column 7.)

Notice that aggregate expenditure increases as income rises. But notice also that the rise in aggregate expenditure is *smaller* than the rise in income. For example, you can see that when income rises from $4,000 billion to $5,000 billion (column 1), aggregate expenditure rises from $5,600 billion to $6,200 billion (column 6). Thus, a $1,000 billion increase in income is associated with a $600 billion increase in aggregate expenditure. This is because, in our analysis, consumption is the only component of spending that depends on income, and consumption spending always increases according to the marginal propensity to consume, here equal to 0.6.

> When income increases, aggregate expenditure (AE) will rise by the MPC times the change in income: $\Delta AE = MPC \times \Delta GDP$.

Notice that we've used ΔGDP to indicate the change in total income, because GDP and total income are always the same number.

FINDING EQUILIBRIUM GDP

Table 4 shows how aggregate expenditure depends on income. In this section, you will see how income depends on aggregate expenditure—that is, how spending determines the economy's *equilibrium income* or *equilibrium GDP*. That is, we are about to use Step 2 of our three-step process: *Find the equilibrium*. As always, the equilibrium will be a point of rest of the economy: a value for GDP that remains the same until something we've been assuming constant begins to change. That part of Step 2 will be familiar to you.

However, be forewarned: Our method of *finding* equilibrium in the short run is very different from anything you've seen before in this text.

Our starting point in finding the economy's short-run equilibrium is to ask ourselves what would happen, hypothetically, if the economy were operating at different levels of output. Let's start with a GDP of $12,000 billion. Could this be the equilibrium GDP we seek? That is, if firms were producing this level of output, would they keep doing so? Let's see.

Table 4 tells us that when GDP, and therefore income, is equal to $12,000 billion, aggregate expenditure is equal to $10,400 billion. Business firms are *producing* $1,600 billion more than they are *selling*. Since firms will certainly not be willing to continue producing output they cannot sell, we can infer that, in future periods, they will slow their production. Thus, if the economy finds itself at a GDP of $12,000 billion, it will not stay there. In other words, $12,000 billion is *not* where the economy will settle in the short run, so it is *not* our equilibrium GDP. More generally,

> *when aggregate expenditure is less than GDP, output will decline in the future. Thus, any level of output at which aggregate expenditure is less than GDP cannot be the equilibrium GDP.*

Now let's consider the opposite case: a level of GDP of $4,000 billion. At this level of output, Table 4 shows aggregate expenditure of $5,600 billion; spending is actually *greater* than output by $1,600 billion. What will business firms do in response? Since they are selling more output than they are currently producing, we can expect them to *increase* their production in future months. Thus, if GDP is $4,000 billion, it will tend to rise in the future. So $4,000 billion is *not* our equilibrium GDP.

> *When aggregate expenditure is greater than GDP, output will rise in the future. Thus, any level of output at which aggregate expenditure exceeds GDP cannot be the equilibrium GDP.*

Now consider a GDP of $8,000 billion. At this level of output, our table shows that aggregate expenditure is precisely equal to $8,000 billion: Output and aggregate expenditure are equal. Since firms, on the whole, are selling just what they produce—no more and no less—they should be content to produce that same amount in the future. We have found our equilibrium GDP:

> *In the short run, **equilibrium GDP** is the level of output at which output and aggregate expenditure are equal.*

Equilibrium GDP In the short run, the level of output at which output and aggregate expenditure are equal.

INVENTORIES AND EQUILIBRIUM GDP

When firms *produce* more goods than they sell, what happens to the unsold output? It is added to their inventory stocks. When firms *sell* more goods than they produce, where do the additional goods come from? They come from firms' inventory stocks. You can see that the gap between output and spending determines what will happen to inventories during the year.

More specifically,

> *the change in inventories during any period will always equal output minus aggregate expenditure.*

For example, Table 4 tells us that if GDP is equal to $12,000 billion, aggregate expenditure is equal to $10,400 billion. In this case, we can find that the change in inventories is

$$\Delta \text{Inventories} = GDP - AE$$
$$= \$12,000 \text{ billion} - \$10,400 \text{ billion}$$
$$= \$1,600 \text{ billion.}$$

When GDP is equal to $4,000 billion, aggregate expenditure is equal to $5,600 billion, so that the change in inventories is

$$\Delta \text{Inventories} = GDP - AE$$
$$= \$4,000 \text{ billion} - \$5,600 \text{ billion}$$
$$= -\$1,600 \text{ billion.}$$

Notice the negative sign in front of the $1,600 billion; if output is $4,000 billion, then inventory stocks will *shrink* by $1,600 billion over the year.

Only when output and aggregate expenditure are equal—that is, when GDP is at its equilibrium value—will the change in inventories be zero. In our example, when GDP is at its equilibrium value of $8,000 billion, so that aggregate expenditure is also $8,000 billion, the change in inventories is equal to zero. At this output level, we have

$$\Delta \text{Inventories} = GDP - AE$$
$$= \$8,000 \text{ billion} - \$8,000 \text{ billion}$$
$$= \$0.$$

What you have just learned about inventories suggests another way to find the equilibrium GDP in the economy: Find the output level at which the change in inventories is equal to zero. Firms cannot allow their inventories of unsold goods to keep growing for very long (they would go out of business), nor can they continue to sell goods out of inventory for very long (they would run out of goods). Instead, they will desire to keep their production in line with their sales, so that their inventories do not change.

To recap,

$$AE < GDP \;\Rightarrow\; \Delta \text{Inventories} > 0 \;\Rightarrow\; GDP \downarrow \text{ in future periods.}$$
$$AE > GDP \;\Rightarrow\; \Delta \text{Inventories} < 0 \;\Rightarrow\; GDP \uparrow \text{ in future periods.}$$
$$AE = GDP \;\Rightarrow\; \Delta \text{Inventories} = 0 \;\Rightarrow\; \text{No change in } GDP$$

Now look at the last column in Table 4, which lists the change in inventories at different levels of output. This column is obtained by subtracting column 6 from column 1. The equilibrium output level is the one at which the change in inventories equals zero, which, as we've already found, is $8,000 billion.

FINDING EQUILIBRIUM GDP WITH A GRAPH

To get an even clearer picture of how equilibrium GDP is determined, we'll illustrate it with a graph, although it will take us a few steps to get there. Figure 5 begins the process by showing how we can construct a graph of aggregate expenditure. The lowest line in the figure, labeled C, is our familiar consumption–income line, obtained from the data in the first two columns of Table 4.

The next line, labeled $C + I^p$, shows the *sum* of consumption and investment spending at each income level. Notice that this line is parallel to the C line, which means that the vertical distance between them—$800 billion—is the same at any income level. This vertical difference is investment spending, which remains the same at all income levels.

The next line adds government purchases to consumption and investment spending, giving us $C + I^p + G$. The $C + I^p + G$ line is parallel to the $C + I^p$ line. The vertical distance between them—$1,000 billion—is government purchases. Like investment spending, government purchases are the same at all income levels.

Finally, the top line adds net exports, giving us $C + I^p + G + NX$, or aggregate expenditure. The distance between the $C + I^p + G + NX$ line and the $C + I^p + G$ line—$600 billion—represents net exports, which are assumed to be the same at any level of income.

Now look just at the aggregate expenditure line—the top line—in Figure 5. Notice that it slopes upward, telling us that as income increases, so does aggregate expenditure. And the slope of the aggregate expenditure line is less than 1: When income increases, the rise in aggregate expenditure is *smaller* than the rise in income. In fact, the slope of the aggregate expenditure line is equal to the *MPC*, or 0.6 in

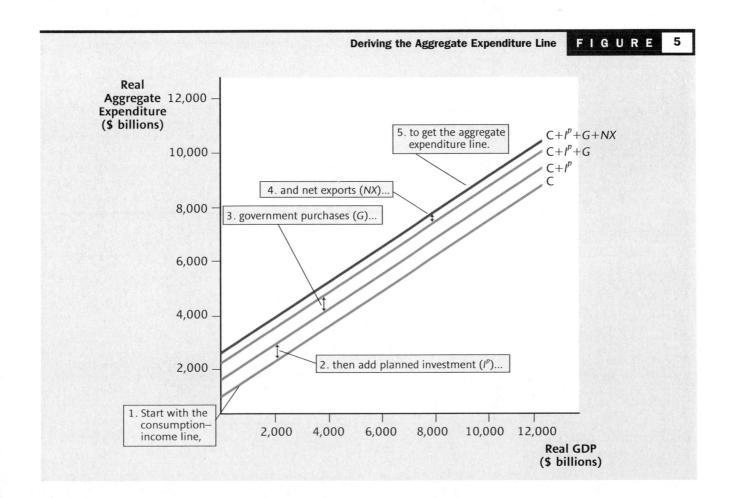

Deriving the Aggregate Expenditure Line   **FIGURE** **5**

this example. This tells us that a one-dollar rise in income causes a 60-cent increase in aggregate expenditure. (Question: In the graph, which of the four components of aggregate expenditure rises when income rises? Which remain the same?)

Now we're almost ready to use a graph like the one in Figure 5 to locate equilibrium GDP, but first we must develop a little geometric trick.

Figure 6 shows a graph in which the horizontal and vertical axes are both measured in the same units, such as dollars. It also shows a line drawn at a 45° angle that begins at the origin. This 45° line has a useful property: Any point along it represents the same value along the vertical axis as it does along the horizontal axis. For example, look at point A on the line. Point A corresponds to the horizontal distance $0B$, and it also corresponds to the vertical distance BA. But because the line is a 45° line, we know that these two distances are equal: $0B = BA$. Now we have two choices for measuring the distance $0B$: We can measure it horizontally, or we can measure it as the vertical distance BA. In fact, *any* horizontal distance can also be read vertically, merely by going from the horizontal value (point B in our example) up to the 45° line.

> A 45° line is a translator line: It allows us to measure any horizontal distance as a vertical distance instead.

Let's apply this geometric trick to help us find the equilibrium GDP. In our aggregate expenditure diagram, we want to compare output with aggregate expenditure. But output is measured horizontally, while aggregate expenditure is measured vertically. Our 45° line, however, enables us to translate output into a vertical distance, and thus permits us to compare output and aggregate expenditure as two vertical distances.

Figure 7 shows how this is done. The blue line is the aggregate expenditure line ($C + I^p + G + NX$) from Figure 5. (We've dispensed with the other three lines that were drawn in Figure 5 because we no longer need them.) The black line is our 45° translator line. Now, let's search for the equilibrium GDP by considering a number of possibilities.

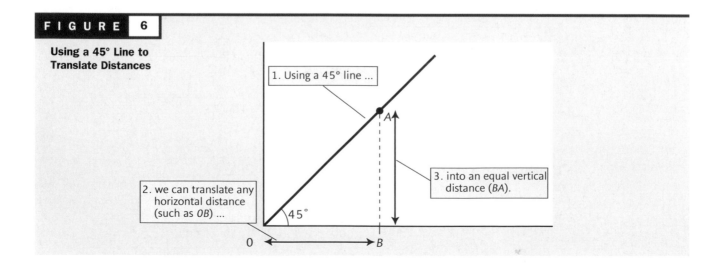

FIGURE 6

Using a 45° Line to Translate Distances

1. Using a 45° line ...

2. we can translate any horizontal distance (such as 0B) ...

3. into an equal vertical distance (BA).

45°

0 — B

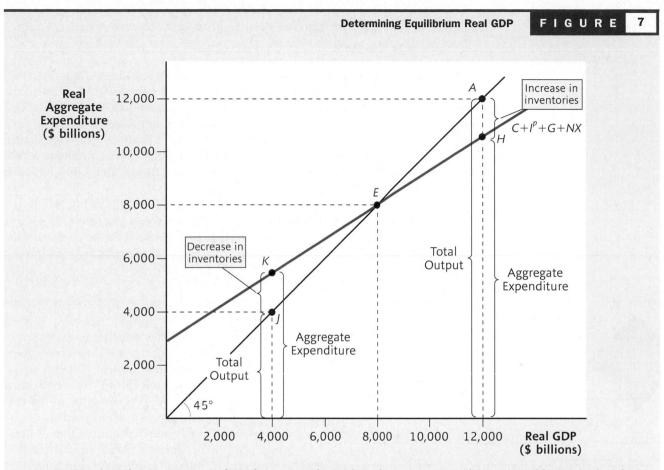

Determining Equilibrium Real GDP   FIGURE 7

At point E, *where the aggregate expenditure line crosses the 45° line, the economy is in short-run equilibrium. With real GDP equal to $8,000 billion, aggregate expenditure equals real GDP. At higher levels of real GDP—such as $12,000 billion—total production exceeds aggregate expenditures, and firms will be unable to sell all they produce. Unplanned inventory increases equal to HA will lead them to reduce production. At lower levels of real GDP—such as $4,000 billion—aggregate expenditure exceeds total production. Firms find their inventories falling, and they will respond by increasing production.*

For example, could the output level $12,000 billion be our sought-after equilibrium? Let's see. We can measure the output level $12,000 billion as the vertical distance from the horizontal axis up to point *A* on the 45° line. But when output is $12,000 billion, aggregate expenditure is the vertical distance from the horizontal axis to point *H* on the aggregate expenditure line. Notice that, since point *H* lies below point *A*, aggregate expenditure is less than output. If firms *did* produce $12,000 billion worth of output, they would accumulate inventories equal to the vertical distance *HA* (the excess of output over spending). We conclude graphically (as we did earlier, using our table) that if output is $12,000 billion, firms will accumulate inventories of unsold goods and reduce output in the future. Thus, $12,000 billion is not our equilibrium. In general,

at any output level at which the aggregate expenditure line lies below the 45° line, aggregate expenditure is less than GDP. If firms produce any of these output levels, their inventories will grow, and they will reduce output in the future.

Now let's see if an output of $4,000 billion could be our equilibrium. First, we read this output level as the vertical distance up to point *J* on the 45° line. Next, we note that when output is $4,000 billion, aggregate expenditure is the vertical distance up to point *K* on the aggregate expenditure line. Point *K* lies *above* point *J*, so aggregate expenditure is greater than output. If firms *did* produce $4,000 billion in output, inventories would *decrease* by the vertical distance *JK*. With declining inventories, firms would want to increase their output in the future, so $4,000 billion is not our equilibrium. More generally,

at any output level at which the aggregate expenditure line lies above *the 45° line, aggregate expenditure exceeds GDP. If firms produce any of these output levels, their inventories will decline, and they will increase their output in the future.*

What About Prices? You may be wondering why, in the short-run macro model, a firm that produces more output than it sells wouldn't just lower the price of its goods. That way, it could sell more of them and not have to lower its output as much. Similarly, a firm whose sales exceeded its production could take advantage of the opportunity to raise its prices rather than increase production.

To some extent, firms *do* change prices—even in the short run. But they change their output levels, too. To keep things as simple as possible, this first version of the short-run macro model assumes that firms adjust *only* their output to match aggregate expenditure. That is, we assume that *prices don't change at all*. In a later chapter, we'll make the model more realistic by assuming that firms adjust both prices and output.

Finally, consider an output of $8,000 billion. At this output level, the aggregate expenditure line and the 45° line cross. As a result, the vertical distance up to point *E* on the 45° line (representing output) is the same as the vertical distance up to point *E* on the aggregate expenditure line. If firms produce an output level of $8,000 billion, aggregate expenditure and output will be precisely equal, inventories will remain unchanged, and firms will have no incentive to increase or decrease output in the future. We have thus found our equilibrium on the graph: $8,000 billion.

Equilibrium GDP is the output level at which the aggregate expenditure line intersects the 45° line. If firms produce this output level, their inventories will not change, and they will be content to continue producing the same level of output in the future.

During the Great Depression of the 1930s, the economy's short-run equilibrium output fell far below potential, and at least a quarter of the labor force became unemployed.

© CORBIS

Equilibrium GDP and Employment

Now that you've learned how to find the economy's equilibrium GDP in the short run, a question may have occurred to you: When the economy operates at equilibrium, will it also be operating at full employment? The answer is: *not necessarily.* Let's see why.

If you look back over the two methods we've employed to find equilibrium GDP—using columns of numbers or using a graph—you will see that in both cases we've asked only one question: How much will households, businesses, the government, and foreigners *spend* on goods produced in the United States? We did not ask any

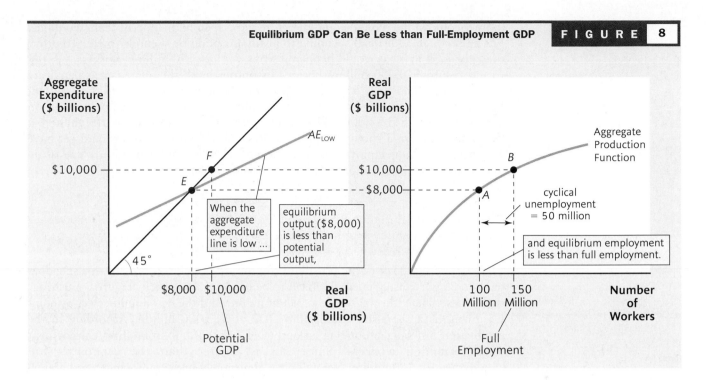

Equilibrium GDP Can Be Less than Full-Employment GDP FIGURE 8

questions about the number of people who want to work. Therefore, it would be quite a coincidence if our equilibrium GDP happened to be the output level at which the entire labor force were employed.

Figure 8 illustrates the connection between employment and equilibrium GDP. We'll be going back and forth between the panels, so it's good to make sure you understand each step before going on to the next. Let's start with the right-hand panel, which shows the economy's *aggregate production function*, introduced earlier as part of the classical model. This curve tells us the relationship between any given number of workers and the level of output, with the current state of technology and given quantities of other resources. In this economy, full employment is assumed to be 150 million workers, measured along the horizontal axis. Potential output— $10,000 billion on the vertical axis—is the amount of output a fully employed labor force of 150 million workers could produce. This is also the long-run equilibrium output level that the classical model would predict for the economy.

But will $10,000 billion be the economy's equilibrium in the *short run*? Not necessarily. One possible outcome is shown in the left panel. The short-run equilibrium occurs at point *E*, where the aggregate expenditure line crosses the 45° line. At this point, output (on the horizontal axis) is $8,000 billion.

How many people will have jobs? We can answer by using the 45° line to convert the $8,000 billion from a horizontal distance to a vertical distance, then (following the dashed line) carrying that vertical distance across to the right panel. The right panel's production function tells us that to produce $8,000 billion in output, only 100 million workers are needed. In short-run equilibrium, then, only 100 million workers will have jobs. The difference between *full* employment and *actual* employment is 150 million − 100 million = 50 million, which is the amount of cyclical unemployment in the economy.

But why? What prevents firms from hiring the extra people who want jobs? After all, with more people working, producing more output, wouldn't there be more income in the economy and therefore more spending? Indeed, there would be. But not *enough* additional spending to justify the additional employment. To prove this, just look at what would happen if firms *did* hire 150 million workers. Output would rise to $10,000 billion, but at this output level, the aggregate expenditure line would lie below the 45° line so *firms would be unable to sell all their output.* Unsold goods would pile up in inventories, and firms would cut back on production until output reached $8,000 billion again, with employment back at 100 million.

In sum: Figure 8 shows that we can be in short-run equilibrium and yet have abnormally high unemployment. The reason: The aggregate expenditure line is *too low* to create an intersection at full-employment output.

> *In the short-run macro model, cyclical unemployment is caused by insufficient spending. As long as spending remains low, production will remain low, and unemployment will remain high.*

What about the opposite possibility? In the short run, is it possible for spending to be *too high,* causing unemployment to be *too low*? Absolutely. Figure 9 illustrates such a case. Here, the aggregate expenditure line and the 45° line intersect at point E′, giving us a short-run equilibrium GDP at $12,000 billion. According to the production function, producing an output of $12,000 billion requires employment of 200 million workers. Since this is greater than the economy's full employment of 150 million, we will have abnormally high employment and abnormally low *un*employment.

> *In the short-run macro model, the economy can overheat because spending is too high. As long as spending remains high, production will exceed potential output, and unemployment will be unusually low.*

FIGURE 9   **Equilibrium GDP Can Be Greater than Full-Employment GDP**

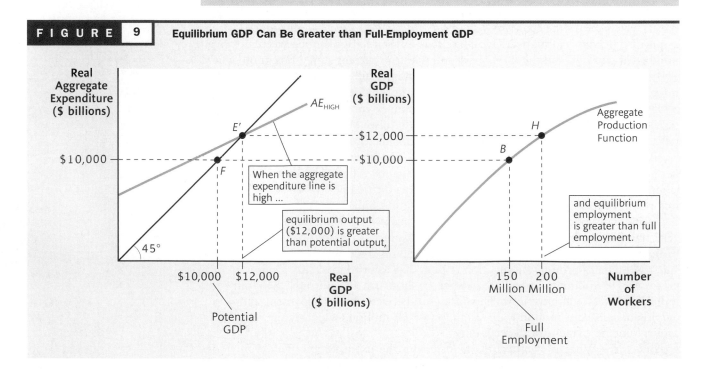

In the previous chapter, we concluded that the classical model could not explain economic fluctuations. The short-run macro model, on the other hand, does provide an explanation: The aggregate expenditure line may be low, so that in the short run, equilibrium GDP is below full employment. Or aggregate expenditure may be high, so that in the short run, equilibrium GDP is above the full-employment level. (Of course, this is just a first step in explaining economic fluctuations. In later chapters, we'll add more realism to the model.)

WHAT HAPPENS WHEN THINGS CHANGE?

So far, you've seen how the economy's equilibrium level of output is determined in the short run, and the important role played by spending in determining that equilibrium. But now it's time to use Step 3 and explore how a *change* in spending affects equilibrium output.

A CHANGE IN INVESTMENT SPENDING

Suppose the equilibrium GDP in an economy is $8,000 billion and then business firms increase their investment spending on plant and equipment. This might happen because business managers feel more optimistic about the economy's future, or because there is a new "must-have" technology (such as the Internet in the late 1990s). Whatever the cause, firms decide to increase yearly planned investment purchases by $1,000 billion above the original level. What will happen?

First, sales revenue at firms that manufacture investment goods—firms like Dell Computer, Caterpillar, and Westinghouse—will increase by $1,000 billion. But remember, each time a dollar in output is produced, a dollar of income (factor payments) is created. Thus, the $1,000 billion in additional sales revenue will become $1,000 billion in additional income. This income will be paid out as wages, rent, interest, and profit to the households who own the resources these firms have purchased.[1]

What will households do with their $1,000 billion in additional income? Remember that with net taxes fixed at some value, a $1,000 billion rise in income is also a $1,000 billion rise in *disposable* income. Households are free to spend or save this additional income as they desire. What they will do depends crucially on the *marginal propensity to consume (MPC) in the economy.* If the *MPC* is 0.6, then consumption spending will rise by 0.6 × $1,000 billion = $600 billion. Households will save the remaining $400 billion.

But that is not the end of the story. When households spend an additional $600 billion, firms that produce consumption goods and services—firms such as McDonald's, American Airlines, and Disney—will receive an additional $600 billion in sales revenue, which, in turn, will become income for the households that supply resources to these firms. And when *these* households see *their* annual incomes rise by $600 billion, they will spend part of it as well. With an *MPC* of 0.6, consumption spending will rise by 0.6 × $600 billion = $360 billion, creating still more sales revenue for firms, and so on and so on. . . .

As you can see, an increase in investment spending will set off a chain reaction, leading to successive rounds of increased spending and income.

---

[1] Some of the sales revenue will also go to pay for intermediate goods, such as raw materials, electricity, and supplies. But the intermediate-goods suppliers will also pay wages, rent, interest, and profit for the resources *they* use, so that household income will still rise by the full $1,000 billion.

TABLE 5			
Cumulative Increases in Spending When Investment Spending Increases by $1,000 Billion	**Round**	**Additional Spending in Each Round (billions of dollars per year)**	**Total Additional Spending (billions of dollars per year)**
	Initial increase in investment spending	1,000	1,000
	Round 2	600	1,600
	Round 3	360	1,960
	Round 4	216	2,176
	Round 5	130	2,306
	Round 6	78	2,384
	Round 7	47	2,431
	Round 8	28	2,459
	Round 9	17	2,476
	Round 10	10	2,486
	. . .	. . .	. . .
	Round 20	0.06	Very close to 2,500

The process is illustrated in Table 5. The second column gives us the additional spending in each round of this chain reaction. The first entry shows the additional spending of $1,000 billion per year from the initial increase in investment. The next entry shows the $600 billion increase in consumption spending, then another $360 billion increase in consumption, and so on. Each successive round of additional spending is 60 percent of the round before. The third column adds up the additional spending created by all preceding rounds, to give the *total* additional spending as this chain reaction continues. For example, total additional spending after the first round is just $1,000 billion. In the second round, we add the $600 billion in additional consumption spending, to get $1,600 billion in additional spending per year. In the third round, additional spending rises to $1,960 billion per year.

Remember that each time spending rises, output rises to match it. Figure 10 illustrates what happens to GDP (at an annual rate) after each round of this chain reaction. When we analyze events like this in the U.S. economy, we find that the successive increases in spending and output occur quickly; the process is largely completed within a year. And at the end of the process, when the economy has reached its new equilibrium, total spending and total output are considerably higher.

But how much higher?

If you look at the second column of Table 5, you can see that each successive round adds less to total spending than the round before. And in Figure 10, you see that GDP rises by less and less with each round. Eventually, GDP rises by such a small amount, and the GDP will be so close to its new equilibrium value, that we can ignore any difference. In our example, when the chain reaction is virtually completed, equilibrium GDP will be $2,500 billion more than it was initially.

THE EXPENDITURE MULTIPLIER

Let's go back and summarize what happened in our example: Business firms increased their investment spending by $1,000 billion, and as a result, spending and output rose by $2,500 billion. Equilibrium GDP increased by *more than* the initial increase in investment spending. In our example, the increase in equilibrium GDP

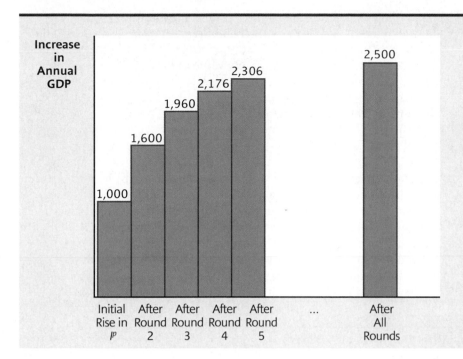

FIGURE 10

The Effect of a Change in Investment Spending

An increase in investment spending sets off a chain reaction, leading to successive rounds of increased spending and income. As shown here, a $1,000 billion increase in investment spending first causes real GDP to increase by $1,000 billion. Then, with higher incomes, households increase consumption spending by the MPC times the change in disposable income. In round 2, spending and GDP increase by another $600 billion. In succeeding rounds, increases in income lead to further changes in spending, but in each round the increases in income and spending are smaller than in the preceding round.

($2,500 billion) was two-and-a-half times the initial increase in investment spending ($1,000 billion). As you can verify, if investment spending had increased by half as much ($500 billion), GDP would have increased by 2.5 times *that* amount ($1,250 billion). In fact, *whatever* the rise in investment spending, equilibrium GDP would increase by a factor of 2.5, so we can write

$$\Delta GDP = 2.5 \times \Delta I^p.$$

In our example, the change in investment spending was *multiplied by* the number 2.5 in order to get the change in GDP that it causes. For this reason, 2.5 is called the *expenditure multiplier* in this example.

> The **expenditure multiplier** is the number by which the change in investment spending must be multiplied to get the change in equilibrium GDP.

Expenditure multiplier The amount by which equilibrium real GDP changes as a result of a one-dollar change in autonomous consumption, investment spending, government purchases, or net exports.

The value of the expenditure multiplier depends on the value of the *MPC* in the economy. If you look back at Table 5, you will see that each round of additional spending would have been larger if the *MPC* had been larger. For example, with an *MPC* of 0.9 instead of 0.6, spending in round 2 would have risen by $900 billion, in round 3 by $810 billion, and so on. The result would have been a larger ultimate change in GDP, and a larger multiplier.

There is a very simple formula we can use to determine the multiplier for *any* value of the *MPC*.

> For any value of the MPC, the formula for the expenditure multiplier is
> $$\frac{1}{(1 - MPC)}.$$

In our example, the *MPC* was equal to 0.6, so the expenditure multiplier had the value $1/(1 - 0.6) = 1/0.4 = 2.5$. If the *MPC* had been 0.9 instead, the expenditure multiplier would have been equal to $1/(1 - 0.9) = 1/0.1 = 10$. The formula $1/(1 - MPC)$ can be used to find the multiplier for any value of the *MPC* between zero and one. If you want to see how this formula is derived, see this footnote.[2]

Using the general formula for the expenditure multiplier, we can restate what happens when investment spending increases:

$$\Delta GDP = \left[\frac{1}{(1-MPC)} \right] \times \Delta I^p.$$

The multiplier effect is a rather surprising phenomenon. It tells us that an increase in investment spending ultimately affects GDP by *more* than the initial increase in investment. Further, it tells us that as long as annual investment spending remains $1,000 billion greater than it was previously, yearly GDP will remain higher than previously—$2,500 billion higher in our example. That is, a sustained increase in investment spending will cause a sustained increase in GDP.

By contrast, a one-time increase in investment—followed by a drop in investment back to its original level—will cause only a temporary change in GDP. That's because the multiplier process works in *both* directions, as you're about to see.

THE MULTIPLIER IN REVERSE

Suppose that, in Table 5, investment spending had *decreased* instead of increased. Then the initial change in spending would be $-\$1,000$ billion. This would cause a $1,000 billion decrease in revenue for firms that produce investment goods, and they, in turn, would pay out $1,000 billion less in factor payments. In the next round, households, with $1,000 billion less in income, would spend $600 billion less on consumption goods, and so on. The final result would be a $2,500 billion *decrease* in equilibrium GDP.

> *Just as increases in investment spending cause equilibrium GDP to rise by a multiple of the change in spending, decreases in investment spending cause equilibrium GDP to fall by a multiple of the change in spending.*

The multiplier formula we've already established will work whether the initial change in spending is positive or negative.

---

[2] To derive the multiplier formula, let's start with our example, in which the change in GDP was:

$$\Delta GDP = (\$1,000 \text{ billion} + \$600 \text{ billion} + \$360 \text{ billion}$$
$$+ \$216 \text{ billion} + \dots).$$

Factoring out the $1,000 billion gives us:

$$\Delta GDP = \$1,000 \text{ billion} \times (1 + 0.6 + 0.36 + 0.216 + \dots)$$
$$= \$1,000 \text{ billion} \times (1 + 0.6 + 0.6^2 + 0.6^3 + \dots).$$

Now, in our example, $1,000 billion was the increase in investment spending and 0.6 was the *MPC*. Generalizing this for *any* change in investment or *any* MPC, we would have

$$\Delta GDP = \Delta I^p \times [1 + (MPC) + (MPC)^2 + (MPC)^3 + \dots].$$

Next, we borrow a rule from the mathematics of infinite sums (such as the sum in brackets): For any value of H between 0 and 1, the infinite sum $1 + H + H^2 + H^3 + \dots$ has the value $1/(1 - H)$. Replacing H with the *MPC* (which is between 0 and 1), we conclude:

$$\Delta GDP = \Delta I^p \times \left[\frac{1}{(1-MPC)} \right].$$

OTHER SPENDING CHANGES

A change in *any* sector's spending will set off a chain of events similar to that in our investment example.

Suppose the government increased its purchases above previous levels. For example, the Department of Defense might raise its spending on new bombers, or state highway departments might hire more road-repair crews, or cities and towns might hire more teachers. If total government purchases rise by $1,000 billion, then, once again, household income will rise by $1,000 billion. As before, households will spend 60 percent of this increase, causing consumption, in the next round, to rise by $600 billion, and so on and so on. The chain of events is exactly like that of Table 5, with one exception: The first line in column 1 would read, "Initial increase in government purchases" instead of "initial increase in investment spending." Once again, output would increase by $2,500 billion.

Besides planned investment and government purchases, there are two other components of spending that can set off the same process. One is an increase in net exports (*NX*). Since *NX* = Exports − Imports, either an increase in the economy's exports or a *decrease* in imports will cause *net* exports to rise.

Finally, a change in *autonomous consumption* (*a*) can set off the process. For example, after a $1,000 billion increase in autonomous consumption spending, we would see further increases in consumption spending of $600 billion, then $360 billion, and so on. This time, the first line in column 1 of Table 5 would read, "Initial increase in autonomous consumption," but every entry in the table would be the same.

> *Changes in planned investment, government purchases, net exports, or autonomous consumption lead to a multiplier effect on GDP. The expenditure multiplier, 1/(1 − MPC), is what we multiply the initial change in spending by in order to get the change in equilibrium GDP.*

The following four equations summarize how we use the expenditure multiplier to determine the effects of different spending changes in the short-run macro model. Keep in mind that these formulas work whether the initial change in spending is positive or negative.

$$\Delta GDP = \left[\frac{1}{(1 - MPC)} \right] \times \Delta I^p$$

$$\Delta GDP = \left[\frac{1}{(1 - MPC)} \right] \times \Delta G$$

$$\Delta GDP = \left[\frac{1}{(1 - MPC)} \right] \times \Delta NX$$

$$\Delta GDP = \left[\frac{1}{(1 - MPC)} \right] \times \Delta a$$

Changes in net taxes, too, have multiplier effects, although they work more indirectly on GDP than the spending changes we've been discussing. A tax cut—by allowing households to keep more of their income—raises disposable income. As a result, consumption spending rises, creating a multiplier effect that increases equilibrium GDP. Similarly, a tax increase lowers disposable income and consumption, creating a multiplier effect that decreases equilibrium GDP. But there is a slightly different multiplier formula that applies to tax changes. We'll discuss the tax multiplier in Appendix 2 of this chapter.

A GRAPHICAL VIEW OF THE MULTIPLIER

Figure 11 illustrates the multiplier using our aggregate expenditure diagram. The darker line is the aggregate expenditure line from Figure 7. The aggregate expenditure line intersects the 45° line at point E, giving us an equilibrium GDP of $8,000 billion.

Now, suppose that either autonomous consumption, investment spending, net exports, or government purchases rises by $1,000 billion. Regardless of which of these types of spending increases, the effect on our aggregate expenditure line is the same: It will *shift upward* by $1,000 billion, to the higher line in the figure. The new

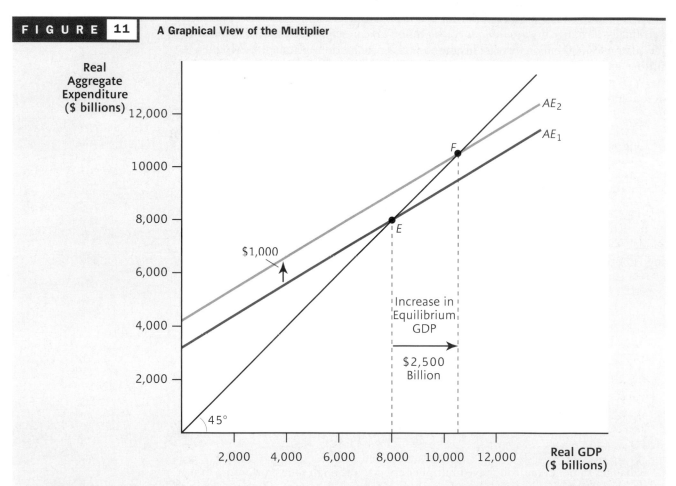

FIGURE 11   **A Graphical View of the Multiplier**

The economy starts off at point E with equilibrium real GDP of $8,000 billion. A $1,000 billion increase in spending shifts the aggregate expenditure line upward by $1,000 billion, triggering the multiplier process. Eventually, the economy will reach a new equilibrium at point F, where the new, higher aggregate expenditure line crosses the 45° line. At F, real GDP is $10,500 billion, an increase of $2,500 billion.

aggregate expenditure line intersects the 45° line at point *F*, showing that our new equilibrium GDP is equal to $10,500 billion.

What has happened? An initial spending increase of $1,000 billion has caused equilibrium GDP to increase from $8,000 billion to $10,500 billion, an increase of $2,500 billion. This is just what our multiplier of 2.5 tells us. In general,

$$\Delta GDP = \left[\frac{1}{(1 - MPC)} \right] \times \Delta \text{Spending}$$

and in this case,

$$\$2,500 \text{ billion} = 2.5 \times \$1,000 \text{ billion}.$$

> *An increase in autonomous consumption spending, investment spending, government purchases, or net exports will shift the aggregate expenditure line upward by the initial increase in spending. Equilibrium GDP will rise by the initial increase in spending times the expenditure multiplier.*

Automatic Stabilizers and the Multiplier

In this chapter, we've presented a model to help us focus on the central relationship between spending and output. To keep the model as simple as possible, we've ignored many real-world factors that interfere with, and reduce the size of, the multiplier effect. These forces are called **automatic stabilizers** because, with a smaller multiplier, spending changes will cause a much smaller change in GDP. As a result, economic fluctuations will be milder.

Automatic stabilizers Forces that reduce the size of the expenditure multiplier and diminish the impact of spending changes.

> *Automatic stabilizers reduce the size of the multiplier and therefore reduce the impact of spending changes on the economy. With milder fluctuations, the economy is more stable.*

How do automatic stabilizers work? They shrink the additional spending that occurs in each round of the multiplier, and thereby reduce the final multiplier effect on equilibrium GDP. In Table 5, automatic stabilizers would reduce each of the numerical entries after the first $1,000 billion, and lead to a final change in GDP smaller than $2,500 billion.

Here are some of the real-world automatic stabilizers we've ignored in the simple, short-run macro model of this chapter:

Taxes. We've been assuming that taxes remain constant, so that a rise in income causes an equal rise in disposable income. But some taxes (like the personal income tax) rise with income. As a result, in each round of the multiplier, the increase in disposable income will be smaller than the increase in income. With a smaller rise in disposable income, there will be a smaller rise in consumption spending as well.

Transfer Payments. Some government transfer payments fall as income rises. For example, many laid-off workers receive unemployment benefits, which help support them for several months while they are unemployed. When output and employment rise, newly hired workers give up their unemployment benefits. As

The Two Kinds of Consumption Changes. Does a change in consumption spending cause a multiplier effect? Or does the multiplier effect create a change in consumption spending? Actually, the causation runs in both directions. The key is to recognize that there are two kinds of changes in consumption spending.

One kind is a change in autonomous consumption spending (the term "*a*" in the consumption function). This change will *shift* the aggregate expenditure line up or down, telling us that total spending will be greater or smaller at *any* level of income. It is the kind of change that *causes* a multiplier effect.

But consumption also changes when something other than autonomous consumption sets off a multiplier effect. This is because consumption depends on income, and income always increases during the successive rounds of the multiplier effect. Such a change in consumption is represented by a movement *along* the aggregate expenditure line, rather than a shift.

Whenever you discuss a change in consumption spending, make sure you know whether it is a change in autonomous consumption (which shifts the *AE* line) or a change in consumption caused by a change in income (a movement along the *AE* line).

a result, a rise in income will cause a smaller rise in *disposable* income in each round, and a smaller rise in consumption.

Interest Rates. In a later chapter, you'll learn that an increase in output often leads to rising interest rates as well. This will crowd out some consumption and investment spending, making the increase in aggregate expenditure smaller than our simple story suggests.

Imports. Some additional spending is on goods and services imported from abroad. That is, instead of remaining constant as in our example, imports often rise as income rises, and net exports therefore fall as income rises. This helps to counteract any increase in spending caused by a rise in income.

Forward-looking Behavior. Consumers may be *forward-looking*. If they realize that the fluctuations in the economy are temporary, their consumption spending may be less sensitive to changes in their current income. Therefore, any change in income will cause a smaller change in consumption spending, and lead to a smaller multiplier effect.

Remember that each of these automatic stabilizers reduces the size of the multiplier, making it smaller than the simple formulas given in this chapter. For example, the simple formula for the expenditure multiplier is $1/(1 - MPC)$. With an MPC of about 0.9—which is in the ballpark for the United States and many other countries—we would expect the multiplier to be about 10 . . . *if the simple formula were accurate*. In that case, a $1,000 billion increase in government spending would cause output to rise by $10,000 billion—quite a large multiplier effect.

But after we take account of all of the automatic stabilizers, the multiplier is considerably smaller. How much smaller? Most of the forecasting models used by economists in business and government predict that the multiplier effect takes about 9 months to a year to work its way through the economy. At the end of the process, the multiplier has a value of about 1.5. This means that a $1,000 billion increase in, say, government spending should cause GDP to increase by only about $1,500 billion in a year. This is much less than the $10,000 billion increase predicted by the simple formula $1/(1 - MPC)$ when the MPC is equal to 0.9.

> *In the real world, due to automatic stabilizers, spending changes have much weaker impacts on the economy than our simple multiplier formula would suggest.*

Finally, there is one more automatic stabilizer you should know about, perhaps the most important of all: the *passage of time*. The impact of spending changes on output is *temporary.* As time passes, the classical model—lurking in the background—stands ready to take over. And if we wait long enough—a few years or so—we will return to our potential output level. So if a change in spending pulls us away from full-employment GDP, the economy will eventually return to full-employment GDP, right where it started. We thus conclude that

> *in the long run, our multipliers have a value of zero: No matter what the change in spending or taxes, output will eventually return to full employment, so the change in equilibrium GDP will be zero.*

Of course, the year or two we must wait can seem like an eternity to those who are jobless when the economy is operating below its potential. The short run is not to be overlooked. This is why, in the next several chapters, we will continue with our exploration of the short run, building on the macro model you've learned in this chapter. We'll be making the analysis more complete and more realistic by bringing in some of the real-world features that were not fully considered here.

COUNTERCYCLICAL FISCAL POLICY

In the classical model, you saw that fiscal policy has no demand-side effects. For example, an increase in government purchases—because it crowds out an equal amount of household and business spending—does not change total spending at all. That is . . . in the long run.

But in the short run, the economy does not operate according to the mechanisms of the classical model. Instead, as you've seen, an increase in government purchases causes an increase in *total* spending and, through the multiplier, raises equilibrium GDP. That is,

> *in the short run, fiscal policy has demand-side effects on output and employment.*

This important observation suggests that fiscal policy could, in principle, improve the path of the economy. The government, by continually adjusting its own purchases or net taxes, could keep the economy closer to potential output and—in theory—smooth out the business cycle. When the government acts in this way, it is engaging in **countercyclical fiscal policy**—a change in government purchases or net taxes designed to reverse or prevent a recession or a boom.

Countercyclical fiscal policy A change in government purchases or net taxes designed to reverse or prevent a recession or a boom.

HOW COUNTERCYCLICAL FISCAL POLICY WORKS

Figure 12 illustrates the idea behind countercyclical fiscal policy. It shows the aggregate expenditure line for an economy that is initially operating at point *A,* producing its potential output of $10,000 billion. Then we suppose that investment or autonomous consumption spending decreases, so the aggregate expenditure line shifts downward, and we end up with an output below potential at $9,000 billion. We are in a recession.

We could wait for a few years, knowing that recessions don't last forever. Eventually, the economy would operate according to the classical model, and we'd be back at our potential output. But why wait for the classical model to "kick in"

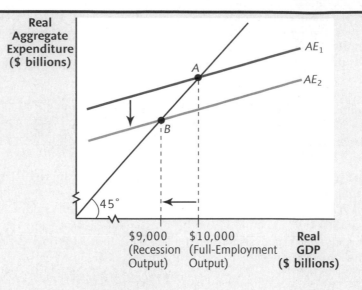

FIGURE 12

Counterycyclical Fiscal Policy

Initially, the economy's equilibrium is at full-employment output of $10,000 billion (Point A). Then a decrease in investment spending shifts the aggregate expenditure line down to AE$_2$, and the economy starts heading toward point B—a recession. The government could shift the AE line back to its original position by increasing its own purchases, or by decreasing net taxes with a change in tax or transfer policies. If the change were enacted quickly enough, the government could prevent the recession.

when we have such a powerful tool—fiscal policy—at our disposal? Why not make things better right away by, say, increasing government purchases?

Let's calculate how much government purchases (G) would have to rise in Figure 12 to bring us back to full employment. We'll start with the equation relating changes in G to changes in GDP:

$$\Delta GDP = \text{Multiplier} \times \Delta G.$$

Let's assume the multiplier in this economy is 2.5. Also, because equilibrium GDP is now at $9,000 billion, and we want it to be $10,000 billion, the required ΔGDP is $1,000. Substituting these values into our equation, we have

$$\$1,000 \text{ billion} = 2.5 \times \Delta G.$$

Finally, we solve for ΔG:

$$\Delta G = \frac{\$1,000 \text{ billion}}{2.5} = \$400 \text{ billion}.$$

This tells us that if the government increases its purchases by $400 billion, it will shift up the aggregate expenditure line by just enough to bring the economy back to full employment. Fiscal policy can cure the recession.

But why not go further and use countercyclical fiscal policy to *prevent* recessions from occurring in the first place? At the first sign of a contraction, the government could quickly increase its own purchases (say, hire more people to work with children in after-school programs) or cut taxes (say, offer everyone an immediate tax rebate). If successful, a government-induced increase in spending would counteract any decline in spending elsewhere in the economy. The recession would never occur.

Indeed, in the 1960s and early 1970s, this was the thinking of many economists. At the time, the popular view was that fiscal policy could effectively smooth out economic fluctuations, perhaps even eliminate them entirely. But very few economists believe this today. Why?

PROBLEMS WITH COUNTERCYCLICAL FISCAL POLICY

While countercyclical fiscal policy is a wonderful idea in theory, it is plagued with practical problems that seriously limit its effectiveness. Here are some of them.

Timing Problems

In most countries, it usually takes many months—or even longer—for fiscal changes to be enacted. Consider, for example, a decision to decrease taxes in the United States. A tax bill originates in the House of Representatives and then goes to the Senate, where it is usually modified. Then a conference committee irons out the differences between the House and Senate versions, and the tax bill goes back to each chamber for a vote. Once the legislation has passed, the president must sign it. Even if all goes smoothly, this process can take many months.

But in most cases, it will *not* go smoothly. First, there is the thorny question of *distributing* the benefits of any total tax cut among different groups within the country—an issue about which Democrats and Republicans rarely agree. And some senators and representatives will see the bill as an opportunity to change the tax system in more fundamental ways, causing further political debate. Because of these problems, the tax cut may not take effect until long after it is needed—stimulating the economy after it has recovered from recession, perhaps even when it is booming.

The same timing problem occurs in the opposite situation—when a tax hike is needed to counteract a boom. And these problems plague fiscal policy whether it is implemented through changes in taxes or changes in government purchases or transfers. Because of the long delays, regular use of countercyclical policy could very well be a *destabilizing* force in the economy—stepping on the gas when we should be hitting the brakes, or vice versa.

Irreversibility

To be effective, countercyclical fiscal policy must be reversible. In our example in Figure 12, suppose the recession was caused by a sudden decrease in investment spending. Then, once investment spending returned to more normal levels, the fiscal stimulation should be reversed as well, so as not to overheat the economy.

But reversing changes in government purchases or taxes is difficult. Spending programs that create new departments or expand existing ones tend to become permanent, or at least difficult to terminate. Many "temporary" tax changes become permanent as well; the public is never happy to see a tax cut reversed, and the government is often reluctant to reverse a tax hike that could provide revenues for new government programs.

The Reaction of the Federal Reserve

In the next chapter, you'll learn about the *Federal Reserve*—a quasi-governmental body responsible for another method of guiding the economy (monetary policy). In recent decades, the Federal Reserve has taken over the main role in reacting to and smoothing out economic fluctuations. And—for reasons you'll soon learn—the Federal Reserve can generally act more rapidly and flexibly than can Congress. In most circumstances, by the time any fiscal change would take place, the Federal Reserve would have *already* taken the steps it thought necessary to adjust aggregate expenditure. Any further changes in spending caused by fiscal policy would then be counteracted and effectively neutralized by the Federal Reserve.

USING THE THEORY

The Recession of 2001

Our most recent recession lasted from March 2001 to November 2001. Figure 13 tells the story. In the upper panel, you can see that investment spending—which had been drifting downward—fell sharply during the second quarter of 2001, and continued to fall throughout the year. The decrease in investment spending shifted the aggregate expenditure line downward (not shown). The middle panel shows the behavior of real GDP, which in normal times would have increased (along with potential output) at an annual rate of $80 billion each quarter. Instead, GDP fluctuated during the year, with almost no growth, and actually fell during the third quarter of 2001. As production faltered, employment fell—as seen in the bottom panel.

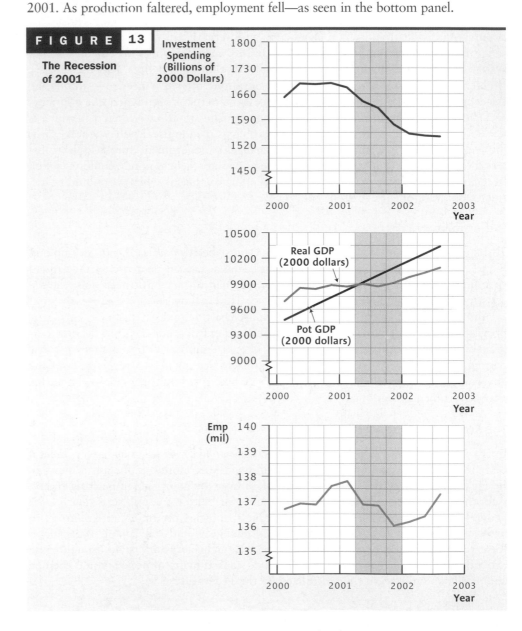

FIGURE 13

The Recession of 2001

What caused the recession of 2001? The simple answer is that the decline in investment spending, through the multiplier process, pushed down real GDP and employment. But what caused investment spending to fall in the first place?

In retrospect, we can see there were at least three causes.

First, during much of the late 1990s, there had been a boom in capital equipment spending as existing businesses rushed to incorporate the Internet into factories, offices, and their business practices in general. Firms like Avis, Wal-Mart, and Viacom needed servers and high-speed Internet connections, and the firms that supplied the new technology needed their own new offices, factories, and equipment. But as 2000 ended and 2001 began, firms had begun to catch up to the new technology. The rush ended, and investment began to fall.

Another reason for the drop in investment spending also had roots in the 1990s. During this period, the Internet and other new technologies made the public very optimistic about the future profits of American businesses, and hungry to own shares of stock in almost any company that had anything to do with the Internet. Share prices rose sky high. The optimism and high share prices encouraged entirely new businesses to start up—businesses that used the Internet to sell pet supplies, prescription drugs, and toys or to deliver videos, groceries, or even fresh hot pizzas. Of course, these new businesses needed their own capital equipment, warehouses, and office buildings, driving investment spending even further skyward in the late 1990s.

Unfortunately, in late 2000 and early 2001, reality set in. Competition was preventing many new firms from earning any profit, and many went bankrupt. Optimism shifted to pessimism. Share prices fell, and new business ventures—especially those having to do with the Internet—came to a halt. And so did the investment spending they had been undertaking.

The final reason for the change in planned investment—more accurately, an exacerbation of the change already occurring—was the infamous terrorist attacks on the World Trade Center and the Pentagon on September 11, 2001. The nation was traumatized by these events. What little optimism was left about the future of the U.S. economy turned to uncertainty and fear. Millions of potential airline passengers no longer wanted to fly, forcing airlines to cancel flights as well as orders for new aircraft. Hotel vacancy rates skyrocketed, and investment in new hotels and expansion of existing hotels came to a halt. Similar decisions were made in other industries, and investment spending fell sharply.

One abnormal feature of the recession of 2001 was the behavior of consumption spending. Ordinarily, as income falls in a

What Makes It a Recession? Newspapers and television commentators often state that a recession occurs when real GDP declines for two consecutive quarters. But this is not correct.

Actually, when a U.S. recession begins and ends is determined by a committee within the National Bureau of Economic Research, an entirely private, nonprofit research organization headquartered in Boston. (For the past few decades, the NBER's Business Cycle Dating Committee has been chaired by Robert E. Hall, a coauthor of this textbook.) The committee makes its decisions by looking at a variety of factors, including employment, industrial production, sales, and personal income, all of which are reported monthly. Even though it is true that each of these measures tends to move closely with real GDP, the latter is measured only quarterly, and plays only a supporting role in dating recessions.

DANGEROUS CURVES

recession, consumption declines along with it. This is a movement leftward and downward along the consumption–income line (such as the line in Figure 3 of this chapter). Moreover, decreases in wealth from falling stock prices, and a sharp drop in consumer confidence after September 11, would ordinarily have caused a decrease in *autonomous* consumption spending (see Table 3), *shifting* the consumption–income line downward. Yet consumption spending (not shown) actually *rose* during every quarter of 2001. Since income fell during this time, the only way that consumption spending could rise was through an upward shift of the consumption–income line.

Part of the reason for the upward shift was a 10-year tax cut that went into effect in June of 2001. While this may seem like a successful example of countercyclical fiscal policy, the timing of the 2001 tax cut was actually a stroke of luck. It had been formulated by presidential candidate Bush in 2000, as a long-run growth measure, well before there was even a hint of a recession on the horizon. Policy moves by the Federal Reserve (which we'll discuss in a later chapter) played a role in boosting consumption as well.

The increase in consumption spending made the recession of 2001 more mild than it would otherwise have been. But it was not enough to prevent the recession from occurring. The decline in investment spending, and the multiplier process it initiated, were too powerful.

Summary

In the short run, spending depends on income, and income depends on spending. The short-run macro model was developed to explore this circular connection between spending and income.

Total spending or aggregate expenditure is the sum of four other aggregates: consumption spending by households, investment spending by firms, government purchases of goods and services, and net exports. Consumption spending (C) depends primarily on *disposable income*—what households have left over after paying taxes. The *consumption function* is a linear relationship between disposable income and consumption spending. The slope of the consumption function is the *marginal propensity to consume*, a number between zero and one. It indicates the fraction of each additional dollar of disposable income that is consumed. The *consumption–income line* is the linear relationship between consumption and income. It has the same slope as the consumption function, but a different vertical intercept. For a given level of income, consumption spending can change as a result of changes in taxes, the interest rate, wealth, or expectations about the future. Each of these changes will shift the consumption–income line.

In this chapter, investment spending (I^p), government purchases (G), and net exports (NX) are taken as given values, determined by forces outside our analysis. Aggregate expenditure (AE) is the sum $C + I^p + G + NX$; it varies with income because consumption spending varies with income.

Equilibrium GDP is the level of output at which aggregate expenditure is just equal to GDP (Y). If AE exceeds Y, then firms will experience unplanned decreases in inventories. They will respond by increasing production. If AE is less than Y, firms will find their inventories increasing and will respond by reducing production. Only when $AE = Y$ will there be no unplanned inventory changes and no reason for firms to change production. Graphically, this occurs at the point where the aggregate expenditure line intersects the 45° line.

Changes in spending will change the economy's short-run equilibrium. An increase in investment spending, for example, shifts the aggregate expenditure line upward and triggers the multiplier process. The initial increase in investment spending causes income to increase. That, in turn, leads to an increase in consumption spending, a further increase in income, more consumption spending, and so on. The economy eventually reaches a new equilibrium with a change in GDP that is a multiple of the original increase in spending. Other spending changes have similar multiplied effects on GDP. The size of the *expenditure multiplier* is determined by the marginal propensity to consume.

There are several important differences between the short-run macro model and the long-run classical model. In the long run, the economy operates at potential output; in the short run, GDP can be above or below potential. In the short run (unlike the long run), fiscal policy can have demand-side effects. A change in G or T can change total spending and change equilibrium GDP. At one time, economists believed that *countercyclical fiscal policy* could effectively prevent or smooth out business cycles. But numerous problems—including timing difficulties, irreversibility, and neutralization by the Federal Reserve—have made economists skeptical about countercyclical fiscal policy.

Problem Set   *Answers to even-numbered Questions and Problems can be found on the text Web site at www.thomsonedu.com/economics/hall.*

1.

Y	C	I^p	G	NX
3,000	2,500	300	500	200
4,000	3,250	300	500	200
5,000	4,000	300	500	200
6,000	4,750	300	500	200
7,000	5,500	300	500	200
8,000	6,250	300	500	200

a. What is the marginal propensity to consume implicit in these data?

b. Plot a 45° line, and then use the data to draw an aggregate expenditure line.

c. What is the equilibrium level of real GDP? Illustrate it on your diagram.

d. Suppose that investment spending increased by 250 at each level of income. What would happen to equilibrium GDP?

2. a. Complete the following table when autonomous consumption is $30 billion, the marginal propensity to consume is 0.85, and net taxes are $0.

Real GDP ($ billions)	Autonomous Consumption	MPC × Disposable Income	Consumption = Autonomous Consumption + (MPC × Disposable Income)
$ 0			
$100			
$200			
$300			
$400			
$500			
$600			

   b. Use your answers in part (a) and assume planned investment is $40 billion, government spending is $20 billion, exports are $20 billion, and imports are $35 billion. Complete the table at the bottom of the page.
   c. Plot a 45° line, and then use your data to draw an aggregate expenditure line.
   d. What is the equilibrium level of real GDP? Illustrate it on your diagram.
   e. What will happen if the actual level of real GDP in this economy is $200 billion?
   f. What will happen if the planned investment in this economy falls to $25 billion?

3.

Y	C	Iᴾ	G	NX
7,000	6,100	400	1,000	500
8,000	6,900	400	1,000	500
9,000	7,700	400	1,000	500
10,000	8,500	400	1,000	500
11,000	9,300	400	1,000	500
12,000	10,100	400	1,000	500
13,000	10,900	400	1,000	500

   a. What is the marginal propensity to consume implicit in these data?
   b. What is the numerical value of the expenditure multiplier for this economy?
   c. What is the equilibrium level of real GDP?
   d. Suppose that government purchases (G) decreased from 1,000 to 400 at each level of income. What would happen to equilibrium real GDP?

4. Draw a graph showing a 45° line and an aggregate expenditure line.
   a. Choose a point where real GDP is less than aggregate expenditure and label it GDPᴬ. Explain what will happen to inventories if the economy is operating at this point. What signal does this send to firms? Is GDPᴬ sustainable?
   b. Choose a point where real GDP is greater than aggregate expenditure and label it GDPᴮ. Explain what will happen to inventories if the economy is operating at this point. What signal does this send to firms? Is GDPᴮ sustainable?

5. Use an aggregate expenditure diagram to show the effect of each of the following changes:
   a. An increase in autonomous consumption spending due, say, to optimism on the part of consumers
   b. An increase in U.S. exports
   c. A decrease in taxes
   d. An increase in U.S. imports

   In each case, be sure to label the initial equilibrium and the new equilibrium.

6. What would be the effect on real GDP and total employment of each of the following changes?
   a. As a result of restrictions on imports into the United States, net exports (NX) increase.
   b. The federal government launches a new program to improve highways, bridges, and airports.
   c. Banks are offering such high interest rates that consumers decide to save a larger proportion of their incomes.

7. Assuming the MPC is 0.8, construct a table similar to Table 5 in this chapter.
   a. Show what would happen in the first five rounds following an increase in investment spending from $400 billion to $800 billion.
   b. If investment spending stays at $800 billion, what would be the ultimate effect on real GDP?
   c. How much would consumption spending rise as a result of the rise in investment spending?

8. Suppose that households become thriftier; that is, they now wish to save a larger proportion of their disposable income and spend a smaller proportion.
   a. In the table in problem 1, which column of data would be affected?

Table for 2(b)

Real GDP ($ billions)	Consumption Spending	Planned Investment	Government Spending	Net Exports	Aggregate Expenditure
$ 0					
$100					
$200					
$300					
$400					
$500					
$600					

b. Draw an aggregate expenditure diagram and show how an increase in saving can be measured in that diagram.

c. Use your aggregate expenditure diagram to show how an economy that is initially in short-run equilibrium will respond to an increase in thriftiness.

9. Calculate the change in real GDP that would result in each of the following cases:
    a. Planned investment spending rises by $100 billion, and the MPC is 0.9.
    b. Autonomous consumption spending decreases by $50 billion, and the MPC is 0.7.
    c. Government purchases rise by $40 billion, while at the same time investment spending falls by $10 billion. The MPC is 0.6.

10. Calculate the changes in real GDP that would result in each of the following cases:
    a. Government purchases rise by $7,500, and the MPC is 0.95.
    b. Planned investment spending falls by $300,000 and the MPC is 0.65.
    c. Export spending rises by $60 billion at the same time that import spending rises by $65 billion, and the MPC is 0.75.

11. [Requires Appendix 2] Calculate the change in real GDP that would result in each of the following cases:
    a. Taxes fall by $30 billion, and the MPC is 0.8.
    b. Government spending and taxes *both* rise by $100 billion and the MPC is 0.9.

12. [Requires Appendix 2] Calculate the change in real GDP that would result in each of the following cases:
    a. Taxes rise by $400,000, and the MPC is 0.75.
    b. Taxes and government spending both fall by $500,000, and the MPC is 0.60.

13. Reread the last few paragraphs of the Using the Theory section. Note that the consumption–income line shifted upward during the recession of 2001. But what happened to the aggregate expenditure line? How do we reconcile the shift in AE with the shift in the consumption–income line?

14. "Saving is good for the economy; it increases GDP." Is this statement true, false, or sometimes true and sometimes false? Explain your reasoning. (Hint: You've now worked with two macroeconomic models: the classical/long-run model and the short-run model of this chapter.)

More Challenging

15. [Requires Appendix 1] Suppose that $a = 600$, $b = 0.75$, $T = 400$, $I^p = 600$, $G = 700$, and $NX = 200$. Calculate the equilibrium level of real GDP. Then check that the equilibrium value equals the sum $C + I^p + G + NX$.

16. [Requires Appendix 1] Suppose that $a = 1,000$, $b = 0.65$, $T = 700$, $I^p = 800$, $G = 600$, and $NX = -200$. Calculate the equilibrium level of real GDP. Then check that the equilibrium value equals aggregate expenditures.

17. The short-run equilibrium condition that $Y = C + I^p + G + NX$ can be reinterpreted as follows. First, subtract C from both sides to get $Y - C = I^p + G + NX$. Then note that all income not spent on consumption goods is either taxed or saved, so that $Y - C = S + T$. Now combine the two equations to obtain $S + T = I^p + G + NX$.

Construct a diagram with real GDP measured on the horizontal axis. Draw two lines, one for $S + T$ and the other for $I^p + G + NX$. How would you interpret the point where the two lines cross? What would happen if investment spending increased?

18. Refer to your answer to problem 12. Will your answer to part (b) change if the MPC is 0.80, rather than 0.60? Use your finding to write a general statement about changes in government spending and taxes, and the resulting change in real GDP.

Finding Equilibrium GDP Algebraically

The chapter showed how we can find equilibrium GDP using tables and graphs. This appendix demonstrates an algebraic way of finding the equilibrium GDP.

Our starting point is the relationship between consumption and disposable income given in the chapter. Letting Y_D represent disposable income:

$$C = a + bY_D$$

where a represents autonomous consumption spending and b represents the marginal propensity to consume. Remember that disposable income (Y_D) is the income that the household sector has left after net taxes. Letting T represent net taxes and Y represent total income or GDP, we have

$$Y_D = Y - T.$$

If we now substitute $Y_D = Y - T$ into $C = a + bY_D$, we get an equation showing consumption at each level of income:

$$C = a + b(Y - T).$$

We can rearrange this equation algebraically to read

$$C = (a - bT) + bY.$$

This is the general equation for the consumption–income line. When graphed, the term in parentheses $(a - bT)$ is the vertical intercept, and b is the slope. (Figure 3 shows a specific example of this line in which $a = \$2,000$, $b = 0.6$, and $T = \$2,000$.)

As you've learned, total spending or aggregate expenditure (AE) is the sum of consumption spending (C), investment spending (I^p), government spending (G), and net exports (NX):

$$AE = C + I^p + G + NX.$$

If we substitute for C the expression $C = (a - bT) + bY$, we get

$$AE = a - bT + bY + I^p + G + NX.$$

Now we can use this expression to find the equilibrium GDP. Equilibrium occurs when output (Y) and aggregate expenditure (AE) are the same. That is,

$$Y = AE$$

or, substituting the equation for AE,

$$Y = a - bT + bY + I^p + G + NX.$$

This last equation will hold true only when Y is at its equilibrium value. We can solve for equilibrium Y by first bringing all terms involving Y to the left-hand side:

$$Y - bY = a - bT + I^p + G + NX.$$

Next, factoring out Y, we get

$$Y(1 - b) = a - bT + I^p + G + NX.$$

Finally, dividing both sides of this equation by $(1 - b)$ yields

$$Y = \frac{a - bT + I^p + G + NX}{1 - b}$$

This last equation shows how equilibrium GDP depends on a (autonomous consumption), b (the MPC), T (net taxes), I^p (investment spending), G (government purchases), and NX (net exports). These variables are all determined "outside our model." That is, they are given values that we use to determine equilibrium output, but they are not themselves affected by the level of output. If we use actual numbers for these given variables in the equation, we will find the same equilibrium GDP we would find using a table or a graph.

In the example we used throughout the chapter, the given values (found in Tables 1, 2, and 4) are, in billions of dollars, $a = 2,000$; $b = 0.6$; $T = 2,000$; $I^p = 800$; $G = 1,000$; and $NX = 600$. Plugging these values into the equation for equilibrium GDP, we get

$$Y = \frac{2,000 - (0.6 \times 2,000) + 800 + 1,000 + 600}{1 - 0.6}$$

$$= \frac{3,200}{0.4}$$

$$= 8,000$$

This is the same value we found in Table 4 and Figure 7.

The Special Case of the Tax Multiplier

You learned in this chapter how changes in autonomous consumption, planned investment, and government purchases affect aggregate expenditure and equilibrium GDP. But there is another type of change that can influence equilibrium GDP: a change in taxes. For this type of change, the formula for the multiplier is slightly different from the one presented in the chapter.

Let's suppose that net taxes (T) *decrease* by $1,000 billion. Since disposable income is equal to total income less net taxes, the immediate impact of the tax cut is to *increase* disposable income by $1,000 billion. As a result, consumption spending will increase by $MPC \times$ $1,000 billion. Using the example in the chapter, with an MPC of 0.6, consumption spending would increase by $0.6 \times$ $1,000 billion = $600 billion. *This is the initial rise in spending caused by the tax cut.* Once consumption spending rises, the multiplier works as with any other change in spending: Consumption rises by another $0.6 \times$ $600 billion = $360 billion in the next round, and by another $0.6 \times$ $360 billion = $216 billion after that, and so on.

Now let's compare the full multiplier effect from a $1,000 billion cut in net taxes with the effect from a $1,000 billion increase in spending, such as planned investment spending. Look back at Table 5. There you can see that a $1,000 billion rise in investment spending causes a total increase in GDP of $1,000 billion + $600 billion + $360 billion + $216 billion + $\cdots$ = $2,500 billion. But when taxes are cut by $1,000 billion, the total increase in GDP is $600 billion + $360 billion + $216 billion + ... These two series of numbers are the same except that for the tax cut, the first $1,000 billion is missing. Therefore, the final rise in GDP from the tax cut must be $1,000 billion less than the final rise in GDP from the increase in investment spending. Since the $1,000 billion rise in investment spending raises GDP by $2,500 billion, a $1,000 billion cut in taxes must raise GDP by $2,500 billion $-$ $1,000 billion = $1,500 billion.

Another way to say this is: For each dollar that taxes are cut, equilibrium GDP will increase by $1.50 rather than $2.50; the increase is one dollar less in the case of the tax cut. This observation tells us that the tax multiplier must have a numerical value *1.0 less than* the spending multiplier of the chapter.

Finally, there is one more difference between the spending multiplier of the chapter and the tax multiplier: While the spending multiplier is a positive number (because an increase in spending causes an increase in equilibrium GDP), the tax multiplier is a negative number, since a tax cut (a negative change in taxes) must be multiplied by a *negative* number to give us a *positive* change in GDP. Putting all this together, we conclude that

the tax multiplier is 1.0 less than the spending multiplier, and negative in sign.

Thus, if the MPC is 0.6 (as in the chapter), so that the spending multiplier is 2.5, then the tax multiplier will have a value of $-(2.5 - 1) = -1.5$.

More generally, since the tax multiplier is 1.0 less than the spending multiplier and is also negative, we can write

$$\text{Tax multiplier} = -(\text{Spending multiplier} - 1).$$

Because the expenditure multiplier is $1/(1 - MPC)$, we can substitute to get

$$\text{Tax multiplier} = -\left[\frac{1}{1 - MPC} - 1\right]$$
$$= -\left[\frac{1}{1 - MPC} - \frac{1 - MPC}{1 - MPC}\right]$$
$$= \frac{-MPC}{1 - MPC}.$$

Hence,

> *the general formula for the tax multiplier is*
>
> $$\frac{-\text{MPC}}{(1 - \text{MPC})}.$$

For any change in net taxes, we can use the formula to find the change in net equilibrium GDP as follows:

$$\Delta GDP = \frac{-MPC}{1 - MPC} \times \Delta T.$$

In our example, in which taxes were cut by $1,000 billion, we have $\Delta T = -\$1{,}000$ billion and $MPC = 0.6$. Plugging these values into the formula, we obtain

$$\Delta GDP = \left[\frac{-0.6}{1 - 0.6} \right] \times -\$1{,}000 \text{ billion}$$

$$= \$1{,}500 \text{ billion}.$$

The Banking System and the Money Supply

Everyone knows that money doesn't grow on trees. But where does it actually come from? You might think that the answer is simple: The government just prints it. Right?

Sort of. It is true that much of our money supply is, indeed, paper currency, provided by our national monetary authority. But most of our money is *not* paper currency at all. Moreover, the monetary authority in the United States—the Federal Reserve System—is technically not a part of the executive, legislative, or judicial branch of government. Rather, it is a quasi-independent agency that operates *alongside* the government.

In future chapters, we'll make our short-run macro model more realistic by bringing in money and its effects on the economy. This will deepen your understanding of economic fluctuations, and help you understand our policy choices in dealing with them. But in this chapter, we focus on money itself, and the institutions that help create it. We will begin, in the next section, by taking a look at the purpose and functions of a nation's monetary system.

THE MONETARY SYSTEM

A monetary system establishes two different types of standardization in the economy. First, it establishes a **unit of value**—a common unit for measuring how much something is worth. A standard unit of value permits us to compare the costs of different goods and services and to communicate these costs when we trade.

Unit of value A common unit for measuring how much something is worth.

The dollar is the unit of value in the United States. If a pair of running shoes costs $120, while a round-trip airline ticket from Phoenix to Minneapolis costs $360, we know immediately that the ticket has the same value in the marketplace as three pairs of running shoes.

The second type of standardization concerns the **means of payment**, the things we can use as payment when we buy goods and services. In the United States, the means of payment include dollar bills, personal checks, money orders, and credit cards like Visa and American Express.

Means of payment Anything acceptable as payment for goods and services.

These two functions of a monetary system—establishing a unit of value and a standard means of payment—are closely related, but they are not the same thing. The unit-of-value function refers to the way we *think* about and record transactions; the means-of-payment function refers to how payment is actually made. The unit of value works in the same way as units of weight, volume, distance, and time.

In fact, the same sentence in Article I of the U.S. Constitution gives Congress the power to create a unit of value along with units of weights and measures. All of these units help us determine clearly and precisely what is being traded for what. Think about buying gas in the United States; you exchange dollars for gallons. The transaction will go smoothly and quickly only if there is clarity about both the unit of fluid volume (gallons) *and* the unit of purchasing power (dollars).

The means of payment can be different from the unit of value. For example, in some countries where local currency prices change very rapidly, it is common to use the U.S. dollar as the unit of value—to specify prices in dollars—while the local currency remains the means of payment. Even in the United States, when you use a check to buy something, the unit of value is the dollar but the means of payment is a piece of paper with your signature on it.

In the United States, the dollar is the centerpiece of our monetary system. It is the unit of value in every economic transaction, and dollar bills are very often the means of payment as well. How did the dollar come to play such an important role in the economy?

A Brief History of the Dollar

Prior to 1790, each colony had its own currency. It was named the "pound" in every colony, but it had a different purchasing power in each of them. In 1790, soon after the Constitution went into effect, Congress created a new unit of value called the dollar. Historical documents show that merchants and businesses switched immediately to the new dollar, thereby ending the chaos of the colonial monetary systems. Prices began to be quoted in dollars, and accounts were kept in dollars. The dollar rapidly became the standard unit of value.

But the primary means of payment in the United States until the Civil War was paper currency issued by private banks. Just as the government defined the length of the yard but did not sell yardsticks, the government defined the unit of value but let private organizations provide the means of payment.

During the Civil War, however, the government issued the first federal paper currency, the greenback. It functioned as both the unit of value and the major means of payment until 1879. Then the government got out of the business of money creation for a few decades. During that time, currency was once again issued by private banks. But in 1913, a new institution called the **Federal Reserve System** was created to be the national monetary authority in the United States. The Federal Reserve was charged with creating and regulating the nation's supply of money, and it continues to do so today.

Federal Reserve System The monetary authority of the United States, charged with creating and regulating the nation's supply of money.

Why Paper Currency Is Accepted as a Means of Payment

You may wonder why people are willing to accept paper dollars—or the promise of paper dollars—as a means of payment. Why should a farmer give up a chicken, or a manufacturer give up a new car, just to receive a bunch of green rectangles with words and numbers printed on them?

In fact, paper currency is a relatively recent development in the history of the means of payment. The earliest means of payment were precious metals and other valuable commodities such as furs or jewels. These were called *commodity money* because they had important uses other than as a means of payment. The nonmoney use is what gave commodity money its ultimate value. For example, people would accept furs as payment because furs could be used to keep warm.

Similarly, gold and silver had a variety of uses in industry, as religious artifacts, and for ornamentation.

Precious metals were an especially popular form of commodity money. Eventually, to make it easier to identify the value of precious metals, they were minted into coins whose weight was declared on their faces. Because gold and silver coins could be melted down into pure metal and used in other ways, they were still commodity money.

Commodity money eventually gave way to paper currency. Initially, paper currency was just a certificate representing a certain amount of gold or silver held by a bank. At any time, the holder of a certificate could go to the bank that issued it and trade the certificate for the stated amount of gold or silver. People were willing to accept paper money as a means of payment for two reasons. First, the currency could be exchanged for a valuable commodity like gold or silver. Second, the issuer—either a government or a bank—could print new money only when it acquired additional gold or silver. This put strict limits on money printing, so people had faith that their paper money would retain its value in the marketplace.

But today, paper currency is no longer backed by gold or any other physical commodity. If you have a dollar handy, put this book down and take a close look at the bill. You will not find on it any promise that you can trade your dollar for gold, silver, furs, or anything else. Yet we all accept it as a means of payment. Why?

A clue is provided by the statement in the upper left-hand corner of every bill: *This note is legal tender for all debts, public and private.* The statement affirms that the piece of paper in your hands will be accepted as a means of payment (you can "tender" it to settle any "debt, public or private") by any American because the government says so. This type of currency is called **fiat money**. *Fiat*, in Latin, means "let there be," and fiat money serves as a means of payment by government declaration.

> **Fiat money** Something that serves as a means of payment by government declaration.

The government need not worry about enforcing this declaration. The real force behind the dollar—and the reason that we are all willing to accept these green pieces of paper as payment—is its long-standing acceptability by *others*. As long as you have confidence that you can use your dollars to buy goods and services, you won't mind giving up goods and services for dollars. And because everyone else feels the same way, the circle of acceptability is completed. But while the government can declare that paper currency is to be accepted as a means of payment, it cannot declare the terms. Whether a gallon of gas will cost you 1 dollar, 4 dollars, or 10 dollars is up to the marketplace.

WHAT COUNTS AS MONEY

Consider what *is* and what is *not* thought to be money in countries around the world. For example, paper currency, travelers checks, and funds held in checking accounts are all considered to be money in nations with well-established banking systems. That makes sense, because all of these can be used as means of payment. Yet credit cards are *not* considered money, even though you can use them to buy things. Why is this?

A more formal definition of money helps to answer questions like this.

> *Money is an asset that is widely accepted as a means of payment in the economy.*

> **Money** An asset widely accepted as a means of payment.

Let's consider this definition more closely. First, only *assets*—things of value that people own—can be considered as money. Paper currency, travelers checks, and funds held in checking accounts are all examples of assets that people own, and these are all considered money in the United States. But *the right to borrow* is not an asset, so is not considered money. This is why the credit limit on your credit card, or your ability to go into a bank and borrow funds, is not considered *money* in the economy.

Second, only things that are *widely acceptable* as a means of payment are regarded as money. Coins and paper currency (usually called *cash*), travelers checks, and personal checks can all be used to buy things or pay bills. Other assets—such as stocks and bonds or even gold bars—can*not* generally be used to pay for goods and services, and so they fail the acceptability test.

MEASURING THE MONEY SUPPLY

As you will learn in the next chapter, the amount of money in circulation can affect the macroeconomy. This is why governments around the world like to know how much money is available to their citizens—the total **money supply**.

Money supply The total amount of money held by the public.

In practice, measuring the money supply is not as straightforward as it might seem, and brings up some conceptual problems. For example, consider funds you might have in a savings account. While you can't use those funds to buy things directly, you can easily *move* the funds *into* your checking account, converting them to money. You might therefore regard your savings account as part of the means of payment that are easily available to you. Should they be included as part of the money supply?

Governments recognize this and other similar sticky questions, and have decided that the best way to deal with them is to have *different* measures of the money supply—in effect, alternative ways of defining what is and what is not money. Each measure includes a selection of *assets* that are *widely acceptable as a means of payment* and, as an additional criterion, *relatively liquid*.

Liquidity The property of being easily converted into cash.

> An asset is considered **liquid** if it can be converted to cash quickly and at little cost. An illiquid asset, by contrast, can be converted to cash only after a delay, or at considerable cost.

Checking account balances are highly liquid because you can convert them to cash at the ATM or by cashing a check. Travelers checks are also highly liquid. But stocks and bonds are *not* as liquid as checking accounts or travelers checks. Stock- and bondholders must go to some trouble and pay brokers' fees to convert these assets into cash.

But notice the phrase "*relatively* liquid." This does not sound like a hard-and-fast rule for measuring the money supply, and indeed it is not. This is why there are different measures of the money supply: Each interprets the phrase "relatively liquid" in a different way. To understand this better, let's look at the different kinds of liquid assets that people can hold.

ASSETS AND THEIR LIQUIDITY

Figure 1 lists a spectrum of assets, ranked according to their liquidity, along with the amounts of each asset in the U.S. public's hands on June 26, 2006. The most

Monetary Assets and Their Liquidity (June 26, 2006) FIGURE 1

Savings-Type
Accounts
($3,558 billion)

Cash in the
Hands of the
Public
($740 billion)

Demand Deposits
($350 billion)
+
Other Checkable
Deposits
($316 billion)
+
Travelers Checks
($7 billion)

Retail Money
Market Mutual
Funds
($763 billion)

Small Time
Deposits
($1,068 billion)

More
Liquid

Less
Liquid

M1

M2

Assets vary according to their liquidity—the ease with which they can be converted into cash.
Assets toward the left side of this figure are more liquid than those toward the right side.

Source: http://www.federalreserve.gov, Money Stock Measures. H.6, Tables 5 and 6.

liquid asset of all is **cash in the hands of the public.** It takes no time and zero expense to convert this asset into cash, since it's *already* cash. In June 2006, the public—including residents of other countries—held about $740 billion in U.S. cash.

Next in line are three asset categories of about equal liquidity. **Demand deposits** are the checking accounts held by households and business firms at commercial banks, including huge ones like the Bank of America or Citibank, and smaller ones like Simmons National Bank in Arkansas. These checking accounts are called "demand" deposits because when you write a check to someone, that person can go into a bank and, on demand, be paid in cash. This is one reason that demand deposits are considered very liquid: The person who has your check can convert it

Cash in the hands of the public
Currency and coins held outside of banks.

Demand deposits Checking accounts that do not pay interest.

into cash quickly and easily. Another reason is that you can withdraw cash from your own checking account very easily—24 hours a day with an ATM card, or during banking hours if you want to speak to a teller. As you can see in the figure, the U.S. public held $350 billion in demand deposits in mid-2006.

Other checkable deposits is a catchall category for several types of checking accounts that work very much like demand deposits. This includes *automatic transfers from savings accounts*, which are interest-paying savings accounts that automatically transfer funds into checking accounts when needed. On June 26, 2006, the U.S. public held $316 billion of these types of checkable deposits.

Travelers checks are specially printed checks that you can buy from banks or other private companies, like American Express. Travelers checks can be easily spent at almost any hotel or store. You can often cash them at a bank. You need only show an I.D. and countersign the check. In mid-2006, the public held about $7 billion in travelers checks.

Savings-type accounts at banks and other financial institutions (such as *savings and loan* institutions) amounted to $3,558 billion in mid-2006. These are less liquid than checking-type accounts, since they do not allow you to write checks. While it is easy to transfer funds from your savings account to your checking account, you must make the transfer yourself.

Next on the list are deposits in *retail money market mutual funds (MMMFs)*, which use customer deposits to buy a variety of financial assets. Depositors can withdraw their money by writing checks. Money market funds held in special retirement accounts—which cannot be accessed before age $59\frac{1}{2}$ without a penalty—are excluded from this measure. In mid-2006, the general public held about $763 billion in such MMMFs.

Time deposits (sometimes called *certificates of deposit*, or *CDs*) require you to keep your money in the bank for a specified period of time (usually six months or longer), and impose an interest penalty if you withdraw early. A *small time deposit* is any amount less than $100,000. As with money market funds, time deposits in special retirement accounts are excluded from the measure. In mid-June 2006, the public held $1,068 billion in these accounts.

Now let's see how these assets have been used to define "money" in different ways.

M1 and M2

M1 A standard measure of the money supply, including cash in the hands of the public, checking account deposits, and travelers checks.

The standard measure of the money stock is called **M1**. It is the sum of the first four assets in our list: cash in the hands of the public, demand deposits, other checkable deposits, and travelers checks. These are also the four most liquid assets in our list.

$$M1 = \text{Cash in the hands of the public} + \text{Demand deposits} +$$
$$\text{Other checkable deposits} + \text{Travelers checks}.$$

On June 26, 2006, this amounted to

$$M1 = \$740 \text{ billion} + \$350 \text{ billion} + \$316$$
$$+ \$7 \text{ billion} = \$1,413 \text{ billion}.$$

When economists or government officials speak about "the money supply," they usually mean M1.

But what about the assets left out of M1? While savings accounts are not as liquid as any of the components of M1, for most of us there is hardly a difference.

All it takes is an ATM card and, presto, funds in your savings account become cash. Money market funds held by households and businesses are fairly liquid, even though there are sometimes restrictions or special risks involved in converting them into cash. And even time deposits—if they are not too large—can be cashed in early with only a small interest penalty. When you think of how much "means of payment" you have, you are very likely to include the amounts you have in these types of accounts. This is why another common measure of the money supply, **M2**, adds these assets to M1:

M2 M1 plus savings account balances, retail money market mutual fund balances, and small time deposits.

$$M2 = M1 + \text{Savings-type accounts} + \text{Retail MMMF balances} +$$
$$\text{Small-denomination time deposits.}$$

Using the numbers for June 26, 2006, in the United States:

$$M2 = \$1{,}413 \text{ billion} + \$3{,}558 \text{ billion} + \$763 \text{ billion} + \$1{,}068 \text{ billion}$$
$$= \$6{,}802 \text{ billion.}$$

There have been other official measures of the money supply besides M1 and M2 that include assets that are less liquid than those in M2. But M1 and M2 have been the most popular, and most commonly watched, definitions.

It is important to understand that the M1 and M2 money stock measures exclude many things that people use regularly as a means of payment. Although M1 and M2 give us important information about the activities of the Fed and of banks, they do not measure all the different ways that people hold their wealth or pay for things. Credit cards, for example, are not included in any of the official measures of the money supply (they are not assets). But for most of us, unused credit *is* a means of payment, which we lump together with our cash and our checking accounts. As credit cards were issued to more and more Americans over the last several decades, the available means of payment increased considerably, much more than the money supply (as measured by M1 and M2) increased.

Cash in Private Banks or the Fed In our definitions of money—whether M1, M2, or some other measure—we include cash (coin and paper currency) only if it is *in the hands of the public*. The italicized words are important. Some of the nation's cash is stored in bank vaults and is released only when the public withdraws cash from their accounts. Other cash is stored in the Federal Reserve or U.S. Treasury for future release. But until this cash is released from bank vaults, the Fed, or the Treasury, it is not part of the money supply. Only the cash possessed by households, businesses, or government agencies (other than the Fed or Treasury) is considered part of the money supply.

DANGEROUS CURVES

Fortunately, the details and complexities of measuring money are not important for a basic understanding of the monetary system and monetary policy. For the rest of our discussion, we will make a simplifying assumption:

> *We will assume the money supply consists of just two components: cash in the hands of the public and checkable deposits, which we'll call demand deposits.*
>
> *Money supply = Cash in the hands of the public + Demand deposits.*

As you will see later, our definition of the money supply corresponds closely to the liquid assets that our national monetary authority—the Federal Reserve—can control. While there is not much that the Federal Reserve can do directly about the amount of funds in savings accounts, MMMFs, or time deposits, or about the ability to borrow on credit cards, it can tightly control the sum of cash in the hands of the public and demand deposits.

We will spend the rest of this chapter analyzing how money is created and what makes the money supply change. Our first step is to introduce a key player in the creation of money: the banking system.

THE BANKING SYSTEM

Think about the last time you used the services of a bank. Perhaps you deposited a paycheck in the bank's ATM, or withdrew cash to take care of your shopping needs for the week. We make these kinds of transactions dozens of times every year without ever thinking about what a bank really is, or how our own actions at the bank—and the actions of millions of other bank customers—might contribute to a change in the money supply.

FINANCIAL INTERMEDIARIES IN GENERAL

Financial intermediary A business firm that specializes in brokering between savers and borrowers.

Let's begin at the beginning: What are banks? They are important examples of **financial intermediaries**: business firms that specialize in assembling loanable funds from households and firms whose revenues exceed their expenditures, and channeling those funds to households and firms (and sometimes the government) whose expenditures exceed revenues. Financial intermediaries make the economy work much more efficiently than would be possible without them.

To understand this more clearly, imagine that Boeing, the U.S. aircraft maker, wants to borrow a billion dollars for 3 years. If there were no financial intermediaries, Boeing would have to make individual arrangements to borrow small amounts of money from thousands—perhaps millions—of households, each of which wants to lend money for, say, 3 months at a time. Every 3 months, Boeing would have to renegotiate the loans, and it would find borrowing money in this way to be quite cumbersome. Lenders, too, would find this arrangement troublesome. All of their funds would be lent to one firm. If that firm encountered difficulties, the funds might not be returned at the end of 3 months.

An intermediary helps to solve these problems by combining a large number of small savers' funds into custom-designed packages and then lending them to larger borrowers. The intermediary can do this because it can predict—from experience—the pattern of inflows of funds. While some deposited funds may be withdrawn, the overall total available for lending tends to be quite stable. The intermediary can also reduce the risk to depositors by spreading its loans among a number of different borrowers. If one borrower fails to repay its loan, that will have only a small effect on the intermediary and its depositors.

Of course, intermediaries must earn a profit for providing brokering services. They do so by charging a higher interest rate on the funds they lend than the rate they pay to depositors. But they are so efficient at brokering that both lenders and borrowers benefit. Lenders earn higher interest rates, with lower risk and greater liquidity, than if they had to deal directly with the ultimate users of funds. And borrowers end up paying lower interest rates on loans that are specially designed for their specific purposes.

The United States boasts a wide variety of financial intermediaries, including commercial banks, savings and loan associations, mutual savings banks, credit unions, insurance companies, and some government agencies. Some of these inter-mediaries—called *depository institutions*—accept deposits from the general public and lend the deposits to borrowers. *Commercial banks* are the largest group of depository institutions. They obtain funds mainly by accepting checkable deposits, savings deposits, and time deposits and use the funds to make business, mortgage, and consumer loans. Since commercial banks will play a central role in the rest of this chapter, let's take a closer look at how they operate.

COMMERCIAL BANKS

A commercial bank (or just "bank" for short) is a private corporation, owned by its stockholders, that provides services to the public. For our purposes, the most impor-tant service is to provide checking accounts, which enable the bank's customers to pay bills and make purchases without holding large amounts of cash that could be lost or stolen. Checks are one of the most important means of payment in the economy. Every year, U.S. households and businesses write trillions of dollars' worth of checks to pay their bills, and many wage and salary earners have their pay deposited direct-ly into their checking accounts. And as you saw in Figure 1, the public holds about as much money in the form of demand deposits and other checking-type accounts as it holds in cash.

Banks provide checking account services in order to earn a profit. Where does a bank's profit come from? Mostly from lending out the funds that people deposit and charging interest on the loans, but also by charging for some services directly, such as check-printing fees or that annoying dollar or so sometimes charged for using an ATM.

A BANK'S BALANCE SHEET

We can understand more clearly how a bank works by looking at its *balance sheet*, a tool used by accountants. A **balance sheet** is a two-column list that provides infor-mation about the financial condition of a bank at a particular point in time. In one column, the bank's *assets* are listed—everything of value that it *owns*. On the other side, the bank's *liabilities* are listed—the amounts that the bank *owes*.

Table 1 shows a simplified version of a commercial bank's balance sheet.

Balance sheet A financial state-ment showing assets, liabilities, and net worth at a point in time.

TABLE	1
A Typical Commercial Bank's Balance Sheet	

Assets		Liabilities and Net Worth	
Property and buildings	$ 5 million	Demand deposit liabilities	$100 million
Government and corporate bonds	$ 25 million	Net worth	$ 5 million
Loans	$ 65 million		
Cash in vault	$ 2 million		
In accounts with the Federal Reserve	$ 8 million		
Total Assets	$105 million	**Total Liabilities plus Net Worth**	$105 million

Bond A promise to pay back borrowed funds, issued by a corporation or government agency.

Loan An agreement to pay back borrowed funds, signed by a household or noncorporate business.

Why does the bank have these assets and liabilities? Let's start with the assets side. The first item, $5 million, is the value of the bank's real estate—the buildings and the land underneath them. This is the easiest to explain, because a bank must have one or more branch offices in order to do business with the public.

Next comes $25 million in *bonds*, and $65 million in *loans*. A **bond** is a promise to pay funds to the holder of the bond, issued by a corporation or a government agency when it borrows money.[1] A bond promises to pay back the loan either gradually (e.g., each month), or all at once at some future date. **Loans** are promises, signed by households or noncorporate businesses, to pay back funds. Examples are auto loans, student loans, small-business loans, and home mortgages (where the funds lent out are used to buy a home). Both bonds and loans generate interest income for the bank.

Next come two categories that might seem curious: $2 million in "vault cash," and $8 million in "accounts with the Federal Reserve." Vault cash, just like it sounds, is the coin and currency that the bank has stored in its vault. In addition, banks maintain their own accounts with the Federal Reserve, and they add to and subtract from these accounts when they make transactions with other banks. Neither vault cash nor accounts with the Federal Reserve pay interest. Why, then, does the bank hold them? After all, a profit-seeking bank should want to hold as much of its assets as possible in interest-earning forms: bonds and loans.

There are two explanations for vault cash and accounts with the Federal Reserve. First, on any given day, some of the bank's customers might want to withdraw more cash than other customers are depositing. The bank must always be prepared to honor its obligations for withdrawals, so it must have some cash on hand to meet these requirements. This explains why it holds vault cash.

Reserves Vault cash plus balances held at the Fed.

Required reserves The minimum amount of reserves a bank must hold, depending on the amount of its deposit liabilities.

Required reserve ratio The minimum fraction of checking account balances that banks must hold as reserves.

Second, banks are required by law to hold **reserves,** which are defined as *the sum of cash in the vault and accounts with the Federal Reserve*. The amount of reserves a bank must hold is called **required reserves.** The more funds its customers hold in their checking accounts, the greater the amount of required reserves. The **required reserve ratio,** set by the Federal Reserve, tells banks the fraction of their checking accounts that they must hold as required reserves.

For example, the bank in Table 1 has $100 million in demand deposits. If the required reserve ratio is 0.1, this bank's required reserves are $0.1 \times \$100$ million = $10 million in reserves. The bank must hold *at least* this amount of its assets as reserves. Since our bank has $2 million in vault cash and $8 million in its reserve account with the Federal Reserve, it has a total of $10 million in reserves, the minimum required amount.

Now skip to the right side of the balance sheet. This bank's only liability is its demand deposits. Why are demand deposits a *liability*? Because the bank's customers have the right to withdraw funds from their checking accounts. Until they do, the bank *owes* them these funds.

Finally, the last entry. When we total up both sides of the bank's balance sheet, we find that it has $105 million in assets and only $100 million in liabilities. If the bank were to go out of business—selling all of its assets and using the proceeds to pay off all of its liabilities (its demand deposits)—it would have $5 million left over.

---

[1] We are using the term "bond" loosely to refer to *all* such promises issued by corporations and government agencies. Technically, a bond must be a long-term obligation to pay back money, 10 years or more from the time the money is first borrowed. Shorter-term obligations are called *notes* (between 1 and 10 years) or *bills* (1 year or less).

Who would get this $5 million? The bank's owners: its stockholders. The $5 million is called the bank's **net worth.** More generally,

$$\text{Net worth} = \text{Total assets} - \text{Total liabilities}.$$

We include net worth on the liabilities side of the balance sheet because it is, in a sense, what the bank would owe to its owners if it went out of business. Notice that, because of the way net worth is defined, both sides of a balance sheet must always have the same total: *A balance sheet always balances.*

Private banks are just one of the players that help determine the money supply. Now we turn our attention to the other key player—the Federal Reserve System.

Net worth The difference between assets and liabilities.

THE FEDERAL RESERVE SYSTEM

Every large nation controls its money supply with a **central bank**—the nation's principal monetary authority and the institution responsible for controlling its money supply. Most of the developed countries established their central banks long ago. For example, England's central bank—the Bank of England—was created in 1694. France was one of the latest in Europe, waiting until 1800 to establish the Banque de France. But the United States was even later. Although we experimented with central banks at various times in our history, we did not get serious about a central bank until 1913, when Congress established the *Federal Reserve System.*

Why did it take the United States so long to create a central bank? Part of the reason is the suspicion of central authority that has always been part of U.S. politics and

Central bank A nation's principal monetary authority responsible for controlling the money supply.

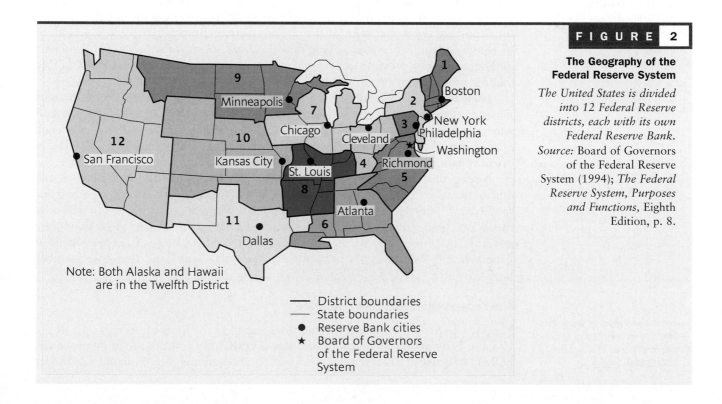

FIGURE 2

The Geography of the Federal Reserve System

The United States is divided into 12 Federal Reserve districts, each with its own Federal Reserve Bank.

Source: Board of Governors of the Federal Reserve System (1994); *The Federal Reserve System, Purposes and Functions,* Eighth Edition, p. 8.

Note: Both Alaska and Hawaii are in the Twelfth District

— District boundaries
— State boundaries
● Reserve Bank cities
★ Board of Governors of the Federal Reserve System

The Federal Open Market Committee meets in this room, inside the Fed's headquarters in Washington, D.C. The meetings are highly secretive. No one from the media, and no one representing Congress or the president, is permitted in the room during the meetings.

culture. Another reason is the large size and extreme diversity of our country, and the fear that a powerful central bank might be dominated by the interests of one region to the detriment of others. These special American characteristics help explain why our own central bank is different in form from its European counterparts.

One major difference is indicated in the very name of the institution: the Federal Reserve System. It does not have the word *central* or *bank* anywhere in its title, making it less suggestive of centralized power.

Another difference is the way the system is organized. Instead of a single central bank, the United States is divided into 12 Federal Reserve districts, each one served by its own Federal Reserve Bank. The 12 districts and the Federal Reserve Banks that serve them are shown in Figure 2. For example, the Federal Reserve Bank of Dallas serves a district consisting of Texas and parts of New Mexico and Louisiana, while the Federal Reserve Bank of Chicago serves a district including Iowa and parts of Illinois, Indiana, Wisconsin, and Michigan.

Another interesting feature of the Federal Reserve System is its peculiar status within the government. Strictly speaking, it is not even a *part* of any branch of government. But the *Fed* (as the system is commonly called) was created by Congress, and could be eliminated by Congress if it so desired. Second, both the president and Congress exert some influence on the Fed through their appointments of key officials in the system.

THE STRUCTURE OF THE FED

Figure 3 shows the organizational structure of the Federal Reserve System. Near the top is the Board of Governors, consisting of seven members who are appointed by the president and confirmed by the Senate for a 14-year term. The most powerful person at the Fed is the *chairman* of the Board of Governors—one of the seven governors who is appointed by the president, with Senate approval, to a 4-year term as chair. In order to keep any president or Congress from having too much influence over the Fed, the 4-year term of the chair is *not* coterminous with the 4-year term of the president. As a result, every newly elected president inherits the Fed chair appointed by the previous president, and may have to wait several years before making an appointment of his own.

Each of the 12 Federal Reserve Banks is supervised by nine directors, three of whom are appointed by the Board of Governors. The other six are elected by private commercial banks, the official stockholders of the system. The directors of each Federal Reserve Bank choose a president of that bank, who manages its day-to-day operations.

Notice that Figure 3 refers to "member banks." Only about a third of the approximately 7,500 commercial banks in the United States are members of the Federal Reserve System. But they include all *national banks* (those chartered by the federal government) and about a thousand *state banks* (chartered by their state governments). All of the largest banks in the United States (e.g., Citibank, Bank of America, and Wells Fargo) are nationally chartered banks and therefore member banks as well.

The Federal Open Market Committee

Federal Open Market Committee (FOMC) A committee of Federal Reserve officials that establishes U.S. monetary policy.

Finally, we come to what most economists regard as the most important part of the Fed, the **Federal Open Market Committee (FOMC)**. As you can see in Figure 3, the FOMC consists of all seven governors of the Fed, along with 5 of the 12 district

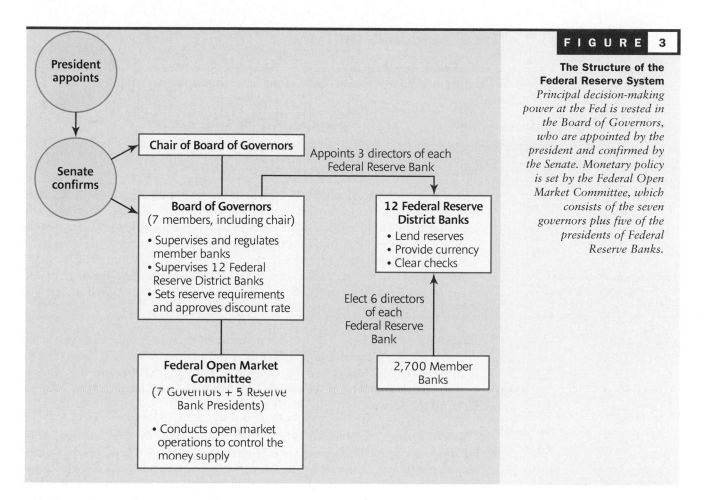

FIGURE 3

The Structure of the Federal Reserve System

Principal decision-making power at the Fed is vested in the Board of Governors, who are appointed by the president and confirmed by the Senate. Monetary policy is set by the Federal Open Market Committee, which consists of the seven governors plus five of the presidents of Federal Reserve Banks.

bank presidents.[2] The committee meets about eight times a year to discuss current trends in inflation, unemployment, output, interest rates, and international exchange rates. After determining the current state of the economy, the FOMC sets the general course for the nation's money supply.

The word "open" in the FOMC's name is ironic, since the committee's deliberations are private. Summaries of its meetings are published only after a delay of a month or more. In some cases, the committee will release a brief public statement about its decisions on the day they are made. But not even the president of the United States knows the details behind the decisions, or what the FOMC actually discussed at its meeting, until the summary of the meeting is finally released. The reason for the word "open" is that the committee exerts control over the nation's money supply by buying and selling bonds in the public ("open") bond market. Later, we will discuss how and why the FOMC does this.

---

[2] Although all Reserve Bank presidents attend FOMC meetings, only 5 of the 12 presidents can vote on FOMC decisions. The president of the Federal Reserve Bank of New York has a permanent vote because New York is such an important financial center. But the remaining four votes rotate among the other district presidents.

THE FUNCTIONS OF THE FED

The Federal Reserve, as the overseer of the nation's monetary system, has a variety of important responsibilities. Some of the most important are listed here.

Supervising and Regulating Banks. We've already seen that the Fed sets and enforces reserve requirements, which all banks—not just Fed members—must obey. The Fed also sets standards for establishing new banks, determines what sorts of loans and investments banks are allowed to make, and closely monitors many banks' financial activities.

Acting as a "Bank for Banks." Commercial banks use the Fed in much the same way that ordinary citizens use commercial banks. For example, we've already seen that banks hold most of their reserves in reserve accounts with the Fed. In addition, banks can borrow from the Fed, just as we can borrow from our local bank. The Fed charges a special interest rate, called the discount rate, on loans that it makes to member banks. In times of financial crisis, the Fed is prepared to act as lender of last resort, to make sure that banks have enough reserves to meet their obligations to depositors.

Discount rate The interest rate the Fed charges on loans to banks.

Issuing Paper Currency. The Fed doesn't actually *print* currency; that is done by the government's Bureau of Engraving and Printing. But once printed, it is shipped to the Fed (under *very* heavy guard). The Fed, in turn, puts this currency into circulation. This is why every U.S. bill carries the label *Federal Reserve Note* on the top.

Check Clearing. Suppose you write a check for $1,000 to pay your rent. Your building's owner will deposit the check into *his* checking account, which is probably at a different bank than yours. Somehow, your rent payment must be transferred from your bank account to your landlord's account at the other bank, a process called *check clearing*. In some cases, the services are provided by private clearinghouses. But in many other cases—especially for clearing out-of-town checks—the Federal Reserve System performs the service by transferring funds from one bank's reserve account to another's.

Controlling the Money Supply The Fed, as the nation's monetary authority, is responsible for controlling the money supply. Since this function is so important in macroeconomics, we explore it in detail in the next section.

THE FED AND THE MONEY SUPPLY

Suppose the Fed wants to change the nation's money supply. (*Why* would the Fed want to do this? The answer will have to wait until the next chapter.) There are many ways this could be done. To increase the money supply, the Fed could print up currency and give it to Fed officials, letting them spend it as they wish. Or it could hold a lottery and give all of the newly printed money to the winner. To decrease the money supply, the Fed could require that all citizens turn over a portion of their cash to Fed officials who would then feed it into paper shredders.

These and other methods would certainly work, but they hardly seem fair or orderly. In practice, the Fed uses a more organized, less haphazard method to change the money supply: *open market operations*.

> *When the Fed wishes to increase or decrease the money supply, it buys or sells government bonds to bond dealers, banks, or other financial institutions. These actions are called **open market operations.***

Open market operations
Purchases or sales of bonds by the Federal Reserve System.

We'll make two special assumptions to keep our analysis of open market operations simple for now:

1. Households and businesses are satisfied holding the amount of cash they are currently holding. Any additional funds they might acquire are deposited in their checking accounts. Any decrease in their funds comes from their checking accounts.
2. Banks never hold reserves in excess of those legally required by law.

Later, we'll discuss what happens when these simplifying assumptions do not hold. We'll also assume that the required reserve ratio is 0.1, so that each time deposits rise by $1,000 at a bank, its required reserves rise by $100.

HOW THE FED INCREASES THE MONEY SUPPLY

To increase the money supply, the Fed will *buy* government bonds. This is called an *open market purchase.* Suppose the Fed buys a government bond worth $1,000 from Lehman Brothers, a bond dealer that has a checking account at First National Bank.[3] The Fed will pay Lehman Brothers with a $1,000 check, which the firm will deposit into its account at First National. First National, in turn, will send the check to the Fed, which will credit First National's reserve account by $1,000.

These actions will change First National's balance sheet as follows:

CHANGES IN FIRST NATIONAL BANK'S BALANCE SHEET

Action	Changes in Assets	Changes in Liabilities
Fed buys $1,000 bond from Lehman Brothers, which deposits $1,000 check from Fed into its checking account.	+$1,000 in reserves	+$1,000 in demand deposits

Notice that here we show only *changes* in First National's balance sheet. Other balance sheet items—such as property and buildings, loans, government bonds, or net worth—are not immediately affected by the open market purchase, so they are not listed here. As you can see, First National gains an asset—reserves—so we enter "+$1,000 in reserves" on the left side of the table. But there are also additional liabilities: the $1,000 that is now in Lehman Brothers' checking account and which First National owes to that firm. The additional liabilities are represented by the entry "+$1,000 in demand deposits" on the right side. Since First National's balance sheet was in balance before Lehman Brothers' deposit, and since assets and liabilities both grew by the same amount ($1,000), we know that the balance sheet is still in balance. Total assets are again equal to total liabilities plus net worth.

Before we go on, let's take note of two important things that have happened. First, the Fed, by conducting an open market purchase, has injected *reserves* into the banking system. So far, these reserves are being held by First National in its reserve account with the Fed.

[3] We'll limit our analysis to commercial banks, which hold demand deposits, although our story would be similar if other types of depository institutions were involved.

The second thing to notice is something that is easy to miss: *The money supply has increased.* How do we know? Because demand deposits are part of the money supply, and they have increased by $1,000. As you are about to see, even more demand deposits will be created before our story ends.

To see what will happen next, let's take the point of view of First National Bank's manager. He might reason as follows: "My demand deposits have just increased by $1,000. Since the required reserve ratio is 0.1, I must now hold $0.1 \times \$1,000 = \$100$ in additional reserves. But my *actual* reserves have gone up by more than $100; in fact, they have gone up by $1,000. Therefore, I have **excess reserves**—reserves above those I'm legally required to hold—equal to $1,000 −$100, or $900. Since these excess reserves are earning no interest, I should lend them out." Thus, we can expect First National, in its search for profit, to lend out $900 at the going rate of interest.

Excess reserves Reserves in excess of required reserves.

How will First National actually make the loan? It could lend out $900 in *cash* from its vault. It would be more typical, however, for the bank to issue a $900 *check* to the borrower. When the borrower deposits the $900 check into his own bank account (at some other bank), the Federal Reserve—which keeps track of these transactions for the banking system—will deduct $900 from First National's reserve account and transfer it to the other bank's reserve account. This will cause a further change in First National's balance sheet, as follows:

CHANGES IN FIRST NATIONAL BANK'S BALANCE SHEET

Action	Changes in Assets	Changes in Liabilities
Fed buys $1,000 bond from Lehman Brothers, which deposits $1,000 check from Fed into its checking account.	+$1,000 in reserves	+$1,000 in demand deposits
First National lends out $900 in excess reserves.	−$900 in reserves +$900 in loans	
Total effect on First National from beginning to end.	+$100 in reserves +$900 in loans	+$1,000 in demand deposits

Look at the highlighted entries in the table. By making the loan, First National has given up an asset: $900 in reserves. This causes assets to change by −$900. But First National also gains an asset of equal value—the $900 loan. (Remember: While loans are liabilities to the borrower, they are assets to banks.) This causes assets to change by +$900. Both of these changes are seen on the assets side of the balance sheet.

Now look at the bottom row of the table. This tells us what has happened to First National from beginning to end. We see that, after making its loan, First National has $100 more in reserves than it started with, and $900 more in loans, for a total of $1,000 more in assets. But it also has $1,000 more in liabilities than it had before: the additional demand deposits that it owes to Lehman Brothers. Both assets and liabilities have gone up by the same amount. Notice, too, that First National is once again holding exactly the reserves it must legally hold. It now has $1,000 more in demand deposits than it had before, and it is holding $0.1 \times \$1,000 = \$100$ more in reserves than before. First National is finished ("loaned up") and cannot lend out any more reserves.

But there is still more to our story. Let's suppose that First National lends the $900 to the owner of a local business, Paula's Pizza, and Paula deposits her loan check into *her* bank account at Second United Bank. The Fed will transfer $900 in reserves from First National's reserve account to that of Second United. Second United's balance sheet will change as follows:

CHANGES IN SECOND UNITED'S BALANCE SHEET

Action	Changes in Assets	Changes in Liabilities
Paula deposits $900 loan check into her checking account.	+ $900 in reserves	+ $900 in demand deposits

Second United now has $900 more in assets—the increase in its reserve account with the Federal Reserve—and $900 in additional liabilities—the amount added to Paula's checking account.

Now consider Second United's situation from its manager's viewpoint. He reasons as follows: "My demand deposits have risen by $900, which means my required reserves have risen by $0.1 \times \$900 = \$90$. But my reserves have *actually* increased by $900. Thus, I have *excess reserves* of $\$900 - \$90 = \$810$, which I will lend out." After making the $810 loan, Second United's balance sheet will change once again (look at the highlighted entries):

CHANGES IN SECOND UNITED'S BALANCE SHEET

Action	Changes in Assets	Changes in Liabilities
Paula deposits $900 loan check into her checking account.	+$900 in reserves	+$900 in demand deposits
Second United lends out $810 in excess reserves.	− $810 in reserves + $810 in loans	
Total effect on Second United from beginning to end.	+ $ 90 in reserves + $810 in loans	+ $900 in demand deposits

In the end, as you can see in the bottom row of the table, Second United has $90 more in reserves than it started with, and $810 more in loans. Its demand deposit liabilities have increased by $900. The money supply has increased once again—this time, by $900.

Are you starting to see a pattern? Let's carry it through one more step. Whoever borrowed $810 from Second United will put it into his or her checking account at, say, Third State Bank. This will give Third State excess reserves that it will lend out. Its balance sheet will change as follows:

CHANGES IN THIRD STATE'S BALANCE SHEET

Action	Changes in Assets	Changes in Liabilities
Borrower from Second United deposits $810 loan check into checking account.	+ $810 in reserves	+$810 in demand deposits
Third State lends out $729 in excess reserves.	− $729 in reserves + $729 in loans	
Total effect on Third State from beginning to end.	+ $ 81 in reserves + $729 in loans	+$810 in demand deposits

As you can see, demand deposits increase each time a bank lends out excess reserves. In the end, they will increase by a *multiple* of the original $1,000 in reserves injected into the banking system by the open market purchase. Does this process sound familiar? It should. It is very similar to the explanation of the *expenditure multiplier* in the previous chapter, where in each round, an increase in spending led to an increase in income, which caused spending to increase again in the next round. Here, instead of spending, it is the *money supply*—or more specifically, *demand deposits*—that increase in each round.

THE DEMAND DEPOSIT MULTIPLIER

By how much will demand deposits increase in total? If you look back at the balance sheet changes we've analyzed, you'll see that each bank creates less in demand deposits than the bank before. When Lehman Brothers deposited its $1,000 check from the Fed at First National, $1,000 in demand deposits was created. This led to an additional $900 in demand deposits created by Second United, another $810 created by Third State, and so on. In each round, a bank lent 90 percent of the deposit it received. Eventually the additional demand deposits will become so small that we can safely ignore them. When the process is complete, how much in additional demand deposits has been created?

Table 2 provides the answer. Each row of the table shows the additional demand deposits created at each bank, as well as the running total. The last row shows that, in the end, $10,000 in new demand deposits has been created.

Let's go back and summarize what happened in our example. The Fed, through its open market purchase, injected $1,000 of reserves into the banking system. As a result, demand deposits rose by $10,000—10 times the injection in reserves. As you can verify, if the Fed had injected twice this amount of reserves ($2,000), demand deposits would have increased by 10 times *that* amount ($20,000). In fact, *whatever* the injection of reserves, demand deposits will increase by a factor of 10, so we can write

$$\Delta DD = 10 \times \text{Reserve injection}$$

TABLE 2 Cumulative Increases in Demand Deposits After a $1,000 Open Market Purchase	Round	Additional Demand Deposits Created by Each Bank	Additional Demand Deposits Created by All Banks
	First National Bank	$1,000	$1,000
	Second United	$ 900	$1,900
	Third State	$ 810	$2,710
	Bank 4	$ 729	$3,439
	Bank 5	$ 656	$4,095
	Bank 6	$ 590	$4,685
	. . .		
	Bank 10	$ 387	$6,511
	. . .		
	Bank 20	$ 135	$8,784
	. . .		
	Bank 50	very close to zero	very close to $10,000

where *DD* stands for demand deposits. The injection of reserves must be *multiplied by* the number 10 in order to get the change in demand deposits that it causes. For this reason, 10 is called the **demand deposit multiplier** in this example.

The size of the demand deposit multiplier depends on the value of the required reserve ratio set by the Fed. If you look back at Table 2, you will see that each round of additional deposit creation would have been smaller if the required reserve ratio had been larger. For example, with a required reserve ratio of 0.2 instead of 0.1, Second United would have created only $800 in deposits, Third State would have created only $640, and so on. The result would have been a smaller cumulative change in deposits, and a smaller multiplier.

There is a very simple formula we can use to determine the value of the demand deposit multiplier for *any* value of the required reserve ratio:

Demand deposit multiplier The number by which a change in reserves is multiplied to determine the resulting change in demand deposits.

> *For any value of the required reserve ratio (RRR), the formula for the demand deposit multiplier is 1/RRR.*

In our example, the *RRR* was equal to 0.1, so the demand deposit multiplier had the value $1/0.1 = 10$. If the *RRR* had been 0.2 instead, the demand deposit multiplier would have been equal to $1/0.2 = 5$. To see how this formula is derived, read this footnote.[4]

Using our general formula for the demand deposit multiplier, we can restate what happens when the Fed injects reserves into the banking system as follows:

$$\Delta DD = \left(\frac{1}{RRR}\right) \times \Delta \text{Reserves}.$$

This formula tells us the change in demand deposits. But because we've been assuming that the amount of cash in the hands of the public (the other component of the money supply) does not change, we can also write

$$\Delta DD = \Delta \text{Money supply} = \left(\frac{1}{RRR}\right) \times \Delta \text{Reserves}.$$

---

[4] To derive the formula for the demand-deposit multiplier, let's start with our numerical example, in which the change in demand deposits (ΔDD) is

$$\Delta DD = (\$1{,}000 + \$900 + \$810 + \$729 + \cdots).$$

Factoring out $1,000 gives us

$$\Delta DD = \$1{,}000 \times (1 + 0.9 + 0.81 + 0.729 + \cdots)$$
$$= \$1{,}000 \times (1 + 0.9 + 0.9^2 + 0.9^3 + \cdots).$$

In this example, $1,000 is the initial injection of reserves, and 0.9 is the fraction of its new reserves that each bank lends out, which is 1 *minus* the required reserve ratio. Generalizing this for *any* change in reserves (ΔReserves) or *any* required reserve ratio (*RRR*), we have

$$\Delta DD = \Delta \text{Reserves} \times [1 + (1-RRR) + (1-RRR)^2 + (1-RRR)^3 + \cdots].$$

Now we use a rule from the mathematics of infinite sums (such as the sum in brackets): For any value of H between 0 and 1, the infinite sum $1 + H + H^2 + H^3 + \cdots$ has the value $1/(1 - H)$.
Replacing H with the value $1 - RRR$ (which is between 0 and 1), we get

$$\Delta DD = \Delta \text{Reserves} \times \{1/[1 - (1 - RRR)]\}$$

or

$$\Delta DD = \Delta \text{Reserves} \times (1/RRR).$$

THE FED'S INFLUENCE ON THE BANKING SYSTEM AS A WHOLE

We can also look at what happened to total demand deposits and the money supply from another perspective. When the Fed bought the $1,000 bond from Lehman Brothers, it injected $1,000 of reserves into the banking system. That was the only increase in reserves that occurred in our story. Where did the additional $1,000 in reserves end up? If you go back through the changes in balance sheets, you'll see that First National ended up with $100 in additional reserves, Second United ended up with $90, Third Savings with $81, and so on. Each of these banks is required to hold more reserves than initially, because its demand deposits have increased. In the end, *the additional $1,000 in reserves will be distributed among different banks in the system as required reserves.*

> *After an injection of reserves, the demand deposit multiplier stops working—and the money supply stops increasing—only when all the reserves injected are being held by banks as* required *reserves.*

This observation helps us understand the demand deposit multiplier in another way. In our example, the deposit-creation process will continue until the entire injection of $1,000 in reserves becomes *required* reserves. But with an *RRR* of 0.1, each dollar of reserves entitles a bank to have $10 in demand deposits. Therefore, by injecting $1,000 of reserves into the system, the Fed has enabled banks, in total, to hold $10,000 in additional demand deposits. Only when $10,000 in deposits has been created will the process come to an end.

Just as we've looked at balance sheet changes for each bank, we can also look at the change in the balance sheet of the *entire banking system*. The Fed's open market purchase of $1,000 has caused the following changes:

"Creating Money" Doesn't Mean "Creating Wealth" Demand deposits are a means of payment, and banks create them. This is why we say that banks "create deposits" and "create money." But don't fall into the trap of thinking that banks create wealth. No one gains any additional wealth as a direct result of money creation.

To see why, think about what happened in our story when Lehman Brothers deposited the $1,000 check from the Fed into its account at First National. *Lehman Brothers* was no wealthier: It gave up a $1,000 check from the Fed and ended up with $1,000 more in its checking account, for a net gain of zero. Similarly, the *bank* gained no additional wealth: It had $1,000 more in cash, but it also *owed* Lehman Brothers $1,000—once again, a net gain of zero.

The same conclusion holds for any other step in the money-creation process. When Paula borrows $900 and deposits it into her checking account at Second United, she is no wealthier: She has $900 more in her account, but owes $900 to First National. And once again, the bank is no wealthier: It has $900 more in demand deposits, but owes this money to Paula.

Always remember that when banks "create money," they do not create wealth.

CHANGES IN THE BALANCE SHEET OF THE ENTIRE BANKING SYSTEM

Changes in Assets	Changes in Liabilities
+ $1,000 in reserves + $9,000 in loans	+ $10,000 in demand deposits

In the end, total reserves in the system have increased by $1,000—the amount of the open market purchase. Each dollar in reserves supports $10 in demand deposits, so we know that total deposits have increased by $10,000. Finally, we know that a balance sheet always balances. Because liabilities increased by $10,000, loans must have increased by $9,000 to increase total assets (loans and reserves) by $10,000.

How the Fed Decreases the Money Supply

Just as the Fed can increase the money supply by purchasing government bonds, it can also *decrease* the money supply by *selling* government bonds—an *open market sale*.

Where does the Fed get the government bonds to sell? It has trillions of dollars' worth of government bonds from open market *purchases* it has conducted in the past. Since, on average, the Fed tends to increase the money supply each year, it conducts more open market purchases than open market sales, and its bond holdings keep growing. So we needn't worry that the Fed will run out of bonds to sell.

Suppose the Fed sells a $1,000 government bond to a bond dealer, Merrill Lynch, which—like Lehman Brothers in our earlier example—has a checking account at First National Bank. Merrill Lynch pays the Fed for the bond with a $1,000 check drawn on its account at First National. When the Fed gets Merrill Lynch's check, it will present the check to First National and deduct $1,000 from First National's reserve account. In turn, First National will deduct $1,000 from Merrill Lynch's checking account.

After all of this has taken place, First National's balance sheet will show the following changes:

CHANGES IN FIRST NATIONAL BANK'S BALANCE SHEET

Action	Changes in Assets	Changes in Liabilities
Fed sells $1,000 bond to Merrill Lynch, which pays with a $1,000 check drawn on First National.	−$1,000 in reserves	−$1,000 in demand deposits

Now First National has a problem. Since its demand deposits have decreased by $1,000, it can legally decrease its reserves by 10 percent of that, or $100. But its reserves have *actually* decreased by $1,000, which is $900 more than they are allowed to decrease. First National has *deficient reserves*—reserves smaller than those it is legally required to hold. How can it get the additional reserves it needs?

First National will have to *call in a loan* (ask for repayment) in the amount of $900.[5] A loan is usually repaid with a check drawn on some other bank. When First National gets this check, the Federal Reserve will add $900 to its reserve account, and deduct $900 from the reserve account at the other bank. This is how First National brings its reserves up to the legal requirement. After it calls in the $900 loan, First National's balance sheet will change as follows:

---

[5] In reality, bank loans are for specified time periods, and a bank cannot actually demand that a loan be repaid early. But most banks have a large volume of loans outstanding, with some being repaid each day. Typically, the funds will be lent out again the very same day they are repaid. A bank that needs additional reserves will simply reduce its rate of new lending on that day, thereby reducing its total amount of loans outstanding. This has the same effect as "calling in a loan."

CHANGES IN FIRST NATIONAL BANK'S BALANCE SHEET

Action	Changes in Assets	Changes in Liabilities
Fed sells $1,000 bond to Merrill Lynch, which pays with a $1,000 check drawn on First National.	− $1,000 in reserves	− $1,000 in demand deposits
First National calls in loans worth $900.	+ $ 900 in reserves − $ 900 in loans	
Total effect on First National from beginning to end.	− $ 100 in reserves − $ 900 in loans	− $1,000 in demand deposits

Look at the highlighted terms. After First National calls in the loan, the composition of its assets will change: $900 more in reserves and $900 less in loans. The last row of the table shows the changes to First National's balance sheet from beginning to end. Compared to its initial situation, First National has $100 less in reserves (it lost $1,000 and then gained $900), $900 less in loans, and $1,000 less in demand deposits.

As you might guess, this is not the end of the story. Remember that whoever paid back the loan to First National did so by a check drawn on another bank. That other bank, which we'll assume is Second United Bank, will lose $900 in reserves and experience the following changes in its balance sheet:

CHANGES IN SECOND UNITED BANK'S BALANCE SHEET

Action	Changes in Assets	Changes in Liabilities
Someone with an account at Second United Bank writes a $900 check to First National.	−$900 in reserves	−$900 in demand deposits

Now Second United Bank is in the same fix that First National was in. Its demand deposits have decreased by $900, so its reserves can legally fall by $90. However, its actual reserves have decreased by $900, which is $810 too much. Now it is Second United's turn to call in a loan. (On your own, fill in the rest of the changes in Second United Bank's balance sheet as it successfully brings its reserves up to the legal requirement.)

As you can see, the process of calling in loans will involve many banks. Each time a bank calls in a loan, demand deposits are destroyed—the same amount as were created in our earlier story, in which each bank *made* a new loan. The total decline in demand deposits will be a multiple of the initial withdrawal of reserves. Keeping in mind that a withdrawal of reserves is a *negative change in reserves*, we can still use our demand deposit multiplier—$1/RRR$—and our general formula:

$$\Delta DD = \left(\frac{1}{RRR}\right) \times \Delta \text{Reserves}.$$

Applying it to our example, we have

$$\Delta DD = \left(\frac{1}{0.1}\right) \times (-\$1,000) = -\$10,000.$$

In words, the Fed's $1,000 open market sale causes a $10,000 decrease in demand deposits. Since we assume that the public's cash holdings do not change, the money supply decreases by $10,000 as well.

To the banking system as a whole, the Fed's bond sale has done the following:

CHANGES IN BALANCE SHEET FOR THE ENTIRE BANKING SYSTEM

Changes in Assets	Changes in Liabilities
−$1,000 in reserves −$9,000 in loans	−$10,000 in demand deposits

SOME IMPORTANT PROVISOS ABOUT THE DEMAND DEPOSIT MULTIPLIER

Although the process of money creation and destruction as we've described it illustrates the basic ideas, our formula for the demand deposit multiplier—$1/RRR$—is oversimplified. In reality, the multiplier is likely to be smaller than our formula suggests, for two reasons.

First, we've assumed that as the money supply changes, the public does *not* change its holdings of cash. But in reality, as the money supply increases, the public typically will want to hold part of the increase as demand deposits and part of the increase as cash. As a result, in each round of the deposit-creation process, some reserves will be *withdrawn* in the form of cash. This will lead to a smaller increase in demand deposits than in our story.

Second, we've assumed that banks will always lend out all of their excess reserves. In reality, banks often *want* to hold excess reserves, for a variety of reasons. For example, they may want some flexibility to increase their loans in case interest rates—their reward for lending—rise in the near future. Or they may prefer not to lend the maximum legal amount during a recession, because borrowers are more likely to declare bankruptcy and not repay their loans. If banks increase their holdings of excess reserves as the money supply expands, they will make smaller loans than in our story, and in each round, demand deposit creation will be smaller.

Selling Bonds: Fed versus Treasury In this section, you learned how the Fed sells government bonds to decrease the money supply. It's easy to confuse this with another type of government bond sale, which is done by the U.S. Treasury.

The U.S. Treasury is the branch of government that collects tax revenue, disburses money for government purchases and transfer payments, and borrows money to finance any government budget deficit. The Treasury borrows funds by issuing *new* government bonds and *selling* them to the public—to banks, other financial institutions, and bond dealers. What the public pays for these bonds is what they are lending the government.

When the Fed conducts open market operations, however, it does not buy or sell *newly* issued bonds, but "secondhand bonds"—those already issued by the Treasury to finance past deficits. Thus, open market sales are *not* government borrowing; they are strictly an operation designed to change the money supply, and they have no direct effect on the government budget.

DANGEROUS CURVES

OTHER TOOLS FOR CONTROLLING THE MONEY SUPPLY

Open market operations are the Fed's primary means of controlling the money supply. But there are two other tools that the Fed can use to increase or decrease the money supply.

- *Changes in the required reserve ratio.* In principle, the Fed can set off the process of deposit creation, similar to that described earlier, by lowering the required reserve ratio. Look back at Table 1, which showed the balance sheet of a bank facing a required reserve ratio of 0.1 and holding exactly the amount of reserves required by law—$10 million. Now suppose the Fed lowered the required reserve ratio to 0.05. Suddenly, the bank would find that its required reserves were only $5 million; the other $5 million in reserves it holds would become excess reserves. To earn the highest profit possible, the bank would increase its lending by $5 million. At the same time, all other banks in the country would find that some of their formerly required reserves were now excess reserves, and they would increase their lending. The money supply would increase.

On the other hand, if the Fed *raised* the required reserve ratio, the process would work in reverse: All banks would suddenly have reserve deficiencies and be forced to call in loans. The money supply would decrease.

- *Changes in the discount rate.* The discount rate, mentioned earlier, is the rate the Fed charges banks when it lends them reserves. In principle, a lower discount rate, by enabling banks to borrow reserves from the Fed more cheaply, might encourage banks to borrow more. An increase in borrowed reserves works just like any other injection of reserves into the banking system: It increases the money supply.

  On the other side, a *rise* in the discount rate would make it more expensive for banks to borrow from the Fed, and decrease the amount of borrowed reserves in the system. This withdrawal of reserves from the banking system would lead to a decrease in the money supply.

Changes in either the required reserve ratio or the discount rate *could* set off the process of deposit creation or deposit destruction in much the same way as is outlined in this chapter. In reality, neither of these policy tools is used very often. The most recent change in the required reserve ratio was in April 1992, when the Fed lowered the required reserve ratio for most demand deposits from 12 percent to 10 percent. Changes in the discount rate are more frequent, but it is not unusual for the Fed to leave the discount rate unchanged for a year or more.

Why are these other tools used so seldom?

First, frequent changes in the required reserve ratio could create problems for the banking industry. Remember that banks earn their revenue by lending out deposits for interest, and that deposits held as reserves pay no interest at all. A rise in the required reserve ratio would immediately require banks to convert interest-earning funds to non-interest earning funds, decreasing their revenue and profits. A drop in the required reserve ratio would have the opposite effect. Thus, if the Fed relied on frequent changes in the required reserve ratio, bank profits would be more unstable.

Changes in the discount rate are problematic for a different reason. Traditionally, bank managers have preferred *not* to borrow reserves from the Fed, since it would put them under closer Fed scrutiny. And in the past, the Fed discouraged banks from borrowing reserves from it, unless the bank was in difficulty. Thus, a small change in the discount rate was unlikely to have much of an impact on bank borrowing of reserves, and therefore on the money supply.

In January 2003, however, the Fed changed its discount policy, and began to *encourage* banks to borrow. It established two different discount rates—one for banks in excellent financial condition and another, higher rate for banks considered more at risk. Banks in sound condition could borrow freely at the lower rate without Fed scrutiny. As a result, the discount rate may become a more effective, and more frequently used, policy tool in the future.

Still, open market operations will almost certainly remain the Fed's *principal* tool for controlling the money supply. The main reason is that they are so efficient in accomplishing the Fed's goals. Open market operations, unlike the other tools, can be adjusted frequently—even minute-by-minute. They enable the Fed to use trial and error—buying or selling bonds and then observing the effects—to fine-tune the money supply to any desired level.

USING THE THEORY

Bank Failures and Banking Panics

A bank becomes *insolvent* when its total assets are less than its total liabilities (or, equivalently, when its net worth becomes negative). When an insolvent bank goes out of business—usually after a regulatory agency steps in—we say that the bank has *failed*. What causes a bank to become insolvent? The most frequent reason is the bankruptcies of businesses and households that have borrowed money from the bank.

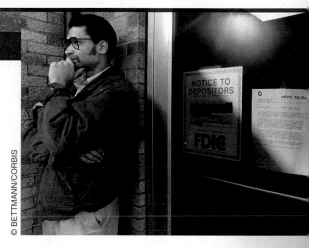

Table 3 shows how such bankruptcies would affect a bank's balance sheet. The original (black-type) entries in the table are taken from the balance sheet in Table 1. Initially, the bank has $65 million in loans that appear on the assets side. These loans—as long as the bank expects them to be repaid—are something of value that the bank owns. Notice that the bank begins with a positive net worth of $5 million. If the bank's owners decided to cease operations and sell off all of the bank's assets and pay off all of its liabilities, the $5 million in net worth would be left, and would go to the bank's owners.

Now suppose that the bank gets some bad news: $15 million of its loans will never be paid back because the businesses and households that owed the money have declared bankruptcy. As a result, $15 million in loans must be "written off" of the balance sheet; they are now worthless to the bank. The new (red-type) entries show how the balance sheet will change. On the left side, outstanding loans are reduced from $65 million to $50 million, so total assets decrease from

Assets		Liabilities and Net Worth		TABLE 3
Property and buildings	$5 million	Demand deposit liabilities	$100 million	**How Borrower Bankruptcies Affect a Bank's Balance Sheet**
Government and corporate bonds	$25 million	Net worth	~~$5 million~~ −$10 million	
Loans	~~$65 million~~ $50 million			
Reserves	$10 million			
Total Assets	~~$105 million~~ $90 million	**Total Liabilities plus Net Worth**	~~$105 million~~ $90 million	

$105 million to $90 million. On the right side, the bank continues to owe the same $100 million to its depositors. The only change is the bank's net worth. Subtracting the bank's liabilities ($100 million) from its assets (now $90 million), net worth has become negative, equal to −$10 million. At this point, even if the bank were to sell all of its assets to other banks, it would not have enough funds to honor all of its liabilities. The bank is *insolvent*.

What will happen?

In the old days, before the banking system was regulated and strict financial reporting was enforced, an insolvent bank could continue to operate for some time. That's because on any given day only a small fraction of its checking account balances would be withdrawn. So as long as the bank had enough cash on hand to meet normal requests for withdrawals, its day of reckoning could be postponed.

Until, that is, word of the bank's insolvency leaked out. At that point, all of the depositors would want to be first in line to withdraw their funds. They would know that banks meet requests for withdrawals on a first-come, first-served basis, and those who wait might not get any cash at all. We call this situation—in which all depositors try to withdraw their funds at once—a **run on the bank.**

Run on the bank An attempt by many of a bank's depositors to withdraw their funds.

Ironically, even a bank in good financial health, with more than enough assets to cover its liabilities, could find itself in trouble from a run on the bank. As you've seen in this chapter, even a solvent bank does not keep enough reserves on hand to cover all of its demand deposit liabilities. Unless it could sell all of its assets quickly and get the cash needed to honor withdrawals, it would have to close its doors and refuse (at least for a while) some of its customers' requests. Thus, a mere *rumor* of insolvency could force a bank to close. And the bank's closure would likely add fuel to the rumors that the bank was in trouble.

Banking panic A situation in which depositors attempt to withdraw funds from many banks simultaneously.

A **banking panic** occurs when a run on many banks occurs simultaneously. In the past, a typical panic would begin with some unexpected event, such as the failure of a large bank. During recessions, for example, many businesses go bankrupt, so fewer bank loans are repaid. A bank that had an unusual number of "bad loans" would be in trouble, and if the public found out about this, there might be a run on that bank. The bank would fail, and many depositors would find that they had lost their deposits.

But that would not be the end of the story. Hearing that their neighbors' banks were short of cash might lead others to question the health of their own banks. Just to be sure, they might withdraw their own funds, preferring to ride out the storm and keep their cash at home. As we've seen, even healthy banks cannot withstand the pressure of a bank run. They, too, would have to close their doors, stoking the rumor mill even more, and so on.

Banking panics can cause serious problems for the nation. First, there is the hardship suffered by people who lose their accounts when their bank fails. Second, the withdrawal of cash decreases the banking system's reserves. As we've seen, the withdrawal of reserves leads—through the demand deposit multiplier—to a larger decrease in the money supply. In the next chapter, you will learn that a decrease in the money supply can cause a recession. In a banking panic, the money supply can decrease suddenly and severely, causing a serious recession.

There were five major banking panics in the United States from 1863 to 1907. Indeed, it was the banking panic of 1907 that convinced Congress to establish the Federal Reserve System. From the beginning, one of the Fed's primary functions was to act as a lender of last resort, providing banks with enough cash to meet their obligations to depositors.

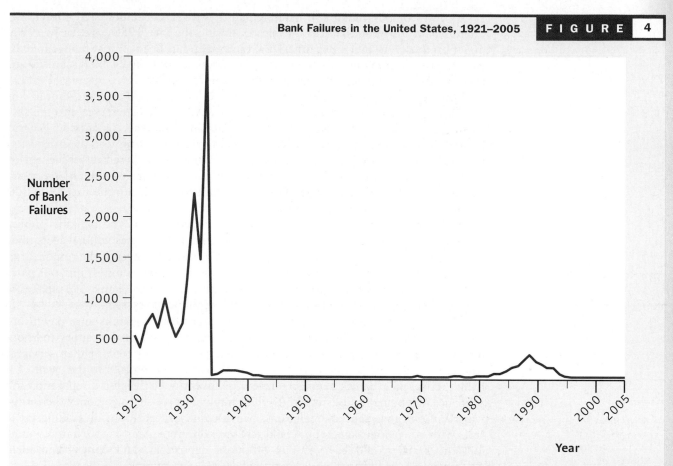

Bank Failures in the United States, 1921–2005 | **F I G U R E** | **4**

Bank failures continued after the Fed was created in 1913. During the Great Depression, a large number of banks failed. The creation of the Federal Deposit Insurance Corporation in 1933 strengthened faith in the stability of the banking system. Few banks have failed since that time.

But the creation of the Fed did not, in itself, solve the problem. Figure 4 shows the number of bank failures each year since 1921. As you can see, banking panics continued to plague the financial system even after the Fed was created. The Fed did not always act forcefully enough or quickly enough to prevent the panic from spreading.

The Great Depression is a good example of this problem. In late 1929 and 1930, many banks began to fail because of bad loans. Then, from October 1930 until March 1933, more than one-third of all banks shut down as frantic depositors stormed bank after bank, demanding to withdraw their funds—even from banks that were in reasonable financial health. Many economists believe that the banking panic of 1930–1933 turned what would have been just a serious recession into the Great Depression. Officials of the Federal Reserve System, not quite grasping the seriousness of the problem, stood by and let it happen.[6]

---

[6] Milton Friedman and Anna Jacobson Schwartz, *A Monetary History of the United States, 1867–1960* (Princeton, NJ: Princeton University Press, 1963), especially p. 358.

As you can see in Figure 4, banking panics were largely eliminated after 1933. There was a moderate increase in failures during the late 1980s and early 1990s (more on this a bit later). But otherwise, the system has been almost failure free. In fact, for the six-year period ending in June 2006, a total of 24 banks failed—an average of just 4 per year. Why the dramatic improvement?

Largely for two reasons. First, the Federal Reserve learned an important lesson from the Great Depression, and it now stands ready to inject reserves into the system more quickly in a crisis. Moreover, in 1933 Congress created the Federal Deposit Insurance Corporation (FDIC) to reimburse those who lose their deposits. If your bank is insured by the FDIC (today, accounts are covered in 99 percent of all banks) and cannot honor its obligations for any reason—bad loans, poor management, or even theft—the FDIC will reimburse you up to the first $100,000 you lose in each of your bank accounts.[7]

The FDIC has had a major impact on the psychology of the banking public. Imagine that you hear your bank is about to go under. As long as you have less than $100,000 in your account, you will not care. Why? Because even if the rumor turns out to be true, you will be reimbursed in full. The resulting calmness on your part, and on the part of other depositors, will prevent a run on the bank. This makes it very unlikely that bank failures will spread throughout the system.

FDIC protection for bank accounts has not been costless. Banks must pay insurance premiums to the FDIC, and they pass this cost on to their depositors and borrowers by charging higher interest rates on loans and higher fees for their services. And there is a more serious cost. If you are thoroughly protected in the event of a bank failure, your bank's managers have little incentive to develop a reputation for prudence in lending funds, since you will be happy to deposit your money there anyway. Without government regulations, banks could act irresponsibly, taking great risks with your money, and you would remain indifferent. Many more banks would fail, the FDIC would have to pay off more depositors, and banks—and their customers—would bear the burden of higher FDIC premiums.

This is the logic behind the Fed's continuing regulation of bank lending. Someone must watch over the banks to keep the failure rate low. If the public has no incentive to pay attention, the Fed must do so. Most economists believe that if we want the freedom from banking panics provided by the FDIC, we must also accept the strict regulation and close monitoring of banks provided by the Fed and other agencies.

Look again at Figure 4 and notice the temporary rise in bank failures of the late 1980s and the early 1990s. Most of these failures occurred in state-chartered banks. These banks are less closely regulated by the Fed, and are often insured by state agencies instead of the FDIC. When a few banks went bankrupt because highly speculative loans turned sour, insurance funds in several states were drained. Citizens in those states began to fear that insufficient funds were left to insure their own deposits, and the psychology of banking panics took over. To many observers, the experience of the late 1980s and early 1990s was a reminder of the need for a sound insurance system and close monitoring of the banking system.

---

[7] If you are fortunate enough to be worried about this limit, keep in mind that it applies to each *account*, not to each household or individual. Anyone can protect more than $100,000 by creating multiple accounts. And in mid-2006, Congress was considering raising the limit to $200,000. The current limits and other relevant facts can be found at *www.fdic.gov/deposit/deposits/insuringdeposits/index.html*.

Summary

A nation's monetary system provides two important functions. First, it creates a *unit of value* that helps us compare the costs of different goods and services. Second, it provides for a generally acceptable *means of payment*. In the United States, the unit of value is the dollar, and the means of payment includes paper currency, checking accounts, travelers checks, and credit cards.

Money is an asset that is also widely accepted as a means of payment. In the United States, the standard measure of money—M1—includes currency, checking account balances, and travelers checks. Each of these assets is liquid and widely acceptable as a means of payment. Other, broader measures go beyond M1 to include funds in savings accounts and other deposits.

The amount of money circulating in the economy is controlled by the Federal Reserve, operating through the banking system. Banks and other financial intermediaries are profit-seeking firms that collect loanable funds from households and businesses; then they repackage them to make loans to other households, businesses, and governmental agencies.

The Federal Reserve injects money into the economy by altering banks' balance sheets. In a balance sheet, assets always equal liabilities plus net worth. One important kind of asset is *reserves*—funds that banks are required to hold in proportion to their demand deposit liabilities. When the Fed wants to increase the money supply, it buys bonds in the open market and pays for them with a check. This is called an *open market purchase*. When the Fed's check is deposited in a bank, the bank's balance sheet changes. On the asset side, reserves increase; on the liabilities side, demand deposits (a form of money) also increase. The bank can lend some of the reserves, and the funds lent out will end up in some other banks where they support creation of still more demand deposits. Eventually, demand deposits, and the M1 money supply, increase by some multiple of the original injection of reserves by the Fed. The *demand deposit multiplier*, the inverse of the required reserve ratio, gives us that multiple.

The Fed can decrease the money supply by selling government bonds—an *open market sale*—causing demand deposits to shrink by a multiple of the initial reduction in reserves. The Fed can also change the money supply by changing either the required reserve ratio or the discount rate it charges when it lends reserves to banks. These tools are used much less frequently than open market operations.

Problem Set   *Answers to even-numbered Questions and Problems can be found on the text Web site at www.thomsonedu.com/economics/hall.*

1. Suppose the required reserve ratio is 0.2. If an extra $20 billion in reserves is injected into the banking system through an open market purchase of bonds, by how much can demand deposits increase? Would your answer be different if the required reserve ratio were 0.1?

2. If the Fed buys $50 million of government securities, by how much can the money supply increase if the required reserve ratio is 0.15? How will your answer be different if the required reserve ratio is 0.18?

3. Which of the following is considered part of the U.S. money supply? (Use the M1 measures.)
   a. A $10 bill you carry in your wallet
   b. A $100 travelers check you bought but did not use
   c. A $100 bill in a bank's vault
   d. The $325.43 balance in your checking account
   e. A share of General Motors stock worth $40

4. Given the following data (in billions of dollars), calculate the value of the M1 money supply and the value of the M2 money supply.

Bank reserves	50
Cash in the hands of the public	400
Demand deposits	400
Retail MMMF balances	880
Other checkable deposits	250
Savings-type account balances	1,300
Small time deposits	950
Travelers checks	10

5. Suppose bank reserves are $100 billion, the required reserve ratio is 0.2, and excess reserves are zero. Calculate how many dollars, worth of demand deposits are being supported. Now suppose that the required reserve ratio is lowered to 0.1 and that banks once again become fully "loaned up" with no excess reserves. What is the new level of demand deposits?

6. Suppose bank reserves are $200 billion, the required reserve ratio is 0.2, and excess reserves are zero. Calculate how many dollars, worth of demand deposits are being supported. If the Fed wants to decrease demand deposits by $50 billion by changing the required reserve ratio, what new required reserve ratio should it set?

7. Suppose that the money supply is $1 trillion. Decision makers at the Federal Reserve decide that they wish to use open market operations to reduce the money supply by $100 billion, or by 10 percent. If the required reserve ratio is 0.05, what does the Fed need to do to carry out the planned reduction?

8. Suppose that the money supply is $3.2 trillion. Decision makers at the Federal Reserve decide that they wish to use open market operation to increase the money supply by $500 billion. If the required reserve ratio is 0.10, what does the Fed need to do to carry out the planned increase? What if the required reserve ratio is 0.15?

9. For each of the following situations, determine whether the money supply will increase, decrease, or stay the same.

a. Depositors become concerned about the safety of depository institutions.

b. The Fed lowers the required reserve ratio.

c. The economy enters a recession and banks have a hard time finding creditworthy borrowers.

d. The Fed sells $100 million of bonds to First National Bank of Ames, Iowa.

10. Suppose that the Fed decides to increase the money supply. It purchases a government bond worth $1,000 from a private citizen. He deposits the check in his account at First National Bank, as in the chapter example. But now, suppose that the required reserve ratio is 0.2, rather than 0.1 as in the chapter.

a. Trace the effect of this change through three banks—First National, Second United, and Third State. Show the changes to each bank's balance sheet as a result of the Fed's action.

b. By how much does the money supply change in each of these first three rounds?

c. What will be the ultimate change in demand deposits in the entire banking system?

11. Suppose accountants at the bank whose balance sheet is depicted in Table 1 discover that they've made an error: Cash in vault is only $1 million, not $2 million.

a. Which other entries in the bank's balance sheet will change as a consequence of correcting this error?

b. If the required reserve ratio is 0.10, does this bank now have excess reserves or deficient reserves? Of what value?

12. Assume that the Fed wants to keep the size of the money supply constant by adjusting the required reserve ratio only. How will it have to adjust the required reserve ratio to achieve this goal if

a. People decide to hold more of their money as cash rather than as demand deposits?

b. Bankers decide to decrease their holdings of excess reserves?

13. Suppose a bank has the following entries on its balance sheet: $20 million in property and buildings; $200 million in government bonds; $300 million in loans; $5 million cash in vault; $95 million in accounts with the Federal Reserve; $550 million in demand deposit liabilities. There are no other entries on the balance sheet except for net worth.

a. What is this bank's net worth?

b. What is the maximum value of the bank's loans that could be "written off" due to bankruptcies before the bank would become insolvent?

More Challenging

14. Sometimes banks wish to hold reserves in excess of the legal minimum. Suppose the Fed makes an open market purchase of $100,000 in government bonds. The required reserve ratio is 0.1, but each bank decides to hold additional reserves equal to 5 percent of its new deposits.

a. Trace the effect of the open market purchase of bonds through the first three banks in the money expansion process. Show the changes to each bank's balance sheet.

b. Derive the demand deposit multiplier in this case. Is it larger or smaller than when banks hold no excess reserves?

c. What is the ultimate change in demand deposits in the entire banking system?

15. Suppose the Fed buys $100,000 in government bonds from Jonathan, and that the required reserve ratio is 0.1. Assume that Jonathan and each additional depositor always hold half of their money as cash.

a. Trace the effect of this open market purchase through the first three banks in the money expansion process. Show the changes to each bank's balance sheet.

b. Derive the demand deposit multiplier in this case. How does it compare with the demand deposit multiplier when depositors hold no cash?

c. What is the ultimate change in demand deposits in the entire banking system?

The Money Market and Monetary Policy

Which of the following two newspaper headlines might you see in your daily paper?

1. **"Motorists Fear Department of Energy Will Raise Gasoline Prices"**
2. **"Wall Street Expects Fed to Raise Interest Rates"**

You probably know the answer: The first headline is entirely unrealistic. The Department of Energy, the government agency that makes energy policy, has no authority to set prices in any market. The Federal Reserve, by contrast, has full authority to influence the interest rate—the price of borrowing money. And it exercises this authority every day. This is why headlines such as the second one appear in newspapers so often.

In this chapter, you will learn how the Fed, through its control of the money supply, also controls the interest rate and uses it to influence real GDP.

THE DEMAND FOR MONEY

Reread the title of this section. Does it appear strange to you? Don't people always want as much money as possible?

Indeed, they do. But when we speak about the *demand* for something, we don't mean the amount that people would desire if they could have all they wanted, without having to sacrifice anything for it. Instead, economic decision makers always face constraints: They must sacrifice one thing in order to have more of another. Thus, the *demand for money* does not mean how much money people would *like* to have in the best of all possible worlds. Rather, it means *how much money people would like to hold, given the constraints that they face*. Let's first consider the demand for money by an individual, and then turn our attention to the demand for money in the entire economy.

AN INDIVIDUAL'S DEMAND FOR MONEY

Money is one of the forms in which people hold their wealth. Unfortunately, at any given moment, the total amount of wealth we have is given; we can't just snap our fingers and have more of it. Therefore, if we want to hold more wealth in the form of money, we must hold less wealth in other forms: savings accounts, money market funds, time deposits, stocks, bonds, and so on. Indeed, people exchange one kind of wealth for another millions of times a day—in banks, stock markets, and bond markets. If you sell shares in the stock market, for example, you give up wealth in the form of corporate stock and acquire money. The buyer of your stock gives up money and acquires the stock.

These two facts—that wealth is given, and that you must give up one kind of wealth in order to acquire more of another—determine an individual's **wealth constraint.** Whenever we speak about the demand for money, the wealth constraint is always in the background, as in the following statement:

Wealth constraint At any point in time, total wealth is fixed.

> *An individual's* quantity of money demanded *is the amount of wealth that the individual chooses to hold as money, rather than as other assets.*

Why do people want to hold some of their wealth in the form of money? The most important reason is that money is a *means of payment;* you can buy things with it. Other forms of wealth, by contrast, are *not* used for purchases. (For example, we don't ordinarily pay for our groceries with shares of stock.) However, the other forms of wealth provide a financial return to their owners. For example, bonds, savings deposits, and time deposits pay interest, while stocks pay dividends and may also rise in value (which is called a *capital gain*). Money, by contrast, pays very little interest (some types of checking accounts) or none at all (cash and most checking accounts). Thus,

> *when you hold money, you bear an opportunity cost—the interest you could have earned by holding other assets instead.*

Each of us must continually decide how to divide our total wealth between money and other assets. The upside to money is that it can be used as a means of payment. The more of our wealth we hold as money, the easier it is to buy things at a moment's notice, and the less often we will have to pay the costs (in time, trouble, and commissions to brokers) to change our other assets into money. The downside to money is that it pays little or no interest.

To keep our analysis as simple as possible, *we'll use bonds as our representative nonmoney asset.* We'll also assume that all assets considered to be money pay no interest at all. In our discussion, therefore, people will choose between two assets that are mirror images of each other. Specifically,

> *individuals choose how to divide wealth between two assets: (1) money, which can be used as a means of payment but earns no interest; and (2) bonds, which earn interest, but cannot be used as a means of payment.*

This choice involves a clear tradeoff: The more wealth we hold as money, the less often we will have to go through the inconvenience of changing our bonds into money . . . but the less interest we will earn on our wealth.

What determines how much money an individual will decide to hold? While tastes vary from person to person, three key variables have rather predictable impacts on most of us.

- *The price level.* The greater the number of dollars you spend in a typical week or month, the more money you will want to have on hand to make your purchases. A rise in the price level, which raises the dollar cost of your purchases, should therefore increase the amount of money you want to hold.
- *Real income.* Suppose the price level remains unchanged, but your income increases. Your purchasing power or *real* income will increase, and so will the

number of dollars you spend in a typical week or month. Once again, since you are spending more dollars, you will choose to hold more of your wealth in the form of money.

- *The interest rate.* Interest payments are what you give up when you hold money—the *opportunity cost* of money. The greater the interest rate, the greater the opportunity cost of holding money. Thus, a rise in the interest rate *decreases* your quantity of money demanded.

The effect of the interest rate on the quantity of money demanded will play a key role in our analysis. But before we go any further, you may be wondering whether it is realistic to think that changes in the interest rate—which are usually rather small—would have any effect at all. Here, as in many aspects of economic life, you may not consciously think about the interest rate in deciding how to adjust your money-holding habits. Similarly, you may not rethink all your habits about using lights and computers every time the price of electricity changes. But in both cases, you may respond more casually. And when we add up everybody's behavior, we find a noticeable and stable tendency for people to hold less money when it is more expensive to hold it—that is, when the interest rate is higher.

The Demand for Money by Businesses

Our discussion of money demand has focused on the typical individual. But some money (not a lot in comparison to what individuals hold) is held by businesses. Stores keep some currency in their cash registers, and firms generally keep funds in business checking accounts. Businesses face the same types of constraints as individuals: They have only so much wealth, and they must decide how much of it to hold as money rather than other assets. The quantity of money demanded by businesses follows the same principles we have developed for individuals: They want to hold more money when real income or the price level is higher, and less money when the opportunity cost (the interest rate) is higher.

THE ECONOMY-WIDE DEMAND FOR MONEY

When we use the term *quantity of money demanded* without the word *individual*, we mean the total demand for money by all wealth holders in the economy—businesses and individuals. And just as each person and each firm in the economy has only so much wealth, so, too, there is a given amount of wealth in the economy as a whole at any given time. In our analysis, this total wealth must be held in one of two forms: money or bonds.

> *The (economy-wide) quantity of money demanded is the amount of total wealth in the economy that all households and businesses, together, choose to hold as money rather than as bonds.*

The demand for money in the economy depends on the same three variables that we discussed for individuals. In particular, (1) a rise in the price level will increase the demand for money; (2) a rise in real income (real GDP) will increase the demand for money; and (3) a rise in the interest rate will *decrease* the quantity of money demanded.

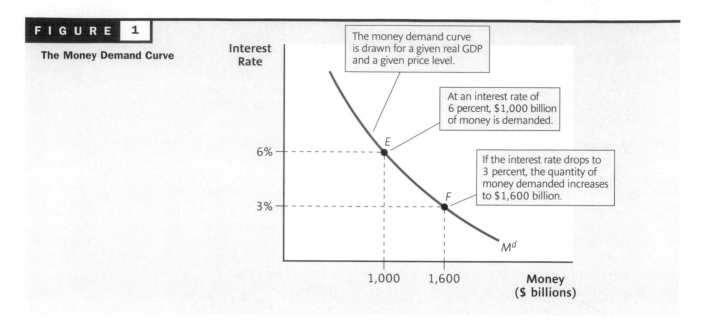

FIGURE 1

The Money Demand Curve

The money demand curve is drawn for a given real GDP and a given price level.

At an interest rate of 6 percent, $1,000 billion of money is demanded.

If the interest rate drops to 3 percent, the quantity of money demanded increases to $1,600 billion.

THE MONEY DEMAND CURVE

Money demand curve A curve indicating how much money will be demanded at each interest rate.

Figure 1 shows a **money demand curve**, which tells us *the total quantity of money demanded in the economy at each interest rate.* Notice that the curve is downward sloping. As long as the other influences on money demand don't change, a drop in the interest rate—which lowers the opportunity cost of holding money—will increase the quantity of money demanded.

Point *E*, for example, shows that when the interest rate is 6 percent, the quantity of money demanded is $1,000 billion. If the interest rate falls to 3 percent, we move to point *F*, where the quantity demanded is $1,600 billion. As we move along the money demand curve, the interest rate changes, but other determinants of money demand (such as the price level and real income) are assumed to remain unchanged.

Shifts in the Money Demand Curve

What happens when something *other* than the interest rate changes the quantity of money demanded? Then the curve shifts. For example, suppose that real income increases. Then, at each interest rate, individuals and businesses will want to hold *more* of their wealth in the form of money. The entire money demand curve will shift rightward. This is illustrated in Figure 2, where the money demand curve shifts rightward from M_1^d to M_2^d. At an interest rate of 6 percent, the quantity of money demanded rises from $1,000 billion to $1,400 billion; if the interest rate were 3 percent, the amount of money demanded would rise from $1,600 billion to $2,000 billion.

In general,

> *a change in the interest rate moves us along the money demand curve. A change in money demand caused by something other than the interest rate (such as real income or the price level) will cause the curve to shift.*

Figure 3 summarizes how the key variables we've discussed so far affect the demand for money.

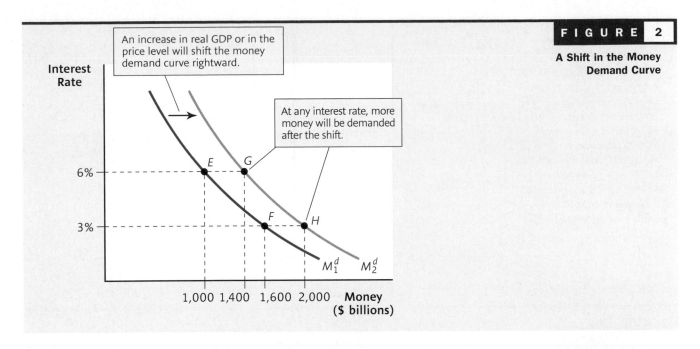

FIGURE 2

A Shift in the Money Demand Curve

An increase in real GDP or in the price level will shift the money demand curve rightward.

At any interest rate, more money will be demanded after the shift.

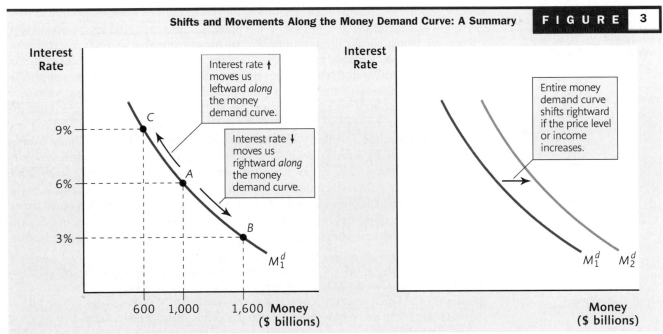

Shifts and Movements Along the Money Demand Curve: A Summary FIGURE 3

Interest rate ↑ moves us leftward *along* the money demand curve.

Interest rate ↓ moves us rightward *along* the money demand curve.

Entire money demand curve shifts rightward if the price level or income increases.

THE SUPPLY OF MONEY

Just as we did for money demand, we would like to draw a curve showing the quantity of money *supplied* at each interest rate. In the previous chapter, you learned how the Fed controls the money supply: It uses open market operations to inject or withdraw reserves from the banking system and then relies on the demand deposit multiplier to do the rest. Since the Fed decides what the money supply will

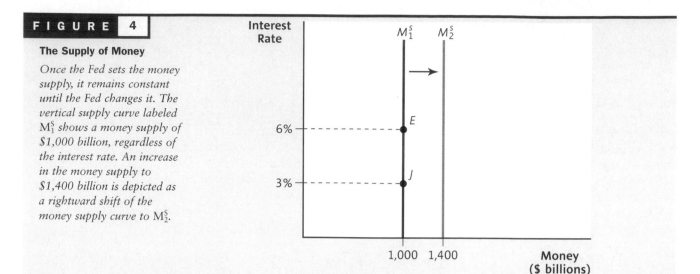

FIGURE 4

The Supply of Money

Once the Fed sets the money supply, it remains constant until the Fed changes it. The vertical supply curve labeled M_1^S shows a money supply of $1,000 billion, regardless of the interest rate. An increase in the money supply to $1,400 billion is depicted as a rightward shift of the money supply curve to M_2^S.

---

be, we treat it as a fixed amount. That is, the interest rate can rise or fall, but the money supply will remain constant unless and until the Fed decides to change it.

Look at the vertical line labeled M_1^S in Figure 4. This is the economy's **money supply curve**, which shows the total amount of money supplied at each interest rate. The line is vertical because once the Fed sets the money supply, it remains constant until the Fed changes it. In the figure, the Fed has chosen to set the money supply at $1,000 billion. A rise in the interest rate from, say, 3 percent to 6 percent would move us from point *J* to point *E* along the money supply curve M_1^S, leaving the money supply unchanged.

Now suppose the Fed, for whatever reason, were to *change* the money supply. Then there would be a *new* vertical line, showing a different quantity of money supplied at each interest rate. Recall from the previous chapter that the Fed raises the money supply by purchasing bonds in an open market operation. For example, if the demand deposit multiplier is 10, and the Fed purchases government bonds worth $40 billion, the money supply increases by 10 × $40 billion = $400 billion. In this case, the money supply curve shifts rightward, to the vertical line labeled M_2^S in the figure.

> *Open market purchases of bonds inject reserves into the banking system, and shift the money supply curve rightward by a multiple of the reserve injection. Open market sales have the opposite effect: They withdraw reserves from the system and shift the money supply curve leftward by a multiple of the reserve withdrawal.*

EQUILIBRIUM IN THE MONEY MARKET

Now let's combine money demand and money supply to find the equilibrium interest rate in the economy (Step two in the three-step process). But before we do, a question may have occurred to you. Haven't we already discussed how the interest rate is determined? Indeed, we have. The classical model tells us that the interest rate

Money supply curve A line showing the total quantity of money in the economy at each interest rate.

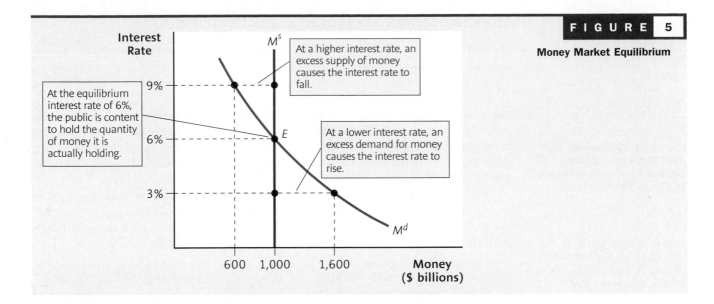

FIGURE 5

Money Market Equilibrium

Interest Rate

M^s

At a higher interest rate, an excess supply of money causes the interest rate to fall.

At the equilibrium interest rate of 6%, the public is content to hold the quantity of money it is actually holding.

9%

6%   E

At a lower interest rate, an excess demand for money causes the interest rate to rise.

3%

M^d

600   1,000   1,600   **Money ($ billions)**

is determined by equilibrium in the *loanable funds market*, where a flow of loanable funds is offered by lenders to borrowers. But remember: The classical model tells us how the economy operates in the *long run*. We can rely on its mechanisms to work only over long periods of time. Here, we are interested in how the interest rate is determined in the *short run*, so we must change our perspective. Toward the end of the chapter, we'll come back to the classical model and explain why its theory of the interest rate does not apply in the short run.

In the short run—our focus here—we look for the equilibrium interest rate in the *money market:* the interest rate at which the quantity of money demanded and the quantity of money supplied are equal. Figure 5 combines the money supply and demand curves. Equilibrium occurs at point *E*, where the two curves intersect. At this point, the quantity of money demanded and the quantity supplied are both equal to $1,000 billion, and the equilibrium interest rate is 6 percent.

It is important to understand what equilibrium in the money market actually means. First, remember that the money supply curve tells us the quantity of money, determined by the Fed, that *actually exists* in the economy. Every dollar of this money—either in cash or in checking account balances—is held by *someone*. Thus, the money supply curve, in addition to telling us the quantity of money supplied by the Fed, also tells us the quantity of money that people *are actually holding* at any given moment. The money demand curve, on the other hand, tells us how much money people *want* to hold at each interest rate. Thus, when the quantity of money supplied and the quantity demanded are equal, all of the money in the economy is being *willingly held*. That is, people are satisfied holding the money that they are *actually* holding.

> *Equilibrium in the money market occurs when the quantity of money people are* actually *holding (quantity supplied) is equal to the quantity of money they* want *to hold (quantity demanded).*

Can we have faith that the interest rate will reach its equilibrium value in the money market, such as 6 percent in our figure? Indeed we can. In the next section, we explore the forces that drive the money market toward its equilibrium.

How the Money Market Reaches Equilibrium

To understand how the money market reaches its equilibrium, suppose that the interest rate, for some reason, were *not* at its equilibrium value of 6 percent in Figure 5. For example, suppose the interest rate were 9 percent. As the figure shows, at this interest rate the quantity of money demanded would be $600 billion, while the quantity supplied would be $1,000 billion. Or, put another way, people would *actually* be holding $1,000 billion of their wealth as money, but they would *want* to hold only $600 billion as money. There would be an **excess supply of money** (the quantity of money supplied would exceed the quantity demanded) equal to $1,000 billion − $600 billion = $400 billion.

Excess supply of money The amount of money supplied exceeds the amount demanded at a particular interest rate.

Now comes an important point. Remember that in our analysis, money and bonds are the only two assets available. If people want to hold *less* money than they are currently holding, then, by definition, they must want to hold *more* in bonds than they are currently holding—an **excess demand for bonds**.

Excess demand for bonds The amount of bonds demanded exceeds the amount supplied at a particular interest rate.

> *When there is an excess supply of money in the economy, there is also an excess demand for bonds.*

To understand this more clearly, imagine that instead of the money market, which can seem rather abstract, we were discussing something more concrete: the arrangement of books in a bookcase. Suppose that you have a certain number of books, and you have only two shelves on which to place all of them: top and bottom. One day, you look at the shelves and decide that, the way you've arranged things, the top shelf has *too many* books. Then, by definition, you must also feel that the bottom shelf has *too few* books. That is, an excess supply of books on the top shelf (it has more books than you want there) is the same as an excess demand for books on the bottom shelf (it has fewer books than you want there).

A similar conclusion applies to the money market. People allocate a given amount of wealth between two different assets: money and bonds. Too much in one asset implies too little in the other.

So far, we've established that if the interest rate were 9 percent, which is higher than its equilibrium value, there would be an excess supply of money, and an excess demand for bonds. What would happen? The public would demand more bonds. Just as there is a market for money, there is also a market for bonds. And as the public begins to demand more bonds, making them scarcer, *the price of bonds will rise*. We can illustrate the steps in our analysis so far as follows:

We conclude that, when the interest rate is higher than its equilibrium value, the price of bonds will rise. Why is this important? In order to take our story further, we must first take a detour for a few paragraphs.

An Important Detour: Bond Prices and Interest Rates

A bond, in the simplest terms, is a promise to pay back borrowed funds at a certain date or dates in the future. There are many types of bonds. Some promise to make payments each month or each year for a certain period and then pay back a large sum at the end. Others promise to make just one payment—perhaps 1, 5, 10, or more years from the date the bond is issued. When a large corporation or the government wants to borrow money, it issues a new bond and sells it in the marketplace; the amount borrowed is equal to the price of the bond.

Let's consider a very simple example: a bond that promises to pay to its holder $1,000 exactly 1 year from today. Suppose that you purchase this bond from the issuer—a firm or government agency—for $800. Then you are lending $800 to the issuer, and you will be paid back $1,000 one year later. What interest rate are you earning on your loan? Let's see: You will be getting back $200 more than you lent, so that is your *interest payment*. The annual interest *rate* is the interest payment over the year divided by the amount of the loan, or $200/$800 = 0.25 or 25 percent.

Now, what if instead of $800, you paid a price of $900 for this very same bond? The bond still promises to pay $1,000 one year from now, so your annual interest payment would now be $100, and your interest rate would be $100/$900 = 0.11 or 11 percent—a considerably lower interest rate. As you can see, the interest rate that you will earn on your bond depends entirely on the *price* of the bond. *The higher the price, the lower the interest rate.*

This general principle applies to virtually all types of bonds, not just the simple one-time-payment bond we've considered here. Bonds promise to pay various sums to their holders at different dates in the future. Therefore, the more you pay for any bond, the lower your overall rate of return, or interest rate, will be. Thus,

> *when the price of bonds rises, the interest rate falls; when the price of bonds falls, the interest rate rises.*[1]

The relationship between bond prices and interest rates helps explain why the government, the press, and the public are so concerned about the *bond market*, where bonds issued in previous periods are bought and sold. This market is sometimes called the *secondary* market for bonds, to distinguish it from the *primary* market where newly issued bonds are bought and sold. When you hear that "the bond market rallied" on a particular day of trading, it means that prices rose in the secondary bond market. This is good news for bondholders. But it is also good news for any person or business that wants to borrow money. When prices rise in the secondary market, they immediately rise in the primary market as well, because newly issued bonds and previously issued bonds are almost perfect substitutes for each other. Therefore, a bond market rally not only means lower interest rates in the secondary market, it also means lower interest rates in the primary market, where firms borrow money by issuing new bonds. Sooner or later, it will also lead to a drop in the interest rate on mortgages, car loans, credit card balances, and even many student loans. This is good news for borrowers. But it is bad news for anyone wishing to lend money, for now they will earn less interest.

Now that you understand the relationship between bond prices and interest rates, let's return to our analysis of the money market.

---

[1] In our macroeconomic model of the economy, we refer to *the* interest rate. In the real world, there are many types of interest rates: a different one for each type of bond, and still other rates on savings accounts, time deposits, car loans, mortgages, and more. However, all of these interest rates usually move up and down together, even though some may lag behind a few days, weeks, or months. Thus, when bond prices rise, interest rates *generally* will fall, and vice versa.

Back to the Money Market

Look back at Figure 5, and let's recap what you've learned so far. If the interest rate were 9 percent, there would be an excess supply of money, and therefore an excess demand for bonds. The price of bonds would rise. Now we can complete the story. As you've just learned, a rise in the price of bonds means a *decrease* in the interest rate. The complete sequence of events is

Thus, if the interest is 9 percent in our figure, it will begin to fall. Therefore, 9 percent is *not* the equilibrium interest rate.

How far will the interest rate fall? As long as there continues to be an excess supply of money, and an excess demand for bonds, the public will still be trying to acquire bonds, and the interest rate will continue to fall. But notice what happens in the figure as the interest rate falls: The quantity of money demanded *rises*. Finally, when the interest rate reaches 6 percent, the excess supply of money, and therefore the excess demand for bonds, is eliminated. At this point, there is no reason for the interest rate to fall further, so 6 percent is, indeed, our equilibrium interest rate.

We can also do the same analysis from the other direction. Suppose the interest rate were *lower* than 6 percent in the figure—say, 3 percent. Then, as you can see in Figure 5, there would be an *excess demand for money*, and an *excess supply of bonds*. In this case, the following would happen:

The interest rate would continue to rise until it reached its equilibrium value: 6 percent.

WHAT HAPPENS WHEN THINGS CHANGE?

Now that we have seen how the interest rate is determined in the money market, we turn our attention to *changes* in the interest rate. We'll focus on two questions: (1) What *causes* the equilibrium interest rate to change? and (2) What are the *consequences* of a change in the interest rate? As you are about to see, the Fed can change the interest rate as a matter of policy, or the interest rate can change on its own, as a by-product of other events in the economy. We'll begin with the Fed.

How the Fed Changes the Interest Rate

Suppose the Fed wants to *lower* the interest rate. Fed officials cannot just declare that the interest rate should be lower. To change the interest rate, the Fed must change the *equilibrium* interest rate in the money market, and it does this by changing the money supply.

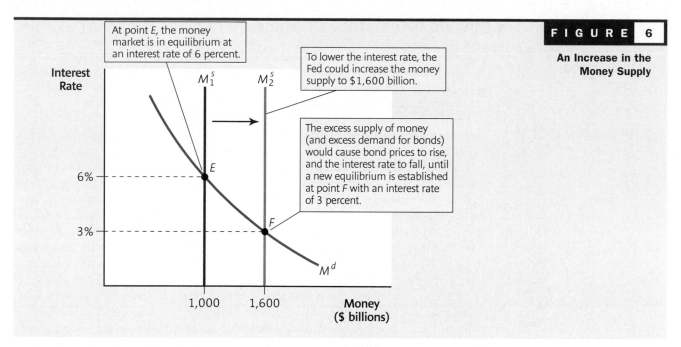

FIGURE 6

An Increase in the Money Supply

Look at Figure 6. Initially, with a money supply of $1,000 billion, the money market is in equilibrium at point *E*, with an interest rate of 6 percent. To lower the interest rate, the Fed *increases* the money supply through open market purchases of bonds. In the figure, the Fed raises the money supply to $1,600 billion, shifting the money supply curve rightward. (This is a much greater shift than the Fed would ever actually engineer in practice, but it makes the graph easier to read.) At the old interest rate of 6 percent, there would be an excess supply of money and an excess demand for bonds. This will drive the interest rate down until it reaches its new equilibrium value of 3 percent, at point *F*. The process works like this:

The Fed can *raise* the interest rate as well, through open market *sales* of bonds. In this case, the money supply curve in Figure 6 would shift leftward (not shown), setting off the following sequence of events:

If the Fed increases the money supply by buying government bonds, the interest rate falls. If the Fed decreases the money supply by selling government bonds, the interest rate rises. By controlling the money supply through purchases and sales of bonds, the Fed can also control the interest rate.

How Do Interest Rate Changes Affect the Economy?

As you've just learned, if the Fed increases the money supply through open market purchases of bonds, the interest rate will fall. But what then? How is the macroeconomy affected? The answer is: *A drop in the interest rate will boost several different types of spending in the economy.*

First, a lower interest rate stimulates business spending on plant and equipment. This idea came up a few chapters ago in the classical model, but we will go back over it here.

Remember that the interest rate is one of the key costs of any investment project. If a firm must borrow funds, it will have to pay for them at the going rate of interest—for example, by selling a bond at the going price. If the firm uses its *own* funds, so it doesn't have to borrow, the interest rate *still* represents a cost: Each dollar spent on plant and equipment *could* have been lent to someone else at the going interest rate. Thus, the interest rate is the *opportunity cost* of the firm's own funds when they are spent on plant and equipment.

A firm deciding whether to spend on plant and equipment compares the benefits of the project—the increase in future income—with the costs of the project. With a lower interest rate, the costs of funding investment projects are lower, so more projects will get the go-ahead. Other variables affect investment spending as well. But all else equal, a drop in the interest rate will cause an increase in spending on plant and equipment.

Interest rate changes also affect another kind of investment spending: spending on new houses and apartments that are built by developers or individuals. Most people borrow to buy houses or condominiums, and most developers borrow to build apartment buildings. The loan agreement for housing is called a *mortgage,* and mortgage interest rates tend to rise and fall with other interest rates. Thus, when the Fed lowers the interest rate, families find it more affordable to buy homes, and developers find it more profitable to build new apartments. Total investment in new housing increases.

Finally, in addition to investment spending, the interest rate affects consumption spending on big-ticket items such as new cars, furniture, and dishwashers. Economists call these *consumer durables* because they usually last several years. People often borrow to buy consumer durables, and the interest rate they are charged tends to rise and fall with other interest rates in the economy. Spending on new cars, the most expensive durable that most of us buy, is especially sensitive to interest rate changes. Since a lower interest rate causes higher consumption spending at *any* level of disposable income, it causes a *shift* of the consumption function, not a movement along it. Therefore, we consider this impact on consumption to be a rise in autonomous consumption spending, called *a* in our discussion of the consumption function.

We can summarize the impact of money supply changes as follows:

> *When the Fed increases the money supply, the interest rate falls, and spending on three categories of goods increases: plant and equipment, new housing, and consumer durables (especially automobiles). When the Fed decreases the money supply, the interest rate rises, and these categories of spending fall.*

MONETARY POLICY

Two chapters ago, you learned that changes in aggregate expenditure cause changes in real GDP through the multiplier process. In this chapter, you've learned that the Federal Reserve, through its control of the money supply, can change the interest rate, and therefore influence aggregate expenditure. Thus, the Fed—through its control of the money supply—has the power to influence real GDP.

When the Fed controls or manipulates the money supply in order to achieve any macroeconomic goal—such as a change in the level of real GDP—it is engaging in **monetary policy.** Let's put all the pieces of our analysis together and see how monetary policy works.

Monetary policy Control or manipulation of the money supply by the Federal Reserve designed to achieve a macroeconomic goal.

HOW MONETARY POLICY WORKS

In Figure 7, we revisit the short-run macro model, but we now include the money market in our analysis. In panel (a), the Fed has initially set the money supply at $1,000 billion. Equilibrium is at point *A*, with an interest rate (*r*) of 6 percent. Panel (b) shows the familiar short-run aggregate expenditure diagram, with equilibrium at point *E*, and equilibrium GDP equal to $8,000 billion.

But notice the new labels in the figure. The aggregate expenditure line has the subscript "*r* = 6%," Why this additional label?

As you are about to see, a change in the interest rate will cause the aggregate expenditure line to shift. Therefore, our aggregate expenditure line is drawn for a particular interest rate, the one determined in the money market, or 6 percent.

Now we suppose that the Fed increases the money supply to $1,600 billion. (Again, this is an unrealistically large change in the money supply, but it makes it easier to see the change in the figure.) In the upper panel, the money market equilibrium moves from point *A* toward point *B*, and the interest rate drops to 3 percent. The drop in the interest rate causes planned investment spending on plant and equipment and on new housing to rise. It also causes an increase in consumption spending—especially on consumer durables like automobiles—to rise at any level of income. This is an increase in autonomous consumption spending (*a*). In the lower panel, the rise in spending causes the aggregate expenditure line to shift upward, setting off the multiplier effect and increasing equilibrium GDP. The new equilibrium in the lower panel is point *F*, with real GDP at $10,000 billion. In the end, we see that the Fed, by increasing the money supply and lowering the interest rate, has increased the level of output.

Shift versus Movement Along the *AE* Line When thinking about the effects of monetary policy, try not to confuse movements *along* the aggregate expenditure line with *shifts* of the line itself. We move *along* the line only when a change in *income* causes spending to change. The line shifts when something *other* than a change in income causes spending to change.

When the Fed changes the interest rate, both types of changes occur, but it's important to keep the order straight. *First,* the drop in the interest rate (something other than income) causes interest-sensitive spending to change, *shifting* the aggregate expenditure line. *Then,* increases in income in each round of the multiplier cause further increases in spending, moving us *along* the new aggregate expenditure line.

We've covered a lot of ground to reach our conclusion, so let's review the highlights of how monetary policy works. This is what happens when the Fed conducts open market purchases of bonds:

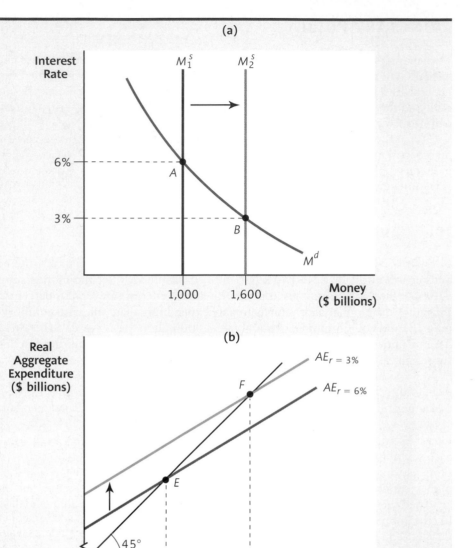

FIGURE 7

Monetary Policy and the Economy

Initially, the Fed has set the money supply at $1,000 billion, so the interest rate is 6 percent (point A). Given that interest rate, aggregate expenditure is AE$_{r=6\%}$ in panel (b), and real GDP is $8,000 billion (point E).

If the Fed increases the money supply to $1,600 billion, money market equilibrium moves to point B in panel (a). The interest rate falls to 3% (point B), stimulating interest-sensitive spending and driving aggregate expenditures upward in panel (b). Through the multiplier process, real GDP increases to $10,000 billion (point F).

Open market *sales* by the Fed have exactly the opposite effects. In this case, the money supply curve in Figure 7 would shift leftward (not shown), driving the interest rate up. The rise in the interest rate would cause a decrease in interest-sensitive spending (*a* and I^p), shifting the aggregate expenditure line downward. Equilibrium GDP would fall by a multiple of the initial decrease in spending.

Feedback Effects?

If you've been paying close attention, you may have a question about Figure 7. We've shown how changes in the upper panel (an increase in the money supply) cause changes in the lower panel (equilibrium GDP rises). But what about effects that go in the other direction? Shouldn't the rise in income in the lower panel increase the demand for money in the upper panel?

In Figure 7, we have ignored this "feedback effect" from changes in income to changes in money demand. Including this effect would make our analysis of monetary policy a bit more complicated, and alter the *size* of the changes in real GDP and the interest rate. But it would not alter the direction of the changes, or any of the conclusions we've reached about monetary policy.

The appendix to this chapter provides a more detailed analysis of monetary policy, incorporating the effect of income on money demand. It also takes another look at fiscal policy, which becomes a bit more complicated when the money market is included.

MONETARY POLICY IN PRACTICE

You've just seen how changes in the interest rate can shift the *AE* line and change equilibrium GDP. It is not surprising that the Fed regards the interest rate as its main policy instrument in influencing the economy.

In practice, the interest rate that the Fed watches most closely is the rate in the *federal funds market*. In this market, banks with excess reserves lend them out to other banks for very short periods, usually a day. The interest rate in the federal funds market is called the **federal funds rate**. Although it is just an interest rate for lending among banks, many other interest rates in the economy vary with it closely. When the Fed changes the federal funds rate, other interest rates—such as those on automobile loans, business loans, mortgages, and home equity loans—change as well. They may change less or more than the federal funds rate has changed, but they virtually always move in the same direction.

During most periods, the Fed tries to prevent unnecessary fluctuations in the federal funds rate in order to avoid unnecessary shifts in the *AE* line. The Fed does this by targeting a specific value for the federal funds rate, and adjusting the money supply as needed to keep the funds rate at the target level.

At other times, the Fed *wants* the federal funds rate (and other interest rates) to change, in order to *cause* a shift in the *AE* line—say, to bring it closer to full employment than it would be otherwise. At such times, the Fed will *change* its target rate.

Note that the money supply itself plays a subservient role in the Fed's thinking about monetary policy. The money supply is simply increased or decreased as needed to keep the federal funds rate at its target. Since 1994, the Federal Open Market Committee has formalized this practice, by publicly announcing its target for the federal funds rate when it meets every six weeks or so. The FOMC then instructs its open market operations desk, operating out of the New York Federal Reserve Bank, to adjust the money supply as needed (with open market operations) to reach and maintain the announced target.

Federal funds rate The interest rate charged for loans of reserves among banks.

To see how this works, let's consider two different situations: one in which the Fed wants to *maintain* the interest rate at its target level, and one in which the Fed wants to *change* the target level.

Maintaining an Interest Rate Target

Figure 8 shows an economy that is initially operating at full employment output. In the upper panel, the money market is in equilibrium at point *A*, with the interest rate (federal funds rate) at its target of 5 percent. The money supply is $1,000 billion, which is just the amount needed to maintain the target. In the lower panel, the

---

FIGURE 8

Maintaining an Interest Rate Target

Initially, the money market in panel (a) is at point A, with the interest rate at its target of 5 percent. In panel (b), this interest rate positions the AE line to create equilibrium output of $10,000 billion, which results in full employment.

An increase in money demand from M₁ᵈ to M₂ᵈ in panel (a), with no action by the Fed, would drive the interest rate up to 8 percent, and shift the AE line in panel (b) downward. To prevent this, the Fed increases the money supply from $1,000 billion (M₁ˢ) to $1,400 billion (M₂ˢ), moving the money market equilibrium to point C. This maintains the interest rate at its target of 5 percent, and prevents any change in equilibrium output in panel (b).

aggregate expenditure line for an interest rate of 5 percent ($AE_{r\,=\,5\%}$) intersects the 45° line to create equilibrium output of $10,000 billion. We assume that this happens to be the economy's full-employment output (Y_{FE}) as well.

Now suppose that public preferences change: People suddenly want to hold more of their wealth in money, which means less in bonds. (Perhaps it's the holiday shopping season, and people need to hold more wealth as money because they are making more purchases.) Because people want to hold more money at every interest rate, the money demand curve shifts rightward. If the Fed did nothing and left the money supply unchanged, the money market equilibrium would move to point B, with an interest rate of 8 percent. But this rise in the interest rate would cause the AE line in the lower panel to shift downward (not shown), and cause equilibrium GDP to fall below Y_{FE}—a recession.

To prevent any drop in GDP, the Fed has a simple task: to maintain its target interest rate. It does so by increasing the money supply (from $1,000 billion to $1,400 billion in the figure), shifting the money supply curve rightward from M^s_1 to M^s_2. After the shift, the new equilibrium in the money market occurs at point C, with the interest rate back to its target rate of 5 percent.

In general,

> to prevent fluctuations in money demand from affecting the economy, the Fed simply adjusts the money supply to maintain its interest rate target.

Changing the Interest Rate Target

Figure 9 illustrates a case where the Fed would want to *change* its interest rate target. Initially, things are fine. In the upper panel, the Fed is maintaining a target interest rate of 5 percent, at point A. In the lower panel, the aggregate expenditure line for that interest rate (AE_1) creates full-employment output of $10,000 billion.

Then something happens: Some sector of the economy reduces its spending. Perhaps pessimism about the future has caused a decrease in investment spending or autonomous consumption spending. Or perhaps the government has increased net taxes. Regardless of the cause, the aggregate expenditure line in the lower panel shifts downward, to AE_2. Equilibrium output falls to $9,000 billion at point F— below potential output. We are in a recession.

The Fed knows that a lower interest rate would stimulate additional investment and consumption spending, and could shift the AE line back up to its original position. So now the Fed will *lower* its interest rate target. For example, suppose the Fed believes an interest rate of 3 percent will move the aggregate expenditure line back to its original position. To achieve this new target, the Fed increases the money supply as necessary (to $1,300 billion in the figure).

In practice, the Fed would use a trial-and-error procedure to find the appropriate target. Every six weeks or so, it would lower the federal funds rate by a small amount, observe how the change is affecting other interest rates in the economy, and try to gauge the ultimate impact on the aggregate expenditure line and equilibrium GDP. This trial-and-error approach is not perfect, and the Fed has made mistakes— overshooting full employment in some periods and not quite hitting it in others. We'll explore some of the Fed's problems in conducting monetary policy in a later chapter.

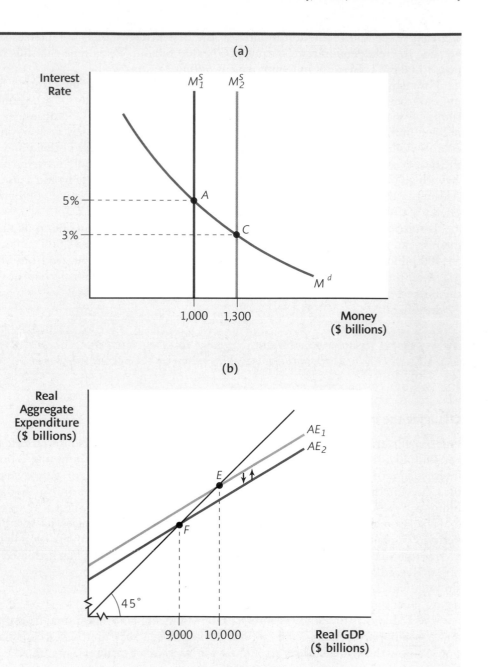

FIGURE 9

Changing the Interest Rate Target to Prevent a Recession

Initially, the money market in panel (a) is at point A, with the interest rate at its target of 5 percent. In panel (b), equilibrium output is $10,000 billion, which is the full-employment output level.

Then, in panel (b), the AE line shifts downward because of a decrease in some sector's spending. With no change in Fed policy, output would fall from $10,000 billion to $9,000 billion (point F). To prevent this recession, the Fed lowers its interest rate target to 3 percent in panel (a), and increases the money supply from $1,000 billion ($M_1^S$) to $1,300 billion ($M_2^S$). This moves the money market equilibrium to point C. The lower interest rate raises consumption and investment spending, shifting the AE line in panel (b) back to its original position.

ARE THERE TWO THEORIES OF THE INTEREST RATE?

At the beginning of this chapter, you were reminded that you had already learned a different theory of how the interest rate is determined in the economy. In the classical model, the interest rate is determined in the *market for loanable funds*. In this chapter, you learned that the interest rate is determined in the *money market*, where people make decisions about holding their wealth as money and bonds. Which theory is correct?

The answer is: Both are correct. The classical model, you remember, tells us what happens in the economy in the *long run*. Therefore, when we ask what changes the interest rate over long periods of time—many years or even a decade—we should think about the market for loanable funds. But over shorter time periods—days, weeks, or months—we should use the money market model presented in this chapter.

Why don't we use the classical loanable funds model to determine the interest rate in the short run? Because, as you've seen, the economy behaves differently in the short run than it does in the long run. For example, in the classical model, output is automatically at full employment. But in the short run, output changes as the economy goes through booms and recessions. These changes in output affect the loanable funds market in ways that the classical model does not consider. For example, flip back to the chapter on the classical model and look at Figure 8 there. Recessions, which decrease household income, would also decrease household saving at any given interest rate: With less income, households will spend less *and* save less. The supply of loanable funds curve would shift leftward in the diagram, and the interest rate would rise. The classical model—because it ignores recessions—ignores these short-run changes in the supply of loanable funds.

The classical model also ignores an important idea discussed in this chapter: that the public continuously chooses how to divide its wealth between money and bonds. In the short run, the public's preferences over money and bonds can change, and this, in turn, can change the interest rate. This idea does not appear in the classical model.

Of course, in the long run, the classical model gives us an accurate picture of how the economy and the interest rate behave. Recessions and booms don't last forever, so the economy returns to full employment. Thus, in the long run we needn't worry about recessions causing shifts in the supply of loanable funds curve. Also, changes in preferences for holding money and bonds are rather short-lived. We can ignore these changes when we take a long-run view.

> *In the long run, we view the interest rate as determined in the market for loanable funds, where household saving is lent to businesses and the government. In the short run, we view the interest rate as determined in the money market, where wealth holders adjust their wealth between money and bonds, and the Fed participates by controlling the money supply.*

USING THE THEORY

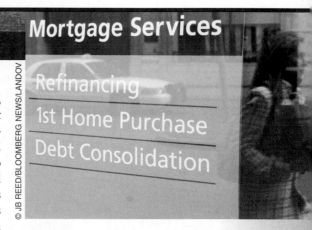

The Fed and the Recession of 2001

Two chapters ago, we began an analysis of our most recent recession, which officially lasted from March to November of 2001. We saw that a drop in investment spending caused a decrease in aggregate expenditure, which in turn caused equilibrium GDP and employment to drop. But we left two questions unanswered: (1) What did policy makers do to try to prevent the recession, and to deal with it once it started? and (2) Why did consumption spending behave abnormally, rising as income fell and preventing the recession from becoming a more serious downturn? Now that you've learned about monetary policy, we can begin to answer these questions.

Starting in January 2001—three months before the official start of the recession—the Fed began to worry. Although the economy was operating at or even above its potential output (the unemployment rate the previous month was 3.9 percent), there was danger on the horizon: Investment spending had declined from the previous quarter. This had started a negative multiplier effect, which was working its way through the economy and could ultimately cause a recession. Other factors made the Fed worry that investment spending could decrease further. And a sharp decrease in stock prices over the previous year—which had destroyed billions of dollars in household wealth—suggested that consumption spending might begin to fall as well.

The lower right panel (d) of Figure 10, which shows the aggregate expenditure diagram, illustrates the situation. Initially, the economy was at point E, with real GDP in January of 2001 (for this example, measured in 1996 dollars) equal to $9,242 billion.[2] The Fed feared that if it did nothing, the investment slowdown would shift the aggregate expenditure line downward, moving the equilibrium to a point like F, with GDP falling (in our diagram) to $9,000 billion.

The Fed decided to take action, indicated in panels (a), (b), and (c) of Figure 10. Panel (a) shows how the publicly announced federal funds rate target changed through the period. As you can see, the Fed repeatedly lowered the target, from 6.5 percent (prior to January 2001) down to 1.75 percent by the end of the year.

The lower left panel (b) tracks the money supply measure M1 (monthly). It shows that the Fed, beginning in January 2001, continually increased M1 in order to hit its (falling) interest rate target.

Now look at the upper right panel (c), which shows a before-and-after view of the money market. In January 2001, the money market was in equilibrium at point A, with the M1 measure of the money supply at $1,093 billion and a federal funds rate of 6.5 percent. By the end of 2001, the money supply had increased to $1,170 billion—just enough to maintain the Fed's federal funds rate target of 1.75 percent (point B).

Finally, look again at panel (d) in the lower right corner. It shows the impact of this monetary policy on equilibrium GDP. Instead of falling to point F, the economy ended up at point H, with real GDP hitting bottom at about $9,125 billion in September 2001. Although the Fed's policy moves did not completely prevent the recession, it no doubt saved the economy from a more severe and longer-lasting one. The lower interest rate was especially helpful in maintaining new-home construction, a category of investment spending that is especially sensitive to the interest rate.

The Fed's policy also helps us understand the other question we raised about the 2001 recession: the continued rise in consumption spending throughout the period. Lower interest rates, as you've now learned, stimulate consumption spending on consumer durables, especially automobiles. Indeed, helped by lower interest rates, auto sales rose in every quarter of 2001.

Moreover, when interest rates drop dramatically and rapidly—as they did in 2001—a frenzy of *home mortgage refinancing* can occur: Households rush to exchange their existing, higher-interest-rate mortgages for new mortgages at a lower interest rate. After a refinance, monthly mortgage payments are reduced, freeing up disposable income to be spent on goods and services. But many households go further, taking advantage of the refinancing to borrow even more than they owed on

[2] This example makes use of monthly real GDP estimates in 1996 dollars provided by Macroeconomic Advisors, a private consulting firm, to the National Bureau of Economic Research (NBER) (available at *http://www.nber.org/cycles/hall.pdf*).

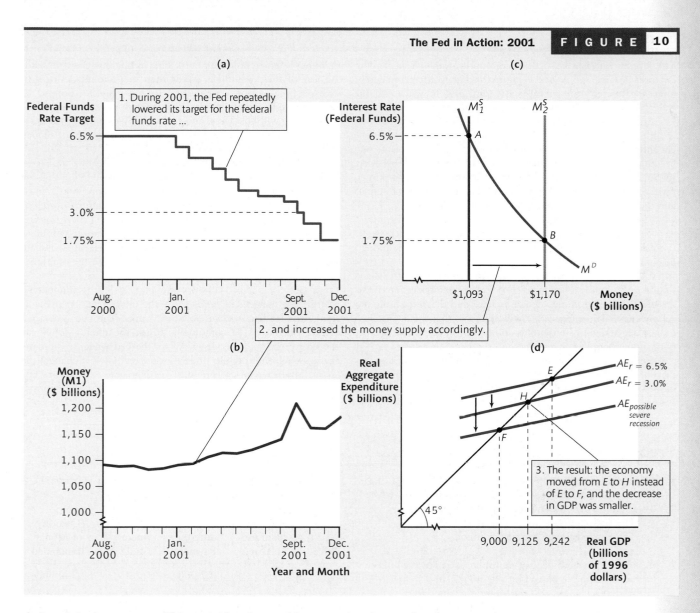

The Fed in Action: 2001   **FIGURE 10**

(a)

Federal Funds Rate Target

1. During 2001, the Fed repeatedly lowered its target for the federal funds rate ...

6.5%

3.0%

1.75%

Aug. 2000   Jan. 2001   Sept. 2001   Dec. 2001

(c)

Interest Rate (Federal Funds)

M_1^S M_2^S

6.5% — A

1.75% — B

M^D

$1,093 $1,170   Money ($ billions)

2. and increased the money supply accordingly.

(b)

Money (M1) ($ billions)

1,200

1,150

1,100

1,050

1,000

Aug. 2000   Jan. 2001   Sept. 2001   Dec. 2001

Year and Month

(d)

Real Aggregate Expenditure ($ billions)

$AE_r = 6.5\%$
$AE_r = 3.0\%$

E

H

$AE_{possible\ severe\ recession}$

F

45°

3. The result: the economy moved from E to H instead of E to F, and the decrease in GDP was smaller.

9,000 9,125 9,242   Real GDP (billions of 1996 dollars)

their original mortgage. This provides them with a one-time burst of cash to spend. Home refinancing and additional borrowing on homes seemed to play a major role in boosting consumption spending during the recession of 2001.

As you've read these pages, some questions may have formed in your mind. Why wasn't the Fed able to prevent the recession entirely? Couldn't the Fed have reduced the interest rate even more rapidly than it did?

There are, in general, good reasons for the Fed to be somewhat cautious in reducing interest rates. Over the next two chapters, you'll learn some of the reasons for the Fed's caution, and why most economists—despite the recession of 2001— give the Fed high marks for its actions during *that year*.

But you'll also learn that Fed policies during the year or so *before* 2001 may have actually contributed to the recession.

Summary

The interest rate is a key macroeconomic variable. This chapter explores how the supply and demand for money interact to determine the interest rate in the short run, and how the Federal Reserve can adjust the money supply to change the interest rate.

An individual's *demand for money* indicates the amount of wealth that person wishes to hold in the form of money, at different interest rates. Money is useful as a means of payment, but holding money means sacrificing the interest that could be earned by holding bonds instead. The higher the interest rate, the larger the fraction of their wealth people will hold in the form of bonds, and the smaller the fraction they will hold as money.

The demand for money is sensitive to the interest rate, but it also depends on the price level, and real income. An increase in the price level, or higher real income, can each shift the money demand curve to the right.

The money supply is under the control of the Fed. Equilibrium in the money market occurs at the intersection of the downward-sloping money demand curve and the vertical money supply curve. The interest rate will adjust so that the quantity of money demanded by households and firms just equals the quantity of money supplied by the Fed and the banking system.

Conditions in the money market mirror conditions in the bond market. If the interest rate is above equilibrium in the money market, there will be an *excess supply of money* there. People are holding more of their wealth in the form of money

than they *want* to hold as money. This means that they are holding less of their wealth in bonds than they would desire. (An excess supply of money means an excess demand for bonds.) As people move to acquire bonds, the price of bonds will rise and the interest rate will fall. Thus, an excess supply of money will cause the interest rate to fall. Similarly, an excess demand for money will cause the interest rate to rise.

The Fed can increase the money supply, creating an excess supply of money. Very quickly, the interest rate will fall so that the public is willing to hold the now-higher money supply.

Changes in the interest rate affect interest-sensitive forms of spending—firms' spending on plant and equipment, new housing construction, and households' purchases of "big-ticket" consumer durables. By lowering the interest rate, the Fed can stimulate aggregate expenditures and increase GDP through the multiplier process.

In practice, the Fed conducts monetary policy by announcing a target for the *federal funds rate*—the interest rate that banks charge for lending reserves to other banks. The Fed uses open market operations to continually adjust the money supply as needed to maintain the target. When the Fed wants to shift the aggregate expenditure line and influence real GDP, it changes the target. Lowering the target shifts the aggregate expenditure line upward and raises real GDP; raising the target has the opposite effects.

Problem Set   *Answers to even-numbered Questions and Problems can be found on the text Web site at www.thomsonedu.com/economics/hall.*

1. Assume the demand deposit multiplier is 10. For each of the following, state the impact on the money supply curve (the direction it will shift, and the amount of the shift).
   a. The Fed purchases bonds worth $10 billion.
   b. The Fed sells bonds worth $5 billion.

2. Assume the demand deposit multiplier is 7. For each of the following, state the impact on the money supply curve (the direction it will shift, and the amount of the shift).
   a. The Fed purchases bonds worth $28 million.
   b. The Fed sells bonds worth $17 million.

3. A bond promises to pay its owner $500 one year from now. For the following prices, find the corresponding interest payments and interest rates that the bond offers.

Price	Amount Paid in 1 Year	Interest Payment	Interest Rate
$375	$500	_____	_____
$425	$500	_____	_____
$450	$500	_____	_____
$500	$500	_____	_____

As the price of the bond rises, what happens to the bond's interest rate?

4. A bond promises to pay its owner $20,000 one year from now.
   a. Complete the following chart.

Price	Amount Paid in 1 Year	Interest Payment	Interest Rate	Quantity of Money Demanded
		$2,000		$2,300 billion
		$1,500		$2,600 billion
		$1,000		$2,900 billion
		$ 500		$3,200 billion
		$ 0		$3,500 billion

   b. Draw a graph of the money market, assuming that it is currently in equilibrium at an interest rate of 5.26 percent. What is the price of this bond? How large is the money supply?
   c. Find the new interest rate and the new bond price if the money supply increases by $300 billion. Show this on your graph.

5. A fellow student in your economics class stops you in the hallway and says: "An increase in the demand for money causes the interest rate to rise. But a rise in the interest rate causes people to demand *less* money. Therefore, increases in money demand largely cancel themselves out, and have very

little effect on the interest rate." Is this correct? Why or why not? (Hint: Draw a graph.)

6. For each of the following events, state (1) the impact on the money demand curve, and (2) whether the Fed should increase or decrease the money supply if it wants to keep the interest rate unchanged. (Hint: It will help to draw a diagram of the money market for each case.)
   a. People start making more of their purchases over the Internet, using credit cards.
   b. Greater fear of credit card fraud makes people stop buying goods over the Internet with credit cards, and discourages the use of credit cards in other types of purchases as well.
   c. A new type of electronic account is created in which your funds are held in bonds up to the second you make a purchase. Then—when you buy something— just the right amount of bonds are transferred to the ownership of the seller. (Hint: Would you want to increase or decrease the amount of your wealth in the form of money after this new type of account were available?)

7. Suppose that you own a bond that matures in one year, and promises to pay you $1,000 at that time. The current one-year interest rate in the economy is 6 percent.
   a. What is the price that someone would pay for your bond?
   b. Suppose that in the next few days, you *expect* the Fed to raise its interest rate target, causing the 1-year interest rate to rise to 8 percent. What is the price that you *expect* someone would pay for your bond after the Fed acts?
   c. If you have confidence in your expectation, which of the following will you want to do *now* (before the Fed acts): (1) acquire more bonds like the one you have; (2) sell your bond now; (3) neither? Explain briefly.
   d. If most other people develop the same expectations about the Fed that you have, what will likely happen to

the money demand curve *now* (before the Fed acts)? Illustrate on a diagram of the money market.
   e. If the Fed wants to maintain the interest rate at its current target level, what must the Fed do? Illustrate by adding to your diagram of the money market.

8. Suppose that, in an attempt to prevent the economy from overheating, the Fed raises the interest rate. Illustrate graphically, using a diagram similar to Figure 7 in this chapter, the effect on the money supply, interest rate, and GDP.

9. In a later chapter, you will learn that a drop in the interest rate has *another* channel of influence on real GDP: It causes a depreciation of the dollar (that is, it makes the dollar cheaper to foreigners), which, in turn, increases U.S. net exports.
   a. When we take account of the effect on net exports, does a given change in the money supply have *more* or *less* impact on real GDP?
   b. Suppose that the Fed wants to stimulate the economy as during 2001. Should the Fed lower the interest rate by more or by less when it takes the impact on net exports into account (compared to the case of no impact on net exports)? Explain.

More Challenging

10. [Requires appendix] As in problem 8, suppose that the Fed raises the interest rate to prevent the economy from overheating. Using a diagram that includes feedback effects (similar to Figure A.1 in the appendix), illustrate the impact on the money supply, interest rate, and real GDP.

11. [Requires appendix] Determine whether *fiscal policy* is *more* or *less* effective in changing GDP when autonomous consumption and investment spending are *very sensitive* to changes in the interest rate, and explain your reasoning.

12. Figure 10(b) shows a spike in money growth during September 2001. Using what you know about bonds versus money and the money demand curve, explain why this spike might have occurred.

APPENDIX

Feedback Effects from GDP to the Money Market

In the body of this chapter, you learned how changes in the money market affect equilibrium GDP. But we ignored how changes in equilibrium GDP affect the money market and cause further changes in the interest rate. In this appendix, we'll incorporate these feedback effects from GDP to the money market into our analysis. This will give us a more complete picture of how monetary policy works. We'll also take another look at fiscal policy, this time incorporating the money market into the analysis.

A MORE COMPLETE VIEW OF MONETARY POLICY

Figure A.1 revisits the economy shown in Figure 7. The upper panel shows the initial situation in the money market. The Fed has initially set the money supply at $1,000 billion, so the money supply curve is M_1^s. The money supply curve and money demand curve initially intersect at point *A*, resulting in an interest rate of 6 percent. But notice the label on the initial money demand curve "*Y* = $8,000 billion." In this appendix, the money demand curve will shift if there is a change in real income. Therefore, our money demand curve is drawn for a particular level of real income—the level of income determined in panel (b) at point *E*. Notice that the aggregate expenditure line in panel (b) has the subscript "*r* = 6%" because that is the interest rate found in panel (a). As you can see, the two panels are *interdependent*: The equilibrium in each one depends on the equilibrium in the other. When we draw the diagrams, we have to make sure that the money demand curve is consistent with the level of income found in the aggregate expenditure diagram, and that the aggregate expenditure line is consistent with the interest rate found in the money market diagram.

Now, let's see how monetary policy works when the two panels are interdependent in this way. Suppose the Fed increases the money supply to $1,600 billion. In the upper panel, the money supply curve shifts rightward, to M_2^s. The equilibrium starts to move toward

point *B*, with the interest rate heading down toward 3 percent.

But it will not actually get there. As the interest rate begins to drop, the aggregate expenditure line in the lower panel begins to rise. This causes equilibrium GDP to rise. As equilibrium GDP (which is the same as income) rises, people will want to hold more of their wealth in the form of money. So, in the upper panel, *the rise in equilibrium GDP shifts the money demand curve to the right.*

Where will we end up? To locate the exact final equilibrium, we would need quite a bit of detailed information about the economy. For example, we would need to know how sensitive aggregate expenditure is to changes in the interest rate, and how sensitive money demand is to changes in income. But even without these details, we know what must be true in the final equilibrium: Income will be higher than initially, because the aggregate expenditure line will have shifted upward. And the interest rate will be lower than initially, because the money supply will have increased.[3] Figure A.1 illustrates just one possibility, in which the new equilibrium is point *C* in the money market (upper panel), and point *H* in the aggregate expenditure diagram (lower panel). At this new equilibrium, the interest rate ends up at 4.5 percent, so our new aggregate expenditure line has the label "*r* = 4.5%." Equilibrium GDP has risen to $9,000 billion, so the new, higher money demand curve has the label "*Y* = $9,000 billion."

If you compare the final equilibrium in Figure A.1 to that in Figure 7, you'll see that the same increase in the money supply (from $1,000 billion to $1,600 bil-

[3] You might think that the interest rate could end up *higher* than initially, if the rightward shift in money demand is great enough—in particular, if the money demand curve shifts by more than the money supply curve. But this cannot happen. The money demand curve can shift rightward *only if* income rises. And income rises *only if* the AE line shifts upward. And the AE line shifts upward *only if* the interest rate falls. And the interest rate falls *only if* the shift in money demand is smaller than the shift in money supply. So to argue that the shift in money demand is so great that the interest rate actually rises is a logical contradiction. It would eliminate the reason for the money demand curve to shift rightward in the first place.

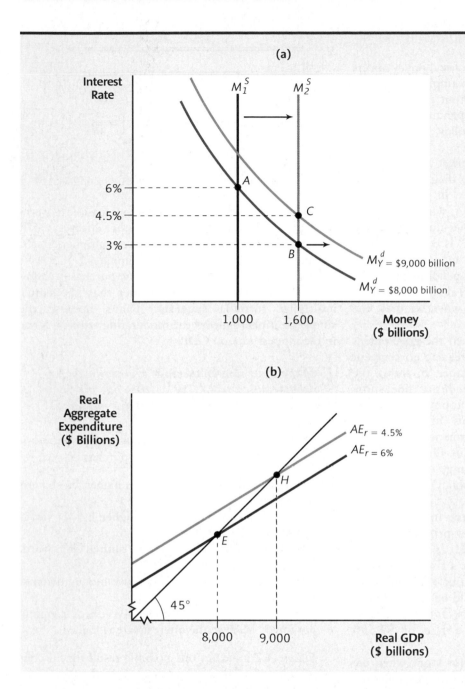

FIGURE A.1

A More Complete View of Monetary Policy

Initially, the Fed has set the money supply at $1,000 billion, so the interest rate is 6 percent (point A). Given that interest rate, the aggregate expenditure line is $AE_{r = 6\%}$ in panel (b), and real GDP is $8,000 billion (point E).

If the Fed increases the money supply to $1,600 billion and the money demand curve did not shift (as in the chapter), the money market equilibrium moves temporarily to point B in panel (a). The interest rate falls, stimulating interest-sensitive spending and shifting up the aggregate expenditure line in panel (a). Through the multiplier process, real GDP increases.

The rise in GDP has feedback effects on the money market in panel (a): The money demand curve shifts rightward, because more money is demanded when income is greater. In the new equilibrium, real GDP is $9,000 billion, and the interest rate is 4.5 percent (point C). Because of the feedback effects from GDP to the money market, the interest rate drops less, and GDP rises less, than when these feedback effects are ignored.

lion) has somewhat different effects. In Figure 7, the interest rate dropped all the way to 3 percent, and real GDP increased all the way to $10,000 billion. In Figure A.1, the interest rate still drops, but by less: to just 4.5 percent. And income still rises, but by less: to just $9,000 billion. Thus, including feedback effects makes monetary policy a little less potent, but it does not really change the way it works. If the Fed wants to hit any given interest rate target (say, 3 percent), the feedback effects will require it to

raise the money supply by more than it otherwise would. But it can still hit any desired target.

When the feedback effects from income to the money market are included, a given change in the money supply will cause a smaller change in the interest rate. Or, equivalently, to achieve any given change in the interest rate requires a larger change in the money supply.

A More Complete View of Fiscal Policy

Two chapters ago, we discussed how fiscal policy affects the economy in the short run. For example, an increase in government purchases causes output to rise, and in successive rounds of the multiplier, spending and output rise still more. Let's revisit fiscal policy, incorporating the money market into our analysis.

Figure A.2 shows the money market and the familiar short-run aggregate expenditure diagram. Initially, we have equilibrium in both panels. In panel (a), the money market equilibrium is point A, with the interest rate at 6 percent. In panel (b), the initial aggregate expenditure line, labeled "r = 6%," is consistent with the interest rate we've found in the money market. As you can see, with this aggregate expenditure line, the equilibrium is at point E, with real GDP equal to $8,000 billion, just as we assumed when we drew the money demand curve in panel (a).

Now let's see what happens when the government changes its fiscal policy, say, by increasing government purchases (G) by $1,000 billion. Panel (b) shows the initial effect: The aggregate expenditure line shifts upward, by $1,000 billion, to the topmost aggregate expenditure line (unlabeled). This new aggregate expenditure line is drawn for the same interest rate as the original line: r = 6%. The shift illustrates what *would* happen if there were no change in the interest rate, as in our analysis of fiscal policy two chapters ago.

As you've learned, the increase in government purchases will set off the multiplier process, increasing GDP and income in each round. *If this were the end of the story*, the result would be a rise in real GDP equal to $[1/(1 - MPC)] \times \Delta G$. In our example, with an MPC of 0.6, the multiplier would be $1/(1 - 0.6) = 2.5$. The new equilibrium would be at point F, with GDP equal to $10,500 billion—a rise of $2,500 billion.

But point F is *not* the end of our story when we include effects in the money market. As income increases, the money demand curve in panel (a) will shift rightward, raising the interest rate. As a result, autonomous consumption (a) and investment spending (I) will decrease and shift the aggregate expenditure line downward. That is, *an increase in government purchases, which by itself shifts the aggregate expenditure line upward, also sets in motion forces that shift it downward.* We can outline these forces as follows:

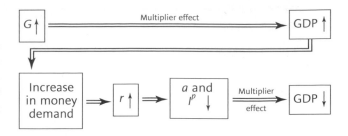

Net Effect: GDP↑, but by less due to effect of r↑

Thus, at the same time that the increase in government purchases has a *positive* multiplier effect on GDP, the decrease in a and I^p have *negative* multiplier effects. But the positive multiplier effect dominates.[4]

Thus, an increase in government purchases causes GDP to rise. But the rise is smaller than the simple multiplier formula suggests. That's because the simple multiplier ignores the moderating effect of a rise in the interest rate on GDP.

> *In the short run, an increase in government purchases causes real GDP to rise, but not by as much as if the interest rate had not increased.*

Let's sum up the characteristics of the new equilibrium after an increase in government purchases:

- The aggregate expenditure line is higher, but by less than ΔG.
- Real GDP and real income are higher, but the rise is less than $[1/(1 - MPC)] \times \Delta G$.
- The money demand curve has shifted rightward, because real income is higher.
- The interest rate is higher, because money demand has increased.
- Autonomous consumption and investment spending are lower, because the interest rate is higher.

Figure A.2 indicates one possible result that is consistent with all of these requirements. In the figure, the new equilibrium occurs at point B in the upper panel

[4] To prove this to yourself, remember that the negative multiplier effect is created *only if* the interest rate rises. And the interest rate rises *only if* the money demand curve shifts rightward. And the money demand curve shifts rightward *only if* income rises—that is, only if the positive multiplier effect is greater than the negative multiplier effect. So to argue that the negative multiplier effect dominates and income falls is a logical contradiction. It would eliminate the reason for the negative multiplier effect to occur in the first place.

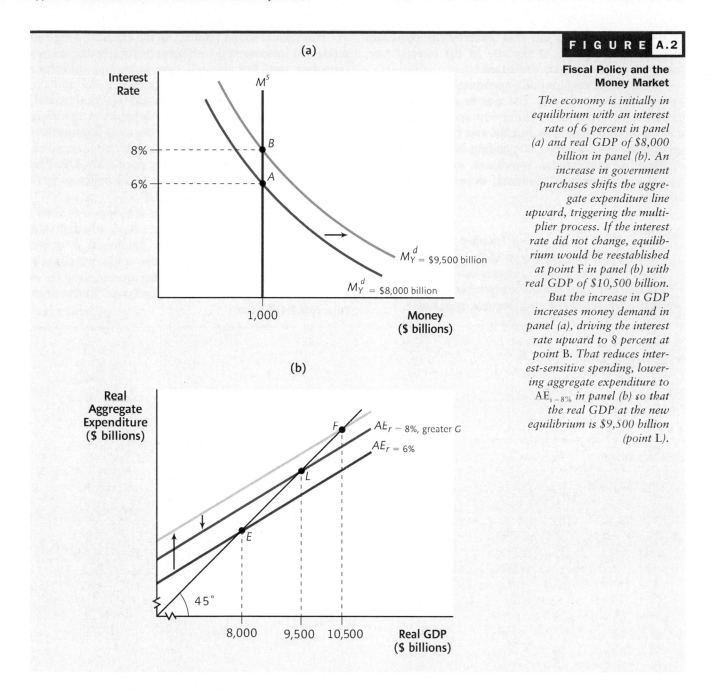

FIGURE A.2

Fiscal Policy and the Money Market

The economy is initially in equilibrium with an interest rate of 6 percent in panel (a) and real GDP of $8,000 billion in panel (b). An increase in government purchases shifts the aggregate expenditure line upward, triggering the multiplier process. If the interest rate did not change, equilibrium would be reestablished at point F in panel (b) with real GDP of $10,500 billion. But the increase in GDP increases money demand in panel (a), driving the interest rate upward to 8 percent at point B. That reduces interest-sensitive spending, lowering aggregate expenditure to $AE_{1-8\%}$ in panel (b) so that the real GDP at the new equilibrium is $9,500 billion (point L).

and *L* in the lower panel. The new equilibrium GDP is $9,500 billion, and the new equilibrium interest rate is 8 percent. Notice that real GDP has risen, but by only $1,500 billion—not the $2,500 billion suggested by the simple multiplier formula. Moreover, the two panels of the diagram are consistent with each other. The aggregate expenditure line (labeled "$r = 8\%$") corresponds to the equilibrium interest rate in the money market.

The money demand curve (labeled "$Y = \$9,500$ billion") corresponds to the equilibrium GDP in the aggregate expenditure diagram.

Crowding Out Once Again

Our analysis illustrates an interesting by-product of fiscal policy. Comparing our initial equilibrium to the final equilibrium, we see that government purchases increase. But because of the rise in the interest rate, *investment spending has decreased*.

What about consumption spending? It is influenced by two opposing forces. The rise in the interest rate causes *some* types of consumption spending (e.g., on automobiles) to decrease, but the rise in *income* makes other types of consumption spending *increase*. Thus, an increase in government purchases may increase or decrease consumption spending, depending on which effect is stronger.

Summing up:

> *When effects in the money market are included in the short-run macro model, an increase in government purchases raises the interest rate and* crowds out *some private investment spending. It may also crowd out consumption spending.*

This should sound familiar. In the classical, long-run model, an increase in government purchases also causes crowding out. But there is one important difference between crowding out in the classical model and the effects we are outlining here. In the classical model, there is *complete crowding out:* Investment spending and consumption spending fall by the same amount that government purchases rise. As a result, total spending does not change at all, and neither does real GDP. This is why, in the *long run,* we expect fiscal policy to have no demand-side effects on real GDP.

In the short run, however, our conclusion is somewhat different. While we expect *some* crowding out from an increase in government purchases, *it is not complete.* Investment spending falls, and consumption spending *may* fall, but together, they do not drop by as much as the rise in government purchases. In the short run, real GDP rises.

Aggregate Demand and Aggregate Supply

Economic fluctuations are facts of life. If you need a reminder, look back at Figure 1 in the chapter titled "Economic Fluctuations." There you can see that while potential GDP tends to move upward year after year due to economic growth, *actual* GDP tends to rise above and fall below potential over shorter periods.

But the figure also reveals another important fact about the economy: Deviations from potential output don't last forever. When output dips below or rises above potential, the economy returns to potential output after a few quarters or years. True, in some of these episodes, government policy—either fiscal or monetary—helped the economy return to full employment more quickly. But even without corrective policies—such as during long parts of the Great Depression of the 1930s—the economy shows a remarkable tendency to begin moving back toward potential output. Why? And what, exactly, is the mechanism that brings us back to our potential when we have strayed from it? These are the questions we will address in this chapter. And we'll address them by studying the behavior of a variable that we've put aside for several chapters: the price level.

The chapter begins by exploring the relationship between the price level and output. This is a two-way relationship, as you can see in Figure 1 in *this* chapter. On the one hand, changes in the price level cause changes in real GDP. This causal relationship is illustrated by the *aggregate demand curve*, which we will discuss shortly. On the other hand, changes in real GDP cause changes in the price level. This relationship is summarized by the *aggregate supply curve*, to which we will turn later.

Once we've developed the aggregate demand and supply curves, we'll be able to use them to understand how changes in the price level—sometimes gently, other times more harshly—steer the economy back toward potential output.

THE AGGREGATE DEMAND CURVE

Our first step in understanding how the price level affects the economy is an important fact: When the price level rises, the money demand curve shifts rightward. Why? Remember that the money demand curve tells us how much of their wealth people want to hold as money (as opposed to bonds) at each interest rate. People hold bonds because of the interest they pay; people hold money because of its convenience. Each day, as we make purchases, we need cash or funds in our checking account to pay for them. If the price level rises, so that our purchases become more expensive, we'll need to hold more of our wealth as money just to achieve the same

FIGURE 1

**The Two-Way Relationship
Between Output and the
Price Level**

level of convenience. Thus, at any given interest rate, the demand for money increases, and the money demand curve shifts rightward.

The shift in money demand, and its impact on the economy, is illustrated in Figure 2. Panel (a) has our familiar money market diagram. We'll assume that, initially, the price level in the economy is equal to 100. With this price level, the money market is in equilibrium at point A, with an interest rate of 6 percent.

In panel (b), equilibrium GDP is at point E, with output equal to $10 trillion. The aggregate expenditure line is marked "$r = 6\%$," which is the equilibrium interest rate we just found in the money market.

Now let's imagine a rather substantial rise in the price level, from 100 to 140. What will happen in the economy? The initial impact is in the money market. The money demand curve will start to shift rightward. For now, we'll assume the Fed does *not* change the money supply, so the interest rate will rise. Next, in panel (b), the higher interest rate decreases interest-sensitive spending—business investment, new housing, and consumer durables. The aggregate expenditure line shifts downward, and equilibrium real GDP decreases. All of these changes continue until we reach a new, consistent equilibrium in both panels. Compared with our initial position, this new equilibrium has the following characteristics:

- The money demand curve has shifted rightward.
- The interest rate is higher.
- The aggregate expenditure line has shifted downward.
- Equilibrium GDP is lower.

Remember that all of these changes are caused by a rise in the price level.

Panels (a) and (b) show one possible new equilibrium that meets these requirements. In panel (a), the money demand curve has shifted to M_2^d. The interest rate has risen to 9 percent. The aggregate expenditure line has shifted downward, to the one marked "$r = 9\%$." Finally, equilibrium output has fallen to $6 trillion.

Now recall the initial event that caused real GDP to fall: a rise in the price level. We've thus established an important principle:

A rise in the price level causes a decrease in equilibrium GDP.

DERIVING THE AGGREGATE DEMAND CURVE

In panel (c), we introduce a new curve that directly shows the negative relationship between the price level and equilibrium GDP. In this panel, the price level is measured

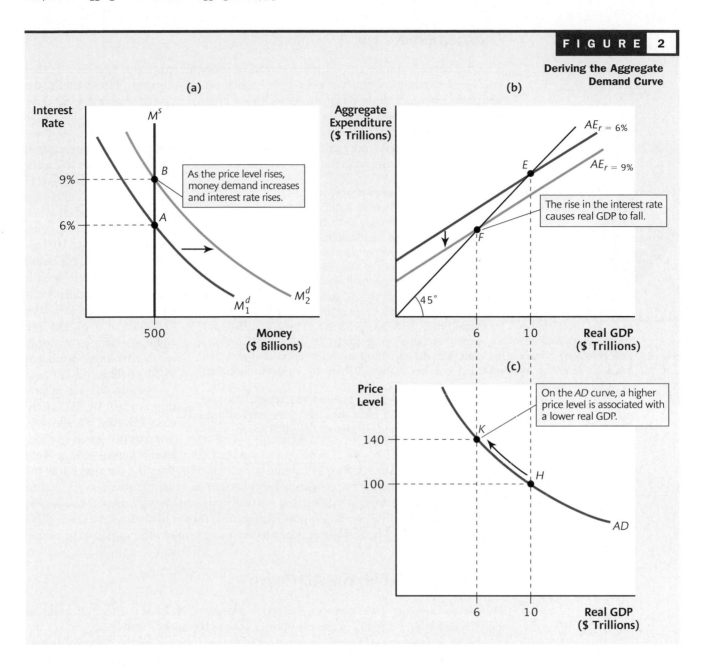

FIGURE 2

Deriving the Aggregate Demand Curve

(a)

(b)

As the price level rises, money demand increases and interest rate rises.

The rise in the interest rate causes real GDP to fall.

(c)

On the *AD* curve, a higher price level is associated with a lower real GDP.

along the vertical axis, while real GDP is on the horizontal. Point *H* represents our initial equilibrium, with *P* = 100 and equilibrium GDP = $10 trillion. Point *K* represents the new equilibrium, with *P* = 140 and equilibrium GDP = $6 trillion. If we continued to change the price level to other values—raising it further to 150, lowering it to 85, and so on—we would find that each different price level results in a different equilibrium GDP. This is illustrated by the downward-sloping curve in the figure, which we call the *aggregate demand curve.*

> The **aggregate demand** (**AD**) **curve** tells us the equilibrium real GDP at any price level.

Aggregate demand (AD) curve A curve indicating equilibrium GDP at each price level.

UNDERSTANDING THE *AD* CURVE

The *AD* curve is unlike any other curve you've encountered in this text. In all other cases, our curves have represented simple behavioral relationships. For example, the demand curve for maple syrup shows us how a change in price affects the behavior of buyers in a market. Similarly, the aggregate expenditure line shows how a change in income affects total spending in the economy.

But the *AD* curve represents more than just a behavioral relationship between two variables. Each point on the curve represents a short-run *equilibrium* in the economy. For example, point *H* on the *AD* curve in Figure 2 tells us that when the price level is 100, *equilibrium* GDP is $10 trillion. Thus, point *H* doesn't just tell us that total spending is $10 trillion; rather, it tells us that when $P = 100$, spending and output are equal to each other only when they *both* are equal to $10 trillion.

Two Misconceptions About the *AD* Curve Watch out for two common mistakes. The first is thinking that the *AD* curve is simply a "total demand" or "total spending" curve for the economy. This is an oversimplification. Rather, the *AD* curve tells us the *equilibrium* real GDP at each price level. This is the level of output at which total spending *equals* total output. Thus, total spending is only part of the story behind the *AD* curve: The other part is the requirement that total spending and total output be equal.

A second, related mistake is thinking that the *AD* curve slopes downward for the same reason that a microeconomic demand curve slopes downward. This, too, is wrong. In the market for maple syrup, for example, a rise in price causes quantity demanded to decrease, mostly because people switch to *other* goods that are now relatively cheaper. But along the *AD* curve, a rise in the price level generally causes the prices of *all* goods to increase *together*. There are no relatively cheaper goods to switch to!

The *AD* curve works in an entirely different way from microeconomic demand curves. Along the *AD* curve, an increase in the price level raises the interest rate in the money market, which decreases spending on interest-sensitive goods, causing a drop in equilibrium GDP.

As you can see, a better name for the *AD* curve would be the "equilibrium-output-at-each-price-level" curve—not a very catchy name. The *AD* curve gets its name because it *resembles* the demand curve for an individual product. It's a downward-sloping curve, with the price level (instead of the price of a single good) on the vertical axis and *equilibrium total output* (instead of the quantity of a single good demanded) on the horizontal axis. But there the similarity ends. The *AD* curve is not a demand curve at all, in spite of its name.

MOVEMENTS ALONG THE *AD* CURVE

Whenever the price level changes, we move *along* the *AD* curve. It's important to understand what happens in the economy as we make such a move.

Look again at the *AD* curve in panel (c) of Figure 2. Suppose the price level rises, and we move from point *H* to point *K* along this curve. Then the following sequence of events occurs: The rise in the price level increases the demand for money, raises the interest rate, decreases autonomous consumption (*a*) and investment spending (I^p), and works through the multiplier to decrease equilibrium GDP. The process can be summarized as follows:

The opposite sequence of events will occur if the price level falls, moving us rightward along the *AD* curve:

SHIFTS OF THE *AD* CURVE

When we move along the *AD* curve in Figure 2, we assume that the price level changes but that other influences on equilibrium GDP are constant. When any of these other influences on GDP changes, the *AD* curve will shift. The distinction between movements along the *AD* curve and shifts of the curve itself is very important. Always keep the following rule in mind:

> When a change in the price level causes equilibrium GDP to change, we move along the AD curve. Whenever anything other than the price level causes equilibrium GDP to change, the AD curve itself shifts.

What are these other influences on GDP? They are the very same changes you learned about in previous chapters. Specifically, equilibrium GDP will change whenever there is a change in any of the following:

- Government purchases
- Taxes
- Autonomous consumption spending
- Investment spending
- Net exports
- The money supply

Let's consider some examples and see how each causes the *AD* curve to shift.

An Increase in Government Purchases

In Figure 3, we assume that the economy begins at a price level of 100. In the money market (not shown), the equilibrium interest rate is 6 percent and equilibrium output—given by point *E* in panel (a)—is $10 trillion. Panel (b) shows the same equilibrium as represented by point *H* on AD_1.

Now let's repeat an experiment from an earlier chapter: We'll increase government purchases by $1 trillion and ask what happens to equilibrium GDP. As we do this, we'll assume that *the price level remains at 100*. If the MPC is 0.6, and our simple multiplier formula applies, the value of the multiplier will be $1/(1 - 0.6) = 2.5$. Therefore, GDP will rise by $1 trillion $\times$ 2.5 = $2.5 trillion. Our new value for equilibrium GDP is $12.5 trillion. This new equilibrium is also shown in panel (a) of Figure 3. The aggregate expenditure line shifts upward to AE_2, and the equilibrium moves to point *F*. With the price level remaining at 100, equilibrium GDP increases.

Now look at panel (b) in Figure 3. There, the new equilibrium is represented by point *J* ($P = 100$, real GDP = $12.5 trillion). This point lies to the right of our original curve AD_1. Point *J*, therefore, must lie on a *new AD* curve—a curve that tells

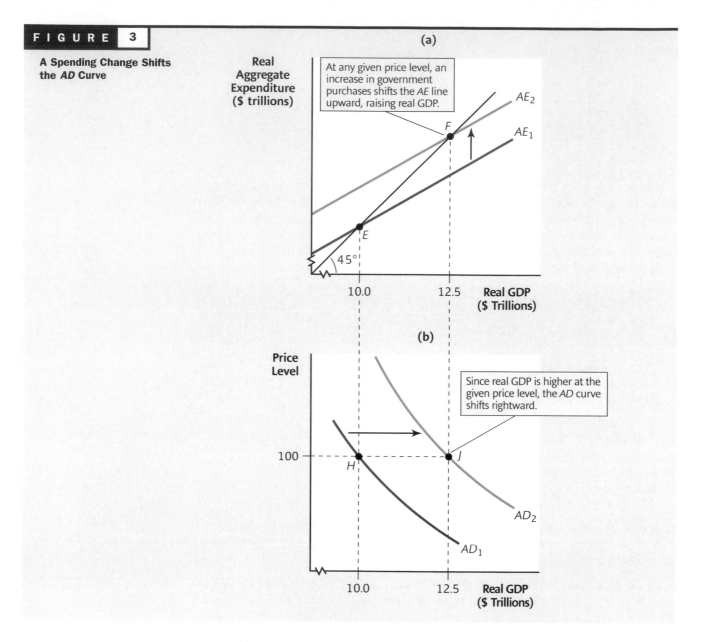

FIGURE 3

A Spending Change Shifts the *AD* Curve

(a)

Real Aggregate Expenditure ($ trillions)

At any given price level, an increase in government purchases shifts the *AE* line upward, raising real GDP.

AE_2

AE_1

F

E

45°

10.0   12.5   **Real GDP ($ Trillions)**

(b)

Price Level

Since real GDP is higher at the given price level, the *AD* curve shifts rightward.

100

H   *J*

AD_2

AD_1

10.0   12.5   **Real GDP ($ Trillions)**

us equilibrium GDP at any price level *after the increase in government spending*. The new *AD* curve is the one labeled AD_2, which goes through point *J*. What about the other points on AD_2? They tell us that, if we had started at any *other* price level, an increase in government spending would have increased equilibrium GDP at that price level, too. We conclude that *an increase in government purchases shifts the entire* AD *curve rightward*.

Any other factor that initially shifts the aggregate expenditure line upward will shift the AD curve rightward, just as in Figure 3. More specifically,

> *the* AD *curve shifts rightward when government purchases, investment spending, autonomous consumption spending, or net exports increase, or when net taxes decrease.*

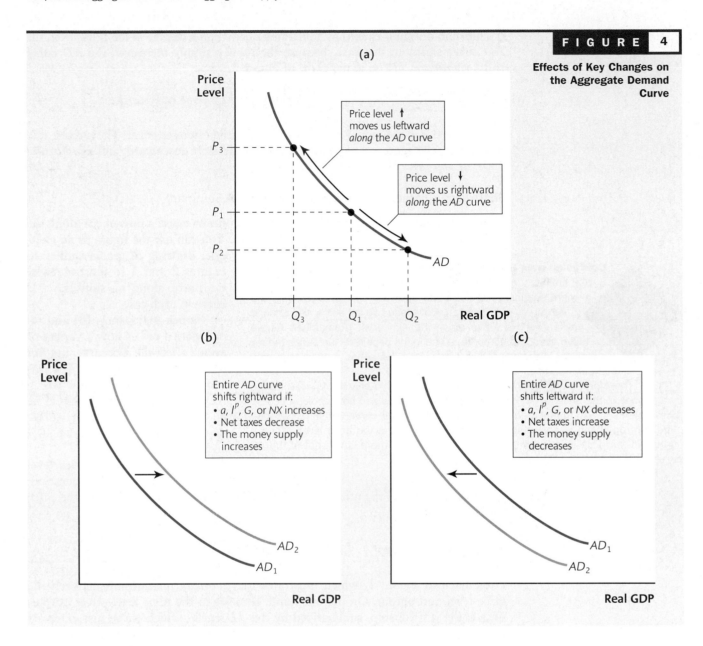

FIGURE 4

Effects of Key Changes on the Aggregate Demand Curve

(a)

Price Level

P_3

P_1

P_2

Price level ↑ moves us leftward *along* the *AD* curve

Price level ↓ moves us rightward *along* the *AD* curve

AD

Q_3 Q_1 Q_2 **Real GDP**

(b)

Price Level

Entire *AD* curve shifts rightward if:
• *a, I^P, G,* or *NX* increases
• Net taxes decrease
• The money supply increases

AD_2
AD_1

Real GDP

(c)

Price Level

Entire *AD* curve shifts leftward if:
• *a, I^P, G,* or *NX* decreases
• Net taxes increase
• The money supply decreases

AD_1
AD_2

Real GDP

Our analysis also applies in the other direction. For example, at any given price level, a *decrease* in government spending shifts the aggregate expenditure line *downward*, decreasing equilibrium GDP. This in turn shifts the *AD* curve leftward.

Changes in the Money Supply

Changes in the money supply will also shift the aggregate demand curve. To see why, let's imagine that the Fed conducts open market operations to *increase* the money supply. As you learned in the previous chapter, this will cause the interest rate to decrease, increasing investment spending and autonomous consumption spending. Together, these spending changes will shift the aggregate expenditure line upward, just as in panel (a) of Figure 3, and increase equilibrium GDP. Since this change in equilibrium output is caused by something *other* than a change in the price level, the *AD* curve shifts. In this case, because the money supply *increased*, the *AD* curve shifts *rightward*, just as in panel (b) of Figure 3.

> *An increase in the money supply shifts the* AD *curve rightward.*

A decrease in the money supply would have the opposite effect: The interest rate would rise, the aggregate expenditure line would shift downward, and *equilibrium GDP at any price level would fall.*

Shifts versus Movements Along the *AD* Curve: A Summary

Figure 4 summarizes how some events in the economy cause a movement along the *AD* curve, and other events shift the *AD* curve. You can use the figure as an exercise, drawing diagrams similar to Figures 2 and 3 to illustrate why we move along or shift the *AD* curve in each case.

Notice that panels (b) and (c) of Figure 4 tell us how a variety of events affect the *AD* curve, but *not* how they affect *real GDP*. The reason is that, even if we know which *AD* curve we are on, we could be at *any point* along that curve, depending on where the price level ends up.

But where will the price level end up? To answer that question, we must understand the other side of the relationship between GDP and the price level.

Confusion over Spending Changes. In this chapter, you've learned that changes in autonomous consumption (*a*) and planned investment spending (I^p), like other spending changes, can shift the *AD* curve. And they can. But these two variables also change whenever we move *along* the *AD* curve. (Remember: As we move along the *AD* curve, a rise in the price level increases money demand, raises the interest rate, and decreases autonomous consumption and I^p).

Therefore, a change in *a* or I^p shifts the *AD* curve only if it is *not* initiated by a change in the price level. For example, if businesses and households become more optimistic and thus increase their spending, the *AD* curve will shift, because increased optimism is something other than a change in the price level. When a change in the price level initiates a change in *a* and I^p, there is no shift of the *AD* curve, but rather a movement along it.

DANGEROUS CURVES

THE AGGREGATE SUPPLY CURVE

Look back at Figure 1, which illustrates the *two-way* relationship between the price level and output. On the one hand, changes in the price level affect output. This is the relationship, summarized by the *AD* curve, which we've just explored in the previous section. On the other hand, changes in output affect the price level. This relationship—summarized by the *aggregate supply curve*—is the focus of this section.

The effect of changes in output on the price level is complex, involving a variety of forces. Current research is helping economists get a clearer picture of this relationship. Here, we will present a simple model of the aggregate supply curve that focuses on the link between prices and costs. Toward the end of the chapter, we'll discuss some additional ideas about the aggregate supply curve.

COSTS AND PRICES

The price *level* in the economy results from the pricing behavior of millions of individual business firms. In any given year, some of these firms will raise their prices, and some will lower them. For example, during the early 2000s, laptop computers and long-distance telephone calls came down in price, while college tuition and the prices of movies rose. These types of price changes are subjects for *microeconomic* analysis, because they involve individual markets.

But often, all firms in the economy are affected by the same *macroeconomic* event, causing prices to rise or fall throughout the economy. This change in the price *level* is what interests us in macroeconomics.

To understand how macroeconomic events affect the price level, we begin with a very simple assumption:

> *A firm sets the price of its products as a markup over cost per unit.*

Fast-food restaurants, like other firms in the economy, charge a markup over cost per unit. The average markup in the economy is determined by competitive conditions and tends to change slowly over time.

For example, if it costs Burger King $2.50, on average, to produce a Whopper (cost per unit is $2.50), and Burger King's percentage markup is 10 percent, then it will charge $2.50 + (0.10 × $2.50) = $2.75 per Whopper.[1]

The percentage markup in any particular industry will depend on the degree of competition there. If there are many firms competing for customers in a market, all producing very similar products, then we can expect the markup to be relatively small. Thus, we expect a relatively low markup on fast-food burgers or personal computers. In industries where there is less competition—such as daily newspapers or jet aircraft—we would expect higher percentage markups.

In macroeconomics, we are not concerned with how the markup varies among different industries, but rather with the *average percentage markup* in the economy:

> *The average percentage markup in the economy is determined by competitive conditions in the economy. The competitive structure of the economy changes very slowly, so the average percentage markup should be somewhat stable from year to year.*

But a stable markup does not necessarily mean a stable price level, because unit costs can change. For example, if Burger King's markup remains at 10 percent, but the unit cost of a Whopper rises from $2.50 to $3.00, then the price of a Whopper will rise to $3.00 + (0.10 × $3.00) = $3.30. Extending this example to all firms in the economy, we can say:

> *In the short run, the price level rises when there is an economy-wide increase in unit costs, and the price level falls when there is an economy-wide decrease in unit costs.*

GDP AND THE PRICE LEVEL

Our primary concern in this chapter is the impact of *total output or real GDP* on unit costs and, therefore, on the price level. Why should a change in output affect unit costs and the price level? We'll focus on three key reasons.

---

[1] In microeconomics, you learn more sophisticated theories of how firms' prices are determined. But our simple markup model captures a central conclusion of those theories: that an increase in costs will result in higher prices.

As total output increases:

Greater amounts of inputs may be needed to produce a unit of output. As output increases, firms hire new, untrained workers who may be less productive than existing workers. Firms also begin using capital and land that are less well suited to their industry. As a result, greater amounts of labor, capital, land, and raw materials are needed to produce each unit of output. Even if the prices of these inputs remain the same, unit costs will rise.

For example, imagine that Intel increases its output of computer chips. Then it will have to be less picky about the workers it employs, hiring some who are less well suited to chip production than those already working there. Thus, more labor hours will be needed to produce each chip. Intel may also have to begin using older, less-efficient production facilities, which require more silicon and other raw materials per chip. Even if the prices of all of these inputs remain unchanged, unit costs will rise.

The prices of nonlabor inputs rise. In addition to needing greater quantities of inputs, firms will have to pay a higher price for them. This is especially true of inputs like land and natural resources, which may be available only in limited quantities in the short run. An increase in the output of final goods raises the demand for these inputs, causing their prices to rise. Firms that produce final goods experience an increase in unit costs, and raise their own prices accordingly.

The nominal wage rate rises. Greater output means higher employment, leaving fewer unemployed workers looking for jobs. As firms compete to hire increasingly scarce workers, they must offer higher nominal wage rates to attract them. Higher nominal wages increase unit costs, and therefore result in a higher price level. Notice that we use the nominal wage, rather than the real wage we've emphasized elsewhere in this book. That's because we are interested in explaining how firms' prices are determined. Since price is a nominal variable, it is marked up over *nominal* costs.

A decrease in output affects unit costs through the same three forces, but with the opposite result. As output falls, firms can be more selective in hiring the best, most efficient workers and in choosing other inputs, decreasing their input requirements per unit of output. Decreases in demand for land and natural resources will cause their prices to drop. And as unemployment rises, wages will fall as workers compete for jobs. Each of these forces contributes to a drop in unit costs, and a decrease in the price level.

Short Run versus Long Run

All three of our reasons are important in explaining why a change in output affects the price level. However, they operate within different time frames. When total output increases, new, less-productive workers will be hired rather quickly. Similarly, the prices of certain key inputs—such as lumber, land, oil, and wheat—may rise within a few weeks or months.

But our third explanation—changes in the nominal wage rate—is a different story. While wages in some lines of work might respond very rapidly, we can expect wages in many industries to change very little or not at all for a year or more after a change in output.

For a year or so after a change in output, changes in the average nominal wage are less important than other forces that change unit costs.

Here are some of the more important reasons why wages in many industries respond so slowly to changes in output:

- Many firms have union contracts that specify wages for up to three years. Although wage increases are often built into these contracts, a rise in output will not affect the amount of the wage increase. When output rises or falls, these firms continue to abide by the contract.
- Wages in many large corporations are set by slow-moving bureaucracies.
- Wage changes in either direction can be costly to firms. Higher wages to attract new workers must be widely publicized in order to raise the number of job applicants at the firm. Lower wages can reduce the morale of workers—and their productivity. Thus, many firms are reluctant to change wages until they are reasonably sure that any change in their output will be long lasting.
- Firms may benefit from developing reputations for paying stable wages. A firm that raises wages when output is high and labor is scarce may have to lower wages when output is low and labor is plentiful. Such a firm would develop a reputation for paying unstable wages, and have difficulty attracting new workers.

For now, we focus exclusively on the short run—a time horizon of a year or so after a change in output. Since the average nominal wage rate changes very little over the short run, we'll make the following simplifying assumption: *The nominal wage rate is fixed in the short run.* More specifically,

we assume that changes in output have no effect on the nominal wage rate in the short run.

Keep in mind, though, that our assumption of a constant wage holds only in the *short run.* As you will see later, wage changes play a very important role in the economy's adjustment over the long run.

Since we assume a constant nominal wage in the short run, a change in output will affect unit costs through the other two factors we mentioned earlier. Specifically, in the short run, a rise in real GDP raises firms' unit costs because (1) input requirements per unit of output rise, and (2) the prices of nonlabor inputs rise. With a constant percentage markup, the rise in unit costs translates into a rise in the price level. Thus,

in the short run, a rise in real GDP, by causing unit costs to increase, will also cause a rise in the price level.

In the other direction, a *drop* in real GDP lowers unit costs because (1) input requirements per unit of output fall, and (2) the prices of nonlabor inputs fall. With a constant percentage markup, the drop in unit costs translates into a drop in the price level.

In the short run, a fall in real GDP, by causing unit costs to decrease, will also cause a decrease in the price level.

FIGURE 5

The Aggregate Supply Curve

DERIVING THE AGGREGATE SUPPLY CURVE

Figure 5 summarizes our discussion about the effect of output on the price level in the short run. Suppose the economy begins at point *A*, with output at $10 trillion and the price level at 100. Now suppose that output rises to $12.5 trillion. What will happen in the short run? Even though wages are assumed to remain constant, the price level will rise because of the other forces we've discussed. In the figure, the price level rises to 130, indicated by point *B*. If, instead, output *fell* to $6 trillion, the price level would fall—to 80 in the figure, indicated by point *C*.

As you can see, each time we change the level of output, there will be a new price level in the short run, giving us another point on the figure. If we connect all of these points, we obtain the economy's *aggregate supply curve:*

Aggregate supply (*AS*) curve A curve indicating the price level consistent with firms' unit costs and markups for any level of output over the short run.

> *The **aggregate supply curve** (or **AS curve**) tells us the price level consistent with firms' unit costs and their percentage markups at any level of output over the short run.*

A more accurate name for the *AS* curve would be the "short-run-price-level-at-each-output-level" curve, but that is more than a mouthful. The *AS* curve gets its name because it *resembles* a microeconomic market supply curve. Like the supply curve for maple syrup we discussed in Chapter 3, the *AS* curve is upward sloping, and it has a price variable (the price level) on the vertical axis and a quantity variable (total output) on the horizontal axis. But there, the similarity ends.

MOVEMENTS ALONG THE *AS* CURVE

When a change in output causes the price level to change, we *move along* the economy's *AS* curve. But what happens in the economy as we make such a move?

Look again at the *AS* curve in Figure 5. Suppose we move from point *A* to point *B* along this curve in the short run. The increase in output raises the prices of raw materials and other (nonlabor) inputs and also raises input requirements per unit of output at many firms. Both of these changes increase costs per unit. As long as the markup remains somewhat stable, the rise in unit costs will lead firms to raise their prices, and the price level will increase. Thus, as we move upward along the *AS* curve, we can represent what happens as follows:

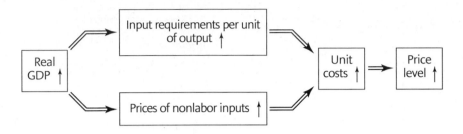

The opposite sequence of events occurs when real GDP falls, moving us downward along the *AS* curve:

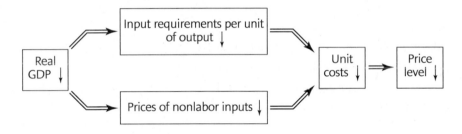

SHIFTS OF THE *AS* CURVE

When we drew the *AS* curve in Figure 5, we assumed that a number of important variables remained unchanged. In particular, we assumed that the only changes in unit costs were those caused by a change in output. But in the real world, unit costs sometimes change for reasons *other* than a change in output. When this occurs, unit costs—*and* the price level—will change at *any* level of output, so the *AS* curve will shift.

In general, we distinguish between a movement along the *AS* curve, and a shift of the curve itself, as follows:

> *When a change in real GDP causes the price level to change, we move along the* AS *curve. When anything other than a change in real GDP causes the price level to change, the* AS *curve itself shifts.*

Figure 6 illustrates the logic of a shift in the *AS* curve. Suppose the economy's initial *AS* curve is AS_1. Now suppose that some economic event *other* than a change in output—for the moment, we'll leave the event unnamed—causes firms to raise their prices. Then the price level will be higher at *any* level of output we might imagine, so the *AS* curve must shift *upward*—for example, to AS_2 in the figure. At an output level of $10 trillion, the price level would rise from 100 to 140. At any other output level, the price level would also rise.

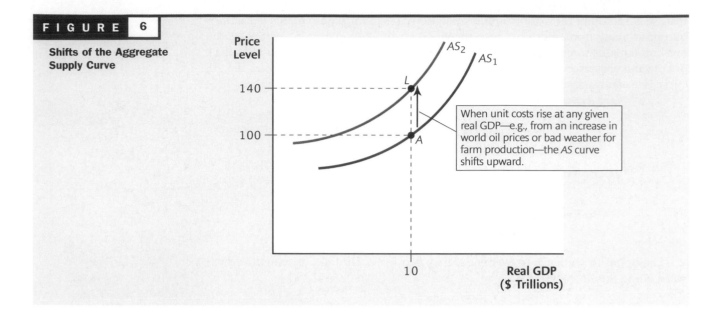

FIGURE 6

Shifts of the Aggregate Supply Curve

When unit costs rise at any given real GDP—e.g., from an increase in world oil prices or bad weather for farm production—the *AS* curve shifts upward.

What can cause unit costs to change at any given level of output? The following are some important examples:

- *Changes in world oil prices.* Oil is traded on a world market, where prices can fluctuate even while output in the United States does not. And changes in world oil prices have often caused shifts in the *AS* curve. For example, from January 2005 to July 2006, the price of oil rose from about $43 per barrel to more than $70. (The reasons included geopolitical instability in the Middle East, and the rapidly rising demand for oil in fast-growing economies such as China and India.) Some firms—especially those that use relatively large quantities of oil, gasoline, or jet fuel (including FedEx, UPS, and American Airlines)—

A Misconception About the *AS* Curve A common mistake about the *AS* curve is thinking that it describes the same kind of relationship between price and quantity as a microeconomic supply curve. There are two reasons why this is wrong.

First, the direction of causation between price and output is reversed for the *AS* curve. For example, when we draw the supply curve for maple syrup, we view changes in the price of maple syrup as causing a change in output supplied. But along the *AS* curve, it's the other way around: A change in *output* causes a change in the *price level*.

Second, the basic assumption behind the *AS* curve is very different from that behind a single market supply curve. When we draw the supply curve for an individual product, we assume that the prices of inputs used in producing the good remain fixed. This is a sensible thing to do because an increase in production for a single good is unlikely to have much effect on input prices in the economy as a whole.

But when we draw the *AS* curve, we imagine an increase in *real GDP*, in which *all* firms are increasing their output. This will significantly raise the demand for inputs, so it is unrealistic to assume that input prices will remain fixed. Indeed, the rise in input prices is one of the important reasons for the *AS* curve's upward slope.

raised prices right away, as did gasoline retailers. If oil prices had remained elevated, many other firms throughout the economy would have raised their prices as well, shifting the *AS* curve noticeably upward, as in Figure 6. (Fortunately, by October 2006, oil prices began coming down again, moderating this upward shift.)

Conversely, oil prices fell sharply during 1997 and 1998. This caused unit costs to decrease at many firms, shifting the *AS* curve downward.

- *Changes in the weather*. Good crop-growing weather increases farmers' yields for any given amounts of land, labor, capital, and other inputs used. This decreases farms' unit costs, and the price of agricultural goods falls. Since many of these goods are final goods (such as fresh fruit and vegetables), the price drop will contribute directly to a drop in the price level and a downward shift of the *AS* curve. Additionally, agricultural products are important inputs in the production of many other goods. (For example, corn is an input in beef production.) Good weather thus leads to a drop in input prices for many other firms in the economy, causing their unit costs, and their prices, to decrease. For these reasons, we can expect good weather to shift the *AS* curve downward. Bad weather, which decreases crop yields, increases unit costs at any level of output and shifts the *AS* curve upward.

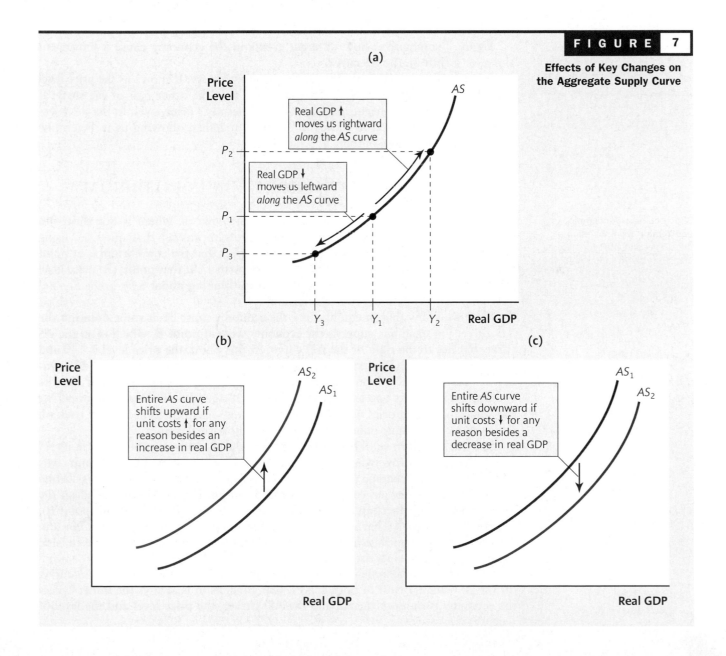

FIGURE 7

Effects of Key Changes on the Aggregate Supply Curve

- *Technological change*. New technologies can enable firms to produce any given level of output at lower unit costs. In recent years, for example, we've seen revolutions in telecommunications, information processing, and medicine. The result has been steady downward shifts of the *AS* curve.
- *The nominal wage*. Remember that in our short-run analysis we're assuming the nominal wage rate does *not* change. As we move along the *AS* curve, we hold the nominal wage rate constant. But later in the chapter—when we extend our time horizon beyond a year or so—you'll see that changes in the nominal wage are an important part of the economy's long-run adjustment process. Here we just point out that, *if* the nominal wage were to increase for any reason, it would raise unit costs for firms at any level of output and therefore *shift* the *AS* curve *upward*. Similarly, *if* the nominal wage rate were to fall for any reason, it would *decrease* unit costs at any level of output and shift the *AS* curve downward. We'll come back to this important fact later.

Figure 7 summarizes how different events in the economy cause a movement along, or a shift in, the *AS* curve.

But the *AS* curve tells only half of the economy's story: It shows us the price level *if* we know the level of output. The *AD* curve tells the other half of the story: It shows us the level of output *if* we know the economy's price level. In the next section, we finally put the two halves of the story together, allowing us to determine both the price level and output.

AD AND AS TOGETHER: SHORT-RUN EQUILIBRIUM

Short-run macroeconomic equilibrium A combination of price level and GDP consistent with both the *AD* and *AS* curves.

Where will the economy settle in the short run? That is, where is our **short-run macroeconomic equilibrium**? Figure 8 shows how to answer that question, using both the *AS* curve and the *AD* curve. If you suspect that the equilibrium is at point *E*, the intersection of these two curves, you are correct. At that point, the price level is 100 and output is $10 trillion. But it's worth thinking about *why* point *E*—and only point *E*—is our short-run equilibrium.

First, we know that in equilibrium, the economy must be at some point on the *AD* curve. For example, suppose the economy were at point *B*, which is on the *AS* curve, but lies to the right of the *AD* curve. At this point, the price level is 140 and output is $14 trillion. But the *AD* curve tells us that with a price level of 140, *equilibrium* output is $6 trillion. Thus, at point *B*, real GDP would be greater than its equilibrium value. As you learned several chapters ago, this situation cannot persist for long, since inventories would pile up and firms would be forced to cut back on their production. Thus, point *B* cannot be our short-run equilibrium.

Second, short-run equilibrium requires that the economy be operating on its *AS* curve. Otherwise, firms would not be charging the prices dictated by their unit costs and the average percentage markup in the economy. For example, point *F* lies *below* the *AS* curve. But the *AS* curve tells us that if output is $14 trillion, based on the average percentage markup and unit costs, the price level should be 140 (point *B*), not something lower. That is, the price level at point *F* is *too low* for equilibrium. This situation will not last long either, since firms will want to raise prices, causing the overall price level to rise.

We could make a similar argument for any other point that is off the *AS* curve, off the *AD* curve, or off of both curves. Our conclusion is always the same: Unless the economy is on *both* the *AS* and the *AD* curves, the price level and the level of

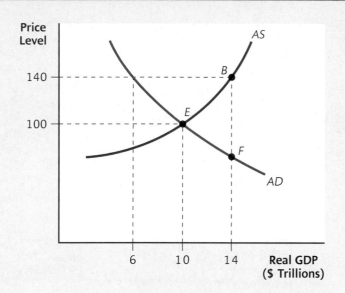

F I G U R E 8

Short-Run Macroeconomic Equilibrium

Short-run equilibrium occurs where the AD *and* AS *curves intersect. At point* E, *the price level of 100 is consistent with an output of $10 trillion along the* AD *curve. The output level of $10 trillion is consistent with a price level of 100 along the* AS *curve. At any other combination of price level and output, such as point* F *or point* B, *at least one condition for equilibrium will not be satisfied.*

output will change. Only when the economy is at point *E*—on *both* curves—can we have a sustainable level of real GDP and the price level.

WHAT HAPPENS WHEN THINGS CHANGE?

Now that we know how the short-run equilibrium is determined, and armed with our knowledge of the *AD* and *AS* curves, we are ready to put the model through its paces. In this section, we'll explore how different types of events cause the short-run equilibrium to change.

Our short-run equilibrium will change when either the *AD* curve, the *AS* curve, or both, *shift*. Since the consequences for the economy are very different for shifts in the *AD* curve as opposed to shifts in the *AS* curve, economists have developed a shorthand language to distinguish between them:

> *An event that causes the* AD *curve to shift is called a **demand shock**. An event that causes the* AS *curve to shift is called a **supply shock**.*

Demand shock Any event that causes the *AD* curve to shift.

Supply shock Any event that causes the *AS* curve to shift.

In this section, we'll first explore the effects of demand shocks, both in the short run and during the adjustment process to the long run. Then, we'll take up the issue of supply shocks.

DEMAND SHOCKS IN THE SHORT RUN

Figure 4, which lists the causes of a shift in the *AD* curve, also serves as a list of demand shocks to the economy. Let's consider some examples.

An Increase in Government Purchases

You've learned that an increase in government purchases shifts the *AD* curve rightward. Now we can see how it affects the economy in the short run. Figure 9 shows

F I G U R E   9

The Effect of a Demand Shock

Starting at point E, an increase in government purchases would shift the AD curve rightward to AD₂. Point J illustrates where the economy would move if the price level remained constant. But as output increases, the price level rises. Thus, the economy moves along the AS curve from point E to point N.

the initial equilibrium at point *E*, with the price level equal to 100 and output at $10 trillion. Now, suppose that government purchases rise by $1 trillion. Figure 4(b) tells us that the *AD* curve will shift rightward. What will happen to equilibrium GDP?

Back in Figure 3, this $1 trillion rise in government purchases increased output to $12.5 trillion. But that analysis did not consider any change in the price level. Thus, the rise in output to $12.5 trillion makes sense *only if the price level does not change*. Here, in Figure 9, this *would* be a movement rightward, from point *E* to point *J*. However, *point J does not describe the economy's short-run equilibrium*. Why not? Because it ignores two facts that you've learned about in this chapter: The rise in output will change the price level, and the change in the price level will, in turn, affect equilibrium GDP.

To see this more clearly, let's first suppose that the price level did *not* rise when output increased, so that the economy actually *did* arrive at point *J* after the *AD* shift. Would we stay there? Absolutely not. Point *J* lies below the *AS* curve, telling us that when GDP is $12.5 trillion, the price level consistent with firms' unit costs and average markup is *greater* than 100. Firms would soon raise prices, and this would cause a movement leftward along *AD₂*. The price level would keep rising and output would keep falling, until we reached point *N*. At that point, with output at $11.5 trillion, we would be on both the *AS* and *AD* curves, so there would be no reason for a further rise in the price level and no reason for a further fall in output.

However, the process we've just described is not entirely realistic. It assumes that when government purchases rise, *first* output increases (the move to point *J*) and *then* the price level rises (the move to point *N*). In reality, output and the price level tend to rise *together*. Thus, the economy would likely *slide along* the *AS* curve from point *E* to point *N*. As we move along the *AS* curve, output rises, increasing unit costs and the price level. At the same time, the rise in the price level *reduces equilibrium GDP* (the level of output toward which the economy is heading on the *AD* curve) from point *J* to point *N*.

We can summarize the impact of a rise in government purchases this way:

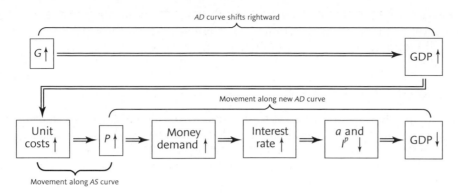

Net Effect: GDP ↑, but by less due to effect of P ↑

Let's step back a minute and get some perspective about this example of fiscal policy. When you first learned about fiscal policy, we used the simple multiplier formula to determine the impact of an increase in G on real GDP. Now you've learned that a rise in government purchases will increase the price level. This, in turn, raises the interest rate in the money market and crowds out some interest-sensitive spending, thus making the rise in GDP smaller than it would be otherwise. We know that the crowding out is not complete, because GDP still rises. This tells us that the drop in consumption and investment spending must be smaller than the rise in government purchases. But this partial crowding out reduces the impact of fiscal policy on GDP. When the partial crowding out of C and I^p is included, the expenditure multiplier is smaller than our simple multiplier formula $[1/(1 - MPC)]$ suggests.[2]

We can summarize the impact of price-level changes this way:

> *When government purchases increase, the horizontal shift of the* AD *curve measures how much real GDP would* increase *if the price level remained constant. But because the price level rises, real GDP rises by* less *than the horizontal shift in the* AD *curve.*

Now let's switch gears into reverse: How would we illustrate the effects of a *decrease* in government purchases? In this case, the *AD* curve would shift *leftward*, causing the following to happen:

Net Effect: GDP ↓, but by less due to effect of P ↓

[2] If you've read the appendix to the chapter on "The Money Market and Monetary Policy," you learned that—even with no change in the price level—there is a feedback effect from the money market to GDP. This effect, too, reduces the size of the multiplier. The partial crowding out described here—caused by a rise in the price level—is *in addition* to the crowding out described in that appendix. It reduces the size of the multiplier further.

As you can see, the same sequence of events occurs in the same order, but each variable moves in the opposite direction. A decrease in government purchases decreases equilibrium GDP, but the multiplier effect is smaller because the price level falls.

An Increase in the Money Supply

Although monetary policy stimulates the economy through a different channel than fiscal policy, once we arrive at the *AD* and *AS* diagram, the two look very much alike. For example, an increase in the money supply, which reduces the interest rate, will stimulate interest-sensitive consumption and investment spending. Real GDP then increases, and the *AD* curve shifts rightward, just as in Figure 9. Once output begins to rise, we have the same sequence of events as in fiscal policy: The price level rises, so the increase in GDP will be smaller. We can represent the situation as follows:

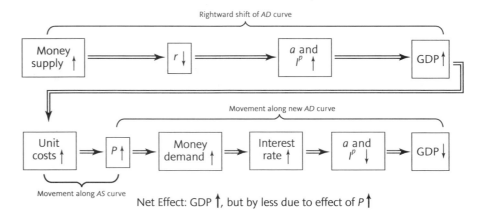

Net Effect: GDP ↑, but by less due to effect of *P* ↑

Other Demand Shocks

On your own, try going through examples of different demand shocks (see the list in Figures 4(b) and (c)) and explain the sequence of events in each case that causes output and the price level to change. This will help you verify the following general conclusion about demand shocks:

> *A positive demand shock—one that shifts the* AD *curve rightward—increases both real GDP and the price level in the short run. A negative demand shock—one that shifts the* AD *curve leftward—decreases both real GDP and the price level in the short run.*

An Example: The Great Depression

As mentioned at the beginning of the chapter, the U.S. economy collapsed far more seriously during the period 1929 through 1933—the onset of the Great Depression—than it did at any other time in the country's history. Because the price level fell during this time, we know that the contraction was caused by an adverse demand shock. (An adverse supply shock would have caused the price level to *rise* as GDP fell, as you will see in a few pages.)

What do we know about the demand shocks that caused the depression? This question has been debated by economists almost continuously over the past 70 years. The candidates are numerous, and it appears that a combination of events was responsible. The 1920s were a period of optimism, with high levels of investment by businesses and spending by families on houses and cars. The stock market soared. In the fall of 1929, the bubble of optimism burst. The stock market crashed, and investment and consumption spending plummeted. Similar events occurred in other countries, and the demand for products exported by the United States fell. The Fed—then only 16 years old—reacted by cutting the money supply sharply, which added an adverse monetary shock to all of the cutbacks in spending. Each of these events contributed to a leftward shift of the *AD* curve, causing both output and the price level to fall.

DEMAND SHOCKS: ADJUSTING TO THE LONG RUN

In Figure 9, point *N* shows the new equilibrium after a positive demand shock *in the short run*—a year or so after the shock. But point *N* is not necessarily where the economy will end up in the long run. For example, suppose full-employment output is $10 trillion, and point *N*—representing an output of $11.5 trillion—is *above full-employment output*. Then, with employment unusually high and unemployment unusually low, business firms will have to compete to hire scarce workers, driving up the wage rate. It might take a year or more for the wage rate to rise significantly (recall our earlier list of reasons that wages adjust only slowly). But extending our horizon to several years or more, if output is above its potential, the wage rate will rise. Since the *AS* curve is drawn for a given wage, a rise in the wage rate will *shift* the curve upward, changing our equilibrium.

Alternatively, we could imagine a situation in which short-run equilibrium GDP was *below* its potential. In this case, with abnormally high unemployment, workers would compete to get scarce jobs, and eventually the wage rate would fall. Then the *AS* curve would shift downward, once again changing our equilibrium GDP.

In the short run, we treat the wage rate as given. But in the long run, the wage rate can change. When output is above full employment, the wage rate will rise, shifting the AS *curve upward. When output is below full employment, the wage rate will fall, shifting the* AS *curve downward.*

Now we are ready to explore what happens over the long run in the aftermath of a demand shock. Figure 10 shows an economy in equilibrium at point *E*. We assume that the initial equilibrium is at full-employment output (Y_{FE}) because—as you are about to see—this is where the economy always ends up after the long-run adjustment process is complete. To make our results as general as possible, we'll use symbols, rather than numbers, to represent output and price levels.

Now suppose the *AD* curve shifts rightward due to, say, an increase in government purchases. In the short run, the equilibrium moves to point *N*, with a higher price level (P_2) and a higher level of output (Y_2). Point *N* tells us where the economy will be about a year after the increase in government purchases, before the wage rate has a chance to adjust. (Remember, along any given *AS* curve, the wage rate is assumed to be constant.)

FIGURE 10

**Long-Run Adjustment After
a Positive Demand Shock**

*Beginning at point E, a posi-
tive demand shock would
shift the aggregate demand
curve to AD$_2$, raising both
output and the price level.
At point N, output is above
the full-employment level,
Y$_{FE}$. Firms will compete to
hire scarce workers, thereby
driving up the wage rate.
The higher wage rate will
shift the AS curve to AS$_2$.
Only when the economy
returns to full-employment
output at point L will there
be no further shifts in AS.*

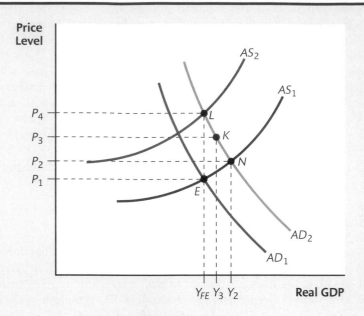

But now let's extend our analysis beyond a year. Notice that Y_2 is greater than Y_{FE}. Eventually, the wage will begin to rise, raising unit costs at any given output level and causing firms to raise prices. In the figure, the *AS* curve would begin shifting upward. Point *K* shows where the shifting aggregate supply curve might be 2 years after the shock, after the long-run adjustment process has begun. (You might want to pencil this intermediate *AS* curve into the figure, so that it intersects AD_2 at point *K*.) At this point, output would be at Y_3, and the rise in the price level has moved us along the new aggregate demand curve, AD_2.

But point *K* cannot be our final, long-run equilibrium. At Y_3, output is *still* greater than Y_{FE}, so the wage rate will continue to rise and the *AS* curve will continue to shift upward. At point *K*, the long-run adjustment process is not yet complete. When will the process end? Only when the wage rate stops rising, that is, only when output has returned to Y_{FE}. This occurs when the *AS* curve has shifted all the way to AS_2, moving the economy to point *L*—our new, long-run equilibrium.

As you can see, the increase in government purchases has no effect on equilibrium GDP in the long run: The economy returns to full employment, which is just where it started. This is why the long-run adjustment process is often called the economy's **self-correcting mechanism.** And this mechanism applies to any demand shock, not just an increase in government purchases:

Self-correcting mechanism
The adjustment process through which price and wage changes return the economy to full-employment output in the long run.

> *If a demand shock pulls the economy away from full employment, changes in the wage rate and the price level will eventually cause the economy to correct itself and return to full-employment output.*

For a positive demand shock that shifts the *AD* curve rightward, the self-correcting mechanism works like this:

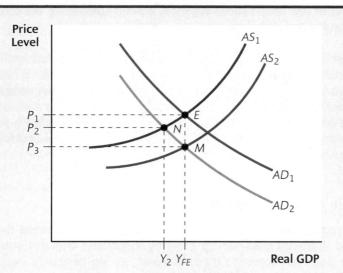

FIGURE 11

**Long-Run Adjustment After
a Negative Demand Shock**

*Starting from point E, a
negative demand shock shifts
the AD curve to AD₂, lowering GDP and the price level.
At point N, output is below
the full-employment level.
With unemployed labor
available, wages and unit
costs will fall, causing firms
to lower their prices. The AS
curve shifts downward until
full employment is regained
at point M, with a lower
price level.*

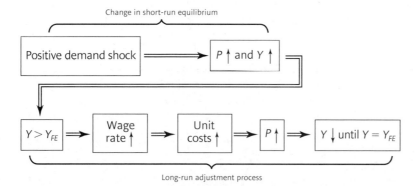

Figure 11 illustrates the case of a negative demand shock, in which the *AD* curve shifts leftward. Starting at point *E*, the short-run equilibrium moves to point *N*, with real GDP *below* Y_{FE}. Over the long run, high unemployment drives the wage rate down, shifting the *AS* curve down as well. The price level decreases, causing equilibrium GDP to rise along the AD_2 curve. The process comes to a halt only when output returns to Y_{FE}. Thus, in the long run, the economy moves from point *E* to point *M*, and the negative demand shock causes no change in equilibrium GDP.

The complete sequence of events after a negative demand shock looks like this:

Pulling all of our observations together, we can summarize the economy's self-correcting mechanism as follows:

> *Whenever a demand shock pulls the economy away from full employment, the self-correcting mechanism will eventually bring it back. When output exceeds its full-employment level, wages will eventually rise, causing a rise in the price level and a drop in GDP until full employment is restored. When output is less than its full-employment level, wages will eventually fall, causing a drop in the price level and a rise in GDP until full employment is restored.*

The Long-Run Aggregate Supply Curve

The self-correcting mechanism provides an important link between the economy's long-run and short-run behaviors. It helps us understand why deviations from full employment don't last forever. Often, however, we are primarily interested in the long-run effects of a demand shock. In these cases, we may want to skip over the self-correcting mechanism and go straight to its end result. A new version of the *AS* curve helps us do this.

Now look at Figure 12, which illustrates the impact of a positive demand shock like the one in Figure 10. The economy begins at full employment at point E, then moves to point N in the short run (before the wage rate rises), and then goes to point

FIGURE 12

The Long-Run *AS* Curve

This figure, like Figure 10, illustrates a positive demand shock, but focuses on the long-run effects. The initial equilibrium is at point E, with output at full employment (Y_{FE}) and price level P_1. After the positive demand shock and all the long-run adjustments to it, the economy ends up at point L with a higher price level (P_4), but the same full-employment output level (Y_{FE}). The long-run AS curve—a vertical line—shows all possible combinations of price level and output for the economy, skipping over the short-run changes. The vertical, long-run AS curve shows that in the long run, demand shocks can affect the price level but not output.

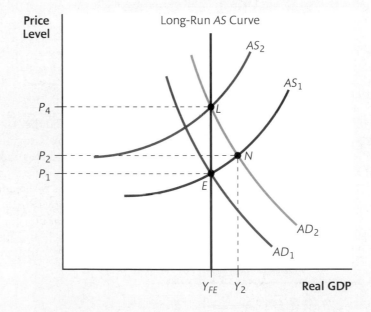

L in the long run (after the rise in wages). If we skip over the short-run equilibrium, we find that the positive demand shock has moved the economy from *E* to *L*, which is vertically above *E*. That is, in the long run, the price level rises but output remains unchanged.

Now look at the vertical line in Figure 12, which shows another way of illustrating this long-run result. In the figure, the vertical line is the economy's **long-run aggregate supply curve**. It summarizes all possible output and price-level combinations at which the economy could end up in the long run. It is vertical because, in the long run, GDP will be the same—full-employment output—*regardless* of the position of the *AD* curve. The price level, however, will depend on the position of the *AD* curve. In the long run, a positive demand shock shifts the *AD* curve rightward, moving the economy from *E* to *L*: a higher price level, but the same level of output. Similarly, in Figure 11, a negative demand shock—which shifts the *AD* curve leftward—moves the economy from *E* to *M* in the long run: a lower price level with the same level of output. (You may want to pencil in a vertical long-run aggregate supply curve in Figure 11 to help you see that it is the same curve as the one drawn in Figure 12.)

The long-run aggregate supply curve tells us something very important about the economy: In the long run, after the self-correcting mechanism has done its job, *the economy behaves as the classical model predicts*. In particular, the classical model tells us that demand shocks cannot change equilibrium GDP in the long run. Figure 12 brings us to the same conclusion: While demand shocks shift the *AD* curve, this only moves the economy up or down along a vertical long-run *AS* curve, leaving output unchanged.[3]

The long-run aggregate supply curve also illustrates another classical conclusion. In the classical model, an increase in government purchases causes *complete crowding out;* the rise in government purchases is precisely matched by a drop in consumption and investment spending, leaving total output and total spending unchanged. In Figure 12, the same result holds in the long run. How do we know? The figures tell us that, in the long run, the rise in government purchases causes no change in GDP. But if GDP is the same, and government purchases are higher, then other components of GDP—consumption and investment—must decrease by the amount that government purchases increased.[4]

> *The self-correcting mechanism shows us that, in the long run, the economy will eventually behave as the classical model predicts.*

But notice the word *eventually* in the previous statement. It can take several years before the economy returns to full employment after a demand shock. This is why governments around the world are reluctant to rely on the self-correcting mechanism alone to keep the economy on track. Instead, they often use fiscal and monetary policies in an attempt to return the economy to full employment more quickly. We'll explore fiscal and monetary policies in more detail in the next two chapters.

Long-run aggregate supply curve
A vertical line indicating all possible output and price-level combinations at which the economy could end up in the long run.

---

[3] Of course, full-employment output can increase from year to year, as you learned in the chapter on economic growth. When the economy is growing, the long-run *AS* curve will shift rightward. In that case, the level of output at which the economy will eventually settle increases from year to year.

[4] Net exports can be crowded out as well. In a later chapter, you'll learn that a higher interest rate causes a currency's value to increase relative to foreign currencies. This causes exports to fall and imports to rise.

FIGURE **13**

The Effect of a Negative Supply Shock

A negative supply shock would shift the AS curve upward from AS₁ to AS₂. In the short-run equilibrium at point R, the price level is higher and output is below Y_{FE}. Eventually, wages will fall, causing unit costs to fall, and the AS curve will shift back to its original position. A positive supply shock would have just the opposite effect.

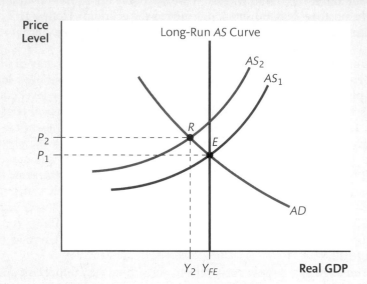

SUPPLY SHOCKS

In recent decades, supply shocks have been important sources of economic fluctuations. The most dramatic supply shocks have resulted from sudden changes in world oil prices. As you are about to see, supply shocks affect the economy differently than demand shocks.

Short-Run Effects of Supply Shocks

Figure 13 shows an example of a supply shock: an increase in world oil prices that shifts the aggregate supply curve upward, from AS_1 to AS_2. As rising oil prices increase unit costs, firms will begin raising prices, and the price level will increase. The rise in the price level decreases equilibrium GDP along the AD curve. In the short run, the price level will continue to rise, and the economy will continue to slide upward along its AD curve, until we reach the AS_2 curve at point R. At this point, the price level is consistent with firms' unit costs and average markup (we are on the AS curve), and total output is equal to total spending (we are on the AD curve). As you can see, the short-run impact of higher oil prices is a rise in the price level and a fall in output. We call this a *negative* supply shock, because of the negative effect on output.

> *In the short run, a negative supply shock shifts the AS curve upward, decreasing output and increasing the price level.*

Notice the sharp contrast between the effects of negative supply shocks and negative demand shocks in the short run. After a negative demand shock (see, for example, Figure 11), both output and the price level fall. After a negative supply shock, output falls but the price level rises. Economists and journalists have coined the term **stagflation** to describe a *stag*nating economy experiencing in*flation*.

Stagflation The combination of falling output and rising prices.

> *A negative supply shock causes* stagflation *in the short run.*

Stagflation caused by increases in oil prices is not just a theoretical possibility. Three of our recessions in the last quarter century—in 1973–74, 1980, and 1990–91—followed increases in world oil prices. And each of these three recessions also saw jumps in the price level.

A *positive supply shock* would increase output by shifting the *AS* curve *downward*. (We call it positive, because of its effect on output.) As you can see if you draw such a shift on your own,

> *a positive supply shock shifts the* AS *curve downward, increasing output and decreasing the price level.*

Examples of positive supply shocks include unusually good weather, a drop in oil prices, and a technological change that lowers unit costs. In addition, a positive supply shock can sometimes be caused by government policy. A few chapters ago, we discussed how the government could use tax incentives and other policies to increase the rate of economic growth. These policies work by shifting the *AS* curve downward, thus increasing output while tending to decrease the price level.

Long-Run Effects of Supply Shocks

What about the effects of supply shocks in the long run? In some cases, we need not concern ourselves with this question, because some supply shocks are temporary. For example, periods of rising oil prices are often followed by periods of falling oil prices. Similarly, supply shocks caused by unusually good or bad weather, or by natural disasters, are always short-lived. A temporary supply shock causes only a temporary shift in the *AS* curve; over the long run, the curve simply returns to its initial position, and the economy returns to full employment. In Figure 13, the *AS* curve would shift back from AS_2 to AS_1, the price level would fall, and the economy would move from point *R* back to point *E*.

In other cases, however, a supply shock can last for an extended period. One example was the rise in oil prices during the 1970s, which persisted for several years. In cases like this, is there a self-correcting mechanism that brings the economy back to full employment after a long-lasting supply shock? Indeed, there is, and it is the same mechanism that brings the economy back to full employment after a demand shock.

Look again at Figure 13. At point *R*, output is below full-employment output. In the long run, as workers compete for scarce jobs, the wage rate will decline. This will cause the *AS* curve to shift *downward*. The wage will continue to fall until the economy returns to full employment, that is, until we are back at point *E*.

> *In the long run, the economy self-corrects after a long-lasting supply shock, just as it does after a demand shock. When output differs from its full-employment level, the wage rate changes, and the* AS *curve shifts until full employment is restored.*

USING THE THEORY

The Story of Two Recessions

The aggregate demand and aggregate supply curves are more than just abstract graphs; they're tools to help us understand important economic events. For example, they can help us understand why the economy suffered its two most recent recessions, and also how and why these recessions differed from one another.

THE RECESSION OF 1990–91

The story of the 1990–91 recession begins in mid-1990, when Iraq invaded Kuwait, a major oil producer. During this conflict, Kuwait's oil was taken off the world market, and so was Iraq's. The reduction in oil supplies resulted in a rapid and substantial increase in the price of oil, a key input to many industries. From the second to the fourth quarter of 1990, the price of oil doubled.

The left-hand panel of Figure 14 shows our *AS–AD* analysis of the shock. Initially, the economy was on both AD_{1990} and AS_{1990}. Equilibrium was at point *E*, and output was at the full-employment level. Then, the oil price shock shifted the *AS* curve upward, to AS_{1991}, while leaving the *AD* curve more or less unchanged. As the short-run equilibrium moved to point *R*, real GDP fell and the price level *rose*. Now look at the left side of the next figure (Figure 15). The upper panel shows the behavior of GDP during the period leading up to, and during, the recession. As you can see, consistent with our *AS–AD* analysis, real GDP fell—from a high of $7.13 trillion in the third quarter of 1990 to a low of $7.04 trillion in the first quarter of 1991 (a decrease of 1.3 percent). The lower panel shows the behavior of the Consumer Price Index (CPI). While the CPI was rising modestly before the recession began, it rose more rapidly during the second half of 1990, as the recession took hold. Once again, this is consistent with what our *AS–AD* analysis predicts for a negative supply shock, such as the rise in oil prices in 1990.

What about the recovery that followed this recession? Once you know what the Fed did, you have all the tools to answer this question yourself. Problem 7 at the end of this chapter takes you through the process.

THE RECESSION OF 2001

The story of the 2001 recession was quite different. This time, there was no spike in oil prices and no other significant supply shock to plague the economy. Rather, there was a demand shock, and a Federal Reserve policy during the year before the recession that might have made it a bit worse.

In earlier chapters, you learned that the major cause of the recession was a decrease in investment spending. To review: In the years leading up to 2001, businesses rushed to acquire and develop new equipment needed to exploit new technologies, such as the Internet and wireless communication. By 2001, many firms had sufficiently "caught up" and the flow of investment spending—while still positive and high—began to decrease relative to previous years. This decrease in investment spending was a demand shock to the economy: In 2001, the *AD* curve shifted leftward.

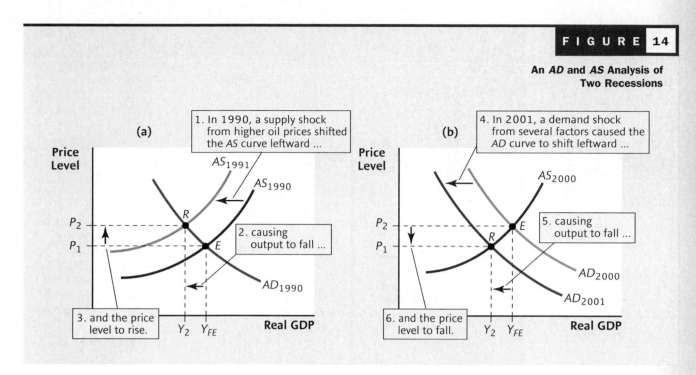

FIGURE 14

An *AD* and *AS* Analysis of Two Recessions

(a)

1. In 1990, a supply shock from higher oil prices shifted the *AS* curve leftward ...

2. causing output to fall ...

3. and the price level to rise.

(b)

4. In 2001, a demand shock from several factors caused the *AD* curve to shift leftward ...

5. causing output to fall ...

6. and the price level to fall.

Now we can introduce another force that may have contributed to the recession of 2001: the policy of the Fed. During the late 1990s, the Fed had become concerned that the investment boom and consumer optimism were shifting the *AD* curve rightward too rapidly, creating a danger that we would overshoot potential GDP and set off higher inflation. The Fed responded by tightening up on the money supply and raising the interest rate. From mid-1999 to mid-2000, the Fed raised its federal funds rate target six times—a total of almost two full percentage points in less than a year. The Fed then held the rate at a relatively high 6.50 percent for another 6 months until early 2001. In retrospect, the Fed may have continued raising and holding the rate high a bit too long, even after the *AD* curve stopped moving rightward. And the effects of this policy may have continued into early 2001, exacerbating the decrease in investment that was occurring for other reasons. In this way, the rate hikes themselves may have contributed to a further leftward shift of the *AD* curve.

The right-hand panel of Figure 14 shows our *AS–AD* analysis of this period. Initially, the economy was on both AD_{2000} and AS_{2000}, with equilibrium at point *E* and output roughly at the full-employment level. Then, the decrease in investment spending—helped along by the Fed—shifted the *AD* curve leftward, to AD_{2001}, while leaving the *AS* curve more or less unchanged. As the short-run equilibrium moved to point *R*, real GDP fell. This is mirrored in Figure 15, where the upper right-hand panel shows the behavior of GDP during the period leading up to, and during, the 2001 recession. As you can see, consistent with our *AS–AD* analysis, real GDP did fall in the first quarter of 2001, although it sputtered upward in the second quarter before falling again in the third.

But what about the price level? Here, we need to recognize that there is a slight difference between what our *AS–AD* analysis predicts and what actually happened.

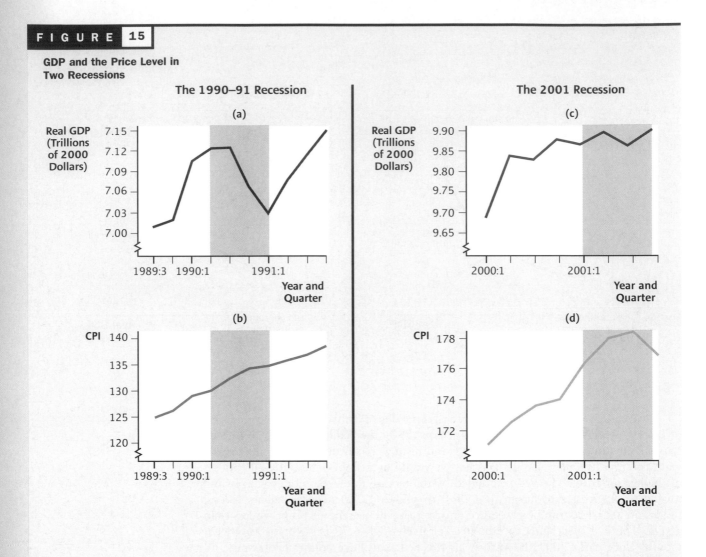

FIGURE 15

GDP and the Price Level in Two Recessions

In the right panel of Figure 14, the price level falls. And indeed, in the lower right panel of Figure 15, you can see that the price level eventually fell—in the fourth quarter of 2001. But for much of the recession, instead of the price level falling we can see that it was rising, but more slowly as 2001 continued. In the next chapter, you will learn that inflation often has some momentum: When it's been rising at a certain rate for some time, then—left alone—it will continue to rise at that rate. The leftward shift in the *AD* curve meant that inflation was *not* left alone in early 2001, so while prices continued to rise, they rose more slowly due to the *AD* shift. And, as you can see, the downward pressure on prices from the shifting *AD* curve eventually overcame the inflationary momentum, causing a drop in the price level toward the end of 2001. This is just what we'd expect from our *AS–AD* analysis.

Summary

The model of aggregate supply and demand explains how the price level and output are determined in the short run—a period of a year or so following a change in the economy—and how the economy adjusts over longer time periods as well.

The *aggregate demand* (AD) *curve* shows how changes in the price level affect equilibrium real GDP. A change in the price level shifts the money demand curve and alters the interest rate in the money market. The change in the interest rate, in turn, affects interest-sensitive forms of spending, shifts the aggregate expenditure curve, triggers the multiplier process, and leads to a new level of equilibrium real GDP. A lower price level means a higher equilibrium real GDP, and a higher price level means lower GDP. A change in government purchases, net taxes, autonomous consumption, planned investment, net exports, or the money supply will cause the AD curve to shift.

The *aggregate supply* (AS) *curve* summarizes the way changes in output affect the price level. To draw the AS curve, we assume that firms set the price of individual products as a markup over their costs per unit, and that the economy's average markup is determined by competitive conditions. We also assume that the nominal wage rate is fixed in the short run. As we move upward along the AS curve, a rise in real GDP, by raising unit costs, causes the price level to increase. When anything other than a change in real GDP causes the price level to change, the entire AS curve shifts.

AD and AS together determine real GDP and the price level. The economy must be on the AD curve, or real GDP would not be at its equilibrium level. It must be on the AS curve or firms would not be charging prices dictated by their unit costs and markups. Both conditions are satisfied at the intersection of the two curves.

The AD–AS equilibrium can be disturbed by a *demand shock*. An increase in government purchases, for example, shifts the AD curve rightward. As a result, the price level rises, and so does real GDP. In the long run, if GDP is above potential, wages will rise. This causes unit costs to rise and shifts the AS curve upward. Eventually, GDP will return to potential and the only long-run result of the demand shock is a higher price level. This implies that the economy's long-run aggregate supply curve is vertical at potential output.

The short-run AD–AS equilibrium can also be disturbed by a *supply shock*, such as an increase in world oil prices. With unit costs higher at each level of output, the AS curve shifts upward, decreasing real GDP and increasing the price level. Eventually, the shock will be self-correcting: With output below potential, the wage rate will fall, unit costs will decrease, and the AS curve will shift back downward until full employment is restored.

Problem Set   *Answers to even-numbered Questions and Problems can be found on the text Web site at www.thomsonedu.com/economics/hall.*

1. Redraw Figure 2, showing how a decrease in the price level will lead to an increase in equilibrium real GDP.

2. With a three-panel diagram—one panel showing the money market, one showing the aggregate expenditure diagram, and one showing the AD curve—show how a *decrease* in the money supply shifts the AD curve leftward.

3. Suppose firms become pessimistic about the future and consequently investment spending falls. With an AD and AS graph, describe the short-run effects on real GDP and the price level. If the price level were constant, how would your answer change?

4. With an AD and AS diagram, explain the short-run effect of a decrease in the money supply on real GDP and the price level. What is the effect in the long run? Assume the economy begins at full employment.

5. Use an AD and AS graph to explain the short-run and long-run effects on real GDP and the price level of an increase in autonomous consumption spending. Assume the economy begins at full employment.

6. A new government policy successfully lowers firms' unit costs. What are the short-run and the long-run effects of such a policy? (Assume that full-employment output does not change.)

7. Make two copies of Figure 14(a) on a sheet of paper. Add curves to illustrate your answer to (a) on one copy and (b) on the other:
   a. What *would* have happened in the years after 1991 if the Fed had done nothing and the economy had relied solely on the self-correcting mechanism to return to full employment?
   b. What *did* happen as a result of the Fed bringing down the interest rate to end the recession?
   c. Is there a difference in the behavior of the price level during the recovery in these two cases? Explain.

8. Make two copies of Figure 14(b) on a sheet of paper. Add curves to illustrate the impacts of Fed policy for (a) on one copy and (b) on the other:
   a. What *would* have happened in the years following 2001 if the Fed had done nothing and the economy had relied solely on the self-correcting mechanism to return to full employment?
   b. What *did* happen as a result of the Fed's actual policy in 2001 (successive cuts in the interest rate throughout the year)?
   c. Is there a difference in the behavior of the price level during the recovery in these two cases? Explain.

9. Increased international trade has forced many U.S. firms to compete with foreign producers. The increased competition has likely affected the average markup in the U.S. economy. Use *AS* and *AD* curves to illustrate the short-run impact on the economy if, at the same time,

   a. The Fed does nothing.

   b. The Fed pursues a policy that successfully achieves the highest possible level of GDP with no rise in the price level.

10. a. Graphically show the effects of a temporary decrease in nonlabor input prices.

    b. How will your results change if this decrease lasts for an extended period?

    c. How would your results differ if the Fed intervened to keep the economy at full employment?

More Challenging

11. Suppose that wages are slow to adjust downward but rapidly adjust upward. What would the *AS* curve look like? How would this affect the economy's adjustment to demand shocks (compared to the analysis given in the chapter)?

12. During the 1990s, because of technological change, the *AS* curve was shifting downward, but—except for a few months—the price level did not fall. Why not? (Hint: What was the Fed doing?)

Inflation and Monetary Policy

In the late 1970s, the annual inflation rate in the United States reached 13 percent. At the time, polls showed that the public considered inflation the most serious economic problem facing the country. From 1991 to 2005, however, the annual inflation rate never exceeded 3.5 percent in any year, and the problem receded as a matter of public concern. Bringing the inflation rate down, and keeping it low, was one of the solid victories of national economic policy.

But in 2006, inflation began to creep up again, reaching 4.9 percent (at an annual rate) during the first half of the year.

Why was the inflation rate so high in the 1970s? How did the Fed bring the rate down? Why did it begin to plague the economy again in early 2006? And finally, how should the Fed respond to future economic disturbances?

In this chapter, we'll be addressing these and other questions as we take a closer look at the Fed's conduct of monetary policy. Our earlier discussions of monetary policy were somewhat limited, because we lacked the tools—aggregate demand and aggregate supply—to explain changes in the price level. In this chapter, we'll explore monetary policy more fully, making extensive use of the *AD* and *AS* curves.

THE OBJECTIVES OF MONETARY POLICY

The Fed's objectives have changed over the years. When the Fed was first established in 1913, its chief responsibility was to ensure the stability of the banking system. By acting as a *lender of last resort*—injecting reserves into the banking system in times of crisis—the Fed was supposed to alleviate financial panics.

By the 1950s, the stability of the banking system was no longer a major concern, largely because the United States had not had a banking panic in decades. (Deposit insurance programs had effectively eliminated panics.) Accordingly, the Fed's objective in the 1950s and 1960s changed to keeping the interest rate low and stable. In the 1970s, the Fed's objectives shifted once again. As stated in the Federal Reserve Banking Act of 1978, which is still in force, the Fed is now responsible for achieving a low, stable rate of inflation, as well as full employment of the labor force. Let's consider each of these goals in turn.

LOW, STABLE INFLATION

Why is a low rate of inflation important? Several chapters ago, we reviewed the social costs of inflation. When the inflation rate is high, society uses up resources coping with it—resources that could have been used to produce goods and services. Among these resources are the labor needed to update prices at stores and factories, as well as the additional time spent by households and businesses to manage their wealth and protect it from a loss of purchasing power.

In addition to keeping the inflation rate low, the Fed tries to keep it *stable* from year to year. For example, the Fed would prefer a steady yearly inflation rate of 3 percent to an inflation rate of 5 percent half the time, and 1 percent the other half, even though the average inflation rate would be 3 percent in both cases. The reason is that unstable inflation is difficult to predict accurately; it will often turn out higher or lower than people expected. As you learned several chapters ago, an inflation rate higher than expected redistributes real income from lenders to borrowers, while an inflation rate lower than expected has the opposite effect. Thus, unstable inflation adds to the risk of lending and borrowing, and interferes with long-run financial planning.

The Fed, as a public agency, chooses its policies with the costs of inflation in mind. And the Fed has another concern: Inflation is very unpopular with the public. Surveys show that most people associate high rates of inflation with a general breakdown of government and the economy.[1] A Fed chairman who delivers low rates of inflation is seen as popular and competent, while one who tolerates high inflation goes down in history as a failure.

FULL EMPLOYMENT

"Full employment" means that unemployment is at normal levels. But what, exactly, is a *normal* amount of employment?

Recall that there are different types of unemployment. Some of the unemployed in any given month will find jobs after only a short time of searching. This *frictional* unemployment is part of the normal workings of the labor market and is not a serious social problem. Other job seekers will spend many months or years out of work because they lack the skills that employers require, or because they lack information about available jobs. While this *structural* unemployment is a serious social problem, it is best solved with *micro*economic policies, such as job-training programs or improved information flows.

Cyclical unemployment, by contrast, is a *macro*economic problem. It occurs during a recession, in which millions of workers lose their jobs and remain unemployed as they seek new ones. This is why macroeconomists use the term "full employment" to mean *the absence of cyclical unemployment*. When the economy achieves full employment according to this definition, macroeconomic policy has done all that it can do.

The Fed is concerned about cyclical unemployment for two reasons. First is its *opportunity cost*: the output that the unemployed could have produced if they were working. Part of this opportunity cost is paid by the unemployed themselves, in the form of lost earnings, and part is paid by people who remain employed but pay higher taxes to provide unemployment benefits to job losers. By maintaining full employment, the Fed can help society avoid this cost.

Second, cyclical unemployment represents a social failure. In a recession, people who have the right skills and who could be working actually *lose* their jobs. Excess

---

[1] Robert J. Shiller, "Public Resistance to Inflation: A Puzzle," *Brookings Papers on Economic Activity,* 1997.

unemployment lingers for several years after a recession strikes. Thus, cyclical unemployment caused by a recession is a partial breakdown of the system. The economy is not doing what it should do: provide a job for anyone who wants to work and who has the needed skills.

But why should the Fed try to eliminate only *cyclical* unemployment? Why not go further and push output above its full-employment level? After all, at higher levels of output, business firms would be more willing to hire *any* available workers. The frictionally unemployed would find jobs more easily, and some of the structurally unemployed would be hired as well. If unemployment is a bad thing, shouldn't the Fed aim for the lowest possible unemployment rate?

The answer is no. If the unemployment rate falls too low, GDP rises beyond its potential, full-employment level. As you learned in the last chapter, this causes the economy's self-correcting mechanism to kick in: The *AS* curve shifts upward, increasing the price level. Thus, unemployment that is too low compromises the Fed's other chief goal by creating inflation. And, as you will see later in the chapter, the Fed cannot keep the economy operating above full employment for more than a short time anyway. In the long run, its attempts to push the economy too hard would only create more inflation and would not succeed in lowering unemployment.

The unemployment rate at which GDP is at its full-employment level—that is, with no cyclical unemployment—is sometimes called the **natural rate of unemployment**.

> *When the unemployment rate is below the natural rate, GDP is greater than potential output. The economy's self-correcting mechanism will then create inflation. When the unemployment rate is above the natural rate, GDP is below potential output. The self-correcting mechanism will then put downward pressure on the price level.*

Natural rate of unemployment The unemployment rate when there is no cyclical unemployment.

The word *natural* must be interpreted with care. The natural unemployment rate is not etched in stone, nor is it the outcome of purely natural forces that can't be influenced by public policy. But it is determined by rather slow-moving forces in the economy: how frequently workers move from job to job, how efficiently the unemployed can search for jobs and firms can search for new workers, and how well the skills of the unemployed match the skills needed by employers.

Still, the natural rate can change when any of these underlying conditions change. And it can also be influenced by government policies that provide incentives or disincentives for workers to find jobs quickly, or for employers to hire them. Indeed, economists generally believe that over the past decade, the natural rate has decreased in the United States—from 6 or 6.5 percent in the mid-1980s to perhaps as low as 4.5 percent today. Meanwhile, in some European economies, the natural rate of unemployment increased during the 1990s and remains stuck at high levels—close to 10 percent in France and Spain. The causes of these changes in the natural rate, as well as the *extent* of the changes, are hotly debated by economists. But there is general agreement that the rate has come down in the United States and remained high in continental Europe.

Why use the term *natural* for such a changeable feature of the economy? The term makes sense only from the perspective of *macroeconomic* policy. Simply put, there isn't much that macroeconomic policy can do about the natural rate. Stimulating the economy with fiscal or monetary policy may bring the *actual* unemployment rate down for a time, but it will not change the natural rate itself. And pushing unemployment below the natural rate would cause inflation. Thus, the natural rate of unemployment can be seen as a kind of goalpost for the Fed. The location of the goalpost may change over the years, but during any given year, it tells us where the Fed is aiming.

THE FED'S PERFORMANCE

How well has the Fed achieved its goals? Panel (a) of Figure 1 shows the annual inflation rate since 1950, as measured by the Consumer Price Index. You can see that monetary policy permitted extended periods of high inflation in the 1970s and

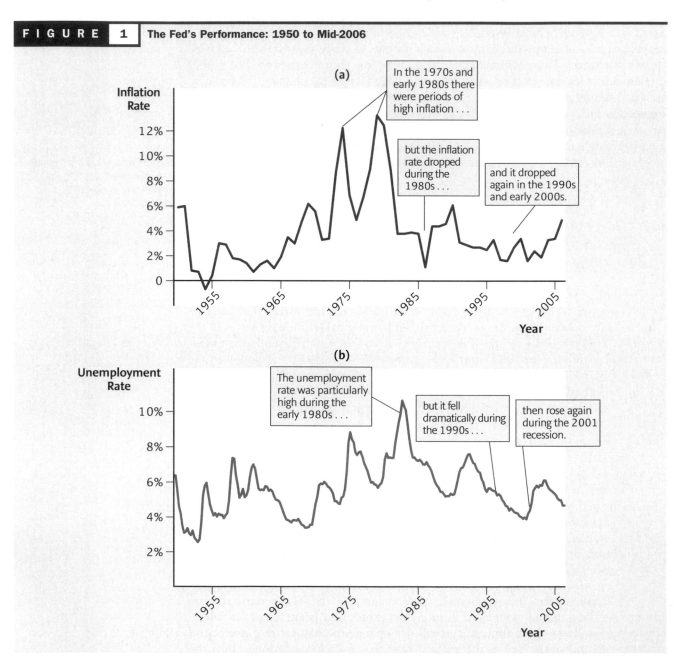

F I G U R E   1   The Fed's Performance: 1950 to Mid-2006

(a)

In the 1970s and early 1980s there were periods of high inflation . . .

but the inflation rate dropped during the 1980s . . .

and it dropped again in the 1990s and early 2000s.

(b)

The unemployment rate was particularly high during the early 1980s . . .

but it fell dramatically during the 1990s . . .

then rose again during the 2001 recession.

early 1980s. You can also see, as noted at the beginning of the chapter, that the Fed has achieved great success in controlling inflation since then. Indeed, in the 20 years leading up to 2006, the annual inflation rate exceeded 4.6 percent only once—in 1990, during the supply shock caused by higher oil prices. And in recent years, inflation near or under 3.0 percent has become the norm.

Panel (b) shows the quarterly rate of unemployment since 1950. Over the last 20 years of that period, the Fed has succeeded in keeping inflation in check. But its performance on unemployment has been somewhat mixed. From mid-1986 to mid-2006, the unemployment rate was 6.5 percent or greater—significantly above its natural rate—more than one-fifth of the time. But notice the remarkable improvement from mid-1992 and after, as the Fed slowly inched the unemployment rate down to 4 percent *without* heating up inflation. The Fed even managed to keep the unemployment rate hovering near 4 percent for more than 2 years until it began to rise during the recession of 2001.

As you can see, the Fed has mostly had a good—and improving—record in recent years. The inflation rate has been kept low and relatively stable, and—except for our most recent recession—unemployment has been near and even below most estimates of the natural rate. How has the Fed done it? Are there any general conclusions we can reach about how a central bank should operate to achieve the twin goals of full employment and a stable, low inflation rate? Indeed there are, as you'll see in the next section.

FEDERAL RESERVE POLICY: THEORY AND PRACTICE

The Fed's job is not an easy one. It must constantly respond to macroeconomic events with its twin goals in mind: low inflation and full employment. In some cases, the correct response—at least in theory—is clear, because the same action that maintains full employment also helps maintain low inflation. But in other cases, the Fed must trade off one goal for another: Responses that maintain full employment will worsen inflation, and responses that alleviate inflation will create more unemployment.

We'll make a temporary simplifying assumption in this section: that the Fed's goal for the inflation rate is *zero*. In reality, the Fed's goal is *low*, but not zero, inflation. Later, we'll discuss why the Fed prefers a low inflation rate to a zero rate, and how this modifies our analysis.

RESPONDING TO DEMAND SHOCKS

In the last chapter, you learned that a demand shock is a change in spending that shifts the economy's aggregate demand (*AD*) curve. Suppose an economy is operating at its potential output, and then it is hit with a *positive* demand shock. The shock might come from fiscal policy (an increase in government purchases or a tax cut) or from the private sector (an increase in autonomous consumption, investment, or net exports). In theory, how should the Fed respond?

Let's consider three possible responses: Maintaining the money supply, maintaining the interest rate, and neutralizing the shock. As you'll see, the first two responses would be poor choices for the Fed. The last one does the best job in achieving the Fed's goals.

Hypothetical Response: Constant Money Supply

Figure 2 illustrates an economy that is initially operating at full employment. Panel (a) shows the money market, with an equilibrium interest rate of 5 percent (point *A*). Panel (b) shows the aggregate demand and aggregate supply diagram. The equilibrium (point *E*) is a price level of 100 and an output of $10 trillion—the assumed full-employment level. Points *A* and *E* represent a *long-run* equilibrium for this economy—with output at its potential and, therefore, unemployment at its natural rate, the economy is at rest.

Then a positive demand shock (an increase in spending) hits the economy, setting off the multiplier process. The *AD* curve shifts rightward, from AD_1 to AD_2. At every price level, equilibrium GDP is greater than before. If, for example, the price level stayed at 100, the figure tells us that equilibrium GDP would rise to $12.5 trillion (point *F*). But that is not necessarily where the economy will end up; it depends on the actions of the Fed.

In the last chapter, we assumed that the Fed's response to a demand shock was to hold the money supply constant and allow the interest rate to rise automatically to its new equilibrium level. That is not a realistic description of Fed policy, but it served as a benchmark case. In Figure 2, we once again explore this benchmark case.

In panel (b), the rise in GDP causes a movement along the economy's *AS* curve, and the price level rises. In the money market in panel (a), the rise in the price level shifts the money demand curve rightward, driving the interest rate up to 7 percent (point *B*). This crowds out some consumption and investment spending, so that GDP does not rise by as much as it otherwise would. But it still rises. In panel (b),

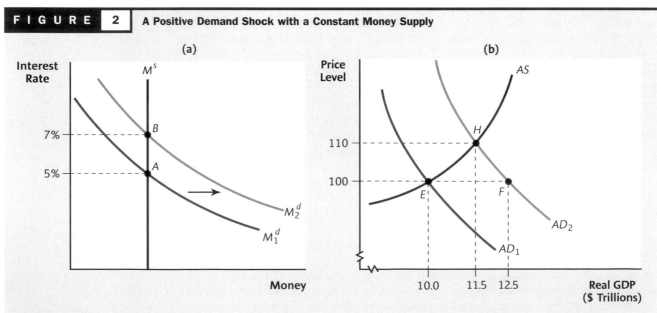

FIGURE 2 | **A Positive Demand Shock with a Constant Money Supply**

A positive demand shock would shift the AD *curve rightward to* AD₂ *in panel (b), causing both the price level and output to rise. If the Fed maintains a constant money supply, the rise in the price level causes the money demand curve to shift to* M₂ᵈ *in panel (a), driving the interest rate up from 5 percent to 7 percent. A higher interest rate causes some crowding out of consumption and investment spending, but not complete crowding out. In panel (b), output ends up higher than initially, and the price level rises as well (point* H).

we end up at point H, with the price level rising to 110, and real GDP rising to $11.5 trillion.

As you can see, the Fed would not want to respond to a positive demand shock by holding the money supply constant as in the figure. Output would rise above potential, bringing the unemployment rate below its natural rate. The price level would rise as well—to 110 in the figure. And in the long run, the price level would rise further, as the self-correcting mechanism returned the economy to full employment (by shifting the AS curve upward—not shown).

> *If a fully employed economy experiences a positive demand shock, and the Fed responds by holding the money supply constant, output will overshoot its potential. The price level will rise in the short run, and rise further in the long run.*

Since we are assuming, for now, that one of the Fed's goals is zero inflation, holding the money supply constant would not be an advisable response.

Hypothetical Response: Constant Interest Rate

Two chapters ago, you learned that, in practice, the Fed conducts monetary policy by setting an interest rate target. It then adjusts the money supply as necessary to hit the desired target. What would happen if the Fed, in response to a positive demand shock, chose to maintain a constant interest rate target?

Figure 3 provides the answer. In panel (a), the interest rate is initially at its target rate of 5 percent. In panel (b), the economy is at full employment with output of $10.0 trillion. When the positive demand shock hits, the AD curve begins to shift rightward in panel (b). We've included AD_2 in the figure, to show where the AD curve would be if the Fed did not change the money supply (as in the last example). But this time, as the money demand curve shifts rightward in panel (a), and the interest rate rises, the Fed increases the money supply (shifting the money supply curve to M_2^s). This will maintain the interest rate at its target of 5 percent (point C).[2]

An increase in the money supply, as you've learned, is one of the factors that shifts the AD curve rightward. So now, in panel (b), the AD curve will shift out further than it did before—all the way to AD_3. (The spending change first shifts it to AD_2; the increase in the money supply shifts it further, to AD_3.) In effect, by maintaining the interest rate target at 5 percent, the Fed prevents *any* crowding out of consumption or investment that would otherwise result from a higher interest rate. Instead, it allows the economy to experience the full effect of the multiplier, so output rises all the way to $12.5 trillion (point J).

But notice the consequence: In Figure 3, the price level rises even more (in comparison with the constant-money-supply policy of Figure 2). By maintaining its interest rate target, the Fed pushes output even further beyond its potential, causing an even greater rise in the price level both in the short run (to 130 in the figure) and in the long run (as the economy self-corrects—not shown).

---

[2] You might have noticed that in panel (a) of Figure 3, the money demand curve shifts out further than in Figure 2. This is because in Figure 3, the price level ends up higher, so the increase in money demand is greater.

FIGURE **3** **A Positive Demand Shock with a Constant Interest Rate**

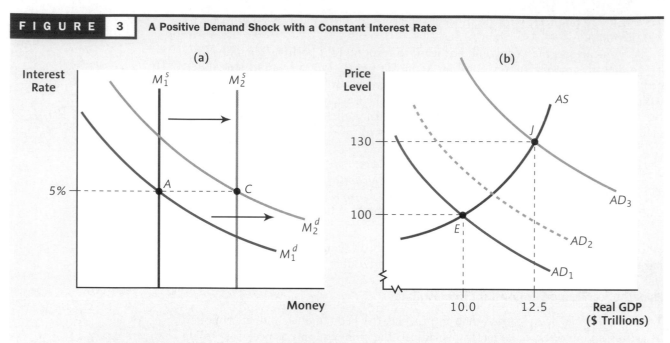

A positive demand shock initially shifts the AD curve rightward to AD₂ in panel (b), causing both the price level and output to rise. The rise in the price level shifts the money demand curve rightward to M₂ᵈ in panel (a), which would ordinarily cause the interest rate to rise. But if the Fed maintains a constant interest rate target, it will increase the money supply to prevent any rise in the interest rate. There will be no crowding out of consumption or investment spending, so the AD curve in panel (b) shifts further rightward (to AD₃). As a result, the economy ends up at point J, with output and the price level rising by more than under a constant-money-supply policy.

> *If a fully employed economy experiences a positive demand shock, a constant interest rate creates an even greater overshooting of potential output than a constant money supply. The result is an even greater rise in the price level.*

You can see that maintaining a constant interest rate would be an even poorer choice for the Fed than maintaining a constant money supply.

Best Response: Neutralization

A third possible response to a demand shock—and the best one—is for the Fed to prevent any shift in the *AD* curve at all. That is, the Fed should completely neutralize the demand shock.

This is illustrated in Figure 4. Once again, in panel (b), an increase in spending begins to shift the *AD* curve rightward (as indicated by the rightward arrow). But this time, instead of keeping the money supply constant (so the interest rate rises enough for *partial* crowding out) or keeping the interest rate constant (preventing *any* crowding out at all), the Fed now creates *complete crowding out*. That is, it raises its interest rate target by just enough to make spending fall as much as it initially rose from the demand shock. In this way, total spending remains unchanged, and the *AD* curve does not shift at all. In the figure, this is indicated by arrows showing the *AD* curve first shifts rightward, and then leftward back to its original position.

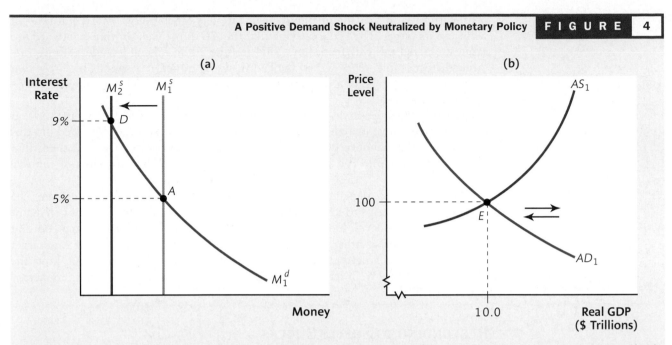

A Positive Demand Shock Neutralized by Monetary Policy   F I G U R E   4

A positive demand shock begins to shift the AD curve rightward in panel (b), which would ordinarily cause both the price level and output to rise. But the Fed can neutralize the shock by increasing its interest rate target enough to cause complete crowding out of consumption and investment spending. To reach the new, higher interest rate target, the Fed must decrease the money supply in panel (a), moving the money market equilibrium to a point like D. This reverses (or prevents) the shift in the AD curve, so the economy ends up at point E in panel (b), at its initial output and price level.

Panel (a) shows what happens in the money market as the Fed raises its interest rate target. In order to neutralize the demand shock completely, the Fed must raise the interest rate *higher* than it rose in Figure 2 (which caused only partial crowding out). In Figure 4, we assume that an interest rate of 9 percent will do the trick. The Fed shifts the money supply curve leftward, from M_1^s to M_2^s, moving the money market equilibrium to point D. Note that the money demand curve does not shift in this case. This is because, in the end, we are back at our original price level.

If the Fed acts quickly enough, it could prevent the demand shock from shifting the *AD* curve at all, keeping the economy at point E in panel (b). The Fed could thus prevent *any* rise in the price level. At the same time, it could keep the economy at full employment.

If a *negative* demand shock hits the economy, shifting the *AD* curve leftward, the Fed should respond with the opposite policy: lowering its interest rate target by *increasing* the money supply. The lower interest rate will stimulate additional consumption and investment spending, and can prevent the *AD* curve from shifting leftward.

> To maintain full employment and price stability after a demand shock, the Fed must change *its interest rate target. A positive demand shock requires an increase in the target; a negative demand shock requires a decrease in the target.*

In recent years, the Fed has changed its interest rate target as frequently as needed to keep the economy on track. If the Fed observes that the economy is overheating—and that the unemployment rate has fallen below its natural rate—it will raise its target. The Fed, believing that the *AD* curve was shifting rightward too rapidly, reacted this way from June 2004 to June 2006, raising its federal funds rate target 17 times in 2 years. When the Fed raises its target, it responds to forces that shift the *AD* curve rightward by creating an opposing force—a higher interest rate—to prevent the shift.

When the Fed observes that the economy is sluggish—and the unemployment rate has risen above its natural rate—the Fed will lower its target. The Fed did this aggressively throughout 2001, dropping its federal funds rate target 12 times that year. In this way, the Fed created a force opposing the leftward shift of the *AD* curve.

As you can see, demand shocks present the Fed with a no-lose situation: The same policy that helps to keep unemployment at its natural rate also helps to maintain a stable price level. However, these shocks present a challenge to the Fed that it doesn't face during other, less-eventful periods. To change the interest rate target by just the right amount, the Fed needs accurate information about how the economy operates. We'll return to this and other problems in conducting monetary policy a bit later.

RESPONDING TO SUPPLY SHOCKS

So far in this chapter, you've seen that demand shocks, in general, present the Fed with easy policy choices. By changing its interest rate target from time to time, it can deal with demand shocks, such as those caused by changes in aggregate expenditure. For demand shocks, the very same policy that maintains a stable price level also helps to maintain full employment.

But adverse or negative *supply* shocks present the Fed with a true dilemma: If the Fed tries to preserve price stability, it will worsen unemployment; if it tries to maintain high employment, it will worsen inflation. And even though supply shocks are usually temporary, the shocks themselves—and the Fed's response—can affect the economy for several quarters or even years.

Figure 5 illustrates the Fed's dilemma when confronting an adverse supply shock. Initially, the economy is at point *E* (full employment). Then, a supply shock—say, a rise in world oil prices—shifts the *AS* curve up to AS_2. One possible response for the Fed is to keep the *AD* curve at AD_1. It would do this by holding the *money supply* constant as the price level rose, allowing the interest rate to rise (not shown) and allowing the economy to move along AD_1. The short-run equilibrium would then move from point *E* to point *R*, and the economy would experience *stagflation*—both inflation and a recession—with output falling to Y_2 and the price level rising to P_2.

But the Fed can instead respond by *shifting* the *AD* curve, changing the money supply in order to alter the short-run equilibrium. Which policy should it choose? The answer will depend on whether it is mostly concerned about rising prices or rising unemployment. Let's start by imagining two extreme positions.

First, the Fed could prevent inflation entirely by decreasing the money supply, shifting the *AD* curve leftward to the curve labeled $AD_{\text{no inflation}}$. This would move the short-run equilibrium to point *T*. Notice, though, that while the price level remains at P_1, output decreases to Y_3, exacerbating the recession.

At the other extreme, the Fed could prevent any fall in output. To accomplish this, the Fed would *increase* the money supply and shift the *AD* curve rightward, to $AD_{\text{no recession}}$. The equilibrium would then move to point *V*, keeping output at its full-

FIGURE 5

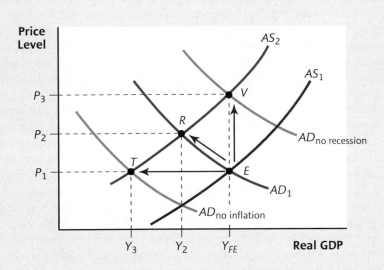

Responding to Supply Shocks

Starting at point E, a negative supply shock shifts the AS curve upward to AS$_2$. With a constant money supply, a new short-run equilibrium would be established at point R, with a higher price level (P$_2$) and a lower level of output (Y$_2$). The Fed could prevent inflation by decreasing the money supply and shifting AD to AD$_{no\ inflation}$, but output would fall to Y$_3$. At the other extreme, it could increase the money supply and shift the AD curve to AD$_{no\ recession}$. This would keep output at the full-employment level, but at the cost of a higher price level, P$_3$.

employment level. But this policy causes more inflation, raising the price level all the way to P_3.

In practice, the Fed is unlikely to choose either of these two extremes to deal with a supply shock, preferring instead some intermediate policy. But the extreme positions help illustrate the Fed's dilemma:

> *A negative supply shock presents the Fed with a short-run tradeoff: It can limit the recession, but only at the cost of more inflation; and it can limit inflation, but only at the cost of a deeper recession.*

The choice between the two policies is a hard one. After supply shocks, there are often debates within the Fed—and in the public arena—about how best to respond. Inflation *hawks* lean in the direction of price stability and are willing to tolerate more unemployment in order to achieve it. In the face of an adverse supply shock, hawks would prefer a response that shifts the *AD* curve closer to $AD_{no\ inflation}$, even though it means higher unemployment. Inflation *doves* lean in the direction of a milder recession, and are more willing to tolerate the cost of higher inflation. They would prefer a response that brings the *AD* curve closer to $AD_{no\ recession}$.

Choosing Between Hawk and Dove Policies

When a supply shock hits, should the Fed use a hawk policy, should it employ a dove policy, or should it keep the *AD* curve unchanged? That depends. Over time, as the economy is hit by supply shocks, the hawk policy maintains more stability in the

Significant supply shocks—which have often been caused by higher oil prices—force the Fed to choose between lower output or a higher inflation rate.

price level but less stability in output and employment. The dove policy gives the opposite result: more stability in output and less stability in the price level. The Fed should choose a hawkish policy if it cares more about price stability, and a dovish policy if it cares more about the stability of output and employment. Or it can pick an intermediate policy—one that balances price and employment stability more evenly.

The proper choice depends on how the Fed weights the harm caused by unemployment against the harm caused by inflation. And since the Fed is a public institution, its views should reflect the assessment of society as a whole. This is why supply shocks present such a challenge to the Fed: The public itself is divided between hawks and doves.

Both inflation and unemployment cause harm, but of very different kinds. Inflation imposes a more general cost on society: the resources used up to cope with it. If the inflation is unexpected, it will also redistribute income between borrowers and lenders. And, as you'll see in the next section, if inflation continues, people will expect it to continue into the future. At that point, prices and wages will begin to rise automatically, even if we are back at the natural rate of unemployment. The costs of unemployment are borne largely by the unemployed themselves—who suffer the harm of job loss—but partly by taxpayers, who provide funds for unemployment insurance. Balancing the gains and losses from hawk and dove policies is no easy task.

In recent years, some officials at the Fed have argued that having two objectives—stable prices *and* full employment—is unrealistic when there are supply shocks. The previous chair of the Board of Governors, Alan Greenspan, asked Congress to change the Fed's mandate to one of controlling inflation, period. But it would be difficult for the Fed to ignore the costs of higher unemployment, even if it were legally permitted to do so. Others have proposed that the Fed follow a predetermined rule, spelling out just how hawkish or dovish its response to supply shocks will be. We'll come back to this controversial idea later in the chapter.

EXPECTATIONS AND ONGOING INFLATION

So far in this chapter, we've assumed that the Fed strives to maintain *zero* inflation, and that the price level remains constant when the economy reaches its long-run, full-employment equilibrium. But as we discussed earlier, this is not entirely realistic. Look again at panel (a) of Figure 1. There you can see that the U.S. economy has been characterized by *ongoing inflation*. Even in the 1990s and into early 2001—with unemployment at (or very close to) its natural rate—the annual inflation rate hovered around 2 to 3 percent. This means that, even though the economy was at full employment (so the economy's self-correcting mechanism was not operating), prices were *continually rising*.

Even when the unemployment rate is *above* its natural rate—as in 2002 and 2003—prices keep rising. Why? And how does ongoing inflation change our analysis of the effects of monetary policy or the guidelines that the Fed should follow? We'll consider these questions next.

How Ongoing Inflation Arises

The best way to begin our analysis of ongoing inflation is to explore how it arises in an economy. We can do this by revisiting the 1960s, when the inflation rate rose steadily, and ongoing inflation first became a public concern.

What was special about the economy in the 1960s? First, it was a period of exuberance and optimism, for both businesses and households. Business spending on plant and equipment rose, and household spending on new homes and automobiles rose as well. At the same time, government spending rose—both military spending for the war in Vietnam and social spending on programs to help alleviate poverty. These increases in spending all contributed to rightward shifts of the *AD* curve; they were positive demand shocks. The unemployment rate fell below the natural rate—hovering around 3 percent in the late 1960s. And, as expected, the economy's self-correcting mechanism kicked in: Higher wages shifted the *AS* curve upward, causing the price level to rise.

As you've learned in this chapter, the Fed could have neutralized the positive demand shocks by raising its interest rate target (as in Figure 4), shifting the *AD* curve back to its original position. Alternatively, the Fed could have allowed the self-correcting mechanism to bring the economy back to full employment with a higher—but stable—price level. But in the late 1960s, the Fed made a different choice: It maintained its low interest rate target. This required the Fed to increase the money supply, thus adding its *own* positive demand shock to the spending shocks already hitting the economy. In Figure 3, this was the equivalent of moving the *AD* curve all the way out to AD_3, preventing any rise in interest rates but overheating the economy even more.

Why did the Fed act in this way? No one knows for sure, but one likely reason is that, in the 1960s, the Fed saw its job differently than it does today. The Fed tried to keep the interest rate stable and low, both to maintain high investment spending and to avoid instability in the financial markets. This is what it had been doing for years, with good effect: Americans had prospered in the previous decade, the 1950s, and financial markets were, indeed, stable.

But even though this policy worked well in the 1950s, it did not serve the economy well during and after the demand shocks of the 1960s. That's because the Fed's policy—year after year—prevented the self-correcting mechanism from bringing the economy back to full employment. Instead, each time the price level began rising, and the economy began to self-correct, the Fed would increase the money supply *again*, causing output to remain *continually* above its potential output. And that, in turn, meant that the price level would continue to rise, year after year.

Now comes a crucial part of the story: As the price level continued to rise in the 1960s, the public began to *expect* it to rise at a similar rate in the future. This illustrates a more general principle:

> *When inflation continues for some time, the public develops expectations that the inflation rate in the future will be similar to the inflation rates of the recent past.*

Why are expectations of inflation so important? Because when managers and workers expect inflation, it gets built into their decision-making process. Union contracts that set wages for the next 3 years will include automatic increases to compensate for the anticipated loss of purchasing power caused by future inflation. Nonunion wages will tend to rise each year as well, to match the wages in the unionized sector. And contracts for future delivery of inputs—like lumber, cement, and unfinished goods—will incorporate the higher prices everyone expects by the date of delivery. For reasons like these,

> *a continuing, stable rate of inflation gets built into the economy. The built-in rate is usually the rate that has existed for the past few years.*

BUILT-IN INFLATION

Once there is built-in inflation, the economy continues to generate inflation even *after* the self-correcting mechanism has finally been allowed to do its job and bring us back to potential output. To see why, look at Figure 6. It shows what might happen over the year in an economy with built-in inflation. In the figure, output is at its full-employment level. But over the year, the *AS* curve shifts upward and the *AD* curve shifts rightward, so the equilibrium moves from A to B and the price level rises from P_1 to P_2. Why does all this happen when there is built-in inflation?

Let's start with the reason for the upward shift of the *AS* curve. Unemployment is at its natural rate, so the self-correction mechanism is no longer contributing to any rise in wages or unit costs. But something else is causing unit costs to increase: inflationary expectations. Based on recent experience, the public expects the price level to rise as it has been rising in the past, so wages (and other input prices) will continue to increase, *even though real GDP is equal to potential output.* Thus,

> *in an economy with built-in inflation, the* AS *curve will shift upward each year, even when output is at potential and unemployment is at its natural rate. The upward shift of the* AS *curve will equal the built-in rate of inflation.*

For example, if the public expects inflation of 6 percent during the year, then contracts will call for wages and input prices to rise by 6 percent that year. This means that unit costs will increase by 6 percent. Firms—marking up prices over unit costs—will raise their prices by 6 percent as well, and the *AS* curve will shift upward by 6 percent.

Explaining why the *AS* curve shifts upward is only half the story in Figure 6. We must also explain why the *AD* curve shifts rightward. The simple answer is: The *AD*

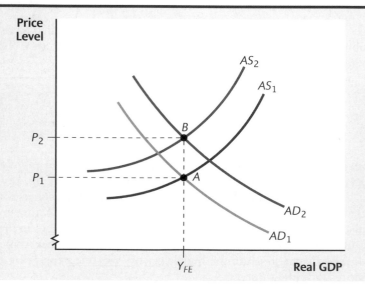

FIGURE 6

Long-Run Equilibrium with Built-In Inflation

During the year, the aggregate supply curve shifts upward by the built-in rate of inflation. To keep the economy at full employment, the Fed shifts the AD *curve rightward by increasing the money supply.*

curve shifts rightward because the Fed increases the money supply. But *why* does the Fed shift the *AD* curve rightward, when it knows that doing so only prolongs inflation? One reason is that reducing inflation would be *costly* to the economy.

Imagine what would happen if the Fed decided *not* to shift the *AD* curve rightward during the year. The *AS* curve will shift upward anyway, by a percentage shift equal to the built-in rate of inflation. This will happen *no matter what the Fed does* because the shift is based on expected inflation, which, in turn, is based on past experiences of inflation. There is nothing the Fed can do today to affect what has happened in the past, so it must accept the upward shift of the *AS* curve as a given. So if, during the year, the Fed maintains the *AD* curve at AD_1, the new equilibrium (not labeled in the figure) will be at the intersection of AD_1 and AS_2. The Fed would achieve its goal of reducing inflation that year—the price level would rise from P_1 to something less than P_2 instead of all the way to P_2. But the drop in inflation would come with a cost: The economy's output will decline below Y_{FE}—a recession.

> *In the short run, the Fed can reduce the rate of inflation below the built-in rate, but only at the cost of creating a recession.*

Would the Fed ever purposely create a recession to reduce inflation? Indeed it would, and it has—more than once. By far the most important episode occurred during the early 1980s. As Figure 1 shows, annual inflation reached the extraordinary level of 13.3 percent in 1979. Soon after, with some support from the newly elected President Reagan, the Fed embarked on an aggressive campaign to bring inflation down. The Fed stopped increasing the money supply and stopped shifting the *AD* curve rightward, and a recession began in July of 1981. Unemployment peaked, as shown earlier in Figure 1, at 10.7 percent at the end of 1982. With tremendous slack in the economy, the inflation rate fell rapidly, to below 4 percent in 1982. The Fed deliberately created a serious recession, but it brought down the rate of inflation.

Creating a recession is not a decision that the Fed takes lightly. Recessions are costly to the economy and painful to those who lose their jobs. The desire to avoid a recession is one reason that the Fed tolerated ongoing inflation for years and continued to play its role by shifting the *AD* curve rightward. We'll discuss other reasons for the Fed's tolerance of ongoing inflation a bit later.

ONGOING INFLATION AND THE PHILLIPS CURVE

Ongoing inflation changes our analysis of monetary policy. For one thing, it forces us to recognize a subtle, but important, change in the Fed's objectives: While the Fed still desires full employment, its other goal—price stability—is not zero inflation, but rather a *low and stable inflation rate*.

Another difference is in the graphs we use to illustrate the Fed's policy choices. Instead of continuing to analyze the economy with *AS* and *AD* graphs, when there is ongoing inflation, we usually use another powerful tool.

This tool is the *Phillips curve*—named after the late economist A. W. Phillips, who did early research on the relationship between inflation and unemployment. The **Phillips curve** illustrates the Fed's choices between inflation and unemployment in the short run, for a given built-in inflation rate.

Figure 7 shows a Phillips curve for the U.S. economy. The inflation rate is measured on the vertical axis; the unemployment rate on the horizontal. Point *E* shows

Phillips curve A curve indicating the Fed's choices between inflation and unemployment in the short run.

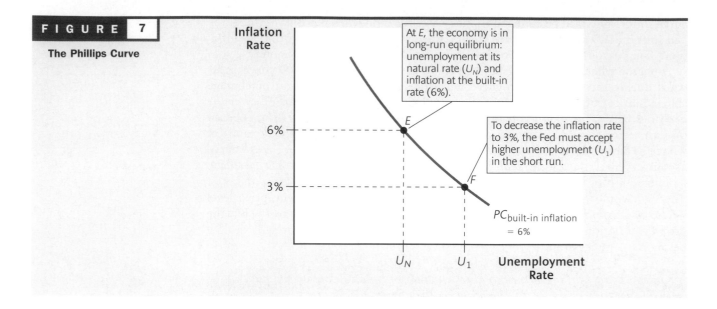

FIGURE **7**

The Phillips Curve

At *E*, the economy is in long-run equilibrium: unemployment at its natural rate (U_N) and inflation at the built-in rate (6%).

To decrease the inflation rate to 3%, the Fed must accept higher unemployment (U_1) in the short run.

the long-run equilibrium in the economy when the built-in inflation rate is 6 percent. At point *E*, unemployment is at its natural rate—U_N—and inflation remains constant from year to year at the built-in rate of 6 percent.

Notice that the Phillips curve is downward sloping. Why? Because it tells the same story we told earlier—with *AD* and *AS* curves—about the Fed's options in the short run. If the Fed wants to decrease the rate of inflation from 6 percent to 3 percent, it must slow the rightward shifts of the *AD* curve. This would cause a movement *along* the Phillips curve from point *E* to point *F*. As you can see, in moving to point *F*, the economy experiences a recession: Since output falls, unemployment rises above the natural rate.

> *In the short run, the Fed can move along the Phillips curve by adjusting the rate at which the* AD *curve shifts rightward. When the Fed moves the economy downward and rightward along the Phillips curve, the unemployment rate increases, and the inflation rate decreases.*

A Downward Shift in the Phillips Curve

Suppose the Fed moves the economy downward along the Phillips curve, from point *E* to point *F*, and then keeps it at point *F*. In the long run, the public—observing a 3 percent inflation rate—will come to expect 3 percent inflation into the future. Thus, in the long run, 3 percent will become the economy's built-in rate of inflation. Figure 8 shows the effect on the Phillips curve. When the economy's built-in inflation rate drops from 6 percent to 3 percent, the Phillips curve shifts downward, to the lower curve. At any unemployment rate, the inflation rate will be lower, now that the public expects inflation of only 3 percent rather than 6 percent.

> *In the long run, a decrease in the inflation rate leads to a lower built-in inflation rate, and the Phillips curve shifts downward.*

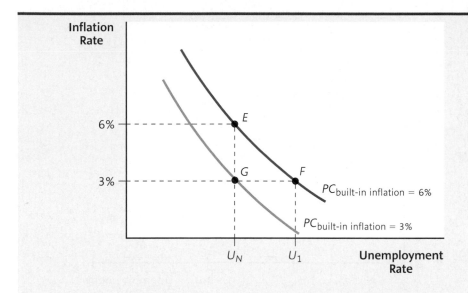

FIGURE 8

The Phillips Curve Shifts Downward

Initially, the economy is at point E, with inflation equal to the built-in rate of 6%. If the Fed moves the economy to point F and keeps it there for some time, the public will eventually come to expect 3% inflation in the future. The built-in inflation rate will fall and the Phillips curve will shift downward to PC_{built-in inflation = 3%}. The economy will move to point G in the long run, with unemployment at the natural rate and an actual inflation rate equal to the built-in rate of 3%.

Once the Fed has reduced the built-in inflation rate, it can locate anywhere on the new Phillips curve by adjusting how rapidly it lets the money supply grow (and, therefore, how rapidly the *AD* curve shifts rightward each year). Therefore, the Fed can choose to bring the economy back to full employment (point *G*), with a new, lower inflation rate of 3 percent rather than the previous 6 percent.

An Upward Shift in the Phillips Curve

The process we've described—moving down the Phillips curve and thereby causing it to shift downward—also works in reverse: Moving *up* the Phillips curve will, in the long run, shift the curve *upward*. Figure 9 illustrates this case. Once again, assume the economy begins at point *E*, with a built-in inflation rate of 6 percent and unemployment at its natural rate. Now suppose the Fed begins to increase the money supply *more rapidly* than in the past, and begins shifting the *AD* curve further rightward than in Figure 6. In the short run, the economy would move *along* the Phillips curve from point *E* to point *H* in Figure 9. The inflation rate would rise to 9 percent, and the unemployment rate would fall below its natural rate—in the short run.

But suppose the Fed keeps the economy at point *H* for some time, continuing to shift the *AD* curve rightward at a faster rate than before. Then, in the long run, the public will begin to expect 9 percent inflation, and that will become the new built-in rate of inflation. The Phillips curve will then shift upward. At this point, if the Fed returns the economy to full employment, we end up at point *J*. The economy will be back in long-run equilibrium—but with a higher built-in inflation rate.

In the long run, an increase in the inflation rate leads to a higher built-in inflation rate, and the Phillips curve shifts upward.

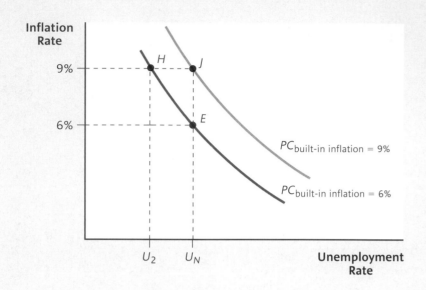

FIGURE 9

The Phillips Curve Shifts Upward

*Initially, the economy is at point E, with inflation equal to the built-in rate of 6%. If the Fed moves the economy to point H and keeps it there for some time, the public will eventually come to expect 9% inflation in the future. The built-in inflation rate will rise and the Phillips curve will shift upward to PC*built-in inflation = 9%*. The economy will move to point J in the long run, with unemployment at the natural rate and an actual inflation rate equal to the built-in rate of 9%.*

THE LONG-RUN PHILLIPS CURVE

Figure 10 combines the previous two figures, showing the policy choices for the Fed and their consequences. We assume, as before, that we are initially at point E on the middle Phillips curve. The built-in inflation rate is 6 percent, and the economy is operating at full employment. In the short run, the built-in inflation rate will remain at 6 percent, so the Fed can freely move along the middle Phillips curve, say, to point H or point F. In doing so, the Fed exploits the short-run tradeoff between unemployment and inflation. But in the long run—once the public's expectations of inflation adjust to the new reality—the built-in inflation rate will change, and the Phillips curve will shift. Indeed, the Phillips curve will *keep* shifting whenever the unemployment rate is kept above or below the natural rate. (To see why, ask yourself what would happen in the future if the Fed tried to keep the unemployment rate *permanently* at a level like U_2—below the natural rate.) Thus, the economy cannot be in long-run equilibrium until the unemployment rate returns to its natural rate, and output is back to its potential level. In the long run, when we are at the natural rate of unemployment, the Fed can only choose *which* Phillips curve the economy will be on.

> *In the short run, there is a tradeoff between inflation and unemployment: The Fed can choose lower unemployment at the cost of higher inflation, or lower inflation at the cost of higher unemployment. But in the long run, since unemployment always returns to its natural rate, there is no such tradeoff.*

Now look at the vertical line. It tells us how monetary policy affects the economy in the long run, without the distractions of the short-run story. The vertical line is the

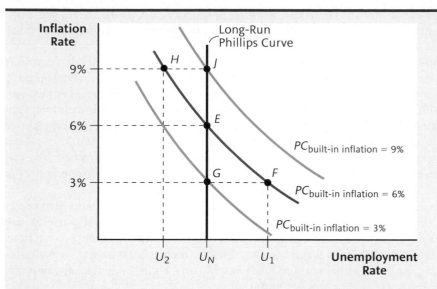

FIGURE 10

The Long-Run Phillips Curve

The vertical line is the economy's long-run Phillips curve, showing all combinations of unemployment and inflation the Fed can choose in the long run. The curve is vertical because in the long run, the unemployment rate must equal the natural rate. Starting at point E with 6% inflation, the Fed can choose unemployment at the natural rate with either a higher rate of inflation (point J) or a lower rate of inflation (point G). But points off of the vertical line are not sustainable in the long run.

economy's *long-run Phillips curve*, which tells us the combinations of unemployment and inflation that the Fed can choose in the long run.

To see why, suppose the Fed moves the economy from point E to point H in the short run. Then in the long run, we will end up at point J on the vertical line: The economy will be back at the natural rate of unemployment, but with a higher inflation rate (9 percent). Suppose, on the other hand, the Fed moves us from point E to point F in the short run. Then in the long run, we will once again be on the vertical line, but this time at point G. Unemployment is at its natural rate, but with a lower inflation rate (3 percent). No matter what the Fed does, unemployment will always return to the natural rate, U_N, in the long run. However, the Fed can use monetary policy to select any rate of inflation it wants.

> *The **long-run Phillips curve** is a vertical line at the natural rate of unemployment. It shows us that, in the long run, the Fed can change the rate of inflation, but not the rate of unemployment.*

Long-run Phillips curve A vertical line indicating that in the long run, unemployment must equal its natural rate, regardless of the rate of inflation.

WHY THE FED ALLOWS ONGOING INFLATION

Since the Fed can choose any rate of inflation it wants, and since inflation is costly to society, we might think that the Fed would aim for an inflation rate of zero. But a look back at panel (a) of Figure 1 shows that this is not what the Fed has chosen to do. In recent years, with unemployment very close to its natural rate, the Fed has maintained annual inflation at around 2 or 3 percent. Why doesn't the Fed eliminate inflation from the economy entirely?

One reason is a widespread belief that the Consumer Price Index (CPI) and other measures of inflation actually *overstate* the true rate of inflation in the economy. As you've learned, many economists believe that the CPI has overstated the true annual inflation rate by 1 to 2 percent—or more—in recent decades. Although the

Bureau of Labor Statistics has been working hard to correct the problem, some significant upward bias remains. Thus, the Fed is effectively eliminating *actual* inflation when it keeps the *measured* rate low.

But some economists have offered another explanation for the Fed's behavior: Low, stable inflation makes the labor market work more smoothly. The argument goes as follows: While no one wants a cut in his or her real wage rate, people seem to react differently, depending on *how* the real wage is decreased. For example, suppose there is an excess supply of workers in some industry, and a real wage cut of 3 percent would bring that labor market back to equilibrium. Workers would strongly resist a 3 percent cut in the nominal wage. But they would more easily tolerate a freeze in the nominal wage while the price level rises by 3 percent, even though in both scenarios, the real wage falls by 3 percent.

If this argument is correct, then a low or modest inflation rate would help wages adjust in different markets, helping to ensure that workers move to industries where they would be most productive as the structure of the economy changes over time. In some labor markets, real wages can be raised by increasing nominal wages faster than prices. In other labor markets, real wages can be cut by increasing nominal wages more slowly than prices, or not at all.

> *The Fed has tolerated measured inflation at 2 to 3 percent per year because it knows that the true rate of inflation is lower, and because low rates of inflation may help labor markets adjust more easily.*

CHALLENGES FOR MONETARY POLICY

So far in this chapter, we've described some clear-cut guidelines the Fed *can* and *does* follow in conducting monetary policy. We've seen that the proper response to demand shocks is a change in the interest rate target. Dealing with a supply shock is more problematic because it requires the Fed to balance its goal of low, stable inflation with its goal of full employment. But even here, once the Fed decides on the proper balance, its policy choice is straightforward: Shift the *AD* curve to achieve the desired combination of inflation and unemployment in the short run, and then guide the economy back to full employment in the long run.

One might almost conclude that monetary policy is akin to operating a giant machine—adjusting this or that knob, and making the occasional repair by consulting the manual. And policy making might appear rather uncontroversial, other than the occasional debate between those who favor hawkish and dovish policies toward inflation after a supply shock.

But the truth is very much the opposite. First, the Fed faces frequent criticism from members of Congress, the business community, the media, and some academic economists—over not just its policy choices but also the *way* it arrives at them. Second, the Fed, rather than operating a well-understood machine, must conduct monetary policy with highly imperfect information about the economy's course and precisely how its policies will alter that course. Let's consider some of the challenges facing the Fed.

INFORMATION PROBLEMS

The Federal Reserve has hundreds of economists carrying out research and gathering data to improve its understanding of how the economy works, and how monetary policy affects the economy. Research at the Fed is widely respected and has made great progress. But because the economy is complex and constantly changing, serious gaps remain. Two of the most important gaps concern the time lag before monetary policy affects the economy, and knowledge of the natural rate of unemployment (or—equivalently—the economy's potential output).

Uncertain and Changing Time Lags

Suppose that we are in the midst of an expansion, and Fed officials begin to worry that the economy is about to overheat. They respond by raising their interest rate target. Eventually, the higher interest rate will dampen planned investment and consumption spending and cool the economy off. But when?

Monetary policy works with a time lag. Even after a rise in the interest rate, business firms will likely continue to build the new plants and new homes they've already started constructing. The most powerful effects on investment spending will be the cancellation of *new* projects currently being planned—projects that *would* have entered the pipeline of new spending many months later. The same applies in the other direction: When the Fed lowers the interest rate to stimulate additional spending, the full effects will be felt many months later, after new investment projects are planned and firms begin making the associated purchases.

The time lag in the effectiveness of monetary policy can have serious consequences. For example, by the time a higher interest rate target has its maximum effect, the economy may already be returning to full employment on its own, or it may be hit by a negative demand shock. In this case, the Fed—by raising its interest rate target—will be reining in the economy at just the wrong time, causing a recession.

Economists often use an analogy to describe this problem. Imagine that you are trying to drive a car with a special problem: When you step on the gas, the car will go forward . . . but not until 5 minutes later. Similarly, when you step on the brake, the car will slow, but also with a 5-minute lag. It would be very difficult to maintain an even speed with this car: You'd step on the gas, and when nothing happened, you'd be tempted to step on it harder. By the time the car begins to move, you will have given too much gas and find yourself speeding down the road. So you try to slow down, but once again, hitting the brakes makes nothing happen. So you brake harder, and when the car finally responds, you come to a dead halt.

The Fed can make—and, in the past, has made—similar mistakes. When it tries to cool off an overheated economy, it may find that nothing is happening. Is it just a long time lag, or has the Fed not hit the brakes hard enough? If it hits the brakes harder, it runs the risk of braking the economy too much; if it doesn't, it runs the risk of continuing to allow the economy to overheat. Even worse, the time lag before monetary policy affects prices and output can change over the years: Just when the Fed may think it has mastered the rules of the game, the rules change.

The Natural Rate of Unemployment

In our Phillips curve analysis, we've assumed that the economy's natural rate of unemployment is known and remains constant, signified by the vertical long-run Phillips curve at some value U_N. In this case, once the economy achieved a long-run equilibrium, the Fed's job would be relatively straightforward: to shift the *AD* curve rightward by just the right amount each period to maintain the natural rate of unemployment with an acceptable rate of inflation.

But even though there is wide agreement that the natural rate rose in the 1970s and has fallen since the late 1980s, economists remain uncertain about its value during any given period. Many economists believe that today the natural rate is between 4.5 and 5 percent, but no one is really sure.

Why is this a problem? It's very much like the two mountain climbers who become lost. One of them pulls out a map. "Do you see that big mountain over there?" he says, pointing off into the distance. "Yes," says the other. "Well," says the first, "according to the map, we're standing on top of it." In order to achieve its twin goals of full employment and a stable, low rate of inflation, the Fed tries to maintain the unemployment rate as close to the natural rate as possible. If its estimate of the natural rate is wrong, it may believe it has succeeded when, in fact, it has not.

For example, suppose the Fed believes the natural rate of unemployment is 5 percent, but the rate is really 4.5 percent. Then—at least for a time—the Fed will be steering the economy toward an unemployment rate that is unnecessarily high and an output level that is unnecessarily low. We've already discussed the costs of cyclical unemployment. An overestimate of the natural rate makes society bear these costs needlessly. On the other hand, if the Fed believes the natural rate is 4.5 percent when it is really 5 percent, it will overheat the economy. This will raise the inflation rate—and a costly recession may be needed later in order to reduce it.

Trial and error can help the Fed determine the true natural rate. If the Fed raises unemployment above the true natural rate, the inflation rate will drop. If unemployment falls below the true natural rate, the inflation rate will rise. But (as we discussed earlier) trial and error works best when there is continual and rapid feedback. It can take some time for the inflation rate to change—6 months, a year, or even longer. In the meantime, the Fed might believe it has been successful, even while causing avoidable unemployment, or planting the seeds for a future rise in the inflation rate.

Estimating the natural rate of unemployment is made even more difficult because the economy is constantly buffeted by shocks of one kind or another. If the Fed observes that the inflation rate is rising, does that mean that unemployment is below the natural rate? Or is the higher inflation being caused by a negative supply shock? Or by the Fed's response to an earlier, negative demand shock? This information is difficult to sort out, although the Fed has become increasingly sophisticated in its efforts to do so.

RULES VERSUS DISCRETION

Over the last several decades, the Federal Reserve has formulated monetary policy using *discretion*: responding to demand and supply shocks in the way that Fed officials thought best at the time. In some cases, this seems to have helped the economy's performance, as when the Fed aggressively cut interest rates during 2001 and helped to make the recession of that year shorter and milder than it would otherwise have been. In other cases, discretion has worked less well. During the late 1970s, frequent changes in monetary policy contributed to wide fluctuations in output and a rapidly rising inflation rate that reached 13.3 percent in 1979. A more recent example is the Fed's policy in 2000. It raised interest rates and, in retrospect, waited too long before bringing them down again, missing an opportunity to begin an early fight against the recession of 2001.

Should the Federal Reserve have complete discretion to change its interest rate target in response to demand and supply shocks as it sees fit? Or should it stick to rules or guidelines in making monetary policy—rules that it announces in advance, with a justification required for any departure? Some economists have suggested that the Fed's performance on average would be better with less discretion and more deference to predetermined rules.

The Taylor Rule

The most often discussed rule for monetary policy is the **Taylor rule**, originally proposed by economist John Taylor. Under this rule, the Fed would be required to announce a target for the inflation rate (say, 2 percent per year) and another target for real GDP (equal to the Fed's estimate of potential GDP in that period). Then the Fed would be required to change its interest rate target by some predetermined amount whenever either output or inflation (or both) deviated from their respective targets.

For example, suppose the economy began to overheat from a positive demand shock. Then at some point either real GDP would rise above potential, or the inflation rate would rise above its target rate, or both would occur. The Fed would then be obligated to raise its interest rate target by an amount that everyone knew in advance, depending on the changes observed in output and inflation. On the other side, if a negative demand shock started to threaten a recession, changes in inflation and/or output would commit the Fed to *lower* its interest rate target, and stimulate the economy back toward full employment.

What about a negative supply shock—such as a rise in oil prices—that causes the inflation rate to rise and output to fall? In this case, inflation would rise *higher* than its target, and output would fall *below* it. But the rule would identify in advance just how the Fed would respond. It would raise or lower the interest rate target depending on which variable—output or inflation—deviated the most, and depending on the response to each variable that the rule calls for. Thus, the hawk–dove debate that follows every supply shock would be settled—publically—in advance.

What would be the advantage of such a rule? First, if the Federal Reserve were committed to respond to the first signs of a boom, the public would know that the Fed would *not* allow the economy to continue overheating. This would discourage the formation of inflationary expectations. In effect, the Fed would be saying to the public, "Even though the inflation rate just rose, you know the rules. We have to bring the inflation rate back down, so don't get any ideas that we're going to let this continue." Similarly, if a negative demand shock sends the economy into a recession, and the Fed begins to stimulate the economy, the public needn't wonder whether the Fed will go too far and create ongoing, higher inflation. The rule says that the Fed will stimulate the economy only until we are back at potential output.

Second, the Taylor rule would give the Fed ammunition to fight inflation with a higher interest rate even when doing so might prove unpopular at the time. The Fed would only be following the rule that everyone understood in advance. This would help discourage the sort of discretion, and political pressure, that contributed to the high inflation rates of the late 1970s.

The Taylor rule is controversial. Opponents argue that it implies more advanced knowledge about the economy—and what an appropriate future response should be—than is realistically possible. And unless the rule were written into law—which only a few economists would advocate—the Fed would not be obligated to follow it. Since the public would know this, the existence of the rule might not be a strong deterrent to inflationary expectations.

Taylor rule A proposed rule that would require the Fed to change the interest rate by a specified amount whenever real GDP or inflation deviates from its pre-announced target.

Interestingly, the Fed's behavior under Alan Greenspan (1987–2005) followed reasonably close to the specific numerical rule that Taylor originally proposed. Whether the economy performed better or worse due to Greenspan's *deviations* from the rule remains controversial.

As you can see, conducting monetary policy is not easy. The Fed has hundreds of economists carrying out research and gathering data to improve its information about the status of the economy and its understanding of how the economy works. And the effort seemed to have paid off during the decade leading up to 2001. But some economists believe that the Fed, in retrospect, could have done more to offset the forces that caused the recession that began in March 2001. They believe that the Fed raised the interest rate too high in 2000 and waited too long before starting to lower the interest rate in January 2001. This is an easy conclusion to come to with hindsight. But given the uncertainties faced by the Fed in conducting monetary policy, most economists have expressed approval of the Fed's performance under the chairmanship of Alan Greenspan. In mid-2006, economists were also giving high marks to Ben Bernanke, who took over Greenspan's job in February of that year.

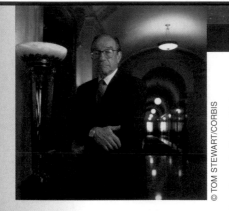

Alan Greenspan, Fed Chair from 1987 through 2005.

© TOM STEWART/CORBIS

USING THE THEORY

Expectations and the Importance of Words

Alan Greenspan—the Chair of the Federal Reserve Board from 1987 through 2005—was famous for his style of speaking. When testifying before Congress, giving a speech, or granting an interview, he spoke in sentences that gave English teachers heartache. They were long, complex, and packed with specifics. At the same time, they seemed carefully designed to allow for multiple interpretations.

A famous example occurred after Greenspan spoke to reporters on June 7, 1995. The next morning, the headline in the *New York Times* was, "Greenspan Sees Chance of Recession," while in the *Washington Post,* it was, "Recession Is Unlikely, Greenspan Concludes." Greenspan's wife, NBC reporter Andrea Mitchell, has said that he had to propose to her three times before she understood what he meant.

Most economists understood why Greenspan spoke in that style—at least about the economy. Words matter. And the words of the Fed chair matter a lot. A Fed chair who speaks *too* clearly and gives *too* much new information about a future change in monetary policy can destabilize financial markets.

To understand why, let's first review how changes in monetary policy affect the bond market. Recall that the interest rate and the price of bonds are negatively related. When the Fed raises interest rates, bond prices drop. Because the public holds trillions of dollars in government and corporate bonds, even a small rise in the interest rate—say, a quarter of a percentage point—decreases the value of the public's bond holdings by billions of dollars.

The stock market is often affected in a similar way. People hold stocks because they entitle the owner to a share of a firm's profits, and because stock prices are usually expected to rise as the economy grows and firms become more profitable. But stocks must offer a competitive rate of return to bonds, or else no one would hold them. The lower the price of a share of stock, the more attractive the stock is to a potential buyer.

When the Fed raises interest rates, and the rate of return on bonds increases, bonds become more attractive to potential buyers. As a result, stock prices must fall, so that stocks, too, will become more attractive to hold. And that is typically what happens. Unless other events are affecting the stock market, a rise in the interest rate causes people to try to sell their stocks in order to acquire the suddenly more attractive bonds. This causes stock prices to fall, until stocks are once again as attractive as bonds.

Thus, a rise in the interest rate (federal funds rate) target—which causes interest rates in general to rise—causes stock prices, as well as bond prices, to fall.

> *The stock and bond markets move in the opposite direction to the Fed's interest rate target. Ceteris paribus, when the Fed raises its target, stock and bond prices fall. When the Fed lowers its target, stock and bond prices rise.*

The potentially destabilizing effect on stock and bond markets is one reason why, in normal times, the Fed prefers not to change its interest rate target very often. Frequent changes in the target would make prices in financial markets less stable and the public more hesitant to supply funds to business firms by buying stocks and bonds.

But financial markets are also affected by *expected* changes in the interest rate target—whether or not they actually occur. If you expect the Fed to raise its target, you also expect stock and bond prices to fall. Therefore, you would want to dump these assets *now*, before their price drops. Similarly, an expectation of a drop in the interest rate target would make you want to buy stocks and bonds now, before their prices rise. Thus, changes in expectations about the Fed's future actions can be as destabilizing as the actions themselves.

Once you understand the Fed's logic in changing its interest rate target, you can understand a phenomenon that—at first glance—appears mystifying: Stock and bond prices often fall when good news about the economy is released, and rise when bad news is released. For example, if the Bureau of Labor Statistics announces a sudden, unexpected drop in the unemployment rate, or the Commerce Department announces that real GDP grew more rapidly during the previous quarter than had been thought, stock and bond prices may plummet. Why? Because owners of stocks and bonds believe that the Fed might interpret the good news as evidence that the economy is overheating. They would then expect the Fed to raise its interest rate target, so they try to sell their stocks and bonds before the Federal Open Market Committee even meets.

> *Good news about the economy sometimes leads to new expectations that the Fed, fearing inflation, will raise its interest rate target. This is why good economic news can cause stock and bond prices to fall. Similarly, bad news about the economy sometimes leads to expectations that the Fed, fearing recession, will lower its interest rate target. This is why bad economic news sometimes causes stock and bond prices to rise.*

Now let's go back to the importance of words. The members of the FOMC are well aware that the public speculates about what the committee will do at its next meeting, and that FOMC announcements and speeches by Fed officials are carefully studied. This creates both an opportunity and a challenge.

The opportunity is that words themselves are another Fed tool (in addition to its interest rate target) for influencing the direction of the economy. For example, if the FOMC hints at a *slight* increase in the likelihood of a lower interest rate target at the next meeting, there will likely be *some* increase in stock and bond buying. Because stocks and bonds are important components of household wealth, households—now wealthier—will increase their consumption spending. In this way the Fed, if it is careful, can gradually shift the aggregate expenditure line by phrasing its announcements carefully. On occasion, the Fed may want to engineer a more dramatic change in aggregate expenditure and will use stronger, more definitive phrasing.

Over the years, the Fed has experimented with different strategies for managing expectations. Greenspan was widely considered a master of this craft. His statements, while complex, often contained hints—sometimes subtle, sometimes more pronounced—of a change in policy.

The challenge for Fed officials—especially the Fed chair—is that if they are not careful, and tip their hand too suddenly or too strongly, there can be huge, undesired price swings in financial markets. Indeed, stock and bond prices often jump around in the days leading up to meetings of the FOMC, as statements made by Fed officials are parsed especially closely.

Ben Bernanke replaced Alan Greenspan as Fed chair in February 2006.[3] And he was quickly reminded about the importance of words. In Congressional testimony just 2 months after taking office, Bernanke—who had promised greater "transparency" about Fed decision making—mused about policy in a rather straightforward manner. Financial market analysts interpreted his remarks to mean that the Fed would not continue its recent interest rate hikes, as had been expected. Stock and bond prices jumped up.

A week later, at a White House correspondent's dinner, Bernanke told CNBC reporter Maria Bartiromo (in what he *may* have thought was a private conversation) that the markets had misinterpreted his testimony. He had been musing only about the *possibility* of a *temporary* pause in rate hikes. Bartiromo, in turn, broadcast her account of the conversation at 3:15 P.M. the next day. Suddenly, expectations changed: Now everyone believed that the FOMC *would* raise interest rates at its next meeting. Stock and bond prices—which had been rising until that very minute—turned on a dime and ended up lower for the day.

A few weeks later, when asked about the incident in a Senate hearing, Bernanke vowed that "in the future, my communications with the public and with the markets will be entirely through regular and formal channels."[4] Those formal channels consist mostly of the carefully worded statements released by the FOMC after each of its meetings. They are most often designed to calm and occasionally nudge—rather than startle or stir up—the financial markets. Typically, that means they must defy clear interpretation.

For example, consider the statement released by the Bernanke FOMC after its meeting on June 29, 2006. Here is the key section that is always studied most closely by journalists and market analysts, who are looking for hints of the Fed's next move. Take a deep breath.

> *Although the moderation in the growth of aggregate demand should help to limit inflation pressures over time, the Committee judges that some inflation risks remain. The extent and timing of any additional firming that may be*

Ben Bernanke became the new Fed Chair in February 2006.

© JOSHUA ROBERTS/REUTERS/CORBIS

---

[3] Before Ben Bernanke was nominated by President Bush, Glenn Hubbard—Dean of the Columbia Business School—was also thought to be a candidate. When Hubbard wasn't chosen, Columbia students made a music video featuring a jealous Hubbard look-alike. It is well worth watching. You can find it at *www.cbsfollies.com*, then find the entry for "Every Breath You Take," and select "View."

[4] Nell Henderson, "Fed Chief Calls His Remarks a Mistake," *Washington Post*, May 24, 2006, p. D01.

needed to address these risks will depend on the evolution of the outlook for both inflation and economic growth, as implied by incoming information. In any event, the Committee will respond to changes in economic prospects as needed to support the attainment of its objectives.

A statement like this does not give much of a hint about the Fed's future moves. It is difficult to read, and even harder to interpret. Alan Greenspan couldn't have phrased it any better.

Summary

As the nation's central bank, the Federal Reserve bears primary responsibility for maintaining a low, stable rate of inflation and for maintaining full employment of the labor force as the economy is buffeted by a variety of shocks.

Demand shocks can shift the *AD* curve, causing output to deviate from its full-employment level. The Fed can neutralize these shocks by adjusting its interest rate target—changing the money supply to shift the *AD* curve back to its original position.

The Fed's most difficult problem is responding to supply shocks. A negative supply shock—an upward shift of the *AS* curve—presents the Fed with a dilemma. In the short run, it must choose a point along that new *AS* curve. If it wishes to maintain price stability, it must shift the *AD* curve to the left and accept higher unemployment. If the Fed wishes to maintain full employment, it must shift the *AD* curve to the right and accept a higher rate of inflation. A "hawk" policy puts greater emphasis on price stability, while a "dove" policy emphasizes lower unemployment.

If Fed policy leads to ongoing inflation, then businesses and households come to expect the prevailing inflation rate to continue. As a result, the *AS* curve continues to shift upward at that built-in expected inflation rate. To maintain full employment, the Fed must shift the *AD* curve rightward, creating an inflation rate equal to the expected rate.

If the Fed wishes to change the built-in inflation rate, it must first change the expected inflation rate. For example, to lower the expected inflation rate, the Fed will slow down the rightward shifts of the *AD* curve. The actual inflation rate will fall, and expectations will eventually adjust downward. While they do so, however, the economy will experience a recession. The Fed's short-run choices between inflation and unemployment can be illustrated with the Phillips curve. In the short run, the Fed can move the economy along the downward-sloping *Phillips curve* by adjusting the rate at which the *AD* curve shifts. If the Fed moves the economy to a new point on the Phillips curve and holds it there, the built-in inflation rate will eventually adjust and the Phillips curve will shift. In the long run, the economy will return to the natural rate of unemployment with a different inflation rate. The *long-run Phillips curve* is a vertical line at the natural rate of unemployment.

In conducting monetary policy, the Fed faces several challenges. It has imperfect information about the time required for its policies to affect the economy, and also about the economy's potential GDP (or its natural rate of unemployment) during any given period. The Fed often faces criticism for using discretion rather than following rigid rules, especially when the economy does not perform well.

Problem Set   *Answers to even-numbered Questions and Problems can be found on the text Web site at www.thomsonedu.com/economics/hall.*

1. Suppose that a law required the Fed to do everything possible to keep the inflation rate equal to zero. Using *AD* and *AS* curves, illustrate and explain how the Fed would deal with (a) a negative demand shock from a decrease in investment spending and (b) an adverse aggregate supply shock. What would the costs and benefits of such a law be?

2. Suppose that, in a world with *no* ongoing inflation, the government raises taxes. Using *AD* and *AS* curves, describe the effects on the economy if the Fed decides to keep the money supply constant. Alternatively, how could the Fed use active policy to neutralize the demand shock?

3. Suppose that initially the price level is P_1 and GDP is Y_1, with no built-in inflation. The Fed reacts to a negative demand shock by shifting the aggregate demand curve in the appropriate direction. The next time the Fed receives data on GDP and the price level, it finds that the price level is above P_1 and GDP is above Y_1. Give a possible explanation for this finding.

4. Suppose the economy has been experiencing a low inflation rate. A new chair of the Federal Reserve is named, and he or she is known to be sympathetic to dove policies. Explain the possible effects on the Phillips curve.

5. "The idea of the Fed having to choose between hawk and dove policies in Figure 5 is silly. All the Fed has to do is

shift the *AS* curve back to its original position, which would prevent *both* recession *and* inflation." Do you agree? Why or why not?

6. Using a graph similar to Figure 9, and some additional curves, show what would happen in the future if the Fed tried to keep the unemployment rate *permanently* at a level like U_2—below the natural rate.

More Challenging

7. Suppose the economy is experiencing ongoing inflation. The Fed wants to reduce expected inflation, so it announces that in the future it will tolerate less inflation. How does the Fed's credibility affect the success of the reduction? How can the Fed build its credibility? Are there costs to building credibility? If so, what are they?

8. This chapter mentioned what would happen if the Fed over- or underestimated the natural rate of unemployment. Using the *AD–AS* model, suppose the economy is at the true natural rate of unemployment, so that GDP is at its potential level. Suppose, too, that the Fed wrongly believes that the natural rate of unemployment is higher (potential GDP is lower) and acts to bring the economy back to its supposed potential. What will the Fed do? What will happen in the short run? If the Fed continues to maintain output below potential, what will happen over the long run?

Spending, Taxes, and the Federal Budget

Almost every year throughout the 1980s and early 1990s, a best-selling book would be published that predicted economic disaster for the United States and the world. In most of these books, the U.S. federal government played a central role. Arguments and statistics were offered to show that federal government spending—which was growing by leaps and bounds—was out of control, causing us to run budget deficits year after year. As a result, the United States was facing a growing debt burden that would soon swallow up all of our incomes, sink the United States economy, and bring about a worldwide depression.

During the late 1990s, as the federal budget picture improved, these disaster books quietly disappeared. Now, the federal government was running *surpluses*—raising more funds in tax revenues than it was spending. Moreover, the surpluses were projected to continue for at least a decade. News articles and public statements described a bright economic future in which our most pressing problem would be: What shall we do with our mounting budget surpluses?

Then, in 2002, another flip-flop: The government began running deficits again, with continued deficits projected through the end of the decade and beyond. Once again, concern over the budget and growing U.S. debt saturated the media, and the word *disaster* reappeared in the media.

What caused these flip-flops in the government's budget? And why should we care?

In this chapter, we'll take a close look at the government's role in the macro-economy. You'll learn how to interpret trends in the government's budget, and how to identify the causes and effects of those trends. You'll also learn how economists differentiate between debt burdens that are not really problematic, those that are cause for concern, and those that can truly be described as disastrous.

THINKING ABOUT THE NUMBERS

Let's start with some simple numbers. In 1959, the federal government's total outlays for goods and services, transfer payments, and interest on its debt was $92 billion. By 2006, the total had grown to about $2,700 billion, an increase of more than 2,800 percent. Does this show that government spending is out of control?

Or consider the **national debt**—the total amount that the federal government owes to the general public from past borrowing in years in which it ran a budget deficit. In 1959, the national debt was $235 billion; by mid-2005, it had grown to $4,900 billion. Is this evidence that debt is crushing the economy?

National debt The total amount the federal government still owes to the general public from past borrowing.

Actually, these figures don't tell us much of anything. First, prices rose during that period, so *real* government outlays and the *real* national debt rose considerably less than these nominal figures suggest. In addition, from 1959 to 2006, the U.S. population grew, the labor force grew, and the average worker became more productive. As a result, real GDP and real income more than quadrupled during this period. Why is that important? Because *spending and debt should be viewed in relation to income.*

We automatically recognize this principle when we think about an individual family or business. Suppose you are told that a family is spending $50,000 each year on goods and services, and has a total debt—a combination of mortgage debt, car loans, student loans, and credit card balances—of $200,000. Is this family acting responsibly? Or is its spending and borrowing out of control? That depends. If the income of the household is less than its spending—say, $40,000—and is expected to remain so, then there is serious trouble. A family that continues to spend more than it earns would see its debt grow every year until it could not handle the monthly interest payments.

But what if the family's income is $800,000 per year? Then our conclusion would change dramatically: We'd wonder why this family spends so *little*. And if it owed $200,000, we would not think it irresponsible at all. After all, the family could pay the interest on its debt with a tiny fraction of its income.

What is true for an individual family is also true for the nation. Spending and debt are *relative* concepts. As a country's total income grows, it will want more of the things that government can provide—education, high environmental standards, domestic security, programs to help the needy, and more. Therefore, we expect government spending to rise as a nation becomes richer. Moreover, as its income grows, a country can *handle* higher interest payments on its debt. Government spending and the total national debt, considered in isolation, tell us nothing about how responsibly or irresponsibly the government is behaving.

> *Budget-related figures such as government outlays, tax revenues, or government debt should be considered relative to a nation's total income—as percentages of GDP.*

Viewing budget-related figures relative to GDP helps to put things in perspective. In 1959, the federal government's total outlays were 19 percent of GDP. In 2006, they were 20.6 percent—reflecting a slight upward drift, but far from out of control. And relative to GDP, the national debt in the hands of the public was lower in 2006 than in 1959, shrinking from about 48 percent to 37 percent of GDP. This doesn't suggest that everything is fine with the federal budget, and we'll discuss some causes for concern in this chapter. But our concerns should be based on, and expressed with, the proper perspective.

In the rest of this chapter, as we explore recent trends in fiscal behavior and their effects on the economy, we'll do so with these lessons in mind. Accordingly, we'll look at fiscal variables as *percentages of GDP*.[1]

---

[1] It makes no difference whether we divide *nominal* government outlays by *nominal* GDP, or *real* government outlays by *real* GDP; we get the same answer for government outlays as a percentage of GDP. When we measure a variable as a percentage of GDP, we are adjusting for inflation *and* for growth in real income at the same time.

THE FEDERAL BUDGET AND ITS COMPONENTS

Our ultimate goal in this chapter is to understand how fiscal changes have affected, and continue to affect, the macroeconomy. But before we do this, some background will help. What has happened to the *composition* of government spending in recent decades? How does the U.S. tax system work, and what has happened to the government's tax revenues? Why has the national debt decreased in some years, risen slowly in other years, and risen very rapidly in still others? This section provides answers to these and other questions about the government's finances. Although state and local spending also play an important role in the macroeconomy, most of the significant macroeconomic changes in recent decades have involved the *federal* government. This is why we'll focus on spending, taxing, and borrowing at the federal level.

GOVERNMENT OUTLAYS

The federal government's *outlays*—the total amount spent or disbursed by the federal government in all of its activities—can be divided into three categories:

- *Government purchases*—the total value of the goods and services that the government buys (corresponding to "*G*" in GDP = *C* + *I* + *G* + *NX*)
- *Transfer payments*—income supplements the government provides to people, such as Social Security benefits, unemployment compensation, and welfare payments
- *Interest on the national debt*—the interest payments the government must make to those who hold government bonds

Government Purchases

Until the mid-1970s, government purchases of goods and services were the largest component of government spending. To understand how these purchases have changed over time, it's essential to divide them into two categories: military and nonmilitary. Figure 1 shows total federal purchases, as well as federal military and nonmilitary purchases, from 1959 to 2006.

One fact stands out from the figure: The federal government uses up only a tiny fraction of our national resources for nonmilitary purposes. These nonmilitary purchases include the salaries paid to all government workers outside the Defense Department (for example, federal judges, legislators, and the people who run federal agencies), as well as purchases of buildings, equipment, and supplies. It also includes the spending of the new Homeland Security Department (established in 2003). Added together, all the different kinds of nonmilitary government purchases account for a stable, low fraction of GDP—about 2 percent.

This strongly contradicts a commonly held notion: that government spending is growing by leaps and bounds because of bloated federal bureaucracies. While it's true that government outlays have drifted upward over the last several decades, nonmilitary purchases have not been the cause.

As a percentage of GDP, nonmilitary government purchases have remained very low and stable. They have not contributed to growth in total government outlays.

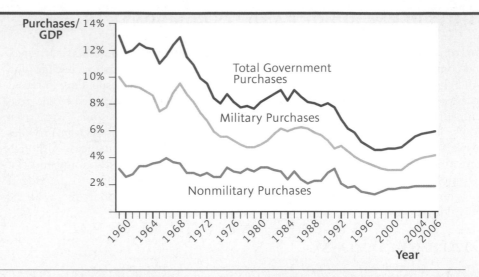

F I G U R E   1

Federal Government Purchases as a Percentage of GDP

Over the last several decades, total government purchases have trended downward largely because nonmilitary purchases remained a stable, small percentage of GDP while military purchases have steadily decreased. Exceptions were the late 1960s (Vietnam War), 1980s (Reagan defense buildup) and the early 2000s (Bush defense buildup after September 11, 2001).

Source for this and most of the other figures in this chapter: Office of Management and Budget, *The Budget for Fiscal Year 2007, Historical Tables* (especially Tables 1.1, 1.3, 2.1, 2.3, 6.1, and 7.1). Data for 2006 are estimates.

What about military purchases? Here, we come to an even stronger conclusion:

> *As a percentage of GDP, military purchases trended sharply downward over the past several decades. Like nonmilitary purchases, they have not contributed to the long-term upward drift in government outlays.*

The decline in military purchases is shown by the middle line in Figure 1. They were around 10 percent of GDP in 1959, fell almost continuously to about 3 percent in the late 1990s, then rose again from 2001 to 2006. In between, there were two large military buildups—one associated with the Vietnam War in the late 1960s and the other during the Reagan administration in the 1980s. But both of these buildups were temporary. From 1959 to 2001, the decline of military spending freed up resources amounting to 6½ to 7 percent of GDP (often called the "peace dividend" from the ending of the cold war). As you can see in Figure 1, the more recent rise in military purchases has taken back only a small part of the peace dividend.

It is too early to say whether the current rise in military purchases will be temporary, or how large it will become. But given the current U.S. role in global politics, significant future cuts seem highly unlikely. The implications are tremendously important for thinking about the recent past and the future of the federal government's role in the economy:

> *The decline in military spending in relation to GDP since the early 1960s has made huge amounts of resources available for other purposes. Because military spending has little room to fall further and is likely to rise over the next decade, there will not be any similar freeing up of resources in coming years.*

The resources released from military spending eased many otherwise tough decisions about resource allocation in the economy. In particular, they made it easy

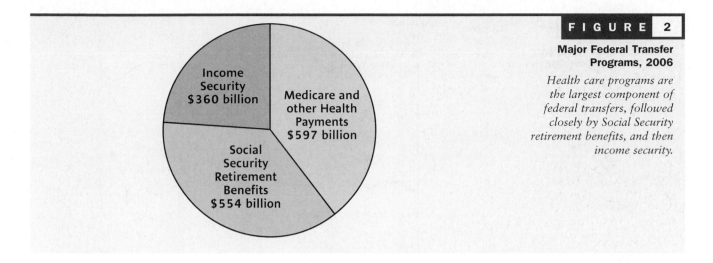

FIGURE **2**

Major Federal Transfer Programs, 2006

Health care programs are the largest component of federal transfers, followed closely by Social Security retirement benefits, and then income security.

for the federal government to provide increases in resources to some parts of the population, through transfer payments. Now that this trend has ended, the government will be presented with difficult budget choices.

Social Security and Other Transfers

Transfer programs provide cash and in-kind benefits to people whom the federal government designates as needing or entitled to help. Figure 2 shows the three major categories of transfers.

The largest category of transfers—and the fastest-growing—occurs in health programs. Medicare (officially part of the Social Security system) provides health-related benefits to everyone aged 62 and over. It covers care at hospitals and nursing facilities, covers outpatient physician services, and began in 2006 to cover prescription medication. Efforts have been made to control Medicare's rapidly rising costs, but they have continued to rise as a percentage of GDP. They are expected to rise even more rapidly over the next decade as the baby-boom generation begins retiring. In addition to funding Medicare, the federal government helps finance state-operated health plans for the poor, through a program called Medicaid. The costs of these programs have been rising rapidly as well.

The second largest category is retirement benefits—the payments made by the Social Security system to retired people. Although the benefits are loosely related to past contributions to the Social Security system, workers whose earnings are low receive benefits that are worth far more than their contributions. And after age 72, even someone with no history of contributions receives the minimum benefit. Social Security outlays have grown rapidly over the last few decades, and are expected to rise even more rapidly as the baby-boom generation begins retiring and collecting benefits around 2010.

Government "Outlays" versus Government "Purchases"
Don't confuse government outlays with government purchases, which are just one component of the government's outlays. The other components are transfer payments and interest on the debt.

DANGEROUS CURVES

The third and smallest of the three categories of transfers is *income security*—a catch-all for some federal retirement programs, as well as programs to help the poor and the unemployed, such as unemployment insurance, food stamps, and welfare.

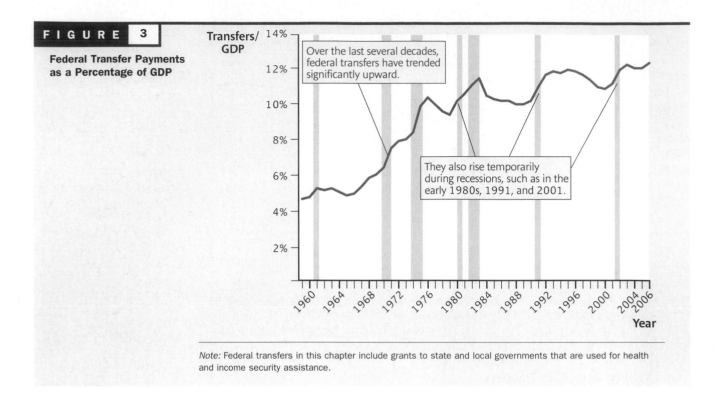

FIGURE 3

Federal Transfer Payments as a Percentage of GDP

Transfers/GDP

Over the last several decades, federal transfers have trended significantly upward.

They also rise temporarily during recessions, such as in the early 1980s, 1991, and 2001.

Year

Note: Federal transfers in this chapter include grants to state and local governments that are used for health and income security assistance.

Have transfer payments been growing as a fraction of GDP? Indeed, they have. All three categories of transfer programs have grown rapidly in recent decades. Figure 3 shows how *total* transfer payments as a percentage of GDP have trended upward.

> *In recent decades, transfers have been the fastest growing part of federal government outlays and are currently equal to about 12.4 percent of GDP.*

Growth in transfers relative to GDP was most rapid in the 1970s during the Nixon administration. During this period, government-financed retirement benefits became much more generous, food stamps were introduced, and Medicare expanded. Since then, transfers have continued to rise modestly but are projected to soar as baby boomers retire and receive Social Security and Medicare benefits.

Notice, too, that transfers are sensitive to the ups and downs of the economy. Transfers as a fraction of GDP rise during recessions, as in 1974, 1981, 1991, and 2001. This is for two reasons. First, the number of needy recipients rises in a recession, so transfer payments—the numerator of the fraction—increase. Second, GDP—the denominator—typically falls in a recession. Similarly, transfers as a fraction of GDP tend to fall during expansions, such as the long expansion that ran from 1991 through early 2001. During expansions, the numerator of this fraction falls (why?), and the denominator rises. We will come back to these movements in transfers toward the end of the chapter.

Interest on the National Debt

Figure 4 shows the behavior of the third and smallest category of government spending: interest on the national debt. As you can see, interest as a percentage of

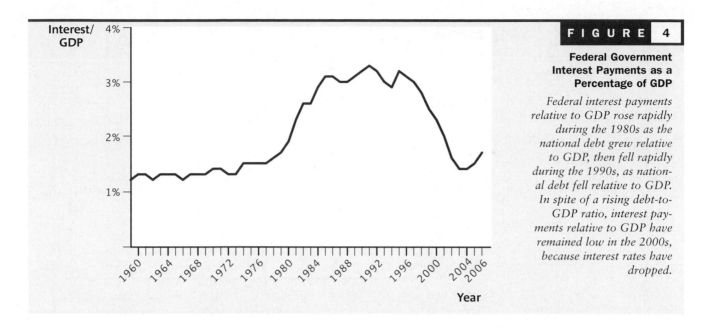

FIGURE 4

Federal Government Interest Payments as a Percentage of GDP

Federal interest payments relative to GDP rose rapidly during the 1980s as the national debt grew relative to GDP, then fell rapidly during the 1990s, as national debt fell relative to GDP. In spite of a rising debt-to-GDP ratio, interest payments relative to GDP have remained low in the 2000s, because interest rates have dropped.

GDP grew rapidly in the early 1980s, when the debt was growing and interest rates were rising. In the 1990s, interest as a fraction of GDP fell slowly at first, as growth in the debt slowed, and then fell dramatically as the national debt dropped from 1998 to 2001. Interest relative to GDP has remained low in the early 2000s even though the national debt has been rising, because the Federal Reserve repeatedly lowered interest rates in 2001, and they remained low through most of 2004.

Total Government Outlays

Figure 5 shows total outlays in relation to GDP over the past several decades. There are two important things to notice in the figure. The first is the *fluctuations* in government outlays over the period. There was a sharp increase in outlays in each recession (shaded) due to the jump in transfers that we saw in Figure 3. The recession of 1981–82 is a striking example. Also visible is the increase in military spending for the Vietnam War in the late 1960s.

The second thing to notice is the trends. First, for several decades up to the early 1990s, federal outlays as a percentage of GDP drifted upward (due mainly to increases in transfers and interest payments). Then, from 1992 to 2000, federal outlays relative to GDP declined (due mainly to the "peace dividend" and falling transfers during a long economic expansion).

However, Figure 5 also shows the appearance of a likely new trend:

> *From 2001 to 2006, due to the ending of the "peace dividend" and continued increases in transfers, federal government outlays as a percentage of GDP have been rising, and seem likely to continue rising through the decade.*

These trends in government outlays have important implications, but they are only half of the story. In order to understand their impact on the budget and the macroeconomy, we must look at the other side of the budget: tax revenue.

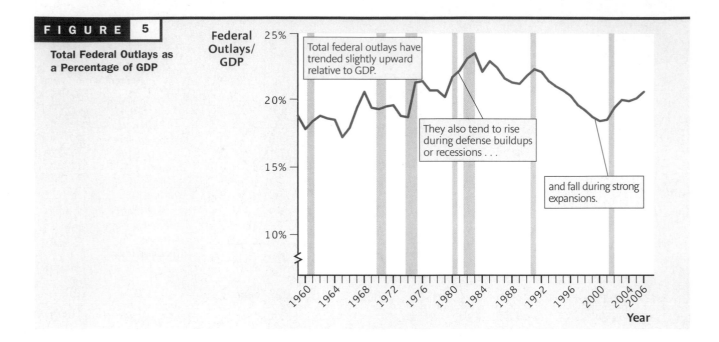

FIGURE 5

Total Federal Outlays as a Percentage of GDP

Total federal outlays have trended slightly upward relative to GDP.

They also tend to rise during defense buildups or recessions . . .

and fall during strong expansions.

FEDERAL TAX REVENUE

The federal government obtains most of its revenue from two sources: the personal income tax and the Social Security tax.

The Personal Income Tax

The personal income tax is the most important source of revenue for the federal government and also the most conspicuous and painful. Almost every adult has to file Form 1040 or one of its shorter cousins. One of the signs of success as an American is seeing your federal tax return swell to the size of a magazine. Proposals to reduce both the amount of taxes people pay and the complexity of the tax forms are immensely popular.

Progressive tax A tax whose rate increases as income increases.

The personal income tax is designed to be **progressive**, to tax those at the higher end of the income scale at higher rates than those at the lower end of the scale, and to excuse the poorest families from paying any tax at all. Table 1 shows how the income tax works, in theory, by computing the amount of tax a family of four should have paid on its 2005 income if it took the standard deduction.[2] The table also shows the **average tax rate**—the fraction of total income a family pays in taxes—and the **marginal tax rate**—the tax rate paid on *each additional dollar* of income.

Average tax rate The fraction of a given income paid in taxes.

Marginal tax rate The fraction of an additional dollar of income paid in taxes.

We can see from Table 1 that the income tax is designed to be quite progressive. In principle, a family in the middle of the income distribution for married couples, earning $65,000 per year, should have paid about 9 percent of its income in taxes, while a family near the top should have paid almost 30 percent of its income in

[2] The federal government allows households to deduct certain expenses (like medical care or the costs of moving to a new job) from their income before calculating the tax that they owe. Alternatively, they may deduct a standard amount (the *standard deduction*) from their income, regardless of their spending patterns.

Income	Tax	Average Tax Rate	Marginal Tax Rate
$ 20,000	$ 0	0%	0%
$ 30,000	$ 723	2.4%	10%
$ 50,000	$ 3,354	6.7%	15%
$ 75,000	$ 7,104	9.5%	15%
$150,000	$ 25,348	16.9%	28%
$250,000	$ 63,092	25.2%	33%
$400,000	$110,563	27.6%	35%

TABLE 1

The 2005 Personal Income Tax for a Married Couple with Two Children

Source: Calculated from the 2005 Form 1040 tax table with the standard deduction of $10,000. First column shows total income before standard deduction or deduction for dependents.

taxes. The table also shows that marginal tax rates on families with the highest income are in the range of 33 to 35 percent.

But the tax system shown in the table does not reflect the ways that people can avoid tax. Many people have deductions far above the standard deduction. Some people earn income that they never report to the government, thereby evading taxes entirely. And people can shelter income in their employer's retirement plan or in a plan of their own. Studies have shown that higher-income households avoid more taxes than poorer families and that the federal tax system—while still progressive—is much less progressive than suggested by Table 1.

Also, remember that we are looking at the *federal personal income* tax only. Households pay other taxes related to their income, some of which are **regressive**—taking a lower percentage in taxes as household income rises. For example, state and local sales taxes are regressive: Lower-income households *spend* a larger fraction of their incomes, so they pay a higher percentage of that income in sales taxes. Another example of a regressive tax is the federal payroll tax, earmarked to fund Social Security and Medicare, which we'll turn to now.

Regressive tax A tax that collects a lower percentage of income as income rises.

The Social Security Tax

The Social Security tax applies to wage and salary income only. It was put in place in 1936, to finance the Social Security system created in that year. Whereas the personal income tax is a nightmare of complex forms and rules, the Social Security tax is remarkably simple. The current tax rate (including the Medicare part of the tax) is a flat 15.3 percent,[3] except for one complication: Most of the tax is applied only on earnings below a certain amount ($94,200 in 2006, although the cap rises each year).

Because the payroll tax applies only to earnings below a certain level, it is regressive. For example, employees earning $94,200 or below in 2006 paid the full 15.3 percent of their income in taxes, while those who earned twice that amount—$188,400—paid only 7.65 percent (since the tax applied to only half of their earnings). The Social Security tax is actually the largest tax paid by many Americans,

---

[3] If you look at your own paycheck, it may seem that the Social Security tax (including Medicare) is only 7.65 percent instead of the 15.3 percent we've just mentioned. The reason is that your employer pays half the tax and you pay the other half. But the amount paid on your earnings is the sum, 15.3 percent.

especially those with lower incomes. These families pay little or no income tax, but pay the Social Security tax on all of their wage earnings. For example, a family with $30,000 of earnings in Table 1 would pay $723 in federal income tax, but Social Security taxes on those earnings would be $4,590.

Other Federal Taxes

The federal government also collects around $503 billion annually from other sources. The most important of these is the *corporate profits tax,* which raised $332 billion in 2006 by taxing the profits earned by corporations at a rate of 35 percent.

The corporate profits tax is often criticized by economists because of two important problems. First, it applies only to corporations. Thus, a business owner can avoid it completely by setting up a sole proprietorship or partnership instead of a corporation. As a result, the tax causes many businesses to forego the benefits of being corporations because of the extra tax they would have to pay.

Second, the corporation tax results in *double taxation* on the portion of corporate profits that corporations pay to their owners. This portion of profits is taxed once when the corporation is taxed and again when the profits are included as part of the owners' personal income. The corporation tax is thus a prime target for tax reform. Almost all reform proposals put forward by economists involve integrating the taxation of corporations into the tax system in a way that avoids these two distortions.

The federal government also taxes the consumption of certain products, such as gasoline, alcohol, tobacco, and air travel. These are called *excise taxes.* Excise taxes raise additional revenue for the government, but they are usually put in place for other, nonrevenue reasons as well. The excise tax on gasoline is seen, in part, as a fee on drivers for the use of federal highways. The taxes on alcohol and tobacco are intended to discourage consumption of these harmful products.

Trends in Federal Tax Revenue

The top line in Figure 6 shows total federal government revenue, as a percentage of GDP, from all of the taxes we've discussed. Until recently, there was an upward trend. More specifically,

> *federal revenue trended upward from around 18 percent of GDP in the early 1960s to around 21 percent in the late 1990s.*

But notice the sharp drop in the early 2000s. This was partly due to the very slow recovery from the 2001 recession, and partly due to significant long-term reductions in tax rates proposed by the Bush administration, and passed by Congress, in 2001 and 2003. We'll have more to say about these tax cuts at the end of this chapter.

Notice, also, that the *composition* of total federal revenue has changed dramatically. The lower two lines in Figure 6 show the part of federal revenue that comes from Social Security taxes and all other taxes. Notice the steady upward trend in Social Security tax revenue. Also notice that all other sources of revenue have trended slightly downward over the same period even before the sharp drop of the 2000s.

Why have Social Security taxes grown in importance? First, a little background. The Social Security system operates on a pay-as-you-go principle: It taxes people who are working now in order to pay benefits to those who worked earlier and are

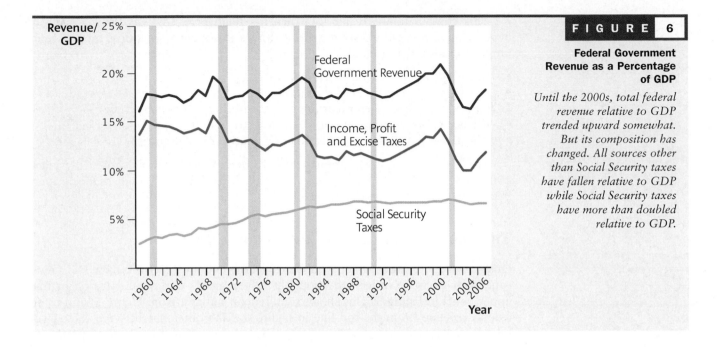

FIGURE 6

Federal Government Revenue as a Percentage of GDP

Until the 2000s, total federal revenue relative to GDP trended upward somewhat. But its composition has changed. All sources other than Social Security taxes have fallen relative to GDP while Social Security taxes have more than doubled relative to GDP.

now retired. For the first several decades after the system was established (in 1935), there were so few retirees that benefits could be funded with very low payroll tax rates on those currently working.

But now, demographic trends are working against the system. First, improved health is allowing people to spend a larger fraction of their lives in retirement. That is good from a human perspective, but from an accounting point of view, it means that the average retiree is drawing more benefits. At the same time, the baby boomers will begin retiring en masse around 2010, which means greater *numbers* of people drawing benefits. Finally, these increased benefits will be funded by a smaller number of working taxpayers.

Anticipating these trends, the government had been raising Social Security tax rates for years, not just to keep the system solvent, but to go further—building up reserves in a separate government account (called the Social Security Trust Fund) for retiring baby boomers. This helped to create the rising Social Security tax line in Figure 6.

But the trust fund has imposed no constraints on Congress, legal or economic. In fact, the reserves built up in the trust fund have been (and continue to be) borrowed by the Treasury and spent on other government programs. Meanwhile, Congress has been (and continues to be) free to raise or lower Social Security benefits as it wishes, regardless of the balance in the trust fund.

Thus, the rising Social Security tax line in Figure 6—while it helped to fund past government outlays—did not "solve" the real Social Security problem. That problem is: Scheduled Social Security benefits as a percentage of GDP will begin rising (due to retiring baby boomers) around 2010. At the same time, payroll tax revenues as a percentage of GDP will begin falling (fewer baby boomers working and paying taxes). Similar but even larger changes will be occurring in Medicare, the government health program for retirees.

This combination—greater total benefits relative to GDP, and lower payroll taxes relative to GDP to pay for them—forces the country to choose among four unpleasant alternatives:

- Raise the payroll tax rate (or other tax rates) on current workers
- Cut future retirement and/or health benefits as a fraction of GDP (say, by raising the retirement age, or cutting projected benefits for each retiree)
- Reduce *other* government outlays relative to GDP to pay the greater benefits
- Allow the overall annual budget deficit relative to GDP to rise

The last option occurs automatically if none of the others is chosen. By mid-2006, it was still unclear which one (or combination) of these unpleasant options the country would ultimately choose.

THE FEDERAL BUDGET AND THE NATIONAL DEBT

Finally, we can bring together what we've learned about the government's tax revenue with what we've learned about the government's outlays. Look first at the upper panel in Figure 7. This shows total federal outlays (from Figure 5) and total federal revenue (from the top line in Figure 6). The difference between these two lines in any year is the federal budget deficit (when outlays exceed revenue) or surplus (when revenue exceeds outlays).

$$\text{Budget surplus} = \text{Tax revenue} - \text{Outlays}$$

$$\text{Budget deficit} = \text{Outlays} - \text{Tax revenue}^4$$

The bottom panel shows the history of the budget in recent decades, with surpluses as positive values and deficits as negative values.[5] The lower panel looks much choppier because the scale of the diagram is different there. But you can see that there was a dramatic change in the behavior of the budget around 1975. Until that year, the government mostly ran deficits, but rarely more than 2 percent of GDP. But from 1975 until 1993, the deficit grew significantly. During that period, it was usually greater than 3 percent of GDP, and often more than 4 percent. Notice, for example, the especially large rise in the deficit that occurred in the early 1980s. This was the combined result of a severe recession, which caused transfers to rise as shown in Figure 3, the buildup in military spending shown in Figure 1, and a large cut in income taxes during President Reagan's first term in office.

---

[4] If we consider interest payments as part of transfer payments, these are the same definitions given earlier in the text. To see this, start with our current definition of the deficit:

$$\begin{aligned} \text{Budget deficit} &= \text{Outlays} - \text{Tax revenue} \\ &= (\text{Government purchases} + \text{Transfers}) - \text{Tax revenue} \\ &= \text{Government purchases} - (\text{Tax revenue} - \text{Transfers}) \\ &= G - T \end{aligned}$$

The last line is the definition for the deficit given in the chapter on the classical model, where G is government purchases in GDP and T is net taxes.

[5] To measure the deficit or surplus, we have included all sources of federal revenue and all types of spending, whether part of the official federal budget or not. In particular, we've included Social Security taxes and Social Security payments even though they are officially considered "off budget" in U.S. government statistics.

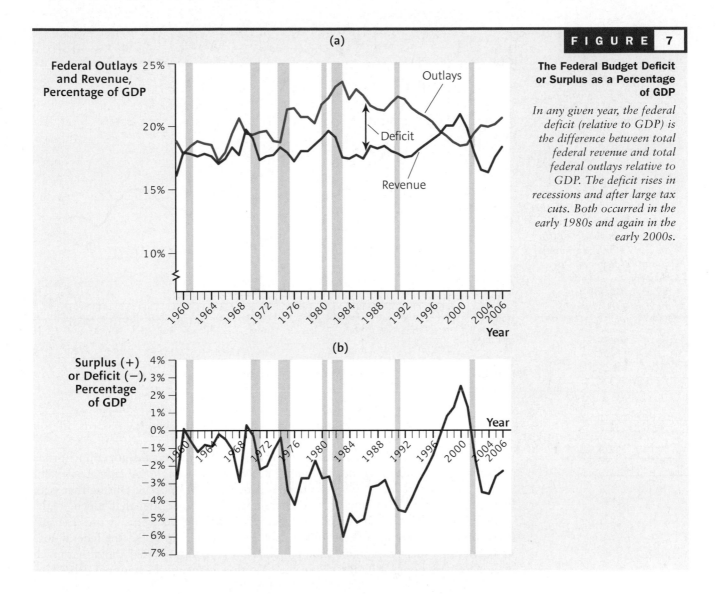

(a)

Federal Outlays and Revenue, Percentage of GDP

Outlays

Deficit

Revenue

Year

(b)

Surplus (+) or Deficit (−), Percentage of GDP

Year

FIGURE 7

The Federal Budget Deficit or Surplus as a Percentage of GDP

In any given year, the federal deficit (relative to GDP) is the difference between total federal revenue and total federal outlays relative to GDP. The deficit rises in recessions and after large tax cuts. Both occurred in the early 1980s and again in the early 2000s.

In the mid-1990s, the deficit began to come down, and finally, in the late 1990s, the federal government began running budget surpluses for a few years. But from 2002 to 2006, the budget was back into deficit, and the deficits were projected to continue through the end of the decade. Even though the world has changed much since the 1980s, the reasons for the recent deficits seem like a repeat of history: a recession, increased military spending, and a sizable, multiyear tax cut.

The National Debt

Before we consider the government's budget further, we need to address some common confusion among three related, but very different, terms: the federal *deficit,* the federal *surplus,* and the national *debt.* The federal deficit and surplus are *flow* variables: They measure the difference between government spending and tax revenue *over a given period,* usually a year. The national debt, by contrast, is a *stock* variable: It measures the total amount that the federal government owes *at a given point*

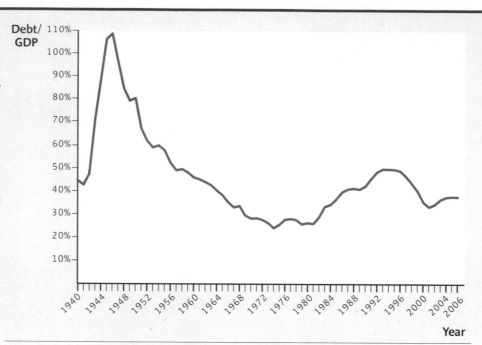

Source: Office of Management and Budget. *Historical Tables, Budget of the United States Government, Fiscal Year 2007*, Table 7.1.

FIGURE 8

Federal Debt as a Percentage of GDP

Federal debt (the national debt) relative to GDP soared during World War II then fell steadily for several decades. It rose during the 1980s due to a combination of tax cuts and defense buildups during the Reagan administration, then fell during the shrinking deficits and expansion of the 1990s. In the early 2000s, a combination of recession and slow recovery, tax cuts, and defense spending caused the debt–GDP ratio to begin rising.

in time. (See the chapter "Economic Growth and Rising Living Standards" if you need a refresher on stocks and flows.)

The relationship between these terms is this: Each year that the government runs a deficit, it must borrow funds to finance it, *adding to the national debt*. For example, in 1996, the federal government ran a deficit of $107 billion. During that year, it issued about $107 billion in new government bonds, adding that much to the national debt. On the other hand, if the government runs a surplus, it uses the surplus to *pay back* some of the national debt. For example, in 2000, the federal government ran a surplus of about $236 billion. That year, it purchased about that much in government bonds it had issued in the past, thus reducing the national debt.[6]

We can measure the national debt as the total value of government bonds held by the public. Thus,

> *deficits—which add to the public's holdings of federal government bonds—add to the national debt. Surpluses—which decrease the public's bond holdings—subtract from the national debt.*

Since the cumulative total of the government's deficits has been greater than its surpluses, the national debt has grown over the past several decades. In the 1980s and early 1990s, it also grew relative to GDP, as shown in Figure 8.

The rise and fall in the national debt also explains another trend we discussed earlier: the rise and fall in *interest payments* the government must make to those who hold government bonds. All else equal, the larger the national debt, the greater

---

[6] The increase or decrease in the national debt is never exactly the same as the annual deficit or surplus, because of accounting details.

will be the government's yearly interest payments on the debt. As you saw in Figure 4, total interest payments rose rapidly during the 1980s—the same period in which the national debt zoomed upward. In the 1990s, as the national debt decreased relative to GDP, so did interest payments on the debt. If you compare Figure 4 with Figure 8, however, you'll see that, as a percentage of GDP, the national debt rose in the early 2000s while yearly interest payments fell. That's because all else was *not* equal during this period: As mentioned earlier, the Federal Reserve dramatically lowered interest rates in the early 2000s, which reduced the government's interest payments on each dollar of newly issued debt.

Now that we've outlined the recent history of federal government spending, taxes, and debt, we turn our attention to the relationship between fiscal changes and the economy.

FISCAL CHANGES IN THE SHORT RUN

In the short run, there is a two-way relationship between the government's budget and the macroeconomy. On the one hand, changes in the economy affect the government's outlays and taxes; on the other hand, changes in outlays and taxes affect the economy. Let's begin by considering how economic fluctuations affect the government's budget.

HOW ECONOMIC FLUCTUATIONS AFFECT THE FEDERAL BUDGET

Economic fluctuations affect both transfer payments and tax revenues. In a recession, in which many people lose their jobs, the federal government contributes larger amounts to state-run unemployment insurance systems and pays more in transfers to the poor, since more families qualify for these types of assistance. Thus, a recession causes transfer payments to rise. Recessions also cause a drop in tax revenue, because household income and corporate profits—two important sources of tax revenue—decrease during recessions.

> *In a recession, because transfers rise and tax revenue falls, the federal budget deficit increases (or the surplus decreases).*

An expansion has the opposite effect on the federal budget: With lower unemployment and higher levels of output and income, federal transfers decrease and tax revenues increase. Thus,

> *in an expansion, because transfers decrease and tax revenue rises, the budget deficit decreases (or the surplus increases).*

Because the business cycle has systematic effects on the budget, economists find it useful to divide the deficit into two components. The **cyclical deficit** is the part that can be attributed to the current state of the economy. We have a cyclical deficit when output is below potential GDP, and a cyclical surplus when output is above potential. When the economy is operating just at full employment, the cyclical deficit is, by definition, zero.

The **structural deficit** is the part of the deficit that is *not* caused by economic fluctuations. As the economy recovers from a recession, for example, the cyclical deficit goes away, but any structural deficit in the budget will remain.

Cyclical deficit The part of the federal budget deficit that varies with the business cycle.

Structural deficit The part of the federal budget deficit that is independent of the business cycle.

Cyclical changes in the budget are not a cause for concern because they average out to about zero, as output fluctuates above and below potential output. Thus, the cyclical deficit should not contribute to a long-run rise in the national debt.

HOW THE BUDGET AFFECTS ECONOMIC FLUCTUATIONS

There are two types of budget changes that can affect the macroeconomy. One is a change in total government purchases or net taxes *not* caused by the business cycle. These are *policy* changes, and they affect the *structural* budget deficit. For example, an increase in government purchases will raise the budget deficit we would have at *any* level of GDP.

As you learned in earlier chapters, fiscal policy can affect total spending and have a multiplier affect on GDP in the short run. In theory, fiscal policy could even change the course of the business cycle itself. However, as discussed in an earlier chapter ("The Short-Run Macro Model"), counter-cyclical fiscal policy is problematic, and is no longer regarded as the most effective tool to counter the business cycle.

A second type of budgetary change that affects the macroeconomy was introduced in this chapter: changes in taxes or transfers that are *caused* by the business cycle itself. These are not policy changes; rather, they occur *automatically* as income rises or falls during the business cycle. They affect the cyclical, but not the structural, deficit.

Such changes in the cyclical deficit have an important impact: They help to make economic fluctuations milder than they would otherwise be. Recall that changes in spending have a multiplier effect on output. The larger the multiplier, the greater will be the fluctuations in output caused by any given change in spending. But changes in the cyclical deficit make the multiplier *smaller*, and thus act as an *automatic stabilizer*. How?

Let's use unemployment insurance as an example. In normal times, with the unemployment rate at around, say, 4.5 percent or lower, federal transfers for unemployment insurance are modest. But when the economy goes into recession, and output and income begin to fall, the unemployment rate rises. Federal transfers for unemployment insurance rise *automatically*. Without assistance from the government, many of the newly unemployed would have to cut back their consumption spending substantially. But unemployment insurance cushions the blow for many such families—at least for six months or sometimes longer—allowing them to make smaller cutbacks in consumption during that time. As a result, the total decline in consumption is smaller and GDP declines by less. Unemployment insurance thus reduces the multiplier.

Other transfer programs have a similar stabilizing effect on output. More people receive food stamps during recessions. Consequently, their consumption falls by less than it would if they did not have this help. And the tax system contributes to economic stability in a similar way. Income tax payments, for example, fall during a recession. With the government siphoning off a smaller amount of income from the household sector, the drop in consumption is smaller than it would be if tax revenues remained constant.

The same principle applies during an expansion. Transfer payments automatically decline, as the unemployed find jobs and fewer families qualify for government assistance. And tax revenues automatically rise, since income rises. As a result, the rise in GDP is smaller than it would otherwise be.

> *Many features of the federal tax and transfer systems act as automatic stabilizers. As the economy goes into a recession, these features help to reduce the decline in consumption spending, and they also cause the cyclical deficit to rise. As the economy goes into an expansion, these features help to reduce the rise in consumption spending, and they also cause the cyclical deficit to fall.*

FISCAL CHANGES IN THE LONG RUN

Fiscal changes have important effects on the economy over the long run. And, as you've learned, the classical model—which focuses on the determinants of potential output—provides a useful framework for analyzing these long-run effects.

Let's first list three important conclusions about fiscal policy in the classical model that you learned in earlier chapters:

- The government's tax and transfer policies can influence employment. For example, higher tax rates on labor income (or household income, generally) or more generous transfers can reduce the employment–population ratio and *decrease* the average standard of living. Lower tax rates or less generous transfers can raise the employment–population ratio and raise the standard of living.
- The government's tax policies can directly influence the rate of investment spending on new capital and R&D. Higher tax rates on the profits from investment projects will lower investment spending and lead to slower growth in the average standard of living. Lower tax rates or other investment incentives will increase investment spending and lead to faster growth in living standards.
- The government's budget deficit can influence investment spending as well. An increase in the budget deficit causes the government to demand more loanable funds. This raises the interest rate, lowers investment spending, and slows the growth in living standards. Lower budget deficits reduce the government's demand for loanable funds, resulting in a lower interest rate, greater investment spending, and faster growth in living standards.

And, from this chapter, you've learned the following:

- Budget deficits add to the national debt.

But what are the *consequences* of adding to the national debt?

THE NATIONAL DEBT

On a billboard in midtown Manhattan, a giant clocklike digital display tracks the U.S. national debt up to the second. In mid-2006, as the clock headed toward $8.5 trillion (rising by $951,000 per minute), the last four digits on the display changed so rapidly that they appeared as a blur.

The national debt clock is one of several public relations campaigns that spread fear among the American public.[7] How can we ever hope to repay all of this debt? Surely, we must be speeding toward a debt disaster.

---

[7] You can find similar debt clocks on the Web (google "national debt clock"). But keep in mind that they all exaggerate the burden by using "total national debt," which includes amounts that one government agency owes to another. In mid-2006, when "total national debt" was approaching $8.5 trillion, the more relevant "publicly held debt" (what the government owed to everyone but itself) was approaching $4.9 trillion.

Economists do have concerns about the national debt. But they are very different from the concerns suggested by the national debt clock or other similar gimmicks.

Mythical Concerns About the National Debt

What bothers many people about a growing national debt is the belief that one day we will have to pay it all back. But although we might *choose* to repay the national debt, we do not have to. *Ever.* Moreover, there is nothing automatically wrong with a national debt that *grows* every year. That may sound surprising. How could a government keep borrowing funds without ever paying them back? Surely, no business could behave that way.

But actually, many successful businesses *do* behave that way. For example, the debt of many major corporations—like Pfizer and Verizon—continues to grow, year after year. While they continue to pay interest on their debt, they may have no plans to pay back the amount originally borrowed. As these companies' bonds become due, they simply *roll them over;* they issue new bonds to pay back the old ones.

Why don't these firms pay back their debt? Because they believe they have a better use for their funds: investing in new capital equipment and research and development to expand their businesses. This will lead to higher future profits.

Of course, this does not mean that *any* size debt would be prudent. Recall the important principle we discussed earlier in the chapter: *Debt and interest payments have meaning only in relation to income.* If a firm's income is growing by 5 percent each year, but its interest payments are growing by 10 percent per year, it would eventually find itself in trouble. Each year, its interest payments would take a larger and larger fraction of its income, and at some point interest payments would exceed total income. But even *before* this occurred, the firm would find itself in trouble. Lenders, anticipating the firm's eventual inability to pay interest, would cut the firm off. At that point, the firm would reach its *credit limit*—the maximum amount it can borrow based on lenders' willingness to lend. Since it could no longer roll over its existing debt with further borrowing, it would have to pay back any bonds coming due until its debt was comfortably below its credit limit.

All of these observations apply to the federal government as well. As long as the nation's total income is rising, the government can safely take on more debt. More specifically, if the nation's income is growing at least as fast as total interest payments, the debt can continue to grow indefinitely, without putting the government in danger.

The federal government *could* pay back the national debt—by running budget surpluses for many years. But the government could also choose to behave like most corporations and *not* pay back its debt. In fact, the government would better serve the public by not paying down the debt if it has better uses for its revenue than debt repayment.

But how rapidly could the government continue to accumulate debt? Or, equivalently, how large could annual deficits be without making the national debt a looming danger?

Let's see. As long as total national income grows at least as fast as interest payments on the debt, the ratio of interest payments to income will not grow. In that case, we could continue to pay interest without increasing the average tax rate on U.S. citizens.

Let's use some round numbers to make this clearer. Suppose that the nominal GDP is $10 trillion and the national debt is $5 trillion. And suppose that annual interest payments average out to 7 percent of the national debt, or $350 billion.

Then the ratio of interest payments to nominal GDP would be $350 billion/$10 trillion = 0.035 or 3.5 percent of GDP. So the government must collect tax revenue equal to 3.5 percent of GDP to cover the interest payments for the year. Now suppose that, over some period of time, both nominal GDP and the national debt double, to $20 trillion and $10 trillion, respectively. Then interest payments would double as well, to $700 billion. But the ratio of interest payments to nominal GDP would remain constant, at $700 billion/$20 trillion = 0.035. The same tax rate of 3.5 percent still covers the interest payments.

More generally,

> *as long as the debt grows by the same percentage as nominal GDP, the ratios of debt to GDP and interest payments to GDP will remain constant. In this case, the government can continue to pay interest on its rising debt without increasing the average tax rate in the economy.*

GENUINE CONCERNS ABOUT THE NATIONAL DEBT

When *should* we be concerned about a growing national debt? Our previous discussion has hinted at three scenarios that should cause concern.

A National Debt That Is Growing Too Rapidly

An important *minimal guideline* for responsible government is that the debt should grow no faster than nominal GDP. Whenever that guideline is violated, interest payments as a fraction of GDP rise, and the average tax burden on the public—taxes relative to GDP—grows. The violation cannot go on forever because the tax burden has a mathematical upper limit of 100 percent of GDP. And even before that limit was reached, tax rates would become oppressive, harming growth and—if pushed too high—actually reducing living standards. However, if the violation of the guideline is temporary, and the debt begins growing at the same rate as nominal GDP again, tax payments as a fraction of GDP could stop rising.

This has two important implications. First, to prevent a long-term disaster after too-rapid growth in the debt, we do not have to run budget surpluses. A surplus is only necessary if the goal is to reduce the *total* debt. But all that is required to put the economy on a *responsible path* is a reduction of the growth rate of the debt back to the growth rate of nominal GDP. After that, we can keep running deficits and the debt can keep rising indefinitely, as long as it rises no faster than nominal GDP.

But there is a second implication as well: Even a temporary violation of the guideline is costly. During the time that debt grows faster than nominal GDP, tax rates must rise to cover the rising interest burden as a fraction of total income. After the debt starts growing at the same rate as nominal GDP again, then the tax rate can stop rising—but *the tax rate will remain at its new, higher level.* Thus, while a temporary violation of the guideline does not mean a disaster, it *does* leave us with a permanently elevated tax burden . . . at least, until we do something about it.

How can the tax burden be brought back down after a temporary violation of the guideline? There are only two basic ways: (1) raise the growth rate of nominal GDP *above* the growth rate of the debt for some time; or (2) lower the growth rate of the debt below the growth rate of nominal GDP for some time. Either of these solutions could return the debt-to-GDP ratio back to its original level, so that interest payments relative to GDP and the tax rate needed to cover them could return to their original levels as well.

But these solutions are costly to society. Let's first consider raising the growth rate of nominal GDP. Since policy has only limited ability to influence the growth rate of *real* GDP over long periods, the only practical method to ensure a higher growth rate of *nominal* GDP is faster growth in the price level. This means allowing the inflation rate to rise for some time. But we've already seen that allowing the inflation rate to rise can be costly for society in numerous ways—including the buildup of inflationary expectations that would be difficult to reverse.

Now consider the second option: slowing down the growth rate of the debt below the growth rate of nominal GDP. The only way to do this is to run *smaller deficits* as a fraction of GDP than we would otherwise be able to run. And the only way to reduce the deficit for some length of time is to raise tax rates or reduce government outlays during that period.

Thus,

> *a debt that rises too fast—faster than nominal GDP—for some period of time will impose an opportunity cost in the future. The cost will be either a permanently higher tax burden, a period of inflation, or a temporary period of reduced government outlays or higher taxes relative to GDP.*

This is not just theoretical, as the U.S. experience during the 1970s and 1980s demonstrates. During this time, nominal GDP was growing at about 9 percent per year—mostly due to increases in the price level. But the debt grew by an average of 11 percent per year, beyond the minimal guidelines for responsible government. The debt-to-GDP ratio therefore rose (see Figure 8) and so did interest payments relative to GDP (see Figure 4). This could not go on indefinitely, or interest payments on the debt would rise to an ever-larger share of GDP, and ever-higher tax rates would be needed to cover them. How did we solve the problem? As we entered the 1990s, we gradually shrunk the budget deficit with higher tax rates and strict limits on the growth of government spending. Fortunately, the 1990s was a period of prolonged expansion and reduced military purchases, so lowering the deficit was not as painful as it might otherwise have been.

A Debt Approaching a National Credit Limit

If debt were to rise *too* rapidly relative to GDP, for *too* long, there is a theoretical danger of reaching the nation's credit limit—the amount of debt that would make lenders worry about the government's ability to continue paying interest. If this credit limit were approached, a nation would be truly flirting with disaster: a tiny increase in the ratio of debt to GDP would lead to a cutoff of further lending and require that the budget be balanced immediately. It could also cause a financial panic, with everyone trying to sell their government bonds at the same time, causing bond prices to fall and household wealth to plummet.

While this is *theoretically* possible, it's doubtful the United States will be anywhere near that type of limit in the next decade. Look at Figure 8. At the end of World War II, the debt reached 109 percent of GDP—almost triple its current percentage. Even then, no one doubted the U.S. government would continue to honor its obligations.

However, since the late 1990s, economists have had another concern: More than half of the national debt held by the public is in foreign hands. While foreigners still have faith that the United States will honor its obligations, they may nevertheless have an upper limit on the proportion of total wealth they want to hold in dollar-denominated assets (say, to limit their risk in case the dollar falls in value against their own currency). If U.S. debt grows too rapidly, and foreigners find themselves with too much dollar-denominated wealth, they could suddenly, simultaneously, begin selling their U.S. bonds.

> *It is highly unlikely U.S. debt levels will approach an absolute credit limit based on loss of faith in the U.S. government. A more realistic concern is that rapidly rising debt causes foreign wealth portfolios to become too "dollar-heavy," leading to a destabilizing sell-off of U.S. bonds.*

We'll come back to this foreign-held debt in the next chapter.

Failing to Account for Future Obligations

Many students reading this book are getting financial help from their parents to pay the costs of college. If so, your parents probably began planning for this obligation very early—perhaps even before you knew what college was. This makes sense: If a family wants to avoid a drastic decrease in its standard of living in the future, it should start accounting for future obligations early.

The federal government is in an analogous situation. It has effectively promised to provide Medicare and Social Security payments to millions of people at some time in the future. If we assume no changes in scheduled benefit policies, and if current cost trends continue, Social Security, Medicare, and Medicaid benefits are projected to rise significantly—from 8.5 percent of GDP in 2005 to around 19 percent of GDP in 2050.[8] (By comparison, remember that *total* federal outlays are currently about 20 percent of GDP.) If the federal government is to act like a responsible household, it should take these future obligations into account in its planning process. Otherwise, we may have to dramatically decrease *other* government outlays, dramatically increase taxes, or have an ever-rising debt-to-GDP ratio, leading to the dangers discussed earlier.

Of course, trying to project total federal revenues and outlays over the next 50 years is guesswork at best. Even official forecasts of *10-year* projections are typically widely off the mark. In 1989, for example, when the government made its fiscal projections for 1990–1999, no one could have predicted the development of the Internet and other technologies, and the rapid economic growth that would accompany them. And in 1999, when projections for 2000–2009 were completed, who could have predicted the events of September 11, 2001, and how they would change our spending on national defense and homeland security?

This uncertainty over future projections has led to divergent views about policy. Some argue that a responsible government should be exceedingly cautious, running

---

[8] *The Long-Term Budget Outlook: A CBO Study,* Congressional Budget Office, December 2005. The 19 percent of GDP figure is actually somewhat conservative. It assumes that medical costs per enrollee will grow 1 percentage point faster than GDP per capita through 2050. From 1970 to 2005, spending per enrollee actually rose 2.9 percentage points faster than GDP per capita.

budget surpluses now, paying down the national debt, and leaving us better prepared for any dramatic future rise in government outlays. Others argue that preparing for the worst would require huge sacrifices in the present—sacrifices that might be unnecessary in hindsight.

These divergent views formed part of the background for the controversy over the Bush tax cuts.

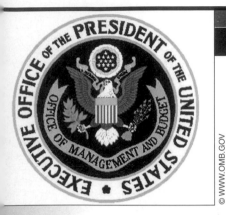

USING THE THEORY
The Bush Tax Cuts of 2001 and 2003

In 2001, the Bush administration cut taxes over 10 years by $1.35 trillion, and in 2003, by another $350 billion. Marginal tax rates were reduced on all income brackets, as were tax rates on capital gains and dividends. There were additional reductions for taxpayers with children, and a reduction of the "marriage penalty" that taxed married couples at higher rates than if they were single. Also, the tax cuts in 2003 accelerated some of the 2001 reductions that had originally been postponed until 2006 and beyond.

Much of the debate over the tax reductions had to do with distribution: whether the cuts were apportioned fairly among different income groups. But they also raised two important macroeconomic issues that we've discussed in this and other chapters.

THE SHORT RUN: COUNTERCYCLICAL FISCAL POLICY?

The tax cuts of 2001 and 2003 seem, at first glance, like perfect examples of well-timed countercyclical fiscal policy. After all, the first cuts were put in place in June 2001—in the middle of a recession that began just three months earlier. And the cuts in May 2003 took effect as the economy was still struggling with a weak expansion. Does this show that countercyclical fiscal policy works?

Not really, because a closer look suggests that neither tax cut was really designed for that purpose. The tax cut of June 2001 had actually been proposed more than 18 months earlier by presidential candidate Bush as a long-run policy measure, to promote growth in potential output. At the time, the economy was in a boom, and the Federal Reserve was actively trying to slow it down. The fact that the tax cut was enacted during a recession was a stroke of luck, not an example of well-timed short-run fiscal policy.

Moreover, remember that countercyclical fiscal policy requires that changes in taxes be reversible when economic conditions change. But both of the Bush tax cuts were *long-term* policy changes: Some of their provisions applied through the end of the decade, and the others were expected to be extended at least that long, and probably beyond.

As so often happens in macroeconomic debates, however, politics took over. As the economy entered the recession of 2001, the debate over the 2001 tax cut quickly shifted to its short-run stimulus potential. And the 2003 cut—weighted heavily toward long-run reforms in the tax code—was both touted and opposed almost entirely on the basis of its ability to create jobs in the short run, during a slow recovery.

In between these two cuts, however, the Bush administration proposed a purely countercyclical, $60 billion tax cut. This was formulated and designed as an emergency measure, shortly after September 11, 2001, to prevent the economy from sliding further into recession. Timing was crucial, and the administration urged quick passage by Congress. If there was ever an opportunity to showcase the effectiveness of countercyclical fiscal policy, this was it. But the tax bill was debated for a full 6 months in the House and Senate, and was not signed by the president until March 2002. During these 6 months of debate, the Fed reduced its interest rate target four times, illustrating the greater flexibility of monetary policy as a countercyclical tool.

THE LONG RUN: THE TAX CUTS AND THE NATIONAL DEBT

Now let's consider the long-run macroeconomic controversies raised by the tax cuts. Table 2 shows two different projections of budget deficits and the national debt, both issued less than 2 months after the 2003 tax cuts were signed into law. It also shows what actually happened during the first 4 years after those tax cuts.

Let's start with the left-most columns in the table, which show numbers released by the Bush administration's Office of Management and Budget (OMB) as part of its midyear budget update in July 2003. The second column shows the projected deficit in each fiscal year, ending in September of the year indicated. For example, back in 2003, the OMB projected a deficit of $304 billion in 2005.

The third column shows the projected national debt as a percentage of GDP at the end of each fiscal year. For the end of 2005, the OMB was predicting the national debt at 40.3 percent of GDP.

Judging by the OMB's numbers, it appeared that the administration's fiscal policy was an example of a temporary violation of the guideline for responsible

	TABLE	2
	Fiscal Projections After the Tax Cuts of 2001 and 2003	

Fiscal Year	OMB Projections Made in 2003		Democratic Caucus Projections Made in 2003		What Actually Happened	
	Federal Budget Deficit ($ Billions)	Debt as a Percentage of GDP	Federal Budget Deficit ($ Billions)	Debt as a Percentage of GDP	Federal Budget Deficit ($ Billions)	Debt as a Percentage of GDP
2002	$158	33.9%	$158	33.9%	$158	33.9%
2003	$455	37.5%	$416	36.8%	$378	36.2%
2004	$475	39.6%	$489	39.4%	$413	37.2%
2005	$304	40.3%	$364	40.5%	$318	37.4%
2006	$238	40.4%	$345	41.3%	$296	37.3%
2007	$213	40.2%	$329	41.8%	—	—
2008	$226	40.1%	$343	42.4%	—	—
. . . .						
2013	—	—	$476	44.3%	—	—

Sources: Office of Management and Budget, *Fiscal Year 2004 Mid-Session Review* (Summary Table 7) and *Fiscal Year 2007 Mid-Session Review* (Historical Tables 1.1 and 7.1), and House Budget Committee, Democratic Caucus, "Deficits Hit Record Levels," Press Release, July 16, 2003. 2002 figures are actual data, known at time of projections.

government: Debt was projected to rise faster than GDP through 2006, and then stabilize and descend through 2008. (Starting in 2003, the administration began issuing only 5-year projections, instead of the usual 10 years, citing uncertainties over the military occupation of Iraq and the war on terrorism.)

What did these numbers imply? Certainly not a debt disaster. But a fiscal policy with future costs. By raising the national debt as a percentage of GDP, interest payments relative to GDP and the tax burden would rise. Afterward, the debt-to-GDP ratio would come down a bit, but not enough to bring the tax burden back to where it was originally.

Where would this rise in the debt come from? Some of the early rise would come from *cyclical* deficits. Because of the economy's slow recovery after the recession in 2001, it was expected to remain below potential even into 2004, with lower tax revenues and higher transfers than would occur at full employment. But the continued deficits in 2006 and beyond—when the economy was assumed to have recovered—would be mostly *structural* deficits. According to the OMB's estimates, the two Bush tax cuts would account for about 25 percent of the total rise in the national debt over the projection period.

Now look at the next two columns. They show the numbers put out by the Democratic Caucus of the House Budget Committee in a press release, within days of the OMB document's release. It shows a more sharply rising deficit, and what looks like a *long-run* violation of the guideline for responsible government. The debt-to-GDP ratio was projected to rise continually, with no end in sight. Note that the Democratic Caucus projected 10 years forward instead of 5. But that accounted for only part of the dramatic difference in the fiscal story each side told. What accounted for the rest?

The answer is: the assumptions behind the numbers. The OMB deficit numbers left out estimates of government outlays for military operations in Iraq or Afghanistan beyond 2003. It also assumed that any provisions of the two tax cuts that were legally set to expire between 2004 and 2008 would, in fact, expire, thereby boosting tax revenues.

The Democrats made different assumptions. On the outlays side, they included the estimated cost of Iraq and Afghanistan from 2004 through 2006, and projected greater increases in other national defense spending. They also added the expenses of the proposed prescription drug benefit plan for Medicare, starting in 2006. (The plan did, in fact, go into effect in 2006.) On the revenue side, the Democrats not only assumed that expiring provisions of the tax cuts would be renewed, but that further changes in the tax code favored by the administration would also be enacted.

Using the Democratic numbers, virtually *all* of the rise in the debt during their 11-year projection period could be attributed to tax cuts of some form—either the original cuts in 2001 and 2003, or expected extensions and further expected reductions.

Note that, based on *either* set of numbers, we would be entering a period of rising debt that would entail the kinds of future costs we've discussed in the chapter. Under the Democrats' assumptions, the path would be unsustainable in the long run: Debt and interest payments would rise faster than GDP for 10 years and perhaps beyond. Under the Bush administration's assumptions, the path would be costly, but sustainable, with debt and interest payments topping out in 2006.

How did the first 4 years of these projections actually play out? Look at the last two columns, which show the actual numbers through fiscal year 2006. As you can see, in each of those years, the budget deficit was actually lower than the Democrats projected, and in some years, even lower than the administration itself projected. Throughout this period, government outlays exceeded what both sides expected, largely because of spending for the war in Iraq and, in 2006, funds spent in the wake of Hurricanes Katrina and Rita. But federal tax revenues also grew faster than expected—so fast, in fact, that the sum of the annual deficits during all 4 years fell below even the administration's own projections.

Now look at the last column, which shows the actual behavior of the national debt as a percentage of GDP. These numbers were also lower than either side expected—significantly so. For 2006, the debt stood at 38.5 percent of GDP, whereas the administration and the Democratic Caucus had forecast 40.4 percent and 41.3 percent, respectively.

What accounts for this disparity? Part of the answer is the smaller deficits just discussed. But even more significant was the behavior of GDP itself. Remember that debt relative to GDP will grow more slowly when GDP rises more rapidly. And during this period, the nation's total output grew much faster than either side had predicted. (Indeed, this was the main reason that tax revenues grew faster than projected.)

But now look just at the last column, and ignore all of the projections. You can see that total debt has been growing faster than GDP in recent years. As a result, the debt as a percentage of GDP rose from 33.9 percent in 2002 to 37.3 percent in 2006. Even if the percentage stays at this level, this past increase in debt has imposed a cost on our society. As you've learned, the cost will be paid in a permanently higher tax burden, a period of inflation, or a temporary period of reduced government outlays or higher taxes to bring the debt-to-GDP ratio back down.

What about the future? In mid-2006, the administration and its critics were once again at odds. The administration, projecting out five years, saw rapidly falling deficits and a rapidly declining debt-to-GDP ratio through 2011.[9] The House Democratic Caucus, projecting out to 2017, saw much larger deficits and only a slow drop in the debt-to-GDP ratio.[10] And neither side's projections included the serious fiscal problem facing the nation beyond 2017, when its ongoing obligations to aging baby boomers will continue to rise.

Clearly, the tax cuts of 2001 and 2003 have created a cost for society. But ultimately, our assessment about any economic policy must compare costs with benefits. And views about the benefits of the administration's tax and spending policies diverge even more widely than views about its costs.

Was the tax cut distributed in the right way? Should the United States have gone to war in Iraq? In the future, how much should younger workers be asked to sacrifice to care for retiring baby boomers? How one answers questions like these ultimately determines whether the costs of higher debt—whatever they turn out to be—are justified. But this is where a purely economic analysis makes its exit, and political and ideological differences take center stage.

[9] Office of Management and Budget, *Fiscal Year 2007 Mid-Session Review*, July 2006, Table S-13.
[10] House Budget Committee, Democratic Caucus, "Administration's Mid-Session Review of the Budget," Press Release, July 11, 2006.

Summary

The U.S. federal government finances its spending through a combination of taxes and borrowing. When government outlays exceed tax revenue, the government runs a budget deficit. It finances that deficit by selling bonds, thereby adding to the national debt. When government outlays are less than tax revenue, the government runs a budget surplus. It uses that surplus to buy back bonds it has issued in the past, thus shrinking the national debt.

Federal government outlays consist of three broad categories: government purchases of goods and services, transfer payments, and interest on the national debt. Nonmilitary government purchases have traditionally accounted for a stable, low 2 percent of real GDP. Military purchases vary according to global politics; in recent years, they have begun rising relative to GDP. Transfer programs—such as Social Security and Medicare—have been the fastest-growing part of government outlays. They currently equal about 12.5 percent of GDP.

On the revenue side, the government relies primarily on personal and corporate income taxes and Social Security taxes. Federal revenue was trending mildly upward until the early 2000s; then it jumped downward, due to a recession and a significant cut in income tax rates.

From 1970 through the mid-1990s, federal outlays exceeded federal revenues every year, so the government ran budget deficits. Particularly large deficits occurred in the early 1980s. But in the 1990s, the deficit declined, and in 1998 the government began running yearly budget surpluses. In 2002, the budget picture flip-flopped again, as deficits were projected for several years.

In the short run, there is a two-way relationship between government outlays and taxes on the one hand and the level of output on the other. In recessions, for example, government tax revenues fall and transfer payments rise. In this way, the tax and transfer system acts as an automatic stabilizer, helping to smooth out fluctuations in output.

Fiscal changes have important long-run effects on the economy. All else equal, we can expect larger budget deficits to slow growth in living standards, and smaller budget deficits or surpluses to speed the growth of living standards.

Over the 1970s and, especially, the 1980s, the average federal budget deficit was so large, and the national debt growing so rapidly, that interest payments were rising relative to GDP. While we were not on the brink of disaster, the deficits and the growing national debt did require a future sacrifice, which we paid in the 1990s by reducing the deficit through tight fiscal policy. The same scenario of high deficits and rising debt-to-GDP ratio occurred in the early 2000s. Even if temporary, it will require future sacrifices.

Problem Set   *Answers to even-numbered Questions and Problems can be found on the text Web site at www.thomsonedu.com/economics/hall.*

1. "The U.S. spends more on national defense than it does helping people who are poor, retired, and unemployed." Was this statement *ever* true during the past five decades? Is it true today? (Hint: Use Figures 1 and 3.)

2. Look at Figures 3, 5, and 6, and project forward for the next several decades. For each figure, what will be the *direct* effects (if any) as the baby-boom generation begins to retire around 2010? (Assume there is no change in policy related to Social Security or Medicare and no change in tax rates.)

3. Use the following statistics, in billions of units, to calculate the real national debt and the debt relative to GDP in 1990 and 2000 for this hypothetical country. Which figures would you use to compare the national debt in the 2 years?

National debt in 1990:	1.2
National debt in 2000:	13.8
Nominal GDP in 1990:	101.7
Nominal GDP in 2000:	552.2
Price index in 1990:	35.2
Price index in 2000:	113.3

4. You are running for president of the small nation of Utopia. You promise to cut tax rates, increase transfers and government purchases, reduce the government's budget deficit, and reduce the government's debt as a fraction of GDP. If elected, is it possible for you to keep all of your campaign promises in the short run? What about in the long run?

5. You are running for reelection as president of the nation of Utopia. Your opponents have criticized you for allowing the national debt to grow by almost 50 percent over the last 4 years. Use the following statistics, measured in millions of dollars, to defend yourself to Utopia's voters:

National debt in year 1 of your presidency:	$152
National debt in year 4 of your presidency:	$200
Nominal GDP in year 1 of your presidency:	$3,042
Nominal GDP in year 4 of your presidency:	$4,098
Price index in year 1 of your presidency:	45
Price index in year 4 of your presidency:	72

6. Suppose there is a country with 30 households divided into three categories (A, B, and C), with 10 households of each type. If a household earns 20,000 zips (the country's currency) or more in a year, it must pay 15 percent of its income in taxes. If the household earns less than 20,000 zips, it doesn't pay any tax. When the economy is operating at full employment, household income is 250,000 zips per year for each type A household, 50,000 zips for type B households, and 20,000 zips for type C households.
   a. If the economy is operating at full employment, how much revenue does the government collect in taxes for the year?
   b. Suppose a recession hits and household income falls for each type of household. Type A households now earn 150,000 zips, type B households earn 30,000 zips, and

type C households earn 10,000 zips for the year. How much does the government collect in tax revenue for the year? Assume the government spends all of the revenue it would have collected if the economy had been operating at full employment. Under this assumption, what is the effect of the recession on the government budget deficit (i.e., the effect on the cyclical deficit)?

c. Suppose instead that the economy expanded and household incomes rose to 400,000 zips, 75,000 zips, and 30,000 zips, respectively, for the year. How much tax would the government collect for the year? What is the effect on the cyclical deficit (assume again that the government spends exactly the amount of revenue it collects when household income is at the values in part (a))?

d. What does this problem tell you about the relationship between shocks to the economy and the budget deficit? The structural deficit?

7. Are either of the following countries violating the minimal guidelines for responsible government as outlined in this text?

Country A
(Figures in Billions of $)

	Debt	GDP
1999	1	100
2000	2	110
2001	3	150

Country B
(Figures in Billions of $)

	Debt	GDP
1999	1,236	1,400
2000	1,346	1,550
2001	1,406	1,707

8. Assume that the unemployment rate in the small country of Economica is currently 6 percent, and that in this country government purchases = $10 million, tax revenue = $17 million, transfers and interest payments = $5 million. Also assume that at full employment, the unemployment rate would be *less* than 6 percent.
   a. Find the size of Economica's budget deficit.
   b. What can you tell about Economica's cyclical deficit and its structural deficit?

9. Suppose a nation's government purchases are equal to $2 trillion, regardless of the state of the economy. However, its taxes and transfers depend on economic conditions. When the economy is at potential output, net taxes (taxes minus transfers) equal $2.2 trillion. However, for each 1 percent GDP falls below potential output, net taxes fall by 5 percent.
   a. Suppose the economy was operating at potential output. What would be the structural deficit? The cyclical deficit?
   b. Suppose that real GDP was 5 percent below potential output. What would be the cyclical deficit? The structural deficit?

10. Complete the table below for the small country of Microland. Assume that Microland started Year 1 with no federal debt. What is the relationship between the deficit and the debt? How can the real national debt fall even in years when the budget is balanced or in deficit? Explain briefly.

[Table for Problem 10]

	Year						
	1	2	3	4	5	6	7
Price index	100	103	105	110	118	133	140
Nominal GDP	$400	$500	$600	$700	$800	$900	$1,000
Outlays	$105	$126	$130	$135	$133	$130	$ 130
Tax revenue	$100	$120	$125	$132	$134	$138	$ 130
Deficit/Surplus							
National debt (end of year)							
Real national debt (end of year)							
Debt to GDP							

More Challenging

11. Suppose the United States were running a budget surplus and decided to eliminate it by increasing government purchases.

   a. Compared to a policy of just accruing surpluses and paying down the national debt, what will this policy do to U.S. real GDP and interest rates in the *short run*? Illustrate your answer graphically. (Hint: Which macro model, and which graphs, should you use to illustrate effects on output and interest rates in the short run? Assume the Fed maintains a constant interest rate.)

   b. Compared to a policy of just accruing surpluses and paying down the national debt, what will this policy do to U.S. real GDP and interest rates in the *long run*? Illustrate your answer graphically.

   c. Going back to the short run, suppose the Fed responds by neutralizing the impact of the fiscal change in part (a). What will happen to real GDP and interest rates in the short run?

Exchange Rates and Macroeconomic Policy

If you've ever traveled to a foreign country, you were a direct participant in the **foreign exchange market**—a market in which one country's currency is traded for that of another. For example, if you traveled to Mexico, you might have stopped near the border to exchange some dollars for Mexican pesos.

But even if you have never traveled abroad, you've been involved, at least indirectly, in all kinds of foreign exchange dealings. For example, suppose you buy some Mexican-grown tomatoes at a store in the United States, where you pay with dollars. A Mexican farmer grew the tomatoes; Mexican truckers transported them to the distribution center in the nearest large city; and Mexican workers, machinery, and raw materials were used to package them. All of these people need to be paid in Mexican pesos, regardless of who buys the final product. After all, they live in Mexico, so they need pesos to buy things there. But you, as an American, want to pay for your tomatoes with dollars.

Foreign exchange market The market in which one country's currency is traded for another country's.

Let's think about this for a moment. You want to pay for the tomatoes in dollars, but the Mexicans who produced them want to be paid in pesos. How can this happen?

The answer: *Someone,* here or abroad, must use the foreign exchange market to exchange dollars for pesos. For example, it might work like this: You pay dollars to your supermarket, which pays dollars to a U.S. importer, who pays dollars to the distributor in Mexico, who—finally—turns the dollars over to a Mexican bank in exchange for pesos. Finally, the Mexican distributor uses these pesos to pay the Mexican farmer.

In this chapter, we'll look at the markets in which dollars are exchanged for foreign currency. We'll also expand our macroeconomic analysis to consider the effects of changes in exchange rates. As you'll see, what happens in the foreign exchange market affects the economy, and changes in the economy affect the foreign exchange market. This has implications for the Fed as it tries to use monetary policy to steer the economy and keep it growing smoothly. Finally, we'll turn our attention to an analysis of the large and growing U.S. trade deficit.

FOREIGN EXCHANGE MARKETS AND EXCHANGE RATES

Every day, all over the world, more than a hundred different national currencies are exchanged for one another in banks, hotels, stores, and kiosks in airports and train stations. Traders exchange dollars for Mexican pesos, Japanese yen, European euros, Indian rupees, Chinese yuan, and so on. In addition, traders exchange each of these foreign currencies for one another: pesos for euros, yen for yuan, euros for yen. . . . There are literally thousands of combinations. How can we hope to make sense of these markets—how they operate and how they affect us?

Our basic approach is to treat each pair of currencies as a separate market. That is, there is one market in which dollars are exchanged for euros, another in which Angolan kwanzas trade for yen, and so on. The physical locations where the trading takes place do not matter: Whether you exchange your dollars for yen in France, Germany, the United States, or even in Ecuador, you are a trader in the same dollar–yen market.

Exchange rate The amount of one country's currency that is traded for one unit of another country's currency.

In any foreign exchange market, the rate at which one currency is traded for another is called the **exchange rate** between those two currencies. For example, if you happened to trade dollars for British pounds on July 28, 2006, each British pound would have cost you about $1.86. On that day, the exchange rate was 1.8629 dollars per pound.

DOLLARS PER POUND OR POUNDS PER DOLLAR?

Table 1 lists exchange rates between the dollar and various foreign currencies on a particular day in 2006. But notice that we can think of any exchange rate in two ways: as so many units of foreign currency per dollar, or so many dollars per unit of foreign currency. For example, the table shows the exchange rate between the British pound and the dollar as 0.5368 pounds per dollar, or 1.8629 dollars per pound. We can always obtain one form of the exchange rate from the other by taking its reciprocal: 1/0.5368 = 1.8629, and 1/1.8629 = 0.5368.

In this chapter, we'll always define the exchange rate as "dollars per unit of foreign currency," as in the last column of the table. That way, from the American point of view, the exchange rate is just another *price*. The same way you pay a certain number of dollars for a gallon of gasoline (the price of gas), so, too, you pay a certain number of dollars for a British pound (the price of pounds).

> *The exchange rate is the price of foreign currency in dollars.*

Table 1 raises some important questions: Why, in mid-2006, did a pound cost $1.86? Why not $1? Or $5? Why did one Japanese yen cost less than a penny? And a Russian ruble about four cents?

TABLE 1 Foreign Exchange Rates, July 28, 2006	Country	Name of Currency	Symbol	Units of Foreign Currency per Dollar	Dollars per Unit of Foreign Currency
	Brazil	real	R	2.1739	$0.4600
	China	yuan	Y	7.971	$0.1255
	European Monetary Union Countries	euro	€	0.7843	$1.2751
	Great Britain	pound	£	0.5368	$1.8629
	India	rupee	R	46.53	$0.02149
	Japan	yen	¥	114.77	$0.008713
	Mexico	peso	P	10.858	$0.09210
	Russia	ruble	R	26.81	$0.03730

The answers to these questions certainly affect Americans who travel abroad. Suppose you are staying in a hotel in London that costs 100 pounds per night. If the price of the pound is $1, the hotel room will cost you $100, but if the price is $5, the room will cost you $500. And exchange rates affect Americans who stay at home, too. They influence the prices of many goods we buy in the United States, and they help determine which of our industries will expand and which will contract.

How are all these exchange rates determined? In most cases, they are determined by the familiar forces of supply and demand. As in other markets, each foreign exchange market reaches an equilibrium at which the quantity of foreign exchange demanded is equal to the quantity supplied.

In the next several sections, we'll build a model of supply and demand for a representative foreign exchange market: the one in which U.S. dollars are exchanged for British pounds. Taking the American point of view, we'll call this simply "the market for pounds." The other currency being traded—the dollar—will always be implicit.

THE DEMAND FOR BRITISH POUNDS

To analyze the demand for pounds, we start with a very basic question: *Who* is demanding them? The simple answer is, anyone who has dollars and wants to exchange them for pounds. But the most important buyers of pounds in the pound–dollar market will be American households and businesses. When Americans want to buy things from Britain, they will need to acquire pounds. To acquire them, they will need to offer U.S. dollars. To keep our analysis simple, we'll focus on just these American buyers. We'll also—for now—ignore any demand for pounds by the U.S. government.

> *In our model of the market for pounds, we assume that American households and businesses are the only buyers.*

Why do Americans want to buy pounds? There are two reasons:

- *To buy goods and services from British firms.* Americans buy sweaters knit in Edinburgh, airline tickets sold by Virgin Airways, and insurance services offered by Lloyd's. American tourists also stay in British hotels, use British taxis, and eat at British restaurants. To buy goods and services from British firms, Americans need to acquire pounds in order to pay for them.
- *To buy British assets.* Americans buy British stocks, British corporate or government bonds, and British real estate. In each case, the British seller will want to be paid in pounds, so the American buyer will have to acquire them.

The Demand for Pounds Curve

Panel (a) of Figure 1 shows an example of a **demand curve for foreign currency,** in this case, the demand curve for pounds. The curve tells us *the quantity of pounds Americans will want to buy in any given period, at each different exchange rate.* Notice that the curve slopes downward: The lower the exchange rate, the greater the quantity of pounds demanded. For example, at an exchange rate of $2.25 per pound, Americans would want to purchase £200 million (point A). If the exchange rate fell to $1.50 per pound, Americans would want to buy £300 million (point E).

Demand curve for foreign currency A curve indicating the quantity of a specific foreign currency that Americans will want to buy, during a given period, at each different exchange rate.

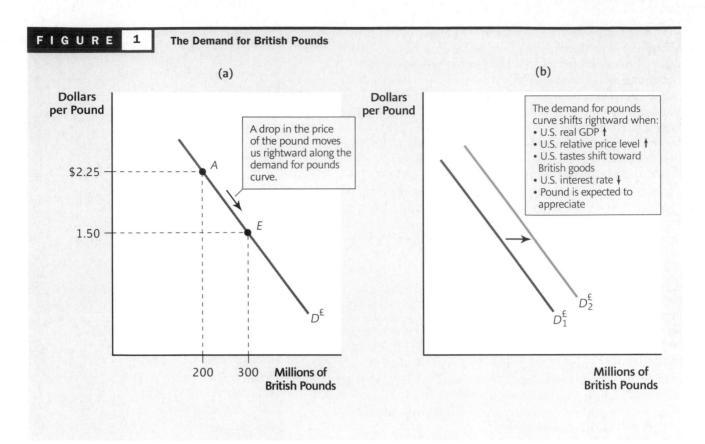

FIGURE 1 The Demand for British Pounds

(a)

A drop in the price of the pound moves us rightward along the demand for pounds curve.

(b)

The demand for pounds curve shifts rightward when:
• U.S. real GDP ↑
• U.S. relative price level ↑
• U.S. tastes shift toward British goods
• U.S. interest rate ↓
• Pound is expected to appreciate

Why does a lower exchange rate—a lower price for the pound—make Americans want to buy more of them? Because the lower the price of the pound, the less expensive British goods are to American buyers. Remember that Americans think of prices in dollar terms. A British compact disc that sells for £8 will cost an American $18 at an exchange rate of $2.25 per pound, but only $12 if the exchange rate is $1.50 per pound.

Thus, as we move rightward *along* the demand for pounds curve, as in the move from point *A* to point *E*:

Price of pounds ↓ ⟹ British goods cheaper to Americans ⟹ Americans buy more British goods ⟹ Quantity of pounds demanded ↑

Shifts in the Demand for Pounds Curve

In panel (a), you saw that a change in the exchange rate moves us *along* the demand for pounds curve. But other variables besides the exchange rate influence the demand for pounds. If any of these other variables changes, the entire curve will shift. As we consider each of these variables, keep in mind that we are assuming that only one of them changes at a time; we suppose the rest to remain constant.

U.S. Real GDP. Suppose real GDP and real income in the United States rise—say, because of continuing economic growth or a recovery from a recession. Then, Americans will buy more of everything, including goods and services from Britain. Thus, at any given exchange rate, Americans will demand more pounds. This is illustrated, in panel (b), as a rightward shift of the demand curve from $D^£_1$ to $D^£_2$.

Relative Price Levels. Suppose that the U.S. price level rises by 8 percent, while that in Britain rises by 5 percent. Then U.S. prices will rise *relative* to British prices. Americans will shift from buying their own goods toward buying the relatively cheaper British goods, so their demand for pounds will rise. That is, the demand for pounds curve will shift rightward.

Americans' Tastes for British Goods All else being equal, would you prefer to drive a General Motors Corvette or a Jaguar? Do you prefer British-made films, like *Pride and Prejudice* or *Harry Potter and the Goblet of Fire,* or America's offerings, such as *Superman Returns* or *Million Dollar Baby*? These are matters of taste, and tastes can change. If Americans develop an increased taste for British cars, films, tea, or music, their demand for these goods will increase, and the demand for pounds curve will shift rightward.

Relative Interest Rates. Because financial assets must remain competitive in order to attract buyers, the rates of return on different financial assets—such as stocks and bonds—tend to rise and fall together. Thus, when one country's interest rate is high relative to that of another country, the first country's assets, *in general,* will have higher rates of return.

Now, suppose you're an American trying to decide whether to hold some of your wealth in British financial assets or in American financial assets. You will look very carefully at the rate of return you expect to earn in each country. All else being equal, a lower U.S. interest rate, relative to the British rate, will make British assets more attractive to you. Accordingly, as you and other Americans demand more British assets, you will need more pounds to buy them. The demand for pounds curve will shift rightward.

Expected Changes in the Exchange Rate. Once again, imagine you are an American deciding whether to buy an American or a British bond. Suppose British bonds pay 10 percent interest per year, while U.S. bonds pay 5 percent. All else equal, you would prefer the British bond, since it pays the higher rate of return. You would then exchange dollars for pounds at the going exchange rate and buy the bond.

But what if the price of the pound falls before the British bond becomes due? Then, when you cash in your British bond for pounds, and convert the pounds back into dollars, you'll be *selling your pounds at a lower price* than you bought them for. While you'd benefit from the higher interest rate on the British bond, you'd lose on the foreign currency transaction—buying pounds when their price is high and selling them when their price is low. If the foreign currency loss is great enough, you would be better off with U.S. bonds, even though they pay a lower interest rate.

As you can see, it is not just relative interest rates that matter to wealth holders; it is also *expected changes in the exchange rate.* An expectation that the price of the pound will fall will make British assets less appealing to Americans, since they will expect a foreign currency loss. In this case, the demand for pounds curve will shift leftward.

The opposite holds as well. If Americans expect the price of the pound to *rise*, they will expect a foreign currency *gain* from buying British assets. This will cause the *demand for pounds curve to shift rightward.*

THE SUPPLY OF BRITISH POUNDS

The demand for pounds is one side of the market for pounds. Now we turn our attention to the other side: the supply of pounds. And we'll begin with our basic question: *Who* is supplying them?

In the real world, pounds are supplied from many sources. Anyone who has pounds and wants to exchange them for dollars can come to the market and supply pounds. But the most important sellers of pounds are British households and businesses, who naturally have pounds and need dollars in order to make purchases from Americans. To keep our analysis simple, we'll focus on just these British sellers, and we'll ignore—for now—any pounds supplied by the British government:

> *In our model of the market for pounds, we assume that British households and firms are the only sellers.*

The British supply pounds in the dollar–pound market for only one reason: because they want dollars. Thus, to ask why the British supply pounds is to ask why they want dollars. We can identify two separate reasons:

- *To buy goods and services from American firms.* The British buy airline tickets on United Airlines, computers made by Hewlett-Packard and Apple, and the rights to show films made in Hollywood. British tourists stay in American hotels and eat at American restaurants. The British demand dollars—and supply pounds—for all of these purchases.
- *To buy American assets.* The British buy American stocks, American corporate or government bonds, and American real estate. In each case, the American seller will want to be paid in dollars, and the British buyer will acquire dollars by offering pounds.

The Supply of Pounds Curve

Supply curve for foreign currency A curve indicating the quantity of a specific foreign currency that will be supplied, during a given period, at each different exchange rate.

Panel (a) of Figure 2 shows an example of a **supply curve for foreign currency**— here, British pounds. The curve tells us *the quantity of pounds the British will want to sell in any given period, at each different exchange rate.* Notice that the curve slopes upward: The higher the exchange rate, the greater is the quantity of pounds supplied. For example, at an exchange rate of $1.50 per pound, the British would want to supply £300 million (point E). If the exchange rate rose to $2.25 per pound, they would supply £400 million (point F).

Why does a higher exchange rate—a higher price for the pound—make the British want to sell more of them? Because the higher the price for the pound, the more dollars someone gets for each pound sold. This makes U.S. goods and services less expensive to British buyers, who will want to buy more of them—and who will therefore need more dollars.[1]

To summarize, as we move rightward *along* the supply of pounds curve, such as the move from point E to point F:

Shifts in the Supply of Pounds Curve

When the exchange rate changes, we *move along* the supply curve for pounds, as in panel (a) of Figure 2. But other variables can affect the supply of pounds besides the exchange rate. When any of these variables change, the supply of pounds curve will shift, as shown in panel (b). What are these variables?

Real GDP in Britain. If real GDP and real income rise in Britain, British residents will buy more goods and services, including those produced in the United States. Because

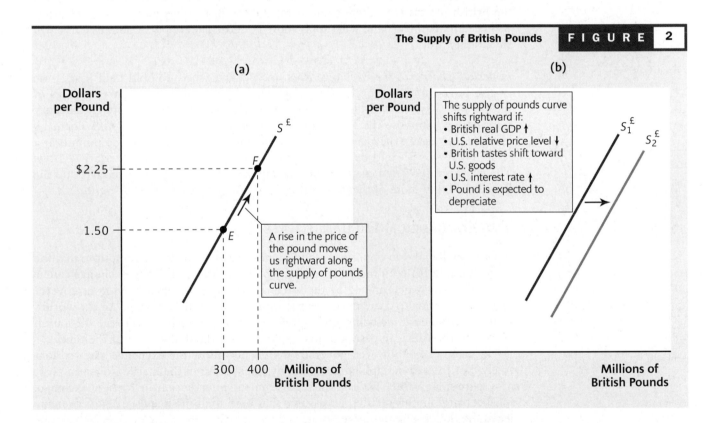

The Supply of British Pounds   **FIGURE 2**

¹ Actually, it is not a logical necessity for the supply of pounds curve to slope upward. Why not? When the price of the pound rises, it is true that the British will buy more U.S. goods and need more dollars to buy them. However, each dollar they buy costs *fewer pounds*. It might be that, even though the British obtain more dollars, they actually supply fewer pounds to get them at the higher exchange rate. In this case, the supply of pounds curve would slope downward. Economists believe, however, that a downward-sloping supply curve for foreign currency—while theoretically possible—is very rare.

they will need more dollars to buy U.S. goods, they will supply more pounds. In panel (b) this causes a rightward shift of the supply curve, from $S_1^£$ to $S_2^£$.

Relative Price Levels. Earlier, you learned that a rise in the relative price level in the United States makes British goods more attractive to Americans. But it also makes *American* goods *less* attractive to the British. Since the British will want to buy fewer U.S. goods, they will want fewer dollars and will supply fewer pounds. Thus, a rise in the relative U.S. price level shifts the supply of pounds curve leftward.

British Tastes for U.S. Goods. Recall our earlier discussion about the effect of American tastes on the demand for pounds. The same reasoning applies to the effect of British tastes on the *supply* of pounds. The British could begin to crave things American—or recoil from them. A shift in British tastes *toward* American goods will shift the supply of pounds curve rightward. A shift in tastes *away* from American goods will shift the curve leftward.

Relative Interest Rates. You've already learned that a rise in the relative U.S. interest rate makes U.S. assets more attractive to Americans. It has exactly the same effect on the British. As the U.S. interest rate rises, and the British buy more U.S. assets, they will need more dollars and will supply more pounds. The supply of pounds curve will shift rightward.

Expected Change in the Exchange Rate. In deciding where to hold their assets, the British have the same concerns as Americans. They will look, in part, at rates of return; but they will *also* think about possible gains or losses on foreign currency transactions. Suppose the British *expect the price of the pound to fall.* Then, by holding U.S. assets, they can anticipate a foreign currency gain—selling pounds at a relatively high price and buying them back again when their price is relatively low. The prospect of foreign currency gain will make U.S. assets more attractive, and the British will buy more of them. *The supply of pounds curve will shift rightward.*

THE EQUILIBRIUM EXCHANGE RATE

Floating exchange rate An exchange rate that is freely determined by the forces of supply and demand.

Now we will make an important—and in most cases, realistic—assumption: that the exchange rate between the dollar and the pound *floats.* A **floating exchange rate** is one that is freely determined by the forces of supply and demand, without government intervention to change it or keep it from changing. Indeed, many of the world's leading currencies, including the Japanese yen, the British pound, the 12-nation euro, and the Mexican peso, do float freely against the dollar most of the time.

In some cases, however, governments do not allow the exchange rate to float freely, but instead manipulate its value by intervening in the market, or even *fix* it at a particular value. We'll discuss government intervention in foreign exchange markets later. In this section, we assume that both the British and U.S. governments leave the dollar–pound market alone.

When the exchange rate floats, the price will settle at the level where quantity supplied and quantity demanded are equal. Here, buyers and sellers are trading British pounds, and the price is the exchange rate—the *price of the pound.*

Look at panel (a) of Figure 3. The equilibrium in the market for pounds occurs at point *E,* where the supply and demand curves intersect. The equilibrium price is $1.50 per pound. As you can verify, if the exchange rate were *higher,* say, $2.25 per

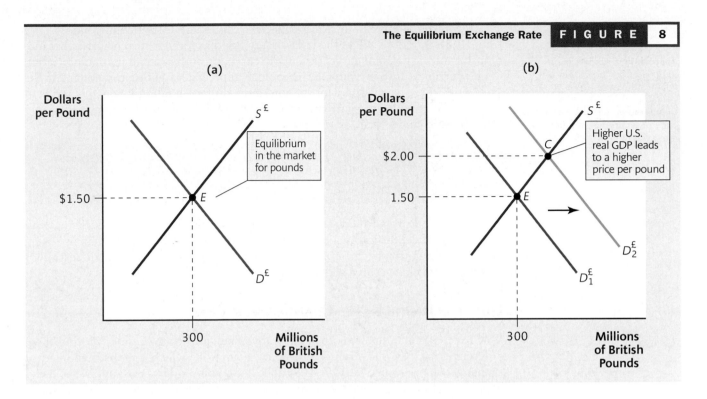

The Equilibrium Exchange Rate **FIGURE 8**

(a)

Dollars per Pound

$S^£$

Equilibrium in the market for pounds

$1.50 ----- *E*

$D^£$

300 **Millions of British Pounds**

(b)

Dollars per Pound

$S^£$

$2.00 ----- *C*

Higher U.S. real GDP leads to a higher price per pound

1.50 ----- *E*

$D_2^£$

$D_1^£$

300 **Millions of British Pounds**

pound, there would be an *excess supply* of pounds, forcing the price of the pound back down to $1.50. If the exchange rate were *lower* than the equilibrium price of $1.50, there would be an *excess demand* for pounds, driving the price back up to $1.50.

> *When the exchange rate floats—that is, when the government does not intervene in the foreign currency market—the equilibrium exchange rate is determined at the intersection of the demand curve and the supply curve.*

WHAT HAPPENS WHEN THINGS CHANGE?

What would cause the price of the pound to rise or fall? The simple answer to this question is, anything that shifts the demand for pounds curve, or the supply of pounds curve, or both curves together. Have another look at the right-hand panels of Figures 1 and 2. They summarize the major factors that can shift the demand and supply curves for pounds and therefore change the floating exchange rate.

Let's illustrate with a simple example. In panel (b) of Figure 3, the initial equilibrium in the market for pounds is at point *E*, with an exchange rate of $1.50 per pound. Now suppose that real GDP rises in the United States. As you've learned (see Figure 1), this rise in U.S. GDP will shift the demand for pounds curve rightward, from $D_1^£$ to $D_2^£$ in the figure. At the old exchange rate of $1.50 per pound, there would be an excess demand for pounds, which would drive the price of the pound higher. The new equilibrium—where the quantities of pounds supplied and demanded are equal—occurs at point *C*, and the new equilibrium exchange rate is $2.00 per pound.

Appreciation An increase in the price of a currency in a floating-rate system.

Depreciation A decrease in the price of a currency in a floating-rate system.

To recap, the increase in American GDP causes the price of the pound to rise from $1.50 to $2.00. When the price of any floating foreign currency rises because of a shift in the demand curve, the supply curve, or both, we call it an **appreciation** of the currency. In our example, the pound appreciates against the dollar. At the same time, there has been a **depreciation** of the dollar—a fall in its price in terms of pounds. (To see this, calculate the price of the dollar in terms of pounds before and after the shift in demand.)

> *When a floating exchange rate changes, one country's currency will appreciate (rise in price) and the other country's currency will depreciate (fall in price).*

As you've learned, there are many other variables besides U.S. GDP that can change and affect the exchange rate. We could analyze each of these changes, using diagrams similar to panel (b) of Figure 3. However, we'll organize our discussion of exchange rate changes in a slightly different way.

How Exchange Rates Change Over Time

When we examine the actual behavior of exchange rates over time, we find three different kinds of movements. Look at Figure 4, which graphs hypothetical exchange rate data between the U.S. dollar and some other currency. We're using hypothetical data to make these three kinds of movements stand out more clearly than they usually do in practice.

Notice first the sharp up-and-down spikes. These fluctuations in exchange rates occur over the course of a few weeks, a few days, or even a few minutes—periods of time that we call the *very short run*.

Second, we see a gradual rise and fall of the exchange rate over the course of several months or a year or two. An example is the appreciation of the foreign currency from point A to B and its depreciation from point B to C. These are *short-run* movements in the exchange rate.

Finally, notice that while the price of the foreign currency fluctuates in the very short run and the short run, we can also discern a general *long-run* trend: This nation's currency seems to be depreciating in the figure. This long-run trend is illustrated by the dashed line connecting points A and E.

In this section, we'll explore the causes of movements in the exchange rate over all three periods: the very short run, the short run, and the long run.

The *Very* Short Run: "Hot Money"

Banks and other large financial institutions collectively have trillions of dollars worth of funds that they can move from one type of investment to another at very short notice. These funds are often called "hot money." If those who manage hot money perceive even a tiny advantage in moving funds to a different country's assets—say, because its interest rate is slightly higher—they will do so. Often, decisions to move billions of dollars are made in split seconds, by traders watching computer screens showing the latest data on exchange rates and interest rates around the world. Because these traders move such large volumes of funds, they have immediate effects on exchange rates.

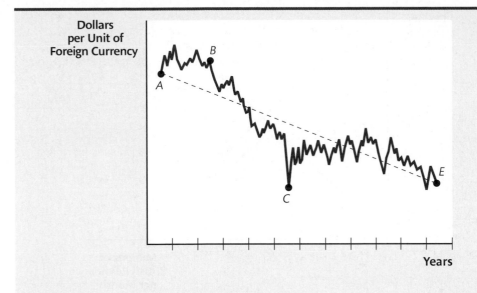

FIGURE 4

Hypothetical Exchange Rate Data Over Time

These hypothetical data show typical patterns of exchange rate fluctuations. Over the course of a few minutes, days, or weeks, the exchange rate can experience sharp up-and-down spikes. Over several months or a year or two, the exchange rate may rise or fall, as in the appreciation of the foreign currency from points A to B and the depreciation from B to C. Over the long run, there may be a general upward or downward trend, like the depreciation of the foreign currency illustrated by the dashed line connecting points A and E.

Let's consider an example. Suppose that the relative interest rate in the United States suddenly rises. Then, as you've learned, U.S. assets will suddenly be more attractive to residents of both the United States and England, including managers of hot-money accounts in both countries. As these managers shift their funds from British to United States assets, they will be dumping billions of pounds on the foreign exchange market in order to acquire dollars to buy U.S. assets. This will cause a significant rightward shift of the supply of pounds curve.

In addition to affecting managers of hot-money accounts, the higher relative interest rate in the United States will affect ordinary investors. British investors will want to buy more American assets, helping to shift the supply of pounds curve further rightward. And American investors will want to buy fewer British assets than before, causing some decrease in the *demand* for pounds. Thus, in addition to the very large rightward shift in the supply of pounds, there will be a more moderate leftward shift in the demand for pounds.

Both of these shifts are illustrated in Figure 5: The supply of pounds curve shifts from $S_1^{\pounds}$ to $S_2^{\pounds}$, and the demand for pounds curve shifts from $D_1^{\pounds}$ to $D_2^{\pounds}$. The result is easy to see: The equilibrium in the market for pounds moves from point E to point G, and the price of the pound *falls* from \$1.50 to \$1.00. The pound depreciates and the dollar appreciates.

Expectations about future exchange rates can also trigger huge shifts of hot money, and Figure 5 also illustrates what would happen if American and British residents suddenly *expect* the pound to depreciate against the dollar. In this case, it would be the anticipation of foreign currency gains from holding U.S. assets, rather than a higher U.S. interest rate, that would cause the supply and demand curves to

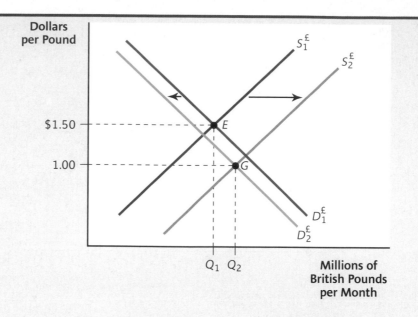

FIGURE 5

Hot Money in the Very Short Run

The market for pounds is initially in equilibrium at point E, with an exchange rate of $1.50 per pound. A rise in the U.S. interest rate relative to the British rate will make U.S. assets more attractive to both Americans and Britons. Hot-money managers in both countries will shift funds from British to U.S. assets, causing a rightward shift of the supply of pounds curve. American investors will want to buy fewer British assets, causing a decrease in the demand for pounds. The net effect is a lower exchange rate—$1.00 per pound at point G.

shift. As you can see in Figure 5, the expectation that the pound will depreciate actually *causes* the pound to depreciate—a self-fulfilling prophecy.

Sudden changes in relative interest rates, as well as sudden expectations of an appreciation or depreciation of a nation's currency, occur frequently in foreign exchange markets. They can cause massive shifts of hot money from the assets of one country to those of another in very short periods of time. For this reason,

> *relative interest rates and expectations of future exchange rates are the dominant forces moving exchange rates in the very short run.*

THE SHORT RUN: MACROECONOMIC FLUCTUATIONS

Look again at Figure 4. What explains the movements in the *short-run* rate—the changes that occur over several months or a few years? In most cases, the causes are economic fluctuations taking place in one or more countries.

Suppose, for example, that both Britain and the United States are in a recession, and the U.S. economy begins to recover while the British slump continues. As real GDP rises in the United States, so does Americans' demand for foreign goods and services, including those from Britain. The demand for pounds curve will shift rightward, and—as shown in panel (a) of Figure 6—the pound will appreciate.

A year or so later, when Britain recovers from *its* recession, its real GDP will rise. British residents will begin to buy more U.S. goods and services, and supply more pounds so they can acquire more dollars. The supply of pounds curve will shift

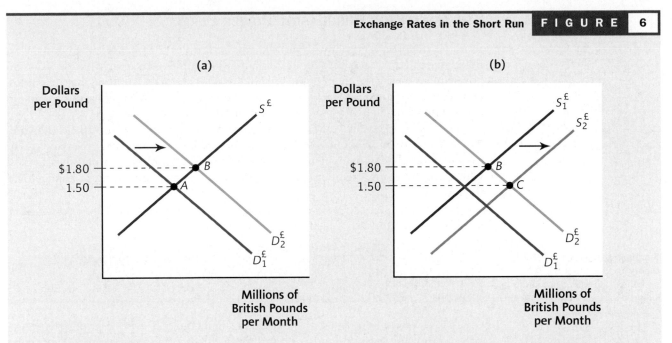

(a)

(b)

Panel (a) shows a situation in which the United States recovers from a recession first. U.S. demand for foreign goods and services increases, shifting the demand for pounds curve to the right. The equilibrium moves from A to B—an appreciation of the pound. Panel (b) shows Britain's subsequent recovery from its recession. As the British begin to buy more U.S. goods and services, the supply of pounds curve shifts rightward. The equilibrium moves from B to C, causing the pound to depreciate.

rightward, and—as shown in panel (b) of Figure 6—the pound will depreciate. Thus,

in the short run, movements in exchange rates are caused largely by economic fluctuations. All else equal, a country whose GDP rises relatively rapidly will experience a depreciation of its currency. A country whose GDP falls more rapidly will experience an appreciation of its currency.

This observation contradicts a commonly held myth: that a strong (appreciating) currency is a sign of economic health and a weak (depreciating) currency denotes a sick economy. The truth may easily be the opposite. Over the course of several quarters or a few years, the dollar could appreciate because the U.S. economy is *weakening*—entering a serious recession. This would cause Americans to cut back spending on domestic *and* foreign goods, and decrease the demand for foreign currency. Similarly, a *strengthening* U.S. economy—in which Americans are earning and spending more—would increase the U.S. demand for foreign currency and (all else equal) cause the dollar to depreciate.

Keep in mind, though, that other variables can change over the business cycle besides real GDP, including interest rates and price levels in the two countries. For example, a recession can be caused by a monetary contraction that raises the relative interest rate in a country. Or a monetary stimulus in the midst of a recession could result in a relatively low interest rate. These changes, too, will influence exchange rates over the business cycle.

THE LONG RUN: PURCHASING POWER PARITY

In mid-1992, you could buy about 100 Russian rubles for one dollar. In mid-1998, that same dollar would get you more than 6,000 rubles—so many that the Russian government that year created a new ruble that was worth 1,000 of the old rubles. (The ruble exchange rate in Table 1 is for the new ruble.) What caused the ruble to depreciate so much against the dollar during those 6 years?

This is a question about exchange rates over many years—the long run. Movements of hot money—which explain sudden, temporary movements of exchange rates—cannot explain this kind of long-run trend. Nor can business cycles, which are, by nature, temporary. What, then, causes exchange rates to change over the long run?

In general, long-run trends in exchange rates are determined by *relative price levels* in two countries. We can be even more specific:

Purchasing power parity (PPP) theory The idea that the exchange rate will adjust in the long run so that the average price of goods in two countries will be roughly the same.

> *According to the **purchasing power parity (PPP) theory**, the exchange rate between two countries will adjust in the long run until the average price of goods is roughly the same in both countries.*

To see why the PPP theory makes sense, imagine a basket of goods that costs $750 in the United States and £500 in Britain. If the prices of the goods themselves do not change, then, according to the PPP theory, the exchange rate will adjust to $750/£500 = $1.5 dollars per pound. Why? Because at this exchange rate, $750 can be exchanged for £500, so the price of the basket is the same to residents of either country—$750 for Americans and £500 for the British.

Now, suppose the exchange rate was *below* its PPP rate of $1.50 per pound—say, $1 per pound. Then a trader could take $500 to the bank, exchange it for £500, buy the basket of goods in Great Britain, and sell it in the United States for $750. She would earn a profit of $250 on each basket of goods traded. In the process, however, traders would be increasing the demand for pounds and raising the exchange rate. When the price of the pound reached $1.50, purchasing power parity would hold, and special trading opportunities would be gone. As you can see, trading activity will tend to drive the exchange rate toward the PPP rate. (On your own, explain the adjustment process when the exchange rate starts *higher* than the PPP rate.)

The PPP theory has an important implication:

> *In the long run, the currency of a country with a higher inflation rate will depreciate against the currency of a country whose inflation rate is lower.*

Why? Because in the country with the higher inflation rate, the relative price level will be rising. As that country's basket of goods becomes relatively more expensive, only a depreciation of its currency can restore purchasing power parity. And traders—taking advantage of opportunities like those just described—would cause the currency to depreciate.

Purchasing Power Parity: Some Important Caveats

While purchasing power parity is a good general guideline for predicting long-run trends in exchange rates, it does not work perfectly. For a variety of reasons, exchange rates can deviate from their PPP values for many years.

First, some goods—by their very nature—are difficult to trade. Suppose a haircut costs £5 in London and $30 in New York, and the exchange rate is $1.50 per pound. Then British haircuts are cheaper for residents of both countries. Could traders take advantage of this? Not really. They cannot take $30 to the bank in exchange for £20, buy four haircuts in London, ship them to New York, and sell them for a total of $120 there. Haircuts and most other personal services are nontradable.

Second, high transportation costs can reduce trading possibilities even for goods that *can* be traded. Our earlier numerical example would have quite a different ending if moving the basket of goods between Great Britain and the United States involved $500 of freight and insurance costs.

Third, artificial barriers to trade, such as special taxes or quotas on imports, can hamper traders' ability to move exchange rates toward purchasing power parity.

Still, the purchasing power parity theory is useful in many circumstances. Under floating exchange rates, a country whose relative price level is rising rapidly will almost always find that the price of its currency is falling rapidly. If not, all of its tradable goods would soon be priced out of the world market.

Indeed, we often observe that countries with very high inflation rates have currencies depreciating against the dollar by roughly the amount needed to preserve purchasing power parity. For example, we've already mentioned the sharp depreciation of the Russian ruble from 1992 to 1998. During those 6 years, the number of rubles that exchanged for a dollar rose from around 100 to about 6,000. Over the same period, the annual inflation rate averaged about 200 percent in Russia, but only about 3 percent in the United States. And in Zimbabwe, which experienced hyperinflation in the early 2000s, the number of Zimbabwean dollars required to purchase one U.S. dollar went from about 1,000 in mid-2002 to more than 100,000 in mid-2006.

GOVERNMENT INTERVENTION IN FOREIGN EXCHANGE MARKETS

As you've seen, when exchange rates float, they can rise and fall for a variety of reasons. But a government may not be content to let the forces of supply and demand change its exchange rate. If the exchange rate rises, the country's goods will become much more expensive to foreigners, causing harm to its export-oriented industries. If the exchange rate falls, goods purchased from other countries will rise in price. Since many imported goods are used as inputs by U.S. firms (such as oil from the Middle East and Mexico or computer screens from Japan), a drop in the exchange rate will cause a rise in the U.S. price level. Finally, if the exchange rate is too volatile, it can make trading riskier or require traders to acquire special insurance against foreign currency losses, which costs them money, time, and trouble. For all of these reasons, governments sometime *intervene* in foreign exchange markets involving their currency.

MANAGED FLOAT

Many governments let their exchange rate float *most of the time,* but will intervene on occasion when the floating exchange rate moves in an undesired direction or becomes too volatile. For example, look back at Figure 5, where the price of the British pound falls to $1 as hot money is shifted out of British assets. Suppose the British government does not want the pound to depreciate. Then its central bank—the Bank of England—could begin trading in the dollar–pound market itself. It would buy British pounds with dollars, thereby shifting the demand for pounds curve rightward. If it buys just the right amount of pounds, it can prevent the pound from depreciating at all. Alternatively, the U.S. government might not be happy with the *appreciation* of the dollar in Figure 5. In that case, the Federal Reserve can enter the market and buy British pounds with dollars, once again shifting the demand for pounds curve rightward.

The central banks of many countries—including the Federal Reserve—will sometimes intervene in this way in foreign exchange markets. When a government buys or sells its own currency or that of a trading partner to influence exchange rates, it is engaging in a "managed float" or a "dirty float."

Managed float A policy of frequent central bank intervention to move the exchange rate.

> Under a **managed float,** a country's central bank actively manages its exchange rate, buying its own currency to prevent depreciations, and selling its own currency to prevent appreciations.

Managed floats are used most often in the very short run, to prevent large, sudden changes in exchange rates. For example, during the week after the terror attacks of September 2001, the Bank of Japan (Japan's central bank) sold 2 trillion yen (about $17 billion worth) in order to stop a rapid *appreciation* of the yen against the dollar. On the other side—and on a smaller scale—Argentina's central bank purchased 15 million Argentinian pesos (about $9 million worth at the time) on January 15, 2002, in order to slow the *depreciation* of the peso against the dollar.

That last example raises a question. When a country—such as Argentina—wants to prevent or slow a depreciation against the dollar, it has to buy its own currency with dollars. Where does it get those dollars? Unfortunately for Argentina, it cannot print dollars; only the U.S. Federal Reserve can do that. Instead, Argentina must use its *reserves* of dollars—the dollars its central bank keeps on hand specifically to intervene in the dollar–peso market.

Almost every nation holds reserves of dollars—as well as euros, yen, and other key currencies—just so it can enter the foreign exchange market and sell them for its own currency when necessary. Under a managed float, periods of selling dollars are usually short-lived, and alternate with periods of buying dollars. Thus, countries rarely use up all of their dollar reserves when they engage in managed floats.

Managed floats are controversial. Some economists believe they help to avoid wide swings in exchange rates, and thus reduce the risks for international traders and investors. But others are critical of how managed floats often work out in practice. They point out that countries often intervene when the forces behind an appreciation or depreciation are strong. In these cases, the intervention only serves to delay inevitable changes in the exchange rate—sometimes, at great cost to a country's reserves of dollars and other key currencies.

FIXED EXCHANGE RATES

Fixed exchange rate A government-declared exchange rate maintained by central bank intervention in the foreign exchange market.

A more extreme form of intervention is a **fixed exchange rate,** in which a government declares a particular value for its exchange rate with another currency. The government, through its central bank, then commits itself to intervene in the foreign exchange market any time the *equilibrium* exchange rate differs from the *fixed* rate.

For example, from 1987 to 1997, the government of Thailand fixed the value of its currency—the *baht*—at $0.04 per baht. The two panels of Figure 7 show the different types of intervention that might be necessary in the baht–dollar market to maintain this fixed exchange rate. Each panel shows a different set of supply and demand curves—and a different equilibrium exchange rate that might exist for the baht. Look first at panel (a). Here, we assume that the equilibrium exchange rate is $0.06 per baht, so that the fixed rate is *lower* than the equilibrium rate. At the fixed rate of $0.04 per baht, 400 million baht would be demanded each month, but only 100 million would be supplied. There would be an *excess demand* of 300 million baht, which would ordinarily drive the exchange rate back up to its equilibrium value of $0.06. But the Thai government prevents this by entering the market and *selling* just enough baht to cover the excess demand. In panel (a), the Central Bank of Thailand would sell 300 million baht per month to maintain the fixed rate.

> When a country fixes its exchange rate below the equilibrium value, the result is an excess demand for the country's currency. To maintain the fixed rate, the country's central bank must sell enough of its own currency to eliminate the excess demand.

Panel (b) shows another possibility, where the equilibrium exchange rate is $0.02, so that the same fixed exchange rate of $0.04 per baht is now *above* the equilibrium rate. There is an excess *supply* of 300 million baht. In this case, to prevent the excess supply from driving the exchange rate down, the Central Bank of Thailand must *buy* the excess baht.

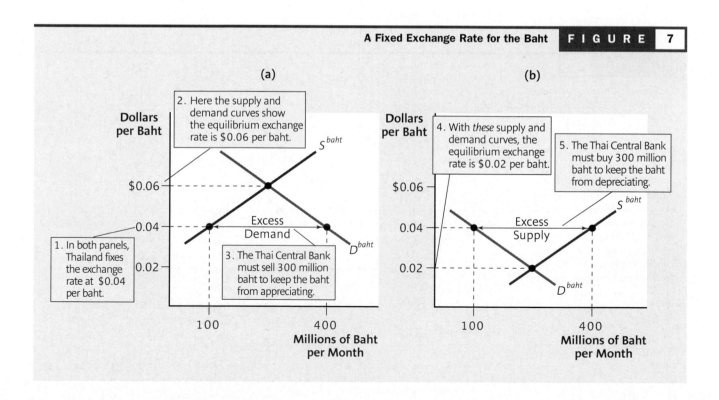

A Fixed Exchange Rate for the Baht **FIGURE 7**

> *When a country fixes its exchange rate above the equilibrium value, the result is an excess supply of the country's currency. To maintain the fixed rate, the country's central bank must buy enough of its own currency to eliminate the excess supply.*

Fixed exchange rates present little problem for a country as long as the exchange rate is fixed at or very close to its equilibrium rate. But when the equilibrium exchange rate moves away from the fixed rate—as in the two panels of Figure 7—governments often try to maintain their fixed rate anyway, sometimes for long periods. This can create problems, especially when the exchange rate is fixed *above* the equilibrium rate.

FOREIGN CURRENCY CRISES, THE IMF, AND MORAL HAZARD

To see how a fixed exchange rate can be problematic, look at Figure 8. Initially, the supply and demand curves for baht are given by S_1 and D_1, respectively, so that the equilibrium exchange rate, $0.04, is equal to the fixed exchange rate. At this point, the central bank is neither selling nor buying baht. Now, suppose that, for some reason (we'll be more specific in a few paragraphs), the supply and demand curves shift to S_2 and D_2, respectively. The equilibrium rate falls, so the fixed rate of $0.04 is above the equilibrium rate of $0.02. The Central Bank of Thailand must now *buy* its own currency with dollars—at the rate of 300 million baht per month. Each baht costs the central bank 4 cents, so as the months go by, its dollar reserves are being depleted at the rate of 300 million × $0.04 = $12 million per month. Once those reserves are gone, Thailand will have only two choices: to let its currency float

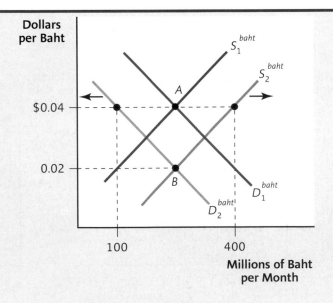

FIGURE 8

A Foreign Currency Crisis

Initially, the baht is fixed at the equilibrium rate of $0.04. When the supply and demand curves shift to D₂ and S₂, the equilibrium exchange rate falls to $0.02. If Thailand continues to fix the rate at $0.04, it will have to buy up the excess supply of 300 million baht per month, using dollars. As its dollar reserves dwindle, traders will anticipate a drop in the value of the baht, shifting the curves out further, as indicated by the arrows.

(which means an immediate depreciation to the lower, equilibrium rate) or to declare a new, lower fixed rate—a **devaluation** of its currency.

Of course, at a certain point, foreign exchange speculators and traders would see that Thailand doesn't have many dollars left. (Most countries' central banks regularly report their holdings of key currencies, and economists can estimate the holdings of countries that don't.) Looking ahead, these speculators and traders will begin to *anticipate* a drop in the baht. And—as you've learned in this chapter—expected changes in the exchange rate *shift* supply and demand curves for foreign currency. In this case, an expected fall in the baht causes the supply curve for baht to shift further rightward and the demand curve to shift further leftward, as indicated by the heavy arrows in the diagram. In Figure 8, these shifts will *decrease* the equilibrium value of the baht, increase the *excess supply* of baht, and make the fixed rate of $0.04 even harder to maintain. The country is now experiencing a *foreign currency crisis*.

> A *foreign currency crisis* arises when people no longer believe that a country can maintain a fixed exchange rate above the equilibrium rate. As a consequence, the supply of the currency increases, demand for it decreases, and the country must use up its reserves of dollars and other key currencies even faster in order to maintain the fixed rate.

Devaluation A change in the exchange rate from a higher fixed rate to a lower fixed rate.

Foreign currency crisis A loss of faith that a country can prevent a drop in its exchange rate, leading to a rapid depletion of its foreign currency (e.g., dollar) reserves.

Once a foreign currency crisis arises, a country typically has no choice but to devalue its currency or let it float and watch it depreciate. And ironically, because the country waited for the crisis to develop, the exchange rate may for a time drop even lower than the original equilibrium rate. For example, in Figure 8, an early devaluation to $0.02 per dollar might prevent a crisis from occurring at all. But once the crisis begins, and the supply and demand curves shift out further than S_2 and D_2, the currency will have to drop *below* $0.02 to end the rapid depletion of dollar reserves.

Our analysis of a foreign currency crisis used the example of the Thai baht for good reason. In 1997 and 1998, Thailand was at the center of a financial crisis that rocked the world.

The crisis began when a lack of confidence in Thailand's financial system led to dramatic shifts in the supply and demand curves for baht—just as in Figure 8. While the *equilibrium* exchange rate fell, Thailand continued to fix the *actual* exchange rate at $0.04 per baht, above the equilibrium rate. As a result, Thailand's central bank was depleting its reserves of dollars and other foreign currencies. This, of course, led currency traders to anticipate a devaluation, shifting the supply and demand curves even further. Finally, in July 1997, the Thai central bank simply ran out of foreign currency reserves, and was forced to let its currency float. The baht immediately depreciated from $0.04 to $0.02.

But this was only the beginning of the story. Many of Thailand's banks—counting on the fixed exchange rate—had borrowed heavily in dollars, yen, and other foreign currencies, but then lent funds to Thai businesses in baht. Once the baht depreciated, these banks were obligated to make unchanged dollar and yen payments on their debts, while continuing to receive unchanged baht payments on the funds they had lent. The problem was that, after the depreciation, the baht coming in would no longer cover the dollars going out. Thailand's banks were in trouble.

And the trouble spread. Investors began to wonder if banks in *other* nearby countries were similarly vulnerable, and began to dump the foreign exchange of

International Monetary Fund (IMF) An international organization founded in 1945 to help stabilize the world monetary system.

Indonesia, South Korea, Malaysia, and the Philippines. Before the crisis ended, it had even spread to several Latin American countries.

What ended the crisis? In large part, the crisis was resolved by the **International Monetary Fund (IMF)**, an international organization formed in 1945 in large part to help nations avoid such foreign currency crises and help them recover when crises occur. In 1998, the IMF—in cooperation with the U.S. government—orchestrated a rescue package of more than $100 billion to cover the Asian economies' foreign debt.

The rescue was controversial, however. Why? Helping a troubled country leads other countries to expect that they, too, will get help if they pursue untenable policies and get themselves into trouble. This is an example of a more general problem which economists call *moral hazard*.

Moral hazard When decision makers—expecting assistance in the event of an unfavorable outcome—change their behavior so that the unfavorable outcome is more likely.

> *Moral hazard occurs when a decision maker (such as an individual, firm, or government) expects to be rescued in the event of an unfavorable outcome, and then changes its behavior so that the unfavorable outcome is more likely.*

Moral hazard plagues the insurance industry (are you as likely to lock your car if you're insured against theft?), efforts to care for the unemployed (will you look as hard for a new job after being laid off if you are collecting unemployment insurance?), and troubled business firms (will mega-corporations be careful not to take risks if they expect the government to rescue them in the event of a disaster?).

But here, our focus is on the international financial system. The problem of moral hazard helps explain the very different response of the IMF when, in late 2001 and early 2002, Argentina faced a somewhat similar foreign currency crisis. Like the Asian countries a few years earlier, Argentina needed billions of dollars of help to prevent it from devaluing its currency and defaulting on its foreign debt. This time, however, it was felt that Argentina's problems were unique, and so its foreign currency crisis—unlike the Asian crisis a few years earlier—was unlikely to spread to other countries. Accordingly, the Bush administration—concerned about the moral hazard problem—encouraged the IMF to take a tough stand. There was no rescue, and Argentina was forced into devaluation *and* default in January 2002.

The IMF headquarters building in Washington, D.C.

EXCHANGE RATES AND THE MACROECONOMY

Exchange rates can have important effects on the macroeconomy—largely through their effect on net exports. And although we've included net exports in our short-run macro model, we haven't yet asked how exchange rates affect them. That's what we'll do now.

EXCHANGE RATES AND DEMAND SHOCKS

Suppose that the dollar depreciates against the foreign currencies of its major trading partners. (We'll discuss *why* that might happen in a later section.) Then U.S. goods would become cheaper to foreigners, and net exports would rise at each level of output. This increase in net exports is a positive demand shock to the economy—it increases aggregate expenditure and shifts the aggregate demand curve to the right. And, as you've learned, positive demand shocks increase GDP in the short run.

> *A depreciation of the dollar causes net exports to rise—a positive demand shock that increases real GDP in the short run. An appreciation of the dollar causes net exports to drop—a negative demand shock that decreases real GDP in the short run.*

The impact of net exports on equilibrium GDP—often caused by changes in the exchange rate—helps us understand one reason why governments are often concerned about their exchange rates. An unstable exchange rate can result in repeated shocks to the economy. At worst, this can cause fluctuations in GDP; at best, it makes the central bank's job more difficult as it tries to keep the economy on an even keel.

EXCHANGE RATES AND MONETARY POLICY

In several earlier chapters, we've explored how the Fed tries to keep the U.S. economy on an even keel with monetary policy. The central banks around the world are engaged in a similar struggle, and face many of the same challenges as the Fed. One challenge to central banks is that monetary policy causes changes in exchange rates, and thus has additional effects on real GDP that we have not yet considered.

To understand this, let's run through an example. Suppose the United States is in a recession, and the Fed decides to increase equilibrium GDP. As you've learned, the Fed—by increasing the money supply—brings down the interest rate. Interest-sensitive spending rises, and so does aggregate expenditure. When we consider the foreign exchange market, however, there is an additional effect on aggregate expenditure.

By lowering the U.S. interest rate, the Fed makes *foreign* financial assets more attractive to Americans, which raises their demand for foreign currency. In the market for pounds, for example, this will shift the demand for pounds curve rightward. At the same time, U.S. financial assets become less attractive to foreigners, which decreases the supply of foreign exchange (in the market for pounds, a leftward shift in the supply of pounds curve). If you sketch out these shifts right now, you'll see that, as long as the exchange rate floats, the result is a *depreciation of the dollar* against the pound.

Now let's see how the depreciation of the dollar affects the economy. With dollars now cheaper to foreigners, they will buy more U.S. goods, raising U.S. exports. At the same time, with foreign goods and services more expensive to Americans, U.S. imports will decrease. Both the increase in exports and the decrease in imports contribute to a rise in net exports, *NX*. This, in turn, increases aggregate expenditure.

Thus, as you can see, the expansionary monetary policy causes aggregate expenditures to rise in two ways: first, by increasing interest-sensitive spending and, second, by increasing net exports. As a result, equilibrium GDP rises by more—and monetary policy is more effective—when the effects on exchange rates are included.

The channels through which monetary policy works are summarized in the following schematic:

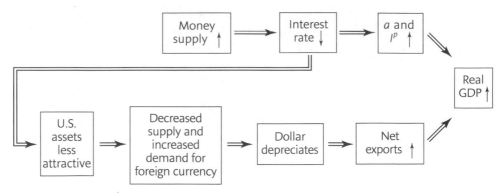

Net Effect: GDP ↑ by more when the exchange rate's effect on net exports is included

The top line shows the familiar effect on interest-sensitive spending: An increase in the money supply causes a drop in the interest rate, which increases autonomous consumption spending (a) and investment spending (I^p). The bottom line shows the *additional* effect on net exports through changes in the exchange rate—the effects we've been discussing.

The analysis of contractionary monetary policy is the same, but in reverse. A decrease in the money supply will not only decrease interest-sensitive spending, it will also cause the dollar to appreciate and net exports to drop. Thus, it will cause equilibrium GDP to fall by more than in earlier chapters, where we ignored the foreign exchange market.

The channel of monetary influence through exchange rates and the volume of trade is an important part of the full story of monetary policy in the United States. And in countries where exports are relatively large fractions of GDP—such as those of Europe—the trade channel is even more important. It is the main channel through which monetary policy affects the economy.

> *Monetary policy has a stronger effect when we include the impact on exchange rates and net exports, rather than just the impact on interest-sensitive consumption and investment spending.*

EXCHANGE RATES AND THE TRADE DEFICIT

The U.S. trade deficit is often in the news. But what, exactly, is it?

The trade deficit is the extent to which a country's imports exceed its exports:

$$\textbf{Trade deficit} = \text{Imports} - \text{Exports}$$

On the other hand, when exports exceed imports, a nation has a trade surplus:

$$\textbf{Trade surplus} = \text{Exports} - \text{Imports}$$

As you can see, the trade surplus is nothing more than a nation's net exports (NX). And when net exports are negative, we have a trade deficit.

The United States has had large trade deficits with the rest of the world since the early 1980s. In 2005, the trade deficit was $716 billion. Simply put, Americans bought $716 billion more goods and services from other countries than their residents bought from the United States.

Trade deficit The excess of a nation's imports over its exports during a given period.

Trade surplus The excess of a nation's exports over its imports during a given period.

Why does the United States have a trade deficit with the rest of the world? A variety of explanations have been offered in the media, including poor U.S. marketing savvy in selling to foreigners, and a greater degree of protectionism in foreign markets.

But economists believe that there is a much more important reason.

THE ORIGINS OF THE U.S. TRADE DEFICIT

To keep our analysis simple, we'll start by looking at the U.S. trade deficit with just one country—Japan—but our results will hold more generally to the trade deficit with many other countries as well.

Before we analyze the causes of the trade deficit, we need to do a little math. Let's begin by breaking down the total quantity of yen demanded by Americans ($D^{\yen}$) into two components: the yen demanded to purchase Japanese goods and services (U.S. imports from Japan) and the yen demanded to buy Japanese assets:

$$D^{\yen} = \text{U.S. imports from Japan} + \text{U.S. purchases of Japanese assets.}$$

Similarly, we can divide the total quantity of yen supplied by the Japanese ($S^{\yen}$) into two components: the yen exchanged for dollars to purchase American goods (U.S. exports to Japan) and the yen exchanged for dollars to purchase American assets like stocks, bonds, or real estate:

$$S^{\yen} = \text{U.S. exports to Japan} + \text{Japanese purchases of U.S. assets.}$$

As long as the yen floats against the dollar without government intervention—which it does during most periods—we know that the exchange rate will adjust until the quantities of yen supplied and demanded are equal, or $D^{\yen} = S^{\yen}$. Substituting the foregoing breakdowns into this equation, we have

$$\left\{ \begin{array}{l} \text{U.S. imports from Japan} \\ + \text{ U.S. purchases of Japanese assets} \end{array} \right\} = \left\{ \begin{array}{l} \text{U.S. exports to Japan} \\ + \text{ Japanese purchases of U.S. assets} \end{array} \right\}.$$

Now let's rearrange this equation—subtracting U.S. exports from both sides and subtracting American purchases of Japanese assets from both sides—to get

$$\left\{ \begin{array}{l} \text{U.S. imports from Japan} \\ - \text{ U.S. exports to Japan} \end{array} \right\} = \left\{ \begin{array}{l} \text{Japanese purchases of U.S. assets} \\ - \text{ U.S. purchases of Japanese assets} \end{array} \right\}.$$

The term on the left should look familiar: It is the U.S. trade deficit with Japan. And since a similar equation must hold for every country, we can generalize it this way:

$$\left\{ \begin{array}{l} \text{U.S. imports from other countries} \\ - \text{ U.S. exports to other countries} \end{array} \right\} = \left\{ \begin{array}{l} \text{foreign purchases of U.S. assets} \\ - \text{ U.S. purchases of foreign assets} \end{array} \right\}.$$

But what is the expression on the right? It tells us the extent to which foreigners are buying more of our assets than we are buying of theirs. It is often called the **net financial inflow** into the United States, because when the residents of other countries buy U.S. assets, funds flow into the U.S. financial market, where they are made available to U.S. firms and the U.S. government. Thus, the equation we've derived—which must hold true when exchange rates float—can also be expressed as

$$\text{U.S. trade deficit} = \text{U.S. net financial inflow}$$

Net financial inflow An inflow of funds equal to a nation's trade deficit.

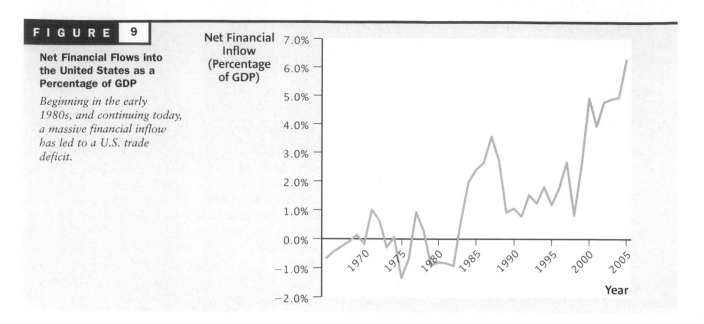

FIGURE 9

Net Financial Flows into the United States as a Percentage of GDP

Beginning in the early 1980s, and continuing today, a massive financial inflow has led to a U.S. trade deficit.

Why have we bothered to derive this equation? Because it tells us two very important things about the U.S. trade deficit. First, it tells us how the trade deficit is *financed*. Think about it: If the United States is running a trade deficit with, say, Japan, it means that the Japanese are providing more goods and services to Americans—more automobiles, VCRs, memory chips, and other goods—than Americans are providing to them. The Japanese are not doing this out of kindness. They must be getting *something* in return for the extra goods we are getting, and the equation tells us just what that is: U.S. assets. This is one reason why the trade deficit concerns U.S. policy makers: It results in a transfer of wealth from Americans to foreign residents.

The second important insight provided by the equation is that a trade deficit can arise *because* of forces that cause a financial inflow. That is, if forces in the global economy make the right side of the equation positive, then the left side must be positive as well, and we will have a trade deficit.

Indeed, economists believe this is just what has happened to the United States: that the U.S. trade deficit has been caused by the desire of foreigners to invest in the United States. The result was a massive financial inflow and trade deficit that arose in the early 1980s, as illustrated in Figure 9. This financial inflow was unprecedented in size and duration, and it reversed a long-standing pattern of ownership between the United States and other countries. For decades, American holdings of foreign assets far exceeded foreign holdings of U.S. assets. But the financial inflows of the 1980s changed that: By 1988, foreigners held about $500 billion more in U.S. assets than Americans held in foreign assets. By the end of 2005, the difference in asset holdings increased more than fivefold, and exceeded $2.7 trillion.

But how do the forces that create a financial inflow also *cause* a trade deficit?

HOW A FINANCIAL INFLOW CAUSES A TRADE DEFICIT

Figure 10 illustrates this process, using the yen–dollar market. We'll assume that initially, neither the Japanese nor the Americans are buying *assets* from the other country. Only goods and services are traded. Point *A* shows the initial equilibrium under

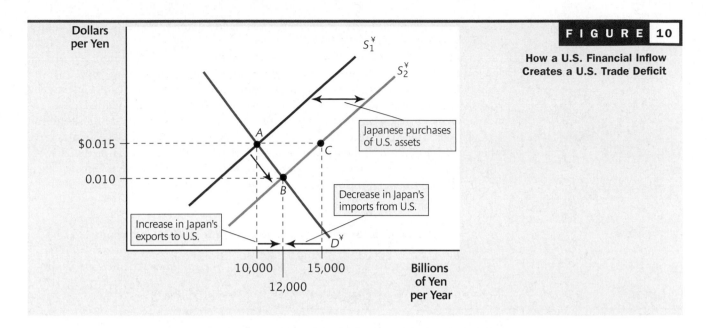

FIGURE 10

How a U.S. Financial Inflow Creates a U.S. Trade Deficit

this special assumption. Under these circumstances, the demand curve for yen would reflect U.S. *imports* of goods and services from Japan, and the supply curve would reflect U.S. *exports* of goods and services to Japan. The exchange rate would be $0.015 per yen (one-and-a-half cents per yen), and each year, 10,000 billion yen would be traded in exchange for $10,000 \times 0.015 = 150$ billion dollars. Since the quantities of yen demanded and supplied are equal in equilibrium, there is no trade deficit: The United States buys $150 billion in goods from Japan, and Japan buys $150 billion in goods from the United States.

Now suppose that the Japanese start to buy U.S. stocks, bonds, and real estate. Specifically, they want to purchase 5,000 billion yen worth of these assets from Americans each year. To do so, they need dollars, so they must supply additional yen to the foreign exchange market to get them. Accordingly, the supply of yen curve shifts rightward by 5,000 billion yen. The market equilibrium moves from point *A* to point *B*, and the new exchange rate is $0.01 per yen. The yen depreciates against the dollar, and the dollar appreciates against the yen.

But something interesting happens in the market as the exchange rate changes. First, there is a *movement along the demand curve* for yen, from point *A* to point *B*. Why? The yen is now cheaper, so Americans—finding Japanese goods and services cheaper—buy more of them. Thus, the movement along the demand curve represents an *increase in Japan's exports to the U.S.* (valued in yen, the units on the horizontal axis). In the figure, Japan's exports—the quantity of yen demanded—rise by 2,000 billion yen as we move from *A* to *B*.

But there is a second movement as well. After the shift in the supply curve, *and at the old exchange rate of $0.015*, the Japanese want to supply 15,000 billion yen to the market (point *C*). But as the exchange rate falls, there is a movement from point *C* to point *B*—the quantity of yen supplied decreases. Why does this happen? Because as the yen depreciates (the dollar appreciates), U.S. goods and services become more expensive to the Japanese. Accordingly, they purchase fewer U.S. goods. Assuming that the Japanese still want to purchase the same 5,000 billion yen in U.S. *assets*, the entire decrease in the quantity of yen supplied as we move from *C* to *B* represents a *decrease in Japan's imports from the United States* (valued in yen). In the figure, Japan's imports decrease by 3,000 billion yen.

Let's recap: Because the Japanese wanted to purchase 5,000 billion yen in U.S. assets (a net financial inflow to the United States of 5,000 billion yen), the yen depreciated. This, in turn, made Japanese goods cheaper for Americans—increasing Japan's exports (U.S. imports) by 2,000 billion yen per year. It also made U.S. goods more expensive in Japan, decreasing Japan's imports (U.S. exports) by 3,000 billion yen per year. Since U.S. imports have risen by 2,000 billion ¥ and U.S. exports have fallen by 3,000 billion ¥, the United States—which initially had no trade deficit with Japan at point *A*—now has a trade deficit equal to 5,000 billion yen. This is exactly equal to the financial inflow—Japan's purchases of U.S. assets.

More generally,

> *an increase in the desire of foreigners to invest in the United States contributes to an appreciation of the dollar. As a result, U.S. exports—which become more expensive for foreigners—decline. Imports—which become cheaper to Americans—increase. The result is a rise in the U.S. trade deficit.*

EXPLAINING THE NET FINANCIAL INFLOW

What explains the huge financial inflow that began in the 1980s and has since grown larger? In the 1980s, an important part of the story was *a rise in U.S. interest rates relative to interest rates abroad,* which made U.S. assets more attractive to foreigners, and foreign assets less attractive to Americans. In the 1990s, however, U.S. interest rates were low relative to rates in other countries, yet the inflow continued. Why?

Even when U.S. interest rates are lower than abroad, it seems that foreign residents have a strong preference for holding American assets. In part, this is because of a favorable investment climate. The United States is a stable country with a long history of protecting individual property rights. People know that if they buy American stocks or bonds, unless they violate U.S. criminal law, the U.S. government is very unlikely to confiscate foreign-owned assets or suddenly impose punitive taxes when foreigners want to repatriate the funds to their home countries. This asymmetrical foreign preference for American assets helps explain why the U.S. net financial inflow has been *persistent*.

But why the recent *surge* in the inflow? One reason is that Americans have been saving less, and foreigners have been saving more. (In Europe and in Japan, aging populations have been saving heavily for retirement, while developing country governments have been reducing debt and building up financial reserves.) All of this new foreign wealth needs to be held in *some* country's assets, and—for reasons discussed earlier—the U.S. seems to be the favorite.[2]

At the same time, the *demand* for loanable funds in the U.S. has been growing rapidly. Part of this greater demand for funds arose from new investment opportunities, causing business firms to issue new shares of stock and new bonds in order to finance projects. This was especially true in the late 1990s, during the Internet boom. And when the boom turned to a bust in the early 2000s, a new demand for funds arose: The government needed to finance large budget deficits.

---

[2] For a complete explanation of this argument, see the speech by Federal Reserve Governor Ben S. Bernanke, "The Global Saving Glut and the U.S. Current Account Deficit," April 14, 2005 (*www. federalreserve.gov/boarddocs/speeches/2005*).

Remember that, under floating exchange rates, the financial inflow equals the trade deficit. Thus, the story of the U.S. financial inflow of the 1980s, 1990s, and early 2000s is also the story of the U.S. trade deficit:

> *We can trace the rise in the trade deficit during recent decades to two important sources: first, relatively high interest rates in the 1980s and, second, a long-held preference for American assets that grew stronger in the 1990s. Each of these contributed to a large financial inflow, a higher value for the dollar, and a trade deficit.*

In addition to a strong desire to buy U.S. assets, a trade deficit can arise from another cause: a foreign currency fixed at an artificially low value. In the minds of many economists, this has contributed to the United States' growing trade deficit with China. We will explore the U.S. trade deficit with China in our Using the Theory section. But first, let's look at why many economists are concerned about the large U.S. trade deficit.

CONCERNS ABOUT THE TRADE DEFICIT

Should we be concerned about the U.S. trade deficit? To most economists, the answer is yes. But the reasons are different from those typically offered in public debate.

To many *non*-economists, the U.S. trade deficit is viewed as bad because it makes Americans poorer. We get VCRs, toys, and T-shirts from the rest of the world. But we don't pay for all of these things with our own goods and services. To make up the difference, we sell assets: We turn over ownership of our factories and real estate to the rest of the world, and also accumulate debt to them (when we sell them bonds). According to this view, the U.S. trade deficit means declining American wealth.

Although the first part of this analysis is correct (the United States *does* finance its trade deficit by selling assets to the rest of the world), it does not necessarily follow that the trade deficit makes American households poorer. That would follow if the total amount of wealth in the U.S. economy were fixed, so that any wealth sold to foreigners meant less wealth in American hands. But, in fact, total U.S. wealth grows every year, as new factories and new homes are built, new intellectual property is developed, and more. And even after deducting the wealth that the rest of the world acquires, what is left in American hands continues to grow every year as well.

What *does* follow from this analysis is that, *because of the trade deficit, U.S. wealth owned by the U.S. public grows more slowly than it otherwise would.* Slower growing wealth is a choice made by U.S. households (choosing to buy more toys and T-shirts instead of saving more) and the U.S. government (choosing to pay for part of its expenditure by borrowing instead of taxing). Economists continue to debate the wisdom or lack of wisdom behind these choices, but slower growing wealth is not the main reason for economists' concern.

The real problem, as economists view it, is the trade deficit's *sustainability.*

Why might the trade deficit not be sustainable? As the U.S. trade deficit continues year after year, foreign holdings of U.S. assets continue to accumulate—rapidly. And the *proportion* of the rest of the world's total wealth that is held in dollar-denominated assets grows as well. At some point, the rest of the world's wealth holders may decide that their portfolios are too "dollar heavy," and that the time

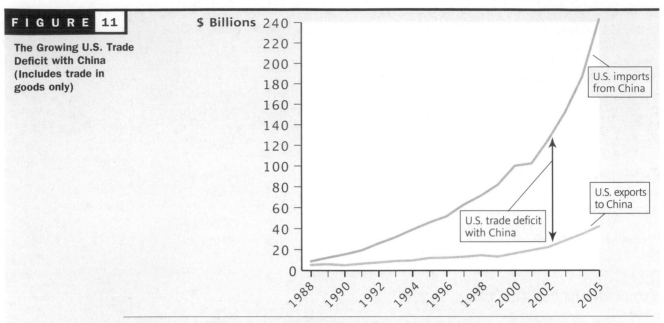

FIGURE 11

The Growing U.S. Trade Deficit with China (Includes trade in goods only)

Source: Wayne M. Morrison, "China-U.S. Trade Issues," Congressional Research Service, Library of Congress, Updated May 16, 2003; *Economic Report of the President,* 2006; and Bureau of Economic Analysis, "U.S. International Transactions by Area."

has come to diversify. This would mean a slowdown—or possibly a halt—in new purchases of U.S. assets. If this occurs, we can imagine two possibilities.

The Soft-Landing Scenario

In the benign, soft-landing scenario, the U.S. and world economies would gradually adjust to a slowdown in foreign purchases of U.S. assets. A decline in the demand for U.S. assets, as you've learned, would cause the dollar to depreciate. Imports would become more expensive for U.S. residents, and U.S. exports would become cheaper to the rest of the world, so the trade deficit would gradually shrink.

At the same time, the U.S. interest rate would rise. (From a long-run, loanable funds perspective, the interest rate would rise because the supply of funds to the U.S. loanable funds market is shrinking. From a short-run perspective, the Fed would raise its interest rate target to prevent the rise in net exports from overheating the U.S. economy.)

The rise in the U.S. interest rate would contribute to the gradualness of the adjustment. First, a higher interest rate would mean more saving by Americans, enabling them to buy some of the assets foreigners are no longer buying. Second, higher interest rates would help make U.S. assets more attractive to foreigners.

The soft-landing scenario would not be painless. It would require structural changes in the U.S. economy as exporting and import-competing industries expanded, while interest-sensitive industries such as home building declined. But it would not be a disaster.

The Hard-Landing Scenario

The more dangerous, hard-landing scenario works much like the soft-landing scenario, except that the changes are much larger and more sudden. Once again, we start with a decline in the demand for U.S. assets by foreigners. Only this time, as the dollar begins to depreciate, foreigners anticipate *further* depreciation in the future. They begin to dump dollar-denominated assets *en masse*, before the anticipated decline in their value. Hot money flows out of the dollar and into other currencies. The dollar doesn't just depreciate—it plummets. And the more it does, the more foreign wealth holders want to get rid of their dollars.

The interest rate would rise. (See the soft-landing scenario.) But in this case, with the dollar depreciating so rapidly, substitute the word "skyrocket" for "rise." With soaring interest rates, spending on interest-sensitive goods, such as new factories and homes, would disappear. Moreover, as you learned a few chapters ago, the rise in interest rates would cause stock and bond prices to fall—a decline in household wealth. Consumption spending would fall across the board.

In the most pessimistic form of the hard-landing scenario, the United States would experience a very serious recession—one that the Fed would be unable to prevent. If the Fed tried to lower the interest rate to prevent the recession entirely, it would have to allow the dollar to continue plummeting. This would make the price of imports rise rapidly and cause unacceptable inflation. And even if the Fed decided to take this course, the dramatic changes in the economy would make any Fed response particularly error-prone.

Which of these two scenarios is most likely to occur? In mid-2006, economists continued to debate the probabilities. Some argued that the hard-landing scenario was unrealistic. It assumes that central banks in the rest of the world would *allow* the dollar to plummet, even though this would devastate their own export industries and decrease the value of their remaining dollar-denominated assets. Surely, so the soft-landers say, these central banks would intervene in the foreign exchange market, by purchasing dollars to prop up its value. If the hard-landing scenario begins to occur, we will see if they are right.

USING THE THEORY

© SUSAN VAN ETTEN

The U.S. Trade Deficit with China

The growing U.S. trade deficit with China has become one of the most controversial issues of U.S. public policy. Figure 11 shows United States imports to, and exports from, China from 1988 to 2005. (The figure excludes trade in services, but this has little effect on the numbers.) Trade in both directions expanded dramatically. But while U.S. exports to China increased tenfold, U.S. *imports* from China increased 28-fold, from $8.5 billion in 1988 to $243 billion in 2005. During this period, China went from being a relatively unimportant trading partner of the United States to the fourth-largest trading partner. In the figure, the growing trade deficit is the increasing distance between the (higher) imports line and the (lower) exports line. In 2005, the United States had a larger trade deficit with China—$202 billion—than with any other country.

The U.S. trade deficit with China has been soaring for a variety of reasons, including special trade agreements during this period that gave China new access to U.S. markets, and Chinese trade policies that have encouraged exports and discouraged imports. But another factor, as mentioned earlier, is China's undervalued exchange rate. China has fixed the value of its currency (the yuan) against the dollar—at about

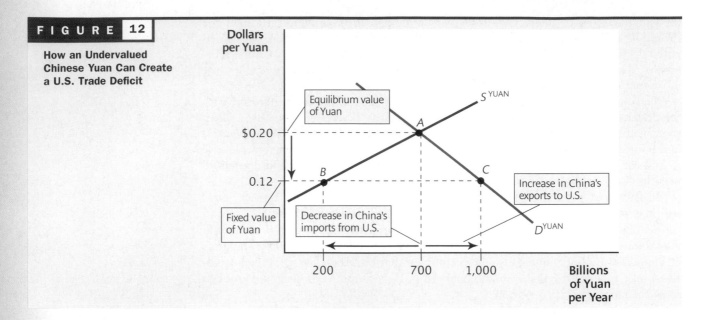

FIGURE 12

How an Undervalued Chinese Yuan Can Create a U.S. Trade Deficit

$0.12 per yuan for most of the past decade. This is widely believed to be far below the yuan's equilibrium value. In mid-2005, China revalued the yuan slightly (by 2.1 percent) and announced that it would move to a managed float, allowing its currency to rise slowly. In fact, the rise has been *so* slow (about another 2 percent from mid-2005 to mid-2006) that, effectively, we can continue to regard the yuan–dollar exchange rate as fixed.

Figure 12 illustrates how an undervalued yuan can create a trade deficit for the United States. We'll assume that if the exchange rate were floating, the market equilibrium would be at point *A*, with an exchange rate of $0.20 per yuan. In this case, 700 billion yuan would be exchanged for 700 × .02 = 140 billion dollars each year.

Now we introduce the lower, fixed exchange rate of $.12 per yuan. Compared to the equilibrium exchange rate, the fixed exchange rate causes a movement along the *demand* for yuan curve, from point *A* to point *C*. The yuan is now cheaper, which makes Chinese goods and services cheaper to Americans, who buy more of them. Measured along the horizontal axis, *China's exports to the U.S. increase* by 300 billion yuan per year.

There is also a move from point *A* to point *B* along the *supply* curve; the quantity of yuan supplied decreases. A lower-valued yuan makes U.S. goods and services more expensive to Chinese households and businesses, so they purchase fewer of them. Along the horizontal axis, *China's imports from the U.S. decrease* by 500 billion yuan.

Since the fixed exchange rate has caused *China's imports from the U.S. to decrease* by 500 billion yuan, and *China's exports to the U.S. to increase* by 300 billion yuan, the U.S. trade deficit with China—valued in yuan—rises by 500 + 300 or 800 billion yuan per year. (If you convert the U.S. trade deficit to dollars, you'll see that our example comes close to the actual U.S. trade deficit with China.)

But wait . . . doesn't the rise in the U.S. trade deficit have to equal the rise in the net financial inflow? Indeed it does. Figure 11 shows an *excess demand for yuan* of 1,000 − 200 = 800 billion at the fixed exchange rate. The Chinese government must supply these yuan, selling them for U.S. dollars. These dollars are then used to purchase U.S. assets, contributing to the U.S. net financial inflow.

> *When a U.S. trading partner fixes the dollar price of its currency below its equilibrium value, U.S. exports—which become more expensive to foreigners—decline. U.S. imports—which become cheaper to Americans—increase. The result is a rise in the U.S. trade deficit.*

China's fixed exchange rate with the dollar is the source of considerable tension between the two countries. On the one hand, it enables Americans to purchase goods from China at even lower prices than otherwise. But rapidly growing trade with China also disrupts production in the U.S. economy, as U.S. businesses that produce sandals, shoes, suits, electronic goods, toys, and textiles find they are unable to compete with cheaper goods from China. The fixed exchange exacerbates their problem. By giving China an even *greater* cost advantage than it would otherwise have, U.S. firms and workers that compete in these markets must adjust more rapidly—and painfully—to the new pattern of international trade.

Summary

When residents of two countries trade with one another, one party ordinarily makes use of the foreign exchange market to trade one national currency for another. In this market, suppliers of a currency interact with demanders to determine an *exchange rate*—the price of one currency in terms of another.

In the market for U.S. dollars and British pounds, for example, demanders are mostly Americans who wish to obtain pounds in order to buy goods and services from British firms, or to buy British assets. A higher dollar price for the pound will lead Americans to demand fewer pounds—the demand curve slopes downward. Changes in U.S. real GDP, the U.S. price level relative to the British price level, Americans' tastes for British goods, interest rates in the United States relative to Britain, or expectations regarding the exchange rate can each cause the demand curve to shift.

Suppliers of pounds are mostly British residents who wish to buy American goods, services, or assets. A higher dollar price for the pound will lead Britons to supply more pounds—the supply curve slopes upward. The supply curve will shift in response to changes in British real GDP, prices in Britain relative to the United States, British tastes for U.S. goods, the British interest rate relative to the U.S. rate, and expectations regarding the exchange rate.

When the exchange rate floats, the equilibrium rate is determined where the supply and demand curves cross. If the equilibrium is disturbed by, say, a rightward shift of the demand curve, then the currency being demanded will *appreciate*—the exchange rate will rise. (The other country's currency will *depreciate*.) In a similar way, a rightward shift of the supply curve will cause the currency being supplied to depreciate.

Governments often intervene in foreign exchange markets. Many countries manage their float, buying and selling their own currency to alter the exchange rate. Some countries fix their exchange rate to the dollar or the currency of a major trading partner.

When a currency depreciates, its net exports rise—a positive demand shock. Monetary policy, in addition to its impact on interest-sensitive spending, also changes the exchange rate and net exports, adding to changes in output. This monetary policy is more effective in changing GDP when its effects on net exports are included.

The United States has had a persistent—and growing—*trade deficit* with the rest of the world. Much of this trade deficit can be explained by the growing U.S. *financial inflow* from the rest of the world. U.S. assets have been consistently more attractive to foreigners than foreign assets have been to Americans. The U.S. financial inflow causes the dollar to appreciate, which decreases U.S. exports and increases U.S. imports. In addition, when an exchange rate is fixed, an undervalued foreign currency can create a U.S. trade deficit. By making the U.S. dollar artificially more expensive to residents of the foreign country, it causes U.S. exports to decline and U.S. imports to rise.

Problem Set   *Answers to even-numbered Questions and Problems can be found on the text Web site at www.thomsonedu.com/economics/hall.*

1. Do the following events cause the dollar to appreciate against the euro or to depreciate?
   a. Health experts discover that red wine, especially French and Italian red wine, lowers cholesterol.
   b. GDP in nations across Europe falls.
   c. The United States experiences a higher inflation rate than Europe does.
   d. The U.S. budget deficit rises. (Hint: What happens to the U.S. interest rate?)

2. Let the monthly demand for British pounds and the monthly supply of British pounds be described by the following equations:

   $$\text{Demand for pounds} = 10 - 2e$$

   $$\text{Supply of pounds} = 4 + 3e$$

   where the quantities are in millions of pounds, and e is dollars per pound.
   a. Find the equilibrium exchange rate.
   b. Suppose the U.S. government intervenes in the foreign currency market and uses U.S. dollars to buy 2 million pounds each month. What happens to the exchange rate? Why might the U.S. government do this?

3. Let the demand and supply of Philippine pesos each month be described by the following equations:

   $$\text{Demand for pesos} = 100 - 2000e$$

   $$\text{Supply of pesos} = 20 + 3000e$$

   where the quantities are millions of pesos, and e is dollars per peso.
   a. Find the equilibrium exchange rate.
   b. Suppose the Philippine central bank wants to fix the exchange rate at 50 pesos per dollar and keep it there. Should the Philippine central bank buy or sell its own currency? How much per month?

4. Suppose the United States and Mexico are each other's sole trading partners. The Fed, afraid that the economy is about to overheat, raises the U.S. interest rate.
   a. Will the dollar appreciate or depreciate against the Mexican peso? Illustrate with a diagram of the dollar–peso foreign exchange market.
   b. What will happen to equilibrium GDP in the United States?
   c. How would your analyses in (a) and (b) change if, at the same time that the Fed was increasing the U.S. interest rate, the Mexican central bank increased the Mexican interest rate by an equivalent amount?

5. Jordan fixes its national currency—the dinar—against the dollar. In June 2006, the fixed rate was 1.41 dinars per dollar.
   a. Draw a diagram illustrating the market in which Jordanian dinars are traded for U.S. dollars, assuming that the equilibrium exchange rate is 1.00 dinar per dollar. (In your diagram, put the number of dinars per month on the horizontal axis.)
   b. Under the assumption in (a), would Jordan's central bank be buying or selling Jordanian dinars in this market? Indicate the number of dinars per month that the central bank must buy or sell as a distance on your graph.
   c. Based on your diagram and your answers so far, could Jordan continue to fix its currency at 1.41 dinars per dollar forever? Why or why not?
   d. Suppose that foreign currency traders believe that Jordan will soon allow the dinar to float. How would this affect the current supply and demand curves for dinars? (Draw new curves to indicate the impact.)
   e. How would the events in (d) affect the number of dinars that Jordan's central bank must buy or sell?

6. As in problem 5, note that Jordan fixes its national currency—the dinar—against the dollar at 1.41 dinars per dollar.
   a. Draw a diagram illustrating the market in which Jordanian dinars are traded for U.S. dollars, assuming that the equilibrium exchange rate is 2.00 dinars per dollar. (Put the number of dinars per month on the horizontal axis.)
   b. Under the assumption in (a), would Jordan's central bank be buying or selling Jordanian dinars in this market? Indicate the number of dinars per month that the central bank must buy or sell as a distance on your graph.
   c. Based on your diagram and your answers so far, could Jordan continue to fix its currency at 1.41 dinars per dollar forever? Why or why not?
   d. Suppose that foreign currency traders believe that Jordan will soon allow the dinar to float. How would this affect the current supply and demand curves for dinars? (Draw new curves to indicate the impact.)
   e. How would the events in (d) affect the number of dinars that Jordan's central bank must buy or sell?

7. Some nations that fix their exchange rates make their currency more expensive for foreigners (an overvalued currency), while others make their currency artificially cheap to foreigners (an undervalued currency).
   a. Why would a country want an overvalued currency? How, specifically, would the country benefit? Would the policy cause harm to anyone in the country? Explain briefly.
   b. Why would a country want an undervalued currency? How, specifically, would the country benefit? Would the policy cause harm to anyone in the country? Explain briefly.

8. If the inflation rate in Country A is 4 percent and the inflation rate in Country B is 6 percent, explain what will happen to the relative value of each country's currency.

9. a. Use the information in the following table to find the exchange rate if the euro and the U.S. dollar are allowed to float freely.

Dollars per Euro	Quantity of Euros Demanded	Quantity of Euros Supplied
$1.20	500 million	2,600 million
$1.10	1,000 million	2,400 million
$1.00	1,500 million	2,200 million
$0.90	2,000 million	2,000 million
$0.80	2,500 million	1,800 million

  b. What will happen to the exchange rate if the demand for euros rises by 700 million at each price if there is no intervention?
  c. Assume that the European central bank currently owns 400 million dollars and the Fed currently owns 300 million euros. If the demand for euros rises by 700 million at each price, what would the European central bank have to do to maintain a fixed exchange rate equal to the exchange rate you found in part (a)? Is this possible?

10. Refer to Figure 10 in the chapter. Remember that there was no trade deficit at point *A*. What is the U.S. trade deficit with Japan in *dollars* at point *B*?

More Challenging

11. It is often stated that the U.S. trade deficit with Japan results from Japanese trade barriers against U.S. goods.

  a. Suppose that Japan and the United States trade goods but not assets. Show—with a diagram of the dollar–yen market—that a U.S. trade deficit is impossible as long as the exchange rate floats. (Hint: With no trading in assets, the quantity of yen demanded at each exchange rate is equal in value to U.S. imports, and the quantity of yen supplied at each exchange rate is equal in value to U.S. exports.)
  b. In the diagram, illustrate the impact of a reduction in Japanese trade barriers. Would the dollar appreciate or depreciate against the yen? What would be the impact on U.S. net exports?
  c. Now suppose that the United States and Japan also trade assets, but that the Japanese buy more U.S. assets than we buy of theirs. Could the elimination of Japanese trade barriers wipe out the U.S. trade deficit with Japan? Why, or why not? (Hint: What is the relationship between the U.S. trade deficit and U.S. net financial inflow?)

12. Suppose that the U.S. government raises spending without increasing taxes. Will there be any effects on the foreign exchange market? (Hint: What does this policy do to U.S. interest rates?) When we add in the effects from the foreign exchange market and net exports, is fiscal policy more effective or less effective in changing equilibrium GDP in the short run?

Glossary

A

Absolute advantage The ability to produce a good or service, using fewer resources than other producers use.

Accounting profit Total revenue minus accounting costs.

Adverse selection A situation in which asymmetric information about quality eliminates high-quality goods from a market.

Aggregate demand (*AD*) curve A curve indicating equilibrium GDP at each price level.

Aggregate expenditure (*AE*) The sum of spending by households, business firms, the government, and foreigners on final goods and services produced in the United States.

Aggregate production function The relationship showing how much total output can be produced with different quantities of labor, with quantities of all other resources held constant.

Aggregate supply (*AS*) curve A curve indicating the price level consistent with firms' unit costs and markups for any level of output over the short run.

Aggregation The process of combining different things into a single category.

Alternate goods Other goods that a firm could produce, using some of the same types of inputs as the good in question.

Alternate market A market other than the one being analyzed in which the same good could be sold.

Appreciation An increase in the price of a currency in a floating-rate system.

Asymmetric information A situation in which one party to a transaction has relevant information not known by the other party.

Automatic stabilizers Forces that reduce the size of the expenditure multiplier and diminish the impact of spending changes.

Autonomous consumption spending The part of consumption spending that is independent of income; also the vertical intercept of the consumption function.

Average cost pricing Setting a monopoly's regulated price equal to long-run average cost where the *LRATC* curve crosses the market demand curve.

Average fixed cost Total fixed cost divided by the quantity of output produced.

Average standard of living Total output (real GDP) per person.

Average tax rate The fraction of a given income paid in taxes.

Average total cost Total cost divided by the quantity of output produced.

Average variable cost Total variable cost divided by the quantity of output produced.

B

Balance sheet A financial statement showing assets, liabilities, and net worth at a point in time.

Banking panic A situation in which depositors attempt to withdraw funds from many banks simultaneously

Behavioral economics A subfield of economics focusing on behavior that deviates from the standard assumptions of economic models.

Black market A market in which goods are sold illegally at a price above the legal ceiling.

Bond A promise to pay back borrowed funds, issued by a corporation or government agency.

Boom A period of time during which real GDP is above potential GDP.

Budget constraint The different combinations of goods a consumer can afford with a limited budget, at given prices.

Budget deficit The excess of government purchases over net taxes.

Budget line The graphical representation of a budget constraint, showing the maximum affordable quantity of one good for given amounts of another good.

Budget surplus The excess of net taxes over government purchases.

Business cycles Fluctuations in real GDP around its long-term growth trend.

Business demand for funds curve Indicates the level of investment spending firms plan at various interest rates.

Business firm An organization, owned and operated by private individuals, that specializes in production.

C

Capital A long-lasting tool that is used to produce other goods.

Capital gain The return someone gets by selling a financial asset at a price higher than they paid for it.

Capital gains tax A tax on profits earned when a financial asset is sold at more than its acquisition price.

Capital per worker The total capital stock divided by total employment.

Capital stock The total amount of capital in a nation that is productively useful at a particular point in time.

Capitalism A type of economic system in which most resources are owned privately.

Cartel A group of firms that selects a common price that maximizes total industry profits.

Cash in the hands of the public Currency and coins held outside of banks.

Central bank A nation's principal monetary authority responsible for controlling the money supply.

Ceteris paribus Latin for "all else remaining the same."

Change in demand A shift of a demand curve in response to a change in some variable other than price.

Change in quantity demanded A movement along a demand curve in response to a change in price.

Change in quantity supplied A movement along a supply curve in response to a change in price.

Change in supply A shift of a supply curve in response to some variable other than price.

Circular flow A simple model that shows how goods, resources, and dollar payments flow between households and firms.

Classical model A macroeconomic model that explains the long-run behavior of the economy.

Coase theorem When a side payment can be arranged without cost, the market will solve an externality problem—and create the efficient outcome—on its own.

Command or centrally planned economy An economic system in which resources are allocated according to explicit instructions from a central authority.

Common resources A nonexcludable and rival good. Generally available free of charge, though efficiency would require a positive price.

Communism A type of economic system in which most resources are owned in common.

Comparative advantage The ability to produce a good or service at a lower opportunity cost than other producers.

Compensating wage differential A difference in wages that makes two jobs equally attractive to a worker.

Complement A good that is used together with some other good.

Complementary input An input whose use increases the marginal product of another input.

Complete crowding out A dollar-for-dollar decline in one sector's spending caused by an increase in some other sector's spending.

Constant cost industry An industry in which the long-run supply curve is horizontal because each firm's costs are unaffected by changes in industry output.

Constant returns to scale Long-run average total cost is unchanged as output increases.

Consumer Price Index An index of the cost, through time, of a fixed market basket of goods purchased by a typical household in some base period.

Consumer surplus The difference between the value of a unit of a good to the buyer and what the buyer actually pays for it.

Consumption (C) The part of GDP purchased by households as final users.

Consumption function A positively sloped relationship between real consumption spending and real disposable income.

Consumption tax A tax on the part of their income that households spend.

Consumption-income line A line showing aggregate consumption spending at each level of income or GDP.

Copyright A grant of exclusive rights to sell a literary, musical, or artistic work.

Corporate profits tax A tax on the profits earned by corporations.

Countercyclical fiscal policy A change in government purchases or net taxes designed to reverse or prevent a recession or a boom.

Coupon payments A series of periodic payments that a bond promises before maturity.

Critical assumption Any assumption that affects the conclusions of a model in an important way.

Cross-price elasticity of demand The percentage change in the quantity demanded of one good caused by a 1-percent change in the price of another good.

Crowding out A decline in one sector's spending caused by an increase in some other sector's spending.

Cyclical deficit The part of the federal budget deficit that varies with the business cycle.

Cyclical unemployment Joblessness arising from changes in production over the business cycle.

D

Deadweight loss The dollar value of potential benefits not achieved due to inefficiency in a particular market.

Decreasing cost industry An industry in which the long-run supply curve slopes downward because each firm's *LRATC* curve shifts downward as industry output increases.

Deflation A *decrease* in the price level from one period to the next.

Demand curve The graphical depiction of a demand schedule; a curve showing the quantity of a good or service demanded at various prices, with all other variables held constant.

Demand curve facing the firm A curve that indicates, for different prices, the quantity of output that customers will purchase from a particular firm.

Demand curve for foreign currency A curve indicating the quantity of a specific foreign currency that Americans will want to buy, during a given period, at each different exchange rate.

Demand deposit multiplier The number by which a change in reserves is multiplied to determine the resulting change in demand deposits.

Demand deposits Checking accounts that do not pay interest.

Demand schedule A list showing the quantities of a good that consumers would choose to purchase at different prices, with all other variables held constant.

Demand shock Any event that causes the *AD* curve to shift.

Demand-side effects Macroeconomic policy effects on total output that work through changes in total spending.

Depreciation A decrease in the price of a currency in a floating-rate system.

Depression An unusually severe recession.

Derived demand The demand for a resource that arises from, and varies with, the demand for the product it helps to produce.

Devaluation A change in the exchange rate from a higher fixed rate to a lower fixed rate.

Diminishing marginal returns to labor The marginal product of labor decreases as more labor is hired.

Discount rate The interest rate used in computing present values.

Discounting The act of converting a future value into its present-day equivalent.

Discouraged workers Individuals who would like a job, but have given up searching for one.

Discrimination When a group of people have different opportunities because of personal characteristics that have nothing to do with their abilities.

Diseconomies of scale Long-run average total cost increases as output increases.

Disposable income Household income minus net taxes, which is either spent or saved.

Dividends Part of a firm's current profit that is distributed to shareholders.

Dominant strategy A strategy that is best for a player no matter what strategy the other player chooses.

Dow Jones Industrial Average An index of the prices of stocks of 30 large U.S. firms.

Duopoly An oligopoly market with only two sellers.

E

Economic growth The increase in our production of goods and services that occurs over long periods of time.

Economic profit Total revenue minus all costs of production.

Economic system A system of resource allocation and resource ownership.

Economics The study of choice under conditions of scarcity.

Economies of scale Long-run average total cost decreases as output increases.

Efficient market A market that instantaneously incorporates all available information relevant to a stock's price.

Elastic demand A price elasticity of demand greater than 1.

Employment–population ratio (EPR) The percentage of the population that wants to be working.

Entrepreneurship The ability and willingness to combine the other resources—labor, capital, and natural resources—into a productive enterprise.

Equilibrium GDP In the short run, the level of output at which output and aggregate expenditure are equal.

Equilibrium price The market price that, once achieved, remains constant until either the demand curve or supply curve shifts.

Equilibrium quantity The market quantity bought and sold per period that, once achieved, remains constant until either the demand curve or supply curve shifts.

Excess demand At a given price, the excess of quantity demanded over quantity supplied.

Excess demand for bonds The amount of bonds demanded exceeds the amount supplied at a particular interest rate.

Excess reserves Reserves in excess of required reserves.

Excess supply At a given price, the amount by which quantity supplied exceeds quantity demanded.

Excess supply of money The amount of money supplied exceeds the amount demanded at a particular interest rate.

Exchange The act of trading with others to obtain what we desire.

Exchange rate The amount of one country's currency that is traded for one unit of another country's currency.

Excise tax A tax on a specific good or service.

Excludability The ability to exclude those who do not pay for a good from consuming it.

Exit A permanent cessation of production when a firm leaves an industry.

Expansion A period of increasing real GDP.

Expenditure approach Measuring GDP by adding the value of goods and services purchased by each type of final user.

Expenditure multiplier The amount by which equilibrium real GDP changes as a result of a one-dollar change in autonomous consumption, investment spending, government purchases, or net exports.

Explicit collusion Cooperation involving direct communication between competing firms about setting prices.

Explicit cost The dollars sacrificed—and actually paid out—for a choice.

Exports Goods and services produced domestically, but sold abroad.

Externality A by-product of a good or activity that affects someone not immediately involved in the transaction.

F

Factor markets Markets in which resources—labor, capital, land and natural resources, and entrepreneurship—are sold to firms.

Factor payments Payments to the owners of resources that are used in production

Factor payments approach Measuring GDP by summing the factor payments earned by all households in the economy.

Federal funds rate The interest rate charged for loans of reserves among banks.

Federal Open Market Committee A committee of Federal Reserve officials that established U.S. monetary policy.

Federal Reserve System The monetary authority of the United States, charged with creating and regulating the nation's supply of money.

Fiat money Something that serves as a means of payment by government declaration.

Final good A good sold to its final user.

Financial asset A promise to pay future income in some form, such as future profits or future interest payments.

Financial intermediary A business firm that specializes in brokening between savers and borrowers.

Firm's supply curve A curve that shows the quantity of output a competitive firm will produce at different prices.

Fiscal policy A change in government purchases or net taxes designed to change total output.

Fixed costs Costs of fixed inputs.

Fixed exchange rate A government-declared exchange rate maintained by central bank intervention in the foreign exchange market.

Fixed input An input whose quantity must remain constant, regardless of how much output is produced.

Floating exchange rate An exchange rate that is freely determined by the forces of supply and demand.

Flow variable A variable measuring a process over some period.

Foreign currency crisis A loss of faith that a country can prevent a drop in its exchange rate, leading to a rapid depletion of its foreign currency (e.g., dollar) reserves.

Foreign exchange market The market in which one country's currency is traded for another country's.

Free rider problem When the efficient outcome requires a side payment but individual gainers will not contribute.

Frictional unemployment Joblessness experienced by people who are between jobs or who are just entering or reentering the labor market.

Full employment A situation in which there is no cyclical unemployment.

G

Game theory An approach to modeling the strategic interaction of oligopolists in terms of moves and countermoves.

GDP price index An index of the price level for all final goods and services included in GDP.

Gini coefficient A measure of income inequality; the ratio of the area above a Lorenz curve and under the complete equality line to the area under the diagonal.

Government demand for funds curve Indicates the amount of government borrowing at various interest rates.

Government franchise A government-granted right to be the sole seller of a product or service.

Government purchases (G) Spending by federal, state, and local governments on goods and services.

Gross domestic product (GDP) The total value of all final goods and services produced for the marketplace during a given year, within the nation's borders.

Growth equation An equation showing the percentage growth rate of output as the sum of the growth rates of productivity, average hours, the employment–population ratio, and population.

H

(Household) saving The portion of after-tax income that households do not spend on consumption.

Human capital The skills and training of the labor force.

I

Imperfect competion A market structure in which there is more than one firm but one or more of the requirements of perfect competition is violated.

Imperfectly competitive market A market in which a single buyer or seller has the power to influence the price of the product.

Implicit cost The value of something sacrificed when no direct payment is made.

Imports Goods and services produced abroad, but consumed domestically.

Income The amount that a person or firm earns over a particular period.

Income effect As the price of a good decreases, the consumer's purchasing power increases, causing a change in quantity demanded for the good.

Income elasticity of demand The percentage change in quantity demanded caused by a 1-percent change in income.

Increasing cost industry An industry in which the long-run supply curve slopes upward because each firm's *ATC* curve shifts upward as industry output increases.

Increasing marginal returns to labor The marginal product of labor increases as more labor is hired.

Index A series of numbers used to track a variable's rise or fall over time.

Indexation Adjusting the value of some nominal payment in proportion to a price index, in order to keep the real payment unchanged.

Indexed payment A payment that is periodically adjusted in proportion with a price index.

Indifference curve A curve representing all combinations of two goods that make the consumer equally well off.

Indifference map A set of indifference curves that represent an individual's preferences.

Individual demand curve A curve showing the quantity of a good or service demanded by a particular individual at each different price.

Inelastic demand A price elasticity of demand between 0 and 1.

Infant industry argument The argument that a new industry in which a country has a comparative advantage might need protection from foreign competition in order to flourish.

Inferior good A good that people demand less of as their income rises.

Inflation rate The percent change in the price level from one period to the next.

Injections Spending from sources other than households.

Input Anything (including a resource) used to produce a good or service.

Intermediate goods Goods used up in producing final goods.

International Monetary Fund (IMF) An international organization founded in 1945 to help stabilize the world monetary system.

Investment Firms' purchases of new capital over some period of time.

Investment tax credit A reduction in taxes for firms that invest in capital.

Involuntary part-time workers Individuals who would like a full-time job, but who are working only part time.

Isocost line A line showing all combinations of two inputs that result in the same given level of total cost.

Isoquant A curve showing all combinations of two inputs that can be used to produce a given level of output.

Isoquant map A diagram showing several isoquants, each for a different level of production.

L

Labor The time human beings spend producing goods and services.

Labor demand curve Indicates how many workers firms will want to hire at various real wage rates.

Labor force Those people who have a job or who are looking for one.

Labor productivity The output produced by the average worker in an hour.

Labor shortage The quantity of labor demanded exceeds the quantity supplied for some period of time.

Labor supply curve A curve indicating the number of people who want jobs in a labor market at each wage rate.

Labor surplus The quantity of labor supplied exceeds the quantity demanded for some period of time.

Land The physical space on which production takes place, as well as the natural resources that come with it.

Law of demand As the price of a good increases, the quantity demanded decreases.

Law of diminishing marginal returns As more and more of any input is added to a fixed amount of other inputs, its marginal product will eventually decline.

Law of diminishing marginal utility As consumption of a good or service increases, marginal utility decreases.

Law of supply As the price of a good increases, the quantity supplied increases.

Leakages Income earned, but not spent, by households during a given year.

Liquidity The property of being easily converted into cash.

Loan An agreement to pay back borrowed funds, signed by a household or noncorporate business.

Loanable funds market The market in which households make their saving available to borrowers.

Long run A time horizon long enough for a firm to vary all of its inputs.

Long-run aggregate supply curve A vertical line indicating all possible output and price-level combinations at which the economy could end up in the long run.

Long-run average total cost The cost per unit of producing each quantity of output in the long run, when all inputs are variable.

Long-run elasticity An elasticity measured a year or more after a price change.

Long-run labor supply curve Curve indicating how many people will want to work in a labor market after full adjustment to a change in the wage rate.

Long-run Phillips curve A vertical line indicating that in the long run, unemployment must eqal its natural rate, regardless of the rate of inflation.

Long-run supply curve A curve indicating price and quantity combinations in an industry after all long-run adjustments have taken place.

Long-run total cost The cost of producing each quantity of output when all inputs are variable and the least-cost input mix is chosen.

Lorenz curve When households are arrayed according to their incomes, a line showing the cumulative percent of income received by each cumulative percent of households.

Loss The difference between total cost (TC) and total revenue (TR), when $TC > TR$.

Lumpy input An input whose quantity cannot be increased gradually as output increases, but must instead be adjusted in large jumps.

M

M1 A standard measure of the money supply, including cash in the hands of the public, checking account deposits, and travelers checks.

M2 M1 plus savings account balances, retail money market mutual fund balances, and small time deposits.

Macroeconomics The study of the behavior of the overall economy.

Managed float A policy of frequent central bank intervention to move the exchange rate.

Marginal approach to profit A firm maximizes its profit by taking any action that adds more to its revenue than to its cost.

Marginal cost The increase in total cost from producing one more unit of output.

Marginal cost pricing Setting a monopoly's regulated price equal to marginal cost where the marginal cost curve crosses the market demand curve.

Marginal factor cost (MFC) The change in the firm's total cost divided by the change in its employment of a resource.

Marginal product of labor The additional output produced when one more worker is hired.

Marginal propensity to consume The amount by which consumption spending rises when disposable income rises by one dollar.

Marginal rate of substitution (MRSy,x) The maximum amount of good y a consumer would willingly trade for one more unit of good x. Also, the slope of a segment of an indifference curve.

Marginal rate of technical substitution (MRTS) The amount by which one input can decrease when another input rises by one unit, while maintaining a constant level of output. Also, the absolute value of the slope of an isoquant.

Marginal revenue The change in total revenue from producing one more unit of output.

Marginal revenue product (MRP) The change in the firm's total revenue divided by the change in its employment of a resource.

Marginal revenue product of capital The increase in revenue due to a one-unit increase in the capital input.

Marginal social benefit (MSB) The full benefit of producing another unit of a good, including the benefit to the consumer and any benefits enjoyed by third parties.

Marginal social cost (MSC) The full cost of producing another unit of a good, including the marginal cost to the producer and any harm caused to third parties.

Marginal tax rate The fraction of an additional dollar of income paid in taxes.

Marginal utility The change in total utility an individual obtains from consuming an additional unit of a good or service.

Market A group of buyers and sellers with the potential to trade with each other.

Market clearing Adjustment of prices until quantities supplied and demanded are equal.

Market consumer surplus The total consumer surplus enjoyed by all consumers in a market.

Market economy An economic system in which resources are allocated through individual decision making.

Market failure A market that fails to take advantage of every Pareto improvement.

Market labor demand curve Curve indicating the total number of workers all firms in a labor market want to employ at each wage rate.

Market power The ability of a seller to raise price without losing all demand for the product being sold.

Market producer surplus The total producer surplus gained by all sellers in a market.

Market signals Price changes that cause changes in production to match changes in consumer demand.

Market structure The characteristics of a market that influence how trading takes place.

Market supply curve A curve indicating the quantity of output that all sellers in a market will produce at different prices.

Marketable public goods An excludable and nonrival good. Generally provided by the market for a price, though efficient would require a price of zero.

Maturity date The date at which a bond's principal amount will be paid to the bond's owner.

Means of payment Anything acceptable as payment for goods and services.

Microeconomics The study of the behavior of individual households, firms, and governments; the choices they make; and their interaction in specific markets.

Minimum efficient scale The lowest output level at which the firm's *LRATC* curve hits bottom.

Model An astract representation of reality.

Monetary policy Control or manipulation of the money supply by the Federal Reserve designed to achieve a macroeconomic goal.

Money An asset widely accepted as a means of payments.

Money demand curve A curve indicating how much money will be willingly held at each interest rate.

Money supply The total amount of money held by the public.

Money supply curve A line showing the total quantity of money in the economy at each interest rate.

Monopolistic competition A market structure in which there are many firms selling products that are differentiated, and in which there is easy entry and exit.

Monopoly firm The only seller of a good or service that has no close substitutes.

Monopoly market The market in which a monopoly firm operates.

Monopsony A labor market in which a single firm is a large-enough employer to affect the market wage. Can also refer to the firm itself.

Moral hazard When decision makers—expecting assistance in the event of an unfavorable outcome—change their behavior so that the unfavorable outcome is more likely.

Mutual fund A corporation that specializes in owning shares of stock in other corporations.

N

Nash equilibrium A situation in which every player of a game takes the best action for themselves, given the actions taken by all other players.

National debt The total amount the federal government still owes to the general public from past borrowing.

Natural monopoly A monopoly that arises when, due to economies of scale, a single firm can produce for the entire market at lower cost per unit than could two or more firms.

Natural oligopoly A market that tends naturally toward oligopoly because the minimum efficient scale of the typical firm is large fraction of the market.

Natural rate of unemployment The unemployment rate when there is no cyclical unemployment.

Net exports (*NX*) Total exports minus total imports.

Net financial inflow An inflow of funds equal to a nation's trade deficit.

Net investment Investment minus depreciation.

Net taxes Government tax revenues minus transfer payments.

Net worth The difference between assets and liabilities.

Network externalities Additional benefits enjoyed by all users of a good or service as the total number of users grows.

Nominal interest rate The annual percent increase in a lender's dollars from making a loan.

Nominal variable A variable measured without adjustment for the dollar's changing value.

Nonmarket production Goods and services that are produced but not sold in a market.

Nonmonetary job characteristic Any aspect of a job—other than the wage—that matters to a potential or current employee.

Nonprice competition Any action a firm takes to shift its demand curve rightward.

Normal good A good that people demand more of as their income rises.

Normal profit Another name for zero economic profit.

Normative economics The study of what *should be*; it is used to make judgments about the economy and prescribe solutions.

O

Oligopoly A market structure in which a small number of firms are strategically interdependent.

Open market operations Purchases or sales of bonds by the Federal Reserve System.

Opportunity cost What is given up when taking an action or making a choice.

P

Pareto improvement An action that makes at least one person better off, and harms no one.

Patent A temporary grant of monopoly rights over a new product or scientific discovery.

Patent protection A government grant of exclusive rights to use or sell a new technology.

Payoff matrix A table showing the payoffs to each of two players for each pair of strategies they choose.

Perfect competition A market structure in which there are many buyers and sellers, the product is standardized, and sellers can easily enter or exit the market.

Perfect price discrimination Charging each customer the most he or she would be willing to pay for each unit purchased.

Perfectly competitive labor market Market with many indistinguishable sellers of labor and many buyers, and with easy entry and exit of workers.

Perfectly competitive market A market in which no buyer or seller has the power to influence the price.

Perfectly inelastic demand A price elasticity of demand equal to 0.

Perfectly (infinitely) elastic demand A price elasticity of demand approaching infinity.

Phillips curve A curve indicating the Fed's choice between inflation and unemployment in the short run.

Physical capital The part of the capital stock consisting of physical goods, such as machinery, equipment, and factories.

Planned investment spending Business purchases of plant and equipment.

Plant The collection of fixed inputs at a firm's disposal.

Positive economics The study of how the economy works.

Potential output The level of output the economy could produce if operating at full employment.

Poverty line The income level below which a family is considered to be in poverty.

Poverty rate The percent of families whose incomes fall below a certain minimum—the poverty line.

Present value The value, in today's dollars, of a sum of money to be received or paid at a specific date in the future.

Price The amount of money that must be paid to a seller to obtain a good or service.

Price ceiling A government-imposed maximum price in a market.

Price discrimination Charging different prices to different customers for reasons other than differences in cost.

Price elasticity of demand The sensitivity of quantity demanded to price; the percentage change in quantity demanded caused by a 1-percent change in price.

Price elasticity of supply The percentage change in quantity supplied of a good or service caused by a 1-percent change in its price.

Price floor A government-imposed minimum price in a market.

Price leadership A form of tacit collusion in which one firm sets a price that other firms copy.

Price level The average level of dollar prices in the economy.

Price setter A firm (with market power) that selects its price, rather than accepting the market price as a given.

Price taker Any firm that treats the price of its product as given and beyond its control.

Primary market The market in which newly issued financial assets are sold for the first time.

Principal (face value) The amount of money a bond promises to pay when it matures.

Principal-agent problem A situation in which an agent maximizes her own well-being at the expense of the principal who hired her.

Principle of asset valuation The idea that the value of an asset is equal to the total present value of all the future benefits it generates.

Private investment (I) The sum of business plant, equipment, and software purchases, new-home construction, and inventory changes; often referred to as just *investment*.

Producer surplus The difference between what the seller actually gets for a unit of a good and the cost of providing it.

Product markets Markets in which firms sell goods and services to households.

Production function A function that indicates the maximum amount of output a firm can produce over some period of time from each combination of inputs.

Production possibilities frontier (PPF) A curve showing all combinations of two goods that can be produced with the resources and technology currently available.

Productively inefficient A situation in which more of at least one good can be produced without sacrificing the production of any other good.

Profit Total revenue minus total cost.

Progressive income tax A tax that collects a higher percentage of total income from higher income households.

Progressive tax A tax whose rate increases as income increases.

Property income Income derived from supplying capital, entrepreneurship, or land.

Protectionism The belief that a nation's industries should be protected from foreign competition.

Purchasing power parity (PPP) theory The idea that the exchange rate will adjust in the long run so that the average price of goods in two countries will be roughly the same.

Pure discount bond A bond that promises no payments except for the principal it pays at maturity.

Pure private good A good that is both rivalrous and excludable.

Pure public good A good that is both nonrivalrous and nonexcludable.

Q

Quantity demanded The amount of a good that all buyers in a market would choose to buy during a period of time, given their constraints.

Quantity supplied The specific amount of a good that all sellers in the market would choose to sell over some time period, given (1) a particular price for the good; (2) all other constraints on firms.

Quota A limit on the physical volume of imports.

R

Rational preferences Preferences that satisfy two conditions: (1) Any two alternatives can be compared, and one is preferred or else the two are valued equally, and (2) the comparisons are logically consistent or transitive.

Real interest rate The annual percent increase in a lender's purchasing power from making a loan.

Real variable A variable adjusted for changes in the dollar's value.

Recession A period of significant decline in real GDP.

Regressive tax A tax that collects a lowest percentage of income as income rises.

Relative price The price of one good relative to the price of another.

Rent controls Government-imposed maximum rents on apartments and homes.

Rent-seeking activity Any costly action a firm undertakes to establish or maintain its monopoly status.

Repeated play A situation in which strategically interdependent sellers compete over many time periods.

Required reserve ratio The minimum fraction of checking account balances that banks must hold as reserves.

Required reserves The minimum amount of reserves a bank must hold, depending on the amount of its deposit liabilities.

Reservation wage The lowest wage rate at which an individual would supply labor to a particular labor market.

Reserves Vault cash plus balances held at the Fed.

Resource allocation A method of determining which goods and services will be produced, how they will be produced, and who will get them.

Resource markets Markets in which households that own resources sell them to firms.

Resources The labor, capital, land and natural resources, and entrepreneurship that are used to produce goods and services.

Rivalry A situation in which one person's consumption of a unit of a good or service means that no one else can consume that unit.

Run on the bank An attempt by many of a bank's depositors to withdraw their funds.

S

Say's law The idea that total spending will be sufficient to purchase the total output produced.

Scarcity A situation in which the amount of something available is insufficient to satisfy the desire for it.

Seasonal unemployment Joblessness related to changes in weather, tourist patterns, or other seasonal factors.

Secondary market The market in which previously issued financial assets are sold.

Self-correcting mechanism The adjustment process through which price and wage changes return the economy to full-employment output in the long run.

Share of stock A share of ownership in a corporation.

Short run A time horizon during which at least one of the firm's inputs cannot be varied.

Short side of the market The smaller of quantity supplied and quantity demanded at a particular price.

Shortage An excess demand not eliminated by a rise in price, so that quantity demanded continues to exceed quantity supplied.

Short-run elasticity An elasticity measured just a short time after a price change.

Short-run macro model A macroeconomic model that explains how changes in spending can affect real GDP in the short run.

Short-run macroeconomic equilibrium A combination of price level and GDP consistent with both the *AD* and *AS* curves.

Shutdown price The price at which a firm is indifferent between producing and shutting down.

Shutdown rule In the short run, the firm should continue to produce if total revenue exceeds total variable costs; otherwise, it should shut down.

Simplifying assumption Any assumption that makes a model simpler without affecting any of its important conclusions.

Single-price monopoly A monopoly firm that is limited to charging the same price for each unit of output sold.

Socialism A type of economic system in which most resources are owned by the state.

Specialization A method of production in which each person concentrates on a limited number of activities.

Stagflation The combination of falling output and rising prices.

Standard & Poor's 500 An index of the prices of stocks of 500 large U.S. firms.

Statistical discrimination When individuals are excluded from an activity based on the statistical probability of behavior in their group, rather than their personal characteristics.

Stock variable A variable measuring a quantity at a moment in time.

Structural deficit The part of the federal budget deficit that is independent of the business cycle.

Structural unemployment Joblessness arising from mismatches between workers' skills and employers' requirements or between workers' locations and employers' locations.

Substitutable input An input whose use decreases the marginal product of another input.

Substitute A good that can be used in place of some other good and that fulfills more or less the same purpose.

Substitution effect As the price of a good falls, the consumer substitutes that good in place of other goods whose prices have not changed.

Sunk cost A cost that has been paid or must be paid, regardless of any future action being considered.

Supply curve A graphical depiction of a supply schedule; a curve showing the quantity of a good or service supplied at various prices, with all other variables held constant.

Supply curve for foreign currency A curve indicating the quantity of a specific foreign currency that will be supplied, during a given period, at each different exchange rate.

Supply of funds curve Indicates the level of household saving at various interest rates.

Supply schedule A list showing the quantities of a good or service that firms would choose to produce and sell at different prices, with all other variables held constant.

Supply shock Any event that causes the *AS* curve to shift.

Supply-side effects Macroeconomic policy effects on total output that work by changing the quantities or resources available.

Surplus An excess supply not eliminated by a fall in price, so that quantity supplied continues to exceed quantity demanded.

T

Tacit collusion Any form of oligopolistic cooperation that does not involve an explicit agreement.

Tariff A tax on imports.

Tax incidence The division of a tax payment between buyers and sellers, determined by comparing the new (after tax) and old (pretax) market equilibriums.

Tax shifting The process by which some or all of a tax imposed on one side of a market ends up being paid by the other side of the market.

Taylor rule A proposed rule that would require the Fed to change the interest-rate by a specified amount whenever real GDP or inflation deviate from their preannounced targets.

Technological change The invention or discovery of new inputs, new outputs, or new production methods.

Technology A method by which inputs are combined to produce a good or service.

Terms of trade The ratio at which a country can trade domestically produced products for foreign-produced products.

Tit-for-tat A game-theoretic strategy of doing to another player this period what he has done to you in the previous period.

Total benefits The sum of consumer and producer surplus in a particular market.

Total cost The costs of all inputs—fixed and variable.

Total demand for funds curve Indicates the total amount of borrowing at various interest rates.

Total fixed cost The cost of all inputs that are fixed in the short run.

Total product The maximum quantity of output that can be produced from a given combination of inputs.

Total revenue The total inflow of receipts from selling a given amount of output.

Total variable cost The cost of all variable inputs used in producing a particular level of output.

Tradable permit A license that allows a company to release a unit of pollution into the environment over some period of time.

Trade deficit The excess of a nation's imports over its exports during a given period.

Trade surplus The excess of a nation's exports over its imports during a given period.

Traditional economy An economy in which resources are allocated according to long-lived practices from the past.

Tragedy of the commons The problem of overuse when a good is rivalrous but nonexcludable.

Transfer payment Any payment that is not compensation for supplying goods, services, or resources.

U

Unemployment rate The fraction of the labor force that is without a job.

Unit elastic demand A price elasticity of demand equal to 1.

Unit of value A common unit for measuring how much something is worth.

Utility A quantitative measure of pleasure or satisfaction obtained from consuming goods and services.

V

Value added The revenue a firm receives minus the cost of the intermediate goods it buys.

Value-added approach Measuring GDP by summing the value added by all firms in the economy.

Variable costs Costs of variable inputs.

Variable input An input whose usage can change as the level of output changes.

W

Wage taker A firm that takes the market wage rate as a given when making employment decisions.

Wealth The total value of everything a person or firm owns, at a point in time, minus the total value of everything owed.

Wealth constraint At any point in time, wealth is fixed.

Y

Yield The rate of return a bond earns for its owner.

Index